W9-BCR-658
SEP 1981
RECEIVED
OHIO DOMINICAN
COLLEGE LIBRARY

THE COUSTEAU ALMANAC

AN INVENTORY OF LIFE ON OUR WATER PLANET

THE COUSTEAU ALMANAC

An Inventory of Life on Our Water Planet

Jacques-Yves Cousteau
and the Staff of The Cousteau Society

MOSE RICHARDS
Editor in Chief

MARY PADEN
Managing Editor

PAULA DIPERNA
Contributing Editor

Doubleday & Company, Inc., Garden City, New York 1981

Library of Congress Cataloging in Publication Data

Cousteau, Jacques-Yves.
The Cousteau almanac.

Includes index.
1. Ecology. 2. Man—Influence on nature.
3. Environmental protection. I. Cousteau Society.
II. Title.
QH541.C67 304.2
ISBN: 0-385-14875-5 (trade)
0-385-14876-3 (paperbound)
Library of Congress Catalog Card Number 79-7862

Printed in the United States of America
First Edition

Editor, MAKING WAVES material: Bruce P. Ballenger

Principal Writers:

Paula DiPerna, Mose Richards, Julie Sullivan, Mary Paden, Kevin Finneran, Laurie Wolfe, Bruce P. Ballenger

Environmental Coordinator: Daniel J. Morast

Art Editor: karin negoro

Assistant Art Editor: Tim Knipe

Researchers:

Carol Sue Davidson, Odile Girard, Tim Corcoran, Darrell Aherin, Bruce Linker

Research Assistants:

Mary Long, Roxanne Davis, Jane Dembner, H. Marla Rybka, Gilbert Cruz

Production Editor: Marta Vivas

Production Assistants:

Esther Holt-Knight, Barbara Stover, Janis Kobran, Gwen O'Hara

Cartoon Editor: Michelle Urry

Cartographer: Rafael D. Palacios

WRITERS' ROSTER

A.L.	Al Lawrence	J.K.	Julie Kosterlitz	P.C.	Peter Campion
A.C.	Anna Collins	J.M.V.	Jo Ann Myer Valenti	P.D.	Paula DiPerna
B.C.B.	Beverly C. Barstow	J.N.	Jeff Nathanson	P.H.	Peter Harnik
B.G.	Brad Gellert	J.R.	June Rogoznica	P.I.	Dr. Pascal J. Imperato
BE.K.	Betsy T. Kagey	J.S.	Julie Sullivan	P.L.	Patricia Logan
B.K.	Bobbi Katz	J.V.	John R. Vallentyne	P.R.B.	Population Reference Bureau
B.L.	Bruce Linker	J.W.	Jane Wholey	P.S.	Peter Stoler
B.M.	Barbara Moynehan	K.F.	Kevin Finneran	P.W.	Patricia Weil
B.P.B.	Bruce P. Ballenger	L.C.	LindaCarol Cherken	R.B.	Rick Bruns
C.F.	Connie Farley	L.W.	Laurie Wolfe	R.C.	Robert Corcoran
C.P.	Carol Pearce	L.Y.L.	Leslie Y. Lin	R.M.	Richard Munson
C.F.C.	Caron F. Chess	M.A.	Mary Azrael	R.N.	Ron Nelson
C.R.C.	C. Ron Carroll	M.C.S.	Mary C. Sherwin	R.V.	Roy Vontobel
C.S.D.	Carol Sue Davidson	M.G.	Marty Gallanter	S.D.	Susan Davis
D.H.	Donald Higgins	M.L.	Mary Long	S.G.	Sarah Geils
D.M.	Diane MacEachern	M.M.	Mike Maza	S.H.	Scott Hempling
D.O.	Dave O'Reilly	M.Mu.	Mary Mushinsky	S.L.	Sheila Liebergott
D.W.	David Weir	M.P.	Mary Paden	S.LY.	Sarah Lydgate
E.B.	Elizabeth Block	M.R.	Mose Richards	T.C.	Tim Corcoran
F.C.S.	Frank C. Shephard	M.S.	Mark Schapiro	T.G.D.	Thomas G. Donlan
F.W.	Fred White	M.V.	Marta Vivas	T.K.	Tim Knipe
H.M.R.	H. Marla Rybka	N.M.	Nikki Meith	W.M.B.	William M. Bloss
J.B.	Jan Brandstrader	O.G.	Odile Girard		

ARTISTS' ROSTER

Brad Gellert: p. 660
Cheryl Ann Regalmuto: pp. 333, 334, 335, 336, 337
Cay Hough: pp. 356, 746
Hal J. Lieffers: pp. 181, 227, 228
John Figurski: p. 6
Joyce Powzyk: pp. 53, 187, 208, 212, 213, 222, 232, 233, 235, 239, 241, 244, 278, 279, 284, 306, 520, 524, 598, 599, 662, 663
Page Ayers: p. 9
Tor Hansen: pp. 54, 285, 287, 321, 323, 383, 415
Tina Salvesen: pp. 10, 102, 259, 365, 366 Right, 367 Top, 369, 370, 374, 385, 386, 387, 388, 389, 536, 537, 637, 666, 667

To the memory of
PHILIPPE COUSTEAU,
who first imagined this book, and
whose life's work continues to be
carried out by the members and staff
of The Cousteau Society.

Acknowledgments

The staff of the *Almanac* would like to thank several people and a handful of organizations for their generous contributions to the book. In particular we are grateful for assistance given us by Norman Solomon (who initiated the project), Susan Schiefelbein, Judith Anderson, Dr. Nancy Kester, Thomas O'Conor Sloane III, Eileen Fallon, Jacques Constans, Robert Heilbroner, Mathilde Camacho, and Dr. Peter M. Sandman.

We are also deeply indebted to the following for their early guidance and later review of the manuscript: the members of The Cousteau Society Council of Advisors, especially Dr. Edward Wenk, Jr., Dr. Elie Shneour, Dr. Gabriel Nahas, Dr. Henry Kendall, Dr. Andrew A. Benson, Dr. H. S. Thayer, and Hazel Henderson; the staff of the Worldwatch Institute, especially Lester Brown, Erik Eckholm, and Bruce Stokes; the staff of the Population Reference Bureau, especially Phyllis Avedon, Sergio Diaz-Briquets, Carl Haub, Arthur Haupt, Thomas T. Kane, Elaine Murphy, Jean van der Tak, and Robert P. Worrall; the staff of the Council on Economic Priorities, especially Stewart Baldwin and Bernard Rivers; Dr. Pascal James Imperato of the Downstate Medical Center of the State University of New York; Patricia Forkan of the Humane Society of the United States; Dr. Thomas Lovejoy of the World Wildlife Fund–U.S.A.; C. Ron Carroll of the State University of New York; James Crowfoot of the University of Michigan; John R. Vallentyne of the Canada Center for Inland Waters; Fran Du Melle of the American Lung Association; Will Pozzi; and the Sierra Club.

Since the compilation of such a large book also involved literally hundreds of members and friends of The Cousteau Society, it would be impossible to acknowledge every contributor. We would like to thank all those who sent us material, as well as the following, whose help was most appreciated: Steve Ainsworth, Bruce Anderson, Dr. George N. Appell, Robert Arbib of the Audubon Society, Isaac Asimov, Jelle Atema, Edward Baer of the Interfaith Center for Corporate Responsibility, David Baker, Deborah Baldwin, Tom Barlow of the Natural Resources Defense Council, Alex Beam, Mrs. E. Beetschen of the American Geographic Association, Judy Berg, Peter Berg, Ellen Bern, Beryl Bernay of the United Nations Food and Agriculture Association, Tom Bieler of the United Nations, Fred Boesselman, Liz Bove, Karen G. Brazeau, Lee Ann Brentlinger, the British Paper Federation, Ruth Brown of the U. S. Environmental Protection Agency, the Carolina Brown Lung Association, Archie Carr, the Center for Investigative Reporting, Bob Clausi, Anna Collins, the Connecticut Citizen Action Group, the U. S. Council on Environmental Quality, Shelton Davis, Ralph De Carpio, Rose DeGregorio, John De Witt of Save the Redwoods, Dr. Sylvia Earle, Kraft Ehricke, Jack B. Elrick, Environmental Action Foundation, Diane M. Eskenasy, J. M. Farrar of Cambridge University, FIND/SVP, the Photo Library of the United Nations Food and Agriculture Organization, Mark D. Freeman of the Mississippi Department of Agriculture, John Frick, Linda Frick, Debbie Galant, Sarah Geils, Edward Glade, Jr., of the U. S. Department of Agriculture, Mary Ann Griffin, Sally Hestad, Karen Hinderstein, Robert J. Hron, Sr., of the U. S. Department of Agriculture, Fred Iannazzi of Arthur D. Little, Inc., the Institute for Local Self-Reliance, the Italian Cultural Center, David Kinley of the Institute for Food and Development Policy, Jerry Kline of the Conservation Foundation, Phil Kreitner, David L. Langston, Charles Le Baron, Jennifer Lee, Dede Letz of Life of the Land in Hawaii, Sam Love, Susan Maggiore, Eileen Mahoney, Laurel Marx, Terry Mayer of the Denim Council, Elizabeth McCarthy, Chuck McCullagh, Dr. Russ McGoodwin, John McPhee, Nikki Meith of the United Nations Environment Programme (UNEP), Michigan Sea Grant, Carmen Miguel of *McCall's* Magazine, Patricia Miller, John Milton, Dr. Edward D. Mitchell of the Fisheries and Marine Service of Quebec–Canada, Dr. John D. Morgan of the U. S. Bureau of Mines, Robert Morris of the Interfaith Center on Corporate Responsibility, Richard C. Murphy, Nancy Naglin,

New York University–Bobst Library, Helene O'Hara, Robert Oldershaw, Paula Osterbrink, Bob Pearlman, Zygmunt Plater, Dr. Peter Pritchard, the Public Media Center, Dr. Robert Pyle, Paul Ress of UNEP, Diane Rhoades, Jess F. Riness, Dr. Arthur Roberts of Fermi National Laboratory, Joseph A. Ross of Motivational Communications, Inc., Dr. Robert R. N. Ross, Debbi Ryan of the UNEP Industry Liaison Office, Polly Pitkin Ryan, Elizabeth Rumbuld of the British Tourist Office, Mike Salzer, Ruth Schaefer, Rusty Schweikert, Leonard Sitomer, Connie Solomon, David Solomon, Ellen Solomon, Babette Soria, Gary Souci, Susan Spencer-Richards, Dr. Robert C. Spindel of the Woods Hole Oceanographic Institution, Saul Steinberg, Bernard P. Stengren of Con Edison, Survival International–U.S.A., Cecile Thiery, Richard Thomas, Cynthia Tovar, UNI-PUB, Emily Van Ness, Marilyn Vogel, Joshua Wanderer, Jayne Wenger-Knipe, Marietta Whittlesley, Richard Willson, the Wind Ship Development Corporation–Frank MacLear, Henry Marcus, and Lloyd Bergeson, World Wildlife Fund–U.S.A., and Joseph Zelvin.

Finally, a sincere thank you to Doubleday editor Joseph Gonzalez, who steered a large ship for a long time.

Contents

Editor's Note

A calendar, a calendar! look in
the almanack; find out moonshine.

WILLIAM SHAKESPEARE
A Midsummer-Night's Dream

It is helpful when a book begins by telling you what it is about.

This book is about the entire world.

For centuries almanacs have helped people find their place in the flow of time and tides, in the circle of the seasons, in the sweep of history. This is an unconventional almanac for uncommon times. It is a planetary inventory of living, an attempt to help people find their place in the great global organism of which we are part, in its flows and circles, and in the sweeping developments that are changing it rapidly in our age.

While it is increasingly clear to all of us that the most important news events of our time are usually linked simultaneously to earth's resources, to population pressures, and to ecological disruptions, there is seldom enough reliable information available in daily reports to give us a thorough understanding of the elements of each crisis, or how it is connected to yesterday's crisis and the inevitable one tomorrow.

We have gathered together some of the seldom-told stories behind the stories of the day, information about the roots of the crises. The book was written in the belief that the common people of the world—all of *us*—can make wise decisions when given the right information.

The *Almanac* is a global book because natural systems know no boundaries. The sea bathes the entire planet with its artery-like currents and its freshwater extensions; the atmosphere is a respiratory system that embraces the entire world. The planetary environment provides a common sustenance; the contamination and depletion of it are common losses. Because the more heavily industrialized nations were the first to encounter and to respond to modern environmental problems, there is more information available from Western countries, but both industrialized and developing countries face these problems, and very few virgin areas remain unthreatened. Fortunately, though, there is a surge of awareness and action around the world, and we have tried here to present international situations.

Some other *Almanac* notes:

- We would like to encourage citizen action, so we have supplied names and addresses of a few organizations as part of selected articles, but space did not allow a comprehensive list of the many important groups working on behalf of nature. A good source of these names and addresses is the National Wildlife Federation's *Conservation Directory,* published annually.
- We believe that protectors of nature should not be concerned with protecting just plants and animals, to the exclusion of people. The *Almanac* is about the human environment, the planet to be occupied by coming generations.
- While we have highlighted worrisome trends and lamented catastrophes, we have also sought out (and found) encouraging developments.
- The problems of the sea cannot be completely separated from those of the rest of the planet, any more than the blood can be separated from the rest of the body. An organization like The Cousteau Society, concerned about the water system, is compelled to deal with all of life. Anyone who traces the causes of ocean problems finds that they lead back to the land. Most of the poisons in the sea came from land-based factories, automobiles, sewage systems. The throngs of people on continents generate needs that play havoc with life in the sea—overfishing, tourism, recreation, petroleum production and transport. Investigating the health of the water system means exploring all of the biosphere—the earth's living skin—because life is organized water, and earth, more than 71 percent covered by the sea, is a water planet. The watery fluid of every cell of every organism is a miniature ocean.

Using the Almanac

The *Almanac* is organized as a reflection of the interplay among all things. The great global membrane called the biosphere is, as ecologist Charles Southwick has described it, a system for capturing, converting, storing, and utilizing the energy of the sun. It is a vast grid of exchanges, changes, births, deaths, dispersions, renewals, all laced together in an intricate pattern that today includes human networks of politics, economics, and technology. Accordingly, *Almanac* chapters are not divided into such traditional topics as energy, population, wildlife, and so on, but according to themes and events that link all of these matters together.

In the long tradition of almanacs, dating back to those printed on Egyptian papyrus by the early Romans, this is a book for browsing. But it is designed for more serious uses, too.

- To extract from the *Almanac* a large picture of life on earth today, read it from cover to cover.
- To pursue the linkages among issues, follow the cross-references inserted throughout the book as a kind of internal map. It is possible to skip back and forth through the book from one connection to another by following suggestions like: (See also "How to Make a Cow," page 590).
- The *Almanac* can also serve as a reference, although that is not its primary goal. To find data about the earth and humanity, turn to Chapter 3, "A Global Census" (page 97). It is a collection of useful statistics and descriptions. To read about a particular subject of interest, consult the index for all of the articles that touch on it.

Finally, there is an effort throughout the *Almanac* to relate stories of environmental heroism. People without great wealth or political power frequently rise to impose common sense on decision-making processes that otherwise, and too frequently, lead to an impoverishment of priceless resources. Profiles of these **"Wavemakers"** are scattered through the book. Their stories point toward the last section of the *Almanac,* which is included for those who believe, as we do, that the intelligent management of such an indivisible planet is the responsibility of all its citizens, not just those in offices of power. If the lamentable trends described by this book are to be reversed, and the auspicious trends encouraged, it falls increasingly to "average" citizens to take action and to wield the power of their numbers. Part VII, "Making Waves" (page 737), is an attempt to provide some answers to the most common question asked by concerned individuals about environmental issues: "What can *I* do?"

To us the word *environment* does not mean something that surrounds us but an organism of all life within which we are fastened. We suggest that the opportunity that confronts the human species, as it relearns its part in the planetary anatomy, is to emerge as a kind of antibody system, neutralizing dangerous matter, preventing disease, protecting, soothing, mending, sustaining. In that spirit the *Almanac* offers facts and behind-the-scenes perspectives to aid the healing process. The notion stems from a thought attributed to Thomas Jefferson: If the people don't have enough information to wield power correctly, don't take the power from them, give them the information.

MOSE RICHARDS

Introduction

By the first week in October the rains are over, the night skies have cleared, and the trade winds blow warm off the Cape Verde Islands. It is 1963. The *Calypso* has sailed past the jagged, perilous coastlines of this archipelago, and now she lies safely at her moorings, her graceful white outline shimmering in the moonlight. Burdened by diving equipment, a few of us climb heavily, awkwardly down her side; then we disappear, swallowed by the dark African waters, and descend dreamily into the deep for a night dive.

Beneath the surface, I languidly kick my fins. A burst of light tumbles from my feet; microscopic water organisms, like undersea fireflies, emit silvery flashes when disturbed—a phenomenon known as bioluminescence, which is beautifully apparent in night waters. I glide downward a few feet and leave what looks like a trail of stardust behind me. By moving my hand in spirals, I conjure up a milky way. Smiling now, I swing my arms about in great wide strokes, and the sea around me brightens with thousands of sparkling lights. I am the creator of a cosmos.

The following evening, I stand at the bridge. Spread out before me is an infinite panorama of space, dappled with darkness and starlight, Hamlet's "majestical roof fretted with golden fire." I am surrounded by semidesert islands that are stopover places for flamingos; yet above me gleam the same constellations that twinkle over cities and towns and farmlands thousands of miles away. I think of the line from *Satyricon:* "Heaven is equally distant everywhere."

My line of thought is interrupted, for a light is moving in the sky above me and I follow it eagerly, thinking for a moment that it is a falling star or a comet. It isn't. This light slides steadily, almost slowly, across the darkened sky; it doesn't travel with the hurtling speed of a burned-out sun. Its brilliance wends its way among the other stars and then finally dips out of sight. Suddenly I realize that this glimmering light is a satellite, the first satellite I have ever seen. The heavens are not so distant after all, I think to myself! Humans can draw circles of starlight in the night skies just as they do in the night waters.

My satellite was only one of many crafts that penetrated the skies in those early days of space travel, sailing through what President Kennedy was to call "the new ocean" of space. By the end of the decade, the Apollo astronauts had established for humanity a lunar observation post, which provided us with a new vision of the universe.

Space exploration has been midwife to the birth of a new global consciousness. Two decades ago, with my first serendipitous sighting of a satellite, I was one of the lucky few to be touched for a moment by this philosophy. The children of the future, however, will be raised with the benefits of these space-age lessons.

The most telling photograph in their textbooks will not be the Apollo crew's snapshot of rocky lunar landscapes but rather their famous photograph of Planet Earth.

What can we learn from that photograph, from that magnificent blue-and-white orb hung in the black eternity of the universe? First, we can see for ourselves that the earth is a water planet. There is a limited amount of water on our globe—no more, relatively speaking, than a single droplet of water on an egg—but nonetheless the earth is the only known planet to be washed with this vital liquid, so necessary for life.

The earth photograph can drive a second lesson home to us; it can finally make us recognize that the inhabitants of the earth must depend upon and support each other. The dust of distant planets has been baked and doused with chemicals in the desperate quest to discover life, but we have discovered only that we are alone in the solar system, and perhaps in the universe.

There is some reassurance in the photograph, however, despite the solitude it so vividly conveys. We are struck by the important difference between the way cartographers map our planet and the way it can be seen, given the perspective of the universe. There are no boundaries on the real Planet Earth. No United States, no Soviet Union, no China, Taiwan, East Germany or West. Rivers flow unimpeded across the swaths of continents. The persistent tides—the pulse of the sea—do not discriminate; they push against all the varied shores on earth.

Mapmakers are not the only ones to have drawn divisive lines; segregation pervades our earthbound vision of ourselves. We are instructed in Western Civilization and Oriental Thought; our education comes in fractions. Even the calendar separates one people from another—solipsistic generations, bereft of connections to the past and the future, feel responsibility neither to ancestors nor to progeny, only to themselves.

As though lacerating time and culture were not enough, we have lacerated the earth as well. Not only have we failed to realize that we are one people but we have forgotten that we have only one planet. The slow dismemberment of the earth is not a recent development; our early forebears began the process thousands of years ago. At one time, for instance, the island of Dia, off Crete, was a paradise covered with woods, refreshed by large rivers, so beautiful, legend says, that Theseus eloped there for his honeymoon with Ariadne, daughter of Minos, after he killed the Minotaur. Then the island was progressively deforested, in order to build or repair ships and to cook meals in thousands of homes. Dia succumbed to overpopulation, probably four thousand years ago, leaving us to decipher a harsh lesson of ecology.

My first satellite danced over sadly denuded lands as well. The Cape Verde Islands were deforested by early settlers, then overgrazed by the goats introduced by burgeoning populations. Deserts now sweep across the low altitudes, and the overgrazed acres are covered, as though in retribution, by thorny, bitter, poisonous plants.

This precedent was set and reset. Nomad communities imposed the burden of their growing tribes on the surrounding environment; when local resources ran short, their people would move to another site. The advent of agriculture, the population explosion, and recently the coming of the industrial age increased the human pressure on natural resources to a dangerous extent. Today, our industries dump arsenic and mercury into our waters; our militaries dispose of their obsolete death machines in the seas. The difference between modern despoliation and the despoliation of nomads is simple but crucial: Today we have nowhere else to go. All the infinity of the universe can offer us no sustenance once we have squandered our earthly resources.

Born of the legitimate struggle for survival, ironically, the pursuit of technology and progress may today endanger the very survival of the human species, as well as that of practically all life on earth and in the ocean. However, those who would denounce technology and progress altogether in an attempt to solve the problem have only a limited vision; and limited vision is sometimes more dangerous than blindness. We must not forget that the same civilization that has clouded our view with toxic smog has also given us the satellite to help us view the planet from high above. The technology that we use to abuse the planet is the same technology that can help us to heal it.

But if we believe in progress, as we should, to whom can we turn to obtain an unbiased evaluation of the risks we can accept, not only for ourselves but also for our children, our grandchildren, and the hundreds and thousands of generations to come? To politically oriented government officials? To profit-obsessed business leaders? To technocrats, to econocrats? No. The true answer is obvious: Average citizens can rely only on their own judgment; their civic duty is to give utterance to that judgment by all means and as loudly as they can.

To judge the problem, first we must understand it, and it is toward this understanding that the *Almanac* is devoted. Fortunately, human beings are endowed with exceptional faculties to study, to assess danger, and to imagine ingenious solutions to the most complex puzzles. Few of us may be blessed with genius, but all of us are blessed with common sense. The ability to reason is equitably distributed among housewives, farmers, accountants, and students, as well as among the Platos and Einsteins in our midst. Facing today's environmental emergencies, the people of the world must use this common sense and arm themselves with better information than ever. Only then can a new concept of progress emerge, based on a better evaluation of the planet's resources, a selfless desire to share these resources more equitably, and our grave responsibilities to future generations, as well as a respect for life on earth—a life that may be unique in the universe.

With this new education, we may provide our progeny with a delight and an insight we ourselves have not yet experienced. When they travel in their spacecraft, creating the illusion of falling stars across the heavens, perhaps they will look down on earth and think, with reverence, of the tiny creatures making stardust in the sea.

A Bill of Rights for Future Generations

While I was in Jamaica recently, studying the coral reefs with *Calypso*'s crew, we were struck by the scarcity of sizable fish along the coast. There were practically none. As we were carrying on our work, I came across a very old man in a small boat—a spectacular Hemingway-type fisherman, like the character in *The Old Man and the Sea.* His name was Moses and his age was impossible to determine. He was hauling in fish traps and in each trap were one or two little fish. I accompanied Moses to shore, where he landed his miserable catch, and when I had looked at the nets of his trap I asked him, "Why do you use such a small-mesh net? You know that by doing this you are eliminating the young, and are compromising the future of fishing." He looked at me sadly, and I will always remember his look as he answered with a grave voice, "I know this is not good, but I have to eat."

He had to eat, and nobody was providing him with the necessary help to get food. It is with a heavy heart that I remember this encounter, because it demonstrates the difficulty we are now in when approximately one billion people in this world do not eat properly, when resources are diminishing, and the world economy precarious.

How can we convince industry to use smoke-purifying devices, farmers fewer chemicals, or fishermen regular-size nets? We cannot do this on a persuasion basis, even with someone like Moses. I talked to him about his children, and he almost cried. He knew he was doing harm to future generations, eliminating the fishery of his children, but he had to eat. This is the tragedy we now face. How can we trust the sweeping, peremptory assertions of the conventional decision-makers whose actions have frequently put selfish interest before environmental concerns—technocrats, politically-oriented government officials, or profit-only-minded big business leaders?

It seems to me that each of us can make sound judgments personally by referring to two basic criteria that are grounded in common sense. In the first place, no risk at all should be taken when survival of the human species is at stake or when the quality of life of future generations may be threatened (we have no moral right to make our children pay dearly for our selfish remissness). Secondly, no chance should be taken on issues that could bring about irreversible damage to the environment in which we live.

The health of the global water system rooted in the ocean is vital to the future welfare of our planet, and is of particular concern to me as an ocean explorer. The future needs of society will be well served, however, only if we change our short-term mentality and often arrogant indifference to the results of our actions and focus on long-term considerations and a sound attitude in the use of *all* our resources. It was with this in mind that The Cousteau Society drafted *A Bill of Rights for Future Generations.* The document is written for adoption by the General Assembly of the United Nations. (*A Bill of Rights for Future Generations* was largely the work of three members of The Cousteau Society Advisory Council—Dr. Gabriel G. Nahas and Dr. E. Allan Farnsworth, both of Columbia University, and Dr. H. Stanley Thayer of the City College of New York.)

J.Y. Cousteau

The Rights of Future Generations

ARTICLE 1

Future generations have a right to an uncontaminated and undamaged earth and to its enjoyment as the ground of human history, of culture, and of the social bonds that make each generation and individual a member of one human family.

ARTICLE 2

Each generation, sharing in the estate and heritage of the earth, has a duty as trustee for future generations to prevent irreversible and irreparable harm to life on earth and to human freedom and dignity.

ARTICLE 3

It is, therefore, the paramount responsibility of each generation to maintain a constantly vigilant and prudential assessment of technological disturbances and modifications adversely affecting life on earth, the balance of nature, and the evolution of humanity in order to protect the rights of future generations.

ARTICLE 4

All appropriate measures, including education, research, and legislation, shall be taken to guarantee these rights and to ensure that they not be sacrificed for present expediences and conveniences.

ARTICLE 5

Governments, non-governmental organizations, and the individuals are urged, therefore, imaginatively to implement these principles, as if in the very presence of those future generations whose rights we seek to establish and perpetuate.

The Cousteau Society

Learn why the world wags and what wags it.

T. H. WHITE
The Once and Future King

THE COUSTEAU ALMANAC

AN INVENTORY OF LIFE ON OUR WATER PLANET

PART I

COMING ATTRACTIONS

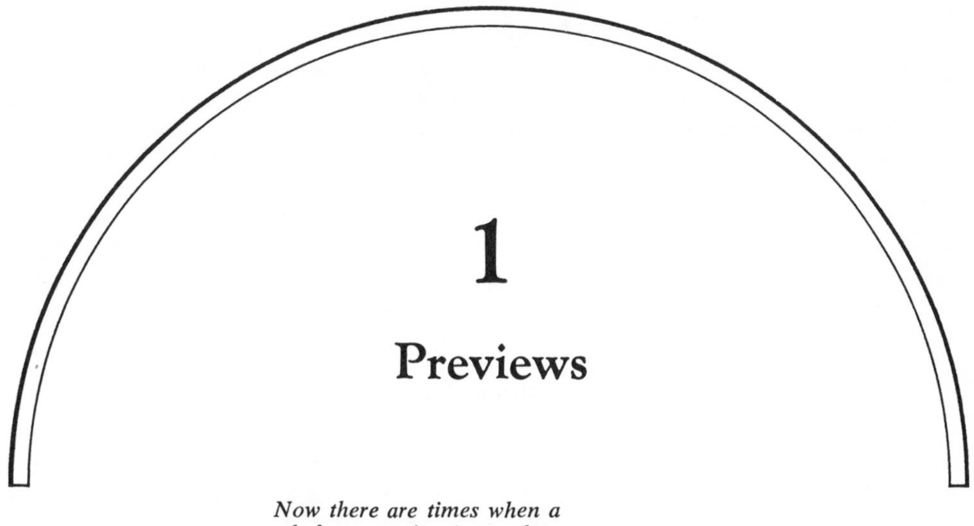

1

Previews

Now there are times when a whole generation is caught . . . between two ages, two modes of life. . . .

HERMAN HESSE
Steppenwolf

A calamity is a time of great opportunity.

CHINESE MAXIM

Predictions about the future usually prove to be wrong, so we have not made any here. Instead, we open the *Almanac* with a catalog of developing gadgets, processes, phenomena, materials—all of which show some promise of becoming commonplace in the future.

Emerging trends and technology pull us along, shift our attention, alter our language, modify our perspective. Sometimes they modify the biological environment, too. A single invention can ripple wildly through human culture and the envelope of nature surrounding it. The invention of the elevator by Elisha Otis suddenly made skyscrapers possible, transforming architecture, transfiguring cities. Galileo's observance of the nature of a pendulum made accurate clocks possible. The cotton gin, a relatively simple device, completely changed the economy of the southern United States. The invention of a powerful fishing pulley, by the American Mario Puretic in 1955, transformed the world fishing industry, making possible vastly increased catches. Peru alone experienced a fivefold growth in its fisheries as a result. The Puretic block, however, by making it possible to pull larger catches into boats, also hastened the overexploitation and eventual demise of many fisheries around the world. Like Trojan horses, many exciting gifts of human creativity seem to carry within them hidden forces of destruction, sometimes even the capacity to unravel the fabric of life.

Developments like these change our political and technological structures without warning, making it difficult to predict the future because it is impossible to anticipate the megasurprises coming. Thus, the predictions of a horrendous plunge toward global doom are as suspect as the visions of a coming golden age.

Barring the monstrous blunder of a nuclear war, the truth of the future probably lies somewhere between a crash to despair and a catapult to paradise. For all of us, time will continue to pass in similar ways, and the changes around us are most likely to be small adjustments in velocity, diversity, flavor, and comfort. We are probably wrong to expect extreme change to take place suddenly, and we also make other assumptions about the future which need reexamining.

The Horizontal Future

For one thing, the future is widely taken to be a horizontal phenomenon. Our language makes travelers of us, headed along a line toward the big foggy uncertainty that is the future. It "stretches before us," "lies ahead," "waits on the horizon." We never seem to be looking down or around or up at the future. The trouble with this linear image is that it fails to account for the trends going on below us, inside us, overtaking us from behind. It encourages us to project the future only from what we see developing in front of us. Thus, in a best-selling book about the future, published in 1971, there is no mention even of a potential oil crisis, a development which emerged with a vengeance only three years later.

Five Billion Futures

Still another misconception about the future is that it will be the same for all of us. While some warn that we are headed for disaster, the fact is that millions of people, perhaps half a billion or more, live disastrously impoverished lives today. Developed nations forget that most of the human race is often uncomfortable, usually hungry. After overseeing the important future study called *Global 2000,* Charles Warren, former chairman of the U. S. President's Council on Environmental Quality, predicted in 1979 that the high-income individual will continue to find life pleasant in the year 2000. In an interview with The Cousteau Society Warren stated: "The wealthy in each nation, regardless of the poverty of the nation, will survive very well. There'll be a higher proportion of people in the low-income regions of the population. For many of these people, life will be very difficult and will involve a question of survival. Anywhere from a billion to a billion and a half people in the year 2000 will find life marginal."

The Climax

Perhaps the most important error in our thinking about the future, however, is the notion that we are going to confront merely *a crisis* or series of crises. The word "crisis," as the British philosopher Eric Ashby has noted, suggests a temporary situation. He proposes to substitute the use of the word "climax," in its ecological sense, suggesting a community of plants and animals that has reached a state of equilibrium through successful adaptation to the environment. We have come to that period when growth is banging into limits—of space, of resources—and this finiteness of the planet cannot be overcome. The situation will persist. The old challenges of frontiers and exploitations are largely past, and the new challenges are mostly ones of adaptation. The work of the coming age will be that of reinvention and reexploration; the systems must be retooled for the long haul, for the generations to come. Whatever develops, the coming age will be one of transition, and history suggests that periods of great change are never easy.

The Limestone Palace

Yet this is also a period of opportunities. We are increasingly aware of how the planet works and how it does not. We are accumulating new facts—about climate, about poisons, about soils, about the sea. We are approaching the point where sufficient knowledge may allow us to evolve a new human society of ecological and economic equilibrium which will work, which will last.

It is possible, because other "climax" systems in nature demonstrate it to be so. The coral reef is an example. Lacking tools possessed by more complex living organisms, such as brains, corals have evolved nonetheless a community in equilibrium with the

(*The Cousteau Society*)

sea. The necessary functions of life proceed in a kind of undersea city. The individuals and the organized groups—corals, sponges, fish, nudibranchs, worms, crinoids, and so on—all manage small enterprises, surviving in an infinite number of small-scale ways. The coral polyps, like small farmers in the sea, harvest tiny plants called zooxanthellae within their tissues. The plants, in turn, aid the coral's nutrition, recycle its waste products, and assist in the building of a skeleton. The community has its developers, its tenants, its commuters, its squatters. It has a system of food and energy exchange that is renewable, and a waste disposal system that is highly efficient. Most of the residents require only minute portions of energy (food), and that is produced by solar power; the corals and most other attaching animals strain plankton from the water, and the plants of the plankton, which form the base of this food source, represent a biomass energy conversion system fueled by the sun. The reef system is characterized by symbiotic relationships, by diversity, by "economies of scale," by beauty. Obviously, human systems are of another order, infused with intellect and creativity. But the elegant coral reef accomplishes what we must in the future. The day-to-day building work of the corals leaves behind a limestone palace for future generations to fasten to or take shelter in, constructed directly in the path of food-bearing currents—solid, stable, fertile with life, and rich with possibilities.

In the chapter that follows, the *Almanac* previews some emerging tools and trends that may work pervasive changes on society in the coming era. Some threaten to fuel social and environmental chaos; but some may provide appropriate building blocks for future human communities in equilibrium with the palaces of nature.

M.R.

KRILL

Euphausiids are small, pinkish, omnivorous shrimplike creatures, found in both deep and shallow ocean waters all around the world. In the waters of Antarctica, where their populations are widely estimated between 220 million and 6.6 billion tons, they are the basic food source for many seals, birds, whales, and species of fish. Deep-ocean currents rise to the surface around the antarctic polar cap, carrying nutrients up from the seafloor, creating rich meadows of vegetable plankton. These plants support varied and abundant marine life, including euphausiids, which can sometimes be seen in swarms so dense that they alter the color of the sea across an area as large as a square mile (2.59 square kilometers). Euphausiids have "frilly" gills and light-producing organs called photophores from which they can emit flashes of blue-green light. One species, *Euphausia superba,* is commonly called krill.

Euphausia superba was first scientifically identified in 1830. One of the largest euphausiid species, averaging 2 inches (5 centimeters) in length when mature, *superba* are also the most commercially useful and abundant. Krill meat, pound for pound, contains as much protein as beef, as well as such minerals as phosphorus, copper, iron, and zinc. It provides calcium, vitamins A and D, and all the B vitamins. Astaxanthin, a carotenoid pigment related to the coloring matter in carrots, lends krill their color. For humans, krill is, potentially, one of the world's most nutritious and important foods. Krill food products—pastes, food enhancers, whole krill, krill tails, even breaded krill sticks—are already available in such countries as the Soviet Union, Japan, West Germany, Poland, Chile, and Norway. Krill by-products, such as fats, pigments, and enzymes, could be used in making dyes, fabrics, adhesives, paper strengtheners, pharmaceuticals, and cosmetics, among others. Limited processing of krill for these items is under way in the United States, Japan, and Chile.

Krill, however, are part of a very simple and therefore fragile food chain, which begins when the krill consume algae and microscopic food particles. The krill position themselves to take best advantage of a water current and filter the food out of the water with the long, finely bristled legs near their mouths.

The well-feasted krill are in turn eaten by the other animals in the ecosystem. The various species of krill distribute themselves at different depths in the sea, and various predator species, like crabeater seals or whales or squid, alternate feeding grounds and feeding seasons, never totally depleting any one area. Whales, especially blues and humpbacks, have been the main predators of krill—in fact, "krill" means "whale food" in Norwegian. These baleen whales skim krill from the surface, or gulp a part of a swarm, forcing water out through the slats of their baleen, swallowing as much as a ton of krill at a time. It is estimated that whales in the Antarctic consume about 50 million tons of krill per year. Given this web of food dependence, any significant decline in the krill population would severely affect other species, just as any significant disruption of the microscopic food supply would severely affect the krill. Whales especially, some of which are enjoying a precarious recovery after decades of unchecked whaling, might be susceptible to a drop in the krill supply. (See "Whales," page 286.)

As of 1981, commercial fishing of krill was limited and marketing restricted by the fact that krill are difficult to keep fresh. However, in Japan and the Soviet Union there is growing interest in krill; paste made from krill is becoming an established product, though a specialty "delicatessen" item for the most part. And though absolutely accurate data are not available, the annual krill catch—22,000 to 44,000 tons—is low in relation to the estimated krill population.

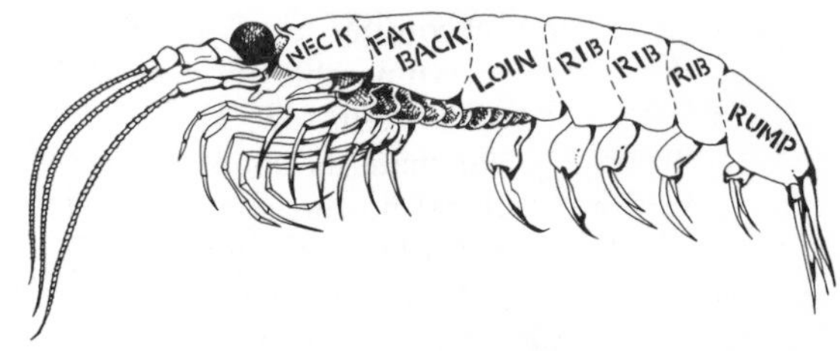

Sirloin of krill? Pound for pound the tiny, shrimplike krill contain as much protein as beef. The 2-inch-long (5-cm) animals are found in dense swarms off the coast of Antarctica. (*Adapted from* The Interdependent)

Ideally, international regulations will prevent krill overfishing. And, before world seafood demand establishes krill as a supermarket staple item, much needs to be learned about the basic habits of the krill. For example, thick krill swarms have been encountered only seasonally so far, suggesting that the total population may be far less than estimates based on these swarms have suggested. Too little of the biology of antarctic krill is known for certain: for instance, their spawning areas, their growth rates, life spans, migration patterns, and density outside the swarms all need further study. It is not even certain whether more than one breeding stock exists.

Much, therefore, remains to be learned about krill, and proper understanding of the species ought to precede its large-scale exploitation, especially when that species may be the dietary mainstay of the entire rich marine ecosystem of Antarctica.

P.D.

MUF

Plutonium, the highly enriched uranium byproduct of nuclear energy, is so powerful that only about 10 pounds (4.5 kilograms) of it is sufficient to build a workable nuclear bomb. Because of inefficiencies in the fission process, significantly less plutonium actually enables the bomb to go off. Only *one gram* of the plutonium packed into Fat Man, the nuclear bomb the United States exploded over Nagasaki, was converted to explosive energy, according to one of the bomb's designers, Dr. Theodore Taylor, in an interview with writer John McPhee. One pound (0.45 kilogram) of plutonium, dispersed as powder, could kill 9 billion people, which is more than twice the population of the world in 1981.

Plutonium, therefore, would be well worth stealing if one had an extremely malevolent motive, as would even "ordinary" reactor-grade uranium.

Given not only the proliferation of nuclear weapons around the world since 1945, but also the spread of nuclear power plants, traffic in potentially explosive nuclear material is frequent, complicated, and, according to many experts and scientists, extremely vulnerable to "unauthorized diversion"—the official term for "stolen."

Thieves of nuclear material could be motivated by cash, fame, political power, or simple insanity. They could attempt to build a nuclear bomb and threaten to detonate it, or they could simply threaten to release the nuclear material into water systems or the atmosphere, greatly increasing the incidence of cancers and death by direct poisoning. Advocates of nuclear energy insist that the odds against a nuclear theft resulting in a serious incident are high enough to render it virtually a "nonpossibility." But the odds were high against the bombing of an Iraq-bound shipment of nuclear equipment by an antinuclear group in the South of France. What were the odds that a frustrated writer would threaten to crash his private Cessna aircraft into the Harcourt Brace Jovanovich building in New York City, resulting in an evacuation of the publishing house and adjacent buildings, including the United Nations? But, despite the odds, in 1979 both of these episodes happened.

The odds were high that a college student with average physics grades could not successfully design a nuclear bomb without access to classified material, but this happened, too, at Princeton University in 1976.

And nuclear "incidents" have also happened. In nuclear energy parlance, when nuclear materials have disappeared from the inventory, the abbreviation used is MUF—Materials Unaccounted For. In the United States, MUFs occur often, in amounts "well within the calculated statistical variability" according to the Department of Energy, which oversees the nuclear energy industry. This means material is lost "in the pipes" or in the bookkeeping system, and therefore the MUF is supposedly nothing to worry about. But MUF quantities over a long period of time are enough to make nuclear weapons, even though over short periods of time the amounts are so small that detection is impossible.

As of the end of 1976 in the United States, according to government statistics secured by New York *Times* reporter David Burnham after two years of investigation, there had been a total of 8,000 pounds (3,629 kilograms) of MUF. There have also been circumstances where large quantities of material have been reported missing. In 1978, to cite only one case, 200 pounds (90 kilograms) of weapons-grade uranium disappeared from the accounting system of a nuclear fuels production company and was believed to have been smuggled from the United States to the Israeli military.

Other incidents have gone by without any public notice. Between 1977 and 1979, for instance, the United States Federal Bureau of Investigation (FBI) received approximately forty-five threats from persons who claimed to possess missing nuclear material ready to be unleashed in one way or another.

These threats have been handled in a variety of ways. The FBI claims to take each one seriously, calling in nuclear experts, psychologists, and criminologists to determine whether the threat could conceivably be legitimate. Could, in other words, the threat really involve nuclear material? Could the bomb the caller claims to have really go off?

To grapple with these questions, the FBI has at its disposal the NEST (Nuclear Emergency Search Team), a small group of nuclear scientists based in Los Alamos, New Mexico, and Washington, D.C. NEST is, officially, a nuclear monitoring team, ready to be deployed in the event of a nuclear threat to provide technical assistance and advice, i.e., to tell the FBI whether the threat is serious. Official records reveal that NEST was deployed in four of the forty-five FBI cases, but much information about NEST's activity is still highly classified. NEST is supposedly a kind of "Mission Impossible" force—a crack technical team able to respond as quickly as presently possible to a nuclear threat. That is, if they are summoned in time.

As of 1979, the Nuclear Regulatory Commission (NRC), which is responsible for safeguarding nuclear materials in the United States, allowed a nuclear facility to take thirty days to complete its routine nuclear materials inventory. These inventories must begin every two months. If there is MUF in excess of approximately 20 pounds (9 kilograms), the facility must be shut down fully until the material is AF (Accounted For). Finding material lost in the plant pipelines or in the accounting system can take up to another thirty days at least. If the material is still missing after the reinventory is completed, the NRC concludes that perhaps an "unauthorized diversion" has occurred. By then, up to ninety days have passed between the beginning of the inventory and the determination that material is indeed missing.

As hypothetical as the scenario sounds, this exact sequence of events took place in Erwin, Tennessee, in 1979. The MUF was never fully accounted for, even after five months of search. An amount greater than 20 pounds (9 kilograms)—the NRC would not say how much—was still missing, but the plant was reopened because it produced nuclear fuel for submarines deemed vital to national security. The plant was exempted from the 20-pound (9-kilogram) limit so that it could return to production. All this, even though Erwin had a ten-year history of problems with MUF.

During the 1979 incident, NEST flew around the Erwin plant in helicopters using radiation sensors to determine whether any nuclear materials were hidden outside or near the plant. But by the time NEST did so, the MUF could have been long gone from the area.

The nuclear security system in the United States is fallible enough, but there is virtually no agency responsible for gathering MUF data on an international scale. Plutonium could be carried in a paper bag through customs, and it would not be detected. There is little or no inventory information available, and the International Atomic Energy Agency, which is supposedly a regulatory body, has no ability, or authority, to collect information on security systems, production, consumption, or shipment of nuclear materials. The possibilities for international nuclear blackmail, the ultimate hijacking involving nuclear bombs or nuclear material traded to terrorists to make bombs, are rife.

The nuclear age has been with us for more than thirty years, but we still don't know *exactly* where and how MUF goes when it goes, or how to keep it from going there.

P.D.

GOSSYPOL

In 1979, the People's Republic of China announced the results of an experiment that could revolutionize population planning: an effective male contraceptive pill. Chinese physicians claimed to have tested the pill with four thousand men between 1972 and 1979, and that it was 99.8 percent successful when used regularly.

The crucial ingredient in the pill is gossypol, a yellow pigment found in cottonseed. (The whole seeds are currently being tested as food additives because of their extremely high protein content—see "Liquid Cycloning," page 9.) Gossypol must be separated from the rest of the seed by a high-speed spinning process, and then treated for safe inclusion in the contraceptive pill.

According to the Chinese researchers involved,

the side effects of the pill have been minimal; low percentages of the test subjects reported fatigue, nausea, and changes in appetite. Six percent reported lower sexual drive, though none reported less sexual "capability." Apparently, the toxic effects of gossypol, which have precluded use of the substance in foods, do not occur at the low doses necessary to provide effective contraception. Moreover, subjects who "went off" the pill in order to father children had no difficulty regaining fertility, and their children have not demonstrated any side effects or birth defects. The Chinese results have been under study in the United States and other countries where other efforts to develop a pill for men have been thus far unsuccessful.

If gossypol really works as a contraceptive for men, it would cause a major sociological change. What was once the almost exclusive province of women—controlling conception—would become a shared responsibility. P.D.

LIQUID CYCLONING

After spinning cotton into cloth for thousands of years, we are now able to spin cottonseed into food. The seeds, long considered refuse of the cotton plant, can be processed through a new spinning technique called liquid cycloning, which produces a nutritious flour consisting of 65 to 68 percent pure protein. The flour, virtually tasteless and colorless, has been approved by the U. S. Food and Drug Administration for use in foods for human consumption, especially to enrich breads, pastries, cereals, and even to extend meats. No special cooking is needed, though in baking, cotton flour must be mixed with about 90 percent wheat flour to permit rising.

Because inadequate protein supply and malnutrition continue to plague many of the world's people, any new source of protein is an exciting development. Since the average annual harvest of glanded cottonseed exceeds 20 million metric tons, a developed cottonseed flour industry could produce *5.5 million tons* of high-quality flour, or approximately 6 percent of the world's protein supply. And this additional food can be available without additional land investment—the land now growing cotton for clothing also grows the cottonseeds needed for flour. Producing cloth and food from the same plant would be an important boon for the cotton industry, which is already in constant competition with soybean producers for arable land.

Cotton flour is already in limited production in parts of Central and South America and Israel, and if the market demanded, widespread production would begin in the United States.

P.D.

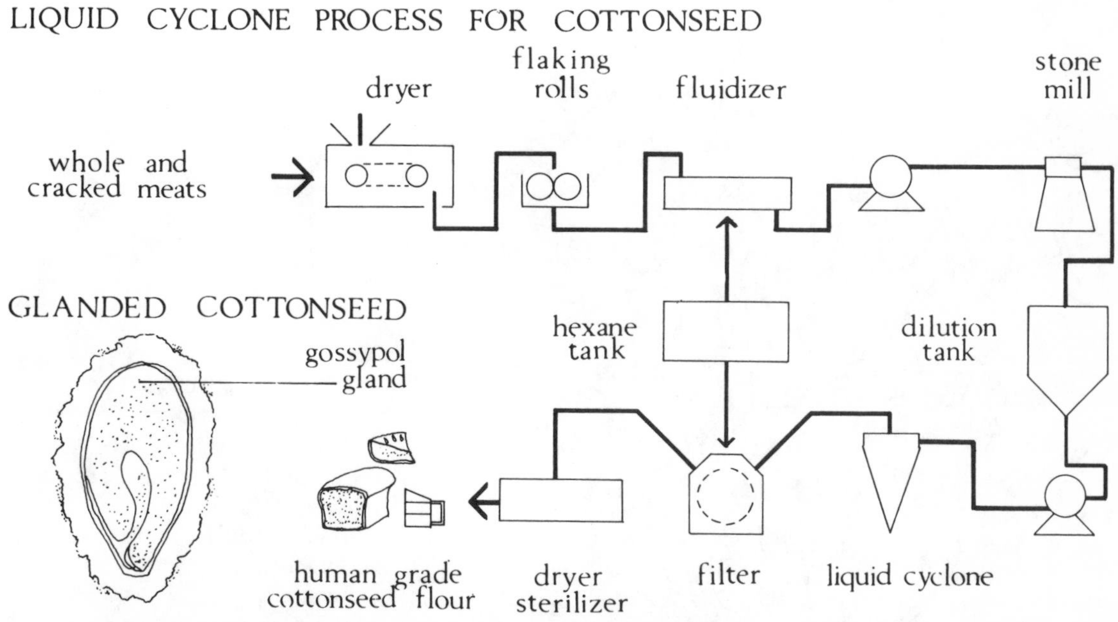

LIQUID CYCLONE PROCESS FOR COTTONSEED

whole and cracked meats
dryer
flaking rolls
fluidizer
stone mill
hexane tank
dilution tank
GLANDED COTTONSEED
gossypol gland
human grade cottonseed flour
dryer sterilizer
filter
liquid cyclone

Two products that can be extracted from the seed of the cotton plant may help humanity overcome two major challenges. A pigment called gossypol in cottonseed may provide the crucial ingredient for an effective male contraceptive pill, and flour made from cottonseed could be a significant addition to the food supply for many nations.

JOJOBA

It is a fascinating parallel of nature that the small brown acornlike seed of the jojoba bush, which has grown wild in deserts for centuries, contains oil that in chemical and physical properties is nearly identical to the oil found in the head of one of the largest sea mammals—the sperm whale. The hunting of this whale, which averages 60 tons in weight and 60 feet (18 meters) in length, accounts for approximately 50 percent of the whaling industry's activities.

Sperm oil, found in the spermaceti organ (the mass of tissue and muscle that constitutes about 80 percent of the whale's head), is used principally as a specialized lubricant and is essential to the high-speed operation of pressurized moving parts, the gears and wheels, of machinery. But it is also an ingredient in a multitude of other products, such as cold cream, lipstick, shaving cream, ointments, leather dressing, dye solvents, dye fixers, powders, pastes, detergents, and alcohols. Though the world whale population is in decline, making whaling generally a less profitable venture, the demand for sperm oil has remained constant. Fortunately there is a remarkable solution at hand, since jojoba oil is a virtually perfect substitute for sperm whale oil.

Jojoba oil itself has been known and used for a long time. California Indians in the eighteenth century were reported to have even used it for cooking. The oil is high quality, able to withstand high pressures and temperature changes. It is clear, nontoxic, and even has a pleasant smell.

The plant is indigenous only to the Sonora Desert region of North America—Mexico, California, and Arizona—though it is being grown experimentally in Israel, the Sudan, and Australia, among other locations. The trees grow to about 10 feet (3 meters) and begin to develop the valuable brown seeds after about five years; once a hearty tree has reached production capability, it continues yielding for up to two hundred years. Each seed consists of 40 to 60 percent oil, and up to 1,500 pounds (750 kilograms) of oil can be produced on an acre of land. A large male sperm whale can yield about 4 tons of oil, so roughly 5 acres (2 hectares) of productive land equals the yield of one sea mammal. While pursuing the whale is a speedier proposition than growing trees, jojoba cultivation seems to be more sensible in

The desert shrub jojoba (*Simmondsia chinensis*) produces seeds that contain valuable oil similar to the oil found in the head of the sperm whale. Left: a jojoba shrub. Right (top to bottom): male flowers, oil-containing seeds on the female bush, female flowers.

the long run when one considers that plants can be farmed while whales, like petroleum, cannot.

That jojoba thrives in deserts is yet another one of its valuable characteristics, since 15 percent of the world's land area is semiarid, and developing countries especially are extremely concerned about finding profitable crops for otherwise unproductive land. Jojoba can be harvested either manually or mechanically, and requires little attention during cultivation and virtually no pesticides or fertilizers.

Other experiments include the possible use of jojoba as livestock feed, as a source of otherwise difficult-to-synthesize chemicals and waxes, even as an appetite suppressant for use in human diet pills. Purposes for this plant seem so endless that the obvious question to ask is why, if it *is* so useful, has its cultivation not been encouraged earlier?

Professor D. Yermanos of the University of California, who is involved in jojoba research, attributes the rediscovery of jojoba to "a convergence of factors" that simply did not take place at earlier points in history. Chief among these was the targeted research of a group of scientists conscious of the need to develop new uses for tropical plants. "We are suddenly concerned with renewable resources, with a lack of water, with endangered species, with pollution, with droughts." In other words, if the time has indeed come for jojoba, it is because we have been pushed to it by environmental conditions. Ironically, this potential major new product of the twenty-first century is a simple desert acorn we might have been farming many years, and many whales, ago.

P.D.

HOT BRINES

In some parts of the ocean, at depths of more than a mile (1.6 kilometers), natural seawater fountains carry tons of minerals into the body of the sea, like spigots connected to the center of the earth. The water at some points is so hot it would boil easily if not for the extreme pressure. Explorers of these hot springs, or "thermal vents," report sightings of strange forms of sea life thriving on the periphery of some of the underwater geysers. They also report vast potential mineral wealth in manganese, iron, lead, and other important substances. The springs may be, in effect, bubbling pots of money. They suggest the future business of deep-sea mineral "farming." And nobody yet even knows how many vents there are.

Hot geysers under the sea were first noted in the Red Sea in the 1880s by Russian sailors who took water samples after noticing unusual temperature and salinity at some points. (Because of the high salinity, Red Sea vents are called "hot brines.") Over the years these observations were corroborated by French, Austrian, German, Swedish, and British research vessels. (In 1959, The Cousteau Society's *Calypso* also did bathymetry in the area, which revealed underwater tectonic activity presumably related to the hot brines.) In 1965 an American vessel, the *Atlantis II* from Woods Hole Oceanographic Institution in Massachusetts, sailed through the Red Sea on its way home from the Indian Ocean. The crew had hoped to collect samples from Discovery Deep, where in 1964 a British investigating team had noted high seawater temperature and salinity. But while the *Atlantis II* was lowering its sampling equipment, the vessel drifted over another, then undiscovered brine. The water was slightly shallower than that of Discovery Deep but hotter —133° F (56° C), compared with the 111° F (44° C) of Discovery Deep. Naming the new site Atlantis II Deep, the scientists set to work.

By comparing samples taken in various parts of the sea and analyzing temperature, salinity, and chemical composition, the *Atlantis II* team reasoned that the Red Sea brines had begun to form 20 million years ago, as the land masses of Africa and Arabia spread apart. This action cracked the earth's crust, releasing heat and gas that met ocean water. Very, very slowly the water began percolating down through the fractured ocean floor, acquiring metals and salts on the way through the "basement rock" that conducted it, migrating in a sense from one part of the Red Sea to another underground, a distance of about 600 miles (about 1,000 kilometers). Eventually, water traveling in this way rises up through the ocean floor again, either to be trapped in trenches like Discovery Deep and Atlantis II Deep or to be dispersed broadly along the seafloor as in the Pacific Ocean off Baja California and the Galápagos Islands. The ages of the vent systems vary, but Atlantis II Deep has been spewing for about 200,000 years, accumulating bottom sediment at a rate of about 2 inches (5 centimeters) per century. The deposit, a black tarlike ooze, contains no oxygen, so no oxidation of the minerals takes place. Consequently, there is reported to be 5,000 times more iron, 25,000 times more manganese, and 30,000 times more lead in Atlantis II's briny waters than in normal seawater, about $2 billion worth of minerals in just the top 30 feet (9.1 meters) of sediment alone—and the sediment may be over 300 feet (91 meters) thick in some areas. And though the vents that release the hot water into these trenches cannot be frequently visited, they are assumed to be constantly depositing new sediment.

Giant red tube worms (*Vestimentifera*) are members of a fantastic community of deep-sea creatures clustered around some mineral-rich thermal vents near the Galápagos Islands in the Pacific. Woods Hole Oceanographic Institution scientists, diving in the submersible *Alvin,* discovered the tube worms in 1979. (*Woods Hole Oceanographic Institution/Kathy Crane*)

At the other vent locations discovered off the Galápagos Islands and at the East Pacific Rise, off Baja California, the discharge of the vents does not accumulate so thickly but scatters across the more level ocean bottom. Here, too, the mineral deposits are highly concentrated and constantly replenishing. At these sites, scientists aboard another Woods Hole vessel, the submersible *Alvin,* discovered a narrow band—only 500 feet (152 meters) across—comprising over twenty-five geysers scattered along thousands of miles of sea. Unlike the Red Sea trenches, the open sea springs areas contain some oxygen and so the Pacific vents are rich with fantastic creatures which seem to thrive on the nutrients available at the edge of the boiling water spray—water so hot that it melted the *Alvin*'s thermometer and threatened its Plexiglas windows. Among these hot spring inhabitants were never-before-seen, brilliant red worms living in protective white tubes attached to rocks. A group of them looks like a head of hair set in curlers hung loosely from the scalp. The worms apparently eat and reproduce without ever leaving the tubes. They appear to have no eyespots, mouth, or digestive system. Other discoveries include 12-inch-long (30-centimeter) clams, foot-wide (30-centimeter) spiders, and unusual sorts of shrimps and crabs.

The abundance of this life in the total darkness of the depths is intriguing, since photosynthesis—the sun-fueled carbohydrate-producing process of plants along the surface of the planet—is impossible here. Scientists believe that the process of *chemo*synthesis takes place instead: Some bacteria produce organic matter using chemical energy liberated by the oxidation of certain sulfur compounds rising in the springs—life without sun. These bacteria sustain the various species of worms and other bottom life. Discovery of strange deep-water creatures and their unique adaptations was one of the most exciting oceanographic events of the 1970s, and pursuing the facts of their world will be one of the most fascinating research prospects of the 1980s.

This complex abyssal life system will need protection, too, especially in view of the commercial interests the hot springs have aroused. The geysers appear to be virtually inexhaustible sources of minerals for land-dwellers to cultivate.

As of early 1980, Saudi Arabia and the Sudan had set an example. These nations have joined in a cooperative venture to exploit the Red Sea brines that lie between their shores. With West German and French technical assistance, they have begun to study ways to recover the briny mineral sediment.

There could be many more vents in the sea, but until the perfection of new technology (see also "Tomography," page 34), finding their locations will be as much a matter of luck as scientific knowledge. And, in the absence of any binding Law of the Sea, the matter of ownership of hot spring wealth will require debate. Unless, that is, what has been quietly churning away for millennia, out of our sight and beyond our common experience, can, in our times, be considered a matter of common heritage. P.D.

MANGANESE NODULES

In 1876, the first ship devoted to oceanographic research returned from its three-year journey through the Atlantic, Pacific, and Antarctic oceans. Among the thousands of new specimens brought back by HMS *Challenger* were numbers of potato-sized reddish-black rocks that had been dredged up from the bottoms of all three oceans. No one was particularly interested in them, and for years they remained unnoticed in the British Museum.

As more was learned about the ocean, these black rocks became an object of study. They are almost wholly made up of hydrated oxides of iron and manganese, along with nickel, cobalt, and copper, the three most valuable components, as well as at least thirty-five other metals. These nodules are scattered across millions of acres of the ocean floor, usually far from any land. They seem to form directly on the ocean floor, where they lie in vast concentrations like oversized gravel.

Although no one knows exactly how manganese nodules are formed, they usually grow in rings around a "seed" of organic material—a piece of shell or a shark's tooth, for example. Scientists believe that the rate of growth of the nodules is exceedingly slow, like most processes at the bottom of the sea. However, sizable nodules have been found growing around spark plugs and shrapnel, which suggests that the metallic oxides can form much more quickly in some parts of the sea.

In 1959 a young graduate engineering student at the University of California, John Mero, wrote an imaginative paper on the benefits of mining these deep-sea nuggets. He estimated their commercial value, described the most likely sites, and suggested ways of mining them at a profit. By the

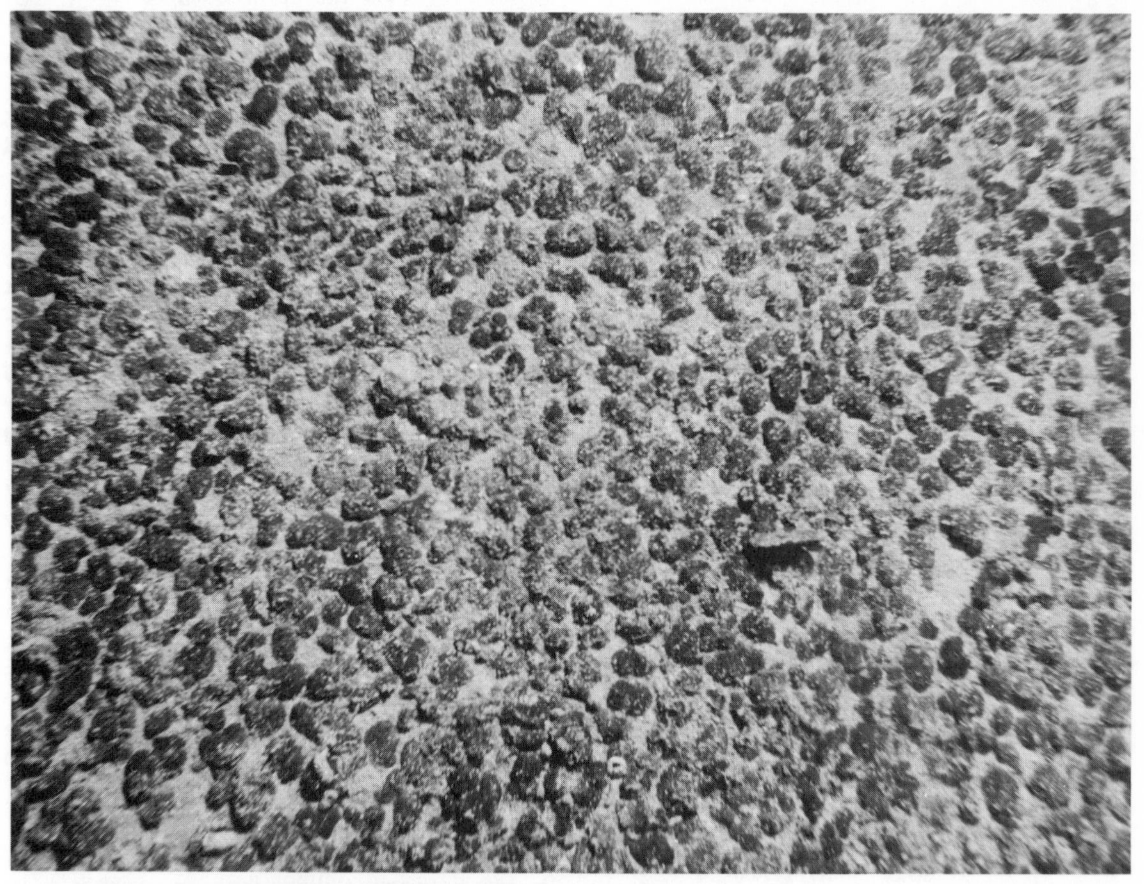

Mineral-filled manganese nodules coat the deep-sea bed in many areas. Discovery of the economic value of the potato-sized lumps has triggered international debate on how to divide the resource. (*Deepsea Ventures, Inc.*)

mid-1960s the prospect no longer seemed far-fetched, and by the late 1970s the nodules had spurred major investments in ocean mining by international consortia. They were also a main subject of contention at the Law of the Sea Conferences; the developing countries, arguing that the ocean is the heritage of all humanity, insisted on international regulations and profit-sharing, while the developed countries fought against such regulation (see "A Law of the Sea," page 568).

The Undersea Consequences

Mining the ocean floor is indeed technologically possible and likely to proceed in the years ahead. But along with the legal and political aspects there are environmental problems to be solved. Mining manganese nodules involves strip-mining the ocean floor. The amount of disruption will depend on the method used to collect the nodules. The continuous-line bucket method, for example, gouges the ocean bottom more than air or hydraulic lifts, which would "vacuum clean" the ocean floor. Self-propelled mining equipment may cut a swath in the ocean floor 36 inches (91 centimeters) wide by 18 inches (46 centimeters) deep. But a dredge head is hard to control from the surface, and its unwieldy sweep may haul in only 60 percent or so of the nodules in an area.

The U. S. Department of the Interior has suggested regulation to require that strips between dredged tracts be left intact so that the bottom can be recolonized by plants and animals from the areas left undredged.

The Plumes of Mud

No one knows the consequences of ocean mining on such a large scale. However, marine scientists have been able to make educated guesses. Their main concern is with the vast quantities of ocean-bottom sediment, sucked up with the nodules, that the mining ships will continually be dumping back into the sea. This dumping will create "plumes" of mud sinking in the wake of the ships.

The plumes will settle slowly, perhaps taking many years to reach the bottom again. Ocean currents will tend to spread the plumes over a wide area. If all the mining projects now envisioned are under way by the mid-1980s, by the end of this century several thousand square miles of the Pacific Ocean will be muddied by the plumes, according to the eminent Yale oceanographer Dr. Karl Turekian.

Other problems may arise. Nodule debris could be absorbed by fish, whales, and other marine life, with unknown results. Or the ocean-bottom sediment may include long-dormant spores or bacteria to which surface creatures have no immunity.

Scrambling Messages in the Sea

As the plume sinks, it will reduce the light filtering through the upper part of the ocean, affecting photosynthesis, the vital process through which plants convert carbon dioxide into oxygen. The plume could also interfere with communications underwater. And according to Dr. John Culliney, a marine biologist who has worked at the Woods Hole Marine Biological Laboratory, the sediment plume may hurt the already endangered whale population by absorbing, scattering, and reflecting their calls to each other. Ironically, there is speculation that the plumes could also interfere with guided missiles suspected of being implanted in the seabed by the U.S. military. If they exist, such missiles are likely to be controlled by sonic signals.

When the sediment plume finally reaches the bottom of the ocean again, it will smother most life forms, according to a study by the Lamont-Doherty Geological Observatory of Columbia University. Since the cycles of sexual maturity and reproduction of abyssal animal species are extremely slow, destruction of life by the falling sediment could render the deep ocean dead for years. Tampering with the ocean bottom could therefore prove reckless, since so little is currently known about the region.

Lastly, the environmental problems continue on land, where the nodule material will be processed and waste discarded. Nickel refining in particular produces toxic emissions, which in some areas near nickel plants have killed almost all trees.

Obviously it will be some time before mining manganese nodules makes environmental and economic sense, but possibly, long before that, the undersea gold rushes will have begun.

J.S., D.W., J.B.

STRATEGIC LUMPS

The most important components of manganese nodules are actually copper, nickel, and cobalt, which make up about 3 percent of the nodules' bulk. Manganese, another potentially important component, is found on land in great supply in various countries around the world, although none has been found in the United States.

Copper, used since antiquity, is the workhorse of the electrical industry because of its excellent conductivity.

Nickel, named for the Devil ("Old Nick"), who supposedly made it so difficult to work with, is used almost entirely in the production of stainless steel and other alloys. It is a strategic metal, included in a wide range of industrial products necessary for civilian and military use.

Cobalt is an ironlike magnetic metal often found with iron and nickel. Its principal uses are in permanent magnets and in heat-resistant, high-strength materials. Jet engines, for example, are made from superalloys that contain as much as 65 percent cobalt.

Manganese is an essential element since it lends steel malleability and durability.

According to a 1979 United States Bureau of Mines estimate, world demand projected to the year 2000 will require the consumption of 83 percent of the presently known world cobalt reserve, 62 percent of the proven world reserve of copper, and 45 percent of the proven world reserve of nickel. The bureau predicts that there will be an adequate supply of manganese by 2000, but it will be highly concentrated in politically "unstable" parts of the world. Most of the reserves of manganese that are not in Eastern Bloc countries are in Africa. For example, a revolution in Zaire, a major supplier of cobalt, forced the price of the metal to skyrocket from $6 per pound ($13 per kilogram) in 1977 to $50 per pound ($110 per kilogram) in 1978. While the price dropped back to $25 per pound ($55 per kilogram) in 1979, there could well be further disruptions in production. Industries using strategic metals might need alternative sources, such as deep-ocean mining.

J.B., J.S.

FIVE BILLION PEOPLE

Editor's Note: *Since it became universally recognized as a serious human problem during the 1960s, the rapid growth of population has fascinated anyone who attempted to project the world of the future. Some observers have gone to bizarre extremes in an attempt to shock—calculating how long it would take humanity's total weight to surpass that of the earth, painting scenes of wretched masses shoulder to shoulder across the continents. Despite these impossible fantasies, population growth is a sobering, exponentially multiplying phenomenon that promises to change the nature of life on earth if not dramatically slowed soon. According to most experts the total world population may reach five billion in 1987. We asked the staff of the Population Reference Bureau in Washington, D.C., to provide the* Almanac *with some perspective on this international problem. Their contributions include the following article, a wealth of statistics* *(see "A Global Census," page 97)**, and some profiles of nations with special population situations* *(see "An Unconventional World Tour," page 63)*.

For more than 99 percent of their time on earth, humans have lived solely as hunter-gatherers. During these long unrecorded ages, the "population problem" was one of simple survival and constant struggle against exposure, wild animals, famine, and disease.

About ten thousand years ago, the first farmers began tilling the land. Farming yielded a far more reliable source of food than hunting or gathering. The small human population began to grow at a quicker pace.

The Great Health Shift

The Industrial Revolution was another great landmark for population growth. It led to improved living standards, including better nutrition, sanitation, clothing, and housing. Later came inoculation against disease, better hospitals, and more advanced health care. During the eighteenth and nineteenth centuries, the mortality rate in Western Europe declined dramatically but the fertility rate remained high—the legacy of centuries when most children did not survive.

With mortality low and fertility high, the population of Western Europe began to surge. The cities grew rapidly as farms were mechanized; family farms, now needing less labor, could not support the larger number of children who survived.

A massive migration to the New World took some of the pressure off Europe's burgeoning cities. And, about 1830, humanity reached the billion mark for the first time.

The Great Family Shift

About sixty years after mortality began to decline in most of Western Europe, fertility also began to drop. Farmers traditionally wanted large families because children helped with the chores, but more and more people now lived in the crowded cities, where children were not the economic asset they were on a farm. By the twentieth century, Europe had completed its two-century shift from high fertility and high mortality to low fertility and low mortality.

The Fifth Billion

Today, the world's population is growing at an awesome rate: 337,000 babies are born every day; 200,000 survive. There are seventy-five people for every square mile of land on earth (twenty-nine per square kilometer). By 1987, if present trends continue, there will be five billion people sharing the same water, air, and land that two billion shared in 1930.

Fertility in most countries in the world is higher today than it was in Western Europe at the time of the Industrial Revolution. The post–World War II decline in mortality in most developing countries has occurred with dramatic suddenness, over a few decades. Unlike the European experience, it is the result of technology rather than economic development—bringing to developing countries sanitation, antibiotics, immunization, insecticides, and campaigns against such major killers as malaria and smallpox. There has been little time for these countries to show the expected response of reducing family size.

With plunging death rates and continued high birth rates, the populations of the developing countries have mushroomed. Although they constitute three fourths of the world's population, developing countries now produce some *90 percent* of current growth. In some countries, populations have doubled in the last twenty to thirty years, wiping out gains from agricultural, educational, and industrial development. Many of these countries, hard-pressed to care for their current citizenry, are projected to double their populations again by the end of this century.

Shantytowns are one result of a burgeoning population. (*EPA Documerica/John Vachon*)

Some Rays of Hope

In developing countries, many women would bear fewer children if they had the knowledge and the means, and if it were culturally acceptable to do so. "Imported" birth-control programs, however, are not the whole answer; studies show that such programs persuade only about 20 to 30 percent of the women in developing countries to become "accepters."

Contraceptive technology is most effective when combined with social change. A recent report on ninety-four developing countries found that while the strength of a nation's family-planning effort was the single most important variable, fertility declined fastest in those countries that also had the greatest socioeconomic development. The most important changes are:

- an increase in school enrollment rates, especially for girls;
- an increase in literacy;
- a decrease in the percentage of females working in agriculture;
- an improvement in life expectancy;

- a reduction of infant mortality;
- an increase in urbanization;
- an increase in per capita gross national product (GNP).

But social changes take time, and time is running short. It took all of human history for world population to reach one billion (in 1830). The second billion took only one hundred years. The third billion took only thirty years, and when in 1975 we reached the four-billion mark, only fifteen years had elapsed. If the fifth billion has been reached as early as 1987, the elapsed time will have been cut to twelve years.

Although there has been a slight downturn in the rate of world growth, the population is so huge (4,470,944,000 in mid-1981) that the 80 million annual increase in 1981 is projected to become an annual increase of 97 million by the year 2000. In numbers only, that is the equivalent of adding more than five new Tokyos to the planet every year!

Such projections are based on the assumption that the basic energy, food, and other natural resources required to support human life will be as available in the future as they have been in the past; in many areas, however, populations are already outgrowing the biological systems they depend on. The implications of the population growth problem touch upon virtually every other environmental issue. Nothing but the specter of war looms so large as a potential threat to the well-being of humanity—and population expansion exerts pressures that could lead to future wars as more people demand more space, more food, more natural resources. No other human environmental issue warrants more attention in the future.

P.R.B.

ELEVEN WAYS OF LOOKING AT ONE BILLION

Editor's Note: *After the world's human population reached four billion in 1975, the following article by Joan Beck appeared in the Chicago* Tribune. *We reprint it here since the number "one billion" can best be comprehended in terms of concrete examples.*

- One billion people is 306 Chicagos—with all of Chicago's need for food, water, electricity, shelter, sewers, jobs, schools, transportation.
- One billion people is more than four times everyone in the United States.
- One billion people is more than all the French in France, the Italians in Italy, the Mexicans in Mexico, the English in England, the Germans in East and West Germany, the Japanese in Japan, and the Indians in India—all together.
- One billion people are all there were on earth in 1830, and it took all the eons in history before the nineteenth century to reach that total.
- One billion people lined up side by side would stretch 568,181 miles (914,203 kilometers).
- One billion people need 875 trillion calories of food each year.
- One billion people should have 1,627,550 doctors if their level of medical care were to equal that in the United States. Yet medical treatment is still inadequate over most of the globe and millions of people now live and die without ever seeing a physician.
- One billion people need 10,169,550 teachers if they are to have the kind of education Americans get now. Yet because of population increases, the number of illiterate adults already is growing, even though the percentage of those who cannot read and write has dropped by half since 1920.
- One billion people would use an average of 150 billion to 200 billion gallons (570 billion to 760 billion liters) of water each day, if their personal and industrial consumption matched that in the United States. Yet water already is in critically short supply in many places in the world and nonreplenishable ground reserves are being used up in worrisome amounts. (See "Not a Drop to Drink," page 616.)
- Electronic population counters tick off an increase in human beings at the rate of about 4 persons every second, almost 200,000 more of us each day. Already, we are a New Mexico bigger than we were five days ago. A year from now, we'll have as many more people as now live in California, New York, Illinois, Indiana, Michigan, Massachusetts, and Ohio. The world will have grown by 264 people in the two minutes it takes to read this column.

SOURCE: By Joan Beck, copyrighted © Chicago *Tribune*.

CERT

For more than a hundred years, many Native Americans have been relegated to barren land that whites didn't want because they thought it valueless. For the most part, reservation land was too dry, too rocky, or too remote to provide resources with which the Native Americans who received it could achieve social or economic standing in the society that developed on richer land around them.

Ironically, Native American lands, which are so poor along the surface, have turned out to be immensely rich beneath. They contain a wealth of coal, uranium, oil, and natural gas that has dramatically changed the position of several reservation tribes.

In an effort to translate these newfound riches into political clout, about twenty-five tribes from the Colvilles in Washington State to the Pueblo of Lagunas in New Mexico formed the Council of Energy Resource Tribes (CERT) in 1976. The goal of the group, often referred to as the "Indian OPEC," is to make certain the Native Americans get their fair share of the mineral revenues and have a say in land reclamation, worker safety, and development around mining areas.

The most plentiful CERT mineral resource is uranium: the tribes hold between *25 and 50 percent* of all uranium in the United States. Their lands also contain about 30 percent of the low-sulfur strippable coal and about 2 percent of all U.S. oil and natural gas.

Before CERT, the U.S. government, which holds title to all Native American lands and acts as a trustee, negotiated leases with mining companies that did not necessarily benefit the Native Americans. Most of the mining contracts set a fixed price per ton and gave mining rights "in perpetuity," thus neither the government nor the Native Americans benefited from the rising market price of fuels. Although many Native Americans were given jobs in mines, even these opportunities were of dubious benefit. Tribes complained of radiation-related illnesses and deaths among workers, despoliation of crop and grazing land from the mining, milling, and disposal of radioactive uranium. Among the Navaho, at least twenty-five deaths have been reported from lung cancer and radiation exposure at the Shiprock, New Mexico, uranium mine, where the Kerr-McGee Corporation began mining in the 1950s.

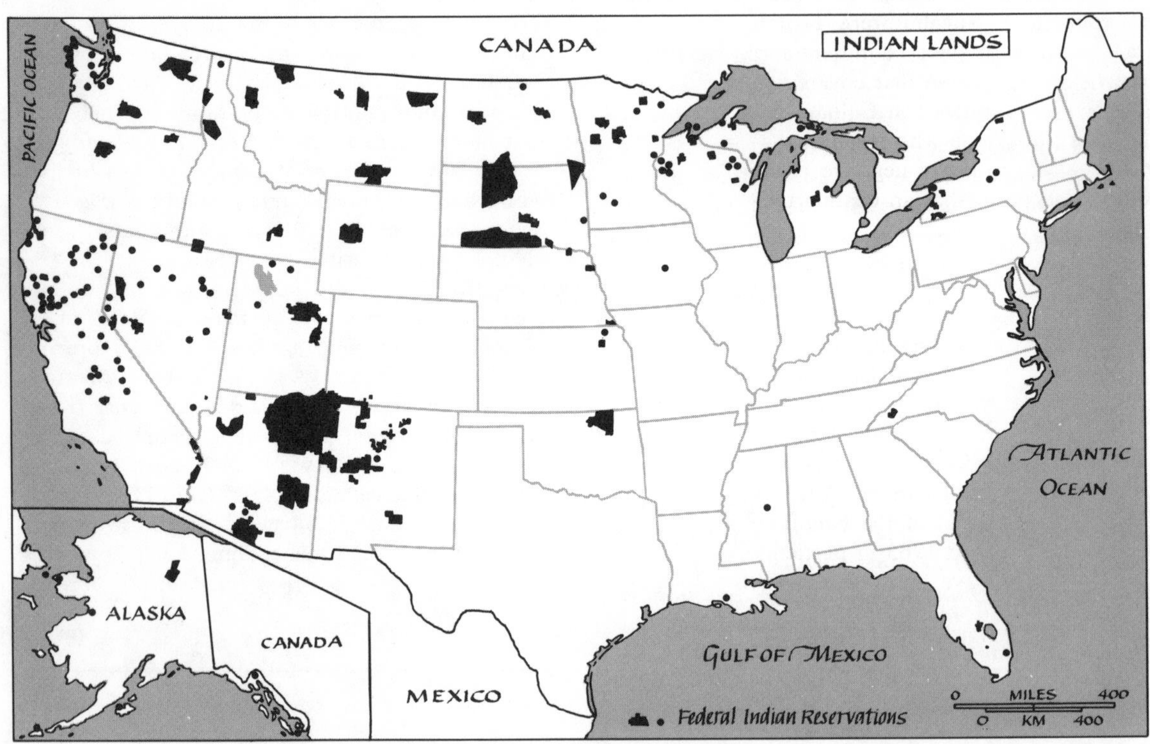

Many Native American lands, though poor along the surface, contain deposits of coal, oil, uranium, or natural gas.

And the energy produced by the exploitation of Native American resources has not often found its way back to the reservation. Many Native American power-plant and mine workers still go home to houses without electricity.

In an attempt to change the situation, CERT, headed by Peter MacDonald, a flamboyant Navaho, hired tough, experienced negotiators to deal with the oil and mineral companies. They included Ahmed Kooros, Iran's former deputy minister for finance and oil, and Charles Lipton, who formerly bargained mineral leases in the international market. MacDonald described CERT tactics: "We said to the companies, 'If you are going to get the coal, you're not going to deal just with the Crow or just with the Navaho or just with the Cheyenne. You've got to deal with the rest of us.' "

So CERT insists on no more perpetuity mining leases, percentage royalties on the mineral yield, a share of the profits, and a say in such issues as land reclamation and the safety of workers. In addition to negotiating leases, CERT has planned educational programs with several western universities to prepare Native Americans for skilled mining jobs that have traditionally gone to whites in engineering, environmental studies, and economics. The organization has helped some tribes obtain financing for their own mining, refining, or power-plant projects. In 1980, for example, MacDonald's Navaho were planning to build a power plant for their 14-million-acre (5.7-million-hectare) reservation that covers parts of Arizona, New Mexico, Utah, and Colorado.

There are those who feel this newfound muscle will have long-range negative effects for the Native Americans, that an obstinate CERT demanding higher prices may trigger a backlash from the government and the public resulting in government takeover of Native American lands.

MacDonald's energy policies have even brought him problems among his own people. In 1978, seven demonstrators known as the Windowrock Seven took over the Navaho Tribal Administration offices in protest of strip-mining projects on tribal lands. Some tribes have initiated lawsuits to stop the mining. Those who have seen the destruction to land and human health that can come from mining, those who are concerned with the depletion of resources on what little land they have, and those who consider that the land has religious sanctity—not to be desecrated in any manner—have other ideas about what should be done.

For example, the 500,000-acre (200,000-hectare) Northern Cheyenne Indian Reservation in Montana contains 23 billion tons of coal, 5 billion tons of which could be mined economically; but the Native Americans there hope to prevent Montana Power Company from developing it. In spite of their high unemployment and low per capita income of $1,700 a year (the 1978 U.S. national per capita income was $7,836), the Cheyenne think clean air and water are more important than coal revenues. They also fear becoming a minority on their own reservation because of an influx of white workers.

Where there are such objections, CERT has backed off, not forcing tribes to exploit their resources. But for tribes interested in development, CERT contends with the big oil and mining companies, the eastern banks, and the Washington bureaucracy.

A.L.

CHANGING CLIMATE

Since the beginning of the twentieth century, the world population has more than tripled. While most of the phenomenal growth is attributed to modern medicine, better famine relief, and more sanitary living conditions, one factor is usually ignored. There has been more food because, during most of the twentieth century, and between 1935 and 1965 in particular, the farmers of the world have enjoyed a uniquely favorable warm, wet, and stable climate.

We have taken this unusual climate for granted. The changes that do come are often so gradual that only a very old person, thinking back to childhood, can recall how things were different. For example, in the 1800s many rivers that are now ice-free all year froze over every winter. During the "little ice age" from about 1600 to 1880, Europe had much harsher winters than at present. Glaciers advanced, some rivers froze solid, and other areas became too cold for agriculture. On the other hand, old documents from China indicate that about 3,000 to 5,000 years ago the climate was significantly warmer than it is now.

When the global climate fluctuates only a few degrees, it can transform the agriculture of a country. To use a common example, it is said that if the world climate were an average of less than 2° F (1.1° C) colder, Canadian farmers could not grow wheat. In general, the warmer the climate, the easier it is to farm. Rains tend to be more reliable, harvests are better, and arable lands spread north and south toward the poles.

In terms of geological time, we actually are living in a "brief" intermission—an interglacial period between the last "ice age" 10,000 years ago and the next one. (These relatively warm interglacial periods rarely last longer than 10,000 to 20,000 years.) Our entire human civilization has developed within the short space of this particular interglacial period.

There is a great deal of speculation as to whether we will enter another "little ice age." Since the late 1940s, world temperatures have become slightly colder, leading some scientists to conclude that our most recent period of fair weather is nearing an end. Because human activity can now be a significant factor in the environment, many scientists believe that we contribute to the changing global climate. Some of our activities seem to be warming the climate, while others seem to do the opposite, leaving scientists in a quandary over predicting future trends.

Humans can affect atmospheric conditions in several important ways, but the consequences are by no means certain. First, overall human actions, like cutting forests, damming rivers, and building large cities, often have changed the local climate. The climate of New York City is about 5° F (2.8° C) warmer than the climate of nearby rural areas. In cities, cement and bricks trap heat and there are few open, grassy areas, which are usually cooler. Deforested areas, too, can have a microclimate quite different from those of similar areas with trees. In the Copper Basin region of southeastern Tennessee, for example, copper-smelting fumes killed all the trees in an area of almost 250,000 acres (100,000 hectares). In the inner part of this desert no vegetation whatsoever survived. In the outer part some grass was retained. A four-year survey of rainfall on the bare area, the grassy area, and a nearby forested area showed that 12 percent less rain fell on the bare area, and 8 percent less on the grassy area, than fell on the forest.

Other activities may be cooling the climate. When particulate material is added to the atmosphere—for example, ash or particulate matter from factories or automobiles—energy from the sun is reflected back and does not reach the earth's surface. Dust and volcanic ash have the same effect. Since 1955, volcanic activity has increased. Some climatologists attribute the cooling trend of world temperatures, a trend which is supposed to have begun in the late 1940s and apparently continues, to a combination of volcanic activity and increased industrial pollution.

Also, the burning of fossil fuels, especially coal and its derivatives, may be warming the global climate. At present levels of consumption of fossil fuels, 11 to 13 million pounds (5 to 6 million kilograms) of carbon particulates are released into the atmosphere each year. The carbon is then oxidized, producing carbon dioxide (CO_2). The oceans and the atmosphere can absorb some carbon dioxide but no one really knows how much.

Since the Industrial Revolution, the levels of carbon dioxide in the atmosphere have risen steadily all over the world. Since 1958, a remote monitoring station on the slopes of Mauna Loa in Hawaii has recorded a steady rise in carbon dioxide levels from 314 parts per million to 335 ppm. Similar rises in carbon dioxide have been recorded in other locations worldwide. Some scientists estimate that atmospheric carbon dioxide may double within the next fifty years.

The significance of an increase in atmospheric carbon dioxide is that carbon dioxide plays a key role in the "greenhouse effect" that keeps the earth warm. Like the glass roof of a greenhouse, carbon dioxide and water vapor in the earth's atmosphere tend to hold in long-wave solar radiation, raising global temperatures because of this back-radiation.

The atmosphere stabilizes what would otherwise be very wide and abrupt changes of temperature, and the greenhouse effect sends more than twice as much radiation back to the earth as is absorbed originally. The well-documented increase in carbon dioxide levels, therefore, may accelerate the greenhouse effect, resulting in warmer global temperatures.

While the ultimate results are unclear, most scientists agree that a global warming is likely if we continue to burn fossil fuels at the current rate. In July 1979, four prominent scientists reported to the United States Council on Environmental Quality (CEQ):

> Man is setting in motion a series of events that seem certain to cause a significant warming of world climates over the next decades unless mitigating steps are taken immediately. The cause is the accumulation of carbon dioxide and other heat-absorbing gases in the atmosphere.

It has been estimated that the average global

temperature could rise as much as 6° F (3.3° C) in fifty years. This warming could mean, according to the CEQ, that "climatic zones will shift, and agriculture will be displaced." Other scientists have even warned that ice covering the North Pole might melt, raising the sea level and inundating coastlines and low-lying coastal cities.

While world temperatures have actually declined, on the average, in the last thirty years, scientists who fear the accelerating greenhouse effect say that the warming of the atmosphere will not be felt for several decades. By then, they warn, it may be too late to reverse the trend. It is possible for carbon dioxide to remain in the atmosphere for as long as a thousand years.

There is obviously a disagreement in the scientific community between those who emphasize that temperatures are declining and those who predict that temperatures will rise. Some scientists even manage to agree with both sides: the world is certainly entering a colder long-term period, they say, but luckily the greenhouse effect of increased carbon dioxide may counteract it and keep us comfortably warm—at least, perhaps, for the near future.

The controversy points up the fact that much is still unknown. Most scientists, however, do agree on one thing. The world climate appears to be entering a period of greater variability. We can no longer count on a fair, predictable climate like that of the past decades.

P.E.W., J.S.

KARAKORAM HIGHWAY

Alas! Behold! How steep! How high!
The road to Shu is hard,
harder than climbing to the sky!
. . . There were landslides, mountains destroyed—
strong young men died
hanging up bridges of stone
and ladders to the sky . . .

Li Po (c. 701–62)

The new Karakoram Highway between Pakistan and China, opened in June 1979, may bring vast changes to "the roof of the world"—the high mountain ranges extending from the Karakoram to the Himalayas. The tribes of Hunza, Chitral, Swat, and other remote regions are now connected by an all-weather highway to the governing centers of Pakistan and to outside influences.

There are few routes from China to Pakistan or India; the highest mountains in the world stand between. But for thousands of years traders made their way through treacherous passes and steep valleys to buy and sell silk, tea, and porcelain from China, gold, ivory, spices, and jewels from the south. The caravans were prey to robbers along the way, but the profits of trade were so high that over the centuries the routes remained well traveled. The first known caravan from China traversed the route of the present highway as early as 53 B.C. Even before that, the army of Alexander the Great supposedly crossed the Karakoram range to conquer northern India; many tribespeople there claim to be descended partly from Greeks who settled in the mountains after the death of Alexander. Genghis Khan traveled in the Karakorams, and so did the Moguls on their way to conquer India. Marco Polo came along the route. Chinese camel caravans continued to travel south along the path of the present highway until 1949, when the border between China and Pakistan was officially closed after the Chinese revolution. The tribes who lived in the northern mountains resisted the forces of the British Empire and later those of Pakistan. Eventually, however, Pakistan asserted its rule over the Karakoram region.

The new highway negotiates some of the highest mountains in the world. The peak K-2, which is only about 1,000 feet (about 300 meters) lower than Mount Everest, is in the Karakorams, along with Nānga Parbat, Gasherbrum, Rakaposhi, and other summits known to all mountaineers. The region is marked by precipitous hillsides terraced for wheat, villages clustered along rushing streams, deep gorges and towering peaks. The ancient caravans often picked their way across swinging rope bridges, with drops of thousands of feet; in certain otherwise inaccessible places, travelers walked gingerly on wood scaffoldings braced into holes in the cliffs.

By 1959, the government of Pakistan had decided to build a road that would connect its remotest regions to the central part of the country. The motivation for building the road was

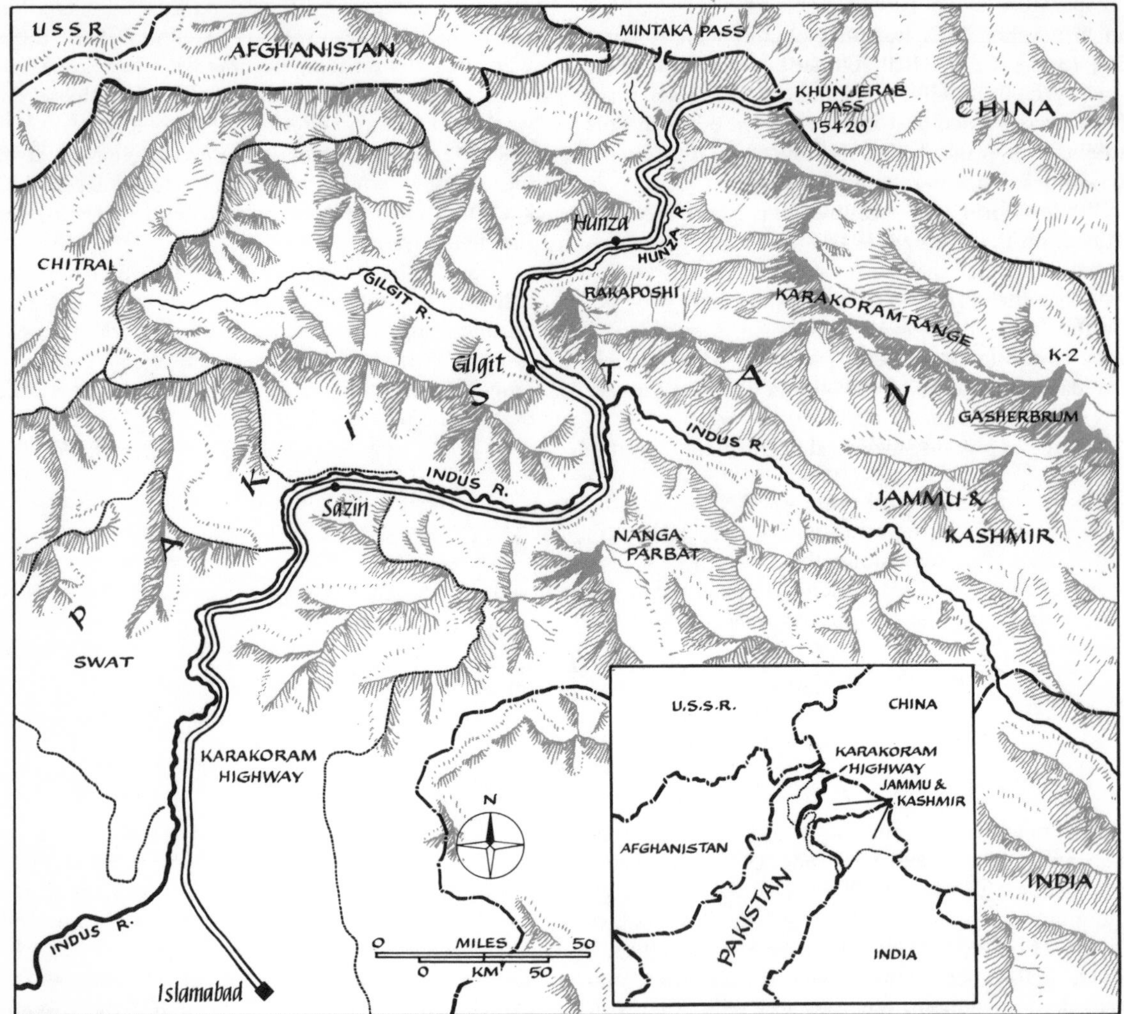

largely strategic and partly economic. The road would allow the distant tribes, who formerly could be reached only after days of arduous travel on foot or by camel, to sell their produce—apples, apricots, and peaches—for better prices in the lowlands, while reducing the high cost of goods from outside the region. However, an even more important consideration was that both India and Afghanistan had laid claim to disputed areas of northern Pakistan, where the highway now runs.

The Pakistani army therefore began drilling and blasting to lay out through the mountains an all-weather road that could be traversed by heavy buses, trucks, and even tanks. In 1964, the Chinese became interested in the project, partly because of their escalating disagreements with the Soviet Union. China shares the longest border in the world with the Soviets; to its south lies another enemy, Vietnam, and the long, high barrier of the Himalayas. A road through the Karakoram range would leave China a southern route to the ocean even if the Soviet Union could blockade all Chinese ports. It would also provide a means of keeping watch on Afghanistan and a link with friendly Pakistan, with whom China shares a common distrust of India.

Twenty-five thousand Chinese and Pakistanis worked together to build the 500-mile-long (800-kilometer) highway that has now replaced the old "Silk Route" of the caravans. Engineers who worked on it consider that no other road has ever been so difficult to build. In one place the road had to be built directly over three glaciers. More than five hundred road workers died in landslides, avalanches, earthquakes, and fights with local tribespeople who often feared the road, resented the many outsiders, or felt they had been cheated out of the land the road was built on. The main danger on the road, however, was and continues to be that it was carved and blasted out of steep, relatively unstable mountainsides at heights of up to 18,000 feet (5,490 meters) above sea level. Every rainfall and every dynamite blast results in some subsidence, and the Pakistanis predict that landslides will continue to endanger travelers on the road for at least a decade.

The opening of the road has brought in money and goods to the Karakoram region on an unprecedented scale. Chinese and Pakistani road workers introduced medical care to the area; for a while, before they were withdrawn at the request of the Pakistan government. Chinese women workers on the road shocked the devout Muslims of the Karakoram with their unveiled faces and their integration with men at the worksites. In some areas along the road, new schools, hotels, clinics, and small factories have opened up —including at least one school for girls, in Hunza.

The trade between China and Pakistan is certain to increase as the road stabilizes. Soon tourists will rival the local and military traffic along the highway. Mountain climbers will have an easier time getting to the mountains, and guides will lead tours through the picturesque streets of once-remote villages, bringing the usual boons and banes of tourism (see "Tourist Detractions," page 712). As there are rubies, iron, mica, sulfur, and other minerals in the Karakoram, it will not be long before mines are built and exploited there, too.

It is hard to judge yet whether the changes caused by the road are for the better or the worse. There are obvious military implications in a region growing increasingly volatile, and there are environmental impacts to be expected, since a roadway into any wilderness is a wedge by which technology penetrates natural systems. Erosion of the Himalayas, for example, is likely to increase (see "The Himalayas," page 189), but the extent of the problem is not obvious yet. Whatever the outcome, the Karakoram Highway is probably the most important single development in the long history of the roof of the world. J.S.

OTEC

Every day the sun's energy warms the surface of the earth, of which about 71 percent is covered by water. The oceans function as a giant solar collector, naturally absorbing and storing this energy. While the surface water warms, the deeper water remains cool, creating a significant temperature difference—in tropical seas the difference between the surface and depths of 3,000 feet (915 meters) is about 45° F (25° C). Year after year the oceans maintain their average temperature, making this thermal gradient relatively constant throughout the world. With a fairly simple turbine generator system, this gradient could be made to produce electricity. In fact proponents project that by the year 2000, Ocean Thermal Energy Conversion, or OTEC, may be able to give us even more electricity than we need.

This is not a new idea. A century ago French scientist Jacques d'Arsonval proposed a system of deriving energy from ocean thermal gradients. As early as 1929, the engineering concept behind OTEC was tried and proven when Georges Claude constructed the first OTEC plant off the coast of Cuba. He was able to generate a 22-kilowatt power output before a hurricane destroyed part of his apparatus. Claude's work was ahead of its time and his invention faded into obscurity. However, in the past few years, as the world has faced serious fossil-fuel shortages, OTEC has resurfaced. Japan, the United States, and a number of Western European and developing countries—all seeking new technology to limit dependence on imported oil—have conducted research, held conferences, and, in some cases, constructed working models of OTEC plants.

The most popular OTEC design circulates a "working fluid," a substance such as ammonia or propane that has a very low boiling point, in a huge closed system of underwater pipes to turn a turbine. Ammonia, for example, has such a low boiling point that it vaporizes when brought into contact with warm, surface water and condenses when exposed to cold water from the ocean depths. In an OTEC plant, surface water flows through a pipe that comes in contact with an evaporator chamber filled with ammonia. The water and ammonia do not mix, but the water's heat is transferred to the chamber, evaporating the ammonia. Ammonia gas rises through a pipe and turns a turbine. On the other side of the turbine the gas flows into a condenser chamber. This

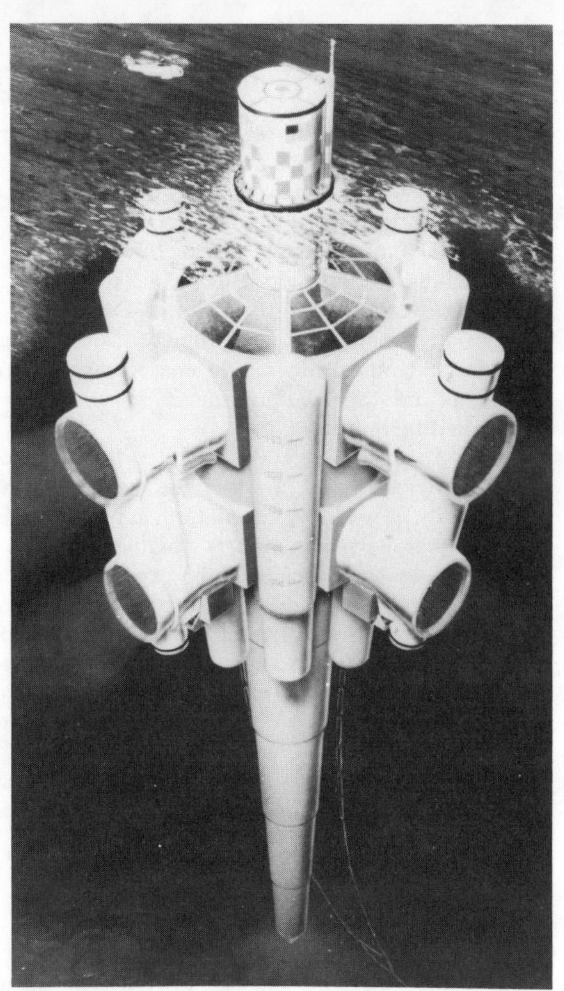

chamber is in contact with another pipe bringing cold water from deeper in the sea. The ammonia is reconverted to a liquid, flows back into the evaporator, and the cycle begins again.

In the United States, three major contractors—Lockheed, TRW, and Westinghouse—are building model OTEC plants. The U. S. Department of Energy, which committed $35 million to OTEC research in 1978, projects the first commercial plant will be operational in the mid-1980s or early 1990s, supplying 400 megawatts of power, enough for a hundred thousand average homes.

An analysis of the energy needed to build and maintain an OTEC plant and pipe the energy to shore through submerged cables, suggests that OTEC is more efficient than nuclear or fossil-fuel power plants. An OTEC plant requires 700 calories of energy to make 1,000 calories available for use, whereas nuclear and fossil-fuel plants require about 3,500 calories to produce 1,000 usable calories of energy.

Artist's concept of an OTEC system, 1,600 feet (480 meters) long and 250 feet (75 meters) in diameter, with turbine generators and pumps attached around the outside. Crews' quarters and maintenance facilities are housed in the surface platform. (*Lockheed Missiles and Space Co./Courtesy DOE*)

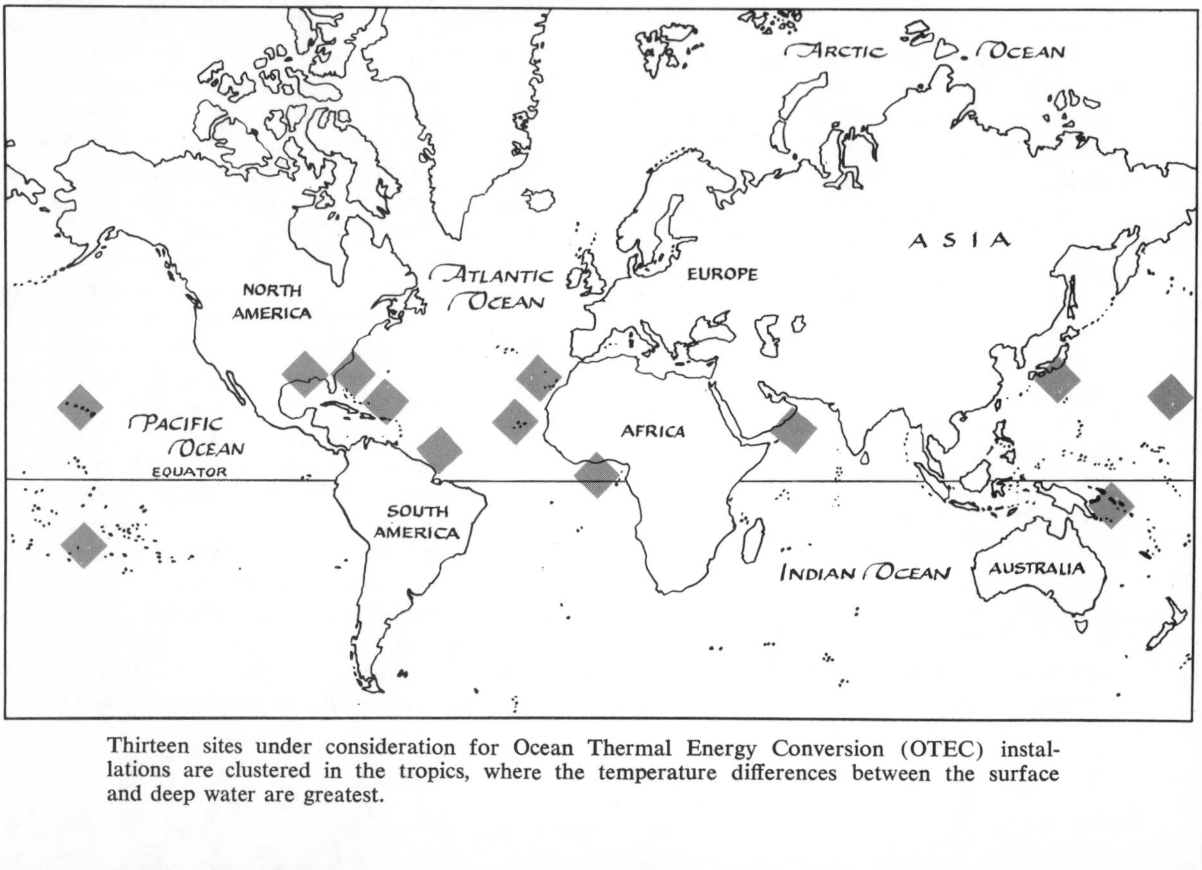

Thirteen sites under consideration for Ocean Thermal Energy Conversion (OTEC) installations are clustered in the tropics, where the temperature differences between the surface and deep water are greatest.

The best sites for OTEC plants are within twenty latitudinal degrees of the equator, where surface waters are warmest; however, power can be generated where the difference in the temperature between surface and bottom waters is as small as 27° F (15° C).

Like an iceberg, an OTEC plant would be largely submerged with only a platform or tower visible on the surface. Designs for the plants would draw on those developed for offshore oil rigs.

Even though OTEC is a very promising energy source, it is not without environmental effects. These are being studied. An ammonia spill could poison marine life in the vicinity, but ammonia is biodegradable and is a nutrient in low concentrations. Fouling ocean organisms, such as barnacles, are likely to enter the workings of the OTEC plant, but any substance used to clean away these organisms would probably affect nearby marine life when flushed into the sea.

The most significant environmental impact under study is the effect of moving large quantities of deep ocean water nearer the surface. Scientists think it would change patterns of ocean life in the immediate area, but perhaps for the better. Areas of natural upwellings of cold, nutrient-rich bottom water are usually very productive. Researchers suggest that the OTEC plants might be good sites for mariculture. Tampering with water temperature is, however, a very serious matter. Marine life is especially sensitive to temperature changes. Should an OTEC plant shut down for cleaning or repair after a new biota had adapted to its flow of cool water, the community could be damaged or destroyed. Perhaps the most serious danger, however, is the possibility that if OTEC plants were to proliferate about the world, resultant water temperature changes could alter the world's weather. While the possibility seems remote, it must be considered before widespread OTEC use is contemplated.

The first model OTEC plant, "Mini-OTEC," began operating off the coast of Hawaii on August 3, 1979, using an open system similar to Claude's ill-fated plant. Other experimental plants were scheduled to begin operation in 1980.

If OTEC proves commercially successful, in twenty years we may be lighting some of our homes and running trains and industries on electricity from the sea.

L.W., M.P.

WINDSHIPS

In recreational boating circles there is a longstanding animosity between the ragmen (sailors) and stink potters (power boaters). Ragmen deplore the noise, smell, and speed of power boats, while stink potters claim that sailboats are constantly tacking into their paths. As fuel prices soared over the past few years, ragmen scored a point while gliding past a power boat owner paying the bill at the fuel dock.

In the late 1970s, the same escalation of marine fuel prices caused a number of ship designers around the world to rethink the potential of commercial wind power; a 1979 symposium in London on the topic, organized by the Royal Institute of Naval Architects, attracted 150 leading shipping figures. A Japanese company is testing a prototype sailing freighter, and the U.S. government is funding a study of commercial sailing. And The Cousteau Society is researching various designs with the goal of replacing the research vessel *Calypso* with an oceanographic ship partially powered by the wind.

Push-Button Sailing

Wind, of course, powered the world's commercial fleets until the steam engine (later replaced by the diesel) took over in the early 1900s. Commercial sailing ships evolved from the tubby square-riggers of the sixteenth century to the sleek, swift clipper ships of the nineteenth century that could cross the Atlantic from New England to Europe in as little as twelve to fifteen days (although their average was closer to twenty-four days). As shipbuilders tentatively installed steam engines, they kept the sails, just in case; but as marine engines were perfected, the sails gradually disappeared, old sailors retired, and the age of sail faded to a romantic memory.

The new breed of commercial sailing-ship designers see no need for crew members to climb the rigging to set the topsail or haul on the halyards to the tune of sea chanties. Sails can be raised and set by push-button power winches. Computerized instruments tuned to satellites aid in navigation, weather monitoring, and ship-to-shore communication. And the diesel engine remains in place. With modern aerodynamically efficient rigs and well-designed hulls, a real fuel-saving synergy can be achieved in light air—a wind of 1–3 miles (1.6–4.8 kilometers) per hour —by motor-sailing as opposed to motoring alone or sailing alone.

The boost in fuel efficiency could be phenomenal. Predictions range from a 10-percent savings during tests on the Japanese prototype vessel to the possibility of 85-percent savings projected for a modern motor-sailing cargo ship equipped with a fore-and-aft boomless rig designed by Frank MacLear of New York. In 1979 ocean shipping consumed *four million barrels* of oil per day, according to Massachusetts naval architect Lloyd Bergeson. Bergeson considers that a savings of 20 percent in consumption of fossil fuels for marine transportation is feasible, and that ultimately reductions of 50 to 75 percent would be possible and may well be necessary as fossil fuels reach scarcity levels.

Bergeson and MacLear teamed up in the fall of 1978 with Dr. Henry Marcus of the Ocean Engineering Department of the Massachusetts Institute of Technology to propose to the U. S. Department of Commerce a three-phase development program leading to the commercialization of sail as a viable means of propelling commercial ships. In the fall of 1979 they formed the Wind Ship Development Corporation. They have since won a government contract covering the first phase of their 1978 proposal. In this phase they will complete a study of the potential of commercial sailing ships on U.S. trade routes as well as an evaluation of different sailing designs.

Reconsidering the Old, Inventing the New

Windship designs range from the familiar to the bizarre. (See "Five Windships," page 27.) The designs share the innovations of automated sail handling and reliance on the engine in unfavorable winds and tight quarters. For example, MacLear estimates that his ship would run one third of the time under sail alone, one third under power alone, and one third under both sail and power, the sails giving the engine a free boost.

Several unconventional concepts would use no sails, but rely on the wind to turn a windmill relaying power to the propellers or a spinning rotor that acts like a sail, the system being tested for the *Calypso II*.

The Routes

While naval architects tinker with designs, Wind Ship Development Corporation is studying sixty-five potential trade routes and three hundred potential cargoes. "We are looking at the wind patterns to see where sailing would be most economical," Dr. Marcus says. He expects that the traditional routes along the east and west coasts of North America and the interisland routes in the Caribbean will be possible opportunities for the first small windships. Some trade patterns have shifted since the heyday of sail, but in the United States the west coast lumber trade and the east coast coal trade have the potential to be readapted to sail. Since even modern sail is slower than power, bulk cargoes that won't spoil, such as coal, lumber, and grain, are the most likely candidates.

The Roadblocks

Wind-power proponents see the transition to wind as only a matter of time, given rising fuel prices. Marcus states that it is possible to have prototype vessels built in the United States by the 1980s and a small fleet in operation by 2000. Designers have addressed many of the initial objections: Yes, the new ships would be able to proceed in adverse or light winds because they will have engines for motoring and motor sailing; No, they won't need a large crew to do dangerous jobs because the sails will be controlled by power winches; Yes, the rigging can be designed so it won't obstruct loading and unloading of cargo. Low bridges in harbors remain a problem. But the major obstacle, according to Marcus, is the understandable reluctance of the maritime industry to innovate in an area that requires long-term investments (a ship lasts about twenty-five years) at a time when shipbuilding is declining after a spurt in the late 1960s and early 1970s. The U. S. Maritime Administration is also somewhat reluctant to pay for an experimental windship, having funded several ships in the past that were not successful, including a nuclear commercial ship and a hydrofoil. The only experimental windship in the water in early 1980 was the junk-rigged 86.2-foot (26.3-meter) *Daioh* being tested by the Nippon Kokan Company of Japan.

So Far, Mixed Results

Meanwhile, smaller-scale entrepreneurs are returning to traditional sail with mixed results. The widely publicized *John J. Leavitt,* a 92-foot (28-meter) replica of a coastal schooner built by Edward A. Ackerman in Maine, attempted a commercial route between New England and the West Indies but was abandoned in a storm off the coast of Long Island on the maiden voyage in 1979. (Unlike the modern designs, the *Leavitt* had neither an engine nor automated rigging.) The same year *National Fisherman* published a design for a sail-supplemented coastal fishing boat for fuel-minded fishermen, and two $6-million junk-rigged, 110-foot (33.5-meter) cruise ships built in Amsterdam began carrying passengers in the Bahamas. In Norfolk, Virginia, when Captain L. A. Briggs found that hoisting a sail on a conventional tugboat saved him 35 percent of his fuel cost, he had a sailing tugboat designed, which he expects will save even more.

Among the best prospects for coastal sailing ships are tropical countries where the winds are steady, where fuel prices are exorbitant for small shippers, and where, in some places, traditional sail never died. Professor Alistair Couper of the University of Wales told shippers at the 1979 London meeting that some of the principal beneficiaries of commercial sail would be jute, coconut, and copra producers whose shipping costs have made their products uncompetitive with synthetic substitutes.

Although they soberly and carefully calculate economics and exploit sophisticated modern technology, the designers of modern sailing ships cannot help but grow impassioned sometimes as they contemplate the white-winged beauty of a commercial sailing fleet. In an article on windships for *Yachting* magazine, MacLear concluded: "The idea is glorious! Will some brave entrepreneur step forward and try again to harness the enormous power of the wind?"

M.P.

FIVE WINDSHIPS

The MacLear Luff Roller Furling Boomless Rig

This design, with a title as long as a supertanker, is similar to conventional fore-and-aft rigged ships except for one important difference: the mainsails have no booms, which allows them to be furled in a flash on a rotating stay at the touch of a button. This eliminates the need for a hard-working crew to raise and lower the sails. Designer Frank MacLear knows the system works because he has installed it on four private yachts. The largest of these yachts (87 feet/26.5 meters) has a sail area of 3,600 square feet (100 square meters), which can be furled in 36 seconds. The rig he and partner Lloyd Bergeson propose for a prototype commercial ship would be about twice that size (180 square feet/54.9 square meters) and include five to seven sails on three masts. In a good breeze, the ship could sail at an average of 11 knots. They also propose evaluation of a cargo-carrying, sailing catamaran of 220 feet (67.1 meters) that would be stabler and faster, achieving a cruising speed of 20 knots and an average speed of 12 knots.

The Dynaship

This square-rigger was designed in 1956 by aircraft designer Wilhelm Prölss, in Hamburg, Germany, and is now being promoted by the Dynaship Corporation in California. All rigging is controlled by hydraulic machinery. Four or more 200-foot (60-meter) masts would be *rotated* at the push of a button to achieve the desired sail-set. Design tests predict that a Dynaship 500 feet (150 meters) long could average 12 to 16 knots and hit a top speed of 20 knots under a heavy wind.

The Daioh

Japan, a maritime country that imports most of its oil, has led the way in developing a prototype sail-equipped cargo ship. The *Daioh* has the hull of a freighter, an engine, and three sails: a rigid square sail, a soft square sail, and a triangular sail. The ship was designed and tested by the Japan Marine Machinery Development Association and Nippon Kokan, a large Japanese shipbuilder. An interim report issued in November 1979 concluded that the sails boosted the power and stretched the mileage of the engine. "Judging from rough calculations we can expect the realization of sail-equipped motor ships in the near future," the report claimed, noting that a 10-percent saving in ship fuel would save Japan as much as 140 million tons of fuel each year.

Windmill and Wind Turbine Ships

This radical concept would eliminate sails and use instead either a huge windmill or a wind turbine with cupped blades to generate power for the ship's propellers. Unlike any other sailing ship,

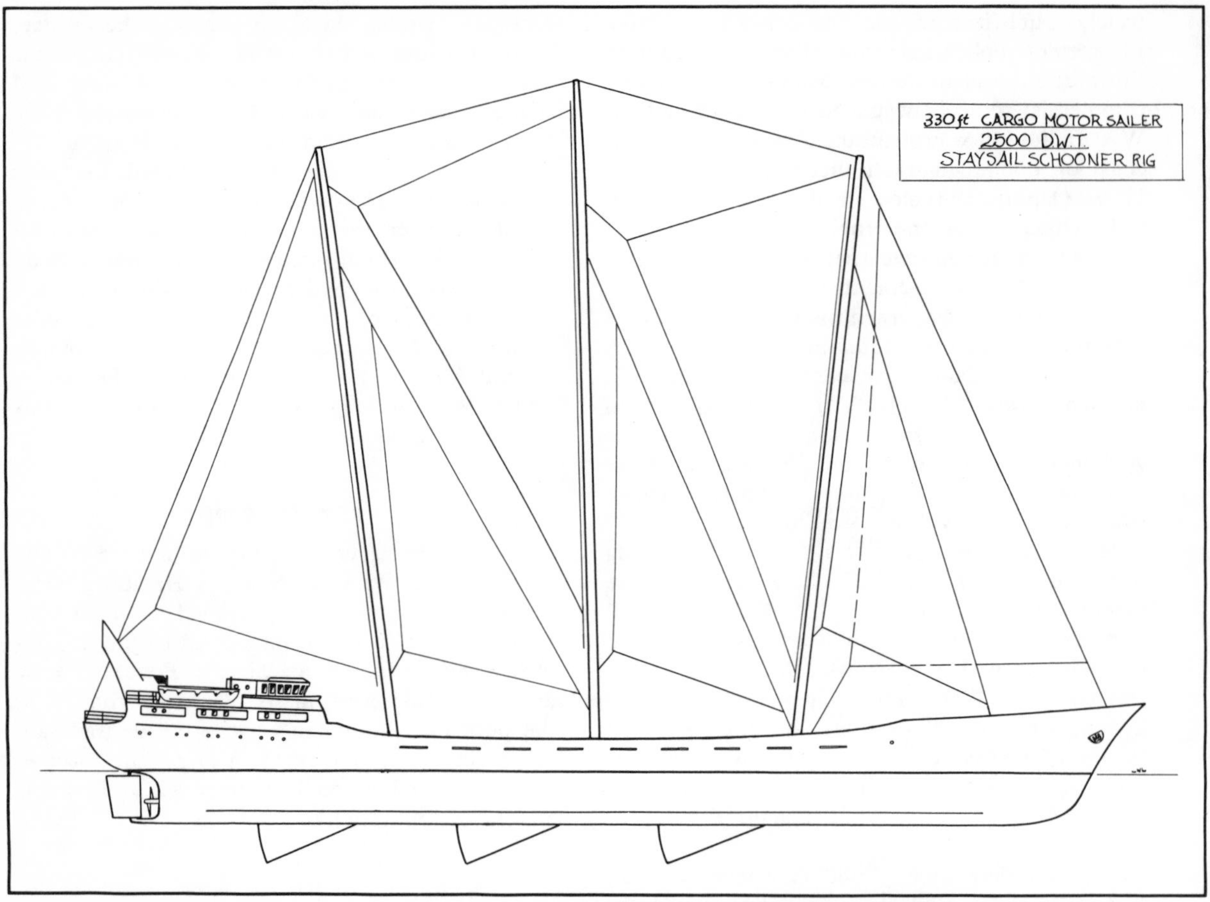

330 ft CARGO MOTOR SAILER
2500 D.W.T.
STAYSAIL SCHOONER RIG

This 330-foot (100-meter), three-masted, boomless schooner designed by Frank MacLear of Wind Ship Development Corp. could provide substantial fuel savings to shippers. Its sails can be furled automatically, reducing the need for a large crew. (Rig by Frank MacLear for *Wind Ship Development Corp.*)

they could travel directly into the wind. The blades of the windmill could be collapsed during extremely heavy weather. In 1979, the St. Helena Shipping Company said it could profitably operate such a ship on a route between Cape Town, South Africa, and the British islands of St. Helena and Ascension in the South Atlantic.

The Rotor Ship

From a distance they look like oversized smokestacks, but they act like sails. The rotor ship is driven by two or more large, vertical cylinders that rotate at 100–150 rpm. Air flowing in the direction of the rotation produces high pressure on one side of the cylinder, which in turn produces a

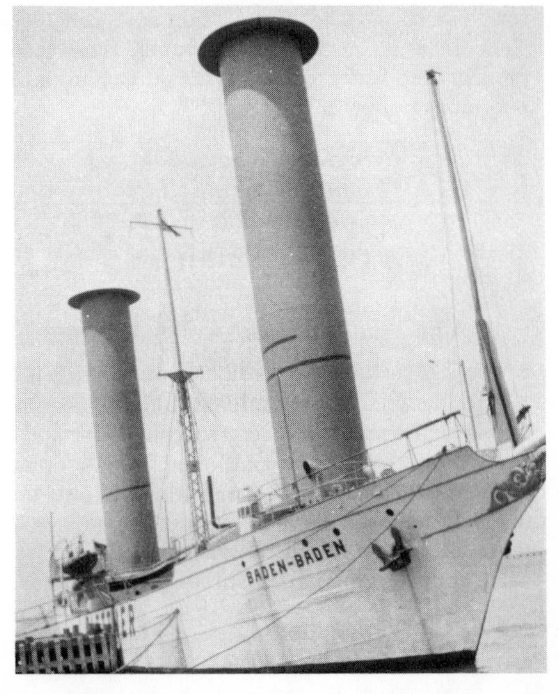

The *Baden Baden,* a rotor ship built by Anton Flettner, sailed across the Atlantic in 1926 and docked at Atlantic City, New Jersey, after its successful crossing. The huge cylindrical rotors act like sails, creating a lift force to propel the ship. (*South Street Seaport Museum/Jack Miller*)

low-pressure lift force on the other side. This pulls the ship forward at a right angle to the wind. The strange design works; a German, Anton Flettner, was the first to build a ship using a rotor system. He crossed the Atlantic in one in 1926. But his design was a victim of bad timing, coming as cheaply fueled steam and diesel ships were ending the age of sail. Now, new technology and the need to conserve fuel have rekindled interest.

The rotor ship has two main disadvantages: first, it cannot head directly into the wind, and tacking is slow because it requires reversing the direction of cylinder rotation; second, the cylinders would present about the same wind resistance as the rigging of a traditional sailing ship, a condition that could cause difficulty in a storm.

The Cousteau Society conducted wind tunnel tests of several configurations of rotors in France in 1980 with the goal of designing a new *Calypso,* partially wind-powered, to serve as a model of a fuel-efficient oceanographic vessel.

M.P.

PHOTOVOLTAIC CELLS

In December 1978, Papago Indians in the remote village of Schuchuli, Arizona, turned on electric lights in their homes for the first time, though there were no power lines leading to the village. Schuchuli is the site of the first totally solar-powered community electrical system. Instead of power lines, an array of photovoltaic cells built by the U. S. Department of Energy supplies an annual output of more than 6,000 kilowatt-hours. Used immediately or stored in batteries, the energy powers small refrigerators and fluorescent lights for all homes, as well as a community water pump, clothes washer, and sewing machine for the village's ninety-six residents. The electricity is very expensive, costing between $1.55 and $1.75 per kilowatt-hour compared with $.10 per kilowatt-hour in much of the United States, but it is cheaper than connecting the village with the closest power company.

Remote villages like Schuchuli promise to be the first communities where sun-generated electricity will be economically feasible. Photovoltaic cells, which turn the sun's light into an electric current, have been technologically feasible for years and were used in the U. S. Skylab space station as a power source. But the Skylab system, which produced enough electricity for three typical U.S. homes, cost $23 million. The price has been reduced by 99 percent, but photovoltaic systems are still more expensive in most of the developed world than conventional electric production. There are still three million villages throughout the world with no electricity, however, and connecting these often small and remote communities to conventional distribution networks is often more expensive than starting fresh with a solar system.

Because photovoltaic systems can be built on a very small scale, they are readily adaptable to the needs of rural villages. Solar-electric water pumps are cheaper to operate and easier to maintain than customary diesel pumps. While initial cost is now greater for solar, as demand for the pumps increases the cost should drop with mass production. Photovoltaic cells are already economical and practical for lighthouses, buoys, rural railway crossing signals, and some other devices.

Although improvements in materials and production methods are needed, the basic technology of solar electricity is understood. The most common photovoltaic cell is made of a thin layer of silicon crystals to which some impurities have been added to produce junctions of intrinsic voltage. Photons of light collide with the silicon atoms to dislodge electrons and leave "holes." The holes act as positive charges, drawing loose electrons back into them. Because the holes and the loose electrons are separated by the intrinsic voltage, an electric current is created. Silicon cells are expensive to make and not very efficient. Costs could soon be reduced by a process that manufactures long ribbons of silicon crystals, and efficiency is being improved by the development of devices that concentrate the sun's rays.

Various other approaches are being pursued. By using silicon that is less pure, costs are cut but so is efficiency. Other materials are also being tested that are either cheaper or more efficient than silicon. A very promising system being developed by Texas Instruments, Inc., immerses tiny silicon cells in an electrolyte solution of halogen acids. This system is inexpensive, requires little maintenance because the silicon cells operate independently, and is capable of storing energy. In addition, the electrolyte solution is circulated through a heat exchanger to capture the thermal

"WHAT'S THE BIG DEAL ABOUT SOLAR HEAT?"

(© *1980 by Sidney Harris*)

energy for space and water heating that is usually wasted in photovoltaic processes.

Advances are coming quickly, but the U. S. Department of Energy (DOE) believes that more basic research is needed to make solar electricity marketable. Photovoltaic arrays were selling for $10 to $15 per peak kilowatt in 1979, and some manufacturers were prepared to produce equipment at $3 per peak kilowatt. The DOE has set a goal of $.70 per peak kilowatt by 1986, and Texas Instruments hopes to perfect its system even sooner. At that price solar electricity will be economically competitive with new coal and nuclear power plants.

And solar electricity already has some very important advantages. Photovoltaic cells do not melt down, vent radioactive gases, generate radioactive waste, or fill the air with particulate pollution. Nor do they require mining practices that scar the earth or endanger miners. There are some questions about the effect of absorbing concentrated solar heat in the earth through solar collectors, and the production of some types of photovoltaic cells does involve the use of possibly dangerous chemicals. However, on balance, photovoltaic cells are, along with wind and hydropower, the most environmentally safe means available for producing electricity. And, of course, the fuel will never run out (well, at least not for six billion years or so). Economic comparisons of energy systems should consider these other "costs."

As solar electricity moves closer to feasibility, a debate is developing over the appropriate scale for the generating facilities. The utility companies argue that large centralized plants that take advantage of existing distribution systems are most sensible. Some space scientists even propose expensive orbiting satellite stations as the best generating facilities (see "Construction in Space," page 49). The advocates of small-scale technology maintain that the beauty of photovoltaic cells is that their efficiency does not change with scale. A little nuclear power plant in your backyard is absurd, but a photovoltaic array is perfectly reasonable. Small-scale systems eliminate the possibility of massive blackouts, and the electricity is free once the system is installed.

The utilities counter that the large systems are cheaper to build, but they are accused of overlooking transmission and distribution costs. Homeowners in the United States spend about 30 percent of their electricity dollar on electricity; 6 percent is profit and the remaining 64 percent pays for the manufacture, construction, and maintenance of transmission and distribution equipment. With centralized solar electricity we could find ourselves paying quite a bit for electricity generated from a free fuel.

As old systems have to be replaced, the use of solar energy will become increasingly prevalent. In developing countries it will certainly grow much faster. The real question is what form the generating facilities will take: centralized behemoths or private and community-owned facilities.

K.F.

TIDAL POWER

"Lunar energy"—derived from the moon's gravitational pull—combines with the pull of the sun and earth to influence the regular rise and fall of the tides. The force of global ocean tides represents a power equivalent to about three thousand 1,000-megawatt nuclear power plants, according to energy expert M. King Hubbert, formerly of the U. S. Geological Survey. Of this, between 10,000 and 60,000 megawatts could be harnessed.

The ancients sometimes used the tide to power mills, and such mills proliferated along coastal areas in nineteenth-century Europe. France built the first commercial tidal electric plant in 1966 in the Rance estuary in Brittany. There a half-mile-long (800-meter) dam spans the estuary, separating it from the sea. The flood tide is allowed to flow into the estuary, then is trapped behind the dam. At low tide the water is released through twenty-four 10-megawatt turbine generators in the dam. The cost of building such tidal plants is high, but the price of power produced can be competitive with some other forms of hydropower, such as those using a seasonal water-storage reservoir.

The technology of tidal power is essentially the same as that for river hydroelectric power. With rivers, however, the water flows in only one direction, while a tidal plant must be adapted for the two-way movement of seawater. A limitation of tidal plants is their inability to generate electricity constantly or on demand—the electricity comes only when the waters rise and fall on their local cycles. An alternative design uses two basins, one higher than the other, both connected by sluices to the sea. By carefully regulating the levels in the basins and generating electricity at the barrier between them, power can be produced continuously, although the output will not always be at the same level. With either method some electricity will have to be stored in order to provide a constant supply.

Economics, however, is the crucial limitation of tidal power for now. The U. S. Army Corps of Engineers estimated in 1979 that a 450-megawatt plant could cost $916 million. Although this price is not competitive with costs of other types of power plants, tidal plants last fifty to one hundred years. Thus if the price of other forms of energy continues to rise, tidal power will grow more attractive. The Canadian government has undertaken a $33-million feasibility study of several sites, particularly Shephody Bay and the Cumberland and Minas basins. Studies are also being done at France's Chausey Islands, England's Severn River, South Korea's Asan Bay, the Soviet Union's Gulf of Mezen, and Australia's Walcott Inlet.

Tidal range, the vertical distance between high and low tide, varies widely from place to place. Because of a plant's high construction cost and because of turbine limitations, a tidal range of 13 to 16 feet (4 to 5 meters) is the minimum needed to provide enough energy to make it economically feasible, and such a wide range is rare. But a new technique developed by Alexander M. Gorlov, an associate professor of mechanical engineering at Northeastern University in Boston, could drastically lower construction costs and thereby increase the number of possible sites. Gorlov proposes replacing the concrete dam with a flexible reinforced plastic barrier that could be raised or lowered. The flow of water would drive an air-compression piston, and the compressed air could be used immediately to drive an air motor to generate electricity or store it for later use. Gorlov claims that his method requires a tidal range of only 7 feet (2 meters) to be feasible, and he is currently investigating possible sites for a pilot plant in Maine.

Engineers in many places are attempting to develop "low head" turbines that could generate power from the flow of water that is only a few feet higher than the turbine. These turbines, while aimed at river hydropower, would be ideal for tidal power.

The environmental impact of tidal power plants has not yet been fully determined. The ecology of coastal basins is complex and the effects of early plants will have to be studied closely. Also, the dam could conceivably alter the tidal range in adjacent areas and even reduce the water flow it is supposed to tap.

The United States began construction of a tidal power plant in Maine's Cobscook Bay in 1935, but Congress cut off funds and the plant was never finished. According to U. S. Army Corps of Engineers calculations, the annual cost of the facility over a one-hundred-year life would have been $2.4 million. If it had been completed as planned, the plant would today be producing electricity at one cent per kilowatt-hour (compared to the 1980 New York City price of ten cents). Considering the rising price of fossil fuel, the hazards of carbon dioxide in the atmosphere, and the drawbacks of nuclear power, we can expect the tide to extend its power far inland in the future.

K.F.

INTEGRATED PEST MANAGEMENT

The Cañete Valley of Peru is an irrigated coastal area that probably had some form of agriculture even before the advent of the Incan empire. Since cotton has long been grown in Cañete, its farmers have had a great deal of experience with the crop's main pests—the boll worm, the boll weevil, and the leaf worm. Until about 1948, these were usually removed by hand or sometimes sprayed with arsenic and nicotine, and the cotton yield remained stable at 400 to 500 pounds per acre (500 to 600 kilograms per hectare). In 1949, however, the yield dropped by nearly half because of a particularly virulent boll worm and aphid infestation. For the first time, DDT, BHC, and Toxaphene were introduced to prevent insect outbreaks, and over the next few years yields returned to their previous level.

As a result, the Peruvian farmers became enraptured with pesticides. Trees and other vegetation were removed so that airplanes could more efficiently blanket the valley with pesticides. The birds began to disappear from the valley, but that was hardly noticed. Then resistance among the pests began to appear. New pesticides were tried. Parathion, an extremely toxic organic phosphate chemical, was sometimes applied on a weekly schedule. We do not know what effect this chemical deluge had on the cotton pickers, but virtually all of the birds and beneficial insects disappeared from the valley, leaving mostly an increasing number of resistant pests. New pests, previously kept under control by birds and other predators, began to appear in the cotton fields. By the mid-1950s, yields dropped to 296 pounds per acre (332 kilograms per hectare) in spite of the use of record amounts of pesticides. The farmers found themselves paying more for petroleum-based chemicals that became less effective with each application.

This scenario—pests that develop genetic resistance to pesticides, the destruction of "nontarget" organisms, the accumulation of pesticides in the food web, and rapidly increasing costs—has been repeated many times throughout the world. (See "The Most-Fertilized Foods," page 601.)

Reviving Traditions of the Ancients

A less anthropocentric philosophy underlies "integrated pest management" (IPM), an old approach recently revived, which recognizes that humans can manipulate but not subjugate nature. IPM does not do away with pesticides, but orchestrates them as merely one tactic among several in a strategy of applied ecology. IPM *does* reduce the use of chemical sprays. Practitioners first establish an economic threshold for each pest population, that is, the population level at which the cost of damage exceeds the cost of control measures. Since pests seldom reach really high numbers, the common practice of routinely using pesticides is wasteful and ecologically unsound. The pest population level, as well as the numbers of their important natural enemies, is regularly monitored so that the crop is sprayed only when the pest reaches the economic threshold.

This approach to pest problems involves an appreciation of certain traditional cultural practices whose value has been obscured by the factory-

The chemical-evolutionary trap: pests resistant to certain pesticides survive the sprayings to breed resistant progeny. Eventually large populations become resistant, rendering the chemicals ineffective. (*UNEP*)

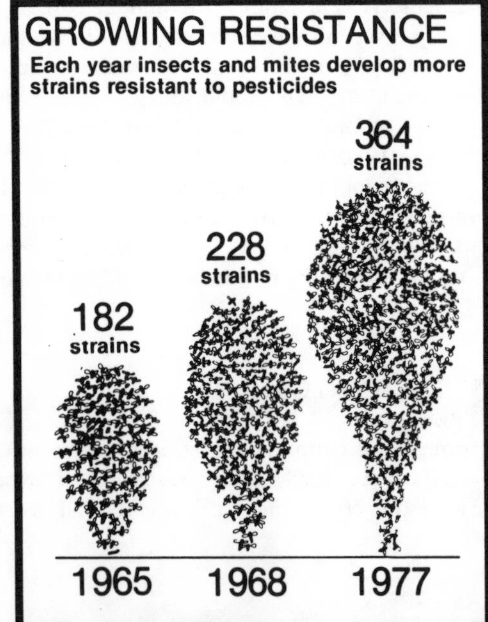

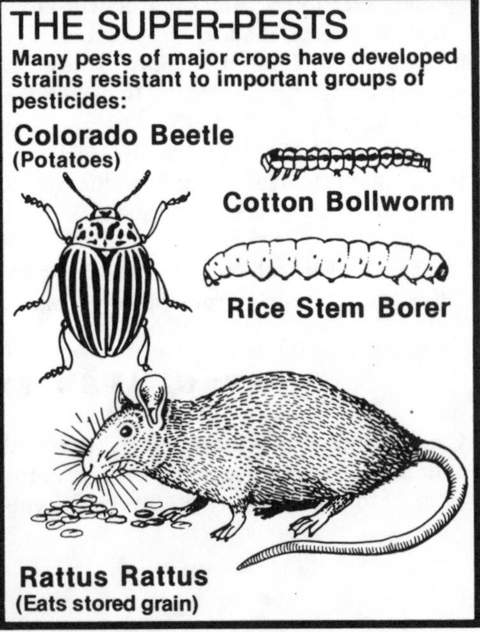

farm method of heavy fertilizer and pesticide use. Crop rotation is a prime example of a valid traditional practice. It not only allows the soil to recover nutrients extracted by a specific crop, but also keeps pests off balance by the periodic removal of their favorite plants. Also, simply timing the seeding and the harvest to avoid certain stages of a pest's life cycle can be effective.

The Use of Sex and Sickness

Parasites and predators have also been collected or raised, then released in infested fields. Trichogrammatid wasps, for example, have long been used with variable success to parasitize the eggs of a number of lepidopteran pests (butterflies and moths). Vast numbers of the pest itself may be reared and the males sterilized by chemicals or irradiation. The male screw worm fly was sterilized and released by the U. S. Department of Agriculture in such large numbers over consecutive years that the natural population of breeding males declined severely. The females laid unfertilized eggs, and this major pest of livestock died out, first on the island of Curaçao, then in Florida and the southern United States, and later in much of the Southwest.

A wide array of pathogens has been employed against insect pests. Spores of *Bacillus thuringiensis* have been sprayed with some success to infect the larvae of a range of butterflies and moths. Insect-attacking fungi have shown considerable promise in limiting certain insect pest populations. Viruses have been employed against the corn earworm and the European pine sawfly.

The Tricking of the Bugs

The most sophisticated controls available to IPM are biological compounds developed over the last decade that are designed to turn the pest's life cycle against itself. These are insect pheromones, substances produced by insects that convey explicit insect messages to the species. If a pheromone released by a female to attract mates can be isolated and manufactured, it can be broadcast into the environment to confuse males, preventing them from locating females. Intensive trapping using pheromones has actually suppressed a wood-boring beetle. Other promising new tactics include the disruption of molting by the use of chitinase, an enzyme that breaks down chitin, the substance that makes up the hard carapace of most insects. Also, hormones can be used to keep the insect pest in an immature form, or to disrupt normal development.

"WHY SHOULD WE HAVE TROUBLE GROWING THE VEGETABLES ORGANICALLY? THE WEEDS ARE ORGANIC, THE BUSHES ARE ORGANIC, THE BUSHES ARE ORGANIC..."

These experimental controls—pathogens, enemy parasites, pheromones—usually kill only the target pest. By contrast, most pesticides affect all insects in the vicinity of application, often creating a prime, predator-free habitat into which a new pest can move. Learning from past mistakes, researchers *are* developing species-specific pesticides, but their work is costly. Also, once developed, species-specific chemicals have a limited market and are therefore less economically attractive.

Back in the Cañete Valley, the bewildered and frustrated farmers turned to the government for help, and a strict IPM program was imposed. The main chemical methods chosen were, ironically enough, arsenics and nicotine sprays, the approach used for generations before modern pesticides were introduced. Alternative crops, such as corn, were planted to allow for a diversification of habitat and alternate hosts for useful predators and parasites. Natural enemies were introduced from other valleys. The traditional practice of growing cotton from old rootstocks, which increased pest populations, was prohibited. In only one year after the institution of the program, the cotton yields nearly doubled, and they have since held to record yields.

R.C., C.R.C., K.F.

TOMOGRAPHY

Tomography, from the Greek word for "slice" or "section," is a three-dimensional surveying technique that makes it possible to look into previously unviewable reaches of the world and of the human body. With tomography it is possible to survey up to 600 miles (1,000 kilometers) of deep ocean without ever taking a water sample, except as a control. It also enables physicians to see the center of the human brain without surgical procedures, and with greater accuracy than any previous X-ray technique. Tomography is an exciting science, for which a Nobel Prize was awarded to an American, Dr. Allan McLeod Cormack, and a Briton, Dr. Godfrey Newbold Hounsfield, in 1979.

In general, tomography involves layers of X-ray images, piled in stacks, projected at different angles. Each image distinguishes one plane of the object or material being tomographed. All the images are collected on a viewing screen, revealing the planes in an accurate three-dimensional array. In the human brain, for example, this means that interior tissue can be examined easily, including the stem and core. Any obstructions or disruptions can be seen well before they would be noticed on conventional X rays. Also, X rays usually cannot reveal lesions in the brain, such as tumors, because the density of a tumor is similar to that of healthy tissue and X rays cannot show the difference. But the CAT (Computerized Axial Tomography) can. Computers reassemble the multitude of bits of visual information into a coherent whole, and all of the mechanisms of deep brain activity can be observed, including potentially dangerous but subtle developments.

When tomography is used in the ocean, a sound-dispersing apparatus is placed at one end of an area to be surveyed, and a receiving apparatus at the other end. The two pieces of equipment can be placed hundreds of miles apart and record conditions at any point in between.

Sound waves are beamed out through the "block" of the ocean in question. Since sound velocity is greatly influenced by such ocean factors as currents, salinity, and, mainly, temperature, the journey of the sound waves depends on the underwater ocean conditions along their path (for example, sound travels faster with the current than against it). By reading tomogram sound velocity maps, scientists can obtain data about the temperature structure of the ocean and can infer information about other conditions. In this manner, deep underwater currents, virtually untraceable by other methods, can be tracked all along their route with relatively few movements of equipment.

The new measuring process promises to revolutionize what has always been a slow, tedious exercise for oceanographers. Previously, a probe was dropped to take a vertical sample and to read the deep-water conditions in one specific area, but then the probe had to be moved to the next sampling site. The difference between this sort of probing and tomography is like the difference between snapshot photography and movies.

With tomography, wide ocean surveys can be done with significantly less equipment, time, and money than previously thought possible. Such detailed readings of the ocean are crucial if we are to understand the health of the sea. It may also reveal new resources in the deep ocean (see, for example, "Hot Brines," page 11). Tomography can trace undersea dynamics, conditions that create perpetually moving, interacting bodies of water that climb, descend, flood, and stream like liquid winds. Studying just the surface, or only a narrow section of the sea's layers, excludes vital information, such as how an oil spill affects deep-water life, or whether alterations in temperature or in the chemical balance of the sea are occurring below the surface, or even, perhaps, whether "hidden" underwater conditions exist that can generate energy (see "OTEC," page 23).

With tomography, we can profile the broadest expanses of the sea, above and below, and finally see what has escaped concern and interest simply because it was out of our sight.

P.D.

SYNFUELS

On July 15, 1979, President Carter proposed that the United States begin a massive effort to create a synthetic fuel industry that would be producing 2.5 million barrels of oil a day by 1990. (This would be about 35 percent of U.S. imports and 12.5 percent of total usage in 1979.) The proposal generated immediate enthusiasm, although no synfuel industry existed in the United States and most people did not even know what synfuels were.

Soon people were praising the ingenuity of Germany's crash synfuel program during World War II and the contemporary example of South Africa, but these "successes" need to be examined closely. Germany's "crash" program actually began in 1923 and, even with this early start, produced a grand total of only 160 million barrels of synthetic fuel—enough to satisfy U.S. needs for eight days. South Africa produces 10,000 barrels of oil a day from coal and hopes to increase production fivefold in the next few years. Even this projected production would supply only one quarter of 1 percent of the U.S. demand. (In addition, South Africa's program would be economically unfeasible without the exploitation of black workers.)

Synfuels may provide a new source of necessary liquid fossil fuels, but their introduction will not be fast or cheap or simple. Synfuels are derived from several very different sources and must be refined by very different processes, most of which are complicated, expensive, potentially hazardous to health and the environment, and as yet commercially unproven.

Heavy Oil

The synfuel source that is closest in chemical composition to conventional oil is heavy oil, which is found in tar sands and elsewhere. Nearly 99 percent of heavy oil reserves are found in the Western Hemisphere (Canada currently produces 150,000 barrels of synthetic crude a day from tar sands). Heavy oil is cheaper and easier to refine than oil shale or coal, but it shares some of their liabilities. Refinement of tar sands requires large quantities of water, produces large quantities of sulfur dioxide, and leaves behind mountains of waste and ponds of oil-covered water that are hazardous to wildlife.

These problems are not as significant to Canada's plants in remote, water-rich Alberta as they would be in the United States. There heavy oil is found in the Rocky Mountains, where water is scarce and the air is already dirty, and in the East, where air pollution is excessive. The problems associated with developing heavy oil are not insurmountable, but they are serious and must be resolved before large-scale production is considered.

Oil Shale

Oil shale is a popular synfuel source in the United States, where 200 billion barrels could be extracted from Colorado, Utah, and Wyoming. (By comparison, total U.S. reserves of conventional crude oil are estimated at 28 billion barrels.) Separating the oil from the rock, however, is problematic. The oil shale must be mined and crushed, heated to 900° F (500° C) in a process called "retorting" to turn solid hydrocarbons to liquid, and further refined until it is acceptable to an ordinary refinery. The spent shale, which retains 85 percent of its original mass and has expanded to 120 percent of its original volume, must be disposed of carefully because it contains alkaline salts and toxic trace elements such as molybdenum, arsenic, selenium, fluoride, and boron. Producing a million barrels of oil a day in this manner would require about 5 million barrels of water and leave behind 2 million tons (1.8 million metric tons) of rock each day. A "modified in situ" process would do the retort stage with the shale still in the ground, thus eliminating much of the surface waste and reducing water use to two barrels per barrel of oil. This process only works with oil shale in the western United States and could pollute the aquifer through leaching of toxic by-products.

Liquid Coal

Coal contains less hydrogen than oil shale and therefore needs more processing to be useful as a liquid fuel. The coal can be processed directly into liquid by "hydrogenation" or first converted into a gas and then into a liquid as was done in Germany and South Africa. Coal can also be "gasified" (mixed with oxygen and steam at high pressure) and then cleaned and purified to produce methane gas. The coal liquefaction process has significant drawbacks. Highly carcinogenic 3, 4-benzo-(a)pyrene is a by-product that is dangerous to plant workers. Coal dust, sulfur dioxide, nitrogen oxides, and carbon monoxide are other by-products that contribute to air pollution. Toxic materials remain in the wastewater and the coal ash. Although coal is plentiful, especially in the United States, the environmental hazards and the social problems associated with short-lived "boom towns" severely limit the possible sites for coal liquefaction plants.

Biomass

A less publicized synfuel, which many people do not consider "synthetic," is ethanol derived from biomass such as agricultural waste and sewage. Ethanol can be mixed with gasoline in a one-to-nine ratio to produce gasohol. The ethanol, produced through fermentation and distillation of waste matter, leaves by-products that can be used as fertilizer and animal feed, and emits fairly easily cleaned gases. The U. S. Department of Energy estimates that 400,000 barrels a day could be produced by 1990. The crucial difference between biomass and other synfuel sources is that biomass can be processed on a small scale from universally available and perpetually renewable materials, so it can be more quickly and more widely used. There is some concern that using biomass for fuel would reduce food availability, but this should be avoidable if the biomass bulk is composed principally of waste products.

Environmental problems are a significant factor in synfuel production, but they are not the only drawbacks. The practical feasibility and economics of synfuels are not really known, because no commercial facilities of the size envisioned (50,000 barrels per day) have been built. And although everyone assumes that synfuels will eventually be cheaper than imported oil, the price has so far remained consistently higher. In 1973 crude oil cost $3.50 per barrel and synfuel oil from shale cost $4.50. The 1979 price of crude oil was $17 per barrel, while synfuel from shale cost $25, and oil from coal was $40 per barrel. Furthermore, these synfuel prices are only estimates and could actually be higher. Oil reserves are running out, but the synfuel substitutes are not ready yet, largely because business interests are not very enthusiastic about a major push for synfuel development. Corporations are reluctant to build too many $1.5-billion synfuel plants until they have seen a few in operation. Yet the efficiency and environmental impact of the various designs of commercial plants will not be known until they are in operation.

Synfuels could play an important role in the world's energy future, but it is difficult to predict how large their ultimate role will be.

K.F.

HELIUM

Helium is what inflates blimps, dirigibles, and zeppelins and what carries toy balloons floating off into the sky. Mixed with oxygen, it permits divers to breathe under water at extreme depths, for extended periods, with no narcotic effects. It is the lightest element except for hydrogen, and though found in only a minute amount in the earth's atmosphere, it constitutes 23 percent of perceivable outer space. Helium liquefies at the lowest temperature of any gas, but it does not freeze at any temperature. At room temperature it is odorless, tasteless, colorless, nontoxic, and nonflammable. Helium transfers heat well, but it is chemically inert. In sum, helium's properties make it unique among the elements. They also make it a resource that may well be crucial to future energy technology, a nonrenewable resource that, because it is not yet precious to us, we waste incessantly.

The most common source of helium is natural gas, which, when burned, releases helium and dissipates it into the atmosphere. Approximately 89 percent of all helium found in natural gas is lost this way, some 13 billion cubic feet a year, a disturbing figure if you consider that 83 percent of the world's known helium reserves are contained in natural gas currently being depleted, or not yet exploited. In the United States, at present rates and patterns of natural gas field consumption, only about thirty years of helium reserves are left. Canada, Algeria, the Netherlands, and Australia have low concentrations of helium available in their natural gas fields. The Soviet Union is another potential source of helium, though the size of its reserves is not known.

Once helium is diffused in the atmosphere, recapturing it using present technology costs about $3,800 per thousand cubic feet, whereas to extract helium from gas before it is burned costs about $13 per thousand cubic feet. By the year 2010, when helium-rich natural gas reserves may be gone, all the helium we need will have to be recovered from the atmosphere. This will be a little like trying to recover oil spilled into the sea.

Part of the problem is that our current helium needs are met and helium-dependent technology is considered a "tomorrow" concept. But while our supply of helium is squandered, the tomorrow in which we will need it appears to be fast approaching. The United States is spending $2 billion a year researching processes that will require helium. The most important of these is superconductivity, a technology not yet fully developed but whose potential is clearly understood. Superconductivity reduces or eliminates the resistance of material to electricity. This means superconductive power lines could transmit ten thousand times the electrical power of today's power lines, and power storage could be achieved with little power loss. Superconductive generators with vastly increased production are also under study. Superconductive magnets could be used to purify water and to manage wastes. They also have a role in the development of computers and nuclear energy, as well as high-speed ground transportation vehicles, some of which will be floated and pulled along by magnetic fields. Certain types of cryogenics, the science of low temperatures that would facilitate superconduction, can best be achieved with helium.

In the nuclear fusion and fission processes, helium is also essential, not only because of the role superconductivity plays but also because helium is the best coolant. Fusion is a controversial source of nuclear energy for which, nevertheless, the United States alone budgeted $376 million on research in 1980. (See "Nuclear Fusion," page 47.)

The U.S. space shuttle, which cost more than $6 billion for research and development, requires helium for pressurizing and purging fuel tanks, and it is vital for stabilizing the air supply of the shuttle cabin.

Helium is also essential to laser technology, leak detection, aerodynamics research, biomedicine, optics, and physics. Dirigibles filled with helium are again being seriously considered as cargo and passenger aircraft (the *Hindenburg,* which burned tragically in 1937 in New Jersey, was filled with hydrogen). Despite its extraordinary potential, helium is not being stockpiled, even though storage in exhausted gas wells is possible.

The reasons for this shortsightedness are purely economic. Natural gas producers do not wish to pay the costs of helium extraction, nor the royalties that would be due land owners who have granted leases only for natural gas production, nor the costs of helium storage, nor storage taxes. They want these charges passed along to consumers, who may balk at paying an increase to natural gas producers that is estimated at $25 per year. In the short run, letting helium escape into the atmosphere now is cheaper and easier for almost all concerned.

Natural gas producers emphasize an important drawback to any helium-preserving steps, and their point is valid. Extracting helium from natural gas, a process involving liquefying the gas to extract helium and then restoring the helium-free liquid to a gaseous state, results in a net loss of 7 percent of the original energy of the natural gas. But regrettable though any energy loss might be, it may not be enough to justify the continued venting of helium into space.

The helium situation is not without precedent. Between 1930 and 1960, because there was little financial incentive to do otherwise, the United States vented and burned off about 119 trillion cubic feet (3.3 trillion cubic meters) of natural gas, regarding it as merely an annoying by-product of petroleum production. That is an amount equal to about 58 percent of the proven U.S. gas reserves as of 1977, or an amount equal to approximately 28 percent of the total natural gas production of the country as of 1979—all wasted natural gas we could be using now.

P.D.

THE JONGLEI CANAL

The long-awaited Aswan dam on the Nile has caused several unforeseen problems (see "The Aswan High Dam," page 173). In 1978, another huge water project was begun on the White Nile in the Sudan. An immense mechanical digging machine is eating its way through 9,000 tons of soil an hour, leaving behind a long ditch that will become the Jonglei Canal. The implications of this project are vast, since it will alter a major wetlands area, will change the amount of fresh water in the Nile, and will change the lives of several tribes.

The White Nile runs north from Lake Victoria to join the Blue Nile at Khartoum, the capital of the Sudan. Before it reaches Khartoum, the White Nile bends and flows into a vast region of swamps, known as the Sudd, where almost half its water is lost through evaporation. More than a million Dinka, Nuer, and Shilluk tribesmen inhabit the area, herding more than 800,000 cattle and growing a few crops.

Because Egypt is running out of water for its projected population of 50 million by 1985, and because the Sudan itself needs more water, the two countries are jointly building a 272-mile-long (438-kilometer) canal between the villages of Bor and Hilet Doleeb. The Jonglei Canal (named after its terminus in the original plan) will cut off about a quarter of the water flowing into the Sudd and send it directly downstream instead, adding an estimated 166 billion cubic feet (4.7 billion cubic meters) a year to the flow of the Nile. This new water supply will be used to irrigate hundreds of thousands of acres of new farmland in dry northern Sudan and southern Egypt.

The canal will also shorten the trip between north and south Sudan by more than 200 miles (322 kilometers), several days by boat. Since north-south, Arab-black relations have always

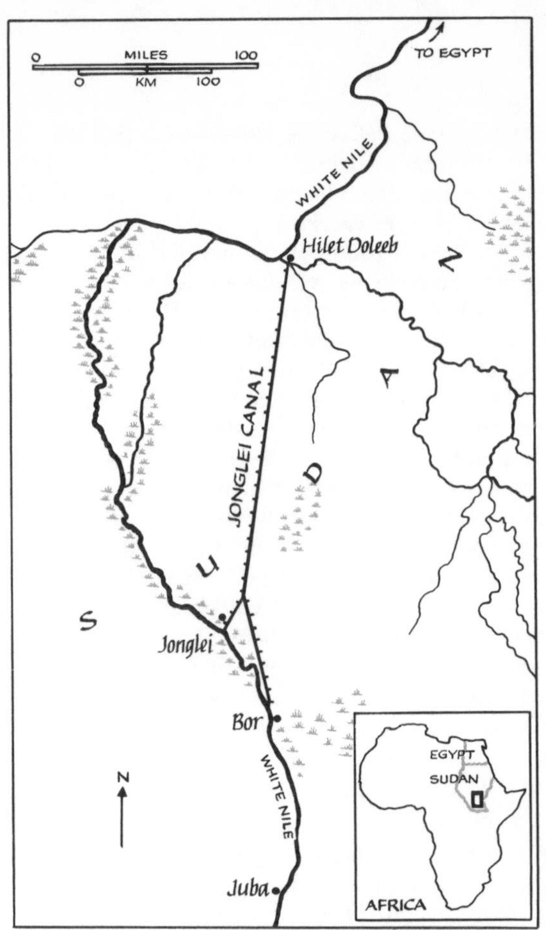

A giant earth mover takes another bite out of the Sudd swampland, giving shape to the Jonglei Canal, which will direct Nile water through the heart of the Sudd, with potentially detrimental effects on its vital wetlands. (*The Cousteau Society/Philippe Cousteau*)

been a problem in the Sudan (a seventeen-year civil war dragged to an end in 1972), government officials hope the Jonglei Canal will lead to better communications.

The Sudanese government also hopes that the smaller amount of water entering the Sudd will allow more land there to be farmed. However, previous plans for large-scale farming in the Sudd have caused problems. In 1974, rumors that 2.5 million Egyptian farmers would settle in the Sudd caused riots in Jūbā, the southern capital; two people were killed, and many jailed. At present, the government plans to emphasize indigenous development, encouraging the Dinka, for example, to raise more cattle for market and helping the Shilluk improve their farming and fishing.

Environmentalists, particularly westerners, have raised many objections to the Jonglei Canal, ranging from its effects on the water table to its destruction of native culture. To its credit, the Sudanese government is making an effort to learn from environmental studies, although it is committed to building the canal, which is scheduled to be finished in 1985. The dubious example of the Aswan dam, which is considered an ecological disaster by many, and the delicate relations between Khartoum and the south since the civil war, have combined to compel the Sudanese to be careful.

One important criticism of the Jonglei Canal seems to be that it will disrupt the lives of the local tribesmen. Sixty-five thousand people and 120,000 cattle migrate during the dry season across the area where the canal will pass. The canal will be from 213 to 328 feet (65 to 100 meters) wide and will interfere with the migration. A few expensive bridges are to be built, but these are not enough, because the separate tribes of the area follow well-defined migration routes and do not tolerate invasion of their grazing land, camping places, water, and fishing by other tribes. To solve this problem, fords will be built in many places so that tribesmen, cattle, and wildlife can cross without interfering with each other. To lessen the impact of the canal on the tribes, the route was shifted to the east after a Dutch study predicted intertribal friction and overgrazing along the original route.

When scientists investigated the people of the Sudd, they discovered the tribes were far less isolated than had been thought. Many of the Dinka already work in towns, and others buy transistor radios and wear city clothes, although they live in the traditional villages. The Sudd is surrounded by more developed regions, and the tribespeople will inevitably become part of the money economy sooner or later. The Sudanese government is anxious to protect the tribes of the Sudd until they enter the modern world, but they will have to enter it eventually.

Another important objection to the Jonglei Canal is that it would have a devastating impact on grazing land and fisheries. Every year, seasonal floods cover the low grasslands of the Sudd. When the floods run off, the grasslands provide pasture for the tribes' cattle and the shallow swamp water is full of fish fry left behind. With water flow through the huge swamp considerably reduced by the canal, these productive lands and wetlands might also decline. (See "Wetlands," page 379.)

Obviously there is no simple solution to the problem of the Sudanese wetlands. Proponents of the canal point out that it will help reduce malaria in the region. Opponents, meanwhile, point to the possible destruction of the huge Bahr al-Ghazāl wetlands, which shelter lions, cheetahs, reedbucks, and white-eared kobs.

The Sudanese government appears to be paying relatively careful attention to the possible environmental consequences of the Jonglei Canal, but that often means simply justifying pro-development decisions, dismissing some consequences as ridiculous (such as the contention that the Sudd could become a desert) and accepting others as a fair price to pay for the benefits of the canal. But, like Aswan, the Jonglei Canal may have some unpleasant surprises to present when it is finished. Whatever the results, it is an important project to be monitored closely during this decade.

J.S.

GASOHOL

Solar panels may heat our homes in the future, the sun, sea, and wind may generate electricity, but most of our machinery and vehicles need liquid fuels that are derived from oil. Gasohol—a blend of gasoline and alcohol—may eventually help conserve oil, since it can be mixed in proportions as high as one part alcohol to five parts gas without any adjustments to an ordinary engine. Gasohol gives good mileage per gallon, and it burns cleanly. In Brazil, where gasohol is readily available, a government official demonstrated just how clean by breathing deeply from the exhaust pipe of an idling automobile fueled by gasohol. He claimed that the car could meet the strictest air pollution control stands without any control devices on the car. But gasohol's main appeal is that we can "grow" it, by growing the crops from which alcohol is derived. Alcohol itself is not a new fuel idea. In the nineteenth century it was used instead of whale oil in lamps, and Henry Ford seriously considered using alcohol in his first cars. Alcohol was used instead of gasoline in many oil-poor regions until the 1930s, when gasoline became cheaper than alcohol almost everywhere. The state of Nebraska has been a friend of alcohol as a fuel all along; in 1935 the state legislature exempted fuel alcohol from taxation, and during World War II a huge grain alcohol plant operated in Nebraska, producing 65,000 gallons (246,000 liters) of alcohol a day for fuel.

Before World War II, Germany and France were leaders in the use of alcohol, and many European countries mandated the use of alcohol in gasoline. During the war, the Germans converted tanks and planes to gasohol when their oil supplies were cut off by the Allies.

After World War II, gasoline became abundant and alcohol/gasohol returned to obscurity for more than twenty years. Alcohol became too expensive to compete with gasoline as a fuel—until gas prices escalated in the early 1970s with the rise of the Organization of Petroleum Exporting Countries (OPEC). The skyrocketing prices and political uncertainty of oil made a homegrown alternative increasingly desirable. Above all, nations began to realize that fossil fuels would not last forever.

A case in point is provided by Brazil. In the early 1970s, the Brazilian economy was booming and the country was enjoying the benefits of a huge trade surplus. That is, until the OPEC oil embargo intervened. Brazil, with almost no fossil fuels, quickly became the largest oil importer among developing nations. Since 1973, Brazil's oil imports have wiped out her trade surplus and made Brazil the world's largest international borrower. So Brazil proceeded with a gasohol development plan at full speed. The country has the advantages of abundant hydropower, cheap labor, and a vast territory for growing plants. The distilleries make alcohol from organic materials, chiefly sugarcane, from Brazil's large sugar industry, and from manioc, a root crop. Since the latter grows on marginal soil that will not support other food crops, the Brazilians hope that using manioc to fuel the distilleries will keep productive farmland free.

The Brazilian program, watched carefully by other countries, has been remarkably successful. According to research compiled by the Worldwatch Institute in 1980, private industry in Brazil claims it can provide 60 to 70 percent of the fuel required to operate the country's automobiles by 1986. Government projections are closer to 30 to 35 percent. Because of a high tax on gasoline, gasohol is cheaper than gasoline in Brazil.

In the United States, gasohol production is under way in several states. In Alabama, a farmers' cooperative, aided by a government grant, is making alcohol from a $12,000 still built of scavenged metal. The farmers (one of whom is a former moonshiner) run their tractors and trucks on alcohol distilled from corn, yeast, water, and enzymes. Their alcohol, they say, costs them less than a dollar a gallon. (See "Distilling High Test," opposite.)

West Germany and the Volkswagen company have successfully tested gasohol in a wide variety of driving conditions all over Europe, and Sweden and Volvo undertook another gasohol feasibility survey, hoping to cut down on oil imports. South Africa, which depends heavily on political adversaries for its oil, is already running many vehicles on gasohol, especially in higher altitudes, where alcohol seems to improve motor performance.

Given all its very positive characteristics, gasohol sounds like a perfect solution to the shortage of liquid fuels, but there are some potential problems. In 1980 there were reports of significant water pollution issuing from gasohol plants into nearby streams in Brazil. Theoretically this problem could be easily solved. A more significant worry involves the diversion of agricultural efforts from food production to fuel production. Farmers would be tempted to sell to the highest bidder, and fuel will command more money than food. So, there is a danger that countries that now export food, like the United States and Canada, will reduce food production, leaving less food in the marketplace, driving up consumer prices. There is also, of course, the problem of world hunger. Many developing nations depend on food imports to feed their people, and those nations that are attempting to achieve food self-sufficiency will be faced with a choice between continuing to try to increase food production or planting more lucrative energy-yielding crops for profit.

If alcohol, however, is produced exclusively

from agricultural wastes, like low-quality or moldy grain, then otherwise useful foodstuffs and food land will not be lost to cars. In fact, the fermentation process could actually improve low-quality grain by removing the toxins, leaving grain suitable at least for livestock. But once the profitability of alcohol versus food is established, it is unlikely that alcohol production can be effectively restricted to use only waste products.

Also, producing alcohol-based fuels, including growing the crop and distilling the alcohol, actually requires more energy than would be saved, unless the initial processing is done in a coal-, hydro-, or solar-powered plant, and unless one includes in the calculations the energy contained in the by-products of the distilling process. So, a net energy saving from gasohol depends on technologies that are not yet broadly in place.

Another objection is that alcohol is less powerful than gasoline. One kind of alcohol, methanol, has only half the energy potential of gasoline, while ethanol has 61 percent. However, the one-to-nine ratio recommended for mixing alcohol with gasoline will make the difference negligible.

Some oil companies claim that fuel alcohol pollutes, degrades car performance, and corrodes the fuel system. The first two claims have been disproven by extensive studies on cars using gasohol, as well as by simple observations by users. The last, that alcohol can damage the fuel system, may or may not be true, depending on the car model. Old cars with parts that are already corroded may need to have some replacements. However, many drivers say they have no trouble with corrosion. In any case, new cars could easily be equipped to handle alcohol with no problems.

As of early 1980 in the United States, it was extremely difficult to set up a small still for alcohol fuel because of federal regulations, expensive bonds, and red tape. Since small stills are practical and inexpensive, a first step toward using alcohol fuels—and conserving gasoline—would be to simplify the application process.

On balance, with proper planning and careful consideration of all the implications of large-scale crop production to produce energy, gasohol could become a key factor in keeping us mobile.

J.S.

Wavemakers:

DISTILLING HIGH TEST

In 1957, when Albert Hubbard stilled his last batch of brew in the Mississippi hills, it was destined for the seasoned gullets of his regular customers. Though Hubbard's backwoods corn whiskey met with the approval of his clients, the U.S. government didn't share their enthusiasm. Hubbard was arrested and, following a well-established Southern tradition, thrown into jail on a charge of illegal "moonshining."

So it was with a certain appreciation and amusement that Albert Hubbard gazed, twenty years later, at an uncompleted alcohol still, quite visible off highway U.S. 80 outside Selma, Alabama. "To be honest," he recalled, "it looked like something out of the funny papers."

Hubbard got to talking with Albert Turner, a husky, black farmer who was directing the construction. The two Alberts quickly became friends, and before long the inelegant distillery—made in large part from junkyard paraphernalia—was producing 186-proof ethanol, more than twice the strength of Jack Daniel's whiskey. For Hubbard it was just like old times.

It wasn't quite. This time around the still had the blessing of the U.S. government, and its product, instead of fueling the passions of local swill-bellies, would fuel a guzzler of a different sort—the automobile.

In 1977, former civil rights activist Albert Turner conceived of the ethanol still as a source of income and self-sufficiency for an economically depressed black farming community outside Selma. At the time he was a pioneer in reapplying the hills technology of moonshining to the new problems of an energy-short age. Gasohol—a blend of gasoline and alcohol—was not a new idea, just a forgotten one. Now Albert Turner, and a growing number of other small farmers around the United States and the world, are demonstrating its attractiveness as a renewable, community-based fuel source.

With an $86,000 seed grant from the U. S. Office of Minority Business Enterprise, Turner and his Southwest Alabama Farmers Cooperative built a still that can produce 2,500 to 3,000 gallons (9,460 to 11,360 liters) of ethanol a week for use in cars and farm machinery. And by using a

wood-burning furnace and minimizing transportation costs, they can produce ethanol for much less than a dollar a gallon.

Turner's still is also pumping new life into the once-ailing co-op. After several years of drought and bad crops, he launched the project as "a combination of trying to find a way to use rotten crops and revive the co-op." Now local farmers are growing corn to fuel the still, and using the mash, a by-product of the distilling process, to feed livestock.

Of course they also come to the Turner still to "fill 'er up." When a local minister dropped by in his Chevy Impala for a few gallons of the special brew, Turner quipped: "Once the preacher gets hooked on this stuff, the whole congregation will go for it." The preacher later returned for more. In 1978, Turner and his cohorts went to Washington, D.C., to convince a different sort of congregation—the U. S. Congress—that community-based gasohol projects are viable. To make his point, Turner, accompanied by a caravan of gasohol advocates, drove his green alcohol-powered tractor to the foot of the Capitol steps. An impressed Senator invited him in to testify before a Senate subcommittee.

With the gradual relaxing of formerly stringent federal laws limiting backyard distilleries, more former moonshiners are bound to go back into business, though their product will find a different use. As Albert Hubbard, the one-time producer of white lightning, put it: "Nobody around here knew I knew anything about it. It's sort of like coming out of retirement."

B.P.B.

SALINITY GRADIENTS

Liquids, nutrients, and gases enter and leave every cell of all living matter through a semipermeable membrane. We know this process as osmosis. It establishes a balance between what is in the cell and what is not, enabling the cell to select from its environment that which it needs to remain healthy. When the balance is disturbed, life is disturbed. For example, if a human being drinks seawater, excess salt is distributed to the cells, interfering with normal osmotic balance, drying body tissue instead of bathing it. The salt water, more concentrated than cell liquid, exerts pressure on the cell wall, and in an attempt to equalize the pressure, the inner cell liquid migrates through the cell wall out into the salt solution, abandoning the cell, shriveling it, eventually dehydrating it.

This same relationship between fresh- and saltwater concentrations is being studied as a potential source of new energy. Where rivers meet the sea, fresh and salt waters interact in "salinity gradients," from which it may be possible to produce electricity.

In this process, fresh water from a river or estuary flows into the lower compartment of a tank. Seawater flows into the upper compartment. The two waters are separated by a semipermeable membrane that allows only fresh water to pass through. The fresh water then flows up into the salty water by osmosis.

The upper water volume, now a mixture of sea and river water at a pressure higher than atmospheric pressure, flows out of the holding compartment, creating a "waterfall" that can be used to drive a turbine, creating electricity. Some of this energy can be diverted to the beginning of the process and used to pressurize incoming seawater so that energy could be generated for as long as rivers flow into the sea. Theoretically it would be possible to create a waterfall at the mouth of every river and wherever water flows over salt flats along desert coasts. Other salinity gradient processes involve using electrochemical solutions, but all depend on the energy potential released during the basic osmotic process.

In theory, the flow of the Congo River could produce salinity gradient power of about 128,000 megawatts, an amount equivalent to the output of 128 large nuclear power plants.

Of course, the environmental impact of salinity gradient installations could be formidable. The required tanks would be enormous intrusions into the natural river systems. There is also the question of intercepting river flow—waters that normally feed the sea would be partially trapped in the salinity gradient generator. No one can predict what the effect of such major interruptions would be.

Finally, there is the question of the effect of wastewaters. At the last stage of the process, there would probably be a release of brackish water into the river. The impact of this is unclear, since animal and plant species that thrive in river waters might not survive should the river become more salty.

The potential environmental problems are not likely to worry anyone for a while, however, because salinity gradient technology is far from upon us. The membrane material needed for the holding compartment must be strong enough to withstand the constant pressure, the flow of water, and the contact with eroding salt solutions, and still be semipermeable. Such a material has yet to be developed.

As of early 1980, experiments with salinity gradients were going on in prototypical tanks, but there were no on-site experiments under way; possible locations are the Congo River and the Dead Sea. But for now, scientists and technologists are cautiously evaluating the potential and the promise of the rather audacious idea of securing usable energy from the mixing of waters.

P.D., L.W.

WATER HYACINTHS

In 1884, at the Cotton States Exhibition in New Orleans, Louisiana, the lavender flowers of the water hyacinth were given away as souvenirs. They were considered exotica, brought especially for the fair from the Orinoco River in Venezuela by a group of exhibitors who had passed through the tropics and thought the plant was lovely. And it was.

But no one who received the flowers in 1884 understood that hyacinths grow prolifically—ten plants can reproduce to cover an acre (0.4 hectare) of water densely in eight months—or that away from their natural environment they were also away from the natural control system of insects and viruses that keep the hyacinth count within limits. So as the gifts from the fair were eventually disposed of, they found their way into U.S. streams, rivers, and canals, multiplying at runaway rates. The plants traveled from Louisiana through Texas and Florida, and by 1905 there was a 100-mile-long (161-kilometer) hyacinth cluster 600 miles (966 kilometers) from the Exhibition site in New Orleans. Such rapid and intense transplantation is possible because the floating plant travels easily, up or down stream, responding to the slightest winds and currents. The plant can even be lifted entirely off the water by a breeze and blown to another breeding ground. Consequently, hyacinths can lodge in the most remote water areas, and there begin new hyacinth colonies. Some hyacinth patches are so thick that humans can walk on top of them without sinking into the water. In Africa, especially on the Nile and Congo rivers, boat traffic has been severely disrupted by obstructive hyacinth mats. The mats also divert valuable irrigation water from cropland—hyacinths are about 95 percent water, absorbing it directly through tubular stems, as if through a straw.

The hyacinth has continued to propagate so steadfastly that it is now one of the world's most costly aquatic plant pests. About $11 million is spent per year in the southern United States alone on hyacinth control. The plant has spread from its native Venezuela to fifty other countries, favoring tropical and subtropical regions but surviving even in some temperate areas such as northern California, Australia, New Zealand, and Argentina. In each country hyacinths are doused with herbicides and hacked with cutting machines, but to date no nation has successfully eradicated the plant. The manatee, an aquatic mammal that dines voraciously on hyacinths as part of its normal diet, is now almost extinct, a factor that has contributed to the hyacinth proliferation, especially in the Caribbean, Florida, and the southeastern United States (see "Manatees and Dugongs," page 305).

But the itinerant hyacinth turns out to have properties unappreciated until recently. In the early 1970s it was discovered that the plant could be extraordinarily useful as a water purifier. The root system is an excellent natural absorber of chemicals and pollutants, including mercury, lead, and strontium-90. These toxic agents have been found in hyacinths in concentrations ten thousand times higher than the source water itself.

The United States National Aeronautics and Space Administration (NASA) established experimental pools to determine exactly how effective the hyacinths could be, hoping that the plants could be used in spaceships to purify water and generate oxygen. In the test system, a series of ponds clogged with hyacinths were interconnected and polluted water was channeled through them. As of 1979, the tests showed that contaminated water entering the pond maze runs clean and odorless at the end of the series. These promising results have led to several water purification pilot projects.

The water hyacinth—pest or water purifier? (*The Cousteau Society*)

Philippe and Jacques-Yves Cousteau survey a mat of prolific water hyacinths in Florida. (*The Cousteau Society*)

In fact, the hyacinth may redeem its reputation on many levels—not only does the plant cleanse water, but it is itself a potentially rich energy and food source. Hyacinths grown in a nontoxic environment can be shredded and fermented into biogas, or methane, and used as fuel. Egypt and the Sudan, for example, have begun a joint hyacinth harvest project on the Nile, and early results have been commercially promising. The sludge that remains from this process can be used as fertilizer. Hyacinths grown in very fertile environments can be used as a nutrient additive for livestock feed, or even as a protein supplement for human consumption.

Though its potential remains to be proved, the hyacinth may well become a valuable all-purpose flower. It is ironic—perhaps even a metaphorical ecology lesson—that water pollution, ugly in concept as well as reality, could be rendered at least partly manageable by a delicate, elegant plant.

P.D.

COGENERATION

In the late spring of 1978, developers renovating a thirty-story New York City office building announced plans to pull the plug on electric and heat service supplied by the local utility company. The office building, they announced, would go it alone and generate its own power and heat.

Faced with the prospect of losing other big customers to such schemes, utility officials were aghast. Not accustomed to calling for public hearings, the utility company demanded one and got it, so they could warn the city against allowing such on-site power generation.

At issue was the resurgence of an old idea, "cogeneration," or simply put, the combined on-site production of heat and electricity—and at least some utilities wish the long-ignored idea would be forgotten again.

Like many other early but promising alternative energy technologies, cogeneration failed to catch on much in the United States after the decline of electric rates in the 1950s. For example, 15 percent of the nation's entire electricity supply in 1950 was generated by industry, not utility companies. But by 1973 that figure had plummeted to 5 percent. It has been a different story in Europe, however, where cogeneration caught on and remains a popular source of power. West Germany is a leader in cogeneration, with industry producing over one quarter of the nation's electric power, while Great Britain's industry generates 20 percent of its electrical needs.

In the face of decreased energy supply and rising costs, cogeneration is being talked about again in the United States. President Carter reintroduced Americans to the term in a 1977 energy speech. Even big business, which obviously has much to gain from cutting energy bills, is tangling with utility officials over the merits of cogeneration. Dow Chemical Company, a giant multinational corporation based in Michigan, predicts in one massive study that U.S. industry could generate up to half its own energy by 1985 using cogeneration. Dow should know—the company currently produces 80 percent of its own power using the technology.

The basics of cogeneration are not complex. It's simply a process that conserves the waste heat normally vented into the air or dumped into rivers and lakes during conventional industrial processes, including power production. Cogenerators retain that heat and use it to warm the building or to run other generators. There are several variations of industrial on-site cogeneration technology. One system uses steam, normally utilized only for industrial processes, to turn a turbine for the generation of electricity. Another cogeneration system taps waste heat from a furnace and instead of sending it up a stack uses it to vaporize a fluid, which in turn drives a turbogenerator.

Cogeneration is not merely an energy technique for industrial and commercial users. Fiat, the Italian car manufacturer, has produced a $3,000 cogenerator for the homeowner. The Fiat cogeneration system, which relies on a small engine normally used in one of its automobiles, can produce both heat and electricity for the home at a cost that is already competitive. The energy efficiency of the Fiat cogenerator (or the portion of the fuel directly converted into usable energy) approaches a remarkable 90 percent.

The specter of rising energy independence has sent shudders through some sectors of the utility industry, and, led by New York's Consolidated Edison Company, they are putting up a fight. Utility officials argue that diesel-fueled cogenerators could cause additional pollution, particularly in urban areas, increased reliance on imported oil, and higher rates for individuals who must assume a greater share of the utility's fixed costs as cogenerating customers pull out of the system.

Cogenerator manufacturers dispute the validity of these claims, arguing that the systems are relatively nonpolluting and are enormously efficient oil burners. Environmentalist Barry Commoner has a more fundamental answer to those questions. He argues that eventually cogeneration systems can be run on readily available methane fuel, resulting in negligible pollution, and since methane is a renewable fuel that can be produced locally, there would be no dependence on foreign energy supplies.

Alden Meyer, utility analyst for the Washington, D.C., Environmental Action Foundation, shares some concern that in the short term consumers might be saddled with an increased rate burden if there is a wholesale shift to cogeneration. He believes, however, that the problem could be minimized if utilities are forced by regulatory agencies to plan for the change. In the United States, with the passage of new federal legislation promoting cogeneration, that regulatory pressure is building. In the long term, Meyer says, cogeneration can only mean large savings for all ratepayers as plans for extremely costly new central power plants, no longer necessary, can be scrapped.

Despite cogeneration's merits as a common-sense technology, there is no guarantee that the United States will catch up to Europe in its application. The obstacles to its development aren't technical anyway. Pointing to the aggressive lobbying and legal campaign being waged by opponents of the widespread use of cogeneration, Meyer predicts, "It will be a huge fight."

B.P.B.

AGROFORESTRY

One third of the land area of the world is still classified as forest, but the eradication of woodlands is proceeding at a tremendous rate in many countries. While industrialized nations anguish over the availability of oil for energy, the world's poorer countries wrestle with a different energy problem. Some experts call it the worst energy problem in the world. In Africa, Asia, and Latin America, wood remains the principal fuel for cooking and keeping warm, as it has been throughout history. In the past the forests were chopped down gradually, over centuries, with little thought given to replanting them. But in the years since World War II, the population of many nations has more than doubled. As a result, more trees are cut down every year in these countries.

Large-scale deforestation initiates a chain of problems:

- In a peasant economy, where wood is necessary every day, the search for wood becomes progressively more time-consuming as the forests disappear. In some areas in South Asia farmers have become increasingly dependent on the use of dried animal dung to cook their food and warm their houses, diverting this land-restoring fertilizer from the soil.
- When trees are cut down on hillsides and annual crops are planted, the soil often erodes, making agriculture eventually impossible. (See "Things Disappearing: Topsoil," page 394.)
- In humid tropical forests like those of the Amazon and the Congo, the soil layer is not very deep. Once the trees are cut, minerals often leach out of the soil within five years, leaving behind a hard, claylike mass where only desert shrubs can grow. (See "Amazonia," page 274.)
- The soil erosion caused by deforestation, especially on hillsides, leads directly to heavy silt loads in local rivers, making them much more subject to flooding downstream than they were before the trees were cut down. (See "The Himalayas," page 189.)

Agroforestry is one possible solution to the problems of deforestation and the use of marginal land. Agroforestry is the growing of trees in an integrated system of agriculture, forestry, and conservation.

Like ordinary forestry, agroforestry is concerned with growing trees for lumber, fiber, and extracts for oil, sugar, alcohol, and drugs. But agroforestry includes many other uses of trees and relates the growing of trees to other aspects of a local environment. For example, trees could be planted constructively to rehabilitate eroded land, stop sand dunes, and fill up gullies. Under a well-managed system of agroforestry, marginal land would be taken out of agricultural use, with its attendant soil depletion, and instead planted with trees and shrubs of economic value.

Many useful trees grow well in dry, hot, windy, cold, or steep areas, where farming is difficult. For example, the pods of drought-resistant carob and honey-locust trees are good livestock fodder. The hardy jojoba shrub, which is a native of the American desert, is a new, valuable substitute for whale oil (see "Jojoba," page 10). Multipurpose trees like the fast-growing eucalyptus provide shelter and shade, forage for bees, and good fuel wood.

Particularly fast-growing tree species would be planted for harvesting as fuel a few years later. Orchards can be established on steep hillsides, substituting soil-binding root systems for the soil-eroding plow often used there now. The same productive trees, planted between fields as windbreaks, have been shown to increase the yield and quality of produce in the fields they shelter.

Another possible application of agroforestry is as a wastewater filter. Recent experiments have successfully employed forest vegetation as a "living filter" for sewage effluent. Irrigating the forest with wastewater makes trees grow faster at the same time that it purifies the water. The trees absorb the nutrients that otherwise pollute streams, rivers, or the ocean. A special advantage is that some industrial wastewater contains potentially dangerous concentrations of certain heavy metals. Tree species that can tolerate these pollutants will effectively lock up the heavy metals they absorb.

Plots of trees and hedgerows interspersed among fields of corn, rice, or wheat can serve as a "pest break" to slow the spread of insects or crop diseases.

Persuading or encouraging the hill and marginal-land farmers of the developing world to substitute agroforestry for plow cultivation is not easy. The gains are not immediate, because trees take longer to grow than annual crops. The future sustained yield of a cash crop may not tempt a farmer whose family is barely subsisting on what they grow from year to year. Short-term exploitation is easier, and many of the farmers do not understand the long-term damage they are doing to their land. For these reasons, it is a hopeful sign that the World Bank has pledged an important increase in its funding of agroforestry projects. Several of these have already been successful in Africa and Asia. A nonprofit agroforestry research group, the International Tree Crops Institute, has been set up in the United States and England.

Although agroforestry requires some investment of time and money to get started, and although it cannot meet world food needs alone, it can be a vital addition to world agricultural production, redeeming and preserving our water and our soil.

J.S.

NUCLEAR FUSION

Nuclear fusion is the primordial process that makes all life possible on earth. It is the basis of solar energy. The mass of the sun creates tremendous gravitational pressure, which pulls hydrogen atoms into its core. Two hydrogen nuclei fuse together to form a helium nucleus. This fusion converts some of the original mass into energy and thus produces the heat of the sun, a temperature of 27 million° F (15 million° C).

Nuclear fission, which is the principle behind currently operating nuclear power plants, produces heat when a nucleus of a heavy atom, such as uranium, breaks into smaller pieces. Fission is a constantly occurring process in the universe. Nuclear power plants merely concentrate the fissile material so that a chain reaction is started that produces enough heat to generate electricity. This process is dangerous, because the necessary radioactive materials and the by-products of fission reaction are harmful, the reaction can get out of control, and a large quantity of long-lived radioactive waste is created. (See "Meltdown, Near Meltdown, and Other 'Events,'" page 451; "Things Accumulating: Nuclear Wastes," page 404; and "The Horses of the Atom," page 447.)

Many scientists see nuclear fusion as a cheaper, more efficient, and less dangerous source of energy than nuclear fission and are trying to find a way to produce and control a fusion reaction. They have already succeeded in generating uncontrolled fusion—the hydrogen bomb.

The fuel for nuclear fusion in the sun is hydrogen, which is abundant on earth. However, fusing hydrogen nuclei requires duplicating the extraordinary temperatures and pressures of the sun's core. One answer to the problem lies with deuterium, an isotope of hydrogen that contains an extra neutron in the nucleus and is more easily fused together than hydrogen atoms. Although only one out of every 6,500 hydrogen atoms is deuterium, the supply is sufficient to provide billions of years of energy at today's rates. Unfortunately, at the present state of the art, even deuterium fusion remains beyond practical application.

Tritium is a radioactive isotope of hydrogen that has two extra neutrons. Scientists are moving closer to fusion reactions containing tritium mixed with deuterium. Tritium, however, rarely occurs in nature and must be manufactured by nuclear bombardment of the metal lithium, which is found in limited quantities. Researchers hope to be able eventually to sustain a fusion reaction without tritium.

Even with tritium as a fuel, commercial fusion plants are not expected to become practical until about 2030, although some scientists maintain that increased research support could make fusion commercially viable as early as 2000. The major obstacle is not control or waste or danger but simply making the process happen. Researchers at Princeton's Plasma Physics Laboratory achieved a temperature of 133 million° F (74 million° C) in 1978, but the pressure was not sufficient to achieve sustained fusion.

Inside a fusion research device at the Oak Ridge National Laboratory in Tennessee, magnetic coils (pictured here) confine and compress fusion plasma. (*Union Carbide/DOE*)

No container can withstand the heat of fusion, and scientists are pursuing two approaches to the problem of keeping the fuel in a limited space so that the nuclei will react with one another rather than dispersing. The first approach is the takomak, a device that holds the nuclei by means of a magnetic field. The second approach is to bombard the fuel with electron beams or lasers under conditions that allow the fusion to take place before the nuclei have time to disperse. The first approach seems the most promising, but the second has certain advantages that deserve to be explored as well.

Fusion power must overcome several obstacles before becoming feasible. Magnetic fields must be improved, and materials for the containment vessel walls must be developed that can withstand the heat and intense radiation without breaking down. The fuel might be cheap eventually, but the power plant itself could be very expensive to build and operate. One significant advantage of fusion is that it is potentially safer than fission. Fusion plants could not melt down, and any explosion would be no more than a small pop. Although waste would be reduced and no uranium or plutonium would be produced, some radioactive materials would be created and the reactor itself would be radioactive.

Even when fusion is achieved in the laboratory, a commercial fusion reactor will be many years away. And after the first commercial reactor is built, many more years will pass before enough fusion plants can be built to make a sufficient energy contribution.

K.F.

TURBINES IN THE GULF STREAM

One of the several thousand schemes the U. S. Department of Energy is studying for alternative energy sources was proposed by AeroVironment Inc., of Pasadena, California: putting huge turbines into the Gulf Stream to generate electricity for much of Florida.

According to AeroVironment, 250 of these huge turbines, each 560 feet (171 meters) in diameter, could supply about 10,000 megawatts a year to customers on shore.

The turbines, held in place by 6,000-ton (5.4-metric-ton) anchors and 2-mile-long (3.2-kilometer) steel cables, would be sunk 25 miles (40 kilometers) off the coast of Florida, in the fastest-flowing stretch of the Gulf Stream. The 4-knot current would rotate the blades of the turbine about once a minute, producing a huge amount of power. The cost per kilowatt-hour, according to AeroVironment, would be less than the cost of power from a new nuclear plant, but more

Artist's rendering of a giant turbine that could be submerged in the Gulf Stream to produce electricity. Conceived by N. J. Mouton and D. M. Thompson, developed by AeroVironment Inc., and funded by Hydro-Energy Associates and U. S. Dept. of Energy. (*AeroVironment Inc./Mark E. McClandish, artist*)

than the cost of power from a new oil-burning plant. The technology for building the turbines is already available.

The major problem with this scheme, however, is the unknown effect these turbines would have on the flow of the Gulf Stream. AeroVironment calculates that 250 turbines would slow the Gulf Stream less than 1 percent—perhaps a negligible slowdown, or perhaps not. The question still remains unanswered.

What would happen if other countries copied these ocean-powered turbines within their own waters and slowed other ocean currents by a few percentage points?

What would happen to the ocean life around these 250 turbines in the fastest part of the Gulf Stream? One can imagine the catastrophe of a whale pod caught in whirling blades, or the disruption of migratory fish schools, but the scope of potential abuses is difficult to determine.

AeroVironment Inc. has a $230,000 contract from the Department of Energy to study this program further and to discover any harmful effects it might have on the Gulf Stream, which affects the climate of the entire North Atlantic region. (The problem is also being mentioned in studies of another ocean energy scheme; see "OTEC," page 23.) Even a slight change could produce severe results. For example, since the Gulf Stream keeps northern Europe warm, a temperature shift of only a few degrees could make England as cold as Labrador and the Yukon, areas at the same latitude that are unaffected by a warming current.

J.S.

CONSTRUCTION IN SPACE

If the National Aeronautics and Space Administration (NASA) has its way, the space near earth will soon begin to sprout all sorts of dreamlike structures. Parasol-type antennas, some 100 feet (30.5 meters) across will pop open in orbit to service an ever-expanding communications system back on earth—a system that will include pocket telephones not much bigger than Dick Tracy's wristwatch. Robot craft called "space spiders" will weave airy, fabulous structures out of materials not much thicker than aluminum foil. Space-suited workers will be busy up there, too. In the apparent weightlessness of space even the scrawniest among them will be able to push around a structure as heavy as a Mack truck on earth. Because these buildings will virtually float in space, humans will have the freedom to extend them in all directions at once—the dream come true of a small child with an erector set.

This grand space show, duly publicized and televised by the space agency for the benefit of fascinated earthlings, will culminate at the turn of the century, or so NASA hopes, in the biggest space structures of them all: solar-power satellites. Each would be nearly as big as Manhattan, a startling 12 miles (19.3 kilometers) long and about 3 miles (4.8 kilometers) across. Shining like synthetic stars at night, these giant platforms would beam energy to earth around the clock.

The first question that obviously comes to mind is: Who needs these structures and who is going to pay for all the cosmic exhilaration? A single solar-power satellite, for instance, will cost somewhere between $2 billion and $20 billion, depending on whose estimate you believe, and the United States would have to have about 100 of them to supply 30 percent of its electric-power needs. NASA's answer is a mixture of the practical and the imaginatively farfetched. Some of the projects can be expected to pay their own way almost from the start, while others are too speculative for any meaningful cost-benefit analysis.

Communications Projects

The practical, near-term projects will be in communications. Satellites that relay signals between points on earth are already a big and worthwhile business, and the first effect of the space shuttle will be to cut launching costs by more than half, from $20 million to $9 million. The cargo bay of the [NASA space] shuttle will house a mechanical arm that can toss satellites out like basketballs or reach out and retrieve them when they need repairs. As the traffic increases, the satellites will inevitably get larger and more powerful. The U. S. Air Force is already designing a dish antenna for radar that will collapse into a trim package for transport aboard the shuttle and then pop open after it is launched.

The most useful space antennas are those in what is called geosynchronous orbit. This orbit, 22,500 miles (36,200 kilometers) up, keeps the satellites above a given spot on earth and so always in a good position to receive and transmit signals. Many of the satellites launched in near-

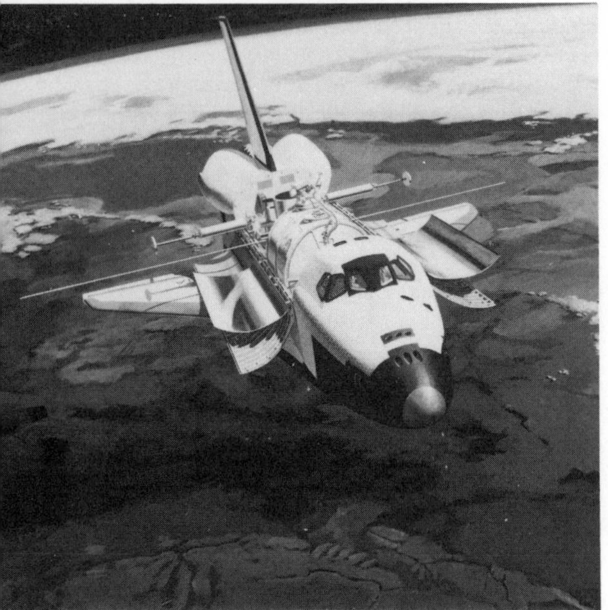

The NASA space shuttle, which would take off and land like a regular airplane, is slated to become the workhorse of the space program, ferrying people and materials from earth to space. In this artist's conception, a crewmember performs extravehicular work outside the cargo bay. (*NASA*)

earth orbit by the shuttle will be equipped with rockets to take them to their stations. Later on, however, as communications needs continue to grow, it will be more efficient to build a great battery of antennas—an antenna "farm," as NASA calls it—in the near-earth orbit to which the shuttle will be confined. The metal skeleton, perhaps 700 feet (214 meters) long, would house as many as thirty large dish antennas. Once completed, it could be towed or propelled up to geosynchronous orbit.

According to a study by Rockwell International, such an antenna farm could simultaneously satisfy many different communications needs. It could easily handle the rapidly growing volume of electronic mail, most of it generated by business. It could accommodate up to five nationwide television channels, though the viewers back on earth would have to buy a one-meter dish antenna at a cost of about $100. Because this transmitter in space would be much more powerful than those now in place, the receiving stations on earth could be simpler—as simple, in fact, as those pocket phones. An antenna farm could service as many as 45,000 private channels, which could handle calls from millions of pocket telephones. Rockwell estimates that the calls, which could also be made to and from conventional telephones, would cost only about twenty cents each.

Rockwell also thinks that inexpensive satellite communication will be of great benefit to the developing world. Paramedics in remote villages would be able to get a diagnosis of difficult cases by pocket telephone, and young people could be taught new skills by television.

It is in building the antenna farms that construction in space will really begin, probably around 1985. To get a jump on some of the problems, however, Grumman Aerospace Corporation has already designed a beam extruder, a later model of which will be carried aboard the shuttle. It can turn out a triangular, interconnected skeleton of thin aluminum at a speed of 5 feet (1.5 meters) a minute. At that rate, the beam builder could cough up a mile-long (1.61-kilometer) structure in less than a day. There will be cherry-picker cranes equipped with their own maneuvering rockets, as well as more mundane space tools such as cable cutters, adjustable wrenches, pliers, and scissors. "You could go to any construction site and see equipment that might be schematically the same as we might use in space," says Allen J. Louviere, chief of the spacecraft-design division of NASA's Houston center. "You'd have to have workers, materials, trucks, an elevator, a crane. We've got to have all those, too, but they may look different and operate somewhat differently because of the unique conditions in space."

The main difference from conditions on earth—the apparent weightlessness—is more an advantage than a problem. Structures won't have to bear the stresses they do on earth and will serve merely as positioning frameworks for the mechanisms attached to them. "You don't have to worry about high winds, or a snowfall that might crush the roof," adds Richard L. Kline, deputy director of advanced space programs at Grumman. "The structure won't rust or corrode, either, the way my car does." Meteorites, however, could strike the structures in space.

The biggest stress these structures will have to bear will be the thrust of the rockets used to move them up to geosynchronous orbit. Once they are 22,500 miles (36,200 kilometers) up and out of the earth's shadow, they will be bathed in continuous sunlight except for a few minutes of eclipse during the days of the spring and fall equinoxes. But the temperature change during an eclipse will be dramatic, as much as 700° F (390° C), and large expanses of thin metal would

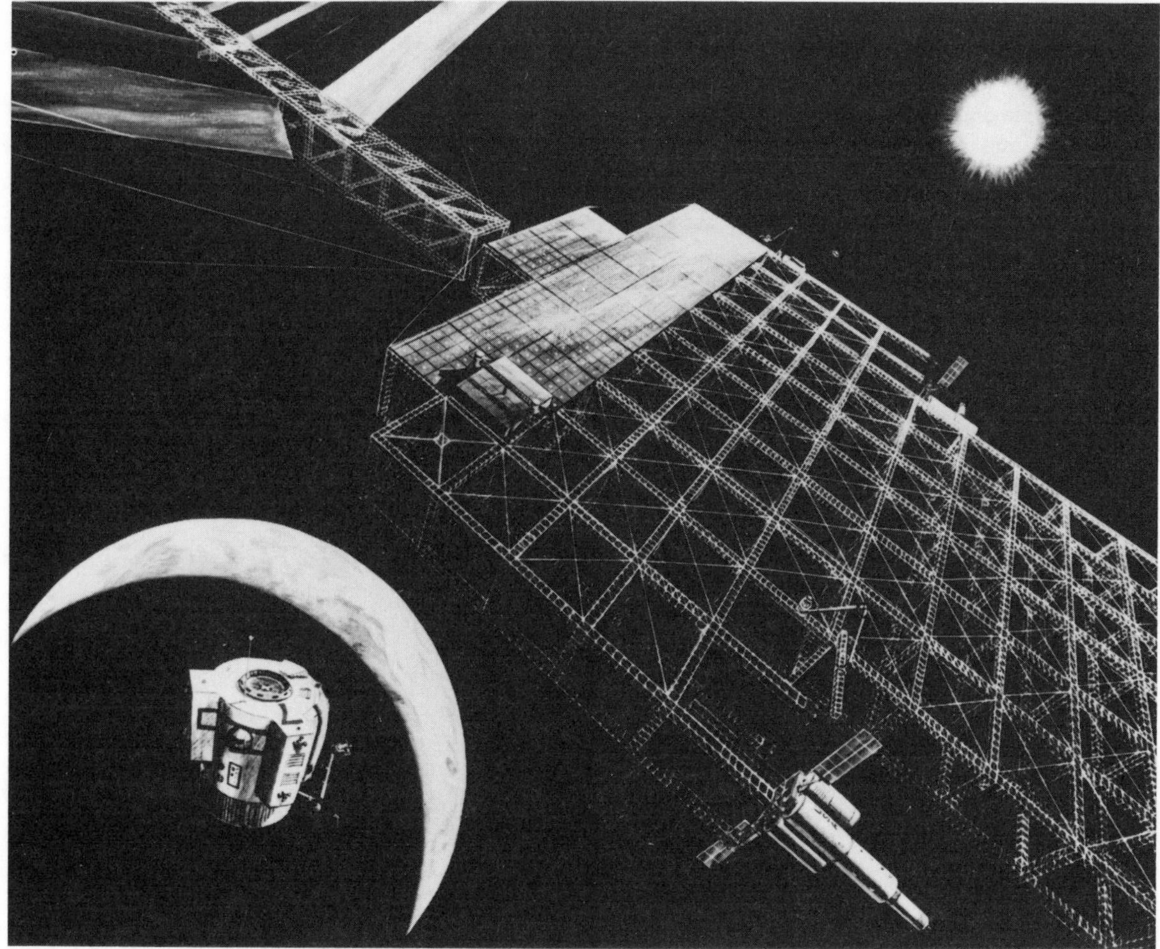

Artist's conception of a solar-power satellite microwave transmission antenna being assembled in orbit 36,000 miles (58,000 kilometers) above the earth. (*NASA/Courtesy DOE*)

tend to curl around the edges. Other materials, such as a composite of graphite and epoxy, will hold up well.

Weightlessness is not quite so congenial to humans. The orbital assembly people will have to have a grip on something solid. Otherwise, says Louviere of NASA, "If the thing you're trying to work on is bigger than you are, you may find that it's turning you rather than you turning it." Space-suited workers are rather clumsy, too, and tire easily, so a lot of mechanical aids will be used. A shirt-sleeved astronaut sitting in a flying robot with mechanical arms will be able to get a lot more work done. The astroworkers will have to be neat: any debris will hang around their work sites to haunt them. If a workman drops a tool up there, it will not fall, of course, but slowly drift away.

As assembly moves farther out, to the geosynchronous orbit where the solar-power satellites are supposed to be built, new hazards will loom. To shield themselves from periodic bursts of potentially fatal radiation from the sun, the astronauts would mostly work inside robot craft or control centers, directing mechanical arms and other automatic equipment.

Energy Projects

Solar-power satellites will be a grand climax to the space show—if they are ever built. Unlike earth-based solar collectors, these satellites would face no vagaries of weather or day-night cycles, and thus would be exposed to ten times the amount of sunlight available on earth. The 36 square miles (93 square kilometers) of solar cells would feed 10 megawatts of electricity into the antenna portion of the satellite, where it would be transformed into microwaves and beamed back to earth. Receiving antennas on the ground would turn the beam back into electricity and put it into the power grid.

What would be an impressive construction job on earth becomes a mind-boggling one in space.

NASA estimates that 550 workers would be needed to build a solar satellite, and some space planners are already worrying about how to keep that many people healthy and happy in space. Each satellite would require 100,000 tons (90,700 metric tons) of materials, much of it exotic composites that now cost as much as $50 a pound ($110 a kilogram). Ferrying up the people, equipment, and supplies would take ten flights a day by the space shuttle or its successor.

The job looks so formidable that some space boosters have seriously suggested using the moon rather than the earth as the main source of raw materials. Because the moon's gravitational pull is weaker than earth's, much less power would be needed to lift off large payloads. In this scheme, the moon's abundant and high-grade ores would be propelled for processing to space colonies in very high orbit or at the so-called Lagrange libration points, 250,000 miles (400,000 kilometers) from earth, where large structures would remain stationary because the gravitational pulls of the earth, the moon, and the sun are equalized there. The Rockwell report gave this plan rather cool treatment, but NASA is still studying it. Sunsat, an aerospace lobby, and L-5 clubs around the United States (named for the fifth libration point) are keeping hope alive.

Apart from the cost of solar-power satellites, there are unresolved questions about just how safe those microwave beams would be for life here on earth. They would be carefully directed into the huge receiving antennas and would harmlessly defocus if a beam got "unlocked" from its antenna. But nearby areas would pick up a low-level dose, and nobody knows yet what long-term effect this would have on animals, plants, and humans.

Advocates of the solar-power satellites point out that the beams would be only about one fourth as intense as sunlight. Unlike sunlight, though, microwave radiation can be highly penetrating even at low intensity. Songbirds, which happen to be about the same size as the wavelength of the radiation, might almost resonate if caught in the beam. They would certainly absorb more microwave heat than humans.

"We need to know whether birds, bats, bees, and other species flying over the receiving antenna will be killed by the microwave beam," says Richard D. Phillips of Batelle Pacific Northwest Laboratories, who managed a study on the potential biological effects of the beam for the Department of Energy. "If the flying biota are killed, it may mean that the solar-power satellite concept, as now designed, is not feasible." Even if the beams are less dangerous than feared, says Phillips, the receiving antennas may have to be situated in remote, sparsely populated areas.

There are also unanswered questions about the beam's possible effect on the atmosphere—in terms of both heating it up and disrupting communications on earth. But the solar-power satellite holds such an enticing promise of unlimited energy that at least it deserves further study. Peter E. Glaser, a vice president at Arthur D. Little, Inc., who first proposed the idea ten years ago, suggests that if the United States finds the costs too much to bear, it might go into partnership with other countries.

Whatever the exact level of funding, power from space, like power from fusion, isn't likely to arrive until the next century.

Condensed with permission from "Space Will Be the Next Big Construction Site," by Gene Bylinsky.

DOLPHINSPEAK

About 50 million years ago a hoofed land mammal returned to the sea. Once there it gradually lost its fur and evolved a thick coat of sleek fat. The body grew streamlined, enabling it to glide through water like a knife. It lost all but internal remnants of its hind legs while developing a powerful tail and modified forelimbs, which it used as steering paddles. In many species a dorsal fin evolved, one final bit of engineering to outfit a superb swimmer.

The Greeks named the animal *delphys.* In their mythology it was the symbol of the womb, as well as the womb "monster" that Apollo defeated at Delphi. Since then, the dolphin has been firmly fixed in art, history, and mythology—our spiritual sibling, some say parent, carrying a small Greek child on its back in play, or a drowning sailor to safety.

Aristotle accurately recognized the dolphin's relationship to whales. He described its anatomy, its ability to hear well, its methods of respiration and reproduction, its amazing speed, its special bond with its offspring, and its gentle "friendship" with humans.

Since antiquity there has been little doubt that dolphins are intelligent. We know that relative to its size and weight, a dolphin's brain is large and as convoluted as the human brain. But just *how* intelligent dolphins are remains a wide-open question. Some suggest the dolphin is at least smarter than any other animal and possibly even smarter than humans. But it is still far too soon to fix dolphin intelligence in relation to anything or anyone else.

Attempting to Bridge Two Worlds

Long-term dolphin observation in the wild is next to impossible. And observation in captivity, beside demanding prohibitive funding, inhumanely limits the animal and possibly the skills it can display. Nevertheless, beginning in the 1950s with Dr. John Lilly's work on the dolphin brain, some interesting and even controversial work has been done to assess dolphin intelligence, social behavior, and communication.

As researchers observed dolphin groups, a definite dominance hierarchy was discovered. When each dolphin was found to have a signature whistle by which it could be identified, group dynamics could be studied. A sophisticated array of interactions was revealed. Besides some now well-known examples of social behavior (protecting an injured group member and even lifting it to the surface to help it breathe), tests showed that dolphins have highly developed learning and memory capabilities. Furthermore, they displayed a remarkable ability to detect differences in sound pitch and surprisingly keen vision, in air as well as in water.

Two aspects of dolphin communication are under study. Scientists are interested in natural dolphin communication within the species as well as a kind of interspecies communication—dubbed "dolphinspeak"—in which humans teach a form of our language to dolphins. In his early experiments Dr. Lilly tried to teach a kind of spoken English to captive dolphins. His meager success was attributed to a possible inability of the animals to hear well within the human speech range and to imitate any sound approaching human speech. With greater success, the Navy tried teaching dolphins human words by translating them through a machine into whistlelike sounds. The animals could easily hear this type of sound and were adept at mimicking it.

Fetch Ball, Touch Pipe

In 1977, Dr. Louis Herman, a professor of psychology at the University of Hawaii, began researching dolphin language. After four months he successfully showed that dolphins can comprehend language to some degree. The commands he gave were limited to two-word sentences consisting of a noun and verb. The animals became familiar with three different nouns and three different verbs, allowing nine possible combinations such as "Fetch ball," "Touch pipe." However, Herman's work was abruptly halted when two employees at the laboratory released the dolphins to "free" them. (Herman believes the dolphins could not have survived in the open sea for very long. Since they had been reared in captivity, they probably did not know how to protect themselves and lacked the essential guidance of a dolphin school.)

In the summer of 1978, Herman acquired two new dolphins, Phoenix and Akeakamai (in Hawaiian, "lover of knowledge"). In terms of comprehension, not vocalization, each animal now has a vocabulary of more than twenty words. Phoenix has learned a computerized language. Sounds within the animal's range have been programmed into a computer. An operator at the keyboard generates sounds to the animal through an underwater speaker. Slowly, so as not to frustrate the animal, Phoenix has been taught to identify certain sounds that are, in fact, different objects and verbs. Akeakamai has been taught a hand signal language similar to the American deaf sign language now being taught to chimps. Each dolphin has responded to its language with about equal success, that is, given forty allowable command combinations, both Phoenix and Akeakamai responded correctly 85 to 90 percent of the time.

Herman's researchers are now up to three-word sentences consisting of a direct object, a verb, and an indirect object, for example, "Ball fetch window." At this command, both animals take the ball to the window. When "Ball fetch pipe" is tried, the animals are again successful. If the syn-

Spotted Dolphin
Common Porpoise
Common Dolphin
Ganges River Dolphin
Bottlenose Dolphin
Bluewhite Dolphin

tax is reversed to "Pipe fetch ball," both dolphins understand and bring the pipe to the ball.

Frisbee Fetch Panel

The next step will be to test the dolphins' understanding of the structure of language and to prove that they have not just memorized how to perform each act, or that they have not outsmarted their trainers. A familiar word like "Frisbee" will be used in a totally unfamiliar context, for example, "Frisbee fetch panel." If the animal follows this command correctly it will exhibit a real understanding of the fundamentals of language.

Using computers, several other marine biologists are working with dolphins with some interesting results. Project JANUS (for Joint Analog Numerical Understanding System), headed by Dr. Lilly, is a five-year program. Minicomputers "translate" the airborne words of humans into water-borne sonar tones programmed to correspond to the language and frequencies dolphins already use. Dr. Lilly hopes to evolve an alphabet consisting of sixty-four distinct sounds that will be enough to begin a dialogue. Lilly's preliminary results indicate that dolphins *can* recognize the frequencies of the human voice range and that they voluntarily modify their own range in a possibly deliberate attempt to communicate.

Should one or more of these experimental programs eventually succeed, the accomplishment would go beyond simple interspecies communication. The achievement would represent communication between two intelligences based on different systems of perception. The dolphin gains most of its information about the world around it acoustically, through an elaborate sonar sense. The human perspective, on the other hand, is largely a visual one. We know what the shape of the world *looks* like; the dolphin knows something of that, too, but knows also what the world *sounds* like (undersea at least). It remains to be seen, if we speak to one another intelligently someday, whether or not we will be talking about the same perceived universe.

Finding Comrades in the Sea

Where is this research headed, and why is it important? There are the common answers: simply to know, to better understand nature, perception, evolution, and the place of language.

But there is a less obvious, more engaging reason, too, as pointed out by Jacques Cousteau: "We need not ask what we would gain if we learned to communicate with mammals in the sea. We are a species alone. Any companionship we find would be a precious reward. We can find that companionship easily by making bonds rather than by practicing butchery; by searching the sea not for captives but for comrades."

L.W., P.D.

The dolphin has long been a symbol of beauty, grace, and intelligence. For centuries sailors have welcomed the appearance of dolphin packs alongside the bow of their ship, and have marveled at the animal's apparent exuberance and joy of life. All of these qualities are symbolized by the dolphin leaping alongside the sea nymph Calypso in The Cousteau Society logo. (*The Cousteau Society*)

GLOBAL EDUCATION

The scene: a class of twenty-five children scampering through a forest adjoining a nature center as a staff naturalist clad in hiking boots and wool shirt points out the scaly bark of the white oak, shows where to look for squirrels' nests, and picks out deer tracks in the mud.

This is the stereotyped image of environmental education, a growing field that is now reaching beyond nature centers, lacing together traditionally separate fields of study, spilling into community political actions, and spreading around the globe into private schools in England, tiny villages in Nepal, and worker groups in the Soviet Union.

While field trips to springtime meadows have not dropped from the repertoire of environmental educators, the discipline has taken on a broader, perhaps more serious mission: exploring with children (and adults) environmental problems that plague the world. Resource depletion, overconsumption, industrial waste, hunger, disease—the list of problems seems endless, but environmental educators hope that teaching schoolchildren, teachers, policymakers, businesspeople, technicians, and communities about the laws of nature will eventually result in a world with fewer problems. Children who grow up with an environmental awareness, they hope, will make more sensible decisions than some of their parents did.

Once restricted to biology classes and summer camps, environmental education is now both global and diverse.

- Children in the schools of Nepal are being taught how to choose the best fuel, a survival skill in a country with rapidly depleting sources of firewood.
- Five thousand students and their teachers are helping U.S. and Canadian scientists conduct field research.
- In an experimental one-year program in Cuba, Panama, Peru, and Brazil, students, teachers, and government officials studied environmental problems including soil erosion and water quality—and proposed solutions.
- In the Jordan Valley, children from three schools joined with adults to press for cleaner drinking water in the region by developing leaflets and posters to explain and demand action on water pollution.
- Educators in Afghanistan launched a three-year project to develop a teachers' package on sanitation, soil conservation, and drinking water and to train teachers to present these topics.
- In Czechoslovakia and the Soviet Union, party youth groups and factory workshops have begun to study environmental problems at their meetings.
- In Ann Arbor, Michigan, environmental education permeates the high-school curriculum. A science class explores the chemical composition of smog, a history class looks at the roots of environmental legislation, a sociology class examines the impact of pollution problems on the quality of life in their community.

These programs are part of a coordinated international effort to heighten human awareness of the fragility of our physical environment and the ways in which we depend on our natural resources. How did environmental education pick up global momentum? Although diverse approaches to environmental education began springing up around the world in the early 1970s, it was the United Nations project International Programme in Environmental Education, founded in 1974, that acted as a global catalyst to encourage environmental education. Two years earlier, in 1972, at the U. N. Conference on the Environment in Stockholm, Sweden, representatives assessed the growing global environmental crisis and decided education was part of the solution.

In 1974, Dr. William Stapp, an innovative educator who had designed an environmental curriculum for U.S. schools and who headed a program in environmental education at the University of Michigan, was asked to take on the staggering task of introducing environmental education to schools and communities throughout the world as director of the newly founded International Programme in Environmental Education. He was given a tiny budget of $65,000 with which to establish a framework to guide the efforts of the world's countries. Stapp opened an office in Paris and began with some tricky initial tasks. For example, just translating the term "environmental education" so that it conveyed the same message in every language was an accomplishment.

Stapp met with a group of twenty education specialists from around the world who suggested holding a conference of government representatives to endorse an international policy for environmental education.

Stapp rejected the idea of exporting the type of environmental education he had devised in Michigan, and instead sent consultants to scores of countries where they met with educators and public officials about their environmental problems and educational needs. Twelve months later, in October 1975, sixty-five specialists from around the world met in Belgrade, Yugoslavia, for a ten-day session where they forged a more detailed set of goals that came to be called the "Belgrade Charter." The charter called for a new global ethic to guide the development of the world's resources. In October 1977, seventy nations sent delegates to a conference, held in Tbilisi, USSR, where they unanimously endorsed a set of guidelines, an international document legitimating environmental education.

Differing perspectives on the environment emerged at each conference—developed and developing nations often found themselves at odds (though a consensus was reached each time). Many developing nations feared environmental concern would slow economic development. There were fundamental differences in point of view. Development, the conferences decided, was not to be opposed, but was to be directed "to ensure maximum human benefits for present and future generations." International environmental education cannot guarantee such a wise development course, but it can clearly be a crucial component in helping both rural and urban residents better understand the environmental challenges they face.

C.F.C.

THE YEAR 2000

Editor's Note: *In the late summer of 1980, the U. S. Council on Environmental Quality (CEQ) issued a long-anticipated study that amounts to a prediction of the state of the planet in the year 2000. The voluminous report, called* The Global 2000 Report to the President, *was immediately attacked by some conservatives as too bleak and by some environmentalists as too rosy. Nevertheless, the study is truly significant, marking as it does the first time the U.S. government and a huge constellation of its agencies have turned their attention to the future of the international environment. What's more,* Global 2000 *officially endorses the gloomy vision common among environmentalists of a more crowded, more polluted, less stable world in the near future—if present trends continue.*

The report's authors emphasize that the goal of the Global 2000 *study, ordered by President Carter in 1977 and coordinated for three years by Dr. Gerald O. Barney, was to determine the quality of the environment at the turn of the century if certain critical trends are not altered dramatically by technological or political developments. The litany of issues is familiar: population growth, energy consumption, industrialization, deforestation, species extinction, desertification, food production, and so on. The unpredictable breakthroughs that* may *alter the global plight could not be factored into the study, of course, so the report represents a kind of dark gauge: if there is little or no progress in creating a more ecology-minded civilization on earth, the distressing scenario of* Global 2000 *could come true.*

We end this chapter on "Previews" with excerpts from the Global 2000 *report because it is perhaps the most thorough study ever undertaken to predict our environmental future, and because, if humanity does not quickly come to grips with disruptive trends and their impact on nature, these trends lead toward global calamity. That is now the opinion not only of the so-called environmental Cassandras but of such diverse U.S. agencies as the Department of Agriculture and the Central Intelligence Agency. The hope is, of course, that if humanity comes to understand that it is drifting toward dangerous waters, decision-makers will devise course corrections. Otherwise, this is possibly what we can expect in the year 2000.*

"Someday, son, none of this will be yours." (© *1980 Eldon Dedini*)

The world in 2000 will be different from the world today in important ways. **There will be more people.** For every two persons on the earth in 1975 there will be three in 2000. **The number of poor will have increased.** Four fifths of the world's population will live in less developed countries. Furthermore, in terms of persons per year added to the world, population growth will be 40 percent *higher* in 2000 than in 1975.

The gap between the richest and the poorest will have increased. By every measure of material welfare the study provides—per capita GNP and consumption of food, energy, and minerals—the gap will widen. For example, the gap between the GNP per capita in the Least Developed Countries (LDCs) and the industrialized countries is projected to grow from about $4,000 in 1975 to about $7,900 in 2000. Great disparities within countries are also expected to continue.

There will be fewer resources to go around. While on a worldwide average there was about four tenths of a hectare of arable land per person in 1975, there will be only about one quarter hectare per person in 2000. By 2000 nearly 1,000 billion barrels of the world's total original petroleum resource of approximately 2,000 billion barrels will have been consumed. Over just the 1975–2000 period, the world's remaining petroleum resources per capita can be expected to decline by at least 50 percent. Over the same period, world per capita water supplies will decline by 35 percent because of greater population alone; increasing competing demands will put further pressure on available water supplies. The world's per capita growing stock of wood is projected to be 47 percent lower in 2000 than in 1978.

The environment will have lost important life-supporting capabilities. By 2000, 40 percent of the forests still remaining in the LDCs in 1978 will have been razed. The atmospheric concentration of carbon dioxide will be nearly one third higher than preindustrial levels. Soil erosion will have removed, on the average, several inches of soil from croplands all over the world. Desertification (including salinization) may have claimed a significant fraction of the world's rangeland and cropland. Over little more than two decades, 15–20 percent of the earth's total species of plants and animals will have become extinct—a loss of at least 500,000 species.

Prices will be higher. The price of many of the most vital resources is projected to rise in real terms—that is, over and above inflation. In order to meet projected demand, a 100-percent increase in the real price of food will be required. To keep energy demand in line with anticipated supplies, the real price of energy is assumed to rise more than 150 percent over the 1975–2000 period. Supplies of water, agricultural land, forest products, and many traditional marine fish species are projected to decline relative to growing demand at current prices, which suggests that real price rises will occur in these sectors too. Collectively, the projections suggest that resource-based inflationary pressures will continue and intensify, especially in nations that are poor in resources or are rapidly depleting their resources.

The world will be more vulnerable both to natural disaster and to disruptions from human causes. Most nations are likely to be still more dependent on foreign sources of energy in 2000 than they are today. Food production will be more vulnerable to disruptions of fossil-fuel energy supplies and to weather fluctuations as cultivation expands to more marginal areas. The loss of diverse germ plasm in local strains and wild progenitors of food crops, together with the increase of monoculture, could lead to greater risks of massive crop failures. Larger numbers of people will be vulnerable to higher food prices or even famine when adverse weather occurs. The world will be more vulnerable to the disruptive effects of war. The tensions that could lead to war will have multiplied. The potential for conflict over fresh water alone is underscored by the fact that out of 200 of the world's major river basins, 148 are shared by two countries and 52 are shared by three to ten countries. Long-standing conflicts over shared rivers such as the Plata (Brazil, Argentina), Euphrates (Syria, Iraq), or Ganges (Bangladesh, India) could easily intensify.

Finally, it must be emphasized that if public policy continues generally unchanged **the world will be different as a result of lost opportunities.** The adverse effects of many of the trends discussed in this study will not be fully evident until 2000 or later; yet the actions that are necessary to change the trends cannot be postponed without foreclosing important options. The opportunity to stabilize the world's population below 10 billion, for example, is slipping away; it has been noted that for every decade of delay in reaching replacement fertility, the world's ultimately stabilized population will be about 11 percent greater. Similar losses of opportunity accompany delayed perceptions or action in other areas. If energy policies and decisions are based on yesterday's (or even today's) oil prices, the opportunity to wisely invest scarce capital resources will be lost as a consequence of undervaluing conservation and efficiency. If agricultural research continues to focus on increasing yields through practices that are highly energy-intensive, both energy resources and the time needed to develop alternative practices will be lost.

The full effects of rising concentrations of carbon dioxide, depletion of stratospheric ozone, deterioration of soils, increasing introduction of complex persistent toxic chemicals into the environment, and massive extinction of species may not occur until well after 2000. Yet once such global environmental problems are in motion they are very difficult to reverse. In fact, few if any of the problems addressed in the *Global 2000* study are amenable to quick technological or policy fixes; rather, they are inextricably mixed with the world's most perplexing social and economic problems.

Perhaps the most troubling problems are those in which population growth and poverty lead to serious long-term declines in the productivity of renewable natural resource systems. In some areas the capacity of renewable resource systems to support human populations is already being seriously damaged by efforts of present populations to meet desperate immediate needs, and the damage threatens to become worse.

Examples of serious deterioration of the earth's most basic resources can already be found today in scattered places in all nations, including the industrialized countries and the better-endowed LDCs. For instance, erosion of agricultural soil and salinization of highly productive irrigated farmland is increasingly evident in the United States, and extensive deforestation, with more or less permanent soil degradation, has occurred in Brazil, Venezuela, and Colombia. But problems related to the decline of the earth's carrying capacity are most immediate, severe, and tragic in those regions of the earth containing the poorest LDCs.

Sub-Saharan Africa faces the problem of exhaustion of its resource base in an acute form. Many causes and effects have come together there to produce excessive demands on the environment, leading to expansion of the desert. Overgrazing, fuelwood gathering, and destructive cropping practices are the principal immediate causes of a series of transitions from open woodland, to scrub, to fragile semiarid range, to worthless weeds and bare earth. Matters are made worse when people are forced by scarcity of fuelwood to burn animal dung and crop wastes. The soil, deprived of organic matter, loses fertility and the ability to hold water—and the desert expands. In Bangladesh, Pakistan, and large parts of India, efforts by growing numbers of people to meet their basic needs are damaging the very cropland, pasture, forests, and water supplies on which they must depend for a livelihood. To restore the lands and soils would require decades—if not centuries—*after* the existing pressures on the land have diminished. But the pressures are growing, not diminishing.

There are no quick or easy solutions, particularly in those regions where population pressure is already leading to a reduction of the carrying capacity of the land. In such regions a complex of social and economic factors (including very low incomes, inequitable land tenure, limited or no educational opportunities, a lack of nonagricultural jobs, and economic pressures toward higher fertility) underlies the decline in the land's carrying capacity. Furthermore, it is generally believed that social and economic conditions must improve before fertility levels will decline to replacement levels. Thus a vicious circle of causality may be at work. Environmental deterioration caused by large populations creates living conditions that make reductions in fertility difficult to achieve; all the while, continuing population growth increases further the pressures on the environment and land.

The declines in carrying capacity already being observed in scattered areas around the world point to a phenomenon that could easily be much more widespread by 2000. In fact, the best evidence now available—even allowing for the many beneficial effects of technological developments and adoptions—suggests that by 2000 the world's human population may be within only a few generations of reaching the entire planet's carrying capacity.

The *Global 2000* study does not estimate the earth's carrying capacity, but it does provide a basis for evaluating an earlier estimate published in the U. S. National Academy of Sciences' report *Resources and Man*. In this 1969 report, the Academy concluded that a world population of 10 billion "is close to (if not above) the maximum that an *intensively managed* world might hope to support with some degree of comfort and individual choice." The Academy also concluded that even with the sacrifice of individual freedom and choice, and even with chronic near starvation for the great majority, the human population of the world is unlikely ever to exceed 30 billion.

Nothing in the *Global 2000* study counters the Academy's conclusions. If anything, data gathered over the past decade suggest the Academy may have underestimated the extent of some problems, especially deforestation and the loss and deterioration of soils.

At present and projected growth rates, the world's population would rapidly approach the

Academy's figures. If the fertility and mortality rates projected for 2000 were to continue unchanged into the twenty-first century, the world's population would reach 10 billion by 2030. Thus anyone with a present life expectancy of an additional fifty years could expect to see the world population reach 10 billion. This same rate of growth would produce a population of nearly 30 billion before the end of the twenty-first century.

Here it must be emphasized that, unlike most of the *Global 2000* study projections, the population projections assume extensive policy changes and developments to reduce fertility rates. Without the assumed policy changes, the projected rate of population growth would be still more rapid.

Unfortunately population growth may be slowed for reasons other than declining birth rates. As the world's populations exceed and reduce the land's carrying capacity in widening areas, the trends of the last century or two toward improved health and longer life may come to a halt. Hunger and disease may claim more lives—especially lives of babies and young children. More of those surviving infancy may be mentally and physically handicapped by childhood malnutrition.

The time for action to prevent this outcome is running out. Unless nations collectively and individually take bold and imaginative steps toward improved social and economic conditions, reduced fertility, better management of resources, and protection of the environment, the world must expect a troubled entry into the twenty-first century.

SOURCE Excerpted from *The Global 2000 Report to the President*, Volume I, Entering the Twenty-first Century; Gerald O. Barney, Study Director.

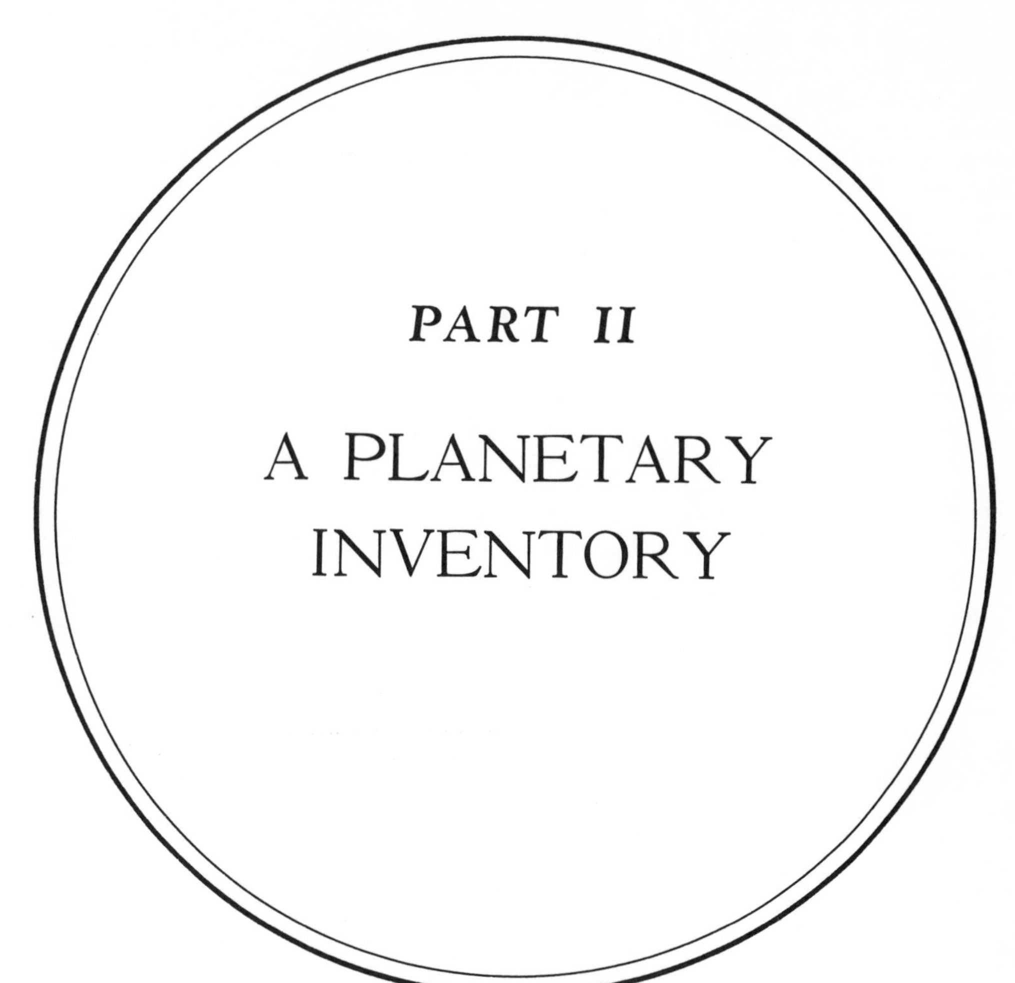

PART II

A PLANETARY INVENTORY

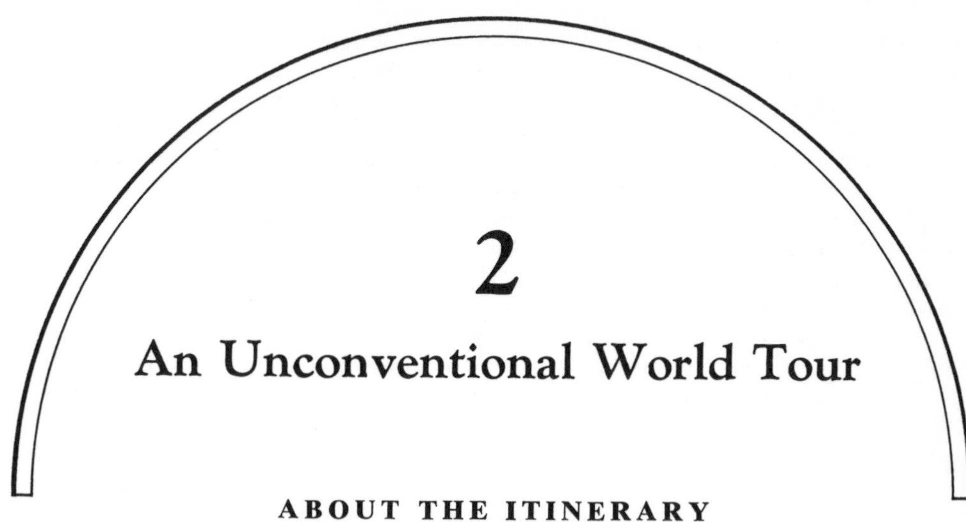

2 An Unconventional World Tour

ABOUT THE ITINERARY

Some time ago the tourism industry developed "special interest" package tours which have grown popular among those who can afford exotic vacations. A gourmet on a *food* tour can revel in epicurean meals at dining rooms across Europe. A wine connoisseur on a *wine country* tour can examine vineyards, cellars, and vintage products of France or California. Amateur archaeologists are guided through digs and museums, art students through museums and birthplaces, music aficionados through birthplaces and festivals.

In this chapter the *Almanac* presents a world tour designed to shed light on the ecological prospects of the planet in general, the human prospects in particular. The premise: What if international environmental scientists were to draw up a "special interest" tour of the world to examine the emerging trends in a global environment rapidly being altered by human endeavor? The package tour would be recommended for decision-makers—heads of state, corporate officers, ministers of planning, commanding generals, religious luminaries, economic advisers—in the hopes that their decisions would then reflect a heightened awareness of the planet's condition.

Except in Voltaire's "best of possible worlds" such a tour is extremely unlikely. Thus, the *Almanac* staff and a handful of experts have put together our own limited tour as an introduction to the themes of this book. The question we asked some specialists was this: If each stop on our unconventional tour were to illustrate an important issue bearing on life and its future environment, where would the itinerary lead?

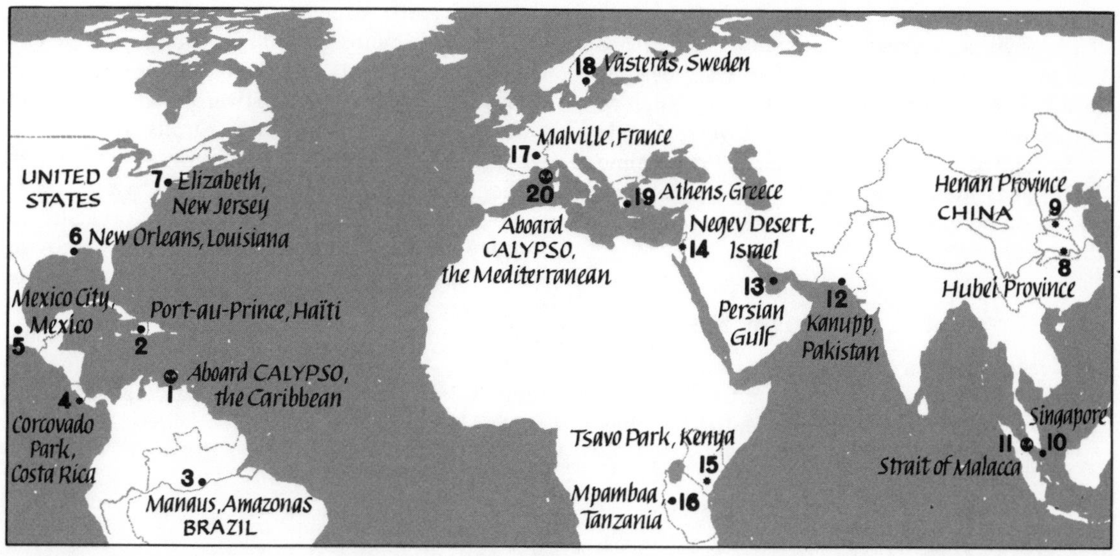

Contributors included the staff of the Population Reference Bureau; Dr. Thomas Lovejoy of the World Wildlife Fund; Dr. Pascal Imperato of the Downstate Medical Center of the State University of New York; food and agriculture researcher C. Ron Carroll of the State University of New York at Stonybrook; staff members of the United Nations Environment Programme in Geneva; and the *Almanac* staff. We reduced one hundred proposed stops to twenty. We chose sites and situations that represent phenomena occurring in many other parts of the world. Some vital regions were bypassed simply because they are thoroughly explored in other chapters of the *Almanac* (Antarctica, the deep seabed, the Himalayas, the Sahel, nuclear waste repositories, and war rooms, for example).

The tours in subsequent *Almanacs* are destined to visit other parts of the planet, as the human world discovers, recovers, develops, destroys, invents, invests, inquires. Gradually we stumble toward the realization that the world is small and its living components inseparable, that life is exuberant but vulnerable, that the whole apparatus of the biosphere must be guarded as the special interest of us all.

M.R.

---

1. ABOARD CALYPSO: THE CARIBBEAN

On its first visit to the Caribbean Sea in 1959, the Cousteau research vessel *Calypso* attempted to photograph with special deep-sea cameras the 26,240-foot-deep (8,000-meter) Puerto Rico Trench. During the ship's second visit, ten years later, the crew explored sunken vessels and studied the behavior of marine animals. It is a measure of the swiftness with which ocean problems have developed that, despite the countless questions still to be answered about the sea's *nature, Calypso* has recently been in the Caribbean off the Venezuelan coast not to explore, but to determine the state of the sea's *health.*

During the past three decades, while science has entered the undersea world to understand it, the waste matter from burgeoning industries, populations, and technologies has entered the sea in such volume as to threaten it. Some scientists worry that marine life will seriously diminish before it can be cataloged, jeopardizing broad global systems, such as oxygen production, which are linked to processes in the sea. The Caribbean is a fitting example, because almost every kind of ocean abuse is occurring in this lovely, fragile sea. The United Nations Environment Programme (UNEP) has described the Caribbean as one of the most polluted and most endangered areas of the world ocean.

Rivers and Fences in the Sea

The nutrient-laden waters that support the abundant tropical marine life of the Caribbean illustrate two aspects of the sea's potential for deterioration. First, the waters of the Caribbean are not efficiently flushed clean by the open sea; they are corralled in large part by the many strings of undersea ridges that occasionally rise above the surface as islands, and they are captured in a number of deep basins below the level of the sills over which water is exchanged with the Atlantic. These static characteristics mean that pollutants can linger for a long period of time once they enter the Caribbean.

While the greater part of the Caribbean's water is penned in by the areas deep seafloor geology, the water surface is alive with equatorial currents. This is the second important phenomenon illustrated by the Caribbean—the nonterritorial, global distribution system of the sea. In a sinuous path that passes northward along the east coast of South America, the Guiana Current collects minerals and organic debris from the Amazon and Orinoco rivers, sweeps westward along the coast of Venezuela, joins the North Equatorial Current, and heads toward the Gulf of Mexico. There these currents find no westward outlet, and they swirl eastward through the Straits of Florida, where they squirt into the Atlantic. At that point, having touched thirty nations, this warm ocean river becomes the Gulf Stream and begins its journey toward Europe. Such endlessly moving waters, obviously, cannot be claimed, tamed, or demarcated by any coastal nation of the world, for eventually the sea's dynamic fluid touches them all, bringing to them not only living resources but, especially in the past few decades, harmful materials as well.

The Fouling of Paradise

Largely as a result of agricultural runoff from the intensely sprayed croplands of Mexico and the United States (41 percent of U.S. land drains down the Mississippi River into Gulf of Mexico/Caribbean waters), the Caribbean is believed by UNEP to be the most pesticide-damaged sea in the world. Island nations of the region contribute to the sea's pesticide load as tropical rains and seaward rushing streams bear the chemical residue from fields of coffee, cotton, bananas, sugar, cocoa, and citrus fruits.

As the small nations of the Caribbean industrialize, the deleterious wastes of industry also enter the semienclosed sea in an increasing volume. Countries rich in natural resources, such as Jamaica, plan to develop heavy industries including petrochemical processing, iron, steel, and aluminum smelting, and caustic soda and chlorine production. Countries without natural resources, such as Antigua and Barbados, construct refineries, pharmaceutical industries, and tourist centers.

The Caribbean is also potentially one of the largest oil-producing areas in the world, with at least thirty-eight new offshore platforms currently under construction. In 1978 offshore sources released an estimated 76.6 million barrels of oil into Caribbean waters, according to UNEP. About 5 million barrels of oil are transported through the region every day, resulting in periodic spills, and as much as 7 million barrels of oily discharge from tank washings can be added to this already high rate of oil pollution in the Caribbean. (See also "The Strait of Malacca," page 80.)

Rapid growth of many Caribbean cities has also meant additional loads of sewage flowing into the sea, and few of the region's cities have proper treatment systems. Havana's sewage streams into the ocean untreated, damaging nearby undersea habitats, and the situation is similar in Kingston (Jamaica), Nassau (Bahamas), Belize City (Belize), Barranquilla and Cartagena (Colombia), and Colón (Panama).

Disassembling the Reefs

Perhaps the most insidious threat to Caribbean marine life is the tourist trade, often financed by foreign investors who reap the profits. Hotels are built along coasts, releasing silt and sewage directly into the richest reef habitats, often smothering them. Tourists invade the reefs, spearfishing and breaking off souvenir pieces of coral, gradually depleting and disassembling the entire coral community. In addition, island residents raid the reefs for coral, starfish, and sea urchins to sell in gift shops or ship to the United States. Rapidly the Caribbean's reef systems are succumbing, and with them the fish and shellfish that depend on shallow reefs for food and shelter and for spawning grounds.

Fortunately, Caribbean nations are belatedly recognizing the danger. Impressive plans for joint action in association with UNEP are being drawn up and several scientific missions to analyze the health of Caribbean waters are under way. As part of this surge of activity, *Calypso* was summoned to the Caribbean between 1979 and 1981

The research vessel *Calypso* explores waters off the Venezuelan coast in 1980. (*The Cousteau Society/Dick Hyman*)

to examine the vitality of many offshore areas. The government of Venezuela is especially interested in finding out if its rapidly expanding coastal developments and its extensive offshore oil platforms (and those of Lake Maracaibo) are contaminating the sea. It is a critical study, since Venezuela is located precisely at the gateway where the northbound currents enter the Caribbean before radiating through it. Aboard the *Calypso* off the Venezuelan coast scientists sample the water at various depths, measure the currents, examine the marine life—take the pulse of the sea. Their findings will offer a glimpse of the worldwide medical examination just getting under way that may tell us if the life of the sea can withstand intensified human insults.

M.R., P.D., N.M.

2. PORT-AU-PRINCE, HAITI

Most North Americans are unaware that a pocket of human and ecological misery, perhaps as intense as that in the most impoverished nations of Africa and southern Asia, exists adjacent to some of the Caribbean's most popular and most plush vacation retreats. The Republic of Haiti, which occupies the western third of the Caribbean island of Hispaniola (the Dominican Republic covers the eastern two thirds), is at once the poorest and most densely populated nation in the Western Hemisphere. It is a ravaged land, nearly denuded of its forests, badly eroded, plagued by famines, nearly unfit for human habitation in many spots. Haiti is a glaring example of the link between the environment, social conditions, and political power. A long tradition of government corruption has produced an atmosphere of ignorance and mistrust among the nation's five million people, effectively hampering almost all efforts to improve the nation's plight. Desperate for survival, thousands of Haitians annually take to the sea in small boats bound for the United States, where they are less than enthusiastically received. With a population growth rate that adds 130,000 new people to the beleaguered nation each year, this flood of emigrants does not seem likely to abate.

The Tree Stealers

Haiti's first liability is its topography. About the size of Maryland, the nation is two-thirds mountainous. What is not hilly is covered by broad plateaus or deep valleys, with only small plains for efficient agriculture. Much of this productive land is not used to produce food for local consumption but coffee and sugar for export. Population growth has now outstripped the capacity of the remaining land to support its people, who have largely clustered around the capital city of Port-au-Prince and a nearby plain called the Cul-de-Sac. About 90 percent of Haiti's once abundant forests—which interested the island's first European visitor, Christopher Columbus, in 1492—have been cut down to clear land for farming, to export as timber (mahogany), and to provide the nation with its main source of heating fuel, charcoal.

The vast majority of the rural peasantry, ignorant of modern conservation techniques and mistrustful of government attempts to reform, have stripped their small landholdings bare of trees, leaving the steep plots vulnerable to the endless cycle of rain erosion and drought that has plagued them for centuries. Studies conducted by the U. S. Agency for International Development (AID) predict that Haiti will be literally devoid of trees within six years if radical measures are not taken at once, and that even with the complete success of such programs, a self-renewing wood source would not result for at least twenty years. That would appear to mean that at least a generation of Haitians will soon become dependent on fuel sources that are far beyond their average annual incomes of about $70. For the relatively cheap charcoal, they are already spending 40 percent of their income, foregoing at least one hot meal per day at the recommendation of the government. The result is that trees planted as part of a government reforestation program are cut down as fast as they are in the ground. Short of posting armed guards at every grove, there seems to be no way to stop this "tree poaching."

A Nation of Suspicions

The roots of Haiti's political and social tensions run deep. Founded in a slave rebellion against French colonists, Haiti has been marked for two hundred years by dictatorships, internal strife, foreign exploitation, bankruptcies, and military domination. The present regime began in 1957 under François Duvalier, known as "Papa Doc." In 1964, Duvalier amended the constitution, making himself president-for-life with the power to dismiss the national assembly and cabinet in times of crisis and to rule by decree. He also established, over the years, a secret police known as the *Tonton macoutes* ("bogeymen" in the island's dominant Creole language), which violently suppressed dissidents. On Duvalier's death in 1971, his son, Jean-Claude, known as "Baby Doc," became president-for-life, and the rule of Papa Doc's authoritarian government continues.

The conditions in Haiti, while dismal for Haitians, can appear bright to foreign business executives. With unemployment in Port-au-Prince running at 60 percent and the minimum hourly wage set at $1.30, some 150 foreign firms established plants in Haiti during the 1970s to take advantage of its cheap labor (textiles, cement manufacturing, light assembly industries). Foreign investments have been swelling, to around $100 million per year, but the new business has not generated a perceptible rise in the per capita income or standard of living of Haiti's poor.

The result of these persisting political and economic exploitations is that the people of Haiti generally view policies aimed at saving their environment as attempts by the urban elite to strip them of what little comfort they possess. Obviously, experts point out, the people's trust must be earned before they will cooperate with plans to radically alter their way of life. If this can be accomplished, Haiti can take the first steps toward survival, exploiting such alternative energy sources as small-scale solar (for heating and cooking) and hydroelectric power, and reforesting the nation's mountainous terrain. However, the outlook, according to AID observers, is exceedingly bleak. The results of centuries of abuse cannot be corrected quickly, and as Haiti runs out of wood, it also runs out of time.

B.J.L., M.R.

3. MANAUS, AMAZONAS, BRAZIL

The setting is lush with superlatives: the Amazon jungle, largest rain forest in the world, containing more species of plants and animals than any other major land habitat on earth; the Amazon River, largest river by volume in the world; both of these giants set principally in Brazil, the fifth-largest country in the world. The question of whether or not Amazonia can survive encroaching development bears on the ecology of the entire planet. The health of the forest is connected to the local climate and oxygen supply, and the health of the river is important to the productivity of the entire ocean (it contributes *one fifth* of all the fresh water entering the sea). But the Amazon rain forest is today under siege by industries (timber, mining, cattle-raising), by a government looking for exportable resources to solve a balance-of-trade crisis, and by an expanding population.

The Goodbye Forests

Amazonia is perhaps the most important example of the increasing destruction of the world's forests, especially its rain forests. A 1980 report by the U. S. National Academy of Sciences warns that 80,000 square miles (200,000 square kilometers) of tropical forest are being converted to other uses each year. That is an area about the size of Kansas. Some estimates are higher. "Even if these rates were constant," says the report, "they would lead to a total destruction of all tropical forests worldwide within fifty years. But the rates are not constant—they are accelerating rapidly." And not just trees are disappearing. According to the report, of the four to five million forms of terrestrial plant and animal life in the world, about three million of them are confined to tropical forests and are destined to be eliminated if their habitat disappears.

The situation in Amazonia, while grander in scope, is typical of most rain forests. Already an estimated 20 percent of the basin has been deforested; an amount of forest equal to the size of England is lost every year. Ecologist Norman Myers, a forestry expert from Kenya, estimates that two species of plants and animals per week are disappearing from Amazonia now, a rate that could increase to *one per hour* by the end of the decade. (For a detailed account, see "Amazonia," page 274.) Also fast disappearing are the Indian tribes of Amazonia, who seem destined to be assimilated or destroyed by invading civilization (see "Native Peoples," page 384).

The Selling of the Amazon

While the forces eating away at Amazonia are similar to those at work elsewhere, the Amazon basin is an especially vivid illustration of the connections between international economics and the environment. Brazil, which contains two thirds of

In a part of the Amazon rain forest north of Manaus, Brazil, a cataloging project is slated to identify and observe the changes among species during the next twenty years in sixty different experimental plots. (*FAO/Peyton Johnson*)

the Amazon rain forest (smaller fragments are divided among Venezuela, Colombia, Peru, Bolivia, Guyana, Surinam, and French Guiana), has developed its economy during the past two decades with an emphasis on automobiles and trucks. Despite the fact that the nation has the ninth-largest automobile industry in the world, it has almost no domestic oil. Brazil must import 85 percent of its petroleum; the result, since oil prices rose in 1973, has been a soaring foreign debt that is now about $52 million, 70 percent of which must be amortized in the early 1980s. With an inflation rate of 80 percent (1979), there is a need for a quick economic fix, which many Brazilian leaders believe lies in the country's greatest resource—Amazonia. The government's Amazon Development Agency is encouraging large-scale enterprise by offering good tax exemptions on lots averaging 250,000 acres (100,000 hectares) to multinational corporations for mining, ranching, agriculture, and forestry. (See "Amazon, Inc.," page 487.) "A few years from now," says a government official, "the Amazon forest is going to be for Brazil what oil is for the Arabs today."

How Big Is Big Enough?

Fortunately, there are those within the government who recognize the deceptive fragility of rain forest ecology—especially the poverty of rain forest soils, which lack the depth and richness of temperate forest soils—and they are pressing for programs that will preserve large portions of Amazonia before it is too late. Just north of Manaus, Brazil's research organization Instituto Nacional de Pesquisas da Amazonas (INPA) and the U.S. branch of the World Wildlife Fund (WWF) have devised a joint plan to determine just how large rain forest refuges will have to be in order to save the most important life within them. The project is a response to recent findings that small parks and refuges often turn out to be death traps for the very species they were designed to protect. Expanding populations may literally eat themselves out of food and shelter (see "Tsavo National Park, Kenya," page 85), or competing species may wipe each other out, or disease may destroy species made vulnerable because they are too confined or too weakened by the effects of inbreeding. And if the area does not contain enough breeding stock of a particular species, the end of the line may be reached when the first generation dies off. Negotiating with land owners, INPA-WWF have obtained 40 square miles (100 square kilometers) of forest north of Manaus. The land is being divided into sixty wilderness preserves of various sizes, and scientists have begun to make complete inventories of flora and fauna. The only drawback to the program is one of time. It may take twenty years to accurately determine the changes in the experimental refuges.

So far, despite these careful investigations, the Brazilian government has actually passed very few solid conservation laws. And one of the most important existing laws—that property owners must leave 50 percent of their land in forest—has a loophole that renders it almost meaningless. Developers may sell their forested half-portions to new owners who may then clear 50 percent of the property and sell to new owners who may then clear 50 percent of the property and sell the remaining half, half of which may be developed, and so on.

In the long run, the Amazon appears destined for major alterations by the year 2000. There is no talk of leaving it alone, only of how its wealth should be harvested. The forces of development propose that "islands" of wilderness be protected, the forces of conservation suggest that vast, continuous forests should surround limited "islands" of cultivation and development. Whatever the course of events in Amazonia, it promises to capture the world's attention during the coming era.

M.R., M.A., T.L.

4. CORCOVADO PARK, COSTA RICA

From the top of Costa Rica's Mount Irazú, an 11,000-foot (3,300-meter) volcano, one can see both the Caribbean Sea and the Pacific Ocean. Only 74 miles (118 kilometers) wide at its narrowest point, this tiny Central American republic is smaller than the state of West Virginia. Yet, despite its size, the country houses a variety and abundance of wildlife unequaled in all of North America. More than perhaps any small developing nation in the world, Costa Rica has acted to prevent ruinous exploitation of this natural treasure. It has become, to international environmental experts, a kind of model for other nations of Latin America, southern Asia, and Africa.

Between Two Worlds

As part of the land bridge connecting North and South America, Costa Rica draws its animal wealth from two continents. From the south come the monkeys, anteaters, and sloths; and from the north come coyotes, foxes, deer, wildcats, and weasels. Naturalists in this small paradise have observed 150 species of snakes and frogs and nearly 8,000 bird species. This is a hundred more kinds of birds than can be found in all of North America above Mexico.

With three fourths of the country covered by virgin forest, plant life is extremely diverse. So far, more than a thousand kinds of orchids are known to grow there. In one Costa Rican rain forest, 1,315 species of trees have been identified, some more than 200 feet (60 meters) high and 6 feet (2 meters) in diameter. In another rain forest a U.S. scientist counted 111 different types of trees on a 2-acre (1-hectare) plot!

Recognizing the intrinsic value of its wildlife, the Costa Rican government, in one decade, has created one of the most important national parks systems in the world. Its twenty parks and biological preserves encompass 3.5 percent of the country's land, a larger percentage than the wealthy United States has dedicated to wildlife. And the Costa Rican parks include a remarkable variety of habitats: Caribbean and Pacific islands, active volcanoes, mangrove forests, cloud forests, tropical rain forests, lowland dry forests, and a coral reef.

The largest and most famous of the parks is Corcovado, a lush tropical rain forest of 89,000 acres (36,000 hectares) on the southern Pacific coast. Corcovado is the home of spider monkeys, peccaries, coatimundis, and six species of rare cats, including ocelot and jaguar, which are extinct in most of Central America. What really distinguishes Corcovado and other Costa Rican parks from those in other parts of the world, however, is not wildlife but dedication to science. Public or private, the Costa Rican parks are primarily tropical ecosystem preserves, not tourist attractions. Having very few roads and only the most primitive accommodations, they are used mostly by rangers and scientists doing research. Of the two hundred annual visitors to Corcovado, more than 90 percent are scientists.

The result of this commitment to scientific examination of the nation's biological diversity is a kind of countrywide naturalist's paradise. Santa Rosa, a smaller reserve north of Corcovado, covers several types of terrain, from beaches

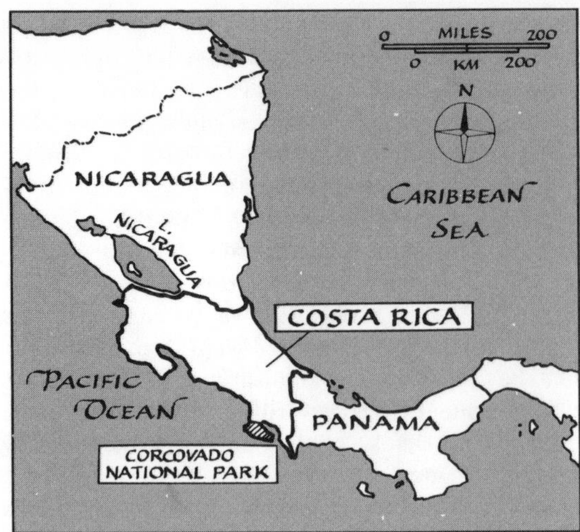

where threatened marine turtles lay their eggs to dry lowland forests sheltering approximately sixty kinds of mammals and two hundred species of birds. On the Caribbean coast, Tortuguero National Park provides one of the last Caribbean refuges for the green turtle (see "Sea Turtle Flotas," page 322), and Cahuita protects the colorful corals and fish of Costa Rica's only reef.

In addition to the national parks, an important cloud forest preserve, Monteverde, was privately established by a nonprofit organization, the Tropical Science Center of San José. Monteverde is the habitat of the quetzal, a rare, spectacular emerald-green bird once sacred to the Maya (see "Endangered Symbols," page 364), and the golden toad, discovered in the 1960s and found nowhere else. Vital to people as well as to quetzals and golden toads, these cloud forests protect the hydroelectric watershed of Arenal, which is one of Costa Rica's few domestic energy sources, and provide a water supply for the dry Pacific lowlands.

Threats Overcome, Threats to Come

Much of the credit for the development of Costa Rica's impressive parks system goes to its first and second directors, Mario Boza and Alvaro Ugalde, two dedicated young men trained in national parks management in the United States. Beginning with no budget and only themselves as staff, the two men lobbied so hard for parks that within five years they had convinced the government to set aside 400,000 acres (160,000 hectares), to give them a healthy budget, and to establish Corcovado. (It cost the government $1.2 million, a huge sum in Costa Rica, just to relocate squatters living in the park.)

One of the first problems Boza and Ugalde faced was the suspicion on the part of Costa Rica's rural population that the parks would threaten their own land. Ugalde nevertheless managed to win over hostile farmers and fishermen in his campaign to establish a park at Cahuita. "After I explained to Cahuitans that the real threat came from the land developers and wealthy people of San José who wanted beachfront vacation homes or land for speculation," Ugalde told *Smithsonian Magazine,* "the local people realized that the park would give the best protection to their way of life." When a vote was taken, Cahuitans decided, almost unanimously, in favor of the park.

Today Costa Rica is feeling the economic stress caused by oil shortages and depressed prices for its main export items, coffee and bananas. Some experts predict that the national parks program will suffer as the government attempts to tighten the budget. Park funds and personnel have already been cut, and with the parks service short of trained professionals, poaching could become a serious problem. Nevertheless, President Rodrigo Carazo Odio remains optimistic enough to approve programs for extensive park expansion and the purchase of private lands within existing parks. As in the past, Costa Ricans appear determined to continue protecting the flora and fauna that are their greatest national treasure and to inspire the entire world, in the process, with their environmental sensitivity and sensibility.

M.A. with T.L.

5. MEXICO CITY, MEXICO

Emerging now as one of the world's most important oil nations, Mexico ponders the future implications of a wealth of proved oil reserves approaching those of Iran and estimated reserves nearly as large as those of Saudi Arabia. But this media-celebrated petroleum treasure and the international power it may confer on Mexico is not the principal subject of the visit here. With 10 million people and a population growth rate of 5.2 percent per year, Mexico City promises to become the largest city in the world by the year 2000. The swelling masses of the city will number *32 million* by then. Such an enormous number of people have never been drawn together in a city before, and the obvious question is: Will such a monstrous agglomeration work, especially in a nation characterized by enduring poverty? The specter of Haiti's plight, across the Caribbean, is a sobering one for Mexican officials.

The battle to be waged in this city during the next two decades pits the skyrocketing human growth against Mexico's efforts to exploit and to distribute the blessings of the nation's natural resources. Except for oil, however, these resources are not abundant. Mexico City may come to represent a kind of acid test for other ballooning cities of the developing world whose profiles are similar except for one crucial factor—without Mexico's projected oil wealth, many metropolises of the future have far less hope. (See "The Most Populous Urban Areas in the Year 2000," page 101.)

The Great Magnet

One in five Mexicans lives in Mexico City, which, set on a high plateau at an altitude of 7,349 feet (2,241 meters), is both an elegant capital and a shanty-ringed behemoth. The country's economic opportunity is concentrated in its "Federal District"—about 80 percent of Mexico's industry is here—and that attracts approximately 800,000 new residents a year, most of them refugees from rural poverty. Thirty percent of the new arrivals live in one-room makeshift huts, without running water, sanitation facilities, electricity, paved roads, or adequate public transportation. Their efforts to rise in the economic strata are usually blocked by the nation's unemployment rate of 25 percent. The result is some 3,600 slum pockets clustered around the city limits, away from the affluent and beautiful parts of town. Thousands of young children, because they neither attend school nor work steadily, roam the streets, begging or performing odd jobs for tourists or the well-to-do. Like all Latin American cities, Mexico City also has its share of *abandonados,* children of elementary school age who have left home to make their own living.

Dispersing the Problem

Throughout this gradual outward sprawl, the city's environment deteriorates. The geographical site is not the most suitable for a mammoth city

An Italian artist's view of Mexico City (date unknown) after the European conquest. The original Aztec "island city" has been covered with Western-style structures, as seen below. (*Library of Congress*)

Modern Mexico City. (*Mexican National Tourist Council*)

anyway. The subsoil is poor, the area is prone to earthquakes, and the air, because of the altitude, is unusually thin, exaggerating what would be a severe air pollution problem anyway. On most mornings smog from the city's two million vehicles and countless factories is so thick that visibility is reduced to a few hundred yards. There is a plan to encircle the city with an oxygen-replenishing "green belt" of trees and grass, but expansion is so rapid and so haphazard that no organized planting can ensue.

Partly out of a genuine will to improve the quality of life and partly because the disparities in Mexico City are an embarrassment for the federal government, a Territorial Deconcentration Program was enacted in 1978. Requiring billions of pesos, the program intends to reduce the concentration of people in Mexico City by attracting the masses away to improved housing, sanitation systems, and public transportation in "underpopulated areas" of the country. Thirteen districts of the nation, including Guadalajara and Monterrey, are marked for federal enhancement programs.

Mexico hopes to finance this economic burst with oil revenues, while continuing to improve on its annual economic growth rate of 6 to 7 percent. Poor Mexicans, however, are skeptical. The top 10 percent of Mexico's population, mostly whites of Spanish descent, chart the nation's development course and are in direct control of half the nation's income.

Like many other emerging megalopolises, Mexico City is today wrestling with ways to control environmental degradation, to stimulate economic development, and to redress social imbalances against a long tradition of laissez-faire business practices and sharp class and ethnic divisions. The traditional political maxim, that a nation's youths represent the hope of its future, has a cruel adverse meaning in the case of Mexico, where more than half the population is no older than fifteen. Amid the jobless and the *abandonados,* the country's young masses await their chance to join the unemployed work force and to start new families.

P.D., J.S., S.L.Y.
with P.R.B.

6. NEW ORLEANS, LOUISIANA, U.S.A.

The empty ships arrive in New Orleans from all over the world and depart with cargoes of feed grain, rice, and soybeans from the southern United States; wheat from Kansas, Nebraska, and the Dakotas; corn from Iowa and Illinois. Most of the ships are headed back to Europe, Japan, or other developed areas, but some will deliver grain to developing countries. The United States is the food-growing center of the planet, especially bountiful in the principal life-sustaining foodstuff of the world—grain. It grows *60 percent* of the grain that is traded internationally. Iowa and Illinois alone grow one sixth of the world's corn. Kansas and North Dakota produce more wheat than all of South America. In 1979 U.S. farmers were able to feed their own country and produce a trade surplus of $15.9 billion, the largest asset in an otherwise declining U.S. trade balance.

A tour stop visiting the so-called bread basket of the world, however, would reveal a number of flaws in the noble picture of U.S. agricultural achievements. The fact is, in countries without the overwhelming farmland resources of the United States, the flow of grains from America has created dangerous dependencies, while the promotion of mechanized farm techniques, inappropriate in many poor parts of the world, has resulted in technological glitches hampering agricultural progress in some countries.

Machines with Claws

Throughout its history the United States has had enviable success with its agriculture because of the continent's excellent land and climate, but its tremendous surplus only came about with the mechanization of farms during the last forty years. (Horses and mules outnumbered tractors until 1955.) Suddenly, the advent of farm machinery rippled through U.S. agriculture in unexpected ways. There were more than 30 million farmers in the United States in 1940; there are only about 8 million now. But there are 4.4 million tractors, 3 million trucks, 535,000 grain combines, 605,000 corn pickers and picker-shellers, 615,000 pick-up balers, and 270,000 field-forage harvesters. In 1950 an average American farm was 214 acres (86 hectares), now it is more than 400 acres (160 hectares). About 6 percent of all farms account for more than half of all farm receipts.

The result of this enormous shift is that in the agribusiness-dominated United States, the age of the integrated farm with a variety of crops and animals is over. The biggest farms often grow only one crop, and animals are raised by the tens and even hundreds of thousands in feed lots (see "How to Make a Cow," page 590). The labor of farm workers has accordingly been replaced by machines and fossil fuels. But while the increase in productivity on U.S. farms has been dramatic, it is not as great as the increase in energy expenditures for agriculture (see "The Oil Diet," page 592). And more machines are being designed.

Tomatoes, prunes, and grapes are already harvested by machine in California. Another machine sorts tomatoes and rejects those that are rotten, green, or blemished. A machine with metal claws is being developed to squeeze oranges on the tree in order to determine whether they are ripe enough. A proposed lettuce-harvesting machine will use a gamma ray sensor to determine maturity. All of these devices mean more energy use and fewer jobs.

Hidden Food Facts

The productivity of U.S. agriculture is often praised as an important asset in the fight against world hunger. Though the notion is defensible, there is more to the story. The income from surplus food production is vital to the economy of the United States. Most of the surplus is sold to those countries that can afford the price, usually the developed countries. Historically, however, developed countries have not always wanted to buy all of the food that was for sale, so the United States has cultivated alternate markets. During the 1950s, when production was high and demand low, U.S. food aid programs began providing cheap food to poor countries, thereby discouraging the development of local agriculture. Eventually many countries became dependent on food from the United States, and when demand was high, they were forced to buy food at regular market prices. Critics claim that U.S. food aid has done more for its own agricultural interests than for the people to whom it was given. (See "Who Produced Your Dinner?" page 597, and "The Grain Merchants," page 483.) But the story doesn't end there. Increasingly, grain is becoming a tool of U.S. foreign policy. The embargoes on grain to the Soviet Union and to Iran are well known, but there are hidden subtleties to U.S. food shipments. Grain is used to win friends and influence governments in a way that calls into question the humanitarian aura that surrounds aid programs. In 1980, for example, of a total of $570 million in food aid to poor nations, $227 million provided wheat for Egypt. As an article in the New York *Times* pointed out, "Some experts question whether that is proportional to its place among needy nations."

Whatever U.S. agriculture may be, however, it is undeniably productive. Much of the credit for the nation's continuous growth in productivity belongs to its universities and colleges, which have developed hybrid crops that are not only more productive but more resistant to pests. Even here, however, there is a shift under way. Increasingly, agricultural colleges take up research on strains that are more suitable for machine harvesting, such as tomatoes with tougher skins, and that are dependent on chemical fertilizers and pesticides. Along with the trend toward mechanized farming has come a disregard for environmental issues. Agriculture in the United States has too often preferred new technology to traditional practices of land management, and the result has been rapid soil erosion and chemical pollution (see "Things Disappearing: Topsoil," page 394; "The Most-Sprayed Foods," page 600; "The Most-Fertilized Foods," page 601). Along with American equipment, chemicals, and techniques, these problems have been exported, via the Green Revolution, around the world. With the rise in fuel prices, it becomes increasingly difficult for a poor nation, enrolled in an agricultural program based on mechanized farming, to afford to feed its people. (See "The Green Revolution," page 177.)

A final note to bear in mind during a visit to this agricultural paradise is the way in which its products are *used*. The remarkable volume of surplus food produced in the United States is almost all feed grains. The food goes to livestock, and only indirectly to people. The animals, of course, provide meat or dairy products for human consumption, but along the way there is a tremendous loss of food potential. Sixteen pounds (7.2 kilograms) of grain protein is reduced to just 1 pound (0.37 kilogram) of meat protein when it is fed to beef cattle. To a world in which people are undernourished, U.S. food production figures may seem less important than the figures on how many people the nation's farms actually feed.

K.F.

7. ELIZABETH, NEW JERSEY, U.S.A.

Elizabeth is a small city on Newark Bay in central New Jersey, an area known for its high concentration of chemical plants and for its high cancer rate. On the morning of April 22, 1980, the residents of Elizabeth awoke to the sound of an explosion. A mushroom-shaped cloud rose from the Chemical Control Corporation, where 24,000 barrels of dangerous chemicals were stored on a 3-acre (1.4-hectare) site. Local officials prepared evacuation plans because the fuel for the fire was special. It included alcohol, solvents, pesticides, insecticides, mercury compounds, and a variety of other toxic chemicals.

The Chemical Control Corporation site is one of at least 30,000 (and perhaps 50,000) hazardous waste dumps in the United States. Most of these dumps are not registered, and their locations are unknown. As many as 2,000 are considered to be imminent hazards. Most of them will not explode but will slowly and silently leak their toxic contents into the ground and contaminate the groundwater. Elizabeth's experience with toxic wastes illustrates a problem expected to grow more severe during the coming decade. It is a grim spinoff from the "miracle breakthroughs" in synthetic materials and industrial processes since World War II, and it is not restricted to the United States. Toxic wastes are accumulating wherever there is heavy industry. That covers an area of the planet that is already large and is expanding.

A Matter of Good Luck

Unlike most waste sites, the Elizabeth dump was well known. The president of Chemical Control had been indicted in 1977 for allegedly dumping wastes in sewers, streets, vacant lots, and creeks around Newark and Elizabeth. He pleaded guilty and promised to inventory the stored waste and to dispose of it properly. In January 1979 state investigators visited the corporation and were alarmed to find about 34,000 drums piled four and five high. Many of them were leaking, some contained explosives, others held extremely toxic chemicals, and some were unlabeled. The dangerous materials included nitroglycerine, cyanide, polychlorinated biphenyls (PCBs), and nerve gas.

The state government took control and began removing the most dangerous drums. Progress was slow because so many of the drums were unlabeled and had to be identified so that they could be safely handled. On two occasions fires burst out spontaneously, but they were extinguished quickly. Between 8,000 and 10,000 drums of the most dangerous materials had been removed by the time of the explosion.

The people of Elizabeth were fortunate. The most harmful chemicals had been removed, and favorable winds blew the menacing cloud out to sea. But the explosion could have occurred two years earlier and the winds might have been blowing the other way. Millions of people in New York and New Jersey, the most densely populated area of the United States, could have been shrouded in a lethal cloud, an environmental disaster of catastrophic proportions.

New Jersey alone produces 5.5 million tons of hazardous waste a year, and the United States total is 35 million tons. The U. S. Environmental Protection Agency estimates that only 10 percent of this waste is disposed of properly. In many countries, especially in the developing world, the situation is worse, and sometimes dumping is completely unregulated. Progress is being made in many countries toward developing guidelines for the safe disposal of chemical wastes, but little has been done to clean up existing sites.

Ironically, the Elizabeth explosion occurred on the tenth anniversary of Earth Day. Ten miles away in New York City, people were gathering to celebrate the success of the first decade of environmental activism. The ominous cloud visible over Elizabeth cast a note of seriousness over the event. Complex problems remain to be solved, and toxic debris is among the most deadly and most difficult.

K.F.

8. HUBEI PROVINCE, CHINA

One out of every four persons alive today lives in the People's Republic of China. For centuries, the country has been marked by poverty, hunger, disease, and environmental decay. Today, as China rapidly industrializes, it faces new problems of pollution not so different from those of New Jersey. But it has also begun to reverse some of its ancient problems, providing encouraging examples of environmental rebirth. China is not the only place in the world where environmental success stories are occurring, as the tour will show, but because it encompasses such a great proportion of humanity, it demands close attention. Accordingly, the tour will make two stops here, each covering a phenomenon that has broad implications for the rest of the world, especially that portion of humanity attempting to rise, like China, from a state of bare subsistence.

In central Chinese provinces like Hubei, along the valley of the Yangtze River, small agricultural communes exist where isolated homesteads were once scattered about the countryside. A stop here, among some of the best rice-producing fields in China, illustrates one of the most important public health problems facing the world today. In 1930, the village of Jentun had 1,000 people. By 1949, only 461 were still alive, of whom all but 12 had schistosomiasis, a waterborne disease that has killed millions of people in the Far East, Africa, the Arabian peninsula, the Middle East, northeastern South America, and the Caribbean. In Jentun, before the disease was controlled, 80 of 244 original families were completely wiped out by the disease. Another Yangtze valley village, Shangyanpan, was called "the village of widows" because most of the men, who did the farming and were in constant contact with irrigation canals, had contracted the disease and died.

China has greatly reduced its epidemic of schistosomiasis, however, through a massive program that international public health experts laud for its ingenuity and scope. At the same time, agencies like the United Nations Environment Programme (UNEP) warn that in most other poor areas of the world schistosomiasis is making advances against humanity.

A Partnership of Snails and Worms

Schistosomiasis, also known as bilharzia, is a bloodworm infection kept alive by poor agricultural practices and unsanitary habits. Adult worms of *Schistosoma japonicum* live in the veins of human intestines, where they lay tremendous numbers of eggs that work their way into the intestinal tract and are eventually passed out in the feces. People in rural China, as in many other areas of the world, defecate in rivers and irrigation canals. Once in the water, each egg hatches into a small worm called *miracidium* which quickly penetrates the body of a snail, maturing and multiplying within it over several weeks, and then producing new worm forms called *cerceriae,* which emerge from the snail into

An Egyptian health worker sprays insecticide on canals in an attempt to kill the snails that cause schistosomiasis. While China has succeeded in diminishing the threat of this waterborne disease, some nations, like Egypt, have experienced explosive increases, largely a result of complications arising from water projects undertaken during the past few decades, which expand the potential habitat of disease-carrying snails. (*World Bank/Ray Witlin*)

the water and penetrate human skin, eventually passing through the heart, lungs, and liver before ending up in the veins of the intestines.

Chinese farmers call schistosomiasis the "big belly" disease because people with the worm infections develop ballooning stomachs caused by water retention, along with large livers and spleens. In 1955, the Chinese government concluded that over ten million people were suffering from severe schistosomiasis and that one hundred million were exposed to the infection, most of the cases appearing in the country's rice-producing areas. Combatting the disease was complicated, since treatment by drugs had produced toxic side effects in other countries, and chemical control of snails harmed other aquatic life.

The eradication of schistosomiasis became a major goal of the country's agricultural development program for the period between 1956 and 1967, and government control centers were set up at 197 sites, run by nearly 30,000 medical and specialized personnel. The thrust of the program was to eliminate snails and to change age-old sanitary habits. Since snails cannot survive when buried under 4 inches (10 centimeters) or more of earth, snail-infested irrigation ditches all over the countryside were drained and filled with earth, and new ditches were dug. Supplementing this program, some swamps were filled in, some snail populations were killed with chemicals, and human feces were treated to destroy eggs.

By 1964, 300,000 acres (120,000 hectares) of farmland had been reclaimed, new sanitary latrines were in place, and the public health was improving. By 1979, the 10 million cases from 1949 had declined to 2 million cases. (In some parts of the world, water projects have enhanced snail habitats, and the disease is on the increase around lakes like Kainji in Nigeria, Volta in Ghana, and Nasser in Egypt and the Sudan. See "The Aswan High Dam," page 173.)

The Price of Progress

While Chinese health officials celebrate their substantial victory over "big belly" disease, however, another health problem is looming on the horizon. Determined to become a major world power by the year 2000, China is committed to a vast industrial expansion. As a New York *Times* article pointed out in April of 1980, Chinese officials have now recognized that rapid development has brought with it serious pollution problems. All of the country's major rivers, including the Yellow (see "Henan Province, China," below) and the Yangtze are "seriously contaminated," according to China's Environmental Protection Office, which has built a research vessel specifically to determine the condition of the Yangtze. Factory workers have been harmed by chlorine gas, fishermen by mercury in the fish they eat, crops by air pollution from factories, shellfish by untreated industrial wastes dumped into the sea. It is, perhaps, an embarrassing situation for a nation that once attributed pollution problems to capitalistic greed. The official state newspaper, *The People's Daily,* once editorialized: "Capitalists make their enormous profits by rampantly discharging harmful substances into the environment at will and in complete disregard for the fate of the people."

More important to Chinese planners than the propaganda, however, is the economics of the pollution problem. The cost of installing antipollution devices on the nation's 400,000 factories could be a serious drain on the already scarce investment funds needed to fuel further industrial growth. What's more, the offending polluters cannot be fined heavily, as a means of raising the funds, because the state owns all of the enterprises. The Chinese are faced with a "Catch-22" situation—they cannot force industries to cut back, because most of the government's revenue comes from the profits of industry. In its struggles to safeguard the health of its enormous population, China seems to present two lessons to the world: first, that citizens acting in concert can correct seemingly insoluble environmental woes, and, second, that some of society's most troublesome new dangers stem not from fervors of ideology but from the fervors of industry, no matter where it is.

P.I., M.R., J.S.

9. HENAN PROVINCE, CHINA

In 1949, a 250-acre (100-hectare) plot of farmland in Henan Province, just south of the fabled Yellow River in central China and today cultivated by the Paichuang Production Brigade of Chaochuang People's Commune, had very few trees. This situation combined with frequent sandstorms and shifting dunes meant that only a little more than 176 pounds of food could be produced annually per acre (200 kilograms per hectare). Today, after nearly twenty years of cultivation and reforestation, the farm's food yield per acre is more than 4,500 pounds per year (5,000 kilograms per hectare). Not only that, but the summer temperatures are 4° F (2.2° C) lower, the winter temperatures 3.6° F (2° C) higher, the wind speed is 30 percent reduced, and the evaporation rate of precious water for irrigation has dropped by 25 percent. All of this improvement can be attributed to one action undertaken by this commune and others throughout China—the planting of trees. Henan today illustrates a trend gaining favor among developing countries around the world—especially those ravaged, like China, by centuries of land abuse—to use trees as the instruments of environmental regeneration and improved agriculture.

Four-Around Trees

When Communist forces took over China in 1949, there were almost no trees left in "China Proper," where more than 90 percent of the population lived. Only about 5 percent of the total land area of the country, which is about the size of the United States, was forested. The plateaus of yellow loess (a fine-grained, wind-deposited soil) in north central China had been almost completely deforested for two thousand years, and the resulting soil erosion filled the Yellow River with the dust that gave it its name. One of the new government's first acts was to nationalize almost all of China's forests, and to create a huge army of forest workers. Trees were planted along deserts and sand dunes, and as windbreaks along the coast. Eroding mountainsides were reforested, and trees were planted between fields for firewood and shelter. The entire nation was urged to "cover the country with green trees," and a program was begun to create shelterbelts "around roads, around waterways, around houses, and around villages"—a movement that came to be known as "Four-Around" tree planting.

The results in Henan Province have been spectacular. Before 1949, 1.6 million acres (667,000 hectares) of land were forested; in 1976 the forest cover had expanded to 5.4 million acres (2.2 million hectares). Nationwide, China's forests have doubled, covering 10 percent of the country's total land area. That is still not a substantial proportion considering China's population of one billion (in contrast, almost 50 percent of the Soviet Union and 39 percent of North America is

Chinese farmers irrigate a communal field in Henan Province. Tree windbreaks have been planted here during the past two decades and, along with other agricultural improvements, have raised the per hectare production of these fields thousands of kilograms per year. (*FAO/F. Mattioli*)

forest), but the Chinese experiment has resulted in new techniques for rehabilitating forests on even the most abused and marginal lands, techniques that may give other deforested regions of the world, written off as useless, a measure of food-growing potential.

To achieve such results, the Chinese government has elevated forests to something approaching a national preoccupation, especially in rural areas. Posters, movies, plays, and radio and television messages urge the Chinese people to protect forests. There are penalties for harming trees, awards for caring for them. Such physical benefits of trees as shelter, fuel, mulch, paper, and cash-producing timber are emphasized in every commune. And this effort, more than the actual planting of the trees, may be the most important thing China has done, infusing among even the poorest members of society an understanding of the balances of nature.

J.S., M.R.

10. SINGAPORE

A tiny island nation, in reality just one sprawling city-state, Singapore is offered by some as a microcosm of the world. The comparison may or may not be apt, but the implications are intriguing. The island's population growth has overrun its environment. Most of the original forest that covered the island has been eliminated for housing developments. Many animals native to the island have almost disappeared, including the leaf monkey, anteater, mouse deer, and wild pig. The last tiger was sighted in 1932. Belatedly, the government established several nature reserves that total about 7,000 acres (about 2,800 hectares), and these protected areas are the only places where most of Singapore's indigenous plants can still be found.

What *can* be found in Singapore is people. The island is the most congested nation in the world (except the British crown colony of Hong Kong). About 2.5 million people live on 226 square miles (585 square kilometers) of land. That is a population only slightly smaller than that of Los Angeles living on less than half the area. With no more space in which to expand, the island's leaders found themselves in a desperate situation fifteen years ago and devised a unique birth control scheme. As a result, while most of the world grapples with uncontrollable growth, Singapore appears to be one of the first nations to succeed at curbing its population explosion.

Two Are Enough

In 1965 Singapore took its first step by calling for population control and setting a goal of "replacement-level fertility" (parents having just enough children—two—to replace themselves). Other nations have declared similar policies, but Singapore went further, establishing a variety of "beyond family planning" measures, seen as "draconian" by those who feel family planning should be a voluntary decision.

In 1966 an act allowing abortion and voluntary sterilization was passed by the parliament. Clinics established by private family-planning organizations were supplemented by government clinics, and a comprehensive set of social policies providing incentives and deterrents was introduced. Among the new measures: higher fees for delivery at government hospitals for more than a certain number of births per couple, paid maternity leave for the first two children only, and income-tax relief limited to families with no more than two children. Subsidized government housing is now available only to small families, priority for choice government schools is limited to families with three or fewer children, and parents who have been sterilized have priority in choosing their children's primary schools. Government clinics collect an attendance fee from pregnant women who already have two or more living children. Delivery charges in government hospitals are waived if certain categories of patients agree to be sterilized, and government workers are given leave with pay to undergo sterilization.

Are the methods justified? Certainly they have been effective; by 1977 Singapore had reduced its growth rate by half. And Singaporeans have generally supported the strict methods. In part this may be a matter of conditioning, since the same discipline demonstrated in its family- and population-planning program characterizes other aspects of life in Singapore. The streets are clean, because anyone caught littering pays a $200 fine. Traffic is carefully monitored; automobiles cannot enter the central city unless *four* people are riding.

Singapore today is far from an ideal human environment; its people live mainly in a crowded, industrialized cityscape. But the slowed growth rate may allow the city to come to terms with its other problems eventually. The economy is prosperous—the world's fourth-largest port is here—and annual per capita income is about $2,800 (slightly higher than Ireland's, slightly lower than Italy's). The island's efforts at self-management promise to attract worldwide attention over the coming decades, perhaps sparking further controversies. Critics continue to charge that Singapore's population laws abridge an individual's right to choose his or her parental life-style. Supporters of the programs, however, argue that a crowded island like Singapore has no choice other than strict disciplinarian measures to ensure that the population doesn't exceed the country's ability to support it, engendering scenes of squalor and misery. They add that, like it or not, the island of Singapore is a harbinger of what earth—the island in space—may someday face if population growth does not reach a leveling-off point.

P.D., M.R. with P.R.B.

11. THE STRAIT OF MALACCA

Located between Sumatra and the Malay Peninsula, the shallow Strait of Malacca is not the safest route between the Indian Ocean and the South China Sea, but it is the quickest, so navigators have sailed through it for centuries. Hindu colonists and Arab traders took this shortcut, and so did Portuguese, Dutch, and British merchants. Today, nearly all of the Persian Gulf oil headed for Japan passes through the Strait of Malacca. Since Japan regularly imports 85 percent of its oil from the Middle East, this volume is enormous. An estimated 4,300 loaded tankers use the narrow waterway each year, carrying more than 300 million tons of crude oil and its derivatives. That means nearly one quarter of the petroleum transported by sea passes through the strait. A 1979

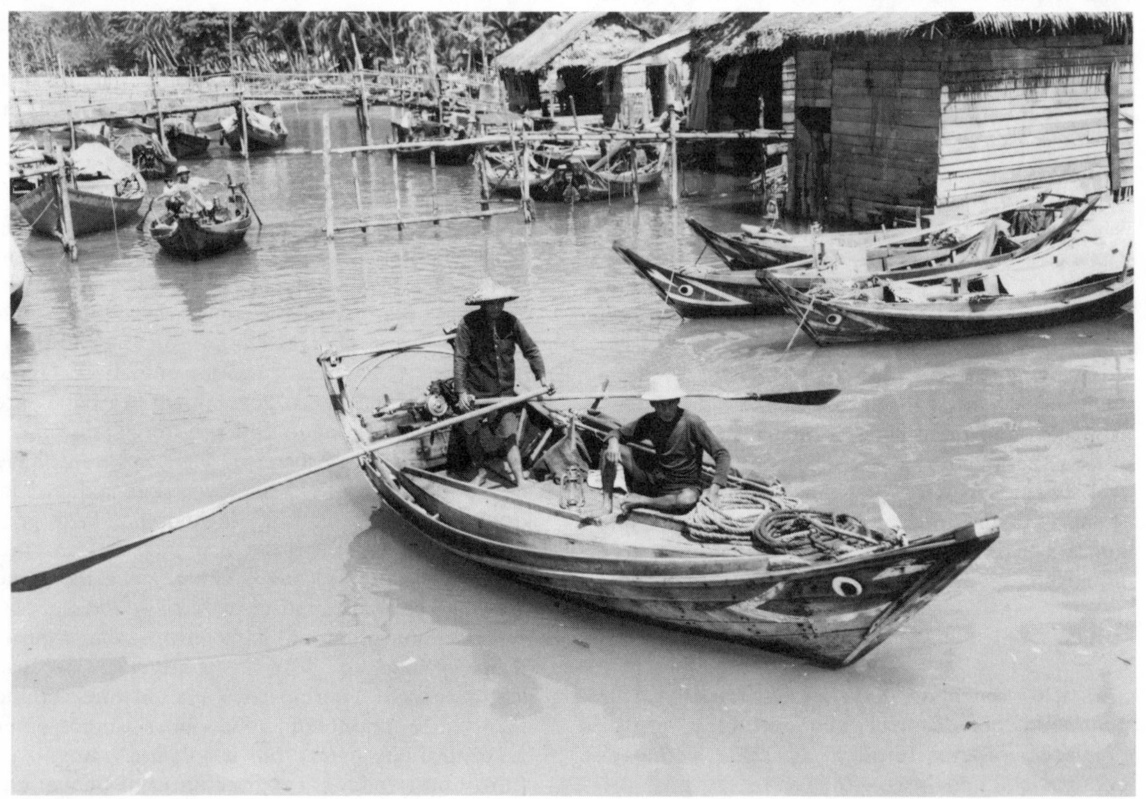

Malay fishermen from Pinang set out in the late afternoon to fish in the Strait of Malacca. The oil lamp will be used to attract fish at night. (*FAO/S. Bunnag*)

report by the East-West Center in Hawaii calculated that if all of the ships that use the strait each year, freighters *and* tankers, were to travel continuously at 15 knots, one vessel would pass another traveling in the opposite direction every nine minutes.

Obviously, that kind of traffic density is dangerous, but the conditions in the Strait of Malacca multiply the hazards. Shaped like a funnel, it narrows to only about 3 miles (5 kilometers) in width at the eastern end. Shifting sands along the bottom form spontaneous, invisible undersea banks. Charts are inadequate, navigational aids sparse. Tides and currents can be peculiar, and there is the occasional threat of heavy monsoon rains. The growing size of tankers further intensifies the dangers, because the larger a ship is, the more difficult it is to maneuver. In a recent eight-year period there were forty-three tanker accidents in the strait, ten of which resulted in lost oil: the Strait of Malacca may now be the most oil-polluted area of the world ocean. But the strategic passageway is more than just a transport shortcut, it is a rich marine habitat, and its undersea problems illustrate the severe impact on the sea of increasing tanker traffic around the world.

Petro Fish

Accidents are not the only way oil is introduced to the waters here. To ride high through the relatively shallow strait, empty tankers are suspected of flushing out oil-contaminated water from their ballast tanks before entering from the east. Prevailing winds and currents may be carrying this oil into the most productive fishing areas in the strait. Since Singapore, at the eastern end, is one of the largest refinery centers in the world, a certain amount of petroleum is also contributed to the sea by routine spills and accidents at coastal docking operations.

The results of all this petroleum are today under examination by the United Nations Environment Programme (UNEP) and the governments of Malaysia and Singapore. There have been reports in local newspapers that more than 50 percent of the beaches along a stretch of the Malay coastline are speckled with tar. More worrisome to government officials, however, are claims by fishermen that their catches in the strait are diminishing.

About 70 percent of Malaysia's total fish catch comes from the Strait of Malacca. In 1978, 400,000 tons of fish were landed by more than 50,000 fishermen. (Included among their catch: sardines, shad, anchovies, eels, horse mackerel, groupers, and silversides.) Authorities fear that smaller catches will mean higher prices for fish, which supplies almost two thirds of the total protein in the Malay diet. A price rise in fish could boost the cost of living significantly and ripple through the region's economy.

Like many other small, semienclosed bodies of seawater around the world, the strait is especially vulnerable. Its waters, protected from the heavy wave action of the Indian Ocean and characterized by relatively weak water circulation, give rise to rich coastal estuaries, which act as nurseries for the developing eggs and larvae of marine populations. Scattered coral reefs in the strait provide food and shelter for fish and shellfish. But the same gentle conditions that foster undersea life ensure that a major oil spill will not undergo the cleansing actions that characterize opensea areas. Subdued waves, winds, and currents in the strait are unlikely to carry away much of the petroleum and are slow to break it up. In 1976 a 6,000-ton spill occurred as a result of a collision between a Philippine tanker, a Soviet freighter, and a Brazilian tanker. Instead of being flushed out to sea, oil was reportedly carried by tides 6 miles (10 kilometers) upriver in the Johor area of the Malay Peninsula, damaging estuaries and river habitats. (For an explanation of the effects of an oil spill on marine life, see "The Business of Supertankers," page 489.)

Fortunately, efforts are being made to study and to improve the situation in the Strait of Malacca. A collection of international agencies—UNEP, the International Oceanographic Commission of UNESCO, the Food and Agriculture Organization—is now convening to draw up pilot study projects in concert with the countries that surround the strait. Meanwhile, like their counterparts in other parts of the world, the fishermen, the tourism community, and the marine scientists concerned about an oily destruction of the strait nervously await a possible catastrophe—the sinking of a supertanker carrying hundreds of thousands of tons of petroleum through the strait. Ironically, the local people, who stand to suffer most from such an accident, are gaining little from the shipping traffic that passes by them. It is nearly all owned by someone else, bound for other nations, providing energy and profits to distant offices where the Strait of Malacca means only a saving of three days' travel time.

M.R.

12. KANUPP, PAKISTAN

At Kanupp, near Karachi, sits Pakistan's only commercial nuclear power plant, a 137-megawatt Canadian heavy-water reactor that began operation in 1972. Pakistan is one of the developing nations that has been interested in nuclear power since the "Atoms for Peace" program began in 1953. Since then Pakistanis have been traveling to the United States, West Germany, Canada, and the Soviet Union for technical training. By 1965 Pakistan had its own 5-megawatt reactor, made in the United States, for research and training, and when the Kanupp reactor began operating seven years later the Pakistan Atomic Energy Commission claimed that the country had 550 qualified nuclear scientists and engineers.

The False Dream

Almost twenty years passed between Pakistan's decision to use nuclear energy and the opening of the relatively small commercial plant at Kanupp. In 1975, Pakistan announced that it would have a new 600-megawatt plant in operation by 1980 and ten more by 1990. But today it appears that Pakistan will be lucky to have one new plant by 1990. The cost of nuclear power has risen dramatically while capital has become increasingly difficult to obtain.

Although proponents of nuclear power claim that it will increase a developing nation's energy independence, it has so far had the opposite effect by making developing nations more dependent on imports. The reactor itself must be imported, as must scarce uranium fuel. Each step of the nuclear cycle requires sophisticated technical expertise and expensive facilities: the uranium needs to be refined, the fuel must be fabricated, and spent fuel must be reprocessed or permanently stored. Developing nations usually cannot afford to build a complete nuclear power system, and therefore become dependent on the developed world for essential materials and services. Moreover, the expense of nuclear power virtually eliminates the possibility of investing in alternate energy systems.

The unreliability of nuclear power plants is a particularly severe problem for countries with limited electrical systems. An average large U.S. reactor operates only a little more than half the time. An installed capacity of 6,000 to 10,000 megawatts from other sources is necessary as a back-up for a nuclear plant so that electrical supply can be maintained when the plant is shut down. Only five developing countries could meet this criterion in 1977, meaning that all others will have to endure regular disruptions in electric supply if they rely on nuclear energy. And most developing countries will not have the facilities to use the generated electricity for years if not decades.

The growing public disaffection for nuclear energy in Europe, Japan, and the United States suggests another aspect of the nuclear energy issue in the developing world. All studies of the potential hazards of nuclear power have been done in the developed countries. The lack of technical expertise would seem to make reactors even more dangerous in the developing countries.

Is the Genie Out of the Bottle?

Unfortunately, electricity is not the only product of nuclear energy. Many developing countries are also eager to gain the prestige of being a nuclear superpower. United States intelligence sources believe, for example, that Pakistan has been working on its first nuclear weapon. Other small nuclear countries are presumably doing the same. (See "Candidates for the Nuclear Club," page 549.)

In 1976, France agreed to sell Pakistan a nuclear reprocessing facility that could extract plutonium from spent fuel and that would move Pakistan one significant step closer to possessing a nuclear weapon. Pressure from the United States delayed the sale, and France eventually canceled the order in 1978. Pakistan, motivated at least partially by India's development of the atomic bomb, was determined to have its own. Denied the opportunity to import bomb-making facilities, Pakistan decided to build its own centrifuge enrichment plant to produce weapons-grade uranium-235. By ordering the needed special materials from a variety of countries, Pakistan managed to circumvent the efforts of those trying to stop nuclear weapons proliferation. A Pakistani scientist, Abdul Qadir Khan, who had worked at a Dutch enrichment plant, managed to obtain the guarded secrets of the enrichment process. Today he is directing the construction of the facility. (For a discussion of atomic energy's role in nuclear proliferation, see "The Horses of the Atom," page 447.)

With its strategic location bordering Iran, China, Afghanistan, and India (in the Hindu Kush region along the northern border with Afghanistan, Pakistan is also only about 20 miles [30 kilometers] from the Soviet Union), Pakistan's campaign for atomic energy and weapons worries many international observers, who fear that a government dominated by military figures and committed to a nuclear defense strategy could one day develop a perceived need to use a nuclear weapon. Pakistan's dedication to its military is as great as that of almost any other nation. In 1978, nearly *30 percent* of Pakistan's central government budget went for military expenditures. Located in one of the "hot spots" of the world and engaged in a serious pursuit of military might, Pakistan promises to attract a great deal of attention in the coming era as an indicator of the fate of nuclear energy in the developing world.

K.F.

13. THE PERSIAN GULF

The Persian Gulf, a politically boiling "hot spot," is also the warmest region of the undersea world—seawater in the Gulf is the temperature of human blood. That irony is compounded by another. While the attention of hundreds of millions of people throughout the industrialized world is sharply focused on the lands around the edge of the Persian Gulf, few people realize that beneath its waters lies one of the most fragile and most endangered ecosystems on earth.

The culprit here is coastal development, a trend that each year eliminates valuable sealife-sustaining estuaries, reefs, and tidal communities around the world. Increasingly, marine scientists are coming to the conclusion that the destruction of coastal habitats, which harbor a high proportion of the next generation of marine creatures each year, is as great a threat to ocean vitality as chemical pollutants (see "Wetlands," page 379). The effects are especially severe in the Persian Gulf because its coastline, according to the United Nations Environment Programme (UNEP), is the most rapidly developing area in the world.

In addition to the Persian Gulf's extraordinary warmth, it is one of the shallowest regions of the sea, a characteristic that is both a strength and a weakness. With an average depth of only 110 feet (34 meters) and with coastal waters that are less than 33 feet (10 meters) deep for miles offshore, the Gulf is penetrated throughout by sunlight. The light fuels plankton production, and the region's high volume of tiny marine plants and animals feeds a large and varied stock of fish and shellfish. Fishing boats exploit rich populations of shrimp, sardines, anchovies, mackerel, and barracudas, as well as many kinds of bottom fish in the areas where the seafloor topography is flat enough for trawl nets.

A Sea of Economics and Politics

But the Persian Gulf's shallowness also makes it a trap for the increasing flow of wastes from new industries and expanding urban centers being built with Arab oil revenues. Unable to discharge its contaminants to the ocean because of the narrowness of the water gateway at the Strait of Hormuz, and too small and shallow to absorb safely the flood of harmful materials, the Gulf accumulates pollution pockets undersea. Waters along the Arabian side and at the northern extreme, which are especially shallow, are also the most damaged.

One unusual aspect of Persian Gulf marine problems is a result of the arid nature of the lands bordering it. The need for drinking water for cities in the region has brought to the Gulf the world's greatest concentration of desalination plants. In the process of creating fresh water for thirsty populations, the plants also discharge enormous amounts of residual brine into the Gulf, a phenomenon that may be changing the salinity of some habitats, thus threatening some species.

The salinity of seawater, like such other variables as temperature and pressure, determines the kinds of organisms that inhabit an area. Having adapted to specific conditions, some species are extremely sensitive to any change. (A fish kill resulting from a sudden release of warm water from a power plant sited alongside an aquatic habitat is an example of this vulnerability.) As yet, the effect of the brine discharges is not known. In fact, the highly charged political situation in the Persian Gulf region has inhibited the kind of exhaustive marine studies needed to determine many other aspects of the Gulf's health.

If the state of the Persian Gulf's marine life cannot be reliably determined because of its internationally strategic location, developments along the coast provide enough clues to worry UNEP and scientists in the area. Urban populations are expected to double within ten years, generating continued alteration of the coast as new marinas and housing units appear.

These trends may not be so important as the unparalleled industrialization, however. Concerned that their oil revenues will one day diminish, Arab nations in particular are rapidly diversifying their economic base by erecting aluminum plants, shipyards, manufacturing centers, stone crushing plants, refineries, and a variety of other profitable operations.

Industrial investment in Saudi Arabia alone was estimated by UNEP in 1976 to total about $160 million per mile ($100 million per kilometer) of coastline, and construction has escalated since then. To carve out new harbors, all eight Persian Gulf nations (Oman, the United Arab Emirates, Qatar, Bahrain, Saudi Arabia, Kuwait, Iraq, and Iran) are dredging huge amounts of seabed material, which is then used for landfill, destroying first the bottom communities disrupted by the dredges, then the shallow water communities covered over to create new building sites and roadways.

Evidence of the disastrous impact of all these activities has begun to accumulate. Recent surveys of Persian Gulf fish have revealed traces of mercury and lead poison, some fisheries appear to be producing smaller catches, pollution-related illnesses have been recorded, and a shrimp fishing ground near Bahrain, according to the English language *Gulf Mirror,* has been destroyed, in part by the construction of a nearby shipyard.

If the situation is more acute here, it is also an unrelenting trend in nearly every other part of the world. Unfortunately, marine creatures, like humans on the land, tend to congregate along coastlines, which have a greater abundance of food, shelter, and light than the deep sea or the open ocean. It is an unfortunate circumstance for both communities. The sea creatures suffer from the human disposal of wastes directly into their habitats, the humans suffer the loss of an important living resource and a fund of diversity and beauty that will become increasingly precious to future generations.

M.R.

14. THE NEGEV DESERT, ISRAEL

The Negev is an exception among deserts in that progress is being made to turn it into usable land. Throughout the arid tropical regions of the world, deserts are fast advancing, eliminating arable farmland, changing microclimates, exacerbating the misery of the peoples who live along and atop them. Wood and charcoal shortages (see "Port-au-Prince, Haiti," page 66) are common throughout North Africa and southern Asia, and as the people in these regions denude the land of its trees, sandy deserts—the obstacles to their progress stripped away—creep further and further each year. Some 680 million people in the world live on land that is desert or nearly so, many of them raising cattle that intensify the problem as they overgraze on scarce vegetation. (See "Engineering a Famine," page 193.) The result is that an area of the world the size of Austria turns to desert each year. The total area of the world threatened by "desertification," according to the United Nations Environment Programme (UNEP), equals the area of the United States, the Soviet Union, and Australia combined. There are many programs to halt encroaching deserts, but none have even approached the stunning successes of Israel's gradual transformation of the Negev into an agricultural oasis. In the process, Israeli scientists and farmers may be devising techniques that could help attenuate both the ominous growth of the world's deserts and the increasingly common global problem of water shortages.

The summer months in Israel are practically devoid of rain, and the winter months are not much better. Since biblical times the country has had to cope with its dry south, the arid Negev Desert. At its formation in 1948, fully 50 percent of Israel's territory was desert, and the influx of Jewish immigrants created tremendous pressures on the country's scarce water supply and scant farmlands. But Israeli scientists, after three decades of experimentation and innovation, are now able to employ over 95 percent of the available water, approximately ten times the amount of available water that is utilized in the United States. So successful have they been, in fact, that the nation not only produces about 80 percent of the food it consumes but exports fruits and vegetables to Europe, and even roses for the flower markets of Amsterdam. That is only the beginning. The nation vows to settle a million people in the Negev—which supported only 14,000 in 1949—by the year 2000.

The Water Network

The "miracle of the blooming desert" has been accomplished by an inspired combination of technology and common sense. In standard irrigation procedures, as much as 90 percent of the water used can be lost, but the Israelis devised a system of "trickle irrigation" that preserves nearly every drop of the water available for irrigation. Plastic pipes with carefully placed holes feed water directly to the roots of plants, dripping at precisely the rate necessary for growth, wasting almost no water. To increase the supply of water, engineers began by building a network of aqueducts, pipelines, and tunnels that convey some 12 billion cubic feet (350 million cubic meters) of water from the more humid north, including the Sea of Galilee. The National Water Project distributes water all the way to the Negev, doubling as a replenishment system by refilling wells and artesian aquifers along the way when there is rain and demand is low.

This flexible water network has stretched the available water about as far as possible, but the Israelis have another plan. About 1,600 feet (500 meters) beneath the desert lie immense artesian reserves of brackish water that have accumulated over thousands of years. The water is too salty for the citrus crops that form the backbone of the country's export earnings, but Israeli scientists are working in two directions. One is a new method of treating the water, the other is the development of crops that would tolerate its salt. (Such experimentation with desert agriculture has even inspired Israeli scientists to attempt to create a substitute for cattle, which cannot adjust to desert conditions well, by developing a breed of camel whose meat is palatable.) And while programs to furnish the desert with more water intensify, Israeli researchers continue to find new ways to produce more food on less water. Consulting the unearthed remains of ancient farms, which appear to have produced crops in areas that may have received less than three inches of rain annually, agronomists have developed new methods patterned after the ones revealed by archaeologists. Pistachio trees and some other crops, as a result, are now being raised on what amounts to four cups of water per plant per year.

Even if all the experiments designed to increase the water supply and reclaim the desert are successful in Israel, there will never be a time when water reserves are sufficient to allow the population to discontinue the most stringent conservation policies, and there will never be a time when the highly vulnerable desert ecosystem is not in danger of being overwhelmed by farming or grazing. In fact, many Israeli scientists today fear that the discovery of new water sources could rapidly inundate the fragile desert with too much water, disrupting the area's natural continuum.

In the long run, however, Israel's intensive studies of dry, nearly marginal lands and previously unusable waters hold great hopes for other desert countries. Unfortunately, politics loom as the greatest threat to the efforts toward desert regeneration. The continual wars of the past three decades have prevented the sharing of Israeli farming successes with surrounding Arab nations, the very people who occupy some of the most rapidly deteriorating desert lands in the world.

B.L., M.R.

15. TSAVO NATIONAL PARK, KENYA

The popular image of Africa is that of "storybook" animals—elephants, zebras, lions, tigers, giraffes. Most of these creatures are not as abundant as they once were, and some are in the process of disappearing; poachers have reduced the number of black rhinos, according to the World Wildlife Fund, by half in the last ten years, and a subspecies of zebra and subspecies of giraffe are threatened with extinction. Although most of the great herds that once existed here are gone, East Africa's wildlife is not undergoing a wholesale extermination, because over the past two decades the government of Kenya has tried to set aside immense wildlife preserves and has banned all "big game" hunting. The situation is neither simple nor entirely encouraging, however. The tour stops in the Tsavo National Park, within sight of Mount Kilimanjaro, because the situation here illustrates the frustrating complexity of trying to save invaluable species in a region of the world where human life also struggles for sustenance.

As It Was, As It Is

At the turn of this century, travelers to Kenya were thrilled by the enormous herds of zebras, wildebeests, ostriches, antelopes, and gazelles roaming the fertile East African plains, hunted by their predators, the lions, leopards, and hyenas. Buffaloes, rhinos, and elephants browsed through the bush. Flamingos by the millions came to feed at Lake Nakuru in the central plateau.

Today the number of humans in Kenya is growing at a rate of 3.5 percent annually, and the population of fifteen million is expected to double within two decades. Nairobi, Kenya's capital, is not simply a staging area for safaris today; there are auto assembly plants, textile factories, chemical industries. Such corporations as Exxon, Firestone, Union Carbide, Del Monte, and General Motors have operations in Kenya, along with 120 other U.S. firms. Even more important to the Kenyan economy, however, is its agricultural output, much of which leaves the country; Kenya's expanding farms and ranches send coffee, tea, and livestock products to Europe and England.

The obvious result of the nation's burgeoning industries, farms, and population is a steady pressure on the habitat shared for millennia by wildlife. Most of the country's wild animals now live in sixteen national parks and twenty-seven game reserves, either bordered or completely surrounded by towns, farms, and ranches. Nairobi National Park, where tourists can see every popular East African species but elephants, lies just outside Nairobi with its population of almost 600,000 people.

Farmers vs. Elephants

At Tsavo National Park, 8,069 square miles (20,900 square kilometers) of flat bush country and semidesert, the problem is too many elephants. Though Tsavo is the largest game park in the world—larger than Kuwait or Israel—it is too dry and barren to support the 30,000 elephants that have crowded into the area because of pressure from farmers and hunters elsewhere. A full-grown elephant can eat 700 pounds (320 kilograms) of grass, leaves, and twigs a day; and Tsavo, with its scant, erratic rainfall, simply lacks

The expansion of agricultural fields, like this one in the Karatina area of Kenya, gradually encroaches on land that formerly supported a variety of wildlife. Often the crops grown, like the coffee in the foreground, are exported to Europe. (*FAO/P. Pittet*)

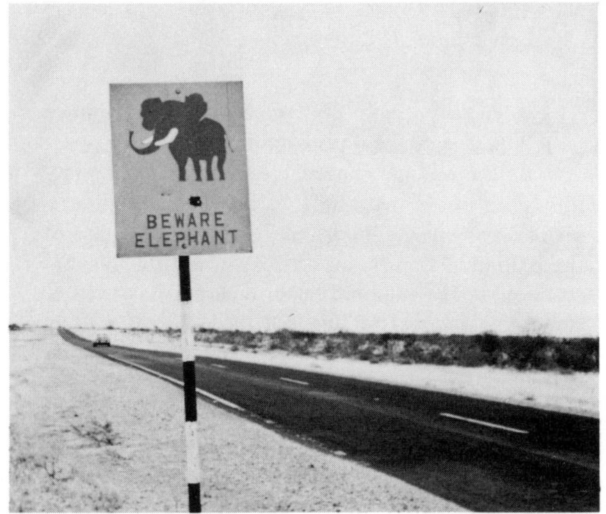

Sign in Tsavo National Park, Kenya. (*Carol Sue Davidson*)

the vegetation to feed more than a few thousand. During the severe droughts that occur there every ten years, animals by the thousands die of starvation. In 1970–71, 6,000 elephants and 600 rhinos perished.

Under natural conditions, elephants will migrate in search of food and water, deserting old feeding grounds for many years until the trees have grown back. But today an elephant leaving the park may be shot by farmers defending their crops. As Boyce Rensberger writes in *The Cult of the Wild,* "East African farmers must contend with raiding elephants the way American farmers contend with raiding rabbits or crows, except, of course, that in a single night one elephant can wipe out a season's efforts on an African farm." So, confined to Tsavo, the herds are stripping away its trees and shrubs, transforming the area into a desert.

A decade ago scientists of the Tsavo Research Project recommended that 3,000 elephants be shot and studied, but the proposal was dropped after outraged protests from some conservationists. Soon afterward drought killed twice that number, most of them females and their young. Now, because of malnutrition and overcrowding, the elephant birth rate has fallen and infant mortality has risen sharply. Somehow, either natural forces or human intervention must limit the size of Tsavo's herds, or overpopulation will destroy first their habitat, then the animals themselves.

Disarming Big Game Hunters

So far the Kenyan government has responded to the problem of wildlife loss by passing laws against hunting. In 1977, after a five-year period in which two thirds of Kenya's animals died from the effects of drought, the parliament canceled all licenses for hunting guns, barred people with weapons from entering the country, and ordered hunting safaris to convert into photographic safaris.

The following year the parliament forbade the sale of wildlife trophies—a measure that increased the effectiveness of the anti-hunting laws. As long as Kenyan shopkeepers were allowed to sell ivory carvings and elephant hair bracelets, zebra drum tables and lion-tooth necklaces, poachers had no trouble unloading their contraband. Now, with wildlife officials spending \$36 million per year to fight poachers, Nairobi warehouses are filled with confiscated goods.

Though the hunting ban has cost Kenya approximately \$1.2 million per year in license and game fees and hunters' expenditures, Minister of Tourism and Wildlife Mathews Ogutu feels that the sacrifice was necessary "to keep the animals alive for future generations to see." The loss seems insignificant at any rate, in the context of Kenya's \$100-million-a-year tourist industry. However, Kenyan officials now realize that protection from the hunter's gun is just the beginning of wildlife management. If the animals are to survive more than another decade, they must have adequate water and food; they must be numerous enough to reproduce without inbreeding, yet few enough to avoid overcrowding. As a first step toward more effective management, Ogutu has announced "a five-year program of monitoring to number each species in a given area and study how to contain them."

The Kenyan government has a strong economic incentive to save its animals: tourism based on wildlife-watching is the country's second-largest industry. Given intelligent programs and sufficient funds and personnel, it may be possible for Kenya to maintain its small but impressive remnant of East Africa's herds. One key factor seems to be funding. There have been appeals during the past few years for financial aid from developed countries to help in the running of Africa's wildlife preserves. Some African leaders feel that the monetary burden of caring for species that are of value to the whole world unfairly falls on their shoulders. Tourism pays the bills now, but as population and development pressures increase, some emerging nations could find themselves in a position of deciding between preservation of wild animals or people. M.A., T.L.

16. MPAMBAA, TANZANIA

Like most of Africa, Tanzania (formed by the union of Zanzibar and Tanganyika in 1964) was controlled for more than a century and a half by European colonial powers, first Germany, then England. As a result, land that for centuries had been cultivated by subsistence farmers was gradually taken over by large landowners for the production of such export crops as cotton, cocoa, tobacco, tea, and coffee. The Europeans prospered while the Africans found it increasingly difficult to feed themselves. Even after most of Africa achieved independence during the 1960s, international aid agencies like the World Bank encouraged the development of corporate farms to raise export crops. Consequently, economic growth rates have soared in many African nations, while much of the continent's population still lives in rural isolation, making inefficient use of land and labor—and battling against hunger.

Julius Nyerere, who became Tanzania's first president in 1964, proposed a different path, a national political system called *ujamaa,* or "familyhood." Unlike European socialism, which is based on class struggle, *ujamaa* is based on the idea of the extended family, an African tradition that has its roots in the regional tribe. Nyerere has tried to make the *ujamaa* village the basic social unit in Tanzania.

Workers at Dodoma, Tanzania, cover sorted sacks of grain with tarpaulins. As part of the nation's attempts to feed itself, the Tanzanian government is building a national strategic grain reserve. Storage buildings will eventually replace these temporary outdoor "warehouses." (*FAO/F. Mattioli*)

Each village is responsible, above all, for feeding itself; only after this is assured can the village turn to the cultivation of export crops. Supporters of the Tanzanian social, economic, and environmental experiment claim that the nation is setting a powerful example for other African nations. It is attempting to avoid total foreign domination, to improve its agricultural practices at an appropriate pace for its people and lands, and to disperse the fruit of its farm production to hungry Tanzanians rather than foreign commodities traders.

Reading, Writing, and a Chicken Chart

In the fields around the village of Mpambaa in the dry central region of Tanzania one can see young children busy at a variety of agricultural jobs. On the wall of the village classrooms are charts that record the egg production, expenses, and income from the school's chickens. The challenge of the day's mathematics lesson is to determine how much feed is required to produce each egg. In 1973 less than half of Tanzania's school-age population was in school. In 1980 almost 90 percent of the seven-to-twelve-year-olds were attending school. And part of this expansion in education has been financed by the agricultural output of the students themselves.

The unusual educational system is part of the *ujamaa* mix of education and agriculture, self-reliance and dependence on the "extended family" of the village. Nyerere's ideal *ujamaa* village has 250 families, each of which works on a large collective farm while maintaining a small individual plot. Each village has its own governing council, school, water supply, health clinic, and agricultural service. Rather than trying to jump immediately from hand tools to tractors (until recently human muscles supplied nearly all of the power for Tanzanian agriculture), Tanzania has encouraged the village groups to begin using oxen because they promise to be more dependable and affordable at this point in the nation's development. Another consideration in the decision to emphasize oxen: they remove the possibility that a dependence would be set up on foreign technicians.

A Fierce Independence

Formulating the *ujamaa* plan, however, has proven easier than making it actually work. While the Tanzanian government has not forced its people to participate in the *ujamaa* network, they *have* compelled rural peasants to abandon their isolated homes and move into villages. Once in the village, peasants are allowed to decide whether to farm individually or collectively. Although 85 percent of the population now live in villages, less than 10 percent of the villages have thus far adopted the *ujamaa* model.

Tanzanian officials explain that implementing the plan will take time, and that it faces two obstacles. The first is the friction of cross-tribal relations that can militate against the cohesion of a village (Tanzania is a nation of more than one hundred different tribes). The second problem is the traditional independence of the farmers who have now been moved into villages. Attempts were made at first to impose collective farming, but they met with little success. The efficiency of farm work diminished because peasants regarded the land as owned by the government rather than the community when authorities forced them to work it.

The thrust now seems to be toward encouraging villages to develop their own agricultural schemes, in the hope these will be more popular than those imposed by the central bureaucracy. When an independent agricultural consulting agency visited a village recently, for example, they brought together various ethnic groups within the village for a discussion of the problem of grain storage. Between 50 and 75 percent of Tanzania's grain is lost each year to pests and mildew during storage. Foreign experts had advised the nation to buy mechanized silos, which were far too expensive for a village. During long meeting sessions with the consultants, the villagers realized that each tribe had its own technique for storage, and that none of these had been shared with others. They soon came up with an effective method based on a combination of traditional practices.

The kind of small-scale farming being encouraged in Tanzania also promises to be more sound environmentally than large-scale mechanized operations, which in many countries have hastened soil erosion and exhausted productive lands. Generally, small farmers tend to have a vested interest in maintaining soils and guarding against their depletion because they lack the freedom of big agribusiness firms to pick up and move elsewhere.

The *ujamaa* program bears close observation in the years to come as Tanzania tries to come up with an African formula for development. The central questions appear to be whether the amalgam of tribes will be cohesive, whether political strife will disrupt the village plan, and whether population pressures will diminish so that the nation's progress is not canceled out by a mass of new mouths to feed each year.

K.F.

17. MALVILLE, FRANCE

Malville is a French village of fifty people on the Rhône River about 30 miles (50 kilometers) east of Lyons. The chickens on the road near the stone farmhouses are in sharp contrast to the giant concrete cylinder under construction nearby. The new building is part of the Super Phénix fast-breeder nuclear power plant. When completed in 1983, the 1,200-megawatt facility will be the world's most advanced commercial reactor, the major achievement of the world's most active nuclear development program.

The new Super Phénix plant rising in Malville illustrates the continuing emphasis on nuclear power among a handful of nations, industrial giants whose huge energy appetites and scarce domestic resources persuade them to choose nuclear power, with its inherent dangers, because it is available immediately. France today races to complete a nuclear power constellation that will make it more independent. Some observers fear the nation will experience a crisis equal to or worse than that at Three Mile Island.

The Super-Nuclear Nation

France has relatively little coal, oil, or natural gas. The implications of this deficiency were underscored during the Arab oil embargo of 1973, which prompted the French government to begin an ambitious nuclear development program. France had only four nuclear plants in operation the year of the embargo; by February 1980 sixteen plants were operating and a new plant was scheduled to open every two months for the next twenty years. In 1980, France got about 20 percent of its electricity and 4 percent of its total energy from nuclear power; by 1985 nuclear power is expected to supply 55 percent of electricity and 20 percent of total energy. That will make France second only to the United States in total production of nuclear energy. (In addition, France has become a major exporter, selling reactors to such buyers as Belgium, South Africa, and South Korea.)

This drive to erect an independent energy program has already led France to develop the most complete nuclear fuel cycle in the world. To avoid being dependent on the United States for enriched uranium, the French are building an enrichment plant at Tricastan, which will supplement already-operating plants and produce enough fuel for *two hundred* reactors. To stretch limited uranium resources, spent fuel is reprocessed in one of the world's largest facilities at Cap de la Hague. But the French see the real hope for the future in breeder reactors such as the Super Phénix and the already-operating Phénix.

Breeder reactors, which are fueled with uranium-238 and plutonium, produce more plutonium than they use and thereby provide a significant saving in fuel costs. The surplus plutonium, however, is a problem, because it can be used to make an atomic bomb. The danger of this plutonium being stolen led U. S. President Carter to oppose the construction of the proposed experimental Clinch River fast-breeder reactor in Tennessee. Although breeder reactors are about 50 percent more expensive to build than other reactors, the French believe they will still prove to be more economical than imported oil and will make France more energy independent.

The French Dilemma

The French nuclear program seems likely to continue growing. All the major political parties support nuclear energy, and even after the accident at Three Mile Island a Harris poll indicated that 57 percent of the French people supported the government's nuclear program. Antinuclear forces have staged large demonstrations and even organized a political party, which was relatively successful initially. But legal and procedural tactics, which have been successful in slowing nuclear development in the United States, have not been effective in France, where the licensing procedure is much simpler and the legal system very different.

Nuclear programs in other industrialized countries are not doing as well as in France. Antinuclear factions in the United States, West Germany, Sweden, Austria, England, and Japan have dramatically reduced the growth of nuclear power, and in the Soviet Union, where there has been no visible antinuclear movement, experts have curtailed their plans for expansion for economic and technical reasons. The continually intensifying energy crisis, however, has convinced many people that nuclear energy is necessary, and no government has decided to completely abandon nuclear power. Antinuclear forces continue to grow in strength, a trend that worries the French and other governments. Not surprisingly, some of the most strident opposition to the French nuclear program has come from people living near existing or proposed plants, particularly near the new Super Phénix in Malville. Committed to its nuclear direction, the government refuses to slow the program and has taken another tack. To weaken local opposition to the plants, French President Giscard d'Estaing announced in January 1980 a 15-percent reduction in the cost of electricity to anyone willing to live near a nuclear plant.

To many opponents of nuclear power around the world, the fundamental issue is not safety but its economic burden. Far from being a relatively low-cost source of power, as its proponents initially suggested during the 1950s and 1960s, it is in fact probably the most costly alternative available when technology, raw material availability, safety, reliability, and waste disposal requirements are included in its price.

K.F.

18. VÄSTERÅS, SWEDEN

Västerås is a typical European industrial city in all respects but one—its clean air. The sulfur dioxide level is only 10 percent of what is usually found in a city of this size. The air is clean because there is no smoke coming from the chimneys of the offices, factories, and homes of Västerås' 120,000 people. The only smoke to be seen is coming from the city's electric power plant, which doubles as the main source of heat and hot water for the entire city. By centralizing these functions, Västerås is able not only to protect the purity of its air but to reduce its energy consumption substantially.

The city is an example of Sweden's intense efforts to conserve energy that, like France's, must be imported. While Sweden *has* begun a limited nuclear energy program, most of its policies of the past few years stand in sharp contrast to other industrialized nations—especially energy-guzzling countries like the United States. Instead of looking for a quick "fix," Sweden looks for ways of reducing its energy consumption.

The Conserver Society

With a comparable standard of living, a much colder climate, and a more energy-intensive industrial sector (particularly the paper industry, which uses 15 percent of the nation's energy), Sweden uses about one third less energy per capita than the United States.

Automobiles squander energy, so Sweden encourages the use of its public transportation system. Gasoline is heavily taxed, as are automobile sales. An annual tax is levied on automobiles, and the tax rate increases with the weight of the automobile. Mass transit, which is comfortable and efficient in Sweden, extends as far as 25 miles (40 kilometers) from the city center. A monthly pass that allows for unlimited use of buses and trains costs only sixteen dollars and half-fare is charged during nonpeak hours. Swedes use public transportation for 45 percent of all trips under 6 miles (10 kilometers); Americans use it for only 10 percent of such trips. (It is not unusual to see a Swedish couple in formal dress stepping off a bus after a night at the opera.)

Through taxes, loans, incentives, and regulations, Sweden has encouraged long-lasting energy savings through building insulation, mass transit, industrial technology, and community cooperation. The techniques for saving energy are taught in all Swedish schools. Factories and offices even have energy committees drawn from workers and management.

Swedish energy efficiency is a result of necessity. With more than 70 percent of its energy coming from imported oil, Sweden has always paid high prices for energy and was particularly hard hit by the 1973 oil embargo. Unlike the United States, Canada, and the Soviet Union, the country has no domestic resources that could be substituted for imports.

The Sharing Society

Fifty percent of Sweden's energy is used for heating homes and workplaces. The Swedish government has provided $1 billion ($125 per person) in loans and grants for the installation of energy-saving measures and has begun a program to improve the insulation in all old buildings. New homes with special energy-saving features are given priority for loans. On the average, home insulation in Sweden is twice as effective as that in the United States. In addition, 58 percent of Swedish families live in apartments (compared to 29 percent in the United States), and apartments need less heat than detached dwellings. The Swedish government is concerned, however, because apartment dwellers usually do not pay for heat separately and are therefore not motivated to save more energy.

Industry in Sweden is also constantly being scrutinized for energy efficiency. Lee Schipper and Allan Lichtenberg, energy analysts for the Energy and Resource Group at the University of California at Berkeley, have found that in virtually every comparable industry Sweden uses energy more effectively than the United States.

And Sweden has achieved this productivity in spite of its heavy use of electricity, an inefficient form of energy for most purposes. Following the lead of the neighboring Finns, Sweden has improved the efficiency of electricity through cogeneration (see "Cogeneration," page 44). Excess heat that is generated for one part of an industrial process is used to drive a turbine to produce electricity needed in another part of the process.

In Västerås, the same notion of conserving wasted energy and using it for an unrelated function is extended to an entire city. Västerås' only power plant, notable along the city skyline because of its tall smokestacks, is the heart of its energy scheme. Beneath the power plant, pipes branch out in all directions beneath the city, carrying hot water under pressure to 98 percent of the buildings in Västerås. Each building contains a heat exchanger that transfers the heat in the most appropriate manner for providing heat and hot water to that building. Ordinarily, two thirds of the energy used in producing electricity is wasted, but Västerås' district heating system recycles and makes use of much of it.

About 25 percent of the cities in Sweden have similar district heating systems, and plans exist to install a system for Stockholm's 1.5 million people. Thirty-five percent of the fuel-generated electricity in Sweden is produced by heat-sharing plants. In addition, 600,000 homes are heated by central plants that produce only heat, but which are still far more efficient than private furnaces.

The advantages of district heating are numerous. Fuel is converted to heat more efficiently in a single large furnace than in many small furnaces, and heat exchangers are smaller, simpler, and cleaner than furnaces in the home. The high chimney of a large plant is better at dispersing the polluting by-products of combustion, and scrubbers and filters are cheaper for one large facility than for many small ones.

Whether Sweden will continue indefinitely to satisfy its energy needs without resorting to nuclear power is questionable. The campaign leading to a referendum on nuclear development in March 1980 prompted pronuclear warnings of lost jobs and factory closures without nuclear expansion. The resulting vote gave a limited "yes" to plans for increasing Sweden's nuclear plants from six to twelve over the next decade. But even this vote illustrated the prevailing Swedish attitude toward nuclear power: a majority of the voters indicated on their ballots a desire to phase out nuclear power within twenty-five years.

K.F.

19. ATHENS, GREECE

The temples of the Acropolis in Athens have long been on the "must see" list of most serious world travelers. For 2,500 years, the temples have been threatened by everything from Turkish soldiers to British archaeologists to American tourists. But none of these human trespassers has done them more harm than an invisible danger they now face. Always a symbol of the creative achievements of civilization, the Acropolis temples have now also become symbols of air pollution. One agent slowly destroying them is acid rain (see "The Trespassing Poison: Acid Rain," page 186)—a phenomenon unheard of until recently, but already a relentlessly expanding threat in the industrial world to lakes and rivers, to fish and other aquatic life, even to some of the most beautiful cathedrals and monuments of Europe, buildings as durable as those on the Acropolis.

A Bloom of Newness

The historian Plutarch, who lived during the first century A.D., wrote that during the fifth century B.C. many Athenian citizens were off fighting wars and carrying out adventurous expeditions, but thousands were left unemployed at home. Pericles, the equivalent of mayor, faced then, as mayors do now, the problem of providing jobs with public funds. So, in an extraordinarily ambitious public works project, Pericles planned elaborate monuments and new buildings.

Of these projects, the temples on the sacred Acropolis are the most magnificent. To build them, Pericles employed "smiths and carpenters and moulders, founders and braziers, stone-cutters, dyers, goldsmiths, painters, sculptors . . . shoemakers, road-makers, miners . . ." according to Plutarch's *Lives of the Noble Greeks*. Cutting and honing and chiseling, carrying and fetching, the people of Athens built the temples of blindingly white marble, every stone so perfectly fitted to the next that no mortar was required. Plutarch, praising the elegance and beauty of the temples, also noted "there is a sort of bloom of newness upon these works . . . preserving them from the touch of time, as if they had some perennial spirit and undying vitality mingled in the composition of them." To a great extent the temples *have* resisted the natural ravages of weather and time, but they are no match for modern threats that Plutarch could not have imagined. As though they were sitting under a tap of dripping acid, the ancient marble temples have begun to melt away.

Monumental Problems

Clouds of sulfur dioxide in the atmosphere around the Acropolis—emitted by cars, trucks, buses, homes, and factories—dissolve in rainwater, turning the rain into dilute sulfuric acid. The porous marble of the monuments soaks up the acidic rain, and eventually the marble can be corroded into powder. This process has especially affected the statues, including the famous Caryatid columns, and the bas reliefs. The effects of acid rain and similar air pollution agents is gradually destroying hundreds of invaluable monuments elsewhere, including many of the great cathedrals of Europe, for example, Rheims, Chartres, and Strasbourg (France); Cologne (West Germany); Lincoln and Wells (Great Britain).

In addition to the problems of acid rains on the Acropolis, metal clamps inserted during the early twentieth century—intended, ironically, to stabi-

The Acropolis, a symbol of Western civilization, is now threatened by technologies that symbolize that civilization today. The Parthenon (center), temple of Athena, guardian of cities, and the Erechtheion, on its left, date from the fifth century B.C. (*Greek National Tourist Organization, New York*)

lize the buildings—have begun to oxidize, a process exacerbated by pollution. Oxidation causes the clamps to expand and decay, adhering to the marble in the process, cracking it open, affecting it like hot coals embedded in ice.

To make matters worse, many of the clamps are inside the marble blocks. In order to discover their location, all the temples have had to be gammagraphed, a process similar to the X ray. Now all the clamps must be painstakingly replaced by titanium alloys, a process somewhat akin to performing surgery on the inside of a table leg.

Recognizing the Acropolis as not only an exemplary work of classical architecture but also an eloquent testimony to the achievements of all humanity, the United Nations Educational, Scientific, and Cultural Organization (UNESCO) and the Greek government have embarked on a project to save the ruins, attempting to clean up the air, stabilize the structures, and prohibiting tourists and their trampling feet from buildings in immediate danger. Traffic has been banned from the Acropolis area, and residents and merchants in the vicinity can no longer burn fuel with a high sulfur content. Saving the Acropolis has become a matter of Greek national pride, and the campaign has focused worldwide attention on both the direct and indirect effects of air pollution. Despite protective measures and major restoration efforts, damage has been severe, and the ultimate solution, halting industries and automobiles, is as unthinkable in Greece as it is elsewhere. It is possible that the Acropolis will eventually be listed as something the serious world traveler *could* have seen in another time.

P.D.

20. ABOARD CALYPSO: THE MEDITERRANEAN

In 1910, Prince Albert I of Monaco built one of the first institutions in the world for the study of the sea. On a rocky bluff above the Mediterranean in the harbor of Monaco, the Musée Océanographique continues to analyze the nature of marine life, working with scientists around the world and with The Cousteau Society's *Calypso*. Because of its collection of ocean specimens, initially begun by Prince Albert himself on pioneering voyages and continued under its present director, Jacques-Yves Cousteau, the museum provides a record of the sea as it was nearly a hundred years ago and as it is today.

The *Almanac* tour ends here, aboard *Calypso* just offshore from the Musée, because the Mediterranean area is now, as it always has been, a focal point of the entire planet, its population a kind of microcosm of humanity. Along its northern coastline lie some of the most heavily industrialized nations in the world, while along its southern shores some of the least developed are struggling with the tensions of the twentieth century. At its eastern end, the major ideologies, religious passions, and economic interests of the modern world are in an uneasy state of coexistence.

Throughout the Mediterranean, hidden from view, the global conflict between human endeavors and the living environment takes its toll on the undersea world. The laboratories of the Musée Océanographique today analyze the artificial chemistry (the result of industrial waste dumping) of a sea long known for the pristine beauty of its blue waters.

Throughout its long history, in fact, the Mediterranean region has served as a kind of ecology textbook. (See "Unlearned Lessons, Unintended Effects," page 167.) The cedar forests of Lebanon were one of the first deforestation catastrophes; the once productive grainfields of North Africa were reduced to deserts long ago. And the deterioration of Mediterranean lands and waters continues, under siege by modern agents of destruction. (The Mediterranean's plight is detailed in "The Mediterranean," page 302.) Coastal development is damaging the sea's fisheries by eliminating the breeding areas that sustain them. Industrial and agricultural chemicals run into the sea from the Po, the Rhône, the Ebro, the Nile. Nuclear power plants rise ominously around the Mediterranean's periphery. Along the fabled Côte d'Azur, where Jacques-Yves Cousteau and his early diving companions first experimented with Aqua-Lungs, the undersea habitat is a veritable wasteland. The animals described in books and films like *The Silent World* have vanished, thanks to intensive commercial fishing, private spearfishing, coastal development, tourism, and the common array of problems that issue from modern industrialism.

Turning the Tide

But for all of its degradation, recent events in the Mediterranean world suggest that most of humanity is finally realizing the importance and urgency of safeguarding the living resources of nature. The eighteen nations of the area, some of them nearly at war with one another, some espousing competing political systems, have grown so concerned about the rapid deterioration of the sea that they have joined together in a common effort to save it.

In January 1975, nearly every Mediterranean coastal nation sent representatives to Barcelona, Spain, to fashion a plan for protecting the Mediterranean Sea from pollution and unwise development strategies.

The governments requested assistance from the United Nations Environment Programme (UNEP) in coordinating the efforts of the region's scientists, economists, and legal experts, as well as a dozen United Nations specialized agencies and other international and nongovernmental organizations.

The strength of the plan they devised, called the Mediterranean Action Plan, is its scientific research and monitoring operation, which aims at pinpointing the sources and types of Mediterranean pollution and the magnitude of their effects. Eighty-five marine laboratories around the sea are taking part in the projects, which analyze the Mediterranean's levels of petroleum, chlorinated hydrocarbons, heavy metals, and pathogenic microorganisms. Obviously, part of the plan is to assess the impact of these on marine communities and human health.

Another major goal of the plan is to encourage economic development that is compatible with environmental precepts and that can therefore be sustained indefinitely. A study of how to accomplish this is under way and has come to be known as the "Blue Plan." In addition, a number of field projects have begun. One, for example, will establish aquaculture centers in selected sites along the coast. Another promotes the use of solar and wind energy for water desalination, distillation and pumping, electricity generation, and heating.

Global Action Plans

The effort to preserve the Mediterranean establishes a model for other regional seas (see "Aboard *Calypso:* The Caribbean," page 64, and "The Strait of Malacca," page 80), but saving the sea is only a part of the problem. Habitats and life-sustaining resources vital to human life are imperiled around the globe. The problems illustrated by stops on the *Almanac* world tour are not unique to their locations. Tropical forests are being lost at a rate of 12 to 25 million acres (5 to 10 million hectares) every year. Deserts grow, replacing arable land by 15 million acres (6 million hectares) every year. The coastal breeding areas for more than two thirds of the world's fisheries are being degraded or destroyed. More than 1,000 animal and 25,000 plant species are in danger of disappearing. Toxic matter accumulates in land dumps and in the sea, amounting to hidden pockets of poison. Such trends cannot continue if human life is to flourish in the future.

While diplomats and scientists were meeting to create the Mediterranean Action Plan in 1975, another program was being discussed that has broad implications. The idea was to invent a grand strategy for the entire world, a checklist of procedures that would enable any nation to develop its potential without destroying its resources in the process. The notion was the product of joint work by UNEP, the International Union for the Conservation of Nature and Natural Resources (IUCN), and the World Wildlife Fund (WWF). The document that resulted, five years later, is called the World Conservation Strategy. It was developed by consensus among more than 450 government agencies and conservation organizations in more than 100 countries. Seven hundred scientists and other experts contributed to the preparation of the strategy.

Among the priorities that the World Conservation Strategy calls for are reservation of prime cropland for crops only (not for shopping centers and highways, for example); vigilant new protective programs for soils, wetlands, watersheds, and forests; and the establishment of a comprehensive global network of protected areas that are ecologically important and/or unique (see "Priority Habitats to Save," page 127). The Strategy makes it possible for governments everywhere to save their own environment and to do so as part of a coordinated plan to save the most critical systems of the entire biosphere.

Another world-encompassing plan was issued by The Cousteau Society in 1979. Called the Global Ocean Policy, the document sets down guidelines for nations to use in protecting their territorial ocean zones, coastlines, lakes, and rivers. At the heart of the plan is the notion that there is only one world ocean, that earth's water supply travels constantly and circulates through

The research vessel *Calypso* with Monaco's Musée Océanographique in the background. (*The Cousteau Society*)

the hydrological cycle. More than perhaps any other resource, the sea needs to be treated as a common treasury and protected commonly.

The Global Ocean Policy proposes, among other items, modification of industrial fishery practices to halt overfishing and safeguards to ensure that deep-sea mining be carried out cleanly and that the profits be shared worldwide, that substantial sections of the planet's coastlines be kept free from any development, and that ocean wastes be stopped at their source before entering the sea, especially permanent or highly toxic pollutants.

We list these new global environmental initiatives to show that solutions to most of the problems illustrated on the *Almanac* world tour are being generated. They will be ignored by some stubborn politicians, greedy business executives, and shortsighted planners; that is inevitable. But the schemes for recovery exist, whether they are sufficiently implemented or not.

Two steps beyond diplomatic talks and scientific studies seem necessary, though, if the new global plans are to turn the tide of environmental destruction. The citizenry of the earth must be thoroughly educated about the connections of natural systems to all of human life—a need that can only be met by the proliferation of environmental education programs throughout the world.

Once armed with the necessary information, the people of the planet must be encouraged to take responsibility for the health of the environment by actively defending it. (See "Making Waves," which begins on page 737.) The technologies and the operations manuals for bringing to a halt the loss of the earth's vitality are available now. The necessary breakthrough is in the collective mind of humanity. It is time to keep the whole planet in mind, time to make peace with nature, time to relearn the facts of living.

M.R. with N.M.

3

A Global Census

In 1967, after ten years of suborbital and orbital space flight, we turned a camera lens in lunar orbit to take the first picture of the whole earth. This simple, beautiful photograph was surprisingly moving, even disturbing. It was difficult, perhaps, to acknowledge that this tiny sphere floating in the vastness of space was the full extent of our world. That first picture of earth became a powerful image for humanity. Everyone could *see* the limits of the planet, the absence of territorial boundaries, and the swirling, life-giving water skin, unique in the solar system. In the eternal night of space, the small Planet Earth was a lonely, wet ornament.

This chapter is another way to view the living earth—through its statistical limits, its eccentricities, its problems. The boundless sea can be measured, even to its dark, cold floor. The great rivers and formidable mountains can be reduced to charts and tables. We know the weight of the earth and its speed, the size of the forests and deserts, the idiosyncrasies of the microscopic organisms. We know how many we are and how hungry and how rich. We can measure the planet's long-held savings of oil and coal and gold. We can even predict, imprecisely, when they will be gone.

That first picture of the planet also unveiled beauty and mystery. The sun reflected off the earth as off a blue diamond. When we focus closely from space, we see the in-

(*NASA*)

tricacy of water-built structures and systems, which we have just begun to understand. We see the richness and diversity of the people, the fauna, the flora. We see the bountiful energy of the sun, wind, plants, oceans, and rivers. And if we are honest as we look at this wealth of information, we notice how little we know.

The common census that follows is only a beginning, a smattering of facts that appear to be important or interesting or both. We know how much food is grown and where, but we do not know how to feed the hungry. We can explain the crucial relationship between water and life, but we cannot keep our waters clean and productive. We can measure the bountiful energy that reaches us every day, but we cannot use it properly yet. There are still places to explore on the planet, spots still unseen. But seeing is not knowing. The inventory is an introduction to the planet, a brief glance. It is a skeleton of facts. To know and understand the living earth one must look also into the flesh, the blood, the organs, the systems—into the whole planetary being that is profiled throughout the *Almanac.*

K.F.

THE VITAL STATISTICS OF PEOPLE

How Many Now?

- On the day *The Cousteau Almanac* was published in the spring of 1981, the population of the world was about 4,470,944,000.
- About 40 percent of these people were children under the age of fifteen.
- About half of these people lived in *four countries:*

China	984 million
India	686 million
USSR	268 million
United States	224 million

How Many in the Past?

- It took thousands of centuries for the human population to reach a total of *one billion* in 1800. By 1930, only 130 years later, the world population had reached *two billion.* By 1960, only 30 years later, the population had hit *three billion. Four billion* was reached in 1975, only 15 years later.

How Many in the Future?

- At the currently projected rate of growth, the world population will reach *five billion* in 1987.
- About five people will be born as you read this sentence. (The rate is almost four births per second.) About 337,000 babies will be born during the next twenty-four hours.
- During the next year, a population about the size of eight New York Cities will be added to the planet (about 80 million more people).
- Predictions about future population growth are legion. Such variables as the spread of education and birth control, as well as the possibilities of major wars and famines, make accurate forecasts difficult. In 1979 the chairman of the United Nations Population Commission, Professor Dirk Jan van de Kaa of the University of Amsterdam, predicted that the world's population will peak in about 2050 at *11.5 billion.*
- If the world in the year 2000 is imagined as a global village of 100 people, then
  58 of these people will be Asian
  14 will be African
  10 will be Latin American
  8 will be European
  5 will be North American
  5 will be Russian

SOURCE: Population Reference Bureau, Washington, D.C.

(*Reprinted with permission of* PLAYGIRL *Magazine*)

NATIONAL DEMOGRAPHIC FIGURES—BY REGION

	Population (Millions)	*Urban Population (% of Total)*	*Life Expectation (Years)*	*Population Increase (% per Year)*
AFRICA	424.0	–	–	2.7
Algeria	17.9	52.0	53	3.2
Angola	5.8	–	39	–
Benin	3.2	13.7	41	2.7
Burundi	3.9	2.2	41	–
Cameroon	6.7	20.3	41	1.9
Chad	4.2	13.9	32	2.1
Congo	1.4	–	43	2.7
Egypt	38.7	43.9	52	2.2
Ethiopia	28.9	12.4	38	2.3
Ghana	10.4	31.4	43	2.8
Guinea-Bissau	4.6	–	41	2.5
Ivory Coast	5.1	32.4	43	2.6
Kenya	14.3	9.9	49	3.6
Lesotho	1.0	–	46	–
Liberia	1.8	27.6	45	2.4
Libya	2.4	29.8	53	–
Malagasy Republic	8.5	14.1	38	3.0
Malawi	5.5	10.1	42	3.2
Mali	5.9	16.6	38	2.5
Mauritania	1.3	22.8	38	–
Morocco	18.2	37.9	53	–
Mozambique	9.6	–	43	2.3
Niger	4.8	–	37	2.7
Nigeria	66.6	–	37	2.8
Rwanda	4.4	3.5	41	2.8
Senegal	4.2	31.7	40	–
Sierra Leone	3.4	–	43	–
Somalia	3.3	–	41	2.7
South Africa	26.1	47.9	51	–
Sudan	16.1	20.4	49	–
Tanzania	16.1	7.3	40	–
Togo	2.3	15.2	35	2.6
Tunisia	6.1	–	55	–
Uganda	12.3	7.1	50	3.4
Upper Volta	6.3	–	32	2.3
Zaire	26.4	30.3	43	2.5
Zambia	5.3	36.3	44	3.6
Zimbabwe	6.7	19.4	51	3.5
NORTH & CENTRAL AMERICA	354.0	–	–	1.5
Canada	23.3	76.1	73	1.3
Costa Rica	2.1	40.6	63	2.6
Cuba	9.5	60.3	70	–
Dominica	5.0	46.8	58	2.9
El Salvador	4.1	38.8	58	–
Guatemala	6.4	36.4	49	2.9
Haiti	4.7	23.7	50	1.7
Honduras	2.8	31.4	48	–
Jamaica	2.1	37.1	65	1.6
Mexico	64.6	64.4	65	3.5
Nicaragua	2.3	48.6	53	3.4
Panama	1.8	50.4	66	3.1
Puerto Rico	3.3	58.1	73	2.8
Trinidad and Tobago	1.1	49.4	66	–
United States	216.8	73.5	72	0.8
SOUTH AMERICA	230.0	–	–	2.6
Argentina	26.1	–	68	1.3
Bolivia	5.9	–	47	2.7
Brazil	112.2	61.2	59	2.8
Chile	10.7	79.2	63	1.9
Colombia	25.1	59.5	61	2.9
Ecuador	7.6	42.4	56	3.4

national demographic figures – by region (continued)

	Population (Millions)	Urban Population (% of Total)	Life Expectation (Years)	Population Increase (% per Year)
Paraguay	2.8	39.6	62	2.9
Peru	16.6	62.5	54	3.0
Uruguay	2.8	83.0	69	–
Venezuela	12.7	75.1	66	–
ASIA (excluding USSR)	2,335.0	–	–	2.2
Afghanistan	20.3	–	49	2.5
Bangladesh	80.6	8.8	36	2.4
Bhutan	1.2	–	44	2.2
Burma	31.5	–	50	2.2
China	865.7	–	61	1.7
Hong Kong	4.5	–	71	1.9
India	625.8	21.2	41	2.2
Indonesia	143.3	18.2	47	2.6
Iran	33.6	46.8	57	–
Iraq	11.9	65.9	53	3.4
Israel	3.6	81.9	72	2.8
Japan	113.9	75.9	75	1.3
Jordan	2.8	42.0	52	–
Kampuchea (Cambodia)	8.6	–	45	2.9
Korea (North)	16.6	48.4	61	2.0
Korea (South)	36.4	14.7	65	1.8
Kuwait	1.1	–	69	6.1
Laos	3.5	14.7	40	2.3
Lebanon	3.1	60.1	63	3.1
Malaysia	12.6	28.8	68	2.8
Mongolia	1.5	46.4	61	3.0
Nepal	13.1	4.0	44	2.3
Pakistan	75.3	25.5	51	–
Philippines	45.0	31.8	58	2.9
Saudi Arabia	9.5	–	45	3.0
Singapore	2.3	–	68	1.5
Sri Lanka	14.0	22.4	65	1.6
Syria	7.8	48.0	56	3.3
Thailand	44.2	13.2	56	2.8
Turkey	42.1	44.6	54	2.7
Vietnam	47.9	–	45	2.9
Yemen	7.1	33.3	44	3.0
EUROPE (excluding USSR)	478.0	–	–	0.6
Albania	2.6	33.8	66	2.9
Austria	7.5	51.9	71	0.2
Belgium	9.8	94.6	72	0.4
Bulgaria	8.8	59.4	71	0.5
Czechoslovakia	15.0	66.7	70	0.7
Denmark	5.1	66.9	73	0.5
Finland	4.7	59.0	72	0.4
France	53.1	70.0	72	0.6
Germany (East)	16.8	75.5	72	–0.2
Germany (West)	61.4	–	72	0.2
Greece	9.2	64.8	69	–
Hungary	10.6	50.6	69	0.4
Ireland	3.2	52.2	71	1.2
Italy	56.5	–	71	0.7
Netherlands	13.9	76.8	74	0.9
Norway	4.0	44.5	75	0.6
Poland	34.7	56.0	70	0.9
Portugal	9.7	–	69	–
Romania	21.5	47.5	69	1.0
Spain	36.4	–	72	1.1
Sweden	8.3	82.7	75	0.4
Switzerland	6.3	54.6	73	0.3
United Kingdom	55.9	77.7	70	–
Yugoslavia	21.7	38.6	68	–

national demographic figures – by region (continued)

	Population (Millions)	Urban Population (% of Total)	Life Expectation (Years)	Population Increase (% per Year)
OCEANIA	22.0	–	–	2.0
Australia	14.0	85.6	71	–
New Zealand	3.1	81.4	72	–
Papua New Guinea	2.9	12.9	48	–
USSR	260.0	62.2	69	1.0

Note: Figures are for mid-1977 (if available) or earlier. No country with population under one million included.

SOURCE: *Demographic Yearbook 1977*, U.N. Department of International Economics and Social Affairs, 1978.

POPULATION DENSITY EXTREMES

	People per Square Mile	People per Square Kilometer
Earth (land area)	72	28
United States	59	23
Australia	4	1
Japan	744	287
Hong Kong	11,383	4,394
Tokyo	20,000	7,722
New York City	26,000	10,039
Manhattan	68,000	26,255

SOURCE: Paul R. Ehrlich, Anne H. Ehrlich, John P. Holdren, *Ecoscience: Population, Resources, Environment,* W. H. Freeman and Company. Copyright © 1977. Adapted from United Nations, *Statistical Yearbook*, New York, 1973: U.S. Department of Commerce, *Statistical Abstract of the United States* Washington, D.C., 1974.

THE MOST POPULOUS URBAN AREAS IN THE YEAR 2000

If present population growth rates continue, the list of largest cities in the world will change during the next two decades, creating several "supercities":

Mexico City	31,616,000
Tokyo/Yokohama	26,128,000
São Paulo	26,045,000
New York/northeastern New Jersey	22,212,000
Calcutta	19,663,000
Rio de Janeiro	19,383,000
Shanghai	19,155,000
Greater Bombay	19,065,000
Peking	19,064,000
Seoul	18,711,000
Jakarta	16,933,000
Cairo/Giza/Imbabah	16,398,000
Karachi	15,862,000
Los Angeles/Long Beach	14,795,000
Buenos Aires	13,978,000

SOURCE: United Nations Department of International Economics and Social Affairs, Population Division.

THE TEN MOST POPULOUS COUNTRIES

1.	China	975,000,000
2.	India	676,200,000
3.	USSR	266,000,000
4.	United States	222,500,000
5.	Indonesia	144,300,000
6.	Brazil	122,000,000
7.	Japan	116,800,000
8.	Bangladesh	90,600,000
9.	Pakistan	86,500,000
10.	Nigeria	77,170,000

SOURCE: The Population Reference Bureau, 1980.

THE SIXTEEN COUNTRIES WITH THE HIGHEST POPULATION DENSITIES

1.	Monaco	41,095.9	9.	Japan	805.9
2.	Singapore	9,873.9	10.	West Germany	640.0
3.	Bangladesh	1,558.8	11.	United Kingdom	592.0
4.	Taiwan	1,256.0	12.	Sri Lanka	572.4
5.	South Korea	985.1	13.	El Salvador	560.0
6.	Netherlands	893.9	14.	India	512.0
7.	Belgium	836.1	15.	Italy	489.5
8.	Lebanon	809.5	16.	Israel	480.4

SOURCE: *Information Please Almanac – 1980*, Copyright © 1979 by Simon & Schuster, a division of Gulf & Western Corporation. Reprinted by permission.

THE TEN MOST POPULOUS METROPOLITAN AREAS

		Millions
1.	Tokyo/Yokohama	19.7
2.	New York	17.9
3.	Mexico City	13.9
4.	São Paulo	12.5
5.	Shanghai	12.0
6.	London	11.0
7.	Los Angeles	10.7
8.	Buenos Aires	10.4
9.	Peking	10.2
10.	Rio de Janeiro	10.0

SOURCE: U.N. Department of International Economics and Social Affairs, Population Division, Nov. 1975.

ANOTHER WAY OF LOOKING AT POPULATION GROWTH

Some Past Disasters	*Approximate Number Killed*	*Present World Population Growth Replaces This Number of People in Approximately*
Pakistan tidal wave, 1970	200,000	1 day
All Americans in all wars	600,000	3 days
Great flood, Yellow River, 1887	900,000	4½ days
U.S. automobile deaths through 1972	1,800,000	1½ weeks
India famine, 1769-70	3,000,000	2½ weeks
China famine, 1877-78	9,500,000	7 weeks
Influenza epidemic, 1918	21,000,000	3¾ months
All wars in the past 500 years (some 280 wars)	35,000,000	6 months
Bubonic plague (Black Death), 1347-51	75,000,000	13 months

SOURCE: G. Tyler Miller, Jr., ***Living in the Environment – Concepts, Problems, and Alternatives***, Wadsworth Publishing Company, Inc., 1975.

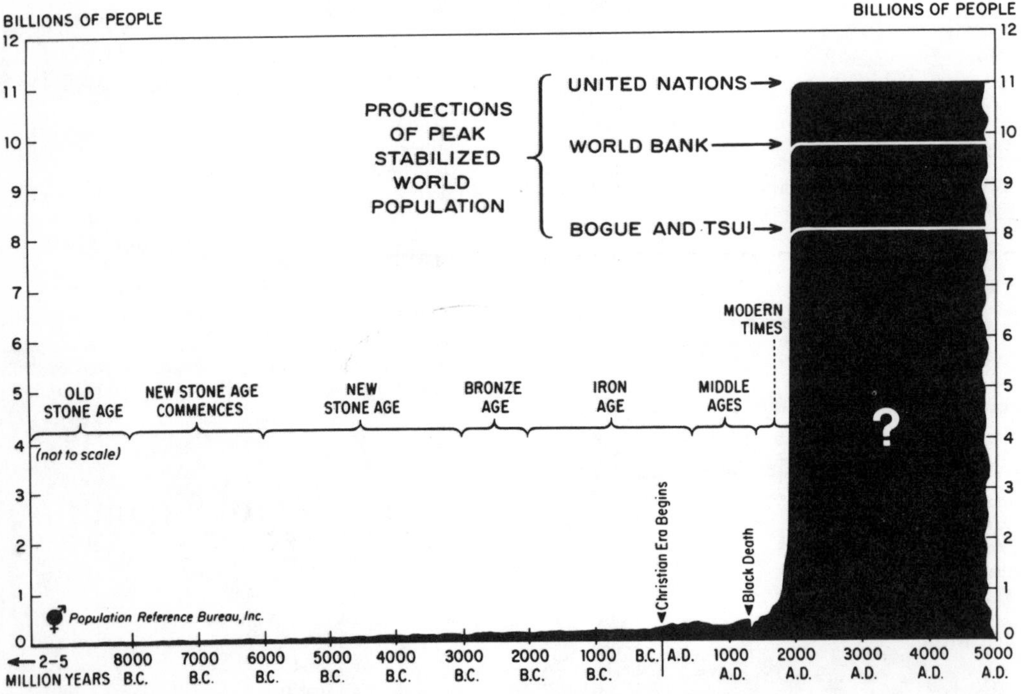

It took 2 million to 5 million years for the human population to reach half a billion, about 1650. The total climbed to 2 billion by 1930, doubled to 4 billion by 1975, and is projected to be up to 6 billion by the year 2000. Current projections of the point at which growth may peak and level off are shown above. University of Chicago demographers Donald Bogue and Amy Ong Tsui project that this point will be reached around the year 2050 at a population of about 8 billion. The World Bank predicts a peak of 10 billion people around 2090; the United Nations says 11 billion about 2125. (*Chart by James O'Brien for the Population Reference Bureau, Inc., 1979*)

CHILD POPULATION 1980

	Children under 15	Percent of Total Population under 15
Canada & U.S.	57 million	23
Latin America	151 million	42
Europe	116 million	24
Africa	212 million	45
USSR	64 million	24
Asia	948 million	37
Oceania	7 million	31

SOURCE: 1980 World Population Data Sheet, Population Reference Bureau, Washington, D.C.

CHILD POPULATION 2000

	Children under 15	Percent of Total Population under 15
Asia	1,120 million	31
Africa	352 million	42
Latin America	221 million	37
Oceania	8 million	26
Europe, Canada, & U.S.	170 million	21
USSR	74 million	24

SOURCE: March 1980 estimates, Population Reference Bureau, Washington, D.C.

PERCENTAGE OF TOTAL POPULATION LIVING IN URBAN AREAS

Area	*1925*	*1950*	*1975*	*2000*	*2025*
World	21	28	39	50	63
U.S. and Canada	54	64	77	86	93
Europe	48	55	67	79	88
USSR	18	39	61	76	87
East Asia	10	15	30	46	63
Latin America	25	41	60	74	85
Africa	8	13	24	37	54
South Asia	9	15	23	35	51
Oceania	54	65	71	77	87

SOURCE: *United Nations Concise Report on World Population Situation in 1977*, U.N. Department of International Economics and Social Affairs, Population Division.

AN UNCOMMON CENSUS OF LIVING

People without a country	10,500,000
Literate adults (15 years and over)	1,830,000,000
Illiterate adults	2,580,000,000
People without access to waste disposal	1,400,000,000
Undernourished people	700,000,000
People with no effective medical service	1,500,000,000
Children under 14 not attending school	250,000,000
People killed each year by waterborne diseases	9,000,000
People without access to clean water	1,200,000,000
Children under 15 who work	55,000,000

SOURCES: The above figures are rough estimates derived from data appearing between 1977 and 1980 in various publications of UNESCO and The International Labor Organization of the United Nations.

The lack of adequate sanitation in many African villages promotes the spread of waterborne diseases, among the most deadly human environmental threats in the world. (*FAO/F. Botts*)

HUMAN LIFE EXPECTANCY

Few subjects are more interesting to most of us than the length of time we will live. In the United States, population experts say, only one person in 2,500 will live to be 95 and only one in 20,000 will live to the age of 100. As of June 1978, there were 11,922 people registered with the U. S. Social Security Administration who were over 100 years old—an increase of almost 50 percent since 1975.

ESTIMATED AVERAGE LIFE EXPECTANCY THROUGH THE AGES

Population	*Years*
Neanderthal	29.4
Upper Paleolithic	32.4
Mesolithic	31.5
Neolithic Anatolic	38.2
Austrian Bronze Age	38
Classic Greece	35
Classic Rome	32
England, 1276	48
England, 1376-1400	38
United States, 1900-1902	61.5
United States, 1950	70

SOURCE: After E. S. Deevey, "The Probability of Death," Copyright © 1950 by Scientific American, Inc. All rights reserved.

COUNTRIES WITH THE HIGHEST INFANT DEATH RATES

	Infant Deaths per 1,000 Live Births
Afghanistan	226
Guinea-Bissau	208
Angola	203
Niger	200
Central African Republic	190
Mali	190
Mauritania	187
Upper Volta	182
Congo	180
Gabon	178
Somalia	177
Laos, East Timor, Guinea	175

SOURCE: World Children Data Sheet, 1979, Population Reference Bureau, Washington, D.C.

COUNTRIES WITH THE LOWEST INFANT DEATH RATES

	Infant Deaths per 1,000 Live Births
Sweden, Japan	8
Denmark, Finland, Norway	9
Netherlands, Switzerland	10
Iceland, France, Luxembourg	11
Australia, Belgium, Singapore, Canada, Hong Kong	12
United States, East Germany	13
United Kingdom, New Zealand	14
Israel, Jamaica, Austria, West Germany	15
Spain, Malta, Ireland	16

SOURCE: World Children Data Sheet, 1979, Population Reference Bureau, Washington, D.C.

SOME RANDOM GLOBAL COUNTS

Mandarin Speakers (Mandarin is spoken by more people than any other language.)	650,000,000
English Speakers (English is spoken in more countries than any other language.)	358,000,000
Russian Speakers	233,000,000
Spanish Speakers	213,000,000
Hindi Speakers	209,000,000
Arabic Speakers	125,000,000
Portuguese Speakers	124,000,000
Bengali Speakers	124,000,000
German Speakers	120,000,000
Japanese Speakers	110,000,000
Christians	954,766,700
Roman Catholics	540,704,000
Muslims	538,213,900
Hindus	524,273,000
Protestants	327,509,100
Buddhists	249,877,300
Confucians	186,104,300
Jews	14,396,000
Teachers (excludes China, North Korea, and Vietnam)	23,850,000
Students (excludes China, North Korea, and Vietnam)	542,761,000
Farmers	1,947,070,000

SOURCES: *World Statistics in Brief*, United Nations, 1978; Stockholm International Peace Research Institute, *World Armament and Disarmament Yearbook*, 1979; *The Book of Lists I*, William Morrow & Co., 1977; Wallechinsky, Wallace, and Wallace, American Jewish Committee, *Britannica Book of the Year, 1979.*

TWENTY COUNTRIES WITH THE HIGHEST NATIONAL INCOMES

Countries with populations of one million or more. GNP per capita rounded to nearest $10. "Real growth" is growth adjusted for inflation.

	GNP per Capita	
	Amount 1977 (US$)	*Real Growth Rates (%) 1970-77*
1. Kuwait	12,690	−0.9
2. Switzerland	11,080	0.1
3. Sweden	9,340	1.2
4. Denmark	9,160	2.3
5. United States	8,750	2.0
6. West Germany	8,620	2.2
7. Norway	8,570	3.9
8. Canada	8,350	3.4
9. Belgium	8,280	3.5
10. Netherlands	7,710	2.2
11. France	7,500	3.1
12. Australia	7,200	1.6
13. Saudi Arabia	7,230	13.0
14. Libya	6,520	−4.5
15. Japan	6,510	3.6
16. Austria	6,450	3.8
17. Finland	6,190	2.8
18. East Germany	5,070	4.9
19. United Kingdom	4,540	1.6
20. New Zealand	4,480	0.9

SOURCE: *The World Bank Atlas*, 1978

TWENTY COUNTRIES WITH THE LOWEST NATIONAL INCOMES

Countries with populations of one million or more. GNP per capita rounded to nearest $10. "Real growth" is growth adjusted for inflation.

	GNP per Capita	
	Amount 1976 (US$)	*Real Growth Rates (%) 1970-76*
1. Bhutan*	80	−0.2
2. Laos*	90	n.a.
3. Bangladesh	90	−0.8
4. Mali	100	0.5
5. Ethiopia	100	0.2
6. Upper Volta	100	0.4
7. Nepal	110	0.6
8. Somalia*	110	−0.6
9. Rwanda	120	1.2
10. Chad	120	−1.4
11. Burundi	120	−0.4
12. Burma	120	0.9
13. Zaire	130	0.4
14. Malawi	130	3.2
15. India	140	0.5
16. Mozambique*	150	−4.3
17. Niger	150	−2.4
18. Vietnam	160	n.a.
19. Benin	180	1.0
20. Afghanistan*	180	2.6

*Estimates of GNP per capita and its growth rate.

SOURCE: *The World Bank Atlas*, 1979

The Grand Illusion

Because birth rates and population growth are highest in the world's developing countries, a mistaken impression persists that developed countries, where growth rates are low, are not part of the population problem. In fact, the lower growth in developed countries may have a greater impact on the environment than even exploding growth in a poor country. Each child born in the industrialized world consumes during his or her lifetime twenty to forty times as much of the world's resources as a child born in the developing world. The relatively smaller population increases in the developed world put about eight times more pressure on world resources than larger increases among poor nations.

According to a study based on data available in 1973, during his or her lifetime one baby born in the United States will:

Require	*Discard*
26 million gallons (98.4 million liters) of water	10,000 no-return bottles
52 tons of iron and steel	17,500 cans
1,200 barrels of petroleum	27,000 bottle caps
13,000 pounds (5,897 kilograms) of paper	2.3 automobiles
21,000 gallons (79,494 liters) of gasoline	126 tons of garbage
50 tons of food	
10,000 pounds (4,536 kilograms) of fertilizer	

SOURCE: G. Tyler Miller, Jr., *Living in the Environment*, Wadsworth Publishing Company, Inc., 1975.

ANNUAL PER CAPITA CONSUMPTION OF STEEL

	Kilograms	Pounds
Algeria	110	242
Belgium	388	855
Brazil	107	236
China, People's Republic of	38	84
Cuba	53	117
Czechoslovakia	700	1,543
East Germany	591	1,303
West Germany	538	1,186
Egypt	26	57
France	368	811
Ghana	11	24
Greece	176	388
Indonesia	8	18
Italy	368	811
Mexico	100	220
Nigeria	27	59
Pakistan	9	20
Spain	249	549
Sweden	463	1,021
United Kingdom	349	769
United States	618	1,363
USSR	567	1,250
Yugoslavia	230	507

SOURCE: *Statistical Abstract of the United States*, 1979, U.S. Department of Commerce.

ANNUAL PER CAPITA ENERGY CONSUMPTION

Given in coal equivalents based on consumption of coal, lignite, petroleum products, natural gas, hydro and nuclear power.

	Kilograms	Pounds
Algeria	729	1,607
Belgium	6,049	13,338
Brazil	731	1,612
Cuba	1,225	2,701
France	4,380	9,658
India	218	481
Iran	1,490	3,285
Italy	3,284	7,241
Mexico	1,229	2,710
Nigeria	94	207
Portugal	1,050	2,315
Sweden	6,046	13,331
United States	11,554	25,477
USSR	5,259	11,596
Zaire	62	137
Zambia	548	1,208

SOURCE: *Statistical Abstract of the United States*, 1979, U.S. Department of Commerce.

FOR EVERY 1,000 PERSONS . . .

in the United States, there are
- 505 automobiles
- 571 television sets
- 721 telephones

in Britain, there are
- 225 automobiles
- 320 television sets
- 394 telephones

in France, there are
- 300 automobiles
- 268 television sets
- 293 telephones

in West Germany, there are
- 308 automobiles
- 306 television sets
- 344 telephones

in Japan, there are
- 163 automobiles
- 235 television sets
- 426 telephones

in Italy, there are
- 283 automobiles
- 213 television sets
- 271 telephones

in India, there are
- 1 automobile
- 3 telephones

in the Philippines, there are
- 9 automobiles
- 12 telephones

in Tanzania, there are
- 3 automobiles
- 4 telephones

(Data on television sets unavailable for last three countries.)

SOURCE: Reprinted by permission of *The Wall Street Journal*,

IN ONE DAY

- The average citizen of the United States generates 3.77 pounds of solid waste, of which only 0.3 pound is recycled.
- About 1,900 gallons of water are withdrawn from the freshwater system for every person living in the United States.

IN ONE YEAR

- The sanitation system of the United States receives (in consumer refuse alone—not counting industrial wastes):
  - 39 million tons of paper
  - 14 million tons of glass
  - 13 million tons of metal
  - 5.3 million tons of plastics
  - 23.8 million tons of food waste
  - 27.3 million tons of yard waste
  - 12.9 million tons of other wastes, including leather, wood, textiles, etc.
- Recyclers recover only 12 million tons of resources from the total 147 million tons of consumer solid waste generated.

SOURCE: Statistical Abstract of the United States, 1979, U. S. Department of Commerce.

ONE U. S. CITIZEN

- In the United States in 1978, each person used an average of:
  - 14 pounds of cotton
  - 0.5 pound of wool
  - 4 pounds of rayon
  - 187 pounds of meat
  - 8 pounds of fresh and frozen fish, 4.6 pounds canned
  - 273 eggs
  - 48 pounds of chicken
  - 9.6 pounds of turkey
  - 20 gallons of milk
  - 17 pounds of cheese
  - 17 pounds of ice cream
  - 84 pounds of fresh fruit, 17 pounds canned
  - 101 pounds fresh vegetables, 54 pounds canned, 10 pounds frozen
  - 122 pounds of potatoes and sweet potatoes
  - 6 pounds of dry edible beans
  - 21 pounds of melons
  - 94 pounds of refined sugar
  - 108 pounds of wheat flour
  - 10 pounds of green coffee beans
  - 0.9 pound of tea
  - 3.3 pounds of cocoa beans
  - 6.4 pounds of shelled peanuts
  - 32 gallons of beer
  - 2.88 gallons of liquor
  - 2.59 gallons of still wine, 0.17 gallon of effervescent wine
  - 3,900 cigarettes, or 195 packs

As Well As . . .

- 650 pounds of paper
- 46 pounds of copper, lead, and zinc
- 18,504 pounds of building materials
- 55 pounds of aluminum
- 1,054 pounds of ferrous metals
- 1,359 pounds of steel
- 15 tons of minerals

And Produced . . .

- 1,376 pounds of solid waste

SOURCES: Statistical Abstract of the United States, 1979, U. S. Department of Commerce; various U. S. Federal Government bulletins.

THE VITAL STATISTICS OF EARTH

- *Weight*—6,586,000,000,000,000,000,000 tons.
- *Measurements*—The earth is not a perfect sphere but what is called an *oblate spheroid,* slightly broader at the equator, with a diameter of 7,926 miles (12,756 kilometers), than at the poles, where the diameter is 7,900 miles (12,712 kilometers).
- *Area*—Total surface area: 196,940,000 square miles (510,074,600 square kilometers).

  Land surface: 57,506,000 square miles (148,940,540 square kilometers). This represents only 29.2 percent of the planetary surface.

  Water surface: 139,434,000 square miles (388,755,999 square kilometers), a total of 70.8 percent of the earth's surface.
- *Age*—Variously estimated at 4.5 billion to 4.7 billion years. In about 6 billion years the sun is expected to swell into a red giant and consume the earth.
- *Speed*—The earth travels at a speed of 66,705 miles (107,351 kilometers) per hour in its orbit around the sun, covering a distance of 580 million miles (933 million kilometers) a year. The velocity of its rotation, which varies according to the latitude at which it is measured, is approximately 1,037 miles (1,668 kilometers) per hour at the equator.
- *Skins*—Air and water: The planet is covered by a dynamic blanket of water and atmospheric gases, which, proportionately, is no thicker than the skin of an apple. This moist shell extends from the deepest trench in the sea to the outer

reaches of the atmosphere. While traces of the earth's hydrogen extend out some 5,000 miles (8,000 kilometers) from the surface, the earth's atmosphere is widely taken to end between 400 and 600 miles (650 to 1,000 kilometers) from the ground. Oxygen disappears above this. Because of gravity most of the atmosphere's mass is concentrated in a thin layer near the surface. Three quarters of it lies below the height of Mount Everest's peak (29,000 feet/8,840 meters). (For a review of the earth's water skin, see "The Vital Statistics of Water," page 114.)

- *Life* — The biosphere represents that relatively narrow band around the surface of the planet within which life is possible. Organisms survive as deep as 656 feet (200 meters) below the surface of the ground, and in the deepest reaches of the sea more than 7 miles (11 kilometers) down. Above ground the biosphere reaches to at least 26,900 feet (8,200 meters), where a bird known as the alpine chough has been found, and it is possible that certain insects and "ballooning" spiders may be carried to greater heights.
- *Soil* — Of the portion of the planet's surface that is exposed, only about 6 percent is land capable of growing crops to support human life. The majority is made up of mountains, rocky areas, deserts, jungles, prairies, and marshlands unsuitable for agriculture and land that is otherwise too dry, too cold, too wet, or too hot to grow food.

M.R.

THE WORLD'S TEN LARGEST COUNTRIES—BY AREA

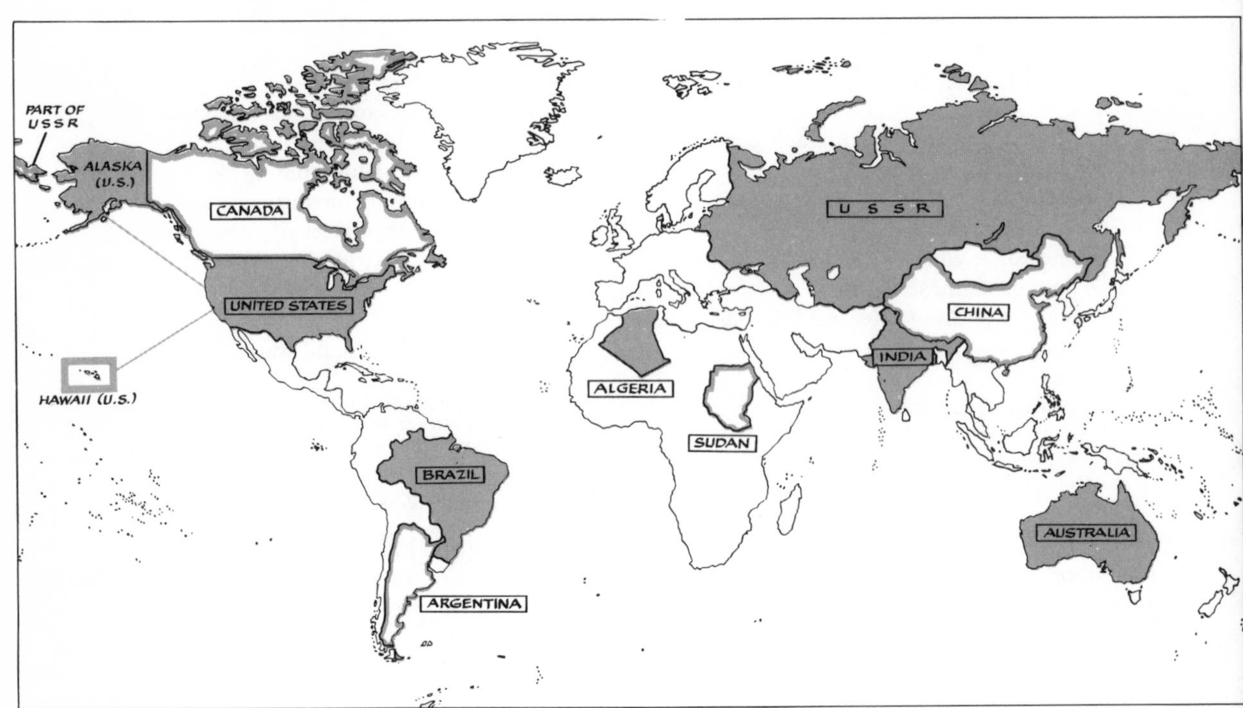

		Area in Square Miles	Area in Square Kilometers	Percent of World Land Area
1.	USSR	8,600,000	22,402,200	14.9
2.	Canada	3,851,809	9,976,139	6.7
3.	China	3,691,500	9,560,900	6.4
4.	United States	3,615,122	9,363,123	6.4
5.	Brazil	3,286,488	8,512,004	5.7
6.	Australia	2,967,909	7,686,849	5.1
7.	India	1,269,346	3,287,590	2.0
8.	Argentina	1,072,763	2,778,456	1.9
9.	Sudan	967,491	2,505,805	1.7
10.	Algeria	919,591	2,381,741	1.6

SOURCE: *Times Atlas of the World*, 1980 edition. Times Books, Ltd., London. Copyright material.

SOME EXTREMES ON EARTH

Rainiest Spot: Mount Waialeale, Hawaii: Annual average rainfall 460 inches (1,168 centimeters). *One-year record:* Cherrapunji, India: 1,042 inches (2,647 centimeters), 1861.

Driest Spot: Atacama Desert, Chile: rainfall barely measurable. (At Calama, Chile, no rain has ever been recorded.)

Coldest Spot: Vostok, Antarctica: −127° F (−38° C), recorded 1960.

Hottest Spot: Al Aziziyah, Libya: 136° F (43° C), recorded 1922.

Northernmost Town: Ny Alesund, Spitsbergen Island, Norway.

Southernmost Town: Puerto Williams, Chile.

Largest Gorge: Grand Canyon, Colorado River, Arizona: 217 miles (349 kilometers) long, 4 to 18 miles (6 to 29 kilometers) wide, 1 mile (1.6 kilometers) deep.

Deepest Gorge: Hells Canyon, Snake River, Idaho: 7,900 feet (2,408 meters).

Strongest Surface Wind: 231 miles (372 kilometers) per hour: Mount Washington, New Hampshire, recorded 1934.

Most Isolated Piece of Inhabited Land: Easter Island in the Pacific Ocean: 1,200 miles (1,931 kilometers) from the nearest human settlement.

SOURCE: *National Geographic Atlas of the World*, 1975.

THE HIGHEST AND THE LOWEST POINTS ON EACH CONTINENT

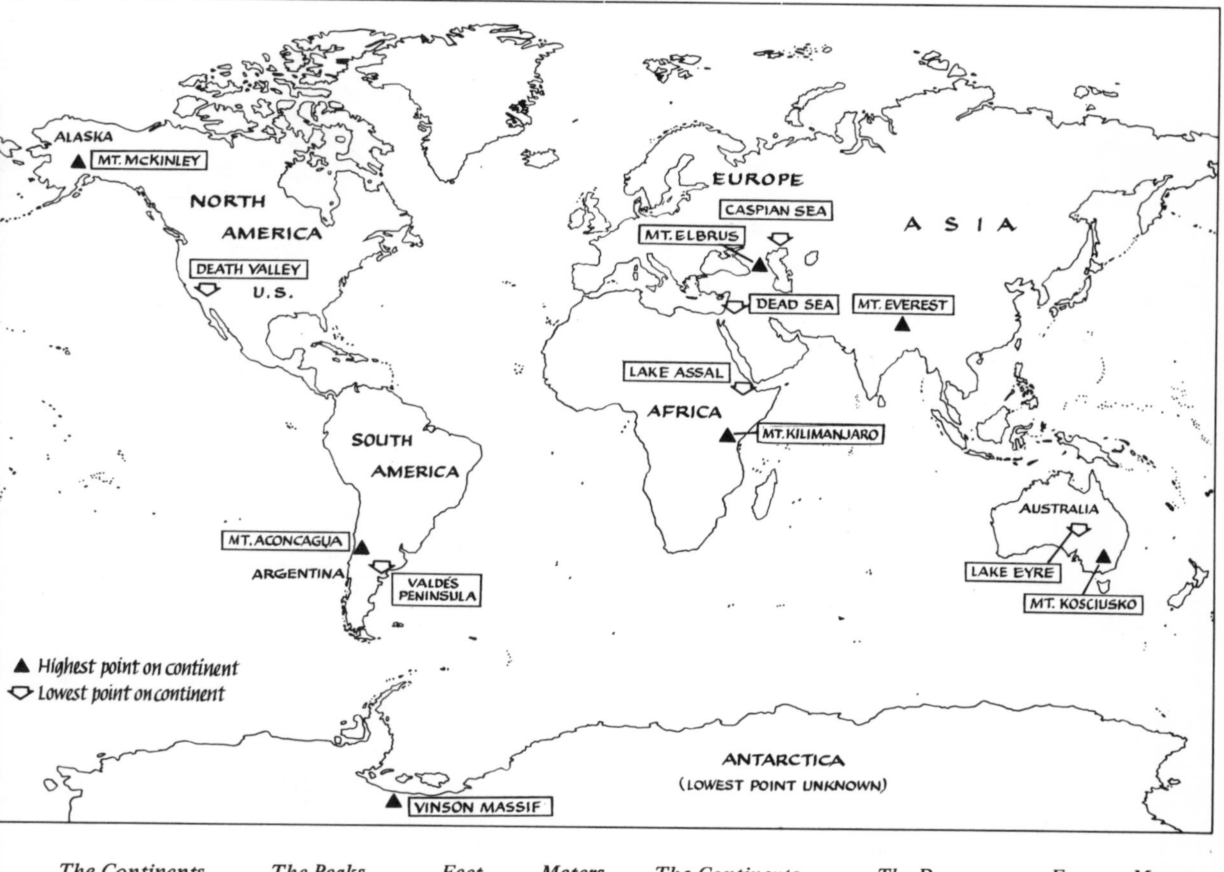

The Continents	*The Peaks*	*Feet*	*Meters*
Asia	Everest	29,028	8,848
Africa	Kilimanjaro	19,340	5,895
North America	McKinley	20,320	6,194
South America	Aconcagua	22,834	6,960
Europe	Elbrus	18,510	5,642
Australia	Kosciusko	7,310	2,230
Antarctica	Vinson Massif	16,864	5,140

The Continents	*The Deeps*	*Feet*	*Meters*
Asia	Dead Sea	−1,302	−397
Africa	Lake Assal	−512	−156
North America	Death Valley	−282	−86
South America	Valdés Peninsula	−131	−40
Europe	Caspian Sea	−92	−28
Australia	Lake Eyre	−52	−16
Antarctica	Not Known		

SOURCE: *Times Atlas of the World*, London

THE TEN LARGEST DESERTS OF THE WORLD

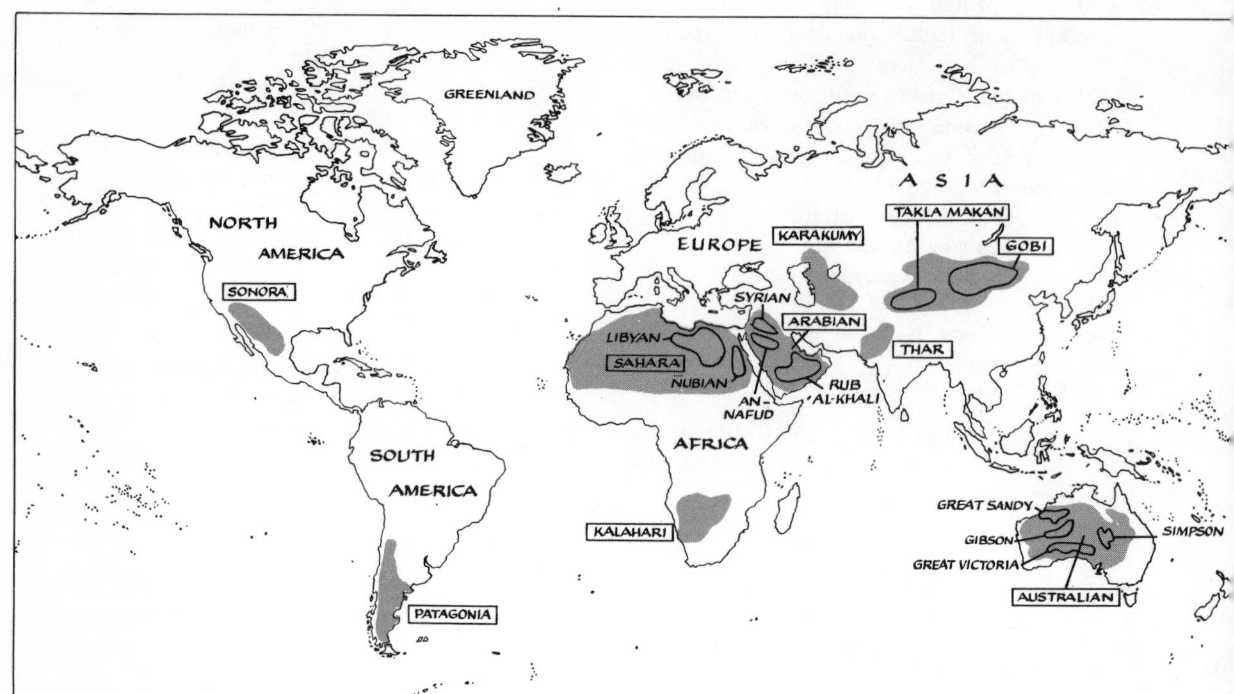

Desert	Continent	Area: Square Miles	Area: Square Kilometers
1. Sahara	Africa	3,500,000	9,065,000
Libyan		650,000	1,683,500
Nubian		105,000	271,950
2. Australian	Australia	600,000	1,554,000
Great Sandy		160,000	414,400
Great Victoria		127,000	328,930
Simpson		120,000	310,800
Gibson		85,000	220,150
3. Arabian	Asia	500,000	1,295,000
Rub al-Khali		250,000	647,500
Syrian		125,000	323,750
An-Nafud		50,000	129,500
4. Gobi	Asia	400,000	1,036,000
5. Kalahari	Africa	275,000	712,250
6. Patagonia	South America	260,000	673,400
7. Takla Makan (Talimupendi)	Asia	127,000	328,930
8. Sonora	North America	120,000	310,800
9. Karakumy	Asia	105,000	271,950
10. Thar	Asia	105,000	271,950

SOURCE: John Paxton, *The Statesman's Yearbook 1976-1977*, St. Martin's Press, New York.

THE TEN LARGEST ISLANDS OF THE WORLD

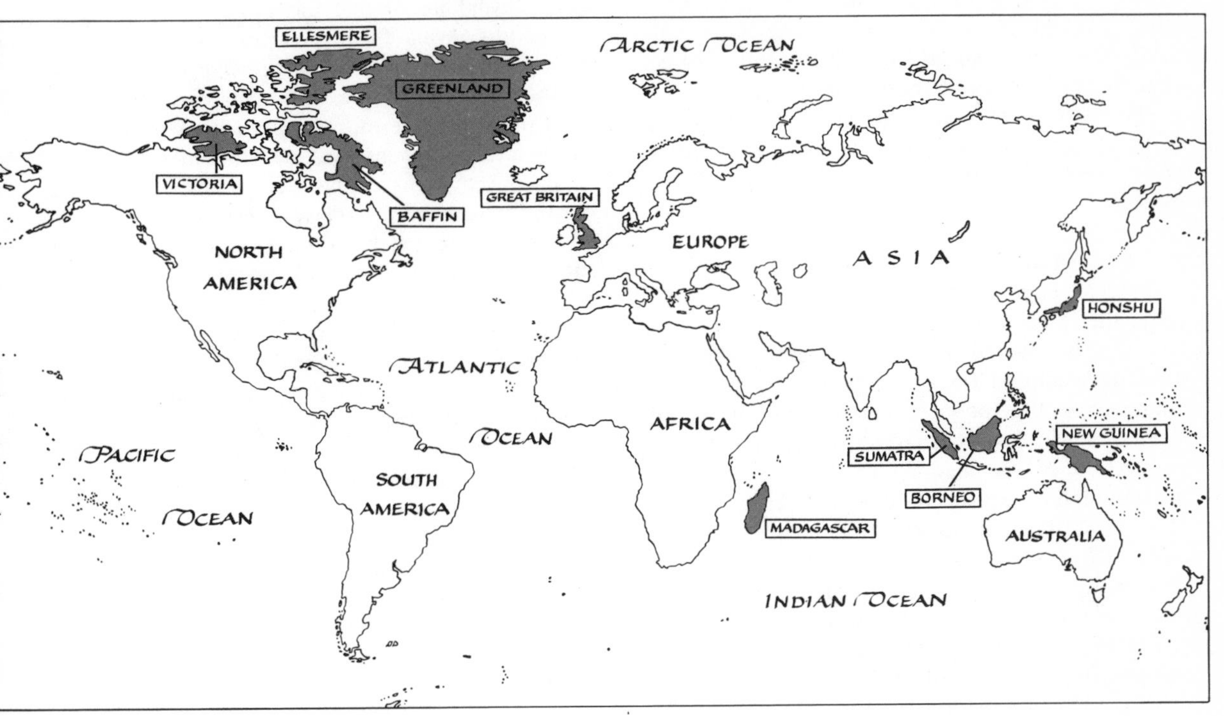

	Island	*Location*	*Area*	
			Square Miles	*Square Kilometers*
1.	Greenland	North Atlantic	839,999	2,175,597
2.	New Guinea	Southwest Pacific	316,615	820,033
3.	Borneo	West mid-Pacific	286,914	743,107
4.	Madagascar	Indian Ocean	226,657	587,042
5.	Baffin	North Atlantic	183,810	476,068
6.	Sumatra	Northeast Indian Ocean	182,859	473,605
7.	Honshu	Sea of Japan – Pacific	88,925	230,316
8.	Great Britain	North Atlantic, off coast of northwest Europe	88,758	229,883
9.	Ellesmere	Arctic Ocean	82,119	212,688
10.	Victoria	Arctic Ocean	81,930	212,199

SOURCE: *Information Please Almanac – 1980*, Copyright © 1979 by Simon & Schuster, a division of Gulf & Western Corporation. Reprinted by permission.

UNEXPLORED AREAS OF THE PLANET

It's a small world, so they say. A world that has decreased in size, thanks to the developments advanced by space-age technology. It is hard to imagine that although we have walked on the moon there are still regions on our own planet that remain unexplored. Expanses of the ocean floor, steamy equatorial jungles, barren, ice-covered Arctic lands, and isles in the Pacific contain thousands of miles of untouched, unmapped terrain.

What wealth of natural resources is hidden in the Himalayas? What will be found under the ice of Greenland? Such questions lure the adventurers and explorers of our age into the unknown.

The Japanese explorer Naomi Uemura is an example of a courageous individual whose curiosity led him, in early 1978, on a fifty-four-day trek across the frozen Arctic Ocean to become the first person to reach the North Pole alone by dogsled (see "Great Adventures," page 723).

John Blashford-Snell, a lieutenant colonel in Britain's Royal Engineers, led the Great Abbai Expedition, which made the first descent of the Blue Nile, in 1978. According to Colonel Blashford-Snell, the equatorial jungles afford the greatest opportunities for the independent explorer.

The following list, adapted from *The Book of Lists,* by David Wallechinsky, is a sample of some of the places awaiting the first footsteps of humanity.

The Ocean Floor

The least-explored region of the planet is, ironically, the largest—the portion of the earth's surface that is covered by the sea. Despite sophisticated technologies for travel that are capable of taking us to the moon, humans have not visited *most* of the ocean floor, which represents almost 71 percent of the land on earth. The first true oceanographic expedition did not set out until 1872, and the knowledge brought back by the HMS *Challenger* trip around the world was obtained in the hit-or-miss fashion of dropping nets and sounding lines over the side of the ship.

The first human to descend very far into the sea was Dr. Charles William Beebe, who was lowered in 1934 to a record depth of 3,028 feet (924 meters) inside a steel ball called a bathysphere. Beebe's descriptions of strange fish and other depth creatures, observed through the porthole of the bathysphere, fueled the interest of others in descending even farther. Trips to the deepest parts of the sea were made possible in the 1950s by the invention of the bathyscaphe, an undersea craft that was little more than a steel ball hanging below a huge tank of gasoline. Burdened by metal weights, the bathyscaphe would sink to the sea bottom; when the pellets were jettisoned, the tank of lighter-than-water gasoline would rise to the surface like a balloon, making the vessel a kind of undersea dirigible.

The deepest dive ever made was a bathyscaphe descent into the Challenger Deep near Guam in 1960. United States Navy Lieutenant Donald Walsh and Jacques Piccard, son of the bathyscaphe's inventor, Auguste Piccard, touched the seafloor at a depth of 35,800 feet (10,919 meters) in a vessel called the *Trieste II*. One mystery was immediately resolved when the *Trieste II* came to a halt on the seafloor. Scientists had long debated whether life could exist in the extreme pressures, the frigid cold, and the total darkness of the abyss. When Walsh and Piccard turned on a shipboard headlight, a small flatfish, similar to a common sole or flounder, rose from the seafloor and darted away.

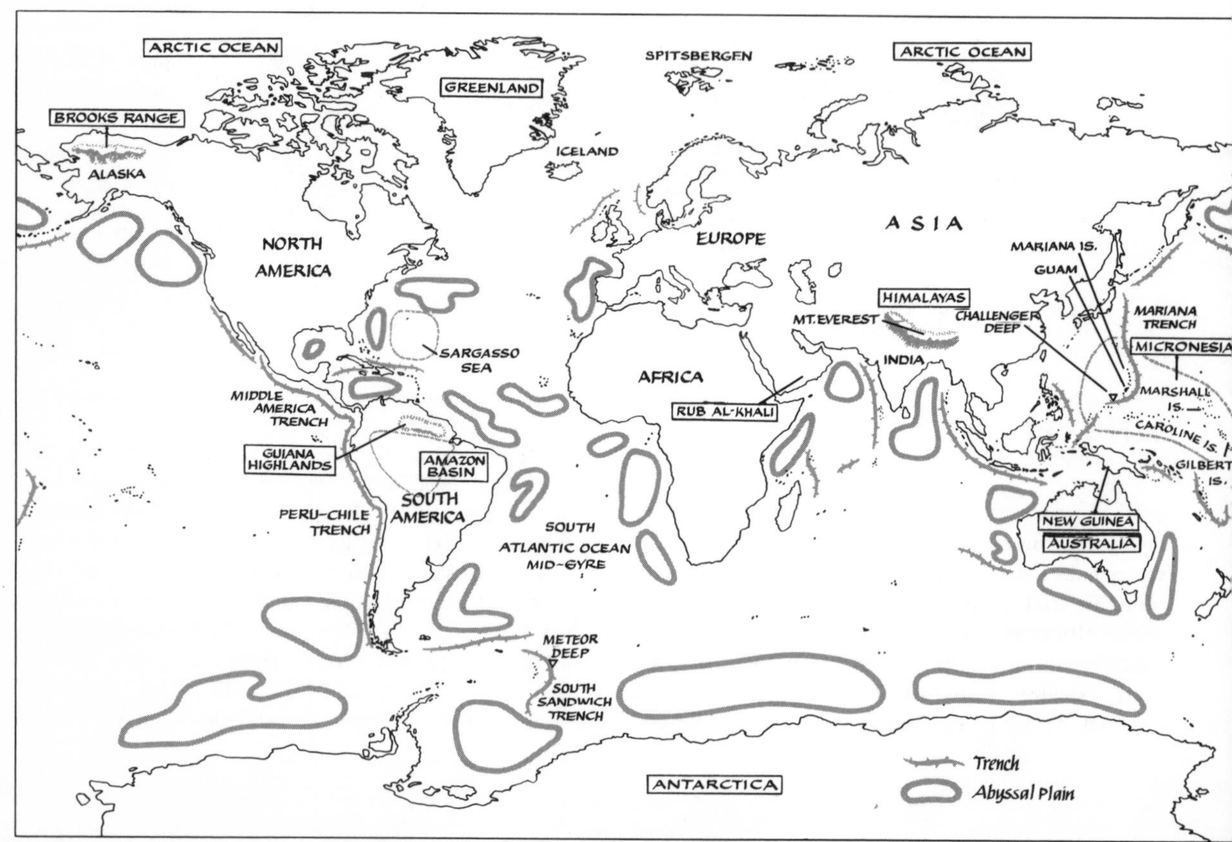

In brief visits like that of the *Trieste II*, humans have dropped to the sea bottom hundreds of times during the past two decades, but these explorations cover only a tiny fraction of the area of the seafloor and the volume of water space above it. For example, scientists studying the undersea mountain ranges that extend around the world, called the midoceanic ridges, estimate that the total area they have explored in submersible vessels represents only about 40 miles (64 kilometers) out of the thousands of miles of ridges. Though they are one of the most dramatic features of the earth's surface, the existence of these ridges was not even known until about twenty years ago.

What knowledge we have of the biology and geology of the seafloor has come largely from sampling instruments, cameras, and sonar scanning devices lowered from surface ships and from echo-sounding equipment. Of the entire world ocean, two of the least-known regions are the floors of the Indian Ocean (which is more remote from major oceanographic institutions than the Pacific and Atlantic) and the Arctic Ocean (which is shielded by an ice cap).

As oceanographic tools become more sophisticated (see " Tomography," page 34), our knowledge of the deep-sea world will expand dramatically. Seafloor mining operations (see "Manganese Nodules," page 13) will also produce new data about the seafloor. But extensive, firsthand investigations of the ocean floor by humans will remain difficult procedures. With an average depth of 12,231 feet (3,729 meters), the seafloor presents a forbidding frontier—where pressures would crush an unprotected human, where sunlight has never penetrated, where the water temperature is just above freezing. Expeditions to this harsh world must be carefully undertaken, and they are enormously expensive.

There are some slightly less formidable regions left to explore.

M.R.

Rub al-Khali

Containing the most arid part of Arabia, Rub al-Khali covers about 250,000 square miles (647,500 square kilometers). Large expanses of this desert have been seen only from the air. Since 1950, the U. S. State Department and the U. S. Geological Survey have cooperated with the Kingdom of Saudi Arabia in conducting surveys of the area's mineral resources.

Himalayas

This perpetually snow-covered Asian mountain range, which stretches uninterrupted for about 1,550 miles (2,495 kilometers), covers an area of about 229,500 square miles (594,405 square kilometers). Mount Everest, the highest mountain in the world, is among the hundreds of peaks over 20,000 feet (6,100 meters) in this range, many of which remain unchallenged and unexplored. Though potentially rich in natural resources, vast parts of the Himalayan range are still inaccessible. (See "The Himalayas," page 189.)

Guiana Highlands

A desolate region of rocky outcrop and dense jungle, comprising about 45 percent of the total area of Venezuela, the Guiana Highlands are the least-known and most sparsely inhabited portion of that country. So forbidding is the landscape that in many places a canoe with an outboard motor is the only means of transportation and communication. Not only the landscape is forbidding in the Guiana Highlands; the fauna living there include caimans (the largest and fiercest of alligators), striped rattlesnakes, and bushmasters, the largest venomous snakes in the Americas.

Amazon Basin

The Amazon River Basin, covering a territory of about 2.7 million square miles (7 million square kilometers), is the largest river basin in the tropical world. Located in northern Brazil, these immense tropical jungles contain one of the world's greatest reserves of natural resources. Many of its flora and fauna have yet to be named. For centuries, few humans other than the native Indians of the region attempted to penetrate these forests. Scientific exploration of the ecosystem and the exploitable resources has intensified in the past decade. (See "Amazonia," page 274, "Amazon, Inc.," page 487, "Daniel K. Ludwig," page 484, and "Amazon Lore," page 278.)

Micronesia

Micronesia, located east of the Philippines and north of the equator, consists of the Mariana, Marshall, Caroline, and Gilbert island groups. There are more than two thousand Micronesian islands, scattered over 3 million square miles (7.7 million square kilometers) of ocean. The combined land area of Micronesia is about 1,055 square miles (2,732 square kilometers), only a little larger than the state of Rhode Island, and most of it is uninhabited wilderness.

New Guinea

Located north of Australia, New Guinea is the second-largest island in the world. Characterized by rivers, steep gorges, and humid jungles, New Guinea's 316,615 square miles (820,033 square kilometers) includes an almost impassable range of mountains. This range, extending from the northwest to the southeastern part of New Guinea, contains many peaks over 12,000 feet (3,660 meters) high.

Greenland

The largest island in the world, Greenland has the greatest ice mass outside of Antarctica. More than 83 percent of its 840,000 square miles (2,175,600 square kilometers) is ice-covered. Tundra vegetation prevails, the climate is bleak, and impenetrable blizzards are common. Although the coastal fringe of Greenland is inhabited, much of the interior has been crossed on the surface only by Eskimos. It is not known what might lie under most of the ice, the average depth of which is 5,000 feet (1,524 meters).

Antarctica

In this virtually lifeless land with an area larger than the continental United States, less than 100 square miles (259 square kilometers) is free from a permanent blanket of ice. Few of the mountainous regions in Antarctica are known in detail, and not all the surface terrain has been seen or reached by people on the ground. Least known is the bedrock terrain that lies under the ice sheets. (See "Antarctica," page 279, and "Antarctic Lore," page 283.)

The Arctic

Warmer than the Antarctic, the Arctic is a less violent, more hospitable place. Drifting ice, 10 feet (3 meters) thick, covers much of the 5,541,000 square miles (14,351,190 square kilometers) of the Arctic Ocean. The Arctic is inhabited by polar bears, seals, reindeer, caribou, and a great variety of birds, and it supports a human population of more than one million. Since the late 1950s, the governments of the United States, Canada, and the Soviet Union have been engaged in a continuous program of investigation in the Arctic region, using drifting stations in addition to airlifted expeditions.

Alaska

Northern Alaska's great Brooks Range is the largest remaining expanse of untouched terrain in the United States. The Notak River and Squirrel River basins in the Brooks Range, constituting about 7.6 million acres (3 million hectares), are virtually devoid of human influence. (See "Alaska," page 297, and "Alaska Lore," page 300.)

S.G.

THE VITAL STATISTICS OF WATER

- Since the surface of the earth is nearly three-quarters water-covered, the misapprehension arises that there is plenty of water on the planet. In fact, if the earth were scaled to a 28-inch (71-centimeter) sphere, all of the water on its surface would fill only a cup.
- Of this total, only about one third of 1 percent is actually available to humans as fresh water for drinking and irrigating (the water in lakes, rivers, and the accessible water table below ground).
- More than three quarters of the fresh water along the earth's surface is frozen in the Antarctic ice cap.
- It has been estimated that as many as nine out of ten organisms in the world live in the oceans.

	Area (sq. mi.)*	*Volume* (cu. mi.)*	*% of Total**
SALT WATER			
The oceans	139,500,000	317,000,000	97.2
Inland seas & saline lakes	270,000	25,000	0.008
FRESH WATER			
Freshwater lakes	330,000	30,000	0.009
All rivers (average level)	–	300	0.0001
Antarctic icecap	6,000,000	6,300,000	1.9
Arctic icecap and glaciers	900,000	680,000	0.15
Water in the atmosphere	–	3,100	0.001
Ground water			
Surface	–	1,000,000	0.31
Deep-lying	–	1,000,000	0.31
Total (rounded)	–	326,000,000	100.00

*All figures are estimated

SOURCE: U.S. Department of the Interior

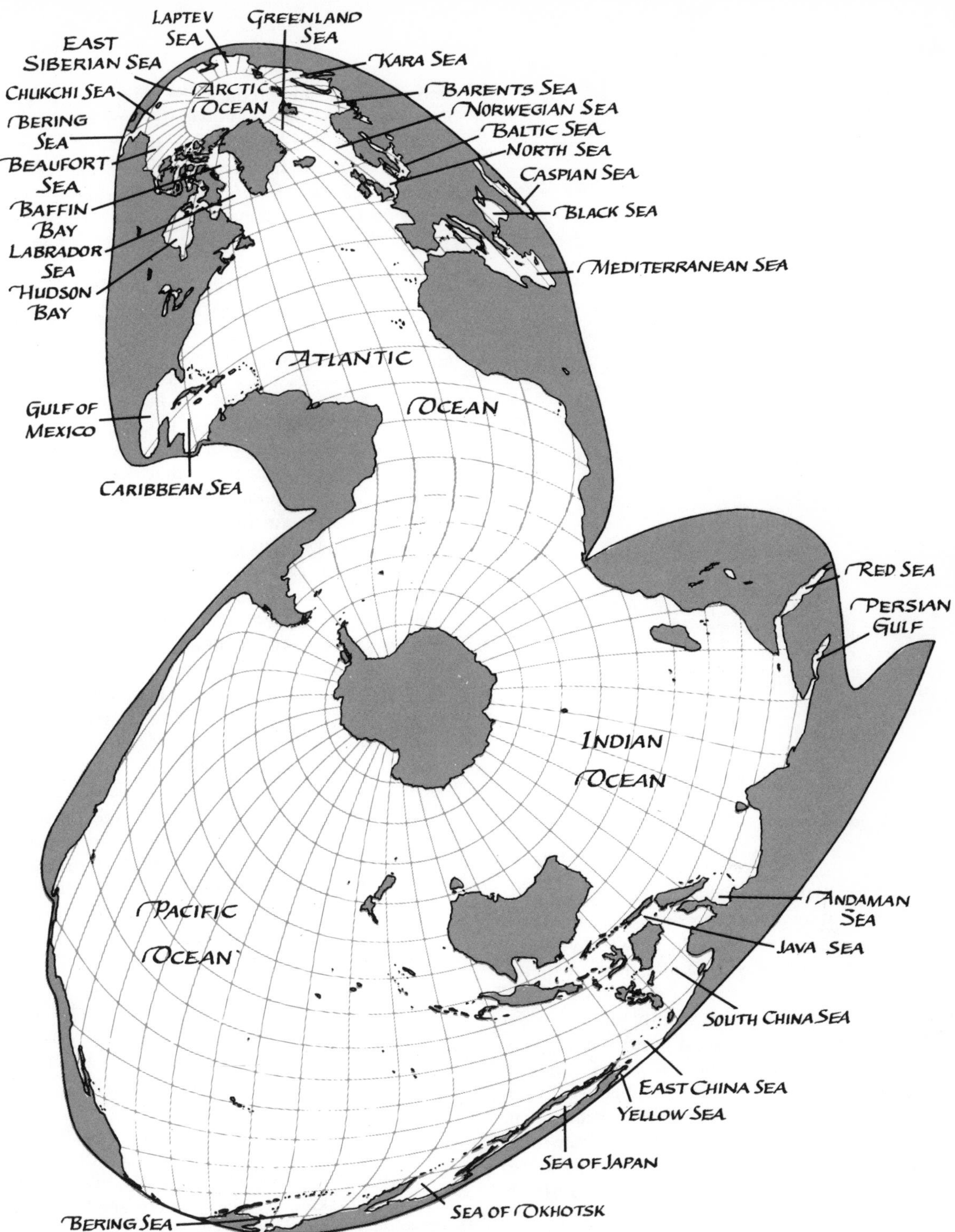

In the past few decades, photos from space have shown us that the earth is a "water planet": more than two thirds of its surface is liquid. From this perspective, the continents are mere islands in a vast global sea. Athelstan Spilhaus, a noted oceanographer, professor, and ocean policy adviser, has recently devised the Spilhaus Whole Ocean Map, shown above, an equal-area projection that minimizes the distortion of ocean areas and reflects the primary importance of the sea to life on earth. No map shows more clearly that the sea is one interconnected body of water—a world ocean—and that the earth is a water planet. (*Adapted from Athelstan Spilhaus, "Whole Ocean Map," and reprinted with his permission. © Athelstan Spilhaus.*)

Nowhere are the three states of water so spectacularly juxtaposed as in the Antarctic. (*The Cousteau Society*)

WATER FACTS

All is born of water, all is sustained by water.

GOETHE

More than perhaps any other element of life on earth, water makes possible the existence of all living organisms. When two hydrogen atoms fasten to one oxygen atom, they create an asymmetrically shaped molecule. The hydrogen atoms are drawn together slightly on one side of the oxygen atom, creating a positive charge on one side of the water molecule and a negative charge on the other. The opposite charges create an effect similar to a magnet—an attraction that bonds water molecules to neighboring water molecules and to other substances. This remarkable chemical circumstance knits together the fabric of life.

The aggregate accumulation of water molecules is a substance that flows at normal temperatures. Most other fluids—sap, milk, blood—are water-based. They are made of nonliquids suspended in water.

Without the motion and the distribution system that moving water provides, the elements of life would never connect, their commingling under sunlight would not produce the complicated carbon compounds that lead eventually to cells, cells would not be able to gather as the moist organized and specialized cell colonies we call tissue, their aggregation would have no exchanging processes, no supply systems of food and breath, the eye would not see, the brain would not compute, the muscle would not move.

By and large, the characteristics of the water molecule that make it life-giving are freakish properties. They are, more often than not, exceptions to basic chemical rules.

- Almost every other substance becomes heavier, smaller, and more dense as it changes from a liquid to a solid. But water expands and grows lighter, so that ice floats. If that does not seem remarkable, it should. If water acted like other substances, its solid form, ice, would sink. The floor of the sea and the bottoms of lakes would accumulate ice. Gradually, winter after winter, the ice would lock up more and more water until there would be none running free on the planet. There would be no life on earth.
- More substances can be dissolved by water than by any other material. The water molecule, with its magnetlike opposite charges, is able to carry other substances suspended within itself, making it a nearly universal solvent.
- Water is able to climb of its own accord, a feat that results in capillary action in soils and in plants. Without this characteristic, water would not travel from the deepest root tip to the highest leaf. There would be no internal flow of nutrients in complicated organisms, and thus no complicated organisms. The trick occurs because the attraction of water molecules to themselves and to other molecules is so strong that they are drawn upward from one foreign molecule to another, always pulling along the adjacent water molecules. The climb is halted only by gravity.
- Great amounts of heat can be absorbed by water, making seas, rivers, lakes, and clouds vast energy storage banks. The release of stored heat from the ocean, for example, moderates climates, making coastal winters milder than those only a few miles inland.
- Human blood, excluding the cells and proteins, has the same general composition as seawater.

Through a fortunate accident, Planet Earth is the right distance from the sun to make the existence of life-giving water possible. Closer to the sun the heat is so intense that water would be vaporized; farther away, water would be permanently frozen. Only Mars, of the other planets in the solar system, is in the narrow temperature band in which water can exist in its three states. But only Earth is blanketed by a living, water-built biosphere, in which the life force itself seems to issue from water's evaporation, precipitation, runoff, seepage, transpiration from plants, respiration from animals, melting, freezing, and flowing. Earth, so far as we know, is the only Water Planet.

M.R.

BODY WATER

Every living creature is made of a tight network of cells bathed in a sea of salty water, what the scientist calls "the internal environment."

Seventy percent of the human body is made of water. In addition to the water that carries red and white cells in our blood vessels, there is the extracellular water in which the 100 million trillion cells of our body exist. Two remarkable features of body water are its purity and the constancy of its composition and temperature: it contains no microbes or viruses, its chemical composition and temperature do not vary.

Our body has millions of filters, a waste disposal system, and thermostats. It also has a unique sterilization plant, the immunity system. The immunity system tracks down and destroys all substances, bacteria, and chemicals that are foreign to the body and that would otherwise pollute the salty waters of our internal environment.

Throughout the millions of years required for the emergence of modern humans, the body had to struggle to preserve itself against the onslaught of bacteria, viruses, and parasites. However, this evolution of human beings took place in an unpolluted environment. The pure waters circulating through the body were not exposed to industrial wastes or pesticides.

By contrast, during the past few decades people have been exposed to an inordinate amount of chemical pollutants, drugs of all sorts (legal and illegal), heavy metals, and ionizing radiations. These chemicals and radiations readily bypass the protective filters of our body. Prolonged exposure to them results in a weakening of our body defenses and a damaging of our cells. Some cancer specialists believe that 80 percent of cancers are caused by environmental factors that could be controlled.

Claude Bernard, the founder of modern medicine and the first scientist to study the internal environment of our body a hundred years ago, concluded his studies by saying: "It is only because all of our cells are bathing in water of constant composition and purity that man may enjoy a free life."

The effort to preserve our water resources has a profound biological basis; it is the prerequisite for the preservation of the purity of our internal environment, which is bound to reflect the composition of our watershed. Our own preservation is closely linked with the preservation of the water from which life evolved three billion years ago.

By Dr. Gabriel G. Nahas, a member of The Cousteau Society Advisory Council.

THE MOVEMENT OF WATER

Except for the small quantities of water carried from the biosphere by astronauts and disposed of in space, nearly every molecule of water present when the seas formed on earth is still present on the planet. Moving from gas to liquid to solid ice, these molecules constitute a dynamic hydrologic cycle that bathes and supports life. A hypothetical example is often used to illustrate the ubiquitous nature of this cycle: in the moisture that bathes your eye there may be a molecule of water from Cleopatra's bathwater, from water drunk by Moses, or from the moist tissue of an octopus that lived in ancient seas.

The molecules of water that blanket the earth move at various speeds from one state and one location to others. Here are some general time schedules:

THE RESIDENCE TIME OF WATER MOLECULES IN THE HYDROLOGIC CYCLE

Location	*Residence Time*
Atmosphere	9 days
Rivers	2 weeks
Soil moisture	2 weeks to 1 year
Largest lakes	10 years
Shallow groundwater	10s to 100s of years
Mixed layer of oceans (top 150 meters)	120 years
World ocean	3,000 years
Deep groundwater	up to 10,000 years
Antarctic icecap	10,000 years

SOURCE: Paul R. Ehrlich, Anne H. Ehrlich, and John P. Holdren, *Ecoscience: Population, Resources, Environment*, W. H. Freeman and Company. Copyright © 1977.

THE RECIPE FOR SEAWATER

- The following table lists the most abundant elements in seawater. The figures represent the number of metric tons to be found in an average cubic kilometer of the ocean.

Most Common Elements	*Metric Tons per Cubic Kilometer*	*Some Selected Elements*	*Metric Tons per Cubic Kilometer*
H_2O	991,000,000	Lithium	175.0
Chlorine	19,600,000	Phosphorus	70.0
Sodium	10,900,000	Iodine	60.0
Magnesium	1,400,000	Arsenic	10-20.0
Sulfur	920,000	Molybdenum	10.0
Calcium	420,000	Copper	3.0
Potassium	390,000	Uranium	3.0
Bromine	67,000	Nickel	2.0
Carbon	29,000	Cesium	0.4
Strontium	8,300	Silver	0.2
Boron	5,000	Thorium	0.04
Silicon	3,100	Lead	0.02
Fluorine	1,300	Mercury	0.02
		Gold	0.004

SOURCE: Edward Wenk, Jr., *The Physical Resources of the Ocean.* Scientific American, September, 1969.

- Water accounts for about 96.5 percent of seawater. About 3.5 percent is dissolved inorganic material. Living particulate matter occurs in traces.
- Rivers are the major sources of sediments (particles) and dissolved elements, adding some 20 billion tons per year to the oceans, of which about 4 billion tons are dissolved salts. The Yellow River of China deposits the most sediment into the ocean: 2.1 billion tons per year. The Ganges is second, adding 1.6 billion tons per year.
- Other sources of matter in the ocean include underwater and surface volcanoes and volcanic vents (lava and hot brines), airborne particles, and particles from outer space (e.g., tektites).

SEA FACTS

- The sea is the principal reservoir for water on earth. Its 317 million cubic miles (1.33 billion cubic kilometers) provide 97.2 percent of the world's entire supply of water.
- The sea's average depth is 2.3 miles (3,729 meters). The average temperature is 38.3° F (3.5° C), but it ranges from below 32° F (0° C) under the ice shelves on Antarctica (the salt content prevents freezing) to temperatures as high as 98.6° F (37° C) in the Persian-Arab Gulf.
- So vast is the world ocean that one of its regions, the Pacific Ocean, is 25 percent larger than all of the land surface of the world combined.
- Immense as the ocean is, however, it is not abundant in life throughout. The great central areas of the sea are sparsely populated water deserts, as are the abyssal depths. It is along the coastal margins, the continental shelves, where 90 percent of the marine life in the world is concentrated. About 98 percent of the world fish catch is taken within 200 miles (300 kilometers) of land.

k.n., M.R.

"My analyst has truly helped me to appreciate the sea." (© *1980 Eldon Dedini*)

OCEANS AND SEAS

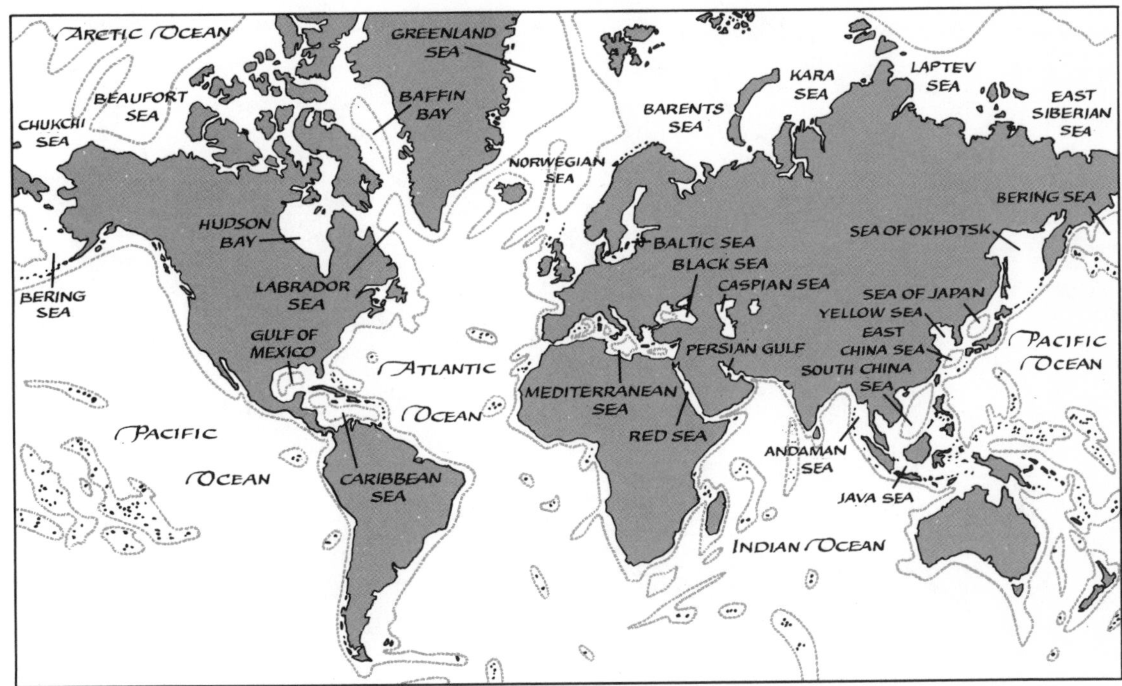

Name	Area: Square Miles	Area: Square Kilometers	Average Depth: Feet	Average Depth: Meters	Greatest Known Depth: Feet	Greatest Known Depth: Meters	Greatest Known Depth: Site
Pacific Ocean	64,000,000	165,700,000	13,200	4,030	37,782	11,022	Marianas Deep/ Philippine Trench
Atlantic Ocean	31,800,000	82,400,000	12,880	3,925	30,246	9,219	Puerto Rico Trough
Indian Ocean	25,300,000	65,500,700	13,000	3,960	24,460	7,455	Sunda Trench
Arctic Ocean	5,440,200	14,100,000	3,950	1,210	18,456	5,625	77°45′N; 175°W
Mediterranean Sea*	1,145,000	2,966,000	4,690	1,430	15,197	4,632	Off Cape Matapa, Greece
Caribbean Sea	1,049,500	2,718,000	8,680	2,650	22,788	6,946	Off Cayman Islands
South China Sea	895,400	2,319,000	5,420	1,650	16,456	5,016	West of Luzon
Bering Sea	885,900	2,292,900	5,070	1,550	15,659	4,773	Off Buldir Island
Gulf of Mexico	615,000	1,592,800	4,870	1,490	12,425	3,787	Sigsbee Deep
Sea of Okhotsk	613,800	1,589,700	2,750	838	12,001	3,658	146° 10′E; 46° 50′N
East China Sea	482,300	1,249,200	617	188	9,126	2,782	25° 16′N; 125°E
Hudson Bay	475,800	1,232,000	420	128	600	183	Near mouth
Sea of Japan	389,100	1,008,000	4,430	1,350	12,276	3,742	Central Basin
Andaman Sea	308,100	797,700	2,850	870	12,392	3,777	Off Car Nicobar Island
North Sea	222,100	575,200	308	94	2,165	660	Skagerrak
Red Sea	169,100	438,000	1,611	491	7,254	2,211	Off Port Sudan
Baltic Sea	163,000	422,200	180	55	1,380	421	Off Gotland

*Includes Black Sea and Sea of Azov.

SOURCE: *Information Please Almanac – 1980*. Copyright © 1979 by Simon & Schuster, a division of Gulf & Western Corporation. Reprinted by permission.

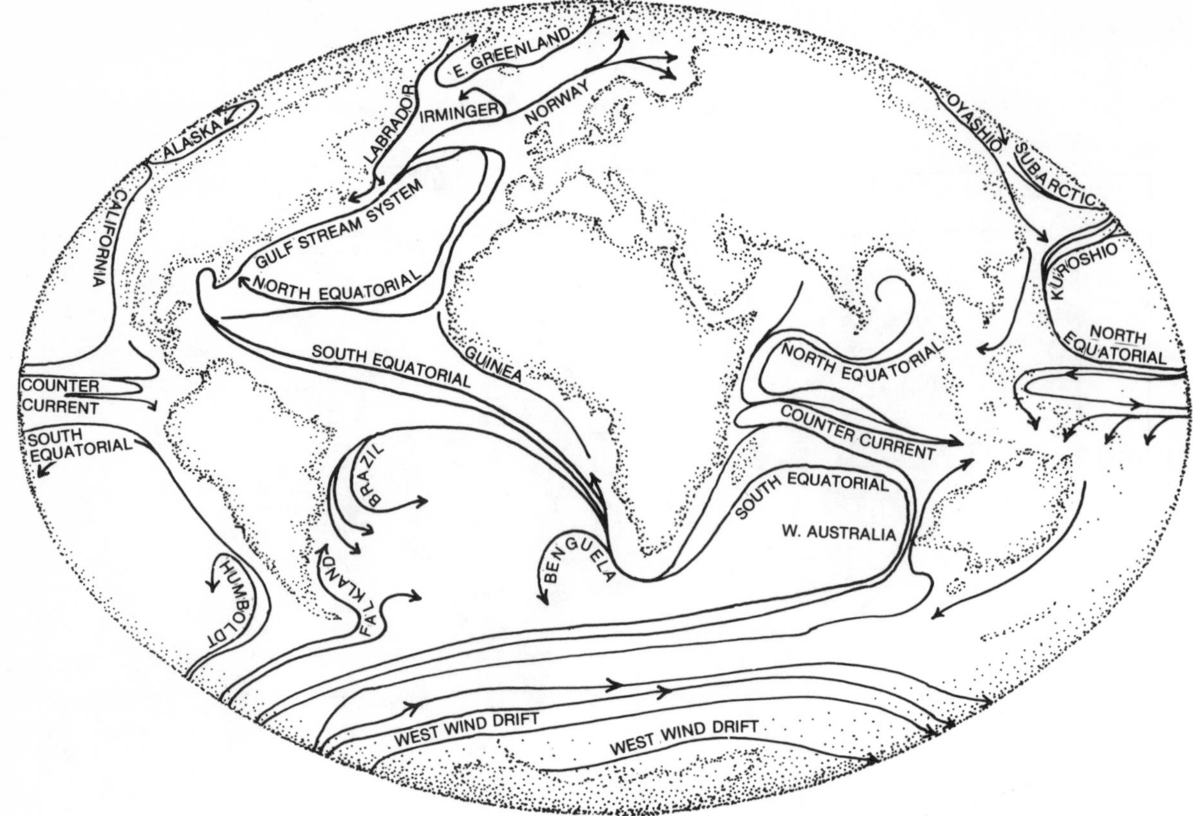

Major Ocean Currents. (*From* The Ever-changing Sea, *by David B. Ericson and Goesta Wollin, 1967, by permission of Alfred A. Knopf, New York*)

SOME WATER EXTREMES

Strongest Currents: The Gulf Stream, traveling north along the east coast of the United States, and the Kuroshio Current, which moves north along the east coast of the Philippines, Formosa, and Japan, each have surface velocities over 7 feet (2.13 meters) per second.

Weakest Currents: Abyssal currents in the Pacific Ocean have been estimated to move hundredths of a centimeter per second.

Highest Waves: Winds of hurricane force have produced waves from 75 to 90 feet high (23 to 28 meters) in the North Atlantic. Storm waves in the Pacific have been measured at more than 100 feet (31 meters). Tsunamis (waves caused by underwater earth movement) rise nearly 200 feet (61 meters).

SOURCE: *The Ocean World of Jacques Cousteau,* Grolier Enterprises, 1975.

THE TEN MAJOR SEDIMENT-PRODUCING RIVERS

	Drainage Area		*Sediment Discharge*
River	*Thousands of Square Kilometers*	*Thousands of Square Miles*	*Millions of Tons per Year*
1. Yellow	666	257	2,100
2. Ganges	945	365	1,600
3. Brahmaputra	658	254	800
4. Yangtze	1,920	741	550
5. Indus	957	369	480
6. Amazon	5,710	2,205	400
7. Mississippi-Missouri	3,180	1,228	340
8. Irrawaddy	425	164	330
9. Mekong	786	303	190
10. Colorado	630	243	150

SOURCE: After J. N. Holeman, "The Sediment Yield of Major Rivers of The World," *Water Resources Research,* 1968. Copyrighted by the American Geophysical Union.

RIVERS

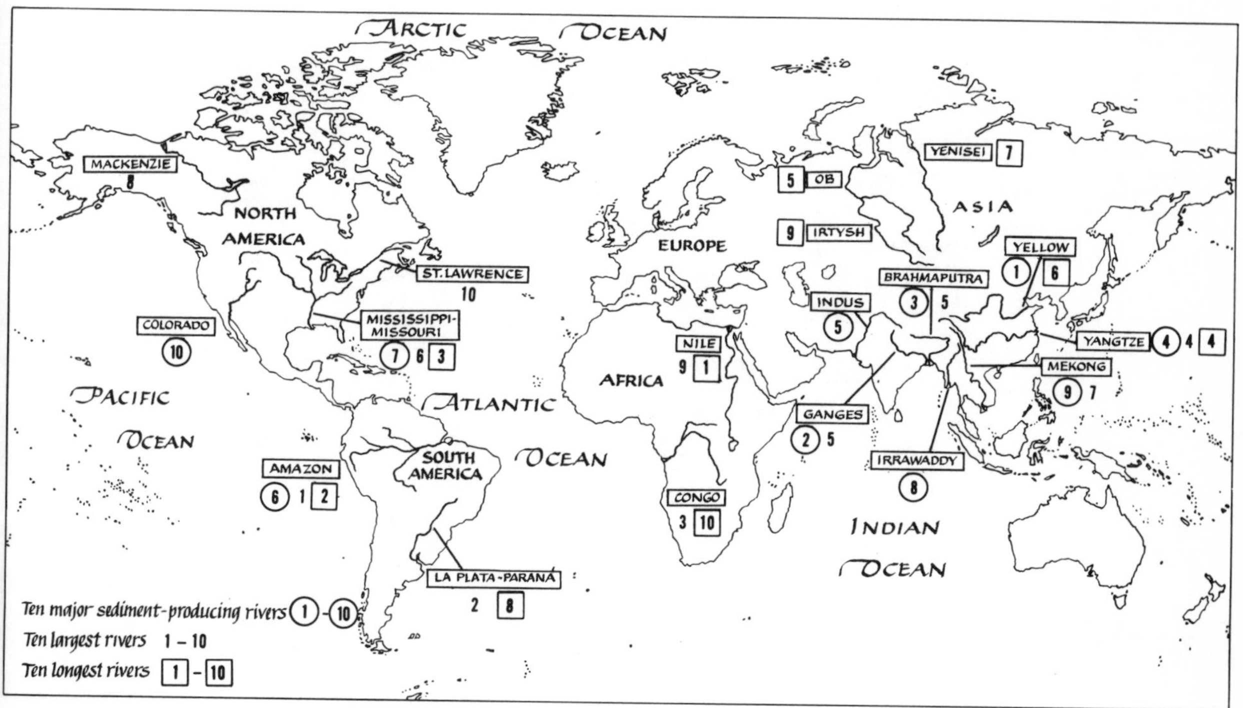

THE TEN LARGEST RIVERS OF THE WORLD

Name	Discharge: Cubic Meters per Second	Discharge: Cubic Feet per Second
1. Amazon	200,000	7,060,000
2. La Plata-Paraná	78,000	2,753,400
3. Congo	56,000	1,976,800
4. Yangtze	22,000	776,600
5. Ganges-Brahmaputra	20,000	706,000
6. Mississippi-Missouri	17,000	600,100
7. Mekong	17,000	600,100
8. Mackenzie	13,000	458,900
9. Nile	12,000	423,600
10. St. Lawrence	11,000	388,300

NOTE: The volume of the Amazon nearly equals that of all the other large rivers combined.

SOURCE: Barry Fell, *Life, Space and Time*, Copyright © 1974 by H. Barraclough Fell. Reprinted by permission of Harper & Row, Publisher, Inc.

THE TEN LONGEST RIVERS OF THE WORLD

River	Approximate Length: Miles	Approximate Length: Kilometers
1. Nile	4,180	6,690
2. Amazon	3,912	6,296
3. Mississippi-Missouri	3,741	6,020
4. Yangtze	3,602	5,797
5. Ob	3,459	5,567
6. Yellow	2,900	4,667
7. Yenisei	2,800	4,506
8. La Plata-Paraná	2,795	4,498
9. Irtysh	2,758	4,438
10. Congo	2,716	4,371

SOURCE: *Information Please Almanac – 1980*. Copyright © 1979 by Simon & Schuster, a division of Gulf & Western Corporation. Reprinted by permission.

THE WORLD'S TEN LARGEST LAKES

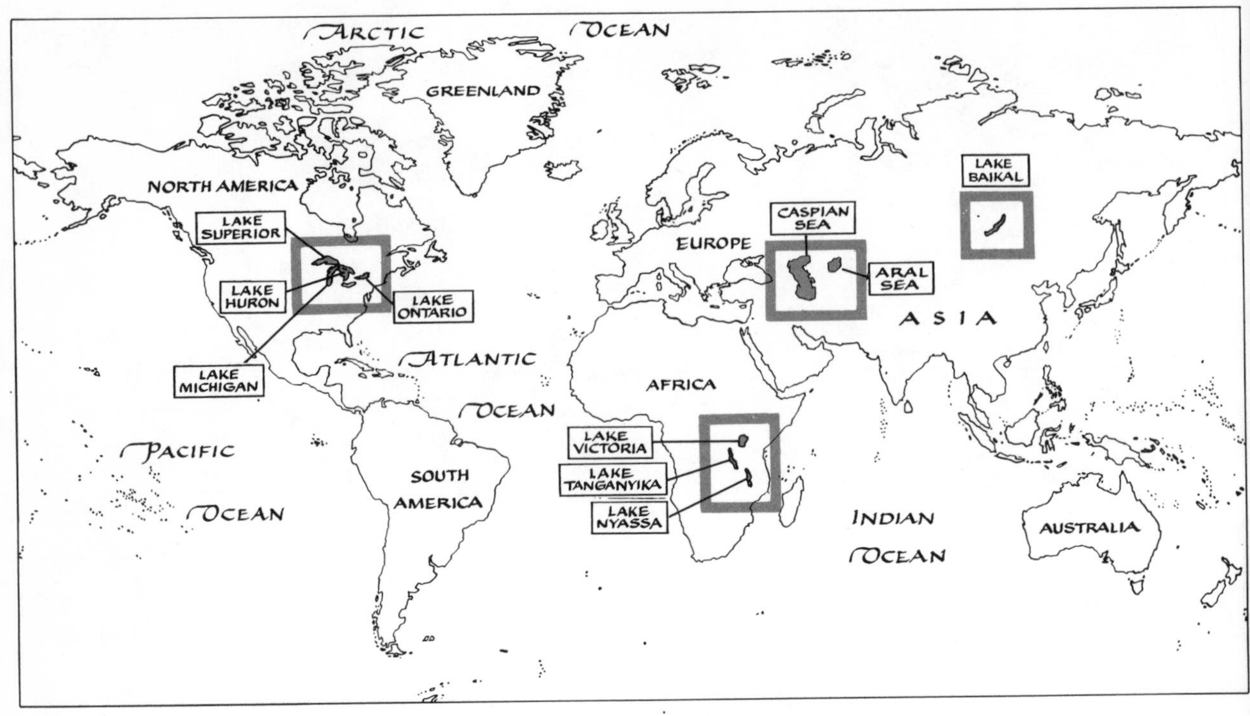

	Volume		Area	
Name	Billions of Cubic Meters	Billions of Cubic Feet	Square Kilometers	Square Miles
1. Caspian	88.0	3,106.4	440,000	169,840
2. Baikal	23.0	811.9	34,700	13,394
3. Superior	12.0	423.6	80,700	31,150
4. Tanganyika	10.0	353.0	31,600	12,198
5. Nyasa	8.0	282.4	28,500	11,001
6. Michigan	5.7	201.2	58,000	22,388
7. Huron	4.6	162.4	59,600	23,005
8. Victoria	2.6	91.7	67,800	26,171
9. Ontario	1.7	60.0	19,500	7,527
10. Aral	0.95	33.5	67,900	26,209

SOURCE: Barry Fell, *Life, Space and Time*, Copyright © 1974 by H. Barraclough Fell. Reprinted by permission of Harper & Row, Publisher, Inc.

SWEET AND SALTY WATER LORE

- *Lake Baikal, USSR.* Among all freshwater lakes, this is the oldest (about 30 million years), the deepest (5,712 feet/1,741 meters), and the greatest in volume (812 billion cubic feet/23 billion cubic meters). It supports the highest proportion (60 percent) of species that occur nowhere else on earth.
- *Bratsk Reservoir, USSR.* Located in Siberia, this is the world's largest reservoir, with a gross capacity of 5.9 million cubic feet (169,888 cubic meters).
- *Caspian Sea.* The world's largest lake has a salinity of 1.3 percent, a surface area of more than 150,000 square miles (388,500 square kilometers), and a volume of about 115 billion cubic yards (88 billion cubic meters). Its surface is about 93 feet (28 meters) below sea level and dropping, in part because of declining inflow resulting from upstream reservoir construction and evaporation of irrigation water.

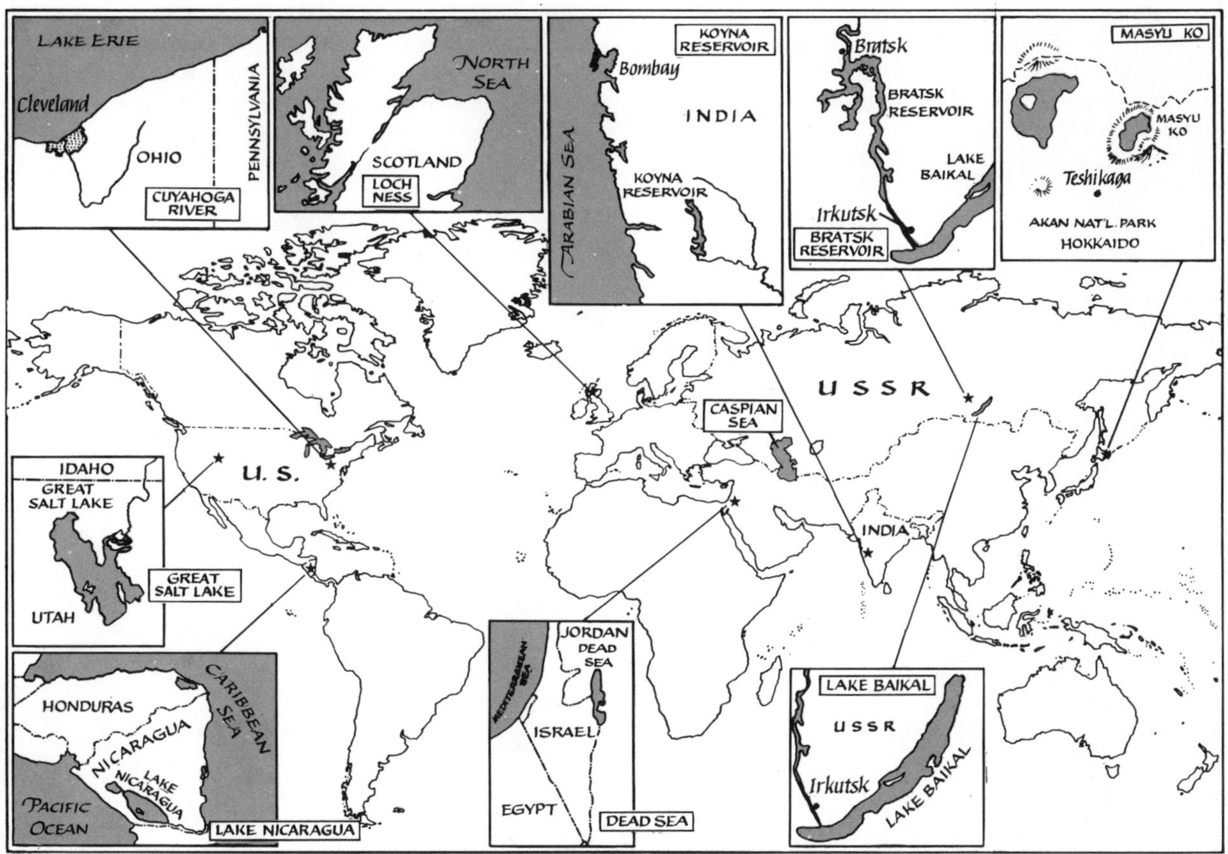

- *Cuyahoga River, United States.* This river in Ohio, tributary to Lake Erie, is so polluted that it caught fire in the 1960s from all the refuse on its surface.
- *Dead Sea.* The world's saltiest lake, with salinity ranging up to 23 percent (as compared to 3.5 percent for ocean water) has an elevation of 1,302 feet (397 meters) below sea level. After water inflow was reduced by diversion for irrigation, the density stratification broke down for the first time in recorded history in the winter of 1978–79, resulting in mixing of the waters from top to bottom.
- *Great Salt Lake, United States.* The most expansive area of salty water on the North American continent, varying in area from 2,300 square miles (5,951 square kilometers) in 1883 to about 1,200 square miles (3,108 square kilometers) in 1940. It contains a few species of algae, some microscopic animal life, a species of brine shrimp, and the larvae of two species of flies. The salinity is variable, averaging about 20 percent.
- *Koyna Reservoir, India.* Large reservoirs commonly induce earthquakes as underlying rocks adjust to the added burden. The Koyna Reservoir caused an earthquake on December 10, 1967, that took 200 lives, injured 1,500, left thousands homeless, and rocked the city of Bombay, 130 miles (209 kilometers) away. Fortunately the dam held together.
- *Masyu ko, Japan.* A volcanic crater (caldera) lake, notable for the clarity of its water—the most transparent of any inland water on record. A Secchi disk, a small white disk first used to determine water clarity by Professor P. A. Secchi in 1865, has been seen from the surface at a depth of 136.5 feet (42 meters). Crater Lake, Oregon, contender for the title, has a recorded Secchi depth of 131 feet (40 meters).
- *Loch Ness, Scotland.* A lake 22.5 miles (36 kilometers) long, averaging less than 1 mile (1.6 kilometers) in width with a maximum depth of 754 feet (230 meters), is famous as the alleged home of the "Loch Ness monster." Evidence used to "prove" the existence of the monster includes photographs, traces on echo sounders, clicks on underwater earphones, and a visual observation of the monster boldly

walking across the road, reported by a London businessman in 1933. The lake is notorious for optical phenomena resulting from varying temperature differences at the air-water interface in different seasons.

- *Lake Nicaragua, Nicaragua.* This 230-foot-deep (70-meter) lake is often discussed as part of a route to connect the Atlantic and Pacific oceans, an alternative to the Panama Canal. It is the home of the world's only freshwater (landlocked) sharks.

J.R.V.

WATER PROBLEMS

EXAMPLES OF INDUSTRIAL AND AGRICULTURAL POLLUTANTS DISCHARGED ANNUALLY INTO THE WORLD'S OCEANS

Pollutant	*Estimated Annual Discharge, 1970-75 (In metric tons)*	*Source*
Petroleum and industrial hydrocarbons	3,405,000	Offshore wells, oil tankers, industrial waste
Airborne hydrocarbons	15,000,000	Vehicles, industries, power plants
Airborne lead	350,000	Vehicles
Mercury	100,000	Industrial operations
Aldrin-Toxaphene (converted to Dieldrin)	25,000	Agricultural and public health operations
Benzene hexachloride	50,000	Agricultural and public health operations
DDT	25,000	Agricultural and public health operations
Polychlorinated biphenyls (PCBs)	25,000	Plastics industries

(For more on ocean pollution see "Wastes in the Sea," page 409.)

SOURCE: Based on data from Charles H. Southwick, *Ecology & the Quality of our Environment*, 2nd edition. Copyright © 1976 by Litton Educational Publishing Company. Reprinted by Permission of D. Van Nostrand Company.

WASTES DISCHARGED INTO ESTUARIES AND THE COASTAL OCEAN

Sources	*Wastes Discharged*
Municipal storm sewers	Waste oils Street washings Raw sewage Suspended sediment
Municipal sewage treatment plants	Nutrients (phosphates and nitrates) Sewage sludges (solids from treatment)
Industrial wastes	Waste chemicals (e.g., acids, petrochemicals) Waste oil
Runoff from agricultural lands	Nutrients from fertilizers Pesticides and herbicides Animal wastes
Electrical power plants	Waste heat Ash (from coal) Chemicals (corrosion-inhibiters, foam-suppressers, biocides)
Dredging operations and construction activities	Suspended sediment Nutrients from sediments
Petroleum production and exploration	Suspended sediment (drilling muds) Crude oil
Ships (commercial and recreational)	Untreated sewage Garbage Waste oil

SOURCE: M. Grant Gross, *Oceanography*, 3rd edition. Copyright © 1976 by Charles E. Merrill Publishing Company. Reprinted by permission.

WATER USE BY INDUSTRY IN THE UNITED STATES

	Billion Gallons per Day
Manufacturing	61 (excluding recycled water, which is roughly equal to the flow of the upper Mississippi River)
Chemicals and allied products	40.1
Primary metals	28.2
Paper and allied products	26.1
Petroleum and coal products	23.7
Food and related products	4.5
Transportation equipment	3.7
Textile mill products	1.7
Irrigation in agriculture	86.4
Livestock in agriculture	1.9

SOURCE: *Nation's Water Resources, 1975-2000* U.S. Water Resources Council.

Discharge from a wood pulp plant pollutes the water of an inlet in Washington State. (*United Nations*)

POLLUTING INCIDENTS IN AND AROUND U. S. WATERS

		Volume	
Item	*Number*	*Gallons (thousands)*	*Liters (thousands)*
SOURCE			
Vessels	3,759	11,928[1]	45,147[1]
Tank ships	590	9,815[1]	37,150[1]
Tank barges	1,112	1,772	6,707
Other	2,057	341	1,291
Land vehicles	532	692	2,619
Onshore facilities	483	968	3,664
Offshore facilities	1,118	81	307
Other facilities	1,027	1,758	6,654
Pipelines	492	2,576	9,750
Marine facilities	742	553	2,093
Land facilities	195	137	519
Miscellaneous/ Unknown	4,496	1,207	4,568
SELECTED TYPE OF POLLUTANT			
Crude oil	2,220	12,232[1]	46,298[1]
Fuel oil	1,018	1,251	4,735
Asphalt or residual fuel oil	132	219	829
Liquid chemical	280	1,428	5,405
LOCATIONS			
Atlantic coast	3,038	1,697	6,423
Gulf coast	4,260	2,919	11,048
Pacific coast	2,326	9,989[1]	37,808[1]
Great Lakes	891	1,057	4,001
Inland U.S.	2,329	4,238	16,041
Total discharges, 1977	12,844	19,900[1]	75,321[1]
Total discharges, 1976	12,655	33,852	128,140
Total discharges, 1970	3,711	15,523	57,737

[1]Includes a 9.6 million gallon (36,336 million liter) spill, *Hawaiian Patriot*, off the Hawaiian Islands.

(See also "Wastes in the Sea," page 409.)

SOURCE: U.S. Environmental Protection Agency, 1977.

THE VITAL STATISTICS OF FLORA AND FAUNA

- Only 10 to 15 percent of the estimated ten million species of organisms in the world have been described by scientists.
- There are more insects in 1 square mile (2.6 square kilometers) of rural land than human beings on the entire earth.
- United States government agencies estimate that as much as 50 million acres (20 million hectares) of tropical forest is disappearing each year. (See also "Manaus, Amazonas, Brazil," page 67.)
- Most of the world's dry lands are considered to be at "high risk" or "very high risk" of losing their ability to support useful species of plant and animal life. As much as 30 percent of the earth's land surface, covering parts of one hundred nations and occupied by one sixth of the world's population, is designated as at least "threatened." (See also "The Negev Desert, Israel," page 84.)
- A large proportion of the world's shared wildlife resources is found in the developing coun-

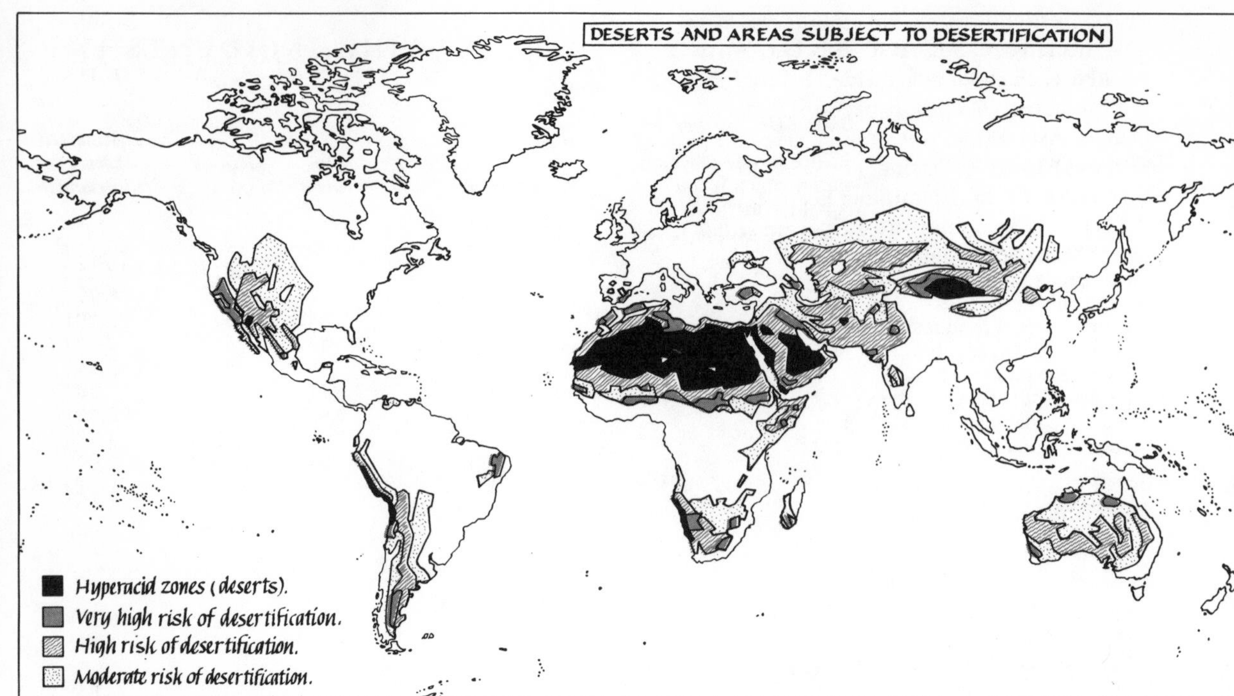

tries. Its protection for the benefit of people throughout the world sometimes poses difficult economic decisions and often requires the commitment of financial resources that exceeds the capability of these countries. (See also "Tsavo National Park, Kenya," page 85.)

- The world's closed forests (mature woodlands with a closed canopy) have been reduced by more than 1.2 billion acres (500 million hectares), an area more than half the size of the United States, between 1963 and 1973. Fifteen percent of the world's total forest was lost in a decade.
- About 630 million people—one seventh of the world's population—live in arid or semiarid areas normally classified as deserts. Of these, it is estimated that 78 million live on land that has been devastated by human-caused soil erosion, dune formation, vegetation changes, and salt formation.
- A report to the United Nations Environment Programme (UNEP) by the Egyptian ecologist Mohammed Kassas claims that 36.3 percent of the earth's surface can be classified as desert (extremely arid, arid, and semiarid). Yet 43 percent of the earth's surface is covered with desertlike soil and vegetation. Kassas claims that the difference between these figures—6.7 percent—represents the amount of the earth's surface that is human-made desert. This is an area larger than Brazil. The land has been degraded to near-desert by deforestation, overgrazing, and poor farming and irrigation practices.
- In 1979, for every person on earth there were approximately 98 cubic feet (2.8 cubic meters) of wood in the world's dense forests (dense forest is defined as land that is 20 percent forest-covered as seen from above). However, at the present rates of population growth, wood consumption, and deforestation, the amount of wood per person will be almost halved by the year 2000.
- About half the wood cut in the world each year is burned as fuel. Eighty percent of the wood used in the developing countries is used as fuel. (See "The Forgotten Energy Source: Firewood," page 157.)
- Although it is estimated that one quarter of the world's land is forested, the figure is misleading. The Soviet Union and Latin America each have approximately 1.7 billion acres (680 million hectares) of forest land—mostly in Siberia and Amazonia, areas that are remote from large population centers. In much of Asia, there is a tiny percentage of forest compared to the total land area.
- The U. N. Food and Agriculture Organization

(FAO) estimates that 9.8 million acres (4 million hectares) of forest are currently being planted each year worldwide. In contrast, 12.3 million acres (5 million hectares) are cut each year in Asia alone, 4.9 million acres (2 million hectares) more in Africa, and 12.3 to 24.6 million acres (5 to 10 million hectares) in Latin America. (See "Port-au-Prince, Haiti," page 66, "Manaus, Amazonas, Brazil," page 67, and "The Himalayas," page 189.)

NAMING AND COUNTING THE CREATURES

Taxonomy, or the systematic classification of living organisms, is not really an exact science. Often experts disagree on an organism's place in the scheme of things. For example, there is no agreement on exactly how many phyla exist. Therefore the following lists are, to a certain extent, arbitrary, but they provide a sense of the incredible diversity of living organisms.

Phylum	*Estimated Number of Species*
Protozoa – single-celled organisms	30,000
Porifera – sponges	5,000
Coelenterata – anemones, corals, jellyfish	10,000
Ctenophora – comb jellies	80
Bryozoa or Ectoprocta } "moss animals"	4,000
Brachioposa – lamp shells	300
Aschelminthes – loosely related wormlike organisms	14,000+
Phoronides – wormlike marine tube dwellers	12
Chaetognatha – arrow worms; active marine creatures	50
Platyhelmintha – flat worms	9,000
Annelida – segmented worms	8,600
Nemertea – proboscis worms	500
Mollusca – mollusks	50,000
Arthropoda - insects, arachnids, crustaceans	1,000,000+
Echinodermata – starfish, sea urchins	5,500
Chordata – vertebrates	43,100

Class	
Pisces (fish)	20,000
Amphibia	2,500
Reptilia	6,000
Aves (birds)	8,600
Mammalia	6,000

SOURCES: Ralph Buchsbaum, ***Animals Without Backbones; New Columbia Encyclopedia; Larousse Encyclopedia of the Animal World; Dictionary of Biology; Phaidon Concise Encyclopedia of Science and Technology.***

NAMING AND COUNTING THE PLANTS

Phylum or Group	*Estimated Number of Species*
Simple Plants	
Chlorophyta – green algae	6,570
Euglenophyta – green or colorless flagellates	450
Cyanophyta – blue-green algae	1,500
Chrysophyta – diatoms of yellow-green algae	16,600
Pyrrophyta – dinoflagellates	1,000
Phaeophyta – brown algae	1,000
Rhodophyta – red algae	2,500
Schizophytala – true bacteria; unicellular thallophytes	1,600
Myxomycota – slime molds	450
Eumyceta – true fungi	46,900
(includes class Lichenes; lichens are a symbiosis involving a fungus and an algae)	16,000
Bryophyta – liverworts and mosses	25,000
Vascular Plants	
Psilopsida – leaves and roots absent; mostly fossil	4
Lycopsida – club mosses, quillworts	951
Sphenopsida – horsetails and kin; mostly extinct	25
Pteropsida	
Filicineae – ferns	11,000
Gymnospermae – conifers, cycads	711
Angiospermae	
Dicotyledonae	200,000
Monocotyledonae	50,000

SOURCES: Wilson and Loomis, ***Botany; Dictionary of Biology; Phaidon Concise Encyclopedia of Science and Technology.***

PRIORITY HABITATS TO SAVE

A new global program aimed at protection of vital habitats has identified regional ecosystems in need of immediate and special attention. Launched in March of 1980, the World Conservation Strategy was developed by the International Union for Conservation of Nature and Natural Resources (IUCN) in association with the United Nations Environment Programme (UNEP) and the World Wildlife Fund (WWF). More than 450 government agencies and conservation organizations in more than 100 countries, employing more than 700 scientists, were involved in the preparation of this global program. The goal of the strategy is to identify important biological areas that do not have adequate protection now, and to propose international programs to ensure that their diversity and balances are not seriously threatened. (See map next page.)

PRIORITY HABITATS TO SAVE

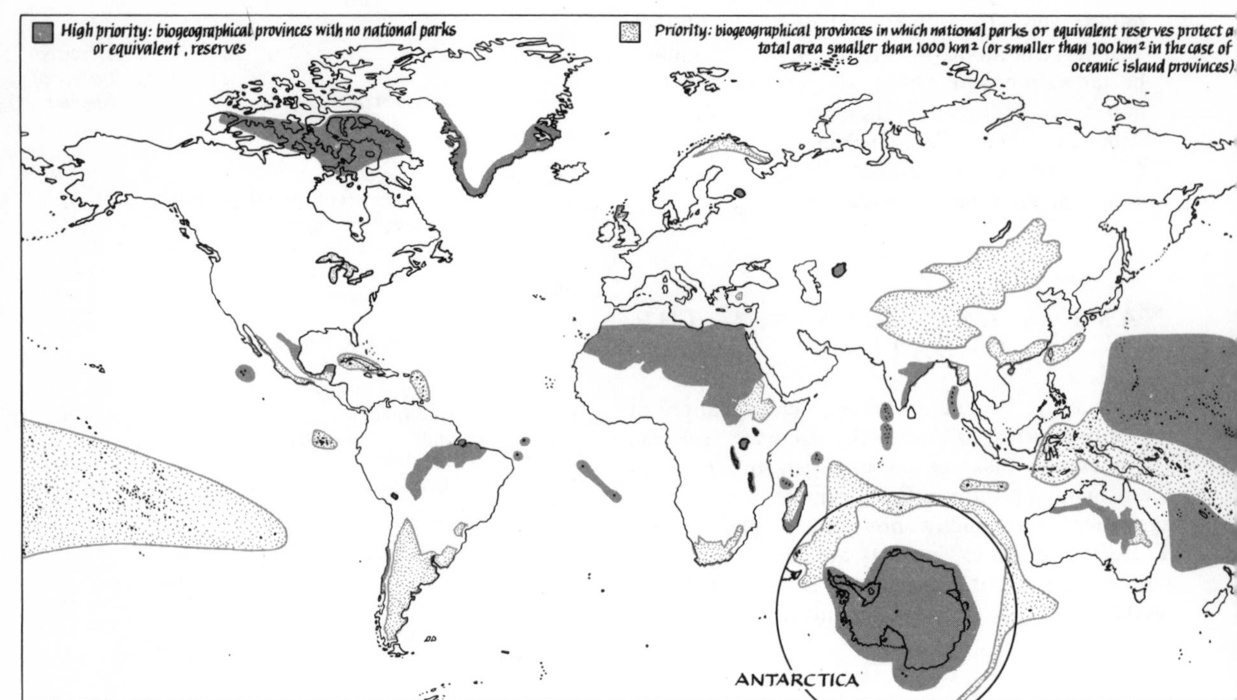

LAND CLASSIFICATION BY VEGETATION

	Total Land Area Occupied		
Type of Vegetation	*Millions of Square Miles*	*Millions of Square Kilometers*	*Percentage of Total Land*
Tropical forest	7.8	20.3	13.6
Coniferous forest	5.6	14.6	9.8
Deciduous forest	2.2	5.7	3.8
Taiga	1.5	3.9	2.6
Semiarid grasslands	8.5	22.0	14.7
Humid grasslands	5.8	14.9	10.0
Wetlands	1.3	3.3	2.2
Cultivated (grain)	2.7	7.0	4.7
Cultivated (other)	2.6	6.8	4.6
Tundra	3.3	8.5	5.7
Desert	8.6	22.4	15.0
Glacier and perpetual frost	7.6	19.7	13.2

SOURCE: After Edward Deevey, "The Human Population," *Scientific American*, September 1960, as adapted by Paul R. Ehrlich, Anne H. Ehrlich, and John P. Holdren in *Ecoscience: Population, Resources, Environment.* W. H. Freeman and Company. Copyright © 1977.

DISTRIBUTION OF THE MAJOR LAND BIOMES

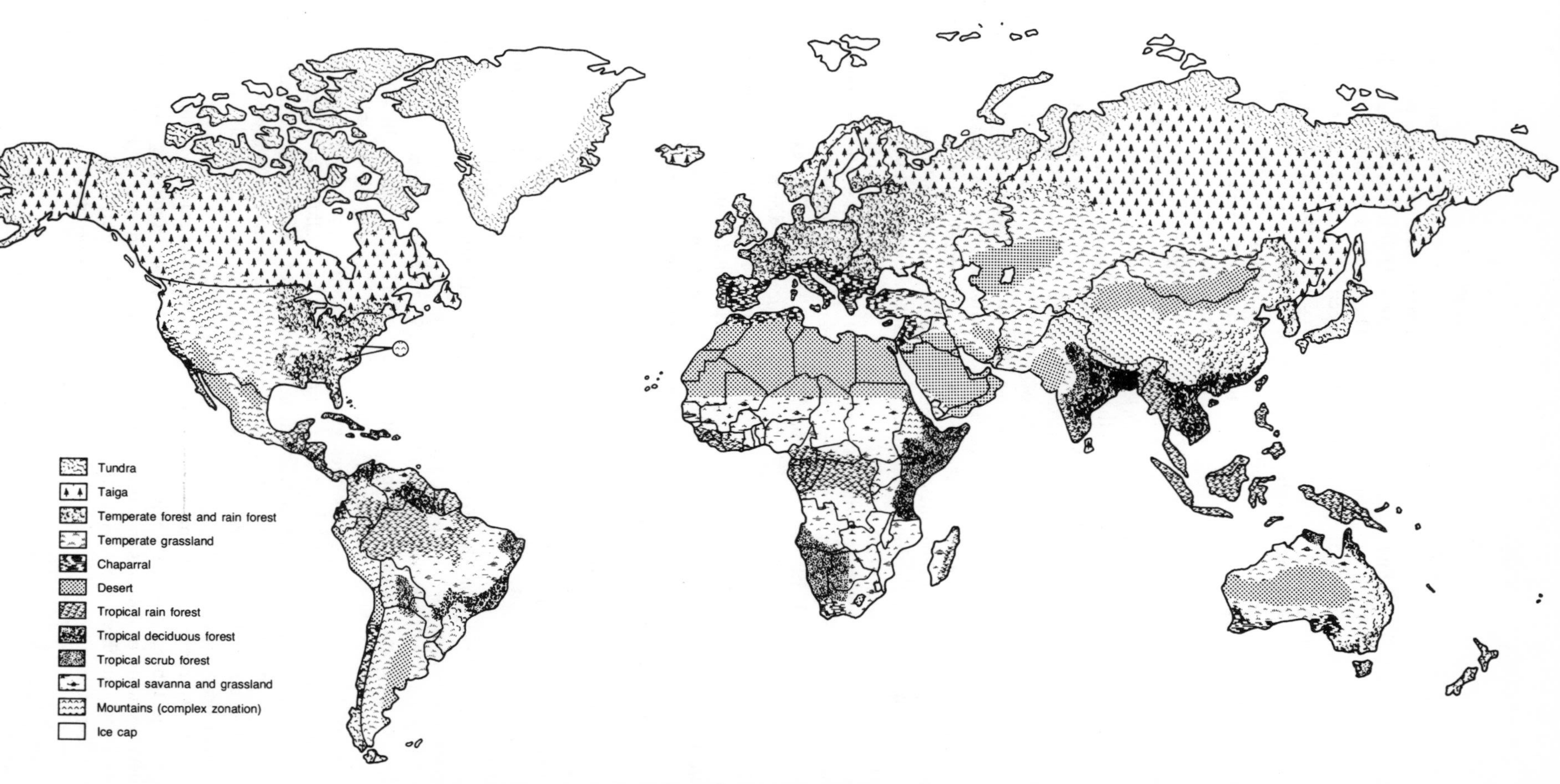

(*Reprinted with permission from* Ecoscience: Population, Resources, Environment, *by Paul R. Ehrlich, Anne H. Ehrlich and John P. Holdren. W. H. Freeman and Company.* Copyright *© 1977, as adapted from Odum, 1971.*)

LAND COMMUNITIES

From the humid, lush, multistoried tropical jungles, gaudy with exotic plants, huge flowers, and colorful birds, to the sweeping emptiness of the frozen tundra, marked by occasional herds of migrating caribou and a soft carpet of lichens and liverworts, the world's ecological communities differ dramatically, and predictably. The type of community that evolves depends on rainfall, soil, and latitude. In the sea, salinity, upwellings, and depth are important factors. Although local communities all differ, certain broad categories can be defined that bear resemblance to others around the world. The taigas (northern coniferous forests) of Canada share many characteristics with those of the Soviet Union. The savannas of South America feature species different from the savannas of Africa, but savanna species of both continents show similar adaptations. Here is a brief description of the world's major biomes, each with its own moods, rhythms, communities —and vulnerabilities. Much of this material was condensed or adapted with permission from *Ecoscience,* a comprehensive ecology text by Paul R. Ehrlich, Anne H. Ehrlich, and John P. Holdren.

Tundra

The treeless plains of the tundra occur where the average annual temperature is below 23° F (−5° C). In the summer the ground thaws to a depth of only 1 meter (3.2 feet). Beneath that is perpetually frozen permafrost, impenetrable to tree roots. The tundra is no skier's paradise. Receiving only about 10 inches (25 centimeters) of precipitation a year, it is more like a cold desert than anything else.

Things change slowly in the frigid tundra. Plants grow and decompose sluggishly. Tracks of vehicles or animals can remain visible for decades. Yet despite the harshness, the tundra springs to life in the brief summer. A thick, spongy mat of lichens, grasses, and sedges grows in low areas. Swarms of insects and blooms of aquatic larvae attract flocks of waterfowl from warmer climates to breed in the tundra. Caribou, wolves, musk-oxen, arctic foxes, rabbits, and occasional polar bears roam the plains.

Because of its remoteness from large human settlements, the tundra was left undisturbed until recent developments of oil and gas resources on North America's northern coast. Any disturbance will take a long time to heal.

Taiga

The northern coniferous forest that stretches across North America, northern Europe, and the Soviet Union is called by its Russian name, *taiga.* The forest is dominated by a few species of evergreen trees, such as spruce and fir. Deciduous trees may spring up but are eventually replaced by conifers. The cold climate and the acids that leach out of the fallen needles keep the soil highly acidic; only herbs and shrubs adapted to acid soil can thrive here.

The diversity of animals and insects is lower than in the deciduous forests to the south. Bears, moose, lynxes, rabbits, squirrels, and an abundance of weasels, martins, sables, fishers, and wolverines inhabit the taiga, as well as a variety of birds, most of them migrating.

The taiga was first exploited by fur trappers, then by loggers. Until recently, most logging operations clear-cut large areas, allowing the thin soil to wash away. Now in many places regulations specify that loggers leave at least a strip of trees along streams to trap eroding soil.

Because large areas of the taiga are composed of the same tree species, they are especially vulnerable to outbreaks of insects that specialize in that species. For example, an outbreak of the spruce bud worm defoliated more than 6 million acres (2.43 million hectares) of forest in New Brunswick, Canada, in the 1950s. Unfortunately, forestry managers often respond with massive applications of pesticides.

Temperate Forest

This is the biome in which most Western and Chinese civilizations developed. It includes the familiar oak and beech-maple forests, which shed their leaves each fall. These forests thrive in areas where the temperature drops below freezing each winter, but that are warmer than taiga regions and have an annual rainfall of 30 to 80 inches (75 to 200 centimeters).

Here the soil is rich: fallen leaves are decomposed by the millions of creatures that churn in the soil's upper layer. Enough light penetrates to the forest floor to support shrubs and herbs, many of which produce berries and seeds that attract a variety of birds and support such mammals as deer, squirrels, shrews, bears, and raccoons.

Much of this forest has been cleared for farms and cities. Removing trees also removes the soil's anchor and one of its sources of nutrients, and without careful soil husbandry a once-productive area can become barren. This happened to many

FORESTS OF THE WORLD

	Total Territory		Total Forest Land		Closed Forest*	
	Millions of Square Miles	*Millions of Square Kilometers*	*Millions of Square Miles*	*Millions of Square Kilometers*	*Millions of Square Miles*	*Millions of Square Kilometers*
Africa	11.7	30.3	3.0	8.0	0.7	1.9
Asia (without USSR)	10.6	27.5	2.0	5.3	1.5	4.0
North America	8.3	21.5	2.4	6.3	2.4	6.3
South America	6.9	17.8	2.8	7.3	2.0	5.3
Central America	1.0	2.7	0.3	0.7	0.2	0.6
Australia and Oceania	3.3	8.5	0.7	1.9	0.3	0.8
Europe (without USSR)	1.9	4.9	0.6	1.7	0.5	1.4
USSR	8.6	22.4	3.5	9.2	3.0	7.7
World	52.3	135.6	15.3	40.3	10.6	28.0

*Land where crowns of trees cover more than 20 percent of area.

SOURCE: Reidar Persson, *World Forest Resources.* Adapted from *Ecoscience: Population, Resources, Environment* by Paul R. Ehrlich, Anne H. Ehrlich and John P. Holdren. W. H. Freeman and Company. Copyright © 1977.

farms in the eastern United States—farmers simply moved to a new "frontier" when the soil was worn out. In more crowded Europe, farmers took more care to replenish soil nutrients, keeping their acreage productive.

Grassland

In climatic areas between forest and desert lie the world's sweeping grasslands, often populated by herds of large animals. Many ecologists believe that these grazing herds maintain the great grasslands by cropping seedlings along bordering forests. Wild horses roam the grasslands of Eurasia; large kangaroos are found in Australia; zebras, giraffes, white rhinoceroses, and a number of antelope species inhabit the African savannas; and before its settlement, buffalo and pronghorn antelope grazed the North American prairie.

In each grassland, predators evolved to prey on the herds: lions, cheetahs, hyenas, coyotes, and others. Burrowing rodents make a home in the deep soil, and insects abound in the grasses. Certain grasshoppers sometimes accumulate a huge population and migrate in masses—a plague of locusts.

The grassland has the richest soil of any biome, about twelve times as rich as temperate forest soils. The interlaced grass roots hold the soil in place and soil organisms constantly return nutrients in dead grass to the soil. The rich soil has attracted farmers to many grasslands, including the American Midwest and the Russian steppes, but, as in the deciduous forest, the soil becomes impoverished without proper management. Plows break up the intricate grass roots, leaving loose soil prey to windstorms, and when crops are removed their nutrients that would otherwise replenish the soil are lost. Chemical fertilizers do nothing to rebuild the soil. Powerful winds whip across the plains, carrying away the loose, dry soil (as happened in the dust bowl of the American Great Plains in the 1930s). A vast productive area can become a wasteland.

Chaparral

Found in places with mild marine climates and winter rains, such as the Mediterranean basin and the southwest coasts of North America, South America, Australia, and the Cape of Africa, the chaparral hosts dry, aromatic, evergreen shrubs and shrubby trees. These plants are adapted to the periodic fires that rage across dry chaparral. Some in fact depend on fire to release their seeds. Others have fire resistant trunks and roots. In places like Southern California, suburban sprawl has overtaken the chaparral, and the inevitable fires sparked in the chaparral take a heavy toll on housing developments.

Desert

Most of the world's deserts are located between 30 degrees North and 30 degrees South latitudes, where the global movement of air masses allows little rain to fall. Lack of moisture is the main factor in shaping deserts; they get fewer than 10 inches (25 centimeters) of rain a year.

Only plants and animals that have evolved devices to conserve water can survive in the desert. Plants often have thick, waterproof outer layers, small leaves to limit the surface area for evaporation, and special hairs that reflect drying sunlight. And since desert animals look to plants for moisture as well as food, many plants are heavily armored or contain toxic substances to deter predators. Many plants have seeds that sprout only after a rain; thus a barren desert can turn miraculously green almost overnight following a storm.

Most desert animals prefer to roam and forage during the cool nights, avoiding the dry heat of the day. And most have metabolisms that conserve water that would be excreted by animals in other habitats.

Although desert plants and animals may thrive in this biome, crops usually do not. Desert soils contain too little water and nitrogen for crops. These can be supplied by irrigation and chemical fertilizers, but these additions are costly and the land usually reverts to desert unless they are meticulously maintained (see "The Aswan High Dam," page 173). Researchers are experimenting with *native* desert crops (see "Jojoba," page 10).

Tropical Rain Forest

Around the equator, in regions with an annual rainfall of about 95 inches (240 centimeters) and a mean annual temperature of 64° F (17° C), cluster areas of one of the world's most diverse habitats, tropical rain forests—the jungles of popular fiction. They once covered much of Central America and South America, central and western Africa, Madagascar, and Southeast Asia, but they are rapidly falling to loggers and developers.

Some trees are enormously tall, about 200 feet (60 meters), and widely spaced, sometimes as much as 1,000 feet (305 meters) apart. Their lofty branches intertwine to form a dense canopy, through which little light penetrates. Unlike the northern conifer or deciduous forests, the rain forests host an amazing number of tree species—more than 20 per acre (50 per hectare) in some places. Since light is screened out by the canopy, there are few shrubs, and trees don't branch below the canopy. Thus one can walk unobstructed through the dimly lit heart of a mature forest. One must look up for the smaller plants; they developed ways to get higher and closer to the light. Vines twine around tree trunks, sending their leaves to the canopy. Epiphytes, which derive their nutrients and moisture from the air, perch on high branches.

The giant trees have shallow root systems that quickly retrieve nutrients from fallen leaves. Thus, unlike temperate forests, the soil is never enriched. Developers in the Amazon basin have found that without protective canopy, the thin soil quickly erodes under the region's heavy rains and cleared tracts turn to wasteland.

The number and diversity of animal species in the rain forest are staggering to biologists accustomed to the temperate zone. In the entire United States, for example, there are about 500 to 600 species of butterflies. That many butterfly species can be found in one remote area of a tropical forest. The rain forests still offer many unnamed species to ambitious taxonomists.

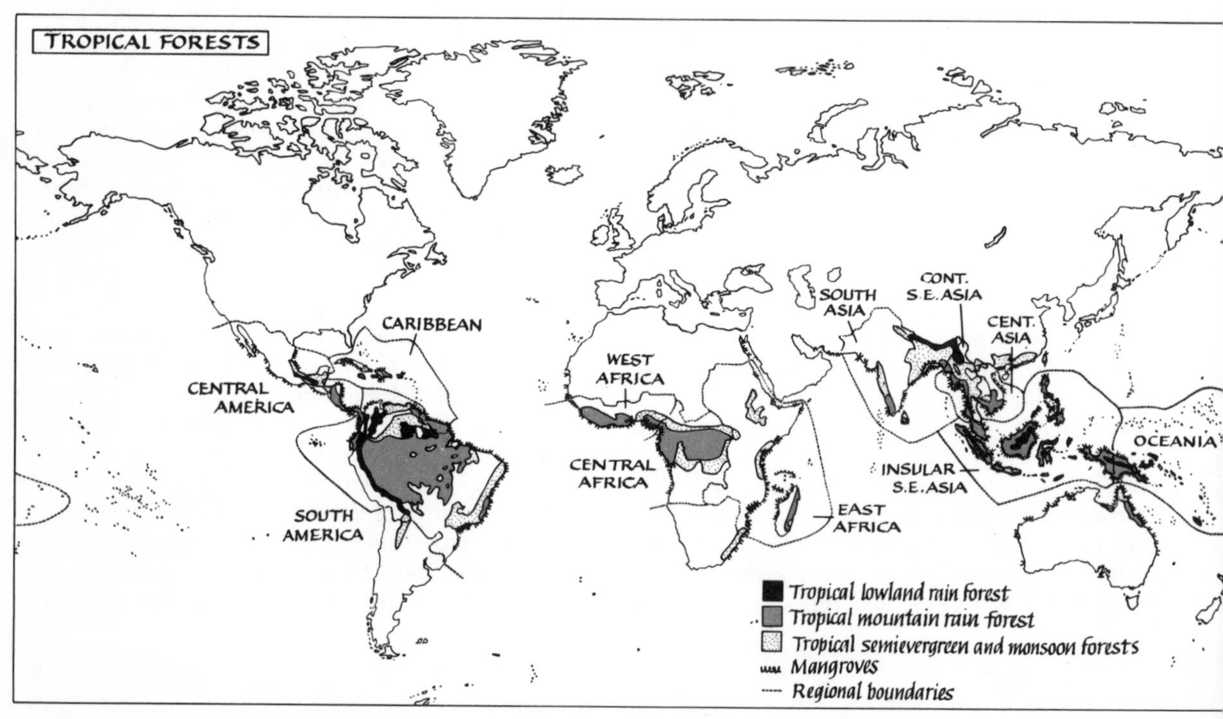

As population and development press on the rain forests, biologists cry out against the loss of this storehouse of diversity, while other scientists warn that the loss of the vast rain forests could alter local and even global climate. (See "Amazonia," page 274, and "Changing Climate," page 19.)

SOIL: KEEPING A LOW PROFILE

Foresters, soil scientists, and some farmers slice into the ground to examine the multihued layers of the soil's "profile." Looking like the layers in an unevenly baked, huge earthen cake, these layers, or "horizons," tell the life story of the soil. Soil scientists have generally classified and mapped soils over most of the world. The soil classification system is modeled on the one developed for plants, with categories from "order" (the broadest group) to "series" (roughly equivalent to species).

Expecting one soil type to perform like another is similar to expecting a lily to perform like an oak; soil types differ as much as plant species and must be treated accordingly. Perhaps because their profiles are hidden and because many developers seldom consider the unique characteristics of an area or consult with ecologists, soil has been much abused. Here are examples of four major soil types and cases in which they have been misunderstood.

Northern Soils (Spodosols)

Under the boreal forest and south of it, in a ring around the Arctic Circle as far south as New England and northern Europe, lie the spodosols, formed from acidic glacial rock. Their upper layers are coarse-grained, allowing water to leach through easily. Spodosols evolve through interaction with the vegetation covering them. As the typically acidic leaves of boreal plants (fir, hemlock, heather) drop to the ground, rainwater carries the acid down through the soil, along the way attracting clay, organic particles, and mineral ions, primarily iron and aluminum, carrying all down to a lower level. This leaves a zone of impoverished soil just below the surface—a starvation zone for new roots attempting to cross it. Minerals may settle at the same level, forming a hardpan layer, which even the strongest roots cannot penetrate, isolating them from water and nutrients below.

Although this leaching (called podzolization) is natural, it can impoverish soil. A classic example is the heathland of Great Britain and other parts of Western Europe. Centuries ago clear-cutting and fires converted forest to heath. Hundreds of years of acid leaching from the heath left a layer of iron pan no root could penetrate. Large trees could no longer grow there.

Desert Soils (Aridisols)

Aridisols, one type of desert soil, are found in areas of northern, central, and southern Africa and South America. About one third of the area covered by aridisols is nonarable (not good for crops) because there is little rainfall. This lack of moisture also prevents the growth of wild vegetation, meaning the soil cannot be enriched by organic matter from decaying plants. Nor do plants shade the soil, helping it retain what moisture there is. The little rainwater that does fall is drawn back to the soil surface and evaporated, leaving a residue of precipitated chemicals, such as calcium and salts.

With sufficient rainfall, aridisols will support enough grass for grazing, and in some cases they can be farmed if irrigated and fertilized. However, because they are dry and contain little organic matter to bind soil particles together, aridisols are highly prone to erosion by wind and occasional floods.

All too often schemes to make the desert into a garden through irrigation have failed because of a poor understanding of desert soils and how they act with water.

For example, after canals were built in Pakistan for irrigation, the water table rose because as much as one third of the channelized water leaked into deeper soil. By 1960, a fifth—over 800,000 acres (2 million hectares)—of the cultivated area in the Indus Plain could no longer produce crop yields equal to previous yields because of either waterlogging or salinity. Desert soils often become saline after irrigation, even if there is very little salt in deeper soils, because the salts are carried to and left in the topsoil as the water moves to the surface to evaporate. Unfortunately, most crops will not tolerate salty soils.

Prairie Soils (Mollisols)

Mollisols and their soil relatives the chernozems form the breadbaskets of North America, central Asia, central Europe, northern China, and Argentina. They have a thick surface layer of organic matter, formed over the ages by layers of decayed prairie grasses, that contains fine, nutrient-binding clay particles trapped by mats of the ancient grass roots. This dark, rich topsoil remains long after the natural vegetation has been destroyed and replaced by crops. Highly productive, mollisols are the world's most fertile soils.

Because the clay and organic matter hold soil particles together, they are more resistant to erosion than lighter soils. But, like all soils, if they're mistreated, disaster follows. In the United States, farmers in the Great Plains suffered from severe erosion during the dust bowl years of the 1930s.

Tropical Rain-Forest Soils (Latosols)

A variety of tropical soils is found in a belt extending about 24 degrees on either side of the equator. One of the most common arises from a limestone base. Latosols (now called oxisols in the U.S. classification system) cover extensive areas in the tropical and subtropical forests of Central America, South America, Southeast Asia, and Africa. In these soils a process similar to the acid leaching of northern soils takes place. The upper layers of latosols are highly porous, allowing nutrients to leach easily through to layers below the reach of plants. However, tropical rainforest trees, surrounded by ample moisture, have no need to penetrate the ground deeply in search of water or nutrients. Their shallow root systems capture rainwater and nutrients from leaf litter as they fall.

But when the rain forest is cleared, the exposed soil loses its input of nutrients from fallen leaves and is exposed to the torrential, seasonal rains of the tropics. As the remaining nutrients and minerals wash downward, the minerals fall out at a certain level where they form a hardpan layer. This process is called "laterization" and the thick layer of mineral-rich red rock that forms is called "laterite."

Schemes to clear-cut huge tracts of the Amazon basin have often proved disastrous. Without its forest cover the impoverished upper layers of the latosol quickly become useless (see "Amazonia," page 274). In some areas erosion has worn away the loose topsoil down to the rocky laterite, leaving a vacant infertile moonscape where once lush jungle thrived.

F.W., M.P.

SOURCE: Adapted from *Ecoscience: Population, Resources, Environment* by Paul R. Ehrlich, Anne H. Ehrlich, and John P. Holdren, W. H. Freeman and Company.

WATER COMMUNITIES

Beneath the surface of the world's oceans, lakes, and rivers lie communities as fascinating and as diverse as those on land. Creatures there live like birds constantly in flight in a three-dimensional world. Some travel long distances, some attach to a rock and never move. Yet the communities of both fresh and salt water are distinct and predictable, depending on the chemistry, depth, and temperature of the water.

Freshwater Communities

Biological communities in freshwater are broadly divided into two groups: those found in running water—rivers and streams—and those found in the standing water of lakes and ponds. Smaller stream creatures depend on nutrients from the land for a great part of their diet, but they can be easily overtaxed by too many nutrients. Most stream animals, from insect larvae to fish, are adapted to a high oxygen level, which is normally the case in running water. They can be seriously threatened by the appearance of oxygen-gulping human wastes in their environment.

Lakes have an intricate seasonal dynamic. All lakes tend to stratify with sun-heated water near the top and colder water along the bottom. As the abundant microscopic creatures of the plankton community in the upper layers die, they drift to the bottom, where, if uneaten by fish, they are decomposed by bacteria into basic nutrients.

As fall turns to winter the surface water cools, becomes heavier, and sinks, mixing the waters, nutrients, and oxygen of the lake. The ice that forms across the lake in winter is lighter than water, but in spring its cold meltwater sinks to the bottom, again forcing a mixing. As long as this cycle is maintained and as long as the lake does not receive excessive nutrients (which cause oxygen-depleting algae blooms), it remains healthy.

Lakes age naturally over thousands of years, gradually filling in with sediment. Human activity along the shores alters the lake balances with eroded soil, sewage, and industrial wastes and greatly speeds the aging process, causing lakes even the size of Lake Erie to choke with nutrients and grow old before their time. Fortunately, the aging process can be slowed if the source of excessive nutrients is cut off.

Fish and other aquatic organisms are adapted to lakes with specific oxygen contents. Sturgeon, trout, whitefish, and salmon, for example, need clean water with plenty of oxygen. They could not survive in the more oxygen-poor lakes and marshes that are the home of carp, catfish, and bass. Two of the most serious problems facing freshwater lakes and streams in the 1980s are toxic chemical pollution and acid rain. Toxic chemicals can affect the breeding cycles and larval stages of freshwater creatures, while acid rain alters water chemistry in a way that native communities cannot tolerate. (See "The Trespassing Poison: Acid Rain," page 186.)

Marine Communities

The ocean, covering about 71 percent of the earth's surface, is the most extensive of the planet's habitats, but like land biomes it is segmented into communities. Most of the ocean is a biological desert. Life is concentrated near shore, along the continental shelves, on the great shoals and reefs, and near upwellings of cold currents that carry nutrients toward the surface from the bottom.

Plankton

The plankton layer that lives in the top few hundred feet or so of the ocean is the most abundant community in the sea, consisting of thousands of species of tiny plants (phytoplankton) and animals (zooplankton). Crustacea, such as shrimp and krill, are examples of the larger planktonic organisms, as are jellyfish and some forms of seaweed. The plankton community is also the temporary home of the tiny larvae of most fish and shellfish. Besides their relatively small, sometimes microscopic sizes, some plankton species are also characterized by their relative immobility, although all zooplankton move in some way. Another trait of the plankton community is the relatively short life span of its members—some plankton live only a few days. Among the species of zooplankton, the most abundant is the tiny copepod. Zoologists estimate that there are more copepods than any other animal in the world.

Plankton are crucial to the food balances of the sea. Phytoplankton trap solar energy and by photosynthesis convert that energy into food for small zooplankton, like copepods, which are in turn food for larger zooplankton, like krill, which are in turn food for fish and larger sea creatures, such as whales. Plankton also support many fixed bottom-dwellers, which comb the passing currents with tentacles to catch tiny organisms gliding by. The type of plankton found in any part of the sea depends on depth, access to light, water temperature, season, even time of day, since all over the world zooplankton migrate toward the surface at dusk. Consequently, plankton communities of the Mediterranean are very dissimilar from those in the South Pacific or the Arctic.

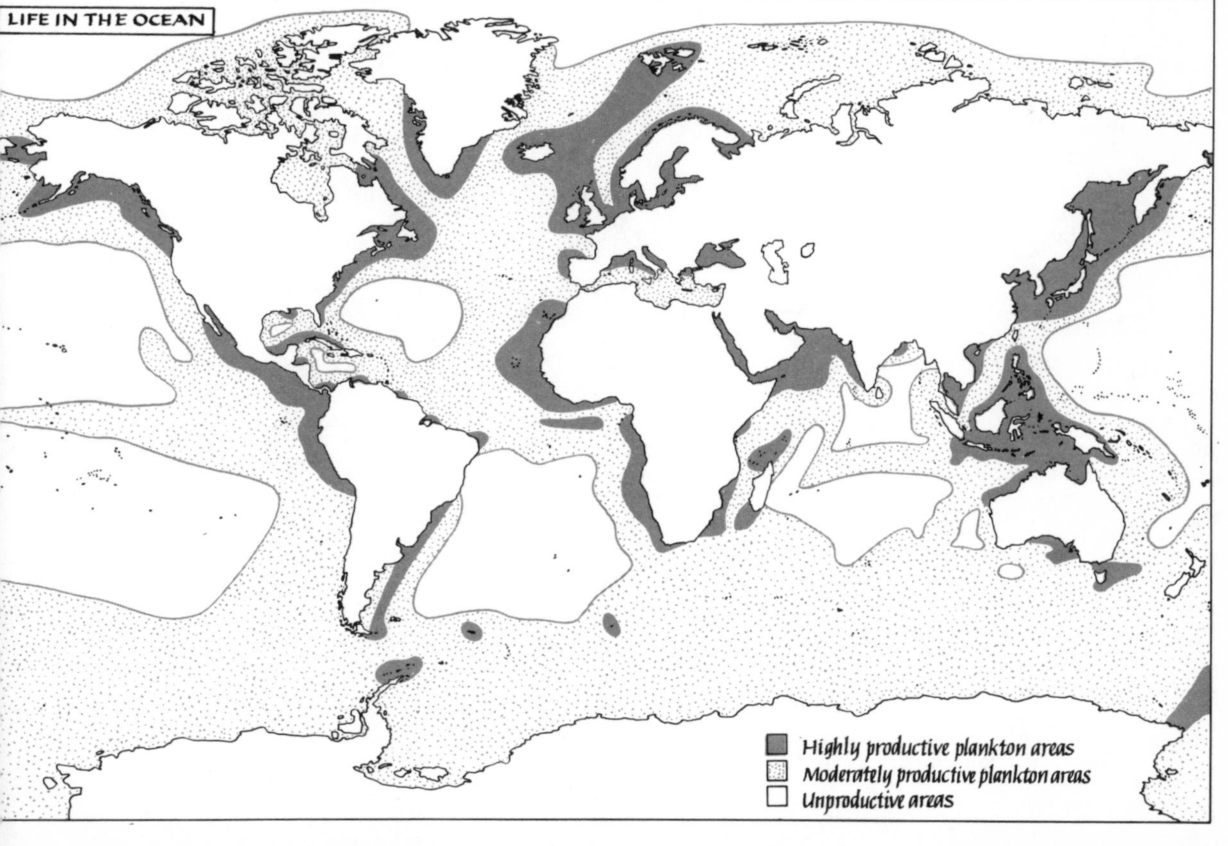

Coral Reefs

Found almost exclusively in subtropical regions where water temperatures are no lower than 64° F (18° C) in winter, the coral reef community is both delicate and diverse. Corals are actually half plant and half animal. The coral polyp, which consists of a sac formed by a double layer of animal cells, designs and deposits about itself a skeleton of calcium carbonate; countless polyps together accumulate their skeletons into great communities growing into a variety of shapes that are efficient for collecting light and food. Each cell of the inner polyp layer contains a single golden-brown alga called a *zooxanthella,* a species of dinoflagellate often known in red-tide organisms. Coral reefs thrive only in low-nutrient areas of the sea where tides, temperatures, and sunlight contribute to the miracle of successful survival in a nutritional desert. (However, if coastal fertilizer runoff increases the nitrogen contact, as on the Great Barrier Reef off Australia, other algae can thrive and displace the corals.)

The symbiotic zooxanthellae avidly consume the animal's waste ammonia and acetate and, with the ample carbon dioxide in seawater, use their photosynthesis skills to produce sugar, glycerol, amino acids, and fats for their hosts. With the efficiency inherent in this tiny closed ecosystem, no nutrients are lost to the clear and barren sea, where it would require too much metabolic work to recover them again. So corals succeed, even without much help from the zooplankton that swarm past their grasping polyps every night. The metabolic success of the coral provides energy for bacteria, clams, and commensal crustaceans, and for the myriads of gorgeous tiny fishes.

The coral skeletons, like apartment houses, create a full community of niches—crevices, shelves, and tunnels—that attract countless animals, which distribute themselves among the reefs at various levels, with low-level dwellers depending for food on what sifts and filters down from above.

Reef areas attract thousands of tourists annually all over the world because of the extraordinary ranges of color and shape found in the coral formations themselves and in the living animal community. Deep-water fish, such as sharks and barracudas, prowl the reef edges like trespassing hunters looking for prey.

Resilient as coral communities are, they are particularly vulnerable to water contamination. Since they survive by absorbing nutrients from the passing currents, almost like a giant, complex sponge, coral reefs quickly assimilate poisonous substances floating in the sea, and they can be

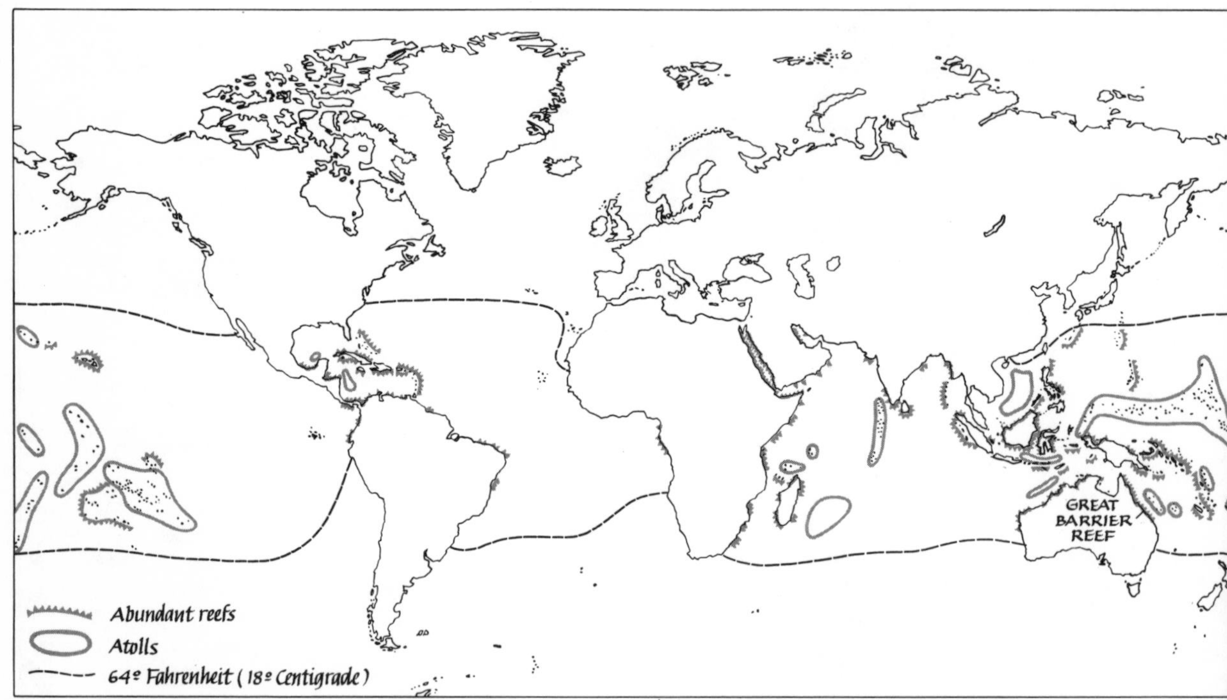

Coral reefs and atolls are rarely found in areas where the water temperature dips below 64° F (18° C) in the winter.

choked by the blanket of silt that usually accompanies heavy shoreline development.

Kelp Beds

These underwater forests consist of masses of large, cold-water algal plants known as kelp, commonly called seaweed. The largest plants in the sea, kelps grow as much as 1 foot (30 centimeters) per day by absorbing seaborne nutrients from the surrounding water, thus eliminating the need for roots, upon which most land plants depend for food. The rootlike series of shoots at the base of kelp columns are actually anchoring devices called holdfasts, which cling to a bottom rock.

Because the plants compete for light with each other, they grow in dense stands that provide animals with hiding places and attract fish, snails, crustacea, worms, mollusks, and other marine organisms. Marine biologists compare the diversity of kelp-bed animal life to a tropical rain forest on land, with each species occupying its niche. Reaching 30 to 80 feet (about 10 to 25 meters), the upper levels of kelp support smaller creatures, like snails and worms, while along the seafloor, bottom fish thrive. On the perimeters of these undersea forests hover such predators as sharks, sea otters, and seals.

Kelp-bed balances are sometimes easily destroyed. Sewage pumped into the sea along the coast of California during the 1960s caused a population explosion among bottom-dwelling sea urchins, which fed not only on the sewage but on kelp holdfasts. The mass of urchins consumed miles of holdfasts, and this, combined with natural stress factors such as temperature and salinity over the previous ten-year period, released 100-foot-long (30-meter) kelp columns that washed to shore. Hundreds of acres of kelp were eliminated, along with the animal life they supported.

Underwater kelp canopies are known to concentrate metals from pollutants, such as cadmium, and they are extremely susceptible to oil slicks.

Intertidal Zones

As the tides rise and fall, they nourish and sustain a marine community unique to the tidal cycle. The elements of the intertidal community are familiar ones—the "sticky" plants that drape beach rocks, the rounded, water-hewn rocks and pebbles themselves, beach sands, the pools of water left behind when the tide washes out, and the myriad creatures that are adapted to live where there are daily extremes of high and low water, changes in temperature, salinity, dryness, and submersion, sand and rocks, fierce waves and gentle washings. It is a community of clingers, like barnacles, and burrowers, like clams. There are armored creatures as well, like the crabs. Certain small, near-shore fish feed off the tiny creatures in the tidal pools, and there is a thriving scavenger group to clean up the debris of animals that have been thrown against rocks, caught under them, or in some other way been victim of the transitions of this environment. The intertidal community is extremely susceptible to the intrusion of people, since it is the marine habitat nearest and most accessible to them, as well as to man-made debris and pollutants, which tides carry and deposit on shore.

Open Sea and Mid-Water

The difference between the quantity of life supported by coastal waters and by the open sea has been compared to the difference on land between a forest and a desert. The various open-ocean species, like the sleek shark, tuna, and barracuda, are well suited for long-distance travel, a necessary adaptation given the relative dispersal of food in their environment. Without the constant nutrient replenishment provided by coastal upwellings, the open oceans support far less biological diversity.

The mid-water areas are the sections of the water column where light penetration is weak, at about 600 feet (about 200 meters). In this transitional zone between surface and abyss, the salinity and temperature of seawater are relatively constant, but food is scarce because of reduced photosynthesis. Very low temperatures prevail below about 300 feet (about 100 meters), and currents tend to be slower. Special trawling equipment has been developed to drag these mid-water areas for fish such as tuna, which swim freely from upper levels to mid-water.

Abyss

The ocean realm below 12,100 feet (3,700 meters) accounts for 90 to 95 percent of the ocean. Marked by incredible pressures, near total darkness, and frigid cold, the abyssal plains, rises, and trenches are essentially unchanging environments, where even the currents move slowly (some at speeds of only inches per hour). Temperatures do not rise above approximately 39° F (4° C), even at the equator. There is no seasonal variation, no light except for the photophores of passing fishes or invertebrates.

Yet despite the cold and darkness, the abyss

sustains an extremely diverse animal population about which very little is known. Many of the denizens have their own bodily lighting systems, similar to that of fireflies. Because comparatively little food drifts down to such depths, bottom-dwelling creatures have evolved sensory mechanisms for discerning food at long distances. Occasionally parts of trees or other shore-based debris will be carried down into the abyss, or a mammal carcass will sink to the bottom, but usually there is little intrusion of surface life. It is theorized that much of the abyssal community survives on the sparse rain of detritus and fecal pellets that descend from surface communities.

The animals that dwell in the abyss have extremely low metabolic rates, and many have extraordinarily long life spans, but most are probably very small. Marine biologists have cataloged inch-long (2.5-centimeter) mollusks that tests showed to be at least 250 years old. Some deep-water life can be found in habitat bands that extend around the world across deep ocean waters—animals collected off the African coast have also been observed off Western Europe. Some abyssal water habitats, however, seem from preliminary investigation to have distinctive local flora and fauna that do not extend beyond the specific area.

In 1979, scientists from Woods Hole Oceanographic Institution discovered previously unknown forms of life in deep trenches off the Galápagos Islands in the Pacific. Clustered around cracks in the earth's crust that spew hot springs rich in minerals (see "Hot Brines," page 11) were communities of giant tube worms and other bottom-dwellers whose food chain appeared to rely on a process called chemosynthesis. While most other known forms of life on earth rely in some way on the fact that plants, through photosynthesis, can turn the sun's energy into food, it appears that in the depths, deprived of light, microorganisms have evolved processes for oxidizing minerals to derive energy for production of food without the sun.

Throughout all of human history, people have done very little damage to the remote communities of the abyssal sea, but that could change in the future as industries enter the deep ocean in search of mineral wealth (see "Manganese Nodules," page 13), or as the deep ocean is used as a dump for noxious wastes.

M.P., P.D.

SOURCE: Adapted from *Ecoscience: Population, Resources, Environment* by Paul R. Ehrlich, Anne H. Ehrlich, and John P. Holdren, W. H. Freeman and Company. Copyright © 1977.

ANIMAL NOTES

The most amazing aspect of life on earth is its diversity. If you can conceive of any way of eating, hunting, moving, perceiving, reproducing, sensing, there is probably a creature somewhere that does it. Humans, sitting atop the evolutionary pyramid, sometimes tend to be smug, forgetting that some creatures do certain things with greater facility than we do. We sometimes think of creatures only in terms of how they can be useful to us, and we miss the chance to explore their fascinating worlds.

The following is a smattering of random items about nonhuman living things.

- The phylum Arthropoda, comprising insects, spiders, crustaceans, and their kin, accounts for four fifths of all known animal species. About 90 percent of these are insects. There are about twenty times as many insects as all of the higher animals. The weight of the insect population is estimated to exceed that of the human population by a factor of twelve! Some scientists claim that Earth is not the planet of humans but of insects.
- A bird sees everything at once in total focus. Whereas the human eye is globular and must adjust to varying distances, most birds have flat eyes that take in everything in a single glance.
- The bird with the largest population in the world is the red-billed quelea (*Quelea quelea*) of Africa. These birds are known to farmers as "feathered locusts" because they travel in flocks of millions, devastating farm fields. The most recent estimate places their population at approximately 10 billion. The only other bird known to have approached this population was the passenger pigeon of North America, which numbered approximately 9 billion in 1840. After eighty years of hunting by humans, however, the passenger pigeon became extinct. (See "Animals You'll Never See," page 333.)
- A robin has about 3,000 feathers. (Even more amazing: Somebody counted them.)
- Scientists discover between 7,000 and 10,000 new insect species every year. (These aren't *new* species, of course; we just didn't know about them before.)
- Insects can perceive a range of light far greater than that discernible by humans. Most insects, for instance, can see ultraviolet light, and many species of beetles can see infrared. Since an insect's eyes are made up of thousands of tiny

six-sided lenses, it does not perceive a single image but sees a staggering number of separate images that would appear to us as a colossal mosaic.

- Insects have lived on earth about 350 million years, compared with about 2 million years for humans.
- A tuna can swim 100 miles (160 kilometers) or more in a single day.
- A species of starfish known as the *Linckia columbiae* can grow an entire new body from a single severed piece of its body less than a half-inch (1.3 centimeters) long.
- The colorful tilefish (*Lopholatilus chamaeleonticeps,* which means "the crested tilus with a head like a chameleon") lives in caves along a narrow band of the continental slope off the east coast of North America. The species suffered one of the major disasters in fish history when an estimated 1.5 billion of them died in 1882. One ship captain reported sailing through waters littered solidly with dead tilefish for 69 miles (111 kilometers). The cause of the tragedy? Scientists theorize that the fish died because the warm Gulf Stream shifted slightly out to sea that year.
- The blowfish, or puffer, found along the coasts of North America and Japan, represents a special challenge to seafood chefs. Although its flesh is tasty, its liver, air bladder, and gonads contain tetrodotoxin, a deadly posion. The same species may be edible in one location and poisonous in another. Although a special school trains Japanese chefs in how to prepare *fugu,* or Pacific puffer, about two dozen deaths occur in Japan each year because of unfortunate mistakes.
- One hundred new species of fish are discovered every year. There are 2,000 species of fish in the Amazon Basin alone, equivalent to one tenth of the world's species.
- Sand crabs are male for the first two years of life, when they mate with older females. At the age of two, they become female and lay eggs.
- When a sea cucumber is threatened by a predator, it is able to shed its intestines and stomach as a distracting ploy. The organs eventually grow back.
- Certain squids have the largest eye in nature—up to 16 inches (41 centimeters) across.
- The shrimp *Acantephyra,* which lives in utter darkness 8,000 feet (2,438 meters) below the surface of the Atlantic, releases clouds of luminescent blue "ink" to distract its enemies.
- The male paper nautilus puts his reproductive organ into a female's mantle pouch, breaks it off, and grows a new one.
- A catfish can taste with its tail.
- Sponges have great regenerative power. After a sponge has been mashed up and strained through cheesecloth, its cells can regroup to form a new sponge.
- During World War II, it was discovered that one croak from a single toad fish was enough to detonate a certain kind of acoustic mine.
- The red sea urchin can drill holes in rock, concrete, and even steel pilings.
- Sharks may have no sense of pain, since fatally wounded sharks have been seen eating their own entrails.
- Yellowfin tuna can travel 45 miles (72 kilometers) per hour at top speed.
- A jellyfish found in the Arctic Ocean, *Cyanea arctica,* grows to 8 feet (2.4 meters) across and has tentacles 200 feet (61 meters) long.

SOURCES: Bernard L. Gordon, *The Secret Lives of Fishes,* Grosset & Dunlap, 1977; *Audubon Magazine; Sport Diver Magazine;* David Louis, *More Fascinating Facts,* Crown Publishers, 1979.

PLANT NOTES

- Seeds of the leguminous Arctic lupine found frozen in northern Canada, and estimated to be 10,000 years old, have been successfully planted and grown by scientists. The seeds of the lotus plant will sometimes germinate after 200 years.
- One of the fastest-growing plants on earth is the yucca kelp (*Macrocystis pyrifera*), which can grow 14 to 16 inches (36 to 41 centimeters) a day and reach 200 feet (61 meters).
- The world's tallest tree is the coast redwood (*Sequoia sempervirens*), which can reach a height of 300 feet (91 meters) or more. The largest redwood, 367.8 feet (112 meters) tall, began its life in 1393, almost a hundred years before Columbus sailed for the New World.
- Although the sequoia is the tallest plant, the *oldest* is the bristlecone pine of the American West; some exceed 7,000 years in age. The shortest life span of any living creature is thought to be that of the colon bacterium *Escherichia coli,* which divides under favorable conditions in twenty minutes. The smallest mammal, at about 0.08 ounce (2.3 grams), is the pygmy shrew, while the nearly extinct blue whale is the largest at about 150 tons.

- There are an estimated 80,000 edible plants on earth, although humankind has used only about 3,000 for food. Only 50 have been cultivated on any major scale, and only 12 of these currently supply 90 percent of the world's food.
- Phytoplankton, the tiny plants living in the upper layers of the sea, produce most of the oxygen in the atmosphere. Their abundance is illustrated by a measurement in the North Atlantic that found more than 12 million individual algal cells in only a cubic foot (0.03 cubic meter) of seawater.
- The skunk cabbage grows so fast it gets warm.
- Sea beans float for months until they find a beach with a freshwater stream where they can sprout and grow to huge vines of *Entada scandens,* producing 4-foot (1.2-meter) bean pods with pocketwatch-sized beans.

SOURCES: *Ocean World of Jacques-Yves Cousteau,* Grolier Enterprises, 1975; John L. Culliney, *The Forests of the Sea,* Sierra Club, 1976; David Louis, *More Fascinating Facts,* Crown Publishers, 1979; Natural Resources Defense Council.

WATER CONTENT OF VARIOUS ANIMALS

Animal		*Percentage of Body Weight*
Jellyfish		95
Codfish		82
Earthworm		80
Lobster		79
Blowfly		79
Frog		78
Chicken		74
Herring		67
Mammals, total body		65
blood	83%	
brain	80	
muscle	75	
skin	70	
bone	30	
fat	10	
Cockroach		61
Flour beetle		59
Bean weevil		48

SOURCE: Knut Schmidt-Nielsen, *Animal Physiology*, 2nd edition, © 1964, p. 48. Reprinted by permission of Prentice-Hall, Inc., Englewood Cliffs, New Jersey.

EXTINCT BIRDS

Bird	*Location*	*Year or Century of Extinction*
△ OSTRICHES		
Arabian ostrich *Struthio camelus syriacus*	Saudi Arabia	20
△ EMUS		
Tasmanian emu *Dromaius novaehollandiae diemenensis*	Tasmania	19
Kangaroo Island emu *Dromaius novaehollandiae diemeniamus*	Kangaroo Island	19
△ PETRELS		
Guadalupe storm petrel *Oceanodroma macrodactyla*	Guadalupe	20
△ CORMORANTS		
Spectacled cormorant *Phalacrocorax perspicillatus*	Bering Island	1852
△ HAWKS		
Guadalupe Island caracara *Polyborus lutosus*	Guadalupe	1900
△ HERONS		
Bonin night heron *Nycticorax caledonicus crassirostris*	Bonin Islands	1889
△ DUCKS		
Indian pink-headed duck *Rhodonessa caryophyllacea*	India	1940
Coues's gadwall *Anas strepera couesi*	Washington Island	19
Labrador duck *Camptorhynchus labradorius*	Eastern North America	1875

Bird	Location	Year or Century of Extinction
Auckland Island merganser *Mergus australis*	Auckland Islands	1901
Crested shelduck *Tadorna cristata*	Korea	1916
△ QUAILS AND PARTRIDGES		
New Zealand quail *Coturnix novae-zelandiae novae-zelandiae*	New Zealand	19
Himalaya quail *Ophrysia superciliosa*	Himalaya	19
Heath hen *Tympanuchus cupido cupido*	Eastern U.S.A.	1932
△ CUCKOOS		
Delalande's Madagascar Coucal *Coua delalandei*	Madagascar	20
△ RAILS		
Red-billed rail *Rallus pacificus*	Tahiti	19
Jamaica wood rail *Amaurolimnas concolor concolor*	Jamaica	1881
Chatham Island banded rail *Rallus dieffenbachii*	Chatham Island	19
Wake Island rail *Rallus wakensis*	Wake Island	20
Auckland Island rail *Rallus muelleri*	Auckland Islands	19
Chatham Island rail *Cabalus modestus*	Chatham Island	19
Laysan Island rail *Porzanula palmeri*	Laysan Island	20
Hawaiian rail *Pennula sandwichensis*	Hawaii	19
Kusaie Island crake *Aphanolimnas monasa*	Kusaie Island	19
Fiji bar-winged rail *Nesoclopeus poeciloptera*	Viti Levu	20
Samoa wood rail *Pareudiastes pacificus*	Samoa	20
Mauritian rail *Aphanapteryx bonasia*	Mauritius	17
Iwo Jima rail *Poliolimnas cinereus brevipes*	Iwo Jima	20
Tristan Island Gallinule *Gallinula nesiotis nesiotis*	Tristan da Cunha	19
White swamp hen *Porphyrio albus*	Lord Howe Island	19
△ SHOREBIRDS		
Tahitian sandpiper *Prosobonia leucoptera*	Tahiti	19
Eskimo curlew *Numenius borealis*	North America	20
△ AUKS		
Great auk *Alca impennis*	North Atlantic	1844
△ PIGEONS		
Mauritius blue pigeon *Alectroenas nitidissima*	Mauritius	18
New Zealand pigeon *Hemiphaga novaeseelandiae spadicea*	Norfolk Island	19
Choiseul crested pigeon *Microgoura meeki*	Choiseul Island	20
Passenger pigeon *Ectopistes migratorius*	Eastern North America	1914

Bird	Location	Year or Century of Extinction
Puerto Rican blue pigeon *Columba inornata wetmorei*	Puerto Rico	20
Bonin wood pigeon *Columba versicolor*	Bonin Islands	20
Dodo *Raphus cucullatus*	Mauritius	17
△ PARROTS		
Norfolk Island parrot *Nestor meridionalis productus*	Norfolk Island	19
Guadalupe parrot *Amazona violacea*	Guadalupe	18
Culebra Island parrot *Amazona vittata graciliceps*	Culebra Island	20
Cuba red macaw *Ara tricolor*	Cuba	19
Puerto Rico Conure *Aratinga chloroptera maugei*	Puerto Rico	19
Carolina parakeet *Conuropsis carolinensis*	Southeastern U.S.A.	20
Mascarene parrot *Mascarinus mascarinus*	Réunion	19
Seychelles Alexandrine parakeet *Psittacula eupatria wardi*	Seychelles	19
Rodriguez ring-necked parakeet *Psittacula krameri exsul*	Rodriguez	20
Mauritius broad-billed parrot *Lophopsittacus mauritianus*	Mauritius	17
Rodriguez parakeet *Necropsittacus rodericanus*	Rodriguez	17
New Caledonian lorikeet *Vini diadema*	New Caledonia	20
Lord Howe Island kakariki *Cyanoramphus novaezelandiae subflavescens*	Lord Howe Island	19
Macquarie Island kakariki *Cyanoramphus novaezelandiae erythrotis*	Macquarie Island	20
Tahiti parakeet *Cyanoramphus zelandicus*	Tahiti	19
Raiatea parakeet *Cyanoramphus ulietanus*	Society Islands	18
△ OWLS		
Rodriguez little owl *Athene murivora*	Rodriguez	17
Guadalupe burrowing owl *Speotyto cunicularia guadeloupensis*	Maria Galante Island	19
Antigua burrowing owl *Speotyto cunicularia amaura*	Antigua and Nevis Islands	19
North Island laughing owl *Sceloglaux albifacies rufifacies*	New Zealand	19
Seychelles Island owl *Otus insularis*	Seychelles	20
△ NIGHTHAWKS		
Puerto Rican nighthawk *Caprimulgus vociferus noctitherus*	Puerto Rico	20
Jamaica Pauraque *Siphonornis americanus americanus*	Jamaica	19
△ KINGFISHERS		
Ryukyu kingfisher *Halcyon miyakoensis*	Miyako Island	19
△ WOODPECKERS		
Guadalupe red-shafted flicker *Colaptes cafer rufipileus*	Guadalupe	20

Bird	Location	Year or Century of Extinction
△ PASSERINES		
Stephen Island wren *Xenicus lyalli*	Stephen Island (New Zealand)	20
Guadalupe wren *Troglodytes musculus guadeloupensis*	Guadalupe	20
Martinique wren *Troglodytes musculus martinicensis*	Martinique	20
Guadalupe Bewick's wren *Thyromanes bewickii brevicauda*	Guadalupe	19
Lord Howe grey-headed blackbird *Turdus poliocephalus vinitinctus*	Lord Howe Island	20
Raiatea thrush *Turdus ulietensis*	Society Islands	18
Kittlitz's thrush *Zoothera terrestris*	Bonin Islands	20
Lanai thrush *Phaeornis obscurus lanaiensis*	Lanai Island	20
Molokai thrush *Phaeornis obscurus rutha*	Molokai Island	20
Oahu thrush *Phaeornis obscurus oahensis*	Oahu Island	20
Laysan millerbird *Acrocephalus familiaris familiaris*	Laysan Island	20
Chatham Island fernbird *Bowdleria rufescens*	Pitt Island	19
Long-legged warbler *Trichocichla rufa*	Viti Levu	19
Eyrean grass-wren *Amytornis goyderi*	Australia	20
Lord Howe Island grey warbler *Gergyone igata insularis*	Lord Howe Island	19
Tongatabu Tahiti flycatcher *Pomarea nigra tabuensis*	Tahiti	20
Lord Howe Island flycatcher *Rhipidura flabellifera cervina*	Lord Howe Island	19
Chatham Island bellbird *Anthornis melanura melanocephala*	Chatham Island	19
Kioea *Chaetoptila angustipluma*	Hawaii	19
Oahu oo *Moho apicalis*	Hawaii	19
Hawaii oo *Moho nobilis*	Hawaii	20
Molokai oo *Moho bishopi*	Hawaii	20
Lord Howe Island white-eye *Zosterops strenua*	Lord Howe Island	20
Hawaiian honey-creepers: 16 forms *Drepaniidae*	Hawaii	19-20
Guadalupe rufous-sided towhee *Pipilo erythrophthalmus consobrinus*	Guadalupe	19
Bonin Island grosbeak *Chaunoproctus ferreirostris*	Bonin Islands	19
St. Christopher bullfinch *Loxigilla portoricensis grandis*	St. Christopher Island	20
Darwin's ground-finch *Geospiza magnirostris magnirostris*	Galapagos	19
Sao Thomé grosbeak weaver *Neospiza concolor*	Sao Thomé Island	19
Réunion fody *Foudia bruante*	Réunion	18
Bourbon crested starling *Fregilupus varius*	Réunion	19

Bird	*Location*	*Year or Century of Extinction*
Lord Howe Island starling *Aplonis fuscus hullianus*	Lord Howe Island	20
Kusaie starling *Aplonis corvina*	Kusaie Island (Caroline Islands)	20
Mysterious starling *Aplonis mavornata*	Society Islands	19
Huia *Heteralocha acutirostris*	New Zealand	20

SOURCE: Vinzenz Ziswiler, *Extinct and Vanishing Animals*. Revised English edition by Fred and Pille Bunnell.

EXTINCT MAMMALS

Mammal	*Location*	*Year or Century of Extinction*
△ MARSUPIALS		
Freckled marsupial mouse *Antechinus apicalis*	Australia	20
Eastern barred bandicoot *Perameles fasciata*	Australia	20
Western barred bandicoot *Perameles myosura myosura*	Australia	20
Gaimard's rat-kangaroo *Bettongia gaimardi*	Australia	20
Gilbert's rat-kangaroo *Potorous gilberti*	Australia	19
Broad-faced rat-kangaroo *Potorous platyops*	Australia	20
Toolach wallaby *Wallabia greyi*	Australia	20
Tasmanian wolf *Thylacinus cynocephalus*	Tasmania	20
△ INSECTIVORES		
Antillean insectivores: 6 forms *Nesophontidae*	Antilles	17-19
Christmas Island musk-shrew *Crocidura fuliginosa trichura*	Christmas Island	20
△ BATS		
7 forms	West Indies	19-20
△ LEMURS		
Hairy-eared mouse lemur *Cheirogaleus trichotis*	Madagascar	19
△ RODENTS		
Spiny rats: 15 forms *Echimyidae*	Antilles	17-20
Hamsterlike rodents: 8 forms *Cricetidae*	Antilles	17-20
Old World rats: 3 forms *Muridae*	Malay Archipelago and Australia	20
Giant rats: 2 forms *Dinomyidae*	Central America and Antilles	19
△ SEA COWS		
Steller's sea cow *Hydrodamalis gigas*	Bering Island	1768
△ CARNIVORES		
Sea mink *Mustela macrodon*	Northeast coast of the U.S.A.	19

Mammal	*Location*	*Year or Century of Extinction*
Grizzly bear: 17 races *Ursus horribilis*	North America	19-20
Atlas bear *Ursus crowtheri*	North Africa	19
Long-eared kit fox *Vulpes macrotis macrotis*	Southern U.S.A.	19
Japanese wolf *Canis hodophilax*	Japan	20
Antarctic wolf *Dusicyon australis*	Falkland Islands	19
Newfoundland wolf *Canis lupus beothucus*	Newfoundland	20
Florida wolf *Canis niger niger*	Florida	20
Eastern cougar *Felix concolor couguar*	Eastern U.S.A.	20
European lion *Panthera leo europaea*	Greece	1-2
Cape lion *Panthera leo melanochaitus*	South Africa	1865
Barbary lion *Panthera leo barbarus*	North Africa	1922
△ HORSES AND RELATIVES (Perissodactyla)		
Syrian wild ass *Equus hemionus hemippus*	Syria, Persia	1927
Algerian wild ass *Equus asinus atlanticus*	North Africa	?
Quagga *Equus quagga*	South Africa	1878
Burchell's zebra *Equus burchelli burchelli*	South Africa	20
△ CATTLE AND RELATIVES (Ariodactyla)		
Arizona wapiti *Cervus canadensis merriami*	Arizona	1906
Eastern wapiti *Cervus canadensis canadensis*	Eastern U.S.A.	19
Schomburgk's deer *Rucervus schomburgki*	Siam	20
Badlands bighorn sheep *Ovis canadensis auduboni*	American middle west	20
Pyrenean ibex *Capra pyrenaica pyrenaica*	Pyrenees	1910
Portuguese ibex *Capra pyrenaica lusitanica*	Western Pyrenees	1892
Rufous gazelle *Gazella rufina*	Algeria	20
Blue buck *Hippotragus leucophaeus*	South Africa	19
Bubal hartebeest *Alcelaphus alcelaphus*	North Africa	20
Aurochs *Bos primigenius*	Europe	1627
Eastern bison *Bison bison pennsylvanicus*	North America	1825
Oregon bison *Bison bison oregonus*	North America	19
Caucasian wisent *Bison bonasus caucasicus*	Caucasus	1930

SOURCE: Vinzenz Ziswiler, *Extinct and Vanishing Animals.* Revised English edition by Fred and Pille Bunnell. Copyright © 1967 by Springer-Verlag New York, Inc.

THE VITAL STATISTICS OF FOOD

Food is obviously essential to human life, and the threat of not having enough to eat is very real to more than a billion people. Indeed, 700 million people are dangerously undernourished. The following tables, maps, and charts provide an overall picture of the world food situation. The surprise for readers in the developed countries may be the significance of grain in the world diet. Meat is clearly a luxury, not a necessity. There is very little equality in the world food picture. The world's wealthiest people eat almost twice as much as the poorest, although we all need about the same amount. (For more information on food see the chapter on "Eating, Drinking, Breathing," page 589.)

WORLD CROP PRODUCTION* 1,000 METRIC TONS

(1 metric ton=1.102 tons)

	1978
Wheat	441,474
Rice	376,448
Barley	196,123
Maize	362,971
Rye	32,389
Oats	50,463
Millet	37,699
Sorghum	69,117
Roots & tubers (total)	522,947
Potatoes	272,975
Sweet potatoes	99,780
Cassava	119,374
Pulses (total)	62,008
Dry beans	17,224
Dry broad beans	11,702
Coconuts	98
Copra	5,032
Tung oil	98
Palm kernels	1,602
Dry peas	16,351
Chick-peas	6,889
Lentils	1,219
Soybeans	80,232
Groundnuts in shell	18,877
Castor beans	921
Sunflower seed	12,705
Rapeseed	10,186
Sesame seed	1,974
Linseed	2,758
Safflower seed	1,101
Seed Cotton	37,792
Cottonseed	1,770
Olives	9,345

(*USDA/Erwin W. Cole*)

	1978
Olive Oil	1,770
Dry onions	18,243
Garlic	2,111
Green beans	2,429
Green peas	4,551
Palm oil	4,029
Hempseed	24,406
Cabbages	32,098
Artichokes	1,254
Tomatoes	47,087
Cauliflowers	4,283
Pumpkins Squash Gourds	4,885
Cucumbers & gherkins	9,819
Eggplants	4,031
Green chilies & peppers	5,999
Citrus fruits	895
Oranges & tangerines, etc.	41,146
Lemons & limes	4,645
Grapefruit & pomelos	4,228
Avocados	1,284
Mangoes	13,782
Pineapples	6,836
Bananas	36,892
Carrots	10,073
Waterlemons	23,635
Cantaloupes & other melons	5,864
Grapes	56,030
Wine	28,641

	1978
Raisins	882
Dates	2,664
Sugarcane	781,291
Sugar beets	289,080
Apples	31,280
Pears	7,651
Peaches & nectarines	6,787
Plums	5,241
Currants	427
Almonds	830
Pistachios	76
Hazelnuts	504
Cashew nuts	498
Chestnuts	501
Walnuts	785
Plantains	20,391
Papayas	1,514
Strawberries	15,644
Raspberries	236
Apricots	1,584
Coffee, green	4,583
Cocoa beans	4,755
Tea	1,833
Hops	111

SOURCE: *Production Yearbook*, U.N. Food and Agriculture Organization, 1978.

*The FAO estimates that a minimum of 10 percent of all food harvested is lost to rodents, viruses, and other causes of spoilage.

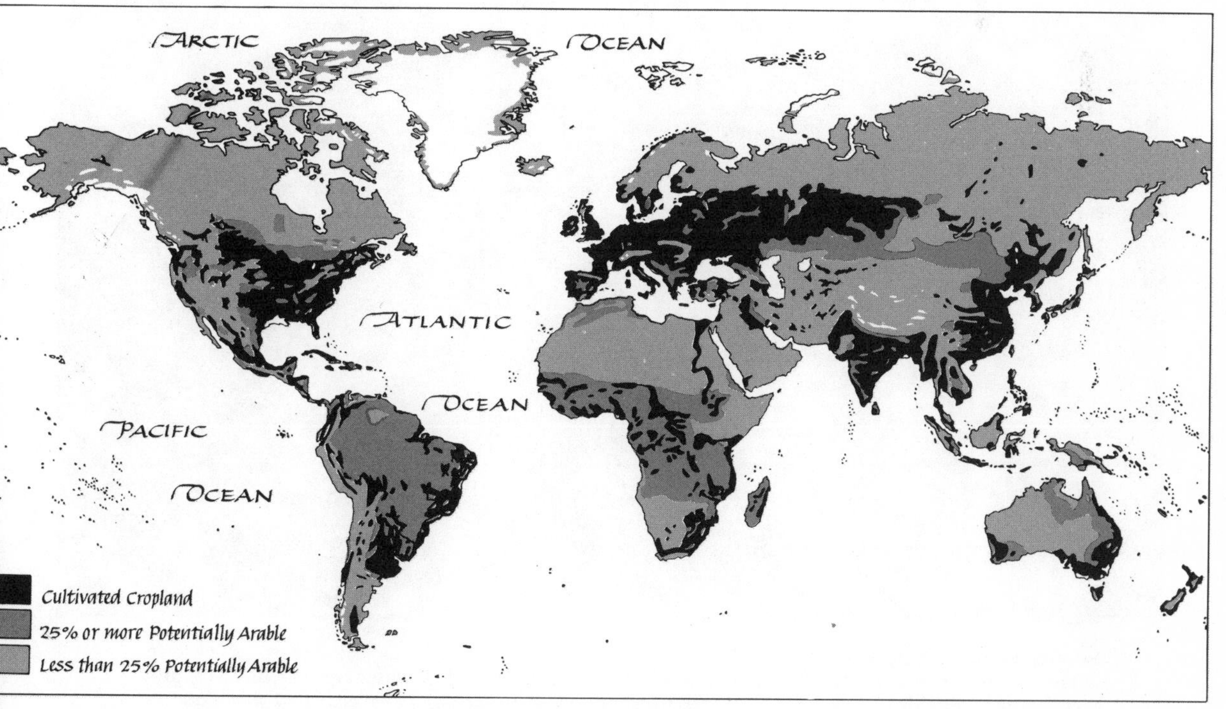

World's productive and potentially productive land.

THE WORLD'S LIVESTOCK

			Livestock Products (1,000 metric tons)
Horses	61,639	All meat	133,438
Mules	11,725	Beef & Veal	46,796
Asses	42,313	Buffalo meat	1,345
Cattle	1,213,092	Mutton & lamb	5,515
Buffaloes	132,425	Goat meat	1,809
Camels	16,991	Pig meat	49,168
Pigs	731,799	Horse meat	525
Sheep	1,055,697	Poultry meat	25,828
Goats	435,352	Cow milk, whole, fresh	415,275
Chickens	6,467,758	Buffalo milk	27,930
Ducks	132,887	Sheep milk	7,328
Turkeys	90,529	Goat milk	6,968
		Cheese	10,483
		Butter & ghee	6,971
		Evapoarted & condensed milk	4,591
		Hen eggs	25,665
		Other eggs	371
		Honey	966
		Fish (1977)	71,898

SOURCE: *Production Yearbook*, U.N. Food and Agriculture Organization, 1978.

Bororo nomadic cattlemen water their zebu cattle at a borehole in the desert of eastern Niger. Tribes in the region engage in a never-ending search for water for themselves and their cattle. Wells drilled as part of Western development programs have provided new sources of water in some areas, but have also brought with them new problems. (*FAO/Banoun/Caracciolo*)

FISH

Fish supply about 13 percent of the world's animal protein—twice as much as eggs and three times as much as poultry. While fewer than 60 million people consume more than two thirds of the world's meat and dairy products, fish are the primary source of animal protein for more than half the world's people. In countries such as Portugal, Japan, India, Chile, and Norway, fish are a crucial part of the diet.

Even in the meat-eating countries fish are important because of the extensive use of fish meal as food for livestock. Only about 35 percent of the total world fish harvest is actually consumed directly by humans. More than 30 percent is used for other purposes that include oil and fertilizer as well as livestock meal. Although fish meal does ultimately contribute to our food supply, feeding fish to livestock is a very inefficient use of protein (see "Meatfacts," page 591). Fish do not provide the answer to world hunger—especially if we continue to destroy their breeding grounds through shoreline development, industrial waste, and offshore oil drilling—but they can play an important role in feeding the world if we make better use of them as a direct source of human food.

WORLD FISH CATCH

Species	*Catch in Metric Tons*
Herring, sardines, anchovies, etc.	13,744,543
Cod, hake, haddock, etc.	11,835,492
Redfish, bass, etc.	4,851,018
Mackerel, billfish, etc.	3,558,760
Jack, mullet, etc.	3,518,503
Salmon, trout, etc.	2,826,398
Tuna, bonita, etc.	1,920,264
Shrimps, prawns, etc.	1,258,570
Squid, cuttlefishes, octupuses, etc.	1,150,812
Flounders, halibut, sole, etc.	1,146,276
Sharks, rays, etc.	564,859

THE TEN LARGEST MARINE FISHING NATIONS

Rank	*Country*	*Catch in Metric Tons*
1.	Japan	10,508,451
2.	USSR	9,876,173
3.	China	6,880,000
4.	Peru	3,447,485
5.	United States	2,798,703
6.	Norway	2,550,438
7.	India	2,328,000
8.	South Korea	2,133,371
9.	Denmark	1,767,039
10.	Spain	1,532,878

SOURCE: *Fisheries Yearbook*, U.N. Food and Agriculture Organization, 1977.

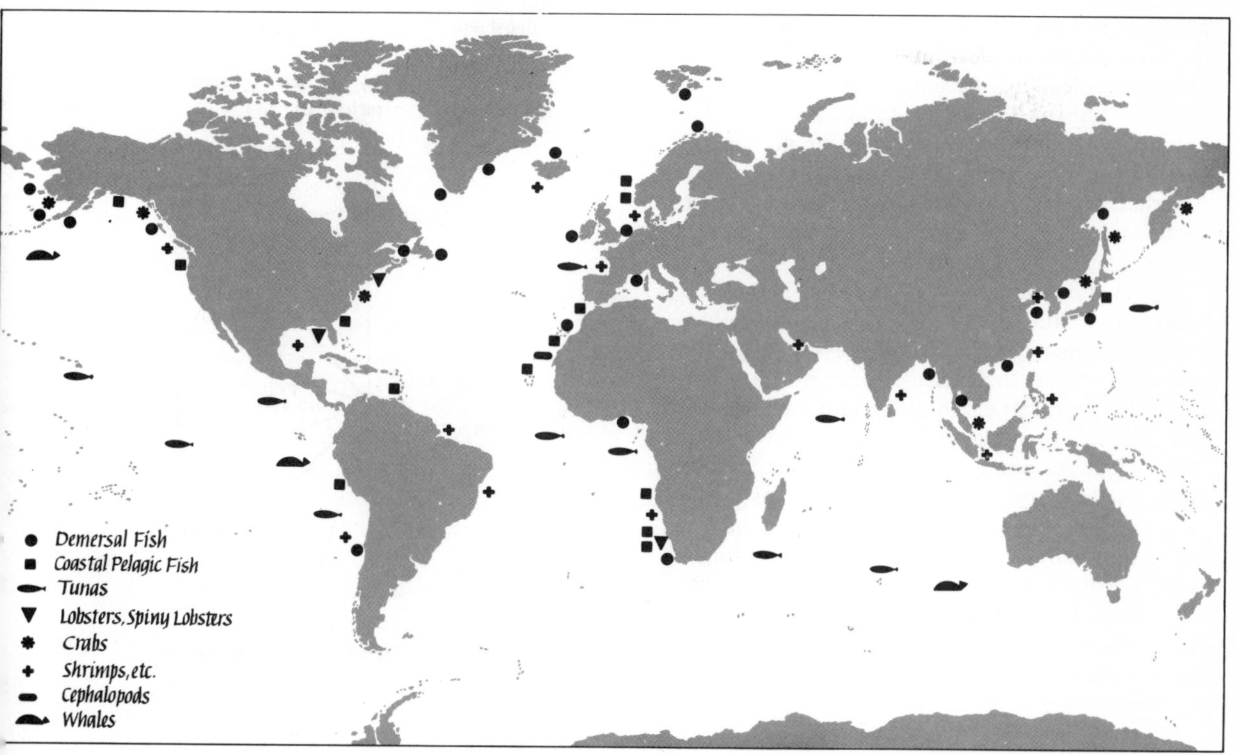

The world's major fisheries. Demersal fish are bottom fish, Coastal pelagic fish are open-sea fish caught offshore, and Cephalopods are members of the squid and octopus family.

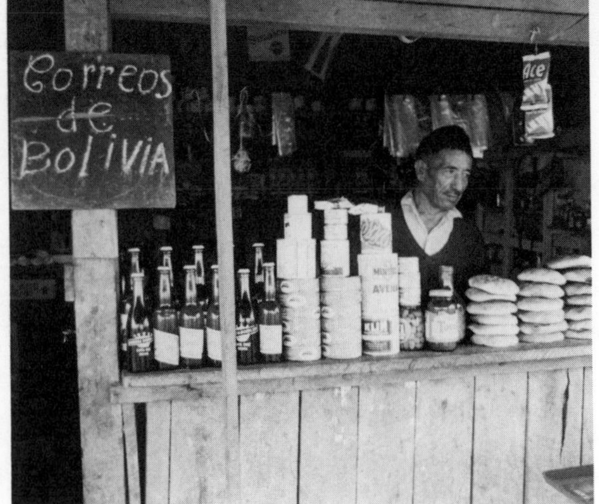

(*FAO*)

FOOD INTAKE AROUND THE WORLD

The following charts reflect the inequities of food distribution and the evidence of widespread hunger and malnutrition. The situation is actually worse than the charts suggest.

When the statistics report an *average* consumption of 2,300 calories (about the minimum to sustain health), it really means that some people are eating much more and that a large percentage of the people are actually eating less. These figures are based on food production and allow for a 10-percent loss to pests and spoilage. In the poorest countries these losses are probably greater. Recommended protein allowances can also be misleading, because they are based on research with well-fed subjects. If a person does not receive sufficient calories to supply energy, the protein will be utilized for energy and not for its crucial function of rebuilding tissues. An underfed person could actually need more protein than the recommended amount.

The final hidden aspect of nutrition is food distribution within the family. Pregnant women, nursing mothers, and children have the greatest and most crucial food needs. Men, who are most often the wage earners in developing nations, usually assume first claim to the available food. When food is short, the women and children suffer, setting up a destructive cycle of undernourished mothers giving birth to sickly children, who are usually susceptible to disease. Continued poor nutrition can produce mental retardation. The ultimate result is the weakening of entire nations. Meanwhile, many people in developed nations suffer from obesity and heart disease caused by overeating.

K.F.

THE TEN COUNTRIES WITH THE LOWEST PER CAPITA CALORIE CONSUMPTION

1.	Chad	1,793 calories/day
2.	Maldives	1,797
3.	Ethiopia	1,838
4.	Kampuchea	1,857
5.	Mauritania	1,894
6.	South Yemen	1,897
7.	Guinea	1,921
8.	Mozambique	1,930
9.	Bangladesh	1,945
10.	India	1,949

SOURCE: *Production Yearbook,* U.N. Food and Agriculture Organization, 1979.

THE TEN COUNTRIES WITH THE HIGHEST PER CAPITA CALORIE CONSUMPTION

1.	Poland	3,647 calories/day
2.	East Germany	3,610
3.	Bulgaria	3,594
4.	Belgium/Luxembourg	3,565
5.	Austria	3,547
6.	United States	3,537
7.	Ireland	3,519
8.	Hungary	3,494
9.	Yugoslavia	3,469
10.	Italy	3,462

SOURCE: *Production Yearbook,* U.N. Food and Agriculture Organization, 1979.

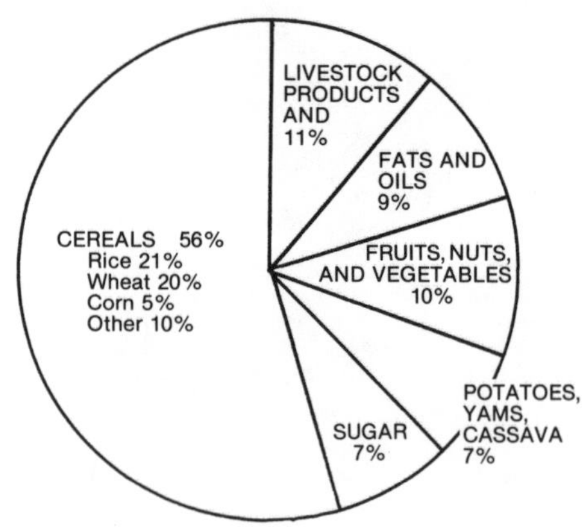

FOODS THAT FEED THE WORLD

Gathering grains around the world: Rice (*above left, World Bank photo by Ray Witlin*), Wheat (*above right, World Bank photo by Thomas Sennett*), Corn (*left, World Bank photo by Jaime Martin*).

THE VITAL STATISTICS OF ENERGY

- Total world energy use in 1976 was about 230 quads (or 230 quadrillion British thermal units), the equivalent of:
  - 40 billion barrels of oil OR
  - 226 trillion cubic feet of natural gas OR
  - 10 billion tons of coal OR
  - 22 trillion kilowatt-hours of electricity
- A human being is a 100- to 150-watt machine. In terms of energy, a person walking into a room is the equivalent of turning on a bright light bulb.
- The energy in one gallon of gas could:
  - — supply a person's energy needs for ten days.
  - — power a fast car for ten minutes.
  - — fly the Concorde SST for a tenth of a second.

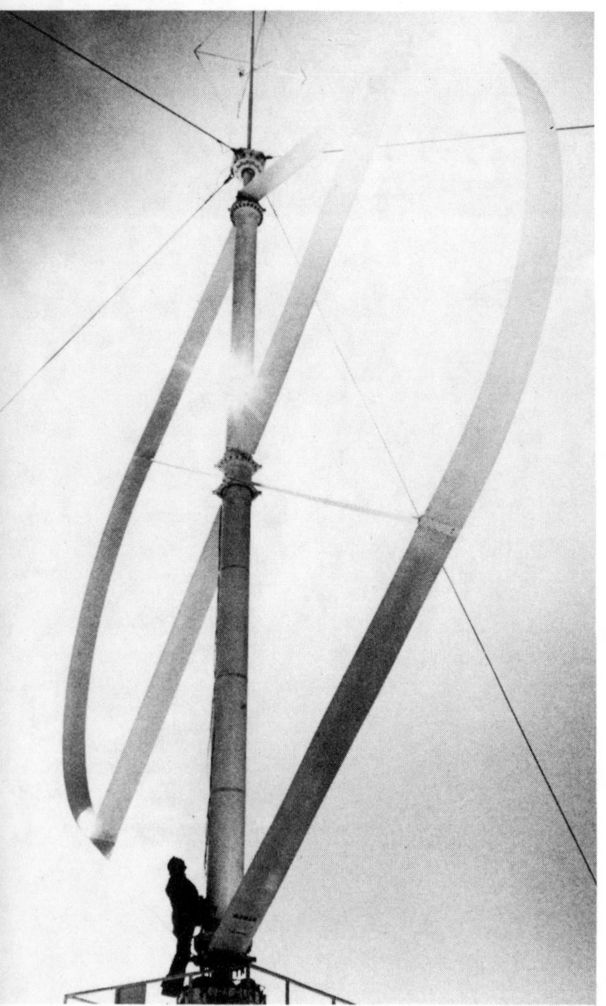

(*Sandia Laboratories/DOE*)

- The following charts and tables dramatically illustrate the growth of world energy use between 1950 and 1976. Energy use more than tripled in twenty-five years, oil consumption quadrupled, and the energy supplied by the Organization of Petroleum Exporting Countries (OPEC) rose almost ten times. During this quarter century, energy became a central focus of world governments.

COMING TO TERMS WITH ENERGY

Energy is the ability to do work. It can exist in many forms—thermal, light, electrical, chemical, mechanical—and can be measured on many different scales. Calories and British thermal units (Btu), which measure thermal energy, are commonly used because heat is our greatest energy need and is involved in so many of our energy conversion processes, such as producing electricity in coal-fired or nuclear plants. The electrical energy produced is then usually measured in kilowatt-hours.

Power measures how fast energy is doing work and is measured in watts or kilowatts. A 1-kilowatt machine uses a specific amount of energy every second: operating that machine for 1 hour uses 1 kilowatt-hour of energy. The wattage of a power plant tells us how fast energy is being produced; the wattage of a light bulb tells us how fast it is being used.

A 100-watt light bulb burning for 10 hours uses 1,000 watt-hours or 1 kilowatt-hour of energy. A 50-watt light bulb burning for 20 hours also uses 1 kilowatt-hour of energy.

ENERGY SOURCES

Estimating how much oil, gas, coal, and uranium can be found in the earth is a difficult but necessary endeavor. Coal resources are easiest to determine because we know most about how coal was formed. Oil is a little trickier, and natural gas is loosely related to oil resources. Uranium is most difficult because it can be found in sedimentary rock in one country and metamorphic or igneous rock in another.

Resources are the quantity of a substance that we can expect with some certainty to find and recover some time in the future.

Reserves are those resources that have already been located with considerable certainty and that can be recovered economically with current technology.

To facilitate comparison, the world total of each source is given in British thermal units (Btu) at the bottom of the following table. Keep in mind that annual world energy use is about 230 quadrillion Btu.

WORLD RECOVERABLE RESERVES AND RESOURCES OF CONVENTIONAL MINERAL FUELS

	Coal (*billion metric tons coal equivalent*)		*Oil* (*billion barrels*)	
Region or Nation	*Reserves*	*Resources*	*Reserves*	*Resources*
United States	178	1,285	29	110-185
Canada	9	57	6	25-40
Mexico	1	3	16	145-215
South and Central America	10	14	26	80-120
Western Europe	91	215	24	50-70
Africa	34	87	58	100-150
Middle East	–	–	370	710-1,000
Asia and Pacific	40	41	18	90-140
Australia	27	132	2	a
Soviet Union	110	2,430	71	140-200
China	99	719	20	b
Other Communist areas	37	80	3	b
TOTAL	636	5,063	642	1,450-2,120
Quadrillion Btu	17,700	140,600	3,700	8,400-12,300

a: included in Asia and Pacific; b: included in Soviet Union.

	Gas (*trillion cubic feet*)		*Uranium* (*thousand metric tons*)	
Region or Nation	*Reserves*	*Resources*	*Reserves*	*Resources*
United States	205	730-1,070	643	1,696
Canada	59	230-380	182	838
Mexico	32	350-480	5	7
South and Central America	81	800-900	60	74
Western Europe	143	500	87	487
Africa	186	1,000	572	772
Middle East	731	1,750	–	–
Asia and Pacific	89	b	45	69
Australia	31	500	296	345
Soviet Union	910	2,850	n.a.	n.a.
China	25	b	n.a.	n.a.
Other Communist areas	10	b	n.a.	n.a.
TOTAL	2,502	8,710-9,430	1,894	4,288
Quadrillion Btu	2,600	8,900-9,700	7,400* 443,200**	16,700* 1,003,400**

*Light water reactors; **Fast breeder reactor.

SOURCE: Sam H. Schurr, *Energy in America's Future,* © 1979 by Resources for the Future, Inc., published by Johns Hopkins Press.

WHERE THE ENERGY GOES

The search for more energy is too often conducted without considering exactly what the energy will be used for. If we are looking for heat and hot water for our homes, we should recognize that we do not need the extremely high temperature of a nuclear reaction. Nuclear power is only useful in the form of electricity, and the chart on United States Energy Use (below) reveals that only 8 percent of U.S. energy has to be in the form of electricity. Almost one quarter of U.S. energy needs to be in the form of heat lower than 212° F (100° C), which can easily and efficiently be provided by solar energy. The source and use chart (below) shows how much energy is wasted in the production of electricity—about two thirds. Using natural gas to produce electricity to heat a home is extremely wasteful when the gas can be used directly. As we work toward solutions to the energy crisis, we should not just look at quads of supply. Energy is like any tool and should be chosen to suit the task.

UNITED STATES ENERGY USE

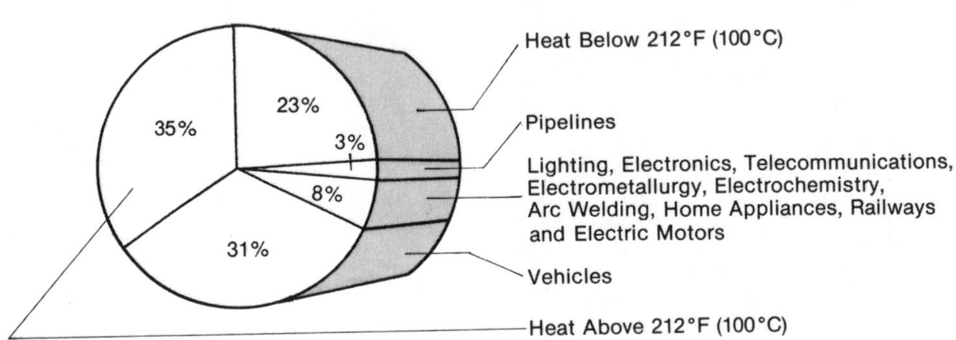

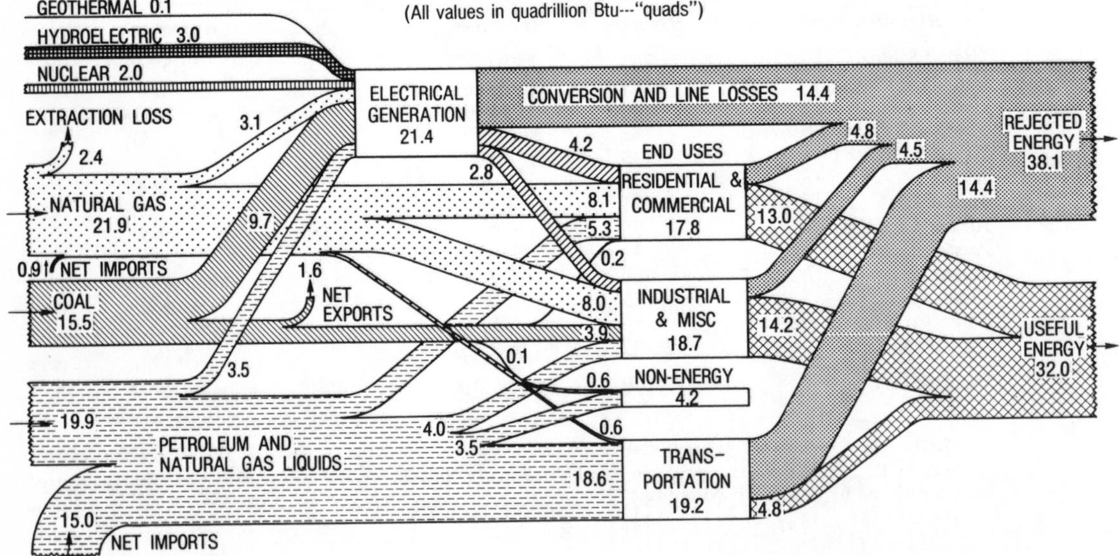

(*Reprinted with permission of Resources for the Future, Inc., from* Energy in America's Future: The Choices Before Us, *Sam R. Schurr, Project Director, Joel Darmstadter, Harry Perry, William Ramsay, Milton Russell, Johns Hopkins University Press for Resources for the Future.*)

HOW LONG WILL THE WORLD'S OIL LAST?

The following table assumes that total world oil resources are 1,952 billion barrels (a relatively high estimate) and calculates how long the oil will last at various rates of increased consumption. If use remains constant, the supply will last 101 years, but if use increases by 1 percent per year, it will last only 69.9 years, and so on. From 1890 to 1970, oil use increased at an annual rate of 7.04 percent.

Annual Percent Increase in Consumption	*Years Until Supply Is Exhausted*
0%	101 years
1	69.9
2	55.3
3	46.5
4	40.5
5	36.0
6	32.6
7	29.8
8	27.6
9	25.7
10	24.1

SOURCE: Albert A. Bartlett, "The Arithmetic of Energy Growth," in *Not Man Apart*, © 1977 by Friends of the Earth.

(*The Cousteau Society*)

U. S. COAL PROJECTIONS

The United States is second only to the Soviet Union in potential coal resources, and many policymakers suggest that the solution to U.S. energy worries is increased dependence on coal. The following table assumes a very high estimate of 1,436 billion metric tons of U.S. coal resources. Far from being an inexhaustible resource, coal will be rapidly exhausted if its use is increased to replace oil or gas.

Annual Percent Increase in Consumption	*Years Until Supply Is Exhausted*
0%	2,872 years
1	339
2	203
3	149
4	119
5	99
6	86
7	76
8	68
9	62
10	57
11	52
12	49
13	46

SOURCE: Albert A. Bartlett, "The Arithmetic of Energy Growth," in *Not Man Apart*, © 1977 by Friends of the Earth.

SYNTHETIC FUELS

The potential energy to be obtained from synthetic fuels is too uncertain to be neatly contained in a chart or table. Estimates vary widely and are constantly changing. (For information on this new energy source, see "Synfuels," page 34.)

NUCLEAR EQUIVALENTS

In the current debate over nuclear power, the nuclear proponents always compare the potential energy from nuclear facilities with the dwindling energy potential of fossil fuels. It is also instructive to compare the potential of nuclear power with the potential of environmentally benign and perpetually renewable energy sources. After more than twenty years of development of commercial nuclear power there are only 233 nuclear power plants in the world, almost all of them having a capacity lower than 1,000 megawatts. The following table expresses the potential power of renewable energy sources in equivalents of 1,000-megawatt nuclear power plants.

Considering the potential dangers associated with nuclear energy and the volume of safe, renewable energy available, it is difficult to justify further development of "nukes." If human ingenuity cannot devise ways to harness enough solar energy to support our needs (only a fraction of the amount of usable solar energy striking the planet), then we are not the masterful technologists we believe ourselves to be.

SOURCES OF THE WORLD'S ENERGY

SOURCES OF THE WORLD'S ENERGY

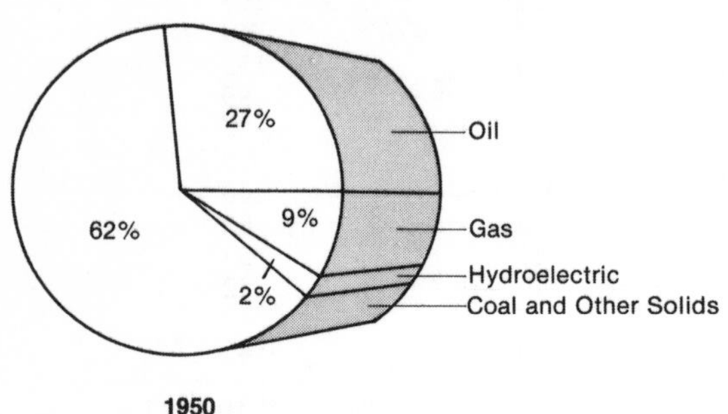

1950

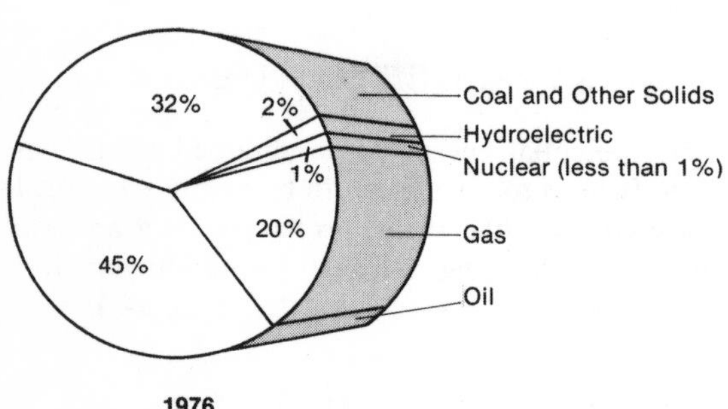

1976

	Nuclear Plants
Current world power use	10,000
Solar energy reaching earth's surface	10,000,000
Photosynthesis (biomass)	10,000
Wind (usable, total is much greater)	1,000
Manure from domestic animals	1,000
Sewage and garbage	10
Geothermal	1,000
Hydroelectric (25 percent now in use)	100

SOURCE: Adapted from "Energy: Natural Limits and Abundances," in Vol. 55 #9, p. 828, *EOS Transactions*, September 1974, © AGU.

OCEAN ENERGY SOURCES

	Nuclear Plants
Thermal gradients	40,000,000
Salinity gradients	1,400,000
Marine biomass	10,000
Marine currents	5,000
Tides	3,000
Ocean waves	2,500

SOURCE: Jacques A. Constans, *Present and Future Possibilities of Energy Production from Marine Sources,* © 1979 by United Nations, published by Pergamon Press.

RENEWABLE ENERGY SOURCES

Hydroelectric

The flow of water from both rivers and reservoirs can be harnessed to generate electricity to a much greater extent than presently. A little more than 2 percent of the world's energy (1.2 trillion kilowatt-hours per year) now comes from hydroelectric power. Potential hydroelectric power is about 5 trillion kilowatt-hours per year, of which South America has 20 percent, Africa 27 percent, and Southeast Asia 16 percent. The major drawback of hydroelectric power is the ecological disruption and loss of farmland resulting from the damming of rivers.

Geothermal

The natural fission of minerals beneath the earth's surface creates heat in the form of dry steam, hot brine, hot dry rock, or pressurized liquid. This heat can be used directly in homes or industry, or used to generate electricity. We currently have only a vague idea of the potential of geothermal energy, which is already being used in Iceland, France, Italy, New Zealand, Japan, the Soviet Union, the United States, and Mexico.

Organic Waste and Refuse

Much of the agricultural waste and sewage that is now a problem throughout the world is a potential energy source. A variety of methods are being developed to produce methane and fertilizer from this waste.

Windmills

Windmills were commonly used to generate electricity in the early twentieth century but were forgotten when large fossil-fuel plants were built. The 2 percent of incoming solar energy that is converted to wind is an abundant energy source that can be used in both small- and large-scale facilities.

The Ocean

Several techniques for obtaining energy from the oceans are currently being pursued. The 240-megawatt Rance River Tidal Plant in France is the largest facility utilizing the continuous ebb and flow of the tides to produce electricity. Two-way turbines in a partially enclosed coastal basin are powered by the movement of massive quantities of water. (See "Tidal Power," page 30.)

Japan uses small 10-watt devices to obtain electricity from the power of the waves. These generators are used as power sources for buoys and lighthouses, and plans for larger facilities are being developed. Some scientists hope to be able to use the prodigious but widely dispersed power of the ocean currents to produce electricity. A more promising source of energy is the temperature differential between surface and deeper water; pilot projects using this approach are already in operation (see "OTEC," page 23). In perhaps twenty-five to fifty years a method of producing energy using the difference in salt content between the sea and freshwater rivers may be perfected (see "Salinity Gradients," page 42).

The Sun

The sun is obviously the greatest potential source of energy for electricity, water heating, home heating, and even industrial heat. (See "Catching the Sun," page 459, and "Photovoltaic Cells," page 29.)

THE FORGOTTEN ENERGY SOURCE: FIREWOOD

One crucial source of energy is always left out of the statistics—firewood. The developed nations (the compilers of statistics) do not analyze fire-

Because of the expanding demands for fuel wood for a rising population, these women from a village in Mali must travel several miles each day to gather firewood for cooking and heating. Each year, a greater proportion of the day is spent searching for firewood as trees disappear. (*WFP/F. Mattioli*)

wood use because they do not use it widely, but firewood provides 96 percent of the energy in such developing nations as Tanzania and Nepal.

Erik Eckholm, noted ecologist, drew the world's attention to some startling facts about firewood. In northern Nigeria, non-firewood commercial sources provide less than 1 percent of total energy. Half the wood cut in the world is used to produce energy, and the supply is dwindling. (See "The Himalayas," page 189.)

Although the energy crisis in the developed nations is undeniably serious, the situation in the developing nations is worse. A shortage of firewood prevents millions of people from cooking or warming their homes. As a result, they are threatened with hunger and disease rather than economic slowdown. Deforestation and its natural corollary, soil erosion, are proceeding rapidly, and the pangs of hunger make efforts to maintain forests extremely difficult.

United Nations statistics indicate that the average U.S. resident uses 957 times as much energy as the average Nepalese, which leads many people to conclude that the Nepalese use little energy. The UN figures, however, do not include firewood as a fuel. When it and noncommercial sources are included, the U.S. resident uses only 40 times as much. As firewood becomes increasingly scarce, the developing nations will be in a precarious position—running out of cheap wood fuel but unable to afford fossil fuels, which will be growing more expensive and less abundant.

Because the developing nations need cheap, renewable energy, governments as different as those of South Korea and China have already begun to support farms of fast-growing trees for fuel, but a worldwide effort is needed. The firewood shortage could be the world's first energy disaster, or it could be the impetus for the world's first step toward a sustainable economy based on renewable energy sources.

K.F.

THE VITAL STATISTICS OF MINERALS

Oil is not the only resource that is dwindling to dangerous levels or is found only in particular parts of the world. Many other minerals are becoming scarce, and the potential for cartels and trade-sanctions diplomacy is becoming more evident.

- *Cobalt,* which is used in jet aircraft engines and mining tools, is found primarily in potentially unstable Zaire. During the past few years, the price has bounced between \$6.40 and \$50 per pound (\$14.08 and \$110 per kilogram) in response to changing political conditions.
- *Manganese,* an essential element in the production of steel, is concentrated in South Africa and the Soviet Union, countries that have been involved in trade boycotts.
- *Chromium,* needed for stainless steel, ball bearings, and surgical equipment, is found primarily in South Africa, Zimbabwe, and the Soviet Union.
- *Titanium* sales were halted in 1979 by the Soviet Union, and the mineral, which is used in jets, missiles, and nuclear plants, rose in price from \$3.98 to \$25 a pound in less than a year.

Possible alternative sources of some of these minerals exist (see "Manganese Nodules," page 13), but as in the case of oil, environmental problems are associated with the development of new sources. United States geologists, for instance, have identified a possible source of cobalt in Idaho—in a wilderness reserve where commercial activity is forbidden. Mining interests are inevitably going to come into conflict with people who want to preserve the natural landscape. Rising prices will make it economical to exploit secondary and tertiary sources where mining is already going on, but that will only postpone the conflict. Obviously, we are going to have to conserve disappearing minerals and work harder to recycle what we have. If we do not, the stage is set for economic warfare or worse on dozens of fronts.

The following charts provide a summary of current mineral reserves around the world and compare projected world use of minerals with current reserves and resources. By 2000 many reserves will be exhausted and even potentially available resources will be dangerously limited.

"Ugor tells me we'll eventually run out of rock." (© *1980 Eldon Dedini*)

WORLD MINERAL RESERVES

Symbols:

c.f. = cubic feet		l.t. = long tons (2,240 pounds)	
fl = flasks (76 pounds)		m.t. = metric tons (2,205 pounds)	
kg = kilograms		s.t. = short tons (2,000 pounds)	
lb = pounds		t.oz. = troy ounces	

A = Adequate   n.a. = Not available   <.5 = Less than one-half unit

Commodity	*Units*	*United States*	*Other North America*	*South America*	*Europe*	*Africa*	*Asia*	*Oceania*	*World Total*
				Metals and Mineral-Forming Elements					
Aluminum	Million s.t.	10	490	1,000	350	2,300	500	1,000	5,600
Antimony	Thousand s.t.	120	300	570	550	350	2,650	200	4,740
Arsenic	Thousand s.t.	400	n.a.	n.a.	n.a.	n.a.	n.a.	n.a.	3,100
Beryllium	Thousand s.t.	28	–	182	67	59	71	12	419
Bismuth	Million lb	20	24	44	20	18	18	40	184
Boron	Million s.t.	22	–	7	16	–	44	–	89
Cadmium	Thousand s.t.	220	169	55	130	40	91	55	760
Cesium	Million lb	–	152	–	–	66	–	–	218
Chromium	Million s.t.	<.5	–	3	14	804	8	–	829
Cobalt	Million lb	–	306	–	500	1,336	–	1,128	3,300
Columbium	Billion lb	–	1	18	n.a.	3	n.a.	n.a.	22
Copper	Million s.t.	93	67	150	70	70	33	20	503
Fluorine	Million s.t.	3	7	2	11	10	4	–	37
Gallium	Million kg	1	7	4	9	45	3	41	110
Germanium	Thousand lb	900	300	300	800	900	600	200	4,000
Gold	Million t.oz.	110	75	25	255	660	40	50	1,215
Hafnium	Thousand s.t.	120	20	20	60	40	40	140	440

Commodity	Units	United States	Other North America	South America	Europe	Africa	Asia	Oceania	World Total
				Metals and Mineral-Forming Elements (continued)					
Indium	Million t.oz.	10	14	4	12	3	4	4	51
Iodine	Million lb	530	–	800	410	–	4,010	–	5,750
Iron in ore	Billion s.t.	4	12	21	39	4	11	12	103
Lead	Million s.t.	28	18	8	25	11	27	19	137
Lithium	Thousand s.t.	410	150	1,420	n.a.	230	n.a.	25	n.a.
Manganese	Million s.t.	–	5	44	700	890	47	160	1,800
Mercury	Thousand fl	410	350	30	3,400	400	620	–	5,210
Molybdenum	Billion lb	8	2	7	2	<.5	1	<.5	20
Nickel	Thousand s.t.	200	8,700	6,400	8,100	2,300	300	34,000	60,000
Palladium	Million t.oz.	<.5	4	–	–	100	90	–	194
Platinum	Million t.oz.	<.5	4	<.5	–	248	45	–	297
Rare earths & yttrium	Thousand s.t.	5,050	250	350	510	70	1,100	400	7,730
Rhenium	Thousand lb	2,600	725	3,000	600	25	50	–	7,000
Rhodium	Million t.oz.	<.5	<.5	–	–	14	3	–	17
Rubidium	Thousand lb	–	1,300	–	–	800	–	–	2,100
Scandium	Thousand kg	230	160	–	50	230	–	100	770
Selenium	Million lb	74	50	100	50	56	26	16	372
Silver	Million t.oz.	1,510	1,560	610	2,000	50	165	205	6,100
Strontium	Thousand s.t.	–	330	7	798	–	20	–	1,155
Sulfur	Million l.t.	205	345	30	400	20	680	20	1,700
Tantalum	Million lb	–	3	7	n.a.	100	18	5	130
Tellurium	Million lb	19	13	30	13	14	8	4	101
Thallium	Thousand lb	192	384	96	240	72	84	132	1,200
Thorium	Thousand s.t.	140	230	70	40	40	220	40	780
Tin	Thousand m.t.	40	25	1,605	920	715	6,535	330	10,170
Titanium	Million s.t.	31	57	70	71	26	59	20	334
Tungsten	Million lb	275	480	130	643	23	2,600	77	4,200
Vanadium	Thousand s.t.	115	–	250	8,000	2,000	100	150	10,600
Zinc	Million s.t.	24	35	16	43	9	18	21	166
Zirconium	Million s.t.	6	1	1	3	2	2	7	22
				Nonmetallic Minerals					
Asbestos	Million s.t.	4	41	2	26	8	13	2	96
Barite	Million s.t.	65	9	25	35	25	35	6	200
Corundum	Thousand s.t.	–	–	–	A	A	A	–	A
Diatomite	Million s.t.	600	–	70	1,330	–	–	–	2,000
Feldspar	Million s.t.	600	110	40	100	50	90	10	1,000
Garnet	Thousand s.t.	700	n.a.	10	500	1,000	10	10	2,230
Graphite	Million s.t.	–	1	–	4	1	4	–	10
Gypsum	Million s.t.	550	600	40	900	80	100	60	2,280
Kyanite	Million s.t.	30	10	–	25	10	25	<.5	100
Mica (sheet)	Million lb	<.5	–	25	–	40	300	–	365
Peat	Billion s.t.	10	1	–	40	–	1	–	52
Perlite	Million s.t.	200	5	–	775	–	20	10	1,010
Phosphate Rock	Million m.t.	3,500	2	80	750	20,000	400	1,000	25,732
Potash	Million s.t.	200	10,000	60	2,630	10	330	–	13,230
Pumice	Million s.t.	1,250	50	15	650	30	40	30	2,065
Talc	Million s.t.	150	10	5	60	5	90	10	330
Vermiculite	Million s.t.	100	5	5	–	75	5	–	190
				Commercial Gases					
Helium	Billion c.f.	149	n.a.	n.a.	n.a.	n.a.	n.a.	n.a.	n.a.

NOTE: The following metals and mineral-forming elements, nonmetallic minerals, and commercial gases have reserves classified as adequate in all areas of the world listed above: Argon, Bromine, Chlorine, Clays, Hydrogen, Lime, Magnesium, Mica (scrap and flake), Nitrogen, Oxygen, Salt, Sand and Gravel, Silicon, Soda Ash, and Stone.

SOURCE: U.S. Department of the Interior, 1976.

HOW LONG WILL THE WORLD'S MINERALS LAST?

The following chart compares the projected demand for minerals between 1976 and 2000 with the estimated reserves and resources.

Resources are the quantity of a substance that we can expect with some certainty to find and recover sometime in the future.

Reserves are those resources that have been located with considerable certainty and that can be recovered economically with current technology.

A ratio of reserves to demand of 1.0 means that all the reserves will be exhausted in the year 2000. A ratio less than 1.0 indicates that the reserves will not last until 2000. For example, a ratio of 0.5 indicates that twice as much as now exists in reserves will be needed by 2000.

Abbreviations used:

s.t. = short tons
lb = pounds
kg = kilograms
t.oz. = troy ounces
m.t. = metric tons
c.f. = cubic feet
A = Adequate
n.a. = Not available
W = Withheld
> = greater than
< = less than

PRIMARY MINERAL DEMAND FORECASTS, 1976–2000

Commodity	*Units*	*Primary Mineral Demand 1976-2000*	*Mineral Reserves 1976*	*Ratio of Recoverable Reserves to Cumulative Demand*	*Identified Mineral Resources*	*Ratio of Identified Resources to Cumulative Demand*
		Metals and Mineral-Forming Elements				
Aluminum (Bauxite only)	Million s.t.	958	5,610	5.8	8,000	8.4
Antimony	Thousand s.t.	2,576	4,740	1.8	5,580	2.2
Arsenic	Thousand s.t.	W	3,100	W	18,000	W
Beryllium	Thousand s.t.	15	419	>10:1	1,218	>10:1
Bismuth	Million lb	283	184	0.7	293	1.0
Boron	Million s.t.	16	89	5.6	–	–
Bromine	Million lb	18,995	A	>10:1	–	–
Cadmium	Thousand s.t.	693	760	1.1	23,000	>10:1
Cesium	Thousand lb	3,730	218,000	A	–	–
Chlorine	Million s.t.	1,141	A	A	–	–
Chromium	Million s.t.	87	829	9.5	n.a.	n.a.
Cobalt	Million lb	2,728	3,300	1.2	9,412	3.5
Columbium	Million lb	1,294	22,000	17.0	30,000	>10:1
Copper	Million s.t.	318	503	1.6	2,453	7.7
Fluorine	Million s.t.	95	37	0.4	75	0.8
Gallium	Thousand kg	680	A	>10:1	–	–
Germanium	Thousand lb	5,437	4,000	0.7	8,500	1.6
Gold	Million t. oz.	1,154	1,215	1.1	1,900	1.6
Hafnium	s.t.	2,310	A	>10:1	–	–
Indium	Million t. oz.	56	51	0.9	109	1.9
Iodine	Million lb	940	5,750	6.0	–	–
Iron in ore	Billion s.t.	20	103	5.1	215	>10:1
Lead	Million s.t.	127	136	1.1	305	2.4
Lithium	Thousand s.t.	260	n.a.	n.a.	n.a.	n.a.
Magnesium	Million s.t.	202	A	>10:1	–	–
Manganese	Million s.t.	390	1,800	4.6	3,000	7.7
Mercury	Thousand fl	6,070	5,210	0.9	17,510	2.9
Molybdenum	Billion lb	10	20	2.1	70	7.4
Nickel	Million s.t.	27	60	2.2	228	8.1
Nitrogen						
fixed	Million s.t.	2,040	A	>10:1	–	–
elemental	Million s.t.	1,328	A	>10:1	–	–
Palladium	Million t.oz.	85	194	2.3	516	6.1
Platinum	Million t.oz.	88	297	3.4	810	9.2

Commodity	Units	Primary Mineral Demand 1976-2000	Mineral Reserves 1976	Ratio of Recoverable Reserves to Cumulative Demand	Identified Mineral Resources	Ratio of Identified Resources to Cumulative Demand
Metals and Mineral-Forming Elements (continued)						
Rare earths and yttrium	Thousand s.t.	966	7,730	8.0	–	–
Rhenium	Thousand lb	306	7,000	>10:1	–	–
Rhodium	Million t.oz.	5	17	3.3	60	>10:1
Rubidium	Thousand lb	106	2,100	>10:1	–	–
Scandium	kg	496	A	>10:1	–	–
Selenium	Million lb	107	372	3.5	1,385	>10:1
Silicon	Thousand s.t.	97,000	A	>10:1	–	–
Silver	Million t.oz.	11,416	6,100	0.5	22,630	2.0
Strontium	Thousand s.t.	678	1,155	1.7	A	>10:1
Sulfur	Million l.t.	1,860	1,700	0.9	–	–
Tantalum	Thousand lb	109	130	1.2	600	5.5
Tellurium	Million lb	15	101	6.6	491	>10:1
Thallium	Thousand lb	112	1,200	>10:1	–	–
Thorium	Thousand s.t.	5	780	>10:1	–	–
Tin	Thousand m.t.	6,600	10,000	1.5	37,000	5.6
Titanium	Million s.t.	81	334	4.1	1,200	>10:1
Tungsten	Million lb	2,931	4,200	1.4	11,900	4.1
Vanadium	Thousand s.t.	1,360	10,600	7.8	50,000	>10:1
Zinc	Million s.t.	201	166	0.8	1,660	8.3
Zirconium	Million s.t.	11	22	2.0	44	4.3
Nonmetallic Minerals						
Asbestos	Million s.t.	201	96	0.5	96	0.5
Barite	Million s.t.	149	200	1.3	420	2.8
Clays	Billion s.t.	18	A	>10:1	–	–
Corundum	Thousand s.t.	385	A	>10:1	–	–
Diatomite	Million s.t.	70	2,000	>10.1	–	–
Feldspar	Million s.t.	134	1,000	7.5	–	–
Garnet	Thousand s.t.	1,031	2,240	2.2	–	–
Graphite	Million s.t.	13	10	0.8	310	>10:1
Gypsum	Million s.t.	2,338	2,280	1.0	–	–
Kyanite	Million s.t.	W	100	W	–	–
Lime	Million s.t.	3,657	A	A	–	–
Mica						
Scrap and Flake	Thousand s.t.	7,500	A	>10:1	–	–
Sheet	Thousand lb	499,200	365,000	0.7	–	–
Peat	Million s.t.	7,355	50,000	6.8	–	–
Perlite	Million s.t.	73	1,010	>10:1	–	–
Phosphate Rock	Million m.t.	3,937	25,732	6.5	75,000	>10:1
Potash	Million s.t.	1,039	12,230	>10:1	151,000	>10:1
Pumice	Million s.t.	714	2,065	2.9	–	–
Salt	Million s.t.	5,630	A	A	–	–
Sand and Gravel	Billion s.t.	n.a.	A	A	–	–
Soda Ash	Million s.t.	835	A	>10:1	–	–
Stone						
crushed	Billion s.t.	254	A	>10:1	–	–
dimension	Million s.t.	1,052	A	>10:1	–	–
Talc	Million s.t.	225	330	1.5	–	–
Vermiculite	Million s.t.	19	190	10.0	–	–
Commercial Gases						
Argon	Million s.t.	24	A	>10:1	–	–
Helium	Billion c.f.	n.a.	n.a.	n.a.	–	–
Oxygen	Million s.t.	2,300	A	>10:1	–	–

Totals may not tally because of rounding. >10:1 = Ratio of more than 10 to 1, involving numbers inexpressible in decimals.

SOURCE: U.S. Department of the Interior, 1976.

ENDANGERED MINERALS

Listed below are the minerals most in danger of being depleted, with their most common industrial uses.

ANTIMONY batteries, semiconductors, ceramics
BISMUTH fire safety devices
CADMIUM low-friction alloys, solders, batteries
COBALT jet aircraft engines, mining tools
COPPER electric wiring and equipment
GERMANIUM semiconductors
GOLD computers, spacecraft, jet turbines
GRAPHITE lead pencils, lubricants, paints
GYPSUM plaster and some cements
INDIUM mirrors, transistors
LEAD storage batteries for transportation, communications
MERCURY thermometers, barometers, batteries
MICA, SHEET insulation, stereo speakers
MOLYBDENUM alloy in steel
NICKEL alloys used in aerospace design for strength
PALLADIUM electric contacts, surgical instruments
PUMICE abrasive, polish
SILVER photography, dental alloys, electrical contacts
STRONTIUM various alloys
SULFUR gunpowder, rubber, insecticides, drugs
TANTALUM light bulb filaments, aircraft, missiles, nuclear plants
TIN anticorrosive in many alloys
TUNGSTEN high-temperature structural materials, electrical elements
ZINC brass, bronze, solders, galvanized iron
ZIRCONIUM ceramics, nuclear reactors

U. S. MINERAL IMPORTS

Mineral	*% Reliance on Imports*	*Major Sources*
Columbium (Niobium) spacecraft	100	Brazil, Thailand, Nigeria
Mica (sheet) insulation, stereo speakers	100	India, Brazil, Malagasy Republic
Strontium various alloys	100	Mexico, Spain
Manganese steel, brass, bronze, glass	98	Brazil, Gabon, South Africa
Tantalum aircraft, missiles, light bulbs, nuclear plants	97	Thailand, Canada, Australia
Cobalt jet aircraft engines, mining tools	97	Zaire, Belgium, Luxembourg
Platinum-group surgical tools, laboratory utensils	91	South Africa, USSR, United Kingdom
Bauxite and Alumina spark plugs, abrasives, furnaces, aluminum	91	Jamaica, Australia, Surinam
Chromium steel, metal plating	91	South Africa, USSR, Turkey
Asbestos fireproof products	85	Canada, South Africa
Tin anticorrosive coating	82	Malaysia, Thailand, Bolivia

PART III

CONNECTIONS

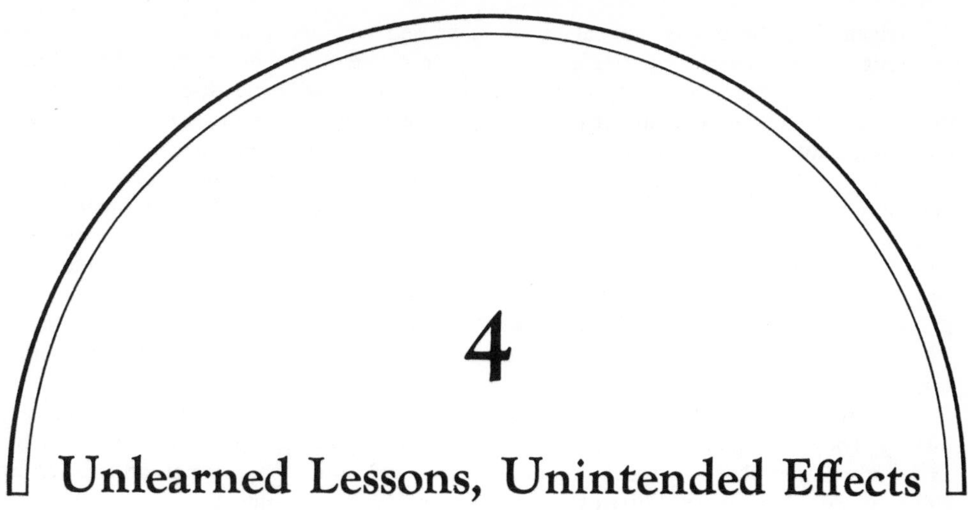

4
Unlearned Lessons, Unintended Effects

Our purpose in compiling the *Almanac* has been, in the words of T. H. White quoted at the beginning, to "learn why the world wags and what wags it." Much of this wagging is predictable—there are repeated movements, predictable cycles, continuing evolutions, notable patterns: Tuesday inevitably follows Monday, low tide unfailingly follows high. So, relying on presumption and experience, we often take nature for granted. We plan on the basis of what we think happened before.

But much more of the world seems to wag unpredictably, jarring our assurance, shaking our preconceptions, giving us pause. We remain largely ignorant of the web of invisible connections that bind life together. What human ingenuity devises to enhance life, with the best of intentions, frequently impairs natural systems and undermines biological networks.

In this chapter, the *Almanac* analyzes some of the history we may have misread and some of the modern phenomena that demonstrate lessons we seem not to have learned, and effects we seem not to have intended.

Often history books describe great ancient civilizations as though a curtain had one day risen on them, and then fallen just as suddenly hundreds of years later. But time-line charts don't account for subtle shifts in conditions that are the true catalysts of history. Ancient Rome did not fall as if from a cliff; it gradually came apart. While there are clearly social and political reasons for the decline, there are environmental reasons as well, which suggest all too bluntly our own possible course. A large part of Rome's dissolution can be traced to its indifferent natural resource management: the agricultural base of the society weakened, combining with other factors, of course, to culminate in the demise of Rome.

It is said the civilization that ignores history is doomed to repeat it. In this chapter, we look for historical precedent on which to base future human planning. The lessons are enlightening—that the Mesopotamians, Phoenicians, and ancient Greeks helped themselves to decline through deforestation, that perhaps the Indus Valley civilization suffocated in preindustrial air pollution, which indirectly destroyed food production.

We look too at previous planners who thought they had a better idea and did not. Some were importers of non-native animal and plant species that created pests and did damage not at all anticipated. Their ill deeds were mainly the result of miscalculation, like not taking into consideration that the mongoose, introduced to the Caribbean islands to prey upon the rat, was innately diurnal which left the innately nocturnal rat bothered hardly at all. Hence, a multitude of mongooses, a multitude of rats. That was a very simple, clear-cut mistake.

Not every venture is as easily judged. The Aswan High Dam, for example, lauded for at last preventing the floods that had bedeviled Egypt for centuries and for allowing irrigation of the desert, appears to have caused negative side effects more serious and long-lasting than the problems engineers were seeking to overcome. Miracle pesticides, meant to free the world from crop loss and insect-borne disease, now invade the tissues of animals and humans and may be instigating illnesses that were not, perhaps could not be, foreseen. High-technology, high-yield farming, expected to feed the millions of unfed, appears now to be contributing ferociously to land abuse as well as indirectly exacerbating the very poverty it was intended to erase. A canal intended to link an ocean with inland water systems became inadvertently a conduit for a parasitic aquatic creature whose behavior destroyed thousands of lake fish. And industries, which for ages seemed to offer hope of improved material goods and comfort, spit poisons into the atmosphere, a side effect that falls as acid rain hundreds of miles away, sometimes over neighboring countries, killing crops, fouling water, poisoning fish.

All of these connections we now understand because they have happened. They are history. They are experience. We have written about them here because they challenge us to admit that there is much we don't know and much we cannot anticipate, let alone control. They remind us to think in the long term, to value the broad outlines of unavoidable ecological reality as highly as the short-term, temporarily profitable innovations of human genius. The machinery of life humbles us in its environmental intricacy. It exhorts us not to be greedy, for though many ill effects are unintended, not all are purely innocent. And still, for all our studying, there is probably just one thing of which we can be sure: Push the world here and, predictably, it will wag over there—somewhere.

P.D.

EASTER ISLAND

Men perish because they cannot join the beginning with the end.
ALCMAEON

(*The Cousteau Society*)

A barren island of lava blemishes the vast expanse of the eastern Pacific. Its desolate coastline is scarred with cliffs that drop abruptly into the sea, their ashen faces of volcanic rock seemingly impervious to the isolation of this lonely landmass, 2,300 miles (3,700 kilometers) from the shores of South America. Scattered shrubs and sparse grasses keep the island's secret well. They give no indication that the place we know as Easter Island—named for the day it was discovered by the Western world—was once an island paradise, so lush, so full of promise, that natives called it Te Pito te Henua, Navel of the World, for it was the birthplace of an advanced civilization.

Today, as the winds blow unimpeded across the bleak, arid rock, it is difficult to imagine that, centuries ago, this forsaken triangle of lava was once shaded by palm trees, or that a burgeoning population, despite the distance from all continents, developed complex social laws here, as well

as religions, technology, and written language. History, in fact, might have overlooked the story of these people had the people themselves not made their story impossible to forget. In every corner of the island, they scattered their ghostly legacies: hidden caches of human bones, a few tablets of unreadable hieroglyphic script, and hundreds of giant statues that now give the island its only fame. Most of these silent Gargantuas have been toppled; others lie unfinished, their eyes not yet carved, stone faces staring blankly, soulless, at the sky. They are a testament both to the birth and to the death of a civilization; just as the island itself is a testament to the theory of cause and effect, to the connections between our actions and their consequences, to what nature can do and what humans can undo.

The Lost Voyagers

No one knows precisely when the first people stepped onto the island or where they came from. According to legend, supported by petroglyphs, in the fifth or sixth century A.D. a group led by King Hotu Matua landed on Easter Island. Some researchers, including Professor Jorge Da Silva of the University of Santiago, postulate they came from the Marquesas Islands, to the west. (Explorer Thor Heyderdahl and other archaeologists posit they came from South America, to the east.) These native colonizers brought with them true treasures of a civilized world—yams, bananas, sugarcane, coconuts, sandalwood seedlings, poultry—all the products of an agriculture to nourish them for years to come.

Landing on the island's only beach, the canoes of King Hotu Matua released into a virgin rain forest one or two hundred voyagers who had suffered storms and thirst and hunger during many weeks at sea. They brought with them a reverence for their ancestors and a resentment of the ocean. While beginning to cut trees and farm the land, they carved small statues, which they systematically erected with backs to the sea. Years passed. When life became easier, the Easter Island people developed a religion and a social structure without equivalent.

The Obsession

According to the theories of the late Dr. William Mulloy, an American anthropologist whom I interviewed on Easter Island, as the rites of their new religion became more strict, the priests became the ruling class, the people became possessed, and the statues grew in size and number. The carvers constituted the second privileged social class, supported, like the priests, by the mass of the "peasants." Heyderdahl's research indicates the lower class may have been a different race, descended from a group of Polynesians who arrived about A.D. 1100. The social rules became rigid and unforgiving. The positions of priest, carver, carrier, and peasant were the only occupations on the now bustling island. Though crossover between classes was unthinkable, all the classes together were singularly engaged in one purpose: the mass production of the statues.

Masterfully carved and beautifully finished in a large quarry called Rano Raraku, the statues were carved larger and larger, until the fifteenth century, when some weighed a massive 80 tons each. The people had artful systems of pulleys and sleds, which they used to drag the statues to the coastline, where they set them up, facing inland, and stood them on *ahu,* low platforms built to support the heavy carvings. Although the statues probably symbolized ancestors, small stone carvings were made of the many "spirits" the islanders believed surrounded them. The highest god in their pantheon was Makemake, the god of nature forces, the god of creation. Beneath Makemake was a long line of other deities, all of them good. The people of the island believed that there was no god of evil—evil, they thought, they brought upon themselves.

A Scourge of People

As time passed, the population exploded; some experts think that as many as 20,000 people scraped a living from the tiny island at once. Frantically, they consumed their scant resources, chopping down more trees, using every square mile of land to support their growing numbers. They furiously deforested their island as their religious zeal became all consuming; they needed wood for sleds, for the giant statues, and for their writing tablets, which they carved with hieroglyphic signs. They leveled more trees to give them space for their agriculture as they wildly increased their numbers year by year. In the seventeenth century, there were no trees left.

Finally—violently—their obsession burst its fragile limitations on the overburdened island. According to research by Dr. Mulloy, the lower classes erupted in a revolutionary reaction to the dictatorial society the islanders had created. In the Rano Raraku quarry tools still lie where they were dropped by the carvers, indicating the peasants revolted almost with a split-second's notice. The most awesome statue of all, weighing about 400 tons, still rests uncompleted in the quarry, a monument to the unimaginable—and unproductive—toil that enraged the workers into a slaughterous passion.

Chaos followed. The priests and the sculptors, who sought refuge in the eastern part of the island, tried to protect themselves behind a long, wood-filled ditch that they set afire. But the majority of the population, peasants and carriers of statues, had been ruthlessly exploited and would not be driven back. The ditch was soon crossed and the priests were exterminated. During the years of chaos that followed, all the standing statues were toppled; the only images that remained upright were the unfinished ones in the quarry, which, having not yet been given eyes, had no religious significance.

Survival Amid the Rubble

Overpopulation had stripped the island of most of its food resources; fires set by the revolutionists burned almost everything else to the ground. The remaining plots of good land, together with the last productive fishing areas, were zealously guarded by feuding families. Intruders were killed and eaten.

Survivors of the increasing cannibalism escaped to the cliffs, where they fashioned crude homes in caves formed from air pockets in the volcanic rock. Spearheads replaced statues as the most massively produced artifacts. The people continued carving wooden statues and tablets, but now they copied hieroglyphics only for ritualistic purposes, for they had forgotten how to read. They burned many of the valuable old tablets when they ran out of fuel. Families hid their prized possessions in caves, many of which were to remain secret forever when death claimed those few who knew the hidden locations.

When the Dutch commander Jacob Roggeveen discovered the island on Easter Day in 1722, the people were in the midst of their civil wars; the population had plummeted from the estimated 20,000 to about 3,000. By 1774, just fifty years later, the islanders had succeeded in wiping out nearly a thousand years of civilization; Captain Cook arrived to find a straggling group of about 600 poverty-stricken people, only 30 of whom were women.

The Denouement

What their own society did not destroy, Western society did. In 1805, Americans kidnapped natives to work on a seal-hunting expedition. Later, whalers raped island women and sent the ones they did not murder back to the island with venereal diseases. Peruvian slavers then took more prisoners; after an international outcry, they released the survivors, about fifteen islanders, who returned home carrying smallpox, which in turn wiped out half the remaining population. In 1872, the famous French author Pierre Loti wrote that "the paths are littered with bones, and whole skeletons are still to be seen, lying in the grass."

Bones clutter the island even today. When Philippe Cousteau and a research team explored the island in 1976 they discovered some of the legendary caves. These rocky crevices still cradle their remnants of human bones, grim reminders of the fate of a society based on exhaustion of natural resources, a society that—except for these traces of skeletons—finally vanished in a calamity of overpopulation, starvation, and hatred. The few natives who remain on the island today know nothing of their ancestry. Even the memories have vaporized.

A Microcosm of the Planet?

"In the dust where we have buried the silent races and their abominations, we have buried so much of the delicate magic of life," wrote D. H. Lawrence. Looking at those bones, I thought about that delicate magic, as I have in a hundred other places in the past. I was reminded that the earth is a living body, an interlocking system of intricately balanced forces endlessly changing—the sea and the cliffs, the tree and the desert. Perhaps, on Easter Island as elsewhere, humans intruded upon a natural process and discovered too late that in nature the injuries we inflict are not always self-healing, or even curable.

The consequences of ignorance, like the consequences of irresponsibility, are fatal. We must learn from the melancholy parable of Easter Island. We must recognize that the resources of our island Earth are equally finite, and that humanity's unparalleled creative gift seems fatally linked to its own self-destruct mechanism. Here, in the endless sea, a vagrant cell of human life anchored itself—with all the vital connections it needed to link it to the rest of the earth—created a civilization, then vanished, leaving a handful of survivors with no conscious recollection that it had ever existed. Shall this happen again, on the larger island Earth? Shall our nuclear power plants melt down, or our toxic wastes infect the waters, or our stockpiles of missiles be triggered, to leave our cathedrals and homes and workplaces empty of life, like the quarry at Rano Raraku? Or shall we pass on the riches of human invention and wisdom to living inheritors? Perhaps the islanders were right—we are not the victims of a god of evil; we are victims only of the evil we bring upon ourselves.

UNEXPECTED CONNECTIONS

- Political instability in Portugal in the mid-1970s caused the postponement of badly needed reforestation projects. The country's cork oak forests were increasingly cut and used for firewood with no replanting. The result was a worldwide cork shortage for wine bottles, leading to the development of half-plastic, half-cork stoppers even for vintage wines.
- In Bavaria, the spawning habits of toads, frogs, and salamanders were seriously disrupted because many amphibians were being killed crossing highways on their way to spawning grounds. The Environmental Ministry built "detours," tunnels and fences that guide the amphibians safely across the road. Auto accidents have also been somewhat diminished since the migrating creatures have been safely rerouted.
- Leonard Silk, of the New York *Times,* reported a "classic case of global interdependence" that occurred during World War II. When the U.S. government allowed hog prices to climb sharply, it became profitable for Corn Belt hog raisers to buy large quantities of corn to feed their animals, creating a corn shortage elsewhere. As a result, livestock raisers in the Northeast had to import Canadian wheat for fodder. This put a strain on Great Lakes iron ore shipping, as shippers gave priority to the wheat. And because so much skim milk was also fed to the hogs, there was a shortage of casein needed for the manufacture of adhesives in many war-related industries, so casein had to be imported from Argentina.
- Twenty-six years after extensive nuclear testing took place in Nevada, U.S. government documents disclosed that the 4,300 sheep that died in the testing area in the spring of 1953 had in fact died from excessively high exposure to radiation.
- The World Health Organization warned in 1979 that spotted grouper, red grouper, and

snapper caught in French Polynesian waters were highly poisonous. The source of the poison was determined to be bacterial dinoflagellates, which grow on coral reefs and attach to the algae fish consume. The dinoflagellates appear to be stimulated to multiply when reef environments are constantly disturbed, as during coastal blasting for construction projects.

- In April 1979, hundreds of thousands of dead fish were washed onto Atlantic beaches of a resort near the mouth of the Rio de la Plata in Argentina. There had been a similar fish kill in November 1977. While the authorities had no explanation, local inhabitants were sure the deaths were attributable to chemicals that had been dumped in the river and settled in bottom silt. Their reason: only fish that feed from the river bottom were among the dead.
- Lead weights left by fishermen on the banks of the River Avon in Stratford, England, have killed many of the famous Stratford swans, who mistook the lead for food or grit and died from lead poisoning.
- Bangladesh exports approximately 1,700 tons of frog legs a year to gourmet markets. According to the Bangladesh Zoological Society, this has also increased the insect population on whom the frogs normally would prey, necessitating increased application of pesticides.
- In Sydney, Australia, and Johannesburg, South Africa, air from the exhaust from vehicles burning leaded gasoline has markedly increased the number of annual cases of lead poisoning in children.
- In Kenya, Western scientists encouraged villagers to dig ponds to cultivate tilapia, a fish high in protein. After 10,000 ponds were dug, the local labor force was deemed insufficient to tend them all properly, and the ponds became breeding grounds for malaria-carrying mosquitoes. In Guyana, the replacement of relatively dry subsistence farming of maize and cassava with water-intensive rice cash cropping had exactly the same unintended effect.
- A farmer, fertilizing his field at the wrong time, killed thousands of birds near Newburgh, New York, in March 1979. Approximately 10,000 birds of varying species were found dead, some hanging from trees and bushes, others lying on the grounds of an elementary school and a local motel. Death was attributed to poisoning from ingestion of powerful fertilizer pellets that were spread over a 3,000-acre (1,213-hectare) area. Because the ground was still hard, the pellets did not sink in, and flocks of migrating birds apparently mistook the pellets for food.
- Copper mining and processing in the Murgal Valley of Turkey has released high quantities of sulfur dioxide into the atmosphere, resulting in serious depletion of natural vegetation, starvation of grazing animals, intensified land erosion, and pollution of underground water systems.
- In the Maldive Islands, rampant cutting of hardwood trees, a secondary export, has removed the food mainstay of rats, who lived on the fruit of some of the trees. The rats, therefore, turned to coconut trees for food, destroying about half the island's coconut crop, which is the country's main export.
- In the People's Republic of China, the hunting of owls, woodpeckers, cuckoos, and other "beneficial birds" has been prohibited because the birds eat insects and vermin that otherwise destroy crops. A Xinhua press release in 1979 reported that one owl eats about a thousand rats, mice, and other rodents in a summer, thereby saving about one ton of grain from destruction.
- In the Philippines, in 1979, river water polluted by upstream copper mining was used to irrigate rice fields and killed approximately 2,500 acres (1,000 hectares) of young rice plants, affecting the livelihoods of two thousand farmers.
- Ten varieties of shade and fruit trees planted in the Philippines for ornamentation have been found also to be extremely capable of filtering harmful sulfur dioxide and nitrogen dioxide from the air.
- The American chestnut tree has almost disappeared because of a blight introduced by a botanical exhibit from Japan on loan to the New York Botanical Garden in 1904.
- Importation to the United States of burl logs from Holland intended to provide veneer for furniture also brought Dutch elm disease, which has killed 13 million trees since 1930.
- Alaskan Eskimos, who eat mainly caribou, were found in 1962 to have high concentrations of radioactive cesium-137 in their bodies. This was blamed on nuclear test fallout that had landed on lichen on which the caribou graze.
- In December 1979, electric power in a region of the Ivory Coast was cut off for four days because a snake had wrapped itself around two high-voltage electricity conductors.
- A windowpane, lampshade, and chandelier shortage could ensue in the Philippines because the kapis shellfish, whose shell is quite impor-

tant in the local variety of these products, is about to become an endangered species as a result of overharvesting.

- The limestone pedestal of the Sphinx in Egypt absorbs underground waters, which evaporate, leaving salt crystals and brittle limestone. The Sphinx, as a result, has become dangerously off balance.
- In 594 B.C., Solon of Greece forbade export of agricultural produce from Athens. This stimulated the planting of olive trees, for which the demand was quite high at the time, in other areas of Greece. Olive trees consume a lot of groundwater but do not hold soil well, and thus the birth of Greece's still primary olive business also introduced land erosion problems that have plagued the country ever since.

P.D.

SOURCES: *World Environment Report,* United Nations Environment Plan; James Trager, *People's Chronology,* Holt, Rhinehart & Winston, 1979; *Translations on Environmental Quality,* 1979; *Worldwide Report,* U. S. Government.

THE ASWAN HIGH DAM

The world's longest river, the Nile, reaches 4,180 miles (6,690 kilometers) from its source in the Luvironza River of Burundi, to its mouth in the Mediterranean Sea. If a single factor could be said to define Egypt, it would be the Nile. Since pharaonic times the river has influenced the country's history, government, and social character. Without it, there could be no Egypt. Now, damming it has presented a host of unanticipated problems.

Early attempts to cope with the Nile's yearly flood gave rise to civilization and government. The Egyptians developed geometry to lay out their irrigation ditches. They developed the calendar to mark the Nile's seasonal changes. The river also served as Egypt's main highway, as well as a place for recreation and sport. But by far the most important aspect of the Nile was the fertility it brought to the land. Each year the flood wrested agricultural land from the middle of the Egyptian desert. Thick with 60 million to 180 million tons of silt, rich in phosphates and nitrates, the river rose each August. The fellahin, traditional peasant farmers, would dam the river

Completed in 1970 on the Nile River, the Aswan High Dam—364 feet (111 meters) tall, 1 mile (1.6 kilometers) at its base, and 2.5 miles (4 kilometers) long—created Lake Nasser (right), which covers almost 2,000 square miles (5,000 square kilometers) of desert. (*The Cousteau Society*)

back until September, then allow it to overflow its banks and cover their fields. When the river receded in November, a thick layer of naturally fertile soil would remain. Wheat, barley, and lentils were planted in April, and a single great harvest would be sufficient to feed 7 million people.

As the Nile's silt-laden waters entered the Mediterranean, they maintained the salinity balance of this ancient sea and nourished marine life. The sediment added to the wonderfully fertile Nile Delta and created natural dikes that prevented erosion by the sea's currents.

But the river could also bring great destruction. Unusually heavy or light rains in the African highlands would result in catastrophic floods or killing droughts. Therefore, attempts to harness the Nile have been going on for thousands of years; Imhotep, the architect of the first pyramid, built earthworks and canals to try to control the Nile's flow in the twenty-seventh century B.C. Efforts continued throughout the centuries. In 1843, British engineers succeeded in building a series of diversion dams on the river, and in 1902 the first Aswan Dam was erected. Still, the force of the river was stronger than any type of containment humans could engineer.

By the 1930s, population growth in Egypt was creating another problem—starvation. The population had swollen to 16 million, and more arable land was needed if the country was to feed itself. Then, in 1938, a flood severely damaged vital irrigation systems. That year, plans were drawn for a much higher second dam south of Aswan.

Political disagreements among Egypt, Britain, and the United States delayed building of the Aswan High Dam. Finally, with Soviet engineering and financing, ground was broken in 1960; and in 1971 the Nile, whose yearly caprices controlled so many aspects of Egyptian life for so many millennia, flooded for the last time. Diesel pumps lifted water from the canals into the fields for the first time. Modern technology had come to the Nile Valley. Perennial irrigation could begin.

The cost of building one of the world's largest rock-filled dams had been $1.5 billion. The High Dam stands 364 feet (111 meters) tall, measures 2.5 miles (4 kilometers) long at its top, and a mile (1.6 kilometers) wide at its base—a marvel of engineering seventeen times larger than the Great Pyramid of Cheops. Behind it is Lake Nasser, filling up and spreading out over 1,930 square miles (5,000 square kilometers) of former desert, stretching its southern third beyond the Egyptian border into the Sudan.

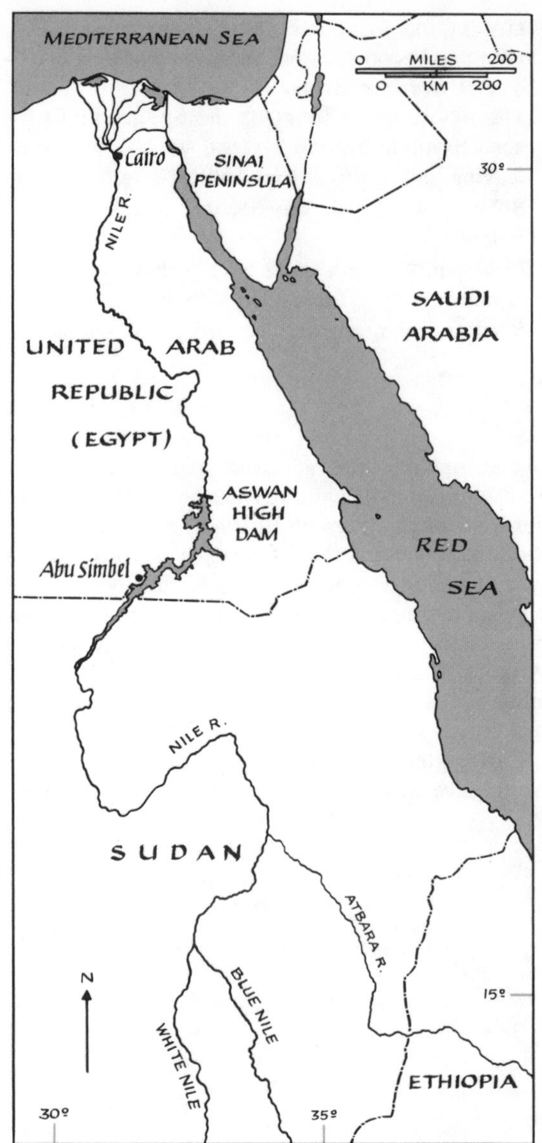

Good News

The dam was hailed as a success. As early as 1964, a potentially disastrous flood was prevented. In 1972 and 1973, low water years, the water stored in Lake Nasser saved $700 million worth of vital crops. Before the High Dam, less than 6 million acres (2.4 million hectares) of land could be irrigated and sown. Since 1970, water provided by the dam has transformed 2.5 million acres (1 million hectares) of desert basin to perennially irrigated farmland. About 950,000 acres (384,000 hectares) of desert were reclaimed for cultivation, although 600,000 acres (242,000 hectares) of agricultural land have since been lost to urban growth and industrial development. In some areas, land that had produced only one crop per year now produces three. And it is possible to plant crops that demand large amounts of water; rice is now harvested in the middle of the desert! Half of Egypt's people work in agriculture. This represents 47 percent of all employment, 30 percent of the gross national product, and 80 percent of export earnings.

Navigation has been improved below the dam. Moreover, a potentially rich fishery resource may be developed from Lake Nasser. The dam is now providing about 50 percent of Egypt's energy needs. It has also provided the power for an aluminum production industry at Qena, the expansion of a nitrate fertilizer plant at Aswan, and the production of iron and steel near Cairo. The power produced by the Aswan High Dam is among the cheapest in the world.

Bad News

In many ways, the High Dam has fulfilled the hopes of its planners. But it has also created serious problems for the people it was built to serve.

To begin with, the High Dam holds silt in Lake Nasser, where it eventually settles to the bottom. The effect has been to unbalance a natural system to which many other systems are connected.

Though three crops a year are produced in areas where one used to be harvested, many farmers complain that the quality of reclaimed soil is poor, as is the quality of crops produced. They blame this on the lack of silt, which acted as a natural fertilizer. Defenders of the dam say this new productivity has just exhausted the soil. In any case, huge amounts of expensive chemical fertilizers must now supplement whatever nutrients may still be supplied by the Nile waters.

Lacking silt, the river has increased in speed, causing greater erosion of its bed. Before the High Dam was built, silt would simply fall into and fill eroded areas. Now, there is nothing to balance the erosion. The Nile bottom deepened by 24 inches (60 centimeters) between 1964 and 1968. This has since slowed down to average about 0.7 inch (1.7 centimeters) per year. However, hydrologists wonder if the rate of erosion might not jump now that Lake Nasser has filled with water.

This scouring process also eats away at the bases of bridges, barrier dams, and all other river installations. To avoid this partially, engineers built the Tuska Canal, into which excess water can be diverted when necessary. However, doing so diminishes the potential for hydroelectric power.

The most serious example of post-dam erosion is occurring on the most fertile agricultural land in the world, the Nile Delta. For thousands of years the Delta slowly grew, thanks to the silt that spilled from the mouth of the river. Now that growth has ceased, and ocean currents eat away at the Delta's edges. Engineers agree it will be necessary to strengthen areas of the coastline to minimize these effects. High quality land on the coast is presently being lost as fast as marginal land in the desert is being gained.

With silt remaining in Lake Nasser, the southeastern Mediterranean food chain has been altered. A major source of organic matter has been lost and, as a result, shrimp and sardines have been deprived of adequate nutrients. Egypt's sardine industry, which used to provide 18,000 tons of fish annually, has disappeared. The entire balance of fish distribution has been upset. So have the coastal fishermen, who have lost a way of life. They have been pressured into either giving up fishing, acquiring the equipment and knowledge for deep-sea fishing, or relocating to Lake Nasser, where a new fishing industry is slowly being built.

Poor drainage of land has posed other problems for the fellahin. Over 1.2 million acres (485,000 hectares) are now so wet or waterlogged they are useless. In some areas the addition of too much water has forced the underground water table to rise, bringing salt up with it. The Nile flood used to flush out the salt, but today large tracts of land are covered by a white crust. Only by building underdrains parallel to irrigation channels can some 400,000 acres (162,000 hectares) of deteriorating land be saved.

The harnessing of the Nile has also had deleterious effects on public health. The annual floods used to cleanse the Nile and its canals, but now industrial, human, and animal pollution accumulates. Noxious algae grow and give the water a foul taste. Water weeds grow in the irrigation systems. Rat and scorpion populations that used to be checked by the flood now proliferate, and residents along the Nile are plagued by them.

Without the yearly periods of dryness there is no check on the spread of schistosomiasis (bilharzia), a tiny worm parasite that lives within certain water snails and causes a debilitating, sometimes fatal disease in humans. Stable water conditions provided by the High Dam create the perfect habitat for these snails, and as they increase so does the incidence of bilharzia disease. The disease has now spread from the Delta, where it has long been a problem, southward into Middle and Upper Egypt, concentrating around Lake Nasser. However, some scientists point out it is impossible to know exactly who or what is responsible for this spread, stagnant water conditions, or the movement of infected humans, or both.

Also, the creation of the High Dam and of Lake Nasser has upset cultures that had remained stable since pharaonic times. Above the dam, nearly 100,000 people had to be relocated from where the lake would form. Half of these were from Egyptian villages, the other half were Sudanese Nubians.

Below the dam, the fellahin culture, which was built around flood irrigation, has been profoundly altered. For example, now that fertilizer and diesel pumps are in demand, money has become far more important. If a fellah cannot afford a pump he must pay for a daily ration of water, or labor by hand with his *shaduf,* a well sweep, through the day. Life is not necessarily easier since the dam. The fellahin no longer work their fields just once a year; now the work is constant and includes a harvest during the hottest summer months. A new class is emerging of peasant entrepreneurs and those who manage to acquire more than their allotted share of land. For some it means being free from poverty at last. For others it means higher expectations, confusion, and frustration.

There may never be a definitive verdict on the Aswan High Dam, but what is certain is that it has changed all that was familiar about the Nile.

L.W.

AN ANCIENT CITIZENS' PROTEST

The Tiber overflowed during Rome's days of glory and the A.D. 15 incident told by historian Tacitus in his *Annals* is a lesson that congressional public works committees might well heed. Overanxious engineers, it seems, are not a phenomenon limited to today.

When the river flooded parts of Rome, engineers were ordered to "control the water level." The question was "whether the Tiber floods should be checked by diverting the streams and lakes which nourished the Tiber. Deputations from the country towns were heard. The Florentines begged that the river Chiana should not be moved from its natural bed into the Arno, with disastrous effect on themselves. Interamna's case was similar—acceptance of the plan to spread the waters of the Nera far and wide in small channels would ruin the best land in Italy.

"The people of Reate protested equally vigorously against the damming of the Velino, since it would burst its banks into the surrounding country. Nature, they said, had done best for humanity by allotting to each river its appropriate mouth, course, and limits too; and respect must be paid to the religious susceptibilities of the inhabitants, who had honored the rivers by their homes with rites, and groves, and altars—and indeed Tiber himself would scarcely be glad to flow less majestically, deprived of his associate tributaries. Because of the pleas from towns, or superstitious scruples, or engineering difficulties, the senate carried a proposal by Gaius Calpurnius Piso that nothing should be changed." Let it flow untouched was the senate's word.

THE CONQUEST OF MESOPOTAMIA

The area surrounding the Tigris and Euphrates rivers (much of contemporary Iraq), which is now dry and barren, was covered with trees and grassland in 7000 B.C. In the hospitable land and climate, shepherds began to raise cattle, sheep, and goats about 6300 B.C. Their success attracted more shepherds, and soon they found it necessary to cut down trees to provide more pasture for their growing herds.

Residential communities appeared about 4000 B.C., and Mesopotamia was born, developing a culture that pitted humans against chaotic nature. Their goal was to impose order on nature. Nature did not provide water when and where the Mesopotamians needed it, so they built irrigation canals. For a while their farms flourished, but they continued to cut trees for lumber and to provide pasture.

Without the trees, of course, the soil began to erode and make its way into the irrigation canals, which became clogged and were continually in need of maintenance. Drainage of farmland was poor, and salt began to build up in the soil. By 3000 B.C. agricultural production was dropping

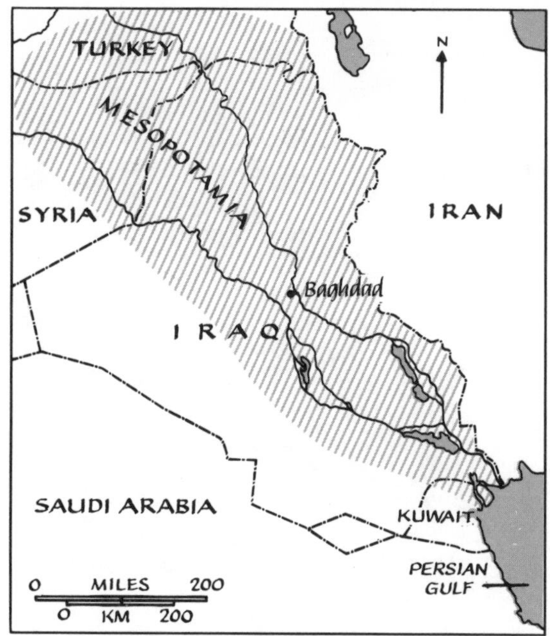

and the pastures were disappearing due to lost topsoil. The canals required more and more work until the efforts of the Mesopotamians to tame nature were not even sufficient to sustain themselves. The canals, which had been built up higher and higher to allow water to flow over the silt would often flood and do extensive damage. The area became prey to successive waves of invaders, each of which remained for a while, continuing the destruction of the environment, until it was conquered by the next wave. A long history of human efforts to manipulate nature has left the area, once part of the "Fertile Crescent," a desolate wasteland today.

The Mesopotamian story was cited in 1980 by the head of the California state resources agency, Huey D. Johnson, as an illustration of what his state could be facing. The so-called breadbasket of California, the San Joaquin Valley, is suffering from poor drainage of irrigated land, overgrazing, and cultivation of highly erodable soils. Salinization of topsoil threatens to turn once-fertile farmland into sheets of salt. The situation brings to mind an ancient aphorism: The more things change the more they remain the same.

K.F.

THE GREEN REVOLUTION

In the decades following World War II, it became apparent to agricultural scientists and politicians that food production was lagging behind population growth in many of the developing countries. Malnutrition was becoming endemic in several Asian and African nations and the amount of exploited farmland was minimal. The threat of widespread famine and social upheaval was seen as very possible.

The general solution to this impending apocalypse was an intensive search for a quick technological remedy. A series of global programs, funded primarily by the Rockefeller and Ford foundations, were initiated to improve the production technology of agriculture. The flaw in this scheme was that no real attempt was made to understand what effects such a program might have on the social and ecological relationships in these countries. The programs focused on farms that had enough capital and land to use the new technology effectively. As a result, a well-meaning program has produced not only tremendous benefits but significant unexpected problems as well.

The production technology was aimed at breeding new varieties of plants, especially wheat, rice, and corn, that would respond dramatically to fertilizers, mechanical tillage, and irrigation. Many of the traditional varieties either did not respond to large amounts of fertilizer or responded by growing spindly and weak. Botanists sought plants that would react by producing more grain.

Great Expectations

The breakthrough came with the development of short-statured varieties, first of wheat and then rice. On experimental plots, spectacular four-fold increases over traditional varieties were sometimes obtained. The press popularized the boundless optimism of several scientists and pronounced a "Green Revolution" that would end the specter of hunger forever. In 1970, the Nobel Peace Prize was awarded to Dr. Norman Borlaug for his success in developing high-yielding varieties (HYV) of wheat in Mexico at the Rockefeller-funded Center for the Improvement of Corn and Wheat. At the awards ceremony, the chairperson enthused, ". . . we do not any longer have to be pessimistic about the economic future of the developing nations."

Thousands of new plow supports await sale in Upper Volta. The Green Revolution sent waves of modern farm equipment, pesticides, and fertilizers to developing countries, with mixed results. (*FAO/J. Van Acker*)

Tricks and Trickles

These new miracle crops were generally made available not to the poor farmers of the world but to wealthier owners of larger farms. Architects of the Green Revolution sincerely believed this would help the poor through the "trickle down" theory of development, in which an infusion of capital into the wealthier classes eventually generates more jobs and opportunities for poorer classes. The opposing theory of development—aiding the poor by giving them capital directly—was not considered until much later. Political considerations, too, played a part in the Green Revolution. Martin Kriegsberg, the director of planning and evaluation of the Foreign Economic Development Service of the U. S. Department of Agriculture, an agency that helped spread the Green Revolution, pointed out that the farmers made wealthy by high-yield crops would become a stabilizing influence on the countries, acting as a counterforce to radical labor groups.

Initially, yields on the better farmlands did rise considerably. In the early 1960s, several nations showed significant increases in grain production. However, these initial spurts in grain yield were not sustained. As more and more land was put into HYV cultivation, the better land was quickly used up and the more marginal lands were cultivated. Suddenly the ecological vulnerability of the HYVs became apparent. Unless the HYVs were pampered with carefully controlled irrigation, large amounts of high nitrogen fertilizer, and frequent application of pesticides, they often produced less than the traditional varieties. These three ingredients were difficult and costly to apply to marginal lands. In the late 1960s in Pakistan, the yields on marginal lands were so low that the national average yield per acre declined by 20 percent.

The Green Addiction

Dependence on costly chemicals and petroleum-based fertilizers turned out to be an Achilles heel of high-yield varieties. When oil prices began to rise in the 1970s, the production costs of these crops, enormous to begin with, soared.

The International Rice Research Institute (IRRI), the agency responsible for developing high-yield varieties of rice, estimates that, before the oil price hikes, farming costs for the new varieties of rice were eleven times greater than the costs for farming the more traditional varieties. Since then the situation has worsened, and not only are the costs greater but the risks are greater. The new varieties have frequently proven to be susceptible to diseases, pests, and drought. For a wealthy farmer with available capital and access to credit and government subsidies, crop failure is a serious event. For the poor farmer, it is a disaster.

The Green Revolution became a kind of high stakes card game with the deck stacked against the poor farmer, who lacked capital, credit, and access to many government price-support and crop-insurance programs. Because of the potentially large profits to be made with HYVs, land prices escalated wildly. In the Punjab of India, land costs in the early 1960s rose nearly 500 percent and the IRRI reported even larger increases in parts of the Philippines. Once a poor farmer lost his farm, land prices made it impossible to acquire another one.

The Big Get Bigger

Large farms also had the advantage of scale. While a tractor is an extravagant expense for a small farm, on a large farm it saves money by eliminating the need for several farm hands. The World Bank estimated that for each tractor purchased in Pakistan, seven to twelve jobs were lost. Also, purchasing tractors apparently gives farm-owners the incentive to expand their farms. The Pakistan study showed that farms that acquired tractors grew by an average of 240 percent within the three years following the purchase. Most of this increase was achieved by evicting tenants. As farms in Pakistan became larger and more mechanized during the 1960s, employment declined by 40 percent.

Indira Rajamaran, an Indian economist, points out that the Green Revolution has increased the need for temporary agricultural laborers at harvest times and greatly decreased the need for full-time agricultural laborers. As a result, bands of migrant laborers, cut off from their families and villages, now roam the countryside. Most rural households below the poverty level are headed by a temporary laborer. Eventually, most of these families move to the rapidly swelling ghettos of the major cities.

The Lean Revolution

The shift to HYVs has actually caused a drop in local food supplies. To earn foreign exchange money, the governments of many developing nations have encouraged the exportation of grain. Since the greatest profits are in HYVs, the production of other basic foods has suffered. In India, the per capita production of protein-rich legumes dropped 30 percent in the ten years following 1961. As the supply of other basic foods declined, the prices increased. While a wealthy farmer is likely to have adequate storage facilities to keep some grains for home use and sell the rest throughout the year when prices are good, a poor farmer must sell everything at the time of harvest when prices are lowest and then purchase higher-priced food throughout the rest of the year.

Finally, the Green Revolution has caused a decline in the *quality* of grains. Researchers have noticed that grains planted close together (this is done to make the application of herbicides easier) have less protein than grains planted farther apart. They have also found that chemical nitrogen fertilizer causes a slightly different distribution of amino acids within the plants than does natural nitrogen fertilizer. The HYV plants are designed to respond to nitrogen fertilizer by producing more protein, but the *quality* of that protein is lower than in traditionally grown crops.

Of course, there was nothing intrinsically wrong with genetically redesigning crops. Farmers have been breeding crops for millennia. As early as the eleventh century, a Sung emperor in China introduced an Indonesian variety of rice that was short-statured and matured in 100 days instead of 180 days, and by the early nineteenth century the Chinese had rice that matured in only 35 days after planting. The unavoidable weak spot in the Green Revolution was the vulnerability of the poorer farmers. As the title of a recent book by Michael Perelman, an agricultural economist, suggests, the Green Revolution was *Farming for Profit in a Hungry World.* There is hope, however—the International Rice Research

Institute in the Philippines and the Center for the Improvement of Corn and Wheat in Mexico have initiated programs to help the small farmer. The new emphasis is on developing cropping systems that are less dependent on capital and fossil fuel. Ironically, the new systems make use of the rich genetic diversity of *traditional* varieties of crops. The redesigned plan is to improve the quality of life by working within the ecological and social framework, not outside it.

C.R.C.

THE RISE AND FALL OF THE ROMAN FARM

The glorious city of ancient Rome began as a community of small farms. As the city grew, so did the farms. Small farmers gradually disappeared, and wealthy farmers, who depended on slave labor, lost sight of the necessity of careful soil management. In a similar trend today, farms are being consolidated and owners are becoming dangerously dependent, not on slaves but on expensive oil-based machinery and chemicals.

In Rome in the first and second centuries B.C., wealthy people acquired tracts of land near the city, which they developed into large farms called *latifundia*. As the demand for food by city dwellers increased, these farmers turned to slave labor to increase their production and their profits. Small farmers, unable to compete with the slave farms, were forced out of business, and many joined the unemployed in the city. A kind of welfare system had to be created in the swelling city, with rations of grain given out to the city poor.

"FROM ALL THE AVAILABLE EVIDENCE, THIS CIVILISATION LASTED ABOUT THREE MONTHS."

Although Roman farmers knew their land had to be left fallow periodically to renew its nutrients, they ignored this precaution as food demand increased. Both native farmland and land in North Africa were pushed to exhaustion to feed the growing empire. As production began to decline, Lucretius, the philosopher and naturalist, observed that the land was dying. Actually, the Romans were killing it.

Columella, a Roman agriculturalist, perceived the problem of the soil and offered a solution: "Come to its aid with manure." His advice was unheeded as Rome watched its valuable sewage flow into the Tiber River.

Rome's efforts to push farm production failed because they ignored the requirements of nature. As Roman armies conquered new granaries far from home, unemployment and food shortages lowered the morale of Romans in the city. The empire, hungry and overextended, moved toward downfall.

The land around Rome has never recovered. It is still dry, rocky, and hard to farm. North African land that once supplied much of Rome's grain is now desert. Tiny, impoverished villages like el Jem and Tisgad are found near the ruins of the large Roman cities of Thysdrus and Thamugadi, sad reminders of the price paid for Rome's days of glory.

K.F.

THE SILENT INVADER

In 1825, great fanfare marked the opening of New York State's Erie Canal to barge traffic. Governor Clinton rode the first barge from Lake Erie to New York City. He carried a keg painted bright green and bound by gilded hoops. When he reached the Atlantic Ocean, he ceremoniously poured the keg's contents, fresh Lake Erie water, into the sea. This mingling of the Great Lakes with the "seven seas" he pronounced as "emblematical of our commercial intercourse with all the nations of the earth."

The commerce he predicted did indeed take place. The Erie Canal linked a hungry world with the vast wheat lands of the American Midwest and the industrial cities of the world with northern U.S. iron and coal. Canal barges dropped the cost of shipping freight from Lake Erie to New York City to $4.00 a ton from an overland cost of $120 a ton. In addition to the traffic in raw materials, the canal provided a westward highway for settlers and manufactured goods.

With all this excitement, nobody paid much attention to something else about to happen because of the new linkage between the Great Lakes and the sea. The stage had been set, the route had been opened, for a major ecological invasion of the Great Lakes by the sea lamprey (*Petromyzon marinus*). The Great Lakes were unprepared for an efficient, prolific predator that would ultimately play a major part in the destruction of fisheries in the lakes.

A sea lamprey attaches with its rasping mouth to a lake trout. It may stick to the fish, feeding from it, until the fish dies.

The sea lamprey is an unusual animal. While it looks like an eel, it actually represents a group of primitive fishes that have no jaws and no hard bone in their skeletons. It is an evolutionary relic that illustrates an important link in the history of vertebrate animals.

In Europe, the sea lamprey has long been part of the cuisine of many cultures. It is mentioned in one of the earliest cookbooks, written by a Greek named Athenaes in the third century B.C., and is depicted in wall murals of Pompeii and Tunisia. The Romans raised lampreys in ponds for food, and even as pets. In later centuries the English regarded sea lamprey as prized gourmet food: King John provided naval escort for lamprey-catching vessels and once traded a horse for a particularly fine specimen, and Henry I actually died of surfeit, apparently from gorging on sea lampreys. Recipes for cooking sea lampreys continue to appear in the regional cookeries of Europe.

In contemporary North America, however, the sea lamprey's reputation is entirely different. Rather than being regarded as a gourmet's delight, it is rarely eaten and is considered a pest, a voracious invader that attacks native fish. Before the Erie Canal was opened, no sea lampreys were recorded in Lake Ontario or the inland lakes of New York State. The first sea lamprey recorded in the Great Lakes was brought to the Royal Ontario Museum in Toronto, Canada, by a commercial fisher in 1835. Biologists speculate that the animal's ancestors entered through the Erie Canal, perhaps taking several generations to move up the waterway. They made several stops along the way, moving into the Finger Lakes of New York before reaching Lake Ontario.

The specimen attracted little attention. It was fifty years before commercial fishers began to notice sea lamprey scars on fish taken from Lake Ontario. Using suction and a rasping tongue and teeth, the adult sea lamprey digs into the flesh of a fish and feeds on its muscle and blood. Often this kills the fish within days—sometimes within hours. One sea lamprey can kill up to 40 pounds (18 kilograms) of fish in its two-year adult life stage. The generation of Great Lakes sea lampreys born in 1956 destroyed almost two million pounds (906,000 kilograms) of fish and scarred many more.

The sea lamprey appears to have stayed in Lake Ontario for several decades, but in 1914 and again in 1932 the Welland Canal connecting Lake Ontario and Lake Erie was widened for ship traffic. The lampreys found their way through the canal into Lake Erie. Conditions in Lake Erie were less suitable for sea lampreys: the water was too warm and shoreline streams lacked the graveled bottoms sea lampreys need for spawning. A population swam on to Lake Huron, where waters were deeper and cooler, streams entering the lake had adequate gravel bottoms, and there was an abundance of lake trout, an ideal prey for sea lampreys.

By 1936 the sea lamprey had populated Lake Huron and spread through the Straits of Mackinac into Lake Michigan. The Soo Locks at the head of the St. Marys River slowed them, but by 1946 lampreys had penetrated the largest and northernmost of the Great Lakes, Superior.

Sea lamprey populations exploded in all three upper Great Lakes (Huron, Michigan, and Superior) during the years that followed, and the sea lamprey was soon accused of destroying the commercial fisheries and of bringing lake trout near to extinction in the Great Lakes. Before the arrival of the sea lamprey, in the good fishing years between 1930 and 1939, fishers took about 14 million pounds (6.4 million kilograms) of trout annually in the upper lakes. The 1960 catch was only 0.5 million pounds (0.23 million kilograms), a decline of almost 97 percent. The lamprey was not the only culprit, however; it was aided and abetted by commercial overfishing, pollution from heavy industry, and invasions of other ocean fish species. (See "The Great Lakes," page 310.)

By the early 1950s, commercial fishers and the public demanded that governments in Canada and the United States do something about the problem. In response, both countries signed a treaty in 1954 to form the International Great Lakes Fishery Commission to control the sea lamprey. The commission's efforts are a rare example of effective international cooperation on a shared environmental problem. Its job was to deal with an unintended effect of canals opened 125 years earlier. Solving the problem has been almost as big a task as building the canal. Almost 30 years and $16 million later, the sea lamprey has been discouraged but not defeated. The story of the struggle illustrates the difficulty of routing an "invader species."

The first control attempt, mechanical barriers to trap adults going upstream to spawn, did not work well. They were easily damaged by floating debris, and during high water the sea lampreys just swam around them.

Next, biologists erected electrical barriers. By suspending electrodes in spawning streams they set up electrical fields that paralyzed the lampreys. Unfortunately, other fish were also paralyzed. Scientists tried and failed to produce a current strong enough to kill younger lamprey without killing fish. Thus, electrical weirs were abandoned.

Finally, scientists turned to chemicals. They sought a chemical that would kill lampreys but not other fish or important stream organisms. The International Great Lakes Fishery Commission financed a massive research effort to test 6,000 chemicals before choosing one called trichloro-3-trifluoromethyl-4-nitrophenol (TFM). TFM kills larval sea lamprey, which bury themselves in the mud after hatching. They remain in the mud four to eighteen years. At this stage they are much more accessible to control methods than the free-swimming adults. TFM kills only lamprey larvae as long as dosages are adjusted to the water chemistry of each stream.

After TFM was discovered and tested, both Canada and the United States began regular treatment of the more than four hundred streams where sea lamprey are known to spawn. Each stream is treated about once every four years at a cost of $10,000 per treatment. TFM has reduced sea lamprey populations from an estimated high of 44,000 in 1956 to 6,000 in 1966. As long as the treatments continue, scientists expect to be able to control the population.

The scientists are aware, however, that the history of most pesticides ends with the pest developing some degree of immunity. Although the sea lamprey has shown no signs of immunity yet, no one will be surprised if that happens.

Another problem is registration of TFM. The chemical was put into use before federal registration of chemicals was required, and the testing necessary now to determine whether TFM is safe is costing millions of dollars. TFM is a phenol, a family of chemicals notorious for their toxicity and their long life in the environment. The chemical is a potent poison; it kills lamprey ammocetes (lamprey larvae) at low concentrations, but it can kill fish at higher concentrations. A few inadvertent fish kills have occurred, proving that careful application is crucial.

Meanwhile, nonchemical controls are being sought. The only permanent solution may be through genetic changes. Researchers are investigating ways to sterilize males or to attract normal males to sterile females. (See "Integrated Pest Management," page 31.)

Governor Clinton certainly could not have imagined the unanticipated invasion of sea lampreys made possible by the Erie Canal. He had no way to foresee that while the canal had made world trade with the Midwest possible, it would also strike a blow to the famous lake trout fishery of the Great Lakes. Nor could he imagine that one of the eventual products of the Erie Canal would be a bureaucracy dedicated to eradicating an ocean pest in the Greak Lakes, costing millions of taxpayer dollars in both Canada and the United States. And ironically, all of this present-day array of scientific research, experimental technology, and wildlife management has been assembled to destroy an animal that other humans in other parts of the world have treasured as a gourmet food.

L.Y.L.

AUSTRALIAN RABBITS AND SOME OTHER INVADERS

When people settle a new place, they often plan to enhance their environment by introducing foreign plants and animals. These introductions can be regrettable mistakes, especially on islands and in isolated ecosystems. Given a favorable climate and no natural enemies, a species may proliferate beyond control. In many cases the result is destructive.

The introduction of rabbits to Australia is probably the most famous of such disastrous interferences with a native ecosystem.

In 1859, a farmer in southern Australia, homesick for England, imported two dozen wild English rabbits and set them free on his land. Within six years, Thomas Austin's twenty-four rabbits had multiplied to 22 *million*. They spread across Australia at a rate of 70 miles (42 kilometers) a year, reaching every corner of the continent by 1907. By the 1930s, the Australian rabbit population was estimated at 750 million!

The rabbits became an enormous plague, eating the best grass, fouling waterholes, devouring crops, gnawing young trees, and contributing to the rapid erosion of soil in many places. The rabbits competed directly with livestock; the sheep population of some areas was cut in half by the rabbit invasion (seven rabbits eat as much as one sheep). It was estimated that half the Australian farmer's dollar spent on machinery, fertilizer, or seeds actually went to feed rabbits.

In the early 1950s, the Australians introduced a disease called myxomatosis to their rabbits. Up to 90 percent of the rabbits in Australia died, and the sheep revived. The wool clip increased by 70 million pounds (31 million kilograms), a graphic illustration of the price that rabbits were exacting from Australia's farmers.

There are many similar examples from around the world.

- The European starling has become a pest in North America, where it was introduced by settlers. A large, greedy, noisy bird, it has driven out the smaller native birds from many areas.
- The Asian mongoose, introduced to Jamaica in 1870 to control rats, has instead killed off several native reptile species.
- European red deer, imported to New Zealand for hunters, increased so fast that they were classified as vermin. The deer are responsible for destroying the ground cover in many watersheds, increasing floods and soil erosion. Except for humans, they have no natural enemies in New Zealand.
- The prickly-pear cactus, brought to Australia from the American desert in the 1800s as a decorative plant, infested more than 62.5 million acres (25 million hectares) of land by 1925. The cacti grew so close together that the land became useless for livestock grazing.
- The Mediterranean tamarisk now lines the banks of the Grand Canyon of the Colorado. The tamarisk drinks up the water supply of the native cottonwood trees, which grow higher up the slopes. The cottonwood trees are dying.
- The kudzu vine, a tenacious, tangly growth from Africa, is now a major problem in the southern United States, where its prolific growth has covered hills, trees, and even roads. (See also "Water Hyacinths," page 43.)

Many introductions have been inadvertent—the rat and mouse must have traveled with the earliest human migrants. Other introductions have been favorable: the honeybee was brought to the Americas, oranges to the Mediterranean, the peanut to Africa, the banana to South America, and so on. But today, in an age of air travel, most countries carefully restrict plant and animal movement across borders. Some important lessons have been learned since Thomas Austin decided Australia needed rabbits.

J.S.

SPRAYING THE WORLD

In 1120, the Bishop of Léon "excommunicated" a plague of crop-eating caterpillars. Since that presumably futile effort at pest control, the arsenal against insects and weeds has grown dramatically. For the most part, we rely on chemical laboratories to provide the newest weaponry. As early as A.D. 100 the Chinese *Pharmacopoeia of the Heavenly Husbandman* recommended the use of mercury to control body lice, but commercial pesticides have been commonly used only in this century. By 1938, pesticides were used so regularly that the U. S. Food, Drug, and Cosmetic Act was passed to regulate the level of acceptable residues in food. In 1939, DDT (dichloro-diphenyl-trichloro-ethane), a chemical known since the previous century, was found to be amazingly effective at killing insects. DDT was first applied to soldiers and citizens during World War II to stop a major outbreak of lice-carried typhus. With proof of DDT's effectiveness, a pest-free world became the goal of many farmers and pesticide manufacturers. What began with the best of intentions, however, has turned into a problem of epic proportions.

Creating Superbugs

The World Health Organization began to use DDT against *Anopheles* mosquitoes, the carriers of malaria. There is little doubt that DDT has saved the lives of millions of people in malaria-infested parts of the world by eliminating mosquitoes. Similar successes were reported for other pests, and the future seemed bright for both the farmers and the pesticide industry until the first warning came in 1947, when houseflies began to develop resistance to DDT. Only insects with genes giving them resistance to DDT survived the massive sprayings in the fields, gardens, and homes. These insects reproduced offspring that were also resistant. As more species of insects evolved DDT-resistant populations, other chemicals were tried, such as organophosphates and carbamates, but many insects developed resistance to these as well. Currently, more than two hundred species are known to be resistant to insecticides. Still, approximately 155 million pounds (70.3 million kilograms) of the active ingredients of insecticides are used annually on U.S. farms,

A crop duster sprays a fungicide over an orange grove near Ft. Pierce, Florida, at a rate of 10 gallons per acre (94 liters per hectare). (*USDA*)

and nearly as much is used by homeowners. This amount is very unequally distributed among the different kinds of crops. For example, soybeans are a major crop but use less than 4 percent of all farm insecticides. Cotton, however, uses nearly half of all farm insecticides. Including herbicides (weed killers), the most rapidly growing pesticide class, the total production in the United States is over 1.5 billion pounds (680 million kilograms), nearly half the world total. (See "The Most-Sprayed Foods," page 600.) The sales value for U.S. pesticides comes to nearly $2 billion. Clearly, selling pesticides is very big business. But are they effective?

What If We Stopped?

David Pimentel, a Cornell University entomologist, has estimated crop losses in dollar value that would result if we stopped all use of pesticides. Overall losses would increase about 9 percent (to approximately 42 percent of production) if pesticides were banned. For food crops the increase is only 2 percent. Grains would be little affected, although there would be significant losses for certain crops such as peaches, plums, and tomatoes unless other control methods were used.

The bald eagle, symbol of the United States, is a victim of the pesticide DDT. DDT apparently caused females to lay extremely thin-shelled eggs, many of which failed to hatch. (*SCS/USDA/Van Dersal*)

Innocent Bystanders

Pesticides are not applied to pests. They are applied to ecosystems that happen to include the pests. In 1962, Rachel Carson forcefully brought this distinction to the public in a book, *Silent Spring,* that documented the ecological problems with pesticides and created an environmental movement. One of the best-documented examples of the ecological effects of pesticides comes from a study of Clear Lake, California. To control annoying gnats at this resort lake in 1949, the pesticide DDD (a relative of DDT) was sprayed in small concentrations of 0.02 and 0.05 parts per million. Over the following few years the gnats were eliminated as a nuisance. Unfortunately, the pesticide's effects weren't limited to the gnats. Fish, feeding on insects, accumulated the pesticide to levels of 600 parts per million. And western grebes, birds which were feeding on the fish, accumulated the pesticide to concentrations of 1,600 parts per million. The grebes disappeared from Clear Lake.

We now know that only about 1 percent of the applied pesticide actually reaches the target pest. The other 99 percent enters the ecosystem. The ecological impact of pesticides has been well documented and the list includes the near extinction of the peregrine falcon, osprey, and bald eagle, as well as many other creatures.

A less-well-known but far-reaching effect of pesticides is on bee populations. As early as 1944, there was evidence that pesticides were seriously affecting honeybee and wild bee populations. Honeybees and wild bees are extremely sensitive to pesticides. In fact, honeybees are so sensitive that the U.S. government has established an indemnity program to protect beekeepers. One report estimated that the poisoning of honeybees and the subsequent losses in pollination of crops and in honey production has cost about $12 million annually.

Human Targets

Humans are also part of the ecosystem. Currently, the average American carries 12 parts per million of DDT in fatty tissues, and agricultural workers may have as much as 1,000 parts per million in body tissue. The social cost of pesticide usage is large and, to a great extent, hidden. According to one study, nearly 100 percent of the people surveyed tested positive for at least one type of pesticide. DDT and related pesticides have been restricted or banned in the United States, but residues occur in milk and in human tissue.

Other, shorter-lived pesticides, such as the organophosphates and carbamates, have appeared. Many of these chemicals and their byproducts are extremely toxic to humans. The U. S. Environmental Protection Agency estimates that about 14,000 people are non-fatally poisoned each year in the United States. Half of these poisonings are serious enough to require hospitalization, and approximately two hundred fatalities occur each year. Yet, these figures may be serious underestimates.

The history of parathion, a particularly common and toxic organophosphate insecticide, provides a glimpse of the complexity involved in estimating the health costs of pesticides. In 1963, peach pickers in several northern California orchards began to report serious symptoms of pesticide poisoning. All of the orchards were complying with the state and federal recommendations for pesticide application times and amounts. None of the fruits contained more than the legal limit (one part per million) of pesticide residues. Yet three fourths of all workers in the fields showed some signs of parathion absorption. Apparently, the workers were not suffering directly from parathion but rather from poisons created as parathion broke down chemically in the fields. One of these molecular spinoffs, paraoxon, is as much as ten times more toxic than parathion.

Farm workers report such symptoms as nausea, eye and skin irritation, chronic headache, and sleeplessness at rates more than fifteen times that of similar nonfarm-worker populations. What's more, studies have shown that farm workers do not always report poisoning symptoms. One study in the *Journal of Occupational Medicine* suggested that less than 2 percent of poisonings were actually reported to physicians, and a 1973 study of California farm workers estimated definite cases of pesticide illnesses at three hundred times the number reported. The low reporting rate seems to issue from a fear of reprisals from employers. A farm worker who reports illegal pesticide use is likely to lose a job and be locally blacklisted as well. Also, many workers simply don't know their rights. Since pesticide poisoning is clearly a job-related illness, all farm workers are entitled to workman's compensation. Yet in one survey 70 percent of the farm workers hadn't heard of workman's compensation and nearly two thirds received no health benefits at all. Thus, a farm worker making a marginal living isn't likely to make a costly visit to a doctor unless the symptoms are severe.

Forty years ago pesticides seemed like an easy solution to humanity's age-old battle with bugs. Scientists have documented the appalling consequences and the unexpected effects of this "easy way out." Although pesticide use has been somewhat restricted in the United States and several other countries, many of the most deadly and least specific of the poisons continue to be used in developing countries. (See "Better Living Through Chemistry?" page 507, and "Come Pollute Us," page 697.)

Fortunately, there are alternatives to chemical pesticides for control of crop pests. Integrated pest management (IPM) is a more ecologically sound method to control pests. This approach attacks insects with a variety of weapons, most of which control the pest without contaminating the ecosystem. (See "Integrated Pest Management," page 31.) C.R.C.

THE TRESPASSING POISON: ACID RAIN

In the early 1960s, Swedish scientists became concerned over a dramatic decline in fish populations in many of their lakes. Their studies showed that the lakes had become highly acidic over the past four decades—so acidic that tiny fish could not survive. Research led into the air and out of the country, to the factories of the English Midlands and the Ruhr Valley of Germany, where oxides of sulfur and nitrogen spewed from industrial smokestacks. These chemicals reacted in the air with oxygen and moisture to form pockets of dilute sulfuric and nitric acid. Downwind from the industrial areas the concentrated acids washed back to earth in rains, snows, hail, or fogs that were often as acidic as vinegar (normal rain is only slightly acidic). Unexpectedly, industry in one part of the world was affecting the health of another part. Reports began to appear in scientific journals that acid rain had harmed lakes in eastern Canada, the north-

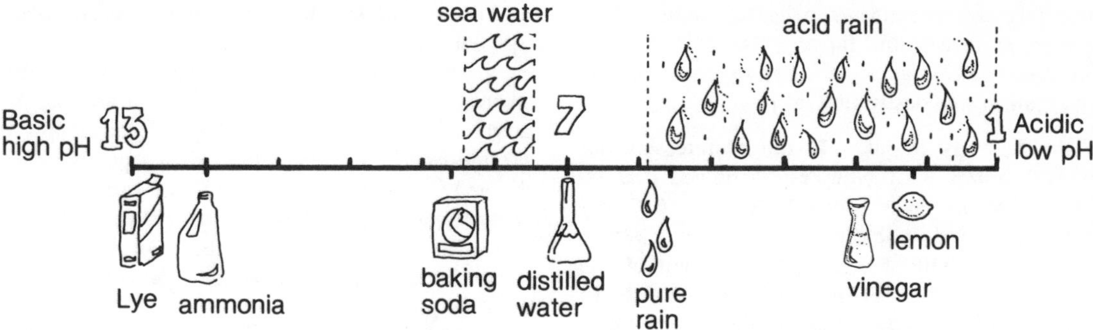

Acid rain on the pH scale—as acidic as lemons and vinegar.

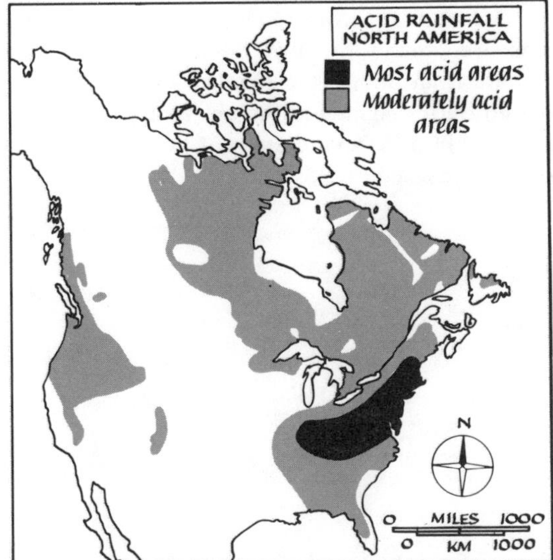

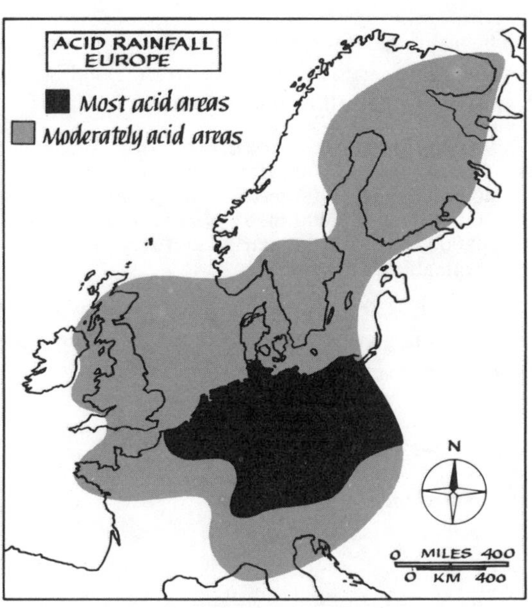

western and northeastern United States, parts of Europe, and Asia.

The best evidence suggests that acid rain derives mainly from vehicle exhaust (63 percent of the nitrogen oxides) and oil- or coal-burning power plants and industries (70 percent of the sulfur dioxides). Coal burning emits more sulfur dioxides than oil burning, thus as coal-rich nations such as the United States switch from oil to coal, the emissions are likely to increase. Ironically, one environmental control may actually increase the problems of acid rain. Tall smokestacks, intended to disperse pollutants away from surrounding cities on high air currents, could be allowing the pollutants to stay airborne long enough to be transformed into acids and to travel thousands of miles before falling to earth as rain or snow.

Airborne sulfur and nitrogen oxides often become trapped in poorly circulating pockets of warm air that travel unpredictably along with frontal systems. At a particular weather station, a rainfall with normal acidity may be followed a few days later by an abnormally high acid rainfall. Until the early 1970s, rain was unsystematically sampled for acidity and pollution levels. During the 1970s, the World Meteorological Organization set up a global system of monitoring stations that now keep track of acid rain.

Though unpredictable, acid rains do follow a general pattern based on prevailing winds and seasonal changes. For example, much of the pollution from Chicago's steel factories follows westerly winds to pollute lakes and streams in Ontario and New York State. The most highly acidic rains fall in early winter and during the transition between spring and summer, meaning that both the melting winter snow and the spring rains are frequently acidic. Poisonous trickles of acid-water flow into streams just as many fish are spawning and along the ground as delicate seedlings are emerging in forests and farm fields.

The effects of acid rain range from killing tiny organisms to destroying crops.

- **Fish** A study of lakes in the remote Adirondack Mountains of New York showed that 90 percent of the lakes above 2,000 feet (610 meters) were highly acidic and had very few fish. Before the 1930s, fewer than 4 percent of the lakes were acidic and they teemed with fish. In these poisoned waters the pH level is below 5 (pH 7 is neutral; 0 is most acid; 14 most alkaline). Most fish eggs and young fish do not develop properly, and thus don't live to adulthood. Many eggs are sterile.
- **Aquatic ecosystem** In addition to its direct effect on fish, acid rain can alter the entire aquatic ecosystem. When the acid level of a lake drops below pH 5, the growth of bacteria and algae is inhibited while fungi continue to flourish. A mat of fungal filaments forms, preventing seasonal turnover of the water, which is necessary to distribute bottom nutrients to the lake's inhabitants. Thus even plants and animals not particularly sensitive to acidity can be starved by the effects of acid rain.

  Increased acidity in the water can unlock toxic heavy metals long ago trapped in the sediments of lake and stream bottoms, including mercury, copper, lead, manganese, nickel, zinc, and aluminum. Once released, these metals move through the food chain, eventually concentrating in large fish. The effect is to recycle pollution that escaped being taken up by the food web when it was first dumped into the water system.
- **Forests** Acid rain is suspected of slowing tree growth and decreasing soil fertility. It also disrupts the sensitive fertilization stage of ferns and lichens.
- **Agriculture** Droplets of acid rain collect on the hairy leaves of soybeans and burn lesions through the leaf surface—a direct wound and an entry point for disease. Some grains, like alfalfa, have shown reduced yields in the presence of acid rain even though there is no visible damage. Spinach, soybeans, and oats are extremely sensitive to the sulfur dioxide in acid rain.

Researchers at the Brookhaven National Laboratory in New York have shown that acid rain even leaches nutrients directly from the leaves of crop plants.

The loss of soil fertility due to acid rain is of special concern to farmers. Acidity upsets the ecology of helpful soil organisms that nourish crops. Such legumes as peas, stringbeans, and soybeans require a symbiosis with a certain nitrogen-fixing root bacteria in the genus *Rhizobium* to produce normal levels of protein. These bacteria are very sensitive to acidity. Since legumes are one of the highest protein-yielding crops, acid rain, if unchecked, could degrade the world's protein supply.

Acid rain also poses some perplexing legal problems, since affected individuals and nations presently have no recourse against the foreign and out-of-state industries wreaking a long-range havoc on their environment. These poisonous rains are among the most noxious side effects of industrialization—the wastes of one region spewed out of sight into the air, migrate with the rain to kill fish and damage forests and crops somewhere else.

C.R.C., M.P.

ACID RAIN "IMPORTS"

The rain that falls over West Germany in one year contains sulfur dioxide from neighboring countries in the following amounts:

90,000 tons (81,000 metric tons) from England
50,000 tons (45,000 metric tons) from France
40,000 tons (36,000 metric tons) from Belgium
30,000 tons (27,000 metric tons) from Holland
90,000 tons (81,000 metric tons) from indeterminable sources

However, West Germany, with its own acid rain output, gives back just about as much as it gets.

P.D.

SOURCE: *Translations on Environmental Quality,* Oct. 23, 1979, Foreign Broadcast Information Service, U. S. Government.

THE HIMALAYAS

Since 1950, the population of Nepal has more than doubled. In the same period, the Nepalese have cut down 75 percent of their trees. Flooding along rivers that originate in Nepal has also become increasingly worse since the early 1950s. These three developments are intimately related, and they point to the growing permanent damage that is being inflicted on the Himalayas—the world's tallest, steepest, youngest, and perhaps most beautiful mountain range.

Most people in Nepal live in the hill country between the icy high peaks and the lowland called the Tarai that borders India. Although the hill country was well forested thirty years ago, it is now so naked of trees that the average family spends a quarter of its time just looking for wood. People have to go farther from home to find trees. At the same time, driven by population pressure to farm new land, farmers have gradually been going higher into the mountains. The steep slopes of the Himalayas are not suited to farming. During the monsoon season, the Himalayas receive more water than any other place on earth. Without trees to hold it in place, soil washes away down the steep slopes at a disastrous rate. Some Nepalese officials have been known to quip that topsoil is one of the country's chief exports.

The loss of topsoil has meant a corresponding decline in farm productivity, at the same time that population is increasing. Very few of the fifty-five hill districts can grow enough food for their people; in some places, a third or more of all land is abandoned farmland. Each hectare (2.5 acres) of good farmland in Nepal must support about ten people—almost the same ratio as in densely populated Java, where the soil is much richer. For almost fifteen years, grain yields per hectare have declined.

The "export" of topsoil by the monsoon rains does double harm, first by denuding the hillsides of Nepal, second by filling the Himalayan rivers with silt. The beds of some rivers now rise a foot every year. The swollen rivers then overflow their

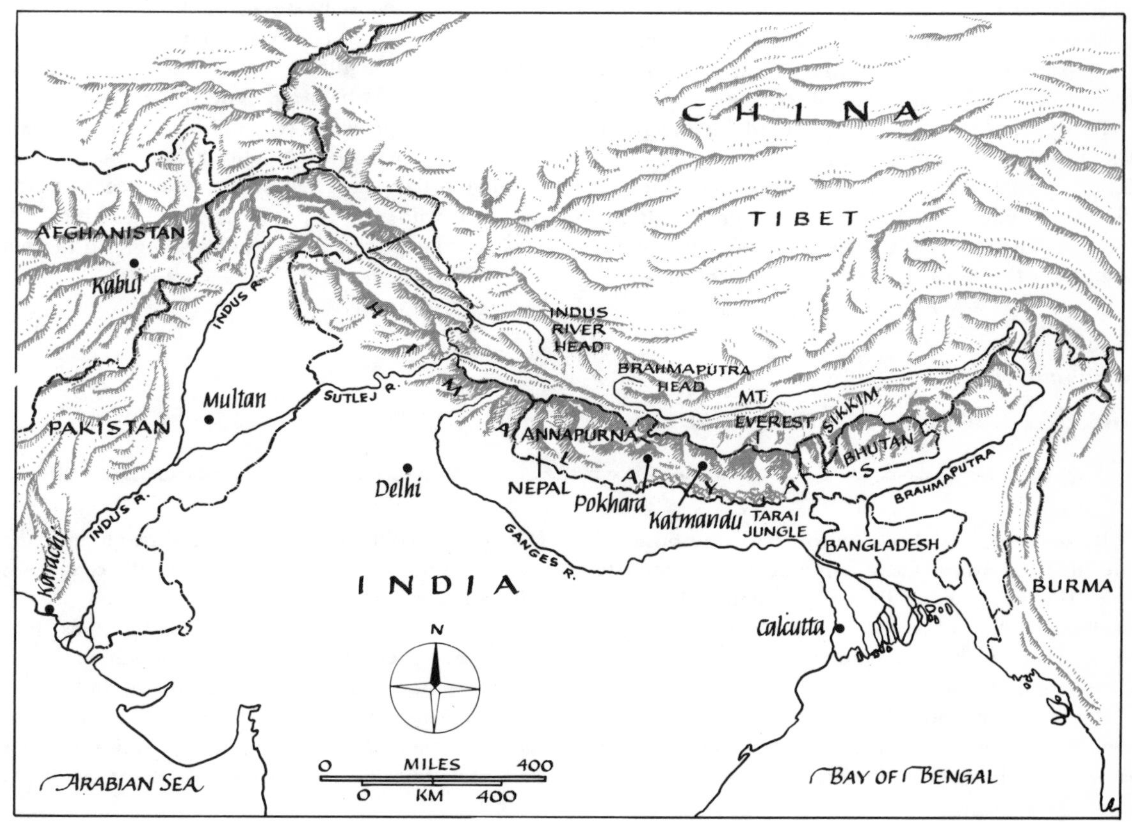

banks to progressively wider levels, sometimes even change course because of the floods and drown the best farmland.

A large corps of foreign advisers has helped the Nepalese destroy their own land. The United Nations Food and Agriculture Organization (FAO) and the World Bank worked together on a project to cut down 35,000 acres (14,140 hectares) of forest in western Nepal. The FAO thought the overgrazed hill country could use 200,000 more sheep. India laid two roads into Nepal; the British bulldozed an airstrip at the foot of Annapurna so that Queen Elizabeth's plane could land there. The United States built several sawmills and an all-weather road deep in the Tarai jungle. The Chinese have built a long road, principally for tourists, from the Tibetan border through Katmandu to Pokhara along the Trisuli River.

The Himalayas are not good mountains for road building. They are steep and tall, so that rock slides tend to be bigger and to travel farther; and the Himalayas are so young geologically—only 20 million to 30 million years old—that they retain a great deal of fragile sedimentary rock that easily washes away. Since these mountains receive more rain than any other range in the world, road building is often accompanied by unusual flooding. The roads cross tectonic faults and unstable hillsides, and they interfere with normal down-slope drainage. The new road to Pokhara has caused landslides all along its route.

Partly because of access afforded by the road, the Trisuli River valley has been deforested up to 8,000 feet (2,438 meters) above sea level. Floods, landslides, and mass wasting have ruined half the land in the once-fertile valley. Farmers are moving closer to the road, hastening the erosion process. The road has not done the Nepalese much good—the tourists it was built for usually fly to Pokhara because of the landslides.

Nepal is not the only country that has been deforesting and misusing its highlands. Overcrowding in the mountain states of India and Pakistan has led to the same problems: deterioration of soil fertility, silting of rivers, and unavailability of firewood.

The major rivers of this part of the world all originate in the Himalayas—the Brahmaputra, the Ganges, and the Indus. Deforestation upstream directly affects the flow of these rivers by swelling the monsoon runoff with silt. Low-lying Bangladesh, at the mouths of the Ganges and Brahmaputra rivers, is particularly subject to flooding, with disastrous results for its large, very poor population. In 1974–75, terrible floods on these rivers covered much of the productive farmland of Bangladesh, and there was widespread starvation and suffering.

The silt carried by the Himalayan rivers ends up in the Bay of Bengal and the Arabian Sea. A series of satellite photographs taken between 1972 and 1977 revealed formation of new land at the mouth of the Ganges River, an "island" about 100 square miles (260 square kilometers) in area. Efforts were being made to "lock in" this new land and use it for cultivation, since it consists of eroded highland topsoil, but it can take up to twenty years for "new" land to be arable.

There is a growing recognition in India, Pakistan, and Nepal that something must be done to prevent soil erosion. However, the needs of the millions who live on subsistence farming will probably keep the Himalayas washing into the sea for years to come.

J.S.

Wavemakers:

THE TREE-HUGGERS OF UTTAR PRADESH

It was late July, 1970, when, with the onset of the monsoon rains, the Alaknanda River began to rise. The residents of Dasholi, a small village in northern India, observed the nearby river's fury with concern but resignation. They were no strangers to disaster.

As the Alaknanda clawed its banks, the land was torn away. Silt-laden streams came rushing down the hills and the mountainsides of the Himalayas, spilling their valuable cargo into the swollen river as it swept toward its confluence with the Ganges.

The Alaknanda had flooded before, as had nearly every other major river in northern India, but never had the villagers seen it rise so high so quickly. Before the river subsided, it had risen 20 feet (6.1 meters), sweeping away entire villages and mountainsides, drowning hundreds of cattle

and causing millions of dollars' worth of property damage. The human toll was variously estimated at two hundred to five hundred lives lost.

The villagers of Dasholi accepted the tragedy as they had so many others. To them its causes remained a mystery. But the sterile and eroded land the flood had left behind made survival an even more tenuous prospect for the people of the already economically depressed region. "The terror of the tiger," said one villager, "has now been replaced by the terror of the landslide."

The life and economy of the Dasholi villagers, and that of the rest of the inhabitants of the northern Uttar Pradesh state in India, are inextricably linked to the forests that dot the surrounding Himalayan hills. The trees provide firewood and building materials, and they provide a protective web for the fragile soil that supports their tiny agricultural plots.

Before 1962 there was little outside interest in massively exploiting that forest wealth, but the strategic and material demands of a border war with China brought plans by the Indian government for a network of new roads in the area and a growing interest in the region's resources. At first, these proposals sparked new hope among the villagers for much-needed employment. Those hopes were soon doused. A tradition of domination by the urban elite from the southern plains continued as outside contractors flocked to Uttar Pradesh to control, and profit from, the new projects. Jobs for the villagers were largely limited to tasks involving heavy labor.

For ten years the people of Dasholi passively observed this economic exploitation. But in 1972, the villagers attempted to reverse this historical domination and formed a labor cooperative to begin on their own road to local economic development. Their first proposal to government officials was a modest one; they asked that the cooperative be allotted a plot of ten ash trees to manufacture agricultural implements for local villagers. With a terse retort Forestry Department officials denied the villagers' request, emphasizing that commercial trees were not for local sale; and, as if to completely smother the villagers' aspirations, the officials quickly sold the ash trees to a sporting goods manufacturer from a city in the plains.

Dasholi residents were stunned. Though they were habitual victims of exploitation, and had for years witnessed the pillage of the forests by "city sahibs," they had not expected that their first collective enterprise would fall so quickly to the ax of bureaucratic arrogance. It was then that the villagers vowed to end their passive witness to the plunder.

Most movements are spawned through endless meetings, and the movement to save the trees was no exception. Every night Dasholi villagers met to plot a strategy to halt the impending felling of the ash trees by the outside lumber crews. All were committed to a nonviolent Gandhian approach, and the options discussed ranged from blocking the loggers' road to burning the trees before they could be cut. No one could agree which tactic was best.

The arrival of officials from the lumber company, a sign the logging operations would soon begin, transformed the villagers' discussions from debate into desperation. But it was in this final hour, shortly before the ax blades were to touch wood, that an effective tactic finally emerged. "Let us tell the [company] officials," suggested a villager, "that when the men raise their axes in the air for striking, they will find each of the tree trunks being hugged by one of us. Before a tree is felled, one of us will be." The Chipko Andolan (the "tree-huggers") movement was born.

As it turned out, the trees were saved without the need of hugging a single tree in the group's first confrontation with the loggers. Intimidated by the spectacle of nearly every villager in the area marching in procession to defend the tiny plot of trees, company officials left angrily without an ax ever being lifted. Their later attempts to log other areas were repeatedly blocked by vigilant tree-huggers. Finally, the company's permit expired without a single tree being felled.

As the Chipko Andolan movement flourished from such victories, the forests took on new importance to the villagers. Though the trees had been traditionally viewed as a resource vital to their subsistence economy, the villagers also began to recognize the critical role the forests play in the fragile ecological fabric of the area. The memory of the tragic flooding of the Alaknanda River several years before gradually led to an environmental awakening among Chipko followers. The villagers came to realize that far from being a "natural" disaster, the unusually high waters were the devastating result of rapid and careless deforestation. What began as primarily an economic movement soon became an ecological one as well.

In 1974 the Chipko movement spread to other areas throughout northern Uttar Pradesh. So when the government announced plans to auction several thousand trees in the Reni Forest, they met Chipko resistance. Though government bureaucrats

and their affluent allies were surprised by the tenacity of the tree-huggers, they were undeterred. The government resolved that the sale of the trees in the Reni Forest would proceed, but a clever scheme would be needed to weaken the resistance.

On March 26 the government announced that a long-overdue payment would be made to the villagers (compensation for land acquired by the military) in a town 44 miles (70 kilometers) away. Few families could afford to spurn the government offer, and as a result Reni was nearly empty on payment day—mostly women and children remained behind. The lumber company quickly took advantage of this convenient opportunity, and the loggers headed in force toward the unprotected Reni Forest. An elderly village woman named Guara Devi noticed these developments with alarm. Quickly she organized a Chipko resistance force, composed exclusively of women, and rushed to the defense of the marked trees. The surprised loggers were once again turned back, and the Chipko movement had a new leader.

As the movement grew in popularity after such episodes, Chipko demands soon found receptive ears in New Delhi. An expert commission appointed by the government to study lumbering in northern forests concurred with their uneducated rural counterparts about the ecological damage of the deforestation. The commission called for—and got—a ten-year moratorium on logging in 464 square miles (1,200 square kilometers) of the Alaknanda watershed.

Chipko calls for replanting of denuded areas also got government action—but the wrong kind. Government afforestation programs substituted more profitable pine trees for the original hardwood forests. Chipko "experts" quickly concluded that the pine trees do not produce humus that can absorb water and retain soil fertility. Taking things into their own hands, the villagers have initiated their own replanting program using primarily broad-leaved trees.

The ecologic—and economic—recovery of northern India is a formidable challenge for this grassroots movement. Experts estimate that over 60 percent of the forests in Uttar Pradesh have been cleared, and if cutting continues at the present rate there are predictions that even worse flooding will devastate the region.

But if anything can halt the havoc and exploitation there, it is a crusade that captures the spirit and will of the Indian people. When Chipko-mentor Mohandas Gandhi launched his nonviolent campaign for Indian independence, he urged his followers to take up the spinning wheel and weave native cloth. This bit of self-reliance, he said, would symbolize the Indian people's resolve to reinstitute the local village economy that had withered away under British influence. Soon hundreds of thousands of Indians, rich and poor, wove in silent protest. Today, that self-determination remains the goal of the growing Chipko movement. Only now the tree has replaced the spinning wheel.

B.P.B.

THE FORESTS OF ANCIENT GREECE

We are all familiar with the splendid heritage of the Classical Greek civilization—its literature, philosophy, art, and architecture. We are much less aware of another legacy, the barren Greek countryside. Today's Grecophiles revel in the unique landscape of mountainous Greece, but the fact is the country's soil severely limits agriculture. Originally, the lands of Greece were forested, and agriculture had been practiced for thousands of years. The rocky, dry land that we recognize as Greece today developed between 600 and 200 B.C.

During this time, the apex of Greek civilization, virtually all the forests of Greece were destroyed. Wood was needed for buildings and ships, for firing pottery and metalwork, for furniture and chariots, for tar and resins. Shepherds actually set fire to forests to create more pasture. Natural regeneration of forests was prevented by the grazing animals that ate the tree seedlings. Without trees the soil eroded, and soon there was nothing for the animals to eat.

The soil was washed from the hills, and the silt accumulated at the mouths of rivers to create swamps, where disease-carrying mosquitoes could breed. Malaria is believed to have reached Greece in the fourth century B.C. Greece ultimately weakened as it became increasingly dependent on imports from its colonies or other countries for the essentials of life.

Some of the Greek forests were casualties of war. Realizing that the country's trees were one of its valuable assets, invading armies set fire to Greek forests and olive groves to wound the Greek state, depriving it of raw materials for shipbuilding and commerce.

Forests that once covered half of Greece now cover only one tenth of the country, leaving a landscape much different from the one familiar to the ancient Greeks.

K.F.

THE CEDARS OF LEBANON

When the Phoenicians began arriving on the coast of Lebanon around 2500 B.C., they found a fertile but narrow coastal plain backed by cedar-covered mountains. The population grew, and the Phoenicians became the foremost seafaring nation in the world from 1000 to 500 B.C. They discovered that the wood from their forests was highly valued by Egypt and Mesopotamia, and an active trade developed. Solomon's famous temple in Jerusalem was built with cedar from Lebanon.

As the Phoenicians prospered, their population continued to increase and the lowlands were no longer sufficient to grow the necessary food. They started farming the hills where the trees had been cut, but the soil quickly washed away. Avid traders, they simply exported more trees and imported food. Like the Greeks, they let goats graze on leveled woodland, thus preventing the forests from growing back.

"But I thought the Enchanted Forest had tight zoning?" (© *1980 Eldon Dedini*)

The Phoenicians did try experimenting with hillside agriculture. In 1500 B.C. they developed the first terraces to prevent erosion of hillside farms. However, the hills were too steep, and the terraces required too much work to maintain. By 800 B.C. the Phoenicians grew practically no food at home and began colonizing other areas to obtain food. Their rivals, the Greeks, however, soon assembled a stronger navy, and the Phoenicians could not maintain their conquests. They continued to export cedar, and when Alexander conquered Lebanon in 332 B.C., the forests were almost gone. The Greeks and Romans later wiped out what remained.

No new culture replaced that of the Phoenicians. The hills were bare, the lowlands littered with the debris of erosion, and the port of Tyre clogged with silt. A few remote groves of cedar can still be found flourishing in Lebanon, suggesting that this wasteland was not created by changing weather patterns, but by ill-informed efforts of human industry.

K.F.

ENGINEERING A FAMINE

The Sahel, where the Tuaregs live and wander, is one of the most desolate regions on earth. It is a great, dry plain, reaching 2,000 miles (3,200 kilometers) from Senegal to Chad, that separates the encroaching Sahara from the tropics to the south. The nomadic Tuaregs long ago mastered the art of living where there is almost no water, shelter, or food, and where, in the spring heat, the temperature commonly rises to 120° F (49° C).

The Tuaregs are herders who live in tents and reckon their wealth in livestock. For centuries they supplemented their living by "taxing" the many caravans that passed through their territory—guarding the merchants for a fee, or robbing them if the fee was refused. The French colonial rulers who eventually succeeded in subduing the Tuaregs described them as chivalrous, shrewd, and greedy, and mentioned that all the other people of the area were afraid of them.

When the French effectively discouraged the Tuareg taxing system, the main source of income, the Tuaregs turned exclusively to herding, traveling from pasture to pasture with their sheep, goats, donkeys, cattle, and their prized camels.

The nomads followed ancient migration routes, each strung along a series of watering holes, driving their herds north into the Sahara in the wet season, returning south for the long dry season. No route was overgrazed because Islamic laws laid down the number of times a route could be traveled before another route must be taken.

In the south, where the Tuareg herders came into settled farming regions, another set of rules came into use. The nomads arrived after the harvest and grazed their cattle on the stubble in the fields. Then the cattle would be corralled overnight in the villages, and the farmers collected their manure to use as fertilizer. The nomads also traded milk and meat for the farmers' grain.

Attempts at Progress

The growing influence of the outside world, however, changed the lives of the Tuaregs as well as the farmers. Political boundaries between countries were laid across the open desert, blocking many of the old migration routes. The nomads were forced to graze their cattle on less land than before.

In the 1950s, the French began a well-intentioned program to improve farming in the Sahel and to aid livestock raising. They sank tube wells for the Tuareg herdsmen; they vaccinated cattle against the rinderpest and other diseases; they encouraged irrigation, mechanization, and the use of fertilizers. But the ultimate repercussions of the attempt to improve the Tuaregs' lot were not based on careful analysis of the Sahelian environment.

The results at first seemed good. The number of cattle shot upward, almost doubling by 1968. Cash crops like cotton and peanuts began to be raised for export, bringing in foreign currency. However, these crops have large water needs and were thus very vulnerable to droughts.

In 1969, such a drought began, lasting until 1974. During the five long dry years, famine killed more than a hundred thousand people according to some estimates, and world attention was drawn to the plight of the nomads, many of whom lost all their cattle and were left with no means of livelihood. Many more people would have died without international relief efforts.

Although initial reports blamed the famine on the perverse Sahelian climate, the Tuaregs could remember weathering other droughts. Drought

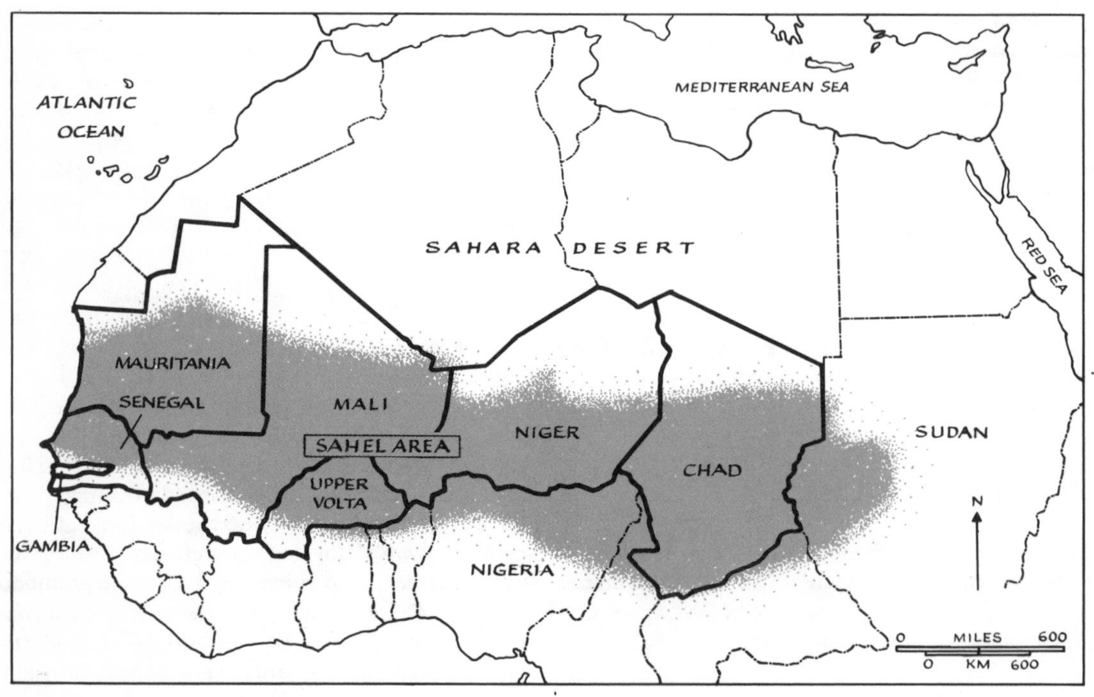

This Tuareg herdsman lost eight of his children, one of his wives, forty camels, forty head of cattle, and a dozen goats to the Sahel famine. Forced to move to the outskirts of the village of Tahoua, Niger, he barely subsists on a daily ration of sorghum. (*UN/CIDA/White,* 1973)

has always been part of the climate cycle, and even five-year droughts have occurred several times in the last two hundred years. Always before, the Tuaregs had survived with little change in their culture. But the drought of 1969–74 was different. In addition to the usual discomfort, it brought death and social disruption. Between half and three quarters of the Tuaregs, many of whom had followed French advice to become farmers or town-dwellers, were uprooted and forced into refugee camps for food. Families broke up and traditional ways of living died.

Part of the blame for the upheaval must go to the very projects the French undertook in the name of "improvement." Irrigation often destroyed the fragile soils of the Sahel by leaching minerals and nutrients, making the soil more acidic. (See "Topsoil," page 394.) Beneath the thin topsoil, and exposed as the topsoil eroded, was an impenetrable layer of hardpan, useless for agriculture.

The Unsupportable Herds

More directly contributing to the disaster, however, were the programs that encouraged the nomads to multiply their livestock herds far beyond the capacity of the land to sustain them. The vaccination programs of the 1950s eliminated the epidemics of animal disease that swept across the Sahel in 1891, 1915, and 1919. These deadly diseases, as well as the recurrent droughts, helped keep the livestock population in balance with the land.

The new wells solved the problem of water but not the problem of pasture for the animals. In the relatively wet years of the early 1960s, pasture was easy to find and herds grew quickly. The nomads clustered their large herds around the convenient new wells. The herds soon overgrazed nearby pasture. During the drought, each well was surrounded by an area of desolate, overgrazed land where livestock could no longer survive. In five years, the Tuaregs lost nearly all of their livestock, and without that source of food people starved.

A Surrounded People

The Sahelian countries are among the poorest in the world, most with annual per capita incomes of less than $200 and very high illiteracy. The officials, in many cases, came from sedentary tribes that cooperated with French control. Because their ancestors had often been victims of the fierce Tuaregs, they had little sympathy for the nomads' present plight—some expressed the opinion that the drought was heaven-sent to destroy troublemaking people. It was not until international aid began to arrive on a large scale in 1973 that the danger of starvation for millions was averted. The Sahel is still recovering from the drought. At least half the Tuaregs were permanently uprooted and now live in the cities or have become peasant farmers—a way of life their tradition despises.

The lesson of the Sahel drought is that technological solutions are not enough; natural limitations of climate, soil, and culture must be taken into consideration. In the absence of storage facilities that can feed people in every bad year, it is a mistake to build up herds in a good year, as if these good conditions were eternal.

J.S., C.R.C.

DES DAUGHTERS

"It should never have happened," said Joyce Bichler, a twenty-five-year-old social worker from New York City, of the cancer she had developed at age eighteen because her mother had taken diethylstilbestrol (DES), a steroid related to cholesterol and sex hormones, while she was pregnant. Bichler is one of an estimated 1.5 million young women in the United States who are "DES daughters." Many of these women have genital abnormalities, and some will develop a type of cancer, clear cell adenocarcinoma, an effect that was certainly unintended when their mothers took DES during pregnancy to prevent miscarriages and other complications. Yet DES was never clearly proven effective for this use, although it was shown as early as 1938 to cause cancer. It is a sad case of a drug rushed into use without adequate consideration of its side effects.

On July 16, 1979, the jury in the New York State Supreme Court agreed with Joyce Bichler's claim: they decided in her favor against Eli Lilly and Company, a major manufacturer of DES, awarding Bichler $500,000 in damages and making her the first woman to win a case involving DES. Ironically, at the same time, DES was still being prescribed for certain uses and was also widely used as a feed additive for livestock. (See "A Hamburger," page 208).

A synthetic estrogen, DES was first developed in England in 1938 by Sir Charles Dodds. Because it was inexpensive to manufacture and thought to be effective when taken orally, it became widely used very quickly, despite its link to cancers in animals that same year. Research suggesting low hormone levels in women having spontaneous abortions led to the frequent prescription of DES in the 1940s and 1950s. Hopes for the drug were such that it was given not only to women with a history of pregnancy problems, but also to those having normal pregnancies. Most women were not told what the drug was; some doctors explained that DES was a "vitamin" or a "hold-the-baby-in pill."

When further studies in Chicago and New Orleans during the 1950s showed DES to have "no therapeutic value in pregnancy" and perhaps actually to encourage premature delivery, use of the drug declined. However, it was still being prescribed as late as 1971, when it was banned as not only ineffective but also as unquestionably dangerous to humans. During those years four million to six million Americans—mothers, daughters, and sons—were exposed to DES.

The daughters are the most certainly and severely affected by their exposure. In 1966, Dr. Arthur Herbst treated a fifteen-year-old girl for clear cell adenocarcinoma of the vagina, a very rare form of cancer that had almost never before been reported in young women. When six more women (ages fifteen to twenty-two) with the cancer came to his attention over the next three years—more young women with this cancer than had ever been reported in worldwide medical literature—Herbst and his colleagues began to search for the source. By 1971, Herbst had examined yet another case, and all but one of the young women were DES daughters. Almost thirty years after its first use, DES became the first hormone product proven to be associated with human cancer.

An adenocarcinoma is a cancer of glandular tissue. Normally the vagina does not have this tissue, but DES can disrupt normal development of the fetus's reproductive system. Later in life, usually at puberty, when hormone levels begin to change in the young woman's body, this glandular tissue is formed and can become cancerous. The DES Task Force, reporting to the U. S. Department of Health, Education, and Welfare in October 1978, confirmed "the association of *in utero* exposure to DES and clear cell adenocarcinoma of the vagina or cervix in the daughter." In

March 1979 a follow-up study estimated the risk of cancer at approximately 1.2 per 1,000 DES daughters, a figure much lower than originally feared.

DES is associated with other complications. Many of the daughters—estimates range from 34 to 90 percent—develop a variety of genital abnormalities including visible changes in the vagina and cervix, and adenosis, which is the appearance in the vagina of glandular tissue that usually occurs only in the cervix and uterus. It appears in almost all the young women whose mothers took DES, even in small doses, during the first three months of pregnancy. Although adenosis is a benign condition, it must be closely watched since no one is yet sure whether or not it is a precancerous condition.

Because the DES daughters are so young, no one knows what the future effects of their exposure might be. The DES Task Force pointed out that a higher frequency of other types of cancer of the reproductive organs, called squamous cancers, may show up as the daughters grow older. The fertility rates, pregnancy outcomes, and long-term effects on their offspring also need to be studied as the DES daughters mature.

As studies continue, investigators are finding even more unintended effects. Studies in Chicago that followed up on the mothers who took DES during the early tests found a higher number of breast cancers among these women. Recent studies also show a higher incidence of abnormalities of the genital and lower urinary tract of DES sons, as well as the possibility of infertility and testicular cancer. And yet, as Joyce Bichler pointed out, these effects "never should have happened." DES had been shown ineffective in 1953, and as many as fifty laboratory tests had shown DES to be carcinogenic before 1947—all before Bichler's mother and many others took the drug. Indeed, many doctors recognized the dangers and stopped prescribing it even then; others did not.

In an interview in 1965, Sir Charles Dodds, who discovered DES, admitted his astonishment that its use spread so rapidly, especially without adequate testing:

> Within a few months of the first publication of the synthesis of [diethyl] stilbestrol, the substance was being marketed throughout the world. No long-term toxicity tests on animals such as dogs were ever done with [diethyl]-stilbestrol. . . . It is really surprising that we escaped major pharmacological disasters until a few years ago.

Questions that the jury had to consider in Joyce Bichler's case included whether a prudent manufacturer should have first tested DES on pregnant mice, whether the tests would have shown cancer in the offspring, and whether a prudent manufacturer would then have gone ahead and marketed the drug. On all three questions the jury found the drug companies at fault for inadequate testing. Although before the drug was marketed tests had shown it was carcinogenic, and although the technology was available to monitor tests on pregnant mice, Eli Lilly and the other drug companies never made the tests.

Nor did federal regulatory agencies act when they could have. Legislation passed in 1962 tightened regulations applying to drugs: they had to be proven effective for human use. In the review of estrogens in 1967, DES was rated "possibly effective," which meant that the companies had six months to prove their claims for DES; they did not. Even though at this point DES was thought to be safe, it could have been restricted by law for use in pregnancy cases simply because it did not work. Yet the Food and Drug Administration (FDA) did not ban DES for this use until 1971, when Dr. Herbst's reports were published linking DES to adenocarcinoma in daughters.

As of late 1979, when DES was clearly associated with cancers, it was still occasionally prescribed as a milk suppressant for new mothers who chose not to breast-feed, as a therapeutic agent for menopausal women, and as the morning-after pill that—although this is an unapproved use of DES—is prescribed through many college health centers. Male workers exposed to DES dust during manufacture have complained of impotence and enlarged breasts; women are affected by menstrual disorders.

Many Americans have also been exposed to DES through residues left in meat, even though more than twenty European countries have banned DES livestock additives, some as early as 1959. Since the 1950s, U.S. health and environmental activists have been denouncing the addition of DES to animal feed. Animals fed DES gain weight faster—in 1974 it made the cattle industry over $90 million—yet no one seems to agree on how DES works. It adds fat to chickens and was used to make them "juicier" until residues found in the meat caused DES additives to be banned for chickens in 1959. Its use in cattle and sheep has seesawed in a scientific and legal battle since that time.

From 1958 to 1962, DES was only partially banned from U.S. livestock feed, despite laws

prohibiting food additives shown to cause cancer in test animals. In 1962, the special Stilbestrol Amendment allowed its widespread use again, providing no residues of DES appeared in meat. Scientists, administrators, industry representatives, and lawyers fought over its use until 1972, when large residues were found in beef, particularly in liver, causing the FDA to ban it completely. Through legal means, however, the industry had that ban overturned in 1974. In 1976 the FDA tried again, calling hearings that resulted in a ban set for July 1979, but a four-month "grace period" followed during which the cattle industry could use whatever DES supplies remained in storage before the food additive was finally banned in November 1979. Just prior to that time 80 percent of the meat and poultry con-
raised on DES feed additives.
sumed in the United States came from animals

No one knows exactly what gives DES carcinogenic properties. Most estrogens have been shown to be associated with cancers, but some scientists suspect DES of changing composition in the body in more complex ways. No one knows what, if any, dose of DES may be safe: some suspect even low doses over extended periods can upset the delicate balance of hormones in the body, others contend that DES residues are "toxicologically insignificant" against natural estrogen backgrounds in the body. No one knows how any added dosage may affect those already exposed to DES, many of whom are unaware of their original exposure. Perhaps in another decade or two we will know more of the possible unintended effects of the continued use of DES.

P.L.

ARCTIC HAZE

Flying over the Arctic Ocean, thousands of kilometers from the murky skies of New York, London, or Hamburg, pilots often spend hour after hour in a haze so thick that any view other than nearly straight down is obliterated. First reported by weather reconnaissance crews in the 1950s, the heavy haze is a regular springtime feature of the Arctic, often reducing visibility aloft to less than 6 miles (about 10 kilometers).

A haze so far from the factories and cars that smudge the air of major cities would seem to require a wholly natural explanation, but evidence has begun to accumulate that a part of the arctic haze may have its origins 6,000 miles (10,000 kilometers) away in the same polluted air that produces acid rain over the United States and Europe (see "The Trespassing Poison: Acid Rain," page 186). Acid rain has wiped out the fish of some lakes and possibly altered forest ecosystems, but the environmental effects of the arctic haze, if any, are as yet unknown. In any case, the existence of significant pollution in the Arctic would greatly extend the documented extent of the long-range transport of pollutant particles in the lower atmosphere.

In the conventional sense, long-range transport has implied the movement of dirty air from, say, the highly industrialized Rhine Valley in West Germany to southern Scandinavia, a distance of about 900 miles (1,500 kilometers). The pollution itself, which includes sulfuric and nitric acids, heavy metals, soot, and organic matter, falls out or is washed out as acid rain all along the way. Likewise, pollutants generated in the eastern United States move similar distances before they rain down on New England and probably Canada. Evidence recorded in ice cores suggests that these pollutants may eventually reach Greenland, a distance of as much as 1,860 miles (3,000 kilometers).

Although some of these pollutants are released as gases, such as sulfur dioxide and hydrocarbons, they are eventually transformed into microscopic particles of sulfuric acid and organic matter through chemical reactions with pollutants and naturally occurring chemicals under the influence of sunlight. If enough of these particles of the proper size are suspended in the air, they become visible as haze.

Atmospheric chemists had generally believed that suspended particles, or aerosols, either fell to the ground from their own weight, stuck to solid objects that they ran into, or were washed out by rain before they could travel much more than about 600 miles (1,000 kilometers). If the arctic haze actually does contain particles derived from the major pollutant sources in the middle latitudes, the distances involved could exceed 6,000 miles (10,000 kilometers), a range not seriously considered possible before for such pollution.

Effects on the weather are possible. The haze might influence cloud properties by changing the concentration of particles that are capable of becoming the nuclei of new ice crystals or cloud droplets. The haze seems to cause a heating effect by absorbing additional sunlight, according to Glenn Shaw [of the University of Alaska]. The problem, he says, is determining exactly how much heating occurs and what, if any, climatic effect it has.

In the case of the arctic haze, the increasingly sensitive tools of atmospheric chemists seem to have revealed a potential problem where it was least expected. In other places considered to be among the cleanest in the world, such as Hawaii, Samoa, Greenland, and Antarctica, apparent excesses of heavy metals, sulfate, and acidity remain to be fully explained. Some of these may in fact be natural, perhaps resulting from volcanic emissions, for example, but the environmental effects, if any, of true pollutants will have to be evaluated. That analysis will undoubtedly be even more complex than unraveling their chemistry.

Condensed with permission from "Global Pollution: Is the Arctic Haze Actually Industrial Smog?" by Richard A. Kerr, *Science,* July 20, 1979. Vol. 205, pp. 290–293.

DRYING OUT THE INDUS VALLEY

Some researchers have suggested the possibility that the affluent and sophisticated Indus Valley civilization, which existed in present-day Pakistan about 2000 B.C., created air pollution severe enough to change its climate and destroy its ecosystem. The civilization ended abruptly about 1500 B.C., and there is no evidence that it was conquered by invaders.

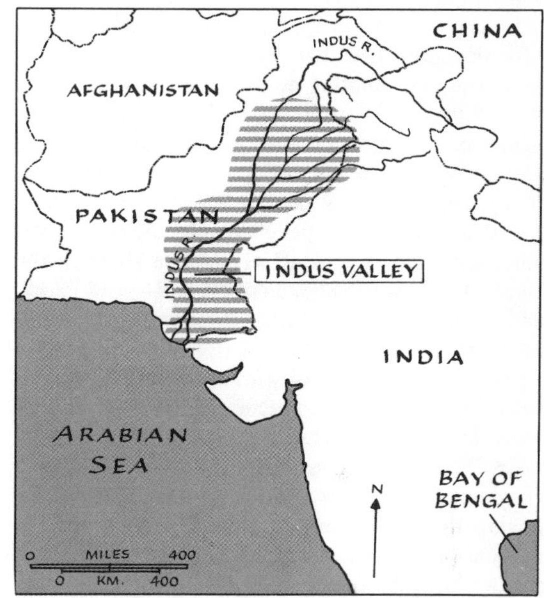

The culture made some obvious ecological mistakes, including deforesting its hillsides and allowing the Indus River to silt up. But some researchers believe the sudden demise of the culture resulted from a drastic change in climate that destroyed food production. They postulate that dust from the eroding land, combined with smoke from wood fires, could have created a permanent haze, like that of Calcutta today. Tiny solid particles in such hazes interrupt the sun's rays before they can warm the land, holding constant heat in the air. This could have changed the daily and seasonal rise and fall of temperature in the area, thus altering rainfall patterns (warm air absorbs moisture that is normally released as the air cools). Without the benefit of life-giving rain, the society would have been doomed.

K.F.

RAINMAKING

Since the earliest times, people have been trying to influence the weather. One famous example, which probably has some base in history, is the sacrifice of Iphigenia in Homer's *Iliad;* the girl was killed and offered to the gods so that the winds would change, allowing the Greek fleet to sail to Troy. A Chinese emperor hoped there would be no droughts and floods during his reign, since they were considered a sign that his rule was corrupt. In North America, Indian rainmakers still dance today.

However, it is only within the last fifty years that there has been a scientific basis for attempts to change the weather. Along with the infant technology of weather modification comes a host of problems that no longer seem hypothetical.

Who owns the clouds, and for whose benefit do humans tamper with the weather? Who is responsible when faltering experiments change the weather in unexpected ways, or in unpredicted places? As one report concluded, ". . . if ever a technology existed which raised major issues for citizen participation . . . it is weather modification."

It is a well-known phenomenon that cities tend to be warmer than the countryside around them, creating what are called "heat islands." Cities, power plants, deforestation, and irrigation, among other human enterprises, are known to modify local weather. We are influencing the weather, involuntarily, in many ways. However, intentional weather modification is another thing entirely, and has caused a great deal of public concern.

In general, "weather modification" refers to cloud and precipitation control. In 1946, scientists showed that seeding clouds, with dry ice or silver iodide, induces precipitation by changing the normal growth processes of the cloud's particles. Cloud seeding is now usually done from a plane, which drops dry-ice pellets, water spray, silver iodide smoke, or even salt as it passes through the cloud. There are also some ground-based cloud seeders that depend on updrafts to carry the seeding agent into the clouds.

The usual purpose of cloud seeding is to increase rainfall, and sometimes snowfall, in an effort to relieve drought, grow more crops, fill reservoirs, and provide more water for hydroelectric power generation. Oddly enough, there is little statistical evidence that seeding clouds does in fact enhance rainfall. Of course, certain claims can definitely be made. A report to the U. S. Department of Commerce states: ". . . supercooled fog and stratus can be seeded to improve visibility; holes can be opened in winter stratus clouds to increase the amount of solar radiation that reaches the ground; . . . rain can be induced from some types of summer cumulus clouds. . . ." The report goes on to caution that weather modification is only one generation from its birth, and that much is still unknown about the atmosphere.

Although results are largely inconclusive, more than a dozen commercial "rainmakers" operate in twenty-three U.S. states, constituting a multimillion-dollar industry. At least seventy-four countries have attempted cloud seeding to induce rainfall. An experiment in Israel from 1961 to 1966 was claimed to have increased precipitation by 18 percent. The Soviet Union claims up to 80 percent success with suppressing hail by seeding clouds.

Unfortunately, when it is most desperately needed—say, during a long drought—rainmaking by cloud seeding is almost impossible, because there are so few clouds in such circumstances. While in certain weather conditions cloud seeding can be relied on, these conditions are not necessarily the most common. For example, the French have successfully seeded clouds to disperse supercooled fog at Orly airport near Paris. Unfortunately there is no proof that cloud seeding works on warm fog, which is far more prevalent.

The effects of cloud seeding are not always beneficial, either. Aside from specific attempts to use weather modification as a weapon (during the Vietnam war, the United States tried to prolong the rainy season—apparently unsuccessfully—to clog the Ho Chi Minh trail), unintended results can be disastrous. A 1972 flood that killed 237 people in Rapid City, South Dakota, has been blamed on cloud seeding. In the Los Angeles, California, area, clouds were seeded just hours before a rainstorm devastated a canyon, killing ten people and doing more than $40 million worth of damage.

Because there is no way to force seeded clouds to stay where they are wanted, the enhanced rain or snow may strike another country or region where it does more harm than good. It costs money to clear snow; and excessive rain can cause floods and accelerate erosion. While natural rainfall and snowfall cause these problems too, people in areas affected unintentionally by cloud seeding do no always appreciate the similarity. There may be some disagreement even if the cloud seeding is needed. For more than ten years, the U. S. Bureau of Reclamation (BOR) has been trying to increase the amount of snow that falls on the San Juan mountains in Colorado. More snow on these mountains would mean that more water eventually finds its way into the BOR's projects on the Colorado River. However, the people who live in the San Juans believe they have more than enough snow already, and they have forced the BOR to place what it considers excessive controls on its cloud seeding.

Many effects of weather modification are still unexplored. Silver iodide, a common seeding agent, may delay decomposition in soil by killing some bacteria (silver is toxic to animals and humans in large quantities), but so far its environ-

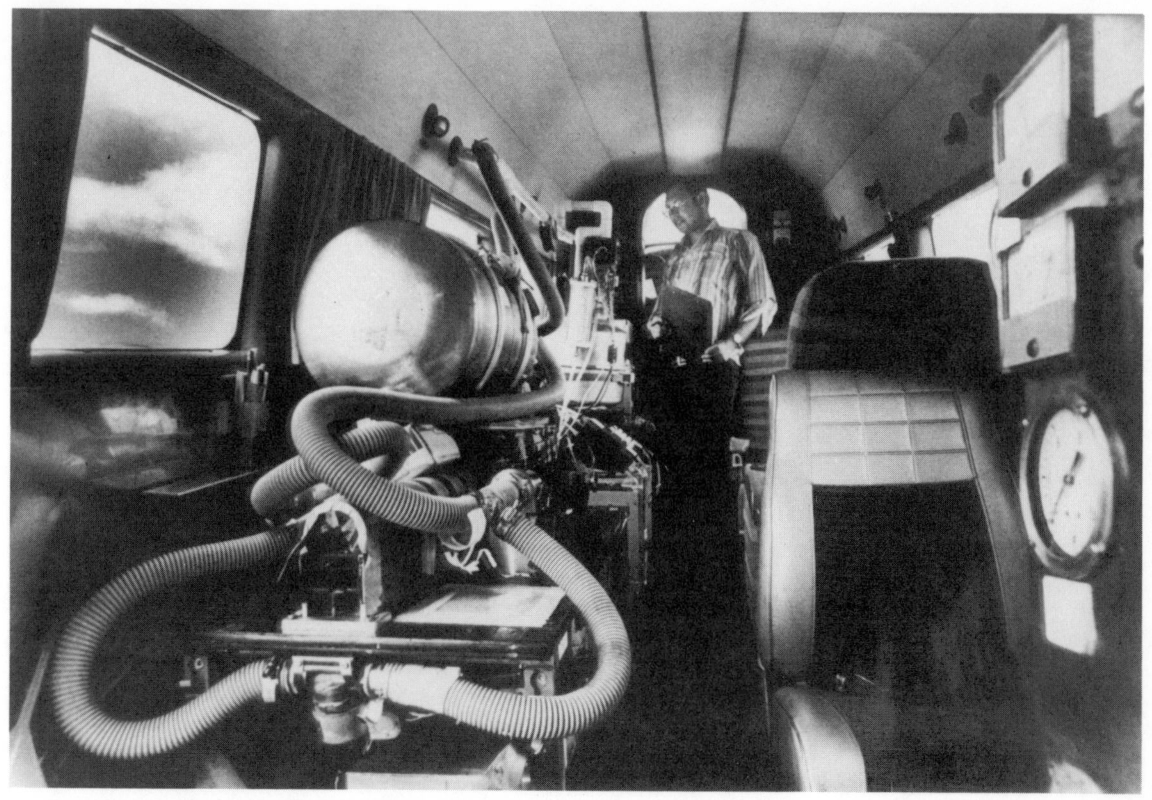

This equipment aboard a B-3 research aircraft is used to measure cloud characteristics, gathering data that could be used in weather modification. (*Denver* Post/*Steve Larson*)

mental effects seem to be negligible. The impact of changing weather on animal populations, according to the Ecological Society of America, would include "shifts of range, local or complete extermination of species, and at least an initial increase in weeds and pests." At a forest site where snowfall was increased, one study found a marked decline of chipmunks and deer mice. Another report predicts that drastically increasing snowfall would probably lower the number of trout in lakes. Other effects may still be unknown.

The environmental, social, and economic (not to mention legal) aspects of "playing God" with the weather that affects every human being are not necessarily simple. Who is to decide between two applicants for one rainfall?

P.W., J.S.

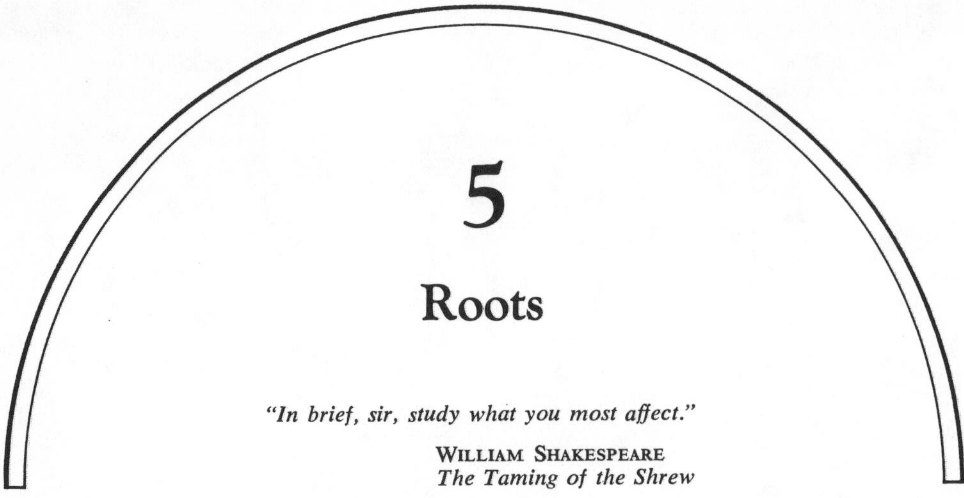

5

Roots

"In brief, sir, study what you most affect."

WILLIAM SHAKESPEARE
The Taming of the Shrew

Once people gathered the materials for living from within about 5 or 10 miles (8 or 16 kilometers) of their dwellings. Whatever grew nearby, or lay exposed, or fell from the sky, or flowed past, they exploited. Some humans still survive on the bounty of their immediate surroundings—out of necessity or, as in some parts of the world today, out of ideological choice. But most of us depend upon products assembled from environmental yields in regions of the world we have never seen.

As a result, we are out of touch with the "roots" of the items that sustain and comfort us day after day. We see the products but not the process. If the mining of the metal that reaches us as a paper clip involves some damage to earth, wind, water, or humanity, we don't necessarily know it. If the raising of a banana results in abandoned patches of ruined land, we aren't told. We know about the grand issues of ecology and economics, but we don't automatically link them in our minds with blue jeans, hamburgers, cigarettes, or the pages of this book.

The background stories of everyday products reveal surprising geographical networks, many of which are enmeshed with social, political, and environmental issues from the morning newspaper. At the dinner table, for example, you may be using stainless steel knives produced with chromium mined in politically volatile South Africa. The bronze candleholder may have been produced with tin extracted from the land beneath a fragile rain forest in Thailand. The pigment in the ceramic dishware may be cobalt from Zaire, whose northern border, the once-impenetrable Congo River, is now targeted for extensive development. The origins of the foods, the fertilizers that nourished them, the pesticides that protected them, the energy that transported them—all of these "biographical" tales would draw us into most of the major global issues of our age, most of them bearing directly on the environment, but these are not facts revealed to us by labels or grocery displays.

Pollution and energy problems are often camouflaged by the patina of a final product, or the images created by its advertising. A common item may not seem to harm people or any natural systems because our own use of it does not. But what of the earliest moments in its genesis, as its ingredients were extracted from something, somewhere, by someone? Along the way, what happens during processing, assembly, packaging, transport?

The foods and the materials of our lives, no matter how modest, have a history—usually surprising, often involving hidden abuses, always fraught with tales of travel and transformation.

There are millions of behind-the-scenes stories we could have told; we chose these—

some because they involve environmental insults, some because they look into pervasive elements in our lives, some because they are just interesting stories. In the main, the tales told in this chapter are histories of the things in our pockets and bedrooms and bellies.

M.R.

THE PAGES YOU ARE READING

The paper on which these words are printed was processed from a blend of hard and soft woods and produced in New York, Ohio, or Pennsylvania. The book cover paper is mainly virgin softwood, either willow or poplar, probably grown in a southern U.S. state, and coated with adhesive plus clay to protect it from the hazards of handling. The trees from which the paper was milled took from twenty to fifty years to grow. The text of each copy is printed on approximately 4 pounds (1.8 kilograms) of paper, representing about 8 pounds (3.6 kilograms) of wood.

The pages of this book have been manufactured to last up to two hundred years. Such long-lived paper results from a process akin in principle to the original two-thousand-year-old Chinese recipe, multiplied many times by technology and speed. Paper is now so readily available that the annual per capita consumption (including cardboard, cartons, and building materials) of an average citizen in the United States has risen to 600 pounds (257 kilograms) as of 1980. That is enough paper to send 60,000 letters, enough paper to cover a road 10 miles (16 kilometers) long.

Of the 600 pounds (257 kilograms) each American consumes, 420 pounds (180 kilograms), or 70 percent, is thrown away. Of what is thrown away, containers and packaging account for approximately 40 percent. This extraordinary quantity of paper represents decades of tree growth, thousands of gallons of water, virtually incalculable labor hours and energy units. We are indiscriminately papering our way through life.

A Novel Pulp

Paper waste is a thoroughly modern phenomenon. Like many items, when first introduced, paper was once painstakingly produced for selective purposes. Most people assume that Egyptian papyrus, the earliest extant example of which dates to 2200 B.C., was the first paper. But papyrus was hardly paper as we now know it.

Papyrus sheets for writing were developed by the Egyptians, adopted by the Greeks and the Romans, and continued in use into the ninth century A.D. Papyrus reeds were cut into strips, arranged in layers, soaked in water, and then pressed until they formed a suitable writing surface. Though the English word "paper" obviously derives from "papyrus," the paper we use is produced by an entirely different process. It results from the pounding and slow cooking of wood and wood fiber, as well as of cotton, rags, and other primary materials containing cellulose. The raw fibers are broken down into a wet pulp, which no longer resembles any of the original materials. The pulp is poured into racks, dried, pressed, and cut into paper sheets, later to be finished or bleached, depending on the type of paper desired.

The invention of this paper process is credited to the Chinese, who in their pre-paper days wrote

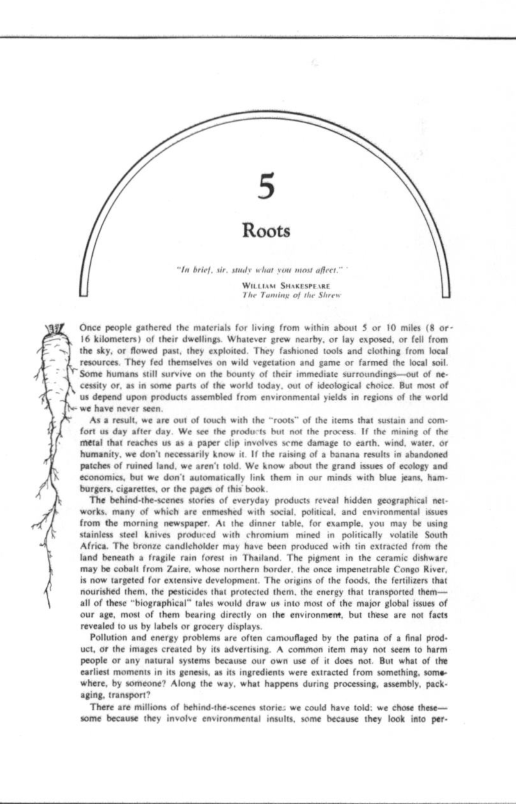

5

Roots

"In brief, sir, study what you most affect."

WILLIAM SHAKESPEARE
The Taming of the Shrew

Once people gathered the materials for living from within about 5 or 10 miles (8 or 16 kilometers) of their dwellings. Whatever grew nearby, or lay exposed, or fell from the sky, or flowed past, they exploited. They fashioned tools and clothing from local resources. They fed themselves on wild vegetation and game or farmed the local soil. Some humans still survive on the bounty of their immediate surroundings—out of necessity or, as in some parts of the world today, out of ideological choice. But most of us depend upon products assembled from environmental yields in regions of the world we have never seen.

As a result, we are out of touch with the "roots" of the items that sustain and comfort us day after day. We see the products but not the process. If the mining of the metal that reaches us as a paper clip involves some damage to earth, wind, water, or humanity, we don't necessarily know it. If the raising of a banana results in abandoned patches of ruined land, we aren't told. We know about the grand issues of ecology and economics, but we don't automatically link them in our minds with blue jeans, hamburgers, cigarettes, or the pages of this book.

The behind-the-scenes stories of everyday products reveal hidden geographical networks, many of which are enmeshed with social, political, and environmental issues from the morning newspaper. At the dinner table, for example, you may be using stainless steel knives produced with chromium mined in politically volatile South Africa. The bronze candleholder may have been produced with tin extracted from the land beneath a fragile rain forest in Thailand. The pigment in the ceramic dishware may be cobalt from Zaire, whose northern border, the once impenetrable Congo River, is now targeted for extensive development. The origins of the foods, the fertilizers that nourished them, the pesticides that protected them, the energy that transported them—all of these "biographical" tales would draw us into most of the major global issues of our age, most of them bearing directly on the environment, but these are not facts revealed to us by labels or grocery displays.

Pollution and energy problems are often camouflaged by the patina of a final product, or the images created by its advertising. A common item may not seem to harm people or any natural systems because our own use of it does not. But what of the earliest moments in its genesis, as its ingredients were extracted from something, somewhere, by someone? Along the way, what happens during processing, assembly, packaging, transport?

There are millions of behind-the-scenes stories we could have told: we chose these—some because they involve environmental insults, some because they look into peron silk, bamboo rods, or slim wood strips lashed together with cord or thread. In A.D. 105, Ts'ai Lun, a court official, invented paper by beating mulberry bark, fish nets, and other scraps of linen and hemp, and mixing the fine bits with water. A cloth-covered frame was dipped into the mixture and left to dry. As the water drained through the mesh of the cloth a thin layer of pulp remained—the world's first sheet of paper. The new item caught on, though it was always considered inferior to silk. In A.D. 142 a letter from one Chinese scholar to another read: "I send you the works of the philosopher Hsu in ten scrolls—unable to afford a copy in silk I am obliged to send you one on paper." By 300, however, paper was generally accepted as a substitute for other writing materials in China. By 875 the Chinese had apparently invented toilet paper; by 969, paper playing cards. By 998 paper money was in circulation.

The Ascent of Paper

Paper moved west to Europe via early Arab travelers, who introduced it in the Middle East and Spain. In 1309, England used paper for the first time. By the time paper had spread this far, the demand for it was substantial and paper mills operated in Spain, Italy, and Germany, where, in 1390, the first recorded labor strike in the paper industry took place.

The first mill in the English colonies opened in 1698 near Philadelphia, and by the time of the American Revolution, papermaking was not only a respected craft but a serious industry. With the invention of the papermaking machine in France in 1798, perfected in England in 1801, paper was producible in quantities unavailable before. But Chinese knowledge of wood as a source of pulp fiber was lost "in transmission" from east to west, and until the mid-eighteenth century in Europe the raw materials used in papermaking were confined to linen, cotton, rags, hemp, and straw. In 1719, the Frenchman René-Antoine de Réaumur took a cue from a "paper wasp." These wasps, of which there are many varieties and whose presence on earth goes back 300 million years, chew wood and grind it into pulp with which they build paper nests. In 1850 a process for grinding wood was developed in Germany, and later English and American inventions made conversion of wood into paper possible.

Once paper was generally available, it was used for a variety of products that today seem outlandish—paper coffins, horseshoes, gas pipes, and boats. There were even paper railway wheels using straw paperboard disks with metal tires, one set of which was reported to have traveled approximately 300,000 miles (482,803 kilometers). An all-paper watch was exhibited in Germany in 1883, and in England in 1895 the town of Downham-in-the-Isle built a cathedral of compressed brown paper reinforced with wire and

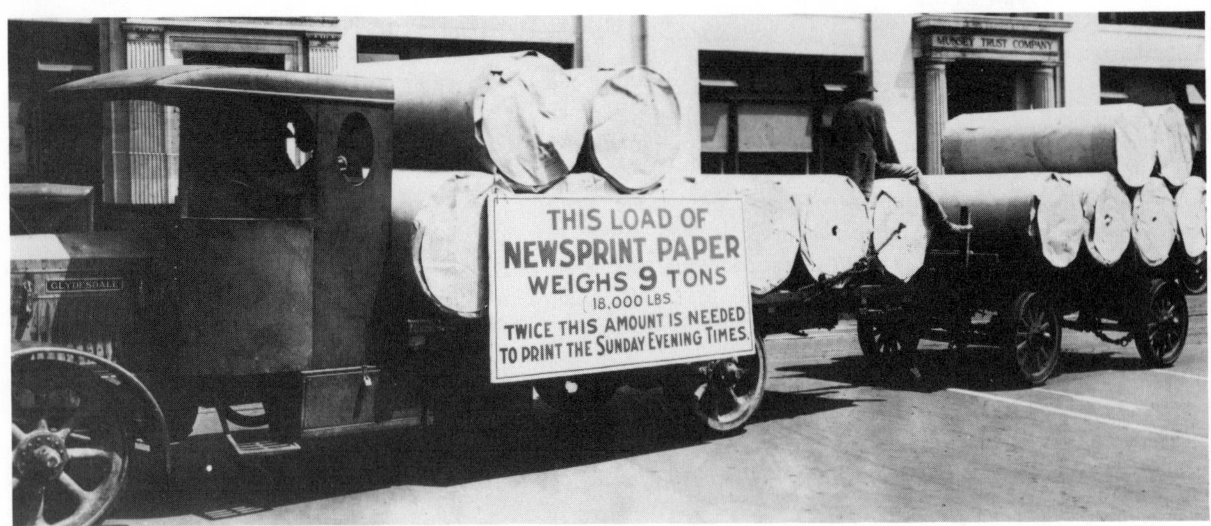

In 1920 it took two truckloads like this of newsprint to produce the *Sunday Evening Times* in Washington, D.C. By 1978, both the size of Sunday editions and their circulation had expanded to the point where it took 184 such truckloads—3,305 tons of newsprint—to produce the Sunday New York *Times*. (*Library of Congress*)

covered with board. The church functioned until 1968, when a population shift away from the area caused it to close. The building was converted to a barn, and except for a few exterior modifications, it remains standing today, structurally unchanged. Ultimately, paper became as common as bread, though the wrapping of bread *in* paper was not common, in the United States at least, until about 1910.

American society in particular became a devourer of paper, using 288 pounds per person per year by 1943. Consumption continues to escalate with a deluge of books, magazines, newspapers, towels, cups, gift wrapping, and everyday items such as shopping bags, commutation tickets, bills and receipts—to say nothing of the tons of documents we print, fill out, study, and file (sometimes in cardboard cabinets).

But this preponderance of paper depends on resources that, though renewable, are today severely strained, and it demands empty land upon which to dump the tide of paper waste. Every sheet of paper relates in some measure to these environmental factors, which begin with the raw wood fiber itself.

Forests to Pages

The paper industry is highly integrated, which means the companies that produce the paper often own the trees. In the United States, corporations that produce paper and other wood products own or lease 14 percent of commercial forest land and produce 30 percent of the wood fiber harvest. Most of these companies systematically harvest and plant so that the forest land yields the maximum amount of wood and fiber per tree.

In the southern United States, where two thirds of the country's paper pulpwood is grown and processed, forest management has become a major industry, employing approximately five thousand professional foresters. But such careful handling of wood resources is a new development. Until about 1950, large tracts of land were clear-cut, left to grow back however they could, leaving an ugly scar on the landscape.

Traditionally, loggers carried away only tree trunks, leaving the leaves and branches in the forest. Today's supersaws vibrate the forests, chomping a whole tree into chips within minutes. The process is more efficient, but it robs the soil of nutrients formerly provided by the decaying "waste" wood. Chipped bark, branches, and trimmed trunks are fed to the mill, where they are either further ground or chemically treated.

Newsprint pulp is produced through a mechanical grinding of the wood. Groundwood pulp, or mechanical pulp, is wood reduced to tiny particles by thrashing it against enormous grindstones, or by applying heat and pressure. The resultant pulp has shorter fibers and therefore less strength, and the paper produced from it is mainly of lower quality. A high percentage of lignin remains, accounting for the yellowing of the paper as it ages.

Higher quality paper is made from chemical pulp in a vat cooking procedure. Wood and other materials such as cotton and rags are immersed in solutions and slowly "churned" like a caustic soup, using abrasive sodas, sulfites, and sulfates to break down the primary fibers. Sixty-five percent of all paper is cooked in sulfate, called kraft pulp, a procedure that yields the widest variety of papers, from unbleached corrugated box material to fine embossed stationery.

Both the chemical and groundwood processes are extremely water-intensive. In fact, the paper industry was the third most water-consuming manufacturing process in the United States as of 1979–80. In the groundwood process, high-speed water jets spin logs and remove the bark. The water then carries off waste material and pushes the clean wood to the next stage. Water also cools the equipment. In chemical pulping, water generally combines with a caustic mix of chemicals. One percent of paper pulp is mixed with as much as 99 percent water at any given point in the process. A ton of kraft pulp uses a maximum of 34,650 gallons (131,150 liters) of water; a ton of sulfite pulp uses 62,700 gallons (237,320 liters) or the equivalent of 2,090 baths.

Spills from the Mills

With all the cleaning, cooking, and carrying away that water accomplishes in the paper process, there is extraordinary potential for water pollution in the water discharge. As recently as 1969, the U.S. paper and pulp industry was responsible for 15 percent of the industrial effluent that entered U.S. waterways. In 1979, the proportion was still between 10 and 20 percent, according to the Environmental Protection Agency.

The effluent can contain bits of wood, bark, uncooked fiber chips, dirt, coloring from inks and paper dyes, bleach, sulfur, chlorine, wax, grease, and oil. One hundred years of papermaking on the shores of New York's Lake Champlain, for example, produced layers of solid waste along the

Foam containing resin and chemicals from this Japanese wood pulp plant coated the waterfront in 1970. Many nations have imposed discharge controls on pulp plants, one of the most polluting of industries. (*UN*)

lake bottom 300 acres (122 hectares) in area and up to 12 feet (3.66 meters) in depth.

Foamy suds, containing resin and chemicals, bubble up from paper plant discharge pipes. The suds in themselves are not very dangerous, but when they coat the water they block sunlight from underwater habitats and interfere with photosynthesis among aquatic plants, thus threatening the food production chain.

The potential impact of paper-mill effluent can be measured by the demand for oxygen by aquatic life. If there is enough oxygen, bacteria normally found in the water can decompose and neutralize the waste. However, when too much waste is dumped, it triggers a multiplication in the normal bacteria populations, which then consume so much oxygen that other aquatic organisms, such as fish, suffocate. This biological oxygen demand (B.O.D.) is a delicate measure of how much oxygen is needed for bacteria to decompose a given amount of waste.

The B.O.D. for one person's daily output of waste is approximately 0.17 pound (0.08 kilogram) of oxygen; for one ton of untreated, bleached sulfite pulp, the B.O.D. is 1,000 pounds (454 kilograms) of oxygen. Therefore, before environmental regulations took hold, a typical sulfite paper mill producing 200 tons (181 metric tons) of pulp a day could create an oxygen demand equal to that of a city of one million people.

Mercury, which can be very toxic to humans when ingested in high concentrations, is used to preserve and bleach paper chips and is often contained in untreated wastewater from paper plants. During the 1960s, the Dryden Paper Company washed 10 to 20 pounds (4.5 to 9 kilograms) of mercury a day into the English Wabigoon River in northwest Ontario, Canada. In 1970 the provincial government warned Indians in the area not to eat fish from that river because they contained poisonous levels of mercury. But many of the Indians, especially those who served as guides for fishing camps, already showed signs of mercury poisoning. (See also "The Dancing Cats of Minamata," page 517.)

As a result of attention focused on the dangers of mercury, the paper industry gradually has begun to find substitute substances. In the late 1970s a survey by the Environmental Protection Agency of one hundred paper plants, representing about one seventh of the paper industry, showed mercury being discharged in only trace amounts. However, mercury persists in the environment, and the effects of previous mercury discharges have yet to be adequately monitored.

Not all water pollution in the paper industry can be attributed to the pulp process. During the printing of paper, when metal plates are etched with the words and letters to be pressed onto paper, water rinses the plates and carries away excess heavy metals such as copper and zinc. As yet, none of this metal has been reclaimed, so it eventually finds its way into the water system.

The production of paper can also significantly pollute the air by releasing airborne particles, gases, and foul-smelling chemicals. The recognizable "rotten eggs" odor of sulfur used in the pulping process can carry as far as 60 miles (96.5 kilometers) from a paper mill. Sulfur dioxide can also do extensive crop damage to areas up to 15 miles (24 kilometers) from the mill location.

The history of the paper industry is not only one of rapid economic growth but also of rampant environmental pollution, which was only recently brought under public scrutiny. In 1969, a major study by the New York-based Council on Economic Priorities exposed the high degrees of air and water pollution around the mills studied, even going so far as to quote the warranty for an auto paint job in Florida, near a mill, which exempted cars constantly exposed to "extreme deterioration such as those caused by acid from a paper mill." Such pollution took place even though the technology existed to clean up approximately 90 percent of the solid-waste emissions and 85 percent of the chemical emissions before any of the pollutants entered the environment.

The U.S. paper industry responded to the public pressure created by disclosure of its pollution record and subsequent legislative demands, and within a few years massive cleanup efforts were under way. Today, public pressure has led to strong legislation in the United States. Other nations have pioneered in paper industry pollution control. In Sweden, for example, paper mills recover up to 90 percent of the chemicals they send into the water system during the cooking process. Advances in bleaching have reduced water consumption from 150 tons of water per ton of pulp to 30. In Mexico, where water is expensive and often scarce, paper mills have had to develop water recycling projects.

Many developing countries, however, continue to produce paper as cheaply as they can, often viewing pollution control as a luxury. In the Philippines, the paper industry admits that unless there is public interest in a cleaner industry, and capital investment to provide it, production will continue much as it always has. In Malaysia, in 1979, where a new paper plant valued at $350 million was proposed for the state of Sabah, the local environmental protection association warned that the plant would cause "great environmental disturbance . . . eating up 45 acres [18 hectares] of tropical forest, including some forest reserve land, as well as draw 200 million gallons [757 million liters] of water a day from a local reservoir."

Paper Mountains

Such a paper mill sounds like an omnivorous and thirsty monster. That this plant and others like it consume valuable natural resources makes casually tossing away paper indefensible, especially when so much of our paper waste can effectively be used again.

While some people view paper recycling as a new idea, it has been among us almost half as long as paper itself, since as early as 1020 in the Orient. Ironically, recycling appeared as paper became more available, around the same time a Persian traveler, Nasiri Khosrau, first noted that paper was being used to wrap food in the markets of Cairo.

As world consumption of paper continues to rise, so the mountain of wastepaper will rise until we literally have no place to put it. As of 1979, municipal trash (residential, not industrial garbage) contained 40 to 60 percent paper products that could have been profitably recycled. They were not recycled for one simple reason: there is no widespread, convenient collection system for recapturing the material. This is unfortunate, since recycled paper can be extremely high quality and the collection and sale of wastepaper can be lucrative. Even in the United States, paper recycling was common until about 1945. Since then, interest in recycling has dropped off, a situation worsened by a tax structure that favors processors of virgin over secondary materials, and by freight rates that make it more expensive to ship secondary materials than virgin materials.

But this situation could easily be reversed, and will eventually have to be. It costs the United States about $4 billion a year to pick up, haul, and dispose of solid waste, of which paper accounts for about 40 percent. Even allowing for the energy consumed in the recycling process, it is less expensive for society to recycle. Revenues of $40 to $80 per ton can be realized when one calculates both the sale of the recovered paper and the decreased disposal costs.

One ready example is office paper, which accounts for approximately 90 percent of all office waste. In the World Trade Center in New York City, one of the world's largest office complexes, a small recycling operation collects about one ton of paper a day, with only approximately 10 percent of the offices in the Center participating. After starting with a small grant of public funds, the operation now breaks even, provides jobs, and, importantly, removes a clog of wastepaper from the waste cycle. Paper users discard paper in conveniently placed containers, separating the paper at the source. Then the material is collected, fine-sorted, bound, sold, and eventually recycled.

Not all paper can be recycled, and in general, recycled paper does not last as long because each recycling stage shortens the fibers and weakens the pulp.

In the future, of course, books and other materials may not even be printed on paper but instead be projected as video, holograms, or other new communications processes. But until the page you are reading can actually come to you on thin air, paper will continue to be the conveyor of ideas, the carrier of words, the wrapper of gifts, the protector of goods—a long way from the mulberry tree bark used long ago for precious manuscripts.

Yet, considering what our paper habit costs, it will be a crazy logic indeed that permits us to continue consuming such a vast quantity of paper, only to throw most of it away. If you subtract this book from your annual consumption, you still have about 599 pounds (257 kilograms) to account for this year.

P.D. with O.G.

A HAMBURGER

There is no food quite like hamburger, quite as popular, quite as available, and, for a hot meal, quite as simple to cook. What was once mainly an at-home dinner has become an outside-the-home phenomenon, an eat-it-standing-up fast food as recognizable as the American flag. The McDonald's chain, for example, boasts that 96 percent of the children in the United States can identify the Ronald McDonald clown logo, and that half the adults in the country eat at McDonald's at least once a month.

The "Big Mac" has traveled to England, France, Japan, Costa Rica, and many other coun-

tries, and every four months McDonald's employees change the signs in front of more than five thousand outlets to indicate that another billion hamburgers have been sold. This, of course, says nothing about the other millions sold by such other favorites as Burger King, Howard Johnson's, Gino's, Wetson's, Wendy's, Carroll's, and Jack-in-the-Box, to name but a few. Together these chains account for tremendous quantities of basic foodstuffs. Each year, the McDonald's chain alone consumes 300,000 cattle, 250 million pounds (113 million kilograms) of flour, 25,000 gallons (94,000 liters) of catsup and mustard, about 60 square miles (155,000 hectares) of forest for paper packaging, and enough electricity to supply Boston, Washington, D.C., and San Francisco.

The hamburger has traveled long and far on its way to success. In medieval Russia the Tartars ate a precursor of the hamburger, which consisted of raw chopped meat with salt, pepper, and onion juice. German sailors brought the idea to Hamburg, where beef was made into patties and broiled. German immigrants in turn brought the hamburger to the United States in the early 1880s, but the American hamburger was officially born at the Louisiana Purchase Exposition in St. Louis in 1904. White Castle became the first hamburger chain in the 1920s, and McDonald's began its proliferation in 1955.

The hamburger has had many promoters in its rise to prominence. In cartoons, Popeye's friend Wimpy maintained his prodigious consumption by offering to "gladly pay you Tuesday for a hamburger today." In the 1960 U.S. presidential campaign, Richard Nixon claimed that his "hamburger" tastes were more appropriate for a U.S. president than the allegedly fancier tastes of millionaire John F. Kennedy. By the 1960s the "chicken in every pot" had become a burger in every bun.

Meat eating has traditionally been associated with prosperity, and every country repeats the pattern. In China, a phrase that translates to "mountains and forests of meat" was used to mean extravagance. The OPEC nations, which have been profiting from increased oil prices, have increased their meat imports from 235,000 tons in the early 1970s to 600,000 tons in 1978, and U.N. experts predict this figure will rise to 1.3 million tons by 1985. The Japanese are willing to pay as much as sixteen dollars a pound for steak.

The appetite for meat in industrialized countries has had an unfavorable effect on poorer countries. Western nations take credit for helping to feed the world's hungry, but for every 3 pounds (1.36 kilograms) of grain protein they export to the developing countries, they import 4 pounds of protein in oilseeds and fish from the very same "underfed" nations. Most of these fish and seeds, including one third of Africa's protein-rich peanuts, are fed to livestock in the American West.

The United States, the world's largest producer of beef, is also the world's largest importer. More than a billion pounds (450 million kilograms) of beef is imported each year, almost half of which comes from the most protein-deficient countries of Central America: Honduras, Guatemala, and Costa Rica. In 1975 Costa Rica, with a population of 2 million, sent 60 million pounds (27 million kilograms) of beef to the United States. That year Costa Rica had a per capita beef consumption of 33 pounds (15 kilograms), 16 pounds (7 kilograms) *less* than its 1950 per capita beef consumption of 49 pounds (22 kilograms). Many Costa Ricans can afford no meat, and one half of the country's children do not get enough food of any type.

The prestige of meat is traditionally explained by its nutritional value. During the 1880s in England, Dr. James Salisbury recommended the unlikely panacea of three meals a day of cooked ground beef with a drink of hot water. Many people still believe that red meat is the best source of protein and absolutely essential to good health. In the United States the average person consumes twice the recommended amount of protein daily *and* actually eats enough protein from nonmeat sources to fulfill the body's needs. The extra protein cannot be used by the body, so the extra 40 to 50 very expensive grams of protein are either burned for energy or stored as fat. Americans could eat less than the 120 pounds (54 kilograms) of beef and 120 pounds of other meats they consume each year without any ill effects, and probably with some benefit.

The U. S. Senate Select Committee on Nutrition and Human Needs warned in 1977 that the consumption of food rich in saturated fat, such as beef, contributed to heart disease and cancer of the colon. The U. S. Surgeon General has also warned that eating too much meat, like smoking, might be hazardous to health.

Children in the United States between the ages of seven and thirteen—a crucial period of growth and development—eat an average of 6.2 hamburgers a week. Their standard meal of hamburger, french fries, and cola is deficient in almost *all* vitamins, iron, and magnesium. For older burger lovers, an additional problem is the meal's almost 1,100 calories, which is high for an average meal. Well-known nutritionist Jean Mayer has characterized the fast-food special as

Beef cattle in Brazil. Many developing countries with suitable land have turned to raising cattle for export to wealthy nations. (*World Bank/Thomas Sennett*)

typical of the diet that leads to heart disease, the leading cause of death in the United States.

Burgers and the Land

The health of the physical environment is also affected by hamburgers. The raising of beef often leads to inefficient use of land, wasted water, enormous consumption of energy, water pollution, and the use of drugs that could have a serious impact on human health. (See "How to Make a Cow," page 590.) U. S. Department of Agriculture scientists Ralph Brand, Roger Drummond, and Nels Konnerup have compared the resources needed to produce 1 pound (.45 kilogram) of beef protein and 1 pound of plant protein. Beef requires approximately three times as much land, ten times as much fertilizer, fifteen times as much water, and eighteen times as much energy. One pound of hamburger requires one third of a gallon (1.2 liters) of gas, three fourths of a pound (.34 kilogram) of fertilizer, 7 pounds (3.2 kilograms) of grain and beans, and 3,000 gallons (11,000 liters) of water.

Many of the problems related to beef production are not *inherent* in cattle raising, but stem from the way cattle are now being raised in the United States and other developed countries. Cattle do not have to occupy valuable land or consume protein that could be fed to people. Most animals require protein to build tissue, but cattle are protein factories. When they eat, the food first passes through the rumen section of the stomach, where nonprotein cellulose and nitrogen are combined to produce microbial protein, which then moves on to the rest of the stomach to be digested in the same way as ordinary protein. Cattle can grow on a diet of protein-free fiber (corn husks or newspaper) and a nitrogen source (urea or uric acid), making it possible to raise them on marginal land that is not suitable for agriculture. The cattle industry, however, has found that it is more profitable to do otherwise, and consumers pay the cost in more ways than one.

After a calf is born, it remains on the ranch for about nine months to graze and gain weight. A "backgrounder" then buys it for about 80 cents a pound and allows it to eat grass and some grain for the next year. (Amounts in this article based on prices at press time.) The grain is expensive, but the steer must grow accustomed to eating grain before it is sent to a feedlot. The young steer, now weighing more than 700 pounds, is sold to a livestock company for about 65 cents a pound and sold again within a few hours to a feedlot operator for about 68 cents a pound.

The feedlot is the most significant step in the process. Over the next four to nine months, the steer will be fed about 2,500 pounds (1,140 kilograms) of grain and 350 pounds (160 kilograms) of soybeans. This diet produces meat that is well "marbled" with fat and therefore more attractive in the U.S. market. In spite of the health dangers associated with saturated fat, consumers are willing to pay more for choice grade meat, which has 63 percent more fat than standard grade.

Cattle gain weight faster on the grain diet, but they are eating protein that could be eaten by people. Sixteen pounds (7.2 kilograms) of grain and beans is required to produce each pound of meat. Frances Moore Lappé and Joseph Collins, in their book *Food First,* maintain that this enables U.S. agribusiness to control the world grain supply by expanding or reducing the amount of grain used as livestock feed. U.S. agriculture officials put it another way. They see cattle as a steady market for grain, assuring stable sales and prices for grain farmers.

The steer gains about 2 pounds (0.9 kilogram) a day on this grain diet, but for the U.S. market, this is not fast enough. Between 1954 and 1979, many cattle were also given the hormone diethylstilbestrol (DES) to speed their weight gain (the additional weight was mostly fat and water). The U. S. Food and Drug Administration banned the use of DES in cattle in 1972, but legal maneuvering by the cattle industry overturned the ban in 1974. In 1979 the FDA banned DES from use in livestock feed. (See "DES Daughters," page 196.)

The cattle are also given antibiotics in their feed to help prevent the spread of disease in the crowded and unsanitary feedlot and to increase weight. Forty percent of the antibiotics used in the United States are given to livestock.

Agricultural scientists are concerned about the long-range effects of this practice. Such widespread use of antibiotics accelerates the evolution of resistant strains of bacteria. If these resistant bacteria infect the cattle or humans, there might be no effective treatment. Six scientists who were studying this problem resigned in January 1979 from the U. S. Council for Agricultural Science and Technology because they thought the council was underestimating the danger of the overuse of antibiotics. A U. S. General Accounting Office report released in April 1979 found that 14 percent of the meat being sold in the United States may contain illegal residues of substances suspected of causing birth defects, cancer, or other toxic effects. It takes from six to twenty-five days after an animal is killed to test its meat for residues, but most meat is sold within twenty-four hours of slaughter.

Cattle serve a valuable function by producing manure, which is an excellent fertilizer and source of methane, but manure in feedlots is practically never used productively. Instead, waste is allowed to break down into ammonia and nitrate, which can leak into ground water and cause dangerously high nitrate levels in wells or can run off into surface water and contribute to oxygen depletion and algae overgrowth.

At the end of its stay in the feedlot, the two-and-a-half-year-old steer is ready to be sold for slaughter at about 64 cents a pound. The steer is killed, and within twenty-five minutes the hide,

Seventy thousand head of cattle at a time can be fattened in the Randall County Cattle Feed Yard, Amarillo, Texas, one of the largest feedlots in the United States. (*USDA/Fred S. Witte*)

head, and all other by-products have been removed. The carcass is ready to be graded by a federal inspector, then sold for about $1.02 a pound. The by-products sell for about $60.

The carcass is trucked to a retailer who sells it to a supermarket, butcher shop, or restaurant for about $1.15 a pound. The carcass is then butchered. About three fourths of the weight can be sold as meat; remaining fat and bone is usually sold to a rendering firm, though some of the excess fat often ends up in hamburger. The meat is then sold for prices ranging from $1.60 a pound for hamburger to $3.50 a pound for porterhouse steak. A large buyer like a fast-food restaurant will obviously pay less. Yet McDonald's "quarter pounder" (which actually cooks down to a sixth-of-a-pounder by the time you get it) was selling in New York City for $1.20 in 1980.

With U.S. per capita meat consumption at 240 pounds (110 kilograms) a year, meat is big business. But that could change. A Roper Organization poll in late 1978 found that 7 million people in the United States identify themselves as vegetarians, and another 37 million are "cautious" about how much meat they consume. During the past decade, vegetarian restaurants have increased in number throughout the country, and vegetarian cookbooks are now common on bookstore shelves. Nutritionists agree that one can satisfy all the body's requirements without eating meat, but fast-food restaurants in the United States are still doing $20 billion a year in sales that usually include a hamburger.

Recent studies suggest that people discover more than something to eat at a fast-food restaurant. Conrad Kottak, writing in *Natural History,* suggests that eating at fast-food chains has many ritual characteristics. Anywhere in the world, in one of many hamburger chain outlets, a meal is comfortingly predictable. Decor and layout are familiar, the menu and prices the same, and the appearance and responses of the sales help as unsurprising as a litany. The hamburger, of course, perfectly replicates billions of others. The advertising reassures you that you will get what you expect and join in an activity shared by millions of others. In an age of divisive social problems, fast-food outlets are a common ground that all U.S. citizens, and increasingly people of other nations, can share—an image of democracy. No ordinary meal, the hamburger is an experience.

There are almost half a million fast-food outlets in the United States, and the connection among almost all of these places is the humble hamburger—satisfying, straightforward, predictable, reassuring.

Inflation and high gasoline prices may hurt some of these enterprises, and doctors and ecologists may convince some people to reduce their meat consumption. And the rising price of oil may finally force the food industry to market more grains and beans. But the sizzling sound of a hamburger cooking will not soon disappear. At home and at barbecues, the hamburger endures as a cheap, convenient, and popular food—an American institution gone global.

K.F., C.R.C., J.S.

A CIGARETTE

In 1492, Christopher Columbus' interpreter ventured into the interior of Cuba and saw with amazement that the natives smoked rolled-up leaves they called *tabacs*. These were the first cigars. Smoking, unknown in Europe, had been important in pre-Colombian culture for thousands of years. A clay pipe found in California has been dated to 7000 B.C. The Aztecs and the Maya ritually blew tobacco smoke at the sun through reeds, and tobacco was necessary for the North American calumet, the peace pipe that sanctified treaties. Archaeologists have suggested

that some Native American tribes settled down from a nomadic life to agriculture so they could have a regular tobacco crop. Tobacco was such an important part of some cultures that in at least one Indian language the word "poor" is synonymous with "no tobacco."

Sailors from Spain and Portugal took tobacco from the West Indies back to Europe, and its use spread rapidly. By the end of the seventeenth century, smoking was a worldwide habit. British colonists transplanted West Indian tobacco to Virginia and the Carolinas, and grew rich on the trade with England.

The English government, deciding that tobacco was harmful, forbade tobacco growing in England in 1620, charged a high duty on American tobacco, and severely limited the importation of tobacco from Spain's colonies in the West Indies. King James I of England hated the smoking habit and declared it "hatefull to the Nose, harmefull to the braine, daungerous to the Lungs," sentiments echoed by the Ottoman emperor Murad IV, who ordered the death penalty for smoking. But early defenders of tobacco countered those opinions, claiming that tobacco smoke cured asthma and soothed the throat. During a plague epidemic in 1603, schoolboys at Eton were ordered to smoke daily to ward off disease. In France, powdered tobacco was used as a cure for migraine headaches. As late as the 1940s, one cigarette manufacturer advertised that cigarette smoke soothed the "T-zone" of a smoker's mouth and throat.

The Endless Tube

Although tobacco had become popular by the eighteenth century, most people smoked it in pipes, chewed it, or sniffed it as snuff. The origin of the modern cigarette is uncertain. Apparently Brazilians were wrapping tobacco in thin paper by the late 1700s, and by the early 1800s cigarettes had come to the Mediterranean area. During the Crimean War, British soldiers took up cigarettes and brought them to northern Europe. (Americans of the nineteenth century preferred chewing tobacco and were notorious for this habit around the world. Every public building in the United States was required to have spittoons.)

By the end of the century, cigarettes were familiar everywhere, and by the middle of the twentieth century more than half the men in several countries were regular cigarette smokers. Social pressures on women not to smoke were strong. An 1897 advertisement showing a woman smoker was a radical departure from the norm, and not another such social gaffe was printed in the United States for more than twenty years. And yet most of the workers who hand-rolled cigarettes in factories were women.

The first commercially produced cigarettes came from a French factory in 1843. The cigarettes had to be hand-rolled, at the rate of twenty every five minutes, and practiced young females were considered more deft than males. In 1884 James Bonsick invented a machine that could roll 120,000 cigarettes a day, and this machine was improved over the years; by World War I, cigarette-making machines could produce 600 cigarettes a minute.

Cigarette factories now are even more automated, at every step of the process. The tobacco that arrives from the farms is processed, blended, and flavored by machine (such flavors as chocolate, licorice, and sugar are regularly added). Then the tobacco goes on a conveyor belt to meet a continuous strip of paper, exactly as wide as the diameter of a cigarette, that endlessly unreels. After an electronic inspector makes sure that enough tobacco is deposited, the continuous rod of paper is sealed and cut into cigarette lengths by self-sharpening knives. Next, the new cigarettes move to another machine that puts filters on them at a rate of 6,000 a minute. Another electronic eye monitors this part of the process.

Finally, the cigarettes are put into packs of twenty, the packs into cartons, and the cartons into cases, all by machine. Electronic inspectors remove imperfect cigarette packs with fewer than twenty cigarettes in them and send them back for reprocessing. The new cigarettes are ready for their trip to the smoker—in some cases, halfway around the world.

The Smoke Giant

The giant American Tobacco Company was broken up in 1911 by the United States Supreme Court for violating the Sherman Anti-Trust Act. Shortly afterward, in 1913, the Reynolds Tobacco Company introduced Camels, the first nationally promoted and distributed cigarette. The extremely successful advertising campaign stimulated sales, and over the next fifty years all cigarette smoking grew at a phenomenal rate. Americans, who had formerly lagged behind the British, the Greeks, and the Finns in per capita cigarette consumption, became the most cigarette-loving people in the world. In 1911, per capita consumption in the United States was 108 cigarettes per year; in 1972, it was 4,040. Although cigarette smoking has declined since then (to 3,900 per capita in 1979), Americans still smoke far more cigarettes than the nearest runners-up, the Japanese (75 percent of Japanese men smoke, but fewer than one in five Japanese women do.)

Smoking Can Be Dangerous to Your Wealth

The increase in cigarette consumption in the United States and Europe was accompanied by a rapid increase in the incidence of lung cancer, which had previously been quite rare. Doctors began to suspect that cigarettes were to blame for their patients' respiratory problems, and athletes were advised not to smoke. In 1962 the Royal College of Physicians in London published a detailed report setting forth the accumulated medical evidence against cigarettes, and in 1964 the Surgeon General of the United States published findings that linked cigarette smoking definitively to cancer of the lung. These two reports, along with many that corroborated them, convinced millions of people that they should not smoke. In the next fifteen years more than 30 million people in the United States alone quit smoking; surveys show that half the college graduates who ever smoked have stopped. Italy, Iceland, Finland, Sweden, Norway, and Singapore banned all cigarette advertisements, and the United States, Soviet Union, Britain, Sweden, and France have launched antismoking campaigns. In most of Europe and North America, cigarette smoking is not allowed—except in special areas—in subways, buses, theaters, and hospitals. Per capita use of tobacco is declining in most developed countries as more people become aware of the danger.

Tobacco companies, jittery at the possible loss of revenue, have been following two strategies: diversifying, by buying into other kinds of business, and expanding, by selling to developing world markets. Their fright is understandable—the chairman of the board of Reynolds Tobacco said in 1978 that if every smoker smoked one less cigarette a day, the industry would lose $450 million a year.

Anticipating a further decline in U.S. cigarette smoking, in spite of the $500 million they spend annually on advertising, U.S. companies are exporting the habit. Philip Morris has increased its overseas cigarette sales at 18 percent a year for each of the last ten years; in contrast, tobacco companies' domestic growth has averaged about 1 percent annually.

The governments of poorer countries often welcome the tax revenues cigarettes generate, and they normally have more pressing concerns than an increase in cancer twenty years in the future. Street urchins from Bogotá to Cairo smoke regularly at the age of eight. In many countries smoking still connotes glamour, sophistication, and flair; many poor people would rather cut down on eating than abandon their cigarettes. Every year the developing world consumes 5 percent more cigarettes than the year before, in spite of such poverty that in many places cigarettes must be sold singly because people cannot afford a whole pack.

Many studies have shown that cigarettes are the first luxury poor people buy. In the prison camps of World War II, the cigarette became a substitute for currency, and after the war a British member of Parliament complained publicly that there was a "cigarette economy" from Paris to Peking. Some American GIs made handsome profits selling one-dollar cartons of cigarettes to Germans in 1947 for ten times that price. Most of the Chinese Communist leaders acquired the cigarette habit during their years of rebellion and deprivation, and Chairman Mao was said to smoke the most expensive blends while leading an otherwise Spartan life.

The Black Leaf

What is it about cigarettes that is so appealing? For one thing, the nicotine in tobacco is addictive, and cigarette smokers, by inhaling, ingest more of it than pipe or cigar smokers. The twenty or thirty minutes between cigarettes for a heavy smoker equals the time it takes for the effect of nicotine on the brain to wear off. The smoker then feels the need for another cigarette to get more nicotine to the brain. Nicotine is not only addictive but also extremely poisonous—it is marketed as an insecticide, for example, under the name Blackleaf 40.

Cigarette smoke is dangerous not only to the smoker but to those around him or her. One survey of eight thousand wives indicated that those married to smokers died, on the average, four years earlier than wives of nonsmokers. In Cleveland, a study of smoke-filled bars demonstrated that a nonsmoking bartender inhaled the equivalent of thirty-six cigarettes during each eight-hour shift.

The children of smokers also suffer. Babies of mothers who smoke weigh less at birth, a factor that affects their survival rates; they also tend to get pneumonia, chest infections, and bronchitis more than other babies, and this in turn may expose them to further danger later on. A controversial German study by Doctors G. Mau and Petra Netter, of the universities of Kiel and Mainz respectively, may demonstrate that men who smoke heavily also risk harming their children.

The chief burden of smoking, of course, falls on the smoker. In any given year, a smoker is much more likely to die than a nonsmoker of the same age, and this fact is so obvious that it was brought up in the 1930s, long before the connection between smoking and lung cancer was proven. Smoking damages many different parts of the body, especially the respiratory system, the heart, and blood vessels.

The disease most commonly associated with cigarettes is lung cancer. As many as 80 to 90 percent of lung cancers are caused by cigarette smoke, and lung cancer is one of the more deadly cancers: only about 10 percent of lung cancer patients survive. Each day, more than 220 people in the United States alone die of lung cancer that was caused by their cigarette smoking. Cigarette smoke has also been implicated in cancer of the mouth, the lip, the larynx, and the bladder.

Smoking is also associated with chronic bronchitis and emphysema. Heart diseases like coronary thrombosis and myocardial infarction are much more common among smokers. So are hardening and obstruction of the arteries of the limbs and head; the heart needs more oxygen just when carbon monoxide from the smoke decreases the amount of oxygen the bloodstream can supply. Smoking also increases blood pressure and heart rate.

A woman who smokes cigarettes and takes birth control pills runs an increased chance of heart attack. Smoking also impairs eyesight, contributes to the development of high blood pressure and of the complications of diabetes and alcoholism. Every cigarette smoked shortens the smoker's life by an average of six minutes.

The cost of hospital bills, disability payments, and lost work time because of cigarette-caused disease was estimated at $18 billion in 1979 for the United States alone. About 360,000 people die annually in the United States because of tobacco use.

The Smoke Screen

Although tobacco is far more harmful than substances that are banned as carcinogenic, the world tobacco industry continues to flourish on the strength of nicotine addiction and the vast sums of money the industry contributes to government. The Chinese, Soviet, and Japanese governments run, as their respective monopolies, three of the world's top five cigarette companies (the other two are British-American Tobacco and Philip Morris). The Indian government depends on tobacco taxes for a substantial share of its revenues.

Tobacco in the United States and Europe is a heavily subsidized crop. In 1977, for example, the United States paid $35 million in direct subsidies

Broad leaf burley tobacco in bloom on a Kentucky farm. (*USDA*)

to the tobacco industry, and underwrote $123 million in loans to foreign countries so they could buy U.S. tobacco. The taxpayers of the European Economic Community (EEC) pay large subsidies —an average of $2,500 per hectare—to the tobacco farmers of Italy and France. In fact, the EEC supplies more than half the farmers' income from tobacco.

Although the United Nations World Health Organization is working to prevent cigarette smoking, other major international forces continue to treat tobacco as just another cash crop, like rubber or bananas. The World Bank, United Nations Development Program, and the U. N. Food and Agriculture Organization, all officially dedicated to alleviating global problems, have helped develop the tobacco industry in Jordan, Yemen, Ethiopia, Uganda, Tanzania, and Zambia. Western cigarette companies have encouraged tobacco growing where it is clearly not suited to the land, in arid northwest Pakistan, for example, where the huge amounts of firewood required to cure tobacco are not readily available and are desperately needed for other, more vital purposes.

The United States government regularly exports tobacco under the aegis of Food for Peace, a program devised to transfer American crop surpluses without lowering domestic prices. This program has the twin effect of supporting tobacco prices at home and encouraging the cigarette habit abroad.

Tobacco companies pour immense sums of money into advertising in the developing world. The Marlboro cowboy rides high in Kuwait, and Gauloises and Gitanes are glamorous in Niger. In South American cities, a higher percentage of the men smoke than in the United States, and the difference is increasing.

In spite of all the evidence against smoking, tobacco companies continue to insist that cigarettes are not dangerous to health. In January 1979 the U. S. Surgeon General issued a new report citing 30,000 scientific papers that add up to "overwhelming proof" that smoking is linked to many diseases, from lung cancer and heart disease to birth defects in children of smokers. The Tobacco Institute, a wealthy lobby for the industry, immediately labeled the report a "publicity stunt." The institute, the New York *Times* reported, "countered that the research results were circumstantial at best."

J.S.

A truckload of tobacco purchased at an auction in Georgia is prepared for the trip to a redrying plant in North Carolina. (*USDA*)

SMOKING LORE

- Some research findings: nine out of ten smokers want to stop; six out of ten have tried and failed; quit-smoking techniques have a 75-percent failure rate; only 2 percent of smokers do not smoke regularly; most teenagers who smoke more than two cigarettes per day become regular cigarette smokers; former drug addicts and alcoholics say it is easier to give up drugs and liquor than smoking.
- Fifty million Americans smoke. One out of six Americans will die prematurely because of cigarettes.
- The U. S. National Fire Prevention and Control Administration says that 13 percent of residential fires and almost a third of all deaths from fire are caused by cigarettes.
- Worldwide, 69 percent of tobacco-growing land is in developing countries. Eleven million acres (4.5 million hectares) of land in the world grow tobacco instead of food.
- More Americans are killed by cigarettes each year than were killed in combat in all of World War II.
- More than 75 percent of Americans who smoke acquired the habit before they were twenty.
- A Harvard study indicates that people who smoke low-tar, low-nicotine cigarettes tend to smoke more cigarettes, inhale deeper, and hold the smoke in their lungs longer.
- Several U.S. and British economic and statistical studies have shown that cigarette advertisement levels influence smoking rates. American tobacco and cigarette companies spend $500 million a year on cigarette advertisements.
- Global consumer expenditure for cigarettes is about $100 billion per year.
- More than one in four U.S. teenage girls smokes, and the proportion is climbing.
- Smokers have 50 percent more abnormal electrocardiograms than nonsmokers.

J.S.

A BANANA

Hanging in supermarkets, unbruised and unblemished, usually sun yellow and bright against a mossy green display background, bananas look so naturally a part of the shopping scene that it is difficult to believe they did not grow right there on the metal hook. But a typical banana shipment travels more than 4,000 miles (6,437 kilometers) to reach its destination. Bananas are picked and packed carefully with these long trips in mind, for banana producing is a sophisticated business. The

fruit is picked green and ripened at high temperatures in special ripening centers located close to the markets. Banana boats, loaded at night by laborers, have been part of the banana trade from the beginning, though mechanization now speeds loading. And speed is especially important in the banana business, since the fruit has only approximately twenty-one days to get from the harvest to the retail shelf before spoiling.

From Malaysia, the Philippines, Central and South America, West Africa, the Caribbean—all hot, humid regions—bananas journey to the distant markets of Western Europe and North America, where about two of every three bananas is consumed, either by the popular hand-held, peel-it-and-eat-it method or in sumptuous banana cakes, shakes, puddings, and whipped creams. Bananas may be the world's most versatile, and most traveled, snack food.

The journeying, however, is only one part of the modern banana's roots system, a history which includes political intrigue, market profiteering, and land abuse. It is a history at once rich and sad.

A Banana by Any Other Name

The banana belongs to the musaceae family of treelike herbs. There are only three major types, but over one hundred subspecies, with as many local names and uses.

In Southeast Asia, shoots and buds of bananas are consumed; in China, the lower heads are pickled; and in Malaysia, immature fruits are added to curries. In Africa, banana beer is brewed in the bottoms of dugout canoes. Pictures of bananas were woven into linen in China as early as A.D. 100, and intrepid Sir Henry Stanley, of "Dr. Livingston, I presume," wrote that banana flour and milk was all the food he could eat during a severe bout of gastritis. In the remote Amazon jungle, rich in banana varieties, the *banana prata* is still used to treat dysentery and vomiting, especially among children. Banana leaves roof houses, and can be formed into umbrellas on a frame of oleander sticks. Rope can be wound from banana stem fiber.

Like today's banana, perpetually headed for market, the original bananas were always being discovered by one group of people and then carried to another. Wild bananas native to Asia were probably eaten by the very earliest people there. Eventually bananas were domesticated along with other early crops. The first recorded mention of bananas is found in a Buddhist canon written in India in the fifth century B.C. In fact, Linnaeus, the founder of botanical nomenclature, named the Gros Michel banana, a once frequently consumed variety, *Musa sapientum,* or "fruit of the wise men," because Indian sages reportedly thrived on them.

By the second century A.D., the banana was notable enough to appear in the *Encyclopedia of Rare Things* written by Yang Fu, a Chinese official. From Malaysia, bananas spread east across the Pacific with the Polynesian migrations, and west, via Arab merchants, to the Mediterranean and the west coast of Africa. The fruit survived such movements because it grows from dry roots rather than seeds that need to be kept fresh.

By the early 1400s, the banana had reached the

Canary Islands, and from there it made its transatlantic crossing in 1516, carried by a Spanish missionary named DeBerlanga to the island of Santo Domingo, now known as Hispaniola and shared by Haiti and the Dominican Republic. Bananas became one of the first crops planted by settlers in the New World, and later explorers of the tropics marveled at the exotic banana, then considered a rare luxury by inhabitants of more temperate zones.

The first bananas imported to the United States arrived in the early nineteenth century, and in 1876 the Philadelphia Centennial Exposition featured the oddity wrapped in tinfoil and sold at what was then considered an exorbitant price of ten cents each.

Banana Business

With the advent of schooner traffic and the expansion of U.S. business, the banana trade picked up. Also, the political milieu in areas naturally suited to banana growing was right for establishing a banana monopoly.

Into this kaleidoscope of changing power entered the United Fruit Company. An American named Minor Keith had traveled to Costa Rica in the hope of building a passenger railroad from the coast to the inland capital of San José. The project was eventually completed at a high human cost; the 25 miles (40 kilometers) of track laid through difficult jungle conditions resulted in the deaths of five thousand men. But there was not enough passenger traffic to keep the line running, so in 1873, Keith began a banana plantation to provide his train with freight.

At about the same time another American named Lorenzo Dow Baker, a schooner captain, took on a cargo of bananas from Jamaica and delivered it with dispatch to the northeastern United States. None of the bananas spoiled. Baker saw the opportunity for a successful banana shipping business, which he called the Boston Fruit Company. Eventually, in 1899, he joined his West Indian operation with Keith's in Central America to form the United Fruit Company. Such were the beginnings of banana power in Central America. United Fruit and a main competitor, Standard Fruit and Steamship Company, still control approximately 70 percent of the world's banana production.

Banana Government

Bananas thus became central to the economies of Guatemala, Costa Rica, Honduras, and other Central American countries, called sarcastically "banana republics," a term reflecting not only the omnipresence of the crop, but the omnipotence of the banana companies. For example, in Guatemala in 1954, the elected Arbenz government, which was promoting agrarian reform, was overthrown by a U.S. government-backed invasion. The invasion followed a large-scale anti-Arbenz public relations campaign waged by United Fruit.

In 1959, *Fortune* magazine reported that United Fruit was the largest private landowner, and the largest employer, in Costa Rica, Guatemala, and Honduras. (By 1976, United Fruit had merged into the conglomerate United Brands.) In 1974, Chairman Eli Black reportedly attempted to win a reduction of the Honduran export tax on bananas by offering a $1.25-million bribe to the president of Honduras, General Osvaldo López Arellano. The result, when word of the arrangement leaked out, was the overthrow of the government of Honduras and the dramatic suicide, once the news of United Fruit's role became public, of Eli Black in New York City.

Banana Land

Though such overt scandals may today be somewhat tempered by tougher local government control over multinational companies, the banana monopoly still has tremendous control over lives and resources. Peel the story further and it reveals tired lands and exploited workers, situations that begin at the banana plantation and persist right through to market.

Banana plants grow in hot, humid regions where winds are light, land drainage good, and moisture abundant. To grow, they require at least 4 inches (10 centimeters) of rainfall per month, or its equivalent in irrigation. Washing bananas to remove sprays, insects, and dust before shipment also consumes large quantities of water.

Banana "trees" grow from an underground stem, or rhizome, that sends up shoots—the "trunks" of the trees. The trunks, wrapped in long leaf stalks, reach 40 feet (12 meters). At the top, the leaves fan out and the slender stem emerges to bend over, laden with a cluster of tubular, yellow flowers that develop, layer by layer, into bananas within three to four months. A stem produces about three hundred bananas, all grown pointing upward, then it dies. It will not produce bananas again. However, the rhizome sends up new shoots, new "trees," as the old ones die. Theoretically, the plant could live forever.

A worker in Ecuador prepares bananas for shipment to distant markets. (*World Bank/Larry Daughters*)

Compared to the long life of the banana plant, the life of the commercial banana plantation is short. A commercial plantation has an average economic life span of about ten years, whereas nonmechanized plantations nearly one hundred years old are known. The difference in the life span has several causes. Mechanical planters lay plants in dense concentrations to squeeze as many as possible into a given plot of land. In addition, hand laborers "rattoon" the plants, cutting back a natural shoot to force a premature second shoot to emerge. Both shoots then mature. This pushing of yield sucks up soil nutrients that are not naturally replenished because banana lands almost never lie fallow. Consequently, tons of oil-based nitrogen fertilizer are applied, sometimes as much as four or five times the maximum commonly applied to other crops—as much as 900 pounds per acre (1,010 kilograms per hectare) per year.

Machines also tread heavily on the soil, compressing and compacting it. Oxygen cannot travel freely through packed soil, so the plants are highly susceptible to diseases from fungus and bacteria that thrive in nonoxygenated ground. Therefore, banana plants grown in heavily mechanized plantations require high applications of pesticides.

Much of the fertilizers and pesticides never reach the plants. Heavy tropical rainstorms, common in banana-growing areas, wash them into streams and rivers, fouling the local water system. Also, deliberate flooding of banana lands to control typical banana pests, such as Sigatoka fungus and burrowing nematode worms, produces chemical wash that meets the already dirtied rain en route to the sea. Fortunately the banana itself is protected from absorbing these chemicals by its tough, thick peel.

Abandoning a spent banana plantation is often cheaper than waiting for the land to renew itself. In Central America, abandoned banana plantations checker the humid lowlands, depleted of banana potential and too abused to grow anything else.

There are alternatives to this exhausting banana monoculture. One system capitalizes on bananas' wide shady leaves, using them as "overstory": bananas grow among other tropical crops that survive in or require shade, like pineapple and sweet potato. The result is a more natural mixed planting system, producing not only bananas but staple crops as well. Bananas have been grown successfully, and commercially, in this way in Africa, though such a system is labor intensive. So far no machine has been designed to cope with the "disarray" of mixed crops in the same row.

On Mindanao, an island in the Philippines where the land well suits banana growing, approximately 35 percent of all cultivated land has been converted to banana production. Banana growers speculate on the land, causing prices to rise, and tenant farmers, who can no longer afford the rent, are displaced. Small landowners are talked into selling out, often at prices far lower than the value of their land. Such diverse crops as rice, corn, coffee, and coconut are uprooted to plant bananas.

Of Mindanao's total 1967 banana crop, less than 1 percent was exported; in 1979 this figure had surpassed 50 percent. Often the displaced farmers work either as stevedores on the banana boat docks or as hands on the plantations. Expanding the banana business into a "cash" crop was supposed to improve their quality of life by providing jobs and bringing in foreign currency. But in 1977, Philippine banana dock workers earned about $5.50 a week, plantation workers approximately $12. The cost of living for a family of six in the Philippines is estimated at the U.S. equivalent of $186 per month. Overall the banana worker received only 1.5 percent of the retail value of the bananas he or she helped produce.

Ironically, when the market for Philippine bananas, mainly in Japan, is low, Philippine banana growers actually dump edible fruit to avoid a market glut and plummeting prices. According to research by the Institute for Food and Development Policy, in 1977 approximately 40 percent of the harvested crop of Mindanao was thrown away!

Banana Food

Though the banana has many useful by-products, none are produced on a commercial scale. And though bananas are the main source of calories in such regions as West Africa and the Amazon basin, they are certainly not a staple food. The weight of the banana is 32 percent refuse; the typical fully ripe fruit is 75 percent moisture, 21 percent sugar, and only 4 percent combined protein, fiber, and starch. For people on restricted diets, bananas are a fine specialty food, since they are low in sodium, cholesterol, and fats and high in phosphorus and potassium, making them particularly helpful for patients taking diuretics. But people who depend on bananas for nutrition soon develop severe deficiencies.

The retail price of the bananas displayed so tantalizingly in supermarkets and groceries is a potpourri of charges, the largest percentage of which is *not* devoted to the costs of growing them. In fact, only approximately 10 percent of the cost is involved in production. The bulk of the cost, approximately 37 percent, is devoted to shipping and on-site ripening. Nineteen percent is taken by the "ripener" for costs, advertising, and profits, and 32 percent by the retailer for the same.

In the United States, where 19.5 pounds of bananas are eaten per person per year, 60 percent of the bananas purchased are bought on impulse. We reach for them casually, four or five at a time, accustomed to their availability, convenienced by their peelability, enamored of their pulpy sweet taste. We have even incorporated them into our speech—we "go bananas," our leaders are "top bananas." (Once in 1979, to avoid using the word "recession," one of the top bananas in U. S. President Carter's administration, Alfred Kahn, called economic downturn a "deep, deep banana.")

Bananas are so commonplace now that we cannot banish them, nor should we want to. But in a world pressed by shortages, to invest so much of a developing country's water, land, labor, and money to produce and transport what is basically a dessert for the rest of the world smacks of "banana wisdom."

P.D., C.R.C., J.S., C.P.

BLUE JEANS

If all the fabric used in an average year in the manufacture of blue jeans and related jeanswear were woven into one length of material, it would stretch around the earth's equator twenty-two times, and still there would be extra yardage, for jeans are probably the most popular form of trousers in the world. But their celebrity is not just a phenomenon of our times. Originally, sailors from Dhunga, India, were recognized by the cotton denim trousers they wore. The sailors, and their pants, were known as Dhungarees. The word "jeans," on the other hand, derives from Italy, where Genoese sailors, and *their* pants, were called "genes." Eventually, the pants made their way to the wild west of the United States, where prospectors, according to blue jeans lore, favored the tough cloth brought by one of them from Nimes, France, serge de Nimes, since Anglicized to "denim."

Using brass rivets, the first jeans designer, Jacob W. Davis, constructed many-pocketed durable pants, perfect for carrying the tools of the gold-rush trade as well as gold nuggets. From these utilitarian beginnings, jeans have captured the center stage of fashion, to the extent that over a half a billion pairs are purchased around the world in an average year. Jeans are worn by farmers as well as fashion designers, workers as well as vacationers, in towns and cities and villages and whistlestops, to cocktail parties and political rallies, and even by schoolchildren to class. They are probably the most universal and ubiquitous item in fashion history.

The blue jeans rage is intertwined with the history of the parent fabric, cotton, a fiber that humanity has known since at least 700 B.C., when it was being cultivated in India. Some studies even place cotton in the Tehuacan Valley of Mexico as

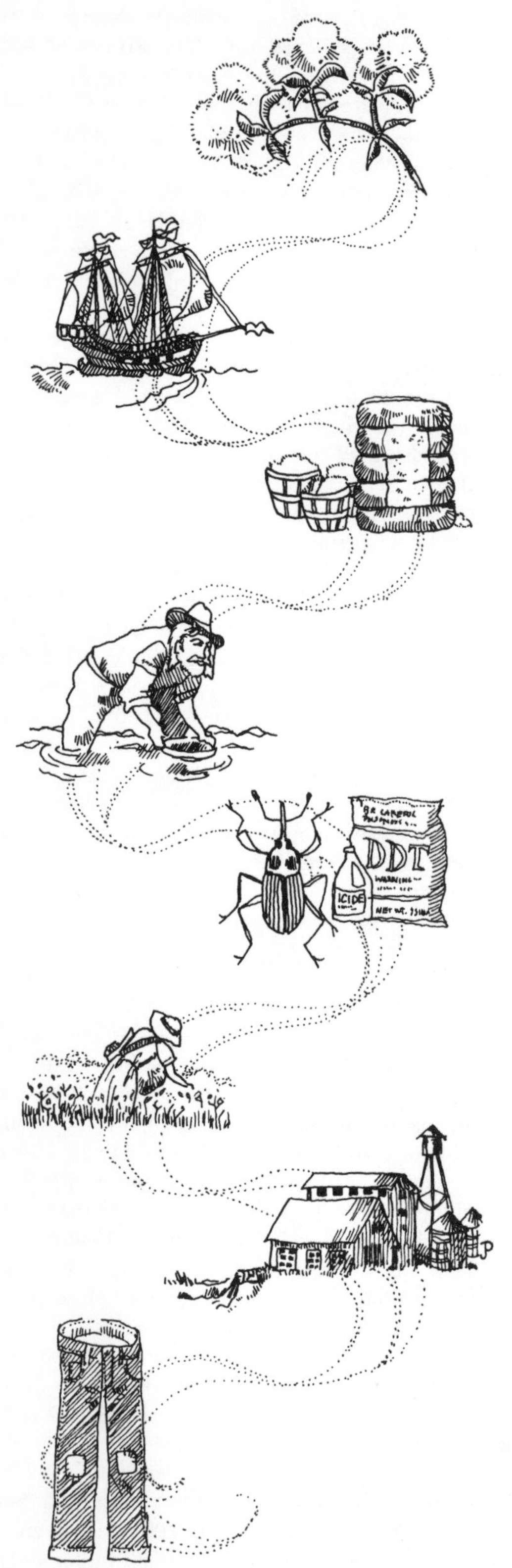

early as 5000 B.C. Certainly, there are written records that the campaigning armies of Alexander the Great noted cotton being traded by Arab merchants as early as 400 B.C. The fabric moved across Europe in various forms: as priestly garments in Egypt, hair nets in Greece, tents and canopies for Roman legions, cotton paper, cotton candlewicks, even defensive pads used by knights in warfare. When Columbus set out to discover a westward route to the Orient, the sails of his ships were sewn from the same kind of serge de Nimes that eventually found its way to the gold rush in California. On a stop in the Bahamas, Columbus encountered yet another form of cotton, unknown in Europe, that grew wild on trees, called sea island cotton today, which yields an especially soft, lovely fabric.

At the time of its first mass use, in the seventeenth century, cotton could be produced more cheaply than wool, leather, or silk, the most common fabrics of the times. Today cotton is itself being challenged by cheaper, synthetic fabrics.

The growth of the cotton industry incited protest among England's wool manufacturers, and in 1700, several laws forbidding the use of cotton were passed to protect the interests of wool merchants. But in the American colonies cotton was introduced successfully in Virginia in 1619, and with the labor of the first black slaves, cotton was well on its way to becoming an agricultural mainstay in the New World. Several inventions appeared in these early years, including yarn-spinning machinery; but it was the 1793 invention of the cotton gin, a device for mechanically separating the seed from the tough fiber, that enabled cotton to become king of the South. By 1860 the United States was providing 75 percent of the world's cotton supply.

Today, cotton is a major world crop, and in 1977, according to the Food and Agriculture Office of the United Nations, 15,748,000 tons (14,290,000 metric tons) were grown worldwide, 5,685,000 tons (5,158,000 metric tons) in Asia alone. The major growing countries are the United States, India, the USSR, and China, but cotton can be found from Mexico to Indonesia, in fact in 125 different countries, accounting for 78.5 million acres (31.7 million hectares) of the world's arable land.

The Seeds of Cotton

Cotton grows best in warm, moist climates, which nurture the fabric's desirable characteristics

—its absorbency, durability, and soft feel or "hand." The growing process is perfectly engineered. The cottonseed sprouts a fiber tube about nine weeks after planting. Each day, an additional layer of fiber forms inside the tube—microscopic filaments padded with cellulose. Eventually, the tube is filled up by these spiral layers and becomes a full boll of cotton. When the boll is mature, long and oval in shape, it breaks open. Approximately thirty layers have formed, and the cotton dries into flat, interlocking threads, which can be processed into yarn.

Much of the cotton-harvesting process has been mechanized, and machines can pick approximately 2,200 pounds (998 kilograms) of cotton per hour, while a laborer can hand pick only 20 to 25 pounds (9 to 11 kilograms). The seed is combed from the cotton and sent to an oil mill to be cracked open and "dekerneled." The fiber is baled—one bale equals approximately 480 pounds (218 kilograms)—and begins its journey through the textile process, to be carded (the initial disentangling stage), drawn, perhaps combed, and drawn further. "Roving" the cotton is usually the last step before spinning, when the strands are twisted slightly and pulled into thinner strands. The roving is then spun into yarn, wound on bobbins, and woven into fabric.

The rough, unbleached cotton fabric, called "greige goods" (pronounced "gray"), then moves into a series of bleaching, dyeing, and preparing processes determined by the nature of the desired end product.

Denim for jeans is woven with the warp yarn dyed indigo; the weft, or filling (horizontal), yarn strands are not dyed. The weave can be any of several constructions but is usually twill, where filling threads pass over one and under two or more warp threads, lending the appearance of diagonal, or broken diagonal, lines.

In 1978 the United States produced 554 million square yards (463 million square meters) of denim, of which 112 million square yards (94 million square meters) were exported. Of this U.S. production, about 90 percent was pure cotton; the rest was cotton blends incorporating synthetic materials that give added strength.

The Food or Fiber Dilemma

The worldwide market for fiber has increased, but the trend has been toward synthetic fibers—petroleum-based—because, despite oil price hikes, they are less expensive than natural fibers. As a result, cotton's share of the world fiber market dropped from 62.3 to 51.9 percent over the ten-year period between 1969 and 1978.

As cotton producers face this competition from synthetics, they must at the same time compete with food crops, especially soybean and sorghum grain. According to the U. S. Department of Agriculture, by the year 2000 the American South, traditionally the world's Cotton Belt, will produce 35 percent of the nation's soybean crop—an agricultural enterprise unheard of in the region until recently. In 1978 the harvest in the South was two to one, soybeans over cotton, but in 1979 cotton was making a strong comeback.

So the cotton producer is caught up in the fluctuations of the market, what has become known as the "food-fiber trade-off," balancing the world's need to eat against its need for clothing. Keeping one eye on prices and the other on the fields, the farmer juggles numbers and economic predictions. Roughly, soybeans become more profitable when their price rises ten times higher than cotton prices. The farmer's return on investment in cotton is a minuscule percentage of the retail price.

For every dollar spent by the consumer on blue jeans—at an average price of $14 a pair—only $.09 covers the farm production costs for the cotton. The other costs are as follows:

$ .42 wholesale and retail costs
.29 apparel manufacturing
.18 textile mill processing and finishing
.01 marketing to mill
.01 ginning

$ .91 plus $.09=$1.00

Cotton Bugs

Since cotton is normally planted as a monoculture, it is especially vulnerable to pests. In fact, it is one of the world's most pesticide-intensive crops. Approximately one third of all pesticides applied in the United States is applied to cotton to eliminate several insects, including the lygus bug, the bollworm, the tobacco budworm, the army worm, and the cabbage looper, to say nothing of the notorious boll weevil. Since it was first noted in the United States in about 1894, the weevil has chewed its way through 600,000 square miles (1.6 million square meters) of cotton in the South and the Caribbean, advancing 40 to 160 miles (65 to 260 kilometers) a year; it had consumed 85 percent of the cotton crop by the early 1920s.

Boll weevil on a cotton plant. About one third of the pesticides sprayed in the United States are directed at cotton pests such as these. (*USDA*)

Pesticide application begets further pesticide application—what is known as the pesticide treadmill—and the process does not necessarily result in fewer pests. (See "Spraying the World," page 184, and "Integrated Pest Management," page 31.)

Chemical spraying continues in all cotton-growing regions (often for merely cosmetic reasons, i.e. to eliminate insect stains). In Guatemala in 1977 so much DDT was used, flash-sprayed by air by private U.S. contractors, to control cotton pests that farmers in the area reported symptoms of severe pesticide poisoning, such as nausea and dizziness. According to reports from the scene, the acrid smell of pesticides clung to the clothing of the local inhabitants. There was DDT in mother's milk and in meat, and because mosquitoes became resistant to the excessive spraying, malaria resurged. Though the Guatemalan government has since banned the import of DDT, Guatemalan growers still rely on heavy pesticide application to control pests. And as U.S. pesticide restrictions tighten, cotton producers shift to the developing world, where restrictions are usually lenient. (See "Better Living Through Chemistry?" page 507.)

Lessons are being learned slowly, and there is some cause for guarded optimism now that several experimental pest-control programs are under way. In the United States, in North Carolina, a pilot program is attempting nothing less than total eradication of the boll weevil through a combination of minimal spraying and the introduction of sterile weevils to the population. In South America and parts of Africa, interplanting of cotton crops, usually in combination with maize and corn, has controlled the bollworm to some extent, but the crucial component in all these programs is to educate cotton growers not to spray at the first sign of an insect.

Cotton Lung

Byssinosis, brown lung disease, can be brought on by the inhalation of cotton dust. First noted in England in the 1800s and named formally in 1877, the disease remains an antagonist to both mill worker and mill owner. In its early stages, after the symptoms of chest tightness and cough are noticed, the disease is reversible. But, eventually, the dust coats the bronchial tubes until they cease to permit the normal passage of air, causing extreme bronchial congestion that can lead to permanent illness or death.

No one is sure what actually causes byssinosis, but the American Lung Association lays the blame on "a chemical agent believed to be located in the bract, that is, the leaf surrounding the stem of the cotton boll. This agent is borne in the air in dust particles, and when inhaled, causes constriction of the small airways." Ironically, there is more bract on the cotton when it is picked by machine. "Break your back hand-picking or risk brown lung" is how cottonmakers describe their predicament.

According to the American Lung Association, approximately 200,000 workers in the United States are considered the "population at risk." Statistics outside the United States are not available, though the brown lung debate has a long history. The cotton industry in the United States has been vigorously accused by labor organizations of deliberately masking the real dangers of brown lung. Industry spokespeople, especially the American Textile Manufacturers Institute, respond that "brown lung" is a catch-all term for many pulmonary disorders that could just as well be related to factors other than cotton dust. They complain that cotton dust factory standards are unrealistically stringent. There are no international dust standards, and an International Labor Organization meeting in 1977 on the textile industry did not explore the issue, nor had the World Health Organization taken it up. In the United States, new dust standards were imposed in 1978, over vigorous industry opposition that resulted in protracted legal battles.

Indigo Blue

No discussion of blue jeans would be complete without a mention of the dyeing process, which lends them not only their color but their character. To many wearers, jeans are not worth putting on until they've been faded and, often, the more faded and well worn the better. Manufacturers even allow for this consumer quirk by prefading the fabric, tagging new jeans with a message to indicate that the "flaws" in the garments are not flaws at all but deliberately introduced "qualities."

Indigo dye, which has been used for at least four thousand years and is possibly the world's oldest known coloring matter, is what puts the blue in blue jeans. Natural indigo derives from a plant genus called *Indigofera,* a member of the pea family native to regions with warm climates, including Asia, Java, Japan, Central America, Brazil, the southern United States, and the West Indies.

Use of the dye was recorded in ancient Sanskrit writings and, like cotton itself, indigo also turned up on Egyptian mummies and in Inca tombs. The Venetians were apparently the first Europeans to use the dye, and by the sixteenth and seventeenth centuries it had become common in the rest of Europe, replacing a locally grown plant called woad, which yielded a similar blue color. The woad industry was so worried about competition from indigo, which had superior dyeing qualities, that it unleashed an anti-indigo advertising campaign, warning potential users off indigo, terming it the "devil's dye." However, indigo prevailed and soon replaced woad almost entirely. Eventually, synthetic indigo was produced in Germany in 1870.

Indigo has a low affinity for cotton, fading quietly with each wash, lending the comfortable, used, well-loved look that accounts for so much of the popularity of jeans. With the beginning of the blue jeans craze in 1970, indigo demand rose. It peaked in 1978 at 14,300 tons (13,000 metric tons) per year and sold at about $16 per pound when supply was lowest and demand highest.

Because the dye has become so expensive, manufacturers are exploring various means of recovering waste dye at the factory. Textile manufacturers have also had to try to find ways to keep denim dye effluents out of the water system in order to meet clean-water standards.

It is the dyeing operation that is the primary source of pollution and wastewater in textile plants, and the indigo-dyeing process, because it requires a high number of rinses, is a major contributor to a textile plant's pollution problems. Typically the wastewater of the textile-dyeing process is highly alkaline and saturated with the dark color of runoff dye. It is generally estimated that the average volume of water effluent is about 10 to 35 gallons per pound (84 to 289 liters per kilogram) of fabric.

Several methods for cleaning wastewater at denim plants are under study, including the use of waste fly ash, a by-product of the combustion of coal, as a color absorbent. In this process, the colored wastewater passes through a bed of ash, to which the color molecules stick. The result is cleaner water, as well as a productive use for fly ash.

Another means of cleaning wastewater involves chemical destabilization. In this process, lime or alum, an astringent used in the manufacture of baking sodas among other things, is chemically treated and added to the wastewater, shattering the existing chemical bonds between the dye and the water. As a result, the water can be vacuum-filtered clean.

The colored sludges left behind by these processes are then landfilled, not an ideal solution, especially since fly ash contains heavy metals, which may leach up through the fill.

But generating residual sludge in the course of cleaning water is part of a possibly inevitable environmental juggling act. It joins a collection of trade-offs, which include choosing between mechanical cotton picking and the risk of brown lung disease, natural and synthetic materials, food and fiber—a fascinating matrix into which the roots of a pair of blue jeans lead.

P.D.

NATURAL RESOURCES USED FOR A BALE OF COTTON

Growing a bale of cotton, 480 pounds (218 kilograms) of fiber, enough to produce 330 pairs of jeans, requires the following:

Production

Input	*Quantity per bale*
Water	105,000 gallons/398,000 liters
Gasoline	8 gallons/30 liters
Diesel fuel	16 gallons/61 liters
Liquid propane gas	2 gallons/7.6 liters
Natural gas	2,300 cubic feet/64 cubic meters
Electricity	60 kilowatt-hours
Fertilizer:	
Nitrogen (N)	31 pounds/14 kilograms
Phosphate (P_2O_5)	15 pounds/6.8 kilograms
Potash (K_2O)	24 pounds/10.9 kilograms

Ginning

Input	*Quantity per bale*
Electricity	65 kilowatt-hours
Natural gas	250 cubic feet/7 cubic meters

Marketing to Mill

Input	*Quantity per bale*
Natural gas (compression)	225 cubic feet/6.3 cubic meters
Diesel fuel (transportation)	3.2 gallons/12.1 liters

Textile Mill Processing and Finishing

Input	*Quantity per square yard*
Water	5.00 gallons/18.9 liters
Electricity	0.79 kilowatt-hour
Fuel oil	0.013 gallon/0.05 liter
Coal	0.20 pound/9 kilogram
Natural gas	3.10 cubic feet/0.087 cubic meter

*Apparel Manufacturing**

Input	*Quantity per pair*
Electricity	1.60 kilowatt-hours
Fuel oil	.007 gallon/0.026 liter
Coal	.008 pound/3.6 grams
Natural gas	8.50 cubic feet/0.238 cubic meter

* Based on an average pair of trousers requiring 2.2 square yards (1.84 square meters) per pair produced.

SOURCE: Fibers and Oils Program Area, Commodity Economics Division, U. S. Department of Agriculture.

FISH-AND-CHIPS

Until 1840, all the fresh fish sold in fish markets were caught near shore. For several hundred years ships had ventured across the continental shelves, where great schools of fish lived, but no one could figure out how to get these fish to port before they spoiled, aside from drying and salting them on board ship.

In 1840 an Englishman named Samuel Hewett had a strikingly simple, but revolutionary, idea. Each day a swift cutter collected fish from Hewett's North Sea trawlers and ran its cargo, packed in ice, to London fish markets.

Hewett's innovation set off a boom in "fast" food. An enterprising London fishmonger, whose name is lost to history, concocted a dish that would become to the British what hamburgers would later become to their American cousins. Vendors sprang up with frying pans, salt shakers, and vinegar to produce "Fish-and-Chips." (The Irish sent a steady supply of potatoes for the

"It's not my factory that's polluting the lake . . . It's all those dead fish that's doing it." (*Reproduced by special permission of* PLAYBOY *Magazine;* © *1974 by* PLAYBOY.)

chips, under pressure from the British, throughout the Irish potato famine of the mid-nineteenth century.)

To a greater extent than the hamburger (see "A Hamburger," page 208), fish-and-chips provided the customer with a cheap, balanced meal, including high-quality protein, most vitamins and essential minerals, fats, and carbohydrates. Deep frying preserved the nutrients as it kept the fish from spoiling.

The Chips

Today, in a time of flaked, pressed, freeze-dried, and reshaped potatoes, the chips in fish-and-chips are still usually real potatoes—a lowly food, but one with a fascinating history. The wild potato, native to the Andes highlands, is a small, unappetizing, black lump. Sixteenth-century Spanish invaders who found the Incas cultivating the plant brought some root stock home to Europe, where the potato was deeply suspect as a food. Its leaves betrayed it as a member of the *Solanaceae* group, of which the most notorious member is the poisonous deadly nightshade, and that also includes the tomato (which suffered from similar disdain). While the edible portion of the potato grows as a tuber in the soil, the fruit resembles a small, unripe tomato and is indeed slightly toxic.

Today the world potato crop exceeds 250 million tons; only the major cereal crops have a higher production. Although fresh potatoes are a nutritious food, the popular forms of processed potatoes have lost many of their nutrients and gained many preserving and coloring chemicals in processing. Yet Americans eat more processed potatoes (a per capita average of 67 pounds/30 kilograms per year in 1975) than fresh potatoes (55 pounds/25 kilograms per year). Potato farming is big business in the United States, with 3 percent of the growers producing more than 95 percent of the potatoes. But the United States is small potatoes in the world market; the Soviet Union is the top grower, producing 30 percent of the world crop.

The potato is such a staple food in temperate climates that most people have a sack of potatoes tucked away in a dark bin. Why in a dark bin? The practice is traditional, but most people have forgotten why potatoes should not be kept in the refrigerator or in sunlight. Stored at temperatures below 50° F (10° C), potato starch converts to sugar, which can carmelize during cooking, turning the potatoes brown. Potatoes stored in sunlight can show an increase of up to 20 percent in solanin, a bitter, poisonous alkaloid, in the peel; those stored in darkness show no increase.

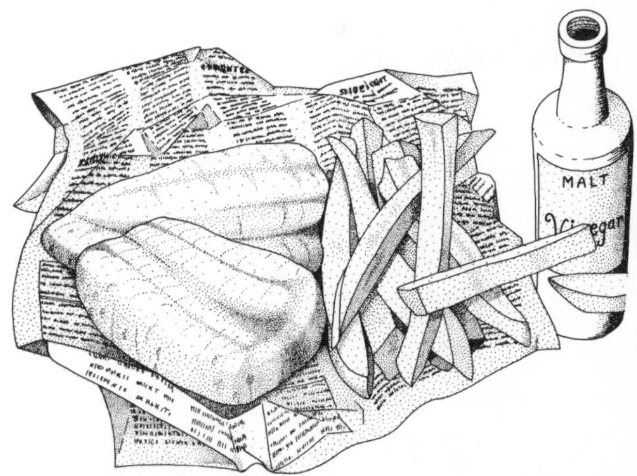

The Fish

Fish, the other half of this commonplace dish, are the world's only major food that are not extensively cultivated or domesticated. Cattle, chickens, pigs—all the land animals we use for food—are carefully bred, fed, fenced, and slaughtered. True, aquaculture farms, especially in China and Japan, breed and feed fish for the killing (see "Aquaculture," page 609), but most of the world's catch is captured on the high seas. Fishers see themselves more as hunters than cattle ranchers.

Nutritionally fish plays a critical role around the world. More than 13 percent of the world's animal protein in human diets comes from finfish and shellfish (a great amount of fish is also used for animal feed). The dependence on fish is especially high in much of the developing world, where 1.5 billion people (one third of the world population) look to fish for more than half their average daily intake of animal protein.

Because people in the developing world eat considerably *less* animal protein than people in developed nations (who consume two thirds of the world's meat and milk) the *quality* of their protein is critical. Fortunately, fish is an especially high-quality protein source, superior in most aspects to beef and other meats. One important factor is lysine, a protein constituent often lacking in vegetarian diets. Fish are remarkably high in lysine. Another important aspect of fish in developing nations is that they are the cheapest animal protein source around—especially herring, sardines, and salt cod. Because of all these traits, dried and powdered fish make up a substantial proportion of food supplied in relief programs to famine-afflicted areas.

The Little Fish That Cod

Most of the fish in fish-and-chips (or any other fast fish food) is cod, long a mainstay of the Atlantic fishery. An adult cod is a rather large fish with mottled spots on its side and a distinctive barbel on its chin. Three dorsal and two anal fins give it a rather finny appearance. Marketable cod range from 2.5 to 40 pounds (1 to 18 kilograms) each, although fishers of the nineteenth century occasionally reported taking huge "whale" cod—the largest was 211 pounds (98 kilograms) and more than 6 feet (1.8 meters) long. But after three hundred years of intense fishing, most if not all of the oldtimers have been netted and no cod now can look forward to such long life.

A pine replica of a cod hangs in the House of Representatives of the Massachusetts Statehouse in Boston. It was placed there in 1784 "as a memorial of the importance of the Cod-Fishery to the welfare of the Commonwealth." Cod has many virtues: it's tasty, easy to salt and preserve, easy to market fresh, and, until recently, easy to catch. Before the Pilgrims landed in America, more than three hundred fishing vessels from France, Portugal, Spain, and England made the arduous trip across northern Atlantic waters to catch cod off the coast of Newfoundland. Now the same waters are scoured by huge fish-factory ships with sophisticated electronic fish-finding equipment.

Schools of cod gather throughout most of the year on the great shoal known as the Grand

Banks, about 100 miles (161 kilometers) southeast of Newfoundland. The Banks are about 100 fathoms deep and about the size of the state of Pennsylvania. Washed by warm, nutrient-bearing currents, the Banks are rich in plankton, the community of tiny plants and animals that form the base of the marine food web. Feeding on small crustaceans here are vast schools of the small, smeltlike capelin, a favorite food of the cod. Although cod are omnivorous, eating almost anything that fits into their mouths, their abundance on the Grand Banks depends on the availability of capelin. For a brief time each spring, mature cod leave the Banks to spawn in inshore waters. Tremendously prolific, a female lays several million eggs, most of which, of course, do not survive to become adult fish. After feeding for a time in shallow waters, the young fingerlings find their way to the Banks, where they take six years to mature.

Fish Centers

The Grand Banks, like other important fishing areas of the world, are productive because their conditions support a rich marine community. Although the ocean covers 71 percent of the world's surface, most of its waters are sparsely populated. The best fishing areas are clustered along the continental shelves and concentrated in areas where currents supply nutrients for the plankton. In the northern Atlantic, rich plankton zones fed by upwellings of bottom currents stretch from New England across the southern tip of Greenland and Iceland to Norway. In the Pacific, one plankton zone stretches from Japan to Alaska, then down the Canadian and U.S. coasts, and another reaches from Southeast Asia along the equator to the coast of Peru. Another plankton band circles the globe in the extreme south, just above the Antarctic. (See map "Life in the Ocean," page 135.)

A second type of good fishing ground is found where two currents of different temperatures meet, forming an environmental boundary. The temperature difference acts as an invisible fence, turning back any fish that attempts to cross. Fish tend to collect near the thermal fence; there are usually more fish swimming along it than there are in the middle of the current. The Pacific coast of Japan, an area fished for hundreds of years, is such an area of contrasting currents.

The third, and perhaps most vulnerable, type of fishing ground is the spawning area. Many fish that spend most of their adult lives in the ocean return to specific areas near shore to spawn in wetlands, estuaries, or rivers. In these nutrient-rich environments their larvae will have an easier time finding food until they grow large enough to join their elders offshore. Much commercial and recreational fishing exploits the annual congregations of spawning fish. Pacific salmon, for example, are easy prey as they crowd into rivers seeking the spot where they were spawned years earlier. And since most spawning grounds are near shore, they are particularly vulnerable to coastal pollution. (See "Wetlands," page 379.)

Mother Ships

The age-old picture of the fisherman is that of a bearded old man, wise in the ways of fish and weather, rowing his wooden dory to the fishing grounds. A more recent image is that of a captain of a 35-foot (11-meter) diesel tug with two or three stalwart crew who venture forth each day and return to port with their catch each night. That is still typical of the near-shore fishery in most countries, but to get a picture of modern, long-distance fishing, one must think on a more grandiose scale. Modern factory ships, ranging from about 300 to about 600 feet (90 to 180 meters) long, can be dispatched on extended voyages to fish anywhere in the world. They are processing plants afloat, able to clean, fillet, and freeze or can fish at sea.

Mother ship. The M.S. *Euo Yuan* is one of three 1,000-ton tuna factory ships purchased by Taiwan with a World Bank loan. The two catcher boats alongside bring fish to the larger ship for processing. (*World Bank/Mary Hill*)

These "mother ships" are accompanied by an entourage of helper vessels. Scouting boats, equipped with Sonar, locate fish by bouncing sound waves off the ocean floor. A passing school of fish will bounce back the sound waves before they hit bottom, producing a different image on the shipboard receiver. Some fishers say they can tell not only the size of the school but the type of fish based on the pattern of the sound waves reflected (different species of fish school in different patterns).

Once fish are located, "catcher" boats are deployed to net them for processing aboard the mother ship. Some factory ships are accompanied by fast transport ships—like Hewett's clippers—to take fresh fish home to port.

The Soviet Union and Japan have made heavy investments in such fishing fleets. The Soviet Union, whose population depends on fish for one third of its protein, began in the 1930s to develop both a long-range fishing fleet and a sophisticated program of marine research. Japan, a nation even more dependent on fish, followed the Soviet example as it rebuilt its fishing fleet after World War II. After exploiting its near-shore fisheries for more than three hundred years, Japan now obtains most of its increased catch from its factory ships. With fishing operations based in fifty countries, Japan takes more than 9.1 million metric tons of fish each year. Other fishing nations—Canada, Norway, Iceland, England, and Spain—also have factory ships. The United States has several factory ships to catch and can tuna, but none that fish for cod.

A heavy consumer of fish and fish products, the United States imports most of its fish from Japan, Canada, Norway, even India (shrimp). There is a large U.S. shellfish industry in bays and estuaries such as Chesapeake Bay and the Louisiana Gulf Coast, and there are fleets of smaller near-shore U.S. vessels. But an American meal of fish-and-chips most likely originated with cod caught by a Canadian or Japanese factory ship on the Grand Banks. (Americans are not big fresh-fish eaters. Most of the fish caught or imported is either shellfish—oysters, crabs, shrimp, lobsters—for the luxury market or "trash" fish that is ground into fishmeal and fed to pigs or poultry, or made into catfood.)

The Grand Banks Robbery

As the factory ships invaded the best fishing grounds, they competed with each other and with boats from bordering nations. In the 1960s, it became apparent that the fish populations in these areas could not withstand the overfishing (see "Ocean Fisheries," page 376). The dwindling populations were not reflected in the annual fish catch data, however, which remained steady or even showed small increases as a result of improved fish catching technology. Even armed with the technology, fishers had to spend more and more time hunting for fish. The huge increases in yearly catches of the 1940s and 1950s were no longer seen.

Several nations made treaties limiting the areas in which foreign vessels could fish or the amount of fish they could take. During the 1970s most coastal nations extended their offshore jurisdiction from 12 miles to 200 nautical miles which enabled them to manage the fishery within that limit by issuing permits to both native and foreign fishers designating the type of fish that could be caught, the type of nets that could be used, and other limitations. (See "A Law of the Sea," page 568.)

Fish like cod are particularly susceptible to overfishing and pollution. Because of their mild, sweet-tasting flesh, they have a good market value in many countries, which leads to intense international competition. Because they congregate in certain feeding areas, they are relatively easy to locate and catch. And because they eat near the top of the marine food web, they are susceptible to disaster from causes other than direct fishing.

Cod are the end result of a long chain of energy transformations. The ocean is somewhat less efficient at making cod than the land is at making a cow. If a cow is simply fed grass or grain, it eats at the second step of the food chain. In the ocean, algae and eelgrass are eaten by small crustaceans, which are eaten by small fish, which may be eaten by medium-size fish, which are eaten by cod—a total of four or five steps. One scientist estimated that to get 2.2 pounds (1 kilogram) of cod requires a base of 220,000 pounds (100,000 kilograms) of algae and eelgrass.

Any major disruption along the cod's long food chain is ultimately felt by the fish. In the past several years, fishing for capelin, the cod's major food, has increased on the Grand Banks and elsewhere. A major oil leak or spill could seriously damage the plankton community, again breaking the chain. Unfortunately, many good fishing grounds—the North Sea and the Gulf of Mexico, for example—also contain oil deposits. Test drilling was under way in 1979 in several more areas along the North American continental shelf, and a large oil field off Newfoundland near the Grand Banks themselves will begin production in the early 1980s.

How Many Fish in the Sea?

The focus of managing a fishery is finding that magic number for each species in each location called the "optimal sustainable yield": the largest number of fish that can be caught each year without endangering the stability of the population. If this number is taken, and no more, there will always be a reliable number of fish, year after year (barring unforeseen disasters). To calculate this number, fishery managers must know approximately the number of fish hatched each year and the number surviving to the age at which they can be legally caught. They must also keep track of such environmental factors as storms, pollution, and human development of spawning areas, which may reduce the number of fish, and know enough about the biology of each fish to determine how many adult fish must be spared to reproduce a sizable next generation.

Fish, unfortunately, are notoriously hard to count. Living beyond our sight in the sea and migrating long distances, they are more elusive than any land animal. Biologists estimate the size of each population by sampling and by examining past commercial catch data, but their figures are often disputed by fishers who almost universally insist there are more fish than the biologists think.

Another problem that plagues fishery managers is the classic "economics of depletion." This problem is illustrated by the cod-haddock fishery off the northeastern coast of the United States. Here haddock, a delicately flavored fish preferred to cod by many U.S. consumers, was a major fishery. Since haddock had a higher retail value than cod on the fresh-fish market, commercial fishers went after haddock and more or less left cod alone. Gradually the haddock populations declined, mainly as a result of overfishing. To the ecologist, the logical thing to do was to ease off on haddock fishing until the species had time to recover. But to the fisher, economics threw a different light on the situation. As haddock became scarcer, their dockside value increased. Even more fishers entered the lucrative haddock business, putting more pressure on the dwindling stocks. The only thing that saves a population at this point is government intervention: setting quotas on the catch.

This, unfortunately, is a classic pattern; as a resource is depleted, its scarcity forces the price up and it is exploited even more heavily. If fishery managers do not step in, fishers will continue to pursue the scarce, valuable fish until the population is so low that it takes more effort than it's worth to find the remaining fish. At this point the population may be so reduced that it cannot make a comeback. The fishers have in effect put themselves out of business. More likely, they switch to fishing another species and the pattern is repeated.

Such scenarios can be avoided if fishery managers have enough information, authority, and credibility to maintain stable fish populations. Usually, though, it takes depletion to stimulate controls. International efforts at managing the high-seas fishery are very young and the problems even more complex than with the inshore fishery.

Sometimes, even in the 1980s, one hears someone speak of the ocean as a "limitless resource"—a phrase that makes ecologists cringe. They remember when the same term was applied to forests that are now deserts, herds of animals now extinct, tracts of wilderness now fully developed, minerals now nearing depletion. The ocean is vast, but not limitless; it's fish are abundant, but not inexhaustible.

Only if we understand this and harvest fish from the sea carefully, rather than in reckless competition, will fish remain a bountiful food resource. If we fail, fish-and-chips could become a luxury for the rich, while the rest of us order chips-and-chips.

L.L., M.P.

A PAPER CLIP

Out of strands of springy stock steel, intricate machines fashion an omnipresent item, cutting off wire lengths and bending them into the basic, everywhere-recognizable, rounded shape of the paper clip. Some machines turn out as many as eight hundred clips a minute, depending on the weight, size, and style of the clip itself, of which there are at least forty-eight varieties. Since the clip was invented, ostensibly in 1899 by a Norwegian named Johan Vaaler, it has become a workhorse of office routine, a lowly item that quite literally keeps the papers of the world together. And, not only do we use paper clips for the purpose for which they were intended, but who among us has not handled, twisted, or unwound a clip during telephone conversations, or when a bit of wire was needed to accomplish something else.

Keeping the United States in paper clips requires 10,000 tons of steel wire annually, according to data collected by the paper clip industry in 1970. And wire represents only one tenth of all the steel produced in the United States. The other nine tenths appear around us in a multitude of things: buildings, cars, airplanes, lightswitch wall plates, eating utensils, watches, nails, door knobs, printing presses, notebook binder rings, furniture, sculpture, thousands of different products made of, or dependent on, steel production.

In the United States, the annual demand for steel is expected to rise to about 18.8 million tons by the year 2000; around the world the demand is expected to be 1.17 billion tons. Transportation, construction, and machinery will account for approximately 79 percent of the demand. Though lighter materials, such as aluminum and plastic, are frequently used as substitutes, steel will probably remain the world's basic building material for some time to come.

Hard Rock

Iron, the fourth most abundant solid element, making up about 5 percent of the earth's crust, is the essential ingredient for steel production. Iron has been an important material for humans since at least 4000 B.C. Mythological pantheons from virtually every culture banner a god who can manipulate metal or iron, who is either revered or feared for the power of changing solid material into shapes ranging from lightning bolts to fine net traps. The Iron Age for humankind began in approximately 1200 B.C., and iron artifacts were commonly used throughout antiquity from China to Western Europe, though in the Western Hemisphere they were unknown until brought there by explorers in the fifteenth century.

It is not possible to speak of a single inventor for steel, since many cultures have known for centuries that some iron-based, or ferrous, metals would become very hard and durable when cooled quickly in water after being extremely hot. The carbon content of the iron permits this hardening, though other factors also influence the type of steel produced. Steel actually is an alloy of iron with 2 percent carbon content.

Methods for steel production developed and changed, but until the discovery of the Bessemer process in the mid-nineteenth century production was confined to the melting of iron and carbon in large clay or graphite crucibles, each of which held 100 pounds (45 kilograms). This steel was mainly used for tools and machinery parts. In the Bessemer conversion technique, a converter blew hot air through molten pig iron, removing excess carbon and preventing the iron from cooling and solidifying. It permitted batches of 25 or more tons and a closer control over carbon content, making possible a range of steel types. Bessemer steel production was eventually surpassed by open-hearth and the basic oxygen processes (B.O.P.), both of which permit even higher grade steel in a wider range of sizes. Most paper clips are made from Bessemer wire.

All steelmaking processes convert molten iron, which has been heated as high as 2,000° F (1,093° C), by refining it and lowering the impurity or "slag" content. Excess oxygen in the steel is neutralized by adding manganese, silicon, or aluminum. The B.O.P. shoots a stream of pure oxygen into the molten metal, producing up to 350 tons of steel in forty-five minutes.

Steel's Hunger and Thirst

Because of the high temperatures involved, steel production consumes tremendous amounts of energy—one ton of steel requires 420 kilowatt-hours of electricity—and tremendous water consumption—one ton of steel requires 34,000 gallons of water. This water not only cools the steel but carries off the slag.

Steel also consumes veritable mountains of raw materials, some two and a half tons to yield one ton of steel.

It was inevitable that an industry so hungry for raw materials and thirsty for water would be one of the most polluting. Since the beginnings of the steel boom in 1901, when United States Steel, Andrew Carnegie's company, became the first billion-dollar corporation in U.S. history, steel mills and their tall furnace smokestacks coughing black exhaust have been symbols of industrial "progress," as were the giant ovens that reduced

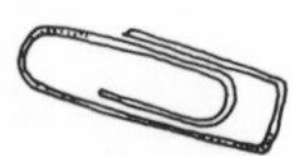

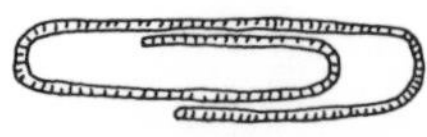

tons of minerals to glowing molten steel. Hot sparks sprayed and the industry grew, but every 1,000 tons of steel left staggeringly dirty by-products: 121 tons of particles spewed into the air; 67.5 tons of dirty water recirculated through the water system; and 3,795 tons of solid waste, including consumer and mining waste, to be hauled, landfilled, or dumped somehow out of the public eye. As of 1968, the industry was responsible for 20 percent of all industrial particulate pollution.

As of 1978, the Mahoning River, which runs between Warren and Youngstown, Ohio, both major steel-producing cities in the United States, was still considered a "classic" illustration of heavy industrial pollution by the President's Council on Environmental Quality. Large quantities of lead, zinc, and other toxic chemical levels were noted.

The Seamy Side

There is pollution potential during each stage of the steel-making process, from the initial grinding and melting of iron ore through the furnace blasts, and on into cutting and molding of steel into its broad variety of shapes. The water must not only be cleaned of excess metals like zinc, manganese, lead, and nitrates—and poisons such as arsenic, cyanide, and cadmium—before being returned to the water system, but the high temperature it acquires must also be eliminated. Dust, gas, vapor, soot, mist, and fumes pour into the atmosphere unless scrubbed out. As one steel industry spokesperson expressed it, "Every time you pour hot metal from one ladle to another there are emissions." One plant in California was slapped with 1,142 violation citations as a result of a four-day inspection by a local Air Resources Board. The ovens of the plant were releasing more than 150 toxic substances, including nine known carcinogens. Not only did these substances escape into the atmosphere, but workers around the ovens were exposed to them in high concentrations.

The wire-drawing process, implicit in the production of all wiring, including paper clips, adds another element to the pollution picture. Pickling liquors used to scrub wire and other steel products clean of gritty iron oxide scale are released into the water. The liquors are highly acidic, though other steel-cleansing processes produce alkaline effluents.

Steel Crazy After All These Years

Despite the extensive pollution potential of their processes, the steel production industry has been one of the industries least responsive to environmental protection laws. Plants resisted cleaning up as long as possible, with the result that as of May 1979, only approximately 12 percent of the more than one thousand steel-processing locations in the United States were in compliance with 1977 regulations. Where water pollution is concerned, the industry's record is somewhat better, though it is required to have the problem fully under control by 1984. Among the promising developments for water clean-up is technology permitting recycling that not only cleans the slag from the water, but reduces the gulping consumption from 34,000 gallons (128,704 liters) per ton to 2,000 gallons (7,571 liters).

Faced with increased criticism and public scrutiny, the steel industry has begun reluctantly to modernize aging equipment, in some cases building new plants altogether. According to industry and government data, steel producers had invested $2.9 billion in pollution control by 1974 and expect an additional investment of $8 billion to $10 billion by 1983. These adaptations could add from 5 to 10 percent to the operating costs of the industry, and indirectly to the price of steel. They will also increase the energy consumption of the industry by 10 percent.

Industry spokespersons claim that pollution control installations account for 25 to 30 percent of all capital investment made by the steel industry. They also predict that this diversion of funds from modernization of equipment programs will result in a shortage of steel by 1985, because producers will not be able to meet projected demands.

One way to offset such a shortage, as well as to limit the natural resource depletion caused by steel production *and* the pollution potential, would be to recycle abandoned steel instead of forging new steel.

The Second Time Around

The recycling of scrap iron to raw steel would eliminate much energy expenditure related to the mining and transporting of iron ore, coal, and

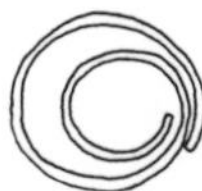
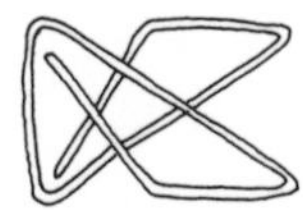

limestone. In fact, though calculations vary, the United States Environmental Protection Agency claims that using scrap iron instead of a combination of raw iron ore and coke to produce raw steel results in:

— 47% reduction in oil consumption (over three million barrels of crude oil)
— 86% reduction in air pollution
— 76% reduction in water pollution
— 40% reduction in water use
— 97% reduction in mining wastes
— 100% reduction in consumer wastes

The amount of metal, especially steel, that is junked each year in the United States is substantial enough to make possible an entire industry in itself. Steel producers recycle scrap to some extent, but in 1978 there were 672 million tons (610 million metric tons) of scrap steel abandoned as waste. That amount is enough to supply the U.S. steel industry (which produced 137 million tons/124 million metric tons of new steel in 1978) with enough raw material to last approximately fourteen years! Each year in the United States, the national backlog grows. In 1978, 66 million tons (60 million metric tons) of steel were discarded, accounted for by, among other things, 29 million major appliances, such as refrigerators, stoves, and washing machines, plus 8 million cast-off cars, buses, and trucks.

All this metal could be baled, sheared, crushed, shredded, and reformed. Not only would steel recycling save energy and resources but the growing mountains of metal garbage would be controlled and disposal costs would be reduced as well.

Steel Blues

But the same obstacles that hinder paper recycling (see "The Pages You Are Reading," page 203) affect steel recycling. The commercial rate structure makes the shipping of secondary materials cost more than the shipping of virgin stocks; tax structures tend to penalize the producer of recyclable materials; and in most parts of the world, recycling waste materials is inconvenient for most people.

In addition, there is the politically and economically sensitive jobs issue—the steel industry employs approximately 450,000 workers in the United States, 1,200,000 worldwide. A shift to recycling would obviously reduce mining jobs, but it would also create many positions in a growing new industry. Whether this would offset the loss of jobs in the steel industry cannot be reliably predicted, but it seems that all too often steel laborers work very hard to produce products that others eventually just throw away.

Even paper clips are not as comprehensively recycled as they might be. Though there is minimal excess in the production of paper clips, once out on the market, three out of every ten clips is somehow wasted. In 1958, the employee's newsletter of Lloyd's Bank of London brought a statistical survey to the attention of the bank's stationery department. According to this Washington study (the most recent one we discovered), of an original batch of 100,000 clips:

3,196	were used as pipe cleaners
5,308	served as nail cleaners
5,434	were used to pick teeth or scratch ears
19,413	were pressed into service as chips in card games
14,163	were broken or twisted during phone calls
7,200	were used as hooks for suspenders, belts, or brassieres

About 25,000 were presumably dropped into office crevices, swept up, or otherwise lost. Only 20,000 were used to clip paper.

P.D.

A FATEFUL CLIP

We do know for certain the fate of at least one paper clip in 1979. Officials investigating the accidental discharge of radioactive gases in September 1979 from the North Anna nuclear power plant in Virginia report that a pencil and a paper clip *wedged into a water control switch apparently were major causes of the accident. It was believed that the switch had been malfunctioning, and a worker used the pencil and clip for a makeshift, temporary repair.*

SOURCE: *The Audubon Leader,* October 19, 1979.

A GALLON OF GASOLINE

An average American car, zipping down the expressway at 60 miles (97 kilometers) per hour, burns a gallon of gasoline every twenty minutes. And on an average day in 1979, 148,345,160 U.S. cars, trucks, and buses were burning 12 million gallons (45 million liters) of gasoline every hour. The fuel flows easily into our tanks. It disappears quickly, propelling us to various destinations. But oil, the inimitable substance that fuels not only the world's machines but now also its political events, flows through complicated pathways. It has simmered for ages within the earth, only to be voraciously extracted in our age for burning, largely as gasoline (in the United States 44 percent of the oil refined is dispensed as gasoline).

If, in 1909, Henry Ford could have foreseen the ramifications of using gasoline to propel his mass-produced auto, he might have selected another fuel (like other car inventors of the time, he did consider alcohol). But he couldn't have known that in only about seventy years—within the life span of the children of his $5-a-day workers—his chosen propellent would also fuel international political intrigue and hostility. Multinational corporations rose to exploit oil from Middle Eastern nations, which soon became defiant and powerful, controlling the black blood of the industrialized world.

The Long Gestation

The oil we use today began to form about 500 million years ago and stayed where it was, for the most part, until the 1940s, when we began to pump it gluttonously. Our generation has used up most of the oil available (oil resource expert M. King Hubbert, formerly with the U. S. Geological Survey, estimated that oil production peaked in 1970).

Back in the days when petroleum was forming, the earth's atmosphere was thin, almost without oxygen, and much of the planet's surface was covered by water. Cycads, primitive fernlike terrestrial plants that grew to heights of 50 feet (15 meters), were the dominant tropical life form. Living and dying generation after generation, cycads released oxygen like all plants. As the amount of oxygen in the atmosphere slowly grew toward its current proportion of 20 percent, oxygen-using organisms evolved. Like the plants that preceded and nourished them, these animals lived, died, and were buried ever deeper under layers of organic matter and sediment.

Millions of years passed. Seas receded. Earth masses shifted. Sediments hardened into sandstone, shale, and limestone. Various in its composition and subjected to varying temperatures and pressures, the organic debris slowly reformed into coal, oil, and natural gas.

Millions more years passed. Under intense pressure, petroleum in solution with groundwater was squeezed here and there. Moving through porous rock or systems of cracks, it migrated until it hit reservoir rock, a formation that held it. Some oil underwent second migrations, pooling in new areas nearer the earth's surface.

Again, millions of years passed.

Humans and oil first crossed paths about 3000 B.C. The Chinese drilled for oil then, and the Babylonians, Assyrians, and Sumerians used petroleum from a natural seep on the Euphrates River for heat, light, medicines, and ship-caulking compound. (A similar surface seep may be seen today at the La Brea "tar pits" in Los Angeles, California.) But the modern petroleum industry is generally considered to date from a well drilled by a railroad conductor, Edwin L. Drake, in Titusville, Pennsylvania, in 1859.

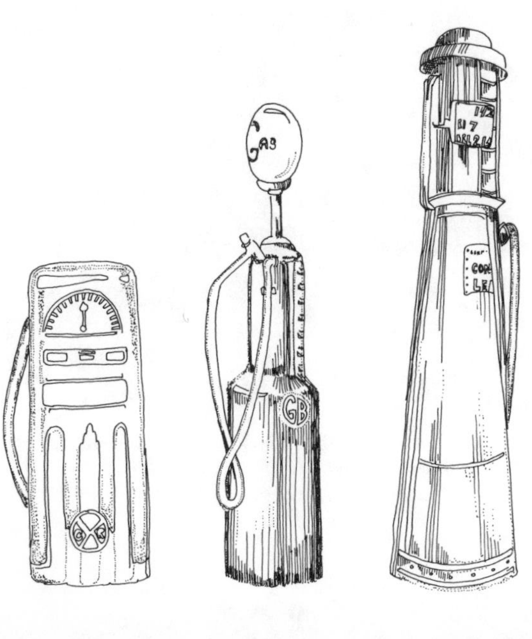

The Gamble

The Pennsylvania Rock Oil Company, Drake's employer, hedged its bets. It picked a drill site near an old oil spring. Later, as geologists gained experience with oil, they learned it was most often found in areas of sedimentary rock formations, especially sandstone and limestone.

Unfortunately for industrialized nations, the world's oil deposits are mostly outside their borders. Sixty-five percent of the known oil reserves are in the Middle East; 10 percent are found in the Americas, mainly clustered in Alaska, Texas, the Gulf of Mexico, and Venezuela; and the other 25 percent is scattered around the world with large pockets under the North Sea, in the Soviet Union, and in West Africa. (Although its conventional oil reserves are thinning, North America contains 98 percent of the world's "heavy oil" in the tar sands of the Canadian and American west. See "Synfuels," page 34.)

Despite huge advances in technology, finding oil today is still something of a gamble. Not that we haven't tried to better the odds. Variations in the earth's magnetic field have been measured. Differences in gravitational pull have been weighed. But the seismograph, originally used mainly to measure earthquake intensity, is now probably the favored instrument of geophysicists who prospect for oil.

If sediments and instruments point to the presence of oil, the ultimate test—drilling—goes forward. But no matter how good it looks, of the wildcat wells drilled in new fields only one in ten will find oil or natural gas. And only one driller in fifty will strike either in commercially significant quantities.

Before drilling begins, however, the site must be prepared. Sometimes this involves widespread clearing and grading of land, the building of roads, fences, and buildings, and the development of power and water supply systems. The petroleum industry has rarely considered the environmental effects of this groundwork. For example, in the 1970s a legal battle between oil drillers and environmentalists raged over the Pigeon River State Forest in Michigan. The environmentalists objected not so much to the danger of a spill but to the effects of roads, clearings, the noise, and the stench of oil drilling on the forest's wildlife and human visitors, who were trying to get away from the roads, clearings, noise, and stench of the city.

The Delivery

From the moment of "spudding-in," until oil is struck or the "duster" is abandoned, drilling for oil is an around-the-clock proposition. The actual boring is done by a drill bit made of very hard steel, often studded with industrial diamonds. The bit is lowered through the derrick floor attached to a string of pipes, each 30 feet (9 meters) long and usually 5 inches (12.7 centimeters) in diameter. The pipe assemblages are long—sometimes wells descend 30,000 feet (9,150 meters)—and high stresses are involved, so both the pipes and the bit must be made of high-quality material.

As the well deepens, a mixture of water, clay, and chemicals, called "mud," is pumped down into the hole. Mud is a multipurpose concoction. Oozing out through openings in the bit, it keeps the cutting edge clean and cool. It cakes the sides of the hole, preventing cave-ins. And by virtue of its weight, mud controls pressures from gas or water encountered by the bit. When disposed of improperly, muds containing toxic substances have been the source of environmental damage.

As drilling continues, bits wear out. Replacing them involves withdrawing the drill string by removing the pipe in 90-foot (27.5-meter) stands, and then dropping it down again. When a bit wears out at 15,000 feet, (4,575 meters) about nine hours are required for a round trip.

Gas station along the Kle-Pujehun road in Liberia. (*World Bank/Pamela Johnson*)

There is, of course, much more to oil drilling; it's daring, dangerous, dirty. For example, blowouts are still a threat to oil field workers and the environment, despite the development of blowout prevention valves, alarm systems, and instruments that monitor the critical aspects of drilling.

Oil from the Bottom of the Sea

Marine drilling is virtually a separate science. In the late nineteenth century, oil wells were drilled from wooden piers extending from the coasts of the Pacific (California), the Caspian Sea, and Lake Maracaibo (Venezuela). In 1938 the first open-water well was drilled in the Gulf of Mexico 1.5 miles (2.4 kilometers) from shore in less than 30 feet (9.2 meters) of water. While most modern offshore platforms are situated in water that is less than 300 feet (90 meters) deep, wells have been drilled off the west coast of Thailand in 3,460 feet (1,055 meters) of water, as far as one 100 miles (160 kilometers) from the coast. More than 12,600 wells have been drilled in U.S. waters alone (a single platform may drill

Offshore oil rig in the Mediterranean. As of 1977 there were about 300 working rigs worldwide and more planned as the search for oil intensified. (*The Cousteau Society*)

between five and fifty wells), and there are today more than three hundred active offshore drilling rigs around the world. Nearly half of these platforms are in the two most exploited areas of the ocean floor—the Gulf of Mexico (off the Texas and Louisiana shores) and the North Sea (the fastest-growing offshore production region).

While the expenses of offshore construction hampered its development for many years, the economics now make it attractive. It is possible that 26 percent of the world reserves of increasingly expensive petroleum are in offshore deposits. The dollar amount this volume represents is astronomical. Untapped seafloor reserves were valued at $1,945 billion in 1976, a figure about equal to one thousand times the income of the world's largest oil company (Exxon) that same year.

Offshore drilling is associated with severe oil contamination of the marine environment—for good reason, as the 1979 Campeche Bay blowout in the Gulf of Mexico demonstrated—but it ranks behind shipping and coastal runoff as a cause of global oil pollution in the sea. (See "Wastes in the Sea," page 409.)

Drilling the Last Drop

Under some circumstances, in wells on land or offshore, oil will gush to the surface when its formation is penetrated. Usually this happens when all of the natural gas in the reservoir is dissolved in the oil. Opening the formation is then like opening a shaken-up bottle of carbonated soft drink. Many wells, however, never flow naturally and must be pumped from the start. Surfacing oil is usually accompanied by water and natural gas. The average ratio is 300 cubic feet (8.4 cubic meters) of gas per barrel of oil (42 gallons or 159 liters).

The life of an oil field, and the amount of oil it will produce, varies. But when oil production drops below the break-even point, the use of secondary recovery methods may be used to increase production, even to double a field's yield. In secondary recovery, water, steam, or gas is pumped into the reservoir to force additional oil from the rock. Even after secondary recovery ends, two thirds of the available oil remains in the ground. Under some conditions, a third, or tertiary, recovery attempt will be made. In one tertiary method, detergents are pumped into the well to reduce the "interfacial tension" of oil droplets clinging to rock particles. These drops flow out of the rock pores and coalesce in a recoverable pool.

Both secondary and tertiary recovery are expensive, tertiary more so because of the cost of detergents, which, ironically, are themselves derived from petroleum. About a half million pounds of detergents are used per acre (560,000 kilograms per hectare) in experimental tertiary recovery; a 20-acre (8.1-hectare) oil field would require more than half the annual output of an average-size detergent plant.

Is it worth it? Primary recovery lifts about 20 percent of the oil in a field. Secondary recovery captures another 13 percent. Tertiary methods could boost recovery by another 7 percent for a total of 40 percent. The rest of the oil stays in the ground, out of reach of today's technology.

Cracking the Goo

Separated from its natural gas, crude oil right out of the ground is barely flammable. You would have to douse it with gasoline to get it to burn. Raw crude is viscous, sticky goo; it might be any color from red to black, depending on its components.

Assuming it travels uneventfully from the wellhead via pipeline or tanker—which is no sure bet (see "The Business of Supertankers," page 489) —crude enters the refinery as a jumble of hydrocarbons. The first task in refining crude is to wash it with water to remove its mineral salts. The second task, which is really a series of tasks, is to separate its hydrocarbons by type. This is done in a series of fractionating columns, vertical steel cylinders divided into a number of sections by horizontal trays. When heated, raw crude is pumped into the column, its light hydrocarbons, those with low boiling points, quickly vaporize and rise to the top. These low boilers are chiefly ethane, propane, and butane.

Middle distillates—gasoline, kerosene, fuel oils, and diesels—bubble only partway up the tower, while heavy residues stay on the bottom. Each of these fractions may be distilled again and again, some under pressure, some in a vacuum, until that crude mixture of hydrocarbons has been sorted exceedingly fine, into propane at one end, asphalt and waxes at the other.

The residues and the heavier fractions may be further refined by "cracking." Using heat and pressure (thermal cracking) or catalysts such as platinum (catalytic cracking), the heavy hydrocarbons can be broken down into simpler, more volatile ones. Cracking processes have doubled the gasoline available from a barrel of oil, and have taken the petrochemical industry from its infancy in the 1930s to its present state as producer of more than 3,000 chemical products. (For a review of everyday products derived from oil, see "Oil Day Long," page 651.)

Hydrocarbons tend to be very accommodating. Refiners can, with very little trouble, alter their production to accommodate winter's demand for home heating oil or the summer's larger rations of gasoline.

There are other, more exotic refining methods that produce gasoline, among them polymerization, alkylation, hydrocracking, and catalytic reforming. According to a 1976 estimate by the American Petroleum Institute, without these cracking and reforming techniques refiners would have to process an additional 3.5 billion barrels of crude a year to meet current gasoline demands.

Finishing Touches

Complex as it may already be, gasoline endures yet another process before it can be fed into an automobile engine. The volatility of gasoline must conform to certain standards and is adjusted according to seasonal and geographic variations. A standard range of volatility is important for the safe transport, storage, and use of gasoline. Other standards govern viscosity, octane rating, and permissible additives. All gasoline brands sold in the United States conform to these minimum standards.

Further refinery work includes adding and then distilling out solvents, which are introduced to remove impurities. Before it reaches the pump, gasoline is filtered several times.

And then there are the additives. Dyes are added to distinguish among end grades of gasoline. Antigum chemicals are added to improve its storage life. Detergents are added to remove and prevent fuel system deposits that might pre-ignite gasoline. Treated alcohols are added because, no matter how carefully refined, gasoline always contains traces of water that may rust engine parts. Tricresyl phosphate is added, another hedge against pre-ignition. De-icing and antistall agents may be added, as well as upper cylinder lubricants.

Getting the Knock Out

Octanes are oily, ring-type hydrocarbon molecules of eight carbon atoms linked to eighteen hydrogen atoms. Varying numbers of octanes are present in all gasolines. A gasoline's octane rating is a measure of its ability to prevent spark-knock. "Knocking" is an undesirable fuel/air explosion prior to the arrival of the spark from a spark plug. To operate efficiently, modern high-compression engines require gasoline with high antiknock characteristics.

Lower-octane gasolines can have their antiknock qualities enhanced by additives. Tetraethyl lead, a petroleum product blended of ethylene dibromide and ethylene dichloride, was found to be a superb antiknock compound back in 1921. In the 1960s, more than 4.1 million pounds (1.9 million kilograms) of highly toxic lead were used in gasoline—all of it eventually exhausted into the atmosphere along with other products of gasoline combustion: carbon, carbon oxides, nitrogen oxides, and water. (See "Why Your Car Pollutes," page 626.)

Since 1975, emissions standards set for automobiles in the United States by the Environmental Protection Agency have resulted in the increased use of unleaded gasoline.

Gas Pains

Refineries tend to stink—especially around their catalytic-cracking units and their sulfur recovery plants. Aside from sulfur oxides, the chemicals that contribute to refinery air pollution are similar to those exhausted from automobiles. Refinery-generated air pollution can be reduced by the installation of vapor-recovery equipment or other control measures. But since most of these controls are expensive or inconvenient, few, if any, refiners have instituted them on their own initiative. Many U.S. refineries have resisted enforcement of antipollution laws. (See "Rating the Refineries," page 496.) But the net effect of refineries upon the environment—in the pollution caused by the gasoline they produce—is not so easily controlled.

A Few Final Facts

Nearly 55 percent of the oil consumed in the United States goes for transportation.

In 1976, 107 billion gallons (405 billion liters) of gasoline were consumed by U.S. motor vehicles. Automobiles used 75 percent of it.

Cars are the least efficient means of using fuel energy—even less efficient than airplanes.

Fill 'er up.

M.M.

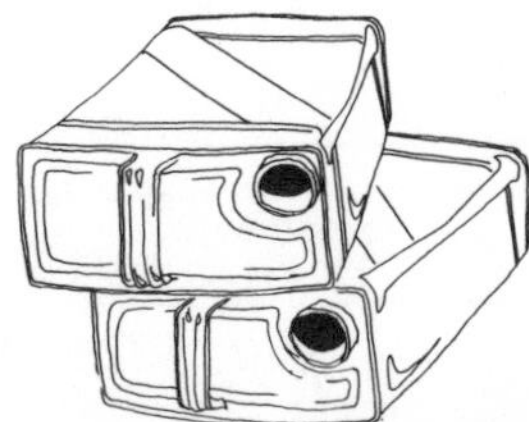

TWELVE WAYS OF LOOKING AT A BARREL OF OIL

A barrel of crude oil, in approximate numbers . . .

- Contains 42 gallons (159 liters), weighs one seventh of a ton (130 kilograms).
- Can be refined into some 21 gallons (79.5 liters) of gasoline, 10.5 gallons (39.7 liters) of home-heating oil, and 10.5 gallons (39.7 liters) of industrial oil. The exact product mix varies widely among types of crude and types of refineries.
- When spilled, covers between 0.5 and 3 square miles (1.3 and 7.8 square kilometers) of water and can poison perhaps 500 pounds (227 kilograms) of clams along with lobsters, finfish, seals, or birds who chance to come in contact with it.
- Contains enough energy to run a typical home furnace for four days of winter use in the northeast United States.
- Gives off about 1 pound (0.45 kilogram) of particulate matter and 6.5 to 20 pounds (2.9 to 9 kilograms) of sulfur oxides. These wastes, along with nitrogen and carbon monoxide, contribute to lung cancer, heart trouble, respiratory diseases, eye discomfort, and metal, stone, and paint corrosion.
- Would generate 500 kilowatt-hours of electricity, assuming a 100-percent efficient generating and transmitting system. This is enough to run an average U.S. home for a month, or an average Soviet home for five months. Given the actual energy losses involved in power generation and distribution, a barrel of oil delivers about 150 kilowatt-hours of electricity.
- Is the energy equivalent of 460 pounds (209 kilograms) of coal, 5,600 cubic feet (157 cubic

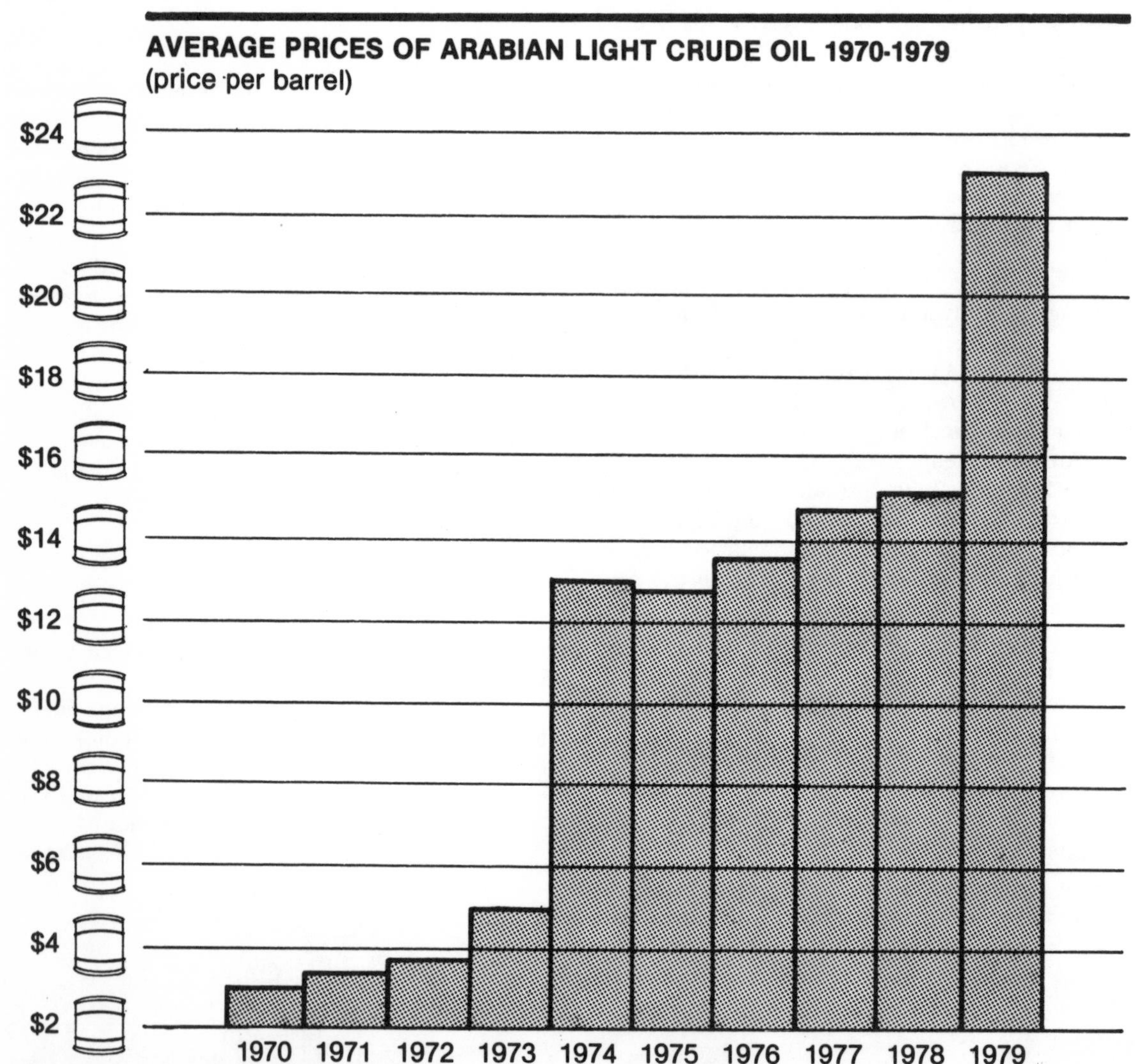

meters) of natural gas, one third of a cord of wood.

- Is 1/16,700,000 of the amount used in the United States in a day.
- Is 1/9,000,000 of the amount produced in the United States in a day.
- Is 1/55,400,000 of the amount used in the world in a day.
- Is 1/100,000,000,000 of the oil produced in the United States to date.
- Is 1/350,000,000,000 of the known U.S. reserves and 1/1,000,000,000,000 of the probable total U.S. reserves, but is only 1/39,000,000,000 of the oil that can be produced from currently installed equipment at known U.S. fields and 1/80,000,000,000 of the amount recoverable from known U.S. fields with maximum applications of current technology.

SOURCE: From "Some Approximate Numbers," p. xi in *Fragile Structures: A Story of Oil Refineries, National Security, and the Coast of Maine* by Peter Amory Bradford. Copyright © 1975 by Peter Amory Bradford. Reprinted by permission of Harper & Row, Publishers, Inc.

A LUMP OF COAL

When Superman squeezed a lump of coal, smoke seeped from his fist, and when he opened his hand, a rough but pure diamond lay in his palm. It was obviously a superhuman trick, the most glamorous transformation possible of an otherwise ordinary dirty black rock.

In theory, anthracite coal can be compressed, heated, and converted to diamond, but only the earth, and science fiction characters, can generate the exeedingly high pressures necessary. For the rest of us, the only result of squeezing a lump of coal will be streaky, sooty fingers. The soot, though, can be appealing. Some of us played in coal bins as children, when coal was the primary home-heating fuel, delighting in the opportunity to get our clothes, hands, faces, and even feet as dirty as possible.

Today, there is a resurgence of interest in coal energy, not only in the burning of coal itself but also in the chemical treatment of it to create synthetic crude oil. Increasingly, coal is viewed as a primary solution to the energy crisis.

Coal power probably dates to the Chou Dynasty of China, where coal was first used on a large scale in 1100 B.C. The Chinese burned a material they called "rock charcoal" to smelt copper and iron, and hundreds of years later they began what was probably the first commercial use of coal in making cast-iron coins for trade. The ancient inhabitants of Europe also knew that coal would burn. Aristotle reported that smiths of his time used a "black, smooth, compact" stone that kindled and burned like wood, and archaeologists have found that the pre-Celtic Welsh used coal for their funeral pyres. The Hopi Indians in the United States independently discovered the use of coal and were burning it at least a thousand years ago. However, coal was never considered as desirable a fuel as wood, and in general it was only used if nothing else was available.

Coal Use Heats Up

England is responsible for the role of coal in the industrial world. The Anglo-Saxon Chronicle of 852 mentions coal as payment for land rent, and monks apparently used to pick up "seacoal" that had fallen from cliffs onto North Sea beaches near Newcastle-on-Tyne. By the mid-thirteenth century, the monks had opened several mines and barged the coal down to London for sale to smiths and other workmen. Since London was already running out of firewood at this time, the coal sold well. However, as the coal smoke mixed

with London fog, it created one of the first air pollution problems, and in 1306 King Edward I forbade coal-burning in London, except by smiths. Coal smoke was also offensive indoors, because very few houses of the time had chimneys; instead, a simple hole in the roof let out the smoke.

In the next few centuries, England's wood shortage grew more critical and coal-burning became a necessity for producing metal goods. Newcastle was a center for a thriving export trade in coal by the middle 1500s, and the expression "carrying coals to Newcastle" came to mean any redundant action. As the British switched their economy from wood to coal—the first nation in the world to do so—the technological innovations that coal inspired led to the Industrial Revolution. The steam engine, powered by coal, made mining more efficient, which in turn made more coal available. The great factories of the English Midlands depended on coal, and the colliers, or coal miners, began to represent the English workman as much as the yeoman had in earlier centuries. The Midland towns were notoriously dreary and filthy; William Blake, who did not live to see the worst, denounced "these dark Satanic Mills" that were defacing "England's green and pleasant Land."

In the United States, coal was not regarded as an important fuel at first, in spite of the vast reserves known to exist there, especially in Pennsylvania. Wood was still abundant even on the eastern seaboard, and coal smoke was not only unpleasant but was even believed to cause epidemic diseases. People were not particularly interested in coal, if they knew about it at all, and coal merchants used to try to drum up business by setting up coal-burning demonstrations on the street.

In 1840, thanks to the development of the American iron industry, the steam locomotive, the growth of the cities, and the depletion of eastern forests, the amount of coal burned in the United States surpassed the amount of wood. With the advent of electricity, coal became even more important; much electricity was—and is—generated from coal-fired steam turbines.

However, the reign of "King Coal" was short in the United States. By the 1920s the price of coal began to fall, as cleaner, more efficient oil and gas came on the market. At the same time, coal miners organized and demanded higher wages and safer working conditions. The market dwindled, especially after World War II. By the 1960s, most coal was used not for direct home heating but by the steel industry and the electric power plants. In the early 1970s environmentalists dealt coal another blow by pushing through clean air legislation that forced many of the remaining coal burners to switch to cleaner and at the time still-inexpensive oil fuel.

Coal: The Future Fuel

In the 1980s, with natural gas and oil expensive and in tight supply, "King Coal" is being touted as an answer to our energy problems. The United States has a reserve of easily accessible coal of 178 billion tons. China and the Soviet Union also have large reserves. Of all the continents, only South America is significantly short of coal.

Around the world, coal is seeing a revival as its exploitation is being pressed by government policies. In West Germany, for example, coal companies now have the right of eminent domain, that is, they are legally entitled to buy any property that lies over coal reserves, whether or not the owners want to sell. In the United States, where the government is pushing coal development as a means to energy independence from Middle Eastern oil, coal companies do not have such rights. (If they own the *mineral* rights, however, they can mine even if it causes the destruction of the surface of the land, which may be owned by someone else. Much of the coal in the western United States lies under ranchland or Indian reservations—see "CERT," page 18.) Most U.S. coal leases have been bought recently by big oil companies, eager to develop the next source of energy as oil becomes harder to find.

Although coal is again receiving much attention, the three major drawbacks historically associated with it remain:

- Underground coal is difficult and dangerous to obtain.
- Coal strip-mining disfigures the landscape and harms the environment.
- The burning of coal is dangerous to human health.

Black Diamond

Coal is a fossil fuel. It is literally composed of fossils, the compressed remains of plants that flourished between 200 and 400 million years ago —although some coal has formed since then—at a time when much of the land surface of the earth was low, marshy, and covered with mosses and ferns. So many plants lived in this warm, lush environment that when they died, some of them were covered with other dead plants before they could decay. As more and more layers of organic material built up, the undecayed plants were compressed until the water squeezed out of them. The peat bog was gradually forced deep into the ground, where the pressure and heat, over the centuries, turned it into coal.

There are at least thirteen grades of coal, ranging from lignite, which resembles peat, to anthracite, which is the hardest and most dense. When anthracite coal is compressed and heated even further, it turns into graphite, which is distantly related to diamonds, a geological fact that inspired the Superman feat.

Anthracite, which burns steadily and with very little smoke, is the most desirable coal for space heating. Bituminous coal, the most plentiful grade, is midway between lignite and anthracite. Unlike lignite, it does not tend to decompose when exposed to air; bituminous coal smokes but produces a good amount of heat. The steel industry uses bituminous coal, and 54 percent of the electricity in the United States is generated from bituminous coal.

There are two main types of coal deposits. The first is a series of coal seams, up to 12 feet (3.7 meters) thick, found in layers throughout clay, limestone, or sandstone deposits. Sometimes thirty coal seams are found in one area within 3,000 feet (915 meters) of the surface. The second type of deposit is a single layer of coal, often of great thickness, found in isolation. In the United States, the first kind of coal deposit is typically found in the east and the second kind in the west.

Coal Casualties

The traditional method of getting to the first type of deposit is underground mining, which has the deserved reputation of being one of the most dangerous of jobs. Cave-ins, fires, suffocation, gas, coal dust, explosions, mechanical accidents, and even drowning (groundwater is a constant problem in some mines) have threatened deep miners. The working conditions in the early days of coal were abysmal. Children, valued for the job because they were small and nimble, commonly put in ten- to twelve-hour days in the coal shafts. Mine owners were generally unconcerned about their miners' health, and workmen's compensation for the inevitable casualties was nonexistent. In the United States the formation of the United Mine Workers in 1890 catalyzed bitter strikes, but improved conditions somewhat. But miners still risk more danger than workers in any other common job, and when they retire from the mines, it is often with black lung disease contracted from long-term inhalation of the coal dust. (See "Are You Dying to Make a Living?" page 685.)

Underground mining often causes the land above it to cave in, a process called subsidence. Since coal mining began in the United States, about 2 million acres (800,000 hectares) of land have collapsed into abandoned mines.

Acid runoff from mines is another problem. About 10 million tons (9 million metric tons) of sulfuric acid run off into streams, lakes, and ponds each year from underground mines in the United States. The acid in the water kills fish and plant life and contaminates drinking water. Unfortunately, after an underground mine is closed the acidic runoff continues unabated. There are several rather effective techniques for countering this problem, but they are expensive.

The Coal War

Surface or strip-mining is the second principal way of getting at underground coal. There is no question that strip-mining is more efficient for simply obtaining the coal. Instead of burrowing into the ground, the surface layer of topsoil and rock is removed as "overburden." One huge machine can move 8,000 cubic yards (6,117 cubic meters) of material in an hour, and can dig out an area to a depth of 182 feet (55.5 meters) while consuming as much power as a city of one hundred thousand people. Strip-mining is obviously a very different operation from deep mining. It uses fewer people and more machinery, and it completely changes the appearance of the land. Strip mines usually leave a barren landscape behind them; mining changes the chemical and physical composition of the soil, which sometimes cannot recover. Every year, 70,000 acres (2,830 hectares) of land in the United States are stripped. The land can be restored by filling, grading, fertilizing, reseeding, and watering, at heavy expense (up to $8,000 an acre/$19,770 per hectare), but the work rarely lives up to the claim of "reclamation."

The strip-mining debate will intensify in the next few years as the energy shortage worsens and the abundant strippable coal in the western United States beckons developers. The arid West is a poor prospect for reclamation, and water pollution from the mining would have a devastating impact on some vital water systems. While some Westerners badly want the jobs and cash coal brings, others understandably fear the boom towns, air pollution, and permanently damaged land that would also result. But 70 percent of U.S. coal is west of the Mississippi, and coal companies press the fight. (In terms of heat produced, however, the poorer-quality western coal is definitely inferior to the eastern.)

The Burning Question

One way or another, our burning of more coal is probably inevitable, and because of the acknowledged dangers of coal-burning, environmentalists are concerned that clean-air standards be kept up. Coal companies, on the other hand, insist that the clean-air laws destroy the efficiency of their operations and cause costs to skyrocket.

Coal is so obviously a dirty fuel that as early as the 1600s a pamphleteer in London inveighed against it: ". . . the very rain and refreshing dews which fall in the several seasons precipitate this impure vapor, which, with its black and tenacious quality, spots and contaminates whatever has been exposed to it." (See "The Trespassing Poison: Acid Rain," page 186.) The famous London fog in which Sherlock Holmes made his rounds was caused by coal smoke; and in 1952, 4,000 Londoners died in a particularly suffocating fog (see "Great Breathing Disasters," page 621). Largely because of this tragedy, laws were passed in Britain to prevent a recurrence, and today London has considerably cleaner air. But there are justified fears that the resumption of coal-burning will bring severe health problems. The particulates, sulfur dioxide, and nitrogen oxide emitted by the coal-burning process irritate the lungs, cause both acute and chronic respiratory diseases, contribute to heart disease, and have been linked to lung cancer.

The coal industry has installed effective but costly "scrubbers" to remove particulates from coal smoke. At present, there is no practical way to control nitrogen oxides. Sulfur dioxide control is controversial because effective scrubbers are extremely expensive, so that to meet clean-air laws, the cost of electricity could be increased by up to a third. Coal smoke also contains traces of mercury, lead, arsenic, cadmium, fluorine, and other elements harmful to human health, as well as some compounds that are very carcinogenic. There is no technology at present to control these emissions.

Another, perhaps more distant, danger from increased consumption of coal was studied by the National Academy of Sciences from 1974 to 1977. The study, by an interdisciplinary panel of scientists, reported that the proportion of carbon dioxide in the earth's atmosphere has increased up to 15 percent since 1860 because of the burning of hydrocarbons. If we keep using fossil fuel at present rates, by the year 2150 there may be up to eight times as much carbon dioxide in the atmosphere as in 1860. This could create a "greenhouse effect" by trapping solar radiation in the atmosphere and raising the average global temperature (see "Changing Climate," page 19). Obviously, this warming could be catastrophic, melting ice caps, raising the level of the sea, disrupting agriculture, and causing other unforeseen problems. The vastly increased use of coal that many people predict, the scientists agreed, may accelerate the greenhouse effect.

The more immediate interests of most governments, however, is coal's availability right now. The United States has enough coal, we are assured, to supply its citizens for several hundred years. There is enough to fill uncountable bins, to send down many chutes, to feed millions of furnaces and machines. Most of the bins won't be in homes this time around, but in factories and at power plants. In the meantime, the world searches for alternatives and examines the net of provisos that constrain our reliance on a "black, smooth, compact" stone.

J.S.

AN ALUMINUM CAN

The taut "ping" of a pop-top can being opened is probably one of the world's most recognizable sounds, testifying to the ubiquitous nature of the can itself. These metal containers carry everything from soft drinks to pet food to agricultural seeds, and probably will be referred to by historians as one of the most representative artifacts of our consumer age. In 1978, approximately 89.5 billion steel cans were shipped in the United States alone. Approximately 30 billion aluminum

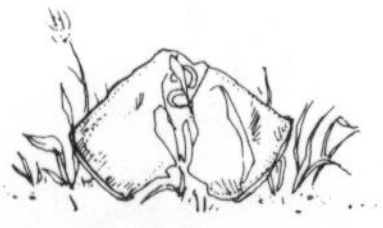

cans were shipped, representing a 710 percent increase in use of aluminum for containers since 1970, and accounting for about 50 percent of the U.S. beverage can market. Nearly 75 percent of all cans are used once and then thrown away, the glinting garbage of highways, river and sea bottoms, beaches, street curbs, and national parks. On can here, another there, and eventually great mountains of cans accumulating in junkyards around the world, monuments to the popularity and convenience of aluminum and to the marketing ingenuity of can producers, who both encouraged and capitalized on the trend toward disposable packaging items.

According to one study of the beverage industry, the proliferation of aluminum cans in the early 1960s saved on warehouse storage space and the cost of labor for sorting and stacking returnables. Aluminum was also lighter, more durable, and easier to handle than glass. It also has the advantage of being noncorrosive. On the other hand, aluminum is one of the most energy-intensive substances we produce.

The Liberated Metal

The existence of aluminum has been known for ages—the Romans used aluminum-based compounds, calling them alum, in their astringents. Aluminum metal itself, however, was not isolated until 1825, by a Danish physicist named Hans Christian Oerstead. The first aluminum produced was shaped into jewelry and fancy dining utensils and was more coveted than platinum, silver, and gold. By 1886, after the aluminum extraction process had been commercialized, the price fell considerably. Napoleon assisted the plummeting price by encouraging experiments with aluminum, believing that the lightweight material would be extremely useful to his marching army.

Aluminum is derived from bauxite, which is named for Les Baux, in southern France, where it was first discovered. It is estimated that bauxite accounts for one twelfth of the earth's crust. It takes, however, a tremendous amount of energy to liberate aluminum from bauxite ore, and, consequently, widespread aluminum production was not possible until the advent of abundant and cheap hydroelectric power. In the United States, aluminum companies were among the first customers of the country's first large-scale hydroelectric plant at Niagara Falls in 1895. By 1939, the aluminum industry had moved to the Pacific Northwest, where fledgling utilities were more than happy to provide long-term, cheap power for large and reliable customers. By 1978, aluminum producers used 1 percent of the nation's total energy consumption, and according to the U. S. Bureau of Mines, producing the light, shiny metal will consume 5 percent of total U.S. energy in the year 2000.

Pandora's Bauxite

The production of aluminum is a three-step process: mining, refining, and reduction. Each step leaves its stain on the world. Most high-grade bauxite is found in tropical areas—Australia, Brazil, and Jamaica, to name a few—where tropical rains have leached minerals, leaving the durable alumina-bearing ore (alumina is an oxide of aluminum used in refining). Bauxite is obtained by strip-mining or blasting, which more often than not permanently alters the ecological equilibrium of the area despite reclamation attempts.

Bauxite is then refined into alumina. For each metric ton of alumina produced, between one third and one full metric ton of "red mud" is generated, which ultimately ends up as the base of a landfill or in the ocean. In most cases, landfills are separated from surrounding land to prevent leaching of pollutants. Two other byproducts of alumina refining are sulfur oxides, suspected to be a cause of acid rains, and fluoride gas, which withers plants and cripples cattle. To avoid lawsuits from farmers, some aluminum companies simply purchase the land around smelters either as buffer zones or for limited agricultural production. It is claimed that fluoride emissions to a large extent can be controlled by antipollution "scrubbers." The Aluminum Company of America (Alcoa) is working on a process at its Palestine, Texas, plant, using chloride instead of fluoride in refining alumina, that could alleviate the air pollution of current methods.

The final step of the production process is the reduction of alumina to aluminum. The typical energy requirement for the production of one metric ton of aluminum is presently estimated to be 18,000 kilowatt-hours, with most of the energy used in the reduction phase of production. Aluminum companies have found it difficult to find new sources of uninterruptible power in the United States and run into local political resistance because current power contracts allow heavy consumption at low rates and are often labeled public subsidies. In July 1979 the Bonneville Power Authority, which serves the Pacific Northwest and provides one third of the total U.S. energy used to make aluminum, cut back on the power available to the industry by 25 percent. Other power systems are raising their rates and some will not guarantee that they will be able to provide the uninterruptible energy flow that is essential for aluminum smelting.

An indication of the problems producers see in obtaining "affordable" power in the United States is that only one aluminum company has recently committed its capital to the construction of a new aluminum smelter within the country. Instead, aluminum producers are now looking to energy-rich Australia, South America (particularly Brazil), and North Africa for the sites of new smelters. One producer estimates that the smelting capacity in these developing countries today is 14 percent of the total capacity of the noncommunist world and will grow to 22 percent by 1985. Nearly $6 billion will be spent by that time to boost Australia's aluminum output sixfold. Australia's chief appeal is an abundant supply of coal-generated electricity. Some companies have reportedly contracted for power from Australian utilities for as low as one half cent a kilowatt-hour. This compares with 1.5 to 2.5 cents a kilowatt-hour often paid in the United States. For a country with plentiful supplies of electricity, aluminum exports are, in effect, energy exports.

This raw aluminum will be used to meet the growing demand for aluminum sheet and plate for cans, cars, and airplanes in the United States, Western Europe, and Japan. Reynolds Metals Company predicts that the all-aluminum can, which in 1979 accounted for about half of the total beverage can market, will hold about 62 percent of that market by 1985. The United States already uses more aluminum in the disposable beverage can than France uses for all its aluminum products. Many say the dependency of aluminum on major sources of electricity will eventually force it out of the packaging market. However, proponents argue that aluminum can be an energy saver, pointing out that the metal's light weight saves on gasoline consumption during transport and reduces the weight—and thus fuel consumption—of automobiles when incorporated extensively into their construction.

Recycling aluminum cans consumes less energy than producing new cans from raw materials. (*DOE*)

Collective Action

At the same time, once made, aluminum can be recycled with minimal loss and with only 5 percent or less of the energy needed for the initial process. Aluminum producers, for whom the cost of energy has been a constant headache in recent years, have long been interested in recycling cans. The problem is that, despite efforts by aluminum companies to provide cash incentives—companies pay approximately 27 cents per pound (60 cents per kilogram) for recyclable aluminum—most cans never find their way back into the production process.

Until fairly recently, many scrap dealers and secondary smelters viewed aluminum can recycling as pure public-relations strategy by aluminum producers to combat a "bad press" for cans. As aluminum cans became more available, littering became more common, and the can itself came to symbolize landscape degradation.

But as rising energy costs forced oil-dependent countries, like Japan, out of the primary aluminum smelting business, the value of aluminum scrap increased. Today scrap dealers who aggressively seek out aluminum garbage can compete directly with primary producers. Alcoa has encouraged entrepreneurs in various recycling schemes, including offering machines that automatically pay consumers for returned cans. Still, the vast majority of cans go uncollected.

Many retail stores resist collecting empty cans for recycling, claiming that they take up too much space and that the residue of beverage left in each can attracts bugs. The other option is for the recycling-minded consumer to take cans to a recycling center, but unless such centers are conveniently located in each community, the consumer could spend more energy in gasoline than is saved by recycling the cans. And many consumers have difficulty distinguishing aluminum cans from steel-based cans (aluminum cans are seamless while steel cans have a vertical seam). Finally, in a voluntary recycling program, the consumer gets no economic benefit; cans made from recycled aluminum are no less expensive than cans made from new aluminum.

Given that the number of cans recycled every year represents only about 27 percent of the number of cans sold, we are throwing away tons of resources that could be used again. For years the U. S. Congress has been considering legislation that would require a 10-cent deposit on all soft drink and beer cans, refundable when the can is turned in to a retailer or to a recycling center. Some states have in fact passed such legislation. We have reached the time when government incentives—in the United States and other countries—are necessary to encourage recycling of this versatile and valuable resource.

J.B.

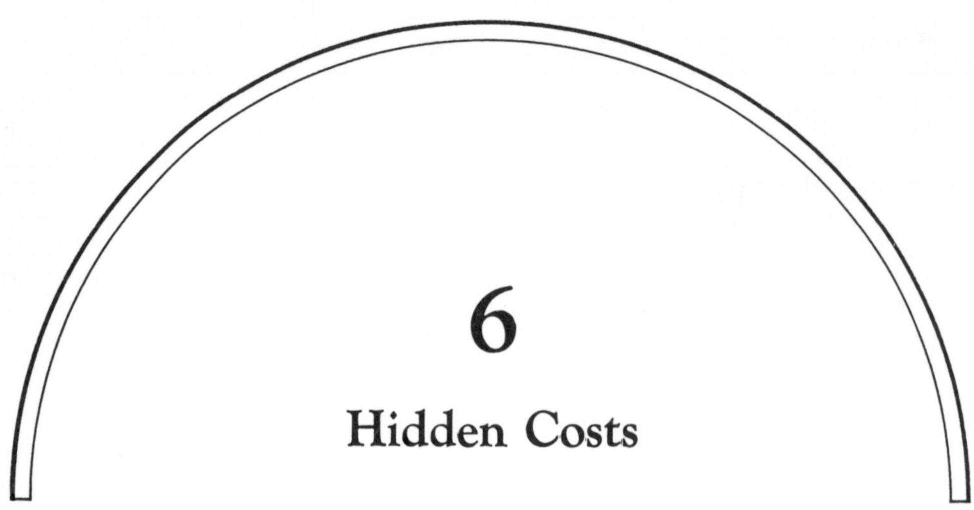

6
Hidden Costs

The costs of human enterprise, especially the social and environmental costs, group in layers. Evaluating these costs means one layer is removed, revealing another, and so on. When we set out to measure the costs of environmental change, we confront underlying numbers and effects, all of which may appear to have nothing to do with the original events.

A river is dammed, eliminating costly annual floods, and the construction requires, say, a hypothetical $100 million. The floods do not recur, irrigation is possible where none was possible before, and the area of expanded arable land is significant. For $100 million, all these benefits have been purchased, and, to boot, hundreds of people have been put to work.

But on the other side of the ledger, we enter the unconsidered costs. Nutrients that were once suspended in the river water and fertilized the flood plain during overflows are now captured by the dam, and their artificial fertilizer substitutes cost money. The nutrients do not flow into the ocean either, as they once did, and the fish that used to feed on them now feed elsewhere. The loss of these fisheries costs money. The boom town created near the dam site no longer has a reason to be. Re-employing and rehousing the workers who were drawn there costs money.

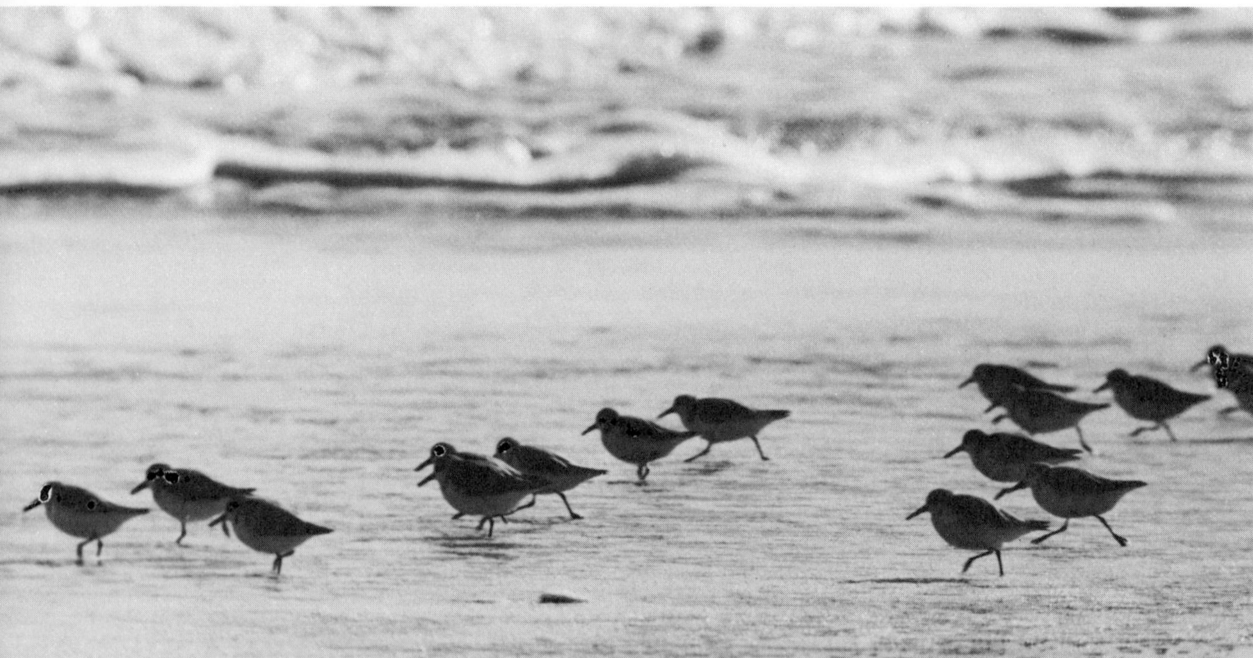

The Aswan High Dam in Egypt, while not a perfectly parallel situation, is an instructive example of hidden costs (see "The Aswan High Dam," page 173). The largely unanticipated costs of that dam may ultimately overrun its benefits—in food and cash—and in fact may do far more harm than anticipated.

In this chapter, we focus on unexpected or concealed costs of various endeavors, both environmental catastrophes and ordinary modern phenomena with broad environmental impact. Many of these costs can easily be computed in current dollars and cents, but the final bills may fall due in a neighboring or distant nation, or a future generation—bystanders removed in circumstance, time, and place from the original causes and effects.

After an oil spill, for example, insurance may cover the loss of cargo, but who is responsible for the loss of fish that could mean lean times ahead for the fishing industry? These secondary costs are often borne by taxpayers because, in the main, local, state, and federal governments pay price supports and unemployment insurance.

The attendant costs of nuclear incidents also ripple frighteningly throughout the economy. The first serious accident was the so-called Three Mile Island "event," in which radiation escaped from an out-of-control nuclear plant. There was no direct loss of life or property, but the incident was costly in many behind-the-scenes ways. Peter Stoler, who covered Three Mile Island for *Time* magazine, revealed some staggering background costs that nuclear plant neighbors and taxpayers may want to consider.

Our own daily actions too have hidden economic consequences. We squander resources, paying constantly rising prices for raw materials while simultaneously paying higher hauling and disposal charges for our garbage, much of which, especially paper and metals, could be profitably recycled and used again.

In this chapter, we also grapple with some concepts of costs that are elusive but important in our time; for example, how much is a seabird worth in dollars? Is that seabird worth anything beyond dollars? Is there intrinsic dollar value to the pristine nature of wilderness?

Here, we consider the question of values beyond money, "noneconomic" components such as natural beauty and cleanliness of air and water. We examine traditional economic measurements, such as the gross national product, and wonder about the elements it excludes from its analysis. We consider other measurements of that intangible "quality of life," indices that attempt to evaluate the goods and services produced by a national economy, against the backdrop of the longevity, health, and education of a nation's people—the items that cannot be conventionally costed.

P.D.

GNP: NOT COUNTING WHAT COUNTS

The gross national product (GNP) measures money. It doesn't measure how clean water is, how literate a population is, whether children have shoes to wear, whether infants die before their first birthday, whether workers are satisfied with their jobs and homes, or whether they receive more than a week's vacation a year. In fact, the GNP leaves out a lot.

The gross national product has long been an internationally recognized economic index. By definition, it is the monetary value assigned to a nation's output of goods and services, including international trade. In 1977, the following GNP scores were recorded by a sampling of countries:

- United States—$2,327 billion
- Soviet Union—$960 billion (1976)
- People's Republic of China—$373 billion
- France—$381 billion
- United Kingdom—$244 billion
- Brazil—$140–$150 billion
- Egypt—$14 billion
- Senegal—$1.7 billion

Several economists, notably John Kenneth Galbraith, the late K. W. Kapp, and Ezra Mishan, have expressed concern that this familiar indicator is far too narrow—that it reflects only pure economic growth, not the nonmonetary costs of that growth. In a way, using the GNP to assess a nation's economic health is a bit like determining a person's overall well-being by measuring his or her height. Height is what we see, indeed often what we notice first, but it certainly does not reflect all the biological and psychological factors that influence health.

Similarly, the GNP does not incorporate all the complexities of a national economy, particularly in a world of diminishing natural resources. Though it may accurately measure the growth of an industry—for example, how many automobiles are produced each year—it does not take into account the impact of the industry on the quality of our lives. In the case of the automotive industry, the GNP distinctly cannot account for how exhaustible the raw materials used in the car might be, or how many people in the country can actually afford to buy the cars, or how satisfied the workers are who assemble the cars.

Paradoxically, as economist Hazel Henderson points out, the GNP adds many of the heavy social costs, such as cleaning up the Love Canal or Three Mile Island, as if those were useful products, rather than subtracting these costs from the GNP. As Ralph Nader has explained, every car accident means a slight rise in the GNP because of increased use of hospital facilities, medical insurance, auto repair shops, to say nothing of the replacement cars that have to be purchased.

A rising GNP tends to symbolize progress and "civilization," and so developing countries tend to emulate industrialized nations. But some of the emulated nations are themselves questioning whether the GNP may need to be supplemented by other measurements.

The NHB

In 1974, Pierre Elliot Trudeau, as Prime Minister of Canada, called the GNP "no measurement of social justice, or human dignity, or cultural attainment." He suggested an alternative called the Net Human Benefit (NHB), which would not only measure growth but would also attempt to calculate the effects of growth on the human condition—the by-products of progress such as pollution and workplace drudgery. But so far the NHB remains just a provocative idea; no attempts to implement it have been made. In Japan, a new indicator, Net National Welfare (NNW) subtracts some social costs, such as pollution cleanup.

The PQLI

The Physical Quality of Life Index (PQLI) was developed to measure the nonincome aspects of a national situation. This averages infant mortality, life expectancy at age one, and literacy. According to the Overseas Development Council, which introduced the index in 1977, "An important advantage of consolidating these three indicators in the PQLI is that such a composite index usefully summarizes a great deal of social performance."

The DRR

The Disparity Reduction Rate (DRR) is used in conjunction with the PQLI to measure a nation's progress toward meeting basic human needs, such as the increase of literacy. It is the rate at which the disparity between a country's current situation and its best expected performance in the year 2000 is being reduced. The "best expected performance" is naturally a subjective matter, but it would be roughly equivalent to what a country calculates it can attain in comparison with developed countries. For example, by 2000 a country might expect to achieve an average life expectancy of seventy years, though currently its life expectancy might be fifty years. The DRR is the rate at which the country is progressing toward its goal. Of course, there are many variables affecting the DRR, and a country can revise expectations constantly to avoid embarrassment if disparities are not being reduced quickly enough, but the concept highlighted by the DRR is an important one.

The Bottom Line

Finally, in talking of the GNP or supplements for it, one must keep in mind the effect of inflation. While the nominal GNP might rise by 9 percent, the real GNP might decline 1 percent if there is a 10-percent inflation rate. It is the real GNP that in fact tells the economic tale.

But telling the economic tale may no longer be telling enough. Factors such as the cost to health of air pollution generated by cars are extremely difficult to quantify and have generally been considered external to the economy. Perhaps the time has come to incorporate some "externals" into our growth models, responding to the very succinct criticism made by the economist

Herman Daly: "The GNP measures only what can be counted, not what counts."

P.D.

POLLUTION CONTROL PAYS

Rough estimates by the Council on Environmental Quality released in April 1980 showed that annual benefits to the United States as a result of air pollution control was $21.4 billion in 1978—in the form of improved human health and reduced damages to crops and vegetation, among other things.

The same study reported annual benefits of approximately $12.3 billion in 1978 as a result of water pollution control, in the form of reduction of some waterborne diseases, reduced water treatment cost, and increased use of lakes and streams for recreation.

TEN HIDDEN COSTS

- According to a study by the Organization for Economic Cooperation and Development (OECD), the hidden costs of automobiles to industrialized societies represent about 5 percent of a country's GNP. The study concludes that congestion, accidents, noise, pollution, and other costs (among those mentioned: disfiguring and occupying open space) amount to a significant drain on the national standard of living. In the United States, the costs were between 4 and 6.8 percent of the GNP, in Japan and Europe the figures were slightly lower. If all of the social costs are totaled, the study says, they amount to two or three times more than road users actually pay.
- The OECD study of automotive hidden costs is substantiated by the case of Dublin, Ireland. Business leaders in the Irish capital claim that traffic jams in the crowded city are costing $4 million (approximately £2 million) a week in wasted fuel and lost business. Business representatives have demanded a new rapid-transit system, which they estimate could pay for itself in two years at the present rate of loss caused by traffic-choked conditions.
- As tropical forests decline (see "Amazonia," page 274), the world loses valuable, sometimes invaluable, species. According to Dr. Norman Meyers of the Natural Resources Defense Council, half of the pharmaceutical drugs purchased today are derived from wild plant or wild animal species, and about one in five come from species in moist tropical forests. Though recent figures are unavailable, in the late 1960s the value of drugs developed from wild species was about $3 billion. Unfortunately, many rainforest species are disappearing before their medicinal value can be analyzed.
- One estimate of the total cost of environmentally induced disease (i.e. health services, loss of wages, compensation, and rehabilitation) is $35 billion per year. At the same time, environmental pollution controls add only about four tenths of 1 percent (or less) per year to the inflation rate.
- The American Lung Association estimates that as much as $10 billion per year is spent to combat the effects of air pollution on health. (See "What's in the Air You're Breathing?" page 629.)
- According to the World Health Organization (WHO), excessive noise costs the United States $4 billion dollars a year in compensation payments, accidents, inefficiency, and absenteeism. Noise depreciation of real estate values mounts into the billions, particularly in the vicinity of major airports.
- Government and private sources in the United

"The quality of life is down 1½ per cent today."

States spent a total of $47.6 billion ($215 per person) in 1978 for air pollution control.

- The annual cost of treating and disposing of hazardous wastes is estimated at $530 million or $23.64 per ton ($21.45 per metric ton). (See "Better Living Through Chemistry?" page 507.)
- A complete animal test for cancer-causing effects of a new chemical costs approximately $300,000 to carry out.
- According to author Michael Harwood, writing in the *New York Times Magazine* in 1971, if all of the copper that is wasted and washed into the sea were sold as wire it would be worth $5 billion a year. Since that time copper has increased in value by about one third.

WHAT CAN YOU BUY FOR A MILLION DOLLARS?

Editor's Note: *Often, in calculating the hidden costs of environmental abuses (to society, to nature, and to taxpayers), the totals reach into millions of dollars. To most of us, a million dollars is incomprehensible. It is an amount that buys a famous athlete for a year, or a popular movie star for one picture, but it is not a sum most of us encounter in our own lives. To give us all some perspective, the* Almanac *compiled a list of things that one million dollars—at 1980 prices—could buy.*

Millionaires are a growing but still fairly rare breed of "fat cat." In 1960 there were only 50,000 millionaires in the United States, but by 1980 there were over 500,000. If you hope to join the club this is heartening news, but if you're already among them, it is distressing. Using the 1967 dollar as a measure, a million was worth $2.38 million in 1940, but by 1978 it had the buying power of only $500,000. Your cool million is cooling rapidly. If you are in a hurry to spend it, here are some ways:

- A million dollars buys only about ten or fifteen minutes of prime time on a U.S. television network. (If you want to start your own little TV network, you can send up a satellite to relay signals for about $50 million, including the hardware and the launching. Or you can rent a channel to bounce your signal off the satellite for up to $1.2 million a year.)
- Since a million dollars doesn't seem to go very far in the electronic entertainment media, perhaps it is better to spend it on that most fundamental investment: education. In the 1979–80 school year, $95.4 billion was spent on public elementary and secondary education in the United States. That's about $2,150 per pupil. Your million will educate 465.17 children for one year.
- If you prefer to travel, you can, with a million dollars:
  —Buy five New York City metropolitan buses and run them for a year.
  —Cart 30,000 tons of garbage to a landfill site.
  —Operate a Concorde for 48,000 miles (77,300 kilometers), or thirty-three hours at top speed.
  —Build 1 mile (1.6 kilometers) of new railroad track to carry coal out of Wyoming.
  —Travel on a U.S. passenger train 175,000 miles (306,000 kilometers).
- How does the U.S. government spend a million dollars? A generalized breakdown of each million it spends would put a quarter million in defense (a million dollars is less than one hundred-thousandth of the annual U.S. defense budget), $430,000 in direct benefit payments, another quarter million in all other programs (e.g., agriculture, environmental protection, law enforcement, education, aid to cities, mass transit, research of all kinds, and the publishing of immense amounts of reports, data, etc.) and $70,000 interest on public debt.
- If you are a terrorist or just paranoid about international aggression these days, you could buy one new MX I tank, with change for spare parts, or twenty Sidewinder missiles mounted on aircraft for a million dollars. Moving up above $10 million, you can buy a MIRV missile with nuclear warheads ($14 million) or an F15 A Eagle fighter ($16.8 million). For $1 billion you can take delivery on a Trident nuclear submarine, which carries twenty-four MIRVs, and at $2 billion, your own *Nimitz*-type nuclear-powered aircraft carrier.
- On the other side of the coin are the opportunities for supporting life on earth with a million dollars. Consider buying food. Twenty grams (.7 ounce) of protein from dry beans cost one cent in 1977, or 2 million kilograms (4.4 million pounds) for your million dollars. This

would provide the protein requirements of 667 million people for one day. (There are about four billion people on earth, one eighth of whom are undernourished.)

- Looking at conservation and pollution cleanup, a million is a drop in the bucket. To clean its rivers, the United States is expected to spend $248 billion by 1984. A million dollars' worth of pollution, on the other hand, can go quite a long way. That much oil, 40,000 barrels of crude at $25 a barrel, is about four days' flow from the Ixtoc I Mexican oil well when it was spilling into the Gulf of Mexico in 1980.
- A million dollars in solar water-heating equipment would cut the fuel bills on four hundred homes by 10 percent. (The $88 billion proposed to develop synthetic fuels in the United States over ten years would solarize 17 million existing houses and all the new houses built in the nation during that same ten-year period at the rate of 1.7 million built each year and $2,500 per house.)
- If your idea is to pay wages with a million, the money will go farther in some countries than in others. In terms of annual per capita income, a million dollars amounts to that of about 300 citizens of the United Arab Emirates, or of 10,000 Ethiopians. In the People's Republic of China, one million dollars represents the annual income of 3,000 people. (In this nation of more than 900 million, half of whom are working, a million dollars would meet the payroll of the entire country for a few minutes of work.) In the tiny principality of Andorra, on the French-Spanish border, a million dollars would pay all the workers (9,500) their wages for a month.
- If you want to gain political power, a million dollars is a pittance. To become president of the United States, in the 1976 election Jimmy Carter gathered $33 million from private and public sources. In pursuit of the same office four years later, several candidates had each collected millions in campaign contributions even before 1980 had dawned. Among those dozen or so men seeking a handhold on the strings of the world's richest purse were at least five millionaires.

R.B.

THE HIDDEN COSTS OF AN OIL SPILL

On March 18, 1967, the oil tanker *Torrey Canyon* ran aground in the English Channel, spilling almost a million barrels of oil that ultimately contaminated beaches in both England and France. The *Torrey Canyon* disaster was a milestone, not only in terms of its size (the largest spill to that date) but because serious attempts were made to control the spill (without much knowledge or success), study the effects of the spill, and collect damages. However, when British and French authorities attempted to collect damages, this is what they found out. Although the *Torrey Canyon* was crewed by Italians, it was registered in Liberia. And although it was registered in Liberia, it was insured in England. And although it was insured in England, it was owned in America. It was being used by the British Petroleum Company via its subsidiary, Petroleum Trading Ltd., which had subleased it from Union Oil Company of California, which in turn had subleased it from Barracuda Tanker Corporation, which in turn was owned by Union Oil which, therefore, must have owned the ship itself. While the sale of the *Torrey Canyon*'s oil might have been everybody's profit, the British and French authorities discovered that the spill was nobody's fault. Eventually,

a sister ship was seized, and the insurer coughed up the rather modest sum of $7.5 million to settle for cleanup costs and other damages.

History Repeats Itself

That was in 1967. In the interim everyone from the Intergovernmental Maritime Consultative Organization (IMCO, which makes rules for vessels like tankers) to the concerned individual has tried to do something about who pays for oil pollution. (See "The Hottest Questions in International Environmental Law," page 572.)

But on December 15, 1976, almost ten years later, the *Argo Merchant* ran aground, spilling her entire cargo of 200,000 barrels of No. 6 fuel oil into a stormy North Atlantic, 25 miles (40 kilometers) south of Nantucket and close to the rich fishing grounds of Georges Bank. The story was the same. The ship was crewed by Greeks and owned by Greeks. Nominally, however, it was owned by a Liberian corporation, Thebes Shipping Company of Monrovia, and, of course, registered there, too. Thebes officers had a total of nine ships registered in Liberia under various corporate names.

The *Argo Merchant* was insured by the Continental Insurance Company of the Bahamas. The insurers promptly denied liability, claiming that the owners had been negligent in maintaining the ship—a claim not without basis, considering that all of the ship's electronic navigational instruments were defunct, and also considering that *Argo Merchant* (in the past also known as *Arcturus, Pemina Samudra,* and *Vari*) had a long history of groundings, as well as breakdowns of boilers, generators, evaporators, and pumps.

Perhaps the owner of the oil could be sued. But was the owner Northeast Petroleum of Massachusetts, the importer; or Holborn Oil Company of Bermuda, the agent; or Coastal States Gas Corporation of Texas, the owner of Holborn; or Cibro Sales Corporation, the original purchasers of the Venezuelan oil; or Cirillo Brothers of New York, the owners of Cibro? All companies vigorously argued about when and where title changed hands, desperate to pass on the hot potato. As well they might—because the public (as well *it* might) has shown a growing impatience with both the spills and the run-arounds, and is now prepared to establish some bases for how much these spills actually cost society, and who will pay for them.

Superfund

For example, legislation developed in the U. S. Congress would establish an oil spill liability fund out of which those damaged could be immediately compensated. The fund (known as "Superfund") would, in turn, pass along costs, to the legal extent that it can, to the original polluter. In order to create such a fund, methods for assessing damage must be established. In 1978, Congress asked the National Advisory Committee on Oceans and Atmosphere to suggest to them how to assess damage from an oil spill. It was another step in an evaluation process that began shortly after the *Torrey Canyon* accident.

The Dollar Value of a Bird

In 1969, a blowout in California's Santa Barbara Channel prompted the first study of the economic effects of an oil spill. In that study, to examine one category of loss, dead seabirds were arbitrarily assigned a value of $1.00. In the words of authors W. J. Mead and P. E. Sorensen, "We know of no objective means by which the economic cost of bird losses may be assessed. We believe that this unknown value is greater than zero . . . and accordingly . . . have arbitrarily assumed that each bird lost involved a social cost of $1.00." Since then, objective (or at least consistent) methods *have been* established. For commercial species, the older concept of fair market value will always suffice even if the value isn't always collected. For noncommercial species, the new concept of "replacement cost" was recently honored for the first time in a U.S. court of law when the Commonwealth of Puerto Rico was awarded $6.2 million to compensate it for the destruction of living resources caused by the spill of oil onto a stand of coastal mangroves. In 1976, the U. S. Department of the Interior, in connection with a Chesapeake Bay oil spill, put replacement costs on dead birds in the range of $10 for a seagull to $200 for a whistling swan. In the case of the Santa Barbara spill itself, the California Department of Fish and Game ultimately sued for a replacement cost of $17 per bird. They settled for $4.5 million in total damages to natural resources—far less than the $54.5 million they had demanded, but considerably more than Mead and Sorensen's initial maximum estimate that total damages to wildlife were less than $35,000. Society had taken a stand.

A Sea of Costs

However, attempting to assess the total damages of something like an oil spill pushes science, society, and its law to the utmost: science because it is asked to expand its findings (based on painfully limited experiments and observations) to an infinite variety of real-world situations; society and its law because the loss of recreational areas or views, or small numbers of a noncommercial and nonendangered species, are utterly subjective valuations, however important. Even the concept of "replacement value" breaks down when there may be no possibility of replacement.

Then there are purely economic problems in attempting to assess the total costs of an oil spill. Does one count "private" costs, for example? A typical private cost would be the losses to a beach-front tourist industry. It is estimated in the case of *Amoco Cadiz* that 1.5 million expected tourists stayed away from the coast of Brittany during the spring and summer following that spill. To economists, this represents a diversion rather than a destruction of resources because it is presumed that those same 1.5 million tourists did indeed vacation somewhere. Nevertheless, such diversions constitute grievous damage to the affected businesses. Obviously such damage should be part of a polluter's liability.

What of imagined consequences leading to real consequences? North Sea fishermen complain that when a North Sea spill grabs the headlines, the market for their fish is temporarily killed, although the fish may not be contaminated, or, indeed, even caught in the same sector of the ocean. Even the actual damages to an ocean fishery are complicated, since the loss may not appear for a year or longer. If an oil spill seriously destroys a wetlands area along the coast, the casualties may be young fish and shellfish that would be lost from a future harvest.

Finally, there are the costs of surveys to assess and levy damages. Small spills are the rule and are so numerous that they can do as much damage as major accidents. There are 2,000 spills per year of 100,000 gallons (380,000 liters) or less in the United States alone. And 7,000 more which are less than 100 gallons (380 liters). But thousands of dollars are required to assess the damages from even a single small spill.

The Bottom Line

Any new oil spill guidelines must necessarily take account of all damage categories where society or its members have truly been harmed. Society must pay for the damage in any event. If strong and comprehensive liability laws are operating, then, via increased insurance premiums to the industry, society will pay at the pump in the form of higher gasoline and oil prices. In the absence of such laws, the cost of damages will be borne disproportionately—namely, by the uncompensated victims who dwell and make their living near the sea. But in either case some grasp of real costs, however imperfect, is essential to making good decisions on energy use and energy alternatives. Such an assessment must take account at least of the following:

- loss of ship and oil
- cleanup costs
- loss of income to those who make their living directly (such as fishermen) or indirectly (such as hotel owners) from the polluted area
- property damage
- loss of use of property
- damage to natural resources

Those who pollute have fought against any liability every step of the way. It was only as a consequence of the *Torrey Canyon* disaster that IMCO instituted a convention on civil liability for oil pollution damage. The convention didn't even come into force until 1975, and while it acknowledged the liability of the ship owner, it also limited liability to a mere $18 million. In 1978, that doubled to $36 million, which is still not enough.

Indeed, the amount will not be sufficient until it compels the oil companies and ship owners to spend enough money on accident prevention to actually prevent accidents, rather than cynically to calculate that it is cheaper to accept accidents and pay off victims (when forced) than it is to act responsibly.

F.C.S.

THE WORLD'S LARGEST OIL SPILL

Ixtoc I, an oil rig owned by Pemex, the national oil company of Mexico, blew out on June 3, 1979, and began releasing crude oil into the open ocean in the Gulf of Mexico. On March 23, 1979, 295 days later, the well was finally capped. As of early 1981, the accident was the largest oil spill on record and had run up these estimated costs:

- $100 million in lost oil, approximately 140 million gallons (3,333,333 barrels) valued at $30 per barrel.
- $365 million in lawsuits pending in courts in the United States for damages, lost oil, etc.
- $21 million for the lost oil rig itself.
- $7 million cleanup costs incurred by the United States.
- $134 million in cleanup and other "response" costs to Mexico.

These estimates, of course, do not account for the monetary losses incurred through related

Oil bubbles up from the Ixtoc I well off the coast of Mexico in a spectacular blowout that spewed 140 million gallons (530 million liters) of oil into the Gulf of Mexico over 295 days in 1979 and 1980. (*U. S. Coast Guard*)

damages to fisheries, to undersea habitats, and to coastal tourism.

Of all the oil spilled, only 4.5 percent was recovered. At the time of the accident, neither Mexico nor the United States had a contingency plan ready for handling the cleanup, nor was there any treaty in force between the two nations to govern settlement of damages. P.D.

SOURCE: Center for Short-Lived Phenomena, Cambridge, Massachusetts.

THE BENEFIT–COST GAME

If a mining company thinks there's gold on your property, how much will it have to pay for the privilege of finding out, in the process putting unsightly holes in your lawn?

If the state wants to build a highway through the middle of your house, how much does it have to pay you to move out of the way?

If the government wants to build a hydroelectric dam in the middle of a national park, how much should it pay the public for giving up the opportunity to enjoy unspoiled natural beauty in the park?

To most economists, all three of these questions are equally sensible. To the rest of us, however, the last may be a little confusing.

We are accustomed to the idea that two individuals will bargain over the price one will pay the other for tolerating a nuisance. We are even used to the idea that the state can take our property for some public purpose if it pays us a fair price for the loss (the law of eminent domain). But we are not accustomed to thinking about balancing the estimable values of electric power against the inestimable values of natural beauty. With benefit-cost analysis, economists have tried to put prices on public projects, even when there is no clear cash value.

Benefit-cost analysis, a standard tool used by business throughout the world, is also used to decide if it makes economic sense to build a new highway—or a new subway system, or a new sewer treatment plant, or a new airport, or a new hydroelectric dam. Sometimes, the calculation is quite straightforward, no different from the kind of private decision that businesses make when they decide whether or not to buy a new machine or build a new factory. The business executive asks if the investment will return a profit; the government wants to know if the revenues from its project will cover its costs.

Many times, with government projects, there are no cash revenues. Still, governments build schools, pay for armies, dig canals, build bridges, subsidize railroads, and so on. Presumably, governments do these things because the benefits to society outweigh the cost. How do they decide? They could just guess. They could poll their citizens. Or they could hire economists.

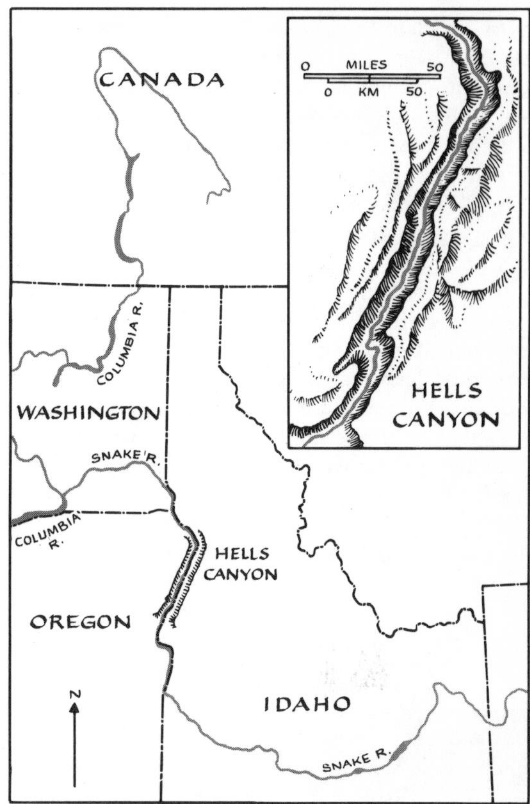

When the U.S. government was considering construction of a giant hydroelectric dam across Hells Canyon on the Snake River in Idaho and Oregon in the 1960s, supporters and opponents brought in hired economists to analyze costs versus benefits. Economists for the dam's supporters calculated the construction cost for the dam and the benefits of having cheap power and better flood control. They found that the benefits outweighed the costs, so they recommended that the dam be built.

Then economists for the dam's opponents tried to tear apart the result of the first analysis. Hells Canyon, they said, has some of the most pristine scenery in the world. It is deeper than the Grand Canyon; the river is rich with salmon and other fish; the surrounding land is an irreplaceable habitat for wild animals; people come from all over the United States to see it. If the dam were built, the canyon would be drowned under an enormous lake. The opponents of the dam tried to put a price on the natural state of Hells Canyon.

To put a price on an elk or an eagle is no simple job. The anti-dam economists began their attempt to put a price on pleasure by estimating what people would pay to maintain the canyon. They looked to Norway, where sports fishermen pay up to $500 a day to fish on privately owned streams. They looked to U.S. hunting clubs, where people pay dues to maintain private land for their sport. They tried to guess what a reasonable admission charge to Hells Canyon might be if it were run like a private preserve. They found out where the people who visit Hells Canyon come from and how much they spend for travel to get there. The opponents produced a report that claimed Hells Canyon was worth considerably more to the people of the United States in its unspoiled state than the people of the country could possibly gain from the benefits of the dam.

Perhaps the study had some influence in the U. S. Congress, which eventually passed a law prohibiting new dams on that part of the Snake River. (More likely the Hells Canyon dam was stopped as a result of a political campaign against the dam by citizens' organizations.)

The Hells Canyon episode is a good example of the power and the weakness of benefit-cost analysis. It can be a fairly simple mathematical exercise to calculate the assumed value of benefits and costs over a long period of time. All it takes is a couple of compound interest formulas like the ones used to figure out home mortgages and a pocket calculator to do the arithmetic. But the result can be misleading, reminding one of the old saying, "Figures don't lie, but liars can figure."

Plugging numbers into a formula and calling it benefit-cost analysis isn't the whole answer. And the benefit-cost procedure ignores the relative distribution of income and wealth. The Hells Canyon calculations excluded completely all those who would have valued the canyon as a national park but who could not afford private fees to visit it. Vague estimates and judgments will always vary; the ultimate worth of projects and the environment they disrupt will never be obvious to all sides.

In the United States and other parts of the industrialized world, arguments favoring development projects are often cloaked in "objective" benefit-cost analysis. Calculations are handed out to the media that try to demonstrate that air pollution cleanup requirements, for example, cost so much that they overshadow the value of the benefits. Environmentalists can overvalue the things they cherish too.

In the Hells Canyon debate there was probably no single answer to the question about the price of pleasure people received from the existence of the unspoiled canyon. And a greater question arose over the human presumption that our pleasure should be the principal criterion in such a decision. The opponents' position—measuring the price people pay for similar things—may have seemed silly to some. But their method wasn't as silly as ignoring the recreational and biological value of the canyon altogether. T.G.D.

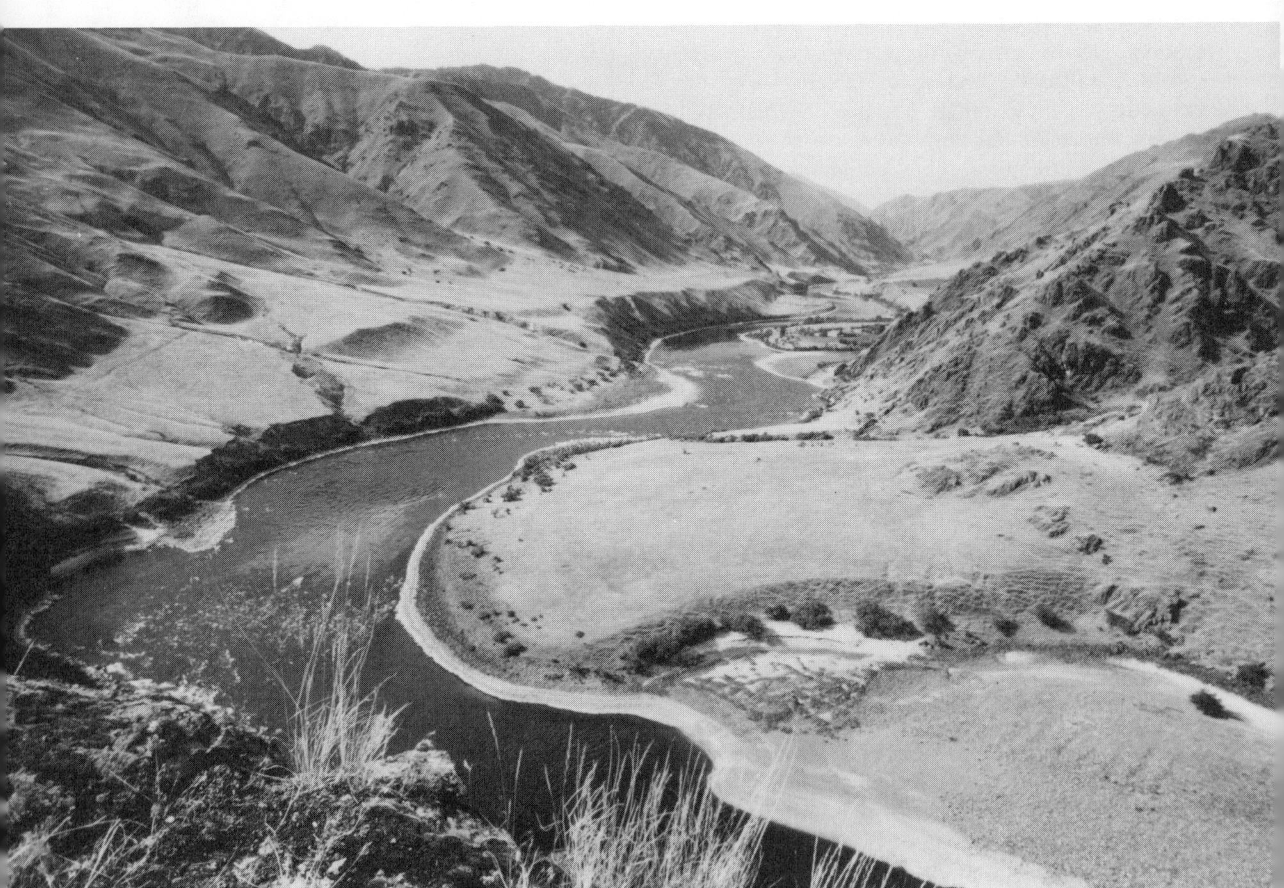

Hells Canyon—worth more without a dam. (*EPA Documerica/Boyd Norton*)

THE HIDDEN COSTS OF FOOD

In February 1979, hundreds of farmers from the American Agricultural Movement drove their tractors along the wide boulevards of Washington, D.C., to dramatize the plight of small, family-owned farms. Consumers, who had watched food prices rise 10.5 percent in the United States during 1978, could not understand why the farmers were unhappy. Most of us make the sensible assumption that most of the money we pay for food goes to the farmer, but the U.S. food system is not that simple.

During 1978, the farmer received only 32.4 cents of every food dollar. Here is where the rest went:

The processor	17.2 cents
The wholesaler	10.0 cents
The transportation firm	5.2 cents
The retailer	35.2 cents

The store that sold the food made more money from it than the farmer who spent months producing it. The basket of food in the supermarket that cost $100 in 1977 cost $110.46 in 1978. Of the additional $10.46, farmers received $1.76, while middlemen collected the remaining $8.70. And 1978 was an unusually good year for farmers. In 1974, by contrast, the average family's food bill increased $105, but only $1.00 went to the farmer. Between 1952 and 1977, the average price per unit paid to farmers rose 6 percent, while farm production costs rose 122 percent.

The Squeezing of the Small Farmer

Many factors have contributed to the problems of farmers. The American people have been buying more prepared and packaged foods, which

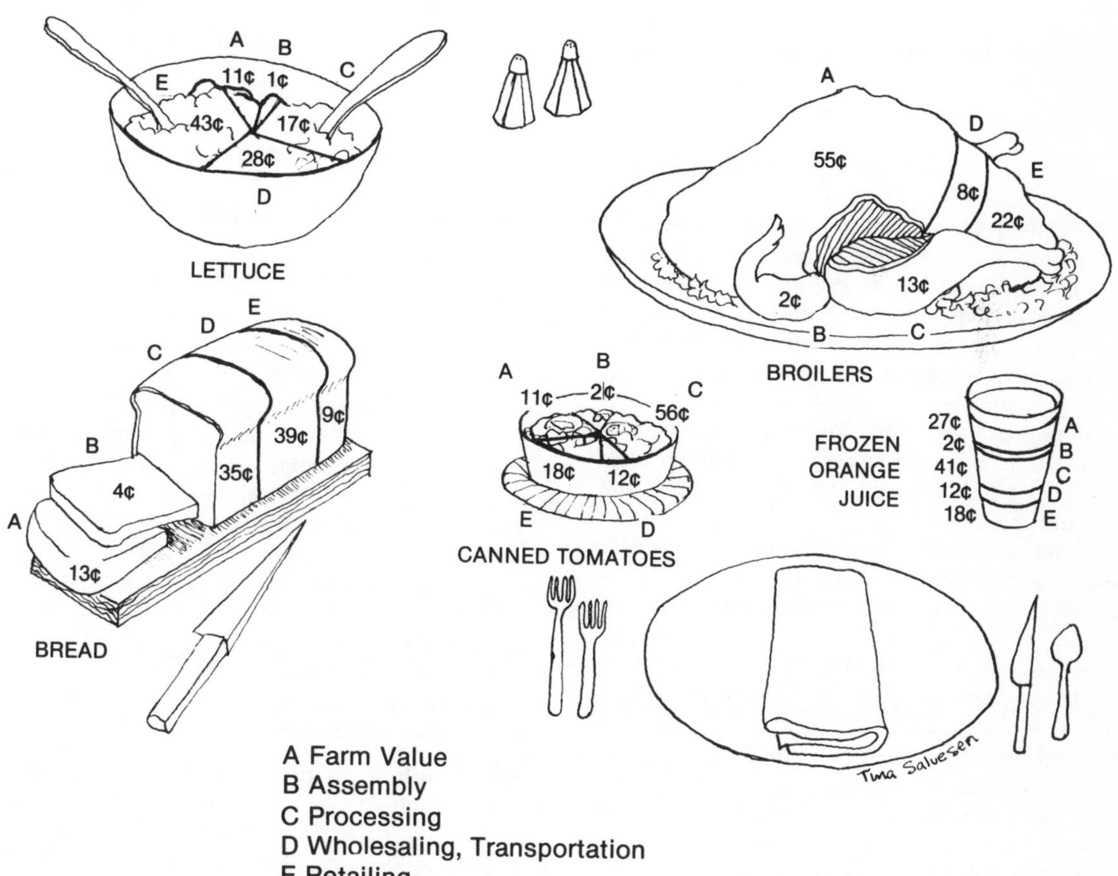

Where Your Food Dollar Goes.

require more processing than ever before. Farmers have been using more fertilizer and pesticides, which require large inputs of fossil fuel in production and are therefore becoming more expensive. (See "The Oil Diet," page 592.) High interest rates have made it difficult for farmers to acquire capital when they need it. Large corporations have developed networks that include farms, transportation, processing, and retailing, enabling them to keep farm prices low and increase profits at other stages of the food cycle. (See "Who Produced Your Dinner?" page 597.)

The Large Corporate Farmers

The farmer and the consumer are at the mercy of powerful economic forces. Corporations like Exxon, DuPont, and General Motors provide essential fuel, agricultural chemicals, and farm machinery. Agribusiness conglomerates like Tenneco and United Brands control marketing and processing. The farmer does not have the cash reserves to battle these giants, and food is too perishable to withhold from sale. This situation helps explain how farmers could be selling wheat for $4.73 per bushel ($0.13 per liter) and beef for $0.52 per pound ($1.14 per kilogram) in 1973, and for $2.50 per bushel ($0.07 per liter) and $0.37 per pound ($0.81 per kilogram) in 1977. While the marketing conglomerates were thus squeezing the small farmer, their own food industry profits rose 73.5 percent.

The accompanying charts illustrate how our food expenditures are divided among the various sectors of the food industry. The farmer's share shrinks a little each year, and so does the number of small farmers. About 6 percent of the farms now do 60 percent of the business. There were 6 million farms in the United States in 1945, 2.3 million in 1978. More than 2,000 farms a week have failed for the last thirty-five years.

Conditions elsewhere are worse. The United States produces almost all of its own food and is the world's leading food exporter. Transportation and distribution costs are minimized for U.S. consumers. Countries that have to import food, including nearly all of the developing nations, have to pay even larger portions of their food expenditures to middlemen. Because they are further removed from the source of food, transportation costs more and more middlemen are involved.

K.F.

THE HIDDEN COSTS OF THROWING IT AWAY

The United States alone accumulates more than 130 million metric tons of municipal solid waste per year. As noted by the President's Council on Environmental Quality, this is enough trash to fill the New Orleans Superdome from floor to ceiling twice a day, weekends and holidays included. And the volume is expected to rise to 180 million metric tons by 1985. This doesn't count industrial waste, which is usually considered separately because it is disposed of by the "generator" at the plant site or elsewhere.

We throw things away for many seemingly good reasons. For one thing, we are told to by the advertisements posted everywhere that encourage us to "replace that worn-out" whatever or "put an end to" something we used to have or used to do. (And many products boast of packaging which is both disposable and indestructible.) Throwing out is a continual purging, a spring cleaning for all seasons.

Our language despises trash: trashy novels are scorned; "white trash" is a slur; to "trash" is to wreck a place in violent protest.

The United States spends about $4 billion a year to carry away society's outcast materials, and precious little of it is redeemed. The municipal solid waste pie can be cut any number of ways to reveal its origins and nature:

- About 70 percent comes from residences, the remainder from commercial and other institutions.
- 63 percent is nonfood: paper, glass, metal, plastic, etc. Over half of this is packaging, and most of it is recyclable. In fact, U.S. trash is full of containers: 75 percent of all the glass manufactured in the United States, 40 percent of the paper, 29 percent of the plastic, 14 percent of the aluminum, and 8 percent of the steel goes into packaging. It is, for the most part, thrown away.
- 17 percent is food waste.
- 19 percent is yard waste.
- 1 percent is miscellaneous inorganic material.

A side dish of municipal sludge derived from sewage treatment cost $635 million per year to dispose of in 1978; disposal of hazardous wastes cost $155 million that year, but may rise to $800 million per year because of stricter environmental regulations. Include as well the average cost of

$1,000 per trash collection employee per year in on-the-job injuries.

Efforts to utilize the resources being thrown away in the United States are minimal. Only 7 percent of municipal refuse was recovered for any purpose in 1977, mostly paper separated before it could enter the waste stream. This includes the 1 percent converted into energy, which compares poorly with the 60-percent conversion of trash into energy in Denmark, or even the 10 percent in England. Using available methods of turning trash into "refuse-derived fuel," enough energy could be produced from the U.S. mountain of waste to supply all the commercial and residential lighting needs of the nation, or 400,000 barrels of oil per day (worth well over $3 billion a year in 1979—almost as much as we pay to get rid of it!).

Recycling (reuse), resource recovery (rescue from the dump), and materials conversion (use of trash in other ways) have been neglected in the United States—which has the world's largest trash mine—because it appears to cost more to retrieve the resources than to manufacture new commodities out of virgin materials. It *appears* to cost more, because we do not assign a cost to the pollution of groundwater by toxic wastes. Nor do we charge ourselves for the economic opportunities lost by covering half a million acres of land with trash. And we have no means of numerically valuing the air polluted, land strip-mined, and forests felled to supply materials already available in the solid waste we generate.

Surveys of disposal costs have been made, however, and reveal how economies could be realized by avoiding the "cheap" solution of throwing things away. In a breakdown of trash collecting and disposal, picking up trash, at about $24 per ton, is shown to be six times as expensive as disposal, at under $4 per ton, which involves, in almost all cases, dumping and covering the refuse with dirt in a "sanitary landfill." Of 17,000 disposal sites identified in a 1975 survey, 75 percent were found to be in violation of environmental standards, but compliance is said to have improved since then. Full compliance could cost municipalities and private operations an additional $1.6 billion a year.

Resource recovery, by comparison with landfilling, costs $8 to $15 per ton after collection. Using only these simple figures, throwing away valuable commodities and getting them back does not appear economical, except where landfill space is very limited (full resource recovery can reduce the volume of trash by up to 90 percent). Unfortunately, local governments have little opportunity to measure the hidden costs of disposal, which may be remote from them, and little motivation to increase local budgets even if there is a long-range savings.

The technological means exist to recapture the value lost in our waste, to turn miscellaneous garbage into fairly clean-burning fuel, to send bottles back to the bottlers, and to mold ground glass into bricks. Solid waste can also be compressed into building materials. In the area of cast-off metals, there is enough scrap iron and steel rusting on the ground now to meet the U.S. demand for fourteen years (over 600 million tons). Only approximately 27 percent of the aluminum cans produced each year are recycled, though the means to reuse the aluminum have existed for decades.

Public perception of the waste of resources and the hazards of waste disposal may lead us to demand biology-imitating systems of genuine sanitation and renewal. The guiding principle is simple: It doesn't make sense to throw away things that can be salvaged, or to produce things to be used once and thrown away.

R.B.

A DAY OF THROWING IT AWAY

Editor's Note: *We asked writer Rick Bruns to keep track of everything he threw away on a typical day. He filed the following report which, while indicating an appalling amount of waste, probably profiles a "throw-away" day not unlike an average day for anyone living in a developed nation.*

After breakfast I throw the empty cereal box away. It is made of cardboard, with a waxed paper bag liner. The garbage can is plastic, with a plastic bag liner. Plastic kitchen garbage bags are sold in a little cardboard box, a "one bag at a time dispenser package." To open, push in along a perforation and pull away the top panel. Throw away the panel. Inside are neatly folded bags and a set of clear plastic tabs for tying the bags shut. When all the bags have been filled with trash and tied with tabs and thrown away, throw away the box.

Time to get dressed in my new shirt. It comes from the store in a plastic bag stamped "Made in Sri Lanka" (referring to the shirt). On the other side it is stamped: "Warning—to avoid danger of suffocation, keep this bag away from babies and children. Do not use in cribs, beds, carriages, or play pens. This bag is not a toy." I throw it away.

Now to find *all* the pins before putting the shirt on: one holds the price tag on (reduced to $5.99), two more keep the lower half tucked up behind the collar—no, three—another holds the shoulders back. The sleeves have fallen loose and released a piece of cardboard whose I-shaped outline precludes it from any other purpose. I throw it away, as well as two accompanying pieces of tissue paper, whose function apparently was to crinkle. Under the collar is a piece of cardboard. A bookmark for the Yellow Pages? No, throw it away. One of the eight pins is bent—away with it—and I am left with a shirt and seven pins from Sri Lanka.

I am preparing for a holiday visit with my family, a thousand miles away in St. Louis, Missouri. On the way to the airport, I buy a gift: cheese from France, wrapped in its own paper and cellophane skin, then wrapped by the man at the deli counter in cellophane again, then in waxed paper and tucked in a brown paper bag. Later in the day, I also pick up a paperback book (in a bag), a candy bar, and a little carton of milk (in another bag). After devouring my snack, I throw away one bag, the waxed paper milk carton, and the candy wrapper. I leave for the airport.

Without throwing away anything else, I take my seat on the plane. I am offered a drink: a bottle containing one tenth of one pint of scotch (with a tiny metal cap), a plastic cup, a small paper napkin, and a cute little plastic stirrer in the shape of a propeller. I toss down the scotch, the rest is gathered by the flight attendant and . . . you know.

Dinner is served. When I have eaten, there remains: a paper napkin, the cellophane wrapper from a piece of bread, the aluminum foil that enveloped a piece of apple pie, the combination plastic and foil thimble-size containers of salad dressing and artificial cream, tiny plastic-and-paper salt and pepper containers (which condiments can cost fifteen times as much in this form as in larger containers), the plastic envelope that held the silverware (*real* silverware), and a paper placemat. All thrown out, except the silverware, three dishes, and the plastic tray, which would live to serve another passenger.

That evening, I snap on the television. The trash list from ads during two hours of prime-time programming is an epic of consumption and disposal. Every product smaller than an automobile is wrapped and boxed and bottled and canned in little containers that can serve no other purpose.

And then at last the ad for plastic kitchen garbage bags. This brand is thicker and stronger, so you can *overstuff* it with your trash and it won't burst. You'll save on bags, so you can throw away more and it'll cost you less. . . .

I am home. I sleep. Tomorrow is the Thanksgiving feast. There will be much to eat and, oh, so much to throw away. R.B.

THE HIDDEN COSTS OF SPRAWL

In every developed and developing country, the migration of rural peoples to urban areas is a continuing phenomenon. The expansion of cities to accommodate this relentless growth has occurred in different ways, but always, as a city fills up, it spreads inexorably into the open areas around its fringes. In developed nations, the newest and poorest arrivals from rural areas are crowded into the city's oldest and least desirable sections, replacing earlier migrants, whose upward social and economic mobility has carried them toward the newly developing fringe areas.

In a sense, perhaps, this outward movement reflects a yearning by urbanized people for their simpler, rural past. But it is a yearning that can only be partially fulfilled, since the newly affluent are tethered to the urban economy. The result is a commuter life-style and a form of development commonly characterized as "sprawl."

Little Boxes on the Hillside

The term sprawl in the United States generally refers to areas of low-density, single-family housing (i.e., two dwellings or fewer per acre of land), often arranged in a grid pattern to keep land development and construction costs low and uniform. These residential tracts, or subdivisions, are frequently located on what was once farmland, usually without regard to existing communities or such public services as transportation, sewers, utility lines, adequate highways, schools, and other elements of the so-called infrastructure. The commercial and industrial development that follows is equally haphazard, spreading strips of shopping centers, office buildings, factories, and retail stores along existing highways or wherever land can be bought reasonably and rezoned easily.

The costs of sprawl, both direct and hidden, are enormous. Its low density uses up land much faster than more concentrated development. Energy use is significantly higher than in downtown areas, on a per capita basis, largely because of the almost exclusive reliance on the private car for transportation.

New suburban shopping and recreation facilities often duplicate existing public facilities that are not far away but are slightly less convenient. The frequent disregard for environmental safeguards in suburban construction creates problems of air and water pollution, flooding, and erosion, which are costly to abate. And, not least, it can cause severe problems of municipal deterioration in the older cities left behind, now shorn of their middle-class tax bases. (See "An Auto Biography," page 432.)

The Advantages of Clustering

The U.S. government has made a comprehensive study of the costs of sprawl compared with those of high-density, planned communities consisting of 40 percent high-rise apartments, 30 percent walk-up apartments, 20 percent townhouses, and 10 percent clustered single-family homes, all grouped in contiguous neighborhoods. The cost differences are dramatic.

When higher-density development is arranged efficiently, it is possible to leave more than half the land area in its natural open state for public use and enjoyment. Sprawl development, on the other hand, uses almost all the land for its low-density spread, leaving only gaps of improved land where a new subdivision has "leapfrogged" over existing development. Furthermore, less land is taken up with roads in a clustering arrangement.

Building costs for high-density development were found to be 44 percent lower than for sprawl. Savings in the cost of roads and utilities amounted to 55 percent when this infrastructure was planned for high-density development. Planning that reduces automobile use can provide a 20- to 30-percent reduction in air pollution. Noise abatement is also possible to a greater extent through skillful planning, despite the fact that clustered developments tend to have more noise sources because of the more concentrated activities.

A Flood of Problems

Water resource problems are exacerbated by sprawl development. The extensive paving, for example, increases the runoff of storm water into nearby water bodies, creating potential flooding problems. Storm water also becomes polluted from street wastes and lawn fertilizers, thereby increasing the pollution in the streams that carry it off. And erosion, too, is made worse by extensive paving, since water is channeled into paths where it is not allowed to soak into undeveloped ground. As a result, considerable local and federal government resources have been committed to correcting flooding, erosion, and water pollution problems caused or worsened by sprawl development. Clustering, on the other hand, concentrates development into smaller areas, making these problems easier to handle and reducing water usage as well.

What effect does sprawl have on the old, established cities? By encouraging city residents to invest in a new home outside, rather than contracting for home improvements to the existing downtown structure, a city's housing stock deteriorates, passing into the hands of successively poorer inhabitants until, finally, it is abandoned as uninhabitable. The deterioration causes mortgage lenders and insurance companies to refuse to do business in such areas, and inner city decline begins to feed upon itself.

Two Alternatives

In a world of more and more people, who are increasingly urbanized, there is no doubt that more land must be consumed for development. But it need not take the form of sprawl.

In the Soviet Union, for example, large cities like Moscow have long planned for the orderly development of their fringe areas. Officials have concentrated new development along existing or extended public transportation lines. They have created new satellite communities specifically related to the metropolitan whole. It has been possible to maintain the inherent cultural, educational, and economic advantages that large agglomerations have over smaller, isolated communities, while at the same time avoiding the problems and cost of sprawl.

In Sweden, the city of Stockholm has practiced some form of metropolitan planning for more than three hundred years. Until about World War II, fringe development was based on the idea that low-density single-family homes should predominate in the city's outer rings. In other words, sprawl was officially endorsed. But the rapid growth of Stockholm after the war caused planners to modify their thinking in the direction of satellite communities built on rail lines extending from the central city. The moderate success of this policy of clustering has recently been threatened by the rapid increase in car ownership in Sweden. However, the long tradition of government planning has enabled the Swedes to hold the costs of sprawl within acceptable limits.

Taming Sprawl

The key to controlling sprawl and its costs is, evidently, increasingly stringent forms of government planning. In many European countries and in Japan, a long tradition of quality public transportation and settlement patterns around rail and other mass transit stations has helped avoid overwhelming dependence on the private car, even in the face of rising personal incomes, thus helping to control sprawl.

Even in the United States, there were signs in the late 1970s that the costs of sprawl were becoming intolerable. Some local building and zoning ordinances were being rewritten to allow various forms of clustering and more efficient land use. Local officials in many U.S. communities raised the planning standard to which builders and developers must adhere. Increasingly, provisions for the costs of sewering, roads, streets, utilities, and other public services, as well as mitigation of environmental damages, were required

"The condominiums are coming! The condominiums are coming!" (*Reproduced by special permission of* PLAYBOY *Magazine; © 1975 by* PLAYBOY.)

in a developer's plans in order to win government approval.

Finally, the tightening screws of a finite world petroleum supply were beginning to make themselves felt in sharply rising gasoline and heating-oil prices. Homes located far from community centers became increasingly difficult to sell. Plans for new shopping centers dependent solely on automobile access were often scrapped in favor of redevelopment of older central cities. Recycling of old buildings became a new form of architecture.

As the cost of nearly everything rose in relentless inflation, people everywhere, and particularly Americans, began to rethink the sprawl life-style based on cheap services, cheap housing, cheap land, and cheap energy.

R.N.

A TAXING PROBLEM

To ensure that those who pollute pay the cost, the advice of many economists has been to create a pollution tax. The tax idea stems from an intriguing notion: that pollution is part of the production system, a by-product of humans and our machines. It issues from the production of things in factories, from transporting ourselves and our goods from place to place, from consuming things and throwing away what we don't want. Technology has enabled us to concentrate these materials, activities, and ourselves so densely that the environment cannot absorb our waste naturally. These are economic activities, and economists have studied them carefully.

Economists recognize that there are real, if rarely measured, costs of pollution. They call them "external costs" because they are outside the accounting system of the polluter. To an economist, the pollution problem is one of getting the polluter to internalize these costs, to recognize them as part of the costs of production. There are really two jobs facing environmental economists. One is to measure the real cost of damage from pollution, including the intangible losses that don't have price tags, like lost beauty and lost enjoyment of nature. The other job is to apply those measured costs to the polluter in a fair way.

But measuring the costs is tricky. And assuming that it would be possible to put a dollar value on pollution damage, how could it be translated into active policies? At this point, most economists part company with most environmentalists. Consider this example.

The Cost-Benefit Equation

If we have figured out that every pound of sulfur dioxide expelled from an industrial smokestack causes $10,000 worth of damage, then the pollution tax on sulfur dioxide should be $10,000 per pound ($22,000 per kilogram). Suppose it cost only $10 to cut emissions by one pound ($22 per kilogram)? The polluter would gladly spend that $10 to avoid $10,000 of tax.

But we know that it gets harder and harder to remove more pollution from the emissions. Suppose that, after the polluter has cut 1,000 pounds (453 kilograms) of sulfur dioxide emissions, he or she finds that to do any better would mean installation of a much more expensive scrubber sys-

Workers stroll by part of the pollution reduction equipment installed at a Union Carbide ferro-alloy plant in West Virginia. The equipment cost $45 million and reduced emissions by 97.7 percent. Eliminating the remaining emissions could be prohibitively expensive. (*EPA Documerica/Harry Schaefer*)

tem. The polluter finds that to remove any more sulfur dioxide would cost $20,000 a pound ($44,000 per kilogram). So no more pollution-control equipment is installed. What has society gained? The polluter removed 1,000 pounds of sulfur dioxide from the air, and on the remaining pollution he's paying $10,000 per pound to the government. The economist is completely satisfied, noting that the price of the factory's product has gone up because of the cost of the pollution tax. "That's fair," says the economist, "people who want that product should pay a price that reflects the true cost of making it."

There is still a lot of sulfur dioxide coming out of the factory, but the economist figures that problem is offset by the good things the government is doing with the money it collects on the pollution tax. If there is too much environmental damage being done by the remaining pollution, the economist advises raising the tax. Trial and error will set the tax at the right rate.

A License to Pollute

Most environmentalists recoil in horror at the pollution tax, because the polluter has the option of paying the tax and continuing to pollute. In the air pollution example, the industrialist made a simple calculation subtracting the benefits of tax avoidance from the cost of installing pollution-control equipment. When the cost outweighed the benefits, the industrialist quit trying to cut pollution and forked over the tax. That left some sulfur dioxide still coming out of the plant. Many environmentalists call that situation "a license to pollute," and so they oppose pollution-tax proposals.

In most industrial countries, environmental lobbies have been winning the battle against the pollution tax and their governments have instead imposed discharge limits. Regulations prescribe the amount of polluting substances that each factory or car or power plant can emit. The limits are usually based on the maximum feasible elimination of pollution. To most economists, these stern limits make little sense, because they ignore the cost-benefit calculation. They say discharge regulations amount to an infinite tax on pollution, since a plant would have to pay any price for control equipment to meet the government limit, even if the equipment cost far more than the losses anyone would suffer if the pollution were allowed to continue. Yet, in many cases, toxic effects of pollution are too dangerous or too delayed, widespread, or unknown simply to use the tax approach.

The Biological Calculations

The argument that pollution controls cost too much for the good they do is fueling an environmental backlash movement, particularly in the United States. Some of the debate is already taking the form of competing calculations of costs and benefits, with environmentalists offering high estimates of pollution damage and low estimates of control costs and their opponents doing the reverse. Some observers see environmentalists losing ground as fewer people are willing to pay any price at all in lost jobs and inflated prices for a clean environment.

Unfortunately, a purely economic calculation of costs ignores one of the biggest pollution problems. Far too often, it's impossible to put the genie back in the bottle. Once released into the atmosphere, sulfur dioxide can't be removed. Once released into a river, polychlorinated biphenyls (PCBs) and many other pollutants inexorably make their way up the food chain, doing irreparable harm all the way. And some effects of pollution are cumulative, so that low-level doses over many years do an unforeseen amount of harm. Environmentalists rightfully distrust the ability of economists and engineers to measure the true costs of pollution over many years.

The Tax That Works

Can the environmentalists and the economists get together on a policy that protects air and water efficiently? There is at least one encouraging example, where the benefits of a tax and the controls of discharge limits have been combined. On the Ruhr River, where 40 percent of West German industry is located, a pollution-tax system has been working for forty years. The volume of waste from coal, iron, steel, and chemical plants often is greater than the natural flow of the river itself in the dry season. But the river is clean enough for people and fish to swim in it.

The Genossenschaften, a system of regional water-quality-control authorities, uses a pollution-tax system to enforce a clean-water standard. If pollution is too heavy to keep the water clean, the authorities raise the tax. They don't try to measure pollution's economic cost to society, they just measure the cleanliness of the water and the health of the fish. But they use the pollution tax as an efficient way to get the message across to polluters. It's more efficient than discharge limits because the authorities don't have to tell industries what methods they should use to clean up their waste. They set a price for pollution and let the industries come up with their own answers. At one point on the river, the cheapest waste-control measure might be for each factory to treat its own effluent. At another spot, the most efficient solution might be for several plants to share the expense of building a common treatment station. The pollution-control authorities are only interested in results.

Used this way, the pollution tax does not provide a license to pollute, because the authorities set a social goal of clean water instead of an economic goal of offsetting financial loss.

T.G.D.

THE HIDDEN COSTS OF A NUCLEAR ACCIDENT

How much would a nuclear accident cost? Too much, as far as U.S. casualty insurance companies are concerned. Faced with official estimates that placed the cost of even a minor nuclear plant accident well up in the millions, and inflation that sees costs increasing with the speed of a free-falling body, American insurance companies decided during the early part of the 1970s that there was no money to be made in insuring nuclear plants—and a lot to be lost. While the probability of an accident was statistically small, the costs of even a small mishap could send an insurance firm down the road to receivership.

Faced with the insurance industry's refusal to cover the costs of nuclear accidents, and recognizing that the U.S. public would be reluctant to accept an uninsured nuclear industry, Congress moved into the gap. In 1975, it enacted the Price-Anderson bill, committing the government to insure against nuclear accidents.

But only up to a point. The bill set a limit of $560 million on the amount the government would pay to the public in the event of a nuclear plant accident.

TMI: The Trial Balance

Is this enough? It might have been in 1975, when an accident occurred (before the passage of the legislation) at the Tennessee Valley Authority's nuclear power plant at Brown's Ferry, Alabama. But it is not nearly enough today, according to studies and investigations following the March 1979 accident at Pennsylvania's Three Mile Island (TMI), which released radiation over a six-county area and where the entire reactor almost melted down.

The costs of the accident, which began on the morning of March 28 (see "Meltdown, Near Meltdown . . . ," page 451), were catastrophic, even if the event itself was not. According to an independent survey conducted for the Nuclear Regulatory Commission (NRC) by Mountain West Research, Inc., the accident drove no fewer than 144,000 people who lived within 15 miles (24 kilometers) of the reactor from their homes. Some fled as far as Oklahoma and California, though the average distance traveled was only 100 miles (160 kilometers). Most stayed away from the area for five days, though a few returned earlier, and a few others decided to move from the area permanently.

The confusing and conflicting reports over the amount of radiation being released by the crippled plant did nothing to help public confidence. Nor were people encouraged to stay by reports that a hydrogen bubble had formed within the overheated reactor. Finally, says the study, the fear that the governor would order an evacuation led many people to "beat the rush" and get out on their own. The study concluded that even more people might have fled, but some stayed because they feared losing their jobs.

The Incredible Expense Account

The flight proved costly. About 19,000 of the evacuees lost wages or commissions as a result of their departure. All incurred out-of-pocket expenses, whether they stayed at hotels or motels or found shelter with friends or relatives. On the average, the study found, these expenses ran to $100 per household. But combined with other losses, they added up. According to Mountain West Research, the Three Mile Island accident cost those who fled a total of $18.2 million in lost wages and special expenses.

These, however, were not the only costs generated by the accident. The plant will eventually be cleaned up, at tremendous expense—and if the utility follows the lead of others, excess costs like this will be passed on to the energy-buying public. Soon after the mishap, officials of General Public Utilities (GPU), the owner of the company that managed TMI, estimated damages to the reactor and the rest of the plant at $140 million. A short time later, GPU upped this figure to $285 million.

A later study, though, showed that even this last figure was unrealistic. The Bechtel Corporation, one of the world's largest engineering firms (see "A Global Company: Bechtel," page 480), studied the situation at the plant and came up with a new figure for getting Three Mile Island cleaned up and back on line. The cost: close to $500 million. According to Bechtel, the cost for the cleanup, including $85 million to replace the damaged reactor core, would come to $405 million in 1979 dollars. GPU promptly added another $25 million to this estimate to cover "possible uncertainties."

What the Taxpayers Pay

But even these figures do not represent the total dollar cost of the accident. As of mid-1980 the Nuclear Regulatory Commission had not released an estimate of its own costs for the personnel and equipment that it sent to Pennsylvania to cope with the accident, but acknowledged that it did have nearly one hundred officials and technicians, not to mention mobile offices and laboratories, on the scene for periods of up to four weeks following the first morning of the crisis. Nor had the government of Pennsylvania come up with a figure for its own costs, for activating its civil defense organization and planning an evacuation, or for dealing with other aspects of the accident.

But government agencies have come up with some estimates of the costs of investigating the accident. According to federal figures, separate U.S. government studies—by a presidential commission, by a congressional committee, and by the NRC itself—cost in excess of $10 million, a figure that includes $96,000 spent by the presidential panel to construct a mockup of the TMI control room. A separate study by the Commonwealth of Pennsylvania cost another $1.5 million.

The costs are likely to climb further, too. A few months after the accident, sixty-eight of TMI's neighbors—among them homeowners, renters, small businesses, and several individuals including at least one pregnant woman, plus fourteen Pennsylvania and New York law firms—brought a class-action suit against GPU on behalf of everyone living within 25 miles (40 kilometers) of the plant. The largest class-action suit ever filed, it charged the company with "negligence or willful misconduct" and sought establishment of a fund to monitor the health of the people in the area for twenty-five years, as well as compensation for out-of-pocket losses and mental anguish resulting from the accident and its aftermath. Those pressing the suit said that they would seek compensation right up to the $560-million limit imposed by law.

Whatever the outcome of various lawsuits, the true costs of the accident will remain untallied, since assessing the hidden expenses from TMI is virtually impossible. Part of the payment is psychological. According to the study conducted for the NRC, fully 22 percent of those responding said that some member of their family had suffered extreme emotional upset during the two-week emergency period. Other studies show an enormous increase in anxiety levels among schoolchildren and others living within 40 miles of TMI, and local psychiatrists reported an increase in psychological problems among those living closest to the plant. P.S.

NO FREE LUNCHES

Editor's Note: *A few years ago ecologist Dr. Barry Commoner spoke to an audience of engineers in St. Louis, Missouri. His theme was the hidden costs of interfering with natural systems. The following is an excerpt from Commoner's speech, as it was reprinted in* Western Electric Magazine.

There is a story economists like to tell. It seems there was a rich sheikh who wanted to figure out what to do with all his money, so he summoned his advisers and told them to produce a set of volumes with all the world's wisdom of economics, or they'd lose their heads. They came back in a year with the volumes and he said, "I can't read all that." And he sent them away and gave them six months to produce one volume. This also proved too much to read, and the process went on and on, until finally he said he wanted all the world's wisdom of economics in one sentence, or they'd lose their heads. So they came back and said to him, "Oh, Sheikh, THERE IS NO SUCH THING AS A FREE LUNCH."

That is a pretty good law of economics, and it is a pretty good law of ecology.

You cannot get away with an intrusion into the ecological system because it's a closed cycle and anything you do to it from the outside is bound to distort it. If you put mercury in, it's going to cause trouble. Or PCBs or DDT. And it's going to cost. That's what's meant when people say that environmental pollution represents a debt to nature.

Let me get to the point of what has happened in this country. We have changed the character of the environment and we have effected most of this change since World War II. Most of our pollution problem didn't exist before then. The first automotive smog was discovered in Los Angeles in 1942. Before 1942 there was no extra phosphate in the water. There was no nylon, no DDT, and relatively little human-contributed mercury in the environment.

In World War II there was a technological revolution and engineers were deeply involved in it. There has been a fantastic transformation of the way in which we do our productive business, not only in industry but also in agriculture.

Some consequences? Look at phosphates. Between 1910 and 1940 the phosphate levels in surface waters doubled due to increased sewage. Between 1940 and 1970 it went up sevenfold. Nitrates: until 1960 there were no changes in levels in Illinois rivers. Between 1960 and the present time, nitrate levels in most Illinois rivers have gone up tenfold.

What factors are involved in these changes since World War II? Some people say it's because there are too many of us and people are the polluters. Well, the population has gone up only 50 percent or less in that time, so that can't account for it. And it's not because of our affluence and our ability to buy more pollutants, because the GNP hasn't gone up that much. The crucial factor is the way in which we produce our goods. For phosphates, the way in which we wash.

In 1946, we produced cleanliness with soap, a natural material that is attacked by bacteria. No bacteria attack detergents, and the extra phosphate all comes from detergents.

From 1946 to the present, detergents took over roughly 80 percent of the soap market. If you were cleanser manufacturers you'd all be sitting here proud and happy, getting awards for cutting costs and introducing new products.

But to what end did we develop detergents? Are we all cleaner than we were? I don't think so, so the social value is about the same. We simply clean differently, using an unnatural material. So here is a technological transformation that was a mistake.

Before the war there was no smog for a very simple reason: auto engines were low compression, they operated at low temperature, and the air taken into the cylinder did not undergo the chemical reaction that produces nitrogen oxide. Now the compression ratio has gone up, engines run hot, nitrogen oxide comes out of the exhaust, is hit by sunlight and turned into a reactive material that combines with waste fuel, and you have smog. (See "Why Your Car Pollutes," page 626.)

What the Detroit engineers did was to produce, among other things, the smog generator.

I don't know of a single instance, during the technological revolution, of an engineering design including an environmental specification as to the impact of the new development on the environment. And it would have been a miracle if, when every engineer sat down to produce a new product, cut costs, and improve convenience—with those criteria to guide him or her—if the engineer were to achieve something which was not only what management wanted, but also fit into the laws of ecology that nobody had bothered to teach. Well, the miracle didn't happen and the result was that a productive technology took a counter-ecological direction. There's no such thing as a free lunch.

Now, how do you answer people who say that all our environmental problems are technology's fault and there's no way out of them? Let me assure you I don't think the answer is in getting rid of technology. I do think we have to redesign technology. A technology that is beautifully—perfectly—based on the laws of physics and the laws of chemistry also has to conform to the laws of ecology. Otherwise, what it does won't fit into the environment, and it's the environment that supports it.

What does redesign mean? For one thing, it means we should get away from non-natural or synthetic materials. (See "Oil Day Long," page 651.) For example, we should not burn up our petroleum—and pollute the air—to make nylon clothes when we can make clothes from cotton which is congealed solar energy. And why should we have synthetic rubber when a rubber tree in Malaysia will do the job perfectly well? The natural rubber supply could fill the demand.

An ecology-minded engineer would consider these facts, too: aluminum consumes a good deal more energy in its manufacture than does steel. Trucks burn six times as much fuel to carry a ton a mile (1.6 kilometers) as do railroads.

I believe we have moved in counter-ecological directions, not because it was ordained by technology but because it served some immediate economic purpose. We've achieved a short-term gain but produced a long-term debt. And that debt has to be paid. And the main way we're going to pay it is by reconstructing our technology.

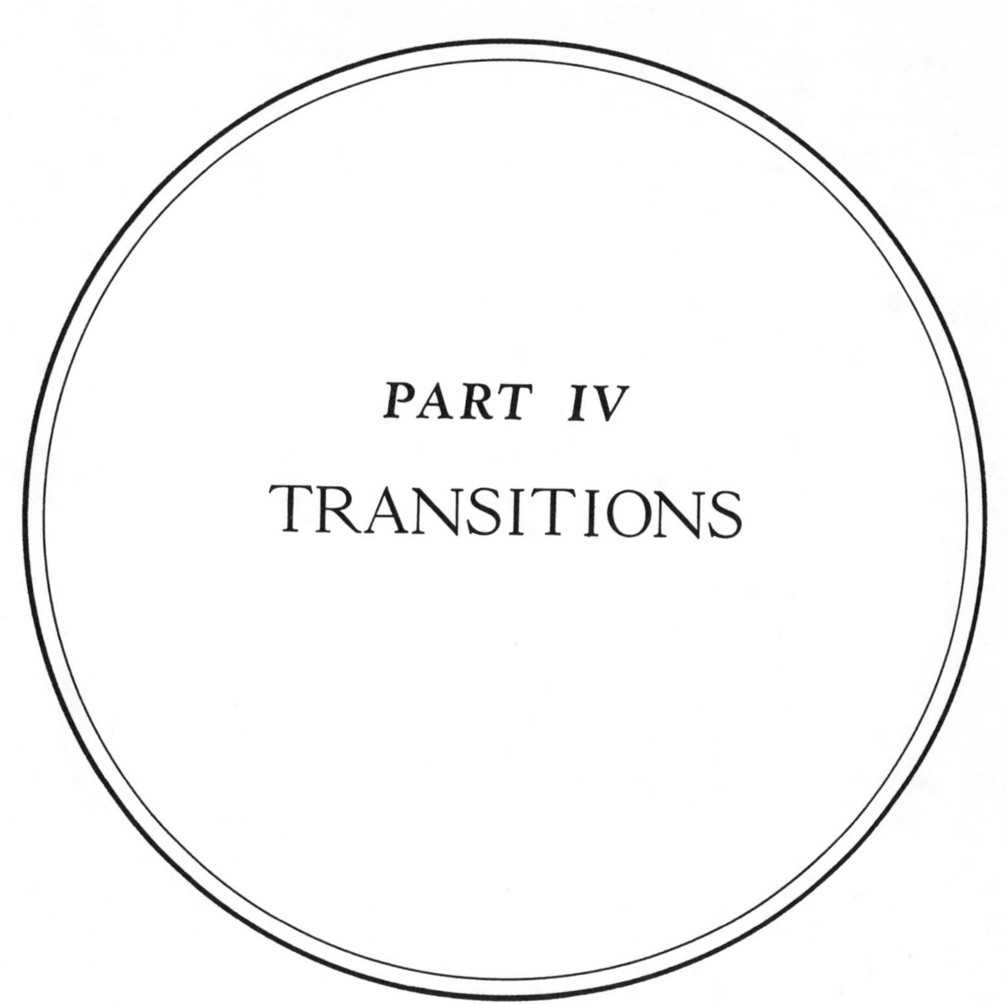

PART IV
TRANSITIONS

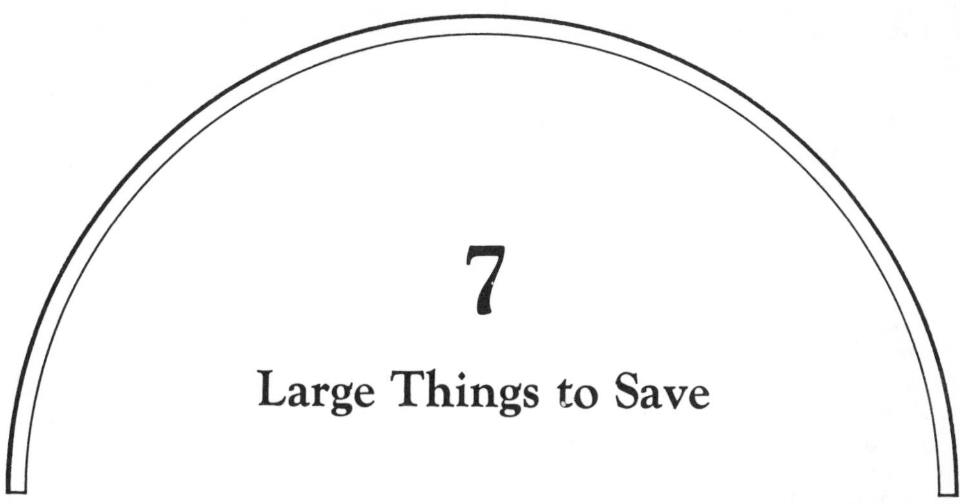

7
Large Things to Save

Flying at the speed of sound we gain a perspective unique to our species. The human scale of life is temporarily suspended. Time is compressed, spatial perception is inflated. In a morning we can glide over centuries' worth of arduous exploration and settlement along the ground. We can see great swaths of territory, a sight beyond the imagination of our ancestors, who pressed inexorably along the surface toward their horizons at a speed measured in generations, across Asia, across the Middle East, across Europe, across the Atlantic, across North America. Unable to see very far or very widely, they recognized only the local impact of their endeavors. From 39,000 feet (9,000 kilometers) in the air, however, we can survey the human imprint broadly —the shorn forests, the piecework quilt of croplands, the constellations of cities marked by smudgy air, the thin but ever-present lace of roadways. The impression one gets from an airplane above an industrialized nation is that the domestication of the entire surface of the planet seems certain eventually, as the slow push continues, as human populations multiply, as technology accelerates development.

The credo of the chapter that follows is this: No matter how thoroughly humanity is capable of altering nature, there are some things that should be saved, whatever the cost. Our collection of priceless assets is an arbitrary one. The list is made up of subjects largely beyond our human scale because of their size, beyond our acquaintance because of their remoteness, or beyond our immediate concern because of their antiquity. While they are threatened to varying degrees, they share a common trait: each belongs to the whole world. The ozone layer is a planetary cloak, the Antarctic continent and its swarming fringe of ocean life belong to no one and to everyone. There are invaluable forms of life on the list, too, which represent extremes of beauty, size, intelligence, or dignity. The demise of these species—to the extent it is human-caused —will impoverish the world to come.

The vastness of Alaska, the Serengeti, or the Amazon could first be grasped with the invention of the airplane, which lofted humanity above the tree lines, above the barrier of mountains to gaze back upon the large things of which humans were a small, if potent, part. Photographs from space expanded the vista to include the entire planet. Today a more subtle kind of revolutionary insight is spreading, as the hidden global network of environmental linkages becomes perceivable through the work of science. We are suddenly aware of the vulnerability of even the largest and oldest elements of life and civilization under the sweep of humanity.

The rise of ecological savvy has enabled our generation, for the first time, to comprehend the biological importance of life beyond our restricted personal range, beyond our scale. So enlightened, we become responsible for initiating movements that will preserve vast if invisible balances and visible if remote beauty. This chapter provides information on some distant places and strains of life that are of inestimable value, that warrant tending as much as the smaller particulars of the local environment that touch our lives more visibly every day.

M.R.

AMAZONIA

Amazonia, the world's largest and one of its oldest rain forests, is facing perilous development pressures. At least a million trees are felled every twenty-four hours, and over one tenth of the forest has already disappeared. A 1975 satellite photograph indicated 62,000 square miles (161,000 square kilometers) of forest had been leveled in a single year. At that rate of deforestation, the Amazon rain forest could virtually disappear by the year 2000.

The Amazon basin, or Amazonia, as it is known to the Brazilians, is drained by the world's largest river and covers 2 million square miles (5.2 million square kilometers) of Brazil and 700,000 total square miles (1.8 million square kilometers) in Bolivia, Peru, Ecuador, Colombia, Venezuela, Guyana, and Surinam. Slightly larger than Australia and more than half the size of Europe, Amazonia contains one third of the world's forest, two thirds of all the river water in the world, and produces one half of all the oxygen generated by land plants in the world.

Amazonia's biological wealth also evokes an unending stream of superlatives. It is a classic jungle with huge trees, liana vines and mosses trailing from their branches, orchids and other flowers of stunning brilliance, a greater variety of mammals with grasping tails (monkeys mostly) than anywhere else in the world, spiders so large they catch birds, catfish so large they have eaten children, butterflies with four-inch wing spans. Amazonia is an untapped well of biologic and ecologic knowledge—one of the few places on earth where new species are still being discovered. Three hundred thousand species of plants have been classified in the world; yet there are probably 80,000 species still unclassified in the Amazonian forest.

Amazon River from space. (*NASA*)

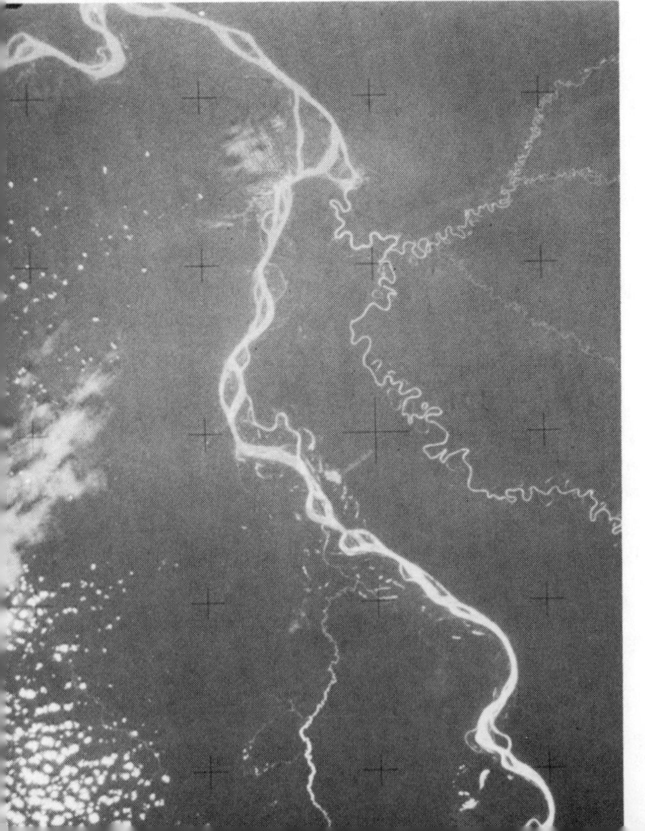

The Living Warehouse

Such amazing diversity is the result of 100 million years of environmental stability. There are only two seasons here, dry and wet. Between 60 and 100 inches (150 to 250 centimeters) of rain fall a year. Because life is difficult on the forest floor, large predators were never dominant. Instead, smaller and lighter animals prospered and evolved in the trees. The result is a fantastically rich gene pool, the major reservoir from which many species were able to recolonize the world after the Ice Ages. Of the roughly three million to ten million species of life now believed to exist on earth, 50 to 70 percent have come from the tropics.

Besides offering extraordinary beauty and the chance to learn how animals, plants, and people evolved, Amazonia could also prove a source of vital new products such as drugs, resins, fibers, spices, and food. Yet, as huge fires are set to clear away the forest for new roads, for pasture and crop land, for mining operations and factories, hopes of understanding and appreciating this wilderness go up in smoke forever.

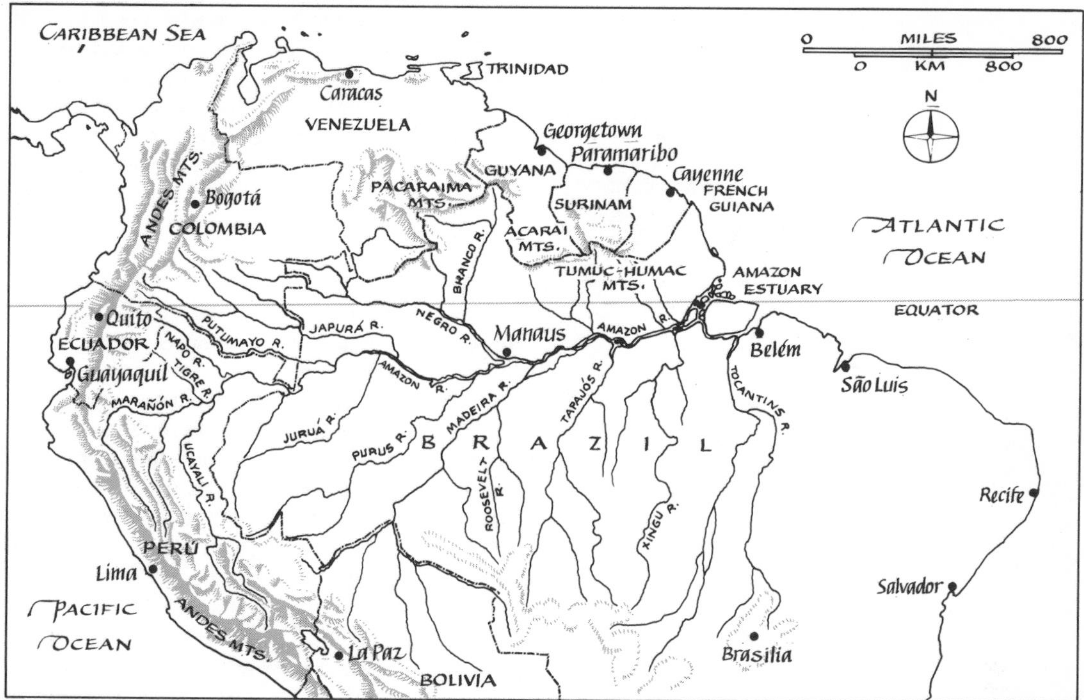

For most of its history, the Amazon remained a mystery, too inhospitable for any but a few hardy settlers and tribes of native Indians. At one time numbering about 270, these tribes were the first successfully to cultivate in the jungle maze. For thousands of years they cut and burned small areas so that the rich ash, mixed with rain, might soak the soil with nutrients. When crop yields fell, they simply moved and repeated the process elsewhere. Meanwhile, the farmed plot was left to return to jungle. Life was, if not easy, at least undisturbed.

The Selling of the Jungle

But after World War II, Brazil began a push intended to take it into the international economic mainstream. Amazonia, with its huge reserves of natural resources, would be a ladder to that position of power. Only one thing stood in the way of Brazil realizing her dreams of exploitation—the forest.

So programs were begun to induce thousands of poor farmers away from the south and northeast and into Amazonia. In most cases, they used a modern version of the traditional "slash-and-burn" technique to clear away the forest cover. Tax incentives, incredibly low land prices, and other favors were used to entice large agribusiness corporations and cattle ranchers into

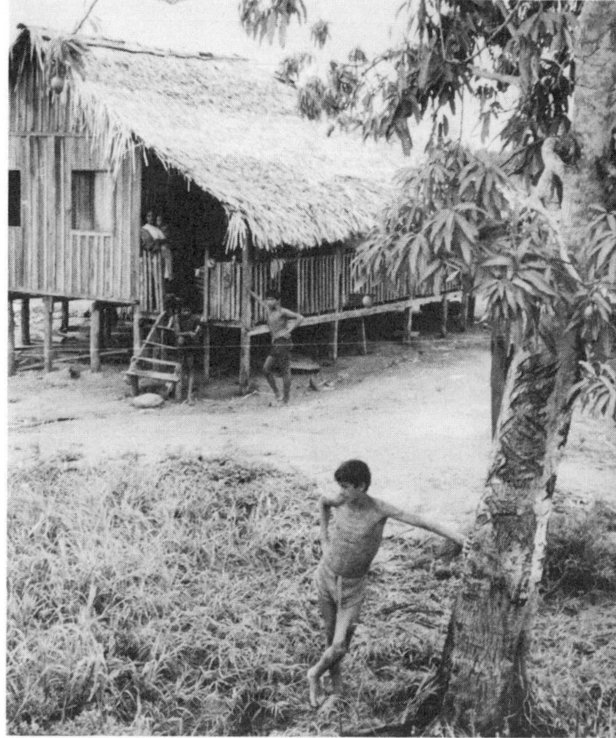

Pioneers on the Brazilian frontier. This family of *caboclos,* people of mixed blood, are settlers, encouraged by the Brazilian government to clear and cultivate the tropical forest in the state of Amazonas. (*FAO/Peyton Johnson*)

This road runs about 125 miles (200 kilometers) from Manaus on the Amazon to the jungle of the interior. It is one of many new roads meant to open Amazonia to development. (*FAO/Peyton Johnson*)

Amazonia. They, in turn, exaggerated the slash-and-burn technique. Tractors rolled through the jungle with massive, hundred-meter chains stretched between them. Every bit of living vegetation could be ripped out. Huge fires were set, so large they were perceptible in satellite photos. Finally, the fields were sown by planes.

Meanwhile, the building of miles of roads began in the middle of the jungle and along its perimeter. The largest, the Trans-Amazonia, would stretch 3,500 miles (5,600 kilometers). Large mining projects were begun throughout Amazonia. Oil was drilled in Bolivia, Ecuador, and Peru. Coal was mined in Colombia, iron ore and bauxite in Guyana, Venezuela, and Brazil. Timber mills, largely owned by Japanese and Western companies, began operating in the middle of the jungle.

The Fragile Giant

But there was one thing the planners, developers, and even scientists at first failed to realize. A tropical rain forest, one of the most fragile ecosystems in nature, lacks the thick, rich topsoil that characterizes most temperate forests. Only by constantly recycling its nutrients (75 to 90 percent of which are not in the soil but in the vegetation itself) can the forest survive. Fortunately, consistently high temperature and humidity promote a high rate of decomposition and regrowth. Dead vegetation falls to the forest floor, where its minerals are quickly taken up by the shallow, spreading root systems of the living vegetation. Only through thousands of years of recycling of nutrients has the thin soil supported the progress from scrub, to grasses, to the complex jungle of today.

The forest canopy prevents the heavy rains from eroding precious soil. But when the forest cover is burned or felled, rainfall leaches away the forest's supply of minerals within a few years, and fertility disappears. Moreover, when much of the Amazon's soil is exposed to the sun, it quickly develops into a hard-packed crust known as laterite. Not only is lateritic soil useless for farming, its inability to absorb moisture promotes the loss of valuable water and heightens erosion. Experiments show that a 2.5-acre (1-hectare) tract of forested land may lose 3 pounds (1.4 kilograms) of soil per year through erosion. Once cleared, the same area may lose 34 tons (30.8 metric tons) of soil a year.

The population of Indians had been small enough to allow the slash-and-burn technique to be used and sustained for thousands of years. But the high population of new immigrants, the efficiency of huge agribusiness corporations, and the demand for grazing land and forest products is now overwhelming the forest's capacity to recover. As millions of acres of forest are burned and cleared away, a vast wasteland is being created, incapable of supporting anything but junk vegetation.

Connections of the Amazon

Deforestation destroys wildlife breeding, resting, foraging, and hunting areas and even disturbs migration routes. It affects the entire ecologic balance within the forest and beyond. Farmers in the midwestern United States must contend with larger insect populations because the birds that used to prey upon them in summer lost their resting sites in the Amazon forest. As these sites were destroyed, the birds died off.

Oil drilling in the forest has created oil slicks on the Amazon River. Not only does this oil seep into the land, it is being washed into the Atlantic. Moreover, industrial waste dumped into the river

An aerial view of the Amazon River as it winds its way through the state of Pará, Brazil, toward the sea. The islands shown here are quite small by Amazon standards. The island of Marajó, near the coast, is bigger than Belgium. (*FAO/Peyton Johnson*)

is spreading out over the flood plain of the basin. Erosion is causing the smaller Amazon tributaries to choke with silt.

Many major food fishes of the Amazon drainage feed primarily on fruits and seeds that fall from the trees during high water. The loss of the forest will ultimately starve off this major source of protein of the Amazon people. And nutrients from the river not only fertilize the Amazon estuary, they also enrich Caribbean waters and ultimately the fishing banks of New England and even the North Sea. Their loss will be reflected in less healthy fish populations and decreased catches.

There is also concern that destruction of the forest will change local climates. Tropical rain forests influence both the balance of carbon dioxide in the atmosphere and the amount of heat reflected from the earth's surface. Evidence in localized areas already suggests that the removal of forest cover has resulted in changes in rainfall—in northeast Brazil, an area that was once rain forest is now a drought-ridden wasteland. One Brazilian study concluded that 50 percent of the rain in the Amazon basin is generated by water evaporating from the forest itself. If the forest is cleared and the rainfall reduced, the entire ecologic balance of the basin would be affected.

Nevertheless . . .

In spite of these findings, the push toward developing Amazonia continues. Recent radar mapping surveys found only about 2 percent of Amazonia's soil fertile enough to support agriculture. Regardless, the pressure for new farmland pushes more settlers farther into the jungle. And as world population increases, so will the demand for agricultural land, timber and forest products, and pasture.

Some scientists have said the clearing of the tropical rain forests is one of the most significant physical changes ever worked on the earth's surface by humans. As we lose the trees, the World Wildlife Fund has estimated that we will also lose up to one million animal and plant species.

Agronomists are trying to come up with alternatives to the intensive farming responsible for so much of this damage. Suggestions have been made that by farming the *varzeas,* or flood plains, that are underwater for half the year, a new type of super-rich tropical agriculture might be developed.

In 1977, all eight countries embraced by the Amazon region pledged to cooperate in developing the basin with due attention to environmental preservation and research. But at the beginning of 1979, Brazilian officials announced they are considering a plan whereby Brazilian and multinational timber companies may sign "risk contracts" for the harvesting of wood on a large scale—100 million acres in total. With a staggering foreign debt of $55 billion as of 1980, Brazil needs the revenue it will be paid for this land. Yet scientists warn that if such large tracts of forest are destroyed, another giant step will be taken toward the creation of a wasteland.

L.W.

AMAZON LORE

- In 1541, Spanish explorer Francisco de Orellana ventured up the Amazon, where he encountered fiercely fighting Indians. Surprised to see Indian women fighting alongside men, de Orellana named the river "Amazonas" after the female warriors of Greek mythology.
- Stretching about 4,000 miles (6,437 kilometers) from its headwaters in the Andes to its mouth at the Atlantic, the Amazon is the widest and second-longest river (after the River Nile) in the world. It has more than a thousand tributaries, several of them more than 1,000 miles (1,600 kilometers) long.
- There are more species of fish in the Amazon Basin than in any other river system on earth, or even in the Atlantic Ocean. More than two thousand species have been classified, but there may be twice that many. Of those classified, five hundred are species of catfish, one of which is able to walk across the ground on its fins.
- There are about forty species of electric eels in the Amazon, some with an ability to generate 800 volts.
- One species of Amazon-dwelling top-minnow has two sets of eyes—one pair for seeing above the water, and one pair for below.
- The largest freshwater fish in the world, the Pirarucú, is an Amazon fish. Reaching 10 feet (3 meters) in length and weighing about 250 pounds (113 kilograms), the Pirarucú is a staple of many Amazon Indian tribes, who use its tough scales as sandpaper and nail files and draw medicines from chemicals in its tongue, as well as obtaining millions of pounds of food from it each year.

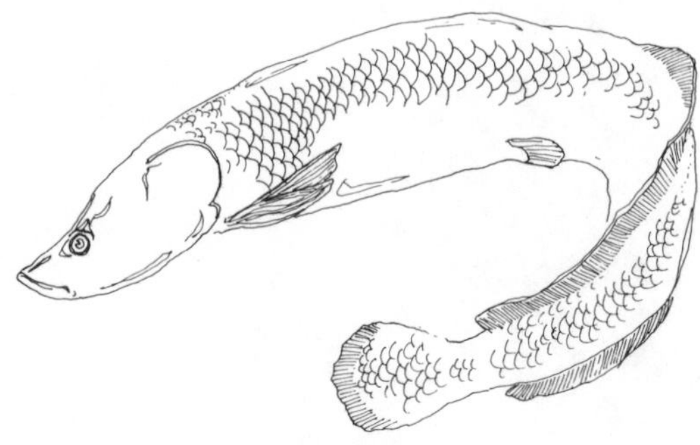

Pirarucú

- Among the mammals that live in or along the Amazon, the largest is the manatee, known locally as the *peixe-boi.* Several tons in weight, this herbivore has been overhunted because of its tasty meat and is considered endangered. (See "Manatees and Dugongs," page 305.)
- Another endangered Amazon mammal is the Brazilian river otter, a strong swimming carnivore that often reaches lengths of 8 feet (2.5 meters). Because its pelts bring hunters more than $100 each, it is "one of the ten rarest animals on earth," according to *Audubon* Magazine.
- The Amazon is also home to freshwater porpoises, a pink species, the *boto,* and a gray species, the *tucuxi.*
- Of more than forty species of New World monkeys, thirty live exclusively in the trees of the Amazon rain forest, mostly in Brazil. They include: the howler monkey, at 20 pounds (9 kilograms) the largest Amazon monkey, whose fierce screams can be heard for more than a mile (it is, ironically, a peaceful vegetarian); the red uakari monkey, whose face is bright red; the bald uakari, whose forehead is hairless and whose pink face turns purple when the monkey is excited; and the pygmy marmoset, the world's smallest monkey and a pet of Amazon Indians, who use the sparrow-sized monkey to pick lice from their hair.

- Amazonian three-toed and two-toed sloths spend their entire lives in the rain-forest trees, eating, sleeping, and even giving birth while hanging upside down. In fact, the three-toed sloth may spend all of its approximately twelve years in and around just one tree.
- The largest rodent in the world, the capybara, lives along the banks of the Amazon. About 4 feet long (1.2 meters) and 150 pounds (68 kilograms), this giant rat is an accomplished swimmer able to remain underwater for several minutes.

Capybara

- There are about one hundred different species of bats in Amazonia, representing a greater variety than any other family of mammals in the vast region.
- There are also more species of butterflies in Amazonia than any other place on earth. Peru alone has about four thousand butterfly and twenty thousand moth species. Brazil boasts a "fragrant butterfly," which has both the color and sweet scent of chocolate.
- Nearly half of the world's total number of bird species are found in Amazonia—more than four thousand. Of these, more than three hundred are hummingbird species. The largest of the world's parrrot species, the macaw, sometimes reaches 40 inches (108 centimeters) in length in the Amazon, but its numbers are dwindling as a result of the pet bird trade.
- The diversity and abundance of Amazonia's tree species is unparalleled. Between 100 and 250 different species of trees can be found in a typical 5-acre (2-hectare) plot. An area of comparable size in a temperate forest would yield only about ten species.
- In the humid Amazon, fungi and other "decomposers" are able to break plant matter down so quickly that its nutrients enter the roots of living plants in only about six weeks. In temperate woodlands this process takes about one year, in northern forests, about seven years.
- The density of the rain forest, however, admits only about 5 percent of the available sunlight to the forest floor. As a result most Amazonian flowers are arboreal. They grow atop trees, usually sprouting from the ubiquitous liana vines that grow up from the ground, sometimes reaching 700 feet (214 meters) in length. On the river itself, giant cup-shaped water lilies sometimes reach 9 feet (2.7 meters) in diameter. The heavy rains would sink them except for one clever trick of nature: the lilies are dotted with tiny notches that allow rainwater to drain through the immense floating disks. C.S.D.

ANTARCTICA

It is one of the last wild places, lying like a slumbering giant, a continent the size of the United States and Mexico combined in the middle of 12 million miles (31 million kilometers) of surrounding polar sea ice. Antarctica. The bottom of the world. Its environment is the most uninviting on earth; *average* temperatures during the coldest month in the interior hover around −95° F (−71° C) and winds sometimes exceed 200 miles (320 kilometers) per hour. Nearly the entire land mass is covered by a mile-thick (1.6-kilometer) sheet of ice, and great mountain ranges thrust above the icy plateaus to heights of almost 17,000 feet (5,185 meters). For millions upon millions of years, Antarctica lay undisturbed while the unique and prolific life that perches on its icy edges and swarms in its frigid waters slowly evolved.

Inevitably, however, humans would come here. In earlier centuries the region was approached only by the hardiest explorers probing the vast reaches of the Southern Ocean. Captain James Cook of England, in his voyage of 1772–75, attempted to penetrate the ring of pack ice but failed. He saw no land. By 1820, both an

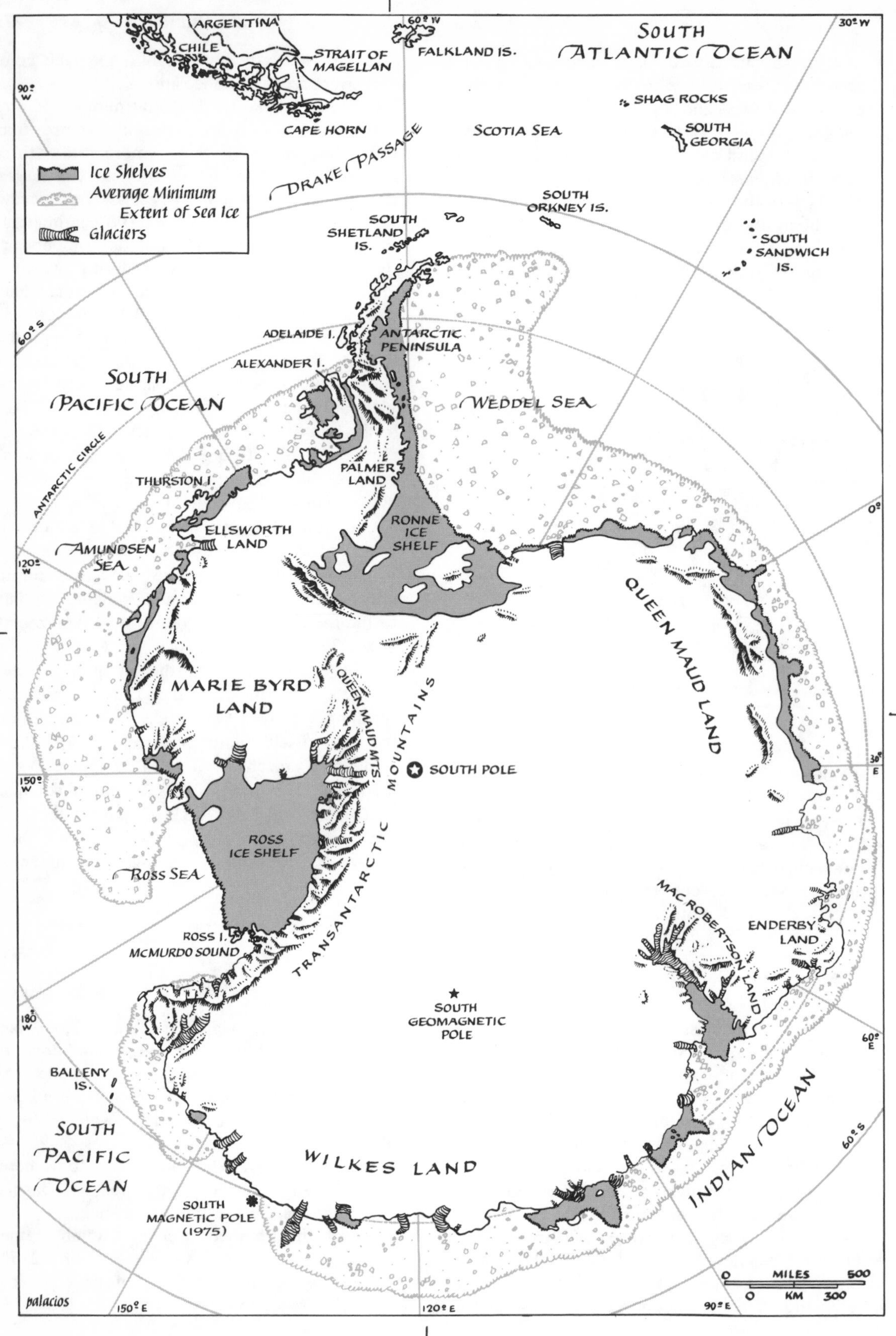

ARGENTINA
CHILE
STRAIT OF MAGELLAN
60° W
FALKLAND IS.
SOUTH ATLANTIC OCEAN
30° W
90° W
SHAG ROCKS
CAPE HORN
SCOTIA SEA
SOUTH GEORGIA
DRAKE PASSAGE
Ice Shelves
Average Minimum Extent of Sea Ice
Glaciers
SOUTH ORKNEY IS.
SOUTH SHETLAND IS.
SOUTH SANDWICH IS.
60° S
ADELAIDE I.
ANTARCTIC PENINSULA
ALEXANDER I.
SOUTH PACIFIC OCEAN
WEDDEL SEA
ANTARCTIC CIRCLE
PALMER LAND
THURSTON I.
RONNE ICE SHELF
0°
ELLSWORTH LAND
AMUNDSEN SEA
120° W
QUEEN MAUD LAND
MARIE BYRD LAND
QUEEN MAUD MTS.
TRANSANTARCTIC MOUNTAINS
SOUTH POLE
30° E
150° W
ROSS ICE SHELF
ROSS SEA
MAC ROBERTSON LAND
ENDERBY LAND
ROSS I.
MCMURDO SOUND
SOUTH GEOMAGNETIC POLE
180° W
60° E
BALLENY IS.
INDIAN OCEAN
SOUTH PACIFIC OCEAN
60° S
WILKES LAND
SOUTH MAGNETIC POLE (1975)
0 MILES 500
0 KM 300
palacios
150° E
120° E
90° E

American sealer, Nathaniel Palmer, and a British explorer, Edward Bransfield, were charting islands just off the Antarctic Peninsula, while the Russian Fabian Gottlieb von Bellingshausen circumnavigated the continent. Another American sealer, Captain John Davis, was apparently the first person ever to set foot on the land of the Antarctic Peninsula on February 7, 1821. Others followed: Lt. Charles Wilkes of the U. S. Navy, 1838–42; Capt. James Ross of England, 1839–43; the Belgian Lt. Adrien de Gerlache in 1898; and many more. Roald Amundsen of Norway reached the South Pole in 1911, followed promptly by British Capt. Robert F. Scott who, on returning, perished with four companions in a blizzard on the Ross Ice Shelf. The airborne exploits of Adm. Richard E. Byrd from the United States came a few decades later.

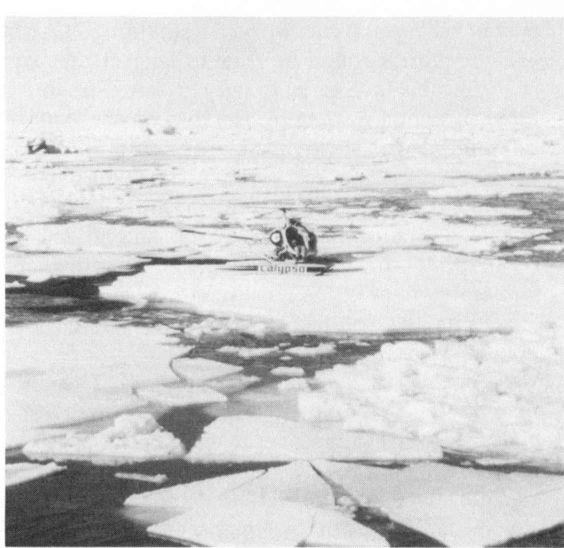

Calypso's helicopter lands on one of thousands of shifting ice floes that surround Antarctica. (*The Cousteau Society*)

The Immense Freezer

Major scientific investigations, such as those of the British research vessel *Discovery,* took place during the first half of this century and in recent decades have intensified to include the work of more than a dozen nations, both in the sea and on the land. Thus, the signs of human activity accumulate. Evidence of early visitors may survive a long time in the Antarctic: Sir Ernest Shackleton's base camp at Cape Royds on Ross Island has been preserved intact, provisions and equipment, since 1907 by the extreme dry air and intense cold. The bones of long-dead whales—and the bones of the recently defunct shore-whaling stations—litter Antarctic islands, mainly on South Georgia. (Whalers have come regularly to Antarctic waters since the turn of the century; during the 1920s and 1930s the catches of the large baleen whales, especially blue whales, were enormous.) Today it is also possible to come upon a lost camera lens cap on these Antarctic islands, for wealthy tourists, too, now visit these once inaccessible shores.

Yet, whales and some other sea mammals ex-

Suspicious of intruders, a male elephant seal challenges a Cousteau diver on an expedition to Antarctica in 1972–73. (*The Cousteau Society*)

cepted, the Antarctic world is still much as the early explorers found it. How to keep it that way is the problem. Energy-hungry nations are interested in the oil-drilling possibilities on the Antarctic continental shelf. And harvesting the most productive marine ecosystem in the world could provide new supplies of protein. But short food chains and the small variety of animal species mean that the ecosystems of Antarctica are vulnerable to even the most minor disturbances.

Despite the continent's remoteness from other land masses, it interacts with global processes in ways no one yet understands very well. The sheer magnitude of the ice, its reflective power especially, creates atmospheric circulation patterns that affect the climates of places great distances away. Deep ocean currents that travel north from the Antarctic, both by their cold temperatures and the nutrients they transport, determine the nature of marine life and of fisheries far to the north, as in Peru. So the exploitation of living and nonliving resources could harm not only the fragile environment of Antarctica but also others many thousands of miles away.

Cold Gold

Environmentalists are becoming especially concerned about two of Antarctica's resources, oil and krill. The latter is a tiny shrimplike crustacean (genus *Euphausia*) and a major component of zooplankton blooms in polar seas (see "Krill," page 6). Although oil is believed to exist in the region, there are no reliable estimates as to the extent of the reserves. Several holes drilled in the Ross Sea floor in 1973 by the deep-sea exploration ship *Glomar Challenger* produced traces of methane, ethane, and ethylene, often indicators of oil and natural gas deposits. But the exploitation of energy resources could endanger the marine systems through oil spills and the pollution of not only fragile coastal areas, but broad stretches of open sea as well. In addition, serious accidents would be likely to occur. Drilling rigs on the deep continental shelf would have to coexist with huge roaming icebergs, sometimes many square miles in area, and large fields of pack ice that may be pushed many miles in a single day by violent storms. Oil tankers, which are wrecked in waters elsewhere, in Antarctica would have to navigate the roughest seas anywhere in the world.

Exploitation of the krill is not without its hazards either. Krill are the almost exclusive food of many large organisms, especially certain fish, some seals, and baleen whales. Humans would now add themselves to this list, and krill fishing by humans would likely occur in the same locations and at the same time of year where the already endangered whales are feeding.

Since virtually all living organisms in Antarctica either exist in the sea or are directly a part of the marine ecosystem, widespread oil pollution poses the area's most dangerous environmental threat. Twenty percent of all oceanic photosynthesis is carried on in the Antarctic by the plant plankton floating in the upper layers of the sea. Oil slicks, by wiping out large areas of this phytoplankton, could affect the oxygen supply. Krill and other zooplankton would also be affected, and subsequently all other animals. Also because of Antarctica's geographical isolation, it has been suggested as an "out of sight, out of mind" disposal area for toxic substances, although such dumping is prevented by international treaty for the time being.

Who Owns Antarctica?

In 1957–58, scientists from twelve nations undertook a highly productive research program in Antarctica, much of it as participation in the International Geophysical Year. In 1959, increased activity on the isolated continent made some form of international agreement seem necessary to regulate research and prevent political squabbles. This led to the Antarctic Treaty, which was ratified in 1960–61 by Argentina, Australia, Belgium, Chile, France, Japan, New Zealand, Norway, South Africa, the United Kingdom, the United States, and the Soviet Union. Seven of these countries have claimed sovereignty over portions of the Antarctic continent, although these claims are not recognized by other Treaty members who have not made claims, including the United States, the Soviet Union, and Japan.

The Treaty, as originally agreed, encouraged scientific research and the exchange of information, and stipulated that Treaty members should focus on preserving the Antarctic environment and resources. Claims to sovereign territory were to be held in abeyance. Unfortunately, no provisions were made in the Treaty to deal with the exploitation of resources or determination of who owns them.

Until it recently became apparent that resources, dwindling in other parts of the world, might be found in great abundance in Antarctica,

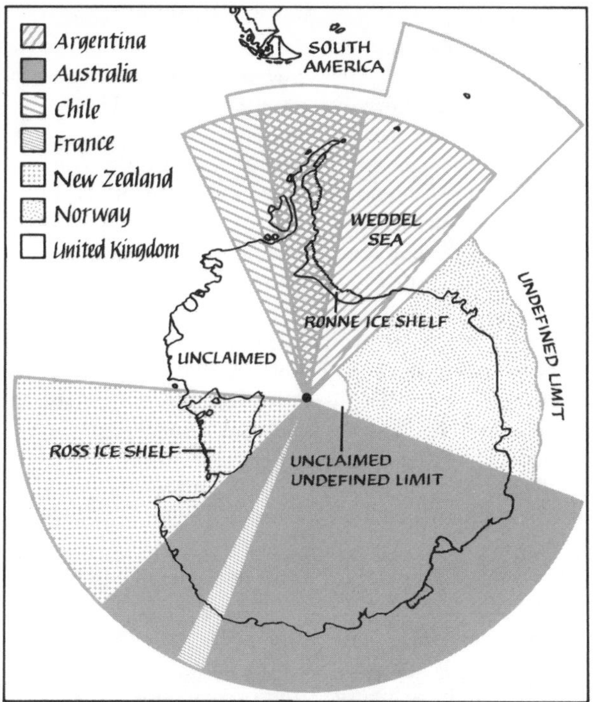

Seven nations have claimed portions of the Antarctic continent, but their claims are not recognized by other major signers of the Antarctic Treaty.

no threat to international cooperation arose. But today the Treaty—and the common sense and good will of the countries involved—are being put to the test. The exploitation of mineral and oil reserves is at the center of the current problems, and the question of who should have access to them is the key issue in negotiations among the Treaty parties. The United States, for one, appears to favor a new agreement that would allow its companies to search for oil anywhere in Antarctica. (See "The Hottest Questions in International Environmental Law," page 572.)

Environmental groups, mainly in the United States, have proposed that Antarctica be declared either a world preserve or an international park under United Nations administration, to benefit all nations. A world preserve would protect Antarctica's potential contributions to science, to food production, and eventually to the energy needs of humanity through safe methods of resource extraction. Events of the very near future will tell whether or not such long-range internationalism is possible.

R.V.

ANTARCTIC LORE

- Beneath the massive ice cover of Antarctica, scientists have found animal and plant fossils that prove the frozen continent was tropical about 600 million years ago, attached to the supercontinent named by scientists Gondwanaland, which included present-day South America, Africa, Arabia, Madagascar, Sri Lanka, India, and Australia. The land mass split apart and Antarctica drifted southward, although there is evidence it was joined to Australia until about 40 million years ago.
- The existence of a great southern continent was first suspected in Greece in the sixth century B.C. as a result of speculations by Pythagoras that the earth was spherical. The reasoning was that large land masses must exist in the Southern Hemisphere to balance those of the North.
- The New Zealand Maoris may have made some kind of early contact with Antarctica—among their legends is a vague one of a white land to the south.
- The lowest temperature on earth was recorded in 1960 by Soviet scientists on the high Antarctic polar plateau—nearly −127° F (−88° C).
- Winds of 100 miles (161 kilometers) per hour are common along the Antarctic coast, and cold air from the interior can whip out toward the coast at windspeeds exceeding 200 miles (322 kilometers) per hour. As a result of these winds, Antarctic seas are the roughest in the world.
- The ice cover blanketing the Antarctic has an average thickness of about 6,900 feet (2,100 meters); in some places it is 2 miles (3.2 kilometers) thick. This massive accumulation of ice has built up from the snowfalls of millions of years, at a rate of only 1 or 2 feet (0.3–0.6 meter) per year. It is so heavy that the land beneath it sinks below sea level in some places.
- The 7.2 million cubic miles (30 million cubic kilometers) of Antarctic ice represents about 90 percent of the glacial ice on earth. If the total world ice cover were to melt, the world's sea level could rise nearly 200 feet (61 meters).
- The surface area of icebergs that break loose from the Antarctic continent is sometimes 100 square miles (259 square kilometers). Some of

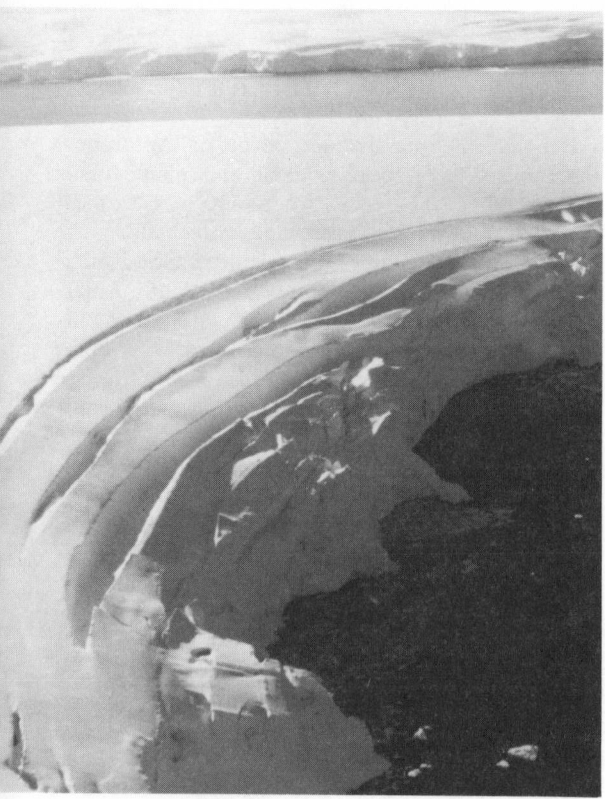

A birthplace of icebergs. Great glaciers flow off the Antarctic continent to the coast, where their leading edges crack and break off, forming beautiful, but to mariners potentially treacherous, ice voyagers. (*The Cousteau Society*)

these floating white islands contain more ice than any of the valley glaciers in the world.

- Algae have been found thriving 20 feet (6.1 kilometers) beneath the permanent ice cover of two freshwater lakes on the Antarctic continent. They receive less than one tenth of one percent of the sunlight that reaches the surface and survive eight months of the year in darkness.
- The living organisms of Antarctica are predominately marine. It is the only continent with no land mammals, although there are about 800 species of plants. Most are lichens and mosses, but there are two flowering plants. Space for plant life is limited, since only about 5 percent of the continent is not ice-covered.
- Some parts of the exposed land surface of Antarctica feature the driest and coldest climates on earth, amounting to frozen deserts. They receive less than 1 inch (2.54 centimeters) of moisture per year, and their life forms are mostly algae, fungi, and bacteria living in the ground.
- The most hospitable environment in Antarctica is in the offshore waters that ring it. Though life undersea in the Antarctic is not generally as diverse as in some regions, it is prolific (one of its most abundant creatures is profiled in "Krill," page 6).
- There are eight seal species that live and breed along Antarctic coasts, about a dozen cetaceans that frequent its shores and floes, and about forty-five species of sea birds that make their home along the edge of this frigid continent.
- One exception to Antarctica's biological lack of diversity is found below depths of 150 feet (46 meters) in the sea, where there are more species of sponges than in tropical waters.
- Two animals that characterize Antarctica in popular literature—penguins and seals—include among their numbers some remarkable divers. The emperor, the largest penguin at 4 feet (1.2 meters) tall and 90 pounds (41 kilograms), can dive to 800 feet (244 meters) and remain submerged for fifteen minutes. The Weddell seal can dive as deep as 2,000 feet (670 meters) and stay under for nearly an hour. It can swim a distance of 5 miles (8 kilometers) below the ice and return to find a small breathing hole gnawed through the ice. It is thought the seals use sonar to accomplish this feat.
- *All* penguins are found in the Southern Hemisphere, and most are found in Antarctica; there are no penguins in the Arctic.

Emperor penguin and chick

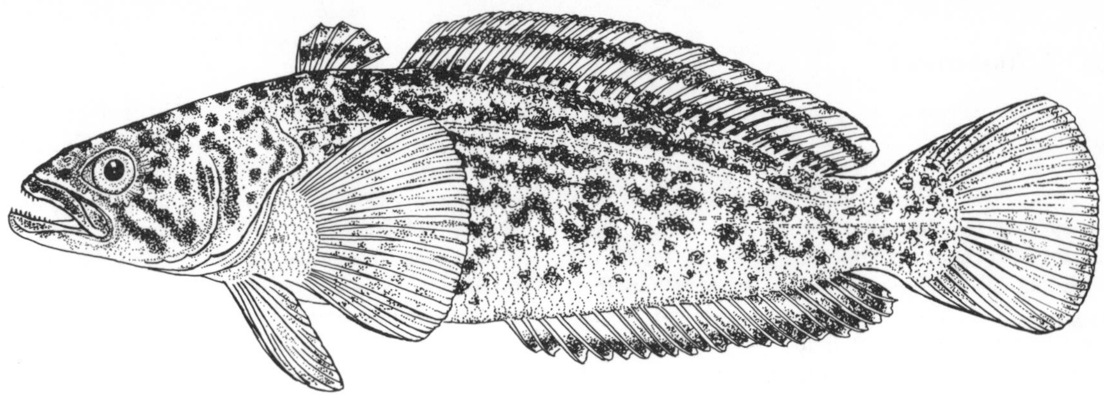

Antarctic ice fish

Underwater, penguins "swim-fly," using their wings as fins, their feet as rudders for steering.

- Though nearly all polar birds breed in mild weather and most penguins breed on the Antarctic mainland, the emperor penguin is an exception. It lays its single egg during the harsh winter, in temperatures as low as −80° F (−62° C), on the floating ice sheets offshore. Another unusual aspect of this creature's reproductive cycle comes after the egg has been produced: the male bird hatches it.
- Besides the deep-diving Weddell seal, other seal species in the Antarctic include: the crabeater, which is the world's most abundant seal (estimated population 30 million) and which actually eats more krill (the shrimplike food staple of Antarctic marine predators) than whales do; the leopard, fiercest of the seals, which is able to jump onto an ice floe to capture and eat penguins and other seals; the Ross, called the "singing" seal because of a cooing sound it makes; and the southern elephant seal (named for the male's ponderous nose), largest of all pinnipeds at a length of about 20 feet (6.1 meters) and a weight of 4 tons (3.5 metric tons).
- Perhaps Antarctica's most unusual creature is the ice fish, *Trematomus*. A remarkable glycoprotein antifreeze in its blood keeps the ice fish from freezing to death in water below 30° F (−1° C)—salt keeps the water from turning to ice. The ice fish also survives without red blood cells, scales, and on a fraction of the oxygen needed by most fish.
- As remote as Antarctica is, winds and ocean currents have carried human pollutants to its waters and creatures. PCBs and DDT have been found in Antarctic snows, and DDT has been found in krill, crabeater seals, fish, and in the flesh and eggs of Adélie penguins.

C.S.D.

THE VOYAGE OF THE TROLLTONGA

The iceberg Trolltonga, also known as 1965A in the numerical nomenclature of iceberg-tracking scientists, broke off the Antarctic ice shelf sometime in 1967. It was about 1,850 square miles (4,792 square kilometers) in size, slightly less than half the size of the island of Cyprus. For a decade the berg drifted quietly off the southernmost tip of South America until, in May 1978, currents carried it into the open sea. By

On its Antarctic expedition, the *Calypso* passes a small iceberg, which, like the Trolltonga, carried penguin passengers. (*The Cousteau Society*)

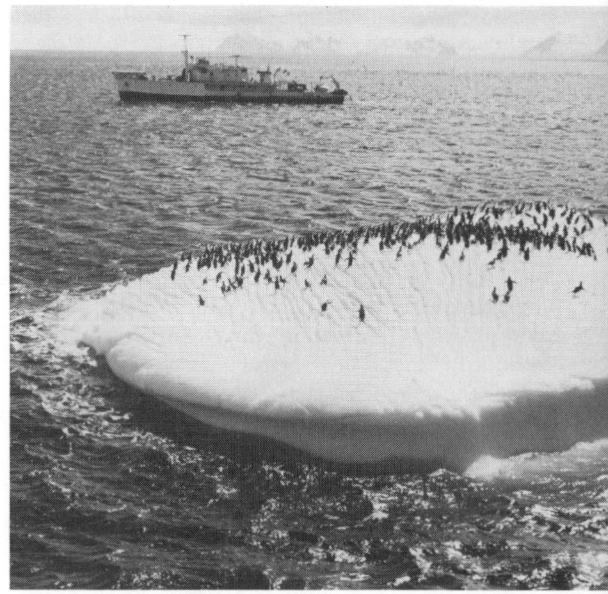

then it had shrunk to 768 square miles (1,989 square kilometers), an area thirty-six times the size of the island of Bermuda. This great mass of ice attracted the attention of a British Antarctic Survey team from Cambridge University, not least of all because it appeared to carry a colony of penguins along its ridges and hills. When the penguins and the iceberg were sighted, they were approximately 200 miles (518 kilometers) northwest of South Georgia island, off the eastern tip of South America.

The berg was monitored by satellite until it drifted out of the tracking path. By then it had traveled a total of approximately 3,500 nautical miles (6,500 kilometers). It is assumed that the penguins traveled on the berg from the beginning, but it is not clear how many penguins started out or how many remained on the berg at the time of sighting. The ice is presumed to have dissolved at sea eventually, and the fate of the penguins remains unknown.

P.D.

WHALES

". . . Within seventy yards of our bow the whale went into its 'flurry' as whalers so aptly call the last heaving convulsions of the great mammal. It turned and twisted and rolled, everything about it shaking, quivering, trembling, and rocking as a mountain of dark African soil caught in an earthquake. Where pearly vapor had recently spurted from its nose, now thick jets of blood, Indian ruby in the sun, burst into the air. Its fluked tail, those delicate, elegant products of the most experienced and loving technology of the Seven Seas, rose to smack the water as if knocking for shelter at the door of a home from which it was locked out."

LAURENS VAN DER POST
*The Hunter and the Whale**

Whales are the largest creatures ever to inhabit the earth, and among the most powerful, the most intelligent, the most far-ranging, the most majestic. There are approximately eighty known species. Sizes range from 4 to 100 feet (1.2 to 30 meters) in length and 160 pounds (73 kilograms) to 150 tons (136 metric tons) of weight. Whales have always been respected, admired, revered, even by those who hunted them. Their irrevocable and indiscriminate slaughter, however, has been among modern humanity's most undignified activities and has, in our times, sparked whale protection movements around the world. In fact, few conservation issues have provoked as much public outrage and concern. The change in attitude, however, was a long time coming.

Commercial whaling began in the ninth century in the Bay of Biscay, when Basque fishers pursued Right whales—the third-largest of the baleen whales—from open boats using hand-held harpoons. As the Right whales declined in number, the Basques stepped up their effort, pushing farther out to sea for larger species. Eventually, the Netherlands and England assumed an interest in whaling, improving techniques to facilitate the catching of even larger species. By the middle of the eighteenth century, whaling was firmly enmeshed in the British economy, and then transferred to North America after the American War of Independence. In New England, for example, whole towns grew and thrived on the industry, described in such powerful works as *Moby Dick*.

The adventurous chased the mammoth whales to produce, among other things, braces for corsets and oil for lamps. The work was dangerous but highly profitable. The taking of a single bowhead whale would finance a whaling ship's entire season. (Today, a factory ship and its catcher boats may have to bring back two thousand whales just to cover expenses.) However, with the growing use of petroleum, which was easier to dig than increasingly rare whales were to catch, and with a turn in fashion trends away from corsets, whaling fleets declined until the new technology of the explosive harpoon gun and the steam engine again made whaling competitive. These inventions permitted the full-scale hunting of species like the blue whale, the humpback, and the fin, which until that point had been very difficult to track and capture with traditional methods.

Of course, during this expansion of the industry, the whale stocks were being radically depleted, but instead of taking action to restore the species in decline, the whaling industry simply stepped up efforts to hunt the ones that were left,

* William Morrow and Company, Inc.

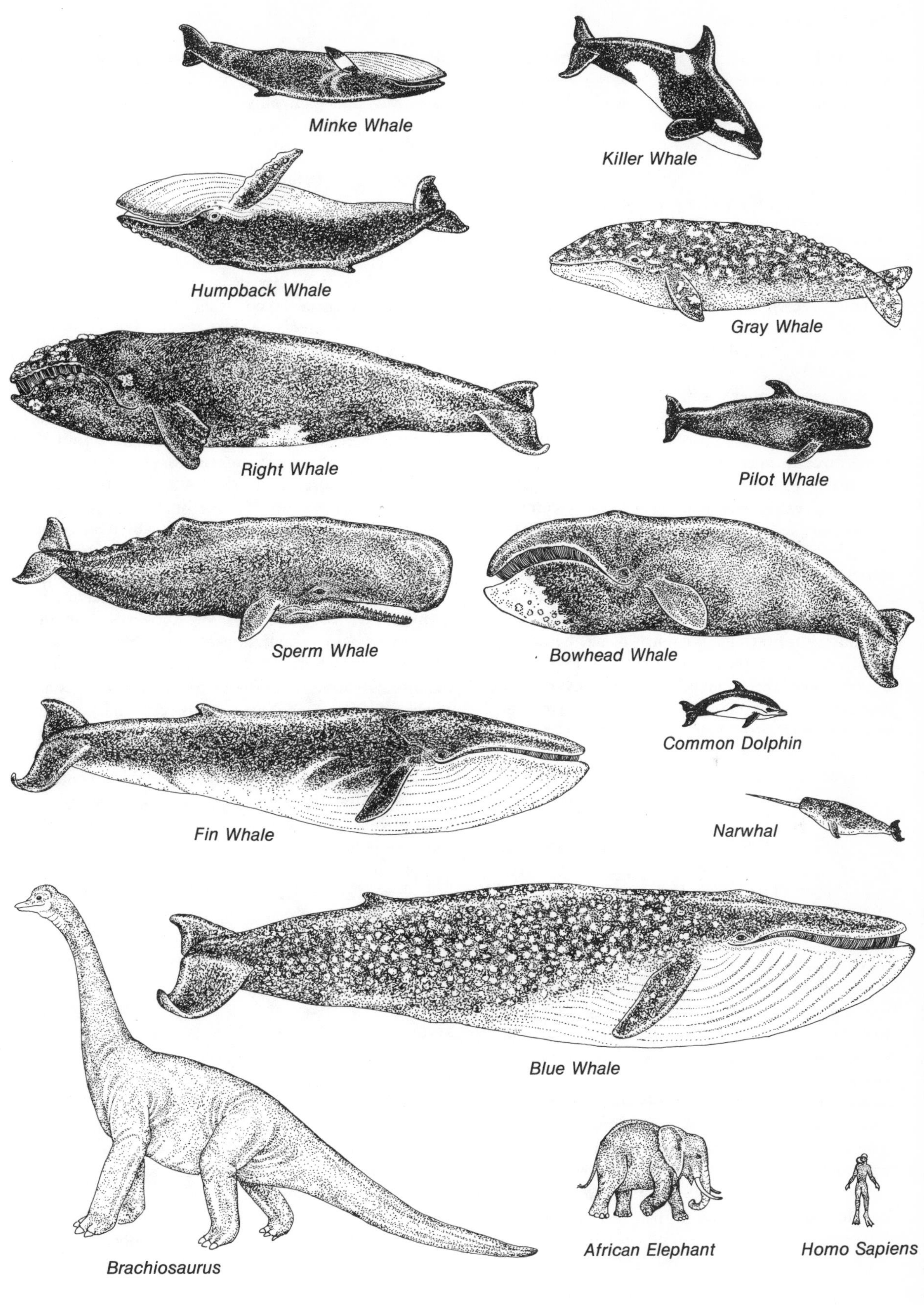
Minke Whale
Killer Whale
Humpback Whale
Gray Whale
Right Whale
Pilot Whale
Sperm Whale
Bowhead Whale
Common Dolphin
Fin Whale
Narwhal
Blue Whale
Brachiosaurus
African Elephant
Homo Sapiens

in a kind of mad race against the process of extinction. Sadly, against the modern techniques that serve this process, the whale had little chance.

Ambushing and Piracy

Using factory ships and harpoon bombs that explode inside the mammal, modern-day whale hunters can reduce an 80-foot (24-meter), 65-ton (59-metric-ton) breathing animal to a mass of oil and other products in less than an hour. When a wounded whale, still in the water, is surrounded by other whales exercising a natural tendency to come to each other's aid, the harpoonists lie in wait for the attending whales to arrive, shooting them too, callously profiting on the whales' cooperative survival instincts.

Statistics prove the law of diminishing whale returns all too dramatically. The 1933 catch of 28,907 whales yielded approximately 2,600,000 barrels of oil. The 1966 catch, however, of 57,891 whales yielded only 1,546,000 barrels of oil. Because the larger species were rapidly disappearing, smaller and smaller whales were being hunted.

Today, the largest whaling fleets belong to Japan and the Soviet Union. (In early 1981 it was reported that the Soviets plan to convert three quarters of their fleet to fishing—a significant development.) Still, there remain pirate whaling ships such as a vessel named the *Sierra,* which employed experienced Japanese whalers. This renegade operation exemplified the difficulty of regulating the whale catch: according to observers, "whale meat is frozen and then labeled 'Produce of Spain' and shipped to Japan via the Ivory Coast." (See "The Whale Defenders," page 291.)

The result of weak regulation of the whaling industry is that the whale population is reduced at a rate of approximately 30,000 per year to supply a $100-million industry. Many products made from whales are distinctly luxurious, like ambergris for perfumes and meat to feed minks on fur farms. Many products, such as inks and industrial lubricants, can be efficiently constituted from other sources, especially the jojoba tree, which itself could prove an important new agricultural crop, since it grows best in deserts (see "Jojoba," page 10). While it is true that whale meat is consumed by humans in some parts of the world, its protein can be replaced by numerous substitutes. For example, in Japan, one of the countries that argues most strongly that whale meat is a crucial diet component, whale meat accounts for only 0.8 percent of protein intake.

Whale Protectors

The record thus far shows that whaling nations and the body set up to protect the resource they exploit—the International Whaling Commission (IWC)—have in most instances been moved to act only when a given whale stock has been reduced so much that it is no longer commercially viable to exploit it. (For more on the IWC, see "Animal Laws," page 576.) The IWC has had its share of problems since its first meeting in 1949. It has managed to infuriate whaling companies and conservationists alike. There are not many international bodies for protecting resources, and the IWC is all the more remarkable because it attempts to regulate exploitation of an ocean resource, which belongs to no one. No member nation is bound by the decisions of the Commission as a whole. Any nation can disregard the findings of the Scientific Committee. And, the lack of knowledge about specific whale populations and about whale biology in general has frequently made the Scientific Committee recommendations unconvincing to some whaling nations, especially when stacked up against the hard facts of the whaling business. Thus, critics say, the IWC has no teeth in its bite and it has only been able to protect severely endangered species after they have been written off as unworthy of consideration by the whaling industry.

Yet, though gloomy, the outlook for whales is not grim. The beleaguered IWC has a number of accomplishments to its credit, and the potential to do more to coordinate whale research and protect whale species is there. The International Whaling Commission is a far different body from what it was when it began, and its proceedings today are scrutinized by anti-whaling lobbyists and environmental groups as never before. The two largest remaining whaling nations, Japan and the Soviet Union, tread more carefully than in 1973, when their rejection of quotas set off a massive international save-the-whales movement. The trend toward extinction, at least of gray whales, blue whales, humpbacks, and perhaps bowheads, appears to be checked at present, although recovery of these animals to numbers of a

Until Canada stopped whaling, workers at several whaling stations such as this along the coast of British Columbia cut whale blubber into chunks to be fed into "digesters." The process resulted in various products—oils, animal food, solubles. At the turn of the century about one thousand whales a year were processed along Canada's west coast. (*FAO*)

half-century ago will no doubt take many years, if possible at all. The scientific data about whale stocks and whale biology grow every year, strengthening the role of the Scientific Committee.

The IWC now appears to have a better balance of anti-whaling and pro-whaling members as well. In 1979, South Korea and Peru joined the pro-whalers, but were offset by the Seychelles, a new member that pushed for the creation of an Indian Ocean whale sanctuary (a proposal that passed), and by Australia, which has banned whaling in its own waters and called for a worldwide ban on all whaling. Bans by countries such as the United States, Canada, and Mexico within their 200-mile (322-kilometer) fishing zones have in effect created sanctuaries in those waters. The Scientific Committee has heard proposals for a total moratorium on commercial whaling for an unspecified period and, in 1979, was considering how such a move would aid the study of whales. And, in 1979, the IWC banned factory ship whaling, a significant development. Such regulatory advances are important, although enforcement remains a critical problem; IWC decisions can be changed from year to year, and, of course non-IWC members are not subject to any regulation.

In the meantime, whale defenders take pride in their victories while remaining mindful of the fact that there are still vast reaches of ocean which seem devoid of whales. Humans still use whale products in some parts of the world, and the huge investments in whaling technology made by the industry will be difficult to abandon. Without continued vigilance, we could still lose the magnificent whales forever.

P.D. and R.V.

UNDERSEA WITH THE WHALE

It is difficult to explain a person's reaction to the sight of a whale underwater. The feeling is one of stupefaction at the size of the animal, for its dimensions go beyond humanity's experience with life forms. Though all our divers agree that the first sight of a whale underwater is terrifying, the more experiences the *Calypso* has had with whales, the less terrifying—and the more intriguing—these leviathans have become.

These remarkable creatures have kept secrets humans would do well to uncover. They can dive to inky depths without risking caisson disease, the deadly ailment also known as the bends. They can go without breathing for an hour and a half. They can communicate with one another and are able to identify one another by voice. And they play a vital role in balancing the ecosystem.

Diving is perhaps one of their more stupendous feats. The sperm whale is the undoubted master, the only whale that can dive 4,000 feet (1,220 kilometers) down, or more. As he prepares to penetrate the depths, he jackknifes with an utter grace—especially in his tail movements, which seem desultory and almost casual. His grace, however, is deceptive; the power in that tail is the estimated equivalent of a 500-horsepower engine.

A more flashy display of a whale's abilities is a stunt called breaching. The whale leaps completely from the water, at a take-off speed of about 30 knots. He does a half roll in midair and falls back, hitting the water with the thunderous clap of massive flesh against the water. The reasons that whales perform this showy trick remain unknown. It could be a sexual rite. One oceanographer I know believes that breaching aids digestion—that whales jump to help the food go down.

Perhaps the most mystifying of the habits peculiar to whales is their "singing." Humpback whales are the most renowned for a wide range of tones, and whole herds often join together in "songs" composed of complete sequences, which, repeated, can last for hours. Some evenings, we listened to the humpbacks starting to make a few sounds, like musicians tuning their instruments. Then, one by one, they began to sing. Underwater canyons make the sounds echo, and it seemed as though we were in a cathedral listening to the faithful alternating verses of a psalm.

One of the most "human" qualities of the whale is its intense devotion to other whales, which is best displayed by the relationship between a mother whale and her calf.

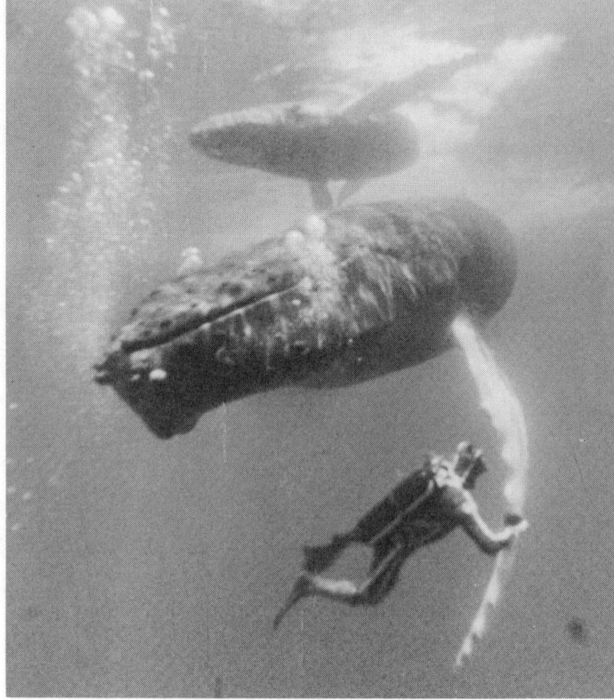

Cousteau diver Bernard Delemotte with humpback mother and calf near Bermuda. (*The Cousteau Society/Philippe Cousteau*)

The mother's first task is to lift her baby to the surface for its first breath. She continues this careful attention to his breathing when she nurses him, all the while cradling the baby in her flippers to keep his head above the surface.

Mothers punish their offspring as well. Once, a crew member on board our ship saw a calf rub against the hull. The mother went after the calf, pushed it far away from the ship, and then struck it several times with her flippers. Never again, that baby was taught, should it confuse a ship with its mother's stomach.

This sort of concern is typical not only of the relationship between mother and calf but also of the relations between members of the whole herd. When a huge sperm whale rammed into our hull one day, the chirping of the herd suddenly became frantic. Whales emerged from everywhere, rushing to the side of the stricken whale to support it at the surface.

Whales are affectionate as well as protective—they love to nuzzle one another, especially as a prelude to mating. Humpbacks actually embrace with their flippers. More than once, flirtatious female whales have rubbed even against our divers. The most touching of our experiences came one day as we were filming. A mother whale and her calf were swimming directly toward Bernard Delemotte, chief diver on our ship. Bernard passed between them with his camera—and the mother gently pulled back a flipper so as not to harm him.

I am touched by a certain sadness, then, when I leaf through volumes of ancient folklore. Rising from the pages are images of monsters from the deep, overturning ships and attacking men. I know that it has been the other way around in real life.

Surely whales have more to offer us than "seafood" for our cats, or stays for corsets, or ribs for umbrellas. *Calypso*'s crew is intensely aware of the whales' true value: we have seen these gray-black cylinders of flesh from underwater; we have been scrutinized by their cloudy blue eyes; our limbs have been spared the crushing impact of a female whale's fin. We have heard the whales sing. And we want to hear them sing again.

Wavemakers:

THE WHALE DEFENDERS

There were early reports that the pirate whalers aboard the ship *Sierra* were arming for the confrontation. Paul Watson, a youthful conservationist, was wary, but he resolved to continue his mission using the vessel *Sea Shepherd* to search out and destroy the outlaw *Sierra* without hurting any of the whalers themselves.

The odds of finding the 683-ton (619-metric-ton) *Sierra,* the most notorious of the whaling ships that wantonly flout international laws regulating the killing of the great mammals, were not good. The ship's hunting ground was vast, and its captain was wily. Setting out from Boston in early July 1979, Watson and his intrepid crew of eighteen knew only that *Sierra* was somewhere between Senegal and the Portuguese port of Leixões. And the crew of the pirate whaler was prepared for the pursuit.

On July 15, as they were scouring the seas off Portugal, the astonished crew of *Sea Shepherd* practically bumped into the *Sierra*. With the environmentalists in hot pursuit, the pirate whaler changed course and steamed toward Leixões. The *Sea Shepherd,* the faster boat, easily passed the whaler, and Watson pondered a first assault. Too risky, he concluded. With rough seas a ramming could endanger lives on both ships.

At Leixões, harbor officials, perhaps trying to defuse the confrontation, boarded *Sea Shepherd* and ordered her into the harbor, promising that the pirate whaler would soon follow. It turned out to be a ruse. As soon as Watson and crew docked, *Sierra* set off for a different port. Realizing that pursuing them would violate the harbor officials' orders to stay put, Watson discharged the captain, who could have lost his master's papers, and set off with a crew of two. The rest opted to stay behind.

Watson found *Sierra* a quarter of a mile (400 meters) away, and crossed her bow at ten knots, damaging the harpoon gun. He then quickly circled, picked up speed to twelve knots, and aimed the *Sea Shepherd*'s bow—which was reinforced with 18 tons of concrete—at the pirate whaler's midships. "We hardly felt the impact on the *Sea Shepherd,*" boasted Watson. "From the bridge I could see that we were practically on top of the whaler, pushing her over to starboard . . . We ripped her open, exposing the whale meat in her guts."

One can imagine *Sierra*'s captain, cursing like Ahab at the white whale, watching helplessly as this band of wild-eyed whale defenders steamed toward his vessel. While he may have muttered unprintable oaths, anti-whaling forces around the world cheered this latest battle in what they often call the "Whale War."

The skirmishes have been going on with increasing intensity since 1975, when a similar band of sea-going environmentalists, belonging to a Canadian-based group called Greenpeace, first buzzed Soviet whaling ships in tiny, inflatable Zodiac boats in an attempt to prevent the killing of sperm whales off the California coast.

For many in the anti-whaling movement, the crusade is something of a holy war—complete with banners, marching songs, and, of course, an environmental navy, sweeping the seas playing music to passing cetaceans, studying their habits, and not infrequently clashing with their human enemies. To the detached observer, these crusaders seem obsessed, almost fanatic about saving whales. But there is something about the massive, mysterious beasts that inexorably attracts many people and at first contact draws them into a profound, almost unexplainable kinship. It is one of the most moving marriages of humans to the sea.

In his book *Warriors of the Rainbow: A Chronicle of the Greenpeace Movement*, activist Robert Hunter eloquently describes an early encounter with a gray whale, capturing, at least a little, the etching of this bond.

> The whale slowed down again and glided to another halt barely two yards away. It hovered there and dimly, through the water, I could see its eyes. We stared at each other—perhaps only for seconds, but my trembling ceased . . . It was not that I was eyeball to eyeball with *something*, but rather with *somebody*.

Nurtured by the growing awareness that whales may be exceedingly intelligent, and mounting evidence that their numbers in the sea are dwindling (see "Whales," page 286), membership in save-the-whale groups has surged, with perhaps hundreds of thousands of activists worldwide. The most famous of these is the Greenpeace Foundation. Founded in 1970, publicity-savvy Greenpeace pioneered environmentalists' use of confrontation tactics when they attempted to sail their ships into nuclear weapon testing sites when blasts were scheduled. The use of similar tactics to defy the whalers on the open sea was a natural sequel.

The save-the-whale movement is anything but

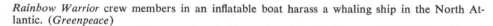

Rainbow Warrior crew members in an inflatable boat harass a whaling ship in the North Atlantic. (*Greenpeace*)

homogeneous in its approach to the crusade. While Greenpeacers are battling at sea, the members of a California group called General Whale are making life-size replicas of finbacks and other species, and plopping them down at demonstrations, in playgrounds, or wherever they will spark appreciation of the great beasts. In February 1978, California sculptor John Perry launched the most whimsical of these whale replicas. "Flo"—short for Flying Leviathan Object—is a 110-foot (34-meter) hot air balloon that bears a remarkable likeness to a humpback whale. Since the launching, Perry has taken Flo on a worldwide tour, from Chicago to Tokyo, to whip up "whalemania." (See "Odd Jobs," page 700.)

While Flo floats about the world as a gentle reminder of the whales' plight, activists are writing angry letters to the International Whaling Commission (IWC), boycotting the products of countries that still have whaling fleets, and signing petitions demanding a ten-year moratorium on all whaling.

On July 11, 1979, anti-whaling activists very nearly got their wish for a moratorium. In a lopsided vote, with Japan and the U.S.S.R. demurring, the IWC resolved to begin a moratorium on factory-ship whaling for all whale species but one (minke). The Commission also declared the Indian Ocean a whale sanctuary for ten years. It was a triumph for environmentalists, and in the words of one activist, "a day of Liberty for the whales."

Despite the victory, the anti-whaling forces admit that they are a long way from winning a total ban on commercial whaling. Patricia Forkan, of the Humane Society of the United States, warns that the battle to protect whales will not get easier. "The only hope is the continuing vigilance and caring of the international whale conservation groups and the continuing strength of the United States to stand firm against objections and any weakening of the recommendations of the Scientific Committee of the Whaling Commission. We are still walking a tight rope of time. It is a fragile lifeline."

"Flo" flying near the capitol in Sacramento, California. (*Greenpeace*)

At least one of the threats to the lifeline will no longer ply the seas in search of whales for the killing. The pirate *Sierra* blew up mysteriously in port after damage from the *Sea Shepherd*'s ramming had been repaired.

B.P.B

HOW TO JOIN THE WHALE CRUSADE

It is common practice among whalers to kill a female whale first, in order to provoke a frenzied charge by the protective bull. Once the bull is disposed of, the pod is leaderless and easier prey to the harpoonist. The members of a 1975 Greenpeace crew, whose mission was physically to obstruct whalers in the North Pacific from doing their deadly business, were forewarned by whale experts to stay clear of the angry bull or "he'll probably turn on you." This advice was quickly remembered when the Greenpeacers—in their small, inflatable Zodiac boats—found themselves caught in the path of a bull charging a Russian whaler that had brutally attacked one of its harem.

Then an unprecedented thing happened. The whale inexplicably veered away from the Greenpeace boat, a maneuver that spared them harm, and then charged the Russian gunner. One of the amazed Greenpeace crew recalled later: "I thought he understood what we were doing."

Whether or not it is really a conscious alliance, whales and their defenders are in a partnership of survival. Many experts agree that where governments fail to provide the remaining whales with protection, environmental organizations play a critical role in providing the leviathans with a fighting chance. What follows is a list of some of the membership organizations around the world that are locked in the struggle to save the whales. They look to you for support.

U. S. Groups:

AMERICAN CETACEAN SOCIETY, P.O. Box 4416, San Pedro, CA 90731, (213) 548-6279.
Publications: *Whalewatcher* (quarterly to members, $15/year)

The American Cetacean Society has "involvement with all matters aquatic," but is particularly interested in whales, dolphins, and porpoises. The Society has eleven local chapters nationwide.

GENERAL WHALE, 1916 MacArthur Blvd., Oakland, CA 94605, (415) 865-5550.
Publications: *Latest Whale News* (periodically to members, $10/year)

Devoted to "an enlightened understanding of whales, dolphins, and porpoises," General Whale produces a broad array of educational materials and exhibits. The group also conducts morphological and behavioral research into cetaceans.

MONITOR, INC., 1506 19th St. NW, Washington, D.C. 20036, (202) 234-6576.
Publications: None

Monitor is a coordinating center and information clearinghouse for member conservation organizations.

PROJECT JONAH, Building 240, Fort Mason, San Francisco, CA 94123, (415) 285-9846.
Publications: Project Jonah Fact Sheet, misc. publications (membership $15/year)

Project Jonah produces educational materials and conducts "observational" research on threatened cetaceans.

OCEANIC SOCIETY, Stamford Marine Center, Magee Ave., Stamford, CT 06902, (203) 327-9786.
Publications: *Oceans Magazine* (bimonthly to members, $15/year)

The Oceanic Society is dedicated to the protection of the world's oceans through research, education, and conservation. The Society combines public information projects with individual involvement opportunities.

WHALE PROTECTION FUND, Center for Environmental Education, 1925 K St. NW, Washington, D.C. 20006, (202) 466-4996.
Publications: *Whale Report* (quarterly to contributors)

WPF conducts research on whale populations, helps coordinate boycott and petitioning activities, and develops educational materials.

THE HUMANE SOCIETY OF THE UNITED STATES, 2100 L St. NW, Washington, D.C. 20037, (202) 452-1100.
Publications: The Humane Society News, Humane Society Newsletter (membership $10/year)
The Humane Society works to end cruelty to and depletion of marine mammals, especially through international treaty and law.

"WE'RE EATEN BY THE MILLIONS, AND THEY'RE CALLED AN ENDANGERED SPECIES."

(© *1980, by Sidney Harris*)

Other U.S. groups involved in defending whales include: Friends of the Earth, Animal Welfare Institute, Animal Protection Institute, Center for Action on Endangered Wildlife, Fund for Animals, National Audubon Society, National Wildlife Federation, Rare Animal Relief Effort, Defenders of Wildlife, Sierra Club, and Environmental Defense Fund.

International Groups:

THE COUSTEAU SOCIETY, INC., 777 Third Ave., New York, NY 10017, (212) 826-2940. Publications: *Calypso Log* (quarterly) and *Calypso Dispatch* (every other month) with individual membership, $15/year; in addition, *Dolphin Log* (bimonthly) with family membership, $25/year

Dedicated to the enhancement and preservation of the water planet, The Cousteau Society conducts research into the marine environment, and produces films, books, and educational materials to inform and alert the public.

THE GREENPEACE FOUNDATION, Building E, Fort Mason, San Francisco, CA 94123, (415) 474-6767; or 2108 West 4th Ave., Vancouver, B.C., Canada, (604) 736-0321. Publications: *Greenpeace Chronicles* (monthly to members, $15/year)

Originally organized in Canada to oppose nuclear weapons proliferation, Greenpeace has since been widely recognized as the most visibly active organization in the save-the-whale movement. Greenpeace has several offices around the world, and local chapters in many nations.

LES AMIS DE LA TERRE / PROJECT JONAH, 14 bis, rue de l'arbalete, Paris 75005, France.

PROJECT JONAH / FRIENDS OF THE EARTH, P.O. Box 34, Leeston, Canterbury, New Zealand.

PROJECT JONAH / FRIENDS OF THE EARTH, 9 Poland St., London WIV 3DG. Three of the many international offices of Friends of the Earth, who are particularly active in protecting whales. FOE has additional offices in Germany, Sweden, Australia, Ireland, Canada, Belgium, Yugoslavia, El Salvador, Switzerland, Italy, Mexico, The Netherlands, and Spain.

WHALE CENTER INTERNATIONAL, 3929 Piedmont Ave., Oakland, CA 94611, (415) 654-4892. Publications: Newsletter and miscellaneous bulletins (membership $15/year)

Whale Center is working for an end to commerical whaling, establishment of whale sanctuaries around the world, and seeks to promote research into whale behavior and biology. Whale Center International has offices in Brazil, Canada, France, Japan, and Mexico.

KEY TO ORGANIZATION SYMBOLS:

 pursues environmental litigation

 has a lobbying program

 engages in public education and/or research

 has local chapters or involved in grassroots organizing

THE OZONE LAYER

Ozone has a pungent odor and is best known as the most damaging ingredient of the famous Los Angeles smog. It cracks rubber, kills plants, irritates lungs, and corrodes metal. But 10 miles (16 kilometers) up, the gaseous shell of ozone that surrounds the planet is a guardian that helps make life on earth possible. Ozone in the troposphere—the air level below the stratosphere—forms a thin, absorbent layer that soaks up 99 percent of the lethal ultraviolet rays that bombard us from the sun. Ultraviolet radiation can destroy DNA, the "building block" of life, and the ozone layer therefore protects all life from genetic damage.

Oxygen gas is found in the atmosphere with two atoms linked together as O_2. Ozone, on the other hand, is an unstable form of oxygen with not two but three atoms, O_3. It is unstable because it is always ready to give up its third atom to other molecules, and thus ozone can be converted back into O_2 fairly easily.

In the early 1970s, scientists analyzing the proposed supersonic transport (SST) came to the disturbing conclusion that the nitrogen oxides and water vapor released by a fleet of five hundred SSTs in a year could destroy half the ozone layer. These frightening predictions helped bring the U.S. production of the SST to a halt. However, supersonic military flights continue to deplete ozone.

There are several other threats to this vital layer. A by-product of the SST investigation was the discovery that nuclear explosions, which produce hundreds of thousands of *tons* of nitrogen oxide, would set off a complex chain reaction, destroying large amounts of ozone over several years (see "The Ultimate Environmental Disaster," page 533). During two years of above-ground nuclear testing by the United States and the Soviet Union, it was estimated, 4 percent of the ozone layer was destroyed. The scientists of the Stockholm International Peace Research Institute (SIPRI) believe that in a nuclear war between the two superpowers the most important damage to the world would be the loss of a large part of the ozone layer for up to ten years.

The nitrogen fertilizers used by farmers also came under examination. These fertilizers release nitrous oxide, which destroys ozone.

But the most surprising enemies of ozone are seemingly innocuous consumer products. The threat was discovered almost by accident. In 1973, two chemistry professors at the University of California decided to find out what happens to chlorofluoromethanes when they rise into the upper atmosphere. These gases, known as CFCs (chlorofluorocarbons), are used as spray propellants in aerosol cans and as coolants in refrigerators and air conditioners.

Sherry Rowland and Mario Molina, the two chemists, knew that CFCs from these relatively new uses had spread everywhere in the world's troposphere. Chlorofluoromethanes do not dissolve in water and are not broken down by chemicals or anything else yet known in the troposphere. So Rowland and Molina guessed that the CFCs would float up to the stratosphere over the years,

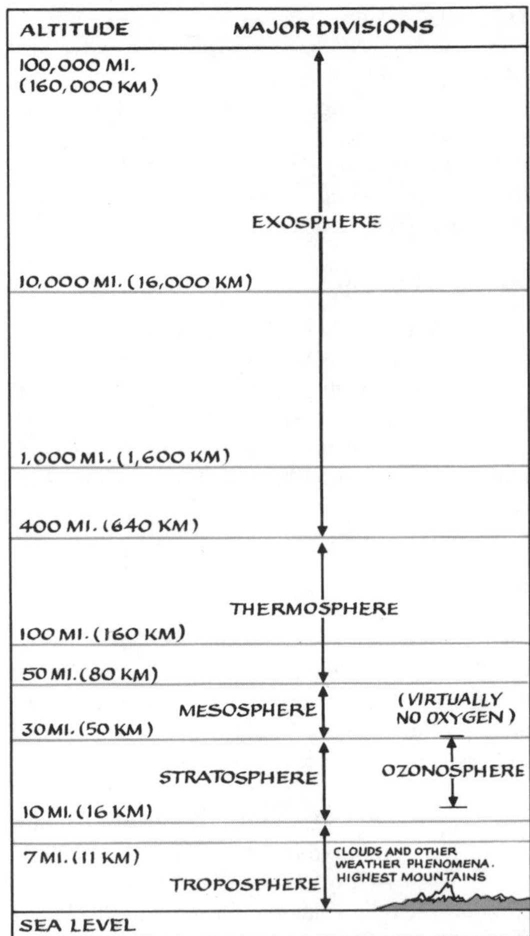

where "hard" ultraviolet light would finally break them down.

When chlorofluoromethanes are broken down, they release free chlorine atoms. The chemists discovered that one atom of chlorine would begin a chain reaction that would "kill" tens of thousands of ozone molecules. Chlorine atoms are six times more destructive of ozone than nitrogen oxides.

Rowland calculated that if chlorofluoromethanes continued to be used at 1974 rates, the chlorine they released could eventually overcome the ozone layer, with disastrous consequences for life on earth. A large decrease in the ozone layer would lead to a noticeable rise in skin cancer, crop damage, genetic mutations, and possibly even to changes in the world climatic pattern.

The chemical industry was predictably outraged when Rowland and Molina published their results in *Nature* in June 1974—fluorocarbons were a $3-billion-a-year industry. But the conclusions of other scientists not only supported Rowland and

Molina, but sometimes went further. In 1978, new calculations predicted that fluorocarbons would have an even worse impact on the ozone than Rowland and Molina had believed—two to three times worse. By 1978, the Canadian aerosol industry had voluntarily eliminated chlorofluorocarbons. The West German industry also agreed to stop using them. Sweden and the United States have banned fluorocarbons in aerosols, although on-hand stocks may be sold until they are gone. (The U.S. ban alone should cut off 25 percent of the total world use.) However, certain uses for these propellants are considered essential and are therefore still legal. Also, fluorocarbons used as refrigerants are not included in these regulations.

Other countries remain skeptical of the danger to the ozone and will probably await evidence of actual damage before they restrict chlorofluorocarbons. Australia, Belgium, Denmark, the Netherlands, Italy, Yugoslavia, Norway, France, Britain, India, China, Japan, and the Soviet Union were still involved in manufacturing or processing fluorocarbons in early 1980.

The problem with waiting for more proof is that it takes from ten to two hundred years for the gases to reach the upper atmosphere where ultraviolet light breaks them down, so that even if all world use of fluorocarbons stopped at the first measurement of an ozone decrease, ozone would keep disappearing for another ten to two hundred years. Two Harvard scientists estimated that if all fluorocarbon production had been stopped in 1975, the ozone layer would still be depleted by 1.5 percent in 1985.

It is extremely difficult to measure reliably the overall rate of ozone depletion, but a U. S. National Academy of Sciences report released in December 1979 described a 16-percent depletion rate over the next fifty to one hundred years attributable to fluorocarbons alone. This was an estimate revised upward from the Academy's 1976 findings.

J.S.

ALASKA

It seems ironic that one of the reasons Russia was willing to sell Alaska in 1867 was a dwindling natural resource in that vast colony. When the land deal was made, Russia's lucrative trade in sea otter fur had ended because the animal was nearly extinct on the Alaskan coast. The other riches locked up in the great northern storehouse, such as oil, were unrecognized.

It is also ironic that the Alaska purchase, at a mere $7.2 million, was opposed so vehemently by a large segment of the public in the United States. It was generally felt at the time that the land was worthless and too remote. It took the gold discoveries of the 1880s and 1890s and the stampede to the gold fields of Alaska and the Yukon Territory to awaken people to the economic potential of the northern wilderness. Today debates flourish in Alaska and in government chambers in Washington, D.C., over what to do with the last great U.S. wilderness or, as some see it, the last U.S. frontier. The lines of battle are drawn between those who want to develop the reserves of oil, natural gas, coal, and other minerals to the fullest, no matter where they might be found, and those who consider the unspoiled land itself a resource and wish to set aside vast tracts of it forever.

The Great North Country

Alaska is a tremendous chunk of country for just one state, 589,757 square miles (1,518,800 square kilometers), well over twice the size of Texas, four times as large as West and East Germany combined. Its population is about half that of the city of Dallas, one fourth that of Munich. Its 47,000 miles (75,623 kilometers) of coast equal the coastline of the entire United States.

Alaska's land mass embraces a wide variety of geography and climate. For example, the southeastern panhandle is a region of magnificent fjords and forests with mild, moist weather. South central Alaska, shielded to a large degree from arctic air masses by the Alaska Range, also has a fairly temperate climate and is the only part of the state where agriculture has been successful. Most of Alaska's population is settled there; 40 percent live in Anchorage alone.

Northward, the various regions become less and less inviting for human habitation. West and north of the Alaska Range lie the central plains, tablelands, and rivers of the interior, one of the last places in North America where wildlife is still abundant. Here grizzlies, wolves, moose, and

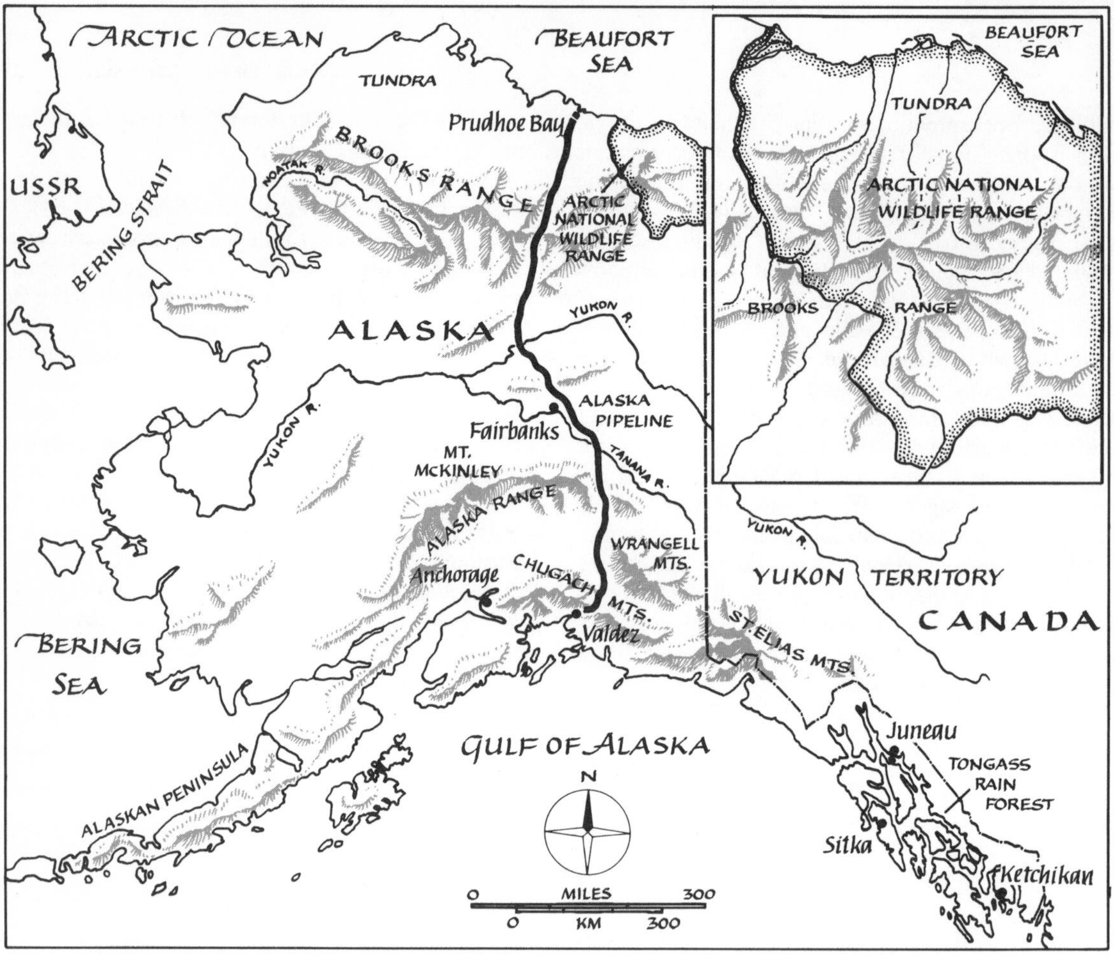

Mount McKinley, highest point in North America, is part of the Alaska Range. (*NPS/M. Woodbridge Williams*)

Valdez—southern end of the Alaska pipeline. Here oil is loaded on tankers for shipment to distant ports. (*EPA Documerica/Dennis Cowals*)

caribou live as they have for millennia. Here waterfowl—geese, ducks, and swans—including one of the largest concentrations of migrating birds in the Western Hemisphere, have their nesting grounds. Through here, too, passes the line of pipe that carries oil from the Arctic coast to ports in the south. Along the route are mud slides and silt-filled ditches that were once clear-running, fish-filled streams—the ravages wrought by the pipeline's construction. Beyond another major mountain chain, the Brooks Range, is the treeless tundra, sometimes known as the North Slope, which stretches to the Arctic Ocean. These polar plains are home to 120,000 caribou, the great "Porcupine" herd, which annually migrate on a round trip of roughly 2,000 miles (3,200 kilometers) between the northern Yukon in Canada and the Arctic National Wildlife Range in Alaska. Unfortunately, the eastern edge of the Arctic Wildlife Range is only some 60 miles (96 kilometers) from Prudhoe Bay, where Atlantic Richfield struck oil in 1968, with deposits measured in billions of barrels. By 1969, petroleum companies had paid the state nearly $1 billion in oil-land revenues.

A young bull caribou looks warily at a photographer near "Mile 0" of the Alaska pipeline. (*EPA Documerica/Dennis Cowals*)

Two Kinds of Problems

The environmental battlegrounds on the Alaskan frontier are numerous. The Wrangell-Chugach-St. Elias Mountains—which contain volcanoes and mighty glaciers (one is larger than the state of Rhode Island)—have been targets for road building schemes and mineral exploration. Conservationists worry about pollution of the Noatak River watershed which, because it is yet entirely undeveloped and untouched by humans, was chosen by the United Nations as an ideal natural water system for scientific study. Anticipated further expansion of the logging and pulpmill operations in the Alaska panhandle near Ketchikan and Sitka eventually led to court actions in the early 1970s as a result of environmentalists' opposition. The unique maritime ecosystems of the Bering Sea islands are also watched carefully by conservationists; the annual Pribilof fur seal harvest created bitter debate, since nearly 60 percent of Alaska's $8-million annual fur production comes from the Pribilof industry.

But it is not necessary to list all of Alaska's environmental problems to appreciate the basic issue in the current land debate. The question seems simple: How much of Alaska should be commercially exploited for the sake of short-term profits and to help meet forever-growing energy needs, and how much should be preserved in its natural state?

There are factors that make this particular land issue unusually complex. They range from the practical to the philosophical. For example, a primary disagreement has arisen over just what the Alaskan resources are (and where they are), since many parts of the state have not even been geologically surveyed. Land ownership patterns, of course, will influence development. When the federal government granted statehood to Alaska, it kept 60 percent of the land under its own jurisdiction. It has earmarked 10 million acres (4 million hectares) of this for preservation. But what was left to the state amounts to far more than that allotted to any other state—over 100 million acres (40 million hectares). Moreover, the state of Alaska has virtually complete control over its entire coastline. Ironically, much of the debate is over land where native peoples of Alaska—Tlingits, Aleuts, and Eskimos—have lived for thousands of years. Today, with traditional life-styles modified by the incursion of industrialized culture, most of Alaska's native peoples suffer from chronic unemployment and poverty. Many welcome revenues from leasing their land to oil companies.

Who Knows Best?

The attitudes of many Alaskans today, especially the most recent settlers, are much the same as those in the nineteenth century when the Great American West was "opened" and "tamed." Their isolation, not only from the rest of the United States but from each other, has bred a fierce independence and resentment of interference from outsiders. Alaskans generally feel they know best what to do with the state and that others are totally ignorant of Alaskan life-styles and Alaskan needs. Yet, while many undoubtedly appreciate that wild and beautiful country, they also came to the north to carve an empire out of that wilderness and to accumulate private fortunes. Thus they are committed to the same course that put the Western prairies to the plow, tied up the plains in barbed wire, created dust bowls, cut down forests, and strip-mined mountainsides.

Frontier spirit looms as the most pervasive threat to the Alaskan wilderness, since it provides an ideal rationale and impetus for the activists of the resource industries, and promotes the promise of immediate prosperity for all. But quick prosperity can be short-lived, leaving a wake of problems. The Alaska pipeline created the need for a large labor force of construction workers, engineers, machine operators, and mechanics. Thousands came, including shopkeepers, tavern owners, gas station attendants, car rental agents, and prostitutes. Before long Alaska experienced the worst inflation anywhere in the United States. In Fairbanks, serious crime increased and pollution rose above levels found in most cities of the world.

A person standing in an Alaskan town can see mountain peaks towering above the building tops and think that beyond them stretches hundreds of thousands of miles with no roads, no buildings, little or no sign of human habitation. With such a vast expanse of land seemingly available, the possibility that Alaska can be forever despoiled seems unduly alarmist. But the American West was once a vast virgin wilderness, too. If strong protective measures are enacted, Alaska can be saved. Otherwise, it is only a matter of time.

R.V.

ALASKA LORE

- Fully a third of Alaska is north of the Arctic Circle. Its most northerly extension, Point Barrow, is second only to Siberia's Cape Chelyuskin as the land mass closest to the North Pole. Point Barrow's winter temperatures dip as low as –40° F (–40° C).
- Mount McKinley, north of Anchorage, is the highest point on the North American continent (20,320 feet/6,198 meters). The aboriginal Alaskans called it Denali, meaning "The Great One."
- The word "Eskimo," which refers to native inhabitants of Alaska and the rest of the Arctic Circle who derive their sustenance from the sea, was brought into common usage by a priest in 1611, who heard them referred to by a

Mount McKinley wildlife: Dall sheep, ewe and lamb. (*NPS/M. Woodbridge Williams*)

neighboring Indian tribe as *eskimantsik*, meaning "eaters of raw flesh." They themselves prefer the term "Inuit."

- Lake Iliamna, the seventh-largest U.S. lake, contains the *only* freshwater colony of seals in the United States. Linked to the Pacific through the Kvichak River, Lake Iliamna also features occasional visits by migrating beluga whales.
- The largest national forest in the United States is Alaska's Tongass, which covers most of the state's Southeast Panhandle. Tongass is actually a northern rain forest, receiving about 200 inches (508 centimeters) of rain annually. It stretches across 16 million acres (6.5 million hectares), 13 million (5.2 million hectares) of it virgin wilderness, and boasts fully two thirds of America's federally owned shorelines.
- Admiralty Island (in Tongass National Forest), near the Alaskan state capital of Juneau, is the prime habitat of the giant brown bear and features the world's greatest concentration of nesting bald eagles; they are drawn to the region by its abundance of salmon. Numbering between 3,000 and 4,000, Admiralty Island's bald eagles represent the highest density of *any* eagle species on earth. Bald eagles mate for life and construct the largest bird nests in the world—5 to 7 feet (1.5 to 2.1 meters) deep, 6 to 8 feet (1.8 to 2.4 meters) wide.
- Misty Fjords, an area of 2.3 million acres (930,000 hectares) in Tongass Forest has some of North America's most striking scenery: sheer granite cliffs, deep canyons, glaciated mountains that reach up to 10,000 feet (3,050 meters), countless waterways, the longest fjords on the continent, old abandoned Indian villages where original totem poles remain standing, thousands of islands, and a virgin rain forest that contains trees more than 200 feet (61 meters) tall, 14 feet (4.3 meters) in diameter, and up to eight hundred years old. It is also the major spawning grounds for all five species of Pacific salmon. In fact, one third of the total U.S. salmon harvest comes from southeast Alaska.
- At least seventeen species of whales (seven endangered) inhabit the area extending from the Chukchi Sea off northwest Alaska to the Gulf of Alaska.
- Glaciers represent only 3 percent of Alaska's land mass, and they are found almost exclusively in the south, near the Alaskan Gulf. Much of the rest of Alaska is green about half of each year. South-central Alaska's glacier system is the most extensive in the United States. It includes North America's largest glacier, the Malaspina, and longest one, the Bering.
- Lake George, about 40 miles (64 meters) from Anchorage in southern Alaska, is the most famous and probably the largest of the world's glacier-dammed lakes. The Knik Glacier holds Lake George's water back except for a period each year when so much rain and melting snow swells the lake that water bursts around the ice barrier, cutting a channel through it and causing an annual flood.
- Among major cities of the world, Leningrad, Helsinki, Stockholm, and Oslo all are farther north than the Alaskan state capital of Juneau.
- Alaska amounts to one sixth of the total U.S. land mass.
- The Eurasians who pursued the woolly

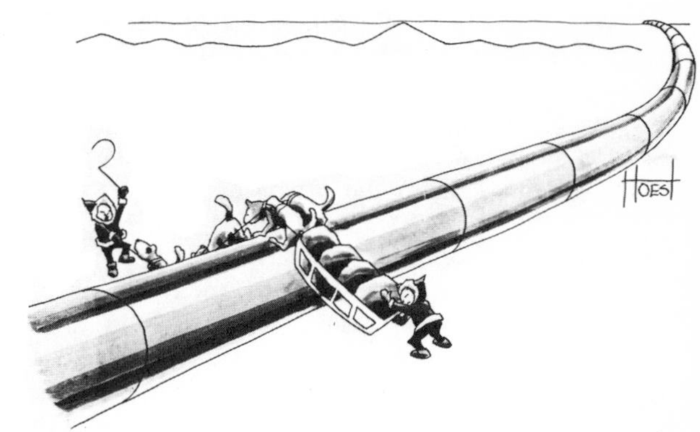

(*TRUE, February 1973*)

mammoth and other Pleistocene mammals across Siberia to Alaska (25,000 to 40,000 years ago) were probably the first humans to cross into the Arctic region.

- The first European to reach Alaska was the Danish mariner Vitus Jonassen Bering, who in 1741 led a Russian expedition that set out to discover if and where Siberia ended. He died that same year on what is now Bering Island (part of the Aleutian chain). Bering Strait and the Bering Sea are also named for him. As a result of Bering's discovery of Alaska, the Russians claimed possession of the country and the Aleutian Islands. The survivors of Bering's expedition sparked an extensive fur-hunting period by Siberians when they returned to Russia with pelts of sea otters. (See also "Return Engagements," page 344.)
- On March 27, 1964—Good Friday—the strongest earthquake ever recorded in North America jolted Alaska, leaving at least 114 people dead, causing serious property damage, and splitting the ground apart in some places.

C.S.D.

THE MEDITERRANEAN

Throughout the four thousand years of recorded history, the Mediterranean Sea has been a central factor in Western culture—the site of migrations, conflicts, commerce, and the rise and fall of varied civilizations. It is still a pivotal region of the world, but today the migrations are made by 100 million sun-seeking vacationers; the commerce centers on fishing and tourism; conflicts arise from tempers frayed by endless traffic jams; and local cultures and traditions are not so much overthrown as overshadowed for the few months each year when some 50 million coastal residents are outnumbered by visitors from around the globe.

In spite of the changes, the Mediterranean remains a source of common identity among its eighteen bordering countries. For all their differing political systems, religions, and levels of development, they share the Mediterranean Sea—united by its riches and by its problems.

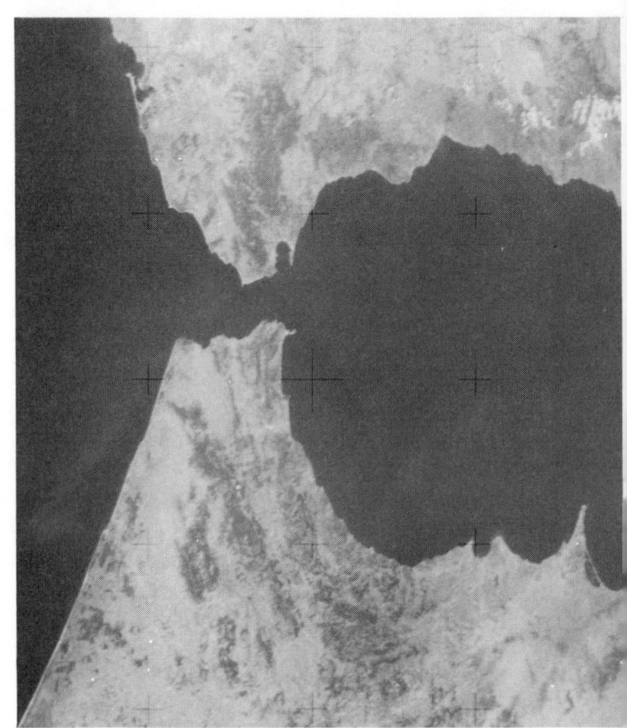

The Strait of Gibraltar, seen here from space, provides the only corridor through which water can flow between the Atlantic and the Mediterranean. (*NASA*)

The Great Sewage Dump

One of the problems is pollution, which threatens the health, economic interests, and quality of life of coastal zone inhabitants and visitors. Although public health problems related to water pollution were probably experienced in ancient times, from the canals of Venice to the Golden Horn of Istanbul, there is evidence that the capacity of the Mediterranean to process waste matter is being strained today as never before, causing the steady deterioration of once beautiful and diverse marine communities. The pollution pours into the sea continuously and from many sources. Most of the sewage from 120 coastal cities enters the Mediterranean untreated or inadequately treated. Thousands of tons of industrial and agricultural chemicals are dumped into coastal waters or carried there by rivers, wind, or rainfall. Ships of every description release their wastes, including oil, directly into the sea.

Anatomy of the Mediterranean

How these substances affect marine organisms, and where they end up, is largely determined by the hydrological nature of the sea. The Mediterranean evolved from an ancient ocean called Tethys; and its present shape results from the interactions of the great prehistoric land masses of Eurasia and Africa as they split away from the supercontinents called Laurasia and Gondwanaland, and the formation of the European Alps in late Cretaceous times. The sea is nearly landlocked, with narrow straits opening to the Atlantic at Gibraltar and to the Black Sea at the Dardanelles and Bosphorus. Its average depth is 4,688 feet (1,429 meters). (For more Mediterranean statistics, see "Oceans and Seas," page 119.)

As water flows into the Mediterranean, it evaporates rapidly, becoming saltier and heavier than the adjacent Atlantic and Black Sea. This dense water sinks, creating deep water masses in the sea's central basins, some of which flow out beneath incoming currents. However, the overall exchange rate is slow and the residence time of Mediterranean water is estimated at eighty to one hundred years.

Whatever the flushing rate of open waters, it is in the coastal zones where pollution causes the most concern, and where fishermen, swimmers, and local residents experience its effects. No doubt many effects have yet to be detected, but those we do know about are disturbing: Diseases which can be transmitted by water or seafood,

A frozen blessing amid the clamor of machinery at a waterfront industrial zone at Taranto, Italy. Near this site *Calypso* researchers found a high concentration of PCBs in the water. (*The Cousteau Society*)

such as viral hepatitis, dysentery, typhoid, and cholera, are endemic in the Mediterranean. Many beaches and recreation areas are public health hazards and have to be closed periodically. In some areas, seafood is often unfit for consumption.

Certain coastal lagoons and estuaries have become algae-ridden and sulfurous due to such phenomena as eutrophication and disruptions caused by the disappearance of species. Some organisms cannot tolerate the polluted conditions and some, being large predators, ingest deadly loads of toxic chemicals as these substances move up the food chain from one organism to another. Clearly, one of humanity's greatest resources is slowly being transformed into an odious symbol of carelessness and neglect.

The Blue Plan

In a recent and encouraging turn of events, the Mediterranean countries themselves have shown an unusual determination to reverse their centuries-old tendency to abuse the sea. The nations around the Mediterranean periphery have joined to create a program called the Mediterranean Action Plan. Scientific research and monitoring are being carried out by laboratories around the sea and a design for environmentally sound development—called the Blue Plan—is being drawn up.

Perhaps the most delicate aspect of the plan is the legal commitment of the Mediterranean countries to live up to their good intentions. By 1978, three treaties had been signed, ratified, and brought into force. The central treaty is a general agreement to refrain from introducing substances or energy into the sea that would threaten human health, fisheries, or marine ecosystems, and to promote regional cooperation on environmental control and management. It is accompanied by two protocols that give the convention its legal "teeth." The first of these forbids the dumping of what are considered the most dangerous substances owing to their toxicity, persistence, and accumulation. This "black list" of chemicals includes mercury, cadmium, DDT, PCBs, some plastics, used lubricating oils, and radioactive wastes. Precise controls are placed on somewhat less noxious materials on a "gray list," including lead, zinc, copper, arsenic, cobalt, silver, cyanide, fluorides, and pathogenic microorganisms.

The second protocol calls for cooperation among the nations in dealing with accidents or other "emergencies" that cause the release of large amounts of oil or other harmful materials into the sea. To provide a means of rapid communication in such instances, and to coordinate contingency plans, the Regional Oil Combating Center was established in Malta in 1976.

A third protocol is likely to be the most important because it deals with the most serious threat to the health of the Mediterranean Sea—the land-based pollution from industries, cities, and modern agriculture practices. A monitoring project completed in 1977 showed that about 85 percent of such pollution is carried to the sea by rivers, notably the Ebro, the Rhône, the Po, the Adige, and the many smaller waterways that drain the continent of Europe.

Paying the Price

Clearly, the legal process of controlling the often-distant inland sources is extremely complicated, often requiring delicate diplomacy. One particularly knotty problem involves the differing levels of industrialization between the northern and southern shores of the Mediterranean. Application of stringent pollution controls on new industry in developing nations, long after the highly developed northern countries have built their profitable and polluting factories, is obviously unfair to developing countries. This particular dilemma was overcome by an agreement to use environmental quality criteria for coastal waters in the place of emission standards for individual factories. What is measured and controlled is the total waste load of the receiving waters. Thus, the relatively few factories in the developing countries will be allowed to emit considerably more waste per factory than the more numerous factories in the developed countries.

Application of this new protocol is going to be extremely expensive for the Mediterranean countries. The latest estimate is that it will cost $10 billion to $15 billion over the next ten to twenty years to limit and control the flow of land-based pollutants into the sea. It is significant, however, that the Mediterranean countries appear willing to pay such a price.

No one knows how successful the Mediterranean plan will be, but the sea will undoubtedly be cleaner than it would have been without these efforts. In one sense the Action Plan is already a success; it is an illustration that otherwise unrelated nations can recognize that their long-term economic interest lies in maintaining the health of an ecosystem they share. In their determination to succeed, the Mediterranean countries—so often in conflict—have overcome age-old obstacles. In the process, the Mediterranean peoples have set a precedent for ecological wisdom that can be emulated around the world.

N.M., L.W.

A TRADITION OF SEA-KEEPING

The precedent-setting Mediterranean Action Plan establishes a claim by the region's governments and scientific institutions to leadership in the movement to protect the ocean, but it is not the first such action to issue from this sea-oriented area of the world. In 1910, Prince Albert of Monaco, a pioneer in oceanography, created the International Commission for the Scientific Exploration of the Mediterranean Sea (ICSEM). The goal of ICSEM was to foster scientific research, to gather existing knowledge, and to encourage exchanges between scientists working on Mediterranean problems. Since its birth, fifteen countries bordering the sea have joined the organization (Spain, France, Monaco, Italy, Yugoslavia, Greece, Turkey, Romania, Cyprus, Syria, Israel, Egypt, Tunisia, Algeria, Morocco), as well as two nonbordering nations: Switzerland and Germany. Now over seventy years old, ICSEM is an active partner in the Mediterranean Action Plan. It has conducted joint workshops with the United Nations Environment Programme (UNEP) on pollution and worked with The Cousteau Society to evaluate the health of the sea. It was under an ICSEM flag that The Cousteau Society's research vessel *Calypso* circled the Mediterranean Sea in 1977 while conducting scientific analyses at hundreds of locations. Presently, the Prince of Monaco is the president of ICSEM and its Secrètary General is Jacques-Yves Cousteau.

M.R.

MANATEES AND DUGONGS

Down to the waist [*the creature*] *resembled a man, but below this it was like a fish with a broad, crescent-shaped tail. Its face was round and full, the nose thick and flat; black hair flecked wtih grey fell over its shoulders and covered its belly. When it rose out of the water it swept the hair out of its face with its hands; and when it dived again it snuffled like a poodle.*

Fisherman's report, Island of Martinique, 1671

The "manfish" creature described above was probably a manatee or dugong, a now rare sea mammal of the order Sirenia. These animals were once plentiful enough to be sighted frequently by homesick sailors who, like the fisherman in Martinique, observed the animals' friendly, "humanlike" behavior, and began weaving an entire mythology of mermaids and mermen around it. It was even reported that the dugong wept when harpooned, and bottled "tears" were sold in Sumatra as charms to bring the purchaser affection.

But neither the manatee nor the dugong has the alluring, seductive physical characteristics of a mythological creature. In fact, except for the approximate location of their mammary glands, and their broad tails—the manatee's is rounded like a paddle and the dugong's split like a whale's fluke—Sirenia bear little resemblance to the popular image of a mermaid.

Both manatees and dugongs, also called sea cows, have thick, bulbous, cleft faces with long coarse bristles covering flexible lip pads and short tusks used for grazing on marine grasses. Dark slate in color, they are bulky and nearly hairless. Probably dugongs and manatees evolved from a four-footed, herbivorous land-dwelling mammal —Sirenia are the only herbivorous mammals in the sea. They have no hind limbs but use their flipperlike forelimbs for sculling and turning while swimming and for sweeping plants like water hyacinths into their mouths.

There is some evidence that Sirenia share an ancestor in common with elephants, and indeed some interesting similarities still exist between today's sea cows and today's elephants. For example, both have continuously growing molars, a unique adaptation that assures replacement of teeth subject to wear from constant grinding. (The teeth-grinding of feeding manatees is quite audible underwater.) It may also be significant

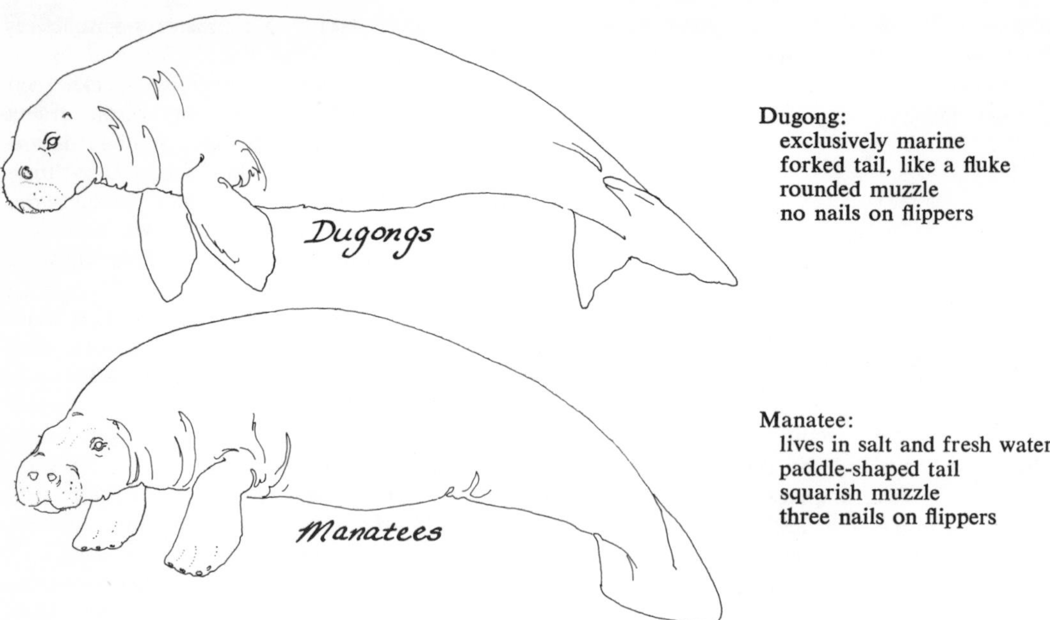

Dugong:
exclusively marine
forked tail, like a fluke
rounded muzzle
no nails on flippers

Manatee:
lives in salt and fresh water
paddle-shaped tail
squarish muzzle
three nails on flippers

that the teats of both animals are in the same relative place—the sea cow's are between its flippers and the elephant's are between its forelegs rather than on the lower abdomen as in cows and other terrestrial mammals.

Though the Sirenia are hardly beautiful in the human sense of the word, their habits and behavior (see "Undersea with the Manatee," opposite) place them among the sea's most appealing and useful creatures. But, due to a variety of factors, they are also among the sea's rarest animal species.

The Cattle of the Sea

Sirenia are ideally adapted for life in calm shallow bays, rivers, and estuaries of the coastal regions of the tropics.

Manatees—there are three varieties—can be found in Caribbean and West Indian waters, in the Amazon and Orinoco river systems of South America, and in West African rivers and coastal regions from Senegal to Angola. There is only one dugong species, which once ranged extensively from the East African coast and the Red Sea to India, Malaysia, the Philippines, Australia, and all the way to the Caroline and Marshall islands in the Pacific. However, like that of the manatee, the dugong's distribution has today declined precipitously. The only concentrations appear to be off Mozambique and Kenya in Africa and around New Guinea and northern Australia.

Like whales, Sirenia have long been hunted for their meat. In some places, such as the Amazon and Orinoco river basins, Mozambique, Sri Lanka, or the Torres Strait off northern Australia, they are still hunted by native peoples, sometimes with government permission but often without. However, these killings are insignificant compared with the mass depletion, especially of the Australian dugong, caused by large-scale hunting by non-natives since the nineteenth century. Now, all dugong hunting in Australia, except by aborigines, is prohibited. Legislation protecting them is comprehensive in the Indian and Pacific Ocean islands, as well as in Sri Lanka and India. East African nations, too, have enacted protective measures, as have Peru, Brazil, Guyana, and others. But, where they exist, laws against hunting are often extremely difficult to enforce because of poor communications in developing countries, lack of education, and local poverty and hunger. Adequate conservation guidelines are often difficult to establish because we lack sufficient scientific information about populations of the animals, their ranges, and where they are most endangered.

Today, where the Sirenians congregate close to the areas of human habitation, their grazing areas are destroyed by herbicide runoff and industrial wastes, as well as by siltation and dredging. They become ensnared and drown in fishery nets or, as in Australia, in shark-control nets. (Large-scale dugong drownings in these nets have prompted the Queensland government to seek other means of protecting humans from sharks.) In the otherwise quiet meandering canals and rivers of Florida or northern South America, Sirenia are battered and slashed by power boat propellers, sometimes even by drivers who deliberately steer their boats close to the animals for sport—a bitter twist for creatures we were once happy to believe were mermaids.

R.V., P.D.

UNDERSEA WITH THE MANATEE

Editor's Note: *Daniel Hartman is a biologist well known for his work with manatees. His observations are mentioned in the following excerpt from an article by Faith McNulty. He has also worked with Cousteau diving teams.*

The manatees' main business in life is peaceful browsing, cowlike, on underwater pastures. Usually, they simply graze, but once in a while they use their flippers to pull food to their mouths.

Manatees nap with closed eyes, sometimes near the surface but more often on the bottom, rising slowly and sleepily every few minutes for a breath of air and then sinking again. Sometimes they are bothered by fish that peck at their hides searching for microorganisms. The manatees flinch, and slap ineffectually with their flippers, like a human bothered by mosquitoes.

Manatees are remarkably supple. Waking from a nap, they may close their eyes and arch their backs, or curl forward like shrimp, emitting a lengthy groan. This stretching may be followed by a back dive to the bottom and a headstand in the sand.

Manatees rub themselves with their flippers as far as they can reach. They also use their flippers to clean their teeth. Apparently, food trapped in a manatee's mouth is irritating, and Hartman saw manatees become almost frantic as they attempted to get rid of it. They also rub their bodies, with apparent pleasure, against such things as rocks and poles and crab traps.

Manatees emit squeals, chirp-squeaks, and screams, which Hartman could hear plainly

Two manatees feed on water hyacinths in a Florida river. (*The Cousteau Society*)

underwater. He saw no air bubbles accompanying these sounds and has no idea how they are produced. Manatees seem to use their voices less to communicate than to express emotion, as in moments of fear, internal conflict, sexual arousal, protest, or play. One manatee squeaked as though with pleasure when Hartman scratched its back, and he heard squealing and chirping as they rubbed themselves on rocks and logs. Sex is accompanied by a medley of sounds, and fright evokes a high-pitched scream. Calves answer the alarm calls of their dams.

Manatees are inquisitive. They investigate oddities encountered in the water by nudging them, licking them, or taking them in their mouths. Hartman saw one manatee chewing on a Coke bottle, another carrying a beer can around, another nudging a log, and so on. Manatees nibbled his flippers, munched on his anchor rope, and tried to carry off his underwater thermometer.

SERENGETI

Wolves and bears were once common in western Europe, while antelope, elephants, and lions roamed the North African coast. Until the 1800s, millions of buffalo grazed on the plains of North America; tigers and wolves thrived in China and India. But civilization advanced, and the numbers of wildlife on every continent have markedly dwindled.

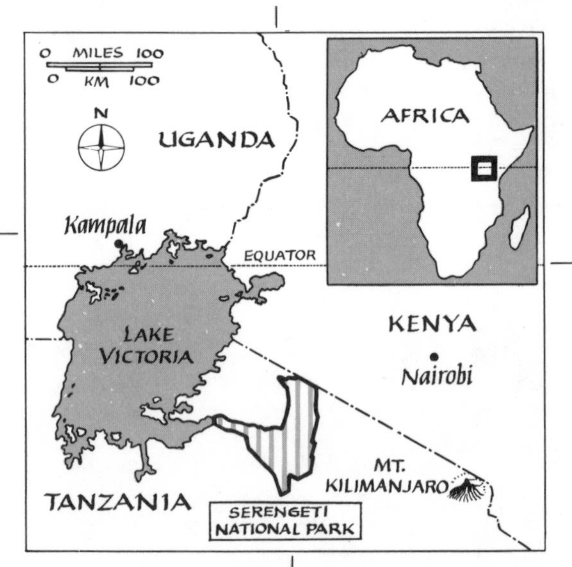

Serengeti National Park, in northern Tanzania, has preserved a window into the past. Serengeti is one of the rare places left on earth where huge concentrations of many species of wildlife still migrate through vast areas with no interference from humans. Serengeti is a resource for the world. The 15,000 square miles (39,000 square kilometers) of the Serengeti Plain (more than one third in the national park, the rest mostly in protected areas) contain literally millions of large wild animals. Enormous herds of wildebeest account for almost half the total number, and during the Great Migration they darken the plain. There are also innumerable other animals—elephants, lions, gazelles, warthogs, giraffes, cheetahs, rhinoceroses, crocodiles, zebras, ostriches, hippos, eagles, and buffalo. Serengeti is one of the most important wildlife reservoirs on earth.

In its modern incarnation, Serengeti is not entirely a natural creation. Although human entrance to the park is now regulated to protect the animals from extinction, humans have always been part of the life of Serengeti. Some of the oldest anthropoid bones ever found come from the Olduvai Gorge near Serengeti. It was there that Mary Leakey discovered *Australopithecus boisei,* a humanoid creature close to two million years old. In those days, too, Serengeti was teeming with wildlife.

The area near Lake Victoria, where Serengeti lies, was one of the last major land regions in the world to be mapped and recorded. Although the Chinese, Arabs, Indians, and Portuguese traded on and colonized the Tanzanian coast, the interior was almost entirely unknown to outsiders, except for slave traders. It was not until the second half of the nineteenth century that German and British explorers began to arrive. In 1860, Richard Burton published his book *The Lake Regions of Central Africa,* in which he described the environs of Lake Victoria. Burton noted that wild game was not particularly abundant and that much of the land was densely populated by agricultural and cattle-herding tribes. Where Burton did find wildlife, he also noticed the tsetse fly.

Lioness, Serengeti National Park. (*Francis P. Bowles*)

The Masai, who gave Serengeti its name, which means "an extended place," had arrived rather recently from the north with their cattle herds. Although the Masai are not predominantly hunters, their cattle were incompatible with wildlife, which were inevitably infested with the tsetse fly. Zebras and wildebeest can live with the fly, but it is deadly for cattle. The Masai and the other tribes of the Serengeti area were gradually eliminating the wildlife, both to clear the land for villages and to get rid of the tsetse fly.

In 1891, Germany officially took charge of Tanzania, including Serengeti. At about the same time, the rinderpest (which spread from Asian cattle brought to Africa by the English and Italians) struck the cattle of all the interior tribes. Famine ensued as the rinderpest killed up to 95 percent of the cattle in East Africa. The Masai, who lived almost entirely by their herds, were in particularly sore straits. A German explorer of the period wrote of walking skeletons followed by swarms of vultures: "They were refugees from Serengeti, where starvation had depopulated whole districts." The eastern Serengeti and the Ngorongoro Crater, which adjoins it, were emptied of people, and the wildlife returned. Shortly after World War I, when the British took over from the Germans, they declared 90 square miles (233 square kilometers) of the Serengeti a game reserve where hunting was prohibited. Since then, first the colonial and then the independent Tanzanian government continued to expand and protect Serengeti.

The Tanzanian government deserves a great deal of credit for maintaining the national park. Tanzania is one of the world's poorer countries and faces a continual pressure of population against limited land and resources. Vaccinations against the tsetse fly and the rinderpest have allowed the tribal cattle herders to return in increasing numbers to the borders of Serengeti, and these tribesmen, who are still often illiterate, see no value in conserving giraffes and warthogs when they desperately want more land for their cattle. To encourage pride in the national heritage, the Tanzanian government takes its schoolchildren on educational tours of Serengeti; Tanzanians gain admission to the park at a small fraction of the fee foreigners must pay. Poaching and trading in wild game is forbidden but still practiced in spite of a relatively effective ranger system, and during the 1979 miniwar with Uganda some soldiers were apparently shooting game in Serengeti.

Serengeti shall not die, as Dr. Bernhard Grzimek, a longtime supporter of the park, proclaimed in the title of a classic book on the park published more than twenty years ago. But it is not fair to expect a developing country like Tanzania to pay the entire cost of maintaining a world reserve of wildlife. Approximately one fourth of Tanzania is set aside as game preserves and national parks, while per capita income is $200. Without help, Serengeti faces an uncertain future.

J.S.

THE GREAT LAKES

Viewed through satellite cameras, when the air is clear and the sun is reflecting off their surfaces, they look like polished diamonds left by ancient, grinding glaciers. Up close they can be tranquil or ferocious: sources of pleasure, means of transportation, monsters clawing at the foundations of buildings, or, in some places, pools of diluted poisons.

Most people think of lakes as small, peaceful bodies of water, with a shore always visible on the horizon. The Great Lakes, as their name implies, are giants among lakes. Called America's "inland seas," they contain 18 percent of the world's liquid fresh water. Their coast is 9,402 miles long (about 15,129 kilometers). If their coastline could be unkinked and stretched taut along the equator, it would reach from the mouth of the Amazon River, across the Atlantic, across the continent of Africa to a point south of the tip of India. Four of the lakes border two countries, the United States and Canada. All five lakes border the Canadian province of Ontario and together they touch eight U.S. states—New York, Pennsylvania, Ohio, Michigan, Indiana, Illinois,

The Greak Lakes touch two countries and eight U.S. states, and contain 18 percent of the world's fresh water.

Wisconsin, and Minnesota. They are connected to both the Atlantic Ocean and the Gulf of Mexico through rivers and canals, forming a seaway that has long carried grain, coal, and ore from the northern and western reaches of the North American continent.

In the seventeenth century, French fur traders first opened this highway for commerce, paddling their canoes a thousand miles along rivers and northern lakes to meet and trade with Indian fur trappers from deep in western Canada. Explorers and missionaries followed. Later settlers came in boatloads—immigrants who had sailed from Europe, up the Hudson River and Erie Canal to Buffalo, where they boarded Great Lakes schooners and steamboats to populate the growing cities like Cleveland, Toledo, Detroit, Saginaw, Milwaukee, and Chicago. In the late 1800s lumberjacks swept through the Great Lakes states, cutting down forests to build cities and leaving behind a legacy of stumps and fouled streams.

Today about 38 million people—one seventh of the U.S. population and almost one third of the Canadian population, live in the Great Lakes basin. The lakes are ringed with manufacturing centers, power stations, and mines. They are also a vacation mecca for millions in the U.S. Midwest and Ontario, who come to fish for lake trout and Coho salmon, to boat, or to lie on the beaches.

More important, perhaps, is the role of the Great Lakes as the largest watering hole in the world, a huge supply of fresh, sweet water. Two hundred years ago you could drink water safely from anywhere in the lakes. Today cities along the shore must extend pipelines farther and farther into the lakes to get beyond the reach of pollution. About 21 million people already drink Great Lakes water, and faraway western states now thirstily eye the great watering hole both for drinking water and water to carry their coal in slurry pipelines to eastern markets. Planners have proposed water pipelines that would carry valuable water west from the lakes just as oil pipelines carry the precious black liquid to where it's needed.

Great Troubles . . .

When Great Lakes scientists gather at conventions they usually have three main topics of discussion: toxic chemicals, both the familiar old ones, such as DDT and PCBs, and an ever-expanding alphabet soup of new ones; the so-far-unknown effects of acid rain on the Great Lakes basins' many streams (see "The Trespassing Poison: Acid Rain," page 186); and the old problems of industrial and municipal pollution. The scum, suds, and slicks of the "dead" Lake Erie of the 1960s are being cleaned up through the efforts of watchful citizens and the imposition of pollution control laws (see "Lake Erie's Crusader," page 312); but the struggle is not over. Detroit, the Lakes' largest municipal polluter (Chicago diverts its sewage south and west to the Mississippi) was taken to court in the mid-1970s by the U. S. Environmental Protection Agency (EPA) for failure to treat its sewage adequately.

Many industries have been recalcitrant in meeting pollution standards. A recent report by the U.S. and Canadian International Joint Commission on the Great Lakes compiles a list of forty-eight major industrial polluters that reads like a Who's Who of midwestern industry: Abitibi Paper, Dow Chemical, American Can, Reserve Mining, U.S. Steel, E. B. Eddy Forest Products, Algoma Steel, Outboard Marine, Esso Chemical, Ford Motor Co., Great Lakes Steel, National Steel, Cleveland Electric Illuminating, Gulf Oil, and Domtar. These polluters contribute phosphorus, phenols, mercury, nitrates, chlorides, ammonia, cyanides, lead, organics, copper, zinc, radioactive wastes, and asbestos to the Great Lakes.

Despite this deluge, much of the flow of wastes has been stemmed, and the lakes, especially the heavily polluted, shallow Lake Erie, have shown hopeful signs of recovery. In the early 1970s Lake Erie's central basin was so choked with waste-fed algae blooms and so lacking in oxygen that many of its native fish died en masse. Now the blighted area is shrinking.

While the lakes respond fairly quickly to a reduction of biological wastes, the invisible toxic chemicals, dumped for years before their effects were known, will linger in the lakes for decades. Laws prohibit dumping these chemicals in the lakes, but they are still flowing in, dumped into streams and rivers by "pirate" waste haulers, who escape the high cost of proper disposal on land. Toxic chemicals are big, and bad, news in Michigan, the state touching four of the Great Lakes. In the past five years the state has been wracked by toxic chemical scandals: PBB, a fire retardant accidentally mixed with chicken and cattle feed, found its way into beef, eggs, human mother's milk, farmland, and streams; Mirex, a potent fire-ant pesticide, contaminated Lake Ontario; DDT and dieldrin from farm fields washed into the lakes; PCBs from industries—and now their relative PCTs (polychlorinated terphenyls)—have found their way into the waters, as well as into fish and the people who eat them. The U. S. Food and Drug Administration (FDA) has banned the commercial sale of several fish species and the State of Michigan warns anglers not to eat more than one meal a week of certain fish species because of chemical contamination. Both DDT and PCB levels in fish have declined in recent years, but scientists and fish managers rejoice cautiously, because new chemicals are continually discovered in the environment.

Rocky shoreline of Lake Superior, Presque Isle City Park, Marquette, Michigan. (*Michigan Sea Grant/ Suzanne Tainter*)

. . . And Great Hopes

But amid the depressing stream of new chemicals is a landmark 1979 court settlement to clean up leaking chemicals involving Hooker Chemical Company, the firm responsible for the contamination of the Love Canal in New York (see "Living on the Love Canal," page 657). A Hooker plant on Michigan's west shore had a massive contamination problem: more than 1.2 million cubic yards (917,520 cubic meters) of contaminated materials had to be isolated from the environment. At the same time more than 20 billion gallons (76 billion liters) of groundwater contaminated with about one hundred different chemicals was flowing toward Lake Michigan. Hooker had been fighting a cleanup in court, and according to several observers had a chance of winning. However, Hooker's parent company, Occidental Petroleum, stepped in and made an out-of-court settlement with Michigan's attorney general that will cost Hooker up to $20 million. The agreement was hailed by scientists and environmentalists as a model for toxic waste settlements.

Many of the Great Lakes' problems are similar to those faced by the Hudson River (see "The Hudson River," page 327), and residents of the two areas have begun to help each other. A small group on Lake Michigan is raising funds for a *Clearwater*-inspired sailing ship to introduce lakeside residents to the history and ecology of their lakes, as the *Clearwater* does along the Hudson (see "Saving a River with a Song," page 329). Other groups, such as the Lake Michigan Federation in Chicago, the Michigan United Conservation Clubs, and many local groups, work to save the lakes for recreation, transportation, and drinking water—and to reinstate their once unblemished natural beauty.

L.Y.L., M.P.

Wavemakers:

LAKE ERIE'S CRUSADER

On the inside of the menu for the Fourteenth Annual Banquet of the Woods and Waters Club of Cleveland was a glowing tribute to the guest of honor.

"It has been several years since our 'Man of the Year Award' Committee has recognized anyone in the field of conservation," it said. "For the year 1964 the selection was easy. . . . That man is David L. Blaushild, who single-handedly, with the utmost sincerity and determinism, has done more than any other person to fight pollution of our lakes and waterways. He has spent a great deal

of his own money backing this campaign; he has pounded on editors' doors and hounded TV and radio people to stir things up. He has spoken before various groups and taken others out into the lake to show them first-hand the cesspool that borders our city . . . and things seem to be working out."

The "cesspool" the menu writer so irreverently referred to was Lake Erie, once by far the most polluted of the American Great Lakes, and that early optimism about "things working out" has proved prophetic.

Today experts say that while Lake Erie faces new threats, particularly from toxic chemicals, the serious degradation witnessed in the 1960s has been reversed.

For David Blaushild, a maverick Chevrolet dealer from Shaker Heights, Ohio, the slow but steady recovery of the mighty lake was gratifying. "It feels good," he said simply.

And so it should. For seven years (from 1964 to 1971), Blaushild was the ailing lake's leading crusader, and his persistent call-to-arms inspired hundreds of thousands to join him in a campaign to prod polluters to begin the cleanup. It was a campaign, he said, that succeeded because it touched people who remember Lake Erie as it used to be, when commercial and sport fishing flourished and bathers flocked to the beaches.

The Moment of Realization

Blaushild's own memory was jogged one summer day in 1963 when he took his eight-year-old daughter to the Shaker Lakes, a series of ponds near Cleveland that eventually find their way to Lake Erie. The ponds were once his boyhood haunt, and he wanted to introduce them to his daughter. Instead, Blaushild had a jarring introduction of his own. Foul-smelling and littered with garbage, the Shaker Lakes had become just another source of Lake Erie's problems.

Lisa Blaushild doesn't remember that trip to the polluted ponds, but she clearly recalls that soon afterward her father was seldom home. Deeply angered by his unpleasant rediscovery of the Shaker Lakes, Blaushild dedicated himself to a nearly full-time crusade to revive Lake Erie and its waterways.

He faced seemingly insurmountable odds. The environmental movement had not yet been born, and the accepted, or rarely opposed, view was that the lake and its tributaries were logical dumping places for untreated industrial and municipal waste. Though there were some antipollution laws, they were largely ignored.

As a result, the lake was moribund. A 1962 government report stated that huge sections of the lake were devoid of fish during much of the year because of the preponderance of oxygen-consuming wastes. Raw sewage and chemicals overenriched its waters, causing massive algae blooms and premature eutrophication. Some alarmed experts said that in a relatively short time the lake had aged ten thousand years. The more pessimistic among them predicted that Lake Erie would be "dead" in a decade.

But this, for Blaushild, was just another challenge to his sales abilities. His instincts told him that the lake needed a bold and effective PR campaign. What was required, he thought, was to sell the public on clean water and then quickly motivate large numbers of people to participate in a highly visible campaign pressuring for pollution control.

Advertising a Lake

In the spring of 1964, Blaushild fired the first publicity salvo. His initial strategy was to turn the public eye toward the lake in order to alert a complacent citizenry to just how bad things were. In the first of a series of newspaper advertisements, Blaushild asked: "Lake Erie is dying. Does anybody care?" followed by brief, trenchant paragraphs that described the appalling condition of the lake.

"If you care about what happens to this area's greatest natural resource," the ads exhorted, "fill in the coupon below and send it to David Blaushild. He'll see that the Governor, the Congress, and others in authority know that you care."

The ads struck a nerve. An avalanche of coupons deluged the automobile agency, many accompanied by moving letters of encouragement. Blaushild replied by sending each respondent petitions and a proposed antipollution resolution for adoption by municipalities along the shore. In an attached appeal, Blaushild called for a massive canvass of citizen support.

"I want 500,000 signatures," he wrote. "This will show the complacent ones that the public, the little guy, is beginning to stir and is indignant at this betrayal of nature's blessing."

To help build the campaign's momentum, Blaushild wangled the free use of fifteen billboards around Cleveland. "STOP KILLING LAKE ERIE. Fight its pollution *NOW*," one sign exhorted passing motorists in bold red letters. Though there were grumblings among some conservationists that the use of billboards was unsavory, the publicity-conscious Blaushild was undeterred.

When he had stirred the public conscience with his first set of ads, Blaushild initiated a new series that were more positive: "Lake Erie is dying. Yes, people do care! What can they do about it?" The ad's text contained pithy and inspiring quotes from some of the many letters he had received from citizens who wanted to do more.

Signature-gatherers appeared on Cleveland streets as Blaushild's campaign took hold. He calculated that nearly five thousand people circulated petitions. One particularly aggressive signature-getter was a local commercial fisherman who claims he personally gathered 37,000 names.

Meanwhile, Blaushild and members of his newly formed Citizens for Clean Air and Water went on a whirlwind speaking tour to Ohio cities along Lake Erie's shore, stumping for enforcement of clean water laws and a crackdown on industrial and municipal polluters. Blaushild estimates he made at least two hundred speeches during the campaign.

"I went to all the Kiwanis and Rotary Clubs," Blaushild recalled. "That's how I learned the words to 'The Star-Spangled Banner.' "

Blaushild and his antipollution forces also attended countless public hearings on Lake Erie pollution. At one hearing, never one to miss an opportunity for good press, Blaushild reached under his chair and offered a drink from a bottle of murky Lake Erie water to a state official who claimed that the lake was "as clear as crystal."

"If it's so clean, here, have a drink," he said, raising the sloshing bottle in the view of TV cameras. The official declined, and Blaushild won new converts.

All this activity did not go unnoticed. As public controversy over the lake's deterioration heightened, formerly complacent elected officials twitched at the brewing political storm.

"Finally, the politicians got wind of it," said Blaushild. "They want to be on the side of the winners, so soon we had them on our side. The only people against us were the heavy industry and the Chamber of Commerce."

The steel industry, economic titans in northern Ohio, gave Blaushild the most trouble. The industry's lobbyists tried to dispute claims that the lake was polluted; they also recited a now-familiar litany of the cost of the cleanup in terms of jobs and money.

When those arguments proved insufficient, the steel industry went after Blaushild. Industry agents infiltrated his antipollution meetings and tried to disrupt them with insults and embarrassing questions.

"What's a car dealer doing leading an antipollution crusade?" industry infiltrators frequently demanded. To this, Blaushild had a pat response: "If I didn't do it, someone else would. And besides, I have the money to fight this thing."

When Blaushild couldn't wangle something for free, he would use his own money. Though his crusade no doubt helped his business by boosting recognition of his name—and that of David Blaushild Chevrolet—it also had some unexpected costs. In the midst of the battle one particularly irked steel company cancelled an order for 168 cars from his agency.

Despite the determined opposition, Blaushild was winning his war against Lake Erie pollution. By August of 1964, three months after the campaign began, Blaushild had collected more than half a million signatures on petitions that he periodically presented to public officials who still needed convincing. Twenty-six towns on Lake Erie's shore had passed Blaushild's resolution by then, pledging to "take every feasible step to reduce, abate, prevent and enjoin any industrial and sanitary pollution . . . into the waters contributory to Lake Erie."

The City of Cleveland held out against the resolution, but finally approved it under heavy public pressure. (Several years later Blaushild took the recalcitrant city to court, and won, charging that officials were not enforcing antipollution laws.)

Blaushild's 1964 crusade did not bring an immediate halt to Lake Erie pollution, but it created a political climate favorable to tougher pollution controls implemented in ensuing years. After 1964, the Citizens for Clean Air and Water continued to push for those new environmental laws, but in a less visible way. In 1971, Blaushild left the group, ending his long crusade, and went back to selling cars instead of clean water. "I was tired," he says, "absolutely tired."

Blaushild's retirement from the clean water crusade did not mark the end of his activism, however. In ensuing years, he lent active support to efforts to pass returnable bottle legislation in Ohio, financed the publication of ads urging efforts to build world peace rather than bomb shelters, and promoted farmers' markets in Cleveland.

On December 20, 1979, David Blaushild's compassionate crusade for a better world came to a quiet end. He died unexpectedly of a heart attack while in the hospital for minor surgery.

Fifteen years earlier a Cleveland editorial writer

mused on the endless energy of this remarkable man, who tirelessly campaigned to clean up Lake Erie. His words are a fitting epitaph.

"So what does it get a man to drive around and implore people to act before it is too late—and too late could be five or twenty years away? He gets the satisfaction of trying to do something for everybody's children and grandchildren. He won't be remembered by a monument or a poet. That's all there is in it for him." For David Blaushild that was enough.

B.P.B.

VENICE

When we think of Venice, we think of gracious curved gondolas, and *palazzi* on canals bridged by elegantly carved walkways. We think of the sea, and the city, and the past.

But Venice, a series of islands dispersed in the lagoon formed by the Po River delta, may well be one of the most futuristic cities we have. For here, the deteriorating (some say dying) city has attracted the most modern technology available in order to save itself. The Venice preservation scheme intends nothing less than to harness and control the sea, correct natural trends of erosion, eliminate air pollution, and revitalize the city's commerce.

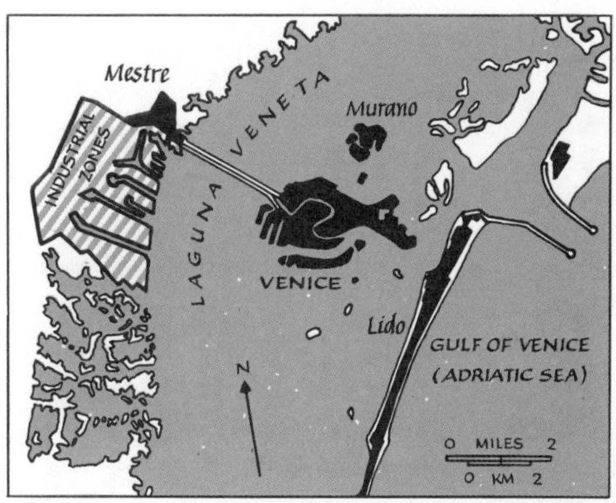

International efforts to save Venice began in 1966 after major floods and *aqua alta* (high water) left the city under more than 6 feet (2 meters) of mud and polluted sea water. At first, relief focused on restoring the artworks that had been soaked or stained—Venice's art inventory includes more than ten thousand monuments and masterpieces, palaces, churches, convents, and other important buildings and artifacts. One hundred million dollars was required to mount the effort. And it was very clear that a long-term solution had to be found, for the floods were just one part of a larger problem involving heavy air pollution from industry that was also ruining the art treasures. Airborne particles clung to buildings, hastening deterioration. The famous bronze horses of St. Mark's Cathedral wore a corroding crust. But any long-term solution requires understanding of both environmental and economic factors. In Venice, these are as related as watchworks.

First, there is the question of jobs. Residents of Venice move to the industrialized mainland, seeking work and an escape from the decay of their homes. Venetians have little left in the city with which to make their livelihood, except the port and the tourist industry, both of which depend on the city's maintaining its traditional charm. Without other viable commercial enterprises, and unless residents perceive preservation of their city as a boon and not a hindrance, the most ambitious restoration plans will fail.

And progress is slow, complicated by contemporary Italian social conditions. As millions of dollars are raised to save artworks, the workers of the Venice region look on scornfully. To them industrialization of the mainland means steady employment, history means poverty. And there is some question too about whether money raised on behalf of Venice actually is spent for this purpose, or whether it is diverted by other ostensibly more pressing needs.

Then there is the question of the water itself—how to secure fresh water and how to control the sea that flows through, around, and under Venice. To provide residents with drinking water, Venice depended on artesian wells, which weakened the city's foundation. So Venice was sinking itself, a process called subsidence. Worse, however, was the water demand of expanding industries along the coast opposite Venice, which required large amounts of fresh water for manufacturing processes. So, ironically, the *sink-*

Venice: The Grand Canal. (*U. S. Library of Congress*)

ing also provided jobs, goods, and services. (According to reports in 1979 by the Italian National Research Council, the subsidence had ceased, but whether it has been permanently arrested remains doubtful.)

Then there is the high water itself, a normal tide accompanying a sea abnormally high due to combined meteorological, lunar, and oceanic conditions. To control this phenomenon, which does not happen often but need only happen once to be destructive, an international team of engineers and architects has suggested such remedies as deepening the Venetian lagoon, narrowing the city's channels, building dikes, establishing a lock system that will regulate itself in relation to the sea, and building inflatable dams, which can be puffed up in time to block the encroaching waters. But, as of early 1980, the long-term solution remains to be found.

When Venice was a powerful independent nation in the fifteenth century, the seat of a wealthy trading empire, one of the highest political offices was held by the *magestero per l'aqua,* the magistrate for the water. He was responsible for monitoring the tides, and maintaining the sea walls and the building foundations. His job was to watch the sea, and his decisions spelled the fortunes of the city. Now Venice is a troubled international monument, but not only the sea needs watching.

P.D.

REDWOODS

The tallest tree in the world has a scientific name, Sequoia sempervirens, *as well as a given name. Nobody uses the given name much. It was named the Howard A. Libby tree when it was measured in 1963, after the chairman of the board of the Arcata Redwood Company, the firm that owned the land on which it stands. Mostly, it is just called "the tall tree." Because it is now inside Redwood National Park, the tree is still there, standing 367.8 feet [112.2 meters] high. . . . The tree, if felled across a football field, would reach from goal post to goal post, and beyond. It is about as tall as a thirty-story building. The tree began its life in the year 1393.*

From Natural Resources Defense Council Report, Marc Reisner

The redwood species indigenous to the northwest United States has been on the earth for approximately 160 million years. At one time, the original redwood forest covered approximately 2 million acres (800,000 hectares) of land, which remained relatively unmolested until the 1850s, when redwood logging began with the development of the American West. By 1925, more than one third of the trees had been logged.

In 1968, Redwood National Park was established to protect the trees, many of which were centuries old and hundreds of feet high, from indiscriminate logging. Ironically, rather than solving the problem of how to protect the trees, the establishment of the park demonstrated that simply "roping off" an area may not be enough to preserve it.

Though the very oldest trees in Redwood National Park in northern California *are* protected, they are as conspicuous on the mountain slopes as a goatee is on the face. They stand, unscathed, surrounded by a war zone of logging, jarred by the metallic buzz of the logger's chain saw.

Conservation groups lobbied, and the park

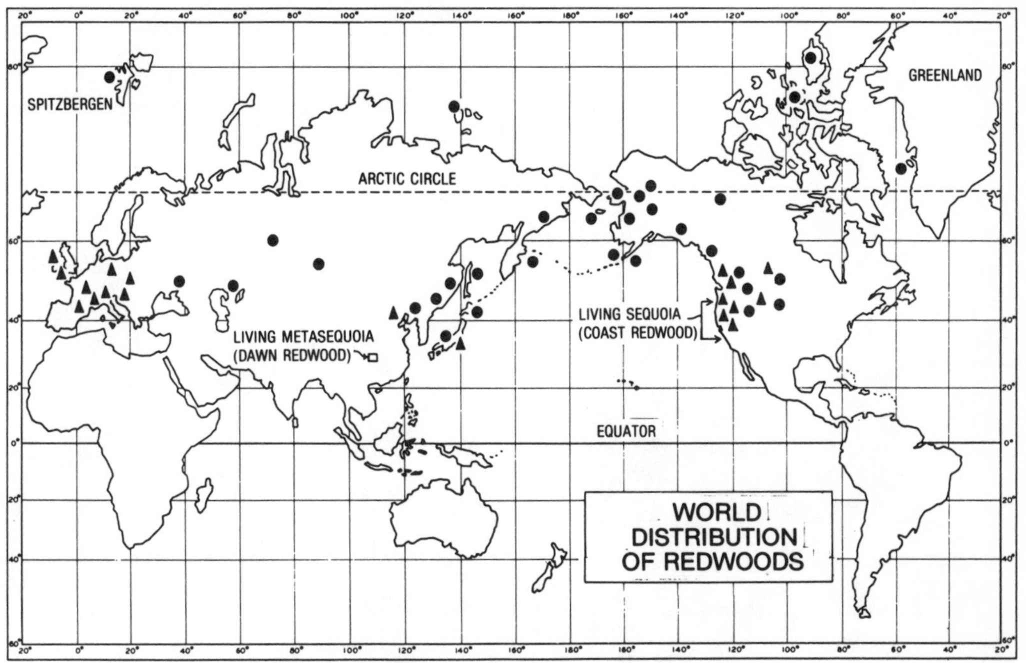

The oldest living sequoias (coast redwoods) are about 2,000 years old; fossil records show that redwoods have existed for 100 million years. Today these giants survive in only two parts of the world. (*Save-the-Redwoods League*)

boundaries were extended in several stages. By 1978, new land had been acquired so that protected areas totaled 218,000 acres (88,000 hectares). However, only 75,000 of these acres (30,300 hectares) were virgin forest, old growth like "the tall tree." The rest is a combination of saplings and stumps that will eventually, in coming generations, also be protected forests. In addition, there is need to acquire about 100,000 more acres (40,400 hectares) as a kind of buffer.

According to the Save-the-Redwoods League, by 1978 only 160,000 acres (64,600 hectares) of the original 2 million acres (808,000 hectares) of old growth remained standing. The rest had been lumbered into construction beams for foundations of buildings, picnic tables, recreation decks, beach walkways, fences, and house decoration—mainly outdoor wood products, for which redwood is ideally suited. The wood is prized for its sheen, its rich colors, and its natural resistance to rot, water, fire, and termites.

The U.S. lumber industry currently cuts about 10,000 acres (4,040 hectares) of redwood per year—about 700 million board feet (214 million board meters). Of this, 10,940,000 board feet is sold to Japan and other nations, sometimes as raw wood that will return to the United States as finished lumber products.

When environmentalists began urging that more land be protected, the timber industry and the loggers who stood to lose their jobs understandably opposed park expansion. A protracted legal battle in 1978 unfortunately pitted conservationists against loggers, and the equation seemed to be that saving trees equalled people out of work. But jobs were already being threatened by indiscriminate cutting; the industry often cut without planning and was therefore eliminating its own supply of new growth. So the park expansion law mandates selective foresting where cutting is permitted, and provides funds for job training and relocation of loggers who might suffer from any loss of work resulting from diminished logging on the park land.

It will probably take about fifty years to acquire the rest of the land needed finally to buttress the park and ensure adequate watershed protection. The land will be purchased parcel by parcel from the timber industry and private owners by the National Park Service, the California State Park Commission, or by citizen groups that will turn the land over to the federal government. The people who have lobbied to save the redwoods probably will not live to enjoy the full-size park or see the trees that are today mere sprouts. Instead they are saving trees for the generations to come.

"I tried to grow trees once, but they never did come out like this." (© *1980 Eldon Dedini*)

P.D.

LAKE BAIKAL

Lake Baikal has been called the blue eye of Siberia. Crescent-shaped and clear, it is an eye fringed with lashes of pine, spruce, and larch. Gazing deeply into Siberia's eye, one can imagine what it has seen: a cataclysmic formation during the days of dinosaurs and giant ferns, aquatic creatures undergoing 25 million years of evolution, a damaging period of pollution, and ten years of restoration efforts.

To the people of Siberia Baikal is a special,

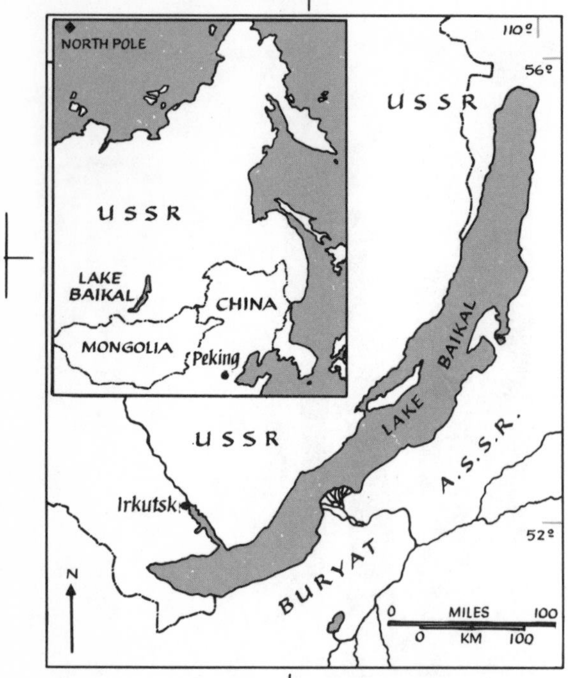

almost sacred place; for limnologists too it is something of a shrine. Most Westerners know it only as the world's largest lake by volume. That is, although it doesn't cover the most area of any lake, it holds the most water: 30 billion cubic yards (23 billion cubic meters) of it, almost enough to fill the basins of all five of North America's Great Lakes. Only 30 miles (48 kilometers) across and about 400 miles (644 kilometers) long, Lake Baikal reaches the incredible depth of 5,314 feet (1,620 meters), more than three times the depth of Lake Superior, the lake with the largest surface area. (See "The Great Lakes," page 310.)

Lake Baikal's trenchlike basin was formed by a massive shift in the earth's crust along a fault line about 25 million years ago, making it also the world's oldest lake. The fault is still active. In 1861 a 70-mile (113-kilometer) section of the eastern shore fractured and sank during an earthquake, drowning more than thirteen hundred people. Some geologists predict the fault will eventually split the northern and southern portions of the Asian subcontinent and Lake Baikal will become a new ocean.

Soviet scientists are more concerned with the immediate future of the lake, which has been threatened by overfishing and by pollution from logging and a paper mill. Although the Soviet Union's postwar push to industrialize met with little opposition from people concerned with protecting natural environments, the threat to Lake Baikal was an exception. In the mid-1950s, Soviet technicians selected the lake as the site for the country's first large, modern pulp and paper mill. It met the requirements of easy access to extensive forests and plenty of water for the thirsty industrial process, as well as hydropower and an adequate transportation system. Logs could be cut from the huge eastern Siberian forest and rafted along the lake or its hundreds of feeder rivers to the mill. But pulp mills are notorious polluters (see "The Pages You Are Reading," page 203), and strong objections were raised by scientists and citizens who regarded the lake with a reverence few Western lakes have inspired; it is known as the "glorious sea" and the "sacred Baikal."

Seals and Caviar

The clarity of the lake is startling. Scientists in helicopters can survey the lake's unique population of freshwater seals simply by looking down and counting; they can see through the water as deep as the seals can dive. The water is so clear because the shore is composed of dense rock, which is not easily broken down and dissolved in water. In some places the shore slopes gently to rocky beaches; in other places it forms sheer cliffs washed by tiny waterfalls and spotted with tenacious trees clinging to thin soil accumulated in cracks.

Swimming in the clear water are creatures with remarkable adaptations evolved over millions of years in the isolated lake. Of the lake's 1,700 species, 1,200 are found nowhere else. Consider the golomyanka, a fish so adapted to living in the lake's cold waters that it will die in temperatures above 45° F (7° C). The golomyanka's body contains so much oil—35 percent of its body weight—that the fish is both extremely buoyant and translucent. Weak and dying golomyankas cast ashore by waves literally melt in the sun, leaving behind only a skeleton. The fish migrate from the depths to the surface at night to feed on plankton. The omul, a foot-long (30-centimeter) member of the whitefish and lake herring family, is the lake's most common commercial catch. Unlike most fish, which struggle silently when hauled out of the water, the omul emits a piercing cry. Baikal's most prized catch is the sturgeon, which can grow to a length of 7 to 10 feet (2 to 3 meters) and weigh more than 500

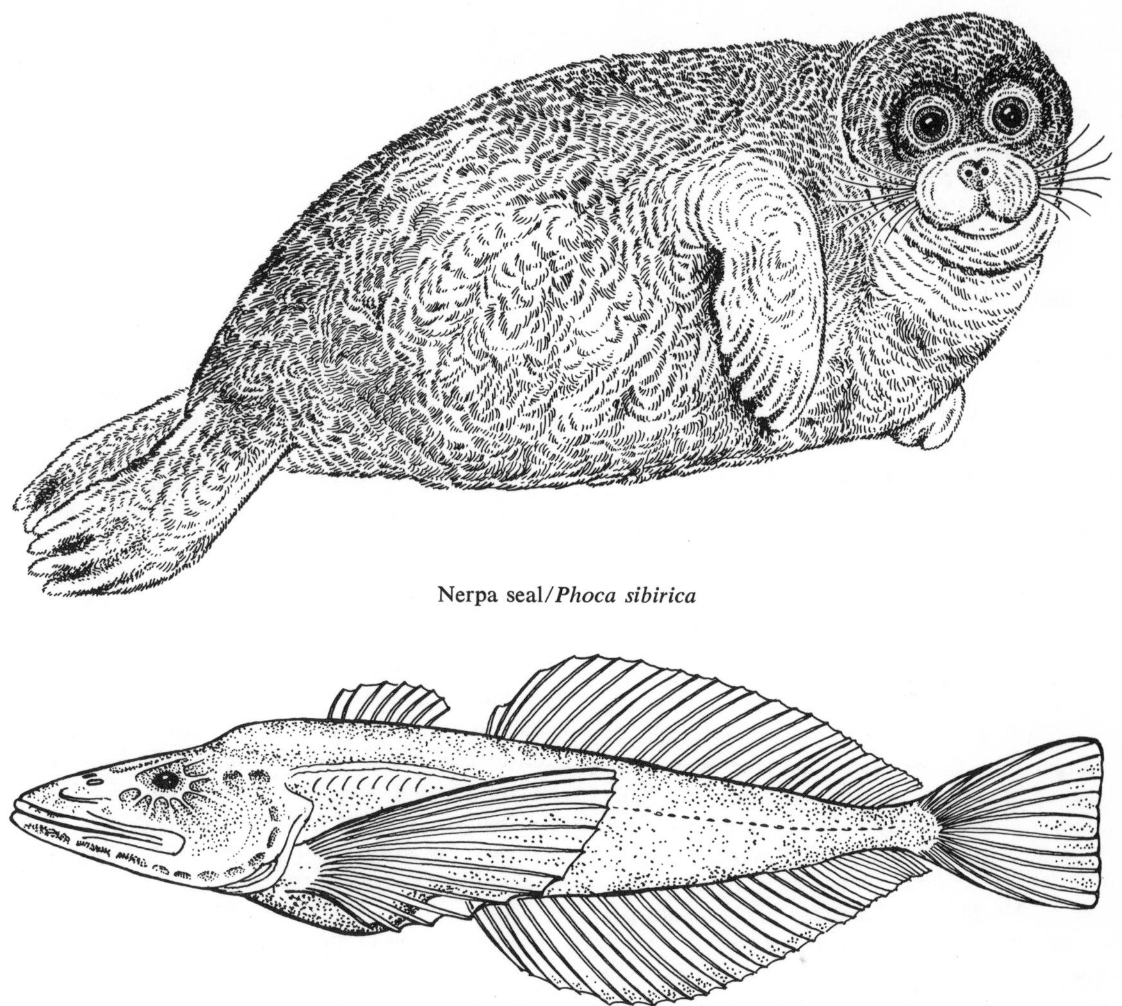

Nerpa seal/*Phoca sibirica*

Golomyanka/*Comephorus baicalensis*

pounds (227 kilograms). Sturgeon meat is popular in the Soviet Union, as are sturgeon eggs—black caviar.

At night, when the golomyankas rise from their deep daytime haunts to feed, they are often attacked by silvery-gray nerpas, Baikal's famous freshwater seal. The nerpa's closest relatives are in the Arctic Ocean, 2,000 miles (3,219 kilometers) away. Scientists speculate nerpas somehow migrated to Lake Baikal from the Arctic eons ago, when land and water patterns were different. Like saltwater seals, they were hunted extensively for their pelts. Now, under hunting limitations, their population is growing slowly.

Lake Baikal's remotenesss protected it until the 1950s. Until then it hosted only a few settlements and fishing vessels. But as fishing cooperatives became more efficient, the sturgeon population was reduced so drastically that scientists doubted it would recover. The once abundant omul catches also became smaller. Part of the fishery decline was attributed to logging. Huge rafts of logs being floated down the lake to mills in the southern factory towns of Irkutsk and Ulan Ude often broke apart in storms. The logs drifted into tributaries and raked the bottom spawning grounds of the omul, and bacteria from decaying logs used up oxygen needed by aquatic organisms. When construction began in 1959 on the modern pulp mill, the lake was already suffering from careless exploitation.

The Sacred Lake in Decline

The mill was located at the town of Baikal, on the southern shore. During its seven-year construction, a controversy raged over its effect on the lake. The plant opened with minimal pollution controls—a filtration system for wastewater—but the debate revealed how little was known about the lake's ecology, and scientists were authorized to make extensive studies. In 1969, three years after the mill opened, the government issued a decree for cleaning Lake Baikal. Omul and sturgeon fishing was banned for several years, log jams were removed, and rafting was prohibited. Although the government hired 150 inspectors to patrol the lake, critics complained that not all the orders were enforced. Effluent from the paper mill, for example, still exceeded government pollution standards in 1978.

Meanwhile, scientists at the Limnological Institute were engaged in a study documenting pollution damage over several years. In 1978, Gregorii Galazii, the institute's director, released the disturbing results. Less than half the pollutants discharged into the lake were being absorbed; the rest fanned out from the Baikal mill in a growing polluted zone at the mouth of the Selenga River, a major tributary, that covered hundreds of square kilometers and reached a depth of 820 feet (250 meters). Fish caught near the polluted zone showed signs of stress, mutations, and behavioral changes. Plankton growth there slowed and bacterial growth increased. Most disturbing, the spawning grounds of the famous (and valuable) omul were seriously affected by mills on the Selenga River. More than 50 percent of the roe was destroyed by pollution. Galazii recommended that the pulp plant cease all discharge into the lake by using a closed-cycle water system and disposing of residual wastes beyond the boundaries of the lake's watershed.

The government responded by declaring that the mills must develop closed-cycle systems by 1985 if they are to continue operating. Part of the impetus to clean the lake comes from a desire to encourage growing tourism to Baikal and the numerous hot springs located nearby.

Recently, scientists discovered phthalate esters in Baikal's sediments, synthetic chemicals used to make brittle plastics more pliable. The compound is not produced near the lake, but is swept in by the wind and rain from distant industrial centers.

"Phthalate esters are not a serious problem in Lake Baikal now," said John Robbins, an American scientist who visited Baikal in 1979. "But they are another example of a high technology pollutant affecting a remote ecosystem. It's like taking a core sample in Antarctica and finding the history of the growth of the auto industry in increasing deposits of lead—lead from auto exhausts halfway around the world. These discoveries always bring a shocking realization of our ability to foul our nest."

The story of Lake Baikal's exploitation, pollution, and cleanup is similar to that of many lakes. But somehow Baikal transcends the familiar story, partly because of its stature among lakes and partly because it so clearly symbolizes the global interconnectedness of the environment.

M.P.

SEA TURTLE FLOTAS

The only pastime we could have was catching tortoises (sea turtles) of which there are vast numbers there. When it is fair, and the sun shines bright, they come out of the water and lie in the hot sand. So when they were all very quiet and settled, we came upon them of a sudden with Sticks and Iron Bars.

Voyage to the East Indies,
Fryke and Schweitzer, 1700

In the Cayman Islands of the Caribbean Sea, a turtle-hunting center that supplied sea turtle meat for merchant cruises in the sixteenth century, iron-bar-wielding crews slaughtered two thousand turtles a night. Ships commonly loaded their decks and holds with as many turtles as they could carry. As a result of mass killings like this, and continued indiscriminate turtle hunting ever since, six of the seven scientifically identified sea turtle species—hawksbill, green, leatherback, Kemp's (or Atlantic) Ridley, loggerhead, Pacific Ridley, and flatback—are officially endangered or threatened in most areas of the world. (There are too few statistics available on the flatback to determine its status.) This is particularly sobering

Ancestral Sea Turtle
Leatherback
Loggerhead
Atlantic Ridley
Pacific Ridley
Hawksbill
Green Turtle

since turtles are the oldest reptiles on earth, having endured for over 200 million years.

Because sea turtles once emerged from the ocean—only to return to it 90 million years ago—they are air breathers, like whales. They are ungainly on land now, but streamlined, flipperlike legs make the sea turtle an expert swimmer. Some species achieve speeds of 10 knots, although the turtle cannot maintain such speeds for long.

The Easiest of Prey

But as well-equipped for its physical environment as the turtle is, evolutionary history ill-equipped these animals to cope with the onslaught of turtle hunters, who take advantage of the turtles' reproductive patterns. Though sea turtles spend their adult lives in the ocean, they return each year to land in search of suitable nesting sites. Their navigational process and endurance on these migrations, sometimes covering hundreds of kilometers of open sea, are considered true wonders of the marine world.

Newly hatched Atlantic (Kemp's Ridleys) head for the sea. Only 1 to 5 percent will survive their first year. (*NPS/Fred Mang, Jr.*)

At nesting time, female turtles "haul out" of the water, often en masse, and crawl awkwardly to the soft, moist sand at the tide's edge to start digging a nest. Once the female has begun nesting, its instincts command. Oblivious to any danger, she lays one hundred or so eggs, which look like soft, wet marbles. At this moment in the female's life, she is extremely vulnerable. In the sea, a mature turtle is formidable simply because of its size. But on land, the turtle is defenseless—a human hunter need merely flip the turtle onto its back, a position from which it cannot right itself, and an easy capture is made. Nesting turtles who manage to escape this fate immediately cover their eggs with sand and lumber back to the sea, leaving tracks that lead straight to the nest.

Unprotected, the nests can be easily raided by hungry animals and human poachers. Surviving eggs hatch forty-five to sixty days after being laid, and the fledgling turtles, guided by instinct, make their first awkward crawl to the sea at the mercy of swooping sea birds. If the tiny turtles reach the ocean, they remain easy prey for diving birds and fish. Only 1 to 5 percent of all turtles hatched survive the natural conditions of their first year of life in the wild.

Turtle Counts

But natural dangers hardly compare to the assaults on turtles made by people. Green turtles, the most commercially valuable species, are hunted for their calipee, the tissue that connects the turtle's belly shell, called the plastron, to the shielding back shell, called the carapace. When boiled, calipee becomes gelatinous and can be used as a base to make the delicacy, turtle soup. Hawksbill turtles are slaughtered for their beautiful spotted shell, from which products such as eyeglass frames, buttons, and jewelry are made. The eggs of virtually all turtle species are hunted for food, and in some areas they are considered powerful aphrodisiacs.

Because of the worldwide market for turtle products, turtle populations have been seriously depleted. The giant leatherback, which weighs roughly three quarters of a ton (700 kilograms), is difficult to count because the males never come ashore, but the breeding female count is approximately 50,000 worldwide. Approximately one quarter to one third of a million hawksbills are slaughtered annually in Japan and the

Indo-Pacific, but population counts of the animals at sea are highly speculative. There are fewer than a thousand mature female Kemp's Ridley turtles today, although in 1947, 40,000 were counted nesting on a single day. This species is particularly vulnerable, since the entire breeding population nests at only one site in the world: Tamaulipas, Mexico. Consequently, hunters have been able to return to the same beach, at the same time each year, and be assured of a massive catch. There are about half a million Pacific Ridleys left, and about the same number of greens, but only about 150,000 loggerheads. There are few statistics on the population of flatbacks, although they are believed to nest and live only around Australia.

Turtle Dilemmas

Fortunately, the turtle's endangered status has been recognized, and Canada, the United States, Costa Rica, Surinam, French Guiana, Nicaragua, South Africa, Australia, and Mexico have developed protection and management programs; some even ban turtle products entirely. But other countries, like Peru, Ecuador, and Guyana, continue rampant turtle hunting.

Conservation laws are undermined by economic and social realities in many countries—two or three easily hunted, quickly gutted turtles can often earn more money for a worker than a week at most other available jobs. Turtle meat and turtle eggs are a vital part of the average diet in some countries, and policing beaches to protect turtles seems a low priority in many countries.

Also, since all turtle species migrate to some extent, effective legislation must be international in application. Protected nests in Surinam, for example, might save turtle hatchlings that could be killed when they land on the beaches of Brazil to nest.

Turtle farming or ranching is considered by some conservationists to be a workable and practical means for both supplying and conserving wild turtle populations. Theoretically, these farms—one was operating in the Cayman Islands in 1979—would take unprotected turtle eggs from the wild, eggs that would otherwise be doomed to predation and poaching, and raise the young turtles through the crucial first years of life. Ideally these turtles would then be released into the wild, and a domestic breeding stock could also be successfully raised. Opponents of the farming idea argue that too little is known about reproductive patterns and populations to justify removing turtles from the wild, and they also warn that turtle farms will only stimulate the market for turtle products by making goods more readily available.

In the meantime, the turtles follow their instincts and nest, on schedule, at beaches around the world, following the reliable rhythms of seasons and sealife, while humans on the land debate how to protect them from humans.

L.W.

Wavemakers:

THE TURTLE LADY

Seventy-six-year-old Ila Loetscher never produced offspring of her own, but she has ten "little children," as she calls them, living on the ground floor of her Padre Island, Texas, home. They live in salt water tanks, because they're sea turtles. Most came to Ila with a serious infirmity—a severed flipper, an injured vertebra. Not only has Ila nursed them back to life, she's probably done more than any human being to focus attention on the plight of the Kemp's or Atlantic Ridley, the smallest, rarest, and most endangered of sea turtles.

One of the turtles, "Dr. Porter," is a strapping twelve-year-old who weighs in at 90 pounds (40.8 kilograms). During 1967, when the animal

Ila Loetscher and "Little Fox," a four-year-old female Kemp's Ridley. (*Evelyn Sizemore*)

was a tiny half-ounce hatchling lumbering down the sand from egg shell to ocean, it was nipped by a crab, breaking a leg. Ila scooped it up and telephoned a veterinarian named Dr. Porter—hence the name—to come and set the limb.

While the little turtle convalesced under Ila's watchful eye, a thousand of its cousins, who hatched at the same time on the same Padre Island beach, were making a go of it alone in the ocean. As Kemp's Ridleys, they shared an extraordinary distinction: they were the first known batch to be born away from the traditional nesting ground, one tiny stretch of beach called Rancho Nuevo, near Tamaulipas, Mexico. Some marine biologists believe that the fate of the Ridleys, whose numbers have shrunk in the last thirty years from 40,000 to about 500, depends partially on programing turtles born on Padre Island to return there and lay more eggs. Dr. Porter's generation was the first step; and if the project succeeds, much credit goes to Ila and her friends, who transported the first lot to Padre Island egg by egg in Styrofoam boxes.

The Turtle Project

In a sense, the whole thing started in 1966 with Ila's friend Dearl Adams. When Adams learned that the Ridleys' numbers had shrunk drastically, he resolved to do something. Researching the problem, he learned that every Kemp's Ridley in the world nested on the same day at the same Mexican beach, and that the rookery had been systematically raided by locals who ate the eggs. (In Mexico, turtle eggs are considered a delicacy and an aphrodisiac.) Coyotes were also contributing to the problem by indulging their equally strong turtle egg habit at Rancho Nuevo.

Adams concluded that Padre Island would make a better nursery for at least some of the vulnerable Ridleys. It's a protected national wildlife sanctuary with a beach similar in slope and grain size to Rancho Nuevo, 40 miles (64 kilometers) to the south. He asked the Mexican government to let him take 2,000 eggs out of the country; they agreed, and he set about gathering a group for the rescue mission. Adams asked Ila, an animal lover and a transplant to Padre Island herself, and she accepted.

In March 1966, Dearl Adams, Ila, and ten others set up a tent caravan on Rancho Nuevo beach. They waited patiently for two weeks, binoculars sighted on the waves, until about three hundred female Atlantic Ridleys finally waddled ashore and laid their eggs. The humans quickly packed up 2,000 eggs and carted them to Padre Island, where they set up camp again for the fifty-day incubation period. No eggs hatched. The next year, 1967, they repeated the trip to Mexico and transported the eggs to Padre by plane. Something worked. The eggs hatched, and Dr. Porter's generation was born.

With Ila at the helm, the group, by now calling itself "the Turtle Project," decided to discontinue the egg transplants for at least seven years, the least amount of time a sea turtle takes to mature and nest. Only if the turtles returned to nest would the project be worth continuing. If the experiment worked, it would be because the Padre "imprinting" had taken effect. Scientists believe that a female hatchling's first contact with sand is so profound that she'll return to the same beach—even if she's wandered as far as the China Sea—to lay her eggs.

With the vigils temporarily stopped, Ila shifted her attention to sick turtles, a service that started when someone gave her three. Word soon got around the Texas coast that a Padre Island woman could work wonders with injured turtles, and before long they started appearing at Ila's door in the arms of shrimpers, biologists, and local children. Droves of children would circle around as she tended to the animals. Eventually, "the turtle lady," as they nicknamed her, started a formal turtle education program that continues to this day.

By 1973, seven years had passed since Dr. Porter's generation had slipped off the Padre Island beach and vanished into the seas. Ila organized a vigil on the chance that the Ridleys might be mature enough to return and nest that year. Four families camped during the entire three-month nesting season. The months passed; no Ridleys. They made plans to meet, same time, same place, the next year.

On March 6, 1974, reports Ila, "Our first little girl came waddling up the beach." Folks from all over Padre Island came for a celebration to view the 80-pound (36-kilogram) guest of honor, who had already laid several hundred eggs. They named her "Alpha," Greek for "the beginning." The next day, apparently unaffected by her newfound fame, Alpha sauntered out to sea again. Ila and her friends had proven a point, and their modest success attracted considerable attention from the media and the scientific community. By 1978, four years after Alpha nested at her Texas birthplace, a million-dollar international campaign got underway to save the Kemp's Ridleys.

The Turtle Man

It would be unfair to say that Ila and her friends were wholly responsible for inspiring the "Kemp's Ridley Project." If Ila is "the turtle lady" to the children of Padre Island, Dr. Archie Carr, a zoologist, is "the turtle man" to the world's scientific community. He has spent his life researching and writing much of what we know about sea turtles. His discovery of the Kemp's Ridleys' Mexican nesting ground in 1953 was the culmination of an eighteen-year search. Though Dr. Carr's professional credibility and lobbying talent were keys to government cooperation and funding, he credits Ila with attracting crucial public support for the campaign. He also credits her and her associates with thinking up the Padre Island connection. The U.S. and Mexican officials controlling the campaign have decided the idea was apt and have pledged to continue the transplants.

The turtle vigils belong to the professionals now, but Ila's work is not over. In late 1979, two college students appeared with an Atlantic green they mistook at first glance for a glob of tar. It was Ila's first casualty from the 1979 Mexican oil spill, an accident she believes will haunt the Ridleys for years to come. Ila persuaded the boys to stay and assist her in treating the year-old turtle with a remedy recommended by a local marine biologist. They bathed its shell in Wesson oil, swabbed out its mouth, and fed it lettuce to clean its intestines. A week later, says Ila, the little turtle was as good as new, almost ready to hit the waves.

Ila's educational work is going strong and expands each year. During the last five-month Padre Island tourist season, about a thousand visitors a month trooped to Ila's home and watched the turtle education program, making Ila very happy. But perhaps the brightest day in her life will be when Alpha's children, as well as Dr. Porter's generation, come home again. Then the turtle lady will be a grandmother, and the species will have inched just that much farther away from extinction.

J.W.

THE HUDSON RIVER

Because early European settlers flocked to its fertile valley and built some of the nation's first industries along its banks, the Hudson River has been called America's first river. Navigable for more than 100 miles (161 kilometers) inland, the Hudson became a principal waterway in the early development of the United States. During the American Revolution, George Washington's troops illustrated its strategic importance by stretching a submerged chain across the river at a narrow spot near West Point Military Academy to snare British ships. It became a principal leg of the Erie Canal. And with the dramatic rise of industry in the twentieth century, the Hudson's banks became studded with waterfront factories.

The convenience the river offered, however—with access to the sea, to New York City, to upland timber and agriculture, and through the Erie Canal to the Great Lakes—gradually became its undoing. By the 1950s the river that once hosted along its edges Indian tribes like the Mohicans (their name meant people-of-the-river-that-flows-two-ways, a reference to the effect of ocean tides that surge over the river's floor to reach far inland), the river that overwhelmed English explorer Henry Hudson with its abundance of fish, oysters, and riverbank game, the river that inspired early American art and literature, became a grossly contaminated waterway.

Once a symbol of U.S. progress, the Hudson River became a symbol of fouled ecosystems, of industrial wastes, of poisoned, inedible fish. The process had begun innocently. By the time of the American Revolution the river was dotted with small cities that used the river as a highway to carry immigrants, raw materials, and manufactured goods north, and grain, produce, lumber, and bricks south to New York City. By the late nineteenth century the steel ribbons of railroads were lining the banks, to be followed a half century later by highways.

The railroad builders filled in marshes, the natural cleansers of Hudson water, creating a filtering problem that would not be recognized for decades. Simultaneously, the additional carrying capacity added by railroads attracted more industry. After World War II, factories with immense polluting potential began to spring up—paper plants, electric plants, plating and metal-finishing factories, plastics industries, and

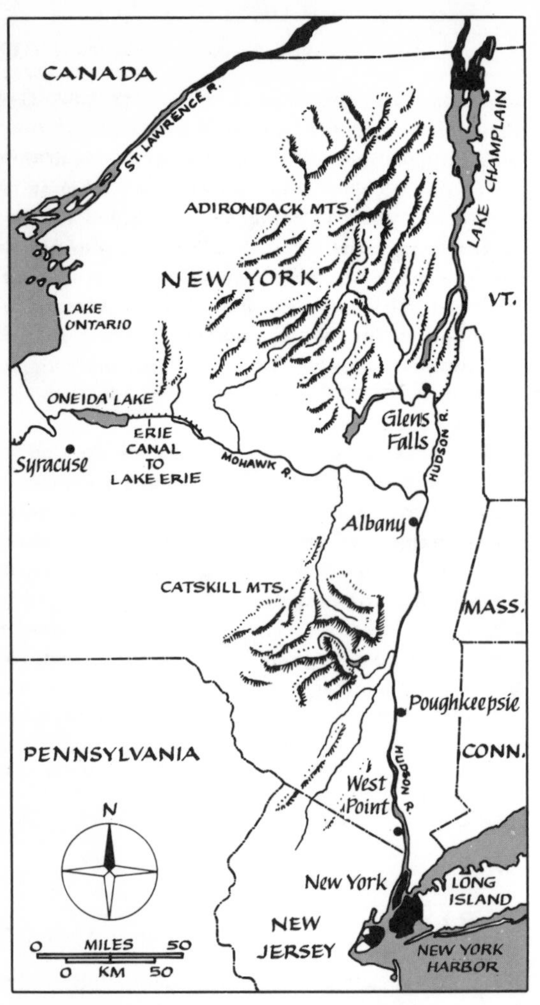

battery factories. In the absence of environmental regulations, they all dumped their wastes into the river. So did the burgeoning cities.

Telltale signs of deterioration soon began to appear. Waste dumping of chemicals and sewage began to taint municipal water supplies drawn from the Hudson. Oil slicks caused by river-borne tanker traffic became common. Along the lower reaches of the river, which slices through the center of the largest metropolitan area in the United States, the river turned into an ugly flow of polluted soup.

New York Harbor bustles with ocean freighters, tugs, barges, and pleasure boats picking their way amid a maze of buoys. It is one of the most polluted harbors in the world. The most populous city in the United States dumps wastes directly into the river, as do a science-fiction array of chemical factories and oil refineries on the New Jersey shore. The mud on the bottom of the harbor is heavy with poisons, which are stirred up whenever shipping channels are dredged.

Robert Fulton's steamboat, the *Clermont,* passing West Point, New York, on the Hudson River, about 1810. (*I. N. Phelps Stokes Collection; Print Collection; The New York Public Library; Astor, Lenox and Tilden Foundations.*)

Fortunately, it is hard to kill life in a river, even one as severely abused as the Hudson. The great oyster beds noted by Henry Hudson's crew are gone, and fish like the shad are not as abundant as they once were, but the river is not dead. In part the Hudson survived because of the residual effects of a shift away from river transport during the 1960s, in part because of citizen anger. As trucks began carrying much of the commerce that once rode the river, many Hudson waterfronts began to decay. While the contamination of the river was only partially visible to its riverbank residents, the deterioration of its commercial structures was an eyesore. Spurred by what seemed a general acceptance of the river's demise, a small core of river residents arose to protest, demanding that its beauty be restored (see "Saving a River with a Song," below). Their efforts were galvanic. Laws requiring sewage treatment were passed, and slowly the foul smell disappeared along most of the waterway.

Gradually, fishing boat crews began to notice more fish, more crabs, more life in general in the Hudson. A few communities built parks on their ravaged waterfronts. As people turned their attention to the river, they made louder demands that it be restored to health.

By 1975 scientists and conservation groups were announcing that the river was getting cleaner. But that year the presence of an invisible, more insidious pollutant was discovered. Scientists found that carcinogenic polychlorinated biphenyls (PCBs), dumped for years in the river by electrical manufacturing plants, had become embedded in Hudson sediments and had worked their way up the food chain into fish. The State of New York announced that some Hudson River fish were unsafe to eat and probably would be for many years. (For more on PCBs, see "The Great Lakes," page 310, and "Wastes in the Sea," page 409.) The more carefully scientists looked for chemical pollution, the more they found, revealing new types of pollutants and a more complex problem than anyone suspected. While pollution from raw sewage can be reversed within only a few years after the sewage flow is halted, recovery from some long-lived chemical pollutants can take decades or longer.

The river continues to be symbolic of the age: America's first river during the country's adolescence, its first industrial artery, one of its first damaged major rivers, and in the years to come, perhaps America's first great river to be restored to the beauty and health of its past.

M.G., M.P.

Wavemakers:

SAVING A RIVER WITH A SONG

At some places along New York's Hudson River, if there are no cars on the bordering highways and no trains passing by, you can stand and enjoy the riverscape of a century and a half ago, a view of clear water. This was not true in the 1960s. Then, the smell of the Hudson water was to be shunned; the river was stained by the sewage and chemical waste of millions that was blithely emptied into it, fouling its waters all the way to the ocean.

Much of the credit for the improved situation goes to a boat—a huge sailboat that regularly journeys up and down the Hudson, as its predecessors did in the nineteenth century. It is one of the most famous boats in the United States, the sloop *Clearwater,* a full-size replica of sailing vessels that were unique to America's "first river." It was conceived in 1966 and born three years later, due mainly to the efforts of social activist, singer-songwriter Pete Seeger, who returned to live in the Hudson Valley during the 1950s. Seeger was touched by the majesty of the river and saddened by the abuses it had suffered.

The idea of building a replica sloop came to Seeger from a friend, Vic Schwartz, a commercial artist and American history buff who read about the great boats in an out-of-print book.

But why build a boat? In 1966, when fund-raising began, parts of the United States were seething with racial tension, and the war in Southeast Asia was headed toward full-scale conflict and national trauma. Was this the time to try to focus attention on a river? The question was resolved quickly when Pete Seeger met with a local millionaire as part of the fund-raising effort. The rich man was interested but had his reservations.

"It's a beautiful boat, all right," he said as he looked at the drawings, "but what do you want to

sail the Hudson for? I do my sailing around the Virgin Islands."

Seeger continues the story.

"I felt my fingers clenching in anger, but I didn't say anything. Unwittingly, he had given us our best reason for building the boat. Cleaning up a river is a cause worth fighting for . . . We had allowed some people to make good profit along the Hudson and then go somewhere else to enjoy clear water."

The theory behind *Clearwater* was simple. When people saw the big, graceful boat gliding on the Hudson, they would be drawn to the riverfront—and its problems—and they might become involved in helping the river back to health.

On May 17, 1969, the *Clearwater* was launched in South Bristol, Maine. That year the Hudson was little more than an open sewer.

The small group around *Clearwater*, made up of people as diverse as IBM executives and counterculture "hippies," started sailing the sloop from town to town and waited for the reaction. The crew, which always included a few musicians, sailed into a community, put up posters, and played music for crowds that gathered. Sometimes scientists, local environmentalists, or river fishermen would follow the songs with short speeches about personal responsibility for pollution and about concern for our natural resources. Occasionally people were asked to sign a petition, or write a legislator, but for the most part the *Clearwater* only reminded them to care, allowing each community to decide for itself how to express that concern.

Over many years the people of the Hudson Valley had lost touch with their river. When the railroads came people no longer had to travel or ship goods by the slower waterways. Bridges spanned the Hudson making the ferry boats obsolete. In time, the waterfront areas of larger cities deteriorated into slum neighborhoods and factories. Industrial and municipal wastes created polluted, brackish water. The Hudson became nothing more than a moat to be crossed now and then. No one swam in it, few fished in it, most ignored it.

The coming of *Clearwater*, however, seemed to work a subtle and exciting change. Local people banded together and these loose organizations, later known as Sloop Clubs, began hanging the posters and opening their homes to the *Clearwater* crews. A string of Sloop Clubs grew along the river and soon they had become the focal point for local environmental campaigns. People began to work for a revival of the Hudson even when the *Clearwater* was not in town.

The *Clearwater*, a replica of a nineteenth-century centerboard sloop, became a symbol of cleaning up the Hudson River. (*Marty Gallanter*)

Initially the gains were small, but each year the list grew longer. More clubs were formed; more towns and cities began to discuss cleanup plans. New legislation was proposed and approved. More treatment plants were built. More riverfront parks were funded, and, most importantly, hundreds of thousands of people became involved with the Hudson once again.

Progress in cleaning up the Hudson was impressive enough to garner national attention, but in 1975 it was discovered that the Hudson and its fish were poisoned by clear, sticky, liquid PCBs (polychlorinated biphenyls) from industries on the upper Hudson. (See "The Hudson River," page 327.)

With the eruption of the PCBs issue, it became clear that cleaning the Hudson was not just a matter of removing surface substances. The threats from riverside industries were highly technical, very pervasive, quietly dangerous, and extremely expensive to eliminate. And few agree even now about which chemicals the river *can* absorb safely and how much of them. But lack of scientific consensus doesn't mean that a historic sailing vessel and a folk song have no place in the campaign to revive the Hudson.

Progress on the Hudson did not begin until local people started to care about the condition of their river. And that did not happen until the *Clearwater* focused the energies of people of the Hudson Valley on the river and on their role in preserving the total ecology of the region. There is continued progress on the river, and little by little the efforts of Hudson Valley residents result in victory. As Pete Seeger puts it in one of his songs, ". . . someday, though maybe not this year, my Hudson and my country will run clear."

M.G.

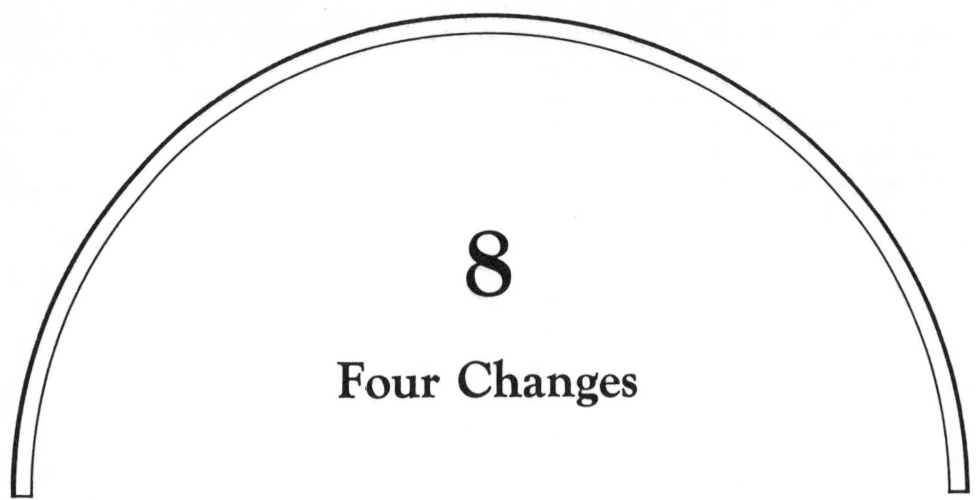

8

Four Changes

The ancient Greeks believed there were four ways in which things changed: in quantity, in quality, in location, and in being—by appearing or perishing. But in the time of Aristotle, humans were observers, by and large. Philosophers could ponder the machinery of life, but they had little access to the controls. Today, humanity can penetrate the most minute bits of matter, even creating new kinds of matter that exist only because of human intervention. We have webbed the globe in technology. We impose new conditions on old, natural systems. Evolutionary ebb and flow is no longer a gradual process directed by nature alone. Humans pull evolutionary switches, accelerating the rise or fall of species, societies, surroundings, circumstances—altering the nature of nature. We affect all of the Greeks' four changes, manipulating the quantity and the whereabouts of organisms and materials, creating and eliminating elements of the biosphere, modifying for good or ill the quality of life. This chapter takes stock of some of the transitions taking place about us, among us, because of us.

It is important to be realistic about change. For example, the inventory of earth's living things has always undergone changes, featuring wildly successful creatures and others that were discontinued. Most of the animal and plant species that ever existed are gone. Something in their nature made them unfit for changing conditions.

Unfortunately, however, the subtle and slow pace of evolution is being overwhelmed by the expanding wave of humans and our virile technology. There have been nearly 2,000 years of animal extinctions since the lion disappeared from Western Europe about A.D. 80. But more than half of these extinctions have occurred since 1900. As a result of lost native habitats, hunting, collecting, and industrial exploitation, we may be heading toward an unintended extermination of about one fifth of all the species on the planet by the year 2000. The loss would mean greatly reduced diversity, which is universally acknowledged as a sign of ecological health, and lost opportunities, since plants and animals produce ingredients for medicines, foods, and other human staples. It would also mean, of course, a further depletion of beauty and ecological exuberance.

Other elements of life on earth are changing, too. There are regrettable losses—acres of topsoil, the natural soundscape, wetlands, fisheries. There are unavoidable deteriorations, including native human societies quickly being consumed by industrial civilization. There are accumulations of new materials, most of them wastes, which threaten to change environments as small as the neighborhood and as large as the sea. But there are enhancing transitions going on, too, and it is these illustrations of human wisdom that offer substantial hope for the future. Species that came close to extinction are returning, diseases are disappearing, rivers are growing cleaner.

The most important transition of our era occurs within the human mind. People are awakening to their destructive potential, to their resource limitations, to their responsibilities. When something catches our imagination, like the beleaguered whale, or offends our sense of natural propriety, like a polluted Lake Washington, or threatens our sense of pride, like a lifeless River Thames, people step out of the passive common quiet to protest, and to correct the situation.

Most of the time there *are* remedies. Concerted action can revive rivers, cities, traditions, life-styles. About the only thing beyond rescue is a strain of life, a species. When the gene pool is gone, the matter is closed forever. The test for humanity is to devise healthy transitions without accelerating the uncorrectable ones, without further diminishing for all time the richness and vitality of the biosphere. We have no rights in this matter, for what we are changing is the future. It does not belong to us. We are living in our children's home.

M.R.

GONE

ANIMALS YOU'LL NEVER SEE

Extinct means gone forever. No one can recreate a dodo or a quagga. Not even advanced genetic engineering can give us another great auk, because we never found out which genes made a great auk a great auk.

Of course species come and go. Darwin taught us that. But recently many have died unnatural deaths: gunned down, bulldozed out of their habitats, poisoned. Many were interesting creatures that might have proved to be of domestic or scientific value. Or they might just have fascinated us by showing us another variety of life. We will never see them, nor will our children. These are some of their stories. (For a more complete list of extinct animals see "Extinct Birds," page 140, and "Extinct Mammals," page 144.)

Dodo (Didus ineptus)

On the isle of Mauritius in the Indian Ocean, 600 miles (966 kilometers) from the nearest populated land, the slow-witted flightless dodo thrived for centuries without a single enemy. The island was discovered by the Portuguese in 1507, and in 1598 Dutch explorers took possession of it, bringing their pet dogs, stowaway rats, and hearty carnivorous human appetites. In 1681 an English traveler saw what may have been the last Mauritius dodo disappear into the woods. Humans and other exotic predators had driven the strange bird to extinction in 174 years.

Seventeenth-century journals describe the dodo as a "very strange fowle" unlike any known to Europeans. "Bigger than the largest Turkey-cock," the great bird carried its bulk awkwardly on short, yellow legs. When it jogged, its plump belly dragged on the ground. The dodo's head was "half covered with a hood of feathers," its bare face dominated by a huge black hooked bill. It had "a small tail consisting of a few soft incurved feathers" and "little hanging wings like short sleeves, alltogether unuseful to Fly withal." Modern ornithologists have placed the dodo in the pigeon family, though it looked more like a vulture than a dove.

Slow and clumsy on foot, unable to swim or fly, the birds had no means of escape from predators. Having lived so long unmolested, they seemed to lack the impulse to flee from danger and offered little resistance when people caught them and clubbed them to death. Portuguese sailors, who enjoyed the taste of dodo meat on their long voyages, added insult to injury when they named the birds "doudo," meaning "dunce." Irresistibly easy prey, most of the world's dodos were eaten—by sailors and settlers, by foraging pigs and monkeys, by dogs and rats raiding ground nests for eggs and chicks. However, a few fine specimens were brought back alive to Europe and presented to royalty. Occasionally people even kept them as pets. But no one thought to try breeding them, and the captive birds died off without hatching a single chick.

By 1638, a mere forty years after the settlement of Mauritius, very few dodos were left. In his diary, an official of the British East India Company reported searching the island for "the strange fowle twice as bigge as a Goose, that can neither flye or swymm" and noted casually that he "mett with None." Neither he nor anyone else seemed aware that extinction was imminent. But within a few years all three related species had vanished, the gray Mauritius dodo, the white dodo of nearby Réunion Island, and a brown dodo called the "solitary" of Rodriguez Island. And half a century later most islanders had forgotten that the bird ever existed.

In Europe, naturalists began to suspect that the dodo was just another fantastic beast created by some traveler's imagination. No scientist had seen a skeleton. And the only stuffed specimen had grown so mangy and moth-eaten in an Oxford museum that the curator burned it as trash. Though the head and one foot survived the incineration, these scraps were hardly convincing evidence.

George Clark, a Mauritian native with an interest in natural history, reasoned that the most likely burial ground for bones on the hard volcanic island would be a marshy delta at the confluence of three large rivers. Washed into the water by torrential rains, the bones would flow with the current and be deposited in the soft mud of the delta. In 1863 Clark searched and found them just where he had predicted. From these scattered fragments he assembled complete skeletons, which he shipped to museums all over the world, including the American Museum of Natural History in New York and the Smithsonian Institution in Washington, D.C. Studying the skeletons against drawings by seventeenth-century artists, scientists agreed that the dodo had, in fact, once lived.

Steller's Sea Cow (Hydrodamalis stelleri)

The only manatee ever found in northern waters, Steller's sea cow was a 30-foot (9-meter) giant with a waistline measuring 22 feet (6.7 meters). From the head to the navel it resembled a seal; from there on, a whale with a powerful flattened tail. It had small lidless eyes, tiny ears concealed among loose folds of skin, and lips covered with bristles, "those on the lower jaw so thick they resembled the quills of fowls." Its hide was black and wrinkled and as tough as cork.

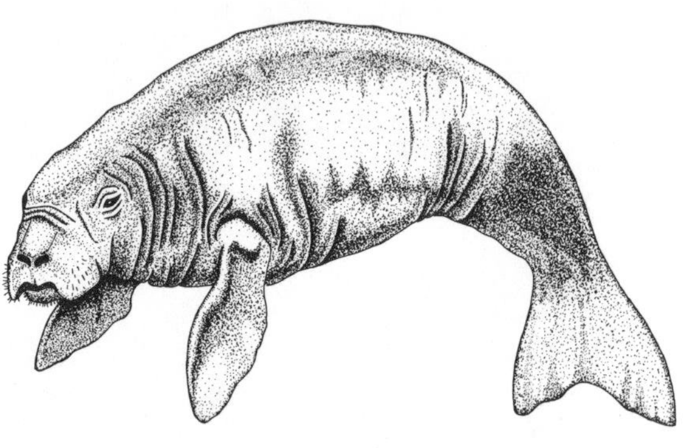

Sea cows grazed in the shallows along Siberia's Kamchatka Peninsula and the islands of the Bering Sea, tearing seaweed from the rocks with their flippers and chewing it endlessly. In place of teeth they had "two wide, longish, flat loose bones on each side of the mouth, one fastened to the upper palate and one to the lower jaw." Each of these "teeth" was a corrugated grinding surface with "obliquely converging furrows and raised welts." The natives of Kamchatka called the beasts "cabbage eaters," for they spent most of their lives supplying their 4-ton bodies with a vegetarian diet. "During the eating they moved their heads and necks like oxen, and after a few moments lifted themselves from the water to inhale with a rasping, snorting sound, after the manner of horses."

We have these descriptive details from the notes of Georg Wilhelm Steller, the only trained scientist ever to see a live sea cow. The young German had joined the crew of a ship under the command of Vitus Jonassen Bering, a Dane employed by the Russian imperial government to sail eastward in search of an unknown continent. When the ship was wrecked in an autumn storm, Steller was one of the few to survive the arctic winter on what is now called Bering Island. Despite hardships that killed his captain and many others, the dedicated naturalist studied the island's wildlife, recorded his observations, and returned to Russia in the spring with a wealth of scientific information . . . and seven hundred sea otter skins.

It was this cargo of pelts that led, indirectly, to the extinction of the sea cow within twenty-six years of its discovery by the Russians. For Bering's party opened a lucrative new source of profits to fur traders, and they lost no time in exploiting it. The northern Pacific was thick with sea otters whose beautiful skins brought high prices in Europe and China. Hunters from three continents joined in the slaughter; and although unrestrained killing nearly wiped out the entire otter population, this little marine mammal was saved by its own intelligence and a timely piece of protective legislation. (See "Return Engagements," page 344.)

The Steller's sea cow was not so fortunate. Slow floating mountains of good red meat and blubber, they were the preferred food of hunters and mariners who found the taste of sea otter and fur seal quite disagreeable. One sea cow provided 7,000 pounds (3,175 kilograms) of meat that "tasted like good beef," and fat, which the hunters boiled and drank by the cupful.

Especially easy to kill, the defenseless giants browsed close to shore, "often so near they could be hit with poles. . . . And they were not afraid of men in the least. . . ." While sea otters learned to hide from ships, the sea cows didn't budge even when attacked.

The enormous creatures made themselves even more vulnerable by their loyalty to one another. When one of them was hooked the others tried to save it by forming a closed circle around its body or attempting to upset the boat. Sometimes they would lay themselves over the rope or try to pull out the harpoon. Occasionally they succeeded, but more often they simply became victims themselves.

When Bering Island became the customary port of call for fur traders in the region, heavy traffic and immoderate killing were more than the small population could bear. Rare to begin with, they had numbered only about fifteen hundred when Bering arrived, and their birth rate was too low to make up for severe losses. In 1755 a Russian geologist searching for copper in the islands noticed that sea cows were becoming scarce and tried to persuade authorities to pass a protective law. But they ignored his petition, and thirteen years later Russian hunters recorded killing a sea cow for the last time.

In 1962, after almost two centuries, the crew of a Russian whaling ship sighted a herd of huge marine mammals—apparently not whales or seals—grazing in the shallows northeast of Kamchatka. They were 20 to 24 feet (6 to 7 meters) long, dark-colored, with large upper lips. Scientists speculated eagerly. Perhaps the world's last herd of sea cows had been living all these years undiscovered in some remote region of the Arctic. But optimism was short-lived. The whalers took no photographs and captured no specimens. And no further sightings have been reported. (For the status of the sea cow's living relatives, see "Manatees and Dugongs," page 305.)

Great Auk (Pinguinis impennis)

The first bird to be called a "penguin" lived in the coastal waters of the North Atlantic and was known to Europeans and Native Americans long before the discovery of the Antarctic bird we today call penguin. Despite a striking resemblance, the two species are not related. The northern penguin was a great auk, largest member of the auk family. Tasty and flightless, living along well-traveled routes, it was hunted to extinction by 1844.

The great auk stood about 30 inches (76 centimeters) tall, with a stocky body, disproportionately small wings, and webbed feet. Its thick, waterproof plumage was gray-black on the back, dark brown on the head, and white on the belly.

During the mating season a large white spot appeared on each cheek. The auk's black bill was as long as its face, curved at the end, and etched with deep white grooves.

Unable to fly and clumsy on land, great auks spent most of their time in the water feeding on fish and crustaceans. They were powerful divers and fast, strong swimmers, able to outlast humans pursuing them in rowboats. Well-adapted to the water, they even slept at sea for most of the year. Unfortunately, however, they had to come ashore to lay their eggs; and it was during the summer nesting seasons that hunters from Europe and America wiped out a population once numbering in the millions.

The slaughter of great auks began in prehistoric times, when their range evidently extended down the North American coast to Florida. Excavations at Indian campgrounds in New England have uncovered heaps of fossil auk bones. Nine hundred years ago, Viking sea rovers also took their toll in the North Atlantic. And then, in the fifteenth century, European fishers sailing west in search of cod began to plunder the auks' nesting colonies.

Auk eggs were a highly prized delicacy, and the birds themselves were fat and delicious. One needed no special skill to club one of these tame, awkward waddlers on its nest and remove its egg, thus destroying two generations with one blow. During the next two centuries the killing increased as people discovered new uses for the birds. Surplus meat was good for bait. The feathers made fine featherbeds. Auk fat was an excellent fuel for lamps and stoves; and the whole dried auk, its body full of oil, could be used as a torch. To make the slaughter more efficient, the hunters built stone corrals into which they drove the birds and clubbed them en masse.

By the late eighteenth century, great auks survived only on the rocky islets around Newfoundland, Greenland, and Iceland and on the isle of St. Kilda near Scotland. The early 1800s saw a rapid decline in their numbers; for, although large hunting parties had stopped, egg hunters still raided nests. After 1821, when the last St. Kilda auk vanished, the birds withdrew, first to the Auk Rocks near the southwest tip of Iceland and then to Geirfuglasker, a remote outcropping where they were finally safe from man. But in 1830 a volcanic eruption led to violent undersea quakes, and Geirfuglasker disappeared beneath the waves. Remarkably, fifty surviving birds found their way to Eldey Island, a small steep mass of volcanic rock nearby. Suddenly naturalists and museum directors noticed that the species, once so abundant, was virtually extinct, and—what they considered most alarming—only two museums had stuffed auks in their collections.

At this point the frantic scramble began as collectors offered great sums for whole skins, skeletons, and undamaged eggs. No one gave a thought to the preservation of the species: by nineteenth-century standards, a mounted specimen was worth more than a living bird. The world's last two great auks earned one hundred crowns apiece for the Icelandic fishers who killed them for collectors.

Quagga (Equus quagga)

When Dutch explorers landed at the Cape of Good Hope in 1652, they found the great plains of South Africa teeming with wildlife. Antelopes, gnus, lions, rhinos, elephants, ostriches, and zebras roamed this enormous expanse of open country with their only human neighbors, the nomadic Hottentots. Today, in all South Africa, large wild animals are found only on private farms and refuges. A number of species have been slaughtered to extinction.

Among the lost creatures was the quagga, a tawny "unfinished zebra" striped only on its head, neck, and shoulders. The rest of its body was a pale chestnut or red-gold, unbroken except for a brown-banded mane, a dark-brown streak down the middle of its back, and flashing white legs. The Hottentots gave the quagga its name, pronounced "quah kah," in imitation of the animal's shrill, barking neigh.

Quaggas lived nowhere in the world but in the South African veld, grazing in small herds with ostriches and white-tailed gnus. Despite competition and numerous predators, their population remained viable until the Dutch and their African-

born descendants, the Boers, began to shoot them. For some reason, as early as 1656 the settlers passed laws to protect a close relative of the quagga, the cape mountain zebra; and though the total world population of these wild horses today is only about two hundred, the species survives, thanks to protective legislation.

But nothing was done to limit quagga hunts, in which animals were rounded up by the thousands and killed. For almost two hundred years the Boers fed their Hottentot slaves quagga meat and used the beautiful quagga hides for shoes and for sacks to store grain. Once the animals disappeared from the Cape Colony, hunters followed the dwindling herds northward. In 1870, the last quagga to be seen in the wild was shot.

If the South African hunters had turned to ranching, they might have saved a useful animal from extinction. For quaggas were more easily tamed than other zebras and often lived long in captivity. The Hottentots occasionally kept them as pets and trained them to guard their domestic sheep and horses against raiding hyenas. During the 1820s a pair of quaggas owned by a rich Englishman learned to pull a carriage around Hyde Park, "as subservient to the curb and whip as any well-trained horses"; and a team of quaggas drew the forage wagon at the London Zoo for years.

The only known attempt to breed quaggas in captivity came too late, when the total world population consisted of a few solitary animals in zoos and private menageries and one pair at the London Zoo. Optimists hoped these two would mate; but the potential father died, leaving only its mate and two other females, one in the Berlin Zoo and one in Amsterdam. By 1883 all three were dead.

Passenger Pigeon (Ectopistes migratorius)

When ornithologist Alexander Wilson heard "a sudden rushing roar, succeeded by instant darkness," he thought a tornado was upon him. What he witnessed in the fall of 1810 was the approach of an estimated *two billion* migrating passenger pigeons as they swept over Kentucky in a flock 240 miles (386 kilometers) long and a mile (1.6 kilometers) wide. In flight, wrote naturalist John James Audubon, "the dense mass which they form presents a beautiful spectacle, as it changes direction, turning from a glistening sheet of azure as the backs of the birds come into view, to a suddenly presented rich deep purple." When they settled down to roost, they "alighted everywhere, one above another until solid masses,

as large as hogsheads, were formed in every tree, in all directions." Such roosting colonies often covered more than 100 square miles (260 square kilometers) and filled the woods with a noise "like a windy rainstorm."

The most abundant birds on earth at the time, these slender, blue-backed, russet-breasted doves ranged over most of North America as far west as the Dakotas. Their extinction was unimaginable. Yet, in 1914, one hundred years after Audubon wrote, the world's last passenger pigeon died at the Cincinnati Zoo. She had outlived her wild relatives by almost a decade.

According to Audubon only "the gradual diminution of our forests" could wipe out these plentiful creatures. And it is true that, as the American population grew from 10 million to 40 million during the middle years of the nineteenth century, vast tracts of wilderness disappeared. Nevertheless, while loss of woodlands certainly disrupted the birds' breeding habits, only relentless slaughtering could have reduced their numbers from the billions to zero in one century.

People killed pigeons on the wing, firing into the dense flocks as they passed overhead, sometimes even knocking birds out of the air with oars, poles, shingles, and other weapons. A Massachusetts man invented an "improved pigeon killer," which consisted of a long, flexible hickory rod planted on a hilltop and vibrated back and forth with ropes. This quick paddling action was deadly and efficient in the midst of a tight mass of low-flying birds.

People killed pigeons roosting: "All one had to do was to reach out and grab them . . . and stick them in the bag," wrote one West Virginian in 1854. And they killed pigeons nesting. The easiest way to get bushels of birds was to chop down trees full of nests and collect the helpless young squabs from the ground.

After hunters had eaten all they could of the succulent dark meat, they salted down tons of birds for shipment to eastern cities, and fattened their livestock on the rest. Audubon saw a farmer who had driven his three hundred hogs many miles to a pigeon roost to eat the surplus birds left on the forest floor.

Throughout the nineteenth century the demand for pigeons grew, boosting the price from a penny apiece in 1805 to a dollar a dozen several years later. As roast pigeon, especially squab, became a fashionable delicacy, huge shipments poured in from rural areas. Between 1866 and 1876, 10 million pigeons per year were shipped to the eastern markets.

Toward the end of the century, "sport" shooting became a popular amusement for city dwellers. Thousands of pigeons were captured in the woods and released to be living targets for shooters. In 1881, 20,000 squabs were taken from their nests and shipped to Coney Island for a pigeon shoot sponsored by, ironically enough, the New York State Association for the Protection of Fish and Game. In 1857, when a bill to protect the passenger pigeon came before the Ohio state legislature, a committee studying the issue concluded: "The passenger pigeon needs no protection. Wonderfully prolific—no ordinary destruction can lessen them." And everyone agreed.

That was just twenty years before the last great nesting colony was obliterated in a big killing spree, near Petoskey, Michigan. In the spring of 1878 an estimated 136 million birds flew into the region and laid their eggs. In one month hunters delivered 300 tons of birds to the marketplace—five freight car loads every day for thirty days.

By this time passenger pigeons had vanished from New York, Pennsylvania, and Massachusetts, and remaining flocks were growing smaller. Oddly enough, they seemed to require an extremely high population density for successful breeding. Without the raucous companionship of millions of other pigeons their fertility decreased. Even in Kentucky, where Audubon had once seen "the air . . . literally filled with pigeon and the noonday light . . . obscured as by an eclipse," only scattered individuals appeared. And hunters picked them off one by one.

The last wild pigeon was seen in Babcock, Wisconsin, in 1899, with only a few unconfirmed sightings after that. This left only one member of the species, a solitary female named Martha who had been born and raised in the Cincinnati Zoo. When she died, the American public began to recognize the importance of thoughtful wildlife management. With the "wonderfully prolific" pigeon extinct, conservationists fought harder than ever to protect other vanishing creatures from the most final death of all—the death of a species.

M.A.

SEVESO, ITALY

It was a lazy Saturday afternoon in the summer of 1976 when the residents of Seveso, Italy, a small, industrial suburb 13 miles (21 kilometers) north of Milan, heard the deep rumbling sound of an explosion coming from a sprawling chemical plant on the northeastern edge of town. It was the noon hour, and most of Seveso's residents were inside eating lunch. Many didn't see a white cloud drifting from the plant in a long plume, slowly settling on 700 acres (283.5 hectares) of their town. If they didn't notice the cloud at first, they quickly became aware of its effects—residents closest to the chemical plant became nauseated and developed headaches, dizziness, and diarrhea. Those who were outside when the cloud descended quickly contracted serious sores (chloracne) on exposed areas of their skin. On July 12, two days after the cloud engulfed Seveso, vegetation wilted, and dogs, cats, rabbits, chickens, and other small animals began to sicken and die.

Nine days later, officials from the chemical plant, the Swiss-owned ICMESA (a company that is in turn owned by the Givaudan Corporation, a subsidiary of the giant Swiss multinational pharmaceutical firm Hoffmann La Roche), notified local authorities that the cloud contained a chemical commonly known as dioxin, one of the deadliest poisons known. Government officials quickly announced the evacuation of 739 Seveso residents in areas most directly affected by the toxic cloud.

The accident occurred when a chemical process

used in the production of trichlorophenol (which Givaudan used to manufacture the antibacterial hexachlorophene) went awry, and the reactor vessel exploded, venting the deadly cloud.

The full impact of the disaster on the human population in the region may not be known for years. But the core of Seveso, a 267-acre (108-hectare) site called "Zone A," which was most affected, remains uninhabitable, and according to some experts it may remain so, forever.

B.P.B.

HETCH HETCHY

Yosemite National Park, established in 1890, is one of the most popular parks in the world. Every year, more than 2.5 million people view the spectacular valley carved out by glaciers, with its waterfalls, flowery meadows under huge granite cliffs, tall trees, and the sparkling Merced River. The economic and aesthetic value of a second Yosemite would be virtually incalculable. Yet there *was* a second Yosemite, which no longer exists.

Twenty miles (32 kilometers) north of the Yosemite Valley, still in the National Park, lies another, forgotten valley, which almost no one visits. Hetch Hetchy, which John Muir called the "Tuolumne Yosemite," after the river that ran through it, was condemned in 1913 to become a reservoir for the city of San Francisco.

Hetch Hetchy Valley had high and wide waterfalls, huge granite cliffs like Yosemite's, and waist-deep grassy meadows full of flowers and tall trees. The Tuolumne River ran through Hetch Hetchy as the Merced still runs through Yosemite. But in the early years of the century there was no law that could protect Hetch Hetchy from the developers. Although the city of San Francisco could have built its reservoir outside the national park, sparing the valley, it was cheaper to put the dam between the narrow granite walls of Hetch Hetchy. John Muir, the Sierra Club, *Century* magazine, and other lovers of Yosemite fought to save the valley, claiming it was protected by its national park status. But Congress decided that the water needs of the many came before the beloved valley of a few.

The destruction of Hetch Hetchy was soon seen as a terrible mistake, and in 1916 the new National Park Act ordered that future parks be left "unimpaired for . . . future generations." However, this Act still holds no guarantee—as recurrent proposals to dam the Grand Canyon prove—that the mistake of Hetch Hetchy will not be repeated.

Although the dam that destroyed the "Tuolumne Yosemite" will lose its usefulness eventually as the reservoir silts up, the lost Hetch Hetchy can never be restored; its former outlines will be buried under 200 feet (61 meters) of silt.

J.S.

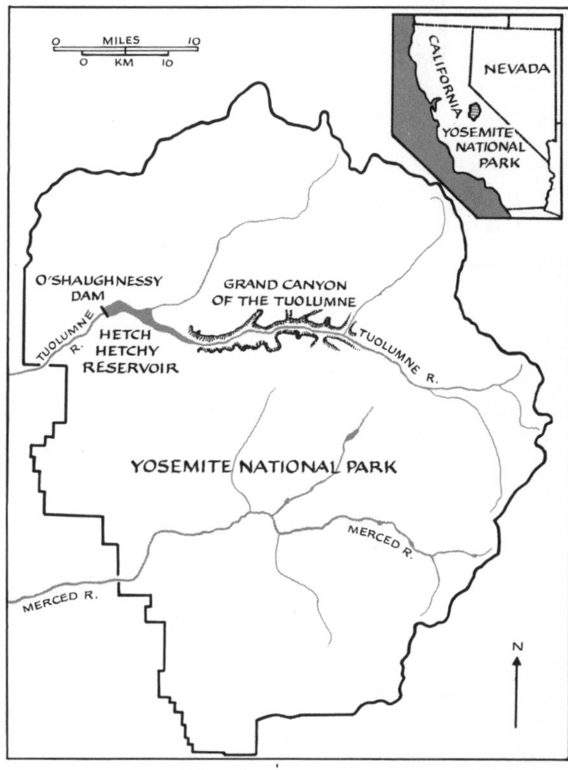

SOME OTHER THINGS GONE

- *Animal Species* More than 99 percent of the animal species that have lived on Earth are extinct.
- *Mammals* Over one half of the mammalian species now extinct have disappeared since the year 1900.
- *Coal* Since a resource consumed is usually a resource gone, one can compute the amount of certain materials "lost" during recent times: 16 billion tons (14.5 billion metric tons) of coal have been burned in the United States alone since 1947. To understand the potential of such an amount of coal, visualize that *one* million tons of coal produces approximately 2.1 billion kilowatt-hours of electricity. That is enough electricity to supply a city the size of Washington, D.C., for fifteen months.
- *Minerals* Approximately $11 billion is spent each year on chemical fertilizers to replace the nitrogen, phosphorus, and other minerals lost through soil erosion in the United States.
- *Forests* Worldwide, about 59,000 square miles (152,810 square kilometers) of forest land is lost every year.
- *Cropland* Between 80,000 and 120,000 acres (200,000 to 300,000 hectares) of cropland is abandoned every year because of waterlogging or excessive salinity caused by improper irrigation practices.

T.C.

"Hadley has alot more to learn about ecology."

RETURNING

THE THAMES

It is the Royal River. It weaves its way through London and through London's history, as vital to the city's character as the Danube to Vienna or the Nile to Khartoum. But the Thames carries other distinctions. In 1950 the river had become so polluted it was officially declared devoid of any life. Today, revived, it is one of the true environmental success stories of the age.

When London was still little more than a bustling town, the Thames had been established as a dumping ground for rubbish and raw sewage.

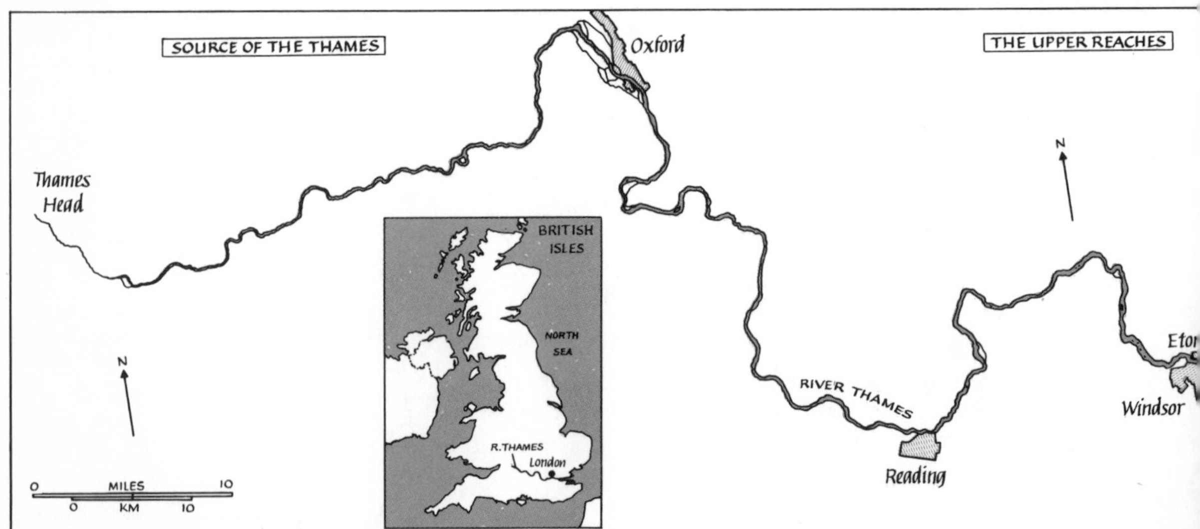

As early as 1357 the condition of the river had declined enough to cause official concern. King Edward III lamented, "Dung and filth has accumulated in divers places upon banks of the river," giving off "fumes and other abominable stenches." But the pattern of abuse had been set and was to remain, for the most part, unalleviated, as the population and industry of London burgeoned through the centuries.

The greatest single blow dealt the Thames was the invention of the water closet. Before that, most of London's waste had simply littered the streets or decayed in some 200,000 cesspools until carted off as fertilizer. With widespread use of the water closet, cesspools became congested. Overflow drains carried raw sewage into the street sewers that ran directly into the Thames. Though there were high salmon catches from the Thames as late as 1810, by 1835, the salmon fishery had been virtually eliminated, and by the 1850s the Thames was almost dead. In the summer of 1856—"The Year of the Great Stink"—the river's overwhelming stench pervaded government buildings and sheets soaked in disinfectant had to be draped over the windows of Parliament.

Only a year before the "Great Stink," Londoners had enjoyed a brief respite when Sir George Bazalgette of the newly established Metropolitan Board of Works, devised a scheme whereby crosstown sewers carried London's wastes past the city to outfalls downstream. There, at Beckton and Crossness, the waste was released on ebb tides, theoretically to be carried out to sea. But Bazalgette made two serious errors. He did not recognize that anything dumped into a tidal river moves seaward very slowly, sometimes at the rate of 1 mile (1.6 kilometers) per day. And, he failed to anticipate the reactions of people living below the outfalls, who were suddenly faced with tons of London's raw sewage floating slowly by their homes.

In 1878 a pleasure boat sank near one of these outfalls and 640 people died. A public inquiry proved that many had lost their lives not by drowning, but by poisoning from the rancid waters. The outcry that followed set the government in motion. Two sewage works were built where solid matter could be settled out, removed, and dumped at sea. Though these measures helped for a short while, ultimately they could not keep pace with a growing industry and a swelling population. New plants and methods of treatment were developed, but new complications arose. Bombing during World War II destroyed or damaged many sewers. A new threat appeared with the introduction of "hard" detergents that would not degrade in bacteriological treatment. In addition, the detergents were toxic to fish, and the foam they created on the surface of the water prevented the natural intake of vital oxygen by aquatic organisms.

By the mid-1950s biologists confirmed what fishermen had known for years. The waters of the Thames were dead. From London to Gravesend, not a single living animal could be found. For nine months of the year a 25-mile (40-kilometer) stretch of river showed absolutely no oxygen content.

Steeped in the lore of the Thames, in its history, in its literature, in the tradition of fishermen, Londoners recoiled at the official death notice of their river. Government, industry, and individuals finally mobilized to bring the Thames back to life. Millions of pounds were committed

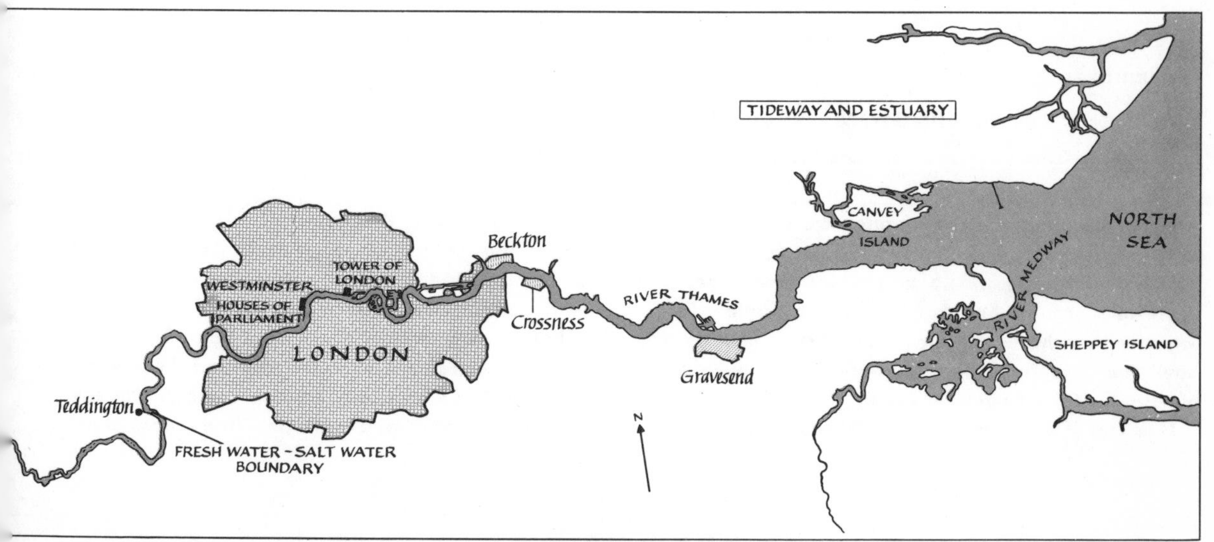

Windsor Castle is one of many historic sites along England's River Thames. Once choked by centuries of pollution, the river is now making a comeback. (*British Tourist Authority*)

to the effort. The Thames became a test case for other major rivers around the world suffering from choking pollution.

To begin with, the detergent problem was attacked. Manufacturers voluntarily phased out hard detergents, replacing them with biodegradable ones. The results were dramatic. The Thames and other British rivers improved immediately. This progress fueled the campaign. Many industries worked at their own expense, and often beyond the demands of the law, to reduce their pollution to a minimum.

By 1961 plans had been drawn up for massive improvements to sewage-disposal facilities. Stringent legal controls were placed on industry, making it illegal to discharge anything but uncontaminated water into the Thames. By 1964, through persistent antipollution measures and the building of a new $24-million treatment plant at Crossness, the first obvious signs of the river's recovery became evident. Beckton became the site of Europe's largest treatment plant. Pouring over 200 million gallons (757 million liters) of treated effluent into the Thames daily, it ranks as the river's most important tributary. By 1978, 470 plants were in operation, and water samples from the Thames were claimed to be clearer than tap water. The investment of taxpayers' money had been hefty, $200 million, but the results were worth it.

Just seventeen years after the commitment to recovery was made, the Thames had been "restored to life." By 1978, the river was supporting an increasing population of ninety-five species of fish. Salmon, a fish especially sensitive to pollution, are now returning. Green algae and seaweed are back, marine worms have recolonized the mud, providing fish with a source of food, and the fish are supporting a renewed population of wildfowl and waders. The river has not been so clean, so alive, for centuries, and London's political establishment, as well as its riverside industry and its citizens, seem bent on keeping it that way.

The Thames, long a symbol of the dark side of industrial progress and of human apathy, is now a symbol of ecological renaissance and wisdom.

L.W.

Wavemakers:

LEADING LAKE WASHINGTON'S REVIVAL

Lake Washington, a glittering, freshwater lake in the midst of urban Seattle, is, to lawyer Jim Ellis, intimately related to an interior landscape, a sense of place. He has spent an entire lifetime living along its shores. He swam and fished in it as a boy, and as a man, he spearheaded a movement to save the lake from near death.

Like many U.S. waters, Lake Washington was a victim of postwar development. Framed by the majestic mountains of the Pacific Cascades and built on land fed by lakes and waterways, Seattle was a boom town of new homes and industries. The burgeoning wastes that accompanied this development were conveniently dumped in nearby waters. By 1953, partially treated sewage effluent, rich in phosphorus and nitrogen, had encouraged

such a profuse growth of plant life and algae that Lake Washington was no longer safe for swimming. Its once abundant fish life—largemouth bass, perch, sockeye, coho, and chinook salmon and cutthroat and rainbow trout—was endangered as eutrophicating algae clogged the coarse sands on the beaches and in the shallow waters that served as spawning grounds.

While other residents of the area deplored the loss of the lake as a natural and recreational resource, Jim Ellis assembled half a dozen people around his kitchen table to explore ways of saving it. Dr. Thomas Edmondson, a limnologist from the University of Washington, assured the group that Lake Washington could be restored to a state of ecological health but that it was going to be a massive and costly task. Although there was no federal legislation at the time to help communities solve their water pollution problems, Jim Ellis and his kitchen cabinet were not about to be stopped.

Marshalling support from citizens throughout the Seattle area, Ellis and his group decided to push for state legislation that would allow Seattle to create a special agency to deal with the situation. Joining forces with the League of Women Voters and the Municipal League, Ellis and his cohorts won passage in 1957 of a measure creating "Metro," an agency empowered to deal with local sewage, transportation, and recreation problems. Jim Ellis became its special counsel.

The fledgling agency quickly became embroiled in controversy when it released a study recommending that twenty-three sewage treatment plants in the Seattle area be totally scrapped.

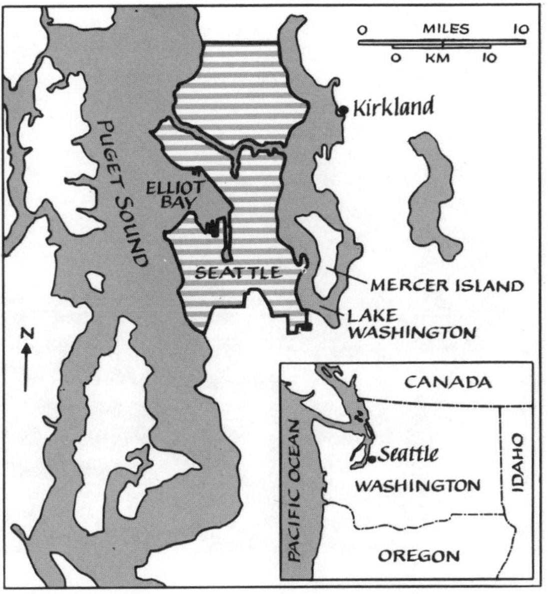

The price tag for new, more effective treatment was high: $125 million for Lake Washington and an additional $40 million for nearby Puget Sound—an enormous tax burden for residents to undertake.

Jim Ellis and his group set about trying to convince them that it was worth it. They spoke to service clubs, homeowner groups, and whoever would stand still long enough to listen, and they published fact sheets on the condition of the lake and what it would take to clean it up. Opposition to the plan came from taxpayer groups, treatment plant engineers, and ultraconservatives who opposed any government interference in their right to use Puget Sound and Lake Washington as a dumping ground for pollution wastes.

The first showdown came in March 1958, when the city held a special vote on a new sewage tax. That initial test of voters' commitment to the cleanup was encouraging: the tax was approved, but too few voters went to the polls, so a second election was scheduled for September. Hoping to pique additional citizen interest in their antipollution crusade, one of Ellis' cohorts came up with a simple suggestion that proved more effective than fact sheets and statistics: a poster of a youngster looking at a sign that said "NO SWIMMING." More voters were quickly won over, and in the second vote, the sewage tax was passed by an overwhelming majority.

Though the cost was high, the cleanup of Lake Washington has produced dramatic results. Two sewage plants have replaced the twenty-three old ones, and their effluent is nearly pure now. The water clarity in Lake Washington, which was 4 to 5 feet (1.2 to 1.5 meters) ten years ago, is now 20 feet (6 meters). The "NO SWIMMING" signs have been torn down and the salmon runs, which had dwindled to several hundred fish, have been restored, so that thousands of salmon now pass through the lake. Beaches and parks provide canoe trails and a variety of recreation. Along the shoreline, marsh lands, wilderness areas, and grassy groundcover provide feeding and nesting grounds for a variety of resident and migratory birds, including an unusually dense flock of Chinese ringneck pheasants.

Jim Ellis credits the Lake Washington success story to the residents of the Seattle area who cared enough about their environment to clean it up. Many of those same citizens remain vigilant defenders of the lake against new threats, including a federal government proposal to construct

two massive piers, which would protrude 470 feet (143 meters) into the lake and could disrupt salmon spawning. Led by a new citizen organization—Save Our Lake Washington—environmentalists are rallying public opposition to the plan.

The environmental crusades of Jim Ellis, meanwhile, have moved from water to land. He is now leading an effort to preserve the Seattle area's remaining farmland from the bulldozers of developers. Meanwhile, the fishing on Lake Washington, he reports, has never been better.

B.K.

RETURN ENGAGEMENTS

These animals came very close to becoming entries on the list of extinctions but were saved by the efforts of concerned people.

Sea Otters (Enhydra lutris)

Smallest of the marine mammals, the sea otter looks like a cross between a weasel and a seal, with a sleek body 4 to 5 feet (1.2 to 1.5 meters) long and an appealing whiskered face. On land, sea otters are somewhat ungainly and easy to hunt, but in the water they're quick and elusive. Powerful swimmers, they move like seals, propelled by strong flipper limbs. Skillful divers, they sometimes plunge to depths of 120 feet (36 meters) in search of shellfish for food. And they belong to that group of clever animals that, like humans, uses tools. Floating on its back, the otter uses its chest as a table and a flat rock as an anvil against which it pounds shellfish to break them open.

For traders of the eighteenth and nineteenth centuries, the sea otter's most attractive feature was its fur, a deep velvety brown, almost black, with long silver guard hairs giving it an unusual sheen. Hunters from Russia, Japan, China, England, and the United States sailed the coastal waters of the northern Pacific, killing otters by the tens of thousands, even enslaving native Aleuts and forcing them to hunt the animals. White traders made ridiculously profitable deals with coastal Indians who, according to Captain James Cook in 1778, were delighted to exchange the finest sea otter skin for two glass beads. A Boston skipper of the same era recorded a trade with Vancouver Indians of "200 skins, worth no less than $8,000, in exchange for an old iron chisel."

The mass slaughter and easy trading went on as long as enough of the animals could be found.

(The Cousteau Society/Philippe Cousteau)

And even as late as the 1880s, when the otter population was very low, U.S. hunters took 48,000 skins during a nine-year period. By 1900, only 127 skins appeared on the market; and though a single pelt sold for $2,500, the business was no longer profitable. The animals were just too rare and too difficult to hunt.

In 1910, with commercial interests out of the way, the United States, England, Russia, and Japan signed a treaty giving sea otters absolute protection from hunters. Since then, seventy islands covering more than 2.7 million acres (1.08 million hectares) have been set aside as the Aleutian Islands National Wildlife Refuge; the animals—more than 50,000 of them—have repopulated much of their old territory. A southern race, the California sea otter, once thought to be extinct, now numbers about 2,000 and is expanding its range southward along the coastline at a rate of 2 miles (3.2 kilometers) per year.

Unfortunately, this success story ends with two question marks. First, the growth of California sea otter herds has created conflicts between hungry animals, which must consume large amounts of food to maintain their body heat, and human industries. Because sea otters do not distinguish between illegal young shellfish and mature ones, they have helped contribute to the demise of the central California abalone fishery. This created an antiotter furor among local abalone fishermen. Now the otters are reaching a famous clam bed near Pismo Beach, threatening, according to local officials, the city's clam-based tourist industry. There is great pressure to relocate or destroy the arriving otter herds.

Secondly, a new industrial menace threatens to undermine past conservation efforts. Oil spills, a hazard for so many ocean dwellers, are deadly for the sea otter because of the nature and function of its fur. Unlike other marine mammals, the otter has no thick layers of insulating blubber and depends entirely on air trapped in its underfur for warmth and buoyancy. If its coat becomes clogged with dirt or oil, the animal cannot survive for very long. In 1965, after a large oil spill near Great Sitkin Island, Alaska, an otter population of six hundred was reduced to six.

American Plains Bison (Bison bison bison)

"The black, shaggy beasts continued to thunder past us in handfuls, in groups, in masses, in whole armies; for forty hours in succession we never lost sight of them . . . a numberless multitude of untamed creatures, whose meat, as we thought, would be sufficient to supply the wigwams of the Indians to all eternity." These are the words of a traveler to the West just after the Civil War, at a time when 60 million wild bison still roamed the prairies.

For centuries the American Plains Indians had depended on these abundant herds for food, clothing, and shelter. They ate bison meat and cured the hides for teepee covers, clothing, and moccasins. They wove bison hair into ropes and belts, treated the sinews for bowstrings and thread, and made spoons and cups of the horns. They regarded the buffalo as their sacred "four-footed relatives." With Indian harvesting, "the numberless multitude" certainly would have sustained itself for centuries longer. But within the twenty years between 1870 and 1890, the great herds were nearly killed off by white buffalo hunters.

Recognizing the dependence of Plains tribes on the bison, white men eager to push their railroads westward through Indian territory saw the destruction of these herds as a means to the defeat of the Cheyenne, Sioux, and others. Following a deadly logic, railroad companies paid hunters to finish off the buffalo while the U. S. Army fought Indians. Between 1872 and 1874, white hunters killed 3.6 million buffalo, leaving the carcasses to rot on the plains. A single man, "Buffalo Bill" Cody, shot 4,280 animals in a year and a half for the Kansas Pacific Railroad. When concerned Texans brought a petition to General

One of several buffalo on the Niabrara Wildlife Refuge, Nebraska. (*USDA/SCS*)

Sheridan to stop the wholesale slaughter, they received this brutal reply: "Let them kill, skin, and sell until the buffalo is exterminated, as it is the only way to bring lasting peace and allow civilization to advance."

Indian fighters attempting to end the destruction of useful animals were no match for the buffalo hunters with telescopes on their guns. By 1889, just before the final defeat of the Sioux at Wounded Knee, no more than 500 of the 60 million wild bison were left in the United States, most of these theoretically under protection in Yellowstone Park. And taxidermists in the illegal business of mounting heads and making robes quickly reduced even this last wild herd to a mere twenty animals.

Fortunately for the bison, in 1905 a group of dedicated conservationists formed the American Bison Society to save the species from extinction. Led by William Hornaday, director of the New York Zoological Society, and supported by President Theodore Roosevelt, they raised money to establish national bison reserves. During the next ten years, largely through the efforts of the Bison Society, the U.S. government set up protected ranges in Oklahoma, Montana, South Dakota, and Nebraska and stocked them with animals from private collections. Provided with shelter and winter fodder, these small herds—fifteen animals in Oklahoma, thirty-four in Montana, twenty-three in Alaska—rapidly increased their numbers.

Today, though wild bison no longer range free on the prairies, more than 10,000 animals live protected in U.S. national parks and wildlife preserves. A small but secure remnant of the 60 million, their herds are flourishing within the narrow limits necessary for coexistence with humanity on a crowded continent.

Trumpeter Swans (Olor buccinator)

Pure white, like some of its smaller cousins, the trumpeter is unique among swans for its great size and distinctive voice. This largest of all the world's waterfowl measures over 5 feet (1.5 meters) from head to tail and an impressive 8 or 9 feet (2.4–2.7 meters) across its wingspread. The loud resonant call that gives the trumpeter its name is produced by a windpipe so long it is double-looped beneath the bird's breastbone: uncoiled, it would extend more than 5 feet.

In American pioneer days the trumpeter was the most common swan in California, Oregon, and Washington. It ranged widely over the interior of North America, nesting in the Northwest and wintering in sheltered areas of the Ohio and Mississippi valleys and Rocky Mountain states. As late as the 1820s, Audubon saw immense flocks of trumpeters on the Mississippi River: ". . . rich creamy white swans by the hundreds, dipping their bills, arching their necks backward, resting with one leg outstretched, and floating and basking in the sunshine."

(Fish and Wildlife Service/Great Bend City Park, Kansas)

Unfortunately these magnificent flocks offered tempting targets for hunters. Audubon witnessed an Indian swan hunt in which "at least fifty birds were brought down by the time the conch-shell horn was blown." A feast of roasted swan followed, but only after the squaws had "skinned the birds of their beautiful feathers intended for the ladies of Europe." Trade in bird feathers was a lucrative business during the nineteenth century. Plumed hats and capes were in demand among fashionable women. Swansdown was ideal for featherbeds, pillows, and powder puffs. And wing quills made excellent pens. Between 1853 and 1877, the Hudson's Bay Company alone recorded sales of 17,671 swan skins.

By 1900 the trumpeter swan had disappeared from most of its old territory in the United States, and ornithologists declared that the bird must be nearly extinct. But even after the Migratory Bird Treaty Act of 1918 banned all traffic in wild birds, people continued to shoot trumpeters illegally. In 1933 at least seventeen of the rare swans were killed by hunters near Yellowstone Park, and by 1935 a census shows only seventy-three surviving birds.

Clearly, hunters were a menace to the dwindling trumpeter population. But the most serious threat eventually came from habitat destruction. With the draining and development of wetlands all over the United States, swans were unable to find the marshy meadows and shallow lakes they needed. By the early 1930s the entire trumpeter population was concentrated in the Yellowstone region of Wyoming and Red Rock Lakes in Montana. Both places offered ideal breeding conditions and unusual thermally heated springs and ponds, so the birds could remain through the winter and avoid the risks of migration.

Because so few suitable habitats remained in the United States, J. N. (Ding) Darling—conservationist, political cartoonist, and chief of the U. S. Biological Survey—recognized the crucial need to set aside inviolate breeding territory for swans wherever possible. One protected habitat at Yellowstone was not enough. Darling worked to establish a national wildlife refuge at Red Rock Lakes, where the resident swan population could breed and flourish undisturbed. And he got what he wanted: an ideal wetland sanctuary of 40,000 acres (16,000 hectares).

Protection at Red Rock Lakes was so successful that by 1958 the refuge had 310 trumpeters, the maximum number it could support. To prevent overcrowding and inevitable losses, the National Audubon Society initiated a program to relocate swans. Captured during the late summer molting season when they were unable to fly, swans were transferred to enclosures on other refuges to be kept wing-clipped and fed through the winter. In spring the birds were released to adapt to their new surroundings.

So far this program has introduced trumpeters to at least six refuges in the United States and Canada: the National Elk Refuge in Wyoming, Malheur in Oregon, Ruby Lake in Nevada, Turnbull in Washington, Lacreeck in South Dakota, and the Delta Waterfowl Research Station in Manitoba. With habitats guaranteed by the government, more than 6,000 trumpeters are thriving in North America today.

Arabian Oryxes (Oryx leucoryx)

Squint at the profile of an Arabian oryx, and you may see a unicorn. Thought to be the source of the ancient unicorn myth, this graceful cream-colored antelope with its long, straight, sharp horns is native to the deserts of the Arabian Peninsula. Well adapted to a harsh climate, the oryx can survive many days without water and endure extreme temperatures ranging from 140° F (60° C) down to freezing. But pressures from human hunting have been almost unendurable.

(Dick George/Phoenix Zoo)

The largest and fastest wild animal in the region, the oryx was admired and therefore hunted by desert tribesmen who believed that any man who killed one would inherit its strength and toughness. Because so many men proved their manhood by slaying oryxes, the animal was already on the way to extinction by the beginning of the eighteenth century. Except for a small herd that the Shah of Persia kept to supply his royal hunts, only about a hundred wild oryxes remained, all of these in Rub al-Khali, "the empty quarter" of Arabia.

For two hundred years the isolated wild herds managed to hold their own. Because so few animals were left in this treacherous land, sheikhs on camels or horseback rarely succeeded in making a kill. But after World War II brought modern technology to the Middle East, wealthy Arab sportsmen gained the advantage. Armed with rapid-fire machine guns, they set out in jeep caravans of several hundred men to shoot oryxes. Finally able to keep pace with the swift-footed animals, hunters all but wiped out the last herds. A search of the Rub al-Khali turned up only two survivors: a male, which soon died of an old bullet wound, and a female that was taken to the London Zoo.

British conservationists of the Fauna Preservation Society realized that the oryx, if not already extinct in the wild, was certainly doomed by these machine-gun safaris. In 1962, with money raised by the World Wildlife Fund, they founded Operation Oryx, an international program to save the species through captive breeding. Their strategy was based on the hope that a small herd still existed, and that if it were protected in a zoo it would produce enough offspring to be returned someday to the native habitat . . . assuming, of course, that a safe habitat could be found.

A search for oryxes for the first captive herd began the same year with seven men in spotter planes covering 6,000 miles (9,654 kilometers) of desert. In this vast territory they found only four animals, one of which died. A second search the following year found no oryxes. A "world herd" of two males and one female did not offer much hope for the future of the species, and Operation Oryx seemed likely to fail. But donations from private collections—one from the London Zoo, one from the ruler of Kuwait, and two pairs, including a pregnant female from the king of Saudi Arabia—brought the total to nine animals.

Well cared for at the Phoenix Zoo in Arizona, this small group has borne more than seventy young, enough to start new herds at other zoos. Both the Gladys Porter Zoo in Brownsville, Texas, and California's San Diego Wild Animal Park, which was established in 1972 expressly for the breeding of endangered animals, now have their own oryxes. Though wild oryxes would be as vulnerable as ever to hunters on the Arabian Peninsula, several protected captive herds exist in Qatar, Oman, Israel, and Saudi Arabia, and Phoenix plans to send some animals to a preserve in Jordan.

Management of the world herd is carried out by a consortium of zoos with trustees who meet annually to plan breeding programs, discuss results, and reset objectives. Members exchange valuable information and even share animals through "breeding loans" of a single male or female to reduce the risks of genetic defects from inbreeding. A useful model of international cooperation in wildlife management, Operation Oryx has assured the safety of one endangered species and shown how effective a worldwide campaign can be.

Nénés, or Hawaiian Geese (Branta sandvicensis)

The Hawaiian islands are the home of more endangered species than any other part of the United States. Even its official state bird, the néné, is on the U. S. Department of the Interior's Endangered Species List. But, despite its threatened status, the néné is a hopeful symbol in the fight against loss of species, for this unique goose has made a remarkable comeback from a mere dozen wild birds in 1946 to more than one thousand in the mid-1970s.

The world's only nonmigratory tropical goose, the néné thrives rather ungooselike away from water. Though domesticated birds will paddle around happily in a pond, wild nénés don't swim at all. They've adapted to the dry lava slopes of volcanic mountains on Hawaii and Maui, have developed long, strong legs with only slightly webbed feet, and get whatever moisture they need from upland berries in summer and rich soft plants of the lowlands in winter.

In 1788, when Captain Cook first landed in these islands, the geese numbered well over 25,000, despite regular hunting by Polynesian natives. But with the coming of the nineteenth-century whaling ships, the néné population declined. Unafraid of humans, they were easily caught,

(U. S. Fish and Wildlife Service/Luther C. Goldman)

especially during the molting season, when all the birds gathered in volcanic craters to drop their wing feathers and wait, flightless, for the growth of new plumage. Whaling crews took advantage of this easy hunting to kill and salt down barrelfuls of geese as provisions for their long voyages. And though the nénés originally had no enemies but humans, Europeans brought in a number of exotic predators—cats, dogs, rats, mongooses—which ate néné eggs and goslings from their ground nests.

By the start of the twentieth century the néné population had fallen so low that the government began to regulate hunting, but with leniency and lack of foresight. A "limit" of six birds per hunter per day could be killed during a four-and-a-half-month open season, which *coincided with the breeding season.* When the hunting of nénés was finally prohibited in 1911 most of them had already disappeared from the wild.

Because nénés were so tame, they seemed likely to breed well in captivity. Herbert Shipman, a rancher from the coastal town of Hilo, was the first to try his luck at raising them; and within a few years his single pair had produced a small flock. The captive nénés continued to thrive and propagate until 1946, when a tsunami engulfed Shipman's estate and carried off thirty-two of his forty-three birds. With only eleven geese left, Shipman recognized the need for more than one sanctuary.

Fortunately, the Hawaiian government agreed to set aside a néné breeding farm on the island of Hawaii. It was here, at Pohakuloa, that keepers discovered a trick to increase the birds' productivity. A female, they learned, would lay as many as three clutches of eggs if her first eggs were removed from the nest. Thus, with the help of incubators, the number of hatchlings could be nearly tripled. This technique and variations of it have worked well, not only with nénés, but with whooping cranes and other captive-bred fowl.

In 1950, Peter Scott, curator of the Severn Wildfowl Trust, decided to try raising nénés in England as insurance against loss in case of another natural disaster in Hawaii. Having obtained what he thought was a breeding pair from Pohakuloa, he soon saw his mistake when both birds laid eggs. Kamehameha, the gander sent by the Hawaiian government to remedy the situation, performed heroically in the campaign to save his species: he sired more than 230 birds at Severn in the decade before his death.

By 1955 most of the world's nénés were living in captivity, as domestic as barnyard chickens, so the emphasis of the program shifted from breeding to reestablishment of the geese in their old habitat. As often happens with animals raised by men, captive-bred nénés didn't know how to live in the wild and fared poorly outside their predator-safe pens. Since it proved impossible to teach these tame geese to be wild, a method was devised whereby captive-bred birds, with their wings pinioned so they couldn't fly, were released into fenced "néné parks" where they could breed safely. Their offspring, reared away from humans, behaved like true wild geese, flew away from the parks, and bred successfully.

The first captive-bred animals to replenish a wild population, nénés were saved from extinction through the initiative of a private citizen, with timely support from his government. Back in their old haunts after a long absence, they can be seen today on the lava slopes of Hawaii in a 600-square-mile (1,551-square-kilometer) region between two volcanoes, Mauna Loa and Mauna Kea, and on Maui near the volcano Haleakala.

Vicuña (Vicugna vicugna)

This miniature cousin of the camel lives high in the Andes, at elevations of 14,000 feet (4,267 meters) and above. Between the timber line and the frost line, the home of the vicuña is bleak and rocky, with sparse vegetation and thin air. The ruggedness of the land has helped to insure survival of the species; for the well-adapted camelid has few nonhuman predators and little competition for the highland's resources.

During the reign of the Incas, the vicuña was worshipped as a daughter of the fertility goddess. Though the Indians prized its soft red-gold fleece as we do, none but the highest officials were allowed to hunt the sacred animals. And vicuña cloth could be worn only by royalty. The hair of the vicuña is so fine—just one fourth the diameter of human hair and half that of the best cashmere of Australian merino—it takes twelve whole fleeces to make a single yard of cloth. Though it was certainly less trouble to kill a vicuña than to catch one and hold it down long enough to shear, the Incas nearly always took fleeces from live animals. Respectful users of wildlife, they collected animals no more than once every four years in a given area, releasing them as soon as they had been clipped.

After the Spanish conquest opened trade with Europe, the vicuña lost its sacred protected status. For traders, it was just another animal to be converted into profits by the quickest possible

(*International Fund for Animal Welfare*)

means: in this case, slaughter. Killing a vicuña, once you come within firing range, is pathetically easy. When a small herd is startled, the dominant male will step forward and freeze—a perfect target. If he is killed, the other animals flee, but return very soon to the same spot where they, too, become victims.

Fortunately, a high reproductive rate kept the population from falling dangerously low despite heavy losses in the nineteenth century. By 1900 a million animals still lived in Peru and Bolivia. But after the turn of the century their numbers declined so rapidly—from 1,000,000 in 1900 to 100,000 in 1950, 10,000 in 1960, and 5,000 in 1970—that conservationists saw the need for strictly enforced laws. Without severe penalties, hunters in jeeps and helicopters would wipe out the last vicuña herds within a few years.

Felipe Benavides, a Peruvian diplomat who gave up his career to work for the preservation of his country's wildlife, was the most famous crusader for this endangered animal. Writing articles, making speeches, enlisting the public support of celebrities, Benavides delivered his message in no uncertain terms: all vicuña trade must stop. The existence of any legal market for any part of the animal anywhere in the world would give poachers a loophole to slip through. "Animals do not respect borders," said Benavides recently, stressing the importance of international consensus; "so when one country says one thing and another says another, there is no conservation. As surely as there is an ecology of nature, there must be an ecology of law."

Though he failed to close every loophole, Benavides' work did bring about some important changes. Because the vicuña have been reluctant to mate in captivity away from their homeland, they needed a large Andean sanctuary. In 1965 Peru established the Pampa Galeras Reserve in the Ayacucho mountains, a day's drive southeast of Lima. There, guarded by armed wardens, a herd of 650 animals has increased to 23,000. In 1969, Bolivia and Peru signed the Act of La Paz, establishing prison terms and fines of $100 for every vicuña killed. Joined later by Chile and Argentina, they also declared a ten-year moratorium on all killing, marketing, and exporting of vicuña. By the early 1970s the U. S. Department of the Interior, the International Union for the Conservation of Nature and Natural Resources (IUCN), and the Convention on International Trade in Endangered Species (CITES) all listed the vicuña as a "rare and endangered species," thus limiting trade to individuals with special permits for scientific work.

A black market centered in Bolivia still operates and vicuña cloth sells for exorbitant prices. But, despite flaws, international legal protection has helped the vicuña population to grow substantially—from 5,000 animals to more than 40,000 in less than a decade. Ironically, the recovering population is overpopulating and overgrazing its reserve. Wildlife advocates and managers now debate whether they can transport some animals to other locations or whether they should reduce the size of the herd by killing some animals.

American Alligators (Alligator mississipiensis)

A century ago American alligators were so abundant in the southeastern United States "you could walk across a lake on their backs," in the words of one old hunter from the Okefenokee Swamp. The great reptiles could be heard on spring nights, roaring for their mates in every river, bayou, and swamp from North Carolina to eastern Texas. On the Red River in Arkansas, Audubon described "'gators' by the hundreds, along the shores or on immense rafts of floating timber, the smaller on the backs of the larger, all groaning and bellowing like thousands of irritated bulls about to fight."

The closest living relative of the dinosaur, this reptile is very similar to an ancient 60-foot (18-meter) cousin, the phytosaur, whose fossil bones have been discovered embedded in the Palisades near New York City and in the Petrified Forest of Arizona, far from any twentieth-

(*National Park Service/Jack E. Boucher*)

century alligator haunts. Outside the southeastern United States the modern world's only alligators live in China on the Yangtze River.

Nine inches (23 centimeters) at birth, the little yellow-banded black lizards grow slowly until they die, reaching a length of 10 feet (3 meters) in ten years. Twenty-foot (6-meter) giants were reported in the past, but now they rarely live long enough to grow beyond 14 feet (4 meters).

With their prehistoric appearance, long jaws, and sharp teeth, alligators have often been accused of aggressive man-eating behavior. Actually, they prefer a diet of small water birds and animals, feasting occasionally on wild pig, dog, or deer; they rarely attack humans unless provoked. Old-timers say you can safely share a waterhole with these forbidding-looking reptiles any time but in the mating season.

As a matter of fact, the alligator has had much more to fear from man than man from alligators. Between 1800 and 1940, hunters killed at least 10 million of the reptiles for their hides. A nineteenth-century mania for alligator shoes, boots, and saddles started the slaughter, and a leather shortage during the Civil War took thousands more skins. Reliable records show sales of 1.5 million hides in Florida alone during the 1930s, many from 3- to 4-foot (0.9- to 1.2-meter) animals not yet old enough to breed. Add to these the large number of babies captured and sold as souvenirs, and one can see why more than nine tenths of all the U.S. alligators were gone by 1960.

As commercial catches grew smaller and smaller, Florida was the first state to outlaw alligator hunting, in 1961, with Louisiana following several years later. By 1969 no alligator could be killed legally anywhere in the United States. But Florida poachers still made big profits. Though game wardens spent almost half their time trying to police the swamps, law-breakers managed to carry on a million-dollar business—50,000 illegal hides—in 1965 in Miami alone.

Alligator protection in Louisiana was more successful, thanks to careful habitat management and strict law enforcement. In 1959 Louisiana wildlife specialists started a program to capture, mark, and release more than two thousand of the reptiles in the Rockefeller Wildlife Refuge on the Gulf of Mexico. Antipoaching laws provided such stiff penalties that one hunter got a five-year prison sentence, the most severe punishment on record for a violation of game laws.

The hardy reptiles responded to protection by repopulating the southwestern marshes of Louisiana with an estimated 200,000 alligators by 1976. Their numbers seemed substantial enough in this region to justify a limited legal harvest. So, their official status having been changed from Endangered to Threatened on the U. S. Department of the Interior's Endangered Species List, the alligators in three Louisiana parishes may be hunted during a sixty-day fall season. Only mature animals 5 feet (1.5 meters) and longer may be taken, and the state wildlife and fisheries commission determines the maximum harvest each year, depending on latest census figures. In the other nine states where alligators live—Florida, North Carolina, South Carolina, Georgia, Mississippi, Alabama, Texas, Arkansas, and Oklahoma—no hunting is permitted at any time.

No longer a severely endangered species, the American alligator is numerous enough to provoke about eight thousand complaints each year from Florida residents who find the reptiles on their lawns and golf courses, in swimming pools, schoolyards, and sewers, or occasionally eating a pet dog. The state game and fisheries commission has specially licensed trappers to get rid of such "nuisance alligators," as they are unofficially designated; but so far Florida is the only state where alligators may be killed for frightening people.

A recent estimate put the number of American alligators at 800,000. With a growing population and a 120-million-year family history, this persistent cousin of the dinosaur seems most likely to survive, as long as there are southern swamps and bayous where hunters can't kill without restraint.

Whooping Cranes (Grus americana)

Since the early 1900s the whooping crane has been declared "on the verge of extinction." A stuffed whooper even appears in a Smithsonian Natural History Museum display entitled "nearly extinct" beside a pair of heath hens, a great auk, and nine passenger pigeons including Martha, the last of her species. All these birds have vanished. But the whooping crane, a rare spectacular relic of Pleistocene times, is still with us, despite the dwindling of its habitat and population. This began long before the arrival of humans on earth but reached a critical point in numbers very suddenly at the end of the nineteenth century.

This large wader, tallest of all the North American birds, needs a special combination of shallow water and grassy marsh vegetation to survive. Though widespread over North America in the prehistoric days of vast inland seas and wet savannas, the cranes were unable to adapt to any other environment and began to die off as the face of the continent changed. By the time Europeans touched these shores, it seems likely that no more than 1,500 birds lived in a narrow range between the Gulf States and Saskatchewan. Then, quickly and drastically, in the thirty years between 1870 and 1900, settlers altered the land through agriculture, cattle grazing, swamp drainage, and building, and 90 percent of the remaining whooper population was wiped out. Hunting and the Victorian hobby of egg collecting took a sizable toll, but loss of habitat was the crucial factor.

The long history of whooping crane protection has really been a series of struggles to maintain small scattered tracts of their territory. It began in 1937 with the establishment of Aransas National Wildlife Refuge, a 47,000-acre (19,000-hectare) wildfowl sanctuary on the Gulf coast of Texas, wintering grounds for the last migratory flock of eighteen cranes. Though a sanctuary should mean safety, conservationists at Aransas have had to guard against oil drilling, dredging, and even U. S. Army bomber practice that took place on or dangerously near the refuge.

At the northern end of the whooping cranes' range, 500 miles (804 kilometers) from the Arctic Circle in Canada, Wood Buffalo National Park provides a remote, secluded nesting ground for the cranes. Originally established as a refuge for endangered bison, this isolated region is the only place where whoopers still breed in the wild. In 1959, when no more than thirty-six birds existed, their privacy was threatened by the Canadian National Railway: the company announced plans to run a branch line through the park within 8 miles (13 kilometers) of nesting sites. After vigorous protests by environmentalists, the railroad took a longer, more expensive route around the park, leaving the birds to breed undisturbed.

The trickiest problems arise during long migrations, when the cranes' "habitat" consists of an unpredictable series of stopping places strung out along 2,500 miles (4,000 kilometers) through North Dakota, South Dakota, Nebraska, Oklahoma, and Kansas. Because they travel in small groups, or even alone, their route is difficult to trace. But a tracking program has recently taken on the task of protecting them while they migrate. As soon as the whoopers leave their refuges, an alert goes out all along the flyway. Sightings are phoned in to the U. S. Fish and Wildlife Service in South Dakota. Communities on the flight path are notified and asked to report any potential hazards, such as oil spills or outbreaks of disease.

At least one disaster has been averted by this relay-alert tactic. In 1975, nine whoopers on their spring migration attempted to land in a Nebraska marsh, but were driven away by low-flying aircraft and firecrackers. The birds went on to another roosting site and thus avoided exposure to fowl cholera, a fatal disease that had swept through the marsh.

The Whooping Crane Recovery Team of the U. S. Fish and Wildlife Service has recommended the protection of "stepping-stones" at 150- to 200-mile (240- to 321-kilometer) intervals along the route. It has surveyed the areas used by cranes, compiled an inventory of the most crucial ones, and worked to have these designated as "critical habitat" and protected under the Endangered Species Act of 1973. After many political and legal hassles, the team has obtained limited assurances that certain vital sandbars and marshlands will not be violated.

With so many vigilant defenders, the whooping crane population has risen slowly but steadily. The latest count showed 115 wild birds, with a record number of eighteen nests in the spring of 1979 at Wood Buffalo Park and with several breeding pairs in zoos in New Orleans and San Antonio. Seriously endangered but still surviving, this stately crane seems to defy extinction. Visit Aransas in winter or find a lucky vantage point along the flyway, and you may still see a tall, red-masked, black-whiskered, yellow-eyed, bugle-voiced whooper.

M.A.

FROZEN TIGER CELLS

Rescue operations to remove rare animals from their endangered habitats have become almost standard procedure during the past two decades. In many cases zoos offer the only safe refuge. Today more Siberian tigers live in captivity than in the wilds of Siberia, and no one expects these captive animals to be returned to their dwindling habitat. Many species now survive *only* in zoos, where, at best, the vanished wilderness can be recreated in miniature to give visitors "the flavor of a world that used to be," in the words of one prominent zoo director. Among the more futuristic conservation efforts is San Diego's "frozen zoo," where cell and sperm samples from endangered species are stored as a precaution against the final disappearance of unique genetic material.

Traditionalists who prefer the idea of real live tigers in real forests to frozen tiger cells in a cell bank have been working since the early 1960s on captive breeding projects aimed at reestablishing animal habitats.

A once rare American bird, the masked bobwhite quail, has been raised so successfully in captivity that, if population figures were the only indicator, one would consider this species saved from extinction. Again, however, the problem is not numbers, but habitat. "We're producing thousands of bobwhites," says a biologist for the Arizona Game and Fish Department, "and we hardly have homes for five." The quail's limited native range in southern Arizona and Sonora, Mexico, has been devastated by overgrazing and drought.

With cooperation between cattle ranchers, who own much of the bird's former habitat, and conservationists, attempts are being made to restore some of the depleted rangelands. Subsidized by government funds, ranchers are clearing mesquite and planting perennial grasses, an improvement that could benefit both quail and cattle.

The latest candidate for captive breeding is the California condor, a victim of urban development and pollution. With fewer than forty condors left in the world, scientists debated the wisdom of capturing these soaring Ice Age giants and rearing them in captivity. But since the birds no longer attempt to nest and breed in the wild, extinction seems inevitable unless the reasons they avoid breeding can be found and corrected.

Even if efforts to breed condors succeed, the birds will not necessarily be out of danger; for their mountain home, the Sespe Sanctuary just north of Los Angeles, is threatened by bulldozers, pesticides, and oil drills. Unless California legislators and scientists can effect significant habitat improvements, the millions spent on captive breeding may be wasted.

"'PRIMATE' MEANS THAT WE'RE NUMBER ONE."

Biding Time

For Ray Erickson, assistant director of the Patuxent Wildlife Research Center in Maryland, and the man responsible for the government's first endangered species programs, survival of condors *in the wild* is "the overriding goal. . . . Captivity is only a means of tiding the birds over a bad period and keeping a gene pool, so that if the environment improves we will have condors to return to the wild. Capture would buy two decades of time in which to clean up the environment."

Efforts are being made to guard against the destructive, sometimes irreversible consequences humans impose on their environment. For example, under the auspices of the United Nations Educational, Scientific, and Cultural Organization (UNESCO), large ecological zones are being set aside as part of a worldwide network of "protected major ecosystem types . . . devoted to conservation of nature and scientific research."

Under this comprehensive program, called "Man and the Biosphere," designated ecological or biosphere reserves are closed to exploitative activities and opened to researchers from all over the world. Selected regions must be large enough to support sizable populations of all resident species, so that animal strains will not be weakened through inbreeding. Where appropriate, the reserves are surrounded by buffer zones to prevent pollution and intrusion from outside. So far, of two hundred proposals, fifty-seven reserves have been certified, including twenty-eight in the United States, several in Poland, Iran, Britain, Norway, Thailand, Uruguay, Yugoslavia, and Zaire.

A successful example of a biosphere reserve, though not part of UNESCO's program, is Corcovado National Park in Costa Rica. Emphasizing scientific research over tourism, the 89,000-acre (35,600-hectare) tropical rain-forest park has no roads and only the most primitive accommodations. Of the two hundred annual visitors to Corcovado, more than 90 percent are scientists. (For further details, see "Corcovado Park, Costa Rica," in the Almanac World Tour, page 69.)

As long as areas like Corcovado can be kept unspoiled, they will provide a standard of comparison for measuring the impacts—negative or positive—of humanity on the natural environment. Clearly, the pressures that endangered animals face from humans cannot be effectively relieved by zoo directors—twentieth-century Noahs, rescuing oryxes and pangolins, orangutans, and gibbons to the safety of zoological gardens. This time we can't just collect the animals two by two and wait for the rain to stop. If rescue is to mean more than just a short reprieve, we must work to protect not only endangered species but their endangered habitats.

M.A.

REUSABLE BOTTLES

As late as 1960, 95 percent of all soft drinks and 50 percent of all beer produced in the United States was sold in refillable bottles. Returning empties and collecting a small refund for them were parts of daily life.

But in the mid-1960s, the beverage industries began to launch seductive advertising campaigns to sell new, more "glamorous" containers. They changed the shape and color of their bottles, boosted aluminum and steel cans, and advertised with both bottles and cans a unique and desirable quality—convenience. One could throw the empty container away, avoiding the inconvenience of returning it to the place of purchase for refill or reuse. Slowly, subtly, the returnables market faded, and the convenient "throwaway ethic" shouldered its way in.

For ten years cans and bottles accumulated as litter along roadsides, beaches, at campsites, and in stadiums. In the early 1970s consumers and conservationists began a fight to return to returnables. But they found the "bottle battle" a difficult one. A major opponent was Keep America Beautiful, Inc. (KAB), a nonprofit group associated with the beverage industry. KAB had a budget of $600 million annually, and formed a lobby to defeat container regulation by promoting litter pick-up through such slogans as "Help Keep America Beautiful" and "People Start Pollution, People Can Stop It." (See "Phony Environmental Groups," page 782.) High-powered lobbyists for the glass manufacturers and the steel workers succeeded in defeating most bottle bills. Between 1953 and 1977, over two thousand pieces of legislation calling for mandatory deposits were introduced in state legislatures across the United States, yet bills passed in only two states—Oregon and Vermont. (See "Building a Coalition," page 765.)

Proponents of deposit laws—environmentalists, public interest groups, and civic groups—turned to the initiative, a process that allowed activists to collect thousands of signatures and thereby put the issue on the ballot for direct vote by the people. Activists in four states, Michigan, Maine,

Colorado, and Massachusetts, decided to put deposit legislation to a popular vote in 1976.

Both proponents and opponents of the bottle bill spent the year prior to the election plotting intense advertising campaigns, compiling information, and conducting public opinion surveys. The campaign budgets of the industry groups far outstripped those of the public interest groups. In Michigan, for example, public interest groups came up with $117,000 for their campaign, while industry spent $1.3 million. But despite the industry's campaign extravaganzas, two states, Michigan and Maine, passed deposit legislation overwhelmingly, and Massachusetts lost by less than 1 percent.

By 1979, seven states had returned to returnables. And legislation is pending in the U. S. Congress that would enact a deposit system nationwide.

Studies on states with returnable bottle laws show the laws do reduce litter, save energy and resources, and create jobs. A report on the progress of deposit legislation shows the following:

- Opposition from grocers, who were among the most active opponents of deposit legislation has all but disappeared.
- Ninety-five percent of all beverage containers are being returned.
- Based on actual beverage prices, a family buying a refillables saves an average of $60 a year on beverage costs. Why? Spokesmen for Coca-Cola of Barre, Vermont, testified before a Vermont legislative committee in May 1974 that by switching to refillable bottles, the company saved about 52 cents per case of soda in operating costs.
- Returnable bottles create jobs. Many retailers and distributors have hired additional people for handling and sorting containers. In addition, since the law was passed, about one hundred redemption centers for beverage containers have opened in Vermont.
- In Oregon, the governor released a report in February 1977 which states that the number of containers entering the solid waste stream has been reduced by 88 percent and that the new system saves 1.4 trillion Btu's per year, enough energy to supply the heating needs of fifty thousand Oregonians.
- Surveys in Maine show that ten months after the law went into effect there, beverage container litter had dropped 77 percent, and that 90 percent of all soda and beer bottles and cans were being returned.
- In Michigan, the state's entire solid waste load is down by 4.5 percent, saving residents $15 million annually in garbage pick-up and disposal costs.
- Finally, the Resource Conservation Committee, an intercabinet agency that spent two years evaluating the deposit concept and other approaches to reducing solid waste, concluded early in 1979 that deposit legislation reduced litter and solid waste more effectively than industry-favored alternatives like shopping center recycling programs and tax assessments to fund litter pick-ups.

D.M.

HYDROPONICS

Before they built a great empire, the Aztecs of Central America were a nomadic tribe. Pressed by ruthless and powerful opponents, the Aztecs roamed the valleys of what is now central Mexico in search of a place to settle. They finally found such a place, on the marshy shores of Lake Tenochtitlán, and set about the task of building a city.

Denied arable land by their aggressors, the Aztecs had the immediate problem of growing sufficient food for the new settlement. Demonstrating their remarkable flair for invention, they looked to the lake for a solution. Lashing rushes and reeds together to make rafts, and covering them with dredged soil, the Aztecs created giant floating islands on which they grew vegetables, flowers, and even trees. The plants, growing through the rafts to the water below, thrived, as did the city, which later became the Aztec capital of central Mexico.

The rafts, called *chinampas,* were invented to stave off starvation, but they proved so successful they were never abandoned as the empire flourished. The *chinampas* were, in fact, one of the early experiments in what we now call hydroponics.

Hydroponics is a method of growing plants without soil in a nutrient-rich solution of water, sometimes with a solid substrate of sand, gravel, or vermiculite to support the plants. Though the technique is not new, it is enjoying a revival as scientists seek ways to grow food in areas with poor soil and landless urban dwellers discover it as a means to a space-saving indoor garden.

The notion of growing plants without soil may seem revolutionary, but it wasn't until the nineteenth century that scientists discovered the

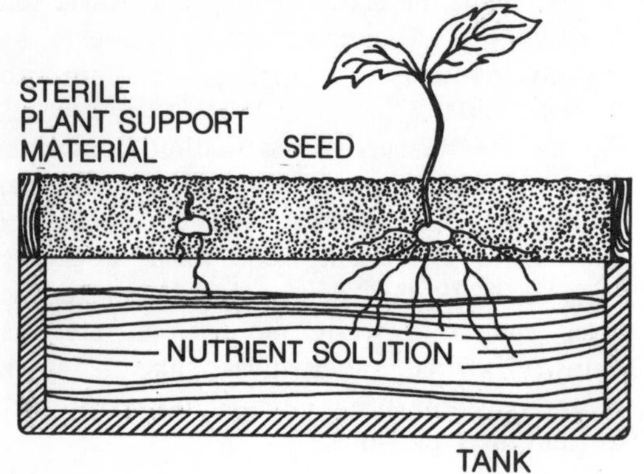

role of soil in plant growth—that it stores nutrients carried by water to plants. Scientists themselves sometimes did without soil, simply adding the necessary nutrients to a water solution for their lab plants. In 1936 one such scientist, Dr. W. F. Gericke at the University of California, grew a 25-foot (7.6-meter) tomato vine in a water solution and posed next to the giant for newspaper photographers. Headlines claimed soilless growing was one of the most important discoveries of the twentieth century, bound to make traditional agriculture obsolete. Dr. Gericke named the method "hydroponics," Greek for "water working."

Thousands of small hydroponic greenhouses and a few major projects were built, but World War II shifted most peoples' minds to other things.

In the late 1970s hydroponics was revived by agricultural scientists and by neighborhood groups. Hydroponics is no replacement for land farming, but it does have certain advantages. Insects, weeds, and disease are kept to a minimum. (Many insects and bacteria pests breed in soil.) It allows more plants to be grown in a given area, because plants can be placed closer together, making the technique useful in areas of limited space. And there is no waste fertilizer runoff. The amount of nutrients added is just what the plants need.

There are major disadvantages to hydroponics, though. It has not been successful in growing grains; it does require a great deal of water; it is not as efficient on a large scale as on a small scale; and it does require chemical fertilizers and pesticides—less than traditional farming but more than organic gardening. The mainstays of organic gardening, compost, manure, and earthworms, are useless in hydroponics.

The technique may find its greatest usefulness in supplying vegetables to areas with poor soil or unfavorable growing conditions, and in providing urban gardeners with a land-free medium to produce their own food. Hydroponics is a simple technology, requiring some knowledge of plants but no extensive equipment when operated on a small scale. In the future, hydroponic greenhouses may aid local food supplies, cutting down the long, energy-expensive transportation routes of many vegetables.

K.F., B.P.B., M.P.

NIGHT SOIL

Twenty-six centuries ago, the Chinese had already learned to use human and animal waste as fertilizer. Horses drawing cartloads of "night soil" went out every day from cities to the countryside nearby, where these wastes were turned into valuable crop nutrients. Night soil is still collected in large "honey buckets" in Chinese cities today, to be composted and spread on farmland. And elsewhere in the world, this ancient fertilizer, in the form of sewage sludge, is being rediscovered.

The ancient Roman writer Columella described how sewage wastes helped crops grow, and early Arab traders sold "poudrette," a fertilizer made of dried and pulverized fecal matter. The seventeenth-century Flemish ordered farmers to use manure from the cities on their fields. In the 1800s, American farmers came into cities with their carts to collect waste from cesspools, privy vaults, stables, restaurants, and markets. Before 1900, London, Paris, Berlin, and many other European cities were operating sewage farms.

By the end of the 1800s, though, the practice of fertilizing farms with human waste had died out in most of North America and Europe. When indoor plumbing came to the city, people started using far more water than before. The runoff flooded the old cesspools, which by now were also known to be breeding places for infectious diseases. When cities of the time built sewer systems, they followed the latest recommendations of Victorian sanitary engineers, who pointed out that running water was a great purifier. As a result, most cities' sewage systems led straight into the nearest stream or river.

Today much raw sewage in the United States is treated before being released into a river. In this process, the raw sewage from a city is separated into wastewater and sludge. Sludge is the solid

A sewage treatment plant aerates sewage to help detoxify it. The remaining sludge can be used for fertilizer. (*EPA Documerica/James H. Pickerell*)

waste that settles out during the treatment process. The wastewater from a treatment plant typically goes back into a river. The newest treatment plants produce wastewater that is relatively clean, which means that the left-over sludge is more concentrated. The plant then faces the problem of what to do with the sludge. Many coastal cities dump their sludge into the ocean. Near Athens, Greece, so much sewage has been dumped into the Mediterranean that methane gas bubbles can be seen on the surface of the water. South of Long Island, in the New York Bight, is an area nicknamed "the Dead Sea," where so much sludge from the megalopolis has been dumped that by the early 1970s the ocean bottom was blanketed with more than 5 feet (1.5 meters) of sludge, which was continuously advancing toward the coast. In June and July, 1976, sewage sludge from the Bight began washing up on the famous beaches of Long Island, polluting them so badly that they had to be closed. The U. S. Environmental Protection Agency promptly ordered an end to sludge dumping in the Bight by 1981. Since most U.S. ocean dumping is done in that area, the order helped considerably to reduce the total amount of U.S. sludge dumping.

Besides ocean dumping, now considered unacceptable for its effects on marine life as well as on the adjacent coasts, there are three other methods to get rid of sludge. The treatment plant can incinerate it; the sludge can be plowed under and compacted with bulldozers as a landfill; or it can be made into fertilizer.

Incineration is expensive, because of the high cost of fuel and of plant operations. Air pollution can be a big problem. These two problems caused Denver, Colorado, for example, to reconsider its sewage-disposal methods.

Landfills are also expensive. Most sanitary landfills have been constructed since World War

II. Recently a new problem has surfaced, literally. Methane gas, which is highly volatile, seeps out of such landfills and can cause explosions. In Richmond, Virginia, a low-income neighborhood was built over a postwar landfill. In 1975, a man and woman were burned when methane gas from the landfill exploded in their living room, blowing out the door and two windows. After inspecting buildings in the neighborhood, fire officials decided there was indeed a major problem from gas leakage. Two schools were closed, and residents were warned to keep their windows partially open at all times to prevent further explosions.

Reusing sewage sludge is by far the most environmentally sound method of disposal. Sewage sludge can replace chemical fertilizer and actually helps build up humus in the soil. In Oregon, sewage sludge was applied to a sand dune that traveled 50 feet (15 meters) a year and threatened to engulf farmland. Within a few months, a grassy ground cover had appeared, halting the spread of the dune.

Brunswick (Braunschweig), a German city of 380,000 people, has been using sludge as fertilizer for years. In Melbourne, Australia, healthy, fat cattle graze in sewage-fertilized pastures. Denver, Milwaukee, and Chicago are among the U.S. cities that turn almost all of their sludge into useful fertilizer. In West Hertfordshire, England, half a million people are served by a successful system that converts sludge to fertilizer.

There are problems associated with using sludge to grow crops, however. In many developing countries that use raw sewage on farmland, there is a high incidence of amoebic dysentery and other diseases spread by fecal contamination. Because of these well-known hazards, many people worry about the dangers of sludge fertilizer. In fact, raw sewage *is* dangerous, but the sludge to be used as fertilizer is not raw sewage.

There are three kinds of sludge. The first, *raw sludge,* is simply the solid waste that settles out of raw sewage by gravity. The second is *digested sludge,* which means sludge that has been anaerobically "fermented" until it decomposes. Digested sludge can be air-dried, heat-dried, or centrifuged to make it solid; or it can be kept liquid to make spreading it easier. *Activated sludge,* the most processed kind, is digested sludge that is put through aerobic secondary treatment, then heat- or air-dried. Activated sludge is so inoffensive that it is sometimes sold in bags as trademarked dry fertilizer.

When sludge is treated properly, contamination by disease is not a problem. A more important problem than pathogen contamination is metal residue. The sludge from urban areas can contain small amounts of heavy metals—zinc, copper, lead, chromium, nickel, and cadmium. The fear is that the metals could be taken in by the growing crops and passed along the food chain to humans. Cadmium is especially troublesome, because the human body cannot metabolize it. However, so far there is no evidence that cadmium in sewage sludge is taken up by crops, and there are no recorded cases of disease from sewage sludge metal in crops. On the other hand, there is considerable evidence that metals in the soil are bound into "unavailable forms" and not taken up by plants. But it is important not to take risks. Sludge should always be analyzed before it is used as fertilizer.

Sewage sludge can be effective both as an economical and efficient substitute for chemical fertilizer, and as a solution to the expensive disposal problems of modern urban sewage systems. The problem left unsolved is the blandness of the name: "Sewage sludge" just doesn't sound as interesting as "night soil."

J.S.

SOME OTHER THINGS RETURNING

- *Solar Water Heaters* In 1891 Charles Kemp patented the first solar water heater. By 1897, 30 percent of the homes in Pasadena, California, had solar heaters, and by 1941, 60,000 had been installed in California and Florida. The current interest in solar energy is actually a return to an old non-oil technology.
- *Bicycles* The bicycle is coming back in the land of the automobile. There were fewer than 24 million bicycles in the United States in 1960. There were 95 million in 1979. Between 1972 and 1978, 5 million more bikes than cars were sold in the United States. The bicycle is still used primarily for recreation in the United States, but people are beginning to realize that bikes are often a faster and healthier way to get to work in cities.
- *Wood Fuel in the United States* Wood has always been the principal fuel for heating and cooking in most of the world, but it had been largely forgotten by the United States during its romance with petroleum. Since 1972, however, the U.S. sale of wood stoves has increased

five times. More than a million U.S. homes were heated primarily by wood in 1979.

- *Windmills* Windmills were first used in Babylon about four thousand years ago. They were common in Persia in the tenth century and spread throughout Europe during the thirteenth century. Six million windmills were sold in the United States between 1880 and 1940. They lost popularity when electricity reached rural areas, but are now enjoying a revival.
- *Ancient Plants* Seeds of the arctic lupine, a small legume found in Canada, have germinated and grown to maturity after being found frozen for up to ten thousand years.
- *Ancient Fish* The coelacanth, a crossopterygian fish believed extinct for almost 200 million years, was rediscovered off the east coast of Africa in 1938 and seems to be a regular, if uncommon, member of the deep water fauna in the area.

T.C., K.F.

DISAPPEARING

ANIMAL SPECIES

"In less than half an hour, we filled two boats full of them, as if they had been stones," wrote the French explorer Cartier in 1543. His cargo: great auks, one of about seventy-five species wiped out by humans during the nineteenth century. (See "Animals You'll Never See," page 333.) So far in the twentieth century, the pace has accelerated, with approximately one species vanishing each year, a rate experts predict will increase drastically by the year 2000. According to a recent environmental study by the U. S. Council on Environmental Quality, called *The Global 2000 Report to the President,* 20 percent of all species on earth could become extinct during the next two decades, a loss "unparalleled in human history." And this, many ecologists feel, is a conservative estimate. Some have predicted half a million extinctions in tropical rain forests alone by the end of the century—an average loss of about one hundred species per day!

Dying in Style

How have we managed to decimate so many animal populations in such a short time? Until recently, overhunting for usually frivolous purposes caused extinctions. When feathered hats were in style in the early 1900s, egret plumes sold for $50 an ounce—and each ounce cost the lives of six courting male birds. Fortunately for egrets, feathers on humans went out of style before all the birds were gone. The black rhino's numbers have been halved over the past decade due to the demands of a market that regards the rhino's horns as a fine aphrodisiac. The little Asian musk deer, extremely shy and rare, has been slaughtered for its "musk," a glandular secretion used to make seductive-smelling perfumes and soaps.

Black rhinos in Ngorongoro Crater, Tanzania. (*Carol Sue Davidson*)

And, of course, people love fur. Before the Endangered Species Act was passed in the United States in 1973, Americans could appropriate the skin of any creature, no matter how rare. An American basketball star was reported to have decorated two rooms of his house with wolf muzzles—seventeen thousand of them. And kangaroo pelts by the millions were imported for athletic shoes, riding boots, furniture, and coats, even kangaroo-paw bottle openers and kangaroo-tail soup.

The Flouted Laws

Laws and treaties like the U. S. Endangered Species Act, the Convention on International

Trade in Endangered Species (CITES), quotas of the International Whaling Commission (IWC), and the Marine Mammal Protection Act (MMPA) restrict the taking of rare animals and plants. (See "Animal Laws," page 576.) More than seven hundred species, including kangaroos and wolves, are listed on the U. S. Department of the Interior's Endangered Species List, with more than two thousand others being reviewed for possible inclusion. Fifty-one nations have ratified the CITES treaty agreeing to prohibit commerce in species threatened with extinction. And the hunting of marine mammals is regulated, for the most part, by quotas and restrictive permits.

Yet, despite this legislation and growing public awareness, world trade in wildlife has increased dramatically since 1973. Imports of animal and plant products into the United States went up an astonishing 9,582 percent in five years, with rare elephants, sea turtles, and wild birds among the species hardest hit.

As the price of ivory rose to ten times what it was ten years ago, the economic incentive for poachers became irresistible: in 1978, between 100,000 and 400,000 African elephants were killed for their tusks.

With over 5.5 million live wild birds sold each year, at least nine species are now listed as threatened or endangered *as a direct result of trade.* Because rare birds must be smuggled across most borders, many die in transit—stuffed in hubcaps or hair curlers, or packed in stockings to keep them quiet between the door panels of cars.

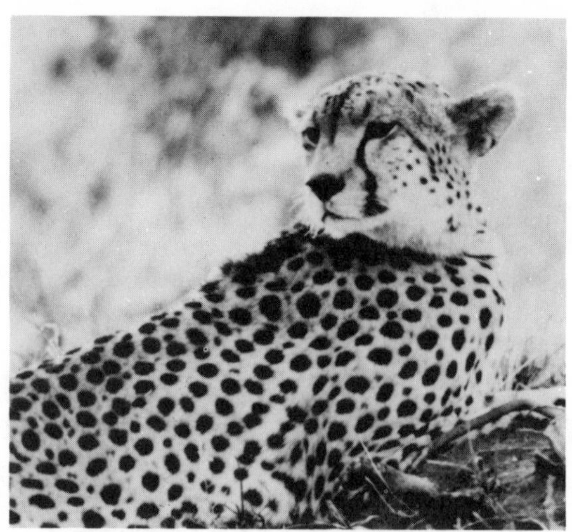

Cheetah (*World Wildlife Fund/Bruce F. Wolfe*)

Animal Cops

According to a U. S. Treasury Department spokesman, the smuggling of endangered animals "rivals the narcotics trade in its scope, methods, and profits." Yet penalties for wildlife smugglers are usually too lenient to hurt overall profits. In January 1979, the Hong Kong Fur Factory, Ltd., illegally imported 319 Ethiopian cheetah skins valued at $43,900, for which it paid a fine of only $1,540. In a major U.S. case, the leader of a smuggling operation was sentenced to four months in prison and fined $10,000 for exporting a shipment of alligator skins—but only after he'd cleared $140,000 on the deal.

Enforcement of the law is difficult, especially with limited personnel. Though the U. S. Fish and Wildlife Service has specially trained wildlife inspectors, there are far too few of them to patrol every U.S. port of entry. When a professional smuggler unloads a crate from Hong Kong marked "Machine Parts" perforated with air holes, when uninformed tourists bring home ivory carvings and turtle shell salad tossers, regular customs officers rarely know enough about wildlife laws to question the legality of the imports. And even if an inspector suspects a violation, very few can distinguish whether an object is made, for example, from a hippo tooth, which is legal, or from an elephant tusk, which is not.

Recognizing the need for knowledgeable enforcement agents, delegates to the 1979 CITES meeting published a detailed wildlife identification manual for customs inspectors. At the same time, the U. S. Customs Service organized a team of specialists in exotic fauna trade to patrol the Los Angeles International Airport. In its first five months of operation, this force intercepted forty-two illegal shipments, including 5,000 pounds (2,270 kilograms) of sea turtle meat and almost 50,000 birds, reptiles, and fish.

Modern Pirates

The marine mammal trade has its poachers and smugglers, too—"pirate" whalers who ignore international regulations and take whales of all sizes, ages, and kinds, even those considered "commercially extinct" and protected. (See "Coming to Terms with Wildlife Managers and Conservationists," page 362, and "Whales," page 286.) Their methods are extremely wasteful: they discard the bulk of every catch, using only choice cuts of meat. They operate in areas that are totally off-limits for IWC whalers. And they disguise responsibility by flying the flags of non-IWC nations though they are often secretly financed, equipped, and supported by IWC members. Though many of these pirate whalers ply the seas with little interference from governments, they are persistently dogged by self-styled enforcers of marine justice. Several conservation organizations sponsor ships of their own to pursue the whalers, and if they get the chance, put them out of business. The Fund for Animals' ship, *Sea Shepherd,* did just that recently—intentionally ramming the *Sierra,* one of the outlaw whalers, off the coast of Portugal. (For more on the *Sea Shepherd*'s high seas confrontation, see "The Whale Defenders," page 291.)

Making Waves

Pressure for short-term profits has traditionally overwhelmed conservationist forces, but today citizen conservation organizations actively monitor world wildlife policy. A coalition of thirty-two citizen groups at the 1979 CITES convention outnumbered lobbyists from the pet and fur industries and effectively blocked several anticonservation moves. The World Wildlife Fund, based in Washington, D.C., has established a privately operated data source, Trade Records Analysis of Flora and Fauna in Commerce (TRAFFIC), that supplies valuable statistics to federal agencies, conservation groups, and all ports of entry.

A Peregrine falcon and chick. Once headed for almost certain extinction, the Peregrine falcon has been the object of conservation programs. The best guess today: it *may* survive. (*World Wildlife Fund/E. Hosking*)

Since the American Bison Society first set out to save the plains buffalo from extinction in 1905 (see "Return Engagements," page 344), private concerned groups have used boycotts, petitions, lobbies, and even flamboyant tactics like the disabling of the *Sierra,* to stop the killing of endangered species. (To find out how to join wildlife protection organizations, see "What to Do About Vanishing Wildlife," page 370, and "How to Join the Whale Crusade," page 293.)

The Roots of Modern Extinction

Where people compete with wildlife for living space, and wastes and pollutants spoil the environment, destruction of wild habitats becomes the major cause of extinction. And some of the world's poorest countries, where competition for land is more intense, contain the last remaining homes of many rare animals.

- In India, a preserve of the last Asiatic lions is located beside the grazing grounds of domestic cattle whose owners would like to see the lions killed or removed. In Africa, protected zebras compete with domestic herds for grazing land, and protected leopards sometimes attack cattle.
- In Thailand, sixteen native species are endangered now and many others are already extinct because of the rapid environmental changes of the last century. A fourfold increase in rice fields, the draining of swamps, and the development of canals have all but wiped out at least seven species of large animals. Three fourths of Thailand's forest cover has been cut, and experts predict that by 1987 the country could be entirely deforested. Extensive barren flatlands exist already where tropical forests stood thirty years ago. Though Thailand has set aside twenty-six national parks and wildlife sanctuaries, these areas may eventually be violated as population grows, as logging, tin mining, and rubber plantations expand.
- In Central America, entire virgin tropical forests have been cut down to create cattle ranches, some of which supply hamburger to North American fast food chains. And in the Amazon Basin, hundreds of Western, European, and Japanese timber companies clear-cut thousands of square miles each year,

devastating whole ecosystems before anyone can catalog what is being destroyed. (See "Amazonia," page 274.)

Paying the Price of Preservation

Pragmatic conservationists suggest that the only real way to save endangered species is to show the economic value of managing a population—killing a certain number each year for profit, but not driving the population to extinction. At a 1979 CITES meeting, delegates decided to permit New Guinea to sell the skins of farm-raised crocodiles, whereas Indonesian wild crocodile skins may not be traded. Breeders of rare fish and butterflies may carry on lucrative commerce in these creatures, as long as trade does not deplete wild populations.

Another CITES decision states that when a protected stock becomes too numerous for its habitat, a carefully determined number of animals may be killed—not by game wardens who would be forced to burn unsaleable carcasses, but by foreign hunters who would pay large fees for the privilege.

Although captive breeding programs and habitat preservation (see "Frozen Tiger Cells," page 353) are also helping to preserve some species, we will be faced with increasingly difficult choices in the future, as population pressure and the need for agricultural land overtake wildlife habitat. We may have to make conscious decisions about whether we are willing to sacrifice certain species. But we must remember that once a species is extinct, it is gone forever.

M.A.

COMING TO TERMS WITH WILDLIFE MANAGERS AND CONSERVATIONISTS

SPECIES: A species, normally the smallest distinct division in biological nomenclature, may be defined as a population that shares the same gene pool and can actually or potentially interbreed. According to Darwinian theory, species are formed as populations become isolated from each other for many generations. Eventually, as the gene pool of each population changes through mutations, separate species emerge.

Here are some terms used to define the status of species:

Endangered: Having so few individual survivors that the species could soon become extinct in all or part of its range.

Threatened: Likely to become endangered within the foreseeable future.

Depleted: Still numerous enough to survive, but declining rapidly.

Indeterminate: Apparently threatened. More information is needed for a reliable assessment of status.

Commercially extinct: Too rare to be profitably exploited by commercial interests; usually refers to whales.

Habitat: Region where a species lives or is usually found, including temporary habitats such as migratory routes, nesting and spawning grounds.

Critical habitat: Habitat that is essential to the conservation of a species. In the United States critical habitats of endangered and threatened species are usually protected under the U. S. Endangered Species Act of 1973.

Maximum sustainable yield (MSY) or Rational sustainable utilization: The greatest number of animals that may be taken (this usually means "killed") from a group without causing a downward trend in population.

Optimum sustainable population (OSP): The ideal number of animals for a given group. If there are too many for the habitat to support or too few to provide a diverse gene pool, the health of the group and the stability of the ecosystem will suffer.

Captive breeding: A conservation technique to increase animal populations by breeding them under safe, controlled conditions in captivity. Often used for endangered or threatened species.

M.A.

THE WORLD'S RAREST BIRDS

Chatham Island black robin
only 7 left (New Zealand)

Kauai oo
fewer than 10 (Hawaiian Islands)

Japanese crested ibis
10 (Japan)

Mauritius kestrel
13 (Mauritius)

Puerto Rican parrot
26 (including 10 in captivity)

Ivory-billed woodpecker
fewer than 30 (U.S.)

Mauritius pink pigeon
24 (Mauritius)

Seychelles magpie robin
36 (Seychelles)

California condor
fewer than 40 (U.S.)

Mauritius parakeet
fewer than 50 (Mauritius)

Kakapo
fewer than 100 (New Zealand)

Whooping crane
115 (U.S. and Canada)

Spanish imperial eagle
150 (Spain)

St. Lucia parrot
150 (Caribbean)

Imperial parrot
150 (Caribbean)

Cahow
200 (Bermuda)

Short-tailed albatross
200 (Torishima, Japan)

Lake Atitlán giant grebe
210 (Guatemala)

Takahe
fewer than 250 (New Zealand)

Monkey-eating eagle
300 (Philippines)

SOURCE: World Wildlife Fund, U.S., 1979.

THE WORLD'S RAREST MAMMALS

Iriomote cat
40–80 (Japan)

Javan rhinoceros
about 50 (Indonesia)

Red wolf
fewer than 100 (U.S.)

Mesopotamian deer
fewer than 100 (Iran)

Rodrigues flying fox
120–125 (Mauritius)

Arabian oryx
about 150 in captive herds

Tamarau
150–200 (Philippines)

Sumatran rhinoceros
fewer than 300 (Indonesia)

Wild Bactrian camel
300–500 (China, Mongolia)

Indus dolphin
450–600 (Pakistan)

Giant panda
low hundreds (China)

Simien fox
fewer than 500 (Ethiopia)

Kuhl's deer
500 (Indonesia)

Golden tamarin
500–600 (Brazil)

Ryukyu rabbit
500–900 (Japan)

Mediterranean monk seal
500–1,000 (Mediterranean and West Atlantic)

Juan Fernández fur seal
700 (Chile)

Calamian deer
fewer than 900 (Philippines)

Hawaiian monk seal
700–1000 (U.S.)

Mariana flying fox
high hundreds (Mariana Islands)

SOURCE: World Wildlife Fund, U.S. 1979.

DISAPPEARING FISHES

Common Name	*Scientific Name*	*Country*
Ala Balik	*Salmo platycephalus*	Turkey
Ayumodoki	*Hymenophysa curta*	Japan
Blindcat, Mexican	*Prietella phreatophila*	Mexico
Bonytail, Pahranagat	*Gila robusta jordani*	U.S. (Nevada)
Catfish	*Pangasius sonitwongsei*	Thailand
Catfish, Giant	*Pangasianodon gigas*	Thailand
Chub, Humpback	*Gila cypha*	U.S. (Arizona, Utah, Wyoming)
Chub, Mohave	*Siphateles mohavensis*	U.S. (California)
Cicek	*Acanthorutilus handlirschi*	Turkey
Cisco, Longjaw	*Coregonus alpenae*	U.S. (Lakes Michigan, Huron, Erie)
Cui-ui	*Chasmistes cujus*	U.S. (Nevada)
Dace, Kendall Warm Springs	*Rhinichthys osculus thermalis*	U.S. (Wyoming)
Dace, Moapa	*Moapa coriacea*	U.S. (Nevada)
Darter, Fountain	*Etheostoma fonticola*	U.S. (Texas)
Darter, Maryland	*Etheostoma sellare*	U.S. (Maryland)
Darter, Okaloosa	*Etheostoma okaloosae*	U.S. (Florida)
Darter, Watercress	*Etheostoma nuchale*	U.S. (Alabama)
Gambusia, Big Bend	*Gambusia gaigei*	U.S. (Texas)
Gambusia, Clear Creek	*Gambusia heterochir*	U.S. (Texas)
Gambusia, Pecos	*Gambusia nobilis*	U.S. (Texas)
Killifish, Pahrump	*Empetrichthys latos*	U.S. (Nevada)
Madtom, Scioto	*Noturus trautmani*	U.S. (Ohio)
Nekogigi	*Coreobagrus ichikawai*	Japan
Pike, Blue	*Stizostedion vitreum glaucum*	U.S. (Lakes Erie, Ontario)
Pupfish, Comanche Springs	*Cyprinodon elegans*	U.S. (Texas)
Pupfish, Devil's Hole	*Cyprinodon diabolis*	U.S. (Nevada)
Pupfish, Owens River	*Cyprinodon radiosus*	U.S. (California)
Pupfish, Tecopa	*Cyprinodon nevadensis calidae*	U.S. (California)
Pupfish, Warm Springs	*Cyprinodon nevadensis pectoralis*	U.S. (Nevada)
Squawfish, Colorado River	*Ptychocheilus lucius*	U.S. (Colorado River System)
Stickleback, Unarmored Threespine	*Gasterosteus aculeatus williamsoni*	U.S. (California)
Sturgeon, Shortnose	*Acipenser brevirostrum*	Atlantic Coast of U.S. and Canada
Tanago, Miyako	*Tanakia tanago*	Japan
Topminnow, Gila	*Poeciliopsis occidentalis*	U.S. (Arizona), Mexico
Trout, Gila	*Salmo gilae*	U.S. (New Mexico)
Trout, Greenback Cutthroat	*Salmo clarki stomias*	U.S. (Colorado)
Woundfin	*Plagopterus argentissimus*	U.S. (Utah)

SOURCE: U. S. Federal Register 40, no. 188 (September 26, 1975).

ENDANGERED SYMBOLS

Animals and birds have appeared on national flags, family crests, and coats of arms, yet ironically some of the animals most commonly revered and employed as symbols are fast disappearing. Here is a sampling of a few from around the world.

The Asian and African Lions (Panthera leo)

Habitat: Lions inhabited eastern Europe and the Middle East until about the second century A.D., when they were eliminated from those regions by hunting and expanding human settlements. They had disappeared from North Africa by about the mid-nineteenth century; now they are only to be found in sub-Saharan Africa and in the Forest of Girnar in northwest India's state of Gujarat. Most African lions now live within the 5,700 square miles (147,000 square kilometers) of Tanzania's Serengeti National Park.

Symbolism: Mentioned more than one hundred times in the Bible; associated with such qualities as courage, strength, power, and nobility. In early Christian symbolism, represented Christ.

Home of the Emblem: Its legendary characteristics have made the lion a ubiquitous symbol. Lions appear on the United Nations coats of arms of more countries than any other animal—on those of India, Kenya, Malawi, Singapore, Burma, Burundi, Senegal, Sri Lanka, Swaziland, and several European nations. Ironically, in most of these countries, lions no longer exist in the wild. Lions are also found on various European royal and aristocratic coats of arms.

Matters of Status: As of 1968, Asiatic lions numbered about 180. Now there are estimates of about 200 to 250 in the Girnar Forest. Lions receive legal protection in India, but habitat loss seriously threatens the Asiatic lion's survival. In Africa, the lion's need for land conflicts with agricultural demands. Also, trophy hunting for skins, claws, and teeth still leads to lion poaching, despite a ban issued by the president of Kenya in May 1977. The reduction in supply of prey, such as zebra and antelope, which are poached for their meat and skins, also threatens the lion's survival, especially in times of drought. The estimated population of African lions in 1979 was 200,000 and decreasing. Oddly enough, there may be more African lions in captivity today than in the wild. They are not listed as endangered by any African government.

Kenya's coat of arms. The Swahili motto means "working together."

Notes and Anecdotes: The male African lion, larger than its Asian cousin and endowed with a heavier mane, is traditionally considered "king of the jungle." In reality, the African lion generally lives on the open plains of the African velds, taking to the trees in sparse forests mainly for shade or rest. The Asiatic lion is specifically a forest dweller. Unlike the other big cats, lions lead social rather than solitary lives.

Although lions are considered skillful hunters, it was recently discovered that they sometimes scavenge the carcasses of animals killed by hyenas, rather than the reverse.

The Tiger (Panthera tigris)

Habitat: The tiger is found throughout Asia, as far as the Caucasus and Siberia.

Symbolism: The tiger is at the top of the forest food chain, and its importance to the ecosystem as well as its strength and grace have long made it a symbol of native independence and might. It is uniquely Asian; only its prehistoric ancestors inhabited other regions of the world.

Home of the Emblem: The tiger appears on the United Nations coats of arms of Malaysia, Singapore, and Malawi, and has traditionally been associated with India.

Matters of Status: India is trying to halt the tiger's decline. Just ten years ago India was exporting three thousand tiger skins annually. Now the government forbids any trade or export of the pelts. Eleven Bengal tiger reserves have been established where hunting is banned. Nepal, Bangladesh, and Bhutan have also adopted protective measures. There are only an estimated 2,000 to 3,000 Bengal tigers left, compared to approximately 40,000 at the turn of the century. The number of tigers in other countries is significantly smaller. According to one authority, the total world population of wild tigers, estimated to be about 100,000 in 1900, is only about 4,000 today (with another 5,000 in captivity). Estimates vary on particular subspecies.

The actually endangered Siberian tiger of North Asia is thought to number no more than 200 to 300 in the wild. The Sumatran tiger, which is still hunted illegally in Indonesia, is very rare, numbering anywhere from 400 to 500. There may be still a few Caspian tigers in eastern Turkey; but the Bali tiger is now considered to be extinct. There are only a few Chinese tigers left; and only 4 or 5 Javan tigers in Meru Betiri National Park. The tiger was last seen in Singapore in 1932.

In 1969, the International Union for Conservation of Nature and Natural Resources declared the tiger an endangered species and encouraged nations to protect it. Joint work by the World Wildlife Fund and the Smithsonian Institution has helped establish protective reserves in India. In March 1972, the U. S. Department of the Interior added all subspecies of tigers to its list of endangered animals, making the importing of their pelts illegal. These efforts have paid off, mainly in areas of strict protection and management. Recent surveys indicated that some subspecies may have a good chance for survival.

Notes and Anecdotes: All tigers lead solitary

The Malaysian coat of arms.

Parrot symbol on the Republic of Dominica flag.

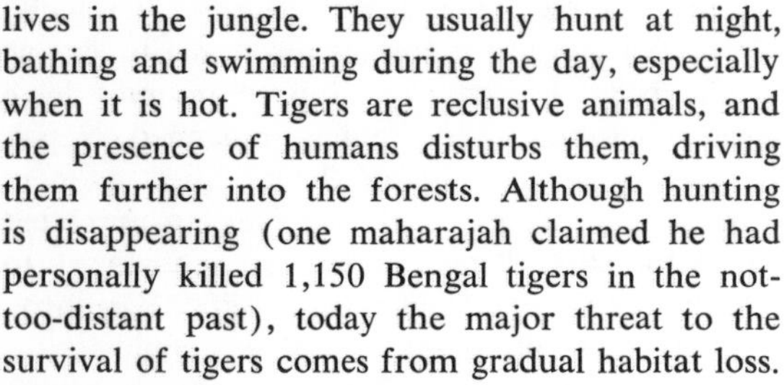

lives in the jungle. They usually hunt at night, bathing and swimming during the day, especially when it is hot. Tigers are reclusive animals, and the presence of humans disturbs them, driving them further into the forests. Although hunting is disappearing (one maharajah claimed he had personally killed 1,150 Bengal tigers in the not-too-distant past), today the major threat to the survival of tigers comes from gradual habitat loss.

Imperial Amazon Parrot (Amazona imperialis)

Habitat: Formerly inhabiting the neighboring islands of Guadeloupe and Martinique, the imperial Amazon parrot disappeared from these areas when they were "developed" and is now found only in the high, remote, rain-forested mountains of Dominica. This shy bird has retreated primarily to the Morne Diablotin mountain in north Dominica, the island's highest peak.

Symbolism: Now that it is restricted to a small part of Dominica, the imperial parrot is considered a "unique national treasure"—a symbol of the last vestiges of island wilderness.

Home of the Emblem: The parrot adorns Dominica's national emblem and flag.

Matters of Status: Out of the 332 parrot species in the world, the imperial, thought to number only about 150 in the wild, is the most critically endangered. The demand for parrots among private zoos and collectors has inflated their selling price to several thousand dollars per bird. Although they do not receive this retail price, Dominicans can still get an impressive amount for a captured parrot, in a country where the average yearly income is less than $1,000. The result is a substantial smuggling operation, in which about four out of every five parrots die in transport.

Notes and Anecdotes: The largest of the Amazon parrots, and one of the more beautiful, the imperial or "Sisserou" parrot is identifiable by its shimmering pink and purple-blue head, neck, and chest; gray beak; and green wings and legs. As part of the parrot family it is naturally equipped to climb trees and to mimic sounds. It is also affectionate with humans, which may be its undoing.

Bald Eagle (Haliaeetus leucocephalus)

Habitat: United States (from Alaska to Florida) and Canada.

Symbolism: The eagle has symbolized strength and courage throughout history. Images of it accompanied Roman legions and Persian soldiers into battle. Indigenous to North America, the bald eagle was soon adopted by the American colonists as a symbol of independence.

Home of the Emblem: In 1782, the Continental Congress chose the bald eagle—over Benjamin Franklin's candidate, the wild turkey—to be the national emblem of the United States. It is found on the Presidential Seal, on U.S. currency, and on top of the silver and ebony mace by the rostrum in the House Chamber of the U. S. Capitol, symbolizing authority.

Matters of Status: Because they live as long as forty years and are high on the food chain, bald eagles concentrate such poisons as DDT, PCB, heavy metals, and dieldrin in their tissues. One possible result has been thinner eggshells and consequent death of eagle offspring. Although the use of DDT was banned in the United States in 1972, and its effects on the eagle population may now be diminishing, other dangers persist, such as shooting by hunters and ranchers, which still accounts for half the mortalities recorded. In addition, bald eagles are faced with the loss of their natural habitats, forests, and with electrocution by contact with high-power wires.

Eagles are on the U. S. Department of Interior's list of endangered species, which makes it unlawful to kill them. Sheep ranchers continue to do so, however, arguing that the eagles threaten their lamb stocks. Biologists claim that the eagle largely restricts its feeding to rodents and carrion. The misunderstanding seems to arise from occasional sightings of eagles feeding on the carcasses of lambs that have died of natural causes.

The largest single grouping of bald eagles in North America is in the Tongass National Forest of southeast Alaska, where there are about 3,000 to 4,000. In the rest of the United States there are an estimated 10,000 or more wintering bald eagles, but not all breeding pairs are producing young, so they are still threatened with extinction.

Notes and Anecdotes: The adult bald eagle is recognizable by its white head feathers. The female, which is larger than the male, can have a wingspan of more than 7 feet (2.1 meters). Male and female bald eagles mate for life; they share the tasks of making the nest and tending the young, and are among the few bird species that have been observed playing.

Seal of the United States.

The Kangaroos (Macropus and Megaleia)

Habitat: The plains of Australia, predominantly, although the kangaroo species are so widely diversified that they inhabit both deserts and forest, some burrowing into the ground, others climbing trees by jumping into them.

Symbolism: Kangaroos are unique to Australia

Kangaroo and emu on Australian coat of arms. (*Australian Information Service*)

(the name "kangaru" is an Aborigine word) and have become, along with the koala bear, a native symbol of the country, described by the Australian Information Service as "fast, free, graceful, and harmless."

Home of the Emblem: The red kangaroo, *Megaleia rufa,* considered the most endangered of the various kangaroo species, is one of the animals featured on the United Nations coat of arms for Australia. The kangaroo is also seen on Australia's coins, banknotes, overseas publications, film titles, the Royal Australian Air Force rondel, and the livery of its international airline.

Matters of Status: About one million kangaroos are "commercially harvested" each year. The government of Australia claims some species are abundant and a threat to ranchers, and therefore tolerates restricted trade in their fur, hides, and meat. There are no effective sanctuaries for kangaroos in Australia. The country has no national parks, and kangaroos are poached in the wildlife refuges. The government is considering the establishment of "biosphere reserves" to further protect them; but meanwhile the laws are lenient and rarely enforced. Until the U. S. Department of the Interior added kangaroos to its "threatened" wildlife list, the American fur industry imported up to 1.3 million pelts per year. Sheep ranchers claim that kangaroos compete for forage with their flocks; but defenders of the kangaroos point out that they eat less and a different variety of grass than the sheep, except in times of severe drought. Nevertheless, ranchers try to eliminate them by shooting, trapping, and poisoning.

Notes and Anecdotes: Kangaroos have several remarkable traits, such as a built-in system to regulate their birth rate—they can delay the development of a fetus while they are nursing a baby. Newborn kangaroos are actually still fetuses when they crawl from the birth canal up to their mother's pouch, where they fully develop. This makes them the smallest newborn mammals in the world, in relation to the size of their mother. Adult gray and red kangaroos attain a height of 7 feet (2.1 meters) and can hop as fast as 30 miles (48 kilometers) per hour.

The Andean Condor (Vultur gryphus)

Habitat: Throughout Chile, Argentina, Colombia, Bolivia, Venezuela, Ecuador, and Peru—from the Pacific to the heights of the Andean Mountains.

Symbolism: For several hundred years the people of the Andean region have worshipped the condor for its sheer size and strength and keen eyesight. The bird is considered a brave "protector" of liberty, watching over the people of Chile from its home high in the Andes.

Home of the Emblem: The condor is found on the United Nations coats of arms of Chile, Bolivia, and Colombia.

Matters of Status: The population of Andean condors has been reduced to a few thousand by trophy hunters and by local people who use the birds for ceremonial purposes.

Since condors are scavengers, they do not prey on live cattle; nonetheless ranchers once offered a bounty of $2,500 per condor. Chile now officially recognizes the condor as an endangered species and has taken steps to assure their protection. Efforts to raise condor chicks in captivity at Maryland's Patuxent Wildlife Center and the New York Zoological Society's Bronx Zoo are successful, and both facilities plan to release young fledglings onto a remote peninsula in northern Peru, where they will be monitored carefully.

The Chilean coat of arms: huemel, a mountain deer, and Andean condor. (*Chilean Embassy*)

Notes and Anecdotes: The Andean condor has a 10-foot (3-meter) wingspan and can easily soar as fast as 80 miles (128 kilometers) per hour on high air currents. It is predominantly black, with a bare head and neck and white neck ruff and wing patches. Condors live as long as twenty years. They mate for life, producing two eggs at a time that must be incubated for up to two months; the young chicks must be tended for a year.

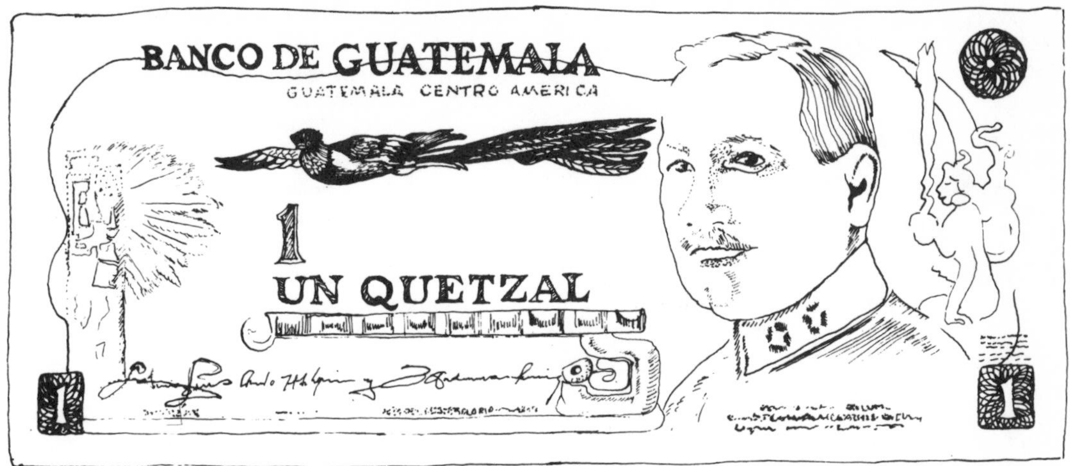

The currency of Guatemala is named after its endangered national bird, the quetzal.

The Resplendent Quetzal (Pharomachrus mocinno)

Habitat: The rain forests of the Central American mountains, from south Mexico to Panama; sometimes in regions 10,000 feet (3,048 meters) in altitude.

Symbolism: The quetzal is the national "bird of freedom" in Guatemala.

Home of the Emblem: It appears on the Guatemalan state coat of arms. The "quetzal" is also the Guatemalan unit of currency.

Matters of Status: A 1978 field study estimated the quetzal population to be decreasing at a rate that qualifies it as endangered. Although legally protected from hunting by the Guatemalan government, the quetzal tempts poachers, who can earn more money selling a pair of live birds to a foreign zoo than they are likely to earn for nearly two weeks of labor. It is estimated that only one out of every fifty captured quetzals survives the ordeal of trapping and transport to reach a zoo or pet shop. The increasing need for more arable land in Guatemala also threatens the survival of the quetzal.

Notes and Anecdotes: The quetzal is noted for its spectacular red-and-green plumage. This coloration is particularly beautiful in the mature male, which also possesses shiny green tail feathers that grow to a length of 2 feet (0.6 meter) and trail gracefully behind in flight. The ancient Aztecs and Mayans used these tail plumes in ceremonies and worshipped the quetzal as the god of the air. They associated the bird with the feathered serpent god Quetzalcoatl, who was also revered as the god of civilization by the Toltecs and, in a related form, as a god of war by the Aztecs.

Giant Panda (Ailuropoda melanoleuca)

Habitat: The bamboo-forested mountains of Szechwan and Kansu in southwestern China and the foothills of the Tibetan Himalayas. The giant panda is specifically indigenous to China, and none are to be found wild outside its borders.

Symbolism: In 1972, this gentle-looking animal became the "symbol of Chinese friendship" when two pandas were presented as a gift to the Smithsonian National Zoological Park in Washington, D.C., by Premier Chou En-lai. It is also recognized as a symbol of the international effort to protect endangered species as the official emblem of the World Wildlife Fund.

Home of the Emblem: The giant panda is frequently employed as a symbol of China in artwork and literature. It appears on China's postal stamps.

Matters of Status: Because their habitat is remote, giant panda populations are difficult to monitor; consequently, estimates of their numbers vary greatly. It is known that they have seriously declined and are now one of the rarest of the world's large mammals. As such they are legally protected by the Chinese government, and are listed as "rare" and "depleted" by the International Union for the Conservation of Nature and Natural Resources (IUCN). The IUCN population estimate in the 1970s was several hundred giant pandas; the Chinese claimed, in 1979, that there were as many as one

A Chinese postage stamp featuring the panda.

thousand distributed in Szechwan Province. But a World Wildlife Fund estimate in 1979 warned that there may actually be no more than sixty giant pandas left in the wild.

Presently China and other nations are attempting to breed the giant panda in captivity. The Chinese have so far produced more than a dozen young pandas, and in 1978, they announced the first birth of a giant panda to result from artificial insemination. In May 1980 the Chinese government announced the designation of a 155-square-mile (401-square-kilometer) protected area near the Tibetan border. In addition to pandas, twenty-five other rare or endangered species have found a home in this rugged patch of mountains and bamboo forest.

Notes and Anecdotes: Although generally considered to be part of the Procyonidae family, of which the raccoon is a member, the giant panda is sometimes classified in the Ursidae family, because of its resemblance to bears. Unlike bears, though, this 6-foot-tall (2-kilometer), 300-pound (136-kilogram) animal is mainly a vegetarian, subsisting primarily on the tender shoots and leaves of the bamboo, along with some fruits, berries, bulbs, and small vertebrates. The giant panda's dependence upon the bamboo plant determines its choice of habitat in the high forests of China.

C.S.D.

WHAT TO DO ABOUT VANISHING WILDLIFE

"The great conservation movements," one encylopedia tells us, "have all been born of fear, after spectacular catastrophes had taken place or were found to be imminent." It must also be said that those movements are born of hope, for lacking that quality they would soon falter and fade away. With the daily assault on the world's wildlife, the conservation movement faces an enormous challenge. But one finds hope in the number and diversity of organizations that work to reverse a sad history of exploitation. This is a list of some of those organizations—several work directly on protection of endangered species, others hope to promote humane treatment of all wildlife, and some work to preserve key habitats. All depend on the support and commitment of the compassionate citizen.

U. S. Groups:

- ANIMAL PROTECTION INSTITUTE OF AMERICA, P.O. Box 22505, Sacramento, CA 95822, (916) 422-1921.
  Publication: *Mainstream* (quarterly, membership $10/year)

  The goal of the Animal Protection Institute is "to eliminate or alleviate fear, pain, and suffering among all animals."

- ANIMAL WELFARE INSTITUTE, P.O. Box 3650, Washington, D.C. 20007, (202) 337-2333.
  Publication: Information Report (quarterly to members, $5/year)

  The Animal Welfare Institute has a particular interest in improving conditions for laboratory animals and endangered species.

- CENTER FOR ACTION ON ENDANGERED SPECIES, 175 West Main St., Ayer, MA 01432, (617) 772-0445.
  Publication: Newsletter (quarterly to members, $10/year)

  The Center develops educational materials, including teaching units, on endangered wildlife.

- DEFENDERS OF WILDLIFE, 1244 19th St. NW, Washington, D.C. 20036, (202) 659-9510.
  Publication: *Defenders* (monthly to members, $15/year)

Dedicated to the preservation of all forms of wildlife, the Defenders of Wildlife promote humane treatment and the elimination of painful methods of trapping, capturing, and killing wildlife.

- ELSA WILD ANIMAL APPEAL, P.O. Box 4752, North Hollywood, CA 91601, (203) 769-8388.
  Publications: *Born Free News, Elsa Echo* (quarterly to members, $10/year)

Founded by the author of *Born Free,* the late Joy Adamson, the Elsa Wild Animal Appeal has a diverse program dedicated to wildlife conservation. The group also sponsors youth conservation groups scattered throughout the United States.

- FRIENDS OF ANIMALS, 11 West 60th St., New York, NY 10023, (212) 247-8077.
  Publication: *Animals* (quarterly to members, $10/year)

The Friends of Animals are dedicated to "regaining ecological balance through preservation of wildlife territory and elimination of human brutality to animals."

- FUND FOR ANIMALS, INC., 140 West 57th St., New York, NY 10019, (212) 246-2096.
  Publications: Newsletter, information pamphlets (membership $10/year)

The Fund for Animals is an advocacy and education organization, pressuring government to develop and enforce measures that preserve wildlife and prevent cruelty to wildlife.

- RARE ANIMAL RELIEF EFFORT, c/o the National Audubon Society, 950 Third Ave., New York, NY 10002, (212) 832-3200.

Staffed almost entirely by volunteers, the Rare Animal Relief Effort aids programs that protect endangered species, especially in tropical America and developing countries.

Other U.S. citizen groups active in wildlife conservation are: Environmental Action (see page 458), Environmental Defense Fund (see page 784), Friends of the Earth (see page 784), Sierra Club (see page 784), Izaak Walton League, Ducks Unlimited, Trout Unlimited, Greenpeace (see page 295), American Cetacean Society (see page 294), Project Jonah (see page 294).

International Groups:

- AFRICAN FUND FOR ENDANGERED WILDLIFE, 1437 Bayhead Road, Annapolis, MD 21401, (301) 974-7818, or P.O. Box 15004, Langata, Nairobi, Kenya, East Africa.
  Publications: Books and occasional newsletters
  The Fund works to safeguard African wildlife and habitat.

- AFRICAN WILDLIFE LEADERSHIP FOUNDATION, INC., 1717 Massachusetts Ave. NW, Washington, D.C. 20036, (202) 265-8394.
  Publication: *African Wildlife News*

AWLF conducts research into wildlife management, training for wildlife officers, and campaigns to stop the poaching of endangered African animals.

- EARTHFORCE ENVIRONMENTAL SOCIETY, Room 18, 2320 Cornwall St., Vancouver, British Columbia V6K 1B7 Canada, (604) 734-4211.
  Publication: *Survival Magazine* (bimonthly)

An international environmental action organization, the Earthforce Environmental Society is involved in direct-action campaigns aimed at protecting African elephants and endangered species in the Arctic and Antarctic.

▪ INTERNATIONAL FUND FOR ANIMAL WELFARE, P.O. Box 1011, New Brunswick, E3B 5B4, Canada.
Publications: Newsletter and miscellaneous educational materials

The IFAW, which works on behalf of many species hunted by humans, has active volunteer chapters throughout the world.

▪ INTERNATIONAL SOCIETY FOR THE PROTECTION OF ANIMALS, 106 Jermyn St., London S.W.1Y, England, or 29 Perkins St., Boston, MA 02130, (617) 522-7000.
Publication: *ISPA News* (quarterly to members, $10/year)

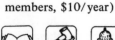

The ISPA, established in 1959, has affiliates in fifty-three countries and maintains international teams to deal with wildlife disasters.

▪ WORLD WILDLIFE FUND, 1110 Morges, Switzerland, or 1601 Connecticut Ave. NW, Washington, D.C. 20009, (202) 387-0805.
Publication: *Focus* (three times yearly to supporters)

The largest private international conservation group, the World Wildlife Fund supports programs around the world to preserve endangered species and their habitats.

KEY TO ORGANIZATION SYMBOLS:

 pursues environmental litigation

 has a lobbying program

 engages in public education and/or research

 has local chapters or involved in grassroots organizing

PLANTS

While the plight of endangered creatures such as blue whales and whooping cranes is widely appreciated, it is less well known that from 20,000 to 25,000 of the world's plant species face extinction.

Recently, the International Union for the Conservation of Nature and Natural Resources (IUCN), an independent organization based in Switzerland, appealed to botanists around the world to supply accurate information about endangered species in their countries. The IUCN's Threatened Plants Committee has assembled the data in a publication to "highlight the growing and continuing threats to the world's natural ecosystems and the diversity of species they contain." Although the *Plant Red Data Book* covers only 250 of the thousands of species the IUCN feels need protection, these species include some of the plants that are in the gravest danger or are particularly spectacular, useful, or interesting.

The plants listed in the book have become endangered for a wide variety of reasons—overgrazing by domestic or feral animals, herbicide spraying, fires, cutting for timber or firewood, damage by off-road vehicles, forest clearing, and collecting by plant fanciers. (Ironically, no plant has become threatened because we eat it—societies maintain their important food plants through careful stewardship.)

The Most Celebrated

Today the most celebrated of all endangered plants is an unprepossessing member of the snapdragon family, Furbish's lousewort (*Pedicularis furbishiae*), which was named for Kate Furbish, an American turn-of-the-century botanical artist of considerable repute. After a careful search, the U. S. Army Corps of Engineers has located only about 1,000 individual plants, all of them along a 120-mile (190-kilometer) stretch of the St. John River in northern Maine and a much shorter stretch of the river in New Brunswick. The surviving louseworts occur in the area of the proposed Dickey-Lincoln hydroelectric project, which, if constructed, would inundate them. Because of the special protection endangered plants and animals have been given in the United States, the future of the Dickey-Lincoln project has been called into question.

The case has aroused intense emotion, both on the part of the environmental groups who want to see the dam halted—the free-flowing St. John not only provides a riverbank habitat for the lousewort but runs through a beautiful 140-square-mile (225-square-kilometer) wilderness area—and of proponents of the dam. The feelings of the latter were articulated in a letter to the editor of *Time:* "For heaven's sake, the species was thought extinct—let's make it official and drown it under a few billion gallons of water." It appears now that the dam will be built, but with special conservation measures to save the plant.

Cape Flora

It is not only in the United States that plants are under pressure. The temperate Cape flora of South Africa, dominated by heaths and porteas—flowers that look like roses made of porcelain—is one of the most varied and spectacular in the world. Yet it has been estimated that approximately 1,500 species in the Cape flora are threatened.

Even more disquieting is the illegal trade in South African cycads. These plants are so coveted by collectors that recently a specimen of *Encephalartos woodii* was stolen from the Durban Botanic Gardens in South Africa and is said to have sold for $65,000.

African Violets

The African violet (*Saintpaulia ionantha*), widely known as a house plant, is exceedingly rare in its native habitat, the damp cliffsides of eastern Tanzania. There its precarious existence is threatened by the removal of forest trees that normally provide the shade in which it grows best.

The Monkey Puzzle Tree et al.

The rain forests of eastern Australia, along the coast of Queensland and New South Wales, are threatened by a number of activities, including replacement of native forests by monocultures of the hoop pine (*Araucaria cunninghamii*), itself an Australian species. A relative of the Australian araucaria that is native to Chile and Argentina, the monkey puzzle tree (*A. araucana*), is being rapidly reduced by the demand for it in the manufacture of plywood. The gigantic Chilean larch (*Fitzroya cupressoides*) may become extinct in ten years, as stands of this tree are being cut at a fantastic rate; all the remaining forests of southern Chile are potential wood pulp for foreign, generally Japanese, paper companies.

The Largest Flower

Japan, the world's largest importer of wood products and pulp, is expanding its industrial timber operations in the forests of Brazil, Borneo, Malaysia, Sarawak, Indonesia, and New Guinea. The chronic and desperate desire for wood and wood by-products is now threatening the Sumatran home of the world's largest flower, *Rafflesia arnoldi.* This rare parasitic plant, which grows on the forest floor attached to roots of tropical grapevines, has a flower that can be 3 feet (1 meter) wide. Its habitats are dangerously near the Japanese timber concessions, and it suffers another threat from the trampling feet of curiosity seekers.

Baobab

The baobab is virtually the botanical symbol of the hot African countries, and traditionally has been protected by taboo because of its prominence in African religious beliefs. At the mouth of the Senegal River the French botanist Michel Adanson, for whom the genus (*Adansonia digitata*) is named, found trees with European names carved in the bark from the fourteenth and fifteenth centuries, and some specimens are reputed to have lived for five thousand years. The baobab's spongy, swollen trunk can be as much as 100 feet (30 meters) in circumference and serves to store water; its imposing stature and shape make it recognizable even on a distant horizon. Unfortunately, these great trees are now being stripped and mutilated by people desperate for fuel.

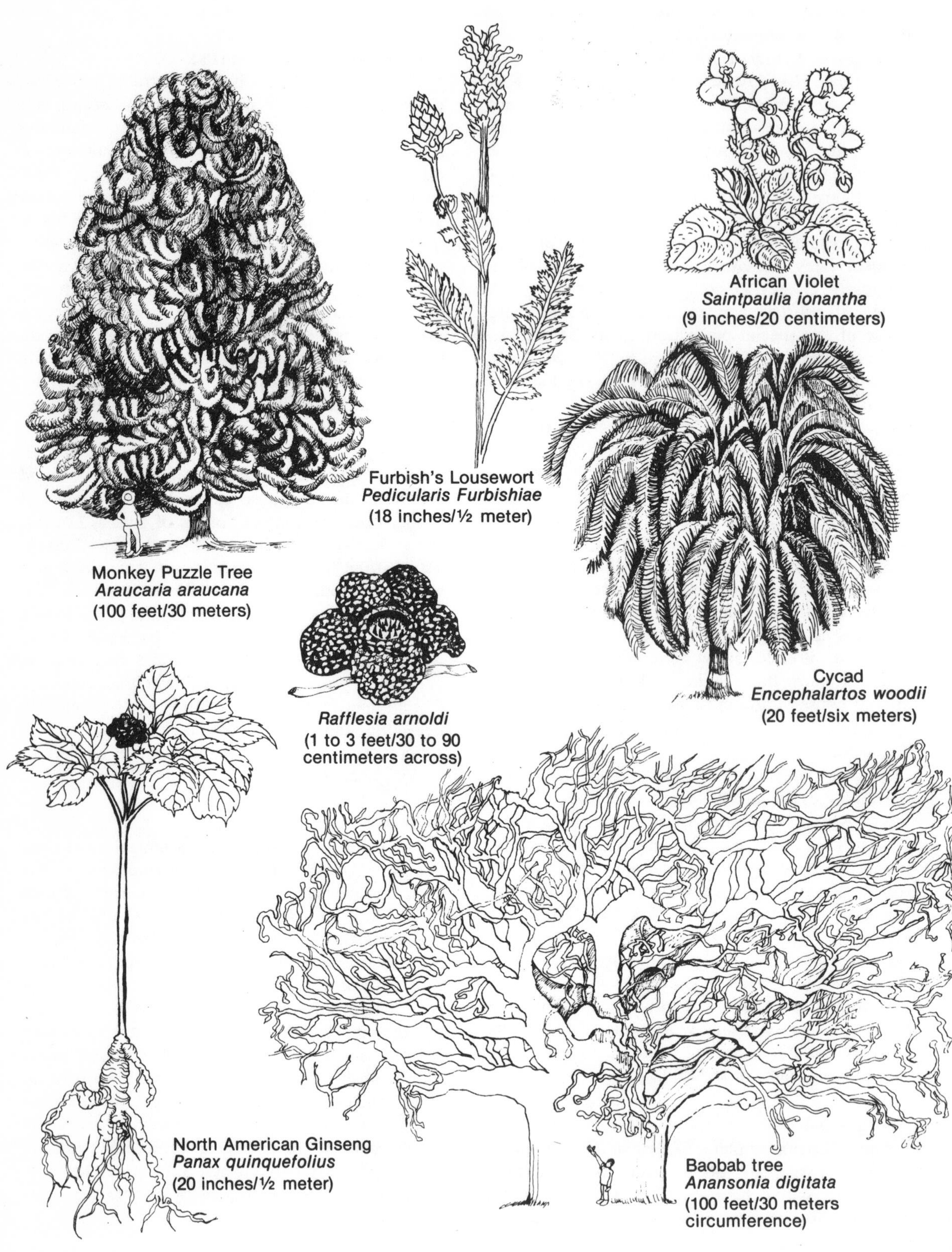

Monkey Puzzle Tree
Araucaria araucana
(100 feet/30 meters)

Furbish's Lousewort
Pedicularis Furbishiae
(18 inches/½ meter)

African Violet
Saintpaulia ionantha
(9 inches/20 centimeters)

Cycad
Encephalartos woodii
(20 feet/six meters)

Rafflesia arnoldi
(1 to 3 feet/30 to 90 centimeters across)

North American Ginseng
Panax quinquefolius
(20 inches/½ meter)

Baobab tree
Anansonia digitata
(100 feet/30 meters circumference)

Ginseng

Throughout the world there has always been a demand for stimulating brews that will restore flagging spirits, cure diseases, and increase sexual appetites. The ginseng root has long been believed to be a source of such powers, and recently there has been an upsurge in its use—and price.

In 1977 the United States exported 380,000 pounds (170,000 kilograms) of ginseng valued at $26.5 million. Of this, about half came from farms in Wisconsin and about half from the wilds, where the plant has been depleted.

Many other plants, of course, are used for their therapeutic values, and this has a twofold effect on the world's flora. On the one hand, the demand for herbs, particularly in parts of Africa and Asia, has brought some plants near extinction. On the other hand, the growing evidence that herbal medicine is not without scientific foundation has made it imperative that no plant species should be wantonly destroyed without analysis of its chemical constituents.

Saving the Plants

To rescue obscure species (that could serve as parental stock for new and strange varieties) a National Seed Storage Laboratory was established in 1958 at Fort Collins, Colorado. It houses more than a hundred thousand samples of all sorts of seeds, and has a capacity for more than half a million. There are seed banks in Mexico that store wheat and corn, a bean bank in Colombia, a bank for pearl millet and pigeon pea seeds in India, and a rice bank in the Philippines.

As populations grow in developing countries, pressures increase on forest and savanna lands. Overgrazing by domestic animals, in particular, is causing deserts to encroach upon grasslands. In North Africa, overgrazing results in the creation each year of 250 *million* acres (100 million hectares) of new desert.

Conservation of the world's flora requires a commitment to preservation of natural landscapes and perpetuation of natural vegetation. This commitment is being made by a number of governments, and also by ordinary people who are simply trying to combat the degradation of their homelands. Last year in India, in order to resist the felling of a forest, the people of the Alaknanda River Basin in Uttar Pradesh peacefully demonstrated against the cutting by joining hands around the trees to ward off the loggers. The forest was subsequently saved. (See "The Tree-Huggers of Uttar Pradesh," page 190.)

Preserving the world's plant resources calls for more protection and management, more research, and an increasing level of public awareness about our vanishing heritage.

The celebrated British tropical botanist E. J. H. Corner related an inspiring incident in Australia: "A few years ago, not a national park but a car park was planned in Sydney. It would have necessitated the felling of some stately trees of the Moreton Bay fig (*Ficus macrophylla*). It was not the officials, however, that saved them, or an august body of scientific representation, but the laborers of the Builders' Federation who threatened to strike if the trees were cut."

Condensed from an article by Edward S. Ayensu in *Smithsonian Magazine,* November 1978. Dr. Ayensu is Secretary General of the International Union of Biological Sciences and the Director of the Smithsonian's Office of Biological Conservation.

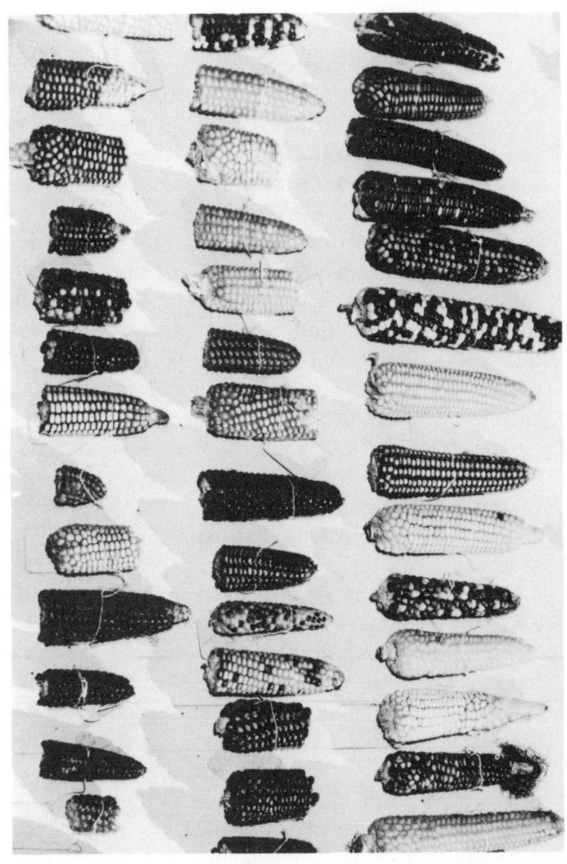

Some varieties of Western Hemisphere maize being preserved as part of the U. S. Department of Agriculture's seed bank program. It is estimated that more than 2,000 types of maize will eventually be collected and kept in refrigerated storage. (*USDA/Mitchell*)

OCEAN FISHERIES

He was an old man who fished alone in a skiff in the Gulf Stream and he had gone eighty-four days now without taking a fish. . . . The old man was thin and gaunt . . . and his hands had the deep-creased scars from handling heavy fish on the cords. But none of these scars were fresh. They were as old as the erosions in a fishless desert.

—ERNEST HEMINGWAY,
*The Old Man and the Sea**

Times have changed since Santiago struggled for his great marlin. Old skiffs are of little use now that fleets of fishing factories sweep across the oceans, and blood-raw bait doesn't lure as many fish as sonar's invisible sound waves can efficiently discover. A hand-held knife is no match against the miles of nets and hooks and lines that capture whole schools of tuna. The only thing that remains of the old man's world is the fishless desert. But now it is dry not just for Santiago; it is drying up for us all. And *salao,* the old man's bad luck, is not so much to blame as is our own careless exploitation of the seas.

About 10,000 B.C. some humans ceased trying to gather enough forage and kill enough wild animals to supply basic food needs. They turned to the farming of selected plants and the breeding of animals. Even then, early humans may have had a dim notion that hunting was living off capital and that farming was living off revenue.

One hundred centuries have passed, and we have yet to apply that simple principle to our oceans. We are living off capital, each year flagrantly withdrawing more. There are those in the fishing industry—not simple Santiagos, but business people with clout—who seem to think that they can ravage the ocean forever.

Ocean fishing today is oceanic anarchy. Nations are scrambling for the dwindling remains in the ocean—Great Britain versus Iceland in the recent Cod War; France versus Brazil in the Lobster War—greedily competing in a senseless game of catch as catch can.

Fishing techniques are about to surpass even science fiction. Special buoys are equipped with "fish calls," played back into the sea, and the lured schools of fish are accurately located. Remote-controlled ships are activated by the telemetric gadgets attached to these instrumented buoys. When fish are in the area, the robot ships approach their prey and catch them with electrically operated nets and automatic suction pumps. Trawl nets, though less sophisticated, are even more damaging, sometimes scraping the sea bottom bare of fixed fauna.

Dramatically underscoring the increased threat to fisheries from massive ships and technological advances, a single Romanian factory ship equipped with modern devices caught in New Zealand waters as many tons of fish one day as the entire New Zealand fleet of some fifteen hundred (mostly traditional) vessels.

These technological "advances" have enabled us to increase the total world catch seventy times over the last century and a half. But the figures are deceiving, and they are beginning to decline. The fact that a great many fish have been taken doesn't mean that many fish remain and of the quantity caught only 71 percent is considered fit for human consumption. The rest are fed to pigs and chickens, made into pet food, or used as fertilizer.

- The North Atlantic, intensely fished to feed Europe and North America, was the first constellation of fisheries to suffer. Overfishing was noticed as early as 1890, when the production of plaice did not rise despite increased fishing. By 1950 the same was true of twelve other North Atlantic fisheries, principally stocks of cod, haddock, herring, and perch. Recent estimates place the number of disappearing or declining fisheries at more than twenty of about thirty traditional grounds.
- The yellowfin sole has been overfished in the Bering Sea. As the stocks of yellowfin sole were depleted, the incidental catch of pollack was discovered. An inexpensive member of the cod family, this fish is especially valuable as a food source because it feeds directly on plankton-eating organisms, thus producing food more directly and efficiently than species at the top of the food web, such as tuna. But in the space of only ten years, Pacific pollack have been so zealously overfished that the catch has declined 76 percent.

A tuna market in Japan. (*Consulate General of Japan*)

- The California sardine fishery, which hit its peak of 1.5 billion pounds (.67 billion kilograms) in 1936, ceased to exist by 1962. Sardines practically vanished as well from such hitherto productive areas as Brittany, Portugal, and Morocco. Such sharp drops in fish stocks can be related to changes in ocean currents and other natural phenomena that fishing fleets often do not take into account. Intense exploitation during a period of current-caused low productivity can quickly deplete a fishery.
- Over the world, more than four million spearfishing enthusiasts, mostly neophytes, ravage coastlines and coral reefs. They spear anything that moves, grab lobsters in their hideouts, and frighten most coastal fish away from their spawning grounds.
- In shameless displays of carelessness, many

A Norwegian trawler hauls in a catch of calypso (or skidfish) in the North Sea. (*UN/Y. Nagata*)

nations continue to practice what they call "pulse fishing." They intensely deplete a stock from some distant shore, then abandon the scene to the locals, only to come back when—and if—the stock makes any sort of recovery.

And so it goes. The Domino Theory of Fish Destruction—overfishing of one species leads to the exploitation of another. The fishing industry of one nation battles against that of another, destroying its neighbor's catch and its own.

Each nation cries out for the simple, and only reasonable, answer: world regulation. Yet no nation wants to be regulated.

In some cases, the situation has become foreboding. Japan, for example, has estimated that if all nations excluded foreigners from within their 200-mile limits, the Japanese fishing catch would be reduced by 45 percent. As pointed out by ecologist Paul Ehrlich, this would result in a loss of half a million jobs (not counting workers in processing, canning, and distribution), a serious wound to a major Japanese industry and a drastic change in the diets of the Japanese people. Most nations with 200-mile limits do allow foreign fishing, but set quotas on the catch and enforce other restrictions.

Yet the drive to "vacuum" the sea of fish stocks does not always spring from such clear-

Anchovies caught by Peruvian fishing boats in the rich Humboldt current are processed, at plants like this, into fishmeal for export. Livestock, especially chickens and pigs, throughout the world are raised on this meal. Shifts in this current, coupled with overfishing, have drastically reduced the Peruvian anchovy fishery, which once made Peru the world's largest fishing nation. (*FAO/R. Coral*)

cut cases of national survival. Japan, whose California-sized land mass cannot adequately feed its 120 million people, has traditionally counted on the surrounding sea and aquaculture to supply sustenance to its population, but the United States is an agrarian nation, the largest producer of food in the world. Nevertheless, passions run deep when it comes to commercial U.S. fishing. Furious that foreign boats have fished herring from its eastern shores, the United States will spend more than $143 million to guard and maintain its self-proclaimed 200-mile zone. Yet for several years American tuna skippers refused to recognize Ecuador's right to issue fishing licenses and proceeded to land a 300,000-ton annual tuna catch. The U.S. government traditionally gave its blessing to American crews who violated the limits of other countries: the Fisherman's Protective Act of 1967 provided that the American fishing industry be reimbursed by the U. S. Treasury (that is, out of citizens' taxes) for fines, confiscated catch, damages, and 50 percent of lost fishing time if they were apprehended on what we define as the "high seas."

Some nations are taking the first steps toward regulating their fisheries. (See "Fish-and-Chips," page 226.) But the task of collecting data on fish populations and of enforcing fishing quotas strains the ability of even the most developed coastal countries. Other countries are limiting their fish hunting and turning instead to fish farming. China, for example, a nation without large offshore fishing vessels, ranks second in world fish production. Most of its fish come from aquaculture operations in its vast network of rivers. (See "Aquaculture," page 609.) Both approaches are crucial if we are to keep ocean fish from becoming another disappearing resource.

We must become stewards of ocean fish, not antagonists who, like Hemingway's old man, confronted with the great marlin, shout in the face of the ocean: "I'll kill him. . . . In all his greatness and his glory . . . I will show him what a man can do."

WETLANDS

The rain-swept bogs of Canada and western Ireland, the lush fenlands of eastern England, the fertile floodplain and estuary of the Rhône Delta in France, the eerie Dismal Swamp of Georgia, and the humid mangrove swamps of the Florida Everglades are all wetlands—lands where a shallow layer of water determines what forms of life will develop or migrate there. As wetlands they have something else in common: they are among the most underestimated and misunderstood areas on the planet.

Early human settlers knew the value of wetlands as food producers, storm barriers, flood protectors. But over the past hundred years, as people and industry elbowed each other for coastal land, the ancient knowledge was lost and we accepted the realtors' definition of wetland as "wasteland." Land was judged according to its suitability for development, and wetlands were difficult places to develop. Of all the wetland's abundant wildlife, humanity focused on one creature: the mosquito. The notion arose that wetlands should be filled and built upon, turning the mosquito breeding grounds into valuable real estate.

The development of wetlands was not a new phenomenon, however. Long ago wetlands fell to farmers, attracted by their fertile soil. The famous diked polders of Holland and Belgium are reclaimed lowlands. (Dikes in the Netherlands date back to 1018.) The rich polderlands provide needed farmland in these small countries, which may now, however, face a choice between grain or fish. Holland's Wadden Zee, a marshy tidal flat, is a primary nursery for North Sea fish and the only North Sea nursery for brown shrimp, a commercially harvested species. New dikes, chemical plants, and oil pipelines planned for the Wadden Zee threaten the nursery.

Tropical mangrove swamps, which filter nutrients and play an important role in marine productivity, are being filled and turned into coconut groves in Sri Lanka and Mozambique. In Thailand and other parts of Southeast Asia, large areas of mangroves have been chopped down for firewood and charcoal.

In 600, Venice was probably the first city to put its roots into the marshy banks of lagoons (see "Venice," page 315). Later, Amsterdam blocked itself from the sea with a dam built in the mid-thirteenth century across the marshy

A productive wetland in South Dakota. The "swamp" is invaluable to waterfowl and aquatic animals, providing both food and shelter. (*USDA/Soil Conservation Service/Jim Hunt*)

Amstel River. But it was the fast-growing United States that filled in the most wetlands in the shortest amount of time. Today, half of the original U.S. wetlands are gone.

Colonial Boston acted early to rid itself of wetlands, setting an example that was to be followed by many American cities. John and Mildred Teal record in *Life and Death of the Salt Marsh* that the first marshes were filled to make the Town Cove in 1641. Dock Square, now a third of a mile (0.5 kilometer) from the nearest waters, was then at the head of the cove. Old Boston was a marsh-surrounded peninsula of 485 acres (194 hectares) jutting between the Charles River and the Atlantic. By filling the marshes the city gained 2,055 acres (822 hectares) increasing its land area nearly three times.

In the mid-nineteenth century the U. S. Congress passed Swamp Lands Acts to encourage the states to "reclaim" wetlands. Anne Simon reports in *The Thin Edge:* "Since then the country has lost half of them through draining, filling, dumping old cars and garbage on them, turning them into something else. In the 1970s, 300,000 acres [120,000 hectares] a year disappeared; the leading cause, according to the U. S. Department of Interior, is housing developments."

Some marshes were turned into cities or subdivisions, others became dumping grounds. "In the period between 1954 and 1965, 45,000 acres [18,000 hectares] of salt marsh were destroyed between Maine and Delaware," the Teals report. "About one third of this amount was suffocated by dredging spoils and navigation channel maintenance." Spoils from dredging the Inland Waterway, a protected channel along the east coast of the United States, has destroyed many adjacent marshes. In Charleston Harbor alone some 10,000 acres (4,000 hectares) of marsh were buried in spoils.

Other wetlands, although untouched by bulldozers, have been choked by sediment deposited from upstream erosion stemming from construction or agriculture along the riverbanks.

A century after the United States began its campaign to reclaim wetlands, scientists discovered that far from being wastelands, they were the most productive ecosystem known. In the 1950s, ecologist Eugene Odum, then a professor at the University of Georgia, measured the production in Georgia's estuaries at 10 tons per acre of dry organic matter. The average wheatfield produces only one and a half tons of wheat.

The productivity of the salt marsh is based on the grass *Spartina,* whose growth and decay produce bacteria and food for detritus-feeding aquatic organisms such as oysters, shrimp, scallops, and crabs.

The coastal marsh is a delicately balanced system dependent on the free flow of the tide and of the rivers and streams that feed it fresh water. These ever-changing but protected waters provide a nursery for birds, mammals, shellfish, and migratory fish. Other research has proved the relationship between healthy estuaries and healthy coastal fisheries: 60 to 70 percent of the fish in U.S. coastal waters depend on wetlands for food, spawning, and shelter at some point in their lives.

Our political boundaries ignore the ancient routes of these migratory fish, making it difficult for local politicians to see the effects of their actions. In the early 1970s, when Massachusetts Senator Edward Kennedy opposed a power plant siting on the Hudson River in New York, some questioned his interest. He was speaking for his constituency who commercially fish the Atlantic off Georges Bank for cod and bass that spawn in Hudson marshes and would have been threatened by the power plant.

Meanwhile, coastal engineers, appalled at flood damage during storms, began to realize the wetlands' role as a sponge to absorb floodwaters before they can reach high ground. Expensive dams, levees, dikes, channels, and seawalls often fail to protect homes as efficiently as marshes did. The United States, where 10 percent of the land is flood-prone, suffers $1.5 billion a year in property damage resulting from floods. Most of the damage is done to buildings on floodplains—areas that flood periodically if not predictably,

A housing development replaces a formerly productive wetland in southwest Florida. Note the small plugs of land at the end of the channels. Because permits to open such channels are hard to obtain, lots are sometimes sold to the unsuspecting, who are assured that the plugs will be removed. By the time buyers realize what is happening, the developer has disappeared. (*EPA Documerica/Flip Schulke*)

such as filled-in coastal marshes and low-lying riverbanks. The capacity of wetlands to control flooding was dramatically illustrated during severe storms in Pennsylvania in 1955. Although many bridges were washed away in developed areas, two survived undamaged. Both were located downstream of an undeveloped floodplain containing a large cranberry bog owned by the Nature Conservancy. The bog acted as an overflow "catch basin" for the floodwater. Only recently have planning agencies realized that it makes more sense to build away from the floodplain rather than to install expensive flood control devices and pay off property owners in federal flood insurance when they fail.

Other investigators found a fourth value in wetlands. As they sponge up incoming floodwaters, wetlands also sponge up outgoing nutrients that would pollute lakes or bays. Wetlands are a natural purification system. Scientists at Brookhaven National Laboratory on Long Island, the University of Michigan, and elsewhere have found that marshes can purify treated sewage. One investigation found a healthy 1,000-acre (400-hectare) marsh can purify the nitrogenous wastes from a town of twenty thousand people. While the marsh concentrates organic waste and uses it to advantage, it also concentrates poisonous industrial wastes. At Cold Spring, New York, a small town 30 miles (50 kilometers) up the Hudson River from New York City, a battery factory dumped cadmium, a highly toxic metal, into a marsh for many years. The marsh sediments trapped the cadmium so successfully that according to Warren McKeon, a local biologist, the metal is now concentrated in commercially extractable quantities.

In keeping poisons out of larger bodies of water the marsh sometimes swallows them to its own detriment. Some toxic chemicals settle into the sediment undisturbed, others work their way up the intricate food chain into waterfowl and predatory fish and mammals. In Japan and in Chesapeake Bay, fishermen found green oysters. The cause: a high concentration of copper from industrial waste.

As the evidence of biologists and the concern of environmentalists reached U.S. policymakers in the 1960s, they began to pass laws to protect wetlands. Most of the laws discouraged development by requiring permits for dredging, filling, or constructing buildings in certain wetlands. However, most wetlands in the United States are privately owned and the economic pressure to turn wetlands into valuable coastal real estate is still stronger in many places than the pressure to preserve them.

To answer the argument over the economic value of developing wetlands, several researchers attempted to figure out how much an undeveloped wetland is worth as a fish hatchery, flood protector, wildlife habitat, and recreation spot.

In 1978, ecologist Eugene Odum figured the value of an acre of marsh under various uses. His estimates point out the economic value of marshes to the public.

Function	*Value per acre/hectare*
▪ Commercial and sport fisheries	$100/$250
▪ Aquaculture potential	$630/$1,550
▪ Waste treatment potential	$2,500/$6,180
▪ Life-support value (ability to absorb carbon dioxide, produce oxygen, harbor wildlife, and provide storm protection)	$4,100/$10,130

A given acre of wetland could be put to more than one of these uses at the same time. This method of accounting puts wetlands in the league with prime Midwestern farmland, which sold for about $2,000 an acre about the same time. However, it does not touch the value of developed shoreline. Along the northeast and southwest U.S. coasts, shoreline property often sold (in 1980) for more than $50,000 per *lot,* only a fraction of an acre.

Ironically, as natural wetlands continue to disappear beneath development, the U. S. Army Corps of Engineers is spending millions of dollars to learn how to plant and restore marshes. Of the Corps' 105 marsh-establishment projects, 96 achieved varying degrees of success. Collecting, transplanting, and fertilizing plugs of the common marsh grass *Spartina* to form a new marsh cost, the Corps estimated, between $2,000 and $5,000 per acre (1 acre = 0.41 hectare). The vegetation becomes established in three to five years, but it takes many more years for the typical marsh fauna to colonize the new site.

As we enact measures to preserve and restore wetlands, a new threat emerges, one that is still not fully recognized by politicians or the public: oil. There is strong evidence that oil is a major threat to wetlands. As we open new ports, build more pipelines from offshore wells, flush out ships and tankers in ports, and wash oil from our city streets, much it finds its way to wetlands. The sight of oil-blackened birds floundering on a beach always arouses sympathy and outrage. But the birds are cleaned; some live. Eventually the oil slick disappears and we forget. But oil lingers invisibly beneath the surface to poison the tiny crustaceans that serve as food for marsh creatures and the minute fish larvae and shellfish larvae in the wetland nursery. Oil even kills the hardy *Spartina* grass that forms the basis for marsh ecology. Scientists found that *Spartina* had failed to reestablish itself eight years after an oil spill in West Falmouth, Massachusetts. (See also "The Hidden Costs of an Oil Spill," page 253.)

Oil and wetlands, though thoroughly incompatible, often meet because harbors and population centers developed around low-lying banks and marshy river mouths, and it's to these places that the oil is delivered and processed. The first major oil refinery to be built on the east coast of the United States in twenty-two years was sited in the heart of the east coast's most productive estuary system, Chesapeake Bay, which hosts an $87-million-a-year shellfish industry. Objecting to the refinery, U. S. Secretary of the Interior Cecil Andrus said the biological and recreational resources of the bay were too important to be subject to the risk of oil spills. His objections were overridden.

Ironically, while the big spills attract attention, most of the damage is done by slow leaks, routine flushings of ship holds, and amazingly, from oil washed from land. Researchers studying the sources of oil entering a wetland found that two thirds came from drainage from land: oil from city streets, gas stations, and industrial plants. It all goes somewhere.

Wetlands are developing a new image in the United States and Europe. They have defenders—scientists, environmentalists, fishers—people who see the connections and the threats. In developing nations the destruction is just beginning and the defenders have yet to assemble.

P.C., M.P.

MESSAGES IN THE SEA

When a human is suddenly deprived of the sense of sight, sound, taste, touch, or smell, living becomes more difficult, but still possible.

In the sea things are different.

Biologists now know that water animals communicate with each other not just by sight and sound, but by pheromones, secreted natural chemicals that convey information. An "alarm" chemical is released from the broken skin of an injured fish. Several feet away, a few molecules of the substance are sensed, through smell or taste, by another fish of the same species. The chemical cue is received, the fish flees.

Pheromones and the ability to sense them give water animals what some scientists refer to as a "chemical language." Though that language is far from being deciphered by humans, there is increasing evidence that animals use chemical signals to guide their migrations, discriminate between individuals, recognize sex and reproductive state, sense aggressors, predators, friends, and their young.

Since vision is difficult in the dense medium of water, in many aquatic animals the receptors and connected brain centers for taste and smell are more important and sophisticated than the optic lobes. Some crustaceans, for example, have chemical-sensitive cells over their entire bodies, allowing them to continuously monitor their environment. Fish have sensitive cells located in their nasal pits, the equivalent of our nostrils. As the animal swims and breathes, these cells are

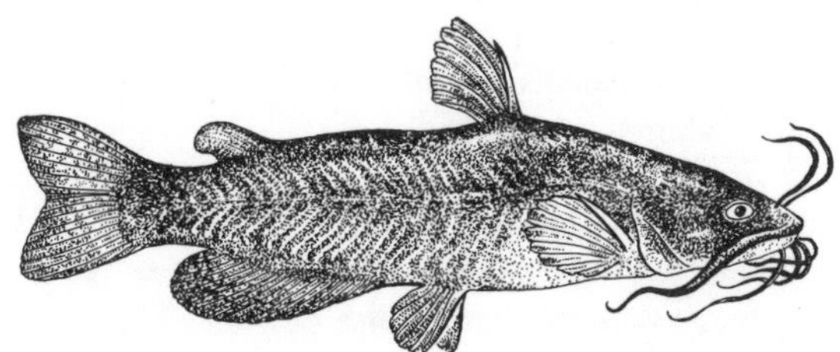
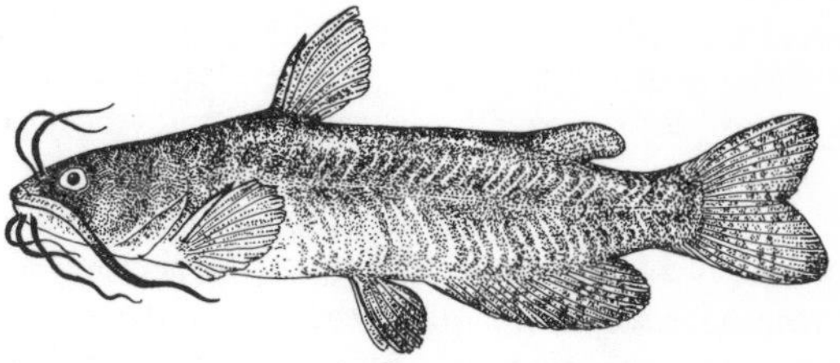

Sensors in the long barbs around the snouts of these Bullhead catfish pick up messages in water around them. Water density and the murkiness created by suspended particles sometimes make the senses of smell and touch more important to aquatic creatures than the sense of vision.

exposed to a constant flow of water. A connecting nerve then carries impulses quickly and directly to the brain. The distribution of taste buds varies with the animal, but many species are known to have taste buds on their outer surfaces as well as in their mouths.

Pollution of the world's water seriously threatens this elaborate sensory system. Small amounts of some chemicals may not be directly poisonous, but they may have indirect, often invisible effects. They may, in part-per-million amounts, destroy, suppress, mimic, or mask vital pheromones, garbling the messages on which aquatic life depends, confusing sea creatures, and altering their behavior. If, for example, that behavior were mating, a generation might be lost even though the culprit pollutant had no perceivable effect on the fish.

Such may be the case with some of the petroleum hydrocarbons and some fluids used in ocean drilling. Experiments have proved that in minute amounts these chemicals alter the behavior of lobsters, mud snails, and crabs. Exposed to kerosene, lobsters may become alternately aggressive and fearful. Worse by far, they are attracted to the kerosene, and even eat it. The amount of oil that affects these animals is so far below the immediately toxic level that scientists are considering using lobsters and mussels as an early warning system for some forms of marine pollution. In the meantime, they ponder the problem of how to protect the delicate receptor organs of billions of aquatic organisms from receiving the wrong messages.

L.W.

NATIVE PEOPLES

Scores of small native cultures around the world are being forced to change traditional ways and conform to the life-styles of encroaching "civilization." Where these minority groups resist integration, they are often physically annihilated.

The cultural machinery of developed nations does not destroy smaller, weaker peoples because it is run by brutes. In most cases, it is not. Most developers, politicians, soldiers, engineers, businessmen, missionaries, and prospectors are trying to accomplish what they perceive as the "right" thing: material progress, discovery of resources, the spread of human comforts, education, religion, elimination of hunger by the opening up of new agricultural areas.

There are several problems with these points of view, though.

- *One:* Many of the native peoples are relatively happy and comfortable without any assistance, their lives entwined with the riches of the wilderness. Although poor by the standards of industrialized nations, they are not impoverished. This is especially true in tropical areas, where many tribes have long harvested the natural bounty of the rain forest—fishing, gathering nuts and fruits, hunting game.
- *Two:* Diseases introduced by newcomers spread among native peoples with lightning speed and violence. Tuberculosis, syphilis, measles, and other virulent diseases amount to unintended weapons of conquest.
- *Three:* The potential agricultural gains from lands occupied by most remaining native peoples are questionable and temporary. The tribes of Amazonia, for example, are being displaced because of many development schemes, which include forest-clearing agricultural projects. Unfortunately, experience has shown that the thin soil of rain forests cannot sustain crop production longer than about five years. (See "Amazonia," page 274.)
- *Four:* Though small societies live amidst valuable resources that fuel the huge technology of the developed world, they will benefit little from the wealth of their territories. The industrialized world will get the energy, the rubber, the building materials, the gold, the diamonds from native peoples in order to keep itself going, to feed and to comfort the expanding populations that live far away from these natives. To justify this, the notion is adopted that life for native peoples will be improved by exploitation.
- *Five:* It hardly ever is. Generally, the peoples are crushed by stress, confusion, and the loss of dignity. Like the Achés of Paraguay, many tribes are dealt with inhumanely, violently. Traditional life-styles like those of the Masai of Africa are disrupted. Art, like that of Africa's Bushmen, is lost to history.
- *Six:* As tribes are lost, so are the cultural and ecological encyclopedias they maintained. Living intimately with nature, tribes develop extensive knowledge of the environment that sustains them. They create elaborate pharmacopoeias from plants, animal substances, minerals. It was Amazonian natives who discovered quinine. The Masai understood the cause of

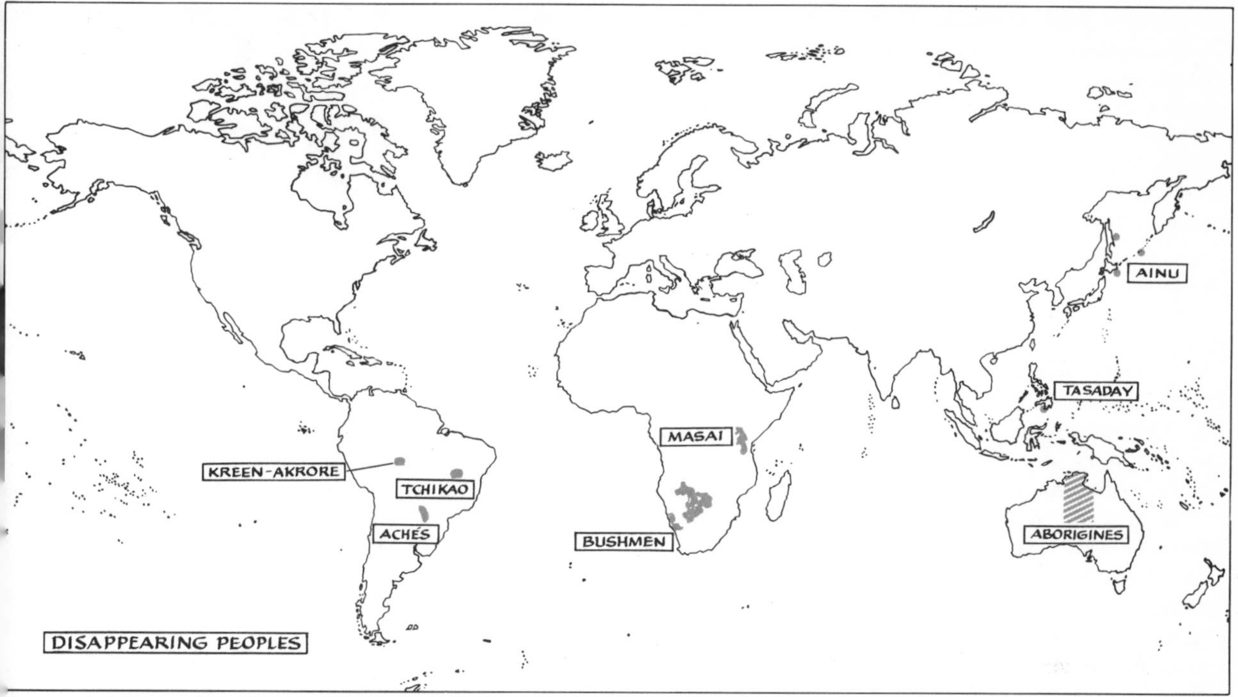

malaria long before Westerners. Since few tribes record the knowledge passed orally from generation to generation, a wealth of information about the environment is lost when the last member of a tribe dies—or the young are absorbed by industrial society before learning the ancient ways.

It is easy to make the mistake of being too naive about native peoples. Some have violent histories. Some have led difficult lives in harsh surroundings. And ultimately, perhaps none will survive "progress." Some are eager to sample its products, from blue jeans to skimobiles. The idea of imposing restrictions on native peoples that ensure their isolation—creating "human zoos"—is not defensible. The best these peoples can hope for, probably, is more time in which to change at a comfortable pace, more enlightened, respectful assistance, and less violence.

There are scores of tribes disappearing today. From these the *Almanac* selected a representative few.

M.R.

The Dream Path People of Australia: The Aborigines

When the Australian natives first saw white men in their tall ships, they thought the Englishmen were the homesick spirits of the dead returning to the land. But they soon realized that these people were not spirits. The English established a penal colony at Botany Bay, near Sydney, in 1788, and the Aborigines began to learn about alcoholism, prostitution, slave labor, and, above all, disease—tuberculosis, leprosy, syphilis, smallpox, influenza, gonorrhea, and the measles, among others.

In 1851 gold was discovered in Australia and the resultant rush eventually deprived the Aborigines of any land that a white person wanted. Unlike the U.S. government, which made treaties with the American Indians and broke them, the British crown seized the Aborigines' land without any sort of acknowledgment. It was only in the most remote and worthless desert that the Aborigines were allowed to wander as freely as in the past.

In the wilderness the Aborigines are a very healthy people. If an Aboriginal child survives its first year, it has a good chance of living to old age. In the reserves and in the city slums, however, the death rate for Aborigines is one of the highest in the world.

The Aborigines believe that the world was created by the dreaming of certain great spirits, who still exist. These dreaming creatures live in sacred places across the land. Today some of the sacred sites of the Aborigines are slated for development as uranium mines. Although the Aborigines are suing the mining companies, the most they are expected to win is a royalty on the mines' profits. Overseas investors on one project were assured by a government official that the Aborigines' land rights were unimportant and would create no difficulties.

Discrimination is officially illegal in Australia, but the years when Aborigines were not allowed or encouraged to go to school, hold a decent job, or even get medical attention have taken a heavy toll. There are now more than 150,000 Aborigines, counting part Aborigines, and while the decimations of the past are over, most of them still live in squalor on reserves or in slums near the big cities. As a tiny percentage of black-skinned people in a predominately white country, they face cultural extinction.

The "Rabid Rats" of Paraguay: The Achés (Guayaki)

The Aché Indians were nomads who roamed the hilly forest of eastern Paraguay in groups of forty to sixty people. They had no tradition of unity. Every tribe of Achés was hostile to every other tribe; each was led by a chief, usually a good hunter with a big family. The Achés had refined their hunting techniques: each band of Achés hunted its territory by rotation through a number of subzones, leaving each area to recover in turn. The Achés had great respect and love for the forest. They believed that the Great Jaguar who created the universe ordered man to hunt, woman to eat the meat, and animals to fight and

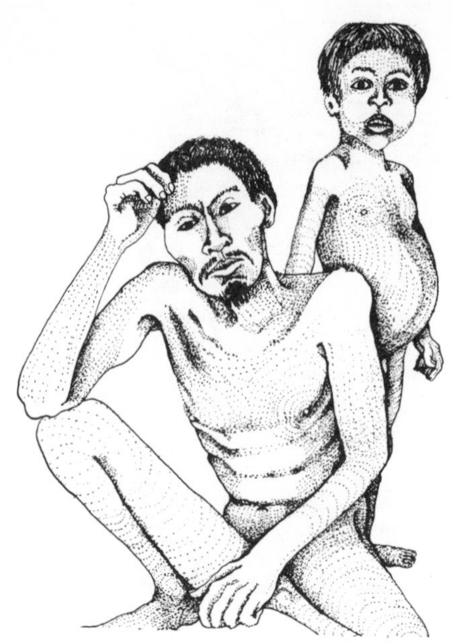

be killed by the hunter. At death, they believed, part of the human soul becomes part of the forest.

From the times of the earliest settlers in Aché territory, the Achés have been in turn hunted, killed, and enslaved.

As the Aché territory shrank and was cut up by roads, the Achés could no longer live on forest game. They began to raid the settlers' cattle. The settlers in turn went on manhunts, hunting and killing adult Achés and selling the children into slavery.

The hunting, killing, and selling of Achés was not prohibited until 1957, but even this law has been ignored. Well into the 1970s these practices were still carried out.

In the early 1960s a reservation for the Achés was founded not far from the range where the Achés once roamed. The National Guayaki Colony ("Guayaki," a name given the Aché by other tribes in the area, roughly translates as "rabid rat") was run for almost fifteen years by a slave trader who bragged openly of killing and raping Achés. The reservation authorities sold their food to settlers for a profit. With no doctor, hundreds died of tuberculosis and other diseases unknown in the wilderness. New Achés were continually being brought in through manhunts, but few survived.

In the forest, the Achés had always respected women greatly, and the chief habitually consulted his mother and wife in important decisions. Now, Aché women were given as rewards to those who helped the reservation authorities. Women who resisted were publicly raped, others were forced into prostitution. Families were forcibly separated.

The Aché men were forced to remove the beta, the lip ornament that was the sign of virility. Men and women were ordered to take Christian names. Since the Achés believed their real names were intimately connected to their souls, many of them now believed they were losing their souls.

On the reservation, they were not allowed to follow their burial customs, to play their music, to have their traditional feasts, or even to wear their hair in the old way. The Aché reservation was referred to as a "graveyard" and "concentration camp."

Finally, the press in Asunción protested the conditions on the reservation. Shortly afterward, the worst offender against the Achés was dismissed from his post. However, Clemens von Thuemen, a German-Paraguayan "Indian specialist," announced that "if they had been left in the forest they would have died anyway"; and the president of the Indigenist Association of Paraguay, nominally responsible for the Achés, described massacres like the Aché manhunts as "problems . . . normal in any part of the world."

With this continuing attitude of government authorities it is not surprising that the few hundred free Achés are still being hunted, and Aché children are still surreptitiously sold and "given away."

The Rock Painters of Africa: The Bushmen (San)

The Bushmen of southern Africa once occupied all the land from the Cape of Good Hope to the Zambezi River, a distance of more than 1,000 miles (600 kilometers). They are the most ancient of all the peoples who now live in southern Africa, going back at least ten thousand years, maybe longer.

The Bushmen were a nomadic people with a superb knowledge of nature. They are highly intelligent, short (5 feet/1.5 meters on the average), and steatopygous (that is, they have unusually prominent buttocks, which may act as a reserve of fat in times of famine, though there is no scientific proof of this). The *labia minora* of the females protrude prominently, and many males have penises that project forward even when not sexually aroused. Bushmen speak a highly unusual language characterized by clicks and whistles unrelated to sounds in any other language.

For two hundred years after the Dutch Afrikaners landed in South Africa in 1652, the

Bushmen were systematically exterminated. Renowned for their courage, Bushmen would die rather than surrender. Unable to bear the "civilized" life of a servant, thousands of Bushmen captured as children escaped to the wilderness or were killed in the attempt.

Today, of an original population numbering in the hundreds of thousands, only about 50,000 Bushmen remain, most as servants or virtual slaves to white or Bantu owners.

There are Bushmen, however, who still lead the old life, traveling, hunting, and gathering for survival, making stone and wooden weapons. Perhaps 2,000 Bushmen live in the wilderness of the Kalahari desert, where, because no one wants the land, they are still free. The Bushmen have adapted to living where other nomadic desert peoples could scarcely survive. They are matchless hunters who can tell an animal's age from its tracks, trot all day after game, run 10 miles (6 kilometers) at top speed in heat of 120° F (49° C), and dance for hours afterward to celebrate the kill of an eland. They hunt with arrows tipped with a homemade poison so strong that they carry the antidote with them at all times.

They know every rock and tree in the desert. In the dry season they can live for months sucking up water from beneath the dried-up streambeds through straws and storing it in ostrich-egg shells. Until the 1950s these sip wells were thought by Westerners to be fantasy.

In the days before the Bushmen were driven into the desert, they were known as artists and musicians. Even today the poorest group of

Bushmen keeps some instrument around. Their exquisite art of rock painting, however, is almost totally lost. In the 1950s, when a visitor showed copies of these rock paintings to a group of Bushmen in Kalahari, only the oldest man and woman in the tribe recognized them as Bushmen paintings. They burst into tears.

The Aristocratic People of Africa: The Masai

The class-conscious British preferred the handsome, aristocratic Masai to all other tribes of east Africa. Because of their reputation and their cooperation, the Masai suffered less than most native peoples. But the same independence that kept their life unchanged under colonialism now threatens them under the Western-educated tribes that rule Kenya.

The Masai, a tall, warlike people who migrated from the Sudan a thousand years ago, were overlords of Kenya for hundreds of years. When the British first arrived in the 1800s, they wrote that the Masai were fierce, savage killers, feared by all other tribes. But when Englishmen met the Masai face to face, they admired the organization and discipline of the warriors and the Masai system of honor, dependability, and courtesy.

At that time, the Masai were in a weak state; a smallpox epidemic had just swept through them, and a plague had wiped out most of their cattle. They were being torn apart by intertribal warfare, raiding, killing, and stealing cattle from one another. Masai elders acknowledge that if the British had not arrived, the Masai would now be splintered into many different warring groups. The intervention of the British, however, cost the Masai a large amount of land, including some of their most sacred places. They were forced to move south of the new railroad that bisected Kenya, giving up their ancient pasture lands near Mount Kenya to white ranchers.

The Masai wanted no part of the British world, and after their forced evacuation they were generally left in peace. When the rare British administrator tried to get a few Masai children to go to school, the Masai would openly buy children from their former tributaries, the Kikuyus, give the children Masai names, and send them off to Nairobi to school.

Although the Masai were forced to give up warfare, for a long time they kept their lion-hunting custom. As lions grew scarcer, this custom was forbidden, but secretly young Masai men still hunt occasionally.

Like many peoples that Westerners have mistakenly considered primitive, the Masai had a great knowledge of their surroundings. Before Europeans discovered that malaria was not caused by "bad air," for example, a Masai elder pointed to a certain mosquito and remarked to a British visitor: "There is the root of the disease." In the great smallpox epidemic, before the British came, a Masai tribesman was inoculating his people—in a crude way, but saving lives.

The Masai were and are master herdsmen, although their food no longer comes exclusively from their cattle. They believed that all the cattle on earth came from the Masai, who were their original owners. Any cattle the tribe seized were only their rightful property, which they were taking back.

In the 1970s the Masai had to face the twentieth century. The Kikuyus, who were once their subjects, now rule Kenya, having taken advantage of the Western education the Masai despised as slavish. The Masai culture is disintegrating as the young turn to modern ways and modern products.

The Earth Spiders of Japan: The Ainu

When the ancestors of the present Japanese arrived in Japan about 1000 B.C., they found a short, hairy people with round eyes and Caucasian features, who spoke a language unrelated to Japanese and whose women decorated themselves with blue tattoos around their mouths and on their forearms and hands. They were called "earth spiders," because they lived in pits in the ground during the winter.

With their superior technology, the Japanese gradually pushed the Ainu out of the more desirable parts of Japan and into the remote, cold, and mountainous north. For centuries the Ainu lived on the northernmost island, Hokkaido, relatively undisturbed. They fished, hunted for bear meat, grew millet and vegetables, and made clothes from the bark of trees and from fur.

The Ainu had a special relationship with the bear, who supplied them with much of their clothing and meat for the long winters. Every year a bear was captured and kept by the Ainu in a cage. For twelve months the bear was lavished with food and gifts. Then, during a three-day ritual, the bear was ceremoniously killed, to depart to the spirit world of bears, where it would spread the word of the Ainu generosity. The Japanese tried for years to forbid this ceremony, considering it an act of cruelty, but bear carvings are still found around Ainu doorsteps or a bear cub is chained nearby. In Hokkaido there still are bears in the mountains who sometimes attack and kill people. These bears, according to the Ainu, are actually evil spirits disguised as animals to carry people away.

The Ainu believed that everywhere in nature there were *kamui,* or spirits. An especially good *kamui* lived in the fire of each household. Today old Ainu people still show reverence for the fire each time they stir the coals in their stove.

The Ainu ways have been disappearing ever since the Japanese began colonizing Hokkaido centuries ago. The Ainu were often so ashamed of their background as "savages" that they adopted Japanese children in an attempt to assimilate. Now all Ainu children have Japanese names and go to Japanese schools. They know their culture is disappearing, but that makes some of them happy. Ainu parents hope their children will marry Japanese and that their grandchildren will no longer be called Ainu.

The Gentle People of the Philippines: The Tasaday

On June 3, 1971, the Tasaday first emerged from the dense forest in a remote area of Mindanao, in the Philippines. Almost overnight, they became famous around the world. Perhaps the last remnant of stone-age people on earth, the Tasaday were living, according to one anthropologist, at a level typical of human society 100,000 years ago.

The first intimations that an undiscovered people might exist on Mindanao came when Manuel Elizalde, a philanthropist from Manila, was visiting the Tboli tribe there. Elizalde had founded an organization called PANAMIN (Private Association of National Minorities) to help the sixty or so indigenous tribes in the Philippines deal with advancing civilization.

While visiting the Tboli people, who had been having some problems with loggers, Elizalde met a wandering hunter named Dafal, who came

from a village so remote there were no roads to it. Dafal was adventurous and often went alone into the jungle for weeks at a time. Dafal claimed that for several years he had been meeting a group of people deep inside the jungle. He was apparently their only contact with the outside world. Dafal said he gave these people gifts in return for food. At first they had been afraid, but now they were friendly.

The people of Tboli, certain the jungle beyond was uninhabited except for ghosts, did not believe Dafal's tales. Elizalde thought there might be some truth and sent a helicopter to scout that area. Satisfying himself that there was some tribe in the remote jungle reaches, Elizalde was able to persuade Dafal to arrange a meeting between himself and a few Tasaday. When this dramatic event took place in a jungle clearing, the Tasaday were not only terrified of Elizalde's helicopter, but they had never even seen an open space as large as the clearing.

Trusting Dafal, these shy people accepted Elizalde, who clowned with them and gave them gifts. Elizalde in turn was amazed. When he finally got an interpreter who could make himself understood, he asked the Tasaday, as they called themselves, if they had any enemies. The interpreter seemed mystified at their answer, but finally reported to Elizalde that the Tasaday had no words in their language for enemies, fighting, war, or weapons. To them there was no such thing as a "bad person." The very concept made them draw back in alarm from the interpreter.

When the Tasaday became more comfortable, they surrounded Elizalde and put their arms around him, just as they nuzzled and touched one another constantly, and unselfconsciously. They were the most affectionate people he had ever met.

The Tasaday were bewildered by the outsider's gifts of rice, tobacco, sugar, corn, cassava, taro, even salt. They had no agriculture and set no traps. Their metal arrowheads, along with all their other metal and cloth, had come from trading with Dafal. These stone-age people were true "cavemen"—they lived in a group of high caves, which could be reached only by climbing trees. Eventually they brought Elizalde and his crew, including anthropologists, to their home deep in the forest.

Because their caves were safe, and on their ancestral grounds, the Tasaday did not travel. Although they lived only about 40 miles (64 kilometers) from the Celebes Sea, their language had no word for "ocean," or even for "lake."

When the outside world learned about the stone-age cave people Elizalde had discovered in Mindanao, proposals came pouring in to PANAMIN's office in Manila. Christian missionaries wanted to clothe the Tasaday and teach them to read the New Testament. Americans proposed to adopt Tasaday children. A lumber company offered to build a school near their caves, in exchange for certain privileges. Meanwhile, logging roads continued to edge closer to the Tasaday's mist-shrouded forest. The Tasaday accepted all the attention with composure.

To Elizalde and others, evidence that other stone-age peoples might still exist even deeper in the jungle made it imperative to protect the Tasaday and their territory from the marauders who had already destroyed other tribes in the Philippines.

During the next few years, the Tasaday became used to visits from helicopters. They built a landing platform out of logs 70 feet (21 meters) above the ground in a tree. A television crew came to film them; tape recorders were left running to capture their conversation at home; anthropologists and archaeologists had a field day with their living Paleolithic informants.

On March 6, 1974, President Ferdinand Marcos of the Philippines signed into law a proclamation protecting the Tasaday and a huge area around them from outside exploitation. The tribes within this municipality, including the Tboli and the Manubu Blit, are self-governing, with their own courts and police force. The Tasaday were given the choice of remaining as they were or of merging with the culture around them.

Although the Tasaday provide such a valuable and hopeful example of what humanity can be—loving, honest, and humorous—it seems unlikely that they will survive as a culture. Among other reasons, modern medicine may allow the small number of Tasaday to increase, and their ancestral caves are not large enough to support many people. As knives and other metal objects are introduced, the art of making stone tools will die.

And finally, the Tasaday tribe is short of women. Intermarriage with other tribespeople is already taking place and will hasten their assimilation with the outside world.

Probably the Tasaday will merge gradually into the surrounding fabric of Philippine tribal society—among the latest, but not the most unlucky, victims of onrushing civilization.

J.S.

Wavemakers:

THE HEROICS OF THE VILLAS BOAS BROTHERS

For Claudio Villas Boas it was a journey back into time, and the Batovi River, a remote tributary that eventually finds its way to the mighty Amazon, was to take him there. The traces of the hidden past were at first fleeting. As Villas Boas reported in the September 1968 edition of *National Geographic,* eight days after he and eight Indian companions left Posto Leonardo, an isolated enclave in the midst of Amazonia's jungles, they discovered abandoned campsites and primitive fishing implements. Two days later they found a bamboo arrow floating in the river. And on the eleventh day of their expedition, the most telling trace of all—a trail, leading from the river into the dense jungle.

It was not an archaeological search that beckoned Villas Boas into the unknown tropical rain forests of central Brazil. He was on the trail of the Tchikao Indians, living remnants of the Stone Age. When he launched this expedition to contact them in 1956, the tribe had never seen the face of civilization. They belonged to another time.

For Claudio Villas Boas, and his brother, Orlando, who worked with him as a fellow *sertanista* (or trained Indian contact-person), the effort to introduce the tribe to the twentieth century was made with great reluctance. It was their belief that primitive Amazonian tribes should, if at all possible, be left in isolation and freedom. But with the increasingly intensified pace of Brazilian development, they realized that the best they could hope for was borrowed time, and, perhaps, a

Orlando Villas Boas (left, in white pants) and Claudio Villas Boas (right, with sunglasses) and a team of Xavante Indians prepare to distribute presents to the Kreen-akrore Indians in 1973. (*Alan Hutchison Library/W. Jesco Von Puttkamer*)

chance for the Indians to make a slow, stable integration into Brazilian society.

That first attempt at contact with the Tchikao in 1956 ended abruptly. After Claudio and his companions followed the newly discovered trail for three hours, the raucous sounds of men's voices led them to the home-fires of a hidden encampment. There, Villas Boas became the first white person to see the primitive Tchikao. As his companions waited down the trail, the unarmed Villas Boas disappeared into the dense vegetation, emerging near the tribe, holding in upraised arms knives, axes and other flashy trinkets of the modern world. He shared a momentary stare with an old Tchikao man. Claudio's brother later wrote of that wordless exchange: "It was as if all the fund of human knowledge, accumulated over thousands of years, lay as a barrier between them."

That barrier, at the outset, proved too great. The terrified Indians leaped to their feet, and while the women and children fled into the forest, angry warriors delivered a wave of arrows in Villas Boas' direction. His waiting party, upon Claudio's signal, fired their guns in the air. The explosive staccato left the jungle silent, and both the Indians and the *civilizados* escaped to the security of their respective worlds.

This encounter was not new to the Villas Boas brothers. For over twenty-five years the two, along with brothers Leonardo, who succumbed to tropical fever in 1961, and Alvaro, who worked for FUNAI (the National Indian Foundation), had championed the cause of Brazil's threatened tribes. Their efforts took on increased urgency as the development-minded government unveiled plans for new highway systems, new settlements, and industrial expansion in the primitive regions of Brazil.

Their work, they say, has two objectives. They accept that development is inevitable in the resource-rich Amazon basin, and that the developers need to be secure from Indian attack. At the same time, the Villas Boas brothers adamantly advocate the protection of the cultural integrity of the Amazonian tribes in the face of the developmental assault on the great interior jungles. "We consider ourselves," wrote Orlando Villas Boas, "first and foremost, protectors of the tribes."

This conviction is firmly rooted in their long experience in the Brazilian jungle (Orlando once spent more than six years, and Claudio more than nine years, in the forest without emerging) and in their own observations of the tragedy that takes place when Indian people are thrust, unprepared, into the glare of the modern world.

The Villas Boas brothers hoped to buy time, for at least a few of the remaining tribes, through the creation of a large park, in which threatened Indians could live traditionally and maintain peaceful, but minimal, contact with the outside world. In 1961, after years of pressuring officials of Brazil's Indian Protective Service (which was replaced by FUNAI in 1967), the Villas Boas brothers' vision became the 8,500-square-mile (22,015-square-kilometer) Xingu National Park in the heart of Brazil.

The park would be a refuge, they hoped, for those tribes directly endangered by development. As Claudio put it: "We do not lead the people of the watery forests into the sanctuary until it is quite clear they cannot survive outside it. And when they are here, our administrative hands are feather light."

In 1964, the Tchikao tribe became one of the many who were urgent candidates for protection. The Villas Boas brothers heard that the lure of gold and diamonds was bringing droves of prospectors into the Batovi River country, perilously close to the haunts of the Tchikao. The prospectors were quickly followed by hunting parties and land surveyors. Civilization, it appeared, had sent its messengers of change.

The brothers resolved to resume contact with the Tchikao. Finding them was, as usual, the first challenge. An air search finally located their village roughly 100 miles (160 kilometers) from Posto Leonardo, near the boundaries of the Xingu National Park. In the autumn of 1964, the brothers embarked in two small planes, to continue what had begun eight years before.

Contact with unknown tribes (or "attraction" in government jargon) has an established methodology. It is a slow, tedious process fraught with uncertainty and danger. First, "attraction posts" are established, sometimes near the Indian village, where *sertanistas* leave gifts. Successful initial contact is confirmed if the Indians take the gifts, and in return, leave some of their own. Next, the Indians are encouraged to come to the *sertanista* camp for further exchanges. And finally, if all goes well, the contact-men visit the Indian village to begin the slow introduction to the modern world.

This process was begun haltingly with the Tchikao. An air drop of presents preceded a landing on a dry flood plain near their village. The planes' engines were kept running, while Orlando Villas Boas, bearing machetes as gifts, approached the concealed Indians. Their frightened cries were peppered with the haunting sound of warriors who, in a show of strength, rattled arrows against their bows. Undaunted, Villas Boas continued to walk slowly toward the commotion. Suddenly, three Indians rushed him, dropped their arrows at his feet, and grabbed the machetes. The Tchikao had made their truce with the outside world.

The outside world proved a cruel partner in this agreement. When the Tchikao were first contacted by Villas Boas, they numbered four hundred. But through violent clashes with prospectors and the resulting spread of civilization's diseases they had dwindled to fifty-three people in 1967. After three years of regular contact with the Tchikao, learning their language and ways, the Villas Boas brothers led the survivors into Xingu National Park.

The future of the Tchikao, and that of the eighteen other tribes that have since settled within the park's boundaries, is by no means assured. The Indians are constantly plagued by diseases, many imported from the outside, such as yellow fever, measles, diphtheria, tuberculosis, and even the common cold. The forest's natural pharmacopoeia, often ill-suited to treat these alien maladies, has been replaced by modern medicines, creating a new dependence on the *civilizados*.

Though the Villas Boas brothers strongly encourage maintenance of traditional life-styles and customs, even to the point of limiting the use of fish hooks and mesh nets in the park, age-old customs are quickly forgotten when a more attractive modern alternative presents itself. A flashlight is a handy replacement for the resin torch, and a gun for the bow and arrow.

Traditional tribal animosities are also aggravated by the relatively close proximity of the Indians in the park and the need to change village sites frequently because the fragile soil is quickly exhausted. To help diminish the potential for such clashes, the Villas Boas brothers promoted Indian leadership and control in the park. A 1972 report by the Aboriginal Protection Society (APS), a group based in the United Kingdom, had high praise for these efforts.

"For the first time in our travels we had arrived at an Indian post where the Indians were actually in charge," wrote APS officials after a visit to Xingu National Park. "Moreover, we felt that their leaders were more capable of meeting the outside world on equal terms than many of those more strenuously 'civilized' Indians we had met elsewhere."

Though the Villas Boas brothers received a Nobel Prize nomination for their work in setting up Xingu National Park, and the two are widely praised as Brazil's most famous *sertanistas*, their approaches are controversial. They have been sharply criticized for "condemning Indians to a primitive life when they want progress," and attempting to keep them "cultural fossils." Pia Maybury-Lewis of Cultural Survival, a U.S.-based group concerned with the social impact of development on ethnic minorities, says that ethnologists are "getting away from the idea" that native peoples should be kept in a kind of "human zoo," completely isolated from the world around them.

"You cannot keep development away, there's nothing you can do to stop it," she says. "One must prepare Indian people to live with the inevitable."

Those inevitabilities are already pressing in on the borders of Xingu National Park. Though it was originally set aside for eternity, a large section of the park has been expropriated for ranches, and a new road put through that violates its boundaries. It was these developments, and weakened health after repeated bouts with tropical diseases, that finally led Orlando and Claudio Villas Boas to resign as administrators of the park in 1975.

The Villas Boas brothers spent their lifetimes attempting to build cultural bridges—sometimes spanning a thousand years of differences—and they remain among the very few who, through understanding and respect for Indian custom, are able to cross that uncertain chasm freely.

In his book *The Rivers Amazon* Alex Shoumatoff describes one such crossing. After three years of attempting contact with the *Kreen-akrore* tribe, which was allegedly responsible for the killing of several whites and scores of other Indians, Claudio and Orlando Villas Boas saw three Kreen-akrore on the other side of a river where gifts had been strewn. The brothers dropped their guns, launched their canoe, and paddled over. Orlando immediately embraced the Indians. One Kreen-akrore, so taken by the scene, made an hour-long speech that neither of the brothers understood. A few days later, forty Kreen-akrore, representing the remnants of the fast-disappearing tribe, appeared in the Villas Boas camp. The immediate surprise and alarm of the brothers quickly dissipated—the Kreen-akrore had come, as it turned out, to dance.

B.P.B.

TOPSOIL

The world's soil is now eroding at the rate of 2.27 million tons a year. If we were *trying* to accomplish this massive transport of soil, every man, woman, and child in the world would have to load 1,375 pounds (624 kilograms) of soil each year, deliver it to the nearest body of water, and dump it in. The rate of soil loss is complicated, however, by differing world situations. In the United States, soil erodes at an average rate of 9 to 12 tons per acre per year. In developing countries erosion rates are twice as high, partly because population pressure forces land to be more intensively farmed. New topsoil is constantly being formed, of course, but at nature's leisurely pace of about 1.5 tons per acre per year (3.4 metric tons per hectare). The difference between creation and loss represents an annual loss of 7.5 to 10 tons per acre (16.8 to 23.5 metric tons per hectare) worldwide.

Because the topsoil is the most nutrient-rich layer of the soil, it is valuable to farmers. Because it is loose and exposed, it easily falls prey to wind and water. Erosion is a natural process, but present rates, speeded by poor farming, overgrazing, ground-clearing for construction and logging or mining practices, are unnatural. It is an alarming situation, especially as food becomes more critical and more expensive. The problem is rooted partly in ignorance, partly in necessity, partly in shortsightedness.

The fact that certain practices speed erosion is no news to most farmers. Poor tropical farmers may know that plowing a steep slope results in yearly soil loss, but they have nowhere else to go. Many were forced from more fertile valleys by corporate farms; increasing population brings more farmers but no more lands. And often poor farmers in developing countries, pushed to hillsides, continue the practices of their ancestors on flatland. But as water drains vertically down a hill, its velocity increases as does its power to dislodge and carry off soil particles. The solution—contour farming, in which horizontal furrows impede the water on a slope—is not practiced in all countries.

Even farmers knowledgeable about soil conservation techniques often choose to ignore them when they conflict with other techniques that offer a higher yield, and a higher profit. For example, fields expanded to accommodate large sprinkler irrigation systems (some center-pivot systems have a radius of a quarter of a mile [.4 kilometer]) are more susceptible to wind erosion, especially in areas with light soils and high winds. Farmers in the American Midwest often sacrifice wind-breaking hedgerows to fit in a few more rows of corn. And farmers who year after year plant only corn, a crop with widely spaced plants, leave a high percentage of their soil bare between rows and highly vulnerable to erosion.

As soil nutrients slip away, farmers are forced to replace them with expensive fertilizers. Calculations based on soil erosion data suggest that more than 50 million tons of plant nutrients are lost annually to erosion. The cost of replacing the lost nitrogen, phosphorus, and potassium in U.S. agricultural soils was last estimated at $7.75 billion by the U. S. Department of Agriculture (USDA) in 1965—and that was before the leap in petroleum prices and the concomitant rise in the price of oil-based nitrogen fertilizer.

Overgrazing and poor logging practices also take a heavy toll on topsoil. Intense grazing has turned many areas of North Africa from grassland to desert. In the United States as of 1974, 50 percent of federal rangelands suffered

Erosion caused by water on a hillside in China. The lost soil, a fine-grain, wind-deposited variety called loess, washes into rivers like the Yellow, which is named for the color of the loess it carries. (*FAO/ Chinese Ministry for Water Conservation*)

Erosion caused by wind on the Great Plains of the United States. Once vegetation is reduced or removed, soil is at the mercy of wind and water, and erosion is virtually assured. (*U. S. Forest Service*)

severe to critical erosion and 32 percent were moderately eroded.

About one and a half billion people depend on wood for cooking and heating, according to the U. N. Food and Agricultural Organization (FAO). Since population grows faster than trees, poor people in Asia and the Indian subcontinent must walk farther and farther to gather enough firewood to cook dinner. Once-forested hills have been stripped bare by peasants and timber companies and are often not replanted. In the richly forested United States and Canada, poor practices such as clear-cutting right up to streams have speeded the loss of soil. In many tropical countries the longstanding practice of slash-and-burn agriculture allowed the soil to regenerate its fertility. Now the same practice, done on a large scale by corporations, and by more and more people as the population grows, is destroying soil. A slash-and-burn farmer clears a plot of forest by cutting and burning trees, a process that releases nutrients from the trees to the soil. The farmer grows crops for a few years, then moves on to another plot, allowing the forest to regenerate. However, the land must rest for ten to fifteen years to regenerate the forest and the soil nutrients. In recent years this rest period is often considerably shortened. Many tropical soils are particularly vulnerable to erosion without their forest cover. (See "Soil: Keeping a Low Profile," page 133.)

There *are* successsful efforts to conserve soil. Because of its sheer magnitude, one of the most striking examples is the Chinese system of agriculture. Mao's China inherited a land of generally salty, worn-out soil. The government built fertilizer plants (and plans on building more), but a decision was made to rely heavily on "green manure" (second-crop legumes plowed back into the soil) and "night soil" (human excreta) to replenish nutrients (see "Night Soil," page 356). Today China is able to feed its population of 900 million and even export food.

Many of the best methods of soil conservation were figured out over generations by local farmers. Soil scientist Pedro A. Sanchez reports in a textbook on tropical soil that in highland areas of South America, extremely sophisticated soil conservation systems, including terracing, have been developed and practiced for centuries. He summarizes that "traditional management systems are well geared toward soil conservation. The problems arise when new practices or new people move into an area or when the old systems break down because of overpopulation."

The Qanat system, used in part of northern Africa and the eastern Middle East, helps collect water for irrigation, reduces flood volumes and velocities, and traps larger soil particles. Farmers build little dams in small valleys between slopes or in riverbeds. When the water flows down the stream, sediment and water collect behind the dam; the water is later tapped through a hole or pipe in the dam. Every year, the farmer raises the dam.

In Pakistan, farmers living on mountainous slopes improved their watershed by planting orchard trees, like apples, apricots, and nuts, with the help of donated food to nourish them until their orchards started bearing food. Plowing the slopes would cause erosion, whereas the orchard trees hold the soil in place.

Experimenting with soil conservation systems has its hazards. When farmers in Tanzania's Uluguru Mountains tried terracing their plots to keep soil from flowing downhill, disaster struck. A heavy rain produced a landslide, collapsing the terraces and exposing infertile subsoil underneath. The farmers later found contour farming and planting orchards more effective.

Allowing soil erosion is supremely illogical: good soil full of nutrients is lost and the nutrients are repaced with expensive, oil-based fertilizers. The valuable topsoil, however, doesn't really disappear. It invades the aquatic environment where it clogs channels and intensifies floods. But it continues to do its work of nourishing plants. It feeds algae, which bloom, die, rot, and rob fish of oxygen—speeding the process of eutrophication. The soil covers and clogs filter-feeding shellfish, often destroying once-flourishing shellfish industries. Around the world, governments spend billions to dredge harbors and channels and restore lakes damaged by topsoil while farmers spend billions to replace the topsoil with chemical fertilizers.

F.W.

THE LAND MECHANISM

The land is one organism. Its parts, like our own parts, compete with each other and cooperate with each other. The competitions are as much a part of the inner workings as the cooperations. You can regulate them—cautiously—but not abolish them. To keep every cog and wheel is the first precaution of intelligent tinkering, but have we learned this first principle of conservation, to preserve all the parts of the land mechanism? No, because even the scientist does not yet recognize all of them.

In Germany there is a mountain called the Spessart. Its south slope bears the most magnificent oaks in the world. American cabinetmakers, when they want the last word in quality, use Spessart oak. The north slope, which should be the better, bears an indifferent stand of Scotch pine. Why? Both slopes are part of the same state forest; both have been managed with equally scrupulous care for two centuries. Why the difference?

Kick up the litter under the oak and you will see that the leaves rot almost as fast as they fall. Under the pines, though, the needles pile up as a thick duff; decay is much slower. Why? Because in the Middle Ages the south slope was preserved as a deer forest by a hunting bishop; the north slope was pastured, plowed, and cut by settlers, just as we do with woodlots in Wisconsin and Iowa today. Only after this period of abuse was the north slope replanted with pines. During this period of abuse something happened to the microscopic flora and fauna of the soil. The number of species was greatly reduced, i.e., the digestive apparatus of the soil lost some of its parts. Two centuries of conservation have not sufficed to restore these losses. It required the modern microscope, and a century of research in soil science, to discover the existence of these "small cogs and wheels" that determine harmony or disharmony between men and land in the Spessart.

Wavemakers:

THE DUNE DEFENDERS

If you ask, Martha Reynolds will take you where desert-loving prickly pear cactus grows in thorny company with arctic barberry, and where a swift lizard—aptly named a six-lined racer—weaves a crooked trail in the sand. Nearby are orchids, she says, that test the imagination, and birds of such diversity that seasoned ornithologists are kept busy searching the pages of their field guides.

Without her help, the untrained eye might miss these things and focus instead on the more obvious elements of the landscape: the towering dunes, the glittering and seemingly endless lake, the sweeping white beaches, and incongruously, looming like a mirage beyond this unspoiled scene, the shadows of the steel mills that are the heart of the second-largest industrial complex in the world.

This uncanny juxtaposition of sand, grass, and blast furnaces is the Indiana Dunes, and to Martha Reynolds, a graying woman who lives alone in an old fisherman's shack at the foot of a giant dune, it is one of the most beautiful spots in the world.

Forged fifteen thousand years ago by the retreating glaciers that gouged the shoreline of Lake Michigan, the third-largest North American lake, the Indiana Dunes are an ecological showcase containing in a very small area a myriad of wildlife as well as 1,300 species of plants, which represent four climatic zones and a variety of habitats including bog, marsh, and woodland. Poet Carl Sandburg described the dunes as "a signature of time and eternity." It is also the site of what American naturalist Edwin Way Teale called "the nation's longest running soap opera," a three-decade battle between well-financed industrialists and committed citizen groups, led by an organization called, appropriately, the Save the Dunes Council.

The struggle to preserve what was once a 30-mile (48-kilometer) strip of rolling dunes and woodland along the southern shore of Lake Michigan began in 1916, when Chicagoan Stephen Mather became head of the newly created National Park Service. Long an admirer of the dunes' beauty and their accessibility as a recreational safety valve for the growing population of nearby urban areas, Mather proposed the creation of a 25-mile (40-kilometer) "Sand Dunes National Park." The idea posed a problem for the conservation-minded agency, however, because unlike many of the vast parks in the West, much of the Indiana Dunes area was privately owned. As a result, Sand Dunes National Park was not to be. Several years later, mounting public pressure, though it was not yet organized, led to the creation of the Indiana Dunes State Park, composed of a mere 3 miles (4.8 kilometers) of shoreline rather than 25.

Meanwhile, a land-hungry Midwest began to nibble away at the dunes. The steel indus-

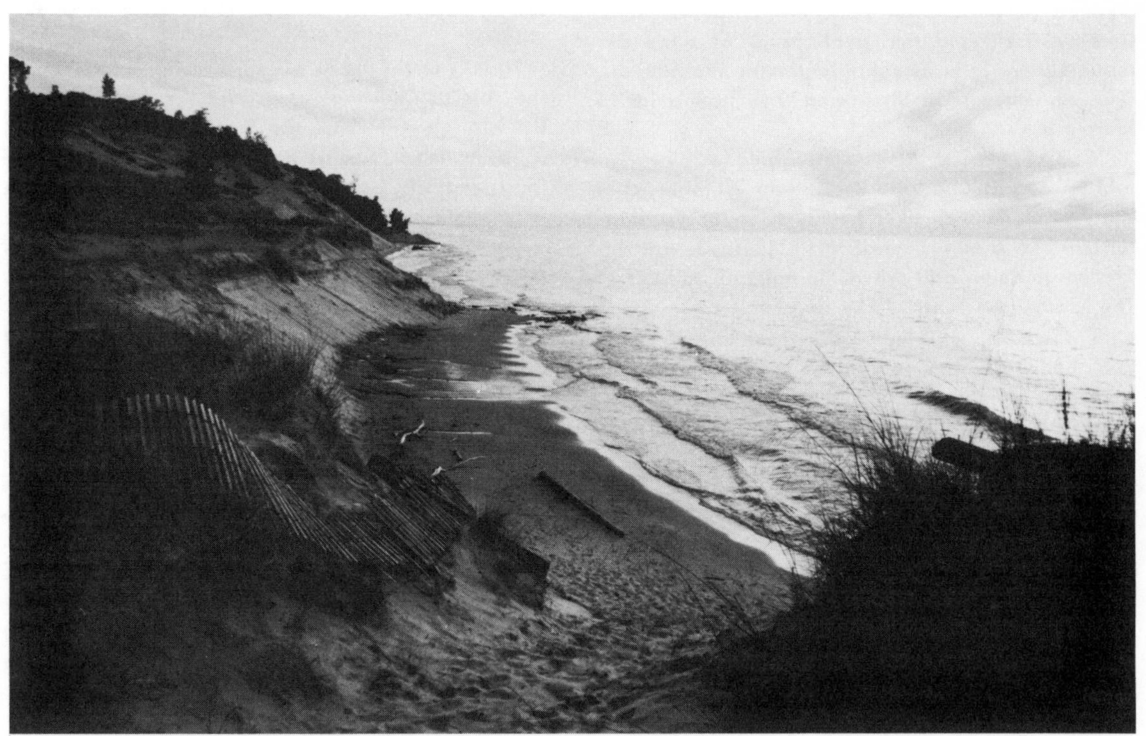

The Indiana Dunes on Lake Michigan: saved from development. (*NPS/Dick Frear*)

try in particular, admiring the shoreline's potential for easily dredged harbors and its proximity to highways and railroads, quietly began to purchase large chunks of the remaining dunes.

It was this familiar chronology that led to the creation, in 1952, of the Save the Dunes Council. Its organizer was a feisty, nearly-seventy-year-old woman named Dorothy Buell, who lived in Ogden Dunes, a small community on the lakeshore. One of the Council's first actions was the purchase of the 56-acre (22-hectare) Cowles Bog, a unique ecological area that was threatened by development. Then the group, composed exclusively of volunteers, set their sights on a much larger objective—preserving the 12,000 acres (4,800 hectares) of unspoiled dunes by expanding the state park.

"In the beginning the idea was that you could get people mobilized to save the dunes by showing them how beautiful they were," recalls Charlotte Read, current director of the Save the Dunes Council and veteran of those early efforts. "That was a naive notion, because what was looming on the horizon was the momentum of postwar industrial development."

The "development at any cost" forces totally dominated Indiana state politics in the 1950s, and Council proposals simply to expand the state park went nowhere. In 1958, the citizen group changed their strategy and decided to back the creation of a national park in the dunes area. Dorothy Buell and her small band of dune defenders were in a new battleground, Washington, D.C., and they soon discovered they had a lot to learn.

"One of the first things we learned was how to lobby," recalls Charlotte Read, who estimates that she has made well over twenty trips to Washington for the Dunes Council. "We learned that we had to go down and prowl the halls of Congress." The group also learned the necessity, when faced with powerful, well-financed opposition, of coalition building. They organized support for their park proposal among other environmental groups, labor unions, community groups, and city officials. The group found a powerful ally in Congress. The late Illinois Senator Paul Douglas, an early member of the Save the Dunes Council, shepherded the park legislation through the Senate. Despite those efforts, industry opposition, led by the steel companies, held environmentalists at bay for eight years, while destruction of the dunes quietly continued.

A low point for the citizen group, recalled one member, was in 1963 when the giant Bethlehem Steel company, beginning construction of a sprawling industrial complex, unleashed a fleet of bulldozers on the tallest and most spectacular of the remaining dunes, "scraping away rare plants without number; a veritable botanist's paradise was destroyed."

Finally, in 1966, following a national campaign orchestrated by the Save the Dunes Council, Congress approved a measure creating the Indiana Dunes National Lakeshore. The bill was a compromise. Instead of 12,000 acres (4,800 hectares), the park was allotted 6,000 (2,400 hectares). And the building of an industrial harbor and complex, which environmentalists had opposed, was allowed in the middle of the park. It was still a remarkable victory for the citizen volunteers. As Charlotte Read put it: "The park never should have happened, everything was against it." At the time, it was the only U.S. national park ever established against the opposition of the Congressman in whose district it is located.

This long-running environmental drama has not yet had its final scene. Despite the addition of 3,660 acres (1,464 hectares) to the National Lakeshore in 1976, three key areas were omitted. A nuclear power plant has also been proposed on the border of the park. If legal challenges are overturned, it will add 450-foot (138-meter) cooling towers to a horizon already cluttered with smokestacks.

Thanks to the funds raised by volunteers through the sale of Christmas cards and the proceeds from the group's gift shop, the Save the Dunes Council persists. Read, who is now the Council's full-time (and modestly paid) director, says the organization is resigned to a long fight.

"I remember meetings after the original park bill was signed when we debated whether we should go out of business," she says. "We quickly learned the difference between getting a bill passed and getting a park. This is a long-term commitment; it's not a flash-in-the-pan."

Martha Reynolds, meanwhile, can be found nearly every morning walking the beach, watching the wind and the water sculpt the sand, as it has for thousands of years. An early participant in the crusade to save the dunes, she now talks of writing a guide to its wildflowers. If you ask her, she will tell you that the campaign to defend the Indiana Dunes has been a long and onerous one. But you know, without her having to say it, that Martha Reynolds thinks it was worth it. B.P.B.

THE NATURAL SOUNDSCAPE

In 1960 an ocean research vessel from Columbia University, the *Vema,* carried out one of the most dramatic sound experiments in history. In order to illustrate how far sound travels through seawater, the ship's crew exploded depth charges in deep water off the coast of Australia. The sounds were picked up in waters off Bermuda—a distance of 12,000 miles (19,200 kilometers), almost halfway around the world.

Because seawater is about eight hundred times denser than air, it carries sound waves more rapidly and far greater distances than the gaseous atmosphere. The velocity of sound in seawater varies according to conditions, but it averages about five times the speed of sound in air. The same water density that enhances sounds interferes with light and vision, limiting visibility to about 100 feet (30 meters). As a result, the most intelligent animals in the sea, whales and dolphins, not only communicate using sophisticated sound systems but directly *perceive* the environment around them acoustically, using sonar transmissions. What they "see" in the distance is a sound image created by echoes from the sonic signals they beam out.

The pervasiveness of sound senses in the sea is not limited to mammals. Fish and many other marine species have sense mechanisms delicately attuned to the sound environment about them. From the ambient music of biological and physical sounds, they learn of predators approaching, of wounded prey, of fishermen, of mates in season to spawn.

Sound is an environmental information system used in all of nature as much if not more than vision. While its role in aquatic surroundings may be more distinctive, all organisms live within an envelope of sounds. Humans tend to take for granted or ignore this veil of surrounding natural sounds.

The Sound News Service

Recently, students of this acoustical environment have begun to call it the "soundscape," comparing its characteristics to the landscape. It has seasons, daily and hourly changes. It has "colors." The soundscape can be as dense in sounds as the tropical forest is dense in vegetation or it can be a sparse acoustical desert. It is alive

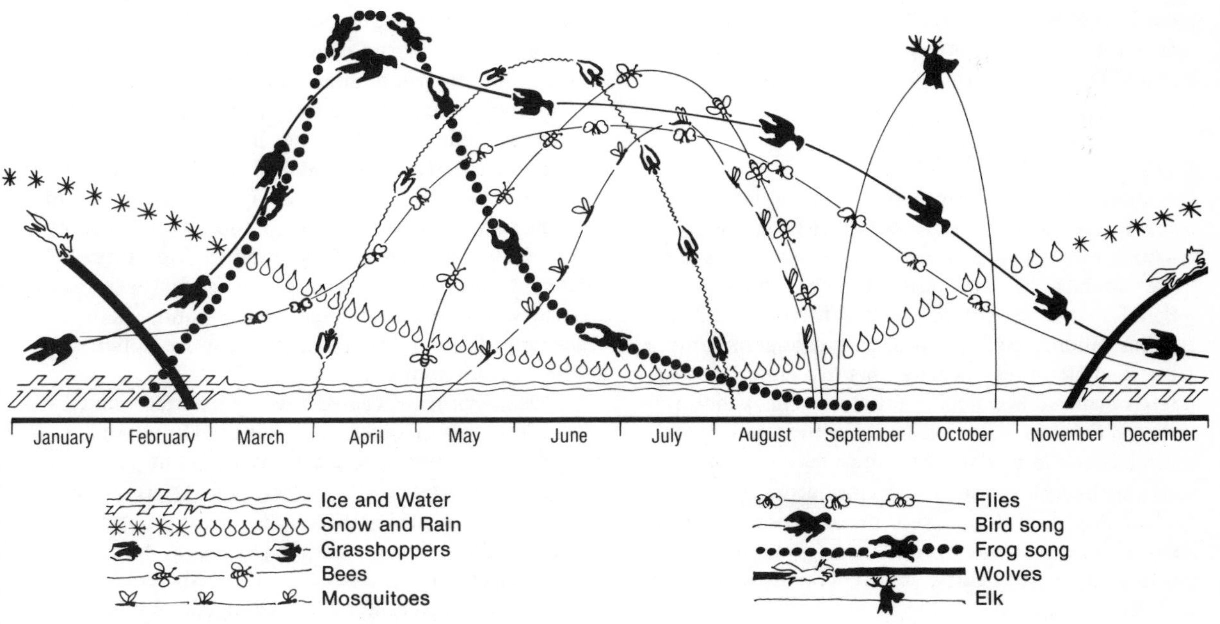

The cycles of the natural soundscape at a point along the west coast of British Columbia, showing the relative volume of sounds during the year (as recorded by R. Murray Schafer). (*Jeff Yates, after R. Murray Schafer,* The Tuning of the World, *Alfred A. Knopf, 1977*)

with biological instruments, with wind, with rain, with human machinery. Until recently the soundscape was dominated by the phenomena of nature, punctuated occasionally by human sounds—the call of a shepherd, the hammering of a blacksmith, the peal of a church bell. To humans of the past these ambient sounds were full of news. When animals could be heard burrowing in the ground, farmers knew the soil had thawed and the spring plowing could begin. The tone and timbre of a faraway sound could reveal changes in air pressure and humidity to a well-tuned ear. The faint sounds of a dog barking signaled a distant arrival. Surf, river, storm, wind, insects, birds—all contributed audible information to a kind of soundscape news service.

Humans have always participated in this flow of sounds, but until the Industrial Revolution perhaps the loudest sound a single human being could produce by hand, not counting a gunshot, was the clang of a blacksmith's hammer or the crack of a whip. The random sounds of human life fit into the natural soundscape in the past, expanding the news service with buoy bells and foghorns, with carriage bells, with factory whistles, with axes striking trees, with calls to prayer by muezzins in Middle Eastern minarets. In much of the world sounds like these are still heard, still noted by people. But for the hundreds of millions of people who live in crowded urban centers, the natural soundscape of the past has disappeared beneath a flood of new sounds that are neither as readable nor as pleasant as previous soundscapes.

The World as Music

One of the leading critics of the modern soundscape is Canadian composer R. Murray Schafer, whose book *The Tuning of the World* discusses the sounds of the past and the present. To Schafer, the world is "a macrocosmic musical composition." But the music is changing rapidly, the discrete notes and rhythms drowning in a surfeit of indiscrete noise. Schafer defines noise as the sounds we consciously or unconsciously learn to ignore: the discordant, abrasive, continuous, or uninformative sounds of modern civilization. "The world suffers from an overpopulation of sound," says Schafer. "There is so much acoustic information that little of it can emerge with clarity."

The Industrial Age worked at least two significant sound changes on society. First, in each city it gathered together so many noise-producing machines that the volume overwhelmed the more delicate sounds of nature and individual humans. Secondly, machinery produced "flat line" sounds: droning, humming, whining sounds that are continuous. These noises fill in the silent gaps between otherwise interrupted sounds, turning the acoustic environment of the world's largest cities into a single great roar that seems to rise up from everywhere, obscuring every sound but the loudest nearby horn, siren, or screeching auto. Noise specialists point to the emotional and physical impact of this new soundscape on people. Emotionally, some believe, it acts like a continuous narcotic on the brain, hindering thought, generating a kind of listlessness in society.

The problem in comparing soundscapes of the past with today's is that no permanent record remains of previous soundscapes. Ancient architecture can be recreated from stone ruins. Primitive humans can be restructured from their skeletal remains. Visual images are recorded in art. But the soundscape disappears in the atmosphere immediately. The only clues to its character lie in the occasional sound descriptions found in literature.

Earwitness Accounts

To reconstruct soundscapes from the past, Schafer and several co-workers created the World Soundscape Project, which was funded by several agencies. They pored over literature, culling references to environmental sounds, assembling a cross-referenced catalog to natural sounds by time and place. Since most of the literature was European or American, the catalog is so far restricted to these areas of the world. They found certain patterns. Of the references to sound they discovered in nineteenth-century English literature, 43 percent referred to natural sounds. In twentieth-century literature, on the other hand, only 20 percent of the sound descriptions were concerned with natural sources.

The literature revealed a more dramatic change in references to quiet and silence. Of all the descriptions of the acoustical environment collected by Schafer's team, 19 percent of the references from the period 1810 to 1830 mention quiet or silence. That figure had slipped to 9 percent in the period from 1940 to 1960. Moreover, the tone of the references had changed. While once the descriptions of quiet evoked moods of peace, sleepiness, or contemplation, more recently they were negative: silences were oppressive, brooding, gloomy, lonely. Having grown accustomed to an overabundance of noise, we are discomforted by its absence, by the permeating silence of the universe, by the pauses that give meaning and shape to natural sounds.

Sound Imperialism

The arrival of loud vehicles and industry quickly obscures wilderness and village sounds, but these developments also work another social change. They eliminate sound "property" rights. Since the acoustical environment cannot usually be delineated on a map or effectively zoned, loud noises flow into space shared by everyone. When the size and sound levels of airplanes increase, the waste noise of a local airport invades ever more distant homes and backyards, an intrusion that may break no law but greatly alters the lives of thousands of people.

Legal attempts to control sound throughout the world are hardly new. Blacksmiths in many thirteenth-century English towns were restricted to designated areas so their clanging noise would not permeate village life. One of the problems with regulation of the modern soundscape, however, is that some of the most ubiquitous sound producers cannot always be restricted; they are the trucks and automobiles that penetrate nearly every city, suburb, and community on the planet, usually producing a deafening roar precisely where the human population is most concentrated.

R. Murray Schafer is trying to draw attention to the problems of the soundscape, suggesting that the vast musical composition around us needs better orchestration. In *The Tuning of the World,* he lists the principles of acoustic design for communities and homes. He calls for the preservation of "soundmarks," particularly distinctive regional sounds. Schafer recommends redesigning the acoustical environment, allowing nature to speak with its own "authentic voices," creating "soniferous gardens" in which sounds are arranged as carefully as the trees, lakes, pathways, and playing fields of a park, and giving greater emphasis to the human need for periods of silence. Most importantly, society needs to learn what the musician knows: all sounds matter. In music, no sound is allowed to thrash about uncontrolled. There is no waste sound, no "noise." There is harmony and balance, pleasure—and an elegant transmission of information without acoustical litter.

The sea still retains this natural, musical soundscape for the most part, giving us both a model of environmental sound and a virgin soundscape to protect. Despite its vastness, however, the buzzing sounds of human machinery invade the ocean along its edges, where boat traffic is heaviest. Perhaps the most poignant evidence of the human threat to the natural soundscape is a tale of the sea. The gentle whales—sensitive to sounds, dependent upon them, masterful at modulating them into songs—can be enraged by the abuse of their acoustic space. Cousteau diving teams have found them especially annoyed by outboard motors, perhaps because the motors' overlapping frequencies interfere with their sonic reception. The whales' sensitivity to sound has been used to their detriment by well-meaning observers who circle the creatures with motor boats. Surrounded by a wall of hostile sound, the animals come to a furious halt. They cannot even dive, since they rely on their sonar to guide them. The intelligent whale, thus stymied and angered, seems not so much a distant marine life form as a close cousin of us all caught up in civilization's blare of noise, which overwhelms natural songs and floods nature's silences.

M.R.

THE SENSE OF HEARING

It is possible to become accustomed to noises that at first seem unbearable. But accommodation to noise is never as complete as many people believe. Noise has subliminal effects on the human body even when it is not overtly annoying. Subconsciously, our bodies react to noise as a threat and prepare for instant flight. The muscles tense; adrenaline is released; blood pressure rises; breathing speeds up. To the ear and the body, noise means danger. In 1979, the United Nations Environment Programme (UNEP) labeled the flood of noise one of the four main "emerging threats" in the world today (the others listed were schistosomiasis, tourism, and the resistance of pests to pesticides). In many countries, the noise level in cities is now two or three times what it was twenty years ago. Sirens must now be louder than before just to be heard above the din of traffic.

There is growing evidence that this noise is physically harmful, not only to the ears but to the entire body. Noise has been shown to increase tension, aggression, fatigue, and irritation in workers. It is well known that noise causes head-

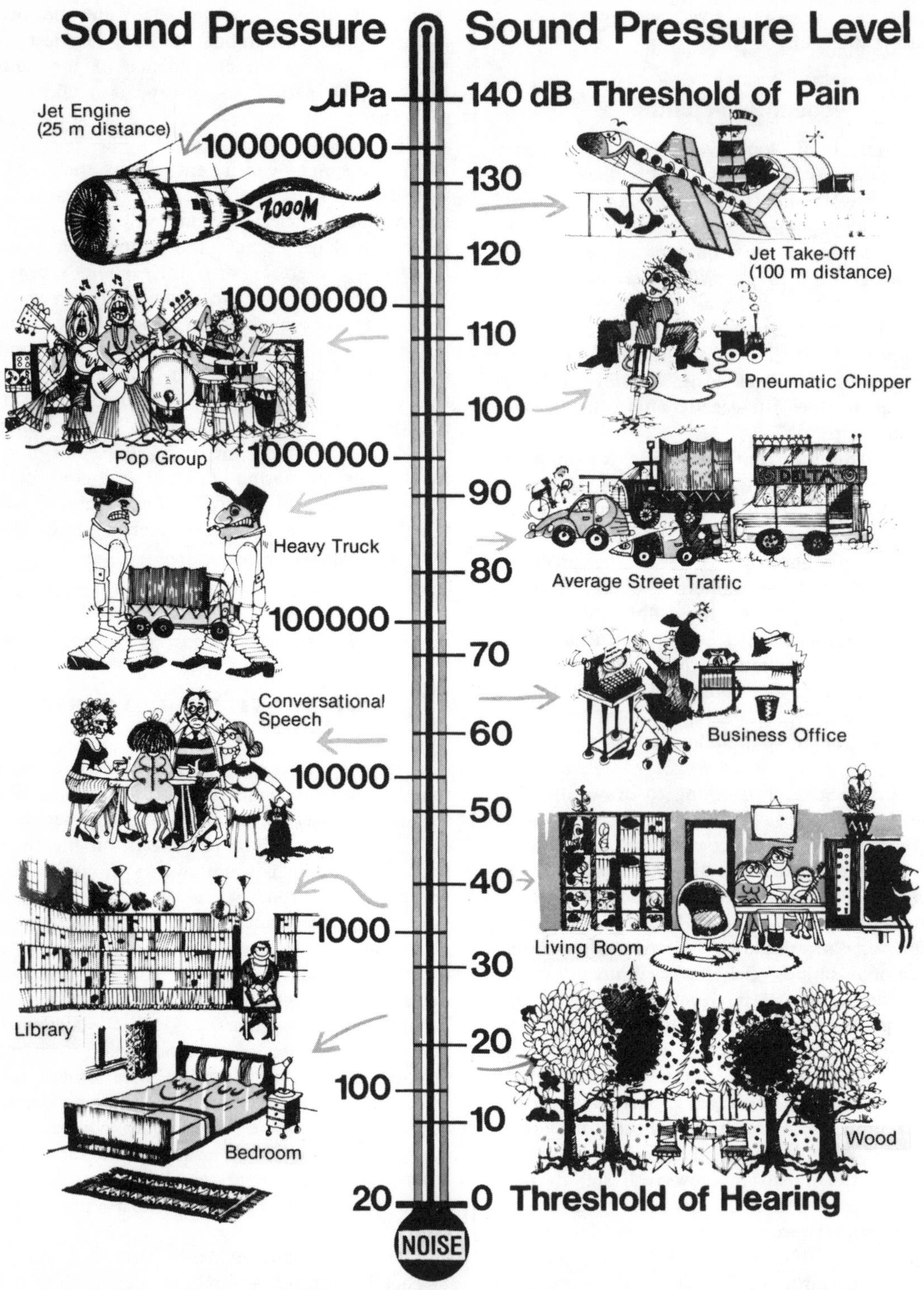

Human hearing range—from rustling leaves to the painful scream of a jet. The decibel (dB) scale (right) measures loudness, beginning with the faintest sound audible to the human ear. The phon (Pa) scale corresponds to the decibel scale and measures sound intensity. (*Brüel and Kjael/UNEP*)

aches, high blood pressure, and an increase in cholesterol deposits, and it has been postulated many times that noise can cause or aggravate mental illness. Other conditions attributed to noise are nausea, sexual impotence and reduction in sexual drive, loss of appetite, nervousness, instability, insomnia, and its opposite, excessive somnolence.

The Unwished-for Silence

The most obvious danger of noise, of course, is loss of hearing. While noise has been considered a nuisance since the beginning of civilization (a denunciation of "the uproar of mankind" occurs in the five-thousand-year-old Epic of Gilgamesh), it is only since the Industrial Revolution that noise was recognized as a real threat. The roaring machines of early industry must have caused premature deafness in thousands of people, although we have few figures. It is now known that continuous noise over 85 decibels often causes deafness ("boilermaker's ear" was a hazard of nineteenth-century riveting factories). Although a temporary exposure to loud noise may cause ringing in the ears, even make the hearer slightly deaf for a while, hearing usually returns to normal before long. But exposure to such noise over a long period of time can damage the inner ear permanently.

Deafness was one of the first recognized legal causes for workmen's compensation, and since the 1930s industry has been forced to quiet down quite a bit. But the sheer volume of general noise has increased, because of both a rising population and a rising standard of living, which means more machines. A New York subway car screeching to a stop has been measured at 100 decibels. Many schools and homes near highways have constant noise levels of from 60 to 80 decibels. In Shanghai, China, some factories in residential neighborhoods produce a noise level outside the factory of 106 decibels; one plant had an exhaust safety valve with a constant noise level of 150 decibels.

The poor level of hearing of modern city dwellers is not caused by simple aging, but by noise. In their silent, desert environment in the Sudan, sixty-year-old men and women of the Mabaan tribe have hearing essentially unchanged from their youth. In contrast, the average New York City dweller begins to suffer hearing loss at the age of twenty-five. J.S. with BE.K.

SOME OTHER THINGS DISAPPEARING

- SALMON FISHERIES . . . The Columbia River in the western United States was once one of the world's great salmon fisheries. Economic exploitation of the river has almost destroyed the fishery. Despite more than $200 million spent to preserve it, the fish yield has dropped 85 percent.
- LIZARDS . . . The tuatara, a sphenodon lizard from New Zealand, is the sole surviving member of the rhynchocephalians, an order that died out during the Triassic period, about 180 million years ago.
- BIRD SPECIES . . . A bird species with an estimated life span of 40,000 years in the seventeenth century would only have a species life span of 16,000 years in the twentieth century. The cause: human destruction of habitats at a pace far greater today than in the past.
- SHELLFISH BEDS . . . More than half the shellfish beds of the Atlantic Ocean have been closed as a result of pesticide, oil, and sewage contamination.
- BARRIER ISLANDS . . . The original character and shape of two thirds of the Atlantic and Gulf Coast barrier islands have been more seriously altered or destroyed by the actions of humanity than by the worst storms.
- CROPLAND . . . Eight billion acres (2 billion hectares) of cropland have been lost since the beginnings of agriculture, one third more than the 600 million acres (1.5 billion hectares) of arable land now on earth.
- WATERFOWL . . . Waterfowl have suffered greatly from habitat encroachment throughout the world; populations in the United States may be as little as one tenth of what they were before the coming of European civilization. For instance, the Redhead, a once popular and fairly common duck species, decreased in numbers from about 100,000 to fewer than 3,000 in the period from 1955 to 1974, a reduction in the population of 97.6 percent.
- SKELETONS . . . Partly because of a ban by India, traditional export leader in the field, there is now a serious shortage of skeletons for medical study. Despite an estimated 10,000 sales per year, supply cannot meet demand, and the price of a good skeleton more than doubled over a two-year span.

T.C.

ACCUMULATING NUCLEAR WASTES

One millionth of a gram of plutonium, if inhaled, is enough to cause cancer. One thousandth of a gram of plutonium, inhaled, will cause fibrosis in the lungs and death within a few hours. Ten pounds (4.5 kilograms) of plutonium is enough to build an atomic bomb. A 1,000-megawatt nuclear power plant creates 400 to 500 pounds (180 to 225 kilograms) of plutonium each year. In 1979 there were 233 nuclear power plants in operation around the world, and 323 more were planned or being built. Plutonium has a half-life of 24,300 years, which means that it will remain a danger to human health for up to half a million years—16,666 generations. Plutonium is only one of many radioactive materials that are accumulating at an increasing rate each year as waste products of nuclear energy and weapons production.

Not all radioactive waste is as dangerous as plutonium, but it is all dangerous. The least powerful but most plentiful form of waste is uranium mine tailings. A ton of uranium ore yields only 4 pounds (1.8 kilograms) of usable uranium; the rest is tailings, which were not considered dangerous in the past and were left uncovered—tailings were even used in building construction in Grand Junction, Colorado. We now realize that tailings emit radioactive radon gas.

Mining the uranium needed to fuel a single 1,000-megawatt nuclear power plant for one year results in 4.6 million cubic feet (130,000 cubic meters) of tailings, enough to build a four-lane highway, 1 foot (0.3 meter) deep for 27 miles (43 kilometers). In the United States there are already 140 million tons of tailings.

Low-level radioactive waste—which includes anything that has picked up induced radiation, such as uranium mining tools, gloves and uniforms of workers in fuel enrichment and reprocessing plants, medical wastes, and cooling water from nuclear reactors—is the next most plentiful form of nuclear waste. The danger of low-level radiation is subject to debate, but there is agreement that these materials have been handled too carelessly in the past. Contaminated tools were dumped outside a uranium mill near Beatty, Nevada, and local people picked up the relatively new, harmless-looking tools. More than a million gallons (3.8 million liters) of low-level waste in steel drums was dumped in the ocean near San Francisco between 1946 and 1962. About 25 percent of the drums are now leaking. (See "Wastes in the Sea," page 409.) The U. S. Environmental Protection Agency (EPA) estimates that there could be as much as 400 million cubic feet (11.3 million cubic meters) of low-level waste in the United States alone by the year 2000.

High-level radioactive waste contains uranium-235 and plutonium-239. It is extremely toxic, can even be used to make nuclear weapons, and is difficult to store because radioactivity keeps it hot and corrosive for hundreds of years. Most of the high-level waste in existence today is a product of nuclear weapons production, a fact often used to minimize the hazards of civilian nuclear power. However, the civilian nuclear waste is a hundred times more concentrated, so that civilian waste in the United States already contains more radioactivity than military waste.

Civilian high-level waste consists primarily of spent fuel rods, and about 3,000 tons of these rods are now being temporarily stored at reactor sites in the United States. Every 1,000-megawatt reactor accumulates about 1,200 cubic feet (about 34 cubic meters) of spent fuel a year. Proponents of nuclear power claim that spent fuel is not waste because it can be reprocessed to recover usable plutonium and uranium-235, but the only operating reprocessing plant (at Cap de la Hague, France) has been plagued by safety problems and political protests. The United States has so far avoided commercial reprocessing because of the danger involved and the fear that the concentrated plutonium and uranium could be stolen too easily and used to make a bomb.

Exact figures on accumulated radioactive waste throughout the world do not exist, but U.S. figures can be extrapolated to suggest the scale of the problem. United States military research and weapons production have produced 10 million cubic feet (280,000 cubic meters) of high-level waste and 50 million cubic feet (1.4 million cubic meters) of low-level waste; the Soviet Union has probably produced an equivalent amount, and the other nuclear powers—France, England, China, and India—proportionately smaller quantities. A large backyard swimming pool 40 feet by 20 feet by 6 feet (12.2 meters by 6 meters by 2 meters) has a capacity of 4,800 cubic feet (135.8 cubic meters). High-level military waste from the United States alone would fill more than 2,000 of these pools.

Each year these totals are growing, and at an ever faster rate. During 1979, the global operation of nuclear reactors (assuming an average capacity of 500 megawatts) resulted in 530 million cubic feet (15 million cubic meters) of mine tailings, 380,000 cubic feet (11,000 cubic meters) of low-level waste, and 140,000 cubic feet (4,000 cubic meters) of high-level waste containing almost 50,000 pounds (23,000 kilograms) of plutonium.

How are we going to handle all of this waste? We're not sure. While radioactive waste continues to accumulate, scientists are still trying to develop safe methods for storage. Radioactivity from unprotected mine tailings that has seeped into water and been scattered by the wind must be sealed from the environment. Tailings need to be buried at least 20 feet (6 meters) underground or put in ditches lined and covered with clay. Both methods are expensive and unpopular with the nuclear industry, which already faces rapidly escalating costs.

Low-level radioactive wastes have traditionally been buried in presumably impermeable clay, but escaped waste at West Valley, New York, and Maxey Flats, Kentucky, has shown that clay is not sufficient. High-level waste is being stored at temporary sites while research on a permanent storage method continues. Commercial waste in the United States is stored at the site of the power plants, but the plants are quickly running out of space. The Hanford storage facility in Washington State, which was built in the 1940s to hold U.S. military waste for decades and possibly five hundred years, began leaking in 1958 and has already leaked 450,000 gallons (1.7 million liters) of waste from steel tanks. Nuclear waste stored at Cap de la Hague, France, has leaked from steel tanks and the radiation level in the storage area had reached three times the acceptable level by 1977. Plutonium has been found on the nearby Normandy coast, and local crabs have developed ulcerous sores as a result.

Plans for permanent storage are abundant, but none is considered satisfactory. Most plans involve solidifying the liquid waste and encasing it in glass or ceramic, and then burying it deep underground in granite or salt. The United States had hoped to have a procedure using glassification and salt burial in operation by 1985, but recent research reveals drawbacks of both glass and salt that may delay the completion of a permanent storage site until 1993. The glass can become permeable under conditions of high temperature and pressure, and the salt beds, which were believed to be water-free, have been found to contain pockets of water that would allow radioactive material to spread if the containers leaked.

The U.S. government has chosen salt formations near Carlsbad, New Mexico, as a permanent waste site, but a broad coalition of Chicanos, Indians, ranchers, unions, and environmentalists is working to prevent waste storage in their neighborhood because of the apparent hazards. (See "Stopping the WIPP Before It Cracks," page 406.)

A recent suggestion involves dropping bullet-shaped waste containers into the ocean, where they will theoretically sink to the bottom of deep basins and embed themselves in red clay deposits. There will be political objections to using international territory for such a risky project and more research needs to be done on the effect of the hot waste on the clay. Any leakage would be a catastrophe for marine life, and currents would circulate the radioactivity throughout the world. It would mean disposing of the containers in proximity to, if not directly in contact with, seawater —one of nature's most powerful dissolving agents. Also, any storage method must allow for retrieval of the waste if leakage is discovered. Retrieval from the ocean floor would be extremely difficult, probably impossible.

No matter which method of disposal is chosen, radioactive waste storage facilities will have to be built to last—tens of thousands of years longer than any building now standing. They will have to be our most permanent creations. The Egyptians are remembered for their pyramids, the Greeks for their temples and stadiums, the medieval Europeans for their cathedrals. Our legacy might be our poisonous radioactive garbage dumps.

K.F.

DEFUNCT NUCLEAR PLANTS

The ultimate waste from a nuclear power plant is the plant itself. A commercial reactor can only operate for thirty to forty years. When it stops operating, 15 to 20 percent of its contents remain radioactive. Andre Cregut, designer of France's Phoenix breeder reactor, thinks that a closed reactor could be even more dangerous than one that is operating, because many of the security devices will have been removed. Cregut believes that dismantling the reactor is the only way to guarantee safety, but no one is certain if dismantlement is feasible.

When a plant closes, it is first mothballed (welded shut with steel), then entombed (completely encased in concrete), and eventually dismantled. Thus far, twenty prototype reactors have been shut down; only five have gone beyond mothballing, and not even one of these relatively small reactors has been dismantled. Because old reactors are so radioactive, the entire dismantling process must be done by remote control and could cost as much as $100 million. While a reactor is mothballed or entombed, it must be guarded for safety. Leaks are likely, and the reactor remains radioactive for up to 250,000 years.

By the turn of the century, one hundred reactors around the world may have shut down, and by 2020 all 233 commercial reactors in operation in 1979 may be ready for the graveyard, even if we are not prepared to bury them. K.F.

Wavemakers:

STOPPING THE WIPP BEFORE IT CRACKS

On July 16, 1945, the sky suddenly flashed over a stretch of New Mexico desert known to residents as the Jornada del Muerto, the Journey of the Dead. To those with security clearance the place had another name—the codeword "Trinity." What happened there that day was the dawning of a new age for modern society. In New Mexico's barren desert the cousin of the atomic bombs sent to Hiroshima and Nagasaki was first tested, and its shock waves are still being felt.

Since that first encounter with the power of the atom, New Mexico has had many others. The state's isolation was a plus for military experimentation in nuclear weaponry, and it even had convenient reserves of uranium. These natural assets quickly made New Mexico the nuclear research hub of the United States. The state is, in fact, so entangled in the nuclear age that government officials expected little opposition to a proposal in 1972 to make New Mexico the nation's nuclear garbage dump.

Proposed disposal site for radioactive wastes near Carlsbad, New Mexico.

The untidy problem of what we do with nuclear wastes has been around since that first bomb test in 1945, but very little had actually been done to solve it. For many years, the U. S. Atomic Energy Commission (AEC) spent less than one tenth of 1 percent of its budget on solving the waste problem. As opposition to nuclear energy and the amounts of wastes accumulating in temporary pools increased, the problem intensified.

It was first thought that the wastes could be stored in dry salt beds near Lyons, Kansas. The site was quickly ruled out however; public opposition was strong and scientists found the beds riddled with oil drilling holes. Northeastern Michigan was the next candidate. After a few short months of discussion, and again, public outcry, the governor of Michigan told the federal officials to look somewhere else. Later, eleven other states followed suit, passing legislation prohibiting the disposal of radioactive wastes within their borders.

So with a great deal of pressure from the beleaguered nuclear industry, the federal Department of Energy (DOE), AEC's successor, selected New Mexico.

The DOE's plan, known as WIPP (Waste Isolation Pilot Plant), proposed to inter permanently millions of cubic feet of radioactive waste in the salt beds near Carlsbad, New Mexico. Although it is called a pilot project, plans are, in reality, full-scale and permanent. The site would be large enough to hold all the commercial and military radioactive wastes produced "well into the twenty-first century."

At first New Mexico residents knew very little about WIPP. Only the federal and state government officials, a few concerned citizens, and public interest groups were even aware of the project. But in 1977 a group of Carlsbad citizens formed the Carlsbad Nuclear Waste Forum in an attempt to find out more about WIPP.

"I was very ignorant about the project," said Roxanne Kartchner, a homemaker and president of the citizen group. "But I thought that whatever was going on should happen only in open discussion. I have a little boy; he is seven years old. It is my responsibility to see that the future is safe for him every way I can. So I got involved. I'm very opposed to the project now. I think the public was deceived."

As the citizens researched WIPP, they found that the U. S. Geological Survey, the U. S. Environmental Protection Agency, and many individual scientists had begun to question the safety of disposing radioactive wastes in salt. They also learned that the New Mexico site, chosen because the salt bed was apparently stable and had minimal water that could corrode the buried waste containers, was very near other deep salt formations that had been dissolved by water intrusions. DOE reports acknowledging that fact, the citizen group charges, were withheld by the agency.

As the group continued probing the WIPP proposal, they uncovered more problems. Seismographic studies revealed that a dangerous fault line runs right through the WIPP site. They also found that some transportation accidents would inevitably occur and no property insurance would cover them. As in other places, property values along transportation routes could decline. Armed with these alarming discoveries, the Carlsbad Nuclear Waste Forum resolved to battle the plan. As it launched its campaign against WIPP, the Forum quickly found natural allies in New Mexico's large Native American and Chicano populations. The history of Chicano, Indian, and Anglo relations have been rocky, and the task of building an antinuclear alliance was formidable, but the groups formed a coalition—Citizens for Alternatives to Radioactive Dumping (CARD)—to coordinate their anti-WIPP activities. The coalition, largely composed of citizens in towns along the routes where the nuclear waste was to be transported, launched a sophisticated media campaign to crystallize public opposition to the project. The campaign included one sixty-second television commercial that aired during the local news, the 1978 World Series, and other programs, fifty radio spots, and twenty newspaper ads. The media messages, one of which won a national award for the best low-budget TV commercial, exhorted New Mexico citizens to question the project and the problems of transportation. Close to one thousand responses were received directly from the media campaign, enlarging and strengthening CARD. The group also initiated a petition drive among the state's 1.25 million people; as of 1979 over 25,000 signatures had been secured, with more on the way. CARD has sponsored rallies, press conferences, door-to-door canvassing, and whirlwind speaking tours to build momentum against the project. These efforts are paying off—recent opinion polls have shown that New Mexico residents line up three to two against WIPP.

The issue is far from resolved. Federal officials remain committed to WIPP, and with equal vehemence citizen groups oppose it. Those groups won a major victory in February 1980, however, when President Jimmy Carter announced his opposition to the Carlsbad waste disposal plan. While the project hangs in the balance, so too, in large measure, does the future of the nuclear industry; the waste issue has become the industry's Achilles heel. Meanwhile, the unlikely citizen alliance battling WIPP in New Mexico remains confident of the outcome. The nuclear industry, which always found New Mexico a tolerant host, has discovered that the "Land of Enchantment" may not be so enchanted with the nuclear age after all.

J.N., B.P.B.

CHEMICAL WASTES

About 35 million tons of hazardous chemical wastes, capable of causing sickness, cancer, immediate death, and birth defects, are produced each year in the United States (see "Birth Defects," page 418). They remain dangerous for thousands of years and are difficult to store without leakage. And in one important way—proliferation—they are at least as much a problem as nuclear radiation. More than 70,000 chemicals are in commercial use, and as many as 20 percent of these are suspected carcinogens. In the United States alone more than 270,000 sources produce hazardous waste, which is transported by 25,000 different companies, to be disposed of at perhaps 50,000 sites.

In the United States, where such chemicals are regulated, accidents are common and thousands of dump sites are considered perilous. Many countries throughout the world lack even minimal regulations for hazardous chemicals. And everywhere dangers of chemical waste are only vaguely understood. One problem is that some substances have catalytic effects: harmless chemicals can become toxic in certain combinations, or a mildly toxic substance can become a thousand times more dangerous in the presence of another chemical. These interactions are very difficult to pinpoint, since a thousand new chemicals enter commercial production each year. The production of almost all of the world's food and the bulk of its manufactured goods involves hazardous chemicals, not all of which can be eliminated. Yet risks can be lessened by safe handling. About 75 percent of the waste can be treated to recover usable chemicals without excessive expense, and many dangerous substances need never leave the plant.

Robert Pojasek, a specialist in hazardous waste disposal, has outlined methods of safer disposal of toxic wastes—methods that are followed by few industries because they are complicated and expensive and because government controls to force industries to abide by safe disposal practices have been extremely lax. (According to the U. S. Environmental Protection Agency, only 10 percent of U.S. waste is safely discarded.)

Pojasek suggests detoxifying certain dangerous chemicals at the plant by mixing them with other chemicals that would lessen their toxicity. These stabilized wastes can then be solidified to prevent them from mixing with water and air and spreading into the environment, where some of them could undergo further reactions and become toxic again. Finally, the solid blocks could be buried in a landfill of impermeable clay, lined with a waterproof, synthetic material to prevent contact with groundwater. Blocks of various substances should be isolated from each other in the burial ground to prevent any possibility of chemical interaction. An accurate record should be kept of what is buried where. Even with all these precautions, the landfills should be monitored for twenty years to detect the escape of any toxic chemicals through the groundwater.

This procedure would certainly increase the cost of disposal; but the "cheap" disposal methods bear hidden costs that later appear in tax bills or medical bills. Cleaning up a chemical dump costs at least ten times as much as properly disposing of the chemicals in the first place.

Other options include incineration for some mildly toxic substances, deep-well disposal in geological reservoirs, and emplacement in stable geological formations. Some of these methods are expensive, others unreliable.

Unfortunately, disposal only applies to waste generated at a specific location, such as a chemical plant. The EPA estimates that 50 percent of water pollution comes from distant, often untraceable, sources, particularly agriculture and urban runoff.

The real answer to chemical pollution is careful testing and regulation before a new substance enters production. Some substances are so toxic and created for such frivolous use that they simply should not be produced. Other killer chemicals do have legitimate uses, but their production, distribution, and disposal must be carefully monitored.

Regulating the chemical industry is no easy task (see "Better Living Through Chemistry?" page 507). Doing so is asking it to restrict production of potentially profitable substances and to bear more of the costs of disposal, now paid for by taxpayers or by the victims of chemical pollution (see "Living on the Love Canal," page 657).

The United States has half-heartedly tried to regulate its chemical industry: during its first eight years of existence, the U. S. Environmental Protection Agency established limits for only four hazardous air pollutants and six toxic water pollutants. Meanwhile the agency is defending itself in two hundred lawsuits filed by industries contesting its regulations.

The EPA withstood strong opposition from the chemical industry when it demanded that industries report what chemicals they were using so the agency could track down the source of toxic chemicals in the environment. Industry claimed that revealing this information would be giving away trade secrets. The EPA has estimated that as many as 2,000 waste dumps could become immediate hazards by 1982, but it hasn't the budget to do anything about cleaning them up.

K.F.

WASTES IN THE SEA

The sea was the first cesspool, the first sewage treatment plant. It has processed the organic waste, the debris, the dead husks of living things since life evolved in its muddy shallows 3.5 billion years ago. The system tolerates, even thrives on this natural excrement. The animal life of the great depths would not survive without the nourishment of waste matter raining down from more populated surface waters. According to John D. Isaacs of the Scripps Institution of Oceanography in California, gray whales contribute more fecal matter to the sea worldwide than the Los Angeles sewer system does; so do anchovies.

Surface wastes foul a harbor in Esberg, Denmark. More damaging wastes often accumulate undersea, where they are invisible to humans. (*UN*)

There are also natural oil leaks in the sea. Seepage from sub-sea deposits wells up in many places around the world. In 1793, Captain George Vancouver noted in his logbook a great oil slick off the California coast near what is now Santa Barbara. This natural seepage contributes about 660,000 tons of petroleum to the sea every year.

A Sea of Misconceptions

Because the sea and its organisms can handle this load of natural wastes very well, the misconception has arisen that there is no limit to what the sea can dispose of in its self-purification systems. The human waste from a large city like Los Angeles may be of a comparable volume to that of certain marine animals, but it is greatly concentrated in one location, not dispersed widely, and it is usually spiked with toxic substances that the sea may be unable to recycle naturally. There *is* natural seepage of petroleum into the sea from ocean floor deposits, but human-caused oil pollution is now about ten times that rising naturally from the ocean bottom.

Perhaps the most pernicious misconception about the sanitation system of the ocean, however, is that coastal dumping is a negligible contribution to an environment so vast and deep, covering nearly three quarters of the planet's surface. The fact is that most of the sea's life is concentrated along the world's coastlines, where nutrient-rich currents pass across convenient hiding and attachment surfaces shallow enough to be touched by sunlight. Of the 140 million square miles (363 million square kilometers) of ocean surface, it is only the 14 million square miles (36 million square kilometers) near shore that contain the sea's most important living habitats. About 90 percent of the world's food fish spawn, mature, and are caught in these coastal areas.

The Crowded Ocean Rim

Unfortunately, the land adjacent to these productive waters is where human populations gather, where many industries locate, where the greatest mass of destructive waste matter is dumped. Of the twenty largest metropolitan areas in the world, sixteen are coastal cities, or cities on rivers that empty relatively quickly into the ocean. About 30 billion gallons (113 billion liters) of industrial and municipal wastes are discharged into the coastal areas of the United States alone every year.

Historically, the world's most extensive industrial activities have been concentrated in Western Europe and the northeastern United States. This means that a disproportionate share of the most dangerous ocean wastes are accumulating in the North Atlantic, carried into it by Western Civilization's most polluted rivers, including the Rhine, the Seine, the Rhône, the Thames, the Tiber, the Delaware, and the Hudson. (There is cause for hope, though, as some of these rivers improve: see "The Thames," page 340, and "The Hudson River," page 327.)

Does all of this mean that the wastes accumulating in the sea are crippling it, poisoning the planetary blood system? Too little is known about the processes of the ocean to be certain. At present, too many materials are entering it at too great a rate from too many dispersal points for science to extract simple answers.

On the basis of the toxicity and the volume of many wastes entering the sea, however, it does seem likely that sea life could be seriously disrupted in some places more than others, but the threat *is* global.

Soils and Spoils

By far the largest amount of "waste" matter entering the sea is sediment from the land. This would not be worthy of mention, since erosion is a vital, natural process, except that human mismanagement of land has greatly escalated the phenomenon into a thick global wave of muddy water that pours into the sea, suffocating life, smothering reefs, clogging the life-sustaining mechanisms of many ocean species.

It has been estimated that the flow to the sea of river-borne suspended solids before humans appeared was about 9.3 billion metric tons per year. Today that figure has risen to about 24 billion metric tons per year.

The load of silt reaching the streams, rivers, and coastal habitats of the United States is about seven hundred times greater than the total sewage discharge of the country. The proof that much of this soil could be saved lies in figures that show how much higher erosion rates become around development projects. Erosion at highway construction sites in an average rainstorm is ten times that of cultivated land, three hundred times that of pasture land, and two thousand times that of a forest area. (See "Topsoil," page 394.)

Of wastes dumped directly and deliberately into the sea, as much as 80 percent consist of "dredge spoils," the materials scraped from river and harbor bottoms to open channels and facilitate navigation. These materials are natural, for the most part, made up of sand, silt, clay, and rock. They are usually barged to offshore areas and dumped, often grossly disrupting these undersea locations for a period of time. Since these "spoils" often include a high proportion of deposited sewage sludge and accumulated industrial waste, the result of dredging is that the original insult to one habitat is compounded by transferring the pollutants—and their potential toxicity—to a second location.

Oil

A 1975 U. S. National Academy of Sciences (NAS) report estimates that about 6 million metric tons of petroleum enter the ocean each year. This appears to be a conservative figure especially in light of growing consumption and transport. Some researchers calculate that tanker contributions alone account for as much as 6 million metric tons—or soon will. But although about half of the oil transported in the world each year is carried by tankers, most of the oil accumulating in the sea does not arrive there as a result of shipping accidents. (More tanker oil is dumped as part of routine operations, such as illegal deballasting and tank washing, which flush oil into the sea.) However, most of the oil in the sea comes from a combination of land-based industrial and municipal sources. As much as 350 million gallons (1.3 billion liters) of used automobile crankcase oil is dumped each year into water drainage systems that reach the sea. About 600,000 metric tons of oil run into the sea each year as a result of petroleum carried into the atmosphere from poorly tuned automobile engines.

Once oil compounds reach the sea, several things can happen to them. Most of the compounds in oil will evaporate, oxidize, or degrade as a result of bacterial action. Some of the petroleum dissolves, some settles or accumulates as tar balls, some becomes a surface film, and some enters marine organisms. In 1975 the NAS estimated that the world's seawater was burdened with 400 million metric tons of dissolved petroleum. Surface films containing hydrocarbons in varying densities are ubiquitous around the world, according to another study, though more common and heavier in shipping lanes. Tar balls have been estimated at 700,000 metric tons with greatest concentrations in the Sargasso Sea, the Mediterranean, the Kuroshio current off Asia, the

Gulf Stream, the Canary and north equatorial current, and the Indian Ocean.

Tar lumps are consumed by some fish (the most extensive study involved sauries, a Pacific and Atlantic fish), but the effects of this ingested oil are unknown. Low concentrations of oil in surrounding waters have been shown to cause anesthesia and drowsiness among fish. (See "Messages in the Sea," page 383.) Young forms of marine life are especially vulnerable. Thick oil clogs the gills of fish and the baleen of whales. (See "The Business of Supertankers," page 489, and "Wetlands," page 379.)

Chemicals

Over 70,000 chemical compounds are sold commercially throughout the world. In the United States alone, 6,000 new chemicals are created every week and about 1,000 enter production every year. Of these perhaps 100 become commercially important. Many of these synthetics—some harmless, some deadly, most unanalyzed for their effects on the environment—eventually reach the ocean.

Many controversial compounds have been banned by individual nations, but few are completely eliminated. DDT production and use continues in some parts of the world, where, in fact, it serves as the most effective means of destroying disease-carrying insects. But as a result of present and past spraying of this persistent pesticide, DDT is still found in plankton samples throughout the world and in the tissues of arctic seals and antarctic penguins. The scattering effect of the atmosphere appears to be the distribution system. DDT sprayed on African fields showed up in 1961 in the Bay of Bengal and the Caribbean. Some scientists believe that two thirds of the 1.5 million metric tons of DDT produced before 1970, when production was uncontrolled, may still be in sediments on the ocean bottom.

Like DDT, the more recently emerging PCBs—chemically related as halogen-containing, polyaromatic organic compounds—are found throughout the world's plankton samples and in arctic and antarctic mammals. PCBs are widely used in electric and heat-transfer equipment, and were formerly used in hydraulic fluids, paints, plastics, and paper products. There are as many as eighty different PCB compounds. Before the dangers of these compounds became widely known in the early 1970s, the United States and Japan, combined, produced more than 50,000 metric tons annually and European nations accounted for about an equal amount. Plankton samples in the Gulf of St. Lawrence, taken during the mid-1970s, contained residues of PCBs as high as 93,000 parts per million. (The FDA has designated 5.0 ppm as the acceptable level of PCBs in fish tissues.) Other areas of alarming PCB concentrations: the coasts of Scotland, California, and Iceland.

The effects of these long-persistent chemical compounds are only now being determined. PCBs appear to cause sea lions to abort, and they kill shrimp when discharged in high concentrations. Mirex, a compound used to combat fire ants and as a flame-retardant in some plastics, has been shown to be lethal to crab larvae and young crayfish. Some of the disposed wastes from polyvinyl chloride production have affected fish in the North Sea.

There are suspicions that many other common chemicals are affecting sea life, including cleaning solvents and the chlorofluorocarbons used as refrigerants and aerosol propellants. (These are the same compounds thought to be endangering the protective ozone layer of the upper atmosphere.) The annual world production is estimated at 1 million tons. (See "The Ozone Layer," page 295.)

The effects of chemicals and other contaminating matter on the vitality of the ocean have drawn the concern of nations throughout the world. As early as 1972 the U. S. Environmental Protection Agency (EPA) was given jurisdiction over dumping off U.S. coasts, in association with the Coast Guard, which acts as the policing force. Over the years their regulatory powers have been strengthened. It is unlawful for municipalities or industries in the United States to dump in the sea without an EPA permit, and permits are not granted if the material involved would adversely affect human health or the marine environment or if there is a feasible alternative dumping site. The EPA encourages dumpers to find land sites, using the sea only as a last resort. A certain amount of industrial waste dumping continues, however, along the east coast (1.7 million tons in 1977) and the Gulf Coast (60,000 tons in 1977), but no dumping at all is allowed in the Pacific (there are more alternative land dumping sites in the West).

Dumping of wastes containing carcinogens or mutagens is illegal in U.S. waters, and while wastes from the manufacture of pharmaceuticals, chemical products, cosmetics, and explosives are occasionally allowed, the EPA monitors the quantities to ensure safety and issues temporary permits with the intention of phasing out these operations.

In 1972, thirty-three nations signed an ocean dumping treaty similar in its structure to the EPA program. The London Ocean Dumping Convention decreed that, beginning in 1975, member nations would restrict marine pollution by requiring permits for dumping of wastes at sea. While dangerous chemicals continue to be deposited in the ocean, there is optimism that unchecked pollution through dumping is on its way out as governments realize the serious implications to the sea and to the future use of the sea as a resource. Hazardous chemicals still enter the ocean through the atmosphere, river systems, and, to an extent, by passing through sewage treatment plants, but direct dumping seems to be a diminishing threat, at least in the nearshore areas of thirty-three nations.

Metals

The effects of accumulating metals in the sea are not well understood. There are documented cases involving mercury (see "The Dancing Cats of Minamata," page 517) and some other trace metals, but there are many mysteries to be unraveled. It is known that about 20,000 metric tons of lead enter the sea each year, most of it from automobile exhaust fumes that wash into the ocean from the atmosphere. About the same amount of lead enters the sea naturally through river discharges of eroded matter. While lead is known to impair human cell metabolism and nervous function, no deleterious effects have yet been proven among ocean animals. Likewise, about 5,000 tons of mercury enter the sea each year, mostly as a result of industrial dumping. This about equals the natural contribution from the land. Mercury can be highly toxic, but it depends on the concentrations and the organisms involved. Sometimes inorganic mercury is altered by natural processes to become poisonous methyl mercury. The case of the Minamata deaths in Japan is an example.

Sewage

The chief danger of ocean sewage dumping lies in the spread of viral and bacterial diseases—directly to bathers, indirectly through fishery products. Persistent viruses and bacteria are accumulated by filter-feeding clams and oysters, which find their way to our tables.

In some parts of the world, the solid sludge residue from sewage processing plants is dumped directly into the sea. Where this matter is produced in great quantities, dumping can create a smothering carpet of muck across large areas of the seafloor. As of 1975, nearly 4 billion gallons (15 billion liters) of municipal waste were being discharged into the coastal areas of the forty-eight contiguous U.S. states every day. The emergence of vile sludge on beaches near New York City in 1976 proved that these materials are not completely eliminated by deep-sea biological processes. United States officials have since acted to control further sludge problems; as of December 31, 1981, sewage sludge cannot be dumped in U.S. waters according to Congressional mandate.

Radioactivity

The entry of significant amounts of radioactive matter into the sea is a potentially catastrophic development, but at present the damage does not appear to be widespread. With the decreases in atmospheric nuclear weapons testing since the 1960s, the inventories of deadly materials such as strontium-90 and cesium-137 have diminished. This situation could take a dramatic turn for the worse, of course, with the advent of even a small-scale nuclear conflict.

There has been and continues to be dumping of low-level radioactive wastes in the sea as a result of nuclear power and weapons production. The United States dumped about 90,000 barrels of radiological wastes in the sea between 1946 and 1970, when this program was halted. The wastes were low-level—contaminated laboratory equipment and clothing, largely—and they were encased in concrete inside 55-gallon (208-liter) drums. There are indications that some of these barrels are corroding and the contents contaminating local areas (the most studied area is off the California coast near San Francisco), but the problem does not seem immediately critical.

The United Kingdom has dumped more than 65,000 metric tons of low-level wastes in the northeastern Atlantic and continues to dispose of waste shipments in the sea, from its own nuclear programs and those of the Netherlands, Switzerland, and Belgium. While these low-level wastes do not pose an immediate threat to marine life and humanity, there are serious future complications. It is unreasonable to expect metal containers that corrode in seawater to withstand deep-sea pressure forever, and when low-level radioactivity is released in the sea, certain marine organisms concentrate it in their bodies. Thus even mild amounts in seawater can become dangerous in seafood.

The planned growth of nuclear power and the resulting (projected) glut of radioactive wastes pose the threat of new proposals to bury these lethal wastes at sea. The disposal could include not only low-level wastes but plutonium (one of the most toxic substances on earth). This presents perhaps the most frightening future danger to the life of the seas and to the human generations dependent upon a healthy ocean.

Garbage

Litter is principally an aesthetic insult to the sea, which our senses and our romantic natures judge to be wrong.

However, there *are* serious problems with solid waste, mostly because there is so much of it. About 6 million metric tons of litter enter the sea each year. By far the greatest contributors of this matter are merchant ships, which cast away rubbish from their cargo packaging—plastics, metal, cloth, glass, and wood. Occasionally deck cargo itself is lost, including timbers and containers large enough to hold three automobiles. This shipping material accounts for about 90 percent of the litter in the sea; the rest can be blamed on commercial fishing boats, recreational boaters, and land-based waste dumps that deposit their loads in the sea. There have even been reports of large areas of the ocean littered with floating plastic sandals—refuse cast away from cruise ships. One problem with the large debris is that it can be hazardous to small ships, while the small pieces of litter can be ingested by fish.

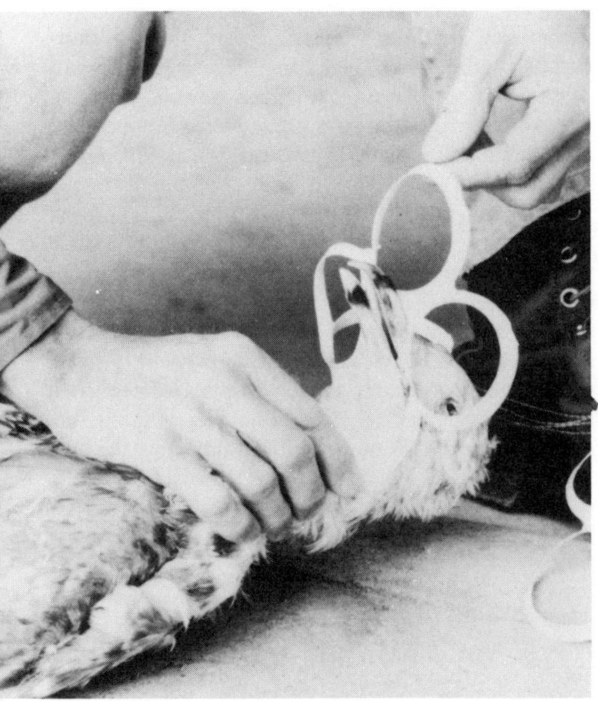

After its bill became entangled in a plastic six-pack holder, this seagull starved to death. (*U. S. Fish and Wildlife Service/John Wilbrecht*)

Weapons

Because it is such a convenient hiding place for wastes, the sea has long been a receptacle for obsolete weaponry. After World War II more than thirty thousand bombs and cannisters containing poison gases—along with other unwanted munitions, mostly German—were dumped into the southern Baltic Sea between Sweden and the Danish island of Bornholm in 295 feet (90 meters) of water. In 1969 these rusting cannisters came back to haunt Baltic shorelines. Leaking mustard gas injured fishermen and panicked bathers along the coasts of Sweden and Bornholm. Danish fishermen caught at least sixteen mustard-gas bombs in their nets. Suspected contamination from these materials caused the boycotting of thousands of tons of fish. There was speculation that currents, tides, or trawler's gear had shifted the cannisters close to shore.

In 1976, mustard-gas bombs washed ashore along the Welsh coast, the deadly debris from the dumping of British chemical munitions off the coasts of Scotland and Ireland between 1945 and 1956.

The United States has disposed of obsolete chemical warfare agents in the sea on at least three known occasions, in 1967, 1968, and 1970. The materials were embedded in concrete within steel vaults and carried several hundred miles out to sea aboard obsolete ships, which were scuttled. The well-publicized 1970 case involved the sinking of a ship about 250 miles (400 kilometers) east of Florida. It contained about 134,000 pounds (60,800 kilograms) of sarin, a lethal nerve agent. Estimates place the 1968 scuttling at 387,000 pounds (175,500 kilograms) of sarin, and the 1967 dumping at nearly 450,000 pounds (204,000 kilograms). The effects these agents might have on the sea is not known.

In the early 1960s, the U. S. Department of Defense began disposing of outdated war materials by loading them aboard World War II "liberty" ships, which were sunk over designated sites offshore. Between 1963 and 1970 nineteen ships carried over 48,000 metric tons of obsolete shells, mines, and solid rocket fuels to the ocean bottom. Approximately 18,000 metric tons of this was composed of explosives and munitions.

Money: The Ultimate Ocean Waste

In an era when the costs of energy and materials are rocketing, when rich topsoil is a precious commodity needed to produce enough food to sustain humanity, when petroleum and other finite resources are rapidly approaching depletion, waste has become unethical. The millions of tons of oil that fouls ocean systems each year is squandered oil and it represents lost money. The lead and copper that leave factories to wash wastefully into the sea have a value. The sewage we dump could be recycled as agricultural fertilizer and, along with sludge and garbage, could be utilized as an energy source.

The profits from revitalized fisheries, were we to halt the seaward flood of sludge, toxic chemicals, industrial poisons, pesticides, radionuclides, and dredge spoils, cannot be accurately estimated, but the increased production of marine systems might be significant. Another immeasurable cost, perhaps the most important, is in human health care as an ocean accumulating poisons returns its diseases to us. Many hazardous substances—DDT, radionuclides, mercury, cadmium, oil derivatives, viral agents, and bacteria—are concentrated into deadly portions as they pass up the food web from plankton to the seafood we consume. The irony is that the valuable resources we disgorge into the sea, when they *do* return to us, come back in destructive ways. In our polluting relationships with the sea, the tide goes out, but it comes back again, sometimes with a vengeance.

M.R.

GHOST SHIPS

Every year about a million tons' worth of ocean-going vessels are lost at sea. As authors Thomas Busha and James Dawson have pointed out, this represents a greater fleet of ships than the individual fleets of nearly one hundred nations of the world. Beyond the potential loss of human life and the localized impact on the seafloor, most of these sinkings do not endanger the sea. The obvious exceptions are those vessels laden with hazardous cargoes, such as chemicals, liquid nitrogen gas, and petroleum. (The United States has now lost at least two nuclear-powered submarines, the *Thresher* in the western Atlantic in 1963 and the *Scorpion* off the Azores in 1968. The Soviet Union may have lost as many as four between 1968 and 1971, two in the Atlantic, one in the Pacific, one in the Mediterranean.)

But there is another problem with lost ships besides their cargoes.

Some of them don't sink.

A Colombian steamer named the *Duarte* disappeared almost thirty years ago. She has been sighted nine times during the three decades since. A cargo ship, the *Dunmore,* has been seen adrift in open waters even more frequently. She was abandoned in 1908 when cargo shifted dangerously across her deck. In 1973 a French ore carrier, the *Montlucon,* was towed into a wrecker's yard after being discovered in the Bay of Bengal. She had been abandoned during a storm in 1951.

The danger is that these "ghost ships," some of them nearly submerged, will be struck by other vessels, perhaps sinking a ship loaded with dangerous substances—or people. In 1974 a cargo vessel, the *Herakos,* was rammed by a drifting derelict ship in the North Sea. The mysterious ship then seemed to disappear; yet a supply ship later sank in the same area and indications were that it too had been struck by some drifting object.

M.R.

Wavemakers:

THE FISH WAR OF WALTER KANDRASHOFF

Walter Kandrashoff, a fisherman for more than twenty years, doesn't fish in Biscayne Bay anymore. The long hours and low prices didn't stop him. It was the fish.

At first he only had to throw back a few fish from each catch. Then the numbers started to increase. Fish with bulging eyes. Fish with dangling tumors. Fish with gross deformities.

Kandrashoff, a blunt man with the observant and meticulous nature of a born scientist, is a native New Yorker who fished his hometown waters for two decades before moving to Florida. He had watched his New York catch diminish to the point where he could no longer support his family. And what was even more ominous, he had caught more and more fish that had "things wrong with them." The snappers feeding near sewage outfalls developed tumors all around their mouths. Like most other fishermen Kandrashoff had just avoided the area. But then he noticed that the fluke he was catching had also developed ragged fins or were missing tails. In New Jersey waters, the fish were swimming around in circles. By 1968 Kandrashoff had had it and moved his family to what he assumed would be the healthier, bluer waters of sunny Florida.

Kandrashoff had a good first year in the South, fishing the waters of Biscayne Bay. Biscayne Bay separates the city of Miami proper from Miami Beach and from the island of Key Biscayne; its shoreline is now home for a million and a half people. Along one side of the bay some pristine areas remain. A few 12-foot (3.5-meter) crocodiles maintain residence in the canals that cool the waters from the Turkey Point nuclear power plant; a bald eagle soars over her nest above Fisher Island's rubble-strewn beach; and, in the Miami River, occasional herds of manatees brave the boat traffic. The bay is still a vital bird feeding ground, rookery, nursery, and winter stop-over. It has been called a birdwatcher's delight. There are supposed to be as many as five hundred species of fish in the bay's waters, and for Kandrashoff, the fish were abundant and seemed healthy.

Kandrashoff's love affair with the area ended abruptly only two short years after his arrival. By early 1970 he was catching emaciated pompano—"just skin and bones." The next year he began finding mullet with tumors. He caught a porgy with a tumor deeply embedded in front of its dorsal fin, and a crevalle jack whose whole body was covered with red sores; near the jack's tail was a spongy tumor the size of Kandrashoff's thumb.

"I'd been a fisherman all my life and I'd never seen anything like those jack," he said. "Something was really wrong."

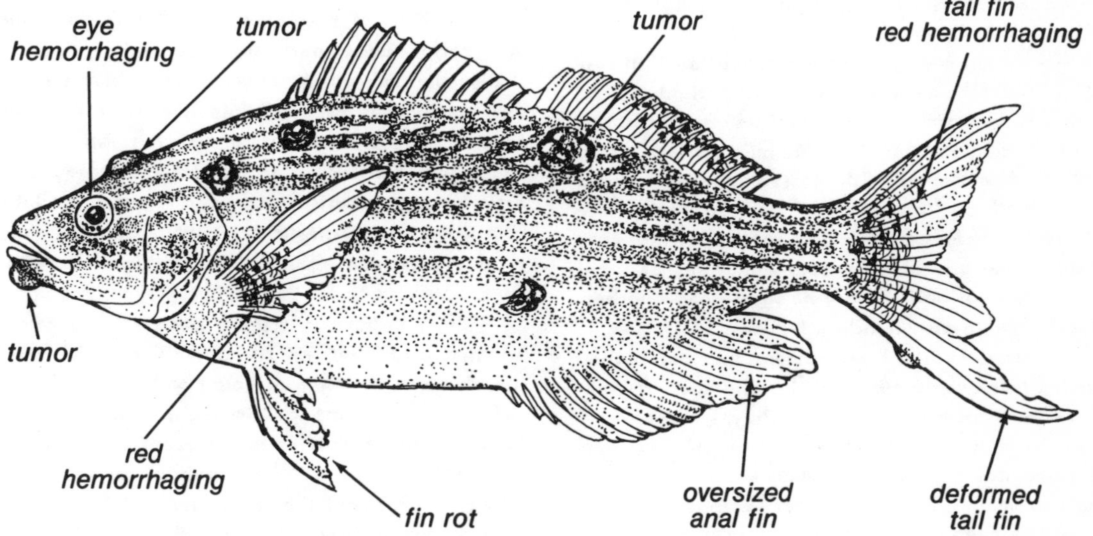

Fish maladies possibly caused by water pollution.

Miami once had seventy outfall pipes spewing raw sewage into the bay. That flow was supposedly halted in the mid-1950s. The bay today meets all state and local pollution standards. However, the director of the county's Environmental Resource Management Department has gone on record saying: "Being a fish in Biscayne Bay is a little like walking around on the streets of New York after dark. It might not kill you, but there are a lot of other places that might be better for your health."

Kandrashoff took his first sickly pompano to the scientists at the University of Miami's Rosenstiel School of Marine and Atmospheric Science. He was told the fish had parasites. "Nothing abnormal," the UM specialists told the unbelieving fisherman. And, besides, where was the baseline data for comparison? After that, Kandrashoff began taking careful notes on all of his catches.

Going door-to-door with his gruesome specimens netted little help. The local scientific community seemed more annoyed by his presence than interested in his findings. When they kidded him about his persistence, he told them, in his loud Brooklyn accent, "I come from a very long line of stubborn people."

One scientist who worked in a UM Medical School lab that Kandrashoff had begun to frequent remembered, "Walter came on very strong. He'd bring in a fish and an hour later he'd call and demand to know what was wrong with it."

Kandrashoff did begin to learn about diseases in fish. Those bloody patches of red he saw on the fish were hemorrhages. The eroded tails he found in New York and then in Biscayne Bay were caused by bacterial fin rot, a disease thought to be influenced by sewage effluent. Armed with his new-found knowledge and the conviction that Biscayne Bay fish were being polluted right out of existence, he stormed into Miami newspaper offices and television stations. One Miami reporter, whose desk had a lot of fish tossed on it, labeled Kandrashoff an "awful pest," but "a really nice guy. He's a street-smart sort of person. Walter saw things in the bay other people didn't see or want to see. He's not half-cocked; he's got good hunches. People need to play hunches."

The Miami Tourist Development members called Kandrashoff an alarmist and the Chamber of Commerce was naturally horrified. They were already upset by area doctors' reports of greater numbers of urogenital infections in young women who had been swimming in Miami area waters. The last thing they needed was this loud fisherman running loose with a bag full of hideous-looking samples. (Kandrashoff had a ploy of showing up at Chamber of Commerce meetings carrying a canvas satchel full of diseased fish he'd caught that day.) The Chamber of Commerce, the Tourist Authority, television, press, everybody did turn up for a "Conference on Fish Pollution" arranged by Kandrashoff and a young intern from the University of Miami Medical School. Kandrashoff and his sole supporter showed maps and slides, and gave a pitch about pollution. But when they finished, a U. S. Marine Fisheries employee arose and proclaimed he had done a survey of all the fish markets in the Miami area and he hadn't found a single diseased fish. The fish markets! Walter was aghast at the official's naivete. Obviously, fishermen were not selling their *deformed* fish to the markets.

In 1973, the University of Miami began studying the bay's fish. The state's Department of Natural Resources also conducted a survey and found that fishermen all along the Florida Gulf Coast were catching fish with tumors. Surveys from Maine to California were uncovering the same horrors Kandrashoff carried around in his satchel.

In 1974, Kandrashoff wrote in his notes: "This year showed not only a continuation of the previous symptoms in many species of fish, but also changes are occurring that, to my mind, are startling. Either the genetic code is being altered or fish show abnormal development in the early stages of life. It is my personal belief that both of these changes are taking place simultaneously."

At first Kandrashoff thought the fish problems were caused by bacteria in sewage. But then he started thinking about chemicals; he'd read and reread Rachel Carson's *Silent Spring*. "I'm not a chemist, I'm not a scientist, but there's something very deadly about pesticides," he said.

Diseased fish in one of America's playgrounds is not something local officials like to talk about. Most of the possible causes of the fish diseases stem from activities that support the state's economy: heavy tourist populations and pollution along the shore, pesticide runoff from the state's orange orchards, industrial wastes from its industries.

"I don't believe in scaring people," one marine scientist said, "but on the other hand, I'm afraid there's some covering up going on."

For the most part, public health officials still behave as though they've never heard about the fish problems. Said the Miami public health director when asked about the consequences of eating fish from Biscayne Bay: "Honestly, this is the first I've heard about it—this is very disturbing news." If

there is a conspiracy of silence, Kandrashoff has been relentlessly blowing his whistle. And yet, all along the causeway over the bay, people can be seen hauling in fish, presumably to take home to the griddle. No doubt, the average tourist fishing Miami's waters doesn't have Kandrashoff's eye for scales gone awry or stripes all out of line. A tumor, however, is a hard thing to miss, but neither the tourists nor the fishing charter boat captains seem disturbed.

Scientists were able to identify every disease that Walter found in his fish. But they couldn't tell him why he was finding so many of them in beautiful Biscayne Bay, or whether or not the fish were fit for human consumption. Kandrashoff decided to stop fishing. "I didn't want to be a fisherman if the fish I was catching might poison someone," he said.

A study recently completed by the University of Miami Medical School shows that the fish in Biscayne Bay—and even the bay itself—may be sicker than even Walter Kandrashoff realized. The study reports that fish in the bay show symptoms of more than forty distinct diseases, including two strains of cholera. That's as high a level as can be found anywhere in the country except perhaps in the Hudson River in New York. The study strongly implicates pollution as the underlying cause of the diseases.

Other surveys have turned up unexplained concentrations of such trace metals as zinc, copper, and mercury. And high levels of pesticides and oil have been found in the sediment at the mouth of the Miami River. Some of the highest concentrations of PCBs found in the country are in the river's bottom mud. For most of its length, the Miami River is unfit for human contact, and this whole witch's brew is eventually dumped into Biscayne Bay.

Contaminated water may flush out of the bay eventually, but the gunk layered on the bottom is persistent. The incidence of disease among bottom-dwelling fish is nearly 100 percent. This bottom bay sediment has been likened to a time bomb that could go off any time it is disturbed by more dredging or by a major hurricane.

"We're living in a stressed environment," Kandrashoff said. "The ocean fish are still good and the Gulf Stream fish are good, but the estuary fish are bad. What's in the estuaries goes into the oceans, you know."

When the fishing goes bad, for whatever reason, commercial fishermen often move on to what they hope will be better waters. Many of Kandrashoff's friends from Biscayne Bay have moved to the Florida Keys. Kandrashoff moved from New York to Biscayne Bay. But there he has stopped to fight. He can't claim victory, and he is discouraged by the powerful forces that refuse to hear his warning. But he forced the scientific community to see and try to explain the sick fish of Biscayne Bay.

J.M.V.

SPACE JUNK

On July 11, 1979, the 85-ton U.S. space-station Skylab disintegrated and fell across an Australian desert, looking, observers said, like a train on fire in the sky. No one was hurt, but Skylab brought the attention of the world to a new problem: the space junk that has begun to ring our planet.

Estimates of the junk in outer space vary widely, because space junk can include discarded equipment and rocket stages as well as dying satellites and spacecraft. It is generally agreed that at least 4,500 pieces of space junk are presently orbiting the earth, and that about 6,900 pieces have already fallen back to earth, usually burning up in the atmosphere, like most meteors.

Still, in the quarter-century since Sputnik I was launched, there have been enough worrisome incidents to show that falling space junk could cause real damage. In 1960, a U.S. rocket exploded over Cuba, sending fragments over easternmost Oriente province and killing a cow. In 1962, 21 pounds (9.5 kilograms) of Sputnik IV fell on a main street in Wisconsin. In 1969, pieces of a Soviet satellite hit a Japanese freighter, and later the same year parts of a U.S. moon-shot booster fell on a German ship. In 1970, five 150-pound (68-kilogram) steel fragments from a Soviet spacecraft fell on Kansas, Oklahoma, and Texas. In 1978, the Soviet Union's satellite Cosmos 954 crashed in the Northwest Territories of Canada. In none of these incidents has anyone been killed or even injured; but the potential for an accident was there.

The Soviet Cosmos crash was controversial in another way. The Cosmos 954, like twenty-five other U.S. and Soviet satellites (nine American, sixteen Soviet), contained a nuclear power reac-

Wastes in space. Artist's conception of the variety of satellites circling the globe. After they outlive their usefulness, they continue on their paths or eventually fall to earth. (*NASA*)

tor that released radiation when it crashed. (The USSR declined to pay Canada for the cost of cleaning up the debris, although it is a party to a U.N. treaty mandating that it do so.) Although the Cosmos fortunately landed in a region that was virtually uninhabited, one more orbit could have brought it directly over New York City.

The Cosmos 954 was designed not to return to Earth for five hundred to a thousand years, but a mechanical failure caused it to fall. On the other hand, Skylab was deliberately designed without a system for keeping it up or returning it to earth, in the expectation that it would stay aloft long enough for the planned space shuttle to rescue it. But Skylab came down prematurely, because of unpredicted sunspot activity affecting the upper atmosphere where it orbited. The dying Skylab, going 17,000 miles (27,000 kilometers) an hour, endangered only areas between fifty degrees north and fifty degrees south latitude—but that is where most of humanity lives.

The growing number of satellites and miscellaneous space junk may cause other problems, according to Donald Nessler and Burton Cour-Palais of the National Aeronautics and Space Administration. The two scientists believe that eventually the earth will be circled with Saturn-like rings composed of debris from colliding satellites. After the first collision, there will be more debris and more collisions, until the earth has its own "asteroid belt" of human-made dust between 310 and 740 miles up (500 to 1,200 kilometers). The scientists believe the formation of this belt can be postponed but not prevented.

The danger of Skylab, even if exaggerated by publicity, was real. If we continue to leave spent rocket stages and other refuse behind to float in space till they fall, we can expect more Skylab-type incidents in the future with increasing chances of damaging impact on earth.

J.S.

BIRTH DEFECTS

Bonnie Hill teaches high school, coaches basketball, and lives on a remote farm surrounded by Bureau of Land Management (BLM) timberland in Alsea, a small logging community in Oregon. In 1975, Bonnie Hill had a miscarriage. Two years later she read some studies of the effects of the herbicide 2,4,5-T and began to wonder about the cause of her miscarriage. She contacted the BLM and was told that the herbicides 2,4-D and silvex (2,4,5-TP) had been sprayed on the lands surrounding her home one month before she miscarried. She remembered hearing of former students in the Alsea area who had also miscarried during the spring of 1975. By talking to these women she learned of still others in the area who had miscarried at the same time.

The developing embryo and fetus can be affected to differing degrees by environmental forces. The critical period is usually the first two months of pregnancy. Birth defects resulting from negative influences during that period can include physical and mental abnormalities apparent at birth, low birth weight (considered a major cause of infant death and childhood disability), and physical and mental dysfunctions that may not become apparent until later in life. The American March of Dimes estimates that roughly one out of every twelve to fourteen babies born in the United States has a birth defect.

Birth defects have a variety of causes. About 20 percent are inherited. Another 20 percent result from the direct exposure of the mother to harmful environmental substances during pregnancy. The remaining 60 percent are caused by an indistinguishable interaction of genetic and environmental factors.

The placenta, the membranous filter that connects the embryo to the life-sustaining systems of the mother, is not the protective "barrier" it was traditionally thought to be. While it affords some degree of protection, most chemicals can cross the placenta to the embryo. All pollutants and toxins absorbed by the mother's bloodstream can reach the growing organism, although the amount of absorption will differ depending on the substance ingested.

But drugs and pollutants do not even need to cross the placenta in order to impair fetal growth. They can affect the mother, who in turn affects the fetus. The placental circulation from mother to fetus is monitored by a "program" in the brain of the mother, and this controls in turn the secretion of hormones from the pituitary. The balanced production of substances that regulate the secretion of ovarian hormones is essential for a proper placental circulation and a good continuous flow of blood and nutrients from mother to fetus. Drugs that act upon the maternal brain (e.g., alcohol, barbiturates, tranquilizers, heroin, marijuana) may affect pituitary and ovarian hormonal production and disturb placental circulation, causing fetal growth to be impaired. Drugs may also act directly in the placenta itself, impairing its normal support function and flow of nutrients.

Radiation

Ionizing radiation has long been known to harm the fetus, either when the mother is exposed to radioactive rays or when she inhales or ingests radioactive particles. The isotope iodine-131 accumulates in the developing thyroid, where it can damage cells and inhibit hormones that control growth patterns and the development of intelligence. Strontium-89 and -90, which chemically resemble calcium, can lodge in bones developing in the last trimester of pregnancy and can contaminate mother's milk. Plutonium, an extremely toxic substance, crosses the placenta to cause developmental defects. Radiation is bioaccumulative, building up in the body with each dose, and no one knows whether there is a safe dose.

Current standards come from studies by the U. S. Atomic Bomb Casualty Commission of 82,000 survivors of the bombings of Hiroshima and Nagasaki in 1945. They showed a significant increase in spontaneous abortions, stillbirths, and infant death rates. Children born of mothers who were near the Hiroshima explosion site developed microcephaly, a defect characterized by abnormally small heads and mental retardation. Of thirty pregnant women near the blast in Nagasaki, seven suffered miscarriages and the babies of six others died. Four of the surviving seventeen children were mentally retarded. Projecting the consequences of a major nuclear power plant meltdown, in which 10 million urban dwellers would be exposed to radiation, a United States Department of Energy report estimates that 100,000 fetuses could be at risk. All could develop cretinism, and fifteen hundred could be microcephalic.

No one is yet certain of the effects of the more typical environmental exposure to low doses of radiation over extended periods. Fallout from weapons testing, emissions from uranium mining, and leaks from power plants, fuel-processing facilities, and waste storage all contribute to environmental contamination. Dr. Linus Pauling, recipient of Nobel Prizes for Chemistry and Peace, wrote to The New York *Times* in 1958 to warn that the radioactive fallout from one year of weapons tests "will ultimately be responsible for the birth of 230,000 seriously defective children and also for 420,000 embryonic and neonatal deaths." In 1975, Joseph Lyon at the University of Utah College of Medicine surveyed the counties most exposed to U.S. bomb testing. He noted a higher incidence of leukemia among those children born during the years of the testing (1951–58) than among those born before or afterward, a rate 50 percent higher than that of the United States as a whole.

There is little a pregnant woman can do to avoid low-level radioactive contamination. However, extensive medical and dental X rays and radiopharmaceuticals are forms of the hazard that can and should be avoided. Studies in the 1920s showed that pregnant women who had X rays of their pelvic regions, even in the later months, had a higher incidence of serious birth defects in their children. British physician Alice Stewart of the University of Birmingham (England) estimated from her 1958 studies that a single pelvic X ray of a pregnant woman increased chances of leukemia in her child by 40 percent. Because X rays are potentially mutagenic, pregnant women should be particularly wary of any radioactive medical procedures.

Chemicals

With the growth of the chemical industry since World War II, pregnant women can be easily exposed to harmful substances through water and air pollution, residues accumulated in foods, and occupational contact.

Pesticides are dusted and sprayed directly into the environment, and while most have not been proven to be teratogenic to humans, many—especially the chlorinated hydrocarbons—are suspected mutagens. The herbicides sprayed near Bonnie Hill's farm are considered particularly dangerous: 2,4-D, 2,4,5-T, and silvex may be teratogenic, and the latter two are also consistently contaminated during manufacture with TCDD, popularly called dioxin. Dioxin is considered to be the most toxic synthetic chemical. It can pass through the skin. It concentrates in the food chain. It accumulates in human fat and has appeared in mother's milk.

Other chemicals contaminate the environment through industrial emissions, leaks, and dumping. In one accident in Japan, polychlorinated biphenyls (PCBs) were found in the placenta and fatty tissues of two stillborn babies. PCBs, passed through the placenta, caused a dark-brown skin stain in infants who also had a high frequency of other abnormalities, including growth retardation.

Heavy metals can cause serious toxic problems. While lead poisoning is usually associated with brain damage in children who have eaten paint chips, pregnant women who have inhaled or ingested forms of lead show a higher rate of abortions, stillbirths, and premature births. Lead from automobile exhaust is a major air polluter, and high blood-lead concentrations have been found in newborns of mothers living near expressways. Organic mercury dumped by a plastics manufacturer in Minamata Bay in Japan between 1953 and 1960 concentrated in fish, the major food source of the area. It resulted in cerebral palsy in infants exposed *in utero,* even when mothers showed no signs of mercury poisoning. (See "The Dancing Cats of Minamata," page 517.)

Combinations of certain apparently harmless chemicals can be dangerous. Even those shown to be safe can combine with other chemicals in the environment or in the human body to become hazardous. More than three hundred chemicals deposited in the Love Canal section of Niagara Falls, New York, in the 1940s were mixed together in a leaking Hooker Chemical Company dump. (See "Living on the Love Canal," page 657.) Health authorities estimate that 10 percent of them are probably teratogenic or mutagenic. Women in the area had three times the normal incidence of miscarriages, and children born there had three and a half times the normal incidence of birth defects.

The chemicals most implicated as teratogenic ("monster-causing," i.e., damaging to the genetic material of embryonic cells) in humans are drugs. Heroin addiction is known to be teratogenic, but many other medications can be toxins: aspirin (which can combine with benzoic acid in food preservatives to cause birth defects), antibiotics (particularly tetracycline), tranquilizers (such as Valium, Librium and Haldol), anticancer drugs, anticonvulsants, anticoagulants, antithyroid drugs, or iodide-containing cough medicines and asthma medications, to name a few. Sex hormones, especially estrogens, can cause cancer in offspring (see "DES Daughters," page 196). Cortisone and drugs for controlling diabetes can also be hazards, as can large doses of vitamin A early in pregnancy.

Babies of alcoholic mothers suffer from fetal alcohol syndrome and many die soon after birth; survivors may show mental retardation, microcephaly, and defects of the head and face. Even "moderate" drinkers have been shown to have babies with abnormalities.

Smoking, however, is perhaps the single most dangerous controllable prenatal hazard. An American Heart Association study released in January of 1979 showed that smoking increased risks of miscarriage, low birth weights, premature delivery, lethal birth defects, and later crib death. The best procedure is never to start smoking; the next best is to stop immediately.

Compared to alcohol and cigarettes, the widespread use of marijuana, especially by teenagers, is a relatively recent phenomenon, thus conclusive scientific evidence is not yet available on its health effects. However, a number of recent studies suggest that marijuana use may produce a number of long-term health problems and could affect developing fetuses. Experiments on four species of animals indicated that marijuana and its psychoactive ingredient THC impair fetal growth and development. Female monkeys treated with THC were four times more likely to abort or to have stillborn infants. Surviving male offspring of THC-treated females showed anomalies of behavior and neuroendocrine function. Studies by Dr. Gabriel Nahas of Columbia University showed marijuana affects the brain's hypothalamus, which directs the pituitary, the master gland that programs the functions of other hormone-producing glands.

The Workplace

One out of every four jobs in the United States exposes workers to hazardous substances. Although the pregnant woman and the fetus are so susceptible to harm, job policy often encourages women to hide their pregnancies, particularly in the first two critical months. No one knows how many pregnant women work, but a conservative estimate is that one million infants were exposed *in utero* to work conditions, safe and unsafe, in the United States in 1970.

Benzene and chlorodiphenyls are suspected of causing fetal damage and stillbirths. A study by Dr. Hildegard Halling (Sodertalje Hospital, Sodertalje, Sweden) of 460 children born to nurses at six Swedish hospitals using soaps containing hexachlorophene, a chemical related to dioxin, showed that 25 had severe congenital defects, a rate fifty times higher than normal.

The traditional solution has been to keep fertile women out of hazardous jobs. Women have already been forced off jobs in lead smelters and in battery manufacturing because of the danger of exposure to lead. Some women have chosen to be sterilized rather than lose their jobs. This policy mistakenly assumes that men can work safely with toxic substances without any effect on their future children, an assumption now shown to be erroneous.

Mutagens can create permanent, irreversible damage to genetic material in sperm cells as well as egg cells, in testes as well as ovaries. The damaged genetic material can be inherited from *either* parent or from both. Environmental mutagens can also prevent conception by causing male sterility, low sperm counts, sperm abnormalities, and loss of sexual drive.

Studies funded by the United Auto Workers show that men working with lead in battery factories or in printing factories have exhibited decreased fertility and a greater likelihood of transmitting birth defects to their children. Their wives have a higher than normal rate of miscarriage. The exposure of the father to hydrocarbons has been linked to a higher incidence of childhood cancers.

Exposure to gas anesthetics has been correlated with higher rates of stillbirths, miscarriages, and malformations in operating room nurses, doctors, and the wives of operating room personnel.

Wives of vinyl chloride workers have fetal death rates two to three times higher than those of control groups. Higher rates of birth defects are showing up in children of Vietnam veterans exposed to dioxins in the herbicide Agent Orange (see "Blowing the Whistle on Agent Orange," page 556). The pesticide dibromochloropropane (DBCP) has been found to be associated with sterility and low sperm counts in workers. Benzene, chloroprene, chlorinated hydrocarbons, cadmium, fluoride, manganese, kepone, and, of course, radiation are also suspect.

In Alsea, Oregon, Bonnie Hill obtained other reports on herbicide spraying from the BLM, the Forest Service, and the timber companies. She made charts correlating the miscarriages to the times and places of the spraying. She noted that each woman lived within a half mile to 2 miles (0.8 to 3.2 kilometers) of a sprayed area. When the suggestions of her "admittedly incomplete data" could no longer be ignored, Bonnie Hill and seven other women sent the evidence to the U. S. Environmental Protection Agency (EPA) in May 1978. When the women's story attracted the support of the media, the EPA started to investigate. On March 1, 1979, the EPA announced an emergency ban on the use of the herbicides 2,4,5-T and silvex while the agency continues its investigation. The women of Alsea have started to stop a poison.

P.L.

For information in the United States on job hazards, write to the National Institute of Occupational Safety and Health (NIOSH), Center for Disease Control, 1600 Clifton Road NE, GA 30333. To initiate an action, write to the Occupational Safety and Health Administration (OSHA), Department of Labor, 200 Constitution Avenue NW, Washington, D.C. 20210.

To get information on particular substances, write to The Environmental Mutagen Information Center (EMIC)/The Environmental Teratogen Information Center (ETIC), Information Center Complex, Information Division, Oak Ridge Laboratory, P.O. Box Y, Building 9224, Oak Ridge, TN 27830. To report a suspected problem write to The Environmental Protection Agency, Washington, D.C. 20460.

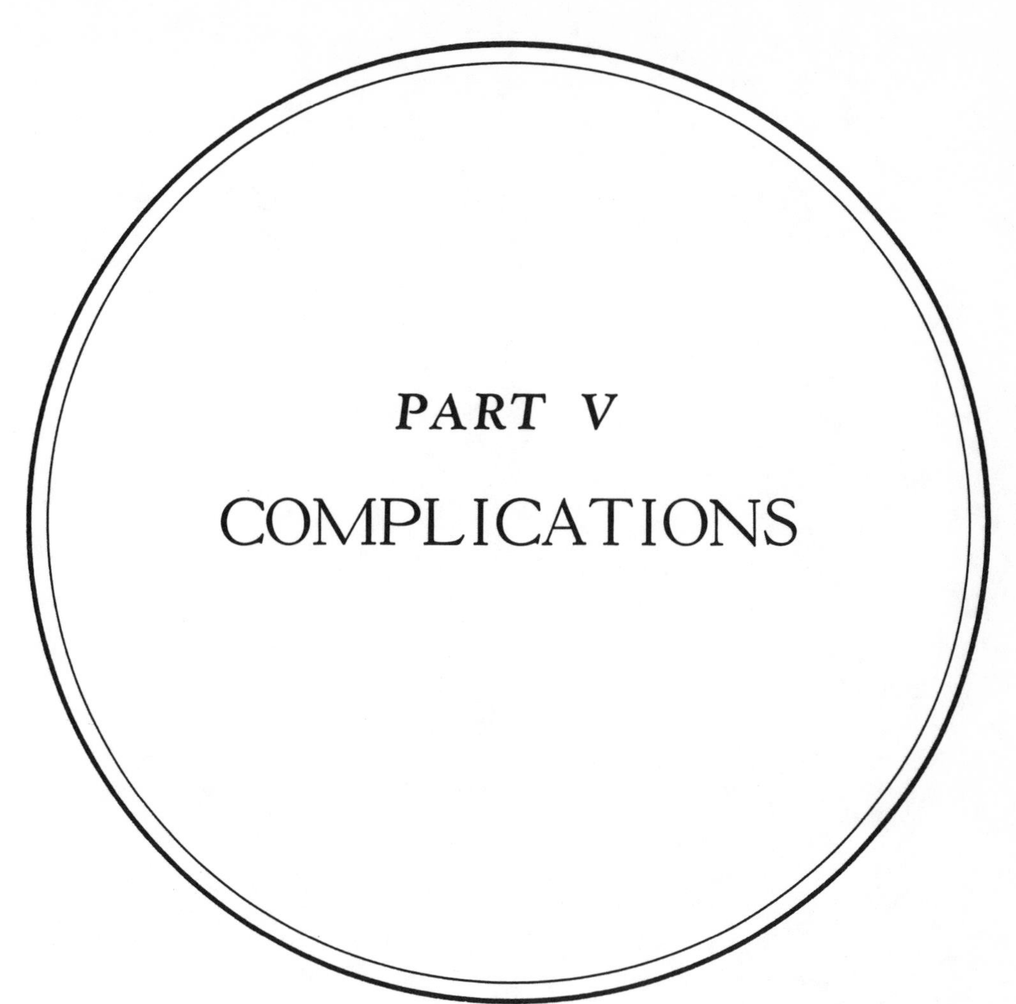

PART V

COMPLICATIONS

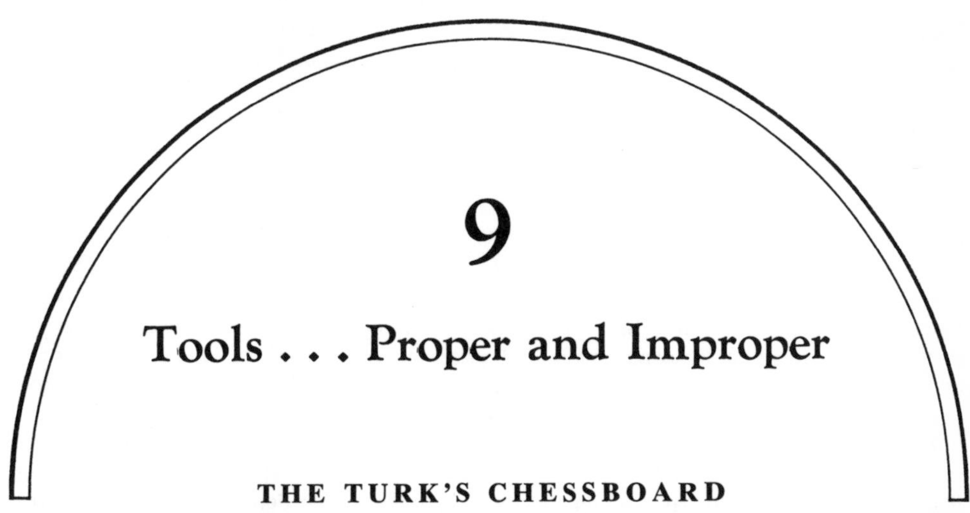

9

Tools . . . Proper and Improper

THE TURK'S CHESSBOARD

It is an axiom of our time that the world has never known such a flowering of inventiveness as the past two or three generations have witnessed, but in fact this is not the only age in which great changes have evoked wonder. During the eighteenth century, when the Industrial Revolution was in crescendo, new mechanical devices seemed to be working a magical transformation over life in Western Europe. The flying shuttle was doubling the output of textile mills. Jethro Tull's seed drill was mechanizing grain farming. The steam engine was generating a new kind of power which made possible the rise of modern factories and, eventually, mass transport.

The sense of human ingenuity was intoxicating to many, and in this atmosphere people were ready to believe that almost anything was possible. A few inventors were moved to take advantage of the public enchantment by creating technological illusions. In 1738 Jacques de Vaucanson amazed Parisians by seeming to bring machinery to life. His invention was an artificial duck. The bird waddled, beat its wings, quacked, picked up grain from the ground, and, after a few moments of whirring, excreted the digested food from the appropriate aperture.

Vaucanson was outdone in 1770, however, by Wolfgang von Kempelen, who exhibited in Vienna a life-size, chess-playing mechanical Turk, suitably outfitted with a turban and a long pipe. On a box before the Turk was a chessboard. Without stirring, the Turk seemed able to move the chess pieces and to do so brilliantly. It defeated nearly everyone it played, a feat that astonished crowds. During each exhibition, to heighten the mystery, Von Kempelen would open the figure, proving that it was empty. The Turk's fame spread. It was taken to Leipzig, Dresden, London, and Paris. It played Napoleon in 1809 and defeated him. What is most interesting, though, is that shortly after the Turk's first appearances, two professors figured out the trick and published pamphlets explaining it to the public. Little attention was paid. Author Joachim Leithauser, who relates the story in *Inventor's Progress,* believes the public ignored the truth because the fiction was more fun. People seemed to want to be overwhelmed by the marvels of the new age of machines, seemed to want to believe technology could outfox nature.

The truth was neither amazing nor very inventive. Before each match, a famous chess expert was hidden in the box beneath the playing board. Magnetic needles dangled from the roof of the box, allowing the expert to follow the game upside down and to move the metal pieces.

Real Turks, Real Gods

The truth of technology today dwarfs the fictions of the past, however, and a non-technician tends to be intimidated by the godlike dexterity and arcane genius of human technology. Soon enough there will be cloned ducks waddling forth from the laboratory of a genetic engineer. Already there are legitimate "Turks," computers able to master the chessboard, even to adjust their acumen to the level of their opponent. Lost in the sea of new gadgets and procedures, however, is the purpose of technology.

What, after all, is technology for?

It seems to have begun as a series of steps to extend the powers of the human body. Time- and labor-saving devices, from the wheel to the Maserati, improve upon the accomplishments of muscles and sinews. Information storage and computation amplify the powers of the brain. Medicine enlarges upon the original function of antibodies, adrenaline, and other bodily nursing systems. The potentials of the human hand are extended by elaborate building and manufacturing equipment; the functions of the eye and ear are expanded by sonar, radar, electron microscopes, laser beams, telescopes, and medical scanners. The act of communication has evolved from guttural signals into television, telephones, and telecommunication satellites.

Today the scope of technology seems to reach far beyond an improvement upon the program of the human body. Tools are appearing that seem extensions of superhuman bodies, carrying out programs as epic as those of the ancient deities. A machine travels to Jupiter, tells us what is there, shows us pictures. A tool, the linear accelerator, neatly cleaves the submicroscopic atom. Machines descend like Poseidon to the bottom of the abyssal sea, and carry messages, Mercury-like, to the edges of the known universe. There are laboratories tinkering with the genetic code, others creating new kinds of synthetic substances—ultimately, science may imitate the powers of Proteus to alter even human forms. There are tools designed as miniature suns to provide nuclear energy on earth, descendants of the fire stolen originally from the sun by Prometheus. There is another fiery tool that will obliterate massive quantities of life in a burst of heat and force. It eclipses, in heinousness and violence, even the imagined powers of Mars, the god of war.

High Tech, Catch-22 Tech

So there is trouble mixed with triumph in this age of clever tools. Sometimes the new advances create new problems, which then force us to invent new cures, never certain that the solutions will not engender another set of problems on a new level. Sometimes it appears questionable whether technology is improving life or fostering its demise. The automobile began as a simple tool that continues to be enormously useful, but it has also become a deadly weapon, a noise and stress producer, a polluter, a city wrecker, a pusher of the global addiction to fossil fuels. Once created it required roads. Roads in turn created new problems, such as sprawl and wilderness deterioration, which demand solutions at a new level—and so on. We seem to be swirling around in a vicious climbing spiral, not yet suffering a fatal mistake, but never quite catching up to guide the rise of technology safely.

Part of the problem may lie in a tendency to deploy any new technology as soon as it is deemed feasible. Individual technicians, specialists in restricted arenas of knowledge, are trained to evaluate whether or not something can be done, not necessarily whether it is desirable. Business experts, in turn, measure a new development by the size of the market and the return on investment. We compare the situation to that of a small child who comes upon a ladder. The child sees that climbing the ladder is feasible and proceeds—never stopping to ponder whether climbing is safe or whether there is anything to be gained by doing so.

In this chapter the *Almanac* looks at some of the tools of our age—not by any means all of them. There are dangerous devices, inappropriate devices, but there are plenty of beneficial ones, too. Since technology permeates our lives, there are other stories about tools scattered throughout the book: some new technologies are described in "Coming Attractions"; specific war tools are mentioned in "War." In the part entitled "Living," we examine the effects of technology on the environment and on living bodies.

The Guiltless Tool

Perhaps the most important point about technology is that, except in the possible case of some weapons, tools are not in themselves evil. The potential for destruction lies in the way a tool is used. The man who shattered Michelangelo's sculpture *The Pietà* at St. Peter's in Rome in 1972 used a hammer, inflicting brutal violence on an invaluable treasure of human art and history. It would be possible for some observers to condemn the hammer as a savage, menacing tool. But it is the same tool that was used by Michelangelo to create the masterpiece in the first place.

The idea is not to attack technology like modern-day Luddites (British workmen who destroyed textile machinery in the early nineteenth century so that factory work would not change and they would not lose their jobs), but to establish ways of sifting through technological developments, evaluating their impacts sufficiently before introducing them, making science and engineering accountable to the public. There are some obvious guiding principles.

A tool should be appropriate to the task and used appropriately. A nuclear power plant is a way of producing energy by heating water. Its use has been compared by Barry Commoner to the employment of a cannon to kill a fly and by Amory Lovins to the use of a chain saw to cut butter. Another illustration comes from a selling trip to China by American agribusiness companies in 1979. Displays of mammoth tractors designed for large-scale farming, equipped with cassette decks and beer coolers, amused Chinese farmers, but no one was buying. The tractors were too huge to use in their fields. Computer data storage, used appropriately, can widely expand human knowledge. Used inappropriately it can facilitate "Big Brother" or fascism through the invasion of privacy. One of the most encouraging trends in technology is in electronics—the miniaturization of components—which means that, in the long run, more people around the world can have access to radios and calculators, for example, at lower prices and with a reduced drain on the earth's diminishing supply of natural resources.

A tool should not pose great risks to people or to the environment, and the risks should be established before the tool is in widespread use. Nuclear power as a theoretical technology is not evil. Perhaps it could be made safe. Perhaps there is a method for disposing of its wastes. Perhaps in another twenty years these vital problems will be solved. In the meantime nuclear plants have been prematurely dispersed throughout the world.

Who Owns Science?

The quality of future life will issue from our ability to impose reason and discretion on inventiveness, without stifling its spirit. There are knotty technological issues to come in our lifetimes, perhaps more marvels ahead than even today's generations have encountered. There are no doubt unforeseen dangers approaching, too. It will take all of the robust genius of scientific and technological minds to explore the infinite dimensions of the universe and simultaneously to enhance human life safely. That enterprise should not be hidden from the public inside a kind of Turk's box of unnecessarily confusing jargon and secretive experiments. The public pays for science; it should be able to see what it is buying and decide if the purchase is a judicious one. That presents all of us with a new responsibility to pay closer attention, to demand layperson's explanations, to study the sciences, and to apply common sense to the technological gifts they offer—some darken the human prospect, but some make it luminous. **M.R.**

THE WIRED PLANET

We are on the brink, futurists tell us, of a revolution in communications. We are about to enter a world in which anyone could have immediate access to the stored knowledge of the ages, to the fast-changing figures from the stock market, or to people in remote places. The new technologies promise to change our lives and our social structures as much as the proliferation of automobiles, telephones, radios, and televisions changed lives during the first half of the century. Our children, futurists contend, will be as lost without these inventions as we would be in a city with no cars, radio, TV, or telephones.

The state of this new wave of telecommunications technologies has been compared to the state of the telephone system in the United States in the early 1900s, when competing phone companies with limited service were developing in major cities. But now, with phone systems unified in many countries and linked by cable or satellite across continents, it's hard to imagine life without them. Likewise we are faced with a smorgasbord of fast-developing and sometimes competing telecommunications technologies—home computers, personal computers, two-way television, worldwide satellite broadcasts—that promise to feed us an indigestible amount of information and to speed it to us in microseconds.

In 1980 there were about 200,000 small, inexpensive personal computers in use in U.S. homes, schools, and factories, and experimental two-way cable TV projects were being tested in England, Germany, Switzerland, and three U.S. states. Even while systems are being tested, the technology is rapidly spinning out faster, smaller, less expensive computers and connectors. Between 1974 and 1979 micro-electronic technology increased the number of components that can be put on a silicon chip (the basic unit of a modern computer) by a factor of 100 with no increase in size or cost, and experts predict that in the next ten years chips will have 10,000 times more capacity. But even this staggering capacity promised to be surpassed by a super-cooled conductor system developed by Nobel Laureate Brian Josephson.

Glass Webs

Technology to carry messages has developed at a similar dizzying rate. The copper-wire cables that connect most telephones and cable TVs has been surpassed by the optical fiber cable. Made of flexible glass one fifth the thickness of a human hair, one fiber can do the work of 10,000 telephone wires or transmit 8,000 TV channels. The fibers allow not only two-way communication between two points, but multi-way communication among several points. Optical fiber bundles have already been used to replace worn copper-wire cable in sections of Atlanta, Chicago, and New York. Communications satellites—there are now about twenty orbiting the globe for public and private use—also offer an incredible number of channels over which to transmit messages.

The sixty-four-thousand answer chip. This tiny IBM memory chip, dwarfed by a thumbnail, can hold up to sixty-four thousand pieces of information. (*IBM*)

Although many of these systems have already become essential to business and government, their popular uses seem like novelties to most. Various systems offer home computer games, up-to-the-minute news, stock market and weather reports, access to limited information banks, current restaurant menus, movie listings, and the opportunity to talk back to a TV show or ad by pressing buttons ranging from "excellent" to "dumb." These systems are fun, interesting, but are they really necessary? Aren't they toys for the affluent?

No, say the experts; they are the fumbling beginnings of what will develop in the next few decades into a pervasive information and communications system. Jon Roland, for example, a Texas microsystems analyst, predicts that "many of these products will become linked together by a worldwide communications system into a vast network that will dominate our lives and fundamentally change the world in which we live."

A Universal Memory

Experts offer a variety of opinions on exactly how telecommunications will change our lives, but they agree it will affect employment, housing, education, transportation, entertainment, and language. They envision a world in which portable or home-based computers are as common as transistor radios are today. These computers would be linked with central information banks, libraries, service industries, offices, and with each other. Much of our commerce would shift from commodities to information, such as computer programs and entertainment packages, and much of our employment and education will shift toward computer design, programming, and information retrieval.

If chores such as banking and shopping can be done by computer, a great number of familiar institutions and jobs will be drastically altered. Education would rely on computerized learning packages and two-way cable TV, and it would be heavily *about* computers. Many children will learn the technology that intimidates their parents today by building and programming their own personal computers as one of their major educational tasks.

Freed from the need to be present physically to shuffle papers or attend meetings, many office workers could "communicate" to work via computer rather than commute to work. They could live where they choose, far beyond commuting distances. A unified system of cables and terminals would even allow social "gatherings." For example, four people in different cities could spend an evening "together" playing electronic bridge over their terminals. Even language could change to suit the medium—perhaps into a sterile, abbreviated "Computerspeak," or perhaps into something richer and more descriptive, as people use words to make up for the absent facial expressions and body language that computers cannot convey.

Telepros and Telecons

The possibilities are intriguing. They raise many questions that futurists now debate and the public may soon debate. The technologies offer us only the potential of access to unlimited information and communication with each other. How we choose to use this technology is a social question. Consider the precedent of another information technology: remote sensing from satellites. By interpreting infrared aerial photos taken from airplanes or satellites, one can gain an immense amount of information unavailable to the naked eye along the ground. (See "Tools in the Ocean of Space," page 467.) Environmental scientists have found remote sensing an invaluable tool for pinpointing sources of pollution, assessing water quality, targeting the source of forest fires and pest outbreaks, and mapping wetlands. It is also an important tool for the military in identifying the location and health of major crops in foreign countries, to facilitate their destruction during war and to benefit from international trade competition. Such satellites can even locate bands of guerrillas in dense foliage by sensing their body heat. Thus the same remarkable tool conveys information that can be used effectively to preserve or to destroy.

(*Jeffrey Seaver*)

The telecommunication network of the future offers governments the opportunity for unprecedented totalitarian control, open democracy, or demagoguery. A government, for example, could use a centralized information bank to compile electronic files of each citizen's personal financial, medical, political, and legal records—information now sometimes computerized but split among many agencies—and use this information as a method of control. (Virtually unbreakable "trap-door" codes *can* prevent unauthorized access to information stored in computers, thus comprehensive computer links do not *necessarily* make all information available indiscreetly.)

Electronic Democracy

On the other hand, computers and multi-way television could allow people to talk back to governments, advertisers, entertainers, and educators instantly, expressing their opinions or voting on policy proposals, candidates, products, issues, entertainment, questions of war and peace. Instant "electronic democracy" is revolutionary to even the most open of traditional democracies based on persuading voters and interest groups (and trading favors) in order to line up votes. Would such a system allow voters to consider issues and products on their merits and respond intelligently? Or would it encourage politicians and advertisers to become even more beguiling? The answer, of course, is not in the technology, but in how it is used and by whom.

Even if none of these extreme developments is realized, the new generation of telecommunications promises to influence our lives in many subtle ways. For example, a computer network would eliminate many of our reasons for gathering in large public groups, including shopping, office work, many forms of entertainment. Would it unite us electronically, but separate us physically from people with different life-styles and cultures? Freed from the need to be physically present in certain places, where will we live? Will we spread out farther onto our shrinking farmland? Cluster in small exurban communities? Retreat to vacation spots? What will happen to the cities?

Teleconservation

Telecommunications technology is for the most part nonpolluting, and it uses fewer resources and less energy than some of the technologies it would partially replace. Producing the tiny computer components is environmentally safer than producing the tons of paper and barrels of oil we now need to transact business. The tiny optical fibers are made from common sand. Moving toward a society that trades largely in information and in tiny chips, disks, and films would certainly conserve resources and energy now used for products that could become obsolete.

One thing is certain: the new communications technologies will speed the course of events as communications developments have for the past century. In the early 1800s it took two weeks to get a message from Europe to the United States via clipper ship, the fastest means available. In 1866 the first transatlantic telegraph cable was laid, and messages flowed at the rate of three hundred letters per minute. Now satellite broadcasts transmit sound and video, and information can be flashed across the ocean by intercontinental computer systems faster than the human mind can comprehend. Instantaneous access to information and communication demands quicker responses, faster decisions. It multiplies the number of actions taken, complicates the texture of life, and speeds the pace of life.

Now fragmented into a variety of systems, the new generation of telecommunications technology promises to become an extraordinary tool that should soon provoke an extraordinary discussion over its proper uses.

M.P.

FUTURE BICYCLES

The bicycle is the most efficient means of converting energy into motion ever invented by humans. It is not easy to improve upon a vehicle that is light, requires little maintenance, provides comfortable travel for short to medium distances, accelerates quickly, pollutes neither air, earth, nor eardrum, and is good for its operator's health.

But the bicycle has certain limitations that have restricted its use where it would do the most good—in urban areas—to relieve noxious, wasteful traffic congestion. Bicycles are not appealing in bad weather; they are unsafe in auto traffic; they can't carry much cargo (like the groceries, briefcase, two children, and dog found in the stereotypical suburban station wagon); and they are not well-suited to the millions of people who are physically disabled or advanced in years.

Renewed interest in building a better bicycle has been the result of current oil shortages. The new designs and new materials being tested today give promise of improvements that will reach to the heart of the bicycle—reinventing its system for transmitting muscle power to mechanical motion and altering its structure. The present chain-drive mechanism, with a selection of gears to adjust the power-speed ratio according to road conditions, requires that all its moving parts—especially the *derailleur* transmission—work perfectly at all times. When well-lubricated it sprays oil, when not, the parts wear; when out of precise adjustment it may jam, damage itself, and bring the rider to a stop—or a fall. Automobile engineers overcame this problem with the introduction of the drive shaft, then relied on better engines to overcome the resulting reduced efficiency. A shaft-driven bicycle first appeared in 1900 and was soon forgotten, but it is now being reconsidered.

A transmission and drive shaft system called the "BioCam," already in limited production, is designed to take advantage of a recent finding that pressure exerted by the legs in pulses, rather than in steady pedaling, can deliver 25 percent more energy to the rear wheel. The sprockets at the BioCam's pedals are heart-shaped, to allow a rest between rotations, and power is "geared" through a wider range. Another answer to the messy, complicated chain is a belt-driven mechanism using a rubber loop with teeth on the inside to mesh with the gears. Holding more closely to present design is the automatic transmission, which shifts gears according to the amount of pedal force exerted by the rider: no hand-levers or guessing involved.

Radical changes in the body of the future bicycle are also in store. A "Bike of the Future" contest, sponsored by the London *Sunday Times* and the British Cycling Bureau in 1979, inspired ingenious bicycle designs for in-town use. The prize-winning bikes could be folded up into a handy package only slightly larger than their wheels (16 inches/40 centimeters in diameter). Smaller wheels, solid rather than spoked, are cheaper to manufacture, stronger, and carry the rider and packages closer to the ground, hence more safely.

Experimentation with the performance of bicycles and human-powered vehicles in general has led to the advantageous repositioning of the rider on the bike. Hunched down with head forward, the conventional bicycle racer reduces wind resistance but increases the likelihood of breaking his or her neck or skull in a fall. The solution is to lean back in the *recumbent* position, with the feet

Professor David Wilson of the Massachusetts Institute of Technology aboard his FOMAC "recumbent" bicycle. The rider who leans back, he says, is safer, more comfortable, and just as efficient as the rider who leans forward. (*Leonard A. Phillips/Technology Review*)

The BioCam Drive delivers 25 percent more power to the rear wheel. (*Facet Cycle, Inc.*)

pedaling out front and the steering column between the knees. The result is greater efficiency, safety, and comfort, because the rider's weight is not resting on the hands and crotch. (The purist bicycle-racing establishment banished the recumbent design in the 1930s, though it set new speed records.) Pursuit of speed has also led to designs for air-foil shells around bicycles, permitting them to approach a speed of 60 miles (96.5 kilometers) per hour.

The result of these advances will be to reduce the objections that have kept bicycling a recreational activity in most people's minds and in most communities. There are exceptional cities and towns in the world where bicycling is an integral part of everyday life (see "Bicycle Cities," page 677), but whether the entire community is designed for bicycle transport or certain pathways are declared off limits to motor traffic, the result is an improvement in the quality of life.

Basic changes in the bicycle itself can bring wider acceptance sooner. The air-foils of today may provide protection from the elements; the smaller, folding bicycle will be carried onto the bus, the train, the airplane; tricycle-vans will carry packages around town; hand-driven models have already put handicapped and senior citizens on wheels; and the recumbent seat will permit bicycle-commuters to travel in heads-up style and comfort. We might even see the bicycle station wagon, with room for the groceries, the briefcase, with everyone pedaling—except maybe the dog.

R.B.

AN AUTO BIOGRAPHY

When Edward Gibbon was writing *The Decline and Fall of the Roman Empire* in the late 1700s, modern Europe was in many ways less advanced than ancient Rome. The Romans had a far better transportation network than existed in Europe until Queen Victoria's time. Travel before the Industrial Revolution was primitive, uncomfortable, and often dangerous. The crude new steam engine promised to change all this. As early as 1769, the French government hired a Swiss engineer named Cugnot to build a self-propelled vehicle to transport cannons. The enormous three-wheeled truck Cugnot invented was heavy, expensive, and less efficient than horses. The government lost interest and Cugnot was dismissed.

Cugnot's engine, however, had proven that a steam engine could push pistons and turn wheels, and other inventors followed with steam carriages. One appeared in Maryland in 1787, another in England in 1801. They were ponderous vehicles, and the invention of the railroad made them seem quaint. The idea of a self-propelled, trackless vehicle attracted no more attention for half a century.

In 1862, a Belgian railway engineer, J.-J. Etienne Lenoir, built an experimental internal combustion engine, powered with illuminating gas, that was small enough to mount on a carriage. In September 1863, Lenoir took the first "horseless carriage" for a spin from rue de la Roquette in Paris to Joinville-le-Pont. The trip took three hours at an average speed of 4 miles (6.4 kilometers) per hour. Czar Alexander II of Russia was sufficiently intrigued by Lenoir's device to place the first order for a motor car in 1864. The car was shipped to Moscow and subsequently disappeared from record.

The Great Grandfather Car

Although Lenoir and Edouard Delamare-Deboutteville, who made the first gasoline-driven car in 1883, contributed greatly to the development of the automobile as we know it, the real

An ancestor of the automobile. Karl Benz's single-cylinder, three-wheeled car traveled at 9 miles (15 kilometers) per hour for about half a mile (1 kilometer) in Mannheim, Germany, in 1886. (*Smithsonian Institution*)

ancestor was built by Karl Benz in Mannheim, Germany, in 1886. His three-wheeled, water-cooled, electric-ignition, single-cylinder car was successfully driven about .6 miles at 9 miles per hour (1 kilometer at 15 kilometers per hour). At almost the same time, Gottlieb Daimler of Cannstatt was building another gasoline-powered car, this one with four wheels. From these two German auto makers, and from many imitators and followers, the modern car developed. By the 1890s, most large cities had a small contingent of motor cars. They were still regarded as freakish toys for the rich, and were subjected to such laws as one in Great Britain that required automobiles to be preceded at all times by a man waving a red flag. However, the technology rapidly advanced, and by 1900 there were over ten thousand cars registered around the world. Already many manufacturers clamored for business. One company catalog assured its customers that its product looked much like a horse-drawn carriage, "relieving the occupants of any sense of embarrassment or conspicuousness." In 1902, Ransom E. Olds began mass-producing the first relatively low-priced car at a rate of about two thousand a year. Olds discovered the mass-market demand by accident, when one of his factories burned down and he could produce only his least expensive model. The one-cylinder runabout inspired one of the most popular songs of the time, "My Merry Oldsmobile."

The automobile did not reach true popularity, though, until the advent of the Model T Ford. Henry Ford's 1913 moving assembly line revolutionized not just the auto industry but industry in general, and Ford factory workers received the then unheard-of wage of five dollars a day. In 1914, for the first time, U.S. production of motor vehicles exceeded production of wagons and carriages. By the end of the next decade, more than half of all American families owned a car. These early popular cars were not noted for their individual styling. Henry Ford remarked that people could order his car in any color they liked "as long as it's black."

The Freedom Machine

Because the coming of the automobile coincided with the consolidation of the North American frontier, the auto had a unique impact on the United States and Canada, more so than on Europe, for example, where cities and roads had long been established. The patterns of growing towns and cities, especially in the American West, took on the configurations best suited to the automobile. At the turn of the century, for every thousand people added to a city's population, 10 acres (4 hectares) were consumed as the city expanded. In 1930, the figure was 30 acres (12 hectares); today, 300 acres (120 hectares). Urban sprawl is directly caused by the automobile. (See "The Hidden Costs of Sprawl," page 263.)

The "Great American Dream Machine" promised Americans the freedom of movement they had prized since frontier days. Before the automobile became common, resorts and national parks were the exclusive playgrounds of the rich, who could afford to get to them. (Before the automobile was allowed, for example, Yellowstone National Park never received more than 35,000 visitors a year; now it has over 2 million visitors annually.) Wealthy people might have one home in the city and another in the country, but the average city dweller never went to the country, and an occasional outing to Coney Island, or a similar destination, was the only escape from the city. With a car, it became possible to live in a suburb, a nice quiet area with green grass and trees, and still commute to the city whenever necessary. Millions of people took this option, especially in the years after World War II; as mortgages became available, the auto became ever more popular, and spending for highways increased.

The millions of individual decisions to move to the suburbs had an enormous impact on American society—much of it negative. Unforeseen problems arose.

The Unintended Effects

Suburbs burgeoned in the 1950s and 1960s as returning World War II veterans sought housing and as affluent families sought an escape from urban pressures. Cities were left to the poor, who had to pay the municipal taxes that were once spread over more people and a broader spectrum of incomes. Commuters, though they depended on the daily use of city facilities, paid no taxes in the cities. The inevitable result was the further decay of the central cities. Meanwhile, as rural areas came to depend more on the car, many poor people were forced to live in the deteriorating cities, where they could get around on public transportation.

But public transportation, too, suffered greatly from the automobile's pre-eminence. Given the choice of the personal, private automobile or the crowded, inconvenient subway or bus, most people chose to drive. The 1970 patronage of public transportation was only half that of 1925. From 1950 to 1970, public transit lost ten billion riders.

By the late 1960s, a new perspective was beginning to develop. Ralph Nader had published *Unsafe at Any Speed,* detailing thousands of examples of the auto industry's disregard for safety. More than fifty thousand people a year died on the highway. The ghetto riots from Newark, New Jersey, to Watts in Los Angeles had focused attention on the declining inner city (the Watts riots were sparked partly by anger over the lack of public transportation). Highways were more and more clogged with cars, and the speed in cities averaged 8 miles (13 kilometers) per hour. For the first time, U.S. oil imports exceeded exports, causing a continuing imbalance of trade, largely because American automobiles annually consume one ninth of all the oil used in the world. Environmentalists pointed to the car as the overwhelming reason so many American cities were plagued with smog.

The Greedy Machine

Each year, 130,000 acres (52,650 hectares) of land—including some of the best agricultural land in the United States—are paved over or in some way consumed for highways and parking lots, displacing more than 50,000 people. Each year more than 7 million cars are abandoned, including more than 70,000 in New York City alone; another 8 million cars a year are brought to auto-wrecking yards and junkyards, which are usually blights on the landscape.

On top of everything else, the automobile is a prime cause of the "American disease"—fat. Most Americans are overweight, and one of the main reasons they get too little exercise is that it is easier to drive.

In the United States, the car has become as much a system of enslavement as a useful transportation tool. Most Americans need their cars for the most basic functions of everyday living—to go to work, to buy food, to visit people. Because their residential areas are typically far from their workplaces, 75 percent of Americans drive to work every day—most of them alone. In the cities that are the commuters' destinations, from 40 to 60 percent of the land surface is devoted to the automobile—to streets, expressways and ramps, garages, drive-ins, parking lots, auto dealers, and gas stations (in Los Angeles alone there are more gas stations than in the entire Soviet Union and fully 60 percent of the city's acreage is devoted to the automobile). The average American spends one quarter of his or her waking hours either driving or working to pay for the car. "In countries deprived of a transportation industry," writes Ivan Illich, "[people walk] wherever they want to go, and they allocate only 3 to 8 percent of their society's energy and monetary budget to traffic instead of 28 percent. What distinguishes the traffic in rich countries from the traffic in poor countries is . . . more hours of compulsory consumption of high doses of energy. . . ." New York City has become strangled with cars. In 1969 architecture critic Ada Louise Huxtable described her way of coping with the city (it is even more applicable today): no crosstown trips at lunch time, no appointments before eleven or after three o'clock, no friendships except within walking distance.

The Planet of the Cars

Although the United States takes car culture to an extreme (almost one out of two Americans has a car), no nation is immune to the problems that attend the automobile. There are huge traffic jams in London, Paris, Rome, Madrid, Lisbon, Athens, Budapest, and Belgrade, in spite of sophisticated public transit networks. It has been estimated that more than 100,000 cars park illegally in Paris every day. In Madrid, in spite of broad avenues and good public transportation, traffic often comes to a dead halt in the center of town. Munich, Stockholm, and some other cities are experimenting with pedestrian malls and closing downtown streets to traffic, but in Rome the piazzas are choked with traffic and the noise level is almost intolerable at times. Cairo, however, gets the prize for being the noisiest city in the world. Drivers there tend to honk several times at any approaching object—even at people on sidewalks—no matter how farfetched the chance of collision. Moscow, concerned about growing auto pollution, recently banned trucks from passing through the city and has begun to install catalytic neutralizers in its municipal buses.

Although the European auto population has exploded in the last ten years, urban areas around the world have the same traffic jams, noise, and pollution. Mexico City is rapidly on its way to becoming the most polluted city in the world. The thin air of its high-altitude natural basin cannot easily absorb or disperse the particulate exhaust from cars. Tokyo's air is so notoriously bad that policemen once had access to sidewalk oxygen machines, and people still occasionally wear gauze masks when on the street to protect their lungs (Tokyo has cracked down on industrial pollution but has done little about the chief cause of its pollution—auto exhausts).

In Caracas, Jakarta, and Hong Kong, the streets are unbelievably congested and traffic increases almost daily. As cars come to seem like a necessity to the middle and upper classes in these cities, the gap between them and the poor grows wider. In Bangkok, where universal flouting of traffic laws makes driving especially hair-raising, the number of motor vehicles goes up 15 to 20 percent a year. Wherever traffic increases, of course, air pollution, noise, and respiratory ailments increase too. (See "Why Your Car Pollutes," page 626.) People want roads to drive on, and in poor countries that means taking money from some other areas where it is vitally needed.

The Biggest Business

The automobile industry is enormous—General Motors has annual sales larger than the gross national product of several prosperous European countries—and its reach extends even further. One out of four jobs in the United States is dependent on the automobile—jobs in making, selling, or servicing cars, and jobs in secondary companies that supply them. Eight of the ten largest American corporations have direct interests in automobile manufacture and supply (General Motors, Exxon, Ford Motor, Mobil, Texaco, Standard Oil of California/SOCAL, Gulf Oil, and Chrysler), and they constitute a mighty lobby, which predictably has been inhospitable to mass transit.

The auto industry deliberately "sabotaged" existing mass-transit systems so that Americans would turn to their automobiles. In 1974, a Senate investigating committee accused GM of having destroyed, between 1932 and 1956, one hundred electric mass-transit systems in forty-five cities.

To illustrate what and how the country lost: In 1940, the Los Angeles freeways did not exist. Pacific Electric, the world's largest interurban electric railway, carried a hundred million passengers a year between fifty-six Southern California towns. In that year, a holding company formed by GM, Standard Oil of California, and Firestone Tire and Rubber began to buy up Pacific Electric. As they gained control, they tore up track—more than a thousand miles of it—to make room for more cars and for GM buses. As cars come to be preferred over mass transit, GM also limited its production of buses and was not particularly interested in improving them.

In 1961, Pacific Electric was finally forced to shut down. As its efficient, smog-free rapid transit disappeared, Los Angeles became both more congested and more polluted. For the next decade, at least, Los Angeles and scores of other cities will be struggling with the legacy of the auto industry's decision to get rid of electric mass-transit systems.

The auto industry is also a staunch supporter of the U.S. highway trust fund, which, until 1973, mandated that all highway-use taxes be turned over to the fund to be spent *solely on building new highways*—any other use whatsoever was illegal. The highway trust fund has spent more than $100 billion since its inception in 1956. This fund is one of the main reasons the United States has the best expressway system in the world—and rundown railways, potholed side roads, and decrepit rapid transit.

The highway lobby, which brought together the auto manufacturers on the one hand and rubber, steel, oil, and other interests on the other, helped suppress legislation affecting auto safety, efficiency, and pollution emission standards for years. By the late 1960s, figures on air pollution and lung disease from automobiles were demanding attention. Los Angeles residents had been making jokes about the smog for years, but it wasn't funny anymore. Periodic smog alerts kept children from playing outside where they could damage their lungs. Orchid growers had once flourished in the pleasant Los Angeles climate, but orchids would no longer grow, so the nurseries had to move to San Francisco—where the smog followed them after a few more years. Rubber tires deteriorated and car paint peeled. On a 1,000-acre (405-hectare) tract of Ponderosa pine in the San Bernardino National Forest, 80 miles (128 kilometers) from Los Angeles, a million trees were killed by smog. In other cities, too, the smog was getting worse. Manhattan dwellers were said to inhale polluted air equivalent to smoking two packs of cigarettes per day. Even the polar bears at the Chicago zoo got emphysema.

In 1970, the U. S. Congress passed the Clean Air Act over strenuous opposition from the highway lobby. Ford, General Motors, and Chrysler signed a consent decree and tacitly admitted they had conspired to keep antipollution devices off the market for seventeen years. Later, the U.S. auto companies fought a long battle to keep their cars big and their gas mileage low.

"Minicars make miniprofits," said Henry Ford II. *Fortune* magazine estimated that a low-horse-power car that cost a thousand dollars less than a high-power car made only half the profit. However, after the oil embargo of 1973 and the worsening energy crisis, American manufacturers increasingly lost business to foreign companies whose smaller cars made excellent mileage—an ever more important consideration. Ford and General Motors came out quickly with their own small cars; the giant Chrysler corporation nearly went bankrupt.

Future Generations of the Auto

The future of the spark-ignition, gasoline-burning automobile is not bright. The fossil fuel on which it has depended is running out quickly, and no easy, cheap alternative is in sight. Some turbo-charged diesel engines appear to be capable of getting as much as 84 miles (134 kilometers) per gallon; but diesel engines produce more particulate pollution than the regular engine, the technology is not proven, and in any case diesels must also use fossil fuel, as do most forms of public and alternative transportation at present. A future automobile may be electric-battery powered: it is already possible to buy a battery-powered, nonpolluting, quiet, small car with a 50-mile (80-kilometer) range and a speed of 40 miles (64 kilometers) per hour, for about $4,000. (See "Reinventing the Automobile," page 438.) Other ideas include gas turbine engines, in which hot gases expand to drive a turbine wheel; Stirling engines, closed systems in which a high-pressure fluid keeps regenerating heat; and even the "Sunwind," which, as it suggests, would be powered by the sun and the wind. Gasohol, a mixture of gasoline and alcohol, offers hope for reduced dependence on oil-based gasoline. (See "Gasohol," page 39.)

None of these possibilities promises much relief before the 1990s, but eventually some substitute for the internal-combustion engine will be acceptable. We may look back with nostalgia on the gasoline-powered auto age, but the chances are we'll be better off without it.

J.S.

AUTO LORE

Opening Moves

- **First Automobile Fatality** On August 17, 1896, at the Crystal Palace in London, Mrs. Bridget Driscoll froze with fright when she saw

A 1930s crack-up. (*Library of Congress*)

an oncoming Roger-Benz driven by Arthur Edsell. She was knocked over and killed as the car wheel fractured her skull. Edsell, who was working for a company that promoted automobiles by offering rides about the city, was traveling 4 miles (6.4 kilometers) per hour at the time of the accident.

- **First Drunk Driving Arrest** Taxi driver George Smith was stopped by an officer of the law on September 10, 1897, in London. He was charged with being "drunk-in-charge" of his electric cab.
- **First Speeding Ticket** On January 28, 1896, a miller named Walter Arnold was fined for "proceeding at about 8 mph," through Paddock Wood, England, thus exhibiting a shocking disregard for health and civility.
- **First Stolen Car** A Peugeot owned by Baron de Zuylen was stolen by his mechanic in June of 1896 in Paris. The culprit and the Peugeot

"I don't know. There's something majestic about it." (© *1980 Eldon Dedini*)

were ultimately located in a small town outside Paris.

- **First Highway** The Avus Autobahn in Berlin opened to traffic on September 10, 1921. It was 6.25 miles (10 kilometers) long and consisted of two lanes covered with tar, separated by a grass divider. This first highway was designed with a second purpose in mind. At each end the builders added a loop, so that the Autobahn could also be used as a race track. It is still in use.
- **First Mass-Produced Gasoline-Powered Automobile** The Oldsmobile. Four hundred and thirty-three were built in 1901. The next year the Olds factory, run by Ransom E. Olds, produced 2,500 cars (this was a year before the Ford Motor Company was organized). Seven hundred and fifty of the cars were sold in New York City. By 1904, the Olds output had topped 5,000. Price: $650.
- **First Suburban Shopping Center** "Suburban Square," Ardmore, Pennsylvania, 1933; 20 acres (8 hectares).
- **First Modern Superhighway** The Pennsylvania Turnpike, a 160-mile (257-kilometer) route between Harrisburg and Pittsburgh, was opened to traffic in October 1940. M.R.

Car Specs

- The world's worst motor vehicle accident occurred in Sotouboua, Togo, on December 6, 1965. Two trucks crashed into a crowd of dancers in a street during a festival. More than 125 people died.
- There are more than 450 million registered motor vehicles in the world.
- On an average day almost a million people use New York City taxis.
- Yearly damage from cars in the United States: $6.5 billion in accidents not covered by insurance; $6.6 billion property damage from auto pollution. Cars annually spew out 80 million tons of pollutants.
- Highest number of deaths annually per registered motor vehicles: Poland with 159 for every 100,000 cars. Highest number of auto deaths per 100,000 people: France and Austria, both with 28 for every 100,000 people (1976 figures).
- Each mile (1.6 kilometers) of four-lane freeway consumes 17.4 acres (7 hectares) of land.
- The average car has 15,000 parts.
- Fifteen million acres (6 million hectares) of land in the United States are paved over.
- Almost 20 percent of the cost of U.S. highways goes for the extra reinforcement needed to make them safe for trucks.
- In the 1960s, San Francisco was the only major U.S. city to turn down freeway funding and freeways; it was also one of the few cities where inner-city retail business did not decline.
- Twenty-five percent of the U.S. population *must* use public transportation to travel—the old, the young, the poor, and the handicapped.
- The dependence of the United States on the automobile is illustrated by the following: 87 percent of Americans travel to work by car; 37 percent of American families have more than one automobile; 75 percent of the nation's freight travels by truck; and 90 percent of America's perishable food is hauled by truck.
- The number of deaths from automobile accidents is closely correlated with the number of cars on the road. No other factor is as relevant.

J.S.

REINVENTING THE AUTOMOBILE

The automobile era was formed and flourished on the assumption of unlimited and relatively inexpensive supplies of gasoline. The consequences of the recent change in that assumption are aptly described by Lester R. Brown, Christopher Flavin, and Colin Norman of the Worldwatch Institute in their book *Running on Empty: The Future of the Automobile in an Oil-Short World.* As world petroleum production levels off and begins to decline during the next twenty years, they explain, governments will have no choice but to allocate the dwindling supply to such high priority uses as food production (for fertilizer and energy), mass transit, the movement of goods, and job-producing industrial activities. In countries where oil is a predominant heating fuel—as it is in many developing countries—that need will be emphasized. Thus, of necessity, already tight gasoline supplies will be increasingly restricted. The reality of the situation hit American auto makers as rising gasoline prices led customers to shun big cars and purchase fuel-efficient imports.

Fine Tuning

Many proposed long-range solutions to this fuel problem are in various stages of exploration or development in several countries. Most tend toward reworking the car's traditional internal combustion engine to wring more miles from a gallon of gas or accept some substitute fuel, such as alcohol or liquid hydrogen. A more radical change would be a shift to electric vehicles (EVs), which run on batteries that so far do not give drivers the peppy performance and pick-up or the driving range of gasoline-powered vehicles. Cars of the future will be smaller and lighter, their fuel may change, and someday stops for a charge-up may replace stops for a fill-up.

Quick Turns

The first steps will involve the use of fuels closely related to gasohol, a mixture of nine parts gasoline to one part alcohol, which can stretch our oil supply (see "Gasohol," page 39). Diesel engines that are up to 25 percent more efficient than standard engines will probably become more common. Someday, we may see cars that go as far as 100 miles (160 kilometers) on a gallon of gasoline refined from shale oil, oil from tar sands, synthetic petroleum made from coal, or one of the other expensive but technologically feasible sources of oil (see "Synfuels," page 34). However, production of these fuels will involve serious environmental problems that may limit their potential.

An Imperfect Perfect Fuel

Hydrogen, many scientists say, is the long-term fuel solution for the automobile, as well as for heating and other energy needs. It is plentifully available from coal or water, has the highest energy content of any fuel, and burns cleanly. Admittedly, hydrogen has some big problems (remember the *Hindenburg?*) that make it a long-term answer, rather than a near-term one.

A Battery of Problems

Electric vehicles could become common by the late 1980s. In fact, they're common now, although not on highways. Electric fork-lift trucks routinely handle goods in warehouses. Electric delivery vehicles are proliferating in London and other parts of Britain. The trouble with EVs is their batteries. They're bulky, low-powered, don't provide jack-rabbit getaways, and don't work very long without a recharge. In addition, recharging the batteries requires the burning of electricity which in turn uses energy and can produce pollution. But none of these problems is beyond solution, and a host of companies, large and small, are searching for the big breakthrough in battery technology that could usher in the era of silent, pollution-free autos.

Juice it up. A General Motors experimental urban electric car receives a charge-up at the first symposium on low-level pollution in Ann Arbor, Michigan, 1973. (*EPA Documerica*)

The World Car

The automobile is gradually becoming cleaner, smaller, and more fuel-efficient, and perhaps slower and safer, but it is still, and will be for quite some time to come, the auto as we know it. One of the principal reasons for a prediction of moderate but not radical change is the nature of the automobile industry. Production is dominated by a few giant corporations who increasingly market more uniform products (there are only about thirty auto manufacturing companies in the entire world). Yet, despite their mammoth size and their reluctance to retool, the big auto manufacturers are being forced to reinvent new automobiles and to do so quickly. As a result of the public's turn to smaller cars at the end of the 1970s, sales of large American cars began to plummet. American auto companies, according to preliminary estimates, lost about $3 billion in 1980. Sales dropped nearly 40 percent during an eighteen-month period beginning in the spring of 1979. The shift caused anguish in Detroit, but euphoria in Japan, where the business of making small, fuel-efficient cars had become an art during the 1970s. In 1980, for the first time, Japan produced more autos than any other nation.

In response, U.S. companies have begun a massive effort to overtake the Japanese by producing standardized, energy-saving small cars—called "world cars"—that can be produced and marketed throughout the world. By 1985 U.S. auto manufacturers will have spent an estimated $80 billion dollars to reassert their dominance over the world auto market. The Japanese and European car makers, meanwhile, are racing to improve their own small cars. Everywhere, the advances in fuel-efficiency during the next decade will be accomplished, in part, by computer technology. The reinvented auto of the future will employ microcomputers and microprocessors to regulate fuel mixtures, to monitor engine performance, and to improve emission controls.

General Motors, the largest U.S. auto maker, gradually reduced the size of its cars during the 1970s, and became the first to introduce a world car in 1979, the "X car." In September 1980 Ford followed by presenting two new world cars, the Escort and the Lynx. Within a month Chrysler introduced its world cars, called the Aries and the Reliant, which the company labeled "K cars." In 1981, General Motors is expected to begin selling its "J cars," which are even smaller than the other alphabet-studded world cars.

The great car hope of the future, of course, is the EV. General Motors promises an electric car by the mid-1980s that will reach a speed of 60 miles (97 kilometers) per hour and run 80 miles (130 kilometers) before needing a recharge. The company estimates that 10 percent of the cars on U.S. highways will be EVs by 1990.

"I THINK OL' GEORGE MAY BE ON TO SOMETHING."

The Automen Empire

As the automobile gradually metamorphoses into a more appropriate vehicle, auto manufacturers plan to reinvent their market strategies as well. Because U.S. sales are not projected to grow at more than 2 to 3 percent annually, even if the world cars catch on, U.S. companies are surveying new markets in Europe, Latin America, Africa, and Asia. The leveling off of U.S. population growth is an important factor in projections of a depressed U.S. market. But developing countries, especially those with expanding economies, present vast new populations to exploit for world car sales. The wasteful, heavy, chrome-embellished cars of the past appear doomed to extinction, but not the automobile itself, which seems on the verge of a revitalization that will mean more cars, better cars, cars in more places, cars making more money.

R.N., M.R.

SUBWAYS AND OTHER WAYS

Old Subways

London

When the first subway, London's Metropolitan, opened in 1863, the future of underground transportation did not look bright. In fact, nothing looked very bright because of the smoke. The electric train had not been developed, and the smoke from the subway's steam locomotive made the air in "the tube" almost unbearable. The first electric train, however, was developed in Germany in 1879, and by 1890 London had the first modern electric subway running through a tunnel under the Thames. London's "Underground" was a great success, and the age of the subway was born.

London's system grew steadily to its present length of 524 miles (844 kilometers) and now carries almost two million passengers a day. A typical ride costs about 30 pence (80 U.S. cents). The Underground has comfortable upholstered seats and provides separate cars for smokers and nonsmokers. It has set high standards of cleanliness and efficiency for other systems to emulate.

Paris

Since its opening in 1900, the Paris Métro system has been called the world's most efficient and most elegant. In addition to carrying three million passengers a day on 109 miles (175 kilometers) of track (which encircles the city), the Métro is a showcase of art and design. The Louvre station displays antiques, Varenne has reproductions of Rodin's sculptures, Gobelins has tapestries, and many stations have eye-catching Art Nouveau iron entranceways. Seated passengers are requested to surrender their seats to disabled veterans and pregnant women when the train is full. A second-class block of ten tickets (called a *carnet*) costs only about $2.50.

The Métro provides a system of electronic maps with which the traveler can find his desired route by simply pushing a button next to the name of the destination.

Boston

The first subway in the United States opened in Boston in 1897, with a design that diminished city congestion by tunneling under downtown traffic (largely horse-drawn in those days) and rising to the surface in less-congested areas. Over the years the system has been expanded to include forty-five stations and 77 miles (124 kilometers) of track, but the fare in the central city is still only 25¢. Nearly half a million people ride the system each day, guided by color-coded lines and murals that help identify stations. One of those stations, at Park Street, is considered a national landmark because of its history and its elegance—an Art Nouveau design of white tile and iron railings.

New York

The world's largest subway opened in 1904, but New York's system developed differently from others. While most cities thought that a single, well-planned subway would be most efficient, New York decided that competition produced the best results. Three competing subways fought it out until 1940 when they were finally merged, which explains the confusion that greets newcomers to a system that does not seem to fit together logically. In spite of its irregular beginning, the New York subway successfully carries three and a half million people daily over 708 miles (1,140 kilometers) of track. Like the city itself, the subway operates twenty-four hours a day. Because of its reputation for occasional violence, screeching cars, and unsightly graffiti, the New York system has its critics, but few deny that the subway generally provides fast, direct transportation in a city that requires a fast, direct method of getting around.

Moscow

The Moscow system, which opened in 1935, with its chandeliers, marble floors, and stained-glass panels, is the last of the great old subways. The automobile had already begun its rise to dominance, which would continue into the 1960s, when the drawbacks of private cars began to become apparent. The Moscow system remains a laudable one—it moves three million people each day at an unbeatable ticket price of 5 kopeks (about 7¢). The suburbs can be reached on one of seven lines that radiate out from the

No, not a ballroom. It's the AVTOVO subway station on the Leningrad Metro. (*TASS from SOVFOTO*)

central city, and there is one circle line connecting the radials. Each station is decorated, some quite elaborately. Every escalator and platform is watched over by uniformed, matronly women guards.

New Subways

Traffic jams, noise, and dirty air opened the public's eyes during the 1960s and 1970s to the advantages of the subway, and a new generation of subways has begun to appear. In most cases, it is too early to rate their efficiency adequately and many have been centers of controversy, but their innovations and the rising problems with autos suggest they will become increasingly important systems.

Tokyo

The image of crowds of Japanese commuters scrambling into subway cars, pushing and shoving, is not without some foundation of truth during heavy rush hours, but the Tokyo subway system is justly famous for the efficient, quiet movement of its crowds during most of the day. A ride on the 102-mile (164-kilometer) system, built just prior to the 1964 Olympic Games, costs about 25¢ for a short trip.

Mexico City

The city destined to be the world's largest in the year 2000 (see "Mexico City," page 71) is well-served for now by a subway system built in 1968. Computer-run and quiet because of its rubber wheels, the subway exhibits the gay colors and brightness of Mexican art, with murals, tiles, and arcades. Nearly two million people use the subway each day and the illiterate among them are guided by graphic illustrations that identify subway stations. The cost of a ride is a little more than a peso, or about 10¢. The Pino Suarez station has an ancient Aztec shrine discovered during construction and preserved by engineers.

Munich

One of the most efficient subways was built in Munich and opened just before the 1972 Olympics. Quiet trains serve clean stations where machines print tickets and make change. The schedules are dependable, the fares cheap, and free transfers are available for the trolley system above ground.

Milan

While the system is a small one, covering only 16 miles (26 kilometers), there are plans for

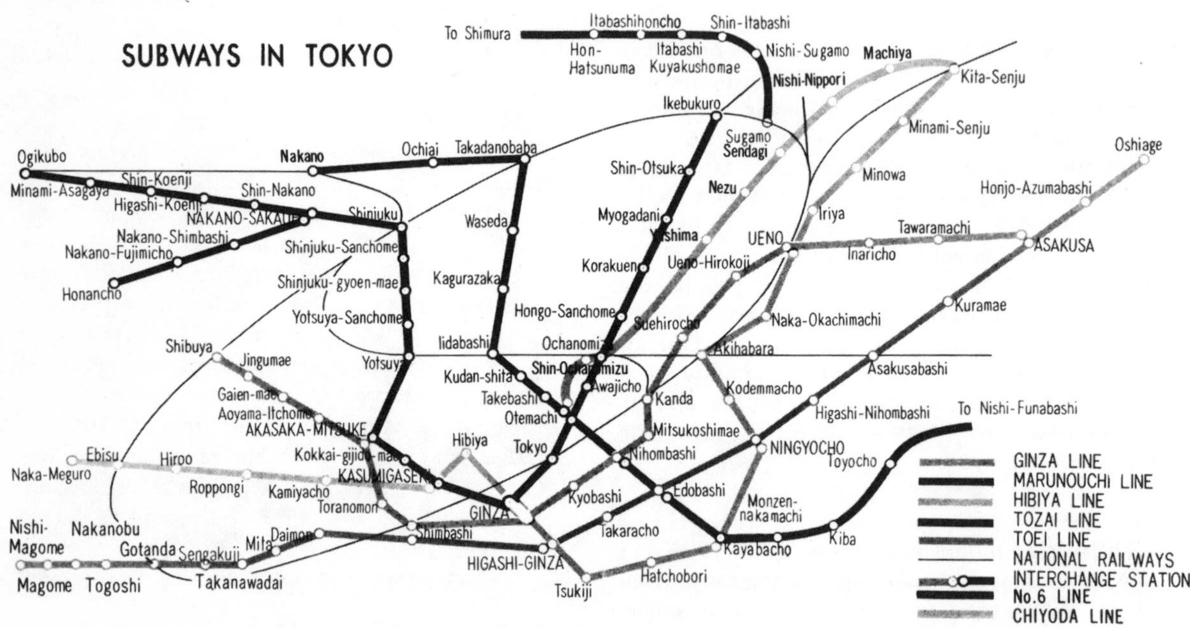

The Tokyo subway system, completed just prior to the 1964 Olympic Games, covers 102 miles (163 kilometers). (*Japan National Tourist Organization*)

A subway stop in Munich, Germany. Passengers enter from one side of the train and leave from the other. (*EPA Documerica/Yoichi Okamoto*)

new lines. Still, four hundred thousand people ride the subway daily, and while waiting for the trains they sit on benches of marble and walk on sound-absorbing platforms, observed by TV monitors for security.

San Francisco

Perhaps the most publicized new subway in the world is the Bay Area Rapid Transit (BART) system, which opened in San Francisco in 1972. The system has had technical difficulties, has not attracted as many commuters as hoped (though this appeared to be changing by 1980), and is losing money. BART took twenty-three years to build but it faced special problems, including construction of the longest vehicular tube in the world—3.6 miles (5.8 kilometers) of tunnel lays 135 feet (41 meters) below San Francisco Bay. One novelty that attracts attention: Automatic train controls that take note of the traffic and adjust speed and scheduling—not a simple feat at speeds as high as 80 miles (128 kilometers) per hour. The trains are supported by air-cushion bellows that eliminate vibration, ensuring smooth rides.

Prague

The Prague system is still expanding from its initial 4.5-mile (7.2-kilometer) route, but what has been built so far is interesting—digital clocks, giant electric signs providing the latest scheduling information, dependable, quiet, and smooth-riding cars. The ticket price is also admirable, amounting to 1 crown (about 10¢).

Other Ways

An automobile requires twice as much energy per passenger-mile as the average subway and three times as much as the new San Francisco trains, so it is not surprising that more cities are putting money into subways. Washington, D.C., is completing its Metro, Stockholm has a new system, New York is adding a new line, and even Los Angeles—the Xanadu of the automobile—is considering one. The resurgence of the subway, however, is not without its setbacks.

A system like San Francisco's BART is destined to have planning problems because of changing conditions. The Washington, D.C., Metro will cost at least twice the anticipated $2.5 billion and cannot handle the crowds that want to use it. The water and sewage pipes, electrical wiring, and phone lines that already lay beneath modern city streets make subway construction slow and difficult. A planned 18-mile (29-kilometer) subway from Los Angeles to the San Fernando Valley will not be finished until 1990. Subways are expensive to build and do not recoup their cost from fares. But neither do highways.

New developments in subway technology indicate that future systems will be more efficient and comfortable. The U. S. Department of Transportation is sponsoring a study of a Uniflo system in which bus-sized cars are held aloft and propelled by air pressure from a "track" below. The system is expensive to build, but the cars will be inexpensive because they will not need motors or mechanical apparatus. Scientists estimate that the cars will use only 12 percent of the energy used by a bus of equivalent size because of the greatly reduced force of friction. The blowers are not sufficiently strong to propel a full-sized train.

The Japanese are developing a "supertrain" that will travel 300 miles (480 kilometers) per hour between Tokyo and Osaka. Repellent electromagnetic forces will lift the train off its track and propel it. Because it does not rattle on the tracks, the supertrain will be quieter than the 120-mile-per-hour (193-kilometer-per-hour) *shinkansen* (bullet train), which is already operating in Japan. Although Japan's supertrain will run on an outdoor elevated track, the principle can be easily adapted to underground trains.

In the United States, Dr. Robert Salter of the Rand Corporation has proposed an electromagnetic subway from New York to Los Angeles. Reducing friction to an absolute minimum by pumping the air from the tunnel would enable the hundred-passenger train to travel at a staggering 14,000 miles (22,500 kilometers) per hour. The trip from Los Angeles to New York would take *twenty-one minutes,* use little fossil fuel, make little noise or air pollution, and save land that might otherwise be used for more highways.

The subways of London, Paris, Boston, New York, and Moscow were very expensive to build, but they have proven their value for more than eighty years and will continue to serve us for many years to come. We can expect new subways to do the same.

K.F.

A PROPER FIT

Technology has been bought and sold around the world like any other commodity, and many times buyers, usually in developing countries, have imported tools that in practice proved to be highly inappropriate or ill-considered. For example, in the late 1960s Pakistan purchased 18,000 tractors with funds borrowed from the World Bank, but the machinery eventually proved useless. No one had the foresight to stock a supply of spare parts, which were difficult to find in Pakistan. Worse, the country's farm-labor needs declined 40 percent, putting large numbers of tenant farmers out of work. In another example, the U. S. Agency for International Development in 1970 built an $80,000 water supply system for 405 families in Ban Ut Kwang, Thailand, but neglected to consider that if the pump broke down, which it did, the villagers could not afford to fix it. Eventually, for lack of a working pump, the water system languished and the villagers returned to their polluted river for water.

Fortunately, fast talk and fast dealing have slowed, and countries everywhere are much more aware of how to evaluate the appropriateness of the tools they develop or import.

- Pakistan's Appropriate Technology Office, in cooperation with local farmers, has designed windmills that pump water for irrigation in the Lower Suid and Mekran Coast areas of the country. The windmills, which can be built by local blacksmiths from locally available materials, cost about $2,400 to make and install, and can pump at least 8,000 gallons (30,000 liters) a day.
- The National Industrial Development Corporation of Swaziland has designed and begun manufacture of the Tinkabi (a Siswati word for oxen), a sixteen-horsepower tractor suited to the needs of the small farmer. Three thousand tractors are manufactured locally each year, and an increasing number of the parts are also being produced locally. Attachments include a plow, planter, cultivator, ridger, harrow, sprayer, circular saw, water pump, hammer mill, sprinkler, sawbench, and electrical generator.
- The International Institute of Tropical Agriculture in Ibadan, Nigeria, has developed a solar-power system for a centrifugal water sprayer. Photovoltaic cells power the rotary disk motor and excess electricity is stored in nickel-cadmium cells for use in cloudy weather.
- In the Soviet Union, photoelectric solar pumps are being used for irrigation and appear to be economical in cases where the nearest water source is at least 18 miles (30 kilometers) away. Also, in the desert, a solar samovar has been developed that will heat water for 6.3 quarts (6 liters) of tea.
- A program to streamline the production of special medicinal herbs is being undertaken in Sri Lanka. Ayurveda, a traditional medicine, is now being actively revived after decades of neglect, notably by the government-supported Ayurvedic Research Institute and the Ayurvedic Drug Corporation.

  According to ayurvedic physicians, only a handful of the island's 2,850 plant species have no medicinal properties, and about 18,500 acres (7,500 hectares) of the nation's forested areas contain abundant supplies of plants that do. Local producers are now being asked to become large-scale suppliers of the plants, and the program is thus creating jobs as well as combating illness, both locally and in government-run hospitals. Areas where the plants grow in abundance are being declared protected reserves.

- A unique biogas plant made out of discarded oil drums has been designed by the Arusha Appropriate Technology Project in Tanzania. It promises to be both cheaper and simpler than the standard Indian-style biogas plant, which ferments human excreta and cow dung into methane gas to be used for cooking, heating, and lighting.

In the standard biogas plant, a drum specially made from steel is used to hold the biogas generated in a fermentation pit. These drums are usually manufactured far away from the village where biogas plants are finally installed. Most developing countries have to import the steel at high prices. This raises the cost of conventional biogas plants beyond the purchasing power of most developing world farmers, unless governments are prepared to subsidize them.

- A Swiss architect and an American anthropologist have jointly designed a revolutionary type of granary for the village of Fatoma in northwest Mali that combines the best elements of traditional architecture with modern materials that can be handled by the villagers themselves.

The new Mali granary is built of *banco,* local clay bricks plastered with sun-dried clay, and lined with ferrocement. It has a precast concrete ceiling, incorporates huge buttresses to withstand the internal pressure, and was built in only forty-two days. Looking like a traditional mosque, the granary holds 32 tons (29 metric tons) and is expected to reduce grain losses to between 5 and 10 percent.

- Egypt produces 8 million tons of waste every year from its four main crops, cotton, corn, rice, and sugar. Research is showing that if these wastes are properly treated they can be mixed with cattle food—the wastes make up to a third of the bulk—to provide excellent fodder. A new plant capable of making a ton of fodder pellets per hour has been designed. Eventually the country could produce 2.5 million tons (2.27 million metric tons) a year—the country's maintenance ration—compared to the 800,000 tons (726,000 metric tons) it now produces. Many other Arab and African nations could benefit from the research.

Among the most sought-after pieces of technology in the world is the transistor radio. Here a teenage boy of the seminomadic Peul tribe of North Senegal listens to a broadcast. (*FAO/Maya Bracher*)

- Medic is a small green weed with yellow flowers found in the Mediterranean region. Scientists at the new International Centre for Agricultural Research in Dry Areas (ICARDA) in Syria believe it could answer many of the problems of farmers in arid areas.

Sometime in the last century medic was accidentally shipped to Australia, where it thrived. Farmers there found that it made excellent grazing for sheep. Furthermore, it is a nitrogen-fixing plant that enriches the soil by adding atmospheric nitrogen to it. Medic could be planted during fallow years, obviating the need for expensive fertilizers.

T.C., K.F.

SOURCE: Several of the above entries have been reprinted with the permission of *Mazingira* magazine.

Wavemakers:

THE NEW ALCHEMISTS

In 1969 John Todd, Nancy Jack Todd, and Bill McLarney were typical of a large number of people who were outspokenly critical of environmental, social, economic, and political conditions in the United States but felt incapable of creating a workable alternative. John Todd notes that their "talk/do" ratio was out of balance, and they decided to do something about it. On some rented land near Wood's Hole on Cape Cod they founded the New Alchemy Institute.

New Alchemy's purpose is to develop ecologically sound models of agriculture, aquaculture, housing, landscaping, and energy production. Unlike many in the "back to the land" movement who rejected modern science and technology, the New Alchemists decided that science was not the enemy, but a valuable ally. The New Alchemists base their work on a biological model of integrated, complementary processes. The New Alchemy Ark is a "bioshelter," a human living system based on an understanding of natural ecology.

The Ark on Cape Cod has a south-facing, double-layered Kalwall (a translucent synthetic) roof, which like the earth's atmosphere, allows sunlight to enter and warm the building during the day and retains this heat during the night. Translucent water tanks are used both to store heat and to grow algae. Tilapia fish eat the algae and become a protein-rich food. As the water accumulates fish wastes, it is pumped by wind power to fertilize and irrigate the indoor garden. Unlike most greenhouse gardens, the Ark garden does not use insecticides and sterilized soil to control pests, but introduces predators to maintain a natural balance. The integrated system produces food throughout the year without any backup heating system. The experimental Ark on Cape Cod does not include living quarters, but a newer Ark on Canada's Prince Edward Island includes 2,000 square feet (180 square meters) of living space. Temperature, humidity, and soil conditions are monitored continuously by a minicomputer. By studying data and food production in the Ark, the New Alchemists are able to alter their design to improve output.

The first few years on Cape Cod were difficult. Local residents told the young experimenters that they could not grow food in such sandy soil, and development money was hard to raise. But years

The New Alchemy Ark, Cape Cod. The south-facing, synthetic roof allows sunlight to warm the building by day and retains the heat at night. (*Kevin Finneran and Patricia Logan*)

of collecting seaweed and organic garbage for composting have built up the soil, and careful attention to gardening methods has dramatically increased yields. An experimental plot of one tenth of an acre, worked one half hour a day, produced enough vegetables for three daily portions for thirteen people for the entire year. Each 66-gallon (250-liter) aquaculture tank produced 50 pounds (23 kilograms) of food in one year—ten times the yield per unit of volume of any other aquaculture project. The secret of their success is simple. By using translucent tanks above ground instead of the traditional pond, and by pumping out waste-polluted water, algae growth was enhanced in increased sunlight and the water was kept clean enough to sustain a greater population density.

The New Alchemists place more emphasis on process than on gadgets. They are more interested in understanding how mulches affect production in the garden than in building a better rototiller. Saving water in agriculture is more valuable than finding a new way to pump water for irrigation. John Todd believes that the root cause of much of the current disenchantment with science is the tendency of people to identify technology only with machinery. Todd counters that technology is actually the knowledge and understanding of how the world works. New Alchemy has not only discovered specific solutions to its own problems, but has gone on to understand the basic principles involved. They not only find which mulch works best in their garden, but why, so that others can use this knowledge to learn what is appropriate to their particular situation. Alternative, small-scale technology must be in tune with local conditions. Agricultural practices especially must be carefully adapted to local conditions. The advantage of small-scale technology is that it can be so readily adapted, but the smallest scale is not always the most appropriate.

Although the New Alchemists use sophisticated scientific knowledge in their research, the methods they formulate require no special training and can be utilized by people at any stage of development. Bill McLarney spends half of each year in Costa Rica developing a center to examine technology appropriate to that area. The Alchemists see themselves doing the research that will enable people throughout the world to meet human needs most economically and most efficiently while protecting the environment.

K.F.

THE HORSES OF THE ATOM

An orange sun rises above the waters of the Sea of Crete, illuminating the activity on *Calypso*'s deck. It is a May morning in 1976 and we are moored near the island of Dia. Three divers and I have already begun an exploratory descent to survey the remains of a Greek ship that sank nineteen centuries ago. Above us the light of the sun appears to shimmer along the water ceiling and I am reminded, as always, of the primal importance of the sun as I leave its warmth to enter the blue darkness below.

We have been immersed for two months not only in the shallows near Greece but in the past. Our ship and this ancient vessel symbolize the odd duality we feel—along the surface we manage a helicopter, a satellite weather forecasting system, and television monitors, on the seafloor below we deal with amphorae, marble artifacts, and Minoan cups. We are intrigued, also, by the mingling in this area of an ancient ideal and a modern dilemma.

The present Greek government, faced with rising electrical demands, is giving consideration to the production of nuclear energy. But citizens of the island of Euboea, only a day's sail from us, are rising in opposition, threatening to block construction near their homes of what they call a "death station." This conflict has erupted as a result of energy decisions throughout Europe and Scandinavia, in the United States, in Australia, and in Japan. It seems particularly ironic in the land of Pericles, because in the long run nuclear power will not be judged as harshly on its accident record, I believe, as on its unintended subversion of democracy and civil liberties.

Suspended in the shallows, I watch a diver rise to the surface like a wingless black bird. Against the flare of the sun, the silhouette of this lone man reminded me of the story of Phaëthon, the mortal son of Helios, the sun god. Foolishly trying to pilot the sun chariot himself, he nearly set the world on fire. The raging horses could not be controlled by anything less than a god, and they raced at will, burning the surface of the world. Today a similar kind of brash confidence has led humanity to take over the reins of other fiery wild horses—those that leap furiously from the heart of matter to scorch the earth.

Among those who oppose nuclear power, the principal fear seems to be that a deadly accident will someday occur, killing or contaminating hundreds of thousands of people. It is a legitimate fear. It presages what may be an inevitable catastrophe approaching us. But grievous as such an event would be, it is not what worries me most.

Peaceful nuclear energy is inseparably forged with our most terrifying weaponry. The decision we made to develop atomic power was, without our knowledge at the time, a decision to distribute atomic weapons throughout civilization. During the years that followed World War II, there was no doubt in my own mind that once again progress born out of the horrors of war would be tamed for peaceful uses. Taming atomic bombs into atomic power was just a modern way to melt swords into plowshares. When President Eisenhower introduced the Atoms for Peace program in the United Nations in December of 1953, the dream was to take the atomic weapon out of the hands of soldiers, "to strip its military casing and adapt it to the arts of peace." The noble metamorphosis would spread the blessings of abundant electrical energy around the world.

From the outset, however, there have been flaws in the Atoms for Peace notion. No one had solved the problem of waste disposal nor designed a fail-safe system to prevent the spread of nuclear weapons, which could accompany the disposal of power plant fuels and wastes. A moral dilemma should have thundered throughout science and government, but it did not. It was a heady time and scientists were swept along to the audacious conclusion that these problems would eventually be solved, that humanity was virtually omnipotent when it came to inventing technological solutions.

Simple basic questions—the problems unsolved when the atomic push began almost thirty years ago—remain unanswered today. Chief among the enduring flaws in nuclear energy are the systems *outside* the power plants, where fuel is enriched, stored, transported, and reprocessed. There are three fissionable, bomb-grade materials in the hands of humanity at certain points along the line from the uranium mine to the accumulation of wastes. Within these substances—uranium-233, uranium-235, and plutonium—abide the fiery horses of our age. The difficult task in building an atomic bomb is the fabrication of these fuels. Once that is done, the production of the weapon can be accomplished *in days* using materials available from a chemical company. The vulnerable points at which these three bomb fuels become most accessible are well known—at enrichment and processing plants, at fuel fabrication plants, at storage facilities handling weapons-quality materials, and during transit of such materials. Already there are twelve countries with facilities housing weapons-grade fuel; soon there will be more. The United States alone has eleven commercial operations handling such material. If a non-nuclear nation or a band of terrorists intercepts the fuel cycle at one of its weak points and obtains only 10 pounds (4.5 kilograms) of fissionable material, the possessors become a superpower.

It would be foolish to assume that security measures will protect every pound of this dreaded material at every facility around the world from every passionate terrorist and despot forever. Civilization today awaits nervously the inevitable day when nuclear-armed radicals take an entire city hostage and issue unthinkable blackmail demands.

The world could begin to change mightily after the first nuclear hostage crisis. When stolen bomb fuel can be hidden in any cellar, democratic governments may be obliged to become police states. Special forces may be created to search for bomb factories. Our rights could be vastly curtailed so that nuclear police could conduct their intelligence, enter private dwellings, seize property, open mail, tap telephones, incarcerate suspects—*and we would probably be glad*. Our civil liberties and human rights would seem a small price to pay for security against loose nuclear weapons with the capacity to obliterate millions of people. Totalitarian regimes could rise, nurtured by a global mood of fear, imposing drastic safeguards on society with ironhanded force. Coercion might spread in the guise of security, proving once more Plato's observation that a tyrant appears first as a protector.

The vision is a sad one. It suggests that in allowing nuclear proliferation, we may be contaminating unwittingly the political systems of our children. We may be building a global prison of potential violence that could subdue future generations, that could smother freedom, humaneness, gentleness. Already there is a Nuclear Emergency Surveillance Team (NEST) in the United States (see "MUF," page 7), and a respected American nuclear scientist has proposed security measures that suggest the inevitable emergence of a militaristic nuclear energy program. To "fix" nuclear power after the events of Three Mile Island, Dr. Alvin M. Weinberg, director of the Institute for Energy Analysis at Oak Ridge, Tennessee, has proposed:

- That nuclear reactors be built in clusters of ten at sites heavily guarded by security forces.
- That they be operated by powerful organizations specializing in nuclear energy.
- And that a cadre of managers, a kind of nuclear priesthood, be trained to run these power bases.

Perhaps this reorganization of the nuclear enterprise would curb some of the dangers, but it would also strengthen the grip on individuals of centralized utility systems, as well as lend power generation the trappings of authoritarianism.

The meticulous care, the massive expenditures, the security shields necessary to protect us from atomic subterfuge will have to accompany nuclear energy as it spreads through the developing world, too. There, the professional training is likely to be less available, the security less stringent. Unfortunately, there is no effective international agency now controlling nuclear expansion. The International Atomic Energy Agency (IAEA) imposes safeguards on nuclear material, but it is a paper tiger without enough inspectors to monitor the world's nuclear facilities and without power to enforce its regulations.

Where did we err, to have invented a technology that evokes fear and threatens to extinguish human ideals as well as human lives? The answer is not that we followed science foolishly, but that we ignored science. There is no tolerance of blind faith among the sacred precepts of the scientific method. This nuclear technology, however, rests on speculation that wastes can someday be disposed of safely, that bomb fuels can always be contained; it is speculation instituted as a massive program. In theory, nuclear energy may be perfectible. There may be safe nuclear designs and fuels. But until the formidable unknowns were resolved we should not have built and activated power plants. The bitter fact is we have made an error of appalling dimensions because we self-confidently implemented an unproven theory. We were wrong; we have set in motion the machinery for a reign of terror in the world we leave our progeny—perhaps even in our own time. We ignored the simple dictum of the scientific and political genius Thomas Jefferson: "Delay is preferable to error."

Can we halt the racing nuclear horses before freedom is trampled and atomic violence destroys the human spirit? We must. Unless we turn the tide of nuclear proliferation we will draw an atomic check on our descendants, endangering and enslaving them. Great sacrifice is called for on the part of our generation—five or ten years of austerity while alternative energy systems are established, three decades before clean, renewable energy can replace fossil fuels forever. The enormous sums invested in the nuclear "cul-de-sac" dry out the possibilities to invest in solar research; but the pressures to adopt nuclear must be resisted. When we talk about the necessity of taking calculated risks in order to benefit from nuclear energy, we are often talking about benefits for *us* and risks for our children.

In the eastern Mediterranean, on a spring morning, as I drift pensively in the sea, a tiny fleck of life catches my eye in the distance, drawing me toward it. Only yards from our archaeological work a small octopus is guarding her cave. Hung from the ceiling like strands of pearls are her developing eggs. No larger than a child's doll, the diaphanous creature is a mute symbol of the drive of the living to protect the unborn. So that her young will not be contaminated by the debris from her meals, the octopus mother forgoes nourishment during the weeks her babies are forming, until they emerge and swim away. Nearly always this means she will starve to death or grow fatally weak in order that her offspring will survive. This instinct to protect the future also drives the salmon upstream, the sea turtle and the whale across thousands of miles of ocean. It may be the most important instinct; it is surely the most beautiful.

I believe that the common sense of the world's human mothers and fathers has begun to awaken. The people of Euboea are joined by millions of citizens whose intuitive response is to protect the future from the horses of the atom. Perhaps this drive, gathering momentum, will hold atomic violence at bay. There is a place in the world for daring, for adventure, for risks, but it is not in the creation of the world our children must inhabit. It is long past time to recognize the proliferation of reactors and of bombs as two intertwined aspects of the same problem, nonproliferation of reactors and reduction of strategic arms as two intertwined solutions.

The toxic and explosive material produced in nuclear plants will have to be isolated from humanity for periods as long as millions of years—far longer than any one human culture has ever lasted. This means that extremely high levels of dedication, vigilance, and quality control must be maintained without interruption, indefinitely, a situation totally alien to the human condition. In other words, safe containment for future generations means all nations participating in the atomic venture will have to be ruled by stable governments, and maintain reliable police forces for millions of years!

Despite the best efforts and intentions of our scientists and political leaders, human society is too diverse, national passions too strong, human aggressiveness too deep-seated, for the peaceful and the warlike atom to stay divorced for long. We cannot embrace one while abhorring the other; we must learn, if we want to live at all, to live without both.

LOOSE NUKES

Most security specialists concede that it is impossible to protect anything from people who wish intensely enough to obtain it. The failure of the international community to halt aircraft hijackings, fiscal embezzlement, bank robberies, and the black market in heroin stand as disquieting reminders—the more so because the open market price of plutonium is comparable to the black market price of heroin, and the black market price of plutonium might be very much higher. Some observers believe that such a black market in strategic materials may already exist.

The fundamental reason that nuclear theft cannot be prevented is that people and human institutions are imperfect. No arrangement, however good it looks on paper, and however competently and devotedly it is established, is proof against boredom, laxity, or corruption. Perhaps a few historical examples relevant to nuclear safeguards might illustrate this conclusion common to everyday experience:

- In 1973 the former security director of the U. S. Atomic Energy Commission (AEC) was sentenced to three years' probation; he had borrowed $239,000 from fellow AEC employees, spent much of it on racetrack gambling, and failed to repay over $170,000.
- A security guard at the former Kerr McGee plutonium fuel fabrication plant in Oklahoma was arrested in connection with an armed robbery of a loan company in which a woman was shot; he was found to be a convicted and paroled armed robber hired under a false name.
- Each year about 3 percent of the approximately 120,000 people working with U.S. nuclear weapons are relieved of duty owing to drug use, mental instability, or other security risks.
- In 1974 several tons of unclassified metal were stolen from the nuclear submarine refitting docks at Rosyth, Scotland, apparently through a conspiracy of dockyard employees. Nuclear submarine fuel, present at those docks, is fully enriched uranium and thus bomb material.
- In 1976 more than a ton of lead shielding was reported missing from Lawrence Livermore Laboratory, a U.S. nuclear weapons design facility.
- Reports persist that materials accountancy records for highly enriched uranium may have been fraudulently manipulated at the Erwin, Tennessee, plant in order to accumulate a surplus with which to cover possible future losses.
- An analytic laboratory used by the Japanese nuclear industry to monitor effluents was shut down by the government for falsifying and fabricating test results.

- During the 1967 Cultural Revolution the military commander of Sinkiang Province, China, reportedly threatened to take over the nuclear base there.
- French scientists testing a bomb in the Algerian Sahara in 1961 apparently had to destroy it hurriedly lest it fall into the hands of rebellious French generals led by Maurice Challe.
- A smuggling ring was found in 1974 to have been selling uranium stolen from an Indian plant to Chinese or Pakistani agents in Katmandu.
- Senior Italian military and intelligence officers were arrested in 1974 for allegedly plotting a right-wing coup in which public panic was to be generated by adding to water supplies some radioactive materials to be stolen from a research center.

SOURCE: Excerpted from Amory Lovins, *Soft Energy Paths: Toward a Durable Peace,* Friends of the Earth International, Ballinger Publishing Co., 1977.

MELTDOWN, NEAR MELTDOWN, AND OTHER "EVENTS"

"Which is worse," asked a journalist who had come to know nuclear power a lot more intimately than he cared to during the days and weeks following the accident at Pennsylvania's Three Mile Island Nuclear Power Station, "to be annihilated by an 'event' or to be totalled by a 'transient'?"

His question is more than merely rhetorical. Regardless of how euphemistically they are described by engineers in the industry (see "Semantic Meltdown," page 454), nuclear accidents are, like Shakespeare's rose, the same by any name. All are potential catastrophes.

All are also much misunderstood. Despite decades of exposure to the nonmilitary uses of nuclear power, the public is still seriously mis- and uninformed about the dangers of nuclear power, both actual and potential, and confused about the real and imaginary risks they face.

The first thing the public must understand is that nuclear power plants are not weapons, even though their waste matter, in some cases, could be fashioned into crude explosives (see "The Horses of the Atom," page 447).

But nuclear plants *can* be dangerous. The history of nuclear power is replete with "events," "incidents," and plain, unadorned "accidents," and while none of these have leveled cities, all, individually and together, provide ample evidence that "nukes" cannot be treated casually.

Windscale

The first of these accidents occurred early in the atomic age. In October, 1957, the atomic reactors at Windscale, a pleasant English town at the edge of the Irish Sea, were operating normally as technicians began the routine process of shutting off cooling systems and allowing the graphite blocks that moderated the plant's nuclear reaction to release the enormous amounts of energy they had accumulated. At first, the process appeared to be proceeding normally. But suddenly, technicians noticed a rapid rise in the temperature of the reactor's fuel rods, and attempted to reinsert the cadmium control rods. Their action appeared ineffective. Throughout the day, temperatures inside the reactor continued to rise. Worse, by the end of the second day, radiation meters near the top of the reactor towers showed abnormally high readings. By the following morning, the situation was worse, with meters outside plant buildings showing a tenfold increase in radiation. The diagnosis, a burning fuel element, was confirmed when an inspection showed the reactor's uranium core glowing red.

When the process started, winds carried the plant's effluent out over the Irish Sea. But by the third night, the winds had shifted, and were blowing the radioactive gases from the plant inland, toward the Lancashire community of Barrow-in-Furness, a town of some sixty thousand. Worse, the reactor continued to overheat, forcing technicians to consider dousing the core with water, risking a steam explosion that could spray the area with some 150 million curies of radium, an amount of fallout nearly equal to that of the Hiroshima bomb. Fortunately, the explosion never took place as workers brought the runaway reactor under control, and no evacuation of the area proved necessary. But the radiation released by the plant forced health authorities to order the dumping of millions of gallons of milk from neighboring farms and to keep a careful watch on the health of thousands of people in the area. The radiation release also showed how far hot particles could carry. At the height of the Windscale emergency, unusually high radiation levels were reported 300 miles (483 kilometers) away.

Idaho Falls

A far more dramatic accident occurred in 1965 at Idaho Falls, Idaho, where the U.S. government maintained a small experimental reactor called the S-L-1. Subsequent investigations have suggested that the mishap may have been due in part to a lover's triangle involving at least two of the S-L-1's three victims. But there is little debate about what happened. As far as investigators were able to determine after the fact, an obstructed pipe caused a loss of coolant, which in turn caused the reactor core to overheat. This overheating then caused a "steam hammer" effect, or sudden buildup of steam within the reactor. The hammer caused the reactor vessel quite literally to jump a couple of feet into the air, spraying radioactive steam into the environment. One man, who was working on the top of the reactor at the time of the accident, was crushed against the ceiling of the containment building and killed instantly. A second, working in the containment building, died a moment later from an intense dose of radiation. A third, who ran into the building to help, succumbed to the high-level radiation before he had managed to take more than a few steps.

None of the radiation released in the Idaho Falls accident spread very far from the plant or endangered the general public. But the incident's gruesome ending still sends a chill through anyone who knows it. The bodies of the three victims were so "hot" that they were buried in lead coffins. The heads and hands of two of the victims were so intensely hot they were amputated and buried separately.

Fermi

A year later, in 1966, a potentially more dangerous accident took place outside Detroit, Michigan, at the $85 million Enrico Fermi Atomic Power Plant. This mishap occurred when a four-by-eight-inch piece of metal plating, originally installed as a safety measure, worked loose and lodged in a coolant pipe, blocking the flow of liquid sodium used to carry off the reactor heat. The coolant cutoff caused two of the plant's one hundred and five fuel elements to melt, releasing radioactive fission products into the coolant.

Despite the popular book that suggests that the Fermi reactor came close to destroying Detroit, the plant never actually came close to melting down. But the accident did contaminate the entire plant, requiring a long, expensive decontamination process that began as soon as things at Fermi cooled down and was not completed until 1974, when the costly breeder was closed for good. It had only operated for a total of thirty days. A conventional reactor was built in its place.

Brown's Ferry

An accident that could have been far more serious occurred in 1975 at Brown's Ferry, Alabama, where the Tennessee Valley Authority operates a

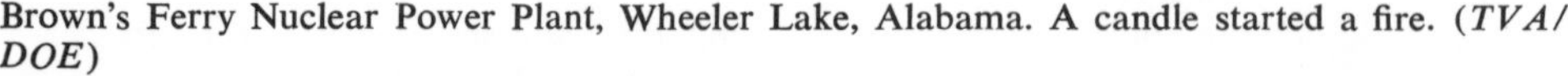

Brown's Ferry Nuclear Power Plant, Wheeler Lake, Alabama. A candle started a fire. (*TVA/DOE*)

reactor that provides people in the area with 750 megawatts of power. This accident happened when an electrician, for reasons that still defy explanation, crawled into a cable tunnel using a lighted candle to check for air leaks. The candle ignited several key cables, shorting out some of the controls used to operate the reactor. Problems then developed quickly. The disabled circuits caused a "loss of coolant" accident, or LOCA, the *bête noire* of reactor operators in which the water used to carry off the heat produced by the nuclear reaction runs out of the reactor faster than it can be replaced. Normally, reactor operators and automatic safety systems respond to a LOCA by activating the plant's emergency core cooling system, or ECCS, which dumps tons of cool water into the reactor. At Brown's Ferry, however, this system was rendered inoperable by the fire, and the reactor core began to overheat and move slowly toward the ultimate consequence of an uncorrected LOCA, a meltdown.

Fortunately, it never happened. Before temperatures in the reactor reached dangerous levels, technicians working around fire fighters battling the electrical blaze managed to rig emergency cooling loops and bring water to the reactor.

Supporters of nuclear power pointed with pride to the fact that no member of the public was exposed to radiation and claimed in subsequent years that the Brown's Ferry accident demonstrated that nuclear plant problems could be contained. For a time at least, the American public seemed satisfied with industry assurances that plants were safe and with government studies suggesting that the chances of being injured in a nuclear accident were smaller than those of being struck by a meteorite.

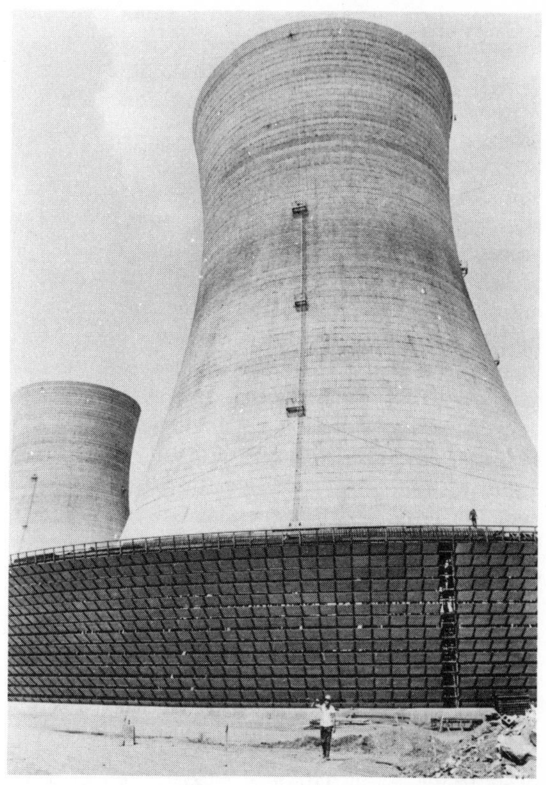

Cooling towers of Unit I nuclear plant at Three Mile Island. Its sister plant, Unit II, suffered a partial meltdown in 1979. (*Metropolitan Edison Company*)

Three Mile Island

This complacency, however, was shattered in the spring of 1979 by an accident in a power plant on Three Mile Island, a site in the Susquehanna River just 10 miles (16.1 kilometers) south of the Pennsylvania state capital at Harrisburg. The antinuclear thriller film *The China Syndrome* was playing at theaters in the area. Something disturbingly close to it was playing at the nuclear plant.

As of early 1981 it was the worst accident in the history of commercial nuclear power, and the first to involve the public. The TMI disaster began when one of the plant's feedwater pumps, which carried water to the turbines, failed, causing the turbines to trip. Normally, such a "transient" would have been temporary; backup systems would have taken over for the disabled pump. But things at TMI were not normal. Two days before the accident, valves leading to the secondary feedwater pumps had been closed during maintenance and left so, although a checklist showed that they had been reopened. Because they were closed, the backup pumps had nowhere to send the water they were pumping and, unable to handle the pressure buildup, also failed, allowing the water in the system to flow into an auxiliary building. At the same time, the water level in the reactor began to drop, raising the possibility of a LOCA and ultimate meltdown, while a relief valve stuck open, allowing radioactive water to escape from the reactor. Misleading instruments further complicated the situation, convincing reactor operators the core was covered when it was not, and leading them to shut off the ECCS prematurely. Core temperatures, normally 600° F (316° C), climbed beyond 2,000° F (1,093° C), causing damage to the uranium fuel rods and leading to a buildup of hydrogen gas, which produced a small explosion within the reactor itself. Relief valves, meanwhile, vented steam and air containing radioactive Iodine-131 and xenon into the atmosphere.

Aided by technicians from the Nuclear Regulatory Commission (NRC), TMI operators finally managed to get the reactor under control, but not before Pennsylvania's governor had ordered a precautionary exodus of all pregnant women and preschool-age children from an area within 5 miles (8 kilometers) of the plant and readied a full-scale evacuation of a six-county area. More than a week passed before technicians were able to say honestly that the situation was stable, more than three elapsed before anyone was even able to initiate the steps to bring the reactor to a condition of cold shutdown. Months after the accident the NRC and other agencies were still unable to agree on how much radiation was released over the lush Pennsylvania Dutch country or how it would affect people and livestock in the area. (See "The Hidden Costs of a Nuclear Accident," page 267.)

Chelyabinsk

A far worse disaster appears to have taken place in the Soviet Union. In 1976, the exiled Soviet scientist Zhores Medvedev shocked his colleagues and journalists alike by reporting that a major nuclear accident had occurred in the winter of 1957–58, killing many people and contaminating an area the size of Rhode Island. At the time, British and American scientists discounted his claim and insisted that if the explosion Medvedev described had actually taken place, it could only have been a weapons test.

The Soviets have yet to concede that anything at all happened near the Ural range community of Chelyabinsk. But Medvedev himself has provided some proof. In a 1979 book entitled *Nuclear Disaster in the Urals* Medvedev presents a compelling compilation of circumstantial evidence, including studies of contaminated lakes and ecosystems and reports from people who had passed through the area. Medvedev's book, which contains CIA documents obtained under the Freedom of Information Act, leaves little doubt that something big happened in the Urals in the winter of 1957–58, and Medvedev, extrapolating from what he has been able to learn, offers a frightening scenario to explain what he thinks took place. According to Medvedev, the Soviets, eager to develop nuclear weapons, rushed into plutonium technology before they had worked out ways of disposing of highly radioactive wastes, and merely dumped these hot by-products into the ground. Eventually, Medvedev hypothesizes, these concentrated wastes went "critical" and cooked off in an explosion similar to that which occurs in a mud-filled volcano. The blast spread radiation over a wide area, filled regional hospitals with victims of radiation sickness, and rendered a large area immediately uninhabitable —and likely to remain so for years.

Medvedev's account of the accident was largely confirmed by a 1979 study conducted by scientists at the Oak Ridge National Laboratory in Tennessee, which was made public in 1980. The scientists admit in an introduction that "we originally believed that Medvedev could have reached completely incorrect conclusions. . . ." After studying CIA documents and Soviet publications, the researchers concluded there was sufficient evidence that a nuclear accident similar to that described had taken place, that it had involved a release of strontium-90 and other radioactive elements through a chemical explosion in tanks containing radioactive wastes from a nuclear weapons program. "The scope of the incident," their report concludes, "in human terms, was not well defined, but appeared to involve some loss of life (magnitude undetermined), the evacuation of the civilian population from a large area, and the appearance of a restricted, radioactive contamination zone." The area covered was estimated at 40 to 400 square miles (100 to 1,000 square kilometers). By comparing high resolution maps of the area before the accident and after, the scientists found that more than thirty small communities had disappeared, suggesting a significant evacuation.

P.S.

SEMANTIC MELTDOWN

The extent to which nuclear power plants endanger public health is a subject of considerable debate. But there is no question that the nuclear industry is a threat to the English language. Every industry has its jargon, designed, it often seems, to separate insiders from outsiders and to help the former retain their control over the situation. But in no industry is the jargon so designed to obscure the facts as it is in the nuclear business.

Take accidents, for example: Other industries may have them, the nuclear industry never does. A malfunction in a nuclear plant is called a "transient," a term that can cover anything from a stuck valve to the ominous failure of the plant's entire cooling system. Unless, of course, it is an "event," which may be anything from a routine turbine trip or an unscheduled shutdown (a "scram") to a complete loss of reactor coolant. A plant system that fails to function as it should does not malfunction but undergoes an "abnormal evolution," which sounds like something Darwin should have studied. The malfunction itself is described as a "normal aberration," which sounds like something out of Krafft-Ebing. A theft of nuclear material is called "unauthorized diversion."

Other potentially dangerous happenings are equally shrouded in euphemism. Fires never occur in nuclear plants, only "rapid oxidation." Out-of-control reactors do not run away, but go on "power excursions" or undergo "unplanned hypercriticality." According to the engineers who struggled with the 1979 accident at Three Mile Island, reactors cannot explode. The worst that they can do is undergo "spontaneous energetic disassembly," a process in which their components can be distributed uniformly over several counties.

Some public officials have tried to end the practice of atomic obfuscation and have urged that those in the nuclear business be required, as a matter of law as well as public safety, to speak plain English. But those who believe in calling an explosion an explosion have their work cut out for them. Some nuclear industry promoters hope, if they can get away with it, to achieve a simple solution to the problem of nuclear waste. To alleviate growing public anxiety about these highly toxic, sometimes bomb-grade substances, they propose a semantic metamorphosis. It really isn't waste at all, they insist; it's "nuclear bonus material." P.S.

ATOM LORE

- The nuclear reactor at the University of Florida had a problem in August of 1977—the cooling system malfunctioned when someone flushed the toilet. The small, experimental reactor had a powerful water-fed cooling system fed by a well for risky experiments. But low-risk experiments were run on a secondary cooling system tied in by a city water main to the toilet. Untimely flushes caused the reactor to be shut down five times in three years, sending students' experiments down the drain. A sign placed on the building's lavatory door read: "Please don't flush the toilet while the reactor is running."
- Marie and Pierre Curie received the Nobel Prize in physics in 1903 for their research with thorium and other radioactive materials. Madame Curie died in 1934 from pernicious anemia brought about by accumulated radiation dosages. (Both had suffered radiation sickness throughout their years of experimentation.) Three notebooks they used in their research are still too highly radioactive to be handled safely.
- In January 1978, the Tennessee Valley Authority announced the reopening of a nuclear power plant that had been closed for seventeen

Bikini Islanders being told they must leave their home so the United States can use their island as a nuclear-bomb test site, 1946. (*National Archives*)

days, at an estimated cost of $2.8 million, because a worker's galosh fell into an atomic reactor. The rubber shoe dropped into a 30-foot-high (10-meter) water-filled container at Unit I of the three-reactor Brown's Ferry Nuclear Plant near Athens, Alabama, while the plant was closed for refueling and modifications. Federal nuclear officials and officials of the seven-state Government utility kept the plant closed until they had figured out a way to assure themselves that the galosh had disintegrated.

- At the San Onofre nuclear power plant in California a shutdown caused by a mysterious electrical short-circuit baffled investigators until several roasted mice were found near the shorted-out wires.
- In 1976, engineers at the Tokai atomic research center in Japan noticed their 90,000-kilowatt reactor was demanding excessive amounts of coolant water—an indication of a leak in the system. They found a foot-long (30-centimeter) crack in a cooling tank which, they determined, had been releasing water for three months. About 960 tons of radioactive water had leaked into the Pacific Ocean as a result.
- On July 16, 1979, a New Mexico dam broke, letting loose 100 million gallons (379 million liters) of radioactive water and 1,100 tons of mill tailings into the Rio Puerco. The spill traveled 60 miles (96 kilometers) downstream before being absorbed into the desert. The pond of tailings above the dam had been filled for two years while the dam was officially considered "under construction" by the State of New Mexico. United Nuclear Corporation, the uranium mining and milling firm responsible, lost $10 million when its milling operations were forced to stop, and sent forty men with buckets and shovels to clean up 1,000 tons of contaminated dirt. Only 8 of the 1,500 people in the area possibly exposed to radiation were tested for the presence of thorium (which has a half-life of 400 years). And signs were placed along the river warning people (including local Navaho children who could not read them) of the danger. R.B.

Wavemakers:

CLAMS AND FRIENDS

Arnie Alpert is a twenty-six-year-old "clam." Alpert is, in fact, one of two full-time staff members of the New England Clamshell Alliance, one of the best-known antinuclear groups in the United States. There are many others, with names drawn from local sea animals—the Abalone Alliance in California, the Crabshell Alliance in Washington state, the Palmetto Alliance in South Carolina, and the Catfish Alliance in Florida. Europe has its share of antinuclear legions, too.

Fueled by the near-tragedy at the now famous Three Mile Island nuclear plant and by growing public concern about nuclear waste disposal, the antinuclear movement has come of age. Its leaders predict that nuclear power will be the biggest issue of the decade. "I do believe," said Richard Pollock, an organizer of a 1979 Washington, D.C., antinuclear demonstration that drew 100,000 protesters, "this will be the major social movement of the 1980s."

Beneath this enthusiasm, however, is a movement struggling for a cohesive political identity in the face of well-financed and determined foes. Despite its broad appeal, the antinuclear movement has yet to harness the collective energy of activists around the world into the coordinated attack on nuclear power that many of the movement's leaders say is necessary to counter the power of the nuclear industry. Others wonder whether the battle against nuclear power can be won unless the movement broadens its focus to include nuclear arms proliferation as well. Some activists worry that such a political expansion of the issue may split the movement.

But Arnie Alpert insists that the fight to curtail the spread of nuclear power has broader implications. He talks of an antinuclear movement that would do more than halt the licensing of atomic power plants. "No nukes is not enough. We're not looking at nuclear power as isolated," he says, "but as one step in the process of creating decentralized energy and economic systems that meet people's needs."

Alpert was a student at Wesleyan University, a small college in Connecticut, when he first noted

growing concern on campus about the hazards of nuclear power. Though he admits being "inclined towards activism," the importance of other issues paled as he studied the nuclear power controversy. He soon became a local organizer for the Clamshell Alliance, founded in 1976 to oppose construction of a nuclear plant at Seabrook, New Hampshire.

The Clamshell, inspired by the occupation by activists of a proposed nuclear plant site in 1975 at Whyl, West Germany, adopted a similar strategy at Seabrook. The first occupation, at the New Hampshire construction site in August 1976, resulted in 179 arrests.

Alpert believes the next occupation was a milestone for the American antinuclear movement. On April 30, 1977, two thousand people, all trained in nonviolent civil disobedience, occupied the construction site. Twenty-four hours later the arrests began. When it was over, more than fourteen hundred protesters were arrested—Arnie Alpert among them—and shuttled off for a two-week stay at a nearby armory. The events at Seabrook are credited with delaying the plant's construction, fueling skepticism about the safety and economics of nuclear power, and drawing the interest of the entire United States to the energy decision making process.

The seeds of protest, however, were planted in Europe as early as 1971. In that year the first European antinuclear demonstration at a plant site in Fessenheim, France, attracted thirteen hundred protesters. Since then, things have been far from quiet on the Western front.

West Germany. In many respects, the Federal Republic of Germany is a nerve center for European nuclear opposition. The first international occupation of a plant site took place there, and subsequent demonstrations in Germany have drawn up to fifty thousand antinuclear protesters from throughout Europe. The movement's leaders estimate that as many as four hundred thousand German citizens are active in local antinuclear "Bürgerinitiativen" (citizen action groups) and involvement is growing. In a nation that once hoped to be 40 percent nuclear by 1985, violent government crackdowns on nuclear demonstrators are increasing, too, according to some activists.

France. The French antinuclear movement, by most accounts, is fragmented. Though fifty thousand demonstrators from throughout Europe gathered at Malville, where the world's first commercial breeder reactor is being built, public pressure has so far failed to slow the French government's ambitious nuclear development program. Organized opposition to that program, to the extent it exists, is largely being led by several French labor unions—particularly CGT and CFDT—whose members have staged walkouts at nuclear plants they consider unsafe.

Sweden. Nuclear power is a politician's nightmare in Sweden, where many observers credit the movement with toppling the forty-four-year rule of the Social Democratic party, which favored expanding the nation's nuclear program. The Center party, which took over the government on an antinuclear campaign platform, moderated its stance once in power and was forced to resign in 1978. A proposal to phase out all nuclear power within ten years lost by less than 1 percent of the vote in a March 1980 referendum. The approved proposal will allow the six existing plants to continue operating and the six plants being built to be finished and eventually operated. No more plants will be built to replace these as they are decommissioned over the next twenty-five years, and alternative energy sources will be developed to replace them.

United Kingdom. In a nation that gave birth to the world's most vibrant antinuclear-arms movement in the 1950s (the Campaign for Nuclear Disarmament), activism against nuclear power has been slow to start. That's due, in part, to the Campaign's call for peaceful uses of nuclear technology—like atomic power—two decades ago. An antinuclear movement does exist, however, though it relies less on mass demonstrations and civil disobedience than on legal intervention and political lobbying.

Japan. Despite the national trauma of nuclear bombing, Japan committed itself to an aggressive nuclear energy program following the war. The country is now the world's second largest producer of nuclear power (the United States is first). The Japanese antinuclear movement has, however, come into its own, with an increasing number of grassroots groups opposing the construction of additional atomic power plants. They face a formidable nuclear establishment. Though officials deny it, there are persistent reports that the government and the utility industry have succeeded in "buying off" local residents and politicians near proposed plant sites with generous cash payments and other rewards. Despite this, antinuclear activists in Japan, perhaps more than in any other country, have succeeded in forging a strong alliance between the nuclear disarmament forces and those opposing atomic power.

Not since the international protests against U.S. involvement in the Vietnam war has an issue so

galvanized political activists around the world. The antinuclear forces, however, must deal with government at multiple levels, with an entrenched industry, with centralized energy systems, and with a worsening global energy crisis. "It's not something that's going to be wrapped up right away," says Arnie Alpert. "The issue is just too big."

B.P.B.

WHAT TO DO ABOUT NUCLEAR POWER

"I think that the antinuclear lobby is very shallow and segmented," announced a nuclear industry lobbyist recently. "I don't feel overwhelmed by the so-called opposition—not by a long shot." The occasion for this remark was an interview in which the lobbyist also spelled out plans by the nuclear industry to launch a new $1.6 million public relations campaign designed to defuse the supposedly "shallow and segmented" critics.

There are so many antinuclear organizations that we can't possibly list them all here. For information about other groups in Europe, write the World Information Service on Energy (WISE), 2e Weteringplantsoen 9, 1017 ZD Amsterdam, Netherlands. For information about other U.S. groups, write the Nuclear Information and Resource Service, 1536 16th St. NW, Washington, D.C. 20005.

U. S. Antinuclear Organizations

Abalone Alliance
452 Higuera
San Luis Obispo, CA 93401

Catfish Alliance
P.O. Box 6306
Dothan, AL 36301

Clamshell Alliance
62 Congress Street
Portsmouth, NH 03801

Critical Mass Energy Project
P.O. Box 1538
Washington, DC 20013

Cactus Alliance
312 Mountain Road NE
Albuquerque, NM 87102

Bailly Alliance
711 South Dearborn
Room 548
Chicago, IL 60605

Paddlewheel Alliance
1426 Highland Avenue
Louisville, KY 40204

Palmetto Alliance
18 Bluff Road
Columbia, SC 29201

People's Power Coalition
260 Lark Street
Albany, NY 12210

Northern Sun Alliance
P.O. Box 8794
Minneapolis, MN 55408

Prairie Alliance
P.O. Box 2424, Station A
Champaign, IL 61820

Oystershell Alliance
1808 Robert Street
New Orleans, LA 70115

Environmental Action Foundation
724 DuPont Circle Building
Washington, DC 20036

Environmental Policy Center
317 Pennsylvania Avenue SE
Washington, DC 20003

Union of Concerned Scientists
1208 Massachusetts Avenue
Cambridge, MA 02138
or
1025 15th Street NW
Washington, DC 20005

Lone Star Alliance
2521 Enfield
Austin, TX 78703

League Against Nuclear Dangers
RR 1
Rudolph, WI 54475

Long Island Safe Energy Coalition
Box 972
Smithtown, NY 11787

Rocky Flats Action Group
c/o Environmental Action
2239 East Colfax
Denver, CO 80206

SEA Alliance
324 Bloomfield Avenue
Montclair, NJ 07042

Organizations Around the World

Australia:
Movement Against Uranium Mining (MAUM)
P.O. Box 196N
Grosvenor Street
Sydney 2000, Australia

Denmark:
Organization for Information About Atomic Power (COOA)
Skindergade 26/DK-1159
Copenhagen, Denmark

France:
Amis de la Terre
117 Avenue de Choisy
75013 Paris, France

Japan:
Gensuikin (Japan Congress Against A- and H-bombs)
4th Floor Akimoto Building
2-19 Tsukasa-cho
Kanda, Chiyoda-ku
Tokyo, Japan

Sweden:
EKOTEKET
S. Jordbrouagen 179 VII
S-136 52 Handen, Sweden

Switzerland:
Nationale Koordination Mombijostr
3011 Bern, Switzerland

Canada:
Canadian Coalition for Nuclear Responsibility
2010 MacKay Street
Montreal, Quebec P.
54-53 Queen Street
Ottawa, Ontario P.

United Kingdom:
Friends of the Earth
9 Poland Street
London W.1.
Scottish Campaign to Resist the Atomic Menace (SCRAM)
2a Ainsle Place
Edinburgh 3, Scotland

Ireland:
Friends of the Earth
17 Arbetus Place
South Circular Road
Dublin 8

CATCHING THE SUN

Despite all the talk of crisis, we are not running out of energy. Theoretically at least, the sunlight that strikes the earth could supply 99 percent of all the energy we need. Unlike fossil and nuclear fuels, sunlight is a flow, not a stock. The sun will continue to shine (and the wind will blow, the plants will grow, and the rain will pour) for a long time to come.

What we are running out of is cheap oil and gas. The United States and other industrialized nations are dependent upon "a long thin line of tankers," in former U.S. President Carter's words, from the unstable Middle East. An assassin's bullet aimed at a Middle East leader or a successful terrorist attack in the Strait of Hormuz could stop the flow of petroleum and shatter the world economy.

Clearly, the world faces a major energy shift away from a petroleum-based economy. A growing body of knowledge holds that the world will eventually obtain almost all of its energy from the sun. But experts debate how quickly we can make the transition to renewable energy resources.

Technical barriers are not the principal inhibiting factors. Every essential technology to harness sunlight has existed for more than a decade, and costs for most are dropping with mass production. We now know how to tap the sun directly and indirectly through the wind, green plants, and running streams. Today the issue is whether we will make the necessary policy decisions to develop these technologies in tandem with conservation techniques.

Catching Heat

Sunlight's most apparent energy contribution is heat. Almost 58 percent of all energy end-use in the United States, for example, is in the form of heat. In fact, 35 percent of the total energy demand is for heat at temperatures less than 100° C (212° F) which are achievable using simple, inexpensive solar collectors.

Put simply, a solar collector is a box that has a black bottom and a glass top and captures the sun's warmth. As it does in a locked-up car on a sunny day, sunlight penetrates the glass and is ab-

A Japanese advertisement for a solar water heating system. (*From* A Golden Thread, *by Ken Butti and John Perlin, 1980.*)

sorbed by the black surface. The glass traps the heat radiation, creating a warm space. Water pumped through the hot collector rises in temperature. The hot water is then piped to a well-insulated storage tank until it is needed. In Israel, 200,000 homes have solar water heaters. In Japan the figure is over 2 million, and the government has established incentives to equip all the nation's thirteen million homes with the devices by 1995.

Direct sunlight can also heat buildings. "Passive" systems shield a building from unwanted summer heat while capturing and retaining the sun's warmth during the colder months. South-facing windows, extra thick walls, and greenhouses are all features of passive solar architecture—beyond a doubt, the most efficient and cost-effective way to heat and cool new buildings. In "active" systems, solar-heated air or liquid is moved from collectors to storage areas by fans or pumps. Energy self-sufficiency from the sun for heating and cooling will require, in most cases, a combination of active and passive features.

Catching Wind

Windpower, another renewable resource, arises from the sun's uneven heating of our spinning planet's land and water, plains and mountains, equatorial regions and poles. Wind machines—commonly known as windmills—played an important role in history, bringing power to rural areas. More than 6 million windmills were built in the United States over the last century (approximately 150,000 of which still spin productively), and new aerodynamic designs are being promoted for "wind farms" situated in particularly windy sections of the world.

Catching Wastes

Bioconversion is the process of converting organic materials such as agricultural wastes (from crops and animals) and urban sewage into usable fuels like methane, alcohol, and oil. China has already built 4.3 million biomass plants to derive methane from wastes. Energy can also be obtained by cultivating crops specifically for consumption or for conversion into fuels. Wood, for example, is biomass.

Biomass can also be converted into alcohol. Brazil hopes to substitute home-grown ethanol for all imported gasoline by the end of the century. In the United States, "gasohol" (alcohol mixed with gasoline) is being sold commercially (see "Gasohol," page 39).

Catching Water

The cheapest undeveloped source of electricity in some nations, such as the United States, may be hydropower. Of the nearly fifty thousand existing U.S. dams over 25 feet (7.6 meters) (built mostly for recreational, agricultural, and flood-control purposes), only eight hundred are licensed to produce power. Many of the existing dams are small and old facilities which were retired when fossil fuels became less expensive and more available. One hundred and twelve such sites have been abandoned in New England since 1940. But as the costs of these fuels have risen and supply has become uncertain, many of these

No spills. An artist's conception of offshore windmills—electricity would flow ashore through underwater cables. (*Westinghouse/DOE*)

dams have assumed new commercial value. According to a 1978 Army Corps of Engineers report an estimated 54 million kilowatts—more power than all U.S. nuclear reactors supplied in 1979—could be harnessed simply by installing turbines at existing dams, assuming environmental and other side effects could be successfully controlled.

Catching Seas

The largest solar collector on earth is the world ocean. Covering nearly three fourths of the planet's surface, it absorbs and stores a proportionate amount of the sunlight striking earth. Schemes to harness this great energy reservoir are detailed in "OTEC," page 23, "Windships," page 25, "Tidal Power," page 30, "Salinity Gradients," page 42, and "Turbines in the Gulf Stream," page 48.

Catching Solar Electricity

The newest solar technology is the photovoltaic cell, which converts sunlight directly into electricity. The solar cell consumes no fuel, produces no pollution while in use, lasts a long time, requires little maintenance, and can be fashioned from silicon (the second most abundant element in the earth's crust) as well as from many other materials (see "Photovoltaic Cells," page 29).

A 1978 United Nations report concluded that solar cells would become cheaper than nuclear power if mass production facilities were built with a total investment of $1 billion—less than the cost of just one large nuclear power plant.

Catching Money

The transition to solar technologies has become a political issue. Competing energy sources are being vigorously defended by powerful vested interests. Bureaucratic inertia and political timidity are also making change difficult, as are government policies that neglect or discriminate against solar energy. And most of the research money that is directed toward solar goes to large corporations rather than the small, independent solar businesses that have mushroomed in the United States (see "The Business of the Sun Also Rises," page 503).

And Finally, Catching Independence

Sweeping social change inevitably attends a shift to a new fuel base. In the eighteenth century, the substitution of coal for wood and for draft animals paved the way for the Industrial Revolution. The shift, just fifty years ago, to petroleum prepared civilization for the jet plane and the automobile, which shrank the world and reshaped its settlements. The coming energy transition will bring far-reaching changes of its own.

According to Denis Hayes, Director of the Solar Energy Research Institute and former chairman of Solar Lobby, the choices are clear: "Tapping some energy sources demands ever-increasing centralization; solar resources are best used at dispersed locations. Some dangerous sources can be permitted widespread growth only under authoritation regimes; solar energy can lead to nothing more dangerous than a leaky roof. Some energy sources invite profiteering cartels; solar sources would tend to narrow the gap between rich and poor—both within and among countries. Some energy sources will tend to reduce the size of the work force; solar sources promise large numbers of new jobs. Some energy sources involve technologies that baffle all but a few specialists; solar energy can be harnessed by individual home-owners with simple devices built of local materials."

Of course, our best energy investments are in improved energy efficiency. Yet no matter how much we conserve, we must develop new sources.

R.M.

THE SUPER-ENGINEERS

In an age of technology few organizations on this planet have acquired a more deserved reputation as "super-engineers" than that branch of the United States Army known as the Corps of Engineers. In peace and war, the Corps has built whole cities, tamed mighty rivers, created harbors, and generally rearranged the landscape at hundreds of points around the globe to suit the diverse interests of human beings. In the process of this herculean construction work, the Corps has also angered many people.

Its plans to create dams on various U.S. rivers for flood control and other purposes have come up against the adamant and not infrequently successful objections of environmentalists. Its schemes to turn such landlocked areas as Oklahoma and the inland portions of Mississippi and Alabama into seaports through construction of great canals have drawn fire from an array of protesters, who see these projects as gigantic boondoggles that waste taxpayers' money.

The Army Corps of Engineers was created in 1775 to design and supervise the construction of fortifications during the Revolutionary War, and entered the civil works field in 1824 with the planning of a national land and water transportation system. Now, a century and a half later, the Corps has grown into an enormous public bureaucracy employing more than 35,000 civilians under the direction of a small corps of military officers. It has hundreds of civilian and military projects worth tens of billions of dollars under construction or on the drawingboards throughout the United States and in many foreign countries.

The Corps has harnessed the nation's rivers, lakes, and harbors for commercial navigation. Digging canals, constructing locks, dredging channels, building dikes and dams, it has created and maintains a vast network of more than 25,000 miles (40,000 kilometers) of navigation lanes interconnecting every region of the United States. Almost a billion tons of domestic cargo move through this system each year, and another billion tons of foreign commerce are handled in the more than 150 U.S. ports and harbors for which the Corps has maintenance responsibilities.

Millions of Americans depend for their water supply and their electricity on reservoirs and hydroelectric power plants built and maintained by the Corps. Millions more swim, fish, and boat at Corps projects nationwide.

Along with its historic mandate to construct great works, the Corps has increasingly become involved in regulatory functions, so that, today, no navigable waterway may be altered, no wetland filled or built upon, no material discharged into the waters of the United States without a consenting permit from the Corps of Engineers.

With such sweeping powers to alter the environment, it is hardly surprising that the Corps has come in for considerable criticism, condemnation, censure, and litigation over its two-hundred-year lifespan. In recent years, the Corps has been widely perceived as a power-hungry, inefficient, insensitive bureaucracy with an awesome ability to move mountains and little regard for the consequences. But the Corps may be slowly changing; it has actually ended up on the same side as environmental groups in recent wetland disputes. The Corps has had its share of cost overruns, boondoggles, preferential arrangements, high-handedness, inefficiencies, and clear-cut waste. But throughout its long history the Corps has built a widely respected reputation for its engineering and construction capabilities, and critics acknowledge that it has probably reflected with considerable accuracy a society that puts stock in action, accomplishment, building, profits, and "progress."

The Corps has been consistently criticized for its relationships with the Congress of the United States, particularly the Public Works Committees of the House of Representatives and the Senate. While Congress controls the purse strings for Corps projects, critics maintain, the Corps controls the data upon which Congressional spending decisions are made, data which the Corps can presumably manipulate for its own purposes and projects. The situation is complicated and largely political. Members of Congress are often judged by their constituents on the basis of what they do for the folks back home. The expenditure of federal funds in a community, particularly for a highly visible construction project that puts money into the pockets of local workers, business people, storekeepers—in short, the local economy—can be a powerful re-election tool.

Environmentalists and other activists have long faulted the Corps for a propensity to dam every river, channel every stream, fill every wetland. It is difficult, however, to identify a Corps project that has not been favored—indeed, promoted—by some influential group or individual in the community, some powerful business interest, some well-entrenched local politician, some well-meaning public official, or, indeed, by a majority who perceive a benefit they equate with the public good. No doubt the question will always be asked: "Engineering power, yes, but exercised for whose benefit?" R.N.

RESHAPING THE GLOBE

Best known for its dams, canals, and harbor projects in the United States, the Army Corps is also engaged in mammoth construction projects around the world. Below is a series of glimpses of the Corps at home and abroad.

- **Building King Khalid Military City in Saudi Arabia.** In 1978, construction began on a brand-new city destined to rise from the middle of the Saudi Arabian desert. Sometime in the 1980s, it will become home for fifty or sixty thousand Saudis and a new axis for this oil-rich kingdom. The huge project is under the planning and supervision of the Army Corps of Engineers. During the next decade, the Corps expects to supervise upward of $20 billion of work for King Khalid.
- **Fifty Years of Technological Research and Experimentation.** Two years after the devastating Mississippi River Flood of 1927 the Corps of Engineers established a Waterways Experiment Station (WES) to study the hydraulics of the river and help develop a comprehensive plan for flood control. During the next fifty years, it grew into the Corps's largest and most diverse research facility, covering more than 685 acres in Vicksburg, Mississippi, and employing more than 1,400 people. Working on assignment for Corps districts, other government agencies, private industry, and even foreign governments, WES has built hydraulic models of the Mississippi River, Niagara Falls, New York Harbor, and other water bodies; developed a new landing gear for the huge C5A military cargo aircraft; studied the effects of waterway dredging and explored new techniques for disposing of dredged materials, including the creation of new wetlands (see "Wetlands," page 379); and performed research in such diverse fields as soil and rock mechanics, earthquake engineering, nuclear weapons effects, and water quality.
- **From the Washington Monument to the Panama Canal.** Throughout its long history, the Corps of Engineers has been involved in projects whose names are now very familiar. In 1876, Corps engineers rescued the problem-plagued Washington Monument construction project and brought it to a successful conclusion. They also built the famous Capitol building dome in Washington. The Corps helped to establish Yellowstone National Park. Army engineers took over and completed the Panama Canal after the French had succumbed to financial reverses, landslides, and disease. The Manhattan Project, a race to develop and produce the world's first atomic bomb, also had a Corps involvement. And the Corps played a

major role in such projects as the Manned Spacecraft Center in Houston, Texas, and the launch facilities at the Kennedy Space Center at Cape Canaveral, Florida. Overseas, the Corps has built suspension bridges in Afghanistan and railroad bridges in Tunisia, aided earthquake victims in Morocco, built a sports field in Germany. It has provided training and technical assistance to numerous other nations. Currently it is working on projects to develop the lower reaches of the Niger River in Africa and the South Han River in South Korea, dredge the Suez Canal, build small dams in Oman, and assist the People's Republic of China to improve its water resources development capabilities.

R.N.

Wavemakers:

TURNING THE TIDE ON THE ARMY CORPS

Marjorie Harris Carr is hardly a little old lady in tennis shoes, but she is "one fiery housewife from Micanopy" who dared take on the formidable U. S. Army Corps of Engineers—and fought them to a standstill.

Since 1962, Carr has been battling the Army Corps' proposed Cross-Florida Barge Canal, which she says is "unjustifiable on environmental, economic, and legal grounds." The struggle is not yet won.

The Cross-Florida Barge Canal is a classic study in bureaucracy. The project was first conceived in the early 1930s, then authorized in 1942. The shortcut through northern Florida would supposedly protect shipments of Texas oil from Nazi submarines lurking near Florida's Atlantic coast. But because of the project's poor cost-benefit ratio, Congress never appropriated the money to build it. The war ended and the project got lost in the confusion. But it never died. Florida congressmen and the Army Corps kept pushing it, and in the early 1960s, Congress finally gave them the money to build the canal.

At a meeting of the Audubon Society in 1962, Marjorie Harris Carr was shocked to discover that the Cross-Florida Barge Canal would alter the Oklawaha River.

The Oklawaha was a beautiful trail of dark water, winding through a lush hardwood forest. The trees were a canopy for the abundant flora and wildlife of the area. Marjorie, who with her husband Archie Carr (See "Sea Turtle Flotas," page 322) lives in Micanopy, Florida, set out to educate the Corps—she has a master's degree in biology—and to offer alternate routes for the canal that would save the river. But no one listened. In 1964, President Lyndon Johnson attended the

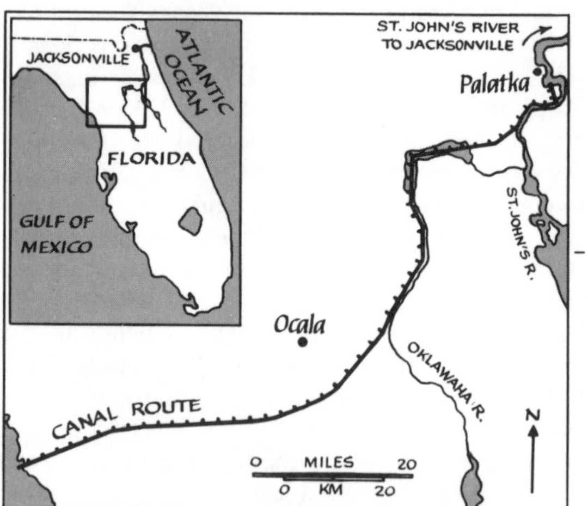

The Cross-Florida Barge Canal. Conceived in the 1930s, authorized in 1942 for military maneuvers, begun long after World War II in the early 1960s, and blocked by environmentalists in the 1970s.

ground-breaking for the canal. He set a match to sticks of dynamite, sending red, white, and blue smoke-puffs billowing into the air. Soon afterward, the Army Corps set to work. They had special machinery built to crush trees into the swamp mud. The Oklawaha began to turn into a straight, flat, barren canal.

Carr did not give up, in spite of the Corps' refusal to consider rerouting the canal. Once, when she was about to give up, an Atlanta, Georgia, magazine ran an article publicizing her losing battle. When Carr read "One Woman's Fight to Save a River," she found new enthusiasm and eventually moved into an office in Gainesville, Florida. In 1969, she formed Florida Defenders of the Environment, Inc. (FDE), with about fifty people

Oklawaha River, lush and winding. The Army Corps proposed to clear the banks and to straighten and dredge the river to form the Cross-Florida Barge Canal. (*Florida Defenders of the Environment, Inc./Archie Carr*)

who had been struggling to save the Oklawaha. Carr and the all-volunteer coalition no longer saw their cause as just saving the river. They wanted the whole canal project stopped.

FDE became a clearinghouse of information about the Cross-Florida Barge Canal project. Carr then orchestrated:

- A monumental report on the Oklawaha region that became a model for future environmental impact statements.
- A letter to then-President Nixon signed by 150 prominent scientists, asking for a moratorium on the canal project.
- A land-use study, by professional planners from Florida, on the future of the Oklawaha with *no* canal.
- A poll of candidates that determined and publicized every politician's stand on the Cross-Florida Barge Canal.
- Extensive use of the media, encouraging reporters to look at both sides of the story.

Carr sought out reporters, shining the media spotlight on her cause. Feature stories like "Rape on the Oklawaha," by James Nathan Miller, in the January 1970 issue of the *Reader's Digest*, inflamed sentiment across the country against the canal. Major newspapers, magazines, and network television news heralded the "big ditch" and the Corps plan to "kill a river in Florida."

FDE grew to hundreds of members, with an active mailing list of two thousand sponsors and supporters. The organization was made up of campers, fishers, scientists, conservationists, and others who were simply fed up with traditional "pork-barrel" projects. Although few opposed the canal in the early days, FDE slowly won over state governors, the entire state legislature, and most of Florida's congressional delegation.

In 1970, the Environmental Defense Fund filed suit against the Army Corps, asking for a permanent injunction against the construction of the canal. FDE was among the plaintiffs. The judge granted a preliminary injunction; before the trial could move much farther, President Nixon halted construction completely with an Executive Order.

Unfortunately, the courts then ruled that only Congress could legally end the project. By 1980, Congress had still not acted. But Carr is optimistic.

The Oklawaha, though much of it has been flooded, is still a beautiful river in parts. Twenty miles (32 kilometers) remain unharmed; of the

16 miles (25 kilometers) of river that have been "engineered," 8 miles (13 kilometers) are devastated. Carr is convinced, and has studies to show, that the ruined areas can be restored. There are plans and money for complete restoration when Congress says the word. Ironically, the Army Corps will be in charge of that, too. New Corps objectives for the area include restoring fluctuating water levels, improving water quality, and enhancing water and related land resources.

For eighteen years, predictions have circulated that the long battle was finally about to end. Yet as of early 1981, the Cross-Florida Barge Canal was still not officially dead. But Carr is so confident that she looks beyond the canal. "As soon as they drain their ditch, we'll have our river back." She predicts that the forest will reseed itself within twenty-five years. Next, she wants to see the Oklawaha declared a wild and scenic river, legally protected by the U. S. Forest Service. She plans to keep watching over the Oklawaha, and hopes the FDE will continue its watchdog role even after the final demise of the Cross-Florida Barge Canal.

J.M.V., J.S.

THE MOON: WAS IT WORTH THE TRIP?

The aerospace technology that sent humans to the Moon also spun off new consumer goods. Here are a few moon tech products.

The Space Roof

In 1967, the National Aeronautics and Space Administration was designing spacesuits for the Apollo astronauts. The suits needed to be durable, noncombustible, yet thin, light, and flexible. NASA contracted for a new fabric woven from ultrafine fiber-glass yarn, then coated with Teflon TFE. The fabric met all NASA's requirements and was tailored to fit the astronauts.

The coated fiber-glass fabric proved so strong that a thickened version is now used in construction to cover fieldhouses, swimming pools, tennis courts, exhibit halls, and schools, among other structures. One example is the stadium roof of the Silverdome in Pontiac, Michigan. The roof is a 10-acre (4-hectare) fabric envelope honeycombed with air compartments kept filled by fans. The lightweight roof lets in sunlight but keeps out the icy Michigan winters, so that the stadium can be used year-round. The new fabric is also much cheaper than conventional roofing. The Silverdome was completed under the budget estimate of $56 million, whereas the steel-roofed New Orleans Superdome cost $168 million.

The Space Guitar

The Ovation guitar, a high-quality guitar with an innovative bowl-like shape, was developed with the help of aerospace technology. A contractor to NASA and the military was conducting research on how to cut down vibration in rotor systems like those of a helicopter. It occurred to the guitar-playing president of the company that the same research could be turned around and used to enhance the vibration in a fine guitar. The bowl-like design that resulted, however, would have been next to impossible to shape in wood, the traditional guitar material. The Ovation researchers found a workable substitute in the bonded fiber glass and carbon graphite used in aerospace flight technology. The resulting guitars take far less time to produce and cost less than conventional instruments of similar quality.

The Space Hospital

Many of the most impressive adaptations of outer space technology are in the field of medicine. Many health-monitoring devices have come from NASA, a result of efforts to carefully determine any health problems during space missions. For example, a new device for measuring blood pressure is now available which does not require special training to interpret. The systolic and diastolic measurements appear clearly on a digital screen.

Another health-related spinoff has probably saved many lives: A radiant warmer made of transparent plastic, which can be positioned over premature infants and over patients with severe burns. NASA used these electrically heated, transparent materials as faceplates for the Apollo astronauts and as cockpit windows in the X-15 supersonic research plane. Layers of clear plastic surround an invisible film of electrically conductive gold.

Earth rises above the Apollo II Lunar Module, which is ascending from the moon's surface to rendezvous with its orbiting command module. (*NASA*)

The cradle warmer for babies fits over a bassinet, emitting low-energy radiant heat all over the child's body. The warmer has a skin sensor which adjusts the temperature to each baby's body. The same kind of warmer is now being used to keep burn patients warm. Serious burns lower a person's body temperature so that extra warmth is necessary, but at the same time sheets and blankets must not touch the burned skin.

Space Miscellany

Industry has especially benefited from much of the technology developed for space exploration. Computer programs from NASA are often used to design and test new industrial equipment, just as NASA simulated new aerospace designs. Miniaturized electrical circuitry, developed for the space program, is being used nationwide to protect people against electric shock by sensing and cutting off current in a faulty circuit. A new kind of burglar alarm has evolved from portable seismic detectors like those left on the Moon by the Apollo astronauts. The small seismic detectors record tiny "moonquakes," and easily register a burglar's footsteps. The alarm can be set for short or long distances—up to 260 feet (79 meters).

Environmental and conservation benefits have also come from moon-race technology. The need for high efficiency in a space vehicle has led to new ways to insulate houses and recycle waste water. We have the space age to thank for the lightweight freeze-dried foods that many hikers subsist on. NASA has also been conducting research on solar energy. The agency has developed a design, originally for use in space, that keeps solar heat from reflecting or escaping from a solar collector.

J.S.

TOOLS IN THE OCEAN OF SPACE

At any given moment there are several hundred satellites, mostly American or Soviet, passing over our heads. They come in every size and shape and serve a bewildering variety of purposes. In some cases, such as reconnaissance satellites, they serve multiple purposes, providing both geological and meteorological information while assisting the military of the two superpowers in their endless attempts to keep track of each other.

Eyes in the Sky

The first weather satellite, Tiros I, was launched in April of 1960 and has been followed by a succession of increasingly sophisticated descendants. Meteorologists, oceanographers, and geographers now have access to a continuous and detailed record of the earth's surface and the dynamic processes affecting it. The current Tyros N and Nimbus G satellites provide data on land and ocean surfaces and, with ultrasensitive instruments, can even detect pollutants in the world's oceans. They clearly showed that much of the garbage dumped daily in the oceans does not disappear, but circulates with the currents. Nimbus photos showed pollution flowing with the Gulf Stream from Cape Hatteras, North Carolina toward Europe. Another photo revealed a trail of acid extending several miles seaward from New York Harbor. The short-lived but effective Seasat A traveled in a circumpolar orbit fourteen times a day, scanning 95 percent of the ocean's surface until scientists at the Jet Propulsion Laboratory in California lost contact with it. Information on wave motion, currents, sea temperatures, surface winds, ice, and storm development was constantly accumulated and returned to the laboratory. The first oceanographic research vessel, HMS *Challenger,* monitored less of the ocean's surface during its historic three-and-a-half-year voyage than Seasat did in just a few hours of flight.

Its companion satellite, Landsat, and various other earth resource satellites, performed similar services, accurately mapping the land surfaces of the world and detailing the effect of land masses on meteorological and agricultural conditions.

Landsat proved an effective spy in the sky for environmental agencies. Its satellite snapshots accurately documented where pollution comes from and where it goes. Using remote sensing (infrared photography) Landsat reveals things invisible to the naked eye. And by manipulating the film with different filters, scientists can bring out different information. For example, a photo can be made to show distinctions among land vegetation, perhaps even revealing an outbreak of pests in a huge forest, or gradations of algae growth in a lake indicative of possible pollution. When Nantucket Island almost fell victim to an oil spill in 1976, NASA used Landsat photos to help the Coast Guard predict the path of the oil slick. The photos were later used to help assess the impact of a potential spill from off-shore drilling. Landsat photos of Chesapeake Bay helped an environmental commission there track down the sources and effects of pollutants.

Other research satellites have turned their attentions away from the earth and looked into

Earthwatching. Satellites linked with land and sea stations of the United Nations Environment Programme's Project Earthwatch monitor climate changes, the condition of the ozone layer, natural resource depletion, and pollution. (*UNEP*)

outer space. The Orbiting Solar Observatory (OSO) and Orbiting Astronomical Observatory (OAO) are the best known of a series of satellites supplied with a variety of astronomical devices for obtaining information on everything from the properties of solar radiation to cosmic rays and the background radiation of the galaxy. The OAO also boasts a 36-inch (91-centimeter) telescope which allows clear viewing of astronomical objects without the distortion created by the earth's atmosphere.

Communication Networks

Communications satellites fulfill the most immediately useful function to the average world citizen. These satellites receive signals from earth, amplify and relay them to other points, providing almost instantaneous communication with any point on the globe. Radio, television, and telecommunications systems now truly link all nations on earth. (For more on future communication systems in space, see "Construction in Space," page 49.)

Spies in the Sky

Approximately 75 percent of the satellites launched since Sputnik I have had military applications. The same sensitive equipment which is used to measure the surface temperature of the ocean from space can be adapted for photoreconnaissance of other nations. The military also has its own navigational, communication, and meteorological satellites. The most distressing military applications of satellite technology, however, are hunter-killer satellites and space-borne ballistic missile systems. (See "Space Wars," page 547.)

Future Satellites

Many new satellite systems are envisioned for the near future. Improvements in satellite technology are progressing rapidly and the new generation of Landsat and Seasat satellites will provide even more detailed information about the earth and its resources. The projected Navstar global positioning system will revolutionize navigation, aviation, and maritime activities with highly accurate computerized position fixing. The Geostationary Orbit Environmental Platform, which would perform a wide variety of environmental monitoring tasks in lieu of numerous specialized satellites, is planned for the 1980s. There are many other ideas which, though not immediately scheduled, present interesting possibilities for both research and practical benefits. A series of solar-powered, electricity-generating satellites could collect energy while in synchronous orbit above the earth and transfer microwaves to properly placed receiving stations on the planet's surface. (For more on the benefits and dangers of these satellites see "Construction in Space," page 49.) Other commercially viable orbital activities include various types of manufacturing processes which could be carried out more cheaply and efficiently in the vacuum of space. NASA plans extensive research into this field in the 1980s and experiments are slated during the Shuttle flights to gain more knowledge in such widely divergent fields as crystal growth and solidification, containerless processing, fluid and chemical manufacturing processes, vacuum research, and pharmaceutical products.

Planetary Probes

We have already seen the surface of Mars and the Voyager satellites have given us our first close look at Jupiter and Saturn. Voyager II may be directed toward Uranus after passing Saturn. It could provide the first detailed glimpse of the solar system's other ringed planet in 1986. Galileo, a combination orbiter and probe, is scheduled to reach Jupiter in 1984, two years after being launched from the Shuttle. The probe will be the first human device to penetrate the misty atmosphere of Jupiter. It will broadcast back biochemical and physical data about the planet, while the orbiter travels around the Jovian system, exploring and photographing the satellites and mapping the planet's radiation belts and magnetic fields.

Two Solar Polar Orbiters, whose launch is planned for early 1983, will be sent toward Jupiter in a spectacular maneuver to take advantage of the giant planet's gravity, which will swing the crafts above the plane of the ecliptic (the plane on which the planetary orbits lie). They will then fall back and eventually pass in orbit over the poles of the Sun. There it is hoped that they will broadcast for at least a year, giving us detailed knowledge of the Sun and its environment.

A probe may be launched in 1985 to rendezvous with Haley's Comet when it returns in 1986 from its long trip into the void. An automated Rover, much like the famous moon buggy used by the Apollo astronauts, may make the trip to Mars and a probe could be sent to Titan, the earthlike moon of Saturn, to study its surface and atmosphere. A semipermanent solar study station could be established on Mercury. T.C.

TOOLS FOR EXPLORING THE OCEAN

The depths of the sea have been shrouded in mystery through most of human history. For ages human knowledge of the oceans was a conglomerate of legend, speculation, and sailors' reports. Even after the Age of Exploration had filled in most of the blank areas on the map of the surface world, our understanding of the depths of the sea was confined to the occasional lucky fisherman's catch or the remains of some undersea creature cast ashore after a storm.

The Voyage of the Challenger

The famous voyage of HMS *Challenger* (1872–76) marked the first serious effort to come to a scientific understanding of the great ocean system. All of the best instruments and techniques of the time, and a variety of untried items as well, were brought to bear in an attempt to wrest from the sea the secrets hidden from humankind.

Vast tracts of the oceans were sounded by the *Challenger,* filling in the first tentative lines on the map of the ocean floor. Water samples were systematically collected, and fifty volumes of scientific literature, concerning hydrology, biology, and marine species scientifically described for the first time, were accurately committed to paper by naturalist-artists. The voyage of the *Challenger* provided a strong foundation upon which was built the modern science of oceanography.

The Aqua-Lung

Many others followed in the wake of the *Challenger,* but for almost seventy-five years the study of the sea was limited by the ingenuity of those who remained on its surface and the daring of those who chose to plunge beneath it in unwieldy and primitive diving suits, tenuously connected to the life-giving atmosphere by a flimsy air hose and completely dependent on their colleagues above for a continuous supply of air.

The first great breakthrough in freeing explorers from their dependence on the surface occurred in 1943 when Jacques-Yves Cousteau and Émile Gagnan, an industrial gas engineer, perfected a regulator which made possible their scuba (or Self-Contained Underwater Breathing Apparatus) gear. Though the basic idea was predicted as early as 1876 by Jules Verne in his classic tale *20,000 Leagues Under the Sea,* it only became a reality with the technical breakthrough achieved by Cousteau and Gagnan. The regulator adjusted the pressure of the air being breathed so that it matched the pressure of the surrounding water. Divers could descend into greater pressures without fear of their chests collapsing. Using compressed air tanks a diver could, for the first time, travel freely underwater for prolonged periods, carrying a supply of atmosphere along, always adapted to the surroundings. (Diving below 100 feet/30 meters, however, remains dangerous to the novice diver.) Obviously this opened up an entirely new world. Explorers, scientists, and photographers were free to remain below for extensive observations of the sea and its life and

Jacques-Yves Cousteau prepares to test the first self-contained underwater breathing apparatus (SCUBA) in a river near Paris, France, in 1943. Cousteau and Émile Gagnan (bending over) invented the device which allowed divers for the first time to explore the undersea world without cumbersome air hoses to the surface. (*The Cousteau Society*)

to travel weightless and horizontal, face-first like fish, in a three-dimensional medium.

The Bathysphere and Bathyscaphe

Diving, however, does have its limitations. The greater part of the ocean's depths lies beneath crushing pressures which no free diver could survive. A free-moving vessel was needed which could not only travel to great depths but perform useful scientific functions. William Beebe had pioneered in this field as early as the 1930s when his bathysphere, a rather confining steel ball, was lowered into the sea near Bermuda in a series of daring dives which culminated in 1934 with a plunge to the then unprecedented depth of 3,028 feet (926 meters). Despite the limited observations possible through the porthole of a bathysphere, dangling into the abyss on a thin cable, Beebe's vivid descriptions of his dives attracted international attention and provided the stimulus for attacking the innumerable problems that still needed to be solved in deep diving. The next step was a free-moving vehicle which did not depend so much on surface support. Auguste Piccard was the great innovator in this phase of ocean exploration with his bathyscaphe *Trieste,* first developed during the 1940s. It resembled an undersea dirigible—the crew quartered in a ball at the bottom, the surrounding vessel filled with lighter-than-water gasoline. It was designed to sink to the bottom carrying lead ballast. To return to the surface, the ballast was released and the ship floated upward when the pilot wished to return to the surface. Piccard and his son Jacques made many improvements in design that culminated in the deepest dive ever made—to the bottom of the Mariana Trench, in the eastern Pacific, in 1960—36,198 feet (11,002 meters).

One of the first bathyscaphes being lowered into the water. The device has allowed humans to descend to the deepest parts of the sea. (*The Cousteau Society*)

The research submersible *Alvin,* operated by the Woods Hole Oceanographic Institution, is one of the new breed of versatile submersibles. Claws on the front take samples of deep-sea flora, fauna, and sediments. (*Woods Hole Oceanographic Institution/John Porteous*)

Submersibles

The 1960s and 1970s saw the development of an array of research submersibles designed for more agility but less depth than the bathyscaphe. The first of these small submersibles, the Cousteau *Diving Saucer,* still in operation after more than a thousand dives, regularly dives to a depth of 1,000 feet (about 300 meters). Submersibles are now commonly used for research, exploration, photography, salvage, deep-sea oil drilling, and submarine rescue work.

Habitats

One important method of ocean exploration remains to be fully implemented, although inroads are now being made. Scientists and researchers have created undersea habitats—environments where divers can live and work at great depths for prolonged periods of time. Projects such as the U. S. Navy's Sealab II experiment off the California coast and Captain Cousteau's three Conshelf experiments in the Mediterranean and Red Sea have shown that humans can survive and work in the sea. These self-contained "houses" allow divers to remain submerged for several weeks without having to undergo daily decompression procedures. Advances in technology have already taken undersea dwellings out of the experimental stage and into the realm of practical use (undersea habitats are used extensively by offshore oil-drilling facilities). The obstacles to wider use of undersea habitats are primarily financial. The support systems necessary to their safe operation are complex and costly.

Dr. Sylvia Earle, encased in an atmospheric diving suit, is carried to a depth of 60 feet (18 meters) aboard a submersible catamaran. At that depth she and the pot-bellied submersible behind her are released to descend farther, to a depth of 1,250 feet (380 meters) in a dive off Hawaii's island of Oahu in 1979—the first open-ocean use of the suit for scientific research. (*Sea Films, Inc./Al Giddings*)

Modern Diving Suits

The sealed, atmospheric diving suit may look like a science-fiction robot, but it is actually a very promising means of working under crushing pressures. Made from a magnesium alloy with articulated joints, it enables a diver to work at depths as great as 1,500 feet (450 meters). It also eliminates the waste of time involved in underwater decompression, since the diver can be raised quickly to the surface. The diving suit and its ever-improving descendants, along with sophisticated heavy machinery for such tasks as laying and burying pipeline on the ocean floor, make working beneath the seas an increasingly practical matter.

Exploring from the Surface

While divers explore the underwater world firsthand, their shipboard colleagues can collect an amazing amount of information by lowering sophisticated instruments into the sea. Underwater stroboscopic light cameras developed by Dr. Harold Edgerton of the Massachusetts Institute of Technology in the early 1950s photograph sites deeper than any diver could go and are frequently used to scout an area before divers are sent to explore further. Seismic techniques actually give us a picture of what lies beneath the *bottom* of the sea and automatic probes can instantly analyze a number of variables including water salinity, depth, and temperature, then relay the data to the surface.

Underwater Photography

Much work in developing underwater photography techniques was pioneered aboard the *Calypso* in the 1950s by Dr. Edgerton and others. Although the first underwater photograph was taken by Louis Boutan around the turn of the century, not until the Aqua-lung gave divers freedom and mobility in 1943 did underwater films become feasible. The first commercial Cousteau film, *The Silent World,* released in 1956, introduced the public to the startling beauty of undersea habitats. Underwater films, closed-circuit television, and still photographs improved as watertight camera housing, lenses, and lighting improved. Today, underwater photography is a fascinating hobby for many, a valuable tool for scientific research, and an indispensable means of revealing to the public the fragile beauty and vulnerability of a world to which they are inextricably linked but may never see.

Sparkers and Boomers

Offshore oil prospectors near the Mississippi delta in 1927 discovered that they could record the pattern of rock and soil layers beneath the ocean bottom by sending a sonic signal through the layers. The signal would bounce back when it hit thick bedrock and could be picked up on a hydrophone suspended from a ship. A sonic signal can be created by vaporizing water, which creates a shock wave—a sonic signal—that penetrates the layers of sediments. Early experimenters created shock waves by exploding dynamite underwater, which was effective, but was also catastrophic for undersea life. More sophisticated emitters (the first developed by Dr. Maurice Ewing of Woods Hole Oceanographic Institute in 1934) harmlessly produce the signal. One version, called "sparkers," consists of cable fringed with filaments which emit tiny sparks to vaporize water and start the shock wave. Another version, called "boomers," consists of a device with two plates that can be suddenly separated to create an implosion. Water rushes into the void and is vaporized.

Both types of seismic devices produce a graphic recording aboard ship that indicates soft sediment, bedrock, salt domes (a formation indicating the possibility of oil and gas), and other features. They are an essential tool in the search for offshore oil and in geologists' quest to understand the history of the seabed.

Automatic Probes

Biologists seeking to measure water salinity, temperature, depth, conductivity, oxygen content, and other parameters, traditionally had to handle several different pieces of equipment, take numerous water samples, and spend days or weeks in the laboratory analyzing samples and charting the results. A device called the automatic probe can now do all these things instantly. The probes are lowered overboard to record data from a vertical water column or can be towed along a prescribed course. One type of probe contains a cassette recording device which, when retrieved, can be hooked up to a computer to produce a numerical printout of the data and a graphic representation. Another type of probe feeds the information directly to the ship as it is being collected. Automatic probes suspended from buoys can even be interrogated by planes passing overhead.

Exploring the Ocean from Space

Navigation, communication, and ocean charting is being made simpler and safer by satellites such as NAVSAT, COMSAT, and remote sensing satellites. NAVSAT permits ships to fix their positions more accurately than they can from shore based signals. COMSAT allows worldwide communication with ships. Other satellites use remote sensing photography to reveal ocean currents, water circulation patterns, algal blooms, and pollution. Remote sensing, which can also be done from airplanes, is one of the most valuable of all ocean tools, providing us with an opportunity to understand the broad global pattern of the ocean. (See "Tools in the Ocean of Space," page 467.)

The development of new tools that penetrate the ocean has escalated in the recent past with the rise of such technologies as computers and holography. (See "Tomography," page 34.) And the process will not end soon. The ocean is so vast and hides so many secrets that solving one riddle merely opens the way for a dozen new questions.

T.C., M.P.

TOOLS LORE

- To build and operate the technological devices of modern life, at least 20 tons of raw materials for every person on earth must be extracted from the ground each year.
- Thomas Edison patented nearly 1,300 inventions during his lifetime, averaging one every five days during one four-year period.
- Perhaps the greatest inventor of all time kept his designs hidden in notebooks and saw few of them produced in even experimental form. During his sixty-seven years, Leonardo da Vinci (who was a contemporary of Christopher Columbus) designed an airplane, submarine, paddlewheel boat, parachute, helicopter, swim fins, a well digger, a water turbine, a water pump, a life jacket, a horseless carriage, a mass production system, shrapnel, a machine gun, and a sprocket chain. He is remembered, of course, as one of the world's greatest painters but he was also an architect, musician, engi-

neer, and scientist. To top it off, he was said to be unusually handsome and charming.

- At the Lawrence Livermore Laboratory in California scientists have succeeded in condensing matter to greater densities and temperatures than exist at the core of the sun. To accomplish this, twenty laser beams focus on areas much smaller than the period at the end of this sentence.
- The "Futurama" exhibit at the 1939 New York World's Fair projected for fascinated spectators what the United States would be like in 1960: "Federal laws forbid wanton cutting of wooded hillsides. People do not care much for possessions. Two-month paid vacations. Cars are air-conditioned and cost as little as $200. The happiest people live in one-factory villages."
- Ten years ago, during the writing of the U. S. Coal Mine Health and Safety Act, it was recommended that the "Auer breather," a device that supplies twenty-five minutes of breath to a trapped miner, be required by law. The lawmakers heard about the Auer (pronounced "hour") breather and ordered the Bureau of Mines to produce what they thought they heard—an "hour breather" that would sustain life for *sixty* minutes. Of course, the Auer breather didn't qualify and was rejected.
- In 1896 a U.S. patent was awarded for a self-tipping hat, which allowed the wearer to politely salute a woman on the sidewalk when his arms were full. The hat tipped, spun around on the head, and then dropped back into place.
- Anxious to exploit the riches of luxuriant Amazon rain forests, the Brazilian government undertook a massive, hurried road-building program—the "Transamazon Highway." In 1970 and 1971 about $115 million was spent and crews worked at breakneck speed to lay 3,500 miles (5,000 kilometers) of road. Unfortunately, the government placed a high premium on time and a low premium on planning. The same meandering river was bridged three times because builders had not checked the maps and diverted the road a few hundred yards. When the highway was completed, designers realized that 105 miles (150 kilometers) of the road will be flooded when a planned hydroelectric power station is built. (See also "Amazonia," page 274.)
- Among the tools designed for war by intrepid inventors: A gun that shoots around corners (so that a soldier could stay safely behind cover); a combined plow and gun for farmers located close to the action; and a combination protective helmet and gun (the soldier could pull a string alongside the head to fire, thus proving the old saying that an infantryman's life is one headache after another).
- Solar panels are hardly a new idea. In 1615 a "solar motor" was designed that pumped water for a fountain. Water in a black metal box was heated by the sun and forced by hot, expanding air into pipes that ran to an indoor fountain.
- One of the first tours to feature the luxury supersonic aircraft Concorde invited passengers to celebrate the New Year at midnight in Paris, then depart to pass another midnight above the Atlantic, and land in New York City before midnight there, in time to ring in the New Year yet a third time.
- In 1882, French engineer Abel Pifre demonstrated a successful solar-powered printing press in Paris. Steam was heated by a large concave mirror, the steam drove a small vertical engine, the engine drove a Marioni-type printing press. The device turned out five hundred copies of a journal per hour, even when the sky was overcast. Newspapers of the day predicted that solar engines would soon be commonplace.
- In the 1930s, before electricity became available through centralized networks, there were 1 million electricity-generating windmills in the United States.
- To minimize the damage caused by a loose pet parakeet indoors, a Wisconsin woman patented sanitary parakeet diapers in 1959.
- A U.S. patent was awarded in 1908 for an invention designed to awaken even the soundest sleeper. At the appointed hour, the clock squirted the sleeper with a cupful of water. Other alarm clock ideas: a device that slapped the sleeper in the face, another that bounced a rubber ball off the face.
- The invention of tools for cemeteries has challenged many clever people. Among devices patented: a casket outfitted with a buzzer enabling the deceased to ring for help, a casket equipped with tubes and mirrors so that the body can still be viewed from above ground.
- Often there is a significant time lag between the conceptualization of an invention and the realization of it. Some ideas take decades to become part of everyday life, others are realized quickly. Here is a list of common products and the interval between the moment of their inspiration and their availability:

Product	*Conception*	*Realization*	*Interval (years)*
Photography	1782	1838	56
Telegraph	1820	1838	18
Zipper	1883	1913	30
Television	1884	1947	63
Radio	1890	1914	24
Flourescent lighting	1901	1934	33
Stainless steel	1904	1920	16
Radar	1904	1939	35
Helicopter	1904	1941	37
Silicone	1904	1942	38
Frozen foods	1908	1923	15
Antibiotics	1910	1940	30
Commercial nuclear energy	1919	1961	42
Nylon	1927	1939	12
Heart pacemaker	1928	1960	32
Automatic transmission	1930	1946	16
Instant rice	1931	1949	18
Instant coffee	1934	1956	22
Xerox copying	1935	1950	15
Ballpoint pen	1938	1945	7
Transistor	1940	1956	16
Long-playing records	1945	1948	3
Roll-on deodorant	1948	1955	7
Videotape recorder	1950	1956	6
Filter cigarettes	1953	1955	2

SOURCE: Many of these facts were extracted from *Isaac Asimov's Book of Facts,* Grosset & Dunlap, 1979, and Stacy V. Jones, *Inventions Necessity Is Not the Mother Of,* Quadrangle/The New York Times Book Co., 1973. The list of inventions and their period before realization is based on an article by Stephen Rosen, the New York *Times,* June 18, 1976.

10

Business . . . As Usual and Unusual

The skirmishes between "business" people and "environmental" people are often bitter, usually hyperbolic, increasingly litigious, and seldom conclusive. The two communities frequently fail to establish a common understanding because they are talking about separate realities, even separate worlds, like two species with different systems of perception.

A business executive lives within a habitat characterized by economic survival, responsible above all to a board of directors and to stockholders. The executive is a kind of hunter and gatherer bringing back profits for the corporate tribe. The system dictates that the size of the catch is a measurement of success. Even though executives may be genuinely sensitive to life, they are not often rewarded professionally for protecting the resources of the planet.

The world perceived by environment-minded critics of the business world is less economic, more biologic; survival is not a drive for earnings but for physical existence. The habitat is seen by ecologists as a vast living grid of exchanges. People are complex and interesting junctures in this living circuitboard. They are not removed from it, not supposed to overwhelm it. To the ecologist everything is connected as *family,* and there is a collective dependence on the family business, which is the biosphere. Maintaining its long-term prosperity is more important than any short-term profits. In this perception of the human habitat, people are meant to husband natural systems, to observe the sanctity of life, to share resources, to ensure that the planetary enterprise is vigorous and healthy when the next generation of stockholders takes over. The corporate world might accept most of these principles but maintain that ecologists lose sight of the day-to-day *reality* of money flow, which, for good or ill, is now a connecting tributary in the planet's resource networks.

As contrasting as these two disciplines appear, both economics and ecology stem from the same ancient concept of grand management of the natural world. Their common prefix—*eco,* from the Greek *oikos*—means "house" and was applied to both in order to denote skilled housekeeping of earth's resources. As sciences, the two are similar in many ways, since they both deal in growth, balances, energy, distribution, seasonal rhythms, raw materials, production, and consumption. But the overriding contrast is one of size and power. The rise of multinational corporations over the past half-century has greatly increased the potential of business for large-scale interruptions of environmental and social balances. While U.S. and European companies bear the brunt of blame for environmental impacts, it is actually a problem of industry in general, not only capitalism. As the world's centrally planned economies intensify industrial production, they encounter the same problems of air and water pollution, for example.

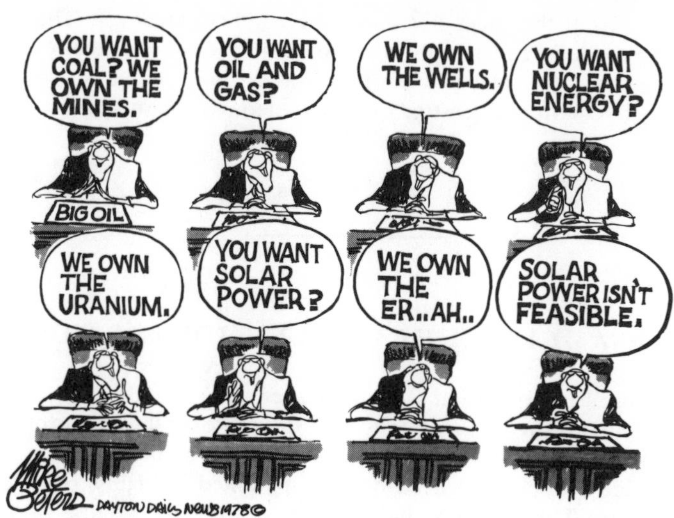

In this chapter, the *Almanac* looks at some industries and some corporations that have altered natural systems as part of their operating procedures. The subjects chosen are not necessarily the worst or the only offenders, but they are interesting representatives of the phenomenon of global enterprise. Some, like the Bechtel Corporation and Daniel K. Ludwig's National Bulk Carriers, are involved in land-modifying schemes so enormous that few governments could attempt them. Others, like companies involved in oil production and transport and companies dealing in the grain trade, exert a critical influence over resources that may mean life or death to millions of people. And some corporations, involved in important but potentially dangerous products or procedures, have the capacity to seriously contaminate life if they are careless.

The world of business is not monolithic, however. There are encouraging attempts, such as Allied Chemical's, to self-impose good housekeeping practices. There are signs that renewable, clean energy systems are becoming profitable business ventures. There are cooperative associations around the world that benefit both consumers and producers, while inhibiting unfair exploitation of either. And there are citizens' "watchdog" organizations keeping tabs on the conscientiousness of business.

It is also important to note that businesses often face tough challenges adapting to environmental regulations that were not even imagined twenty or thirty years ago, when many existing plants, products, and processes were instituted. Awareness of ecological problems came like a flood during the 1970s and, as a result, many attempts to regulate and revise business have been confusing and contradictory. It will take time to make business accountable to the planetary good without suffocating it; but the process has begun at least. The problem for regulators is to identify those enterprises that, out of callousness, greed, or ignorance, abuse their power and abuse the planet. In some cases, the product generated by certain companies may be so harmful that the firm's very existence must be called into question. But as Dr. John T. Funkhouser of Arthur D. Little and Company, a well-known consulting firm, puts it: "There is a wide range of companies, just like there is a wide range of people. You just can't oversimplify these issues." Most executives admit that no business likes to make "nonproductive investments"—pollution controls, for example, are in themselves not directly profit-generating—but they argue that they are moving toward new, longer-term definitions of productivity. If a company's public image is ruined by its pollution record, that's bad for business. If a company recklessly depletes a raw material on which it depends, that is bad for business. If employees picket a factory to protest unsafe working conditions, that, too, is demonstrably bad for business.

It is slowly becoming apparent to most people that what is good for the environment is good for business, but that does not mean the conflicts are over. The clash between profit-seekers and earth-defenders will be a continuing one. Eventually, as society adjusts to the limits of the planet, the two forces may move closer to the idea at the core of their common ancestry, of simultaneous economic and ecologic housekeeping.

M.R. with P.D.

THE ALLIED CHEMICAL TURNAROUND

In 1975, Allied Chemical Corporation, the fifth-largest chemical company in the United States, became notorious overnight as the producer of kepone, a pesticide that has since been banned in the United States. The chemical had been identified as the probable cause of sterility and neurological disturbances in male workers at a plant in Hopewell, Virginia, that made kepone under contract to Allied. In addition, it was discovered that Allied had illegally dumped stocks of kepone in 1972 in the James River near the plant. These incidents ultimately cost Allied approximately $15 million, including a $5-million federal government fine, an $8-million donation to develop an environmental research center in Virginia, and $2 million in settlements to kepone victims.

Five years later, in 1979, a chastened Allied had earned accolades in the New York *Times* for its environmental consciousness. The company has been called "a model for industry." To achieve this dramatic turnaround, Allied hired the management consulting firm Arthur D. Little and Company, Inc., of Boston. As a result of new attention to the health and environmental implications of its chemical production, Allied Chemical

- spent $250 million on antipollution equipment to improve the performance of its coke and chemical plants;
- appointed a highly regarded vice-president for environmental affairs, who was given direct responsibility for the company's environmental policy, as well as high-level management responsibility;
- established a Toxic Risk Assessment committee, which includes lawyers, physicians, and scientists, to review possible hazards referred to it by Allied employees;
- discontinued or delayed development of several new products because they produced negative effects in laboratory animals in preliminary testing;
- based one third of all plant managers' salaries on the safety records of their plants; and
- reduced its on-the-job safety record from 8.1 injuries per 100 workers in 1975 (considered an extremely high rate) to 1.78 per 100 workers in 1979, well below the industry average of 4.56.

P.D.

SOURCE: Adapted from an article by Thomas C. Hayes in the New York *Times*, Business Section, January 16, 1980.

THE TWENTY-FIVE LARGEST INDUSTRIAL COMPANIES IN THE WORLD

1979 Rank	*Company*	*Headquarters*	*Sales (thousands of dollars)*	*Net Income (thousands of dollars)*
1	Exxon	New York	79,106,471	4,295,243
2	General Motors	Detroit	66,311,200	2,292,700
3	Royal Dutch/Shell Group	The Hague/London	59,416,560	6,474,283
4	Mobil	New York	44,720,908	2,007,158
5	Ford Motor	Dearborn, Mich.	43,513,700	1,169,300
6	British Petroleum	London	38,713,496	3,439,582
7	Texaco	Harrison, N.Y.	38,350,370	1,759,069
8	Standard Oil of California	San Francisco	29,947,554	1,784,694
9	Gulf Oil	Pittsburgh	23,910,000	1,322,000

1979 Rank	*Company*	*Headquarters*	*Sales (thousands of dollars)*	*Net Income (thousands of dollars)*
10	International Business Machines	Armonk, N.Y.	22,862,776	3,011,259
11	General Electric	Fairfield, Conn.	22,460,600	1,408,800
12	Unilever	London/Rotterdam	21,748,583	920,320
13	ENI	Rome	18,984,960	89,040
14	Standard Oil (Ind.)	Chicago	18,610,347	1,506,618
15	Fiat	Turin (Italy)	18,300,000	NA
16	Française des Pétroles	Paris	17,305,220	1,137,282
17	Peugeot-Citroën	Paris	17,270,104	254,318
18	International Telephone & Telegraph	New York	17,197,423	380,685
19	Volkswagenwerk	Wolfsburg (Germany)	16,765,683	371,534
20	Philips' Gloeilampenfabrieken	Eindhoven (Netherlands)	16,576,123	308,701
21	Atlantic Richfield	Los Angeles	16,233,959	1,165,894
22	Renault	Paris	16,117,376	241,520
23	Siemens	Munich	15,069,575	361,938
24	Daimler-Benz	Stuttgart	14,942,324	347,794
25	Hoechst	Frankfurt	14,785,464	141,684

SOURCE: *Fortune* Magazine, August 11, 1980.

GOING, GOING, GLOBAL

A multinational company is defined by the United Nations as any company with assets in more than two countries. The phenomenon is not exclusively American, although the "global reach" business style was certainly developed in the United States and maintains its headquarters there.

The following is a list of sixteen companies not based in the United States that have very definitely gone global.

Company	*Country*	*Products*	*1979 Sales (millions of dollars)*
Petróleos de Venezuela	Venezuela	Petroleum	14,115,899
Petrobrás	Brazil	Petroleum	10,278,517
Pemex	Mexico	Petroleum	7,290,691
Hyundai Group	South Korea	Shipbuilding transportation	4,303,841
Kuwait National Petroleum	Kuwait	Petroleum	3,832,233
Indian Oil	India	Petroleum	3,533,032
Samsung Group	South Korea	Industrial equipment, electronics, textiles	3,409,700
Chinese Petroleum	Taiwan	Petroleum	3,097,506
Haci Omer Sabanci Holding	Turkey	Textiles	2,628,662
Korea Oil	South Korea	Petroleum	2,315,841
CODELCO-CHILE	Chile	Mining and metal refining (copper)	2,071,369
Zambia Industrial & Mining	Zambia	Mining and metal refining (copper)	1,886,105
The Lucky Group	South Korea	Petroleum, electronics appliances	1,760,362
Steel Authority of India	India	Metal refining (steel)	1,758,056
Koç Holding	Turkey	Motor vehicles	1,569,902*
Philippine National Oil	Philippines	Petroleum	1,547,022

* *Fortune* estimate

SOURCE: 1980 *Fortune* Directory;

A GLOBAL COMPANY: BECHTEL

Editor's Note: *Privately owned corporations, or "family businesses," generally are not obliged by law to publish an annual report, nor are they required to provide the public with detailed information on corporate activities. The Bechtel Corporation, based in San Francisco, is such a company, and its activities often directly affect the environment. The following reprinted article profiles this immense corporation and suggests the potential for environmental alteration that rests with companies operating outside the public consciousness and conscience. While Bechtel's impact on the environment can be substantial, the company's inclusion in the* Almanac *is not meant to imply that it is the only or the most important private corporation altering the environment.*

Today, Jubail is a sleepy little fishing village on the Persian Gulf. By 1994 it will be a major industrial city the size of Toledo, Ohio, with oil refineries, steel mills, a deep-water port, hotels, hospitals, an international airport, several power plants, and the world's largest desalinization complex. This mammoth engineering feat is at the heart of Saudi Arabia's plan to transform itself from a nation of desert nomads into a major industrial state. Jubail is far and away the largest single construction project in history. The entire city is being built by a family-owned business in San Francisco whose name is familiar to prime ministers and presidents around the world: the Bechtel Corporation.

Bechtel would be important if for no other reason than its sheer size. If privately held firms were listed among the Fortune 500, Bechtel would rank about twenty-fifth—bigger than Coca-Cola, Lockheed, or American Motors.

Few unnatural forces have altered the face of this planet more than the Bechtel Corporation. Following its slogan, "Bechtel Builds," the company has undertaken as projects the world's first nuclear power plant (Arco, Idaho, 1951), the Hoover Dam, the San Francisco Bay Bridge, the Alaska pipeline, the Washington, D.C., Metro, the San Francisco Bay Area Rapid Transit system, and the 1,100-mile [1,771 kilometer] Trans-Arabian Pipeline. Bechtel has built the world's tallest earth-filled dam (Swift Dam in Oregon), Central America's first oil refinery (in Panama), the biggest copper complex in the world (Bougainville, Papua New Guinea), the first and biggest coal-slurry pipelines, and the largest U.S. nuclear power plant (San Onofre, California). With one major construction project, Bechtel doubled the energy output of South Korea.

Started by an immigrant muleskinner named Warren "Dad" Bechtel in 1898, this "little family business" has grown to be the largest engineering and construction company in the world. Bechtel's son Steve, 77, remains the senior director of the Bechtel domain. Steve's fifty-three-year-old son, Stephen Jr., is now chief executive officer.

Built by Bechtel—the Hoover Dam spans the Colorado River between Nevada and Arizona. (*Bureau of Reclamation/DOE*)

A Confidential Memo

As of late 1980 Jubail was Bechtel's largest current project, but far from its only one. More than 26,000 full-time employees in about twenty-one permanent offices and thirty-odd subsidiaries are busy at work on elaborate oil and gas pipelines in Indonesia, a pet-food plant in Missouri, a trade center in Moscow, and a copper complex in South Africa.

Bechtel also has salesmen out hunting for new business. Unlike other construction companies, however, which seek out single-item projects—a $2-billion nuclear plant here, a $70-million shopping center there—Bechtel has taken to proposing the building of entire cities like Jubail, or the installation of industrial infrastructures for entire nations.

Jubail is only a sample of what the company has in store for countries like Nigeria, another oil-rich country that today stands on the brink of industrialization. "Using criteria starting with oil," begins a March 4, 1977, company memo on International Job Strategy, "we have selected nine countries, including four where Bechtel could exploit good current positioning and five where we suggest business-development positioning should begin or be intensified. Heading the list of the latter five is Nigeria." (The others: Iraq, Malaysia, Algeria, and Indonesia.)

This confidential memo goes on to say that Bechtel has learned from U.S. foreign-service intelligence sources that Nigeria is planning to spend $50 billion on industrial development.

Bechtel's political clout in Nigeria is underlined in the memo by its reference to the ease with which a meeting can be arranged with the chief of state.

Secrecy Pays

Secrecy has been a continuing theme for the Bechtel family. The company, like most of the other great American empires, could have gone public years ago. It undoubtedly could have had its stock listed on the New York Stock Exchange. New York analysts estimate that Bechtel shares would trade publicly at about nine times the current value now arbitrarily placed on each tightly held share by the family-dominated stock-evaluation committee.

But the Bechtel family has deliberately exchanged higher stock prices for greater advantages. They are happy not to be listed with the Fortune 500, or indexed in Standard and Poor's, or registered with the Securities and Exchange Commission (SEC).

What appears to an outsider as an almost paranoiac preoccupation with privacy is instead a strategic business policy with several motives:

- Privately held companies are not subject to SEC regulation. So Bechtel does not have to file lengthy and revealing financial reports with the government and is thus correspondingly immune from inquiring federal investigators.
- All Bechtel shareholders (about fifty-six at last count) are either company vice-presidents or their wives (wives' shares are held in trust by their husbands, who retain voting power). Each shareholder agrees to sell his stock back when he leaves the company or dies, at a price determined by the owners of 66 percent of the company's stock.
- Most foreign governments and corporations would rather deal with a U.S. corporation than a government agency, and particularly with one that is immune from government surveillance.

Buying Clout

Hiring people in high places to deal with others in high places is nothing new for U.S. corporations. The revolving door between big business and government is well documented. But Bechtel seems to hire higher. When it needs financial connections it hires the Secretary of the Treasury. When it needs nuclear technology, it hires the general manager of the Atomic Energy Commission. When it needs international clout it hires an undersecretary of state. And when it needs expertise to run the bureaucracy it is becoming it hires the secretary of Health, Education, and Welfare.

Names like George Shultz, Caspar Weinberger, Cordell Hull, Rear Admiral John Dillon, and William Hollingsworth (former general manager of the AEC) have been found sprinkled through the Bechtel directory at one time or another.

A look at one of Bechtel's strategic hires, George Shultz, reveals the advantages of this business practice. Leaving the Treasury Department for Bechtel, Shultz joined the boards of Morgan Guaranty, J. P. Morgan Company, the International Monetary Fund, the World Bank, the Inter-American Development Bank. These connections, combined with the occupation of other bank boards by members of the Bechtel family and other Bechtel directors (Crocker National, Wells Fargo), cover the financial markets fairly well. Under such circumstances Bechtel is in a position to channel long- or short-term finance capital anywhere in the world.

Bechtel's access to capital has placed the company in a unique bargaining position. If it can assure a developing country of U.S. financing of a major project, it doesn't have to worry much about competition. Since most developing nations can't afford to pay out billions for roads, power plants, ports, or refineries, U.S. financing is the *sine qua non* of development. Bechtel arranges the financing, Bechtel gets the job.

Nuclear Power . . . and Beyond

Bechtel saw the profits in nuclear power early on and quickly moved to become a dominant company in the field. The company hired W. Kenneth Davis, head of reactor development at the AEC, along with a handful of his top aides. They began to push nuclear power as the salvation of the modern world. Bechtel pumped money into campaigns for this "clean and safe" source of energy, helped finance the opposition to antinuclear referenda, and began building nuclear plants all over the world.

However, all has not gone smoothly for Bechtel's nuclear business in recent years. The directors of Consumers Power in Michigan sued the company for $300 million in 1974, when the Palisades nuclear generator broke down shortly after opening. The suit was filed when a number of metal steam-generator tubes corroded, allowing radioactive water to leak into the steam-generating system. Bechtel settled with Consumers Power for $14 million in cash and a promise to fix the problem.

Another Bechtel nuclear trouble spot has been its Tarapur reactor in India, which has been plagued with breakdowns, radioactivity leaks, and unexplained deaths among former employees. An AEC inspector called the plant "a prime candidate for nuclear disaster."

Such problems have put a damper on Bechtel's nuclear business in the last few years. But because the company doesn't own the plants it builds, it doesn't have to worry about being saddled with billions of dollars' worth of obsolete and dangerous machinery. Leaving that problem to its customers, Bechtel has quietly changed directions and set its sights on coal.

Once Bechtel decided to move into coal, its first step was to join a consortium to buy Peabody Coal Company from Kennecott Copper for $1.2 billion. Peabody owns by far the largest coal reserves in the United States.

The second step was to join with Lehman Brothers, the New York investment banking firm, and the Kansas Nebraska Gas Company to form something called Energy Transport Systems, Inc. (ETSI). Bechtel initiated the joint venture, bought 40 percent of ETSI, and made its own vice chairman, Jerome Komes, the chairman of ETSI.

After Bechtel pioneered slurry systems—pipelines that pump large quantities of pulverized ore or coal suspended in water from one point to another—ETSI proposed to build thousands of miles of coal-slurry pipelines criss-crossing the United States. To the present day, Bechtel has built 70 percent of the world's slurry lines, pipelines that service copper mines in Venezuela and Indonesia and carry coal from Black Mesa, Arizona, to the California border.

The slurry project that ETSI/Bechtel is now pushing hardest for is a 1,000-mile (1,610-kilometer) line that will move 25 million tons (22.7 million metric tons) of coal a year from the huge strip-mining area along Wyoming's Powder River to White Bluffs, Arkansas, where Arkansas Power and Light wants to build a large coal-fired generator.

With formidable opposition from farmers who fear dust bowls and cattle deaths from the loss of scarce groundwater, environmentalists who claim that water that has been used for slurrying becomes toxic, and the railroads that will lose billions in freight revenue, ETSI/Bechtel faces an uphill battle for its proposed pipeline.

The day after ETSI was incorporated, Bechtel wrote an unsolicited letter to the Interior Department's Office of Coal Research proposing to do a study of different coal-transportation methods. Bechtel did not mention its ETSI partnership in the letter. Bechtel was granted the contract and promptly began its coal-transportation study. The study concluded that of all possible coal-transportation methods, the most economical was—slurry pipelines.

SOURCE: Condensed from "The Bechtel File," by Mark Dowie, Center for Investigative Reporting, *Mother Jones*, September/October 1978.

THE GRAIN MERCHANTS

In the late nineteenth century, the heyday of "captains of industry" in the United States, families like the Rockefellers, Carnegies, and Vanderbilts dominated major U.S. industries and wielded unprecedented economic power. But those days are largely gone. Most U.S. corporations are now publicly owned and controlled by stockholders. The world grain trade, however, remains a stronghold of old-fashioned family-dominated industry: Continental Grain of New York is owned by the Fribourgs, Cargill of Minneapolis is owned by the Cargills and MacMillans, Bunge of Argentina by the Hirsches and Borns, Andre of Switzerland and Louis-Dreyfus of Paris by families of the same names. Outside of the grain business and the upper echelons of government, few people realize that such an important, life-sustaining commodity is controlled, essentially, by seven families.

Because the grain companies are privately owned, they do not have to make public their sales and profits, despite the fact that they control billions of dollars in grain, cooking oil, and animal feed. Cargill has a larger volume of sales than Sears, Roebuck and makes more profit than Goodyear or RCA. Bunge, with fifty thousand employees, may be the world's largest private company.

Interestingly, none of these companies grows any grain. They simply buy grain where it is available and sell it where it is needed, profiting in good crop years and bad. Their knowledge of technology, communications, and distribution networks makes them indispensable.

The Hidden Addiction

The grain trade has increased fivefold in the past forty years, with the result that more nations are becoming dependent on imported grain. A good example is South Korea, the second-largest recipient of U.S. food aid. The United States loaned Cargill $2.4 million in 1968 to help establish a poultry industry in South Korea (with the late President Park as a partner). By 1972 the operation was still not making a profit because South Korean import restrictions hampered Cargill's grain trade. Cargill used its influence to convince the U. S. State Department to encourage South Korea to change its policies. Finally, the United States deferred Cargill's payment of the original loans.

Meanwhile, South Korea was adjusting its agriculture and diet to accommodate the new source of food. Imported U.S. grain fed the poultry, and bread made from imported wheat began to replace rice at meals. Feed-grain imports rose from zero to a million tons a year, and the South Koreans could not turn back, even as prices increased 350 percent between 1970 and 1974. Local agriculture declined, but cheap food subsidized by the United States helped low-paid urban workers. South Korea eventually was importing almost half its food and has purchased more U.S. agricultural goods than any other developing nation. There have been similar developments elsewhere. Food aid programs also turned the Taiwanese from rice to wheat and made Colombia and Bolivia dependent on imported food.

The principal benefactors of increased trade have been the grain merchants. Dan Morgan of the Washington *Post,* one of the first to investigate the grain companies, reports that Bunge and Cargill doubled or even tripled their net worth between 1972 and 1977. The United States is the source of half of all the grain traded, and the increased trade is one of the few growing assets in the U.S. trade balance.

From Dust to Dust

Grain prices rose throughout the 1970s as demand increased, and the press for profits led to an environmental problem. Those who *could,* increased their planting, spreading their fields to marginal land that requires extra water and fertilizer. Twenty million additional acres (8 million hectares) were planted throughout the midwestern United States after the 1973 grain price increases. Trees that had been planted in the 1930s to prevent soil erosion were cut down to facilitate the use of mobile irrigation devices. As a result, the topsoil eroded and some of this land has been abandoned again. Bare sand has appeared again in many areas where the thin topsoil blew away.

Farmers should know better. In the United States between 1917 and 1920, grain prices reached record high levels and farmers rushed to plant crops on marginal lands to produce as much as possible as quickly as possible. By the mid-1930s, the exhausted soil had washed and blown away, leaving a ravaged Dust Bowl. After being nursed back to limited productivity, some of these same lands in Oklahoma and Kansas are again being exploited, and the levels of underground water tables are beginning to fall.

More significant than the grain that is being grown, however, is the grain that is not. Many developing nations are now importing grain and are instead using land that once grew domestic grain to raise luxury export crops. (See "The Green Revolution," page 177, and "What's on Land That Could Grow Food?" page 594.)

The U. S. Department of Agriculture estimated in 1974 that 460 million undernourished people would have an adequate diet if they had an additional 500 calories a day. This would require 21.9 million tons (19.9 million metric tons) of grain, about 2 percent of annual world production. The grain dealers, whose businesses are no different from any other commercial enterprises, cannot be expected to feed the world's undernourished people. They do not intentionally foster human hunger. But grain trading does involve a product immediately essential to life, so that some profit-oriented decisions must come under careful scrutiny.

K.F.

DANIEL K. LUDWIG: GLOBAL BUSINESSMAN

Daniel K. Ludwig is estimated to have a net worth of $3 billion or more, making him one of the richest men in the world. Yet his business ventures are so secretive that his name and face are unfamiliar to most people, even on Wall Street. At the age of eighty-three, Ludwig continues quietly to direct and even expand his empire with the energy and vision of a much younger man. He has already established himself as the third-largest independent shipping magnate in the world. Added to that are major holdings in twenty-three countries that include real estate (of which the Princess Hotel chain is but a part), mining (oil, coal, bauxite, and a variety of minerals), insurance, savings and loan associations, banking, and agriculture. And, he has purchased a tract of the Amazon jungle in Brazil four fifths the size of the state of Connecticut, spending approximately $180,000 a day to reap a profit eventually from developing this vast parcel of rain forest.

His is a rags-to-riches story, a textbook example of the enterprising youth whose intellect and business daring transform him into one of the world's most powerful people. Born in Michigan and raised in Texas, Ludwig began entrepreneuring at the age of nineteen with $5,000 borrowed on his father's credit. He used the money to convert a broken-down side-wheel steamer into a barge for hauling molasses. His profits were modest, but enough to enable him to begin slowly buying up other old tugs and barges. With the skill he acquired as a ship's mechanic he later converted surplus vessels, bought from the government after World War I, into cargo ships. These he chartered out under the name National Bulk Carriers (NBC), the company that became the "flagship" of his growing enterprises.

Perhaps Ludwig's greatest personal asset was his ability to foresee future trends. While in his mid-thirties he shifted from ship chartering to building oil tankers. Lacking collateral, he came up with an ingenious system for financing ships that would later be adopted by Stavros Niarchos and Aristotle Onassis. First he would obtain a long-term charter contract from major oil companies for tankers he had yet to build. He used these contracts as collateral against loans that provided the capital needed to build the ships. Ludwig then turned the oil company's monthly charter fee directly over to the lending bank to pay off the loan. In effect, the oil company's credit financed Ludwig's venture, with minimal risk to Ludwig. The bank got its money, the oil company got its oil, and Ludwig got the ships.

During World War II, the U.S. government hired Ludwig to build much-needed oil tankers, and he modernized the industry with a simple process. Instead of riveting a ship's plates together, he welded them, an innovation that made the ships stronger and allowed them to be built faster. At the end of the war, according to his original agreement with the government, all the tankers Ludwig built were returned to him.

Ludwig saw an advantage in moving his operation to countries where labor was cheaper and unorganized, where raw material prices were lower, and where the governments would welcome him. Moving to Japan, he leased the Kure Shipyard, where he eventually built the largest ships in the world—100,000-ton supertankers. Again, Ludwig had managed to be ready when a need arose. With the closing of the Suez Canal, oil from the Mideast had to travel all the way around Africa's Cape of Good Hope. Only very large ships could make such a long trip profitable.

Today, National Bulk Carriers, Inc., manages the third-largest private fleet in the world, with more than fifty tankers and dead-weight tonnage of about 6.5 million. Under the NBC banner, Ludwig has amassed a complex of other companies and holdings in different parts of the world. In order to avoid government interference, or the threat of antitrust action in certain markets, Ludwig has registered his ventures under different national flags.

Ludwig has managed to stay almost totally out of reach of public opinion, and this may be his most powerful advantage. His businesses do not have to advertise because they do not involve consumer goods. But the unique aspect of Daniel Ludwig's operation is that he is in total control of his empire. He is a one-person multinational corporate force. National Bulk Carriers has no board of directors, no stockholders, no annual reports. All decisions of consequence rest with Ludwig alone, a situation that allows his corporations to move quickly on one of Ludwig's educated hunches. A true venture capitalist, Ludwig has built his fortune not on shipping alone, but on investing huge sums in maverick schemes and being willing to wait years for what he believes will be a handsome return. Much more often than not, Ludwig's guesses have been correct.

For example, a friend once sent Ludwig a gift of oranges. Ludwig was so impressed with their flavor that he immediately dispatched his agronomists to find out where they had been grown and how. When he learned they'd come from Panama, Ludwig moved to establish Citricos de Chiriqui, a $25-million orange plantation on 10,000 Panamanian acres (4,040 hectares). Eventually he developed the entire area, parceled the land, built roads and bridges. He planted 800,000 Valencia orange trees and created the largest such plantation in the world.

But Ludwig's greatest venture by far, both in terms of capital and imagination, has been his Jari Forestry and Ranching Company, spread over an incredible 3.7 million acres (1.5 million hectares) of Amazonian jungle in Brazil. The original idea for Jari grew out of his belief that a worldwide paper shortage was imminent. Deforested and replanted with the proper type of tree, this gigantic piece of property could gain Ludwig control of the world's paper market. And, according to those who know him, Ludwig sees Jari as an achievement that will be his own living monument.

After reportedly spending an initial amount of only $3 million for the Jari land in 1967, Ludwig has poured from $780 million to $1 billion into the project, investments which have taken him far beyond his initial plan of producing pulp.

Ludwig has clear-cut at least a quarter of a million acres (100,000 hectares) of forest. Since the indigenous trees grow in such variety and so few have commercial value, Ludwig and his botanists decided to replant two imported species: *Gmelina arborea* from Africa and a *Pinus carybea* from Honduras. Both are quick-growing, especially the *Gmelina,* which is ready for harvest within ten years. In the early 1980s Ludwig expects to have 145 million trees growing on about 247,000 acres (100,000 hectares).

Perhaps Ludwig's most spectacular success at Jari is the pulp mill he built to process Jari's wood. His investigators advised him that building such a giant plant on site would be too expensive. Roads were not yet adequate nor were the cargo-handling facilities. Undaunted, Ludwig assembled a $250-million plant in his Japan shipyard, then had it towed, fully assembled, by giant barges on a 15,000-mile (24,000-kilometer) journey half way around the world. Then, the mill and its 55,000-kilowatt power plant were pulled up the Amazon and the Jari River and floated into place atop 4,000 submerged pilings.

Ludwig has also been trying to raise cattle, but has been running into difficulty. When the Vene-

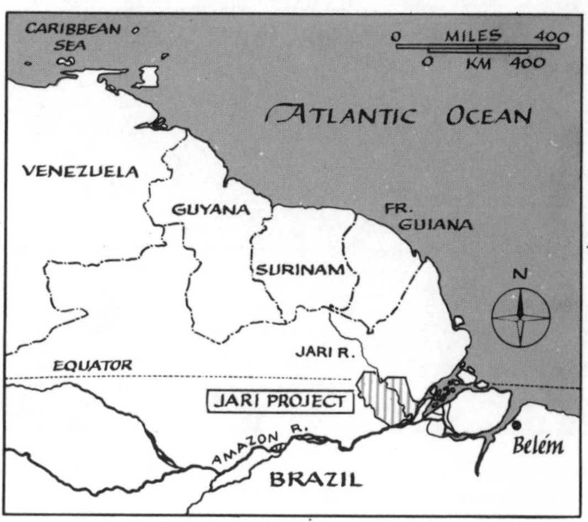

zuelan government refused to allow him to transplant the herd from his 650,000-acre (263,000-hectare) Venezuelan ranch, he began breeding humpbacked cattle from India at Jari. Eventually the herd should be large enough to feed his workers and also be exported to Europe and the United States—on Ludwig ships.

Ludwig has also begun experimenting with a new strain of high-yield rice. Eight thousand acres (323 hectares) are now under cultivation, aided by a system of dikes that control water levels. Current output is about 30,000 tons and growing. Another 27,000 acres (11,000 hectares) are planned for future cultivation, making Jari the world's largest rice project. Jari farms also grow soya beans, corn, castor oil plants, fifteen varieties of sugarcane, and twenty-two of manioc. Ludwig is also planting the world's largest palm-tree plantation, from which he intends to produce palm oil and lubricants. No one is sure where these will be exported.

When Ludwig purchased the Jari tract, it was already known to have diamonds, gold, tin, and bauxite, the raw material from which aluminum is made. In addition, a rare mineral, kaolin, which is used in the bleaching of paper, has been discovered at Jari. The Jari deposit is one of the largest in the world. Since Ludwig was already equipped with a shipping network, he built a $24-million factory for processing kaolin. Annual exports of 220,000 tons are expected, each ton to be sold at approximately seventy dollars. Ludwig has also built at Jari a hospital, schools, stores, recreation facilities, three small airports, thousands of miles of roads, and a railroad. About 30,000 workers live in Jari's five towns, Monte Dourado being the largest.

The environmental impact of Jari is extremely difficult to assess. Though Ludwig claims to be avoiding significant damage and even to be improving the rain forest's soil while protecting it from erosion, ecologists worry. (For more on Amazonia's delicate soil structure see "Ama-

Jari. In the heart of the Amazon jungle Daniel K. Ludwig is carving out a rice and timber plantation the size of the state of Connecticut. (*FAO/Peyton Johnson*)

zonia," page 274.) Dr. Howard S. Irwin, president of the New York Botanical Garden, warns that the method Ludwig uses will eventually desertify the land. Others though, like Dr. Ghillian Prance, also of New York Botanical Garden, are ambivalent. They point out that Ludwig's tree forests have produced high yields, but that such tree monocultures are susceptible, especially in tropical areas, to disease and therefore potential ruin. The diking off of the floodplain must also be regarded with caution. While on the one hand Ludwig's project appears likely to provide tons of rice in a region where food has never been grown in such quantities (in a country with a rapidly expanding population), manipulating the traditional ebb and flow of the Amazon's water systems could seriously affect fish and other life forms that depend on them. Also, projects of the scope of Jari, which require importation of vast labor forces and the construction of support systems as vast as those of a major city, are bound to have devastating effects on the immediate jungle environment.

Some visitors to Jari, like Dr. Gary Hartshorn, a forest ecologist at the Tropical Science Center in San José, Costa Rica, have clearly been impressed. "We are still a long way from answers about the long-term consequences of Jari's forestry operations. At this time [early 1980] it appears to me to be heading toward success primarily because of the unusually good soils being planted to *gmelina.*"

As ecologists study the impact of Ludwig's project, many remain fascinated by Ludwig himself. About the only certainty is that at this stage in his life Ludwig is motivated by something beyond profit, and that he intends to crown his life with projects, like Jari, that have truly global significance. It remains to be seen whether Jari will be considered a valuable monument or a regrettable legacy.

L.W.

AMAZON, INC.

The economic boom in Brazil, largely imported, has brought fortune to the rich and middle classes, continued poverty to the poor, disease to many Indians, and ecological ruin to some of Amazonia. In spite of assessments by Brazil's own federal agencies that only 2 percent of the Amazon is suitable for agriculture, vast tracts of land continue to be razed for plantations, small farms, and cattle ranches. An area the size of Texas has been deforested, mostly in the last ten years (this is still only about one tenth of the Amazon forest area).

While the word "fragile" has been overused by those concerned with conservation, the Amazon jungle deserves it fully, as the Brazilians are finding out to their dismay. "A cattle ranch in the Amazon is like a marriage. It all goes well the first few years, and then the problems begin," one large cattle rancher who got out of the business complained. The lush rain forest does not grow on lush soil. Once the trees, with their life-giving, nutrient-filled organic litter, are gone, the soil quickly degenerates in many parts of the Amazon to a barren expanse where only a few tenacious grasses will grow. In at least one area the size of Maryland, much land that was once rich rain forest is now a true desert of rock and soil that won't hold water.

In spite of the bad examples, the development of the Amazon proceeds apace. The last twenty-five years have brought accelerated exploitation, under circumstances that have left many Brazilians particularly bitter. Foreign business interests now control 100 percent of Brazil's auto industry, 82 percent of its rubber industry, and 54 percent of its chemical industry. Foreign corporations account for 50 percent of all manufacturing and 50 percent of the country's largest firms. Much of the foreign business interest in Brazil centers on vast, still unexploited Amazonia.

Before 1956, the resources of the tropical rain forest were guarded by strongly nationalistic policies. But the forest was a "barrier" to development. Few people had been able to penetrate it, much less extract and remove its resources. Juscelino Kubitschek was elected president in 1955 with a motto: "Fifty years in five." Deciding that Brazil needed technology and capital it just did not have, he reversed former policies. The Free Trade Zone of Manaus was established, and by decree the Amazon River was made international waters. Amazonia's tropical rain forest was open for business.

After a military coup in 1964, the new government extended Kubitschek's policies. Instituting legal and fiscal incentives, they literally and figuratively paved the way for foreign investment in the Amazon. Restrictions to foreigners buying undeveloped land were removed if the buyers would agree to begin development within ten months. Land prices were so low, payment was more symbolic than real. United States companies were given a guarantee against nationalization. Labor legislation was altered, and the government gained more control of wages and forbade the right to strike.

Industry from southern Brazil (much of it foreign-based) was enticed into the Amazon by a fiscal incentive plan too generous to refuse. The income tax payable on 50 percent of their profits could be placed in the Amazon Development Bank, where it was readily available to them for the financing of cattle ranches. (There are now, as a result, about three hundred cattle ranches in the Amazon.)

Exploratory mining projects were favored by all kinds of help: research assistance from Brazilian geologists, access to maps, and even the providing of extensive aerial photographs. The government reimbursed the cost of unsuccessful explorations and gave immediate revolving credit to those who made strikes. Tax breaks and a 20 percent mineral depletion allowance were offered.

With the blessing of the government, foreign companies and consortia joined Brazilian firms. Mining, timber, agribusiness, and cattle-ranching multinational companies formed, bankrolled by international lending agencies eager to get into the act. Obviously, investment in the Amazon had been turned into a very attractive proposition, as the following companies are finding out.

VOLKSWAGEN, Wolfsburg, West Germany

Automobiles, yes, but a cattle ranch, too. In 1974, the German auto-making firm purchased a 345,000-acre (140,000-hectare) ranch on which they plan to have 112,569 head of cattle by 1984. The Volkswagen scheme provides an interesting case history of Amazonian economics. The purchase of cattle represents about 40 percent of their costs. Turning the forests into grazing land will make up another 20 percent. But the purchase of land—at about $4.75 per acre ($11.75 per hectare)—represents less than 9 percent of Volkswagen's total investment.

LIQUIGAS, Milano, Italy

The deal made by Volkswagen is actually eclipsed by a land sale made to a subsidiary of this Italian conglomerate. It is estimated that Liquigas got between a half million and a million acres (200,000–400,000 hectares) in the Suia Missu Ranch, the largest in the Amazon, for 21,000 English pounds. Even based on the smaller estimated area, that works out to about $.98 an acre ($2.42 per hectare). The government has aided in another way, by constructing a "cattle integration road" that will run 1,200 miles (1,930 kilometers) to Belém, enabling these firms and others (including ranch-owning Caterpillar Tractor) to transport their beef and corned beef to the coast. A city, Liquilandia, was built for the ranch's twenty thousand workers.

NATIONAL BULK CARRIERS, flagship of billionaire Daniel K. Ludwig, New York City.

Ludwig is a breed apart. Single-handedly he has gained control of more than 3.7 million acres (1.5 million hectares) of Amazonian forest. (The Ludwig story is told in detail in "Daniel K. Ludwig: Global Businessman," page 484.) Few national governments could afford to initiate a project with the large scope of Ludwig's.

MINERAÇAO RIO DO NORTE, The Trombetas River Project, Para, Brazil.

Formed in 1973, the Trombetas project is targeted to produce 8 million tons (7 million metric tons) of high-grade bauxite annually, making it one of the largest aluminum mining operations in the world. Many foreign corporations hold nearly a 60-percent interest in Mineraçao Rio do Norte: Alcan Aluminium Company of Canada, Aardal of Sunndal Verk of Sweden, Norsk Hydro of Norway, the National Institute of Industry of Spain, Reynolds Aluminum Company of the United States, Rio Tinto Zinc of Britain.

COMPANHIA VALE DO RIO DOCE, Brazil

Owned by the Brazilian government, this is one of the largest mining companies in the world. It is exploiting the world's greatest known reserve of iron ore, more than 18 billion tons (16.3 billion metric tons) of 66 percent pure ore located in the Carajas region. Originally working in alliance with United States Steel, Vale do Rio Doce is now associated with a Japanese company.

A Few of the Others:

British Steel, Bethlehem Steel, Hanna Mining Company, Kaiser Aluminum, Reynolds Metals, Mitsubishi, Maruben, Thyssen, Hoesch, Krupp, International Nickel of Canada, W. R. Grace and Company, the Anglo-American Corporation, and Union Carbide. According to a 1976 New York *Times* article, "The iron ore, bauxite, copper, nickel, and scores of other minerals have attracted every major metals company in the industrialized world as well as those in Eastern Europe." L.W.

THE BUSINESS OF SUPERTANKERS

The birth of the giant supertanker is a near-perfect illustration of the interconnection between business, foreign relations, consumers, and a deteriorating environment. The massive ships were not created out of simple cleverness or naked greed but out of economic and political necessity. The consumption of petroleum has regularly grown by almost 10 percent per year for more than half a century. More than half of the world's proven oil reserves are located in one part of the world—the Persian Gulf area. These unavoidable facts of oil demand and location have dictated many of the world's political gyrations for decades.

Thus, when conflict broke out between Israel and the Arab nations in 1956 and 1967, the oil shipping business was vastly changed. The closing of the Suez Canal blocked the busiest oil tanker shipping lane in the world, forcing tankers to journey all the way around the southern tip of Africa to deliver their cargoes to Europe and the United States. The only way to make these imperative but costly trips profitable was to enlarge the carrying capacity of each tanker. As a result, the 50,000 dead weight ton (dwt) tankers of the 1950s doubled in size, then expanded to become Very Large Crude Carriers (VLCCs) in the early 1960s, capable of carrying 200,000 to 400,000 dwt, then grew to become Ultra Large Crude Carriers (ULCCs) in the late 1960s, some of which exceed 500,000 dwt. A ship of this size is about a quarter of a mile (0.4 kilometer) long, 200 feet (60 meters) across the beam, with a draft of nearly 100 feet (30 meters).

But if the reason for creation of supertankers is historically defensible, the way they are designed, run, and maintained is not. Unlike ordinary freight and passenger ships, supertankers have none of the internal integrity and strength provided by many separate decks. Their only structure is provided by the tank bulkheads themselves, and an exterior shell plating to give the ship its shape. The extreme length of these ships results in their alternately "sagging" between successive swells that support them fore and aft, and "hogging" or "bowing" across a single swell that supports only the midships. In addition, the low freeboard (the distance between the water line and the uppermost deck) allows an enormous weight of water to smash across the deck during storms. Such repeated stresses explain why structural failure is responsible for fully a third of the oil accidentally spilled at sea.

Flags of Convenience

In the mid-1980s, the VLCCs built in the late 1960s will be at least fifteen years old. Many of these ships, extremely difficult to maneuver in the best of circumstances, are from the beginning inadequately equipped with navigational instruments and have but a single engine, propeller, rudder, steering system, radio, and gyro. Usually only one officer will be on duty at any given time. (Contrast this with the redundancy of crew, equipment, and power required of an airplane.) As the ship ages and weakens, it is disposed of by the original owner, sold to an independent shipper who, operating with tighter margins, less responsibility, and greater anonymity, will sail the ship under a "flag of convenience" by registering it in Liberia or Panama, or in any other country

Ultra Large Crude Carriers (ULCCs) are about a quarter of a mile (0.4 kilometer) long. Small craft skippers have been known to mistake their bow and stern lights for two separate ships at night and collide with them amidships. (*The Cousteau Society*)

whose rules and regulations are either lax or circumventable. The new owners will protect themselves by assigning nominal ownership to a corporation whose only role is to limit the real owners' liability, and which can dissolve in bankruptcy in the face of a disaster induced by structural collapse or failed equipment or the errors of an inept crew, sometimes ill-trained and under orders to cut costs by cutting corners. In fact absence of traffic discipline—e.g., refusal to honor right-of-way—navigational errors, and other failures in professional standards are partially implicated in 85 percent of all ships' mishaps.

Getting Worse Before It Gets Better

The wild building spree of the 1960s, induced by profits of $4 million to $7 million per voyage, has resulted in an oversupply of tankers. In the face of an economic crisis brought about by inflation and laid-up but unpaid-for ships, tanker owners are more reluctant than ever to spend the money required to upgrade their ships, equipment, or crews. In the absence of stiff countermeasures, the world can expect the supertanker spills of the 1980s to be both bigger and more frequent than ever before.

What are the consequences of the supertanker business likely to be for the sea and its inhabitants? The only clue we have is found in the few studies made of tanker accidents of the recent past.

More Than They Bargained For

The largest supertanker accident as of early 1981 was the wreck of the *Amoco Cadiz,* which ran aground off the north coast of Brittany on March 16, 1978, and in breaking up lost its entire cargo of more than 1.5 million barrels of crude oil to foul more than 100 miles (160 kilometers) of shoreline, kill thousands of birds, ruin an entire harvest of oysters, lobsters, fish, and seaweed, and ultimately to cause an estimated 1.5 million tourists to take their vacations elsewhere.

Editor's Note: *The largest oil* spill *so far recorded was the blowout of the Ixtoc I well, owned by Petróleos Mexicanos (PEMEX), which occurred on June 3, 1979, and was not capped until March 23, 1980.*

The complete circumstances surrounding the wreck of the *Amoco Cadiz* may never be known, but it has been alleged that, after the failure of its steering systems, the ship went aground while the captain and a salvager haggled over the price of towing the vessel to safety. The tugboat's owners deny that service was withheld during bargaining, but no one denies that three hours elapsed between the time the tug arrived and the time it secured permission to tow. By then, the single tug proved inadequate and no others were available. The Bretons then had to helplessly endure a long list of injuries, while those companies and individuals at fault rested securely behind disclaimers of responsibility, limitations of liability, and international legal barriers. (See "The Hidden Costs of an Oil Spill," page 253.)

A Disaster Inventory

Major disasters, like the wreck of the *Amoco Cadiz* or the Ixtoc blowout, steal the headlines, but pollution on a smaller scale is continuous and unrelenting. For example, there are now about 7,000 tankers worldwide. During the five-year period from 1973 to 1977 these ships were involved in 5,000 separate incidents, resulting in the total loss of 90 ships and death or injury to more than 1,000 persons. Included in those casualties are 464 strandings, 1,488 collisions or rammings, and 339 fires or explosions. On average during this period such incidents occurred two or three times a day. Only 22 accidents in the same period involved spills of more than 20,000 barrels.

A typical event was that of the *Esso Bernicia,* which, following engine failure in one of its tugs, plowed into a dock at Sullom Voe (Scotland) on December 30, 1978, rupturing a tank and spilling about 4,000 barrels of fuel oil into the harbor. Thereafter followed a series of mishaps that ended with the failure of two booms deployed to contain the spill, the release of oil into Yell Sound, the contamination of miles of coastline, the deaths of hundreds of shore birds, and the begriming of 2,000 sheep that had grazed near the strand. One angered sheep farmer described the tankers entering and leaving Sullom Voe as "floating disasters waiting to happen."

Intentional Discharge

Unfortunately, the accidents, frequent as they are, are only a small part of the story, because at present most oil pollution is a fully intentional discharge of some kind. According to figures from the U. S. National Academy of Sciences, oil attributed directly to accidents of all types (that is, with both tankers and production facilities) only accounts for about 5 percent of the some 50 million barrels, or better than 2 billion gallons (7.6

billion liters), of hydrocarbon pollutants that enter the marine ecosystem each year. A full 50 percent of the total pollution occurs after the human utilization of petroleum products; pollutants enter the sea as oil particles found in air pollution that drifts out to sea, as municipal and industrial sewage, and as runoff crankcase oil from automobiles. (See "Wetlands," page 379, and "Wastes in the Sea," page 409.)

While pollution from these sources will ultimately have to be controlled, production and transportation of petroleum account for a full third of the total amount of oil entering the sea each year, most of it highly concentrated. Much of this pollution could easily be prevented by making and enforcing tougher regulations. Routine tanker operations—not accidents—account for almost 18 percent of the annual oil pollution in the sea. Most of it occurs during tank cleaning, when seawater is used to hose down the slimy residue that clings to the tank walls and is then discharged immediately or held as ballast to be discharged upon taking on a new load. Though using seawater for this purpose saves money and time, the practice is now being restricted in designated areas by the United Nations Intergovernmental Maritime Consultative Organization (IMCO). Ninety-five percent of all spills are less than 1,000 gallons (3,785 liters). Such small amounts may appear to do no harm, yet chronic low-level pollution of coastal areas is more damaging than a single big spill from which an area, given time, can recover.

How Damaging Is Oil?

The oil companies are quick to point out that petroleum is biodegradable, meaning that it is immediately attacked by microorganisms (it can be, in fact, a bonus source of nutrients for some microorganisms, enriching the sea to a certain extent); also, that it is far less toxic than many other pollutants, and that natural underwater oil seeps already occur. (Natural seeps add an estimated 600,000 tons of oil to the sea each year according to the U. S. National Academy of Sciences.) The truth is, petroleum can cause great damage before being degraded, and the effects of an oil spill are almost impossible to generalize. They will depend on the composition and concentration of the original oil, the rate at which the spill spreads and disperses, and the sensitivity of the surrounding ecosystem. One effect is the immediate poisoning of exposed organisms by lightweight, toxic petroleum fractions. Larger organisms, including many fish, are somewhat resistant to lethal effects because of their size and ability to avoid the spills, but smaller and less mobile organisms are inevitably subject to heavy losses. These include the zooplankton on which the larger fish feed, and the larval stages of both fish and shellfish. Dissolved alkanes can inhibit primary production of the phytoplankton for weeks or months, thus interfering with the food chain on the most fundamental level.

Another initial effect is the coating, by thicker petroleum components, of birds, fish, shellfish, and seaweed, many of which will die from a variety of direct causes. It is estimated that 40,000 to 100,000 birds died following the wreck of the *Torrey Canyon* in the English Channel in 1967. Such deaths are induced by ingestion of oil, by suffocation after surfacing under a slick, or by exposure or drowning due to the disruption of insulation and buoyancy normally provided by the birds' feathers. Because sea birds are frequently long-lived, slow-reproducing creatures with fixed breeding locations, an oil spill at the wrong time and place, or a series of spills in the same place, could seriously reduce a population. Several Atlantic bird species presently face extinction from repeated oil pollution events.

As an oil slick begins to weather, volatile fractions evaporate, soluble fractions dissolve out, and the oil thickens to heavier emulsions and tar balls. Much will collect on suspended particulates and sink. Eventually, most of the oil will end up on the bottom. But, in the water and on the bottom, it will continue to exert numerous secondary effects whose consequences are far from being fully understood. It enters the food chain with effects that include tainting, interfering drastically with local fishing industries, posing a possible carcinogenic threat to eventual consumers, and synergistic effects that interfere with reproductive, chemosensory, and orientation mechanisms. (See "Messages in the Sea," page 383.) Possible effects on the ecosystem include changes in species ratios, reductions in number of species, and shortening and simplification of food chains. Such consequences could be especially disastrous in areas already marked by low species diversity, where the removal of one or two species could result in the destruction of an entire ecosystem because of a complete rupture in the food chain.

The Long Term

In September 1969 the barge *Florida* ran aground off West Falmouth, Massachusetts, spilling about 4,000 barrels of Number Two fuel oil. Strong winds over Buzzards Bay pushed the slick into the West Falmouth Harbor and the Wild River estuary. The West Falmouth oil spill, in spite of its modest size, has been the subject of intense and continuing study over the years because of its proximity to both the Woods Hole Oceanographic Institution and Marine Biological Laboratory.

Soon after the spill, the shoreline was littered with the carcasses of fish and invertebrates. However, within a week, as the carcasses rotted and dispersed with the waves and tides, visible evidence of this massive kill had disappeared—an important point in attempting to assess the impact of such a spill. But in some areas of the harbor, mortality was nearly 100 percent. Oil sucked from the sandy sediment and carried ashore on high tides continued to kill new marsh grass for several weeks. For the next several years oil in the bottom sediments continued to seep and spread, vastly increasing the polluted area. Six years after the spill, fiddler crab larvae still could not survive in many areas of the marsh, and other species were still not behaving normally. Eight years after the spill, oil would still pool in the footprints of those walking through the exposed marsh at low tide, and clam flats remained closed to shellfishing because of tainting.

The Finite Sea

Another argument of the oil companies and tanker owners is that the ocean is vast enough to accommodate the oil that is spilled without great or permanent damage. Strictly speaking this might be true if oil and biota were uniformly distributed, but of course they are not. Most of the open ocean is a desert. The small population that does exist there is almost all contained in the photic zone—in the upper layer through which light can penetrate. This layer is a maximum of 650 feet (200 meters) deep. Unfortunately, oil, at least initially, is buoyant, so pollutant and biota are confined to the same very restricted space. Thor Heyerdahl, traversing the Atlantic on his papyrus raft, the *Ra II,* reported seeing evidence of oil pollution on forty-seven of his fifty-seven days at sea.

Even the photic zone of the open ocean is relatively devoid of life compared with the rich areas along the coasts and continental shelves. It is the photic zone of these regions that contains 90 percent of all marine life, although it comprises less than 0.5 percent of the oceans' total volume. Unfortunately it is also these same areas, close to the shores and harbors, that receive the great bulk of all pollution, not only from ships' operations, but from municipal and industrial runoff, outfalls, and dumps. It is in these areas where tanker lanes are most concentrated and where most offshore drilling takes place.

While much remains to be learned about the consequences of an oil spill, enough is already known to conclude that under temperate conditions, an ecosystem can take ten years or more to recover. Under worse conditions there may be no recovery at all. For example, a spill under Arctic ice could be catastrophic. Since the oil could not be cleaned up, nor could it evaporate, it would remain toxic indefinitely. Bacterial degradation would be extremely slow. Such a spill could conceivably destroy a large section of the Arctic's already fragile ecosystem. And it is not only remote polar areas that are vulnerable. Semi-enclosed ocean areas like Puget Sound in the Pacific Northwest are not quickly cleansed by the heavy wave and tidal action of the sea. A major spill in relatively calm waters like these could take decades to disappear completely. (See "The Strait of Malacca," page 80.)

With polar regions now under the active scrutiny of the oil companies, with the strategic availability of oil creating situations in which profits may be even greater and precautions less common, the need for tighter regulations and greater margins of safety in the supertanker business has never been more pressing. F.C.S.

CLEANING UP

In a world in which some oil companies and shipping lines wield more influence and money than many nations, it is easy to conclude that these businesses are beyond regulation, that marine oil pollution must be accepted as a contemporary fact of life. Fortunately, however, countermeasures can be and are being taken, as a result, to a large degree, of the urgent calls to action issued by individuals and groups. Such lobbying can pay off. Indeed, in the absence of lobbying the likelihood of effective action has been practically nil.

Remedies

The steps required to reduce significantly the international and accidental pollution by tankers have long been known. Seawater ballast, carried by tankers on their return voyages, must be stored in separate tanks to prevent its contamination by oily residue. The explosive atmosphere of the nearly empty oil tanks must then be replaced with inert gas; for example stack gas, deoxygenated during combustion in the ship's engines. Smaller ships should, at the very least, have tank spraying and cleaning systems that allow collection, separation, and storage of oily residues. Ports must include facilities for the discharge and recovery of such residues as well as the bilge water from all ships. Full double hulls, or at least double bottoms and bows should be required of newly built tankers. Tonnage should be limited. Double engines and steering facilities should be required in addition to redundancy in navigational and alarm systems. Maintenance and inspection schedules should be stiffer, as should training and licensing requirements for crew and officers. There should be a mandatory record and report system that would allow any prospective client to examine a ship's history of rule violations, warnings, and accidents.

The Laws

These and similar recommendations have been bandied about since the late 1960s, when the stranded *Torrey Canyon* spilled nearly a million barrels of crude in the English Channel. Public pressure from that disaster and others prompted the Intergovernmental Maritime Consultative Organization (IMCO), a United Nations agency based in London, to call an international conference on marine pollution in the fall of 1973 to revise the ineffectual 1954 standards, which prohibited little more than dumping oil in coastal waters. Even that proscription was ignored because there were no mechanisms to identify or prosecute offenders. While the 1973 convention did require segregated ballast on new tankers larger than 70,000 dwt, it contained no provisions concerning older tankers, nor did it adopt any of the other measures so clearly necessary actually to prevent pollution. It wasn't until a rash of six disasters in the United States in the space of twenty days, beginning with the breakup of the *Argo Merchant* off the New England coast on December 15, 1976, that public pressure forced U.S. officials and legislators to act. Their uncomfortable choice was then to take strong unilateral action applicable only to U.S. waters or to attempt to persuade IMCO to take stronger international action. In the end, IMCO did act.

In February of 1978 a new protocol required all existing tankers of at least 40,000 dwt to segregate their ballast, and smaller tankers to install tank-washing systems. Inert gas systems were required along with two independent steering

After a long history of groundings and breakdowns, the *Argo Merchant* went aground near Nantucket Island, Massachusetts, in December 1976, spilling 200,000 gallons (758,000 liters) of oil near the rich fishing grounds of Georges Bank. (*U. S. Coast Guard*)

mechanisms and radars. Most significant of all, the delegations, breaking with tradition, established an early target date (1981) for ratification, and invited governments to unilaterally enforce the protocol without waiting for ratification. Then, in the summer of 1978, IMCO drew a new convention on the training and certification of seafarers.

More to Do

Matters cannot rest here. Offenders must be spotted and penalized—actions that IMCO itself cannot take. Central to effective enforcement is the concept of "port state jurisdiction," by which any state where a ship is docked can seize it and prosecute for violations committed elsewhere. Such questions of jurisdiction and law enforcement are now under discussion in the U. N. Conference on the Law of the Sea (see "A Law of the Sea," page 568). Until these questions are resolved unilateral action remains the only possibility for enforcing compliance with IMCO's latest protocols.

Another problem is the monitoring of ship traffic in such a vast expanse as the world ocean. Some conservation groups, including The Cousteau Society, are hopeful that satellite "cops in the sky" may one day patrol the seas, making it difficult for ships beyond sight of shore to empty their ballasts, a practice that is virtually impossible to monitor now.

Controlling the routes and speeds of larger ships—always in the harbors and channels, and perhaps on the high seas as well—will be a blow to ancient and venerable marine traditions. But it is simply unavoidable today, when the ships are too large, the cargoes too dangerous, the routes too crowded, the owners too unaccountable, and the oceans too vulnerable, too small, and too precious. F.C.S.

Spilled oil can coat and kill marine creatures, including large animals like this penguin. The effects on plankton and larvae are less obvious, but even more detrimental to the food web. (*U. S. Coast Guard*)

HOW BIG OIL BEGUILED IRAQ

Nationalism, religion, conflicting ideologies, and above all oil have kept the Middle East a global "hot spot" for the past decade. Confronted with hostile rhetoric and actions, people in many Western countries have reacted in kind. Western political cartoonists responded to oil price hikes by the Organization of Petroleum Exporting Countries (OPEC) with caricatures of fat, greedy Arabs victimizing Western consumers. In 1979, Islamic militants took American hostages and chanted bitter slogans in the street, and Americans responded with equally bitter anti-Islamic demonstrations.

There are obviously huge gaps of understanding between the highly industrialized, largely Christian West and the newly rich, rapidly developing, Islamic Middle East—gaps both sides will be forced to bridge if they are to avoid open conflict over their shared dependence on oil resources. One small story from the history of Middle Eastern oil development helps to explain some of the current hostility.

No deep knowledge of Islamic culture is necessary to understand what was basically a "sting" operation in which Western oil companies held back the development of Iraq's oil resources for decades for fear of glutting the world market with oil, thus forcing prices down. Iraq had trusted a consortium of foreign oil companies to develop its oil resource, and the consortium claimed it was doing just that while secretly keeping a lid on production. Iraq watched its neighbors growing rich from their oil royalties unaware that it was being tricked. It's a common strategy among monopolies and oligopolies, and in the long run, a world resource manager might say, it was just as well the supply of oil wasn't higher and the price lower or industrial nations would have had even more trouble adjusting to the inevitable price hikes of the 1970s and 1980s. But for Iraq it was simply a bad deal. When it realized the scheme, it reinstated control over many of its fields with a bitterness toward Western oil companies that has persisted.

Tracing the story requires a glimpse at the history of Iraq and a closer look at the history of oil exploration in the Middle East beginning around the turn of the century.

Aside from its oil, Iraq is a poor, dusty agricultural country of about 13 million people. Although a highly advanced civilization existed in Mesopotamia by 4000 B.C., the last prosperous period for the area ended more than seven hundred years ago when the Mongols took Baghdad. For hundreds of years afterward, Persia and Turkey contended for Iraq, with first one then the other claiming sovereignty. By the 1800s the Ottoman Turks had a firm grip, which they maintained until World War I.

In the early 1900s the petroleum industry, which began in the United States, was spreading to other industrialized countries and young oil companies were beginning the global search for black gold. Oil was discovered in Russia, Borneo, Sumatra, Burma, and Iran, with the rest of the Middle East holding promise of vast oil reserves. In 1914 the British Petroleum Company (BP), Royal Dutch Shell, and the German Deutsche Bank joined with an Armenian entrepreneur named Calouste Gulbenkian to form a syndicate called the Turkish Petroleum Company to look for oil in the Ottoman Empire. After World War I, when the British and the French superseded the Ottoman Empire in the Middle East, the syndicate concentrated its search in Iraq, renamed itself the Iraq Petroleum Company (IPC), and contracted to give the Iraqi government a 20 percent concession on the oil production. Over the years, IPC gradually changed: the Germans sold their shares and were replaced by the Compagnie Française des Petroles (CFP), and two American companies—Exxon and Mobil—bought in. In 1928 IPC negotiated a new agreement with the government of Iraq, giving it a fixed fee rather than its former 20 percent royalty.

For the next thirty years IPC ran the oil business in Iraq with a dictatorial hand. IPC was legally required to report each new oil field to the Iraqi government and to develop production as fast as possible, but it did not. Although huge oil strikes were made in Iraq as early as 1927, commercial production did not begin on a large scale until 1950. IPC intentionally drilled dry holes to mislead the Iraqi government about the amount of oil in its fields and in several cases capped potentially productive wells rather than build pipelines to transport the oil. (These and other activities were revealed in U. S. Senate subcommittee hearings on multinational corporations in March 1974.) IPC's strategy was to hold back Iraqi oil from the world market to keep prices up—the same strategy now used by OPEC nations that so enrages Western consumers. The same oil companies involved in IPC were also drilling and making profits from oil in neighboring Arab countries. As Iraqis watched Saudi Arabia and Kuwait grow rich on oil revenues, they grew restless with IPC. In the late 1950s the Iraqi monarchy was overthrown and the new government asked IPC to give up parts of its concession. IPC refused.

In 1960, afraid to be undercut by cheap Soviet oil, the big oil companies cut their oil price by ten cents a barrel, without consulting the producing countries. Because so many Middle Eastern countries are dependent on oil revenues for large portions of their national income, this unilateral step infuriated them. Iraq, which had lost billions of dollars because of IPC's self-serving inactivity there, convened four other oil-exporting countries in Baghdad a month after the oil companies slashed prices. This was the birth of OPEC.

The increasingly angry Iraqis passed a law that withdrew IPC's right to all areas within Iraq where the company was not already producing oil. This amounted to more than 99 percent of IPC's concession, including wells capable of producing 50,000 barrels of oil a day that IPC had plugged and kept secret.

IPC never recovered from this blow, although for ten years it negotiated with Iraq, while at the same time trying to keep the country's oil off the market. In 1972, Iraq finally nationalized all of IPC's concessions.

For fifty years, Western companies had exploited, dominated, cheated, and lied to Iraq. IPC was Iraq's main contact with the West for most of those years. It is not surprising, because of these circumstances, that Iraq was probably the first to suggest the oil embargo of 1973. Although to some extent its economy, like those of other Arab oil producing nations, is tied to that of Western nations, Iraq remains militant, and it will be a long time before the legacy of IPC is forgotten.

J.S., M.P. with H.M.R.

THE PROBLEM THAT CROSSES IDEOLOGIES

Cartoonists, satirists, and social critics often depict multinational corporations as insatiable predators pursuing profit without human or environmental sensitivity. The need to pay shareholder dividends often takes the blame for the lion's share of global pollution, and the public perception is that any corporation that can get away with being dirty will do so, because cleaning up cuts into profits. Whatever the truth of corporate malfeasance, centrally planned budgets also wrestle with the need to show profits, if only to plow them back into the state economy. Socialist industries too are caught dumping illegally. They face the same challenge capitalists do: maintaining economic growth within a healthy natural environment. The *Almanac* scanned international press coverage from some socialist countries, and turned up a few interesting reports:

- In the Soviet Union, where environmental regulations are tough, enforcement is a problem. In July 1979, the State Committee on Labor and Social Questions passed a resolution ordering that plant "directors, deputies, and main engineers, as well as general employees . . . guilty of not fulfilling plans and measures to protect the environment . . . are to lose completely or partially the bonuses awarded for the basic results of economic activity." (*Gudok,* Moscow)
- Soviet managers have also been fined personally for violating pollution law, and at least one plant director has been sentenced to a year's corrective labor for violating environmental law. (*Izvestia*)
- In Hungary, journalists have blamed increasing pollution on "too-late government intervention," and criticize subsequent attempts to silence journalists who discover the violations. Pollution incidents are officially described as "mistakes." (*Magyarorszag*)
- In Czechoslovakia, the director of the National Department for Protection of Living Environment, Miloslav Hudeč, when interviewed in 1979 about how to reconcile the needs of the economy with ecology, said: "It is apparent that the living standard and the living environment are two important factors, and one could not exist without the other." He urged citizens to adopt personal habits that were consistent with a healthy environment and suggested that "the workers must judge their plants also from the standpoint of environmental protection. They must apply pressure for efficiency and for the observance of environmental regulation." (*Pravda*)
- In the People's Republic of China, the goal of the government has been to establish the country as a first-rank industrial power by the year 2000. But the drive to achieve this goal has produced extreme environmental pollution—air quality in some Chinese cities is worse than in many of the worst-polluted cities in the United States; waterways are severely contaminated by industrial chemicals, pesticides, and human wastes (one river was so coated with pollutants that it caught fire when hit with a spark), and coastal pollution appears to be a major hazard. In the late 1970s, realizing that they had been virtually ignoring their environmental degradation, the Chinese government enacted tough pollution control laws. Problems were not only blamed on technical and economic difficulties, but on the indifference of industrial managers. Li Hungyuan, an official of the national Environmental Protection Agency, was quoted in the New York *Times* in April 1980: "There is often a contradiction between production and protecting the environment. Some factory directors think only of increasing their profits."

P.D.

RATING THE REFINERIES

The petroleum industry is one of the most important polluters of air and water in the United States. Its refineries rank among the top five industrial offenders.

A Council of Economic Priorities study (December 1975) of sixty-one refineries run by the eight largest U.S. oil companies concluded that "the single greatest determinant of pollution control is government enforcement of regulation." Simply put, the companies operate cleaner refineries where state and local laws are more stringent; they do not control pollution well in areas where laws are more lenient. *Every* Los Angeles refinery, for example, had better control over air pollution than *any* refinery in Illinois. The difference is due mostly to the Los Angeles County Air Pollution Control District, which strictly monitors industrial emissions in that area.

The sixty-one refineries studied had 54 percent of the total refining capacity of the United States. These refineries also tended to be located in densely populated parts of the United States. As of early 1981, the 1975 CEP study had not been updated to reflect any recent changes in company performance. The study is included here because researchers claim there has been little movement toward corrective measures since it was completed. It should be kept in mind, though, that specific problems mentioned here may have been resolved or improved since the study was made.

The study focused on four major air pollutants:

- sulfur oxides, which can be toxic in sufficient concentrations to both plant and animal life and can react in the atmosphere to become sulfuric acid;
- carbon monoxide, which diminishes the oxygen-carrying ability of the blood;
- hydrocarbons, which can combine with nitrogen oxides in sunlight to form smog; and
- particulates, which are microscopic bits of any material released primarily when fuels are burned, and which are harmful substances that can lodge deep in the lungs.

The study also considered five types of water problems:

- biochemical oxygen demand (BOD), and
- chemical oxygen demand (COD), both of which result in the consumption of oxygen that organisms need in order to resist other harmful pollutants, and which may in extreme cases suffocate aquatic organisms outright;
- oil and grease, which coat the gills of fish and the bodies of other animals and can interfere with the reproductive ability of some species;
- phenols, a family of organic compounds that are toxic in sufficient concentrations and in the presence of chlorine give water a very foul odor and taste; and
- ammonia, a nitrogen-containing compound that acts as a fertilizer in some aquatic ecosystems

This Exxon refinery at Baytown, Texas, had good water-pollution control, but not-so-good air-pollution control, according to a Council on Economic Priorities study. (*Exxon Corporation*)

and causes an explosion of algal growth that depletes the dissolved oxygen supply.

The study's report on company performance follows.

Atlantic Richfield Corporation (Arco)

Arco had the best control of air pollution, in general, of any company. Although none of its five refineries did an outstanding cleanup job, they were consistently controlled. Arco had the best control of hydrocarbons of any company. And while its water-pollution record is not so good, Arco still ranked third in water-pollution control. Overall, it was the best performer of all eight companies.

Exxon

Exxon had good water-pollution control but a poor record on air pollution. Its refineries at Benicia, California, Billings, Montana, and Baytown, Texas, all had excellent water-pollution control. But none of Exxon's five refineries had good control of particulates, hydrocarbons, or carbon monoxide.

Gulf

Gulf's water pollution was the worst of all the companies. The Port Arthur, Texas, refinery was one of the two worst water polluters in the entire survey. Gulf did fairly well controlling air pollution.

Mobil

Although Mobil had some of the best refineries in controlling water pollution, it also had the very worst at Paulsboro, New Jersey. Mobil controlled particulate emissions better than any other company and also did well in carbon-monoxide control.

Shell

Shell had the top water-control ranking. Its eight refineries were still only fair on air-pollution control.

Standard Oil of California (Socal)

Socal had a good record on air-pollution control, perhaps largely because its home state, California, had the nation's strictest laws. The company, however, had a bad record of water pollution, and its El Segundo plant on the Southern California coast was one of the worst in the survey.

Standard Oil Company of Indiana (Amoco)

Amoco's eight refineries were nearly all bad air polluters. Amoco had the worst overall particulate control of all eight companies in the study. Amoco had not kept pace with water-pollution control, either.

Texaco

Overall, Texaco was the worst air polluter of the eight companies studied. Although carbon monoxide is the easiest refinery pollutant to control, every Texaco plant had a CO pollution problem. Texaco management seemed to resent federal interference in its water pollution as well; it has questioned the federal government's right to require submission of water pollution data at all.

POLLUTION CONTROL PERFORMANCE RECORD

	Air	*Water*
1 (best)	Arco	Shell
2	Socal	Exxon
3	Mobil	Arco
4	Gulf	Amoco
5	Shell	Texaco
6	Exxon	Socal
7	Amoco	Mobil
8 (worst)	Texaco	Gulf

J.S.

SOURCE: Council on Economic Priorities Newsletter, December 15, 1975.

RATING THE UTILITIES

In December 1977 the Council on Economic Priorities (CEP) published its second survey of the environmental impact of fifteen major electric utilities in the United States (the first was in 1972).

To meet new legal standards for cleaner air and water, the electric-power industry may need to spend more money than any other industry. Power plants use fossil fuels predominantly—gas, coal, or oil—and they rank with the automobile as the leading cause of air pollution in the United States.

CEP's updated analysis produced the following overall performance ranking, from best to worst, of the fifteen U.S. utilities surveyed:

AIR AND WATER POLLUTION EMISSION RANKING*

Pacific Gas & Electric (4.23), San Francisco, Ca.
Southern California Edison (4.97), Rose Meade, Ca.
Florida Power & Light (5.84), Miami, Fla.
Consolidated Edison (6.04), New York, N.Y.
Pacific Power & Light (9.35), Portland, Or.
Baltimore Gas & Electric (9.67), Baltimore, Md.
Duke Power (10.01), Charlotte, N.C.
Virginia Electric & Power (10.11), Richmond, Va.
Pennsylvania Power & Light (11.83), Allentown, Pa.
The Southern Company (14.03), Atlanta, Ga.
Commonwealth Edison (14.70), Chicago, Ill.
American Electric Power (15.17), New York, N.Y.
Northern States Power (16.26), Minneapolis, Mn.
Union Electric (18.36), St. Louis, Mo.
Tennessee Valley Authority (21.55), Memphis, Tn.

* Based on computed 1975 average emissions measured in pounds per megawatt-hour (lbs/Mwh) generated for three air pollutants—particulates, sulfur dioxide, nitrogen oxides—plus a factor derived from the percent of generating capacity with adequate thermal control equipment. The lower the number the better.

The companies improved their performance, over the period from 1972 to 1977, in the following order (from most to least improved):

1. Florida Power & Light
2. Commonwealth Edison
3. American Electric Power
   and
4. Virginia Electric & Power
5. The Southern Company
6. Northern States Power
7. Pacific Gas & Electric
8. Southern California Edison
   and
9. Consolidated Edison
10. Baltimore Gas & Electric

Five other utilities were not listed in the 1972 analysis. It is important to remember that the latest CEP study was in 1977; some of the situations may have changed, some of the problems may have been remedied since then. Company by company, here is what the Council on Economic Priorities had to say about each utility at that time.

American Electric Power

AEP's plant at Muskingum River, Ohio, was one of the very worst air polluters of the entire 119 plants operated by the fifteen utility companies. AEP showed good gains in controlling particulate and thermal pollution, but sulfur dioxide and nitrogen oxide emissions were as bad as 1972.

Baltimore Gas & Electric

The Federal Energy Administration forced plants in the Baltimore area to convert from oil to coal. BG&E did not upgrade its pollution-control equipment to deal with the dirtier coal, so it showed a decline in particulate control. SO_2, NO_x, and thermal pollution have not improved since 1972.

Commonwealth Edison

In 1975 the company's plant at Kincaid, Illinois, was the largest (output-adjusted) polluter of both SO_2 and NO_x in the study. The company's overall NO_x pollution rate is second worst. Other air-pollution and thermal-pollution control showed some improvement.

Consolidated Edison

Con Ed, along with Union Electric, was the very worst thermal polluter in the study. Con Ed's pollution control improved in only one area, No_x; all others got worse.

Duke Power

Duke's eight major plants emitted a large amount of particulates. However, Duke's power plant system was the most energy-efficient in the study. It used less fuel, and consequently polluted less, than a less efficient company would producing the same amount of electricity.

Florida Power & Light

The company is relatively good on air-pollution control, but by 1977 it had not tried to reduce its NO_x emissions from the 1972 level. It made good gains, however, in controlling thermal and SO_2 pollution.

Northern States Power

NSP had problems with SO_2 and NO_x control. It improved moderately in controlling particulate and thermal pollution, but the company's A. S. King plant in Minnesota emitted the third-largest amount of NO_x in the study.

Pacific Gas & Electric

The company's worst pollution problem was thermal. It fought the EPA over installation of cooling towers at several plants. Nevertheless, PG&E was one of the top companies for controlling all three air pollutants.

Pacific Power & Light

The company had a good record in using thermal-pollution-control equipment, and it was the highest-ranked of the major coal-burning utilities. Its Dave Johnston plant in Wyoming had a big problem with particulate emissions, but new equipment to reduce particulate discharge was installed in 1976.

Pennsylvania Power & Light

Penn P&L had an excellent water-pollution-control record, and its particulate control was also good. The company's main problem was SO_2 emissions, caused by its extensive use of local medium-sulfur coal.

Southern California Edison

SCE had a fairly good record in both air- and water-pollution control. However, it is part owner of the Four Corners plant in the Southwest desert, still a major polluter.

The Southern Company

SoCo had made substantial improvements in thermal-pollution control, but it had a low rank in particulate control and also had a serious problem with SO_2. The company's Barry plant in Alabama was the third-largest particulate emitter in the study.

Tennessee Valley Authority

TVA was one of the worst particulate polluters in the survey and had a poor record on thermal pollution too. Because of its use of high-sulfur coal, TVA had the worst SO_2 control in the study.

Union Electric

UE used high-sulfur coal and had SO_2 control problems. It had the worst record among all utilities studied in controlling thermal pollution.

Virginia Electric & Power

Vepco had a relatively strong particulate-control program. It improved in control of SO_2 and thermal pollution.

The CEP study concluded that the electric-power industry, with few exceptions, does not clean up after itself unless legally required to do so—and not always even then.

Company	*Overall Air and Water Pollution Control Rank*	*Pollution Control Improvement Rank*
American Electric Power	12	3
Baltimore Gas & Electric	6	10
Commonwealth Edison	11	2
Consolidated Edison	4	8
Duke Power	7	*
Florida Power & Light	3	1
Northern States Power	13	6
Pacific Gas & Electric	1	7
Pacific Power & Light	5	*
Pennsylvania Power & Light	9	*
Southern California Edison	2	8
The Southern Company	10	5
Tennessee Valley Authority	15	*
Union Electric	14	*
Virginia Electric Power	8	3

* Improvement rank not applicable; company not included in the original study.

SOURCE: Council on Economic Priorities Newsletter, December 7, 1977.

J.S.

Wavemakers:

PRODDING THE CORPORATE CONSCIENCE

On the ninth floor of a low-rent office building in New York City, surrounded by the citadels of American big business, a small group of people quietly and diligently investigate the morality of the corporate world, frequently exposing irresponsibility at high levels.

The staff of the Council on Economic Priorities (CEP) assembles facts—carefully substantiated data

about the social and environmental performance of U.S. corporations. Since 1970, those facts have served to topple managements, prompt legislation, and prove that responsibility can coexist with profit.

The Council's purpose is to investigate company performance in areas that have included environmental impact, consumer health and safety, political influence, and military production. The published data are received by the Council membership, corporate subscribers, libraries, environmental organizations, stockholders, consumer groups, and government agencies.

The Council, says a brochure, "presents the data, and lets the facts speak for themselves." The simple formula has worked. The Council "has never had an instance where a significant finding in one of its studies has been successfully challenged," according to Stuart Baldwin, the Council's marketing director.

The group points to three examples of its success:

- After a 1970 Council report entitled "Paper Profits" ranked twenty-four paper companies in their compliance with pollution-control regulations (see "The Page You Are Reading," page 203), the family owners of one low-ranked company summarily fired its top management. The company now rates its managers according to their sensitivity to environmental impact.
- When a 1975 study, "Military Maneuvers," turned up conflicts of interest between the U. S. Defense Department and defense contractors, legislation was passed to close the "revolving door" between jobs in both workplaces.
- Amendments to the Mineral Leasing Act were passed over former President Gerald Ford's veto after a 1974 Council study, "Leased and Lost," found that coal on public land was being leased for private speculation.

Ironically, in the style of its daily operations—cool, businesslike, and academic—the Council might be an investment firm or the research arm of a major corporation.

In fact, the Council's founder and president, Alice Tepper Marlin, was a securities analyst for a Boston brokerage firm when, in 1969, she was inspired to begin the Council. She was asked by a synagogue to develop a "peace portfolio" of nonmilitary stocks. After a *Wall Street Journal* advertisement drew six hundred responses, "I started thinking of how to expand to cover other social problems," she recalled. Clearly, her thinking was sound; in the Council's first eight years, as a result

As marketing requested it

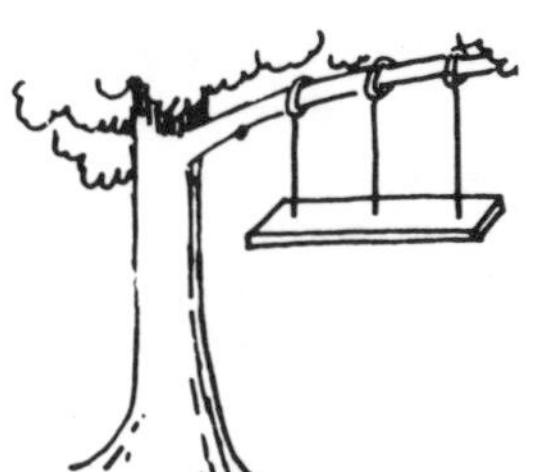

As sales ordered it

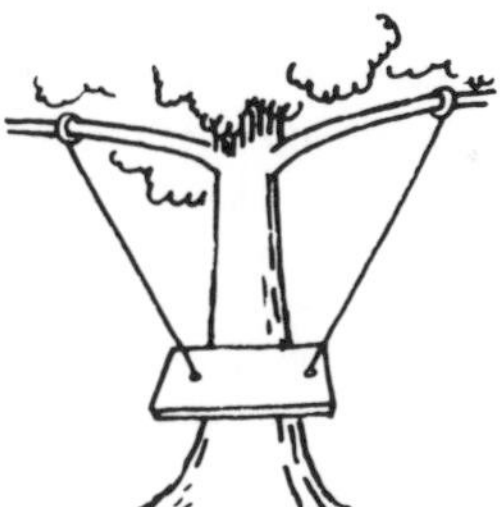

As manufacturing built it

As supply delivered it

As plant installed it

As advertising sold it

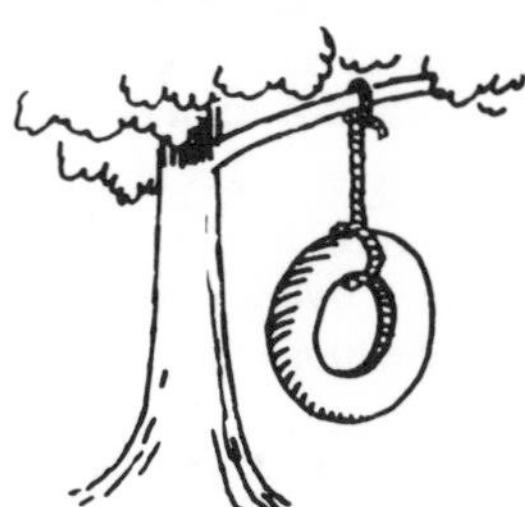

What the customer wanted

(*World Press Review*)

of growing corporate subscriptions and donations, her budget jumped from $30,000 to half a million dollars.

A look at some members of her staff provides insight into what moves the organization.

Marketing Director Stuart Baldwin was a seventeen-year-old Boy Scout competing in a speech contest on "Youth's Role in the Environmental Crisis" when he was noticed—and hired—by one of his judges, Jim Kollegger, founder of New York's Environment Information Center.

Baldwin wears several hats. Besides being the marketing director, which gives him responsibility for the earned income that comprises one third of the Council's budget, he is also a member of the executive staff, is the elected staff liaison to the Board of Directors, and managed a study of the ethical implications of investments by the California state employees' pension fund.

The pension fund project was an unusual one for the Council because "state governments are not generally beating down our doors to give us $60,000," says Baldwin. It's important for the future, he explains, because in the country at large, $500 billion is invested by pension funds, which own 20 percent of all New York Stock Exchange securities and 40 percent of all corporate bonds. "My own feeling is that pension funds will be the battleground of social responsibility in the 1980s," he says.

Another staffer at the Council is comptroller Dorothy Elliot, a thirty-nine-year-old mother, who once handled finances for a Rhode Island advertising firm. "I was having a really easy life," she recalls. One day she started asking questions about the company's principal clients—chemical companies. "Nobody ever told us what the detrimental aspects of those chemicals were. Here I was helping to sell chemicals without knowing their effect."

She began making significant changes in her life, which led to a job with the Environmental Action Coalition, then to CEP.

Besides her job at the Council and her maternal duties, Elliot handles some of the antinuclear finances of Musicians United for Safe Energy (MUSE). Does she feel the Council's work is effective? "You can see it in the studies and reports," she said. "They are being used by the government. Like the 'B-1 Bomber' (a 1976 study of the bomber's strategic, economic, and employment impact). President Carter read it, and his advisers read it, and that's one reason he decided not to build it.

"I think corporations aren't ignoring the issues as much anymore. We know that some of them are taking us seriously because when we go back for follow-up studies a few years later, we can see changes."

Gordon Adams, thirty-eight, is a research fellow at the Council. An assistant professor in Political Science at Rutgers University, Adams joined the Council to research military spending. He's working now to investigate the feasibility of converting defense contracting to other forms of manufacturing. (See "Swords into Plowshares," page 561.)

Adams says of his work at the Council, "A lot of people spend a lot of time in universities thinking but not doing. And a lot of people in action groups don't have time to think." At the Council, "the thinking you're doing is relevant to change in American society, and that's very personally satisfying to me.

"In the energy area, for instance, one of the problems politically is the very common expectation in American society, and among labor unions particularly, that further advances in high-level technology industries are going to create unemployment. One of the very important contributions the Council can make is to provide some data showing that the employment situation in the United States is going to be better off with renewable resources development than it would with nuclear power."

The work of the Council is effective, according to the people who work there. But is overall change occurring? Are corporations in general becoming more responsible?

Stuart Baldwin thinks they are. "The biggest change I've seen is the institutionalizing of what used to be only external social issues," he says. "It's a rare company that would actively condone discrimination now. There's a whole apparatus that's grown in the area of equal employment. The same could be said for pollution control.

"There are still going to be disputes between reasonable people about how to address the issues, but the idea that a company is in business solely to make money is, if not a dead concept, a dying concept."

B.C.B.

HOW TO JOIN CEP

COUNCIL ON ECONOMIC PRIORITIES (CEP), 84 Fifth Avenue, New, York, NY 10001, (212) 691-7506
Publications: CEP Newsletter, numerous reports (newsletter free to members, $15/year)

CEP produces a broad range of reports dealing with issues of corporate accountability. In addition to supplying information to interested individuals, CEP also provides full research services to institutions.

B.C.B.

THE BUSINESS OF THE SUN ALSO RISES

When the sun shineth, make hay.

JOHN HEYWOOD
Proverbs (1546)

There are at least two things upon which most energy specialists agree: one, that someday we will learn to handle solar power so well it will dominate our energy sources; and, two, that it will take a lot of money to make this happen. The technological breakthroughs necessary to turn sunbeams into electrical power *cheaply* and to capture the solar energy in the wind and sea will demand expensive research, development, and implementation. Two sponsors of such programs are usually mentioned as sources of "megabucks"—government and big business.

Solar energy advocates have proposed that the U.S. government begin nurturing solar energy by purchasing it for military installations and other government facilities. By creating a demand, the funds and market would generate new developments while reducing prices of existing devices. Other solar advocates claim that small solar companies could initiate a Solar Age if they were given government grants and incentives. Still other solar advocates believe that the only realistic route to renewable energies such as solar is through the existing structures—and investment capital—of the large energy corporations, especially the oil companies. In the long run, the debate may be academic, because major corporations have already begun a drive to capture the initiative (and the control) in solar development.

Item: Of the nine firms producing photovoltaics (small solar cells that convert sunlight directly into electricity), eight have been purchased by large corporations, five of those by major oil companies. Between them, Exxon and Atlantic Richfield control approximately half the industry. (See also "Photovoltaic Cells," page 29.)

Item: Essential for the construction of solar collectors, copper stands to become an increasingly valuable resource. Through recent acquisitions, the oil industry has gained control of 33 percent of all U.S. domestic copper production.

Item: In 1978, Southern California Gas and Electric installed demonstration solar hot-water heaters in several homes. Residents objected when the private utility placed meters on the collectors. They were outraged when they discovered that the price of free sunlight was being pegged to that of natural gas.

Item: Twelve of the top twenty-five solar companies are owned by firms with annual sales greater than $1 billion, including Exxon, General Electric, General Motors, Alcoa, and Grumman. Other solar vendors such as Westinghouse, Bechtel, and Lockheed are not far behind the twenty-five leaders.

The New Sun Kings

United States government antitrust experts, intent on preserving competition in the solar industry, are troubled by oil company involvement. They fear oil companies may hold back on the pace of development of alternative fuels in order to protect oil and gas reserve value, or that supply of alternative fuels could be restricted by a lack of competition.

A very troubling argument against major oil company involvement in solar development has been presented by the Federal Trade Commission (FTC): "The trend toward diversified energy companies, if allowed to continue, threatens to limit decision-making in the crucial energy market to a few powerful firms." The giant oil com-

"THE WAY I UNDERSTAND IT, SOLAR ENERGY TAKES FROM THE RICH, AND GIVES TO THE POOR."

panies already control a great proportion of U.S. energy resources. According to a 1979 congressional study, the eight largest oil firms control 64 percent of all proven oil reserves, 60 percent of all natural gas, and 45 percent of all known uranium reserves. The FTC's Dougherty is concerned that "the oil companies' substantial political and economic power . . . has apparently been abused in a variety of ways, ranging from bribery to political interventions in the internal affairs of foreign nations."

Solar Power Plays

Regrettably, the U.S. government is doing little to encourage competition within the solar industry. Some solar advocates even contend that the Department of Energy (DOE) is, in effect, handing over the solar industry to the large energy firms. In 1978, five large corporations won 70 percent of the government's energy research and development funds. A single company, Rockwell International, received close to a quarter of the research and development budget. According to the House Committee on Small Business, DOE

The "big business" approach to solar energy is to orbit huge solar satellites that would transmit energy to earth via microwaves. The transmission could be expensive and environmentally disruptive. (*NASA/DOE*)

gave only 0.7 percent of its total solar obligations to small businesses in the first six months of fiscal year 1979.

Besides funding research, the federal government purchases solar equipment, and these funds are also directed toward large firms. Almost 70 percent of the $6 million available through the Department of Housing and Urban Development's solar demonstration program for 1977 went to seven major corporate solar manufacturers. All but two were solar subsidiaries of large U.S. corporations.

Besides favoring large companies, DOE's solar office favors large solar projects, to the dismay of solar advocates who warn that such centralized generating stations eliminate a major attraction of solar: energy independence from large utilities. Fifteen percent of DOE's total solar budget goes for the "Power Tower" in California's Mojave Desert, a project consisting of 2,200 giant mirrors that focus sunlight on a boiler atop a 500-foot (152-meter) concrete tower. The $130-million project is being constructed by McDonnell-Douglas and will produce electricity for Southern California Edison. The White House Office of Science and Technology describes the project as "economically unpromising."

Sunsat

But some firms want the Department of Energy's solar office to think even bigger, to produce a satellite that would be history's largest energy-production facility. "Sunsat," a 72-square-mile (186.5-square-kilometer) satellite, larger than Manhattan, would beam microwave radiation down to huge reception and relay stations on earth. (See "Construction in Space," page 49.) Sunsat's supporters say one of the system's dozen space stations could produce almost twice the power of a major dam. At any rate, industry wants to use government money to find out. Many of the largest aerospace firms (including Boeing, Lockheed, McDonnell-Douglas, General Electric, Westinghouse, and Martin Marietta) are lobbying for federal money to cover the initial investments in Sunsat.

Sunsat's critics contend that the microwaves are harmful, that the $60-billion price tag is out of bounds, that the satellite would be difficult to protect from sabotage or attack, and that the energy required to build and launch the satellite would exceed the amount it could produce for many years. The most vehement opposition, however, is aroused by the prospect that a solar/microwave satellite would be another centralized technology controlled by large corporate interests.

Avoiding Sun Business Burns

The transition to a solar society will not be easy, cheap, or quick. And the crucial developments may not be technological ones. Decisions over the economics and the control of the emerging solar industry may determine its nature in the future. If corporate clout prevails, the dream of small-scale solar advocates could be extinguished. Their work is rooted in the belief that solar technologies offer us the chance to phase out the use of energy sources that are environmentally damaging, vulnerable to interruption, and controlled by a few corporations. R.M.

"Power Tower" amid a field of sun-reflecting mirrors or "heliostats." Artist's rendering of a project being constructed in the Mojave Desert near Barstow, California, to produce solar electric power. (*Martin Marietta Corp./DOE*)

SOLAR VELVET

The textile industry is one of the most water-intensive industries in the United States (see "Blue Jeans," page 221), and much of the water it uses must be extremely hot, consuming vast amounts of energy. The U. S. Department of Energy (DOE) has calculated that if the entire industry could switch to solar hot water heating, it could save 8 million barrels of oil each year.

A full switchover will not be possible for several years, but one textile company, the Riegel Textile Corporation, has installed a model solar unit at its La France velvet upholstery plant in South Carolina. The unit is a joint project of Riegel, the DOE, the Environmental Protection Agency, and the General Electric Company to gather data on how solar might best be adapted to the textile industry.

Experimental projects like this, with government funding and analysis, help overcome the reluctance of many businesses to invest in new, low-energy technology. Once a system proves workable and economical, the investments follow. At the velvet plant, although results of the experiment were mixed, the chairman of the company remains enthusiastic about solar.

The La France unit, 6,800 square feet (632 square meters) of collection area spread over 396 panels of collectors, heats water to be used in the dye-fixing process to just about the boiling point of 210° F (100° C) and has hot storage capacity for approximately 8,000 gallons (30,280 liters) of water, and so the hope is to maintain the storage tank nearly full all the time.

The unit, which cost $300,000 to install, requires little special maintenance and, depending upon the weather and the time of year, provides 50 to 70 percent of the heat required for one dyebeck (the machine where hot water, dye, auxiliary materials and fabric are mixed to produce dyed fabric). Since the La France plant has 17 dyebecks, the solar unit is a long way from carrying all the plant's heating needs, but, according to Robert Coleman, chairman of Riegel Textile, "We went into the project to learn what can and cannot be done with solar in terms of water volume, temperature, and how power can be stored. It will take a few more increments in the price of fossil fuels, or a great reduction in their supply, before solar is economically justifiable, but I am a long way from convinced that solar energy has no role to play in our industry. We have some skeptics in this company, but I keep reminding them to put the Kitty Hawk against the 747, and then they can see how fast technology develops. Then you can see the possibilities for solar energy."

P.D.

Wavemakers:

THE CREATIVE CRANK

For the beaten, the timid, and the irresolute, Charles MacArthur offers this anecdote: "It took Thomas Edison four thousand light bulbs to come up with one that worked. In our society the man on the street doesn't try anything new because he's afraid of failure or he thinks that because he doesn't have a PhD, he can't succeed."

"Everyone," says the fifty-three-year-old MacArthur, "ought to be into things up to their ears."

MacArthur, American inventor, businessperson, but most of all, practical-minded environmentalist, has been completely submerged in "things" since 1970, when, as an avid balloonist, he designed a lighter, more energy-efficient hot-air balloon.

It was those silent journeys in his hot-air balloon that led to MacArthur's environmental awakening. "Flying at low altitudes I began to see that the woods in the continental United States were filled with overturned cars, like dead cockroaches. This was the handiwork of man, if you want to call it that."

Inspired by the notion of wresting the automobile from its addiction to gasoline when the 1973 energy crunch arrived, MacArthur (who has a degree in English, not engineering) took time off from his Connecticut blueprinting business to invite seventeen other energy conservation enthusiasts to negotiate the road up New Hampshire's highest peak. Though the first annual Mt. Washington Alternative Vehicle Regatta did not capture the attention of Detroit motor moguls, it was a fertile testing ground for a new breed of environmental

inventor. Electric motorcycles, an electric VW bug, and others hummed their way up the 8-mile (12.8-kilometer) road to the summit, where a waiting wind-powered electric generator offered a "refill."

For MacArthur, promoting the development and eventual marketing of alternative vehicles was but one part of his evolving vision of how to survive and prosper following what he believes is an imminent "energy apocalypse."

"The cost of energy is climbing so high," he says, "that the whole country will have to restructure everything back to a local and regional basis."

A devoted adherent to the "small-is-beautiful" philosophy of E. F. Schumacher, the British economist who urged a return to community-based, self-sufficient economies, MacArthur sold his blueprint business in 1977 and moved to Maine, a place with a history of nurturing Yankees with ingenuity.

It was there, in Dover-Foxcroft, a small economically depressed town of four thousand, that MacArthur found a new testing ground for his concepts. On the north bank of the Piscataqua River stood a 112-year-old wool mill. Once a nucleus of employment for the community, Brown's Mill was now an empty symbol of better times.

In that sprawling 92,000-square-foot (8,500-square-meter) mill, MacArthur envisioned "a hatchery" for environmentally sound small businesses. So, with a $100,000 mortgage, MacArthur became landlord of Brown's Mill, which came complete with its own hydroelectric dam and a cigar-chewing Yankee by the name of Hermie Nutter, a janitor and chief engineer, who had been a fixture in the place since 1939.

Today, visitors to Brown's Mill can witness MacArthur's version of "post-petroleum age" business in full swing. By renting space in the mill for $1 a day, which includes heat and light produced by the building's own wood-burning boiler and hydroelectric dam, MacArthur has managed to fill the entire building with small cottage industries. His only criteria: "New businesses will be encouraged to utilize local resources, avoid desecration of the environment, and produce products with real utility in an energy-short future."

MacArthur's own enterprises include a unique assortment of alternative vehicles that run on fuels ranging from charcoal to waste fat from McDonald's hamburgers, as well as the production of "earth closets"—indoor toilets that combine waste with clay, moss, and soil, turning it into fertilizer. His latest venture is building life-size inflatable models of the blue whale—all 110 feet (33.6 meters) of it—that can pop out of a suitcase to be used in educational demonstrations.

To MacArthur, "appropriate technology" concepts are not just a business, they are also a crusade. To help spread the word he has started live-in courses in low-energy technology at the mill. At his "dirty fingernail" seminars he exhorts his students to engage in creating "hardware, not hogwash."

"Each applicant will be encouraged to grab a wrench in the conversion of a Volkswagen into a low-energy electric car." Budding MacArthurites also tinker with solar collectors, a sawdust-fired furnace, biological waste disposal systems, and some of the eighty-six other projects now underway.

Though MacArthur's mill may be a "rural Disneyland" demonstrating workable applications of his decentralist environmental economics, he is an inventor who still must go through a lot of light bulbs before he comes up with one that works. But he tackles the task with dogged enthusiasm that his mentor Edison would admire.

"We just tried a new solar-powered car, and some people were disappointed that it only went about 200 yards [183 meters] and then stopped," says the creative crank with a chuckle. "I was elated that it got as far as it did." B.P.B.

BETTER LIVING THROUGH CHEMISTRY?

Every year some 70,000 chemicals are synthetically produced around the world. The United Nations' International Register of Potentially Toxic Chemicals lists 30,000 that are toxic, 2,200 of which are suspected carcinogens.

We hear about chemicals when they spill dramatically, but the most insidious effects are invisible: they leach into the environment slowly and subtly by several routes. Some, like fertilizers and pesticides, enter through direct application to the soil and are consumed by people as residues in food and water. (See "The Most-Fertilized Foods," page 601, and "The Most-Sprayed Foods," page 600.)

Some chemicals, like polyvinyl chloride and benzene, are critical ingredients in fabricated products (automobile parts and pipes, for example), and enter the environment more slowly as they age and break down. Some can even be transmitted directly into the bloodstream when synthetic clothing interacts with the oil on the skin of infants and adults. Others are released during the manufacturing process itself, like arsenic, which is extracted from copper during smelting and inhaled by workers and by neighbors downwind from the smelter.

The Chemical Makers

The chemical industry is enormous and highly profitable. The Chemical Manufacturers Association lists four hundred chemical companies in the United States and Canada and their total gross is $115 billion a year; but the real power, according to the United Nations Conference on Trade and Development, lies with only twenty-five United States and European companies that dominate the worldwide chemical trade. West Germany and Great Britain boast some of the world's largest chemical corporations—Germany's Hoechst and Britain's Imperial Chemical Industries (ICI)—while the United States is easily the biggest chemical consumer, accounting for approximately 30 percent of the world's total. Italy and a number of Eastern European countries are notorious for producing low-priced versions of chemicals whose patents have expired in other countries and now are manufactured with impurities that increase their potential toxicity. Industrializing developing countries, especially in Latin America and the Far East, have attracted numerous new chemical industries, which routinely operate unimpeded by even the most minimal regulations. (See "Come Pollute Us," page 697.)

Most of today's chemicals did not exist before the beginning of the great plastic and synthetic boom right after World War II. Scientists are now observing for the first time the chronic, long-term effects of chemical exposure, which can take from twenty to forty years to appear. A U. S. National Cancer Institute study in the late 1970s gives a frightening glimpse of those effects: in thirty-nine counties across the United States with petrochemical industries, the rates of lung, skin, and other cancers were significantly higher than rates in the general population.

The Cancer Connection

"The distribution and use of toxic chemicals is a worldwide problem," said one World Health Organization (WHO) official. WHO estimates that 75 to 80 percent of all cancers are triggered by environmental pollutants, foremost among them industrial chemicals. Multinational chemical producers like Great Britain's ICI, France's Rhône-Poulenc, and Switzerland's Ciba-Geigy operate unimpeded by national boundaries, with manufacturing and distribution facilities in countries around the world. United States companies like American Cyanamid, a major producer of pesticides and synthetic fibers, garner as much as one half of their total earnings from abroad.

One of the largest multinationals, Royal Dutch Shell, has seventy-eight chemical factories in twenty-one different countries. Over a million tons a year of benzene, for example, are produced by Shell in France, India, West Germany, Japan, Great Britain, Canada, and the United States. Benzene is derived from coal and is a prime ingredient in paints and gasoline, as well as being one of the most widely used intermediate substances for producing other chemicals. The U. S. Environmental Protection Agency (EPA) found that repeated exposure can cause leukemia and chromosome damage in both workers and consumers who inhale it. Even filling a car tank with gasoline can expose motorists and service station attendants to potentially harmful levels of benzene, say EPA officials.

Toxic Agents in Plastics

Many of the chemicals now known to be hazardous were developed during the post-World War II years as derivatives of petroleum. The petrochemical industry supplies us with synthetic substances for manufacturing everything from gasoline to resins to household appliances to plastic, the most widely used petroleum-based synthetic on earth.

Polyvinyl chloride (PVC), for example, is produced from petroleum and is the world's second most popular source for plastic products; it is fabricated into a wide range of everyday things like food wraps, home furnishings, phonograph records, apparel, automotive parts, packaging film, and bottles. (See "Oil Day Long," page 651.) When five vinyl chloride workers at a B. F. Goodrich plant in Kentucky died of an extremely rare liver disease (angiosarcoma), scientists were alarmed. Subsequent cases of the fatal illness turned up at Union Carbide's PVC plant in West Virginia and Firestone's plant in Pennsylvania. From West Germany, Romania, and Japan came further reports of PVC-induced angiosarcoma, as well as restricted blood circulation. (See "Are You Dying to Make a Living?" page 685.)

The U. S. National Institute for Occupational Safety and Health (NIOSH) concluded that PVC is a potent carcinogen and has been keeping tabs on PVC-related deaths. It now records eighty-one deaths from angiosarcoma. Seven hundred thousand people may be exposed to PVC's harmful effects through manufacturing processes that use the chemical, and many more will be exposed by its breakdown in the environment.

The controversy set off by PVC forced B. F. Goodrich to halt its plans to open a plant in New Zealand after local citizens organized strenuous opposition. In 1980 Goodrich planned, according to a company spokesman, to double its U. S. PVC production by 1985.

Polyvinyl chloride is an organochlorine chemical and a relative of the infamous DDT and other pesticides. What particularly disturbs scientists about the organochlorines is that their unique chemical combination—hydrogen, carbon, and chlorine molecules—is rarely found naturally in living organisms, making them highly toxic when introduced into the environment and extremely difficult to decompose.

SOME OF THE WORLD'S MAJOR PVC PRODUCERS

United States
Dow Chemical
B. F. Goodrich
Monsanto
Stauffer Chemical

Japan
Nippon Zeon
Mitsubishi Chemical

West Germany
Hoechst

Britain
ICI
British Petroleum

Netherlands/Britain
Royal Dutch Shell

Belgium
Solvay & Cie
(Europe's largest PVC producer)

Bitter By-Products

Sometimes toxic materials are created during the manufacturing process rather than being integral to the end product. Poisons can infiltrate the environment through the processing of metals and minerals, such as asbestos, mercury, and arsenic.

Arsenic, one of the more infamous poisons known to humans, is a by-product of the smelting of nonferrous metals, primarily copper, as well as lead and zinc. Areas surrounding some of the largest refining plants—those belonging to Kennecott Copper in New Mexico and Utah, Asarco in Washington and Texas, Anaconda Copper in Montana, and Phelps Dodge Corporation in Arizona—have extraordinarily high rates of lung cancer, according to the U. S. National Cancer Institute. Most of the arsenic is discarded in waste dumps, but Asarco's Tacoma, Washington, plant sells 18,000 tons a year of arsenic to pesticide, electronic product, and glass manufacturers. Asarco's plant emits about 200 tons per year of arsenic, and children living near the plant have been found to have high levels of the poisonous substance in their urine, teeth, and hair. The fifteen copper-smelting companies in the United States claim that the costs of reducing their arsenic emissions through pollution control would force them out of business.

The Direct Dump

Ultimately the chemical age reaches its quintessence in pesticides, the only type of toxic substance spread purposefully and directly onto the earth. Pesticides present caricatures of the perfect ecological circle, returning to us in the form of residues on our fruits and vegetables, in our meat and dairy products from cattle that were fed pesticide-treated crops, and in groundwater contaminated by chemical seepage. Take the organochlorines, for instance, a pesticide family tree that begins with DDT. They are not readily degraded in nature. Substantial amounts of carcinogenic organochlorine pesticides—heptachlor, chlordane, lindane, dieldrin, and DDT—have been found in mother's milk and human fat tissue in the general population of North and Central America.

A new family of phosphate-based pesticides was developed after considerable controversy in the 1970s led to the banning of many of the organochlorines in the industrialized nations. But these organophosphate pesticides, designed to break down more quickly in the environment, pose a new twist to an old problem: their biodegradability also makes them easier for the human body to metabolize. Thousands of farm laborers and factory workers have suffered severe nerve and brain damage after exposure to pesticides like Parathion and Malathion.

Multinational pesticide-makers are based in the United States and Europe, but they push pesticides with aggressive advertising campaigns on a global scale. In many developing countries, pesticide company representatives are the only people farmers may go to for crop advice. And some will never know whether a pesticide is dangerous.

Even if a pesticide is banned in a particular country, that does not prevent it from being sold elsewhere. A provision of U.S. law explicitly states that pesticides banned in the United States may be exported to other nations; and every pesticide banned in the United States *has* been exported.

Take the case of Phosvel, an organophosphate nerve toxin that attacks the human body like rattlesnake venom. The EPA never allowed Phosvel to be sold in the United States after workers at Velsicol's Texas factory suffered serious nerve damage, becoming known as the "Phosvel Zombies." Velsicol, one of the most scandal-ridden of the chemical companies, was also behind the Michigan PCB poisoning in 1977, Tris-treated baby clothes found to be flammable, and the United States' biggest mercury-waste dump in Woodbridge, New Jersey. And with Phosvel, Velsicol sold the pesticide to such developing countries as India, Pakistan, Brazil, Colombia, and Indonesia. In Egypt, one thousand water buffalo and an untold number of humans were killed by Phosvel exposure.

This is only one small example of the long shadow cast by pesticide use around the world. About 500,000 people are poisoned each year by pesticides, 5,000 of them fatally, according to WHO.

Chemical Combos

Problems with toxic chemicals are compounded by their synergistic effects. Chemicals have become so pervasive that they mingle in the air and in the water to form new substances that are often toxic even if the original materials were not.

At Hooker Chemical's notorious Love Canal dump, for instance, the deadly chemical dioxin—a contaminant produced during the manufacture of the pesticide 2,4,5-T and normally insoluble in water—was made more soluble after combining with benzene that was also leaking from the dump site. Once made soluble, the mutagenic and carcinogenic dioxin migrated through the groundwater, oozing into the basements and backyards of the surrounding neighborhood.

"Cancer doesn't cost those who cause it," commented Anthony Mazzochi, vice-president of the Oil, Chemical, and Atomic Workers Union in 1979. The union represents workers who are most often the first to feel the toxic effects of chemicals, and Mazzochi has been a leader in the movement to ensure greater health and safety for chemical workers and residents who live near the chemical plants. "The industries make money and the population subsidizes them with their health—short lives, illnesses, cancer."

Regulation Roulette

Powerful industry lobbies apply pressure to discourage government regulation, often employing complicated and expensive legal maneuvers to hold up the regulating process. The American Petroleum Institute, for example, representing B. F. Goodrich, Union Oil, Dow, and other U.S. benzene producers, delayed the Occupational Safety and Health Administration's (OSHA) proposed 90-percent reduction in the benzene workplace standard for two years while battling the regulation in court.

On the other hand, a growing number of "public interest" environment and health groups are by lobbying, rallying public opinion, and instigating lawsuits against the government and individual companies to ensure stricter control of chemical releases. The 1979 bans on the pesticides DBCP and 2,4,5-T were largely the result of pressure from such citizens' groups.

Countries like the United States, Japan, Russia, Denmark, and West Germany lead the field in regulating toxic substances, but serious regulation is still a fledgling effort. In the United States, increasing scrutiny is being paid by NIOSH and the National Cancer Institute to environmental causes of disease, while OSHA is drawing up criteria for identifying carcinogens and limiting worker exposure. In 1976 the Toxic Substances Control Act (TOSCA) was passed to require the manufacturer to test all new chemicals for toxic effects, signaling a shift to preventive, rather than crisis-oriented, regulation. TOSCA gives EPA the power to ban or restrict a chemical's use.

But the sheer magnitude of the regulator's task illustrates the frightening extent to which chemicals are infiltrating our lives: in addition to the 70,000 existing chemicals, 6,000 new chemicals are invented every week in the United States alone, and, of those, 1,000 are introduced into the market each year.

The European Economic Community (EEC) wrote its own version of TOSCA; and coordination with the United States' regulating efforts were begun. Some EEC countries had already imposed constraints on their own toxic chemical industries. Denmark pioneered toxic chemical regulation by establishing rules in 1953 to restrict pesticide production. The Netherlands passed a bill similar to TOSCA in 1980, while West Germany's National Allowable Concentration in the Environment Act sets up standards and tolerances for toxic chemicals in the environment.

"You have Sweden and Japan taking strong actions with mercury," says Maureen Hinkle of the Environmental Defense Fund, a lobbying group in Washington, D.C. "England is strong with chemical poisoning; Germany is strong with thalidomide. But it's very uneven and unpredictable—and then there are the multinationals, which transcend all of the national efforts."

Increasingly, multinationals—notably the asbestos, copper, lead, and pesticide industries—have been circumventing regulations by shifting their enterprises to developing countries. Dr. Trent Lewis, Chief Experimental Toxicologist for NIOSH, recalled: "We've had people come through from Africa and Asia. They have tremendous potential problems, with different genetic predispositions and different diets than in the United States. Some compounds may be more toxic to them than to us. But they have few resources for regulating; their first inclination, for the most part, is to bring industry on line to their countries."

The developing world may make the same mistakes that developed countries have already made in allowing the toxins of "progress" to permeate their environment and damage the health of their people. Since the global ecosystem does not recognize political boundaries, this is as much a problem for the developed nations as it is for the developing nations. Today's chemical time bombs have twenty-year fuses; and we may not even hear the sound of their ticking.

M.S.

THE CHEMICAL PLANET

The threat to human health and the environment posed by the rapidly proliferating chemical industry has only recently been widely recognized. In fact, a 1979 survey by the Center for International Environment Information was the first attempt to collect worldwide information on existing chemical hazards. The survey is far from comprehensive, but it suggests the extent and the seriousness of the problem and the failure of governments to act to protect their people.

Latin America

In much of Latin America pesticides are a serious hazard. Many chemicals banned elsewhere, such as DDT, are still in use. General pesticide poisoning is common. In the United States there are about two poisonings per million people each year; in El Salvador and Guatemala there are 3,600 poisonings per million people.

Many Latin American countries attempting to industrialize quickly cannot afford to protect the environment adequately. Serious problems exist in Mexico, Colombia, Venezuela, Argentina, and northeast Brazil. Many of these countries dump untreated waste directly into rivers and the ocean. In the Valley of Mexico, 80 percent of industry lacks minimum safety or emergency plans. Regulations are lax throughout Latin America and even when they do exist, enforcement is minimal.

Europe

The situation in Europe is very different. Most countries recycle waste or at least detoxify it before dumping. In Britain, burial of wastes, which has proved unreliable in the United States, is the most common means of disposal. France is developing uniform national guidelines for chemical waste disposal. In 1979, mining industry experts located thirty-three uncontrolled raw toxic waste dumps in France that pose a serious threat of pollution; the country has fifteen regulated waste treatment centers for toxic waste. Clandestine dumping is also a problem in the Netherlands. West Germany lacks thorough regulations, and one German firm accepted waste kepone from the United States to be buried in salt mines in Hesse. Spain has relatively little industry but its dumping regulations are very lax. The fine for illegal ocean dumping is only 25,000 pesetas ($357). The European Community, recognizing these growing problems, is in the process of developing uniform guidelines for testing and regulating chemicals for member nations.

The Soviet Union

The Soviet Union also suffers from chemical pollution. The Volga River is not as polluted as the Rhine or Mississippi, but it does carry half of the Soviet Union's industrial effluents into the Caspian Sea. Partly as a result of this pollution, the sturgeon catch has decreased by 80 percent. Runoff of agricultural chemicals causes water pollution in several areas. For example, the Sea of Azov was seriously polluted when dust storms blew fertilizer mixed with topsoil into the water.

Africa

In Egypt, industrial waste is dumped into agricultural canals and ends up in soil used for farming. In South Africa, occupational health problems, many related to use of agricultural chemicals, are common for the mainly black work force.

Middle East

Conditions in the Middle East have not been closely examined, but rapid expansion in petroleum and other industries is likely to cause problems. In Turkey, the wastes from the textile, chemical, plastics, pesticide, and mining industries are usually dumped into rivers or the ocean.

Asia

India does virtually nothing to control chemical dumping of its fertilizer and petrochemical plants. Serious accidents have occurred, but little has been done.

Hong Kong has no regulations governing effluent pollution. Largely agricultural China has a thorough program to recycle agricultural wastes into fertilizer, and is a leader in developing biological pest management. Because there was little industry in China until recently, industrial pollution has only recently become a problem (see "The Problem That Crosses Ideologies," page 496). But industrial growth has accompanied recent modernization, and the government has ordered 170 factories to install pollution-control equipment or shut down. The government also promised to provide the requisite funds and equipment.

In Taiwan, pollution is caused by waste from petrochemical, steel, and fertilizer production.

Japan has more than its share of environmental problems because of its population density and heavy industrialization. Serious health damage occurred at Minamata, Hokkaido, and Yusho. (See "The Dancing Cats of Minamata," page 517.)

Industrial wastes are dumped into offshore waters in the Philippines with disastrous results.

Oceania

In Australia, air and water pollution are tightly regulated but there is little legislation to protect the land from chemical dumping. Toxic wastes are stockpiled but not inventoried.

Awareness of the potential danger of chemical wastes has led many countries to enforce stricter regulations. But often, economic progress is traded off against the goal of providing people with a safe place to live. K.F.

Wavemakers:

OVER THE COUNTER

"Mexaform?" The Tamil clerk nods and swiftly produces ten tablets sealed in plastic on a card. The drug is a dysentery remedy known elsewhere as Enterovioform—and often cited for its harmful side effects. It is banned in Japan, off the market in the United States.

You can get it in Malaysia and many other countries, though. Only pharmacies are entitled to sell the drug here, but this little general store, at a dusty crossroads near a fishing village, has Mexaform and a lot of other surprising items for sale.

There are locally made eyebrow pencils laden with lead; mosquito coils impregnated with DDT (they have been banned here since 1972); baby bottles of polyvinyl chloride (they melt in the water boiled to sterilize them); condensed milk, loaded with sugar, that is sold as food for infants; ginger candy whose cherry color usually is derived from Red Dye No. 2 (banned in the United States as a possible carcinogen).

All-Purpose Cure

Does the clerk have penicillin? He turns to root through a drawer behind his counter, and finding no pills, only penicillin ointment, offers a consolation: a bottle of colorless liquid that, according to its label, contains dissolved rhinoceros horn. (A chemical analysis, however, showed no trace of rhinoceros.) It promises immediate relief from "malaria, high-temperature fever affecting heart and four limbs, climate giddiness, insanity, toothache, etc."

"Most people get sick, they take this," the clerk says.

So it is with consumer protection in the develop-

ing world. Malaysia is one of those developing nations rich enough to make or import the whole range of consumer products but not quite developed enough to be concerned with effectively screening out their evils.

Life here on any level has grown complicated. Plastic wrap, with its problems of disposal, has supplanted banana leaves. People sit on chairs rather than their haunches, making low-back pain a common ailment. The Malaysian marketplace now is fraught with the new and the unknown. The consumer, largely uninformed and unprotected, is a sitting duck.

"We haven't reached affluence," says Mohammed Idris, "but we already suffer from all its ills."

Nader of the East

Mr. Idris, an Indian Muslim merchant, is Malaysia's answer to Ralph Nader. He is a founder and president of the Consumers' Association of Penang, by many accounts the largest and loudest consumers' group in the developing world. For ten years the association has been keeping track of septic tanks and polluted waters, potholes and weevily rice. It has been blowing the whistle on bogus job agencies, unlicensed optometrists and moonshine, and pushing the panic button on flammable teddy bears, deforestation, war toys, and broken glass in bottled drinks.

Working under spinning paddle fans in an old British bungalow, on an annual budget of $75,000, Mr. Idris's staff of thirty churns out press releases, a weekly national newspaper column, a monthly newspaper (circulation 30,000), and a radio show. They investigate two thousand complaints a year and inundate business and government in a steady downpour of angry letters.

In fact, rising prices and a dawning suspicion of technology's consumer spinoffs have helped spawn such groups in nearly every developing country, from Barbados to Bangladesh. The concern has become pronounced enough for the United Nations Commission on Transnational Corporations to consider including an international consumer-protection clause in its proposed code of conduct.

Building Pressures

The Consumers' Association of Penang declines to accept public money and has no political affiliation. "It is a way for people to express their views in Malaysia without being hit on the head," says Anwar Fazal, president of the Hague-based International Organization of Consumers Unions. "It gets results."

"We create pressures within the bureaucracy," explains Martin Khor, research director for the Penang group; he has a master's degree in economics from Cambridge University. Mr. Khor asserts that "if we educate the public, the bureaucrats will have to listen."

It isn't as if Malaysia's government had totally failed the consumer. There are laws against phony discounts and short-weighting, plus rules covering labels, preservatives, food coloring, and installment buying. Malaysia has an Environmental Quality Act and a Price Control Act. A UN survey shows that its consumer laws cover much the same ground as those of Japan, Canada, and West Germany. But, except for a new seat-belt ordinance, the laws aren't overly strict, and they don't seem to be applied with much vigor.

In September 1977, the Consumers' Association weighed loaves of bread from nine Penang bakeries. Each fell short of the government standard. A fuss was made at the Department of Weights and Measures, and the bakeries agreed to conform. In February 1979, ten samples were tested. Nine were below weight. Nine brands of rice sold in "39-pound" (17.6-kilogram) bags also were caught short. And of eleven brands of soy sauce, six bottles held half what the labels claimed. Western esoterica like shelf-life limits and unit pricing are unheard of here; at one Penang supermarket, codfish fingers cost more per ounce in the ten-ounce box than in the six-ounce box.

In Malaysia, shrimp paste has a warm brown color that comes, says the Consumers' Association, from rhodamine-B, a chemical long banned by the government. The pale yellow color of bean curd is imparted by metanil yellow, also banned.

The maker of Woodward's Celebrated Gripe Water, a British concoction for infant discomforts, legally lists ingredients on its Malaysian label in Latin. In Britain the label is in English, and it sets a limit of eight doses a day. (A consumers' group in neighboring Singapore reported a year ago that Gripe Water sold there contains almost twice the 4.9 percent alcohol declared on the label, perhaps explaining why it puts baby to sleep.)

Brand's Essence of Chicken, another British import, is sold in minute bottles (to fit minute budgets) and heavily promoted as concentrated protein. A consumers' group in the Malaysian state of Selangor found a few years ago that this protein costs 130 times more than the protein in a local fish called whitebait. It didn't matter. Essence of Chicken and products like it remain popular.

A Long Time

The Malaysian government has written a code of ethics for companies selling powdered infant formulas. But there are no restrictions on the sale of sweetened condensed milk, which contains 45 percent sugar by weight and, in 1976, was declared "highly unsuitable for infants and young children" by the UN Protein-Calorie Advisory Group. In Malaysia, it is commonly used for bottle-feeding babies, and it is sold in cans showing pictures of babies accompanied by instructions for infant feeding. (See also "Unsafe Water, Unsafe Milk," page 515.)

Products recognized as dangerous in the West may be even more unhealthy in their developing world formulations. One is Benson and Hedges cigarettes, made by B.A.T. Industries Ltd. In the British home market, this cigarette has a tar content of 17 milligrams. But a 1978 study by the U.S. government's Smoking and Health Program found that the same brand sold in Malaysia had 30 milligrams of tar per cigarette, a 76 percent increase.

In London, a B.A.T. spokesman says, "It's merely a reflection of consumer taste." In developed countries, he explains, consumers have shown a preference for lower tar levels. But this trend isn't evident in the developing world because consumers there smoke fewer cigarettes per day, so they "tend to prefer more taste."

B.A.T. disputes the UN figure of 30 milligrams for the Malaysian Benson and Hedges. "Substantially too high," says an official. But the company says it can't reveal the real figure. That is "a commercial secret."

Dieldrin, aldrin, heptachlor, and chlordane, highly toxic pesticides that are banned in the United States, are freely marketed in Malaysia, along with other chemical and pharmaceutical items restricted in advanced economies. The International Organization of Consumers Unions has put together a sampler from the Drug Index for Malaysia and Singapore, for example, of eight drugs off the shelves elsewhere and approved here.

Besides clioquinol, the chief ingredient of Mexaform, they include chloroform, which has been ordered removed from over-the-counter remedies in the United States, and dipyrone, which has been removed from cold medicines in the United States.

Problem for Teeth

The antibiotic tetracycline is distributed here by Dow Chemical, listing dosages for children. Other international distributors warn that the drug can cause teeth discoloration in children and shouldn't be used by women in the second half of pregnancy or by children under eight. Dow makes no mention of the hazard in its package inserts distributed in Malaysia.

"The literature has to conform to local registration regulations, which aren't up to international standards sometimes," says Jackie Tay, Dow's pharmaceutical division representative in Kuala Lumpur, the Malaysian capital. "There isn't much on the insert. The literature leaves much to be desired. We have marketing communications people pursuing this matter right now. These things don't get done overnight."

The drug Depo-Provera, made by Upjohn Company, is used by the Malaysian government in birth-control programs. Given by injection, it is said to be effective for three months or more. But in the United States, the Food and Drug Administration (FDA) has declined to license it for birth-control uses. The agency cited evidence that the drug causes menstrual difficulties in women and breast cancer in animals. Upjohn is challenging the FDA stand in court.

The FDA found that in the United States the risks outweighed the benefits of using Depo-Provera as a contraceptive (it is approved for use as an anticancer drug). In the developing world, however, the risk-benefit calculation is different, and some experts suggest that even a risky drug might be worthwhile if it had a great effect on the population-control problem.

Martin Khor of the Consumers' Association objects violently to Depo-Provera's use here, calling it "grossly irresponsible" of the government to "distribute to our Malaysian women a drug which has been banned in the Western countries where it originated."

The industrialized nations clearly aren't straining to curtail exports of products that they restrict at home. Very often, government agencies don't have the power to do that. The U. S. State Department does provide an informational service, issuing notices of bans and recalls through its embassies, but these are less than comprehensive.

Whether Malaysia's government allows such

items in by design or neglect is difficult to fathom. According to Tey Boon Hwa, head of the consumer-affairs division in the Department of Trade and Industry, the country is kept informed by its trade commissions overseas. "I wouldn't say regularly," he concedes. "On and off."

The Consumers' Association of Penang, meanwhile, isn't notified of anything by anybody. Its staff watches the newspapers, roots through fifty consumer magazines from around the world, follows up complaints and tries to let the public know what's going on. "We've had an impact," says its president, Mohammed Idris. "A small impact."

By Barry Newman. Reprinted with permission from the *Wall Street Journal,* April 8, 1980,

UNSAFE WATER, UNSAFE MILK

Without clean water, parents can't mix healthy milk from premeasured powder. Illiterate parents can't properly follow instructions on a formula can. The result: malnourished infants—and controversy. International protests have arisen since the mid-1970s against the indiscriminate sale of infant formula products. Ironically the formula feeding of infants—once considered a sign of social progress—has become a threat to health in some developing countries. The chemical composition of the products themselves is not the danger. Rather, it is the improper use of the formula, stimulated, in many cases, by improper sales campaigns.

For example, the Nestlé Company, based in Vevey, Switzerland, a leading producer of these products, has been the object of world-wide consumer boycotts since 1977 because of its formula marketing policies, and Nestlé's is not alone.

Several corporations with both pharmaceutical and food-processing operations are involved, among them Abbot Laboratories, Bristol-Myers Company, Wyeth International, and the Borden Company.

Because disclosure of sales figures is not required by most countries, accurate data are difficult to obtain. However, an economist who studied the industry for the Rockefeller Foundation valued the market for infant formula at approximately $1.5 billion in 1978. Forty to fifty percent of the market is in Latin America, Africa, the Middle East, and Southern Asia. Population specialists predicted that by 1980 the developing nations alone would be spending about $1 billion per year on infant formula and powdered milk.

The History

The first infant formula products were marketed commercially in 1867 by Henri Nestlé and were widely used in hospitals in the United States during the early twentieth century. The industry was spurred, however, by World War II, which had created a need for dried and evaporated food products for military rations and the technology to produce them in bulk. In developed countries there was a marked decline in breastfeeding after the war, and it is estimated that in the United States alone 75 percent of all babies born were being bottle-fed. Scientifically constituted formula was perceived as healthier and more nutritious than mother's milk, although in most cases, human milk *is* indeed the best food for human infants. Formula, previously intended as a supplement to mother's milk or as a substitute only in cases where breast milk was insufficient, thus became the mainstay of many American infants' diets. Slowly it began to be marketed and exported to postwar Europe and elsewhere.

It is usually impossible to say whether a product follows demand or creates it. However, in developing countries, where the infant formula controversy is most pronounced, there is little question that the availability of the products and their vigorous promotion created a demand where little demand existed before.

So What?

The central conditions of the controversy are as poignant as they are disturbing. A mother gives birth in a hospital or with a visiting midwife, medical institutions in which she is predisposed to have faith. She sees posters advertising powdered milk or formula that picture beautifully healthy babies. She may receive free samples. The advertising effect known as "transfer" occurs—healthy babies must equal infant formula. If the mother is only marginally literate, she cannot fully understand formula labels. Even though a label may *say* breast milk is better and that the formula is intended as a supplement, the mother probably asks herself why, if breast milk is *really* better, "they" let her buy formula in the first place?

Often the mother is completely illiterate, dependent on pictorial labeling and her memory of hospital classes on how to use the formula. Beyond illiteracy, the biggest problem is that in many towns and villages a public tap supplying impure water is the only freshwater source. For example, it is estimated that in rural Colombia 72 percent of the rural population do not have access to potable water. So, as a result, the odds are very high that the formula mixture will be unhealthy. Even if the mother understands the need for sterilizing the milk, she may be reluctant to do so when it means burning expensive gas fuel needed for cooking. In rural areas, sterilizing milk may mean gathering wood and building a fire. Inevitably, unless mothers have the conveniences of a modern kitchen, babies are exposed to all sorts of water-borne diseases through bad water mixed with formula. Also, in many cases, the valuable formula is diluted to stretch it, further threatening the infant. Infant milk products are very expensive in relation to local income. In Liberia, where the average wage is $1 per day, formula costs approximately $18 per month per child. In Peru, six months of infant formula would cost about 23 percent of an average annual family income; in Nigeria, 47 percent; in Pakistan, 62 percent.

The results are severely undernourished infants infected with dysentery, typhoid, or any of a host of other diseases. According to a leading nutritionist, Dr. Derrick B. Jelliffe of the University of California, an early critic of infant formula, "It has been estimated that some ten million cases of marasmus and diarrhea occur annually in infants in developing countries, related in part to inadequate bottle feeding." (Marasmus is progressive emaciation of the body.) Though most obvious in developing countries, these bottle-based diseases are also found among the poor and uneducated in developed countries.

Fighting Back

The bottle-baby problem is not new. In the early 1970s attention was called to the controversy by noted nutritionists and medical personnel who charged that, because of declining birth rates in developed countries, producers of infant formula needed to expand their markets to make up for lost profits. Thus they introduced the product to populous developing countries where its use could not be adequately monitored and where it led to a decline in breastfeeding, generally agreed to be the best form of infant nutrition, even when mothers themselves are undernourished. By 1974 the World Health Organization had passed a resolution calling for countries to "review sales and promotion activities on baby foods and introduce remedial measures where necessary."

Still, the problems persisted and public criticism of the infant formula companies mounted. Subject to particular attack were ad campaigns in the local mass media and the use of "mothercraft nurses," company employees dressed in white uniforms, hired to promote infant-formula products in hospitals and rural villages. Also denounced were the payment of royalties to doctors who prescribe formula products and the financing of parties and educational seminars to promote infant formulas.

In 1974 Nestlé sued the Third World Action group, a political organization active on behalf of the poor in developing nations, for defamation and libel. After several hearings, Nestlé dropped three out of four charges. The suit was settled in 1976 when a Swiss judge ruled that a statement made in a Third World pamphlet, "Nestlé's Kills Infants," was indeed libelous. But the judge added, "The verdict is no acquittal" and recommended that Nestlé "fundamentally rethink" its advertising policies. In 1978 the United States Congress held hearings on the subject, even though it has jurisdiction only in the United States over U.S.-based companies.

As a result of citizen action and public pressure, formula companies did officially eliminate mass-media advertising, and most of them eliminated mothercraft nurses. Local investigators have turned up cases of continued advertising though; the most notorious was a large-scale "baby show" in the Philippines. When the formula companies were questioned, they called the violations "regrettable exceptions," arguing that they cannot strictly monitor local distributors.

Pass the Bottle, Pass the Buck

The industry contends that formula products fill a need. They also argue that they intend their products to be used *only* as a substitute when breast milk is unavailable. Finally, they claim they cannot be responsible if local governments do not closely monitor distribution, and that the illness and death of infants is related not to their product, but to local conditions of illiteracy and dirty water. Poverty and underdevelopment are the real villians, they argue. And, they ask, what about the people who *do* understand how to use the products properly and who legitimately want to purchase them?

These arguments, which have a certain merit, evade the crucial question of moral responsibility. Can any company, in good conscience, introduce a product that depends on clean water and an understanding of the concept of sterilization, knowing that most mothers in the area have access neither to the water nor to the concept? And while one does not expect a private company to assume all the educational and environmental responsibilities of a local government, someone must accept the blame when a baby suffers from malnutrition or dies because its well-meaning mother has been very effectively taught how to buy a product but not how to use it.

P.D.

THE DANCING CATS OF MINAMATA

When the Chisso Chemical Corporation opened a plant in 1932 to produce fertilizer in the town of Minamata on Kyushu, the southernmost island of Japan, the area was noted for its beauty, its fishing boats on Yatsushiro (the Sea of Mysterious Fire), and groves of mandarin orange trees on the hills surrounding the city. The population was composed of hard-working fishermen and farmers. Now, nearly fifty years and between 200 and 600 tons of mercury later, Minamata is a city in anguish. Its fishing boats are idle. Its orange groves are untended. Although Chisso no longer dumps chemicals into the surrounding waters, the number of victims of the painful and often fatal Minamata disease, methyl mercury poisoning, is increasing.

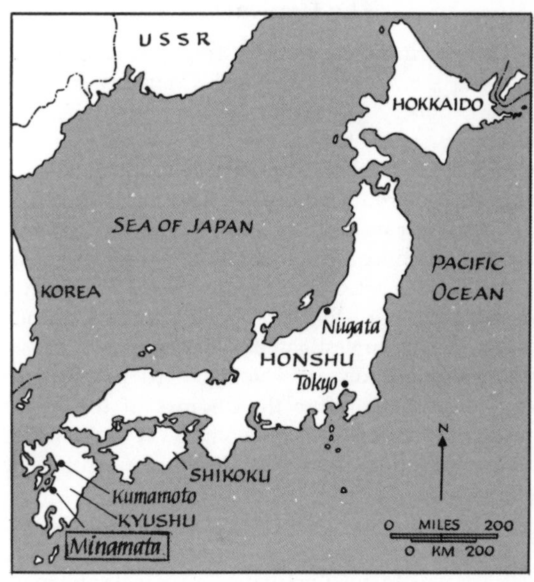

Unlike the thousands of synthetic industrial toxic chemicals, mercury occurs naturally. It is a heavy, silver-white, poisonous, metallic element that is liquid at normal temperatures. Small amounts are commonly found in soil, rocks, fresh water, and the ocean. In 1714, German physicist Gabriel Fahrenheit discovered its now most-famous use as the temperature-indicating liquid in the thermometer.

Mercury is released from fossil fuels when they are burned, but the most serious cases of mercury contamination come from industries that use mercury in the manufacture of chlorine and caustic soda, paper and paper products, and, as in the case of Minamata, fertilizer. When inorganic mercury is released into water, microorganisms convert it to lethal methyl mercury. Scientists estimate that methyl mercury remains in the environment from seventy to a hundred years. While natural mercury does not seem to move up the food chain to concentrate in fish, methyl mercury does. Neither freezing nor any form of cooking reduces the methyl mercury content of fish. Natural mercury is quickly excreted by the human body in urine; methyl mercury is quickly absorbed by the body. To humans, it is nerve poison. The people of Minamata, dependent on fish for such a large percentage of their diet, were to learn these scientific facts all too well.

The Cats

At first the Chisso plant, which was eventually to employ about one third of Minamata's workforce, seemed a boon to the city. However, in 1950 an unusual number of dead fish began to wash ashore, and in 1952 a bizarre affliction sent cats into convulsive spasms that left most of the pets dead. Between 1953 and 1956 the symptoms of the "dancing cats" began appearing in people. Their limbs became twisted and spastic. They suffered convulsions, tunnel vision, blindness, madness, and incredible pain. Some died. The doctors of Minamata, alarmed by these symptoms and fearful that the disease might be infectious, formed an investigating team. It did not take long to discover that the victims were being poisoned by chemicals in the fish they ate from local waters, which were being polluted by the Chisso factory. While they speculated that mercury was probably the culprit, they wavered from this theory when Chisso, after first blocking their efforts to get information, finally published a list of the materials used in the manufacturing process. Mercury was not included. Industrial chemists know that mercury is a commonly used catalyst in the processes the factory was using. One of the Chisso chemists made a deathbed admission that he had withheld this information for years.

The Cynical Gifts

The investigation was frustrated at every turn by both the Chisso Chemical Company and Japan's Ministry of Welfare. The latter blocked funds for the Kumamoto University medical school when a school research team attributed the disease to mercury poisoning. The ministry set up its own researchers appointed by the government's pro-industry Economic Planning Agency. With the support of the Japan Chemical Industry Association, Chisso set up yet another study group, which investigated other possible causes for Minamata disease. Neither group produced any evidence to refute the findings of the Minamata doctors or the researchers at Kumamoto medical school. Mercury discharges from the plant continued.

Meanwhile, based on the limited Kumamoto findings, the Minamata fish cooperative refused to sell fish caught in Minamata Bay. Unemployment was added to the misery of illness.

In 1956, after several thousand angry fishermen and families of victims stormed the Chisso plant, the Chisso Corporation—without admitting guilt—began to offer an annual "gift" of about three hundred dollars to afflicted adults and one hundred dollars to children. In cases of death the "gift" to the survivors was one thousand dollars. The string attached to the "gift" was a contract in which the victims agreed not to seek further compensation, regardless of future evidence. Impoverished by hospital bills and unemployment, many signed the contract. It was not until 1968, when the Japanese government declared the Chisso plant responsible for Minamata disease, that the discharge of mercury was stopped.

A Portrait of Suffering

A former *Life* photographer, the late Eugene Smith, and his wife, Aileen, traveled to Minamata and recorded the on-going story of human suffering and courage as well as the indifference of industrial executives in a series of powerful, sensitive photographs that drew the attention of the world to Minamata. Severely beaten by company thugs while he was attempting to photograph a demonstration against Chisso, Smith lost his sight for several years, but he returned to Minamata after successful treatment in the United States.

One of Smith's friends in Minamata, Tsuginori Hamamoto, a former fisherman struck with the disease, became a protest leader who dedicated his life to fighting mercury pollution. Both of his parents died from the disease. Financed by a group of private citizens, he told his story at the United Nations Conference on the Environment in Stockholm in 1973. At the trial against Chisso, Hamamoto painfully struggled into court every day. He expressed this wish:

> If only I may live long enough to get out into the world, using my own body as an example, and demonstrate to everyone . . . what our planet earth would come to if we don't stop industrial pollution and the decimation of our rivers and coastal waters . . . but I fear I may crumble at any moment.

By 1976, 120 Minamata residents had died of mercury poisoning and 800 had mercury-caused brain damage. By 1978, 8,100 residents claimed health damage, and about 1,500 of them had been examined and certified as cases of mercury poisoning.

On March 22, 1979, the former president of Chisso, age 77, and the former plant manager, age 68, were sentenced to two years in prison and three years probation for professional negligence at Minamata. Twelve victims of the disease, plaintiffs in the case, were awarded a total of $725,000.

Today, fetally damaged children and other victims continue to seek relief from pain in Minamata, years after they have stopped eating contaminated fish.

More Minamatas

Minamata was the first and most famous case of mass mercury poisoning from industrial effluent. Since then there have been others.

In 1965, when residents of another Japanese village, Niigata, near the Showa Denko Chemical factory, showed the same symptoms as the residents of Minamata, the same slow process of industry-biased investigation began. An outraged group of young lawyers—with little support from the government—represented the victims. In 1972, after a four-year trial, the courts ruled that organic mercury caused the disease and ordered Showa Denko to pay $710,000 in compensation to the plaintiffs.

In the spring of 1970, the government of Ontario, Canada, alerted fishing camps and Indians living along the English-Wabigoon River in northwest Ontario not to eat fish from the river. For a decade a paper plant in the area had dumped mercury waste into the river, contaminating the fish. A long-term medical study was undertaken of the people of the White Knolls and Grassy Knolls and White Dog reserves to determine if a rash of health complaints stemmed from mercury poisoning. Dr. Masazumi Harada of Kumamoto University, which had investigated the Minamata poisonings, flew to the site. He reported that thirty-seven of the Indians he examined had neurological damage symptoms similar to those in Minamata victims.

B.K.

MAKING WASTES MAKE MONEY

The United States is plagued by festering illegal dumps, guarded landfills, and warehouses full of useless, often poisonous, chemicals. (See "Elizabeth, New Jersey," page 75, and "Living on the Love Canal," page 657.)

Increasingly, however, companies worried about legal liabilities from leaking chemical drums, or from landfills like the one on the Love Canal near Niagara Falls, New York, are trying to detoxify the wastes by chemically converting poisonous compounds back into harmless components. They're being joined by environmentalists concerned about contamination of groundwater.

"If you have to store toxic wastes, you're just postponing a solution. If you develop a detoxification scheme, then you have a system that is an effective solution," says George Pierce, a researcher for Battelle Laboratories in Columbus, Ohio, who is working to develop detoxification methods.

"Detoxification clearly will become more and more important," says Stephen Lingle, chief of the technology branch in the Environmental Protection Agency (EPA) hazardous waste section. It will also be more attractive as the costs of chemical landfills go up, says Joan Berkowitz, a chemist at Arthur D. Little Inc., a Cambridge, Massachusetts, research and consulting firm. Those costs are soaring, partly because the trucking of chemicals to special waste dumps is increasingly expensive.

Extracting Poisons

Some chemical wastes can't be handled except by detoxification—polychlorinated biphenyls (PCBs), for example, were once widely used in electric transformers and heat-transfer fluids. But several years ago, environmentalists became concerned that PCBs don't break down in the environment. (See "The Hudson River," page 327.) Instead, they collect in tissues of fish, later to be eaten by humans.

PCBs were banned by the government and aren't made anymore in the United States. But thousands of pounds of the chemicals remain in hundreds of industrial products that are still being junked. EPA requires that they be stored in drums or burned in approved incinerators capable of destroying the ordinarily fire-resistant chemicals, but the agency has yet to approve any incinerator for PCBs.

In August 1980, Goodyear Tire & Rubber Company said it had developed a detoxification system that can remove low concentrations of PCB contaminants from oil-based heat-transfer fluids used in its industrial processes. Dane K. Parker, a research scientist who developed the system, says Goodyear "wanted to remove the trace amounts of PCBs and reuse the oil," which costs more than $10 a gallon. Essentially, a sodium compound is mixed with the contaminated oil; chlorine is stripped from the carbon chain and then is bonded to the sodium to form sodium chloride—common table salt.

The EPA hasn't approved the process yet, but an agency scientist says it has the advantage of using "known chemistry." The process is only economical with the very valuable heat-transfer fluids and works only with low concentrations of PCBs. But scientists say similar processes could work for other toxic, long-lasting chemicals, such as polybrominated biphenyls, or PBBs, the fire retardants that poisoned thousands of cattle and chickens in Michigan when they were mixed with animal feed, and even DDT that remains in the environment a decade after its use was banned.

A Case in Point

SCA Services Inc., a Boston waste disposal company that operates two hazardous-waste landfills, has decided to emphasize detoxification. The company bought an old chemical plant in Newark, New Jersey, in 1978 and has converted it to process waste chemicals. Richard Moon, a chemist who heads the operation, says his goal is to recover anything of commercial value from the wastes. Where there's nothing worthwhile, SCA Services tries to detoxify them. Maine, for example, sent the company a hundred barrels of a highly flammable tear gas called chloroacetone that had been dumped in the woods. SCA chemically converted the gas into hydroxyacetone, which is odorless, nontoxic, and completely biodegradable.

When a rail car full of sodium trichloride was pierced in Somerville, Massachusetts, in April 1980, it released clouds of poisonous gas. The Boston & Maine Railroad hired SCA Services to treat contaminated liquid that leaked from the car. Using an expensive process developed at its Buffalo, New York, research laboratories, SCA was able to transform the liquid into a neutral brine solution less salty than the ocean.

Some wastes can't be detoxified completely. When SCA Services got a contract to handle 600,000 gallons (2.23 million liters) of water contaminated with arsenic, it devised a process for precipitating out the poisonous chemical element, cleaning the water. But the resulting arsenic-laden sludge had to go to a company landfill.

The hazardous nature of such wastes also can be limited. "There are half a dozen companies in the United States that offer solidification," says Jesse R. Conner, president of Solidtek Inc., of Morrow, Georgia, which is one of the companies. Using combinations of silicates, such as cement, Solidtek can create a claylike material that will hold wastes so they can't be leached out by rainwater, Mr. Conner says. "For most industrial wastes, we can come up with a product that will be suitable for putting into a regular landfill."

SOURCE: A *Wall Street Journal* article by William M. Bulkeley, September 26, 1980.

WHO IS THE FUR INDUSTRY?

From the otter-skin skirts of American Indians to the ermine and sable robes of European kings to the colorful, long-haired "fun furs" of the 1970s, fur garments have long been worn for their warmth, beauty, and prestige. Once, they were simply the sensible garments of northern tribes, but in the past few centuries an explosion in demand for fur has opened new lands, built empires, and driven a number of fur-bearing species to extinction. (See "Disappearing: Animal Species," page 359.)

Early European explorers of North America sought and found riches in the continent's abundance of fur-bearing creatures. French and English entrepreneurs set up trade networks with Native Americans that stretched over thousands of miles from the east coast of what is now the United States and Canada to the rugged western land now British Columbia. Beaver was the prize, and thousands of pelts packed in canoes headed east along wild rivers, then across the Atlantic to become much-coveted beaver hats in Europe.

Great fur companies emerged—the North West Company, the royal-chartered Hudson's Bay Company, John Jacob Astor's American Fur Company—many of them still powerful today. Settlements founded around the companies' trading posts later became cities such as Albany, Detroit, and St. Louis, all fur centers still.

In the 1960s, conservationists and animal lovers branded the fur industry an exploitative, inhumane, and frivolous business. Furriers, threatened by slowing sales as a result of the attack, re-

sponded with a high-powered and successful advertising campaign to improve their image.

Whatever the fur industry is, it is private. Most major companies are privately owned and thus do not report their earnings publicly. Industry trade association spokespeople are still defensive when speaking to environmental groups, and government officials watchdogging the industry hint at international financial intrigue, but few studies have examined the fur industry's inner workings. One that did, however, was a 1978 doctoral dissertation by Russell Taylor of Western Colorado University. Much of the information that follows is drawn from Taylor's study. He concluded that although trapping has changed little over the past hundred years, the number of fur-garment manufacturers has dwindled dramatically since the 1940s. The United States, dominant in the industry between the 1920s and 1950s, slipped to second position behind the Soviet Union in fur export, and second to West Germany in retail sales. The actual number of fur garments sold in the United States in 1977 was less than one third the 1947 total. Still, profits are high because of inflated prices.

Who's Who

THE ANIMALS The first distinction among animals exploited for their furs is between those caught in the wild and those raised on commercial fur ranches. In 1976–77, 17 million *wild* animals were killed in the United States alone to supply pelts for the fur industry. The greatest number of these were muskrats (6.5 million), rabbits (3.5 million), raccoons (3.2 million), nutrias (1.6 million), opossums (729,000), foxes (406,000), minks (235,000), coyotes (174,000), and beavers (171,000). Others killed by the thousands included skunks, bobcats, Alaskan fur seals, badgers, otters, ermines, martens, and lynx. The *ranch-raised* pelts account for a much smaller proportion of the U.S. fur market. More than three million additional skins came from ranch-raised minks, and an unspecified number from farm-raised chinchillas and foxes. Of all these, the rare bobcat had the highest-priced hide ($275) and the opossum the lowest ($4.50–$5.50).

Like many figures released by the fur industry, these do not match statistics published by government agencies. For example, according to the U. S. Fish and Wildlife Service, 1977 exports of bobcat and river otter skins were three times higher than industry-reported kills.

TRAPPERS Most of the 825,000 trappers in the United States today are nonprofessionals, described by a fur industry spokesman as "a mixture of rustic individuals such as rural students, farmers, gas station attendants, post-office workers, or anyone who can spare some time during winter months laying out a few traps and making periodic rounds to reap the harvest."

Only half the trappers in the United States are licensed. Among these are the federal government's predator control agents who, on an annual budget of $11 million, kill about 100,000 wolves, coyotes, foxes, and bobcats. To help pay for this costly program, many of the pelts are sold to furriers at government auctions.

COUNTRY FUR COLLECTORS Country collectors visit the trappers yearly and pay them cash for their pelts, which they resell to fur merchants. There are about 25,000 country collectors in the United States.

FUR RANCHERS The richest and most numerous fur ranchers in the United States are the mink ranchers. Of 1,100 mink farms in the northern states (from New England westward to the Great Lakes states, Wisconsin and Minnesota especially), one of the largest is Lester Bennett's thousand-acre (400-hectare) farm in New York State, with a breeding stock of 18,000 animals and an operation worth about $3.5 million. The animals are well-fed, vaccinated against diseases, then slaughtered and skinned in late autumn by migrant workers, most of them Algonquin Indians from Canada.

Because novelty brings high prices, many mink ranches specialize in the inbreeding of animals to produce new color strains. A recently developed apricot shade, called "Fun-Glo," sold at auction for $320 per pelt.

The mink ranchers have three large cooperative marketing associations: Emba Mink Breeders (1,064 members), the Great Lakes Mink Association (540 members), and Amerimink (220 members). These groups maintain a strong lobby in Washington and have helped to stimulate the fur market through nationwide prestige advertising. Large foreign ranchers' associations are based in Ontario, London, and Oslo.

AUCTION COMPANIES The auction house, which earns a 9 percent commission on sales of pelts, is the marketplace of the fur industry. The Hudson's Bay Company in New York is the oldest and largest of three U.S. companies that offer periodic auction sales for pelts. Part of the fur-trading company founded in 1670 by the British, Hudson's Bay is now a major corporation with fur offices in the United States, Canada, and England, and substantial investments in retail stores (326 retail outlets), oil and gas, and real estate companies.

The other American auction houses are the Seattle Fur Exchange and the New York Auction Company in Minneapolis. Leningrad, London, Montreal, Copenhagen, Helsinki, and Stockholm are also fur auction centers.

DEALERS Any firm or individual owning pelts and selling them for a profit is called a dealer. "It's the dealers who get the big returns," says Murray Scheflin of New York-based Scheflin-Reich, the largest mink dealer in the United States. His company may buy 100,000 pelts per year directly from ranchers, but most of its stock comes through auction houses in New York and Copenhagen, another major mink-ranching center. "I can sit down in a day and spend $2 million or $3 million at one auction," says Scheflin, whose firm sells $20 million worth of fur in a season.

Dealers tend to keep a significant portion of their wealth in fur inventories, which they depreciate periodically to conceal profits and reduce their taxable income. Because raw pelts may be stored indefinitely in deep-freeze vaults, dealers can create shortages and cause prices to escalate by hoarding large quantities of a single type of fur.

Most of the 109 dealers listed in the 1978 Directory of *Fur Age Weekly,* a trade publication, are located in New York City.

BROKERS Acting as agents or commissioners, brokers buy and sell furs for others. There are forty-eight such "pelt brokers" in New York City who deal in all of the major fur centers of the world.

MANUFACTURERS The manufacturers buy raw pelts from dealers, send them out to be dressed and dyed, then make them into clothing. The labor is done by hand in small shops usually having fewer than twenty employees, some with only one or two fur-sewing machines in a basement, attic, or garage. The average age of fur workers today is sixty. Union members, represented by the Furriers Joint Council of New York, make up less than half of the work force. Most employees are Greek and Asian immigrants.

The number of American manufacturers dropped from more than 2,000 in 1947 to 663 in 1977; and imports of garments—from Canada, Hong Kong, Korea, Taiwan, Greece, and Italy—rose almost 500 percent between 1972 and 1977. Prominent American manufacturers are beginning to establish factories abroad, in Korea, for example, where labor is cheap.

RETAILERS Most fur garments are sold by furriers in specialty shops. Because few department stores can afford the million-dollar inventory necessary today for a fur salon, many have stopped selling furs. Those that still handle the expensive garments usually lease their fur departments to specialists, who supply the merchandise, cover all operating costs, and pay rent based on a percentage of sales.

CONSUMERS Leading the foreign market, West Germany, Switzerland, and Japan import millions of dollars worth of U.S.-made fur clothing annually. Of the 630,000 fur garments sold in the United States during 1977, most were bought by women over thirty-five years old with incomes above $25,000. The industry has tried to broaden its markets by pursuing foreign customers, young people, and men (through "macho" ads featuring athletes wearing fur coats—a New York Knickerbocker basketball star who posed for one of these ads now has two mink, two seal, an otter, and a raccoon coat, says furrier Ben Kahn.)

The Industry Under Attack

When conservationists and animal welfare groups spoke out against inhumane and ecologically unsound killing of animals for commercial purposes, the fur industry was a principal target. And the steel leghold trap, the most common tool of the fur trapper, was condemned as an unnecessarily cruel device, causing painful injury and prolonged suffering to its victims.

While the U. S. Department of the Interior stated that the leghold trap was the most humane device available, many foreign governments disagreed. Austria, Chile, Denmark, Norway, Switzerland, West Germany, the United Kingdom, and Sweden have banned the leghold trap and replaced it with snares that kill instantly or hold animals unharmed.

Responding to pressure from humane societies, the Fund for Animals, Defenders of Wildlife, and many other groups, the fur industry, in cooperation with federal and state agencies, launched a public relations campaign promoting the leghold trap as "a wildlife management tool." The Ohio Department of Natural Resources, for example, published a document that declared: "Without trapping as a wildlife management tool, cruelty to animals would occur in the form of starvation and disease." (However, as ecologists point out, starvation and disease tend to eliminate the weakest animals from a group, thus maintaining a strong breeding stock, whereas traps kill at random.)

Though most states do regulate trapping seasons and the numbers of animals that may be taken, the rules are almost impossible to enforce. Wardens cannot effectively police large wilderness areas. Pelts are slight and easy to smuggle. And, with the high price of skins, there are strong financial incentives to break the law.

Bobcats and Harp Seals—Fair Game or Endangered Species?

In the early 1970s, when animals threatened with extinction gained legal protection under the U. S. Endangered Species Act of 1973 and the Convention on International Trade in Endangered Species (CITES), furriers began to regard *themselves* as an endangered species. Having fought successfully against endangered species bills since 1968, the industry suddenly faced restrictions on the types and numbers of animals it could kill. High-priced exotic cat skins, for instance, were now off limits. Though cheetah, leopard, jaguar, and ocelot fur could still be obtained illegally with relatively small risks, dealers found it less troublesome to exploit "legal" fur-bearers.

The North American bobcat, long considered worthless, gained status in the fur industry for its black-spotted rufous hide. As the price of its fur climbed as high as $400 a pelt, conservationists claimed that unregulated trapping (100,000 cats in 1977–78) would lead to extinction; and the President's Council on Environmental Quality agreed. But when the Endangered Species Scientific Authority (ESSA), a "watchdog" agency created in the U. S. Fish and Wildlife Service, tried to ban the export of bobcat skins in 1978, state agencies fought to prove that their bobcats were numerous enough to supply foreign markets. As a compromise, ESSA assigned national and state export quotas, which are notoriously easy to violate.

Still battling over the bobcat's hide, conservationists and furriers confronted each other at the 1979 CITES meeting. When a coalition of fur industry groups, state wildlife agencies, and the U. S. Fish and Wildlife Service tried to have all bobcat quotas abolished, Defenders of Wildlife threatened to sue. As a result of this angry opposition the Fish and Wildlife Service issued a temporary restraining order forbidding export of bobcat hides. The industry, however, continues to lobby for unlimited trapping and export of this threatened species.

Another bitter fight between the fur industry and wildlife defenders concerns the killing of baby harp seals. Each year, Newfoundland sealers club 180,000 of the helpless, white-coated pups during their first eighteen days of life, before their fur darkens. White fur is especially valuable because it can be dyed any color (disguising it from customers who are boycotting sealskin). Though some biologists say that the annual kill quota is too high, the Canadian government supports the sealers.

Members of Greenpeace, the Fund for Animals, and the International Fund for Animal Welfare have tried to stop the hunt by chaining themselves to sealing ships, spray-dyeing pups green to destroy their commercial value, and flying news people to the scene to cover the violence of the seal hunt. The Fund for Animals also organized a tourist boycott of Canada. Emphasizing the clubbing techniques used by the sealers, these groups aroused worldwide public sympathy for the appealing baby animals. As a result of the unfavorable publicity, the Canadian government has improved its supervision of the seal hunt, but as of 1980, wildlife groups said the quota was still too high.

Fake Fur—A Real Alternative to the Real Thing?

In 1950, George Borg, the inventor of the automobile clutch, found a way to make a textile product closely resembling sheared beaver. Since then, manufacturers have simulated leopard, seal, mink, and many other types of fur, creating an industry furriers regarded as a serious threat to their business. Conservationists and humane societies quickly joined forces with synthetic fur manufacturers in an attempt to convince consumers to buy the imitation and save animals' lives. Friends of the Earth called for an international boycott of fur products; and ads featured glamorous movie stars, chic but humane, wearing fake furs.

Though this fashion revolt shook the fur industry for several years, businesspeople today claim that the 2.5 million synthetic furs sold annually compete only with the lowest-priced furs. The wealthy consumer who is willing and able to pay $70,000 for a Russian sable coat won't be likely to buy fake fur no matter how real it looks.

The Fur Industry Fights Back

In response to all this anti-fur publicity, the fur industry established a unified front to revive prestige and stimulate sales. In 1971, all branches of labor and management joined to form the American Fur Industry, Inc. (AFI), an umbrella organization that handles industry-wide advertising and public relations.

With an annual budget of $1 million contributed by manufacturers, labor, retailers, buyers, auction companies, dealers, and ranchers' organizations, AFI pays for media advertising, press shows, and local TV appearances. Its public relations program emphasizes the value of trapping to maintain an ecological balance, and tries to make consumers feel that buying fur products fulfills an ecological responsibility.

The industry also set up a Fur Conservation Institute (FCI) to act as an "early warning system" against unfavorable legislation. FCI monitors the activities of conservationist groups and sends lobbyists to international wildlife conventions because it sees the "anti-fur" arguments of conservationists as the most formidable threat facing the industry.

M.A., S.L.

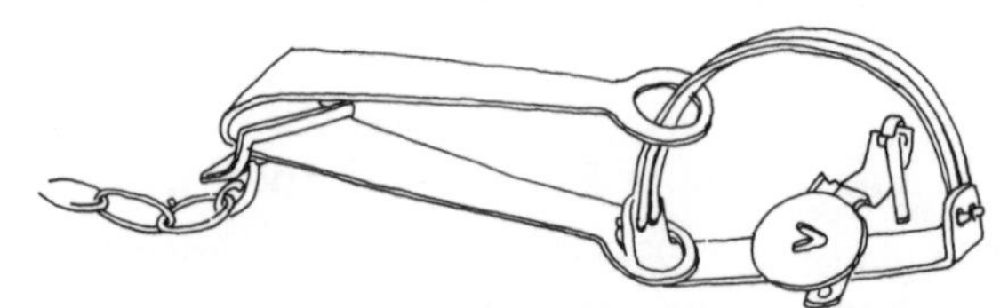

The controversial leg-hold trap.

CO-OPS: THE BUSINESS OF SHARING

Two hospitals near Seattle, Washington, have eliminated unnecessary surgery: their doctors are staff members who receive a flat salary, rather than a fee for each surgical procedure. The result is a rate of surgery about half that of the general U.S. population.

This innovation was conceived by no standard medical establishment; it is part of a unique health care system in which patients set the rules because they own and direct the hospitals.

The Group Health Cooperative of Puget Sound is an example of consumer cooperatives, companies that are owned and controlled by their own customers who wish to receive high-quality goods and services at the cheapest possible price. Co-ops have existed worldwide for hundreds of years and now almost 300 million people find co-ops a money-saving alternative to paying for someone else's profits.

The best known are food co-ops, whose members share the benefit of small price markups by eliminating middlemen and contributing work to lower overhead. But co-ops now operate in virtually every market, including housing, utilities, credit, and health.

Whatever the product or service delivered by a co-op, the general rules are the same: each member pays a fee and gains a share in the company, a vote for the board of directors, and a portion of the money left after operating expenses are paid. Crucial to success is a true spirit of cooperation among members, and motivation to volunteer a lot of time and energy.

The system can produce fine results. When The Group Health Cooperative of Puget Sound began in 1947, it had six hundred members; now it boasts over two thousand members, two hospitals, nine clinics, a full staff of doctors, and an annual budget of $70 million.

During the early nineteenth century in Europe, various groups tried organizing co-ops as a way to fend off financial insecurity, only to see failure because of internal strife. Then in 1844, a group of striking weavers in Rochdale, England, opened a small food co-op that succeeded where others had failed, by establishing a set of rules: one member, one vote; limited interest on shares; and savings returned to members. The Rochdale Principles still govern co-ops.

A major stumbling block to founding co-ops in the United States has been difficulty in finding financial backers. Banks traditionally saw co-ops as credit risks and have been reluctant to lend them money. The Small Business Administration viewed them as threats to small businesses and has likewise refused them funds. But in 1978, after a decade of increasing support for consumer legislation, Congress passed the National Consumer Cooperative Bank Act, which set up a federally funded bank to promote the development and expansion of consumer co-ops.

In contrast to the consumer co-op, in which

consumer members organize to cut costs in buying goods and services, the producer co-op is jointly owned by workers and entrepreneurs who want to reduce costs of *selling* goods and services. Producer co-ops account for more than half the 700,000 co-ops in the world, and the ratio is much higher in the United States: of its 9,000 co-ops (excluding credit unions) 8,000 are producer cooperatives. Most are agricultural cooperatives, or "farm co-ops," with names like Land O' Lakes and Sunkist. Together these farmers harvest, process, and market their crops. There are 17,000 fishing cooperatives in the world (100 in the United States). In addition, there are also arts and crafts co-ops and industrial co-ops such as the plywood co-ops in America's Pacific Northwest, which are owned and operated by workers who distribute profits among themselves in proportion to their contribution of labor.

The founder of the first successful consumer co-op in the United States was none other than Benjamin Franklin, who, in 1736, began a fire insurance company called the Philadelphia Contributionship. Still in existence, the company was a forerunner of the mutual insurance companies of today that return profit to "member" clients.

American consumer co-ops during the twentieth century experienced cycles of success and failure. After initial interest, which peaked around 1920, the cooperative movement fell into a lull until the Depression, when it saw another major growth period—again temporary. Then in the late 1960s, concern about ecology triggered a boom in co-ops focused on recycling and health foods. Though many failed because of poor management and lack of cooperative education, the continuing interest in conservation and nutrition kept the movement alive through the 1970s.

The latest wave of food co-ops was set off by consumers' desires to control the contents and quality of the products they buy. Art Danforth of the Cooperative League of the U.S.A. described this philosophy: "The name of the game is controlling the food and the additives and chemicals that go into it. With organized purchasing power we could, for example, go to somebody in Detroit and say, 'We want you to produce a car that has this and this.' The extent to which an automobile is engineered for safety and mileage could be greatly affected."

The versatility of the co-op concept and its benefits to members have attracted 35 million people in the United States alone. Here are some examples of the major types of co-ops and their organizational structures.

Housing

As of 1980 there were 2,500 housing cooperatives in the United States and 62 million worldwide, all tenant-owned buildings where one mortgage is held on the entire property, unlike condominiums whose residents hold separate mortgages on each unit. Part of the monthly rent is applied to the mortgage payment, thereby increasing the equity returned to each departing tenant. Board of directors decide whether shares may be sold for an inflated market price.

In the United States, housing co-ops come in three types: converted, in which buildings are turned cooperative after construction and developers pass along often-inflated mortgages to members; consumer-built, where a group arranges a mortgage to build housing units; and federally-funded, in which cooperatives are built by private developers wih low-interest mortgages from the Department of Housing and Urban Development, then a share of the mortgage is turned over to each tenant.

Food

As of 1980, there were about one thousand co-op food stores in the United States, owned and operated by members, paying reduced food prices after initial joining fees. Food co-ops often unite regionally to form a distribution cooperative in order to shave transportation and warehousing costs and to produce "house" labels under contract with manufacturers.

Similar to food co-ops, though far more numerous and virtually uncountable because they tend to be temporary operations, are "buying clubs." Here, groups of people, usually neighbors or work colleagues, pool their marketing lists, buy cheaply in bulk, and divide the purchases, all with minimum overhead since shopping and distribution duties are shared by members of the club.

Health Care

As of 1980, fifteen health co-ops in the United States offered comprehensive care to 400,000 members. Although membership fees are comparable to health insurance premiums, co-ops offer all medical services, a reduced rate of surgery, and an emphasis on preventative medicine.

Credit

With 32 million members as of 1980, credit unions account for 91 percent of co-op membership in the United States. Although usually formed by companies to provide their employees the benefit of low-interest loans, credit unions are also formed by church groups and other organizations. They may be started by any group that shares a common purpose.

Other Types

Co-ops have been formed over the years to meet virtually every need. In the United States, as of 1980, they included the following types: electricity (930 co-ops with 8 million members) and telephone (240 co-ops with 1 million members), mainly in rural areas where utility companies found population densities too low to make service installation profitable, and where co-op members secured financial aid and technical assistance to provide themselves with electric and telephone services; nursery schools (1,700 co-ops with 68,000 members), in which programs and staff are supervised by parents; legal (5 with 8,000 members), which offer counseling, education, and assistance in areas of "volume law" such as real estate and divorce; auto repair (12 with 24,000 members), offering self-help preventative maintenance; and fuel oil, in which contracts with distributors save members one or two cents per gallon. Recreation Equipment, Inc., Co-operative, with outlets in six U.S. cities, enrolled its millionth member in 1980.

Co-ops Around the World

The encouragement given by most European countries to consumer co-ops of all types has spawned a broader system. Sweden's consumer co-op system is the world's most successful, accounting for 15 percent of the country's retail sales and one third of its food sales. In England, consumer co-ops account for 9 percent of retail sales but, unlike Sweden, prices there are marked higher to provide a greater investment return to members.

Other countries prominent in co-op organization are Holland, where four thousand people belong to a taxi co-op, and Canada, which leads the world in the variety of its co-ops.

Starting Out

The Cooperative League of the U.S.A. provides information on all types of co-ops and offers helpful tips on how to start one. For information on where to find co-ops of a similar nature and on how to organize one, prospective co-op founders can write the League at Suite 1100, 1828 L Street NW, Washington, D.C. 20036.

The National Consumer Cooperative Bank (2001 S Street NW, Washington, D.C. 20009) offers similar services and subsidizes technical assistance and provides loans for co-op development.

A VISION OF THE FUTURE OF BUSINESS

Editor's Note: *In the* Almanac *we have tried to avoid rigid predictions, but we are fascinated by educated guesses. Robert Heilbroner, the noted economist, has written that, by his educated guess, the world economy as currently constituted faces at best only twenty-five more years of growth as we now define it. He anticipates a major shift among economic institutions of the West toward greater planning. Heilbroner's reasoning follows in an excerpt from an article tying current economic problems to considerations of the environment.*

To justify an argument for a drastic change in institutional arrangements, we must be able to discover some element in the present crisis that is quantitatively large enough and qualitatively different enough to warrant another major restructuring of the capitalistic framework. I suggest that there is such an element in the challenges posed to the process of capitalist accumulation by what we loosely call "the environment"—the complex and interconnected constraints of our energy supplies, our resource availabilities, our pollution dangers. The problems of the environment are now so generally familiar that I shall not try to marshal the standard facts and figures. Let us instead consider the ways in which some of these constraints impinge on the capitalist process. Here we might begin again with oil shock, which has already dealt the system a serious, although certainly not fatal, blow. But present-day oil shock is not the full measure of the problem. Today's oil prices are artificially maintained by the coordinated action of the OPEC cartel, not by the pressure of demand against supply. Meanwhile, demand is steadily increasing and the day will come when it is the pull of demand, and not the prop of a cartel agreement, which sets the price of oil. Moreover, the difference between the most optimistic and the most pessimistic dates for that "cross-over" point —optimistic dates assuming a high rate of new oil discoveries and effective conservation plans, and pessimistic dates assuming the opposite—is surprisingly small. In both cases, cross-over is expected to occur during the next twenty years. Thereafter, demand will be in charge and we can expect the price of oil to rise steadily, with no help from OPEC at all, unless we find substitutes for gasoline and heating oil.

The coming rise of oil prices is only the leading edge of a series of such changes that will affect the very possibility of economic growth, interfering with the process of capital accumulation, in a hitherto unknown way. The stringency of worldwide resources, while not imposing anything like an oil bottleneck, will nonetheless be sufficiently great during the coming years of this century to necessitate vast investments in mineral extraction and food production. According to a study of global needs conducted for the United Nations by Wassily Leontief, a Nobel laureate in economics, the consumption of common minerals must rise fivefold, food fourfold, if a moderate rate of global growth is to continue. All this will require stupendous economic, and no less stupendous social and political, commitments.

Finally, the newly apparent fragility of the atmospheric mantle poses perhaps the most formidable obstacle of all. Human activity, especially in the industrial regions where its effect on nature is most concentrated, is at the verge of creating violent and irreversible effects on the planet. The immense magnitude of technological assault on the environment is indicated by the ongoing debates over the possibility of carbon dioxide creating a "greenhouse effect" that would alter the temperature of the entire earth [see "Changing Climate," page 19]; the possibility that massed industrial heat could change the patterns of air circulation and of precipitation on a continental scale; the possibility that the release of chemical waste might contaminate the ground water of a large region; and the possibility that the volume of nuclear wastes might constitute a hazard for an entire city or state.

All these new constraints point in the same direction. They indicate the need for an unprecedented degree of monitoring, control, supervision, and precaution with regard to the economic process. Some of these safeguarding functions can perhaps be performed by the marketplace itself, particularly as far as the allocation of scarce resources is concerned. But the market will not monitor safety, nor will it impose decisions about the rate of growth, or its sharing within or among nations, which accord with the moral and political, as well as the economic, desires of peoples and nations. Thus, the constraints of our time, the need for which will steadily intensify as far ahead as we can see, imply a powerful, and I think irresistible, force for planning the economic process in a way that has never before been necessary.

What is new about the emphasis on planning is its purpose. Its essential purpose will be not to remedy the various failures that capitalist growth has brought but to direct, and at bottom to protect, the very possibility of such growth, as long as that can be. This will certainly require the formulation of strict policies concerning the use of energy. It must embrace an ever wider range of considerations affecting the environment. The processes of scientific development and technical application must likewise fall more and more under the guidance and, where necessary, the veto power of government. All this may require allocations of materials, prohibitions against certain kinds of investment or consumption activities, international arrangements, and a general sticking of the public nose into private life wherever that life, left to itself, threatens the very survival of the system.

We can anticipate that the new planning effort, despite its inevitable mistakes, inefficiencies, wastes and irritations, will prevent an interruption from bringing the system to a halt. We can anticipate as well that the planning effort, mounted as it will surely be by an uneasy partnership of big business and government, will look like socialism from one angle, like "fascism" from another. It may well contain elements of both, but I think it should be called what it is—planned capitalism.

And in the end? No doubt there will be still another deep crisis. Moreover, it may come rapidly, for the pace of change seems to be quickening. Branko Horvat, a widely known Yugoslavian economist, has pointed out that the era of so-called competitive capitalism lasted almost two hundred years, from roughly 1700 to 1875; the era of monopoly capitalism fifty-five years, from about 1875 to 1930; welfare capitalism forty-three years, from 1930 to 1973. Assuming that I am right, and that we are now entering the era of planned capitalism, how long will it last?

That is a question to which we can give only the most tentative answer. The constraints of the environment, which are the great determining element in the era into which we are moving, suggest that we will have perhaps twenty-five years of "safe," although increasingly difficult, growth (as the Leontief study also suggests), followed by curtailments that promise to be more and more drastic. But, meanwhile, there are other contradictions and barriers and hindrances that may induce a crisis before we reach that winding down of growth that, by its very definition, would pose a truly historic challenge to capitalism. There is, for example, the suffocating growth of bureaucracy, itself the by-product of the welfare state and the planned state—another "contradiction," if you will. There is the rampant expansion of industrial technology, bringing not only the ever greater socialization of the economic structure but what seems to be a concomitant disaffection, indifference, and antipathy of a population unable to find satisfaction in the plastic wealth or the impersonal employments that industrialism generates. There is the lingering, always explosive problem of the distribution of wealth, justice, and decency within the rich nations, and between the rich nations and the poor ones. There is the unsettled state of the economic world, with capitalist nations hesitating between live-and-let-live and beggar-my-neighbor philosophies, and developed nations and developing ones eyeing one another in mixed need and hatred. And there is violence and despair and the slow erosion of order-maintaining behavior. Any of these may become the entering wedge of a new crisis, pushing for further adaptations that may ultimately exceed the capabilities of the system.

But this is still some distance into the future, I think. History has shown capitalism to be an extraordinarily resilient and tenacious system, perhaps because its driving force is dispersed among so much of its population rather than concentrated solely in a governing elite. In pursuit of the privileges, the beliefs, and above all the profits of capitalism, its main protagonists have not only created the material wonders that Marx marvelled at but have shown a capacity for change that even he, who never underestimated the self-preserving drive of capital, did not fully anticipate. Thus, it is still too soon to write "finis" to the present era, for in our time capitalism has yet another sub-chapter within its power to create, and perhaps others after that. But already we can see more clearly than past generations that the chapter cannot go on forever, and that in our own time, even if the system survives, we will have to live through periods of wrenching change.

THE THIRD CENTURY FUND

When meat prices rose dramatically in the United States in 1973, a nationwide meat boycott was organized to help drive the price down. When lettuce pickers went on strike to protest wages and working conditions, they enlisted support for a consumer lettuce boycott. Whale products are boycotted on a worldwide basis by those who wish to save the whale, and other international boycotts have been organized around political issues, like apartheid in South Africa or the marketing of infant formula products in developing countries. The boycott, in short, is a confrontational tool used to bring pressure and force a change in consumer habits or commercial policy. Some view it as the means of last resort.

Others view the boycott as economic violence, as radical, unruly behavior, and seek more traditional methods for bringing about social change. For those who choose to work within the system, ethical or "alternative investments" may be a more acceptable tactic. The idea is to use the existing financial mechanisms, instead of bucking them.

Moral Investments

Investment in "clean" companies will generate "clean" profits, or at least that is the hope of several investment and philanthropic ventures. They attempt to use wealth conscientiously, for socially responsible purposes, by investing only in companies that can point to a record of fairness, honesty, lawfulness, and respect for the environment.

One example is the Third Century Fund, a mu-

A company's pollution control performance is one criterion considered by alternative investors. (*EPA Documerica/Marc St. Gil*)

tual fund with assets of about $40 million administered by the Dreyfus Fund in New York City. The fund buys stocks on behalf of investors only in companies that have positive ratings for equal opportunity employment, occupational safety and health, consumer protection, product purity, and environmental protection. The ratings are derived from questionnaires developed by the Fund's officers working with consulting experts in each field.

Researchers for the Fund claim to conduct on-site interviews and to rate companies on the basis of day-to-day operations, rather than simply on press releases and company self-praise. To weed out offensive companies, the researchers use an equation developed for each industry. First, companies are scored and ranked within each industry, then a cut-off score is established. Companies with marks below the cut-off point are excluded from the Fund.

Just Making It

There are limits to the Fund's exclusiveness, of course. It does include companies in controversial fields like off-shore drilling, or nuclear fusion research, or industries that are polluting virtually by definition, like the paper industry. Some fast-food companies, too, are included. In these cases the Fund researchers choose the companies that have the best records among their peers. For example, no company that is a flagrant violator of environmental control laws would be included in the Fund, but one that had a better than average pollution record for its industry might be included if it had an exceptionally good record in equal opportunity employment or product purity or occupational safety as well. All companies included, obviously, must be deemed positive financial risks. Some companies in the Fund, as of early 1980, are United Airlines, Kaiser Aluminum, Teleprompter Corporation, Fairchild Camera and Instrument Corporation, John Wiley publishers, the New York Times Company, Envirotech Corporation, and Peabody International.

Moral Profits

The idea is to encourage companies to upgrade their social performance, the incentive being to lure new investors and avoid bad press. Investors by the same token can be selective about where they put their money, avoiding companies whose profits are made at the expense of social responsibility.

In the five years between 1974 and 1979, the Fund showed an average 275.33 percent increase in the value of shares owned. By comparison, the overall average for all mutual funds was 143.43 percent. (For more information, write Third Century Fund, 600 Madison Avenue, New York, New York 10022.)

Other Alternative Investments

The Pax Fund

A smaller portfolio of $2.5 million, this fund was established to "encourage investment in companies which provide constructive rather than destructive goods and services." The fund excludes companies that are Department of Defense contractors, as well as companies in the liquor, tobacco, and gambling businesses. In 1979, the fund paid a return of 8.6 percent per share. (For more information, write The Pax Fund, 224 State Street, Portsmouth, New Hampshire 03801.)

The Institute for Community Economics, Inc.

This Boston-based organization works for the creation of community land trusts, housing cooperatives, and small business ventures. (For more information, write The Institute for Community Economics, Inc., 120 Boylston Street, Boston, Massachusetts 02116.) P.D.

11
The Dogs of War

The unleashed power of the atom has changed everything except our way of thinking.

ALBERT EINSTEIN

AHAB'S PURSUIT

"War's a game," said William Cowper. It is "grievous," lamented Homer. "War is hell," declared General Sherman; "a contagion," said Franklin Roosevelt. More recently, someone observed that war is the ultimate pollutant. That is the purpose of this section of the *Almanac,* to look beyond the obvious facts of war—the body counts, the rubble, the shifting borders—to the unspoken and unrecognized effects of violent conflict on the theater of nature in which war is played out.

While the vitality of ecological systems is the first consideration in nature's strategy of life, it is usually the last consideration in humanity's strategy of war. Sometimes the destruction of the environment even becomes part of the war plan, as in Indochina, where U.S. forces burned large forest tracts during the Vietnam War in an attempt to eliminate the wooded hiding places of the Vietcong. (See "Vietnam: The Green War," page 554.) Herbicides were sprayed aerially first, to kill leaves and twigs, building up an adequate supply of kindling. Then massive fires were initiated with the aim of destroying nearly 20,000 acres (8,000 hectares) at a time. Three major actions designed to create ecological catastrophes in Vietnam went under the code names "Operation Sherwood Forest," "Operation Hot Tip," and "Operation Pink Rose." During World War II, the Japanese made repeated attempts to ignite large forest fires in the western United States by releasing long-range balloons carrying incendiary devices. At least one of these attacks *did* result in forest fires in Oregon, though the destruction was negligible.

Sometimes the effects of war on the adjacent environment are unintended. In 1979, as a result of the continuing war between Ethiopia and South Yemen, government agents were not able to enter the "horn" of Africa, where they annually conduct a census of the breeding population of locusts. Thus, they did not discover the presence of an extraordinarily large locust population that year and were unprepared when the locusts gathered in a huge, dense cloud resembling a tornado and began traveling north toward the Indian subcontinent, ravaging crops along the way. The farmers of North Africa, the Arabian peninsula, and India, all vulnerable to this plague, were luckily spared devastation when unusually strong winds carried the locust cloud out to sea.

But these disruptions are dwarfed by the prospective environmental effects of a

(*Lookout Mountain Air Force Station*)

major nuclear war—the ultimate ecological catastrophe. If a nuclear bomb is ever detonated again in a major city of the world, there will be adequate statistics available to calculate quickly, on the basis of the megatonnage, how many people were killed, how quickly, and precisely where. That information is well publicized.

But a more prodigious, longer-term destruction could be just getting under way as the fireball darkens. The environment of much of the planet, perhaps all of it, could be seriously distorted. The climate could be altered, with ominous implications for vital food-growing regions and the billions of people dependent upon them. The ozone layer could be thinned, allowing intense ultraviolet rays to strike the earth, causing a vast increase in skin cancer. Important long-term genetic effects would begin brewing in the cells of great populations of people, animals, and plants, with unpredictable Frankenstein possibilities for future generations. These effects are rarely discussed.

Perhaps that is because our warriors still think only along lines of tactics and strategies, as the ancient geniuses of war did when the results were tabulated *only* in losses of lives and territory—and that meant soldiers' lives mostly and political territory. The great military inventions of the distant past were mostly human maneuvers: the Alexandrian phalanx, the forced marches of Caesar, Hannibal's outflanking and enveloping movements at the battle of Cannae. The old wars, though colored with "pale fear" and "black death," as Homer described them, were based on classical models, on the "art" and "principles" of war.

The facades and the posturing of traditional warriors continue today, but the events of war are different. Hecuba could mourn for the women and children left behind during ancient war, but now the wars come home to them. The "innocent" are spared no violence, and neither is the environment. The military inventions of today are mostly inhuman devices and chemicals and other phenomena—mostly indiscriminate, mostly horrible. But locked up in the old thought patterns of conflict, we fail to see that a pitched battle at Agincourt did little damage beyond the battlefield while a nuclear exchange could warp life everywhere forever.

If the bomb never drops again, it has still violated lives by inspiring runaway armament programs that divert money, energy, brainpower, and resources—all precious commodities—from programs of sustenance and education for people, the very things that offer the only hope for eradication of the disease of war. As the American ecologist Charles Southwick has pointed out, the nations of the world spend over ten thousand dollars per year training each soldier and less than one hundred dollars per year educating each child. Political scientist William Ophuls estimates that the U.S. defense establishment probably uses 10 percent of all petroleum consumed in the United States.

Wars can be a terrific business. Writer Paul Erdman has estimated that of Iran's annual oil income of about $20 billion in the late 1970s, the Shah spent about $6 billion to $8 billion on military hardware from the United States, where weapons production is just another business. Eighteen of the twenty largest U.S. companies are major participants in the weapons industry. Representative John F. Seiberling of Ohio pointed out in 1970 that the Pentagon had three thousand people working on arms sales to other countries while the Arms Control and Disarmament Agency had twelve people monitoring arms sales. "That gives you an idea of where the executive branch priorities are," said Seiberling.

In the same international spirit of business, nations export nuclear-energy technology, and with it the starter kit for war materials that will eventually enable the least developed and the least stable countries to join the nuclear-weapons club. After reaching this conclusion, the 1976 report of the United Kingdom's Royal Commission on Environmental Pollution (known as the Flowers Report after its chairman, Sir Brian Flowers) observed: "We see no reason to trust in the stability of any nation of any political persuasion for centuries ahead."

Unfortunately, for some of the most powerful elements of human society, the exercise of war, or at least the anticipation of it, is an adventure. War is a great unpredictable beast. And, like Captain Ahab in *Moby Dick,* who pursued the embodiment of evil in the white whale, we are coming to wonder if it is perhaps we, rather than the beast, who are caught up in something evil. Like children with war games and war toys, purchased at "weapons fairs," we blindly play a game of chance with a future that does not belong to us.

In the coming age, human society must grapple not only with its poised weaponry but with increasing *reasons* to go to war. As access to petroleum and certain minerals becomes more strategic, as food production lags further behind the demand for it, as living space grows more precious, the opportunities for conflict will increase. These factors are significant in the light of history. Quincy Wright's *Study of War* counts 278 major wars in the world between 1480 and 1940. Of these, 64 percent were the result of territorial expansion and jockeying for dominance. Twenty-eight percent were civil wars. Eight percent, almost all the others, were the result of errors in communication, hardly a reassuring statistic in a time when the greatest missile flight time between two locations on the planet is about thirty minutes. Some believe this time frame makes a war decision at the head-of-government level effectively impossible. They advocate giving the decision about retaliation to computers, or to the people who would first detect the approach of missiles—radar technicians. This incredible notion is the latest generation of the protective strategy devised in the 1950s: *mutual assured destruction,* long known by its perfectly appropriate acronym, MAD.

So, as humanity wrestles with political, economic, and environmental strains that call for greater cooperation, the dogs of war whine louder than ever. We are, like Ahab, caught up in a dangerous chase, flirting adventurously with a terrible fury that can rise up and sink us. It is, like Ahab's pursuit, a journey toward a large unpredictable killing.

M.R.

ONE-MINUTE BRIEFING ON WAR

- The world spends more than $1 billion a day (more than $400 billion per year) on the military. That is about $1 million every ninety seconds.

- Development aid extended to developing countries amounts to about 5 percent of what the military budgets total in industrialized nations.

- The nations of the world today spend thirty times as much of their budgets on the military as they did in 1900.

- About 130 wars have been fought since World War II, according to the Hungarian professor Istvan Kende, an expert on world conflict. These wars have been played out in some seventy countries; they have killed more people than the combined fatalities of World War II.

- Since World War II, there has not been a single day when the world was free of war.

SOURCE: Alva Myrdal, *The Game of Disarmament.*

- More than half of the physical and engineering scientists in the world—some half million people—work only on military research. They are funded by about $35 billion a year, far more than is spent on peaceful research.

- "We have this new profession that has started since World War II, the defense intellectuals, who have never seen a weapon or warfare, and who are really more troublesome than the uniformed military. . . . In the Soviet Union there are enormous numbers of academics who are paid by the military budget, and they want their funding to continue. . . . It is about the same in the United States, which, all in all, employs more civilians than soldiers on defense activities. Worldwide there are 26 million people in uniform but there are an equal number of people not in uniform who are paid on the military budget. Of course that is a tremendous political constituency. . . . What the nuclear weapon did was to reduce security. . . . The United States was absolutely secure in World War II. The chances of its territory being bombed in any serious way, except perhaps the coasts, were nil. Whereas now you could eliminate every American in thirty minutes. . . . So American security has gone from 100 percent to 0 in thirty years. Only a handful of people realize that; the average American feels very secure."

SOURCE: Dr. Frank Barnaby, director of the Stockholm International Peace Research Institute (SIPRI), during an interview in 1979 with Ruth Link for *Seven Days* magazine.

THE ULTIMATE ENVIRONMENTAL DISASTER

Beyond the calamity of millions of dead or dying human beings in the event of a full-scale nuclear exchange, there are momentous ecological disruptions to consider. While this may seem obvious, not until 1975 did the United States Arms Control and Disarmament Agency undertake a detailed evaluation of the long-term environmental consequences of multiple nuclear weapons explosions. The analysis was done by the National Research Council, in association with the National Academy of Sciences (NAS). In a cover letter submitted with the completed report, NAS president Philip Handler described the hypothetical nuclear event they had studied. To begin with, the report assumes that the two warring nations will both be in the Northern

Hemisphere. About half of all nuclear weapons in strategic arsenals (of the United States and the Soviet Union, the report implies) would be detonated. That means 500 to 1,000 large weapons yielding ten to twenty megatons per bomb (each of them approximately the equivalent of 750 to 1,500 Hiroshima bombs) and another 4,000 to 5,000 lesser weapons of one or two megatons (75 to 150 Hiroshima bombs). The total explosive power is the equivalent of 10 billion tons of TNT.

The study does not say this is a "probable" nuclear exchange, but by working from this as a base it suggests that military strategists consider it a highly possible event. Since only half of the available weapons are used in this scenario, some specialists point out that emotional decisions and unforeseen events in the midst of an actual nuclear war could result in a far greater exchange.

The following article, based on the National Research Council report, describes the environmental aftermath of a full-blown nuclear war.

M.R.

The possible effects of a nuclear war are often written about as if they concerned only the United States and the Soviet Union. The truth is that nuclear war, directly or indirectly, threatens almost every nation on earth.

In a thermonuclear conflict between the United States and the Soviet Union, great damage, of course, would be done to both countries. Since most U.S. missile sites are in the northern Plains states, radioactivity from an attack meant to destroy them would almost certainly wipe out the U.S.—and probably Canadian—grain harvest. Since the United States and Canada export twice as much grain as the rest of the world (some of it to the Soviet Union), the impact would be felt in hungry, populous countries far from the fighting. Most Soviet targets are also near the western, grain-growing region of the nation. There would be widespread famine both in the immediate countries affected and around the world.

The breakdown of international trade would have severe consequences for all industrial countries and for all countries that depend on imports for vital parts of their economy. Supply lines for certain raw materials, machinery, and food would be disrupted. Pesticides, fertilizer, seeds, tractors, and fuel would be scarce, making large-scale farming difficult.

Millions of people would be thrown out of work. In areas where a large proportion of the land is devoted to luxury cash crops for export, the precipitous drop in the demand for coffee, bananas, or pineapples could destroy the economy. In cities everywhere, factories, stores, and other businesses would have to close when deprived of their usual commerce with affected countries.

The changes that would immediately occur in world trade, because of global interdependence, would be accompanied by other, more ominous, physical changes. Even if a large-scale nuclear exchange were confined to the Northern Hemisphere, its effects would soon spread to other parts of the world.

Dust raised by the explosions would circumnavigate the earth and stay in the atmosphere for several years. There would be a worldwide reduction in the light and heat reaching the earth, although probably not more than a one-degree decrease in temperature. After a year or two, most of this atmospheric dust would be removed by precipitation.

Unfortunately, although it would produce spectacular sunsets for a few years, dust from an atomic explosion is radioactive. Much of the radioactive fallout from a nuclear war would reach uninvolved countries. About a third of all fallout from the Northern Hemisphere would reach the lower latitudes of Africa and South America within a year, carrying lethal doses of strontium-90. Atmospheric patterns would cause the majority of the fallout to land between 30 and 60 degrees north latitude, an area that encompasses most of the United States, Canada, Europe, North Africa, the Soviet Union, and the People's Republic of China. In general, areas between these latitudes that normally have a high annual rainfall would receive the brunt of radioactive fallout, since most fallout descends with ordinary rain or snow. A deadly rain could fall on "hot spot" regions thousands of miles from the explosions. Unpredictable freak concentrations of radionuclides can occur at very great distances from the scene of the attack.

Vegetation near an explosion would be exposed to ionizing radiation and to fallout. Many crops would be killed instantly, many surviving plants would suffer chromosome breakage and genetic mutations. In the past, scientists have demonstrated that relatively low doses of radioactivity can triple the mutation rate of some plants. Although farmers would be able to control most damaging crop mutations with selective breeding from undamaged plants, there is a danger that new plant diseases could develop.

The ocean would also be damaged by nuclear

Nagasaki, Japan, after it was hit by a U.S. nuclear bomb on August 9, 1945. The United States bombed Nagasaki and Hiroshima with nuclear weapons only three weeks after the first successful bomb test. The destructiveness of the new weapon forced Japan to surrender, ending World War II. (*National Archives*)

More than a third of Nagasaki was devastated by the atomic bomb blast; 75,000 people were killed or injured. (*National Archives*)

war over land. The soluble radionuclides in fallout would eventually find their way to the ocean, where plankton would accumulate them in a relatively high concentration. Because plankton are at the bottom of the oceanic food chain, and because of their widespread distribution, their contamination means that many other forms of marine life could be endangered. Five months after the nuclear test on Bikini atoll in March 1954, radiation-contaminated tuna were caught 1,000 miles (1,600 kilometers) away, near Japan, one of the first indications of the damage that could be done far from the actual site of the explosion.

In general, primitive life forms are more resistant to radioactivity than complex forms—the cockroach, for example, is eminently suited to survival. Among aquatic animals, freshwater fish are the most sensitive. Radionuclides tend to concentrate in the fish, so that eating fish from contaminated water would probably harm humans more than drinking the water itself.

In 1975, when the National Research Council sponsored their study of the subject, scientists concluded that the most important long-term effect of multiple nuclear-weapons detonations would be the worldwide increase in ultraviolet radiation because of reduction of the stratospheric ozone layer.

A nuclear explosion releases a large concentration of oxides of nitrogen into the stratosphere. These immediately begin to break down the ozone. A 50 percent reduction in the ozone layer over the Northern Hemisphere would be possible in the first year after a nuclear exchange; by the third year afterward, the entire globe could experience a 20 percent decrease in total ozone. It would take ten to twenty years for the ozone layer to regenerate. Meanwhile, severe effects of ultraviolet radiation would appear worldwide. The ozone layer protects DNA, the basic material of life, from almost all ultraviolet rays. The reduction of ozone would lead to an increase in skin cancers, lethal sunburns, genetic mutations

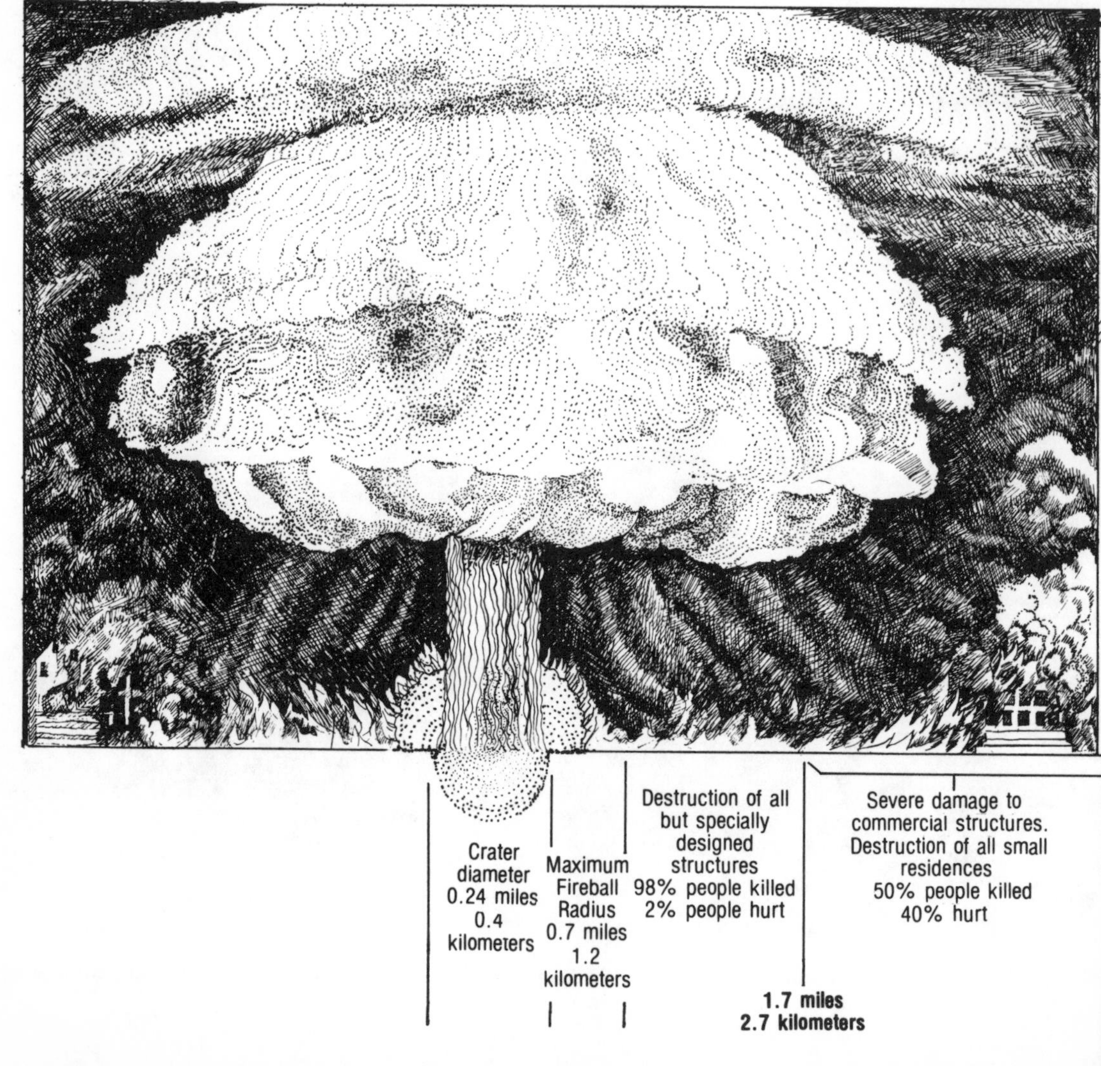

in plants and animals, and even the destruction of some species. Snow blindness in northern regions would become common during the most severe phase of ozone depletion. Anyone who worked outside would have to be protected from incapacitating sunburn.

The National Research Council report concluded that, in the event of a large-scale nuclear war in the Northern Hemisphere, *Homo sapiens* would definitely survive—but civilization might not. J.S.

WEAPONS EFFECTS

Little Boy, of Hiroshima, was a thirteen-kiloton bomb. It killed nearly a hundred thousand people —a fact later filed under "weapons effects." The most densely populated sector of the world is the part of Manhattan island synecdochically known as Wall Street, where, in a third of a square mile, the workaday population is half a million people. If all the people were to try to go outdoors at the same time, they could not do so, because they are too many for the streets. A crude bomb with a yield of only one kiloton could kill a couple of hundred thousand people there. Weapons effects. Because the tall buildings would create something known as "shadow effect," more than twenty-five kilotons would be the yield necessary to kill almost everybody in the financial district.

High dams taper, are thinner at the top. One kiloton would destroy at least the upper half of any dam in the world. Hoover Dam has the biggest head of water in the United States. A bomb dropped behind it into Lake Mead and set to go off at a depth of fifty feet (fifteen meters) would pretty much empty the lake. Weapons effects.

The yield necessary to kill everyone in the Rose Bowl is a fizzle yield, something on the scale of one fiftieth of a kiloton—so little that it would not be shock or fire but gamma rays that did the killing. A tenth of a kiloton detonated outside an electric-power reactor could breach the containment shell, disable the controls, and eliminate the emergency core-cooling system. There is more long-lived radioactivity in a reactor that has been running for a year than there would be in a bomb of a hundred megatons. A bomb with a yield of a fiftieth of a kiloton exploded just outside the spent-fuel pools at a reactor or a reprocessing plant could send downwind enough strontium-90 alone to kill tens of thousands of people. The placement of an explosion—where it happens—is what matters most, and that depends on purpose.

The Hiroshima and Nagasaki bombs were exploded 1,850 feet (563 meters) in the air, because the guess was that from that height the bombs would accomplish the most damage through shock, fire, and radiation effects. A low-yield bomb exploded inside one of the World Trade Center towers could bring it down. The same bomb, if exploded outside, would perform erratically. The Pentagon is a hard target, because it is so spread out. A low-yield bomb exploded in the building's central courtyard would not be particularly effective. To crater the place and leave nothing but a hole in the ground, a full megaton —set off in the concourse, several levels un-

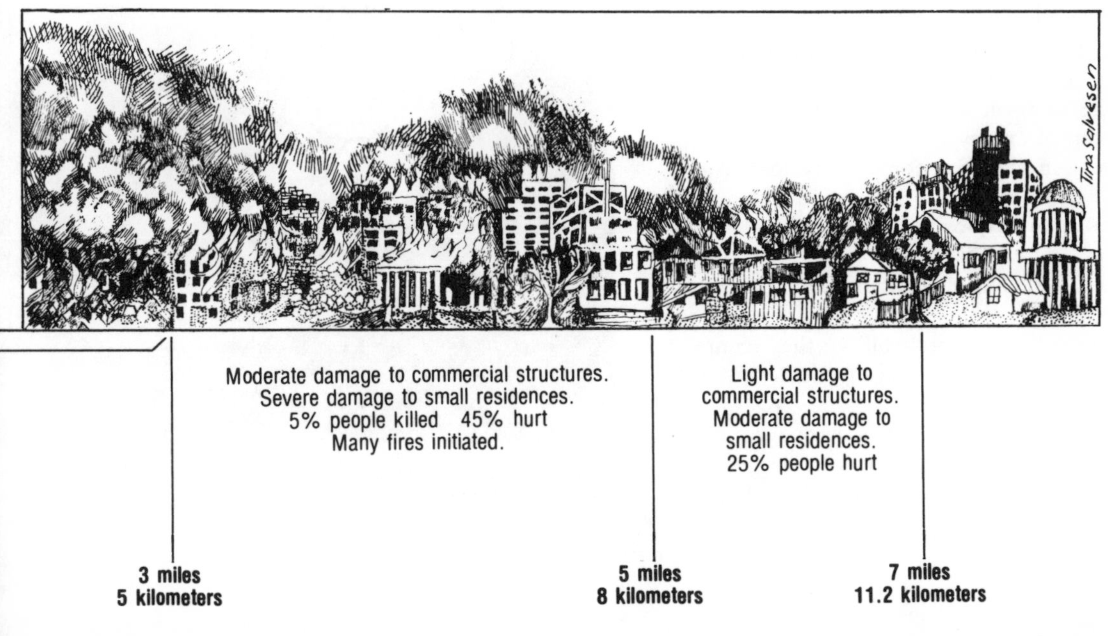

der the courtyard—would be needed. Weapons effects.

A one-fiftieth-kiloton yield coming out of a car on Pennsylvania Avenue would include enough radiation to kill anyone above the basement level in the White House. A one-kiloton bomb exploded just outside the exclusion area during a State of the Union Message would kill everyone inside the Capitol. "It's hard for me to think of a higher-leverage target, at least in the United States," Ted Taylor (a nuclear physicist who has worked at the Los Alamos Scientific Laboratory, where he was a conceptual designer of nuclear bombs) said one day. "The bomb would destroy the heads of all branches of the U.S. government—all Supreme Court justices, the entire Cabinet, all legislators, and, for what it's worth, the Joint Chiefs of Staff. With the exception of anyone who happened to be sick in bed, it would kill the line of succession to the presidency all the way to the bottom of the list. A fizzle-yield, low-efficiency, basically lousy fission bomb could do this."

COMING TO TERMS WITH WARRIORS

For some time many people have suspected that defense establishments have specialists closeted away whose only purpose is to think up confusing initials for what the military is doing. This admittedly incomplete glossary may help the reader find his or her way through the maze of defense literature.

MAD Mutual assured destruction, the guiding premise of the global arms race. Essentially it seeks to ensure that, in the event of a first strike by one side, the other will still retain sufficient retaliatory ability to inflict unacceptable damage in return, thereby (theoretically) inhibiting either side from starting World War III.

STRATEGIC NUCLEAR WEAPON A long-range, high-yield nuclear weapon.

TACTICAL NUCLEAR WEAPON A short-range, low-yield nuclear weapon.

THERMONUCLEAR WEAPON A fusion, or hydrogen, bomb. A very high temperature is created by the detonation of a fission bomb, which in turn initiates a fusion reaction in which two light nuclei unite to form a heavier atom, releasing a large amount of energy.

KILOTON An explosive force equivalent to one thousand tons of TNT.

MEGATON An explosive force equivalent to one million tons of TNT.

GROUND ZERO The detonation point of a nuclear explosion.

CEP Circular error probability, the accuracy radius within which 50 percent of missiles fired at a particular target will fall.

YIELD The explosive force of a nuclear blast, usually measured in megatons or kilotons.

NATO/WTO The North Atlantic Treaty Organization and the Warsaw Treaty Organization, the two sides of the nuclear fence.

ICBM Intercontinental ballistic missile, the basic strategic nuclear weapon. The most important of the U.S. ICBMs are the Titan and Minuteman, while the Soviet Union's equivalent weapons are generally referred to as the SS series.

ABM Antiballistic missile, an anti-ICBM weapon.

CRUISE MISSILE A jet-powered missile with remote control guidance that can alter course as the need arises. It can be launched from the ground, air, or by submarine.

SLBM Submarine-launched ballistic missile. The U.S. SLBMs are the Polaris and Poseidon,

Cruise missiles on an A-6 Intruder aircraft. (*U. S. Navy/PH2 Matthews*)

which are gradually being phased out in favor of the newer Trident series. The Soviet equivalents are the SS-N series.

MIRV Multiple independently targeted reentry vehicle, a weapon with several independently guided warheads.

MX MISSILE A newly developed MIRVed ICBM system concealed on movable cars in long underground tunnels, to make it more difficult for an enemy to target them. The Soviet Union is developing a similar system known as the SS-X-16.

NEUTRON BOMB An enhanced-radiation, reduced-blast thermonuclear weapon, not yet deployed. The weapon would kill living organisms while leaving property such as buildings relatively undamaged. It is the subject of much controversy because of its frightening selectivity.

BW Biological warfare.

CW Chemical warfare.

ASAT Antisatellite weapon.

ACDA U. S. Arms Control and Disarmament Agency, the U.S. agency responsible for keeping track of developments in the arms race.

NORAD North American Air Defense Command, located in Colorado, the nerve center for the United States defense and early warning system.

SNS Strategic nuclear submarine.

ASW Antisubmarine warfare.

T.C.

THE LIQUID BATTLEFIELD

The time when armadas engaged one another at sea is past and the days of destroyers maneuvering to fire artillery at one another seem to be fading, but the importance of the ocean to military strategists is actually on the increase. Since the 1960s there has been a marked acceleration in the growth rate of the fleets operated by the world's fifty-one navies. Ronald Huisken, a war analyst with the Stockholm International Peace Research Institute (SIPRI), estimates that the naval "stocks"—a complicated measurement combining the number of vessels, their tonnage, and their military capabilities—have doubled since World War II. According to SIPRI, there are presently about 2,300 large and small naval vessels afloat.

To some extent this trend may reflect an increasing awareness around the world of the future importance of marine resources, such as seabed minerals, but it is principally a result of a shift in strategies by the two superpowers, the Soviet Union and the United States, which account for nearly three fourths of the world's naval stock.

An important part of the mutual deterrence idea involves using the world's oceans as a vast hiding place for weapons. This largely undersea gamesmanship between the two superpowers, and in fact a great proportion of the expansion of naval activity, is mostly attributable to one type of vessel. In military parlance it is referred to coolly as the SNS, the strategic nuclear submarine.

The Ultimate Spear Gun

If a major nuclear war erupts someday, it is likely that the instruments of greatest violence will not surge out of holes in the ground or drop from the bellies of planes but emerge from the liquid camouflage of the sea. Submarines provide near-perfect deterrence because, equipped with nuclear power plants, they can cruise for long distances underwater and remain at sea for prolonged periods of time. They can hide anywhere in the upper 10 percent of the ocean's volume, making them almost impossible to keep under surveillance. With advances in submarine weapons systems, they are also tremendously powerful.

The new Trident submarine, which NATO forces hope gradually to substitute for the older Poseidon and Polaris submarines, carries upward of two hundred warheads: twenty-four MIRV (multiple independently targeted reentry vehicle) Trident missiles with eight to ten warheads each. The missiles have a range of 4,350 miles (7,000 kilometers) and an accuracy within 547 yards (500 meters) of their target. One half to three quarters of the fleet could be kept at sea to ensure an adequate strike force. Only *one or two of the Tridents would carry enough firepower to destroy all major Soviet cities.*

The virulence and invisibility of SNSs has led to an almost astronomical rise in their deployment. In 1960 strategic nuclear submarines constituted only 1.8 percent of world naval stocks, but by 1976 they had mushroomed to 28.2 percent. The United States presently has forty-one strategic nuclear subs. Britain and France have four each. The Soviet Union has seventy-two, but this superiority in numbers is balanced by the greater firepower of U.S. submarines. It is estimated that the Soviets have about 800 warheads installed on submarines, while the United States has some 5,000 independently targetable nuclear warheads on SNSs. Among both superpowers, these figures are expected to grow. With the addition of the Trident fleet to U.S. forces, the number of submarine warheads is likely to double during the 1980s. Although Soviet ships are not as advanced, the USSR is believed to be escalating its submarine production and adding MIRVs.

The Game of Hide and Seek

The number of strategic nuclear submarines in the world does not entirely reflect the impact of these weapons on naval operations and on the sea. Their development has spawned elaborate, expensive, and enormous new systems designed to track and to destroy them. This technology is known by another set of military initials, ASW—antisubmarine warfare. It is not a new idea. During World War I British hydrophones (underwater listening devices) and aircraft were used to locate German U-boats. Today, however, detection is more complex. Planes and helicopters bristling with the latest electronic equipment now fly regular patrols in search of enemy submarines. Well over a hundred "hunter-killer" submarines (subs without ballistic missile armaments) are now being adapted to the role of stalking other subs with acoustic detection devices, long-range homing nuclear torpedoes, and cruise missiles. New types of weapons for surface ships, including nuclear depth charges, are being developed. The United States has sunk a series of ultra-sensitive detection devices along the perimeter of its Atlantic coastline. The Soviet ASW program is believed to be less sophisticated than that of the United States, relying mainly on naval helicopters and long-range, land-based aircraft capable of finding and sinking strategic submarines.

NATO efforts at ASW are assisted by the geography of the Soviet Union, which has relatively few ocean ports. The USSR operates four separate fleets, but two of these are based in the Baltic and the Black seas, rendering them almost completely blocked in, and the other two must return to ports that are relatively easy to monitor with new detection equipment.

The Unintended Victim

While the nuclear squadrons and their chasers accumulate above and below the sea surface, at least two possibilities grow. One is the risk of a nuclear war erupting. The other is a potential for severe, perhaps catastrophic damage to the marine environment.

Launched in 1954, the USS *Nautilus* was the first U.S. nuclear-powered submarine. It is shown here on an early cruise through New York Harbor. (*U. S. Navy/DOE*)

Nuclear-powered submarines and surface ships routinely release a certain amount of radioactivity into the sea; the quantity is probably insignificant, at least when compared to the potential contamination that could result from an accidental or intentional sinking. The long-lived isotopes produced in a reactor build up while a submarine is in continuous operation. Arthur H. Westing, an ecologist who has conducted research for SIPRI, has calculated that if a nuclear submarine were to sink after about fifty days of continuous operation, it could contaminate the sea with long-lived radioactivity equivalent to what a twenty-kiloton atomic bomb would release (the Hiroshima bomb was thirteen kilotons). This calculation, of course, does not account for the possibility that nuclear warheads aboard the vessel could be detonated or that, in the case of an intentional sinking, nuclear-armed torpedoes or missiles might have been the enemy's offensive weapon.

There are today about 260 large nuclear submarines in operation (about 240 of them U.S. or Soviet) as well as seven nuclear-powered surface ships (all U.S.). As this fleet expands, the possibilities for accidents multiply. Already at least six nuclear-powered submarines have been lost. Two U.S. nuclear subs have sunk in the Atlantic (the *Thresher* in 1963 and the *Scorpion* in 1968), and it is believed the Soviets lost as many as four between 1968 and 1971, two in the Atlantic, one in the Mediterranean, and one in the Pacific.

The effects of wartime nuclear contamination in the sea could be formidable. Long-lived radioactive products would be distributed by ocean currents throughout the sea, compounding the obvious catastrophes of initial death and destruction. Several of these radioactive products are taken up by marine organisms and distributed through the food web, especially strontium-90, which follows the same course in organisms as calcium, and cesium-137, which acts like potassium. Plutonium is also taken up by many marine organisms, some of which concentrate it to levels from a thousand to as much as ten thousand times higher than its initial concentration in seawater.

Nuclear ships sinking, or nuclear weapons being used as torpedoes and as depth charges, could diminish life in the sea, disrupt delicate balances, contaminate ocean fisheries, perhaps even warp the nature of undersea life indefinitely.

T.C. and M.R.

MORE EFFECTS OF WAR ON THE UNDERSEA WORLD

- Undersea explosions, whether from depth charges, torpedoes, conventional or nuclear bombs, or sea mines, take a serious toll on marine animals, especially ray-finned bony fish (which comprise about 95 percent of the fish in the sea). The air bladders of these fish, which give them buoyancy, are easily ruptured by underwater explosions. In addition, some of the materials used in explosives are poisonous. One important explosive, cyclonite, is a nerve poison sometimes sold as rat killer.
- During World War II, 152 U.S. oil tankers were sunk as a means of impairing the Allied war effort, and there may have been another 450 tankers sunk belonging to other nations. With the enormous increases in tanker size since the 1940s, and with the emplacement of vulnerable offshore oil platforms around the world, oil contamination of the sea could be significant in a major war.
- As a result of massive herbicide spraying of mangrove forests along the coast of South Vietnam during the Vietnam War, coastal habitats were devastated. (See also "Vietnam: The Green War," page 554.) Scientists surveying offshore areas found that the loss of these marine nurseries and breeding grounds had caused a severe decline in the populations of fish, planktonic organisms, and shellfish. Recovery, they estimated, could take more than a hundred years.
- The testing of nuclear weapons since the 1940s has been associated directly with the sea. More than 1,000 nuclear bombs have been detonated; of these, 373 were exploded in the atmosphere (about 80 percent of the long-lived components of these blasts probably reached the sea), 35 were exploded along the sea surface, and 6 were detonated undersea. (The remainder were exploded underground.)
- Ironically, despite the sobering potential for marine destruction that is associated with the world's military forces, there are also at least two benefits. A substantial proportion of the ocean research under way around the world is supported by navies and carried out by naval scientists (often, unfortunately, as part of the strategic submarine programs), and . . .
- During times of war, some detrimental ocean activities cease. After World War II, for exam-

ple, fish catches along the Atlantic coast of Europe were as much as three times greater than before the war. The lack of access to fisheries had allowed stocks in these intensely exploited areas to build up. This benefit can be negated, however, by the dumping into the sea of obsolete weapons once war is over, a practice that endangers fisheries and creates problems for fishermen (see "Wastes in the Sea," page 409).

M.R.

SOURCE: Most of the above information was extracted from "Military Impact on the Sea," by Arthur H. Westing, in *Ocean Yearbook I,* the University of Chicago Press, 1978.

HOT SPOTS: THE NEXT WARS?

Cry "Havoc!" and let slip the dogs of war.

WILLIAM SHAKESPEARE
Julius Caesar

When going to war, nations have traditionally rationalized their aggressive actions, unfurling banners of religion, politics, philosophy, and national defense to inspire the masses. However, the underlying reason for war is often the struggle for environmental resources. Since the end of World War II there have been about 130 wars. All have in common nation-states grabbing limited resources by force. Unless we learn to husband our resources and to share them more equitably than we do now, the opportunities for conflict stand to increase in the future as resources become ever more precious. One or more of the following hot spots may soon occupy too prominent a place on the world stage.

SPANISH SAHARA Located on the northwest coast of Africa, the Spanish Sahara is an arid land thinly populated by a mixture of Arabs and Berbers along with a seasonal influx of pastoral nomads. Some of the world's richest deposits of phosphates can be found spread over the surface of this otherwise inhospitable land. Phosphates have various industrial uses, but their greatest importance is their use in fertilizers. By the year 2000, modern agriculture may demand 30 to 40 million tons of phosphates each year to enrich soils and sustain high yields. The raw material is consistently in short supply on the world market, and recent years have seen prices skyrocket.

The Spanish were ousted from their former colony in 1957 but, with the aid of European allies, regained power in 1958. The Polisario guerrilla movement gained momentum in the early 1970s in reaction to the presence of the colonial power. They received backing from neighboring Algeria and, more recently, from Libya and the Soviet Union. As the Spanish attempted to divest themselves of their colonial headache, Morocco and Mauritania each laid claim to parts of the territory, but Mauritania withdrew because internal problems made any attempt to press its dubious claim ineffective. Still, a number of contenders remain to scramble for the valuable phosphate resources. Armed conflict has spilled over the border into Morocco while attempts at a referendum to determine the area's future have repeatedly failed.

Morocco has recently attempted to obtain quantities of U.S. arms to continue the conflict, but the United States has resisted being drawn into the conflict. Forces in the U.S. government are sharply split on whether to supply the Moroccans, who have backed American Middle East policy but seem to have no legitimate claim in the Spanish Sahara. An early 1980 sale of helicopters and airplanes was approved under a long-standing agreement that Morocco may use weapons purchased from the United States only for national defense. However, it is difficult to guarantee that this agreement will be honored. The prospect of future sales is the only leverage the United States can bring to bear to ensure that Morocco will abide by the agreement.

RUSSIAN-CHINESE BORDER A long-standing animosity exists between the Soviet Union and China over a border zone that is cold, sparsely populated, and generally unproductive. The last ten years have seen cycles of escalated tensions and troop buildups. The quarrel seems senseless until one looks at a map of mineral resources. Stretching along the southern part of the border are some of the richest uranium and thorium deposits in the world. These deposits, all confined to a relatively narrow strip of terrain a few hundred miles wide, represent an invaluable resource, and both nations, wishing to avoid a nuclear war, would find the land there ideally suited to a large-scale military confrontation. Both sides have extremely large conventional forces waiting in the wings and have shown no inclination to seek world opinion or outside mediation in the dispute.

CHILE AND ARGENTINA In a flareup of a hundred-year-old dispute, Chile and Argentina have been building up their armed forces in expectation of war. The tension is centered on three small islands, Picton, Nueva, and Lennox, which lie off the tip of Tierra del Fuego. The islands themselves contain nothing but a few sheep, cattle herds, and herders. But the nation that owns the islands controls the sea for 200 miles (322 kilometers) to the south and east, along with oil and mineral rights and rich antarctic fisheries.

The islands were first awarded to Chile by international mediation in 1896, and more recently a British-led international commission again awarded them to Chile. But Argentina continues to balk at these decisions, and war has at times seemed imminent as troops were deployed along the 2,600-mile-long (4,184-kilometer) border and each nation spent hundreds of millions of dollars to strengthen its armed forces.

In 1978 Pope John Paul II took the unusual step of dispatching a special envoy to mediate the dispute. Both countries are overwhelmingly Roman Catholic, and in January 1979 Chile and Argentina signed an agreement not to use force and asked the pope to determine ownership of the islands. Whether any decision by the Vatican would carry more strength than previous resolutions remained to be seen in early 1981. Meanwhile Chile had begun pumping 36,000 barrels of petroleum per day from platforms in the Strait of Magellan in the hope of producing 45 percent of its oil from the Strait by 1983.

SOUTH AFRICA From a moral point of view, it is easy to condemn the white government of South Africa for resisting peaceful transition to majority rule. Faced with the active hostility of its black African neighbors as well as increasing sanctions against it from the rest of the world community, South Africa appears to be powerfully armed and prepared to resist as long as the present government wishes. Events in this nation might seem remote to the citizens of industrialized northern nations, but in fact there is a direct linkage. A violent changeover in government could have worldwide economic repercussions. Political and social problems aside, South Africa is a land blessed with an abundance of natural resources that play a significant role in the world economy. It is one of the world's leading suppliers of gold, uranium, platinum, chrome, gem diamonds, and several other precious or industrially valuable minerals. Because of its apartheid policy, the South African government has trained few blacks in the technical and administrative skills necessary to run these industries. In the event of a violent change of government, these industries could fall into disarray, not only severely depleting South African revenue but disrupting world commerce and particularly affecting the world money standard if the flow of gold were interrupted.

THE MIDDLE EAST The dangers inherent in the Middle East situation are all too clear. It is and will probably remain the hottest spot in the world. Oil, a not merely valuable but absolutely necessary resource, is at stake. The matter is further complicated by a complex web of bitter racial and religious hatreds. Economic blackmail, terrorist activity, and military force are all standard means of problem-solving. Obviously, unless cool heads prevail and an attempt is made to find realistic solutions to the many economic and social issues that have destabilized the area, the Middle East situation may erupt with devastating force, especially if nuclear weapons are introduced to the area.

T.C.

WAR LORE

- The pyramid of Ramses II, commemorating his victory over the Hittites at the Battle of Kadesh, is a hoax. Recent archaeological evidence indicates that the Egyptians lost that one.
- During World War II it cost the United States an average of $225,000 to kill each enemy soldier.
- Lieutenant Hiroo Onada of the Japanese Army spent thirty years in hiding in the Philippines and discovered only in 1974 that World War II had ended. Curiously enough, he had originally been sent there to gather intelligence.
- The first recorded use of a "secret weapon" was in the campaign of the Hyksos against Upper Egypt in the second millennium B.C. The new technology was the horse-drawn chariot.
- During the Vietnam War, American forces made eleven assaults in ten days on a plot of Vietnamese land known as Hamburger Hill. It

was held for eight days and then abandoned because of its lack of strategic significance.

- Herodotus tells us that about 6,400 Persians and 192 Athenians fell at the rather one-sided Battle of Marathon in 491 B.C. By World War I technology had advanced to the extent that there were 600,000 Allied casualties at the Battle of the Somme alone.
- The artist Frederic Remington was sent to Cuba by the New York *Journal American* shortly before the outbreak of the Spanish-American War. Finding nothing newsworthy there, according to a popular story, he asked publisher William Randolph Hearst, known as the father of yellow journalism, whether he might return. Hearst telegraphed this reply: PLEASE REMAIN. YOU FURNISH PICTURES. I WILL FURNISH WAR.
- The story of an elderly resident of Belfast who assaulted a British soldier with her umbrella recently points out how long people can hold a nationalist grudge. She passionately informed him that his army was a disgrace for its conduct at the Massacre of Drogheda, an action that took place in 1647.
- During the Spanish conquest of Mexico, Cortez and his Conquistadors used the fat of Indians killed in battle as a salve for their wounds.
- American journalist Ambrose Bierce once defined a battle as "a method of untying with the teeth a political knot that would not yield to the tongue."
- On July 30, 1972, fifty-three caribou were found dead of unknown causes near an army base in Alaska that housed a laboratory for chemical and biological warfare experimentation. The post commander speculated that they'd all been struck by lightning.
- Contemporary accounts of victories by the Ch'in Dynasty of China (A.D. 265–420) generally conclude with the adage ". . . and a hundred thousand heads were lopped off."
- During World War II the commanding general of all Allied forces, Dwight Eisenhower, transmitted the following note of caution to his troops: "Do not needlessly endanger your lives until I give you the signal."

T.C.

"WE INFILTRATE THEIR ECONOMY. WE HELP THEM BUILD STEEL MILLS, REFINERIES, AND POWER PLANTS. THEY POLLUTE THEMSELVES INTO SUBMISSION."

(© *1980 by Sidney Harris*)

TRYING TO DEFUSE THE BOMBS: ARMS CONTROL AGREEMENTS

Since World War II international wariness of a potentially devastating new global holocaust has moved the major world powers to enter into a series of agreements concerning the use of certain potent weapons. While these agreements have not led to the destruction of a single weapon, not even a pistol, as Paul Ehrlich points out in *Ecoscience,* they do represent steps in the right direction.

The main arms control agreements concluded to date have had the following goals:

- prevention of the militarization, or military "nuclearization," of certain areas or environments;
- freezing or limiting the numbers and characteristics of nuclear delivery vehicles;
- restricting weapons tests;
- preventing the spread of specified weapons among nations;
- prohibiting the production, as well as eliminating stocks, of certain types of weapons;
- prohibiting certain methods of warfare;

- observing the rules of conduct in warfare;
- notifying one another of certain military activities.

Here is a list of the major arms control agreements either completed or under negotiation:

The Antarctic Treaty has declared that Antarctica shall be used exclusively for peaceful purposes. It is an important demilitarization measure, but the question of territorial sovereignty in Antarctica has not been definitely resolved.

Signed: 1 December 1959; Entered into force: 23 June 1961.

Number of parties as of 31 December 1979: 20.

The Partial Test Ban Treaty has banned nuclear weapon tests in the atmosphere, in outer space, and under water. It has helped to curb radioactive pollution caused by nuclear explosions. But testing underground has continued, making it possible for the nuclear weapon parties to the treaty to develop new generations of nuclear warheads.

Signed: 5 August 1963; Entered into force: 10 October 1963.

Number of parties as of 31 December 1979: 111.

The Outer Space Treaty has prohibited the placing of nuclear or other weapons of mass destruction in orbit around the earth and also established that celestial bodies are to be used exclusively for peaceful purposes. But outer space has remained open for the passage of ballistic missiles carrying nuclear weapons, and the deployment in outer space of weapons not capable of mass destruction is subject to no restrictions.

Signed: 27 January 1967; Entered into force: 10 October 1967.

Number of parties as of 31 December 1979: 80.

The Treaty of Tlatelolco has prohibited nuclear weapons in Latin America. It has thus established the first internationally recognized nuclear weapon-free zone in a populated region of the world. Also non-Latin American states are obliged to keep their territories which lie within the zone free of nuclear weapons (Protocol I), while the nuclear powers undertake not to use or threaten to use nuclear weapons against the zonal states (Protocol II). But Argentina and Brazil, the only countries in the area with any nuclear potential and aspirations, are still not bound by the provisions of the treaty.

Signed: 14 February 1967; Entered into force: 22 April 1968.

Number of parties as of 31 December 1979: 22.

The Non-Proliferation Treaty has prohibited the transfer of nuclear weapons by nuclear weapon states and the acquisition of such weapons by non-nuclear weapon states. The latter are subject to international safeguards to prevent diversion of nuclear energy from peaceful uses to nuclear explosive devices. The treaty grew out of the realization that the possession of nuclear weapons by many countries would increase the threat to world security. But it is being eroded because of the inconsistent policies of the nuclear-material suppliers, as well as the non-fulfillment of the disarmament obligations undertaken by the nuclear weapon powers.

Signed: 1 July 1968; Entered into force: 5 March 1970.

Number of parties as of 31 December 1979: 111.

The Sea-Bed Treaty has prohibited the emplacement of nuclear weapons on the sea-bed beyond a twelve-mile zone. But the treaty presents no obstacle to a nuclear arms race in the whole of the marine environment.

Signed: 11 February 1971; Entered into force: 18 May 1972.

Number of parties as of 31 December 1979: 68.

The Biological Weapons Convention has prohibited biological means of warfare. But chemical weapons, which are more controllable and predictable than biological weapons, and which have been used on a large scale in war, are still the subject of disarmament negotiations.

Signed: 10 April 1972; Entered into force: 26 March 1975.

Number of parties as of 31 December 1979: 87.

The SALT I ABM Treaty has imposed limitations on a specific type of U.S. and Soviet antiballistic missile defense. But the development of new ABMs continues.

Signed: 26 May 1972; Entered into force: 3 October 1972.

The SALT I Interim Agreement has frozen the aggregate number of U.S. and Soviet ballistic missile launchers. But it has not restricted the qualitative improvement of nuclear weapons, and the number of nuclear charges carried by each missile has been allowed to increase.

Signed: 26 May 1972; Entered into force: 3 October 1972.

The Threshold Test Ban Treaty has limited the size of U.S. and Soviet nuclear weapon test explosions to 150 kilotons. But this threshold is so high that the parties can continue their nuclear weapon development programs without experiencing onerous restraints.

Signed: 3 July 1974; **Not** in force by 31 December 1979.

The Document on Confidence-Building Measures contained in the Final Act of the Conference on Security and Co-operation in Europe provides for notification of major military maneuvers in Europe, but it does not restrict these activities. Military movements, other than maneuvers, do not have to be notified.

Signed: 1 August 1975.

The Peaceful Nuclear Explosions Treaty regulates the U.S. and Soviet explosions carried out outside the nuclear weapon test sites and therefore presumed to be for peaceful purposes. But, apart from being a complement to the 1974 Threshold Test Ban Treaty, it has no arms control value.

Signed: 28 May 1976; **Not** in force by 31 December 1979.

The Environmental Modification Convention (ENMOD) has prohibited the hostile use of techniques which could produce substantial environmental modifications. But manipulation of the environment with certain techniques which can be useful in tactical military operations has escaped proscription.

Signed: 18 May 1977; Entered into force: 5 October 1978.

Number of parties as of 31 December 1979: 27.

The SALT II Treaty sets equal ceilings on the aggregate number of U.S. and Soviet strategic nuclear missile launchers and bombers and imposes sub-limits on certain categories of strategic nuclear arms. It also sets limits on the number of warheads per missile. However, the treaty will have only a minor impact on the relevant military programs on both sides; it will not slow, much less halt or reverse, the qualitative nuclear arms race. Current weapons may, with minor restrictions, be modernized, and some completely new

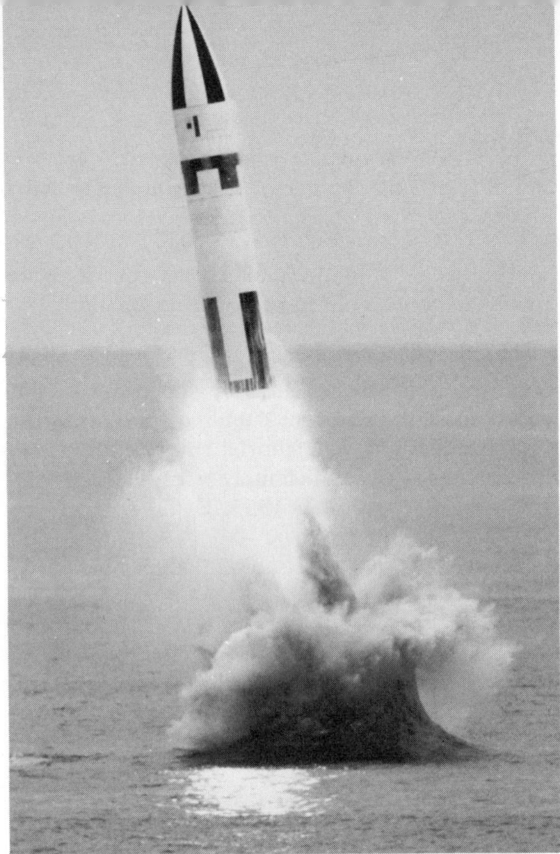

Polaris missile fired from a submarine. (*U. S. Navy*)

weapons may be introduced. The treaty is accompanied by a protocol dealing with mobile intercontinental ballistic missiles and cruise missiles and a joint statement of principles and general guidelines for subsequent, SALT III, negotiations. The sides have also exchanged data on the number of strategic arms they possess in certain categories limited by the treaty. In addition, the USSR made a statement outlining Soviet intentions concerning the production rate and other characteristics of the Soviet Backfire (Tu-22M) bomber.

Signed: 18 June 1979; Not in force by December 1980.

Current negotiations

The present arms control negotiations deal mainly with the following subjects:

- Ban on all nuclear weapon tests,
- Prohibition of the possession of chemical weapons,
- Prohibition of radiological weapons,
- Security assurances for non-nuclear weapon countries,
- Mutual force reductions in Central Europe.

SOURCE: *Armaments or Disarmament? SIPRI Brochure 1980,* Stockholm International Peace Research Institute. Reprinted by permission.

SPACE WARS

It's a hundred billion dollars
Every year at your expense,
For the Pentagon to gadget up
Our national defense.

But it's comforting to know that
In the up and coming war,
We'll be dying far more safely
Than we ever died before.

E. Y. HARBURG
"Fail Safe"*

Space Spying

During 1978, 112 military satellites were launched, about one every three days (91 were Soviet, 19 U.S., 1 Chinese, and 1 was launched by the United States for NATO). This brought the total of military satellites launched to 1,601, about 75 percent of all the satellites launched.

Soviet satellites are more numerous because they are generally relatively short-lived. But the Soviet Union is beginning to launch longer-lived ones. The life of some of its photo-reconnaissance satellites, for example, has increased from 13 to about 30 days.

Over 50 percent of military satellites are for reconnaissance, and about 25 percent for military communications. The rest are for geodesy, navigation, early warning of attack, and meteorology.

In May 1978, the Soviet Union launched a hunter-killer satellite as part of a program to test the feasibility of intercepting hostile satellites in space. This goal is dangerous, since it would threaten the other side's reconnaissance and early-warning satellites. The United States and the Soviet Union are, however, currently discussing ways to control antisatellite activities.

SOURCE: Excerpted from an article by Frank Barnaby, director of the Stockholm International Peace Research Institute, in *The Bulletin of the Atomic Scientist*.

Space Zapping

Soviet and American scientists are busily and discreetly investigating the possibilities of lasers and charged-particle beams as space-borne defense systems against nuclear attack. If they succeed in developing weapons based on these principles, claim defense strategists, nuclear warfare could become a thing of the past. There is a less optimistic outlook however: mastery of these techniques might actually hasten this worst of all possible disasters.

Lasers generate energy through chemical reactions and focus a powerful beam of light on a target. The perfection of focusing power over distances of thousands of miles would make the laser a very efficient weapon of war. The second technology, particle-beam weapons, would project a stream of charged subatomic particles capable of disrupting any matter in their path. Placed in orbit around the earth, weapons based on these principles could disrupt an enemy's war effort by destroying its surveillance and communication satellites. More importantly, if coupled with the most sophisticated sensory equipment, they could destroy ICBMs while these missiles were being boosted into orbit and before they had locked onto their target sites.

The SALT II treaty forbids development of these weapons but does not ban basic research into the problem. Such weapons could theoretically be completely designed on paper and stay within the letter, if not the spirit, of the SALT agreement, up until the time when an actual prototype weapon is built. Why restrict such a defensive weapon? The first country to develop such a device would obviously tip the balance of power in its favor, perhaps far enough to make it trigger-happy in a nuclear war. Unless both sides perfected and deployed laser or particle-beam weapons simultaneously, the country that could prevent a nuclear attack by its enemy through a space defense system would essentially have won the war.

Governments and research scientists are being very circumspect about the extent of their involvement in laser and particle-beam research. Yet there is little doubt that they are pursuing these aims. The U. S. Defense Department's 1981 budget authorized $108.6 million for development and improvement of "space defense systems." They will become a reality in the near future. The question is whether they will finally free us from the fear of nuclear destruction or whether cynical governments will employ them strategically to force their own ideologies and economic systems on the world. T.C.

*From *At This Point in Rhyme*.

THE NUCLEAR CLUB

Some analysts, urging us to lean back and enjoy the inevitable, take the imaginative view that a world of sixty nuclear-weapons states will somehow be more stable or more just than a world of six.

AMORY LOVINS
Soft Energy Paths

The United States started the nuclear club in the 1940s, planning to keep it quite exclusive. But by the end of the 1970s, the Soviet Union, Great Britain, France, India, and China were all members, and forty more countries may join by the end of the century.

The spread of the "peaceful atom" and of reactor-grade plutonium has meant that all over the world there are people with the technological know-how to build an atomic weapon. Much of this knowledge is in the public domain. In the United States several students and at least one magazine writer have described the makings of a "homemade bomb." It now seems as likely that nuclear catastrophe could originate with a small group of terrorists or with a developing country as with the two military superpowers.

Since the 1950s, world military spending has doubled, to more than $400 billion a year. The global arms trade is now worth $20 billion a year, and most of the weapons sold go to developing countries, especially to Iraq, Israel, South Korea, Saudi Arabia, India, and Libya.

The race for more and better armaments inevitably leads to nuclear weapons. Although no nuclear power deliberately distributes information or material for nuclear weapons, the spread of nuclear reactors and plutonium often has exactly the same effect. All power reactors produce strategic materials that can be used in simple but destructive bombs.

Richard Betts of the Brookings Institution has invented three categories to identify countries he thinks most likely to develop or obtain nuclear weapons: "pygmies," small countries with large, powerful, unfriendly neighbors (e.g., Pakistan); "paranoids," opponent nations that are roughly equal and in constant fear of disequilibrium (e.g., North and South Korea); and "pariahs," states largely shunned by the world community and threatened by opponents dedicated to their destruction (e.g., South Africa).

Some apprehensive governments in these and other categories may indeed come to believe that they should attack their weaker enemies soon, while time is still on their side. The white South African government, for example, has access to one of the world's largest uranium reserves, and is developing a plant that could process uranium for nuclear weapons. South Africa currently has both the technology and the motivation to develop nuclear weapons.

Israel is another state frequently mentioned as a possible nuclear agressor. The Arab nations outnumber Israel and for the most part are determined enemies of the Zionist state. Muammar al-Qaddafi of Libya has repeatedly vowed to destroy Israel and offered to buy nuclear weapons, presumably for that purpose, from anyone who will sell them. Libya, Egypt, and Algeria all have nuclear reactors and the potential for developing a bomb. At present, Israel's technological and military capability is greater, but in time Arab nations will achieve parity. The Israelis, like the South Africans, have more incentive than most countries to push atomic development. As early as 1968 the U. S. Central Intelligence Agency (CIA) secretly reported to President Lyndon Johnson that Israel already had nuclear weapons. By 1976 the CIA claimed that Israel had built at least ten nuclear weapons.

The CIA also predicted as early as 1974 that Taiwan could have the bomb within five years. Taiwan has placed great emphasis on atomic energy and has a very high level of technology, much higher at present than that of the People's Republic of China. With their official abandonment by most other countries and by the United Nations, the Taiwanese may be tempted to use their present advantage in an emergency.

In the world today, it is a mark of national prestige to belong to the nuclear club. Each new member of the club accelerates nuclear proliferation, since no unarmed nation feels comfortable when its neighbor has the bomb. The continuation of this trend would mean nuclear power in every world capital. Since about 130 wars have been fought since World War II, almost all in the developing world, that is a terrifying prospect.

J.S.

CANDIDATES FOR THE NUCLEAR CLUB

This table considers technical capability only, rather than the political motivation to develop nuclear weapons.

A. Countries that appear technically capable of detonating a nuclear device in the short term (within one to three years of a decision to do so):

Argentina	Italy
Canada	Japan
Republic of China (Taiwan)	South Africa
West Germany	Spain
Israel	Sweden

B. Countries that appear technically capable of detonating a nuclear device in the intermediate term (within four to six years of a decision to do so):

Belgium	The Netherlands
Brazil	Norway
Czechoslovakia	Pakistan
East Germany	Poland
South Korea	Switzerland

C. Countries that appear technically capable of detonating a nuclear device in the longer term (within seven to ten years of a decision to do so):

Austria	Mexico
Denmark	Portugal
Egypt	Romania
Finland	Turkey
Iran	Yugoslavia

SOURCE: U. S. Energy Research and Development Administration, April 1977.

PRIORITY NUCLEAR TARGETS IN THE UNITED STATES

The Russians have a joke about their ubiquitous civil-defense drills: "When you hear the alarm, put on a sheet and crawl slowly to the cemetery."

"Why slowly?"

"So no one panics."

In a nuclear attack, depending on its size, nearly the entire population of the United States could be killed. However, the United States Defense Civil Preparedness Agency (DCPA) suggests that only 134 million people (population figures from 1970 census) are living in the four hundred areas it pinpoints as particularly "high-risk." Considering the difficulties in moving urban populations rapidly should an emergency arise, most of these people could not escape during a major attack. The Stanford Research Institute concluded that the evacuation of New York City alone would take at least a week, and is essentially impractical in case of nuclear attack.

The DCPA has designated fifty-three "Priority One" targets, sites that could respond to a nuclear attack. These are top military targets—with civilians nearby, of course—such as the intercontinental ballistic missile bases (in Tucson, Little Rock, and McConnell Air Force Base in Kansas), Strategic Air Command bomber bases, and strategic-missile submarine bases.

"Priority Two" targets include other high-value military installations or places of military value, and strategic cities. "Priority Three" includes industries and facilities basic to the U.S. economy, and cities of at least fifty thousand people.

Some of the safest places, according to the DCPA, are likely to be:

Oregon (except the northwest part of the state)
Idaho (except the Boise area and along the border near Spokane)
Wyoming (except the southeast)
Texas (the Panhandle and Brownsville areas)
Missouri (southern)
North Carolina (coast)
Vermont and New Hampshire (northern)

J.S.

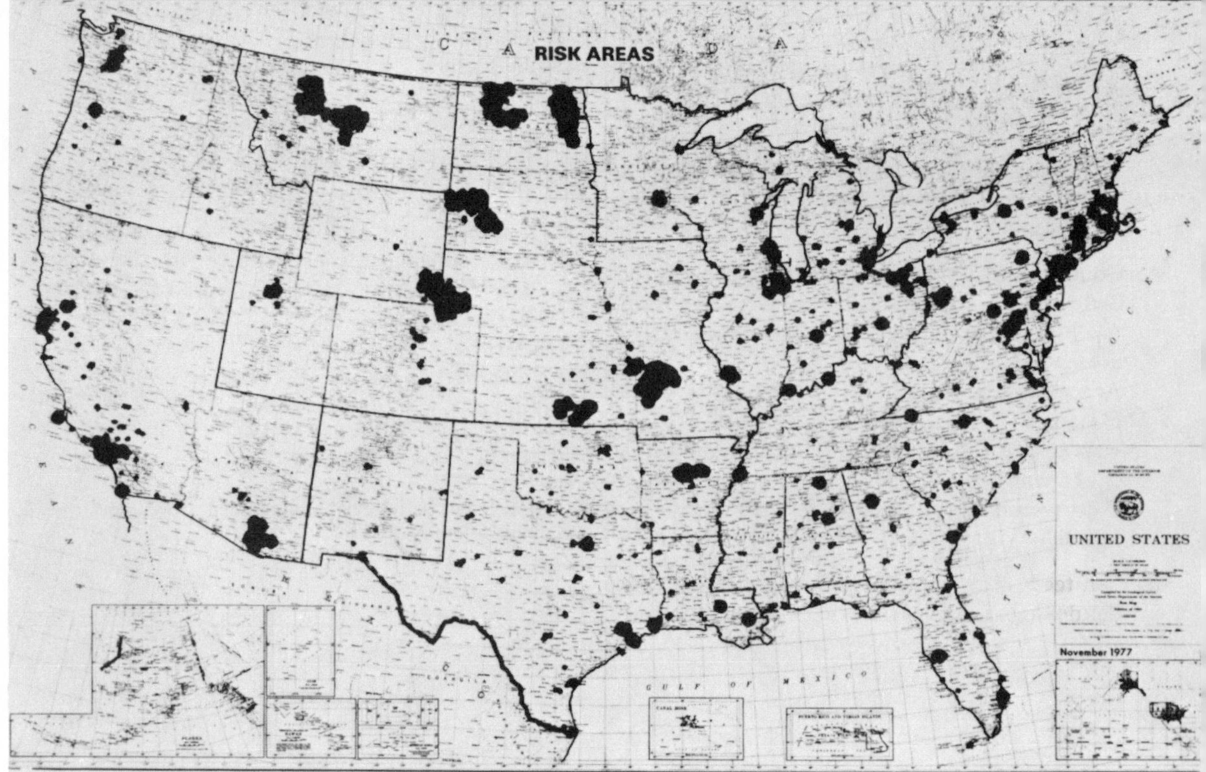

Priority nuclear targets in the forty-eight contiguous U.S. states. (*Defense Civil Preparedness Agency/Federal Emergency Management Agency*)

WHAT HAPPENS TO THE U. S. PRESIDENT IN A NUCLEAR ATTACK?

If U.S. missile-detection equipment in Colorado Springs suddenly transmitted a warning that an attack by nuclear weapons was imminent, what would happen to the President?

A detailed plan of action exists, but because it has never been rehearsed, no one knows how well it will work in an emergency.

The President is always accompanied by someone who carries the nuclear-war codes. He is always within reach of a special helicopter. If word of an attack should come—reaching him in minutes, if all went as planned—the President would leave immediately in the helicopter for the nearest airport.

Three huge Boeing 747s have been specially outfitted to serve the President in a wartime emergency. One of them is always on a runway, waiting. These planes, which cost $117 million apiece, serve as airborne command posts. They are each equipped to fly for four days straight (with in-flight refueling) while the President directs the course of the war.

Suppose that the warning has come. A nuclear attack has been launched against the United States. The President is whisked from the White House to his jet. The jet takes off—just in time, too, because Washington, D.C., is high on the list of likely targets. To avoid detection and radiation, the President's airborne command post will fly in a random pattern across the country, 7 or 8 miles (11 or 12 kilometers) up. The pilot will stay a good distance from areas known to have been hit by nuclear warheads.

An elaborate communications system keeps the president informed of the extent of the disasters on the ground. Since the atmosphere the plane flies through may at times be highly radioactive, one component of the communications system is designed to work best in high radioactivity. Another component will transmit military orders,

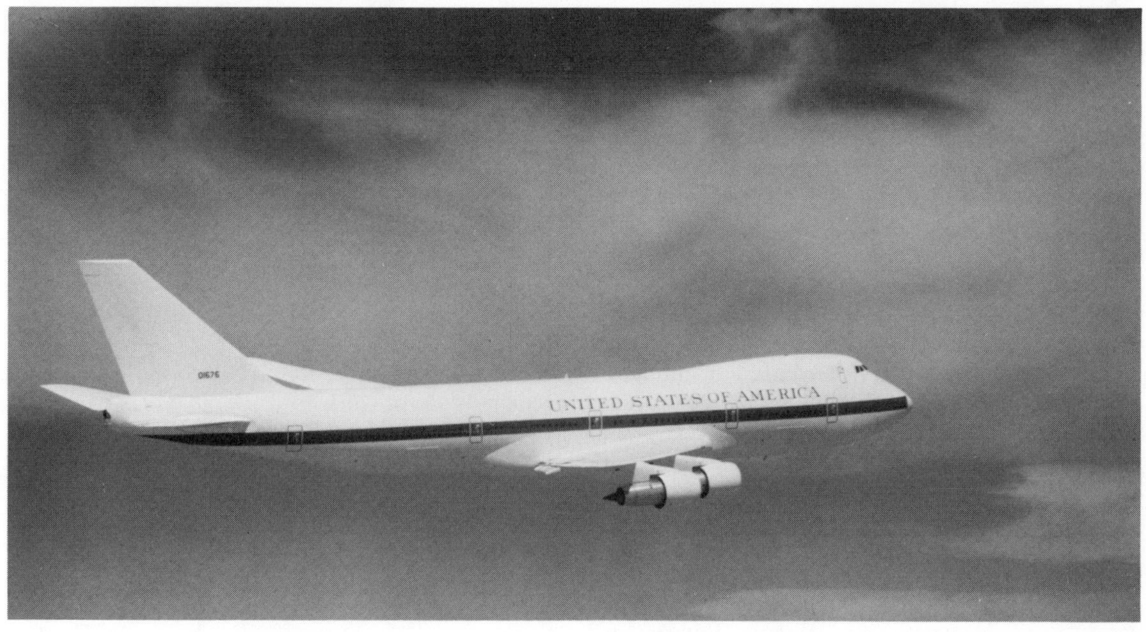

Airborne command post Boeing 747: presidential office of last resort. (*U. S. Air Force*)

even if the rest of the system fails. A slow-speed teletype backs up the radio in case radio transmissions become jammed by radiation. A 5-mile-long (8-kilometer) antenna streams behind the plane to collect transmissions from other military command planes from Europe to the Pacific.

The President's plane is not the only one. Since 1961 the Strategic Air Command has kept one or another of its own command posts in the air at all times. There are also planes, sent up at the first sign of an attack, whose sole purpose is to relay messages between command posts that can't communicate with each other. Navy planes would be sending messages to submerged missile-carrying submarines.

Inside his plane, the President, with his immediate family and a few close advisers, shares the battle-staff work area with fifteen military experts. There is a rest area, a briefing room, and a conference room. The President has his own work area. The military advisers are absolutely necessary, because there is no computer on the plane. There appears to be some fear that conditions during a hot war could damage or distort computers, making them less than totally reliable. Instead, the advisers have carried aboard an enormous load of computerized battle plans, which they have to sort out manually.

At this point, the President can't do much to help the ravaged country. But he still has the power to take revenge—and any order to retaliate must come directly from him. He can launch missiles by remote control, even if all the missile crews are dead in their underground blockhouses. The President can, if he wants, take over and give orders personally to individual bomber pilots and

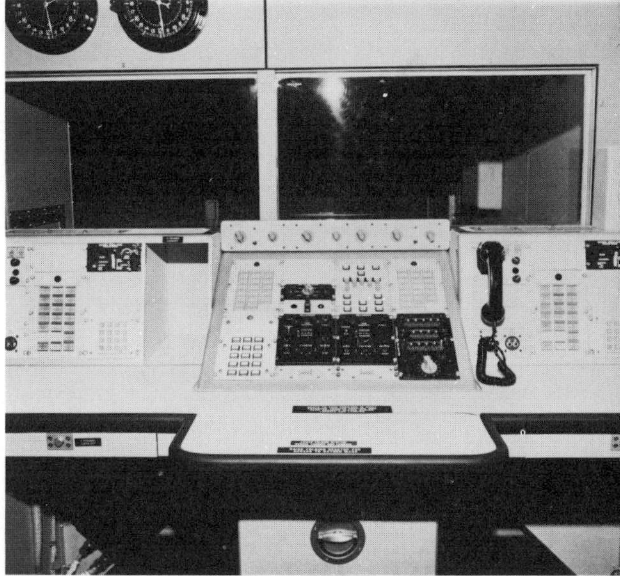

Communications area of the President's airborne command post. (*Department of Defense/U. S. Air Force*)

submarine skippers who command nuclear weapons. He can order attacks overseas individually or in "packages"—all-out war on the enemy's home front, strategic bombing of certain areas, or an attack on a particular category of target.

Checks and balances are built into the system. Except for the President's own orders, every step must be duplicated before the next step can occur. It is not clear how much presidential authority has been delegated, in case of an emergency, to people who are not next in line of succession to the presidency. The commander of the North American Air Defense Command (NORAD) has some authority, and evidently the Secretary of Defense has also been delegated some presidential power, but the details are sealed away and kept in the hands of a few key military commanders.

If the President himself should die or become incapacitated, the authority structure of the government would be in jeopardy. Others in the line of succession could be away from the capital or dead. The Vice President might not be available. Officially, there are special government evacuation plans for people in line for the presidency, for important congressmen, and for the Supreme Court. There are shelters sunk deep in the Appalachians at Mt. Weather, Virginia, for government personnel, with power plants, wells, water-storage tanks, sewer systems, laundries, kitchens, and dormitories, and special bunkers for VIPs in hidden locations. But no one really knows if there will be time for people to get to them in the mass panic of a nuclear alert.

Should the elaborate, airborne command scheme fail or prove to be inappropriate, the President does have another option. According to a White House spokesman, there is a shelter somewhere below the White House for the presidential family. Whether it is equpped for national command, and whether or not it could house staff and advisers are carefully guarded pieces of information.

J.S.

NUCLEAR EXPLOSIONS, 1945 TO 1978 (Known and Presumed)

I. 16 July 1945–5 August 1963 (the signing of the Partial Test Ban Treaty)

USA	USSR	UK	France	Total
293	164	23	8	488

II. 5 August 1963–31 December 1979
a – atmospheric
u – underground

USA		USSR		UK		France		China		India		Total
a	u	a	u	a	u	a	u	a	u	a	u	
0	360	0	262	0	7	41	37	21	4	0	1	733

TOTALS:
16 July 1945–31 December 1976

USA	USSR	UK	France	China	India	Total
653	426	30	86	25	1	1,221

SOURCE: Stockholm International Peace Research Institute, "World Armaments & Disarmament," SIPRI Yearbook, 1980.

TRUST US WITH YOUR LIFE: NUCLEAR WEAPONS ACCIDENTS

Most of the speculation and strategy surrounding the effects of a nuclear explosion assume that the weapon will be dropped on purpose. But over the past three decades bombs have been dropped accidentally, and the following list suggests that the possibilities are real. It also suggests, rather convincingly, that the people entrusted with the care of the bomb are capable of the same kind of everyday slapstick mistakes that plague us all. Somehow, though, there is a difference.

Here are some instances when bomb guardians somehow fumbled:

- As a result of mid-air collisions or malfunctions of the equipment that locks a bomb in place within a bomber, several nuclear weapons have been dropped accidentally, though none has exploded. In a two-month period in the winter of 1958, part of one atomic bomb was dropped accidentally in Georgia, another was jettisoned off the Georgia coast, and another was inadvertently jettisoned over South Carolina.

- On June 8, 1960, a fire and two explosions at McGuire Air Force Base in New Jersey severely damaged a "Bomare" surface-to-air missile that carried a nuclear warhead.
- In June of 1962 the United States attempted to carry out two high-altitude nuclear test explosions, each with a warhead yield of about one megaton. Both weapons were to be carried by Thor ICBMs, to altitudes of 30 miles (48 kilometers), in one case, and 200 miles (322 kilometers) in the other. Neither was successful and both weapons were destroyed in flight. Presumably, the weapons or the fallout from them contaminated parts of the Pacific.
- Air crashes have resulted in the accidental dropping of several atomic weapons termed by the military "unarmed," meaning that in each case the triggering device was not in place, so the bomb could not have exploded. Such crashes have occurred since 1952 in Louisiana, North Carolina, California, Kentucky, Georgia, and Indiana. A bomb accidentally dropped in New Mexico in 1956 was never categorized by government sources as either unarmed or armed.
- In January 1966, a U.S. B-52 and a KC-135 refueling tanker collided in mid-air near Palomares, Spain. The B-52 was carrying four unarmed hydrogen bombs, which separated from the aircraft during the collision. One landed intact in a dry riverbed. The second and third bombs released radioactive material in a populated area. The fourth was retrieved three months later in the ocean after an intensive search. The U.S. government has not released information about the yield of the four bombs, but press reports claimed that all four were in the range of 1.5 megatons, and one report claimed that the bomb found in the ocean was a 20-megaton weapon.
- Two years after the Palomares crash, a second B-52 was lost near Thule, Greenland. According to government spokespersons, all four thermonuclear bombs were lost.
- On September 19, 1980, a Titan 2 missile exploded in an underground silo near Damascus, Arkansas. The force of the explosion blew away the silo's 750-ton door and violently ejected the missile's nine-megaton nuclear warhead. Although one U.S. airman was killed and twenty-one others were injured by the explosion, the 6,000-pound (2,722-kilogram) warhead did not detonate. Fears that the weapon was leaking radioactive material caused the evacuation of 1,400 area residents. The bomb was disarmed and removed to Little Rock Air Force Base three days later. The incident was triggered when a workman dropped a heavy socket wrench that fell seventy odd feet and punctured one of the missile's fuel tanks. Leaking fuel exploded eight hours later.

SOURCE: Adapted from a list of nuclear weapons accidents compiled from government sources by the Stockholm International Peace Research Institute (SIPRI).

BIG ARMIES, LITTLE ARMIES

TEN NATIONS IN WHICH PERCENTAGE OF GNP SPENT ON THE MILITARY EXCEEDS 10 PERCENT

	Percentage of GNP (1977)
1. Oman	42.7
2. Israel	28.4
3. United Arab Emirates	22.3
4. North Korea	19.6
5. Saudi Arabia	15.7
6. Syria	14.2
7. Soviet Union	13.3
8. Iran	10.5
9. Iraq	10.5
10. Egypt	10.4

TEN NATIONS IN WHICH PERCENTAGE OF GNP SPENT ON THE MILITARY IS BELOW 1 PERCENT

	Percentage of GNP (1977)
1. Japan	0.9
2. Jamaica	0.9
3. Liberia	0.9
4. Guatemala	0.8
5. Mexico	0.7
6. Panama	0.7
7. Sri Lanka	0.7
8. Swaziland	0.7
9. Malta	0.5
10. Iceland	.0

TEN NATIONS WITH LARGEST PERCENTAGE OF TOTAL POPULATION IN ARMED FORCES

	Percent in Armed Forces (1977)
1. Israel	4.51
2. United Arab Emirates	3.20
3. Qatar	3.18
4. North Korea	2.95
5. Syria	2.86
6. Cyprus	2.81 (1976)
7. Republic of China (Taiwan)	2.73
8. Mongolia	2.40
9. Kuwait	.885
10. Portugal	.604

TEN NATIONS WITH SMALLEST PERCENTAGE OF TOTAL POPULATION IN ARMED FORCES

	Percent in Armed Forces (1977)
1. Fiji	0.183
2. Benin	0.096 (1976)
3. Upper Volta	0.094
4. Rwanda	0.093
5. Kenya	0.091
6. Iceland	0.090
7. Barbados	0.074
8. Niger	0.071
9. Jamaica	0.046
10. Lesotho	0.046

SOURCE: *World Military Expenditures and Arms Transfers 1968–1977* (Washington, D.C.: U. S. Arms Control and Disarmament Agency, 1979).

VIETNAM: THE GREEN WAR

During the Second Indochina War in Vietnam, the United States used an unprecedented barrage of environmental weapons against the Vietcong. Unwilling to wage a slow land-war campaign, the United States attempted to win the guerrilla war through high technology. Basically, U.S. strategy was to interfere with Vietcong operations by cutting the guerrillas off from food, shelter, and supplies.

This strategy of "area denial" specifically focused on forests and croplands. About 90 percent of all U.S. munitions during the war were used against rural areas, mostly "nonspecific" targets where enemy activity was suspected. Since almost two thirds of Vietnam was forested, the U.S. military concentrated on destroying the forest itself when they believed guerrillas were using it for cover. Long-term area denial also included killing crops so guerrillas would have no food, removing the rural population to U.S.-controlled areas, and bombing roads and bridges that led to guerrilla strongholds.

In *Ecological Consequences of the Second Indochina War,* the botanist Arthur Westing describes the three main methods the United States used to render rural areas useless: high-explosive munitions (bombs and shells); chemical antiplant agents (herbicides); and mechanized land-clearing (with bulldozers).

From 1965 to 1973, the United States used 14 million tons of munitions in Vietnam, mostly in South Vietnam. (During two months at Khe Sanh in 1968, more explosives were dropped on the Vietcong than all the nonnuclear explosives dropped on the Japanese throughout World War II.) Almost every bomb and shell dropped on Vietnam left a crater. Of course, every war in which heavy ammunition is used hurts the environment: the craters left by shelling at the battle of Verdun in World War I are still, almost seventy years later, only sparsely grown over. But in Vietnam the extent of the problem is vast. Almost a half million acres (200,000 hectares) of land in Indochina is taken up by craters. About 32 billion square feet (3 billion square meters) of soil was displaced by the explosives, and permanent craters of one size or another number about 250 million. Besides disrupting agriculture until they are filled in, craters in many areas of high rainfall have become small ponds, breeding mosquitoes that carry malaria.

The problems caused by the craters are intensified because some areas of Vietnam were hit far more frequently than others. Most of the attacks were on South Vietnam, and an area called Military Region III, near Saigon, was particularly hard hit. The B-52 attacks alone devastated 11,200,000 acres (4,500,000 hectares) of South Vietnamese land. The damage to the land was so great that the countryside after bomber and artillery attacks was often compared to a moonscape. The jungle was blasted loose, trees tossed into the air, undergrowth torn up by the bombs. The land itself was pulverized. In War Zone D, a large region near Saigon, it was estimated that more than four fifths of the trees were either killed or struck by shrapnel. Another estimate is that during the war more than 45 million trees were killed by high explosives in Indochina.

Since gunpowder was brought to the West from the Orient, every war has involved the latest technology in explosives. But the use of herbicides as a weapon was without precedent. Since technically herbicides are classified as chemical warfare and outlawed by the Geneva Protocol of 1925, an international outcry arose when it became evident that the United States was spraying Vietnamese vegetation. U.S. authorities promptly began a propaganda campaign (which has been continued since the war) to the effect that the herbicides were not poisonous to humans and therefore did not come under the heading of chemical warfare. Reports of deaths of Vietnamese peasants after the spraying of crops near their villages were ignored, even though some of these deaths were independently documented by neutral European medical observers.

The main herbicides used against the Vietcong were Agent Orange, Agent Blue, and Agent White (named for their color-coded containers). Although in civilian use these herbicides would have had more specific applications, the U.S. military sprayed them in such high concentrations that their poisonous effects were less selective. By far the most common was Agent Orange (see "Blowing the Whistle on Agent Orange," page 556), which kills plants by changing their metabolism. Agent Orange was predominantly used to kill forests, although it was also sprayed on crops. About 11,714,000 gallons (44,338,000 liters) of Agent Orange were used in Vietnam between 1962 and 1970, killing millions of trees and destroying vegetation on thousands of hectares of land.

The mangroves that line many of Vietnam's waterways were worst affected by the herbicides. Whereas in most kinds of forest it took more than four sprayings to kill all the trees, the mangroves were so susceptible to the herbicides that one spraying usually destroyed them. Much of the Vietnamese forest has recovered to a large degree from the herbicides in the years since the war, but the mangroves have disappeared wherever they were sprayed. Since mangrove forests are a vital breeding and nursery area for marine animals, the offshore impact of the spraying program was devastating.

Ironically, the herbicides, with their great destructive powers, did not even accomplish their goals. The Vietcong continued to hide in the forest, and the forces of the South Vietnamese government complained that spraying the areas around the main roads only made it easier for the Vietcong to ambush them, as they had no cover. And while spraying croplands took food away from the Vietnamese peasantry, it hardly hurt the Vietcong, who were mostly young, well-armed men. When food is short, as every investigation has shown, soldiers are the last to suffer from hunger. "Starving the enemy" inevitably means starving children, old people, and pregnant and nursing women.

The last and probably most effective method of "area denial" practiced by the United States was land clearing with Rome plows, huge bulldozer-type machines that scraped every tree and shrub off the land in question. Once a Rome plow had cleared the forest, it was impossible for anyone, peasant or guerrilla, to live there any longer. Toward the end of the war, the U.S. military began to prefer land clearing to herbicides as more effective, cheaper, and less internationally controversial. By 1973, 2 percent of South Vietnam had been cleared in this way, mostly near Saigon.

The total impact of the U.S military tactics on the land of South Vietnam has been devastating. Much of the area has not yet recovered and perhaps will not in this century. Unexploded bombs remain a hazard to farmers and to children playing. About 5 percent of the forest in South Vietnam was completely destroyed, and 54 percent was severely damaged. Herbicides not only killed mangroves on more than 370,650 acres (150,000 hectares), destroyed forests, and ruined cropland, but they remain in Vietnam's soil and water. Agent Orange has been blamed for teratogenic (monster-causing) effects in fetuses and for damaging the health of the exposed general population. It is not only the Vietnamese who complain of the long-term effects of the herbicides. Thousands of United States army veterans who were ordered into sprayed areas were also affected. In environmental warfare, there is no sure separation of victims.

J.S.

Wavemakers:
BLOWING THE WHISTLE ON AGENT ORANGE

War heroes traditionally were made during battles. The Vietnam War, in many ways an untraditional war, produced some heroes of a different nature. A few of those heroes are people who, years after the battle ended, stood up for the rights of soldiers who were unknowingly exposed to dangerous chemicals while they were dodging bullets.

Maude de Victor has never been to Vietnam, but as a counselor at the Chicago regional office of the United States Veterans Administration (VA), she became involved with many of its victims.

In 1978 she began gathering data on Agent Orange (a mixture of 2,4-D and 2,4,5-T that is often itself contaminated with another extremely toxic chemical commonly called dioxin), which was used extensively in Vietnam as a defoliant.

Agent Orange was sprayed from August 1965 through February 1971. The more De Victor researched the herbicide, the more alarmed she became. A startling correlation began to emerge, she says, between the use of Agent Orange and the illnesses of some Vietnam veterans, including cancer, lung and liver problems, chloracne, sterility, and psychological problems.

"It all happened because I am basically nosey. There was no flash of thunder. I picked up the phone one day and a sobbing woman just struck at my heart, like a Cinderella. She told me her husband was dying. He had served in Vietnam, and he was convinced that his illness was because of chemicals sprayed there. When they were in Los Angeles he told her the smog there looked like Vietnam after they sprayed. I just told her I'd try to help," De Victor says of the phone call she received from Mrs. Charles Owens in June 1977. Mr. Owens died of cancer two days after the call.

Four months later, De Victor found out that Mrs. Owens was not receiving the widow's benefits she was entitled to; the VA denied her claim that her husband's cancer and death were service-related. De Victor decided to handle the appeal. She had routinely been handling appeals for veterans and their families since she became a claims counselor at the VA in July 1974. De Victor says: "I was like an in-house nonlicensed attorney. It was my duty to advise vets and to help them beat the VA."

At first the Owens appeal seemed easy. "I called Washington and asked about a chemical used by the Air Force that looked like smog. I figured if this guy was in the Air Force for twenty-three years, whatever he came in contact with they would know about. They called me back and told me that the chemical was dioxin," recalls De Victor.

At that point her supervisor told her to do research on the chemical. She made 364 phone calls and gathered a boxful of supporting documents. As part of her research, De Victor polled every Vietnam vet she met about dioxin symptoms, even those who came in to file for a change of address. By March 1978, in two months, she had logged twenty-seven other Vietnam vets in the Chicago area who suffered from dioxin poisoning symptoms: chloracne (which can be caused only by chemical exposure), reduced libido, cancer, sterility, and the parenting of children with birth defects. She also found thirty other possible victims.

During this time, De Victor kept working to get Mrs. Owens's benefits. The rating book, used to determine payment to vets and their widows, had no reference to biological warfare, but De Victor fought "tooth and nail" and won. Washington rendered the benefits for Mrs. Owens because there was "doubt" as to the cause of her husband's cancer.

The implications of that victory were great, since other veterans alleging illness from the chemical might use the Owens case as a precedent. Since there were 2 million people, including military personnel, press, and civilian support, in Vietnam, the cost of settling those claims could be astronomical.

At this time the medical evidence about the harmful effects of dioxin was mounting. A Swedish study showed a ninefold increase in birth defects among children born of mothers who had been exposed to dioxin. Dr. Ton That Tung of Vietnam released a study showing an increased incidence of liver cancer and birth defects among exposed Vietnamese. A report on the effects of a dioxin cloud was compiled following an explosion of a factory near Seveso, Italy. Studies of the people in the area revealed a high incidence of chloracne, spontaneous abortions, loss of sexual drive, and liver damage. (See page 338).

The VA wanted the investigation into Agent Orange slowed down. De Victor continued. On a television news special produced by the CBS affiliate in Chicago on March 23, 1978, she told the public what she had learned about Agent Orange and its effects. From this local show, the Associated Press and other news agencies picked up the story for national distribution. Also, De Victor says, "People in Chicago spoke with relatives and said, 'Hey, that's why cousin Ralph isn't right.' " The response was enormous. When De Victor got to work the next day, she was flooded with phone calls from vets, government officials, the press, and environmentalists.

Officials at the VA, however, did not share the enthusiasm for her new notoriety. When she got to work one morning in April, her desk had been relocated; she was placed between two supervisors, and her phone rang less frequently. Calls about Agent Orange were being put through to other counselors. De Victor explains that "the girl at the front desk was told not to give me Orange calls. They didn't want veterans to have access to me. Other counselors may have meant well, but I was on this from the start." Undeterred, De Victor continued to work on Agent Orange. She gave information to the press whenever they asked, and spoke with vets and their families whenever they called, even late at night from hospital rooms.

When the VA couldn't stop the calls, she said, an official "called me in and said they didn't care if I was talking to the Oval Office. If I was on the phone for over fifteen minutes, they would deduct the time from my vacation pay." Her bosses were aware that she had no vacation time left after a four-month medical absence for cancer surgery.

Then VA officials rewrote De Victor's job description. She was assigned to operate a computer that emitted a low level of radiation. Though she had letters from doctors pointing out that proximity to the machine might aggravate her own cancer, the VA tried to fire her for her refusal to operate it. They accused her of "insubordination."

De Victor and VA officials came to what she terms a "Missouri compromise." They lowered her rank, which put her on a lower pay and retirement-benefit scale, and moved her upstairs to the loan department "as a symbol to the others," she says. Despite her B.A. degree in sociology, training as a prison counselor, and experience at the VA, her supervisors thought she was more qualified to authorize loans than to counsel vets.

"And they harassed me at work. They accused me of stealing documents. So, I called Max Cleland (the national Administrator of the Veterans Administration) and told him what was happening. I said I set two parameters for myself. I wasn't going to end up like the guy in Watergate who found the door open and hasn't worked a day since, because I am no martyr and no scapegoat. And I have a son, so I would not allow disgrace to my family name."

De Victor has remained at the VA partly because she needs the money to support her son; she is divorced. She is also committed to continue helping veterans. Thanks to her work there, untold numbers of hospitalized vets can understand the cause of their suffering. The gauntlet has also been taken up by organizations such as Agent Orange Victims International and Citizen Soldier, formed to assist the victims of the herbicide. These groups have joined other veterans' groups in a class-action suit against the Dow Chemical Company, the world's largest manufacturer of Agent Orange. They also plan to propose a resolution to the United Nations to ban Agent Orange.

Although her new job classification has restricted her budget and her working conditions are unpleasant, the woman whom Frank McCarthy, president of Agent Orange Victims International, calls "the mother of Agent Orange in America" has no regrets over what she did and no plans to quit the VA. De Victor says, "I did the work as part of my job. And I had to go public because I was paid by taxpayers' money. I had a responsibility. I had information involving four and a half million people. And I had seen these people, talked with guys that were dying and didn't know why. It's like one vet said: 'I was killed in Vietnam and I didn't know it.' "

S.D.

THE DOG BENEATH THE SKIN

Small arms have been the instruments of most of the wars since World War II, from Lebanon to Biafra, from Yemen to Katanga, and they have been the greatest cause of loss of life. The trade in rifles, machine guns, or mortars reveals the cold heart of a business in which diplomacy and wars are translated into orders, balance sheets, and profits.

Near the center of Manchester, in the middle of Victorian industrial Britain, is an unpretentious brick warehouse, alongside the ship canal and adjoining a fine Gothic church. Its only distinguishing marks are a heavy stainless-steel door and big letters across the top of the building saying INTERARMS. This is the biggest private arsenal in Europe. It is the British headquarters of the most successful of all the small-arms dealers, Sam Cummings, the chairman and principal shareholder in the Interarms Company. Six stories of the warehouse contain no fewer than 300,000 weapons, stacked as densely as wine bottles in a cellar, waiting to be shipped to whatever government or company may want them.

Upstairs is a row of cheerful offices, with a small exhibition of machine guns on the floor by the entrance. Cummings himself comes over once a month from Monte Carlo to take stock of his empire here. He is a relaxed, chubby-faced man, who looks much younger than his forty-nine years: his style is genial and innocent, with a beatific smile, like that of a boy who has been a gun freak and has suddenly found all his wishes come true—which is, more or less, what he is. He talks quietly and courteously and dresses in a clerical black suit. He does not smoke or drink, and he travels as little as possible, economy class.

Cummings talks about his trade with such loving attention to detail and technicalities that he succeeds, like all good arms dealers, in making it sound as boring as machine tools or camshafts. But he also offers himself as the philosopher of the business, like a Greek chorus that has sadly discovered the secrets of human motivation, and he likes to provide aphorisms to make his points. "The arms business," Cummings told me, as he had told senators and congressmen, "is founded on human folly. That is why its depths will never be plumbed and why it will go on forever."

"All weapons," he says, "are defensive, and all spare parts are nonlethal."

For his company Cummings has adopted the classical-sounding slogan "The Arms of Man." And for his motto, he takes that of his own American private school, the Episcopal Academy in Philadelphia: *Esse Quam Videri*—"To be rather than to seem." The motto sums up well enough the recurring attitude of arms dealers. Others may talk about peace and disarmament, but they, the arms merchants, know that human nature is based on aggression and violence and that that will never change. They have seen the dog beneath the skin.

Gun dealer Sam Cummings. (*Susan Heller Anderson/N.Y.T. Pictures*)

Cummings' own adventurous career provides a kind of pocket history of small-arms trade over the last quarter century. He was brought up in Philadelphia, the son of a once prosperous father who had lost his fortune in the great crash. He was fascinated by guns from the time he acquired an old German Maxim gun at the age of five. When he was drafted into the army after World

War II, he became a weapons instructor and made money on the side by selling old German helmets.

Cummings established his first private arsenal in Alexandria, Virginia, outside Washington, D.C., and found customers for his wares among the regimes of Latin America. After the right-wing revolution in Guatemala in 1954, he supplied the new government of Carlos Castillo Armas with American Garand rifles, which he had bought in Britain. In the Dominican Republic, he became friendly with the dictator, Trujillo, and supplied him first with machine guns, then (in one of his most remarkable deals) with Vampire jet fighters, which he bought in Sweden. In Costa Rica in 1955, when exiles tried to invade their homeland, both sides were armed with machine guns bought from Cummings. In Cuba he was believed to have supplied the Castro forces before the revolution, and also some of the anti-Castro invaders for the Bay of Pigs fiasco.

In the meantime, Cummings was able to replenish his growing private arsenal with huge quantities of surplus from Europe and the Middle East. After the Suez war of 1956, for instance, he bought two thousand Russian small arms captured by the Israelis from the Egyptians. In the late 1950s he bought nearly a million Lee-Enfield rifles from the British government, which kept him in stocks for some years: most of them were sold to Americans as sports guns, others to Kenya and Pakistan.

By the end of the 1950s Cummings was established as the world's leading private arms dealer. He soon had the advantage of sheer size, and he is now reckoned to have 90 percent of the small-arms trade. He has built up huge stocks in the United States and Britain—now augmented by another arsenal in Singapore—from which he can quickly supply customers throughout the world, and he has agents and offices in every major capital. He has a personal fortune and runs his companies from his large flat in Monte Carlo, where he now lives with his Swiss wife.

Cummings' total world sales, he insists, are still tiny compared to those of the big aerospace companies: he has never exceeded an annual turnover of $100 million, which is less than the cost of a squadron of fighters. But, as an individual entrepreneur, he remains a kind of weather-cock of the arms trade. His thirty years in the business have given him a unique experience, and as he walks round his Manchester arsenal he can portray the history of the world in terms of the much-traveled weapons, which provide a melancholy museum of warfare.

Here, he points out, is a stack of American Garand rifles that were first exported to Germany in the 1950s for the first German rearmament. When Germany got more advanced weapons in the late 1960s, Garands were transported to Jordan, and when Jordan got more advanced weapons they were bought by Cummings and shipped to Manchester. From there many of them were shipped to the Philippines, to help in the fight against Muslim rebels financed by Libya. A few remain in Manchester waiting for customers.

Here, just next door to the Garands, are some British Enfield rifles that were captured by the Japanese in Indochina, then taken over by the Americans and used in Vietnam before they were bought by Cummings.

Here are some Springfield rifles first supplied to the French in Indochina in the 1950s. Here are Mausers brought over to Taiwan by General Chiang Kai-shek when he left the mainland in 1949. Over there are German ME 42 guns left by Hitler's troops in Greece, Swedish guns made under license in Egypt and captured by the Israelis, British Sten guns dropped by parachute during World War II for the French Maquis, American Brownings from the Dominican Republic, Belgian Mausers from Venezuela, American M-16s from the Chilean army.

Cummings likes to present his arsenals as an index of the world's folly; their stocks go up and down according to the state of war or peace. "Of course I'd like to see this building filled up with arms," he said. "World peace would give me the chance to build up my inventory. But people are always ordering more arms, which runs down the stocks again. I don't see any prospect of that changing. There are huge new markets opening up; soon there will be rearming of China, which everyone in the business knows will happen. That will bring the story round to full circle since Chiang Kai-shek left twenty-five years ago. And then Russia. And then Europe again. There's never any end to it."

THE BUSINESS OF WAR: THE TOP TWENTY U. S. DEFENSE CONTRACTORS

The following companies were the leading suppliers to the U. S. Defense Department in fiscal year 1978. The listing includes the dollar volume of their contract awards for that year and some major items they were contracted to supply (it should not be interpreted as a complete listing of the services they have provided).

Some of this information was made available in a Department of Defense publication, *100 Companies Receiving the Largest Dollar Volume of Military Prime Contract Awards;* some was provided by the companies themselves.

1. GENERAL DYNAMICS CORP. $4,153,547,000
F-16 jet aircraft, cruise missiles, the Trident submarine, "Stinger" portable anti-aircraft systems, "Viper" anti-tank rocket.
2. MCDONNELL-DOUGLAS CORP. $2,863,294,000
F-15 "Eagle" Air Force interceptor, F-18 "Hornet" Navy fighter-bomber, "Harpoon" anti-ship missile, C-9 multipurpose jet aircraft (employed for cargo and hospital duty).
3. UNITED TECHNOLOGIES CORP. $2,399,789,000
Pratt and Whitney jet engines, Sikorsky transport helicopters, airborne radar systems, solid fuel rocket boosters.
4. LOCKHEED AIRCRAFT CORP. $2,226,431,000
TR-1 tactical reconnaisance version of the U-2 aircraft, P-3C "Orion" and the S3A "Viking" anti-submarine warfare aircraft, Trident and Poseidon missiles, C-5 and C-130 transport aircraft, RPV remote-control reconnaisance aircraft.
5. GENERAL ELECTRIC CO. $1,786,448,000
Jet engines, medical systems, telemetry equipment.
6. LITTON INDUSTRIES, INC. $1,557,134,000
LHA (Landing Helicopter Assault) ship, second-largest ship in the U. S. Navy, Spruance-class destroyers, "Hawk" ground-to-air missile defense systems, various electronic equipment.
7. BOEING CO. $1,524,454,000
AWACS (Airborne Warning Air Command System), Minuteman and MX ICBMs, B-52 Avionics Improvement Program.
8. HUGHES AIRCRAFT CO. $1,488,558,000
Laser weapon systems, land-mine warfare systems, satellite navigation components, radar equipment.
9. RAYTHEON COMPANY $1,306,783,000
"Sidewinder" heat-seeking missile, "Patriot" air defense system, "Dragon" anti-tank missile, advanced radar and sonar guidance equipment.
10. GRUMMAN CORP. $1,180,032,000
F-14 "Tomcat" fighter, "Prowler" electronic countermeasure aircraft (employed in jamming enemy radar), A6E "Intruder" Navy attack aircraft.
11. ROCKWELL INTERNATIONAL CORP. $890,204,000
On-board navigation computers and ordnance for the Army and Air Force.
12. TEXTRON INC. $867,517,000
Manufacturer of Bell helicopters.
13. CHRYSLER CORP. $742,489,000
Army M60-A3 and XM1 tanks, expanded mobility truck (in development).
14. SPERRY RAND CORP. $612,020,000
"Univac" computer systems, fluid power hydraulic systems, guidance and control mechanisms for both missiles and aircraft.
15. NORTHROP CORP. $586,049,000
F-5 fighter aircraft, guidance system for MX missiles, F-18 fighter aircraft, electronic countermeasure equipment.
16. RCA CORP. $585,214,000
Naval air and missile systems, communications satellites, electro-optical devices.
17. HONEYWELL INC. $544,703,000
Sonar systems, MK 46 torpedo, combat fire control, various guidance systems for ships.
18. WESTINGHOUSE ELECTRIC CORP. $539,187,000
Radar systems for AWACS and F-16 fighter planes, launch canisters for Trident submarines and MX missiles, three-dimensional land-based radar, electronic components for defense meteorological satellites.
19. MARTIN MARIETTA CORP. $539,181,000
"Pershing" tactical missile, "Copperhead" laser-guided artillery shell, "Titan 3" missile, "Missile X."
20. FAIRCHILD INDUSTRIES INC. $507,866,000
Air Force A-10 "Thunderbolt" attack jet (an infantry-support aircraft), cryptographic computer systems, 30mm. Gatling gun, subcontractor for various aircraft modifications.

B.L.

SWORDS INTO PLOWSHARES

It is a city that indulges itself in a glittery, show-biz tradition and boasts of its flamboyant disregard for convention. Undeterred by smog, mudslides, or earthquakes, the city is, to many of its advocates, secure in its Manifest Destiny. Los Angeles may be all of this, but it is also host to the realities of this military planet. It is the arms capital of the world.

Most of the big names are there—Lockheed, Rockwell, McDonnell-Douglas, and Northrop—in sprawling complexes and towering buildings. Twenty-three percent of the total U.S. defense contracts were awarded in California in 1976, far more than any other state in the union, and Los Angeles is the heartland of its military industry. These contracts mean jobs to California. The state's two single largest employers are defense companies; in the aerospace industry alone, whose backbone is military production, about a half million people are employed.

While many celebrate the social freedom and independence that has been called characteristically Californian, the economic future of much of the state's work force is decided beyond its boundaries, by those who control the American defense dollar. Californians are not alone in this uncertainty. New York, Missouri, Texas, Massachusetts, and Connecticut all received significant shares of the $116 billion that the Defense Department spent in 1978 on military research and development.

The ebb and flow of jobs—and the fates of the communities that depend on them—has long been recognized as one serious result of defense spending; in 1961 the Department of Defense created the Office of Economic Adjustment to help smooth out some of the difficulties. But some economists and peace activists believe that military spending has a more subtle, but equally disruptive, effect. They argue that massive defense expenditures create a severe undertow, which is the major force pulling the American economy down into inflation, slow growth, and unemployment.

"When the United States, for the first time in history, entered into a protracted era of high military spending following the close of World War II," says Lloyd Dumas of Columbia University, "it sowed the seeds of the economic decline whose bitter harvest it is just beginning to reap." According to Dumas, defense spending fuels inflation because it puts large amounts of money in the hands of the military producers whose products are removed from the general economy. He also says that since military producers don't worry much about cost overruns, they tend to hike prices of goods and labor.

Despite this, table-pounding Congress members often demand increased defense expenditures in their districts. The reason is simple: jobs. But here too critics cite statistics revealing that military expenditures are among the lowest in creating jobs. According to the U. S. Department of Labor, with $1 billion to spend you can create 87,000 jobs by giving the money to state and local governments, 92,000 jobs if it goes to transportation, 139,000 jobs in the health-care industry, and 187,000 jobs in education. That same $1 billion, however, if spent by the Department of Defense, would create only 76,000 jobs. The U. S. Bureau of Labor Statistics reports that a $10-billion shift in government spending from military to other areas in the federal budget would result in a net increase of 245,000 jobs.

Besides the job costs, critics argue that civilian technological development also suffers from high military spending. With as many as one third of all engineers and scientists in the United States involved in defense-related work, the technological development is skewed toward militarily useful products. As one critic put it: "A Grumman F-14 'Tomcat' can fire at six targets simultaneously and track twenty-four others, but aging mass-transit cars screech by on outmoded tracks, and the steel industry slowly strangles on antiquated equipment, unable to compete in world markets."

What, then, is the solution? A growing number of military-spending critics think there is one—and they call it economic conversion. Quite simply, economic conversion is the transfer of workers, capital, and technology from military to civilian economy. ("Peace" conversion advocates take economic conversion several steps further; they see it as an opportunity for increased worker control and substantive economic restructuring.)

Some proponents see conversion as an economic necessity. In the words of Seymour Melman, a Columbia University economist and early architect of the conversion concept, the options are "Go civilian or go broke." The idea also has some strong backers from at least two major unions with a substantial membership in military-related work, the United Auto Workers and the International Association of Machinists. It is also being pushed by a variety of peace organizations.

According to Lloyd Dumas, effective economic conversion would require major planning and preparation, in which the federal government would play a major role. The process, he says, involves three basic steps. First, civilian alternatives must be identified for defense industries; then planning for the conversion would take place, perhaps through the establishment of local commissions composed of workers as well as community and industry representatives; and, finally, social-service support would be provided to the workers during the transition, which would include any necessary retraining.

Such advance planning is already taking place in several communities. California's Mid-Peninsula Conversion Project, for example, has completed a detailed study outlining how Santa Clara's workers could be employed in the solar industry. In Connecticut, where 28 percent of the work force is involved in military-related activity, the state government is developing economic tools to promote conversion, including loans, mortgage guarantees, training programs, and tax breaks. Federal legislation has also been introduced to require the preparation of alternative-use plans for military facilities prior to plant closings.

There are clearly plenty of nonmilitary activities to which the defense industry could convert, including mass transit, housing, refuse disposal and recycling, and environmental protection. But some major obstacles remain. One problem is that many defense industries, accustomed to a single customer (the Defense Department) who is relatively unconcerned about cost, manufacture nonmilitary products that are too complicated and too expensive for the commercial market. This could perhaps be overcome, but the basic problem is that military-industrial firm managements are, by and large, uninterested in planning for economic conversion.

Another nagging question, raised by defense-spending advocates, is whether such a reordering of priorities would endanger national security. A recent study by the Boston Study Group, a research organization, suggests that U.S. defense needs could be fully met with only 60 percent of the resources now spent by the Department of Defense—at a saving of $50 billion.

B.P.B.

THE MOST IMPORTANT ARMS EXPORTERS

	U.S. Dollars (1977)
United States	$6.9 Billion
USSR	$5.2 Billion
France	$1.3 Billion
United Kingdom	$825 Million
West Germany	$800 Million
Czechoslovakia	$470 Million
Italy	$320 Million
Poland	$310 Million
China	$ 90 Million
Canada	$ 70 Million

SOURCE: *World Military Expenditures and Arms Transfers 1968–1977* (U. S. Arms Control and Disarmament Agency, 1977)

Wavemakers:

ONE MAN'S WAR ON WAR

When Matthew Meselson went to work at the Arms Control and Disarmament Agency (ACDA) for the summer of 1963, he was neither a crusader nor an expert on military matters. A biologist from Harvard University, he knew little about disarmament and the ways of world politics, but as an ACDA observer he was able to scrutinize the defense establishment. It was a crucial time in the nuclear test ban negotiations, and almost everyone's attention and energy were focused in that direction, leaving Meselson on his own to dig into whatever interested him. Being a biologist, he naturally looked to what he knew best and began to investigate the murky world of biological weaponry. He did not like what he found at all.

Meselson had many conversations with the officers involved in the planning of biological warfare (BW), and he intensively studied the literature of the trade, particularly Army Field Manual 3-10, the bible of biological warfare. He discovered that, the moral question aside, biological weapons are an ineffective and unpredictable method of waging war or deterring it. They have no real function in the field of defense, yet large stocks of

lethally dangerous organisms exist. Armed only with rationality and a single-minded determination to succeed, Meselson set out on the Herculean task of changing the defense establishment's mind.

He began systematically to expose the irrationality of BW policy, both publicly through the media and activist organizations and privately whenever he could get the attention of the policymakers. His demand was simple: the complete and unilateral abandonment of stocks of biological agents in the United States. The main points of his argument were first proposed publicly in 1965 at a meeting of the Pugwash Conference, an international scientists' group concerned with peace activism; military officers, government officials, and scientists soon heard them with monotonous frequency. Meselson knew whom he had to influence in order to change things, and he kept driving home the point that biological weaponry is fundamentally unsuited to a policy of deterrence. First, the possession of biological weapons is in no way a defense against employment of them by a hostile power; existing nuclear stockpiles are more than enough of a deterrent, if "deterrence" really exists. Biological weapons are also particularly dangerous in a suicidally escalating arms race: they are cheap, readily manufactured, and well within the technological reach of most small nations and even individual terrorist groups. Finally, biological weapons are among the most unreliable and uncontrollable weapons systems ever devised. A sudden change in wind or a mutated strain of an organism could create a totally indiscriminate and horrible disaster. Clearly they stem from no known military tradition; they are useful only for destroying innocent noncombatants while conveying no strategic advantage to the user. Couldn't the United States simply stop without waiting for other countries to follow suit? This was the question Matthew Meselson repeatedly asked the American public and their civil and military leaders.

Frequently coincidence is the prime mover in making history. In 1968, Richard Nixon was elected president of the United States and appointed an old colleague of Meselson's as his National Security Adviser. Henry Kissinger had worked right next door to Meselson and had followed his campaign with great interest. There was a mutual respect between the two men, and the scientist from Harvard realized that he finally had a strong lever to apply to the dead weight of government policy. Nixon and Kissinger saw the strength of Meselson's arguments and were also naturally aware of the advantage in world opinion that could be gained by an unprecedented unilateral abandonment of one of the deadliest forms of warfare. In November 1969, President Nixon announced that the United States would destroy its stockpiles of biological weapons and convert its laboratories to open programs of medical research. He then invited the Soviet Union to follow suit.

In diplomacy one is never supposed to negotiate from such a position of weakness, and some American leaders expressed their doubts about the move. But evidently the Soviet Union was convinced of the sincerity of the American position, or elements in their own government had already come to similar conclusions. General Secretary Leonid Brezhnev signed a pact in the summer of 1972, agreeing to dismantle the Soviet biological warfare program. In the space of only nine years, Matthew Meselson had taken a major step toward removing the ever-present threat of death, in at least one form, from all our lives.

Editor's Note: *Unfortunately, the U. S. Department of Defense, as of early 1981, was preparing to reactivate some biological warfare programs.*

T.C.

WHAT TO DO ABOUT WAR

"The central question," Adlai Stevenson once said, "is whether the wonderfully diverse and gifted assemblage of human beings on this earth really knows how to run a civilization." The list that follows is a diverse assemblage of organizations that are trying to help humanity chart a course toward peace. Some attempt to influence policy, others educate, and a few provide direct support to local groups and individuals plotting a similar path.

U. S. Groups:

THE CENTER FOR DEFENSE INFORMATION (CDI), 122 Maryland Avenue NE, Washington, D.C. 20002, (202) 543-0400.
Publication: *Defense Monitor* (newsletter, $10/year).

CDI is a research organization that supports a strong defense but opposes excessive military expenditures. The group makes available reports on defense programs and expenditures.

FEDERATION OF AMERICAN SCIENTISTS (FAS), 307 Massachusetts Avenue NE, Washington, D.C. 20002, (202) 546-3300.
Publication: *FAS Public Interest Report* (monthly newsletter, $20/year).

FAS is a public interest lobbying organization for scientists; it is primarily interested in nuclear power, strategic arms limitation, and arms proliferation.

FRIENDS COMMITTEE ON NATIONAL LEGISLATION (FCNL), 245 Second Street NE, Washington, D.C. 20002, (202) 547-4343.
Publication: *FCNL Washington Newsletter* (monthly except August, $10/year).

FCNL is a Quaker lobbying organization concerned with peace, human rights, and social justice. They have worked with other organizations to reduce military spending and are also involved in the struggle for the rights of Native Americans.

INSTITUTE FOR POLICY STUDIES (IPS), 1901 Q Street NW, Washington, D.C. 20009, (202) 234-9382.
Publication: Conference Newsletter (bimonthly, $5/year).

IPS is a research organization that believes a transformation in our institutions and assumptions is necessary to achieve a democratic and equitable society. They are concerned with the relationship between the multinational corporations and the military.

MILITARY AUDIT PROJECT (MAP), 1028 Connecticut Avenue NW, Washington, D.C. 20036, (202) 337-6065.
Publication: *Military Audit* (quarterly newsletter, free to contributors).

The Military Audit Project was founded in 1975 to "find and expose areas of doubtful or illegal behavior by the Department of Defense and/or its corporate suppliers in the performance of federal contracts."

NATIONAL ACTION/RESEARCH ON THE MILITARY INDUSTRIAL COMPLEX (NARMIC), American Friends Service Committee, 1501 Cherry Street, Philadelphia, PA 19102, (215) 241-7175.

Since it was established in 1969, NARMIC has conducted research into the role of U.S. corporations in weapons production. Along with a series of reports and slide shows, NARMIC has recently produced a set of maps illustrating the location of U.S. nuclear facilities.

PACIFIC NORTHWEST RESEARCH CENTER, P.O. Box 3708, Eugene, OR 97403, (503) 686-5125.
Publication: *Northwest Bulletin* (monthly newsletter, $5/year).

Founded in 1971, the Pacific Northwest Research Center conducts studies of the "economy, industries, corporations, and politics of the Pacific Northwest." The Center also assists community groups and citizen organizations with needed research.

SANE, 318 Massachusetts Avenue NE, Washington, D.C. 20002, (202) 546-4868.
Publication: *SANE World* (monthly newsletter, $15/year).

SANE, which was founded in 1957, is a citizen-education center working for a nuclear test ban treaty. Its program has also grown to include various concerns about the military and civilian uses of nuclear power.

AMERICAN FRIENDS SERVICE COMMITTEE, 1501 Cherry Street, Philadelphia, PA 19102, (215) 241-7000.
Publication: *Quaker Service Bulletin* (three times yearly to contributors).

A Quaker group with a long history of activism for peace both in the United States and throughout the world.

COALITION FOR A NEW FOREIGN AND MILITARY POLICY, 120 Maryland Avenue NE, Washington, D.C. 20002, (202) 546-8400.
Publications: Various "Action Guides."

The Coalition, a merging of two antiwar groups, is concerned with disarmament, human rights, and federal spending priorities.

Other U.S. groups involved in peace efforts include Mobilization for Survival, Council on Economic Priorities (see page 503), and the Union of Concerned Scientists (see page 784).

International Groups:

INSTITUTE FOR WORLD ORDER, 777 United Nations Plaza, New York, NY 10028, (212) 490-0010.
Publication: *Transition* newsletter (quarterly to members, $15/year).

Founded in 1961, the Institute for World Order attempts to advance the values of peace, social justice, economic well-being, and ecological balance through research and education.

FELLOWSHIP OF RECONCILIATION, Box 217, Nyack, NY 10960, (914) 358-4601.
Publication: *Fellowship Magazine* (ten times yearly, $8/year).

Established in 1914 on the eve of World War I, the Fellowship hopes to promote nonviolent solutions to world problems and campaigns for disarmament.

WOMEN'S INTERNATIONAL LEAGUE FOR PEACE AND FREEDOM (WILPF), 1213 Race Street, Philadelphia, PA 19107, (215) 563-7110. International office: Centre Internationale 1, rue de Varembé, 1211 Geneva 20, Switzerland.
Publication: *Peace and Freedom* (quarterly, $15/year to members).

With chapters around the world, WILPF works for world disarmament and peace conversion. The group was founded in 1915 by Nobel Peace Prize winner Jane Addams.

STOCKHOLM INTERNATIONAL PEACE RESEARCH INSTITUTE (SIPRI), Sveavagen 166, s-113 46 Stockholm, Sweden.

SIPRI is an independent institute for research into the problems of peace and conflict, with particular attention to the problems of disarmament and arms regulation. The organization was established in 1966 to commemorate Sweden's 150 years of unbroken peace. SIPRI publishes a variety of books and reports, including a comprehensive yearbook, *World Armaments and Disarmament.*

KEY TO ORGANIZATION SYMBOLS:

 Pursues environmental litigation

 Has a lobbying program

 Engages in public education and/or research

 Has local chapters or is involved in grassroots organizing

WAR BACKWARDS

Editor's Note: *Billy Pilgrim, the central character in Kurt Vonnegut's novel* Slaughterhouse Five, *has survived some of the most brutal moments of World War II in Europe and has experienced, as a result, a mental collapse and shock treatments. Years later his mind is still unstable. He travels at will through his past and future. He can see events happen backwards. He is crazy, of course, but through the wild eyes of this gentle, shell-shocked man come sane perceptions. In the following excerpt, Billy Pilgrim sees a vision of war as all reasonable people would like to see it, as it ought to be. It is our last word on war.*

Billy went into the living room . . . turned on the television. He came slightly unstuck in time, saw the late movie backwards, then forwards again. It was a movie about American bombers in the Second World War and the gallant men who flew them. Seen backwards by Billy, the story went like this:

American planes, full of holes and wounded men and corpses took off backwards from an airfield in England. Over France, a few German fighter planes flew at them backwards, sucked bullets and shell fragments from some of the planes and crewmen. They did the same for wrecked American bombers on the ground, and those planes flew up backwards to join the formation.

The formation flew backwards over a German city that was in flames. The bombers opened their bomb bay doors, exerted a miraculous magnetism which shrunk the fires, gathered them into cylindrical steel containers, and lifted the containers into the bellies of the planes. The containers were stored neatly in racks. The Germans below had miraculous devices of their own, which were long steel tubes. They used them to suck more fragments from the crewmen and planes. But there were still a few wounded Americans, though, and some of the bombers were in bad repair. Over France, though, German fighters came up again, made everything and everybody as good as new.

When the bombers got back to their base, the steel cylinders were taken from the racks and shipped back to the United States of America, where factories were operating night and day, dismantling the cylinders, separating the dangerous contents into minerals. Touchingly, it was mainly women who did this work. The minerals were then shipped to specialists in remote areas. It was their business to put them into the ground, to hide them cleverly, so they would never hurt anybody ever again.

KURT VONNEGUT, JR.

12

The Human Laws of Nature

In ancient Athens the punishment for anyone found polluting the public water supply was often death. Almost every civilization throughout recorded history, in fact, has had laws to protect the public health and the environment. Some of these laws were extreme, odd, or ineffective, but the force of law has always been a tool, sometimes weak, sometimes powerful, to prevent wanton destruction of resources.

In the past ten years, especially in the United States, environmental laws have proliferated as have environmental lawsuits. Part of this growth in legal action can be traced to the United Nations Conference on the Human Environment held in Stockholm, Sweden, in 1972. At this meeting, an international Declaration, the world's first, was drawn up to proclaim the need for individual nations to take action to protect the environment. This Conference also was the origin of the United Nations Environment Programme, which has since catalyzed many resource protection plans and helped publicize the need for legislative action.

The United States and other countries have passed volumes of antipollution laws in the face of rampant industrial pollution. But other kinds of environmental regulations have appeared, too—laws protecting endangered species, laws attempting to regulate the proliferation of synthetic chemicals, laws to preserve open space, laws in response to each newly perceived problem. The laws themselves, in fact, sometimes seem to complicate matters. At the same time that Americans, for example, point with pride to improvements brought about by their environmental laws, they bemoan the entangling technicalities, the complicated regulations, the unrelenting challenges to industry, the ongoing lobbying these laws entail. (See "Environmental Mediation," page 747.)

This chapter, however, is not about the legislation of new law; rather, it is an examination of international law, which is not law as most people think of it, but a web of negotiated—often unenforced—agreements; and case law, i.e., the court battles that grab headlines for a few weeks then fade from public attention, leaving behind, however, important precedents that influence the next similar case.

Though nations may gradually accumulate a body of law to guard the environment within their national boundaries, sweeping environmental problems disregard borderlines. Ocean pollution; acid rain; nuclear proliferation; dwindling populations of migratory animals; the development of resources in areas that belong to no nation, such as the deep sea, Antarctica, and outer space, are all problems that can only be solved through global cooperation—which is the goal of international law. The machinations of international bodies formed to forge agreements is sometimes frustrating, sometimes comical, sometimes confusing, sometimes hopeful. Here we will explore some of their achievements and failures.

Court cases often make good stories because they involve conflict, drama, and a concrete resolution. Several U.S. cases profiled here not only raise important environmental issues but are also interesting from a legal point of view.

In law, as in other endeavors, there are heroes. The judge of the small Italian village of Otranto is one. Through the use of legal tools and through sheer perseverance he succeeded in defusing a sunken, toxic time bomb that threatened his town.

To nonlawyers the law may seem formidable, intimidating, decisive. But a much-celebrated recent case reminds us that the law can be less powerful in some conflicts than political or economic tools. The case of the Tellico Dam was such a reminder. Opponents of the dam won in court and in the tribunal of a special commission, but lost ultimately to political and economic interests.

Nevertheless the law can be a great equalizer. In democratic countries people can influence what laws are passed and insist that powerful industries as well as private citizens obey them. Of course, there are complications, but the law, combined with other tactics, remains a forceful tool to shape the future of the environment.

M.P.

A LAW OF THE SEA

In the early eleventh century, so the legend goes, Canute, the Danish king of England, set his chair on the seashore and commanded the ocean to retreat. When the tide rose, wetting his royal gown, Canute cast off his crown, renouncing it forever as a lesson to his court that there exist on earth powers far greater than those of any king.

Canute knew that the ocean is impervious to human law, but some nine and a half centuries after his reign, the sovereign political powers of the world assembled to impose laws on the ocean—to decide who shall have authority over it and what kind of authority shall be had, to decide who shall have access to the sea's bounteous wealth.

The United Nations Third Law of the Sea Conference convened representatives of as many as 158 nations, twice yearly, for the better part of a decade to hammer out agreements concerning nearly every imaginable use of the ocean. It has been the largest, longest, most complex international conference the world has known. And it has been among the most important and controversial proceedings in the history of international relations.

At stake were an interrelated complex of economic, political, and environmental issues of enormous magnitude. The outcome of the Law of the Sea Conference will have a decisive impact on the future well-being of the ocean, and on the world inherited by future generations.

The Grotian Principle

Until the mid-1940s, Law of the Sea was based on the age-old principle of "freedom of the seas." The principle has probably existed since humankind first set boats on the ocean, but it was periodically overruled whenever one nation gained sufficient naval power to rule a broad area of the sea as its exclusive province. In the sixteenth and seventeenth centuries, when European kingdoms were battling one another to establish naval supremacy and claiming sovereignty over as much of the ocean as they could defend, a young Dutch jurist named Hugo Grotius argued in support of the "free-seas" principle, and became perhaps its most celebrated champion. In 1609 he published a treatise called "Mare Liberum" ("Freedom of the Seas"), a document that has inspired international maritime law to the present day.

Slowly Grotius' ideas came to be accepted, and by the eighteenth century, they were practiced by most nations. The seas were to remain free to all comers, except within a narrow belt of water immediately adjacent to a nation's shoreline. Called the "territorial sea," this strip would fall under the control of the nation whose territory it adjoined in order to facilitate national defense, fishing, customs, and trade. There was no fixed limit on the territorial sea, but many nations accepted a limit of three nautical miles, safely out of range of an enemy ship's cannon.

Beyond the territorial sea, the so-called "high seas" were to remain free. Even within the territorial sea, custom dictated that foreign ships be granted "rights of innocent passage"; that is, minimal restrictions provided their missions were peaceful.

Freedom of the seas became international law by virtue of customary practice rather than explicit agreement of all nations. Then as now, international law is binding only on those who agree to be bound by it. Without an international body whose authority is greater than that of individual nations, there is no way of enforcing international laws. So Grotius' ideas prevailed as long as they served the needs of the international community.

But these ideas had been founded on the twin notions that the seas were boundless, and that their living resources were inexhaustible. Grotius, of course, could not have imagined a time when nations would squabble over minerals found miles below the ocean's surface, when fishermen would command floating factories capable of processing thousands of tons of fish on board and preserving them over a voyage of several months, when schools of fish would be tracked down with the aid of helicopters and sonar equipment. Grotius could not have dreamed, either, of a time when human beings could so foul the ocean with wastes as to render areas of the sea nearly moribund.

The Big Grab

The new era in ocean law dates from 1945, when the U. S. President, Harry Truman, claimed the continental shelf resources along the country's coast on behalf of the nation. The reason for this unprecedented action was not very complicated. U.S. oil companies believed that oil deposits lay beneath the shelf and technological advances would soon put the United States in a position to exploit them.

The U. S. President's action touched off a series of claims by other nations to a larger territorial sea. Truman had claimed exclusive jurisdiction over the continental shelf, and all the resources it contained, but not the waters above it: these were to remain the free "high seas." But the claims that followed were frequently more concerned with important fishing grounds, rather than oil, which no other country at the time had the technology to exploit. In the early 1950s, for example, Chile, Peru, and Ecuador extended their sovereignty over waters out to 200 nautical miles from shore; other nations followed suit, although most stopped far short of the 200-mile mark.

Fishing matters were further complicated in the 1950s, when the appearance of the new, far-ranging Soviet and Japanese "supertrawlers" marked the transformation of fishing into a modern, mechanized industry (see "Fish-and-Chips," page 226). As the dimensions of world fishing changed, more countries acted to protect their national fishing industries from foreign competition by extending their authority further out to sea.

Who Owns the Sea?

Concerned about the steady erosion of the Grotian principle, the United Nations called its first conference on Law of the Sea in 1958 to obtain agreement on certain principles and specific rules of ocean use. The conference did succeed in getting considerable agreement on some issues, but it failed to resolve two critical points: the maximum seaward limit of the territorial sea, and the rights of coastal states to fisheries beyond their territorial sea. A second Law of the Sea Conference, convened by the United Nations in 1960 to resolve these two issues, also failed.

In the absence of international agreement, individual nations proceeded on their own with offshore development. The result, not surprisingly, was conflict as nations disagreed over boundaries, rights, and duties. In the early 1970s, for example, it was reported that in the twenty-odd years since Peru and Ecuador had claimed their 200-mile limits, the two countries had seized some 150 U.S. tuna boats and levied a total of $6 million in fines against them.

By the mid-1960s, private companies had developed the technology to extract mineral-rich manganese nodules from the floor of the abyssal plains some two to three miles below the surface of the "high seas" (see "Manganese Nodules," page 13). With the ability to mine the deep seabed came a whole new set of questions which, like those raised by the Truman proclamation, Grotius' simple dictum was unable to resolve.

To whom did the deep seabed and its riches belong? The high seas, Grotius had said, were to be free to all. Did that include the seabed? If so, did it mean that these belonged to no one in particular and were therefore fair game for anyone with the ability to get at them? Or did "free to all" mean that the deep seabed was to be held in *common* by all human beings? And, if this were the case, what exactly did it mean for something to be owned by everyone on earth? What did it mean, for example, to the private companies with over $100 million invested in deep-sea mining equipment—or to a child in the arid African Sahel? During the mid-1960s such questions became increasingly relevant.

A Voice in the Marine Wilderness

In 1967, Dr. Arvid Pardo, U.N. ambassador from Malta, addressed the U. N. General Assembly on these very issues. The deep seabed, he suggested, should be regarded as the "common heritage of mankind." As such, it should be used only for peaceful purposes, and for the benefit of all. In particular, he suggested that the wealth of the deep seabed be used to foster the economic progress of the world's poorer regions.

The resolution was supported by an overwhelming yes vote, and in 1970, with attention focused on ocean matters, the U.N. decided to hold the Third Law of the Sea Conference.

By the time the Conference was convened in 1973, the list of issues to be considered had grown enormously. Dr. Pardo had addressed himself principally to the question of the seabed. Now the conference proposed to consider items ranging from the deep seabed to the air-space above the oceans, and every imaginable use of the oceans in between.

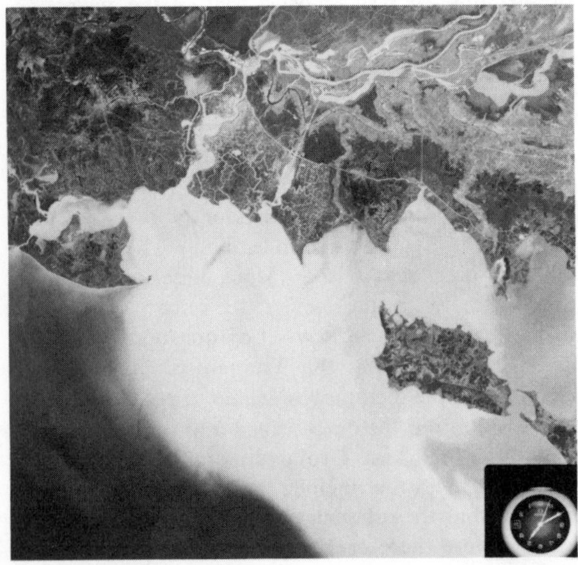

Water pollution knows no boundaries. This satellite photo shows sediments and pollution in waters off the coast of Louisiana. (*NASA*)

The conference opened amid great expectations and the hope it would produce a definitive "Constitution for the Sea." Great expectations aside, the task at hand was enormous: from 114 to 158 nations—more than double the number that had attended the 1958 conference—were to consider twenty-five items, sixty-one subitems and nineteen sub-subitems all highly interrelated and complex. The conference items addressed five major issue areas: the deep seabed, navigation, fishing, pollution, and scientific research.

The Politics of the Sea

It quickly became clear that progress, if there was to be any, was going to be much slower than had been anticipated. The difficulty lay in the high degree of factionalism caused by political blocs and interest groups. In this respect, the conference was worlds away from the previous two conferences under U.N. auspices. But political realities in the international sphere had changed radically since 1958.

Whereas the 1950s and early 1960s had been dominated by the East-West polarization of the superpowers, the international scene of the late 1960s and early 1970s had come increasingly to be dominated by a so-called "North-South" polarization between the wealthy industrialized countries and the poor, nonindustrialized countries. The latter were, by and large, former colonies which had gained political independence during the 1960s. They had not even existed at the time of the 1958 conference, and did not feel bound by its provisions.

The Law of the Sea Conference quickly became something of a tug-of-war between North and South. The two blocs disagreed principally over items in the deep seabed negotiations, probably the most complicated and controversial issue before the conference. How was the deep seabed to be managed so that all nations and particularly the economically disadvantaged, would benefit from its exploitation?

Both sides agreed that an international authority should be created to manage the resources of the deep seabed, but differed over the specifics: the South favored broad powers for the authority, the North wanted a minimum of interference with its ability to mine.

The tensions present in these negotiations were in no small measure heightened by an awareness that several consortiums or private companies from various developed countries were sitting on the sidelines ready to proceed with mining preparations should the talks falter, or stray too far from their interests. Within the North versus South political cast of the conference, other issues became surprisingly controversial. Certain pollution control measures, for example, were seen by many developing countries as a challenge to their political sovereignty, or as posing yet another constraint to economic advancement. Scientific ocean research, almost exclusively the preserve of wealthy industrialized countries, was regarded with considerable suspicion by the poor nations.

Strange Seabed Fellows

But the North-South split was not the only one in evidence at the conference: As negotiations proceeded from the broad issue areas to the more particular concerns, the conference fragmented into a variety of partnerships of temporary convenience, which frequently cross-cut major political groupings.

Some interest groups were based on geographical concerns, like the group of landlocked countries. Twenty-nine of the world's nations, ranging from Switzerland to Upper Volta, have no direct access to the sea. When it appeared the conference favored giving generous zones of exclusive economic control to coastal states, the landlocked countries banded together to demand certain rights in these areas too.

Similar concerns about the proposed economic zones brought a very mixed group of nations together as an association of "Geographically disadvantaged states"—nations that stood to gain less than others from these proposed zones because of the peculiarities of their coastal geography (nations with short coastlines, for example).

The seabed issue brought out an interest group composed of land-based producers of minerals, like Zambia and Chile (copper) and Indonesia (nickel). Concerned that seabed mining would damage their mineral industries, these nations pushed for controls.

Trade and defense concerns made naval bedfellows out of old ideological foes: the United States and the Soviet Union, both major maritime powers and strong supporters of navigational freedoms. Specifically they wanted to make international waterways out of some one hundred narrow straits and archipelagic waters that would otherwise become territorial waters under the conference's plan to extend the territorial limit to twelve nautical miles.

This "crazy-quilt" pattern of negotiations prolonged the conference. So too did a "Gentlemen's Agreement" made early in the conference, obliging participants to seek consensus on every item before attempting to adopt the treaty as a whole. With this provision, the power to withhold approval of any given item thus became a bargaining chip in itself. Still, the specter of individual countries and mining companies poised to take independent initiatives spurred the negotiations onward.

The Scorecard Today

In August 1980 the negotiating text was finally approved in Geneva, to be presented for final approval at meetings in New York and Caracas in 1981. While only relatively minor issues remain to be worked out, the process of approving the treaty could take years—and the governing structure it creates will undergo a long, possibly controversial formative period. The treaty includes the following items of broad agreement:

- The territorial sea has been set at twelve miles. Narrow straits and some archipelagic waters have been declared international passageways free to foreign vessels.
- Coastal nations have been given "Exclusive Economic Zones" extending 200 miles seaward and ownership of the continental shelf where it extends beyond two hundred miles. In such cases, nations have been given a choice of two methods for determining the outer boundary of the shelf. Between them, they effectively give some nations a 350-mile limit, and in some cases, even more. Exploitation of resources on the continental shelf beyond the 200-mile limit is to be taxed by an international authority, and the proceeds to be used for the benefit of developing states, with preference given to least developed and landlocked states.
- Landlocked nations have been granted limited rights to fish in the Exclusive Economic Zones of coastal nations, but details of application have been left largely up to the coastal nations.
- An International Seabed Authority is to be established, and will be composed of a council, assembly, secretariat, and an operational arm, called the "Enterprise." The Authority will have the power to license private companies to mine the seabed, as well as to undertake its own mining operations on behalf of the nonindustrialized nations. Private companies wishing to

mine must select two sites of comparable value; the authority chooses one of the sites to mine or to hold in trust, the other site is mined by the company, which must also pay royalties on mineral production.

- Controls on pollution from ships have been strengthened. Nations are also obliged to control land-based pollution, although the specifics of that control have been left largely to individual nations. Possible pollution resulting from seabed mining is to be monitored closely, and mining halted if deemed necessary.
- Permission to conduct scientific research within the 200-mile economic zone must be obtained from the nation having jurisdiction over the waters. Nations were urged not to refuse permission groundlessly, and scientists were urged to involve the host nation in its activities and share all findings with it.
- An international Tribunal for the Law of the Sea was established to provide a mechanism for the settlement of disputes.

Sinking Ideals

Most critics of the Law of the Sea Conference point out that national priorities have been the overriding concerns of the sessions, not the original goal of a "common heritage." For example, granting 200-mile "exclusive economic zones" to every coastal and island nation has effectively removed one third of total ocean space from the areas to be held commonly. This third is estimated to contain nearly all significant oil deposits and most of the world's major fisheries.

Some observers, including Dr. Pardo, fear the results of the Conference will increase rather than reduce the threat of conflict among nations. Slight changes in the projection of a boundary can mean the difference between owning huge oil reserves, for example, or watching a neighbor exploit them. To many students of the Law of the Sea Conferences, the actual language of the treaty contradicts the principles of interdependence and common heritage that gave rise to the sessions. The initial suggestion by Dr. Pardo for a World Authority to control even coastal resources and habitats was dropped early in the negotiations. Some characterize the treaty as an important missed opportunity.

J.K.

THE HOTTEST QUESTIONS IN INTERNATIONAL ENVIRONMENTAL LAW

Acid rain is the most serious environmental threat facing Canada, declared Canadian Minister of Environment John Frasier at an international conference in November 1979. It's a problem that Canada both imports and exports. The sulfur-dioxide fumes that cause acid rain waft across the border from Canadian smokestacks to the United States, just as U.S. factory fumes migrate to Canada. "The problem cannot be solved without an agreement between the two countries," Frasier pointed out.

Frasier made his remarks at a New York convention of seven hundred scientists gathered to discuss the impact of acid rain, the newest international pollution threat. (See "The Trespassing Poison: Acid Rain," page 186.) Like air pollution and ocean pollution, acid rain ignores national boundaries. What goes up as smoke in one country comes down as poison in another. And possible solutions fall into the equally hazy area of international environmental law. This is not law as most people think of law: not a clear-cut set of rules like speed limits, with prescribed punishments for violators. This is the law of treaties and promises, of diplomatic, sometimes undecipherable codes. Although nations have been attempting to develop a workable international law of pollution control for more than forty years, their efforts have been hamstrung by mistrust, competition, and economic expedience. While jurists have drawn up treaties, formed commissions, and convened numerous boards of review, an increasingly complex array of chemicals and technologies have rendered their piecemeal efforts hopelessly inadequate. Ironically, Minister Frasier's warning came forty-four years after an international tribunal rendered judgment in a strikingly similar dispute between the United States and Canada over damages caused by airborne pollution drifting across the border. The judgment, known as the *Trail Smelter* decision, was hailed as a landmark in international jurisprudence. But more than four decades later stacks are still smoking, fish are still dying, and politicians, scientists, and jurists are still talking.

The questions are difficult, the process is slow, the issues often seem remote from our daily lives. But the basic question of how well we can cooperate on crucial planetary matters may in large part determine whether we can safeguard the sweeping systems of the environment or not. Described below are some of the major questions in international environmental law.

Trans-boundary Pollution

International law regarding a country's liability for environmental damage beyond its borders is in its infancy. However, clear-cut assignment of responsibility has been made in specific treaties between nations sharing a border, and the principles involved in these treaties may be recognized as a basis for international standards of liability in the future. Perhaps the most effective has been the International Joint Commission (IJC), established under a 1909 boundary waters treaty between the United States and Canada. Though limited to an advisory and investigatory role, and armed with little more than the force of publicity, the IJC has been able to implement its findings on several occasions, most notably in the *Trail Smelter* case in 1935, which, as of 1980, was the only international adjudication of a pollution dispute. In the *Trail Smelter* case a metal refinery in British Columbia was found to have emitted sulfurous gases, damaging the crops of farmers in the State of Washington. An international tribunal, composed of an American, a Canadian, and a Belgian, found the Canadian government liable, largely on the basis of evidence presented by the IJC, for damages of $350,000.

The importance of the *Trail Smelter* decision is twofold. First, it demonstrates the ability of an international commission to investigate a case. (Subsequent to *Trail Smelter,* the recommendations of an IJC investigation into marine pollution were also put into effect in the 1972 Agreement on Great Lakes Water Quality.) More important, the principles of the *Trail Smelter* decision have been recognized by international conventions, most notably the Stockholm Conference on the Human Environment of 1972 held under the auspices of the United Nations. The Conference declared that member states should "cooperate to develop further international and regional liability and compensation for the victims of pollution and other environmental damage caused by activities within the jurisdiction or control of such states to areas beyond their jurisdiction."

Maritime Safety and Pollution

Since the turn of the century nations have gathered at conferences to attempt to regulate shipping, perhaps the most international of industries. Not until 1959 was a permanent organization—the Inter-Governmental Maritime Consultive Organization (IMCO)—formed under the auspices of the eleven-year-old United Nations, to forge agreements on maritime safety and pollution. IMCO, headquartered in London, has one hundred and six members, including most of the major maritime nations. Members meet every two years to discuss problems of vessel safety, navigation, and pollution. Agreements must be ratified by a specified majority of members, a process that can take from ninety days to several years. Even then enforcement is left up to the nation whose flag is flown by the offending ship.

IMCO agreements on safety—aimed at preventing accidents at sea—have, for example, established traffic lanes in congested areas and required safety inspections. One agreement authorizes port authorities to detain foreign vessels they deem unseaworthy. Much of IMCO's attention has focused on preventing marine pollution from oil, chemicals, sewage and other substances and of compensating nations that suffer the damages of oil spills from foreign vessels. (See "The Hidden Costs of an Oil Spill," page 253.)

Although public attention focuses on oil spills, much of the more than 6 million metric tons of petroleum hydrocarbons that enter the oceans each year come from routine shipping operations such as the release of oily ballast water, according to a 1975 National Academy of Sciences study. Shipping accounts for 35 percent of the oil entering the sea and of that only 10 percent comes from accidents. However, the concentration of oil from a spill, especially one near shore, can be devastating to local marine life. Early IMCO agreements attempted to restrict routine discharges by limiting the amount of oil a ship could discharge to a small percentage of its cargo capacity and prohibiting all discharge within 50 miles (80.5 kilometers) of land. They also restricted the size of oil tanks on ships to limit the size of a spill if the hull was punctured.

In 1973 IMCO adopted a more comprehensive agreement to prevent ship pollution, but as of 1980 the agreement was still awaiting the endorsement of member nations. The agreement would further restrict the amount of oil that could be routinely discharged, designate special areas such as the Mediterranean, Black, Baltic, and Red Seas where no discharge would be allowed, extend controls to other hazardous substances such as sewage and garbage, and require new ships over 750,000 dead weight tons to install separate ballast tanks to keep the ballast water free from oil contamination. Specifically exempted from discharge restrictions are wastes associated with deep-sea mining. (See "Manganese Nodules," page 13.) Another agreement that has not yet been ratified would establish a fund to pay for oil spill cleanup costs that rise beyond the amount covered by insurance—up to $56 million per spill. Contributions to the fund would come from nations that receive oil by sea. The United States has refused to endorse the agreement saying the limit is too low; cleanup costs after the *Amoco Cadiz*, a 230,000-dead-weight-ton carrier that spilled 1.5 million barrels of oil off the Brittany coast in 1978, came to more than $84 million.

Meanwhile the United States and other countries have passed their own laws governing responsibility for pollution from ships and off-shore oil wells (wells are not included in IMCO agreements). The U.S. government has a $35 million fund for cleanup and the U.S. oil industry maintains a $200 million cleanup fund as required by federal law.

Violation of IMCO agreements carry no set penalty. When a violation occurs the offended nation sends its complaint and evidence to the nation whose flag is flown by the ship in question. Enforcement and penalties are up to the flag nation. IMCO requires only that a copy of the proceedings be sent to it and to the nation that filed the complaint. Although several nations, such as Liberia and Greece, that allow foreign shippers to fly their "flags of convenience" belong to IMCO, these nations tend to be lax in their regulation of shipping—one of the reasons, of course, why shippers seek their flags in the first place.

Nuclear Energy

There are two major areas of concern to international jurists in the field of nuclear energy: the testing of weapons and the operation of reactors. Because of the obvious gravity of the problem, the years since 1945 have seen a series of conventions and agreements aimed at controlling the power of the atom. However, as in all areas of international law, the treaties suffer from the lack of an effective system of enforcement.

Control of nuclear weapons testing dramatizes the classic conflict between national sovereignty and international control. Nothing separates the "haves" from the "have nots" in the realm of military power more than possession of a nuclear weapon. Nations possessing the bomb are referred to as a "club," an exclusive group seeking to limit membership and maintain control over a vital resource. (See "The Nuclear Club," page 548.) With weapons already stockpiled, they have declared nuclear testing dangerous, and seek international agreement in limiting its practice. The irony is obvious, and France and China, two important military powers, are among the more than fifty nations that have refused to sign the nuclear test ban treaties.

The Non-Proliferation Treaty (NPT) was drawn up in 1968, twenty-three years after the United States first dropped the atomic bomb on Japan. Approximately two years after the treaty was drafted, a sufficient number of nations had signed the pact to put its strictures into effect. Of course, most of the nations did not have the technology necessary to develop a bomb, and hence were placing academic restrictions on themselves. They promised not to develop nuclear weapons, and not to obtain them from other countries. Furthermore, they pledged to allow inspection of their "peaceful" nuclear activities to ensure that nuclear materials are not diverted for the manufacture of nuclear explosives. These inspections were assigned to the International Atomic Energy Agency, a Vienna-based organization with membership of over one hundred nations.

Facilities of nations possessing nuclear weaponry are off limits to the inspections under the terms of the Treaty, a clause that angers developing countries. To meet the objections of the nonnuclear countries, the British and Americans declared their intention to allow inspection of their nonmilitary nuclear facilities (but the U. S. Senate has yet to approve this). Military installations, however, would be off limits. The Soviet Union declared that it would not, under any circumstances, permit foreign inspection of any of its nuclear installations.

To gain the support of the nonnuclear nations the nuclear powers agreed in the Treaty to "undertake to facilitate, and have the fullest possible exchange of equipment, materials, and scientific and technological information for the peaceful uses of nuclear energy." The superpowers also agreed to negotiate in good faith the cessation of the nuclear arms race. Neither of these promises, which were the only major concessions of the nuclear powers, have been kept.

Although the nuclear powers have been willing to sell nuclear power plants to other countries, they have been much less anxious to give them the uranium enrichment, fuel fabrication, and reprocessing facilities that are essential parts of the nuclear cycle. The United States in particular has opposed the export of these auxiliary technologies on the grounds that they will make it easier for other nations to develop nuclear weapons. The U. S. Nuclear Non-Proliferation Act of 1978 seemingly violates the intent of the NPT by unilaterally limiting the export of nuclear technology, especially technology that could produce bomb-grade fuel. Of course, by denying this technology to other countries, the United States guarantees itself a market for its nuclear fuel industry.

Those nonnuclear nations that agreed to the NPT did so in the hope that by accepting as permanent the existing military domination of the world by the nuclear powers, they might gain energy independence and the reassurance that the potential for a nuclear conflict would be diminished by partial disarmament. The suspicions of the countries that did not sign the Treaty seem to have been justified.

During the past decade the Non-Proliferation Treaty has been a valuable deterrent to the spread of nuclear weapons, however, and technology sharing has made nuclear power safer in countries with limited technical backgrounds. But dissatisfaction with the NPT is growing among the nonnuclear states. The nuclear powers will have to be more responsive to the needs and fears of the other countries if this crucial effort to avert the horrors of a nuclear war is to be successful.

Access to New Resources

In relatively unexploited areas, such as Antarctica, the deep sea, and outer space, international agreements have attempted to set forth guidelines to prevent a repetition of the "land grabs" of powerful nations in the nineteenth century. Since the economic value of these areas is still unproven, there are as yet few vested interests to conflict with the forces of cooperation.

The Antarctic Treaty, adopted in December of 1959 by Southern Hemisphere nations nearest Antarctica as well as nations interested in doing scientific research there, bans all nuclear explosions in the area and provides for regular scientific consultations to share the results of antarctic research. (See "Antarctica," page 279.)

The discovery of manganese nodules, a potential mineral resource in the deep sea, has set nations to debating the meaning of treaty language regarding holding the area "in common." The Law of the Sea Conference has worked out a scheme in which countries able to mine must share the resource with a consortium of countries that don't have the necessary technology, but a great many questions remain. (See "A Law of the Sea," page 568, and "Manganese Nodules," page 13.)

Although several nations have sent satellites into space and two nations have landed on the Moon, so far no one has the technology to seriously exploit other planets. In advance of such exploitation, nations have agreed that none will claim a piece of the heavens. Moreover, and perhaps more immediately relevant, nations with the ability to launch space vehicles have agreed to accept liability for damage caused by their rockets or satellites that crash to earth. The agreement was tested in 1979 when falling remnants of the U. S. Skylab struck a rural section of Australia and the United States paid for the damages. The Soviet Union, on the other hand, refused to pay damages when its nuclear-powered satellite *Cosmos 954* crashed in northwest Canada in 1978 (see "Space Junk," page 417).

The treaty on the exploration and use of outer space was adopted by the U. N. General Assembly in 1963 and put into force in October 1967 showing that humans can plan for international cooperation in advance of irreparable, irreversible damage.

B.L., M.P., K.F.

ENVIRONMENTAL LAWS AROUND THE WORLD

- Switzerland, where smog does not hamper the view of distant mountain peaks, possesses a unique air pollution code. Once an industrial air polluter is convicted, the court hires a contractor to correct the problem to its satisfaction. The offending company is billed for the work.
- Norway has passed a regulation to limit home

energy use. It requires that all private homes be built with chimneys for fireplaces or stoves, as well as with an alternate heating source.

- In South Korea extraordinarily strong environmental legislation has been directed at motorists. Stringent new laws define permissible levels of exhaust emission. Motorists whose cars are found to exceed these levels face whopping fines of up to $30,928 and a three-year jail sentence. Violators with cars that were in use prior to the legislation fare a little better. They face only one year in prison.
- West Germany is another country in favor of imprisonment as a penalty for crimes against the environment. A bill under consideration in 1980 would set penalties of up to ten years in prison for intentional damage to the environment.
- Understanding the intricacies of the voluminous Russian Environmental Code is an exercise in confusion for the average Soviet citizen. Among the most interesting are the regulations governing fishing. Two categories of fish have been created: "Valuable" and "Game Species." Catching game fish without a proper license will result in fines based on how much damage was done to the river by the taking of that particular species. However, if valuable fish are caught—sturgeon heads the list—the penalty is imprisonment.
- In Kenya there is no legal definition of "environment" and no national environmental protection act. Dealing with environmental problems is left to local governments, which have the power to prevent any pollution they deem harmful to the health and welfare of the people in their jurisdiction.
- The element of surprise characterizes South Korean industrial pollution inspections. Government officials drop in unannounced at various industrial plants and take a look around. The success of this campaign can be measured in numbers; since the practice began, 152 business licenses have been revoked, 155 businesses were ordered to leave the country, and 874 were ordered to make changes to reduce pollution.
- A recently enacted environmental law of China is a good example of the use of incentives rather than penalties. Enacted in September 1979, the law provides rewards for various achievements in environmental protection, generally in the form of tax breaks and exemption. For example any industry that recycles waste as a raw material is not only given tax exemptions but, in some cases, allowed more freedom in the pricing of their products.

T.K.

ANIMAL LAWS

International Whaling Commission

Membership (1979–80): 27 nations

WHALING NATIONS—Brazil, Chile, Denmark, Iceland, Japan, South Korea, Norway, Peru, Spain, USSR

NONWHALING NATIONS—Argentina, Australia, Canada, France, Mexico, Netherlands, New Zealand, Panama, Seychelles, South Africa, Sweden, United Kingdom, United States

WHALING NATIONS WHICH ARE NOT MEMBERS—Cyprus, Portugal, North Korea, Taiwan

The IWC is a self-regulating association of whaling and nonwhaling nations established in 1946 to preserve world whale stocks. (See "Whales," page 286.) Its principal job has been to assess whale populations and set regional hunting quotas for each species. Though it is virtually impossible to make accurate whale counts, a Scientific Committee, composed of scientists nominated by member nations, analyzes data and recommends quotas. Members may challenge the Committee's findings but rarely do.

Quotas have dropped steadily over the last decade, from a worldwide total catch of over 40,000 in 1969–70 to 15,853 in 1979–80. Several species—the blue, gray, humpback, right, bowhead—are considered to be "commercially extinct" and may not be hunted at all. A controversial exception to this total protection is the small quota for bowheads and grays permitted to North American and Siberian Eskimos engaging in traditional subsistence hunting.

Effective hunting quotas must be based on *accurate* population counts and biological studies but because it is so difficult and expensive to observe submarine creatures—especially those that migrate thousands of miles along unknown routes—scientists often disagree about the status of particular stocks. Hampered by insufficient funds, they are often forced to make decisions based on incomplete information.

Important IWC resolutions have prohibited the sale of whaling equipment or technology to non-IWC nations, forbidden the use of factory ships (highly efficient plants able to process one 80-foot [24-meter] whale per hour while at sea), and declared the entire Indian Ocean a sanctuary for whales until 1985.

Subject to commercial pressures, Japan and other members have consistently ignored IWC rules that cut into profits. If quotas were too low, whalers simply made new ones. When regulations were too stringent, subsidiaries of Japanese whaling companies set up operations in South America, where they killed thousands of endangered whales each year, more than half of them undersize.

In an attempt to end such abuses the United States recently threatened to impose trade sanctions against any country that undermines an international fisheries conservation program. Specifically, violators of IWC rules could be denied fishing rights within U.S. 200-mile coastal limits. Neither Japan nor the Soviet Union, another major whaler, can afford to lose fishing grounds in the North Pacific. Possibly because of this, the Japanese Parliament finally passed a law forbidding the import of non-IWC products.

Unfortunately, the IWC has no enforcement powers. Though IWC observers may board whaling ships of member nations, adherence to quotas and resolutions is strictly voluntary. At present, public sentiment is the most effective means of pressure for compliance.

For current information on IWC actions, contact:

The Whale Protection Fund
1925 K Street NW
Washington, D.C. 10006
Tel. (202) 466-4996

CITES
Convention on International Trade in Endangered Species of Wild Fauna and Flora

Membership (1979–80): 51 nations

MAJOR WILDLIFE-TRADING COUNTRIES WHICH *are not members:* Japan, Italy, Belgium, Spain, the Netherlands, Mexico, Bolivia, Colombia, the Philippines, Sudan, Thailand

The CITES convention, drawn up in Washington, D.C., in 1973, was the first major worldwide effort to regulate trade in rare animals and plants, now a multimillion-dollar business. The treaty's import-export restrictions cover nearly a thousand species, which are listed in three appendices according to their conservation status.

Appendix I includes more than 600 species threatened with immediate extinction—among them, the orangutan, Asian elephant, snow leopard, the Guadalupe fur seal. CITES forbids *all* commercial trade in these species or any products derived from them. Noncommercial trade for scientific purposes is allowed only if it can be proven not to threaten the survival of the species.

Appendix II lists 250 plants and animals which could become threatened with extinction if trade were not regulated. These species—including the bobcat, gray wolf, polar bear, and American ginseng plant—may be traded in limited numbers with special permits. All birds of prey and all cetaceans not on Appendix I are listed here.

Appendix III contains nonendangered species which individual countries wish to protect within their borders.

Each member nation has an independent scientific authority which determines status of species and allowable purposes of trade, and a management authority which enforces regulations.

Originally funded by the United Nations Environment Programme (UNEP), the Convention plans to be self-supporting by 1983 through voluntary contributions of members.

For further information about CITES, contact:

CITES Secretariat
IUCN
CH-1110 Morges
Switzerland

MMPA
Marine Mammal Protection Act (United States)

The U. S. Marine Mammal Protection Act was passed by Congress in 1972 to establish humane and scientific guidelines for the management of marine mammal populations. The Act created a three-member Marine Mammal Commission with a board of nine scientific advisors to study the health, numerical distribution, and habits of marine mammals, and to recommend government conservation policies.

Though the Act imposed an indefinite moratorium on the taking and importing of all marine mammals, the Secretary of Commerce and the Secretary of the Interior, advised by the Commission, may waive the moratorium and issue permits. Seeking a responsible balance between commerce and conservation, permits restrict the number, size, age, and sex of animals taken, as well as the time and place of hunting. No pregnant, nursing, or endangered mammal may be taken, except for scientific purposes which may benefit the species; and the law absolutely prohibits any inhumane method of capture or killing.

The first major conservation act to be based on ecosystem principles, the MMPA introduced the wildlife management concept of "optimum sustainable population" or OSP. The Act defines OSP as "the number of animals which will result in the maximum productivity of the population or the species, keeping in mind the optimum carrying capacity of the habitat and the health of the ecosystem of which they are part." Though this definition has been called vague and unworkable, the ultimate objective of the MMPA is to determine and maintain the OSP for all marine mammals.

Endangered Species Act of 1973 (United States)

The most comprehensive of all U.S. wildlife laws, the Endangered Species Act attempts to halt the extinction of species in the United States and worldwide. The Act requires the Secretary of the Interior, after public notice and hearing, to publish annually a List of Endangered and Threatened Wildlife and Plants, which indicates whether a species is "endangered" or "threatened" (see "Coming to Terms," page 362) and specifies the region where it is protected.

With limited exceptions for scientific or conservation purposes, the Act prohibits the taking, importing, and exporting of any listed species or its products. To "take" is broadly defined to cover not only capture and killing, but also pursuit and harassment, and even *attempts* at these activities. Violators may be fined, imprisoned, and deprived of import and export permits.

Because survival of a species in the wild depends upon protection of its habitat, the Secretary, whenever possible, designates "critical habitats" (see "Coming to Terms," page 362) which may not be destroyed or modified by any federally funded project or agency. Because ecological and economic interests often conflict, the Secretary must consider not only biological data but "other" impacts as well. However, an area may be excluded from critical habitat if economic considerations outweigh ecological ones.

Even after the designation of critical habitat has been made, a cabinet-level Endangered Species Committee may review proposals and grant exemptions for projects of regional or national significance which are clearly in the public interest.

Anyone may obtain a copy of the Endangered Species List by writing to:

The Director, Office of Endangered Species
U. S. Fish and Wildlife Service
U. S. Department of the Interior
Washington, D.C. 20204

M.A.

Wavemakers:

THE COURAGEOUS JUDGE OF OTRANTO

On July 14, 1974, two ships collided off the Italian coast, and a Yugoslavian freighter, *Çavtat,* sank in 320 feet (100 meters) of water. Since the wreckage of a foreign ship in Italian waters is covered by Italian law, Judge Alberto Maritati, the young magistrate of the district, heard the case to decide the matter of responsibility. Immediately Maritati took a special interest in the case. The *Çavtat* was well-known. It was no secret she often carried contraband, including armaments. What, Maritati worried, was now tossing about on the seafloor, three miles from his village of Otranto and in the path of its fishing boats?

Three days after the wreck, as part of a routine procedure, Judge Maritati was informed of the nature and quantity of the cargo. Approximately nine hundred drums—600,000 pounds (270,000 kilograms)—of tetraethyl and tetramethyl lead had gone down with the *Çavtat*. Though Maritati had never heard of these chemicals, he had an understanding of ecologic systems and a concern for the environment. Urgently, he dispatched telegrams to

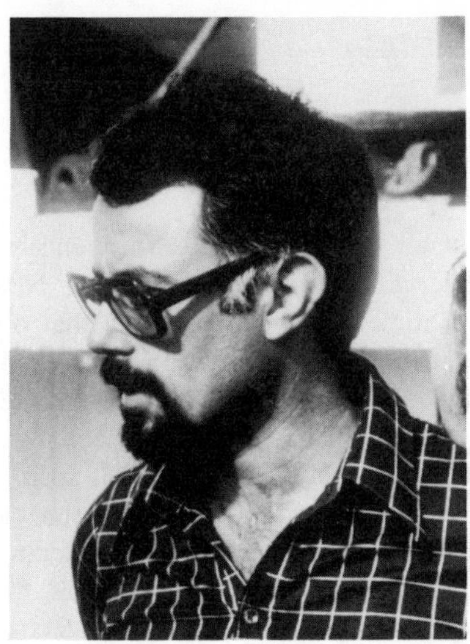

Judge Alberto Maritati. (*The Cousteau Society*)

marine institutions asking if the lead compounds were poisonous and whether marine and human lives were in danger. The answer came back an unequivocal "yes."

Little was known about the action of these chemicals in seawater and their effects on the marine life. But their effects on humans were documented. Exposure to even a small and very dilute amount could cause insomnia, emotional instability, and hallucinations. Direct contact with the undiluted chemicals could be lethal. Undoubtedly some of the drums had been crushed or punctured in the accident. Ocean swells could push one of these ashore. Eventually, the saltwater environment would corrode others, allowing the poisons to spill into the sea. Recovery should begin immediately, the scientists advised.

But it did not begin. Instead the Italian and Yugoslavian governments quibbled back and forth, each refusing to assume responsibility. Acting alone, Maritati had researchers sample the water and mud around the *Cavtat*. He ordered the wreck site encircled with buoys as a warning to passing boats and ships. Fearing contamination, he forbade fishing in the immediate area. For two-and-a-half years he sent letters to the appropriate ministries, urging action, suggesting what should be done, learning about the chemicals and passing it on. He did not receive a single reply.

Hoping public pressure might force officials into action, he sought publicity, hammering away at the government's negligence, warning of its consequences. Slowly, the campaign of a small-town magistrate became news. Captain Jacques Cousteau and The Cousteau Society helped publicize the incident internationally. But the publicity had an adverse affect on Otranto's main livelihood—tourism. Fishermen, too, were feeling a financial pinch because of restricted fishing. When the government continued to ignore Maritati, his neighbors began to suspect he had exaggerated the danger. As popular support grew for Maritati abroad, it declined in Otranto.

Finally, Maritati gained proof, in a roundabout way, that officials considered the sunken chemicals life-threatening. After finally agreeing to recover the lead compounds, the government of Yugoslavia abandoned the effort, saying it was much too dangerous to touch the drums. The safest place for them was exactly where they were. Maritati suspected his neighbors in Otranto would not agree.

In the spring of 1976, Judge Maritati gained access to classified papers that gave him the evidence he needed to start legal action against the *Cavat*'s captain. Setting a judicial precedent, he sequestered the wreck, putting it and the cargo solely under his court's jurisdiction. Supplying expert testimony to the Italian government, Maritati convinced officials the lead compounds were indeed poisonous. The government approached NATO with the situation. The Superior Council for Health agreed to support Maritati's efforts.

By January of 1977, Maritati had grown impatient. Though Parliament had not yet voted the necessary funds for recovery, he ordered SAIPEM, a privately owned company, to commence recovery efforts. Without guarantee of payment, SAIPEM provided an off-shore platform, a launch, and one hundred and twenty crew plus specialized divers. Eleven months and $12 million later, the last drum was lifted from the floor of the Adriatic, a testimony to the curiosity, courage, and tenacity of an obscure Italian judge. Without him there would have been no one chipping away at the icy indifference of two governments, and the people of Italy, Yugoslavia, Albania, and Greece would still be threatened by the deadly contents of nine hundred drums of poison.

L.W.

CASES IN POINT

Lawsuits not only settle disputes but often focus issues as squabbling parties are forced to present their case clearly and persuasively. Beneath the legal jargon of writs and briefs, often, lies the framework for tough decisions. The six recent U.S. lawsuits outlined here—some very convoluted—set forth difficult issues in environmental law.

Case law builds on itself. Legislators pass laws, but the courts interpret them, using the rationale of each decision to help make the next decision. Thus cases such as these may not only settle current arguments, but also influence the outcome of similar disputes in years to come.

M.P.

Oil vs. Fish

Georges Bank juts out from the continental shelf of the northeastern United States near Cape Cod in the shape of a huge thumb. Eons ago it was part of the coast, accumulating rich sediments from river drainages and the decayed remains of prehistoric plants and animals. After being swept by waves of glaciers over thousands of years, Georges Bank ended up underwater, a relatively mild and shallow environment for cod, haddock, herring, shrimp, scallops, lobsters, and other marine life.

The bank's history provided it with two important resources. The first is fish: the bank is one of the most productive and most fished areas in the world. The second is oil: buried in the rich sediments—25,000 feet (7.6 kilometers) thick in places—there are probably pockets of oil, according to geologists. They estimate the amount at a half-billion barrels, enough to fuel the energy-hungry United States for only six days.

With proposed oil drilling would come inevitable small seepages and the risk of a major spill that could devastate the fishery. Given the toll oil spills have taken on fisheries in other areas (see the following stories: "The Business of Supertankers," page 489, and "The Strait of Malacca," page 80), environmental organizations, fishing industry groups, and several New England states questioned whether oil drilling can coexist with fishing. They filed a suit in U. S. Federal Court.

The states of Maine and Massachusetts, and the Conservation Law Foundation of New England, plaintiffs in the action, argue that oil spills, likely during both exploration and production, could have a severe impact on the New England fishing industry. Spills could kill the planktonic eggs and larvae of lobsters and fish such as haddock and herring which spawn on the bank. In addition, certain compounds in petroleum attract lobsters. Seepage or a spill on the bank, biologists fear, might confuse and distract lobsters crossing the bank on their annual spawning migration.

The plaintiffs did not seek an absolute bar to exploration or production of oil, but they insisted on further study before any drilling, or construction of platforms was begun. Their suit initiated a protracted legal battle.

In 1979 and 1980 Atlantic Richfield and the score of other oil companies named as defendants in the action won a significant victory when a U. S. Circuit Court of Appeals judge lifted an injunction against sale of Georges Bank leases by the federal government to the oil companies. About half the leases were sold in December 1979 for $800 million, including $200 million in cash. Production in the lease area, however, would not begin before 1985.

The plaintiffs had insisted, unsuccessfully, that the sales were illegal, arguing that the oil companies' environmental impact study failed to consider suitable alternatives to the exploration plan, that the U. S. Secretary of the Interior failed to meet his duty to protect the fishery from unreasonable risk of harm by allowing the project to proceed, and that the federal government has violated the Endangered Species Act by committing itself to the exploration without seeking an opinion on possible effects on endangered species in the area.

But Georges Bank could be as rich an area for litigation as it is for fish or oil. Although the plaintiffs failed to get the lease sales rescinded, they did win concessions that will allow them to closely monitor exploratory drilling and plans for oil production in preparation for possible future legal challenges to actual oil production.

The Georges Bank choice between oil and fish is likely to occupy the court for some time to come.

C.F.

A Bird's Day in Court

In 1979 a federal court in Hawaii ordered the state to protect the Palila—a small blunt-billed bird on the Endangered Species list. The decision itself, requiring the state to rid the Palila's habitat of sheep and goats which were threatening its feeding and nesting areas, was unremarkable in most ways. However, one of the parties to the lawsuit was rather remarkable. The Palila, named individually in the legal papers as a plaintiff, may be the first animal to get its own day in court.

Attorneys for the Sierra Club Legal Defense Fund and the Audubon Society, which initiated the suit, had hoped to provoke a ruling on the legal issue of "standing to sue" for animals and other natural objects. Traditionally, human beings have been able to get standing—the right to sue—when they are able to prove they have suffered damage to their health, property, finances, or reputation. But if a group of environmentalists wanted to file a suit to prevent the development of a public wilderness, it would have difficulty proving that the development would cause them any personal harm in the traditional legal sense. That was the situation in *Sierra Club* v. *Morton,* a 1972 U. S. Supreme Court case that denied standing to the Sierra Club, which sought to protect the Mineral King Valley in California from developers' bulldozers. In the dissenting opinion to that case, the late Justice William O. Douglas suggested that Mineral King itself should have been the plaintiff. He cited arguments from legal scholar Christopher Stone, who has proposed that animals and natural objects should have recognized legal rights. Stone argues that corporations—nonhuman entities—have the right to sue and be sued and to have humans represent their interests, so why not allow the same rights for natural objects?

In *Palila* v. *Hawaii,* however, the attorneys for the state did not challenge the Palila's standing and the district judge did not rule on whether the Palila was a proper plaintiff. Thus, although no clear precedent was set, the Palila may have cracked the courthouse door for other such litigation.

Although it may take years for court decisions to establish a ruling on standing for natural objects, several U.S. states have attempted to solve the problem of standing through legislation. In 1970 the State of Michigan passed a landmark Environmental Protection Act that gives any citizen the right to sue anyone who is polluting, impairing, or destroying the environment. Several other states have passed similar legislation offering residents a powerful tool to help protect the environment.

C.F.

Legal Meltdown

Minimizing the seriousness of a nuclear accident may maximize the cost to those responsible for it.

That's the way things seem to be turning out in Harrisburg, Pennsylvania, where the first lawsuits to compensate victims of a nuclear accident were filed as a result of the release of radiation at the nearby Three Mile Island nuclear plant in 1979.

The Federal Price-Anderson Act provides for more or less automatic payments of up to $560 million per occurrence to people injured in a nuclear accident. The law requires defendants in such an action to waive their legal defenses, thus making it much easier for victims to collect damages. The hitch is that Price-Anderson is only invoked if the Nuclear Regulatory Commission (NRC) deems an accident an Extraordinary Nuclear Occurrence (ENO).

The NRC has decided that the radiation released at Three Mile Island was not substantial enough to be classified as an ENO. That's not necessarily bad news for victims, however, because although the scores of plaintiffs in the pending lawsuits will not have the advantage of an automatic finding of liability under Price-Anderson, they will now be free to seek damages in excess of the $560 million ceiling set by the law.

What amount—if any—will eventually be awarded hinges on how a number of legal questions are decided, among them, what kinds of damages are compensable in the relatively new field of nuclear negligence. Can plaintiffs collect damages for the emotional trauma of simply living through the crisis; for cancer or birth defects that may show up years from now; for loss of real estate values or economic loss from business shutdowns during the crisis? Courts have not always been sympathetic to such claims in analogous cases in the past—such as certain economic damage from oil spills or long-latent cancers from industrial hazards.

Some of the claims will be dealt with in a planned, massive class-action suit. In mid-1980 legal observers were predicting that claims would far exceed the Price-Anderson limit. Although there may be some question as to whether the nuclear occurrence at Three Mile Island was "extraordinary," it appears that the damages sought because of it may be.

C.F.

The Case of the Seeping Chemicals

Three hundred miles northeast of Harrisburg, the city of Niagara Falls, New York is the scene of what may be another first in environmental litigation. Attorneys for the federal government are suing Hooker Chemical and Plastics Corp. and its parent, Occidental Petroleum, for $117 million in damages from toxic wastes leaking out of several dump sites in and around the city. The most notorious of the dump sites is the Love Canal, a neighborhood built on a Hooker landfill, which was found to be so dangerous that hundreds of families had to be evacuated.

The Love Canal neighborhood with the Niagara River in the foreground. (*John Kudla/Niagara* Gazette)

The lawsuit, the largest federal suit filed against a toxic waste dumper as of mid-1980, attempts to establish that manufacturers are responsible for the disposal of their toxic wastes even if they have broken no statutory law. During the 1970s, as toxic wastes from dump sites caused damage to the environment and to humans living near them, the federal government passed increasingly strict regulations for the disposal of such wastes. Hooker and other chemical companies claim that these laws should not apply retroactively to chemicals dumped before the laws were passed—though in many cases it is these chemicals that are now seeping into adjacent land and drinking water supplies causing health problems.

The government is claiming that Hooker violated a number of specific waste disposal laws, but it is also accusing Hooker of violating *the common law*—a body of law that is not written down as statutes but which developed from a series of judicial decisions, the first of which dates back to English courts before the United States was founded. In this case the government claims that Hooker violated the common law of nuisance by dumping its toxic chemicals in landfills and allowing the chemicals to leach out and contaminate other areas. Calling a deadly waste dump a "nuisance" may seem like an understatement, but the term has a specific legal meaning—generally that a person cannot do something, even on his or her own property, that creates a substantial nuisance for neighbors. Under this common law, for example, one could sue neighbors for consistently playing the stereo loudly at night. In one landmark environmental nuisance case a New York Court of Appeals judge ruled that the Atlantic Cement Company near Albany, which spewed out cement dust that coated homes in the neighborhood, was creating a nuisance.

As of mid-1980 few substantial government suits had been filed against toxic waste dumpers, and only a few of these invoked common nuisance law. If the government wins its case against Hooker or a similar case based partly on common law, it could establish that manufacturers are responsible for dumping that took place before specific laws were passed and that dumpers are responsible for chemicals that leach onto property adjacent to dumps. Such legal precedent could also broaden the possible penalties the court could impose on dumpers. Statutory law usually imposes specific penalties—usually fines—on violators. Common law leaves the penalties to the creativeness of the plaintiffs and the decision of the judge. In the Hooker case, government lawyers are asking that Hooker be ordered to set up a $117 million trust fund to pay for, among other things, relocation and lifetime health monitoring for residents on the Love Canal and several other sites, insulation of nearby homes and a water treatment plant, perpetual monitoring of the soil, air, and water in the area, and the installation of barriers to prevent chemicals from migrating through the soil and groundwater to other areas. (The government is also asking for civil penalties of $10,000 a day for each day Hooker violated the Federal Clean Water Act and restitution of at least $7 million spent by the government for emergency remedial action.) In a separate action the State of New York filed an even larger lawsuit—$635 million—against Occidental and Hooker over the dumps.

The Federal Hooker case covers four dumpsites, at which chemicals including deadly carcinogens—dioxin, chloroform, and tetrachlorethylene—were disposed of from the company's chemical manufacturing plant. In addition to the Love Canal, the sites include a dump 200 yards from the city's drinking water treatment plant, and two others in industrial areas where the chemicals have migrated to nearby streams that ultimately pass through residential areas on their way to the Niagara River.

The action against Hooker is part of a blitz of lawsuits begun in the late 1970s by the U.S. government against creators of hazardous waste dumps. The Hazardous Waste Section of the U. S. Justice Department expects to initiate up to fifty similar cases soon under a new get-tough approach to chemical dumping. It should find no shortage of dumps. The U. S. Environmental Protection Agency estimated in 1979 that there were between 30,000 and 50,000 hazardous waste landfills in the nation—2,000 of which may be dangerous to the public or the environment.

C.F., M.P.

Treaty on Trial

Three little words written into an 1854 Indian treaty have provoked a bitter, decade-long battle over fishing rights and conservation more than a hundred years later.

The Nisqually Indians, in what is now western Washington State, gave up their rights to much of their tribal land when they signed the Treaty of Medicine Creek with the U.S. government on December 26, 1854. In partial return, they were guaranteed the continued right to fish at their usual inland and coastal fishing sites "in common with" citizens of the territory—a provision included in similar treaties signed in the region at the time.

But what exactly were the Indians' rights under the treaties? Were they granted merely a right of equal access to the fish "in common with" the territorial settlers? Or were those three nebulous words intended to guarantee to the Indians a portion of the annual fish run?

One hundred and twenty years after they were written, a federal district court judge decided the language of the treaties allotted the Indians roughly 50 percent of the harvestable fish passing through their traditional off-reservation fishing sites. Noting that at the time the treaty was made Indians outnumbered territorial settlers by three to one and caught most of the fish consumed by both themselves and the settlers, the court reasoned that the treaties were intended to protect the major source of the Indians' livelihood—fishing. The circumstances under which the treaties were made, coupled with the literal meaning of "in common with," dictated an equal division of the resource between the two groups, the court said.

In 1974 Washington's 6,600 non-Indian commercial fishermen were upset that half the harvestable fish in parts of the state were allocated to the 800 Indians who make their livelihood fishing. But the consternation was even greater among the 280,000 licensed sportsfishermen, mostly non-Indians, whose allocation of fish was also cut in half. State officials worried that the treaty rights would threaten fish management and conservation measures, drastically reduce revenues from sportfishing, and hurt the well-established commercial fishing industry.

A series of Washington State court decisions followed, which attempted to thwart the federal court decision. The state departments of Fishery and Game refused to enforce the federal orders and for a time the federal court took control of Washington's fisheries. Violence erupted frequently between Indian and non-Indian fishermen.

Finally, early in 1979, in *Washington* versus

Washington State Commercial Passenger Fishing Vessel Association the U. S. Supreme Court overruled the state court decisions and endorsed the 50 percent allocation plan of the district court. The high court was quick to point out that "harvestable fish" meant those left after the necessary numbers of fish were allowed to escape for conservation purposes and that the state still has the power to regulate the amount of fish Indians take to ensure that enough fish remained for a breeding stock. About half the fish in question do not even pass through the Indian fishing sites and so are exempt from the order anyway, the court noted.

In a grudging, but somewhat conciliatory acceptance of the Supreme Court decision, the Washington State Supreme Court late in 1979 ordered the state to begin allocating the fish runs and it appeared that the state would comply.

C.F.

THE TELLICO DAM

In 1979 the snail darter, a three-inch-long member of the perch family, had been known to exist for six years. But in those six years the fish became the symbol of an incredible legal, political, and financial whirlpool that involved farmers, Indians, environmentalists, lawyers, politicians, bureaucrats, the U. S. Supreme Court, the U. S. Congress, and the U. S. President. The controversy precipitated a landmark court decision, but ended with a stroke of politics by which the farmers lost their land, the Indians lost their sacred grounds, and the snail darter may cease to exist.

The snail darter became a household word in the United States during 1978 and 1979 as newscasters reported the legal battle to halt construction of the Tellico Dam, which would destroy the last habitat of the snail darter, on the Little Tennessee River. Most of the stories carried headlines on the order of: "Little Fish Stops Big Dam." Environmentalism has gone too far, responded many businessmen and politicians, when federal law (the U. S. Endangered Species Act) can stop "progress" for the sake of a tiny, obscure fish.

That was the very surface of the Tellico Dam story, much of which, despite extensive coverage, remains untold. The story of the snail darter is only one fascinating chapter in the story of the dam.

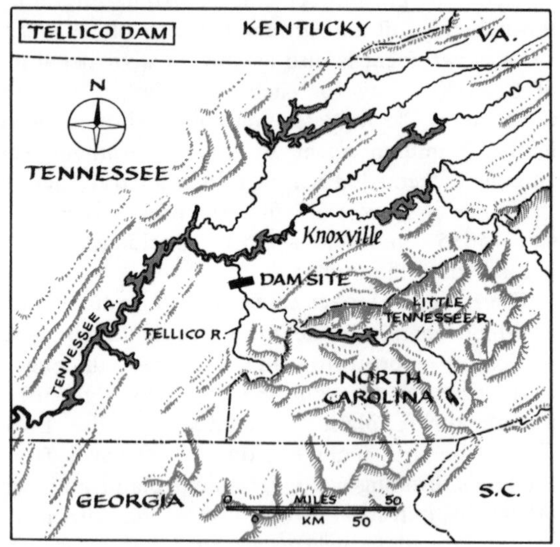

Minor Dam, Major Controversy

The legal battle to halt the dam began six years before the snail darter was discovered. Tellico Dam was one of sixty-nine dam projects born during the depression of the 1930s to provide hydroelectric power to rural homes and to attract industry to eastern Tennessee. The dams, constructed along various tributaries of the Tennessee River, were administered by the Tennessee Valley Authority (TVA). The other dams were built, but Tellico lagged behind. It was a minor dam, containing no generating capacity, but intended to slightly increase water flow to another dam with a generator downstream. However, it would create a reservoir and the TVA envisioned the land around the reservoir as valuable for industry and recreation. It justified the project economically based on revenues from the sale of this land. Tellico was funded in 1966 and construction began the following year. Three years later citizen groups filed suit claiming that TVA had not complied with the National Environmental Policy Act's requirement for a detailed study of possible environmental impacts of the project. The basis of the suit was a technicality: the citizens knew the environmental effects. The project would flood 16,000 acres (5,000 hectares) of rich farmland and condemn 38,000 acres (15,000 hectares), displacing two hundred farmers whose families had been there for generations. It would flood fourteen historically and archaeologically important Cherokee Indian village and meeting sites, including one called Tanasi which was the capital of the Cherokee nation until 1725 and from which the State of Tennessee took its name. It would dam the last free-flowing river in that section of the state. For what? The amount of power generated by increasing the flow of water to the downstream dam was equivalent to 22.8 megawatts, less than one tenth of 1 percent of the annual power generated by TVA. Only $5 million of the $150 million project was needed to build the dam. Most of the remaining money was to purchase surrounding land and build roads. But no industries were lined up to locate at the new reservoir and opponents pointed out that there were twenty-four similar reservoirs within 60 miles (100 kilometers) of the Tellico Dam site. A subsequent land-use study showed the area could employ more people without the dam than with it by sticking to agriculture and by attracting tourists to the river, a rarity in that heavily dammed area.

Construction continued. In mid-August 1973, Professor David Etnier, an ichthyologist at the University of Tennessee, and a former graduate student were fish collecting in the Little Tennessee River. Etnier noticed a slender, brown and gold fish—drab, but unfamiliar—swimming near the sandy bottom. After months of further collections and identification he classified it as a new species, Percina Tanasi (*Percina* for the perch family and *Tanasi* in honor of the Cherokee capital)—commonly called the snail darter, since it was a darter that fed on snails.

Darting and Bulldozing Ahead

The fish had once bred throughout several tributaries to the Tennessee River, ichthyologists postulated, but had disappeared as the rivers were dammed. None could be found outside the Little Tennessee. In 1976 the snail darter was placed on the Endangered Species list, providing citizens opposing the dam with a new legal tool. The act flatly states that no project can knowingly eliminate a species. Zygmunt Plater, law professor and volunteer attorney for the citizens group, filed suit and asked for an injunction to halt work pending the outcome of the case. But between the time he was denied an injunction in U. S. District Court and the time he was allowed to argue before the U. S. Appeals Court, the TVA stepped up its land-clearing effort, bulldozing throughout the area, including the ancient, sacred sites of Tanasi.

During the last half of the 1970s Plater was consumed by the Tellico case, preparing legal papers, arguing the case all the way to the nation's highest court, trying to convince the news media that there was more to the case than a small, drab fish, and arguing with other environmentalists who begged him to stop the case fearing that if he lost, the Endangered Species Act would be gutted.

"We thought long and hard before filing the lawsuit," Plater said. "If it was just the fish alone, perhaps Tellico wouldn't have been a wise case with which to test the Endangered Species Act. But we had all the biological and economic common sense on our side. A lot of environmentalists are still understandably bitter that we brought the case."

The Public Be Dammed

How Plater and the Tellico opponents lost is a lesson in politics. They won in the U. S. Supreme Court. But as a result of the decision Congress amended the Endangered Species Act to create a seven-member committee to settle "unresolvable" cases in which an endangered species stood in the way of a construction project. The committee was charged to seriously consider all alternatives, but to balance the merits of the endangered species against the benefits of the project. In 1978 Tellico opponents won again as the committee unanimously decided that the dam could not be justified economically. Not only was the entire $150-million project uneconomical, but even the cost of finishing it, with the dam already 95 percent complete, was uneconomical, they concluded. They won twice more in Congress by blocking attempts by Tennessee congressmen to exempt the Tellico project from the committee's ruling.

But ultimately they lost. In late summer 1979, Tennessee Senator Howard Baker, then a candidate for the Republican presidential nomination, and Representative John Duncan slipped an amendment on the 1980 Public Works Appropriations bill, exempting the Tellico Dam from the Endangered Species Act and five other federal laws the TVA admitted the project violated. In September, President Jimmy Carter, who had earlier opposed the dam, signed the bill into law. Just after he signed it, Carter called Plater and several other leading environmentalists who had opposed the dam to explain. He didn't like to do it, he said, but he was trading the Tellico Dam for congressional votes on two other concerns: the Panama Canal treaty and the creation of a Department of Education. It was the first time, Plater pointed out, that a public official had made a conscious decision to risk extinction of a species.

How could a project clearly declared uneconomical by both the Committee on Endangered Species and the Government Accounting Office, uniformly opposed by environmental lobbyists and twice rejected by Congress suddenly pass? Pork barrel, says Plater. Land speculators in the area are very close to the political machine. A number of local politicians, real estate developers, influential business people, many of them alleged to be friends of Baker, had bought up land around the perimeter of the project area. If the TVA does bring in industry to that area they stand to make some money, he said.

In November 1979 the TVA closed the flood gates on the Tellico Dam, backing water up along a 33-mile (53-kilometer) stretch of the Little Tennessee River to create a lake 50 feet (15 meters) deep. The farmers had left bitterly. The Cherokees had failed in a last-minute lawsuit. The snail darter had been transplanted to a nearby river, but it was not known whether it would survive there. "There is an acid manufacturing plant nearby and a railroad that runs along the river," Plater says of the snail darters' new habitat. "Every so often a tank car carrying acid falls into the river. It appears that will have some deleterious effect on the snail darter."

Although they had biological and economic common sense on their side, Tellico Dam opponents were caught in a web of local financial interest, foreign policy concerns, and presidential politics.

M.P.

"What surprised me was not that we're an endangered species but that we're snail darters."

(*Drawing by Modell.* © *1978* New Yorker *Magazine, Inc.*)

PART VI

LIVING

13

Eating, Drinking, and Breathing

Fresh, wholesome food; clear water; crisp, clean air—the essentials of life. These humble pleasures, which all people should be able to enjoy, are becoming increasingly difficult to find. "Health food" is now distinguished from "food" as each day brings new warnings of the dangers of eating. Much of the world lacks clean drinking water. Air quality is improving in some places, but continues to decline in others.

Frightening headlines have appeared regularly in newspapers for the past few years, at first alarming us but increasingly just dulling our sensibilities. We have heard so many warnings, we no longer respond. The 1979 attempt of the U. S. Food and Drug Administration (FDA) to ban saccharin as a possible carcinogen actually met with public hostility. The unending, and too often undifferentiated, barrage of warnings has made us cynical. If everything causes cancer, why not just enjoy? Why worry?

This chapter attempts to sort through the frightening headlines and put them in perspective. We also look at some stories behind the headlines: the concentration of power in the food industry, the inefficiency of the meat diet of the industrialized countries, and the waste of energy in modern agriculture—all crucial problems in the world food system. And we look as well at the threats to our drinking water through contamination and depletion, many of which are unseen and silent, with effects that are all too long-lasting.

Air pollution was one of the first noticeable effects of industrialization, and here we look at some of the large- and small-scale problems, as well as the personal and political action we can take to improve air quality.

Eating, drinking, and breathing are the activities essential to maintaining all life, and they must be protected from environmental abuse and thoughtless exploitation. We hope alarmism and despair can be replaced, however, with good sense and information.

K.F.

HOW TO MAKE A COW

The following recipe will feed a thousand people. It requires more than two years of preparation, some unusual ingredients, and a substantial amount of expense and trouble. But people enjoy it. The dish: an American cow.

Ingredients

1 80-pound calf
8 acres grazing land
1.5 acres farmland
12,000 pounds forage
2,500 pounds grain
350 pounds soybeans
125 gallons gasoline and various petroleum products
170 pounds nitrogen
45 pounds phosphorus
90 pounds potassium
pesticides
herbicides
hormones
antibiotics
1.2 million gallons water, to be added regularly throughout.

The first step is simple. Allow the calf to nurse and eat grass for six months. At the end of this period the calf should be weaned.

Cattle pens at the Union Stockyards, Omaha, Nebraska. (*USDA/Herman Postelthwaite*)

Continue to allow the calf to graze. At nine months it should weigh 400 pounds. At sixteen months it should be 650 pounds. Most of the 12,000 pounds of forage is eaten during this time.

While the young cow is grazing, you should be preparing the stuffing. Begin by using about 25 gallons of petroleum to make the fertilizer. (Each time you use this recipe, increase the amount of fertilizer.) Add the fertilizer to the 1.5 acres of land. Set aside the remainder of the gasoline to power the tractors and other machinery, produce electricity, and pump water for irrigation.

Plant the corn and soybeans. Prepare the insecticides and herbicides. It's hard to know how much insecticide to use, because many insects have developed resistance. Herbicide 2,4-D is the most popular in the United States, but it now seems that it increases the number and size of certain pests. Some people worry about the harmful effects of these chemicals, but symptoms won't appear until long after the cow has been consumed.

Start feeding small amounts of the grain and soy stuffing to the cow at twenty months to prepare it for the feedlot stage.

At the end of twenty-four months you are ready for the crucial stage, which will transform your lean cow into a luscious, fat-marbled piece of meat. Squeeze the cow into a feedlot with perhaps 200,000 other cattle. Since the purpose of the feedlot is eating, give the cow some MGA to kill its sex drive, which can be distracting. Feed the cow all the remaining stuffing of grain and soy, mixed with some roughage. It will gain as much as 2 pounds a day.

A potential problem arises at this point. Disease can spread quickly among so many cattle living in such proximity and mired in their own waste, but antibiotics mixed into the stuffing should protect them. Another problem: the waste itself, which your animal has been creating each day at a rate equivalent to that of twenty people. The waste can be used to make methane, or recycled to produce feed for other livestock, or used as fertilizer, but most people simply allow it to leach into groundwater or to wash into streams and rivers.

After four months in the feedlot your cow weighs about 1,000 pounds and is ready for slaughter. Cut away all the inedible parts, and you will have about 440 pounds of meat—a thousand 7-ounce servings. Unfortunately, not all this will be steak. In fact, only 16 pounds will be T-bone steak. The rest will be pot roast, chuck, stew meat, and other less cherished cuts, but enough for a good meal for a thousand people. If you are in the mood for something simpler, you could just bake the 2,500 pounds of grain and the 350 pounds of soybeans into bread and casseroles (add a few vegetables). With this recipe you can feed 18,000 people each a one-cup serving.

K.F.

MEAT FACTS

- One third of the world's grain is fed to livestock, but animal foods account for only one tenth of the world's caloric intake.
- The world produces enough grain to provide every person with 2 pounds (almost 1 kilogram) of grain a day, which would provide 3,000 calories.
- In the United States, about two thirds of the harvested acreage is used to grow food for livestock.
- Western developed nations export 3 million metric tons of grain protein to underdeveloped nations and import 4 million metric tons of protein in oilseeds and fish from these countries. Most of the oilseeds and fish is fed to livestock.
- One third of Africa's protein-rich peanuts end up being fed to European livestock.
- To produce 1 pound (.45 kilogram) of meat protein, one must feed cattle 16 pounds (7.2 kilograms) of grain; pigs, 6 pounds (2.7 kilograms) of grain; turkeys, 4 pounds (1.8 kilograms); and chickens, 3 pounds (1.4 kilograms).
- To feed the entire world an average American diet would require twice the world's existing arable land and 80 percent of the world's energy.

K.F.

Wall-to-wall nine-week-old chickens, specially bred as "meat-type birds." (*USDA*)

"WE DO NOT DISCUSS SOYBEANS ON THESE PREMISES, MRS. GROMMET."

(© *1980 by Sidney Harris*)

THE OIL DIET

The most frequently and proudly quoted statistic of U.S. agribusiness is the increase in output per farmer. A single farmer could feed five people in 1900, ten people in 1940, twenty-five people in 1960, and about sixty people in 1978. Some of this increase in productivity can be attributed to advances in agricultural science, such as the development of new varieties of plants. Most of the increase, however, is simply the result of using more technology, more energy, and fewer farmers. Machinery powered by gasoline or electricity has replaced many workers. Fertilizers, pesticides, and herbicides, largely derived from fossil fuels, have increased yields while decreasing the need for human labor.

The statistics are misleading because they do not include farm support workers, many of them former farmers, who build the machinery and manufacture the chemicals; David Pimentel, director of a research project in energy use in agriculture at Cornell University in New York, estimates there are two farm support workers for every farmer. Nor do the statistics include workers in the food processing and distribution industries. Only the primary metal, chemical, and petroleum-refining industries use more energy than food processing.

Carol and John Steinhart, energy analysts, have calculated how much energy U.S. farmers use. Producing one calorie of food energy required less than one calorie of energy in 1910, about four calories in 1940, and almost ten calories in 1970. American corn production increased by 240 percent between 1945 and 1970, which seems to be a remarkable improvement in efficiency, but during the same period the quantity of fossil fuel used to produce each bushel of corn increased by more than 30 percent: technological advances resulted in a decrease in energy efficiency.

Farming, like so many other aspects of industrialized life, became increasingly mechanized and energy intensive during the years of cheap and plentiful energy. Recent energy scarcity will force the food industry, which consumes 15 percent of the fossil fuel used in the United States, to make major changes.

The problem with such a food system is striking when you view it in a global context. Pimentel estimates that food production requires the equivalent of 330 gallons (1,249 liters) of gasoline per person each year in the United States. In order to feed the entire world this way, 80 percent of all energy would be needed for food production, and if petroleum were the only source of this energy, all known reserves would be exhausted in thirteen years. Although this exaggerates the actual situation, it does emphasize the importance of energy efficiency in agriculture.

This John Deere 430 Diesel tractor consumes 70 to 80 gallons (265 to 300 liters) of fuel during a day of heavy work. (*USDA/David F. Warren*)

The Green Revolution of the late 1960s was an attempt by developed nations to help the underdeveloped nations produce more food. It saw only limited success because it encouraged farmers to grow high-yield hybrid plant varieties unsuited to local soil and climate, therefore requiring extensive irrigation, fertilization, and protection from pests, weeds, and disease. Labor-saving machinery was encouraged in countries too poor to buy fuel and already suffering from high unemployment. (See "The Green Revolution," page 177.)

America's faith in the virtues of mechanized farming has created problems at home as well as abroad. Farmers are encouraged to grow one crop and only one variety of that crop to facilitate mechanical planting and harvesting. This monoculture farming puts a severe strain on soil fertility, so more fertilizer is required. The traditional practice of rotating crops to rebuild soil has nearly been forgotten. A monoculture is also more vulnerable to pests and disease, thus requiring more extensive use of pesticides and fungicides. This vulnerability was apparent in the Irish potato famine of the 1840s and the leaf blight that destroyed 15 percent of the U.S. corn crop in 1970.

Many hybrid varieties are developed to work best with heavy applications of fertilizer and pesticide. Plants could be bred instead for qualities of hardiness and resistance, allowing a reduction in the extensive use of herbicides and pesticides, which are energy intensive and dangerous to health. Where the use of pesticides and herbicides is unavoidable, properly protected farm workers could apply them by hand and only where necessary, eliminating the wasteful application by machines, which must spray an entire crop. One application of herbicide to corn by tractor requires 18,000 kilocalories per acre; by hand this same process would consume only 300 kilocalories per acre. Cheap energy made spraying from planes and tractors more economical in the past, but this situation is quickly changing. Integrated pest management, a method that uses a combination of biological and chemical pest controls, promises to use less energy and be even more effective than current methods (see page 31).

Nitrogen fertilizer accounts for the single largest energy expenditure on the farm. Pimentel has estimated the energy savings with different types of fertilizer. Manure fertilizer from a nearby source, less than a mile (1.6 kilometers) away, requires less than a third of the energy of chemical fertilizer. Planting a nitrogen-fixing legume crop will save even more energy. Although crop rotation is best, the legume can be planted between rows in late August, left in the ground during the winter, and plowed under in the spring. This method uses only 7 percent as much energy as chemical fertilization and helps prevent soil erosion during the winter. Both manure and legumes also help to rebuild topsoil, while the chemical fertilizer does not.

Faced with rising food prices, many Americans are growing some of their own food in home or community gardens. The potentials of this private agriculture are enormous. A substantial portion of the country's 19 million acres (7.6 million hectares) of private lawns, heavy consumers of fertilizer, herbicides, and pesticides, could provide a significant, energy-efficient source of food. John Jeavons, director of an agricultural research program in California, has suggested gardening techniques that use little or no energy and produce enough food to feed one person for a year on a plot of 2,500 square feet (226 square meters), the size of a large backyard, with only a half-hour's work a day. By comparison, American energy-intensive farming methods require 10,000 square feet (930 square meters) per person. Home gardens also eliminate the cost and energy consumption of transportation, processing, and packaging.

Food packaging uses about 10 percent of the energy in the United States food system. The average American purchases 58 pounds (26 kilograms) of paper, 80 pounds (36 kilograms) of glass, 42 pounds (19 kilograms) of steel, 8 pounds (3.6 kilograms) of aluminum, and 6 pounds (2.7 kilograms) of plastic in food packaging each year. Beer and soft drinks account for 43 pounds (19 kilograms) of glass, 16 pounds (7.2 kilograms) of steel, and 4 pounds (1.8 kilograms) of aluminum. Returnable bottles and recycling can provide considerable savings. Home refrigeration and cooking use more than 20 percent of the food system energy, which could be reduced through the use of fewer and more efficient appliances. For example, a frost-free refrigerator uses 50 percent more energy than a standard model.

Reducing energy use in the food system does more than save oil. Fertilizing with manure and rotating crops help slow the erosion of topsoil. The distribution of dangerous pesticides in our food, and in the water system, would diminish. The mounds of garbage that accumulate around us would be reduced. Agriculture might even be a source of more jobs for the growing number of unemployed.

The decreasing supply of fossil fuel makes an energy-intensive food system ecologically and economically unsound. We cannot afford to have food costs directly related to rapidly increasing oil prices. We need to find a better way.

K.F.

FOOD FACTS

- Half of all the trucks in the United States are used to transport food and agricultural products.
- There are about 80,000 species of edible plants, but only 50 are cultivated on any sizeable scale anywhere in the world, and that number is decreasing.
- Ninety percent of the world's crops come from only twelve species.
- Half of the nitrogen fertilizer used in the United States is applied to corn.
- It takes three times more energy to process and deliver most foods than to produce them.
- Eighty percent of the energy used in the United States food system is used to cultivate corn, wheat, and soybeans.
- In the United States, 49 percent of all fruits processed—grown, canned, frozen, packaged—are oranges.
- The transport of tomatoes within California accounts for approximately 25 percent of the total number of miles traveled by fresh fruits and vegetables in the entire United States.

P.D.

California tomato field planted on the contour. The fruit of fields like this is shipped throughout the United States. (*SCS–USDA/Robert Branstead*)

WHAT'S ON LAND THAT COULD GROW FOOD?

Only about 28 percent of the earth's surface is not covered by water, and only about 11 percent of this land surface is arable. Ironically, even with so little usable land available, much of the farmland that does exist is growing nonfood crops. Pictures taken by land-monitoring satellites from space show vast tracts of land growing tea, coffee, cocoa, flowers, sisal (a fleshy plant that yields a stiff fiber used in cordage and rope), and sugarcane—crops with little nutritional but high cash value. These export crops sustain many tropical nations' economies, but in the process make them largely dependent on developed, temperate zone countries—primarily the United States and the Soviet Union—for their shipments of daily bread.

Meanwhile, the developed, grain-growing countries, blessed with fertile soil and favorable weather, are slowly and steadily losing some of their best land to soil erosion (See "Topsoil," page 394) and urbanization. The U. S. Department of Agriculture tells farmers they are

Indonesian tea pickers, West Java. (*World Bank/ Thomas Sennett*)

edging toward the upper limits of land readily available for crop production. Other marginal land would require huge investments in irrigation or fertilizer to become productive. Globally, farmers stand to lose about 7.5 million acres (3 million hectares) to urbanization by 2000, according to the United Nations.

In their popular and controversial book *Food First* (Houghton Mifflin, 1977), Frances Moore Lappé and Joseph Collins argue that there is enough cropland to feed the world, but that people in less developed countries still go hungry because so much of their land belongs to the rich and the rich grow luxury "cash" crops for export to the middle and upper classes in more developed countries—a pattern established by colonial rule in the seventeenth and eighteenth centuries. Population control alone won't solve the problem, Lappé and Collins argue; even if developing nations could achieve zero population growth tomorrow, the poor would still go hungry unless the land were distributed to local farmers and cash export crops replaced by local food crops.

Do wealthy landowners in developing countries really control so much land for export crops? Statistics appear to bear this out. More than half the arable land in the Caribbean is planted with cash crops for export: sugar, cocoa, bananas, tobacco, coffee, and vegetables. In Guadeloupe more than 66 percent of the cropland produces similar export crops, in Martinique more than 70 percent; 77 percent of the arable land in Barbados is planted in sugarcane.

A pod of cocoa beans. Grown primarily in poor, tropical countries, cocoa is used to make soap, cosmetics, and nonnutritious candies and confections, most of which are consumed in wealthier nations. (*USDA*)

In Colombia, according to a World Bank study, most prime cropland is owned by absentee landlords who use it largely for grazing cattle. These landlords control 70 percent of the country's farmland but cultivate only a small fraction of it. And little of the beef raised on the land ever reaches the poor classes of Colombia. In the Andean region of South America, almost four times as much land is used for cattle grazing as is devoted to food crops, and the ranches usually occupy the best land. Much of this South American beef is exported to the United States.

Africa and Asia show similar patterns. Coffee production in Africa has increased fourfold in the past twenty years, tea production sixfold, sugarcane output has tripled, and cocoa and cotton production has doubled. All are export crops; none is produced for local consumption. In Bangladesh, only about 7 percent of the farms occupy 31 percent of the farmland. Here, in one of the most crowded countries in the world, two thirds of the rural population are landless or own less than 2.5 acres (1 hectare) per household. About one fourth of the farmland is worked by sharecroppers, who must give most of their crop to absentee landlords. In East Java, where cash crops for export are also increasing, the government requires that as much as 30 percent of the land be used to grow sugarcane. In less developed nations as a whole, production of luxury crops is expanding much faster than local food crop production.

Meanwhile, farms in developed nations face the threat of overdevelopment. Early settlers, when choosing a site for a town, used the proximity of good farmland as a prime criterion. As the towns grew into cities surrounded by suburbs, which often merged with suburbs of the next city, this carefully selected farmland succumbed to a network of roads, parking lots, and buildings. In the 1970s, the United States saw a shift in population from large cities to small towns and rural areas, where the pattern is repeated. As a result, the United States loses about a million acres (405,000 hectares) of farmland each year to development; that's slightly more than 4 square miles (10 square kilometers) a day.

Development pressure is especially heavy in sun belt states, where northern urbanites seek refuge from harsh winters and high fuel bills. California is at once the salad bowl of America and one of its fastest-growing states. By 1979, California's urbanization and suburbanization had spread over 20 percent of the acreage that produced food in 1945. Officials predicted that within seven or eight years another million acres of good farmland would be swallowed by pavement. San Diego County alone, according to local authorities, could lose 27 percent of its 200,000 acres (81,000 hectares) of good cropland by 1985. Despite rigid growth controls, county supervisor Lee Taylor admitted in 1979 that "agriculture is being phased out in our county, giving way to development pressures, and will soon disappear." San Diego is following the pattern set in most metropolitan areas; as development potential increases, land values soar, forcing up taxes. Farmers sell to speculators who subdivide and sell to developers. Everyone makes a profit, but another farm is lost. Government programs that give farmers a tax break if they promise to keep farming the land for a certain number of years have not managed to stop the bulldozers.

Yearly loss of farmland to urbanization is greater in smaller industrialized countries than it is in the United States. For example: The United States, .08 percent; Norway, .15 percent; Austria, France, and the United Kingdom, .18 percent; Germany, .25 percent; Denmark, .30 percent; the Netherlands, .43 percent; Japan, .73 percent; Belgium, 1.23 percent. If these estimated figures don't appear serious at first glance, think of them compounding every year for ten to twenty years. If the loss rates continue unabated, they could mean a sizeable drop in domestic food production, especially for land-poor countries like Belgium and Japan.

We are left with an ironic but serious situation: developing countries grow sugar and flowers for the tables of developed nations, but produce far too little food for their own populations. At the same time, the United States and other "breadbasket" nations pave over their prime cropland.

D.H. with F.W.

VERY SMALL FARMS

On a small piece of ground in California, a systems analyst is developing crop-raising methods that he hopes may revolutionize agriculture yields and bring hope to a world facing massive undernourishment.

By combining new tools and techniques with age-old organic farming methods, John Jeavons is harvesting crops at a consistently higher yield than county, state, or national averages for commercial agriculture, according to a report that appeared in *Science 80* magazine in November 1979. Many of his crops have produced yields four or more times higher than commercial averages. His cucumber crop has been nine times the county average, his zucchini squash yield is more than sixteen times the average.

Jeavons's methods, pioneered by British horticulturist Alan Chadwick, have drawn attention from such groups as the League for International Food Education, a consortium sponsored by the U. S. Agency for International Development. The method is being tested in several developing countries including Honduras, Colombia, and Indonesia.

Fundamentally, the technique includes cultivation of raised beds to depths up to 24 inches (61 centimeters) for drainage and aeration of the soil; tight planting to increase yield and provide a microclimate under a leaf canopy; planting several varieties for increased soil and plant health; lots of natural compost; and frequent light watering.

With tools he's designed to improve his methods even further, including a "U-bar" for deep cultivation, a bicyclelike thresher, and a new watering nozzle, Jeavons expects it will be possible for a person with a four-month growing season to raise a complete year's vegetarian diet on only 2,800 square feet (78.4 square meters) of land. In southern temperate regions where two crops per year are feasible, he estimates a need for only half that amount of land.

But it's Jeavons's predictions about the time needed to grow food that are the most interesting. He claims a person using his methods can grow a year's complete diet with only three hours of work each day. "By 1982," he said, "we expect to be able to demonstrate that it need take no more than twenty-eight minutes a day to grow a complete diet." L.B.

WHO PRODUCED YOUR DINNER?

At first glance the food industry seems to encompass inconceivable diversity and complexity, thousands of products, brands, farms, dairies, ranches, feedlots, processors, packagers, truckers, butchers, bakers, grocery stores, and supermarkets. The United States has 32,000 food companies. But closer inspection reveals that a handful of corporations control almost every aspect of this vast U.S. industry; fifty corporations reap about 75 percent of the profits.

The Del Monte brand name is familiar as the world's largest processor of fruits and vegetables. It is no surprise that Del Monte cans a large quantity of food, but that is a fraction of Del Monte's kingdom. Del Monte maintains its own seed farm and six research laboratories with a total staff of five hundred. Its fifty-five farms, ranches, plantations, and orchards encompass 132,700 farmed acres (53,700 hectares) in the United States, Canada, Kenya, Latin America, and the Philippines. Ten thousand "independent" U.S. farmers are under contract to sell their crops to Del Monte.

When the food leaves the farm, Del Monte's fifteen can-manufacturing plants and two label-printing plants supply its fifty-nine canneries, three dried-fruit plants, and fifteen snack-food, specialty, and frozen food plants. The products are transported by Del Monte's seven trucking operations to Del Monte's fifteen warehouses.

Del Monte is typical of the food conglomerates in the United States. United Brands, General Foods, Campbell's, Borden, Beatrice, Pet, Kraftco, and a few others are "vertically integrated" to control food production and marketing from seed to table.

The only other significant force in the food industry is the supermarket system, and it is also becoming vertically integrated. Safeway has 2,400 stores, 109 manufacturing and processing plants, 16 produce-packaging plants, 16 bakeries, 19 milk and 16 ice cream plants, 4 soft drink bottlers, 3 meat processors, 3 coffee-roasting plants, 2,100 tractor-trailer trucks, and 60 warehouses. Southland Corporation controls 4,800 small retail shops including 7-Eleven and Gristede's. And these are just the food companies. Giant nonfood corporations like ITT and Tenneco have also begun to enter the food business.

These conglomerates exert an overwhelming influence over food. They decide what to put in food and how much it will sell for. Although we might seem to have freedom of choice in our giant supermarkets, often one company has a virtual monopoly on a product. In the United States, Gerber sells 60 percent of all baby food, Lipton sells 70 percent of all dried soup and 50 percent of the tea, Campbell's has 90 percent of the canned soup business. Many other foods are controlled by a small group of corporations. At least 50 percent of the U.S. market for each of the following products is controlled by no more than four large companies: butter, cheese, milk, ice cream, condensed and evaporated milk, canned specialties, dehydrated fruits and vegetables, breakfast cereals, blended and prepared flour, biscuits and crackers, raw cane sugar, chocolate and cocoa products, malt liquor, distilled liquor, shortening and cooking oils, and food preparations.

Many small farms are under contract to sell their crops at a predetermined price to a food processor. Contracts cover 95 percent of the sweet corn, 92 percent of the broiler chickens, 90 percent of the snap beans, 50 percent of the cantaloupes and honeydews, and 95 percent of the tomatoes.

Because of their size and diversity, these huge corporations can afford to sustain large losses in one product or at one stage of a process in order to crush their competition—once the competitor is gone, they are free to maximize profits by manipulating prices. They also control the quality of food. The trend toward more highly processed and chemically treated foods is an outgrowth of the centralization of the food industry. Fresh food is perishable and expensive to transport. Large-scale, centralized food production requires ingredients that will not spoil and products that will last a long time and are easily shipped. Preservatives and chemical additives are crucial to this type of operation.

The food industry is able to conceal its concentration by using many brand names without mentioning the name of the parent corporation. Many popular, homey-sounding brands are actually subsidiaries of the food giants: Mogen David (Coca Cola), Hebrew National Kosher (Riviana Foods), Hostess (ITT), Hawaiian Punch and Chun King (R. J. Reynolds), Old El Paso Mexican (Pet, Inc.), and San Giorgio (Hershey). In addition, almost all the major U.S. food conglomerates also own restaurants and fast-food chains. Pillsbury owns Burger King, General Foods owns Burger Chef, Ralston Purina owns Jack-in-the-Box, Heublein owns Kentucky Fried Chicken, Pepsico owns Pizza Hut.

The following menus provide two ways of seeing the role of giant corporations in the food industry. The first menu suggests a day's diet that seems to include many food companies but actually involves only Beatrice Foods, which sells five thousand items under about one hundred different names. The second indicates how much of your food dollar can go to corporations that you probably didn't know were in the food business.

(For more information, contact the Agribusiness Accountability Project, P. O. Box 5646, San Francisco, CA 94101, 415-626-1650.)

K.F.

THE BEATRICE FOODS MENU

(All the foods listed below are actually sold by Beatrice Foods)

BREAKFAST

Meadow Gold Milk
Eckrich Sausage Links
Butter Krust Bread

MORNING SNACK

Milk Duds

LUNCH

Lambrecht Pepperoni Pizza
Rainbo Sweet Gherkins
Dannon Yogurt

AFTERNOON SNACK

Kitchen Fresh Potato Chips

DINNER

La Choy Frozen Egg Rolls
Rosarita Frozen Enchilada Dinner
Aunt Nellie's Pickled Beets
Kobey's Shoestring Potatoes
Louis Sherry Ice Cream

TV SNACK

Fisher's Mixed Nuts
Lowrey's Beef Jerky

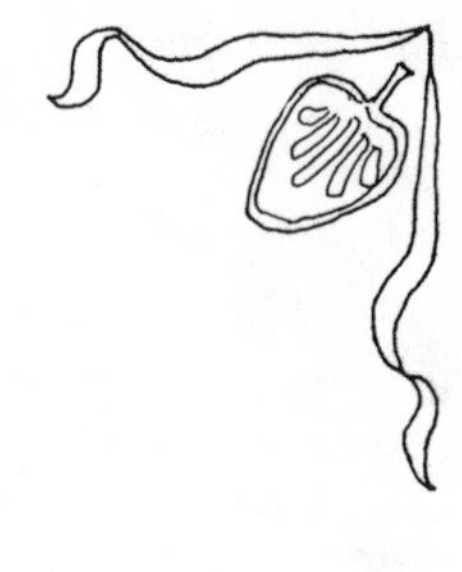

A CORPORATE MENU

APPETIZERS

Sautéed Mushrooms by Clorox
wrapped in Bacon by ITT
Salmon by Unilever

SALADS

Lettuce by Dow Chemical
and Tomatoes by Gulf+Western
Avocados by Superior Oil

ENTREES

Turkey by Ling-Temco-Vought
Ham by Greyhound
Roast Beef by Oppenheimer Industries

SIDE DISHES

Artichokes by Purex
Carrots by Tenneco
Potatoes by Boeing
Apple Sauce by American Brands
Deviled Eggs by Cargill
Olives by Zapata Oil

BEVERAGE

Wine by Heublein
Citrus Juice by Pacific Lighting Corp.

AFTER DINNER

Peaches by Westgate-California Corp.
Almonds by Getty Oil

SOURCE: James Hightower, *Eat Your Heart Out,* Crown Publishers.

THE MOST-SPRAYED FOODS

Each year 1 pound (454 grams) of pesticides is used on crops, parks, forests, and lawns for each person on earth. In the United States, 6 pounds (2.7 kilograms) per person is used. The UN World Health Organization estimates that half a million people are poisoned by pesticides each year, and five thousand die. Although developed nations like the United States have restricted the most dangerous chemicals, they do not forbid their production for export. More than 140 million pounds (63 million kilograms) of restricted or unregistered pesticides were exported by the United States in 1976. Though its use is banned in the United States, DDT is still produced for export and traces of it can be found on most coffee beans imported into the country. More than 800 million pounds (360 million kilograms) of pesticides are used in developing countries that lack the resources or expertise to evaluate their safety.

As pesticide use increases, so does resistance among pests. (See "Spraying the World," page 184.) Pesticide use is then increased or new poisons are found to fight these new pests. The following charts provide a picture of the extent of pesticide use, but they do not tell the full story of decreasing effectiveness, rising costs, and harm to animals and people. The alternative is a more limited use of pesticides, combined with sophisticated biological controls (see "Integrated Pest Management," page 31).

"Don't eat one of them—they're loaded with additives and preservatives." (*Reproduced by special permission of* PLAYBOY *Magazine. © 1979, by* PLAYBOY)

PESTICIDE USE IN THE UNITED STATES, 1976

FUNGICIDES, HERBICIDES, INSECTICIDES

Crop	*Percentage of crop's acreage treated with pesticide*	*Amount of pesticides applied (in millions of pounds)*	*(in millions of kilograms)*
corn	92%	239.1	108.5
cotton	95	82.4	37.4
wheat	48	30.0	13.6
sorghum	58	20.3	9.2
rice	83	9.0	4.1
other grains	41	6.0	2.7
soybeans	90	89.0	40.4
tobacco	97	4.7	2.1
peanuts	99	12.6	5.7

U.S. PESTICIDE USE BY TYPE, 1976

	Total		*Farm*	
	(in millions of pounds)	*(in millions of kilograms)*	*(in millions of pounds)*	*(in millions of kilograms)*
fungicides	110	49	43	20
herbicides	555	252	410	186
insecticides	350	159	208	94
	1,015	460	661	300

(Worldwide use of pesticides amounts to approximately 4 billion pounds (18 billion kilograms) annually).

SOURCE: "Farmers' Use of Pesticides in 1976," U. S. Department of Agriculture.

THE MOST-FERTILIZED FOODS

Although chemical fertilizers have been used as a supplement to traditional fertilizers since the 1860s, it is only since the 1940s that the developed nations have begun using them as a substitute. As a result, the traditional method of using manure, organic waste, and crop rotation to enrich soil has given way to excessive use of chemical fertilizers that require large quantities of fossil fuel in their production. The multibillion-dollar fertilizer industry, found primarily in developed nations, prospers with the development of new crop hybrids that are genetically designed to grow well only with massive applications of fertilizer. Unlike traditional methods, chemical fertilizers do not rebuild topsoil, thus each year farms become more dependent on increasing applications of fertilizer.

The accompanying charts detail fertilizer use by crop in the United States and total use in various parts of the world.

K.F.

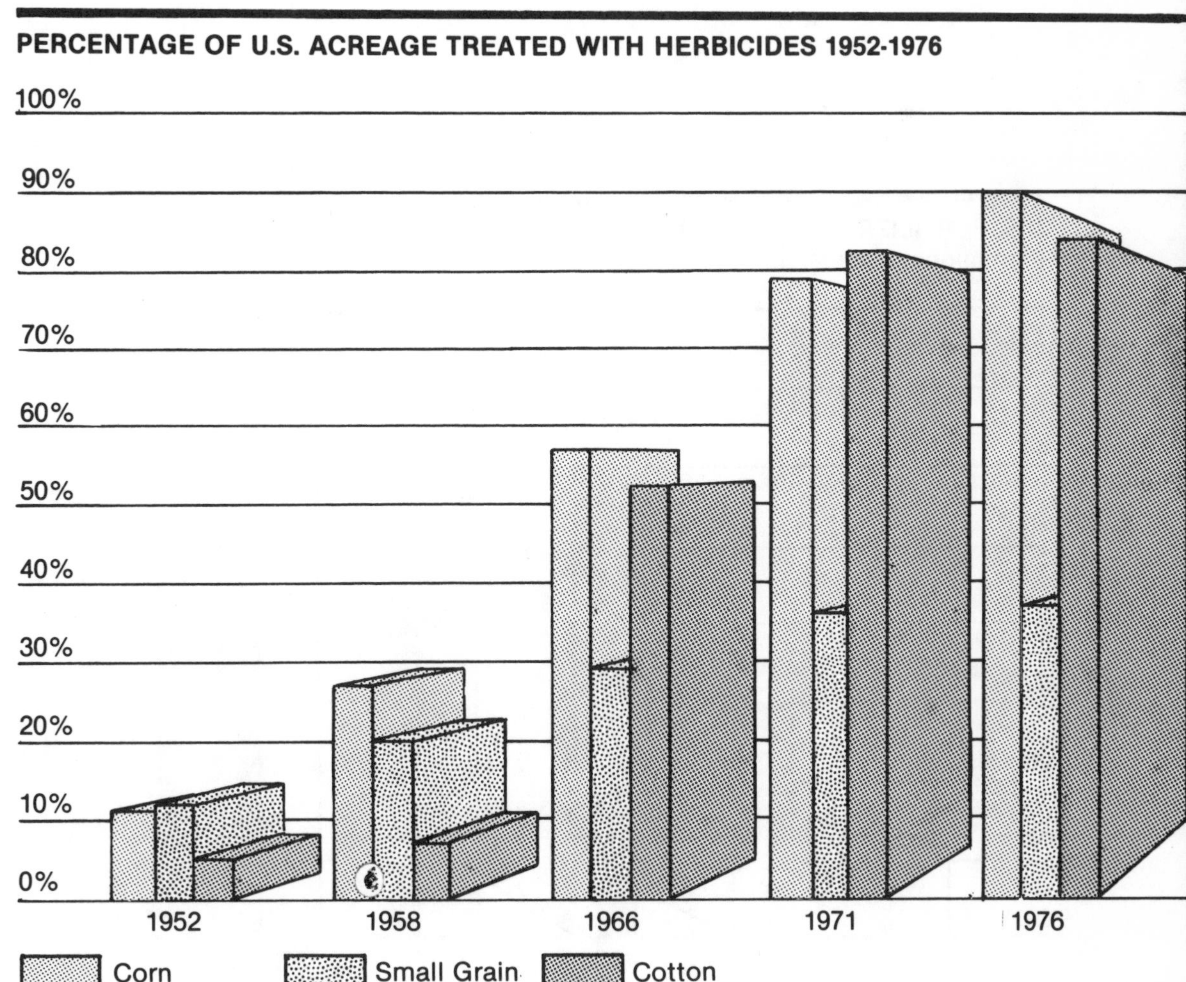

SOURCE: U.S. DEPARTMENT OF AGRICULTURE, *Farmers' Use of Pesticides in 1976.*

FERTILIZER USE IN SELECTED COUNTRIES, 1976

Country	*Fertilizer Use*	
	Pounds/Acre	*Kilograms/Hectare*
Angola	1.0	1.1
Egypt	192	210
U.S.	97	106.5
USSR	66	72.7
Ireland	448	489.7
East Germany	323	352.9
Japan	393	430.5
Tanzania	4.3	4.7
World Average	58	63.6

SOURCE: FAO Fertilizer Review, 1977, United Nations.

FERTILIZER USE IN THE UNITED STATES, SELECTED CROPS, 1974

		Fertilizer Use	
Crop	*Yield (tons)*	*Pounds/ Acre*	*Kilograms/ Hectare*
corn	11,834,744	385	432
sorghum	1,010,597	192	216
soybeans	1,728,123	241	271
wheat	3,270,880	169	190
cotton	1,673,987	343	385
tobacco	785,242	1,873	2,104
hay	1,462,985	290	326
vegetables	1,091,912	818	919
orchards	1,155,441	732	822

SOURCE: U. S. Census of Agriculture, 1974.

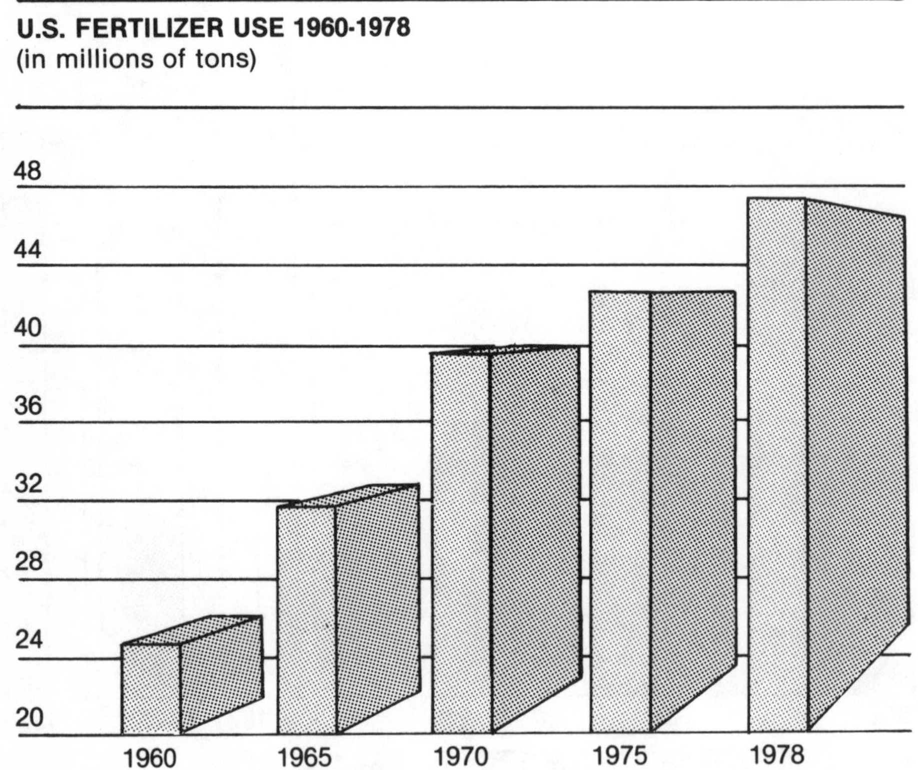

SOURCE: U.S. Department of Agriculture

Wavemakers:

WALNUT ACRES—FOOD FOR THOUGHT

It is the spirit of optimism that brought Paul and Betty Keene to their farm, nestled in a valley of central Pennsylvania, in 1946. The couple had little more than $200 and a team of horses. More than thirty years later, the Keenes' dream of raising fresh food and a family in the country "far from the madding crowd's ignoble strife," has burgeoned into one of the largest and most famous organic farms in the United States.

Today the farm, christened Walnut Acres by an earlier inhabitant, sprawls across 500 acres (202 hectares) the Keenes have acquired over the years and produces "without chemical or poisonous sprays" a wide variety of organic vegetables and grains as well as cattle and chickens. The farm provides many of the raw materials for the two hundred natural foods carefully produced in small batches at the Walnut Acres plant, which houses thousands of feet of refrigerated storage rooms, mills, food-processing equipment, cannery, office space, and a store. Flours, baked goods, peanut butters, cereals, soups, sauces, and stews that come from the fields and kitchens of Walnut Acres, as well as three hundred items produced by other sources (ranging from toothpaste to cookies), are shipped to 35,000 mail-order customers who are the backbone of the Walnut Acres business. It is a $2.5-million-a-year enterprise.

But to the Keenes and the seventy staff members who form the Walnut Acres "extended family," producing natural foods is more than a business. The 5-pound (2.25-kilogram) bags of flours and grains that line the shelves of the store are discretely packaged, each bearing a sprig of walnut leaves and one of a variety of quotations that represent the guiding philosophy of Walnut Acres. On

The early years. Betty and Paul Keene, their children, and other relatives, 1946. (*Walnut Acres, Inc.*)

Raisin Bran Granola: "If the doctor of today does not become the dietician of tomorrow, the dietician of today will become the doctor of tomorrow"—Dr. Alexis Carrel. On cracked millet: "Nature and wisdom always say the same"—Juvenal. The label on the jar of a peanut butter-coconut mixture echoes a similar sentiment, in Paul Keene's own words: "Here in the quiet countryside on our old farms and in the old barn, we do wondrous things in co-operation with nature."

At a time when fertilizers and pesticides are often considered as necessary to farming as soil and sunshine, the Keenes have found it "a blessing to skip over the age of chemicals." As Keene explains, "Instead of telling nature what we want her to do, we listen to her. That's the whole basis on which we operate."

Paul Keene points to the surface of a newly plowed strip of soil littered with enough stones to frighten away most gardeners. But nearby, thriving on the same rocky soil, which has never known chemical fertilizers, are rows of lush tomato plants. Keene turns over a rock and feels the cool, damp dirt beneath, an illustration, he says, of the benefits of "rock mulch," which helps retain the soil's moisture.

As for the tomato hornworm, the bane of many a gardener, Keene has never seen one. "If the soil is well-balanced, you get well-balanced plants. Insects will not grow and multiply to harmful levels," he says. As far as Keene is concerned, "This makes sense, it ought to work, and it does work."

The oats, rye, and soybeans growing on the hillside of a farm belonging to Walnut Acres are living proof of the success of Keene's methods. The Soil Conservation Service told Keene that the soil on the slopes was the poorest in the county, but over the past twelve years Keene slowly "rescued" the hills, with such soil-saving techniques as planting crops in narrow strips so soil wouldn't wash down the hillside, rotating crops, growing a mixture of grass, alfalfa, and clover two years out of four to let the land rest and, of great importance, manuring. A single year may see a thousand tons of manure added to Walnut Acres soil.

As a boy, Paul Keene did not aspire to the life of a farmer. But as a young man, the head of the mathematics department at a small New Jersey college, Keene was "stirred by discontent" and "the feeling that life could hold something better." He took a two-year leave of absence to teach at a missionary school in India, using every spare moment to travel throughout the country and acquaint himself with local people. He found his own goals seemed "incomplete and provincial" contrasted with those of the Indians, who led "a life based on the simple, elemental—some would say monotonous—kind of diet." But they worked out an accommodation to life and knew where they belonged in the universe. Walnut Acres is modeled on this philosophy.

Their life at Walnut Acres has not been without difficulty. As Keene puts it, "When you are dealing with nature you hardly ever know what's going to happen." However, in the same breath he adds, "It's so great to roll with the punches and be faced with solving the problems. That's the way life was meant to be."

The Keene's ability to roll with the punches was sorely tested in their early years at Walnut Acres. The surrounding community's antagonism toward newcomers flared at the arrival of the unconventional couple. Keene recalls a fiery cross smoldering on their property, threats of tar and feathering, and nights spent sleeping in the barn with shotguns. But he smiles when he adds that, "gradually you feel the change." Keene points to their founding of the community library, a Boy Scout troop, and his recent election as township supervisor as measures of acceptance by the community. As he drives the country roads, greeting neighbors by name and chatting briefly, it is difficult to imagine that there ever was any enmity.

One of the Keene's first major undertakings was making old-fashioned apple butter. The Keenes accumulated 500 quarts (470 liters) of apple sauce made from unsprayed but worm-free apples cooked and stirred over an open fire, then placed ads for their "Apple Essence" in the newly founded *Organic Gardening* magazine, now the monthly bible of many organic farmers.

Paul Keene remembers keeping the requests that slowly filtered in by mail in an old shoe box. After "Apple Essence" found its way into an article in the New York *Herald Tribune,* the shoe box overflowed. The Walnut Acres mail order business sprouted and grew rapidly as customers demanded more products.

Next came fresh produce—potatoes, carrots, beets, eggs, and even chickens shipped through the mail. Then marinara sauce, apple sauce, honey, and peanut butter, shipped to customers as far away as South America and Africa. Then, as Keene says, "The country awakened in the 1950s and 1960s. There was more demand than we could keep up with."

The Keenes incorporated Walnut Acres in 1963 as a cooperative that makes full-time employees stockholders who are granted more shares each

year. The same year they started the Walnut Acres Foundation, setting aside a certain percentage of their income, Keene says, as "a tithe owed to the surrounding community and wherever there is need in the world." Walnut Acres' customers respond generously with contributions. Among the foundation's efforts: relief in Bangladesh, a hostel for homeless children in India, and a community center in the village of Penns Creek. The Keenes take the same care in choosing foundation projects as they do in selecting products for their catalog.

The Keenes' "larger Walnut Acres family" responds to their generosity and homely style in kind. Tacked on the bulletin board in the rear of the store are letters from customers thanking the Keenes for "their beautifully expressed sentiments" and "quality products." The snapshots sent in by "family members" of their new-born babies, growing children, weddings, and get-togethers testify to the fact that in a world where millions are now spent promoting phony "all-natural" enterprises, the Keenes are the real thing. C.F.C.

THINGS YOU DIDN'T KNOW YOU WERE EATING

In nineteenth-century England, beer was hardened with sulfuric acid, and ferric sulfate was added to enhance the head; green tea was colored with a toxic dye; and bread contained alum, chalk, and carbonates of magnesium of aluminum. At the same time in the United States, copper sulfate, a powerful emetic, was used to make canned vegetables greener, while borax and formaldehyde were added to a variety of foods. No one regulated food additives then, but that changed in the early 1900s. As a result, today we *know* that our food is adulterated.

We have become accustomed to seeing ingredients listed on packages. We are no longer surprised to find calcium propionate or butylated hydroxytoluene (BHT) included in the list. We even accept vague references to "artificial flavor" and "artificial color." The labels would be far more difficult to read if the 31 artificial colors and more than 2,000 artificial flavors were actually listed. A single flavor of ice cream can contain as many as 55 different additives. In all, 2,800 substances are intentionally added to food in the United States. Not all of these substances are dangerous; many are safe, even beneficial in some ways. But there *are* hazards among them.

The additives serve four general purposes.

- Vitamins and minerals are added to replace nutrients lost in processing or as dietary supplements.
- Preservatives and antioxidants are added to extend the shelf life of products by inhibiting spoilage and discoloration.
- Emulsifiers, stabilizers, thickeners, texturizers, pH control agents, humectants, maturing and bleaching agents, dough conditioners, and anticaking agents are used in food processing to guarantee a uniform and reliable product.
- Flavor enhancers and colors are added to improve the product's appeal to customers.

Many of these additives, such as dough conditioners, do not have to be listed and are almost universally used. Some foods—ice cream is an example—are exempt from the U. S. Federal Food Packaging and Labeling Act that requires all ingredients to be listed. And food that is purchased in restaurants and fast food outlets (more than 30 percent of U.S. food expenditures) contains no list of ingredients. The purpose of all of these additives is to make it easier to mass-produce prepared foods, to extend the shelf life of products and thus expand their potential market, and to make life easier for people who don't want to bother preparing fresh food themselves.

Confronted with fearsome lists of ingredients, consumers need to know what to look out for. The safest approach is obviously to avoid foods with additives, which is not easy because many foods advertised as "natural" are anything but natural. Tang, with "natural orange flavor," does indeed have some orange oil extract added to its long list of artificial ingredients. Hawaiian Punch, with "seven real fruit juices and other natural flavors," is actually only 10 percent fruit juice. If you must buy food with additives, it is difficult to know which chemicals might be harmful.

The Delaney Clause of the U. S. Food, Drug, and Cosmetic Act forbids the use of any additive that has been proven to cause cancer in humans or animals, and the U. S. Food and Drug Administration does exercise control over the use of additives, but many scientists believe that it is not sufficiently strict. The Center for Science in the Public Interest has classified food additives according to their relative safety. The following lists will help you to select among processed foods without getting a degree in chemistry.

(For more information, contact The Center for Science in the Public Interest, 1757 S Street NW, Washington, D.C. 20009, 202-332-4250.)

K.F.

FOOD ADDITIVES TO AVOID

(Poorly tested and potentially dangerous)

Blue #1 (artificial coloring) — beverages, candy, baked goods

Blue #2 (artificial coloring) — pet food, beverages, candy

Citrus red #2 (artificial coloring) — skin of some Florida oranges

Green #3 (artificial coloring) — candy, beverages

Orange B (artificial coloring) — hot dogs

Red #3 (artificial coloring) — cherries in fruit cocktail, candy, baked goods

Red #40 (artificial coloring) — soft drinks, candy, gelatin desserts, pastry, pet food, sausage

Yellow #5 (artificial coloring) — gelatin desserts, candy, pet food, baked goods

Brominated vegetable oil or **BCO** (emulsifier, clouding agent) — soft drinks

Butylated hydroxytoluene or **BHT** (antioxidant) — cereals, chewing gum, potato chips, oils

"DO YOU REALIZE WE'VE JUST PROVEN THAT FOOD CAUSES CANCER?"

Quinine (flavoring) — tonic water, quinine water, bitter lemon

Saccharin (synthetic sweetener) — diet products

Sodium nitrate (preservative, coloring, flavoring)—bacon, ham, hot dogs, luncheon meats, smoked fish, corned beef

FOOD ADDITIVES TO USE CAUTIOUSLY

(Poorly tested and may be unsafe, or present in foods we eat too much of)

Yellow #6 (artificial coloring) — beverages, sausage, baked goods, candy, gelatin

Butylated hydroxyanisole or **BHA** (antioxidant) — cereals, chewing gum, potato chips, vegetable oil

Corn syrup (sweetener, thickener) — candy, toppings, syrups, snack foods, imitation dairy foods

Dextrose, glucose, or **corn sugar** (sweetener, coloring agent) — bread, caramel, soft drinks, cookies, many other foods

Heptyl paraben (preservative) — beer

Hydrogenated vegetable oil (source of oil or fat) — margarine, many processed foods

Invert sugar (sweetener) — candy, soft drinks, many other foods

Monosodium glutamate or **MSG** (flavor enhancer) — soup, seafood, poultry, cheeses, sauces, stews, and many others

Phosphoric acid, phosphates (acidulant, chelating agent, buffer, emulsifier, nutrient, discoloration inhibitor) — baked goods, cheese, powdered foods, cured meats, soft drinks, breakfast cereals, dehydrated potatoes

Propyl gallate (antioxidant) — vegetable oil, meat products, potato sticks, chicken soup base, chewing gum

Sulfur dioxide, sodium bisulfite (preservative, bleach) — sliced fruit, wine, grape juice, dehydrated potatoes

ADDITIVES THAT APPEAR TO BE SAFE

Alginate, propylene glycol alginate (thickening agents, foam stabilizer) — ice cream, cheese, candy, yogurt

Alpha tocopherol or **Vitamin E** (antioxidant, nutrient) — vegetable oil

Ascorbic Acid or **Vitamin C, erythorbic acid** (antioxidant, nutrient, color stabilizer) — oily foods, cereals, soft drinks, cured meats

Beta carotene (coloring, nutrient) — margarine, shortening, nondairy whiteners, butter

Calcium (or **sodium**) **propionate** (preservative) — bread, rolls, pies, cakes

Calcium (or **sodium**) **stearoyl lactylate** (dough conditioner, whipping agent) — bread dough, cake fillings, artificial whipped cream, processed egg whites

Carrageenan (thickening and whitening agent) — ice cream, jelly, chocolate milk, infant formula

Casein, sodium caseinate (thickening and whitening agent) — ice cream, ice milk, sherbet, coffee creamers

Citric acid, sodium citrate (acid, flavoring, chelating agent) — ice cream, sherbet, fruit drinks, candy, carbonated beverages, instant potatoes

EDTA (chelating agent) — salad dressing, margarine, sandwich spreads, mayonnaise, processed fruits and vegetables, canned shellfish, soft drinks

Ferrous glucanate (coloring, nutrient) — black olives

Fumaric acid (tartness agent) — powdered drinks, puddings, pie fillings, gelatin desserts

Gelatin (thickening and gelling agent) — powdered dessert mix, yogurt, ice cream, cheese spreads, beverages

Glycerin or **glycerol** (maintains water content) — marshmallow, candy, fudge, baked goods

Gums: guar, locust bean, arabic, furcelleran, ghatti, karaya, tragacanth (thickening agents, stabilizers) — beverages, ice cream, frozen pudding, salad dressing, dough, cottage cheese, candy, drink mixes

Hydrolyzed vegetable protein or **HVP** (flavor enhancer) — instant soups, frankfurters, sauce mixes, beef stew

Lactic acid (acidity regulator) — Spanish olives, cheese, frozen desserts, carbonated beverages

Lactose (sweetener) — whipped topping mix, breakfast pastry

Lecithin (emulsifier, antioxidant) — baked goods, margarine, chocolate, ice cream

Mannitol (sweetener, other uses) — chewing gum, low-calorie foods

Mono- and **diglycerides** (emulsifiers) — baked goods, margarine, candy, peanut butter

Polysorbate 60 (emulsifier) — baked goods, frozen desserts, imitation dairy products

Sodium benzoate (preservative) — fruit juice, carbonated drinks, pickles, preserves

Sodium carboxymethylcellulose or **CMC** (thickening and stabilizing agent, prevents sugar from crystallizing) — ice cream, beer, pie fillings, icings, diet foods, candy

Sorbic acid, potassium sorbate (prevents growth of mold and bacteria) — cheese, syrups, jelly, cakes, wine, dried fruits

Sorbitan monostearate (emulsifier) — cakes, candy, frozen pudding, icing

Sorbitol (sweetener, thickening agent, maintains moisture) — dietetic drinks and foods, candy, shredded coconut, chewing gum

Starch, modified starch (thickening agent) — soup, gravy, baby foods

Vanillin, ethyl vanillin (substitute for vanilla) — ice cream, baked goods, beverages, chocolate, candy, gelatin desserts

SOURCE: Center for Science in the Public Interest, 1978.

CHEMICAL CONSCIOUSNESS QUIZ

Can you match the product to its contents?

A Cool Whip Topping
B Country Time Lemonade Drink
C Listerine Mouthwash
D Dove Soap
E Gaines Burgers
F Carnation Instant Breakfast
G Massengil Disposable Douche
H Hershey's Syrup
I Kellogg's Frosted Flakes
J Hartz Hamster & Gerbil Munch
K Coffee-Mate Non-Dairy Creamer
L Sure Anti-Perspirant Roll-On
M Farmer John Liverwurst
N Fresh Horizons Bread
O d-Con Rodent Poison
P Schilling Imitation Bacon Bits
Q Herb-Ox Beef Bouillon Cubes
R Pepsodent Toothpaste
S Orange Juice
T Preparation H Ointment

1. Meat By-Products, Soybean Grits, Sucrose, Soybean Meal, Propylene Glycol, Wheat Flour, Corn Syrup, Soybean Hulls, Chicken Digest, Salt, Dried Whey Product, Calcium Carbonate, Water, Beef, Vegetable Oil, Mono Calcium Phosphate, Iron Oxide, Potassium Sorbate, Animal Fat (with BHA), Ethoxy-

quin, Zinc Oxide, Ammoniated Glycrrhizin, Vitamins, Calcium Pantothenate, Ethylenediamine Dihydriodide.

---

2. Corn Syrup, Water, Sugar, Cocoa, Salt, Mono and Diglycerides from Vegetable Oil, Xanthan Gum, Polysorbate 60, Vanillin.

---

3. Water, Sugar Syrup, Citric Acid, Sodium Citrate, Vegetable Gum, Natural Flavors, Potassium Sorbate, Sodium Benzoate, Vitamin C, Glyceryl Abietate, Artificial Color, BHA.

---

4. Sodium Cocoyl Isethionate, Stearic Acid, Sodium Tallowate, Water, Sodium Isethionate, Coconut Acid, Sodium Stearate, Sodium Dodecylbenzenesulfonate, Sodium Cocoate, Fragrance, Salt, Titanium Dioxide.

---

5. Live Yeast Cell Deriviate, Shark Liver Oil, Phenylmercuric Nitrate.

---

6. Soy Flour, Vegetable Oil, Salt, Natural and Artificial Flavors, Caramel, FD&C Red No. 3, BHA, BHT.

---

7. Milled Corn, Sugar, Salt, Malt Flavoring, Vitamins, BHA.

---

8. Hydrolyzed Vegetable Protein, Salt, Sugar, Onion, Autolyzed Yeast, Beef Fat, Malto-Dextrin, Celery, Caramel, Beef Extract, Disodium Inosinate, Disodium Guanylate.

---

9. Zirconium-Aluminum-Glycine-Hydroxychloride Complex, Water, PEG-40 Stearate, Glyceryl Stearate, Glycerin, Refined Paraffin, Isopropyl Palmitate, Magnesium Aluminum Silicate, Fragrance.

---

10. Non-Fat Dry Milk, Sugar, Cocoa, Corn Syrup Solids, Lactose, Isolated Soy Protein, Sodium Caseinate, Lecithin, Magnesium Hydroxide, Ammonium Carrageenan, Artificial Flavors, Sodium Ascorbate, Ferric Orthophosphate, Vitamin E Acetate, Vitamin A Palmitate, Niacinamide, Copper Gluconate, Zinc Oxide, Calcium Pantothenate, Thiamine Mononitrate, Pyridoxine Hydrochloride, Folic Acid.

---

11. Water, Hydrogenated Coconut and Palm Kernel Oils, Sugar, Corn Syrup, Sodium Caseinate, Dextrose, Natural and Artificial Flavors, Polysorbate 60, Sorbitan Monostearate, Xanthan Gum, Guar Gum, Artificial Color.

---

12. Pork, Pork Livers, Pork Snouts, Bacon (cured with Water, Salt, Sodium Phosphate, Soy Sauce, Flavoring, Sodium Erythorbate, Sodium Nitrate), Salt, Corn Syrup, Spices, Flavoring, Hydrolyzed Vegetable Protein, Monosodium Glutamate, Sodium Nitrate.

---

13. Corn Meal, Vegetable Oil, Artificial Meat Flavors, Salt, Artificial Coloring.

---

14. Water, Alcohol, Thymol, Eucalyptol, Methyl Salicylate, Menthol, Benzoic Acid, Poloxamer 407, Caramel.

---

15. Corn Syrup Solids, Partially Hydrogenated Vegetable Oil, Sodium Caseinate, Mono and Diglycerides, Dipotassium Phosphate, Artificial Flavorings and Colors.

---

16. Orange Juice

---

17. Water, SD Alcohol 40, Lactic Acid, Sodium Lactate, Octoxynol-9, Cetylpyridinium Chloride, Sorbic Acid, Disodium EDTA, Fragrance D&C Red No. 19.

---

18. Homogenous Mixture of Cereals (Corn, Wheat, Rice), Wafarin.

---

19. Sorbitol, Water, Alumina, Hydrated Silica, Glycerin, PEG 32, Sodium Lauryl Sulfate, Dicalcium Phosphate, Cellulose Gum, Flavor, Titanium Dioxide, Sodium Saccharin, Sodium Benzoate.

---

20. Water, Flour, Powdered Wood Cellulose, Wheat Gluten, Brown Sugar, Yeast, Lactalbumin, Calcium Sulfate, Sodium Stearoyl-2-Lactylate, Mono and Diglycerides, Polyglycerate 60, Polysorbate 60, Potassium Bromate, Artificial Flavor, Vitamins and Calcium Propionate.

Answers: 1-E; 2-H; 3-B; 4-D; 5-T; 6-P; 7-I; 8-Q; 9-L; 10-F; 11-A; 12-M; 13-J; 14-C; 15-K; 16-S; 17-G; 18-O; 19-R; 20-N.

AQUACULTURE

There are still some unexploited fisheries and aquatic species, ignored in the past, that may be exploited if the world grows hungry enough. But for the most part the world's commercial fishery is approaching, and may have already exceeded, its limit. Even huge investments in far-ranging factory ships and electronic fish-finding equipment no longer produce proportionate increases in the overall catch. (See "Ocean Fisheries," page 376, and "Fish-and-Chips," page 226.) As our ancestors abandoned hunting on land and turned to agriculture as a more reliable and efficient means of supplying food, so we may someday abandon the traditional sea hunt to farm the oceans.

An Ancient Practice

Humans have been successfully farming a few freshwater species of fish for thousands of years. In 460 B.C., a Chinese scholar named Fan Li described how his people cultivated carp. A bas relief on the wall of a four-thousand-year-old Egyptian tomb depicts the harvesting of fish from a small, artificial pond. About the same time, the Japanese, Greeks, and Romans were successfully cultivating oysters.

In general, however, the development of aquaculture has been much slower than the development of agriculture. We are just beginning to understand the requirements of aquatic species in terms of water chemistry, temperature, salinity, food supply, and reproduction and their susceptibility to disease and predators. But in recent years aquaculture has made significant progress. In 1976, aquaculture produced about 6 million metric tons of fish and shellfish, compared to 600,000 metric tons in 1965. Aquaculture presents many biological and engineering problems, but it holds the promise of surpassing agriculture in the amount of protein it can produce per acre.

Aquaculture is most widely practiced in Asian

Fish ponds near Hong Kong. Government officials turned to developing fish ponds in the early 1960s as an effective way to feed Hong Kong's swelling population. (*FAO/J. Olsen*)

countries where fish is traditionally the primary source of protein. In India, the contribution aquaculture makes to the total fish supply is 38 percent; in Indonesia, 22 percent; in Japan, 13 percent; in the Philippines, 10 percent; in China, 40 percent.

The Aquaculture Capital

In total aquaculture production, China may exceed the rest of the world combined. Here, as in other Asian countries, the majority of aquaculture enterprises raise freshwater species on small-scale farms for markets usually no larger than a few families or a village. To the Chinese, the fish pond is considered an integral part of each farm. Each pond is stocked with a number of species to achieve ecological balance and greater production. For example, a single pond may have six species of carp, each with different habitat and feeding requirements. The grass carp lives near the surface and feeds on large aquatic weeds. The bighead carp filters out microscopic zooplankton, which are dispersed throughout the water column. The silver carp, also a filter feeder, dines only on planktonic algae. Meanwhile, the bottom-dwelling common carp eats almost everything. When the proportion of carp species is just right, the pond becomes self-sustaining. Almost every organic product in the pond is used as food. The metabolic wastes of the fish serve as nutrients for the algae, which in turn serve as nutrients for the fish. The result is one of the most efficient, low-cost, low-energy methods of protein production. One pond can support a very large and self-sustaining population; yields of 8,000 pounds per acre (3,600 kilograms per hectare) have been achieved.

The Problems to Overcome

The United States is showing increasing interest in aquaculture; already 99 percent of the rainbow trout consumed are raised on fish farms. Under controlled conditions, the fish grow six to ten times faster than in the wild. Catfish farming is also an expanding industry in the southern United States. (See "Odd Jobs," page 700.) But despite the capital and technology available, U.S. aquaculturists still don't get yields comparable to the Asian carp farmers. A productive catfish pond may yield less than half the pounds per acre produced by an average carp pond. Part of the problem is simply that feed costs are much higher for catfish and trout, which require a diet high in animal protein, while some carp survive well on planktonic algae. But most important, U.S. farmers are not yet adept at diversifying and controlling the ecology of their ponds. As a result, production is lower and more money must be allotted for nutrients and pesticides.

A different set of problems must be confronted when culturing marine animals. Saltwater environments are far more complex, hence more difficult to define and control, than freshwater. Though authors have imagined submarine "cowboys" rounding up pods of whales, the ocean is just too vast and complicated an environment to be fenced, farmed, or easily regulated. Most open-ocean fishes, for example, are unsuitable for aquaculture simply because they demand large quantities of food and much space for maneuvering. This effectively rules out some of the most popular fish species, such as tuna.

Health is also a serious problem in marine aquaculture: thirty diseases have been identified in oysters, at least fifty parasites attack sockeye salmon. In crowded pens the animals are even more susceptible to disease. Feeding marine animals can be particularly expensive because, as the young grow, they pass through a number of stages, each of which may require a different, sometimes live, food.

Liquid Roundups

Still, aquaculture of marine animals is becoming more successful. The simplest methods are undertaken in shallow marshy and brackish areas, such as mangrove swamps, where the young of many ocean fish species and invertebrates spend a part of their life cycles. A coastal farmer will dig out a pond, and mullet, milkfish, or eels, for example, will swim in. The farmer then closes the entrance to the pond, adds fertilizers to produce algae, and some months later harvests the fish. This type of aquaculture uses land that is useless for conventional agriculture; however, it could disturb some coastal wetlands, rich nursery grounds for many species, which are already under heavy development pressures in most parts of the world. Another disadvantage is the lack of control over breeding. The real aim of aquaculture is truly to farm animals, that is, to control the entire life cycle to maximize efficiency and production.

Most U.S. aquaculture research has been devoted to farming those marine creatures with the highest market value: lobsters, shrimp, salmon, and oysters. Lobster culturing is just now meeting with some success, since an inexpensive, fully adequate diet has been found. Shrimp farmers have also had success, since shrimp grow to marketable size within ninety days on a cheap diet. However, they have so far refused to breed in captivity, and the process of collecting egg-bearing females and then caring for the hatchlings during the first tenuous weeks of life is difficult and expensive. If captive breeding becomes possible, the shrimp industry will definitely prosper. Of all the attempts at aquaculture launched in the United States, oyster raising, for which the techniques were established and refined long ago, has been the most successful. Since oysters feed on phytoplankton and grow rapidly while fixed on the bottom, costs are low.

"Ocean ranching," "sea farming," or "culture-based fisheries" have already been successful with anadromous fish such as salmon, which travel up river to spawn. Hatchery-reared salmon fingerlings are conditioned in fresh water near the mouths of rivers before being released into the open ocean, where they complete their growth cycle and return to their "home river" to spawn. When the adults return for spawning, they are caught and prepared for market.

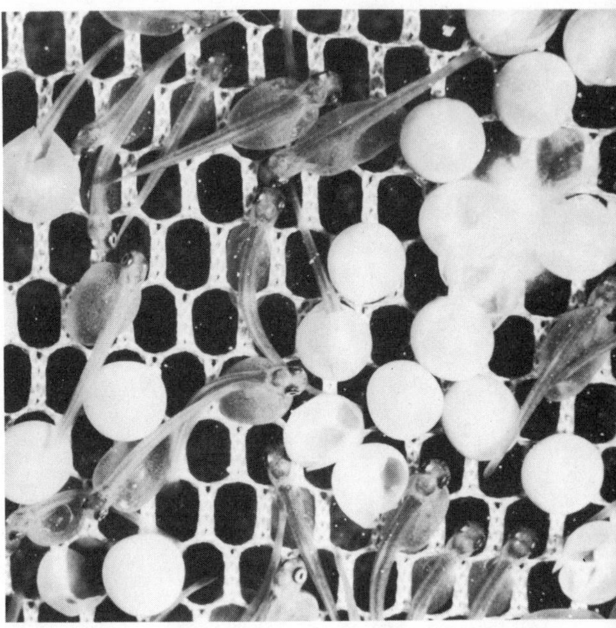

Young salmon fry emerging from eggs in aquaculture hatchery near Ketchikan, Alaska. (*Richard C. Murphy*)

Raising Food or Profits?

Overcoming the scientific challenges to aquaculture will demand huge investments of capital available only from governments and large corporations. Corporations may be attracted only to the high-profit species, such as oysters and lobsters. The real danger in this approach is that it bypasses the world's hungriest people in favor of the affluent who have developed a taste for luxury fish and shellfish.

Aquaculture provides a rare opportunity to make technology and economics serve the majority of the world's people. Aquaculture researchers should direct a large part of their work toward breakthroughs in the production of mass quantities of inexpensive protein, not limited supplies of expensive delicacies.

There is an old saying, "If you give a man a fish he will have food for a day; if you teach him how to fish he will have food for a lifetime." An aquaculturist might add, "If you teach him how to *raise* fish, he will have food for his grandchildren and generations of children to come."

L.W.

THE NEW ORLEANS COCKTAIL

The basin of the Mississippi is the body of the nation. All the other parts are but members, important in themselves, yet more important in their relations to this. . . . As a dwelling place for civilized man it is by far the first upon our globe.

"Editor's Table," *Harper's* Magazine, February 1863

The water of the Mississippi River system, including its main branch, the Missouri, is North America's greatest transport system. The river is burdened with human shipping, but that is insignificant compared to the natural freightage from the land. Across the surface of 40 percent of the United States, Mississippi-bound moisture loads up with nutrients, minerals, salts, and soil, as well as the seeds, eggs, and larvae of things commencing life and the dead husks of things de-

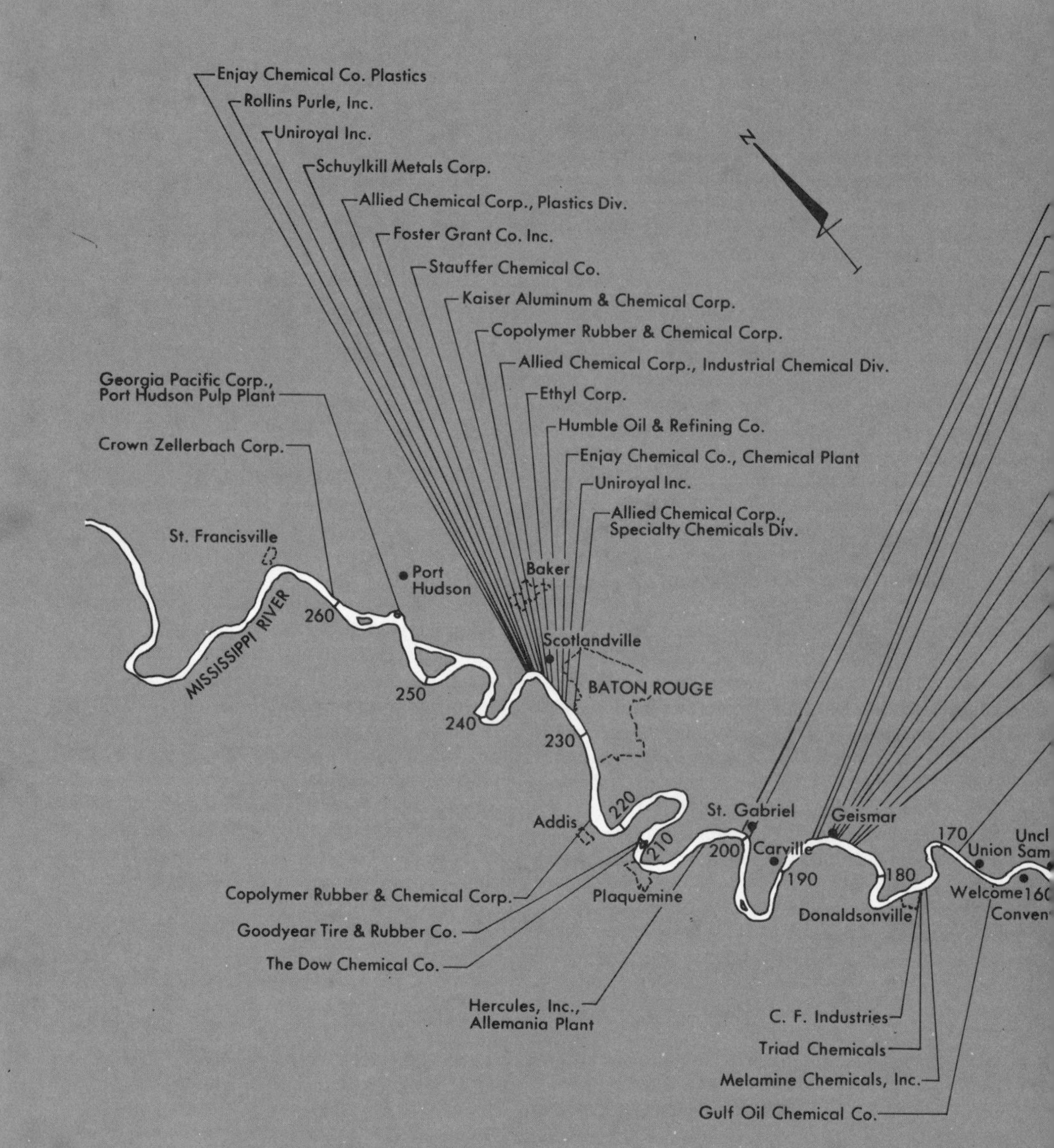
Enjay Chemical Co. Plastics
Rollins Purle, Inc.
Uniroyal Inc.
Schuylkill Metals Corp.
Allied Chemical Corp., Plastics Div.
Foster Grant Co. Inc.
Stauffer Chemical Co.
Kaiser Aluminum & Chemical Corp.
Copolymer Rubber & Chemical Corp.
Allied Chemical Corp., Industrial Chemical Div.
Ethyl Corp.
Humble Oil & Refining Co.
Enjay Chemical Co., Chemical Plant
Uniroyal Inc.
Allied Chemical Corp., Specialty Chemicals Div.
Georgia Pacific Corp., Port Hudson Pulp Plant
Crown Zellerbach Corp.
St. Francisville
Port Hudson
Baker
Scotlandville
BATON ROUGE
MISSISSIPPI RIVER
260
250
240
230
220
210
200
190
180
170
Addis
St. Gabriel
Geismar
Carville
Plaquemine
Donaldsonville
Union Sam
Welcome
Copolymer Rubber & Chemical Corp.
Goodyear Tire & Rubber Co.
The Dow Chemical Co.
Hercules, Inc., Allemania Plant
C. F. Industries
Triad Chemicals
Melamine Chemicals, Inc.
Gulf Oil Chemical Co.
N

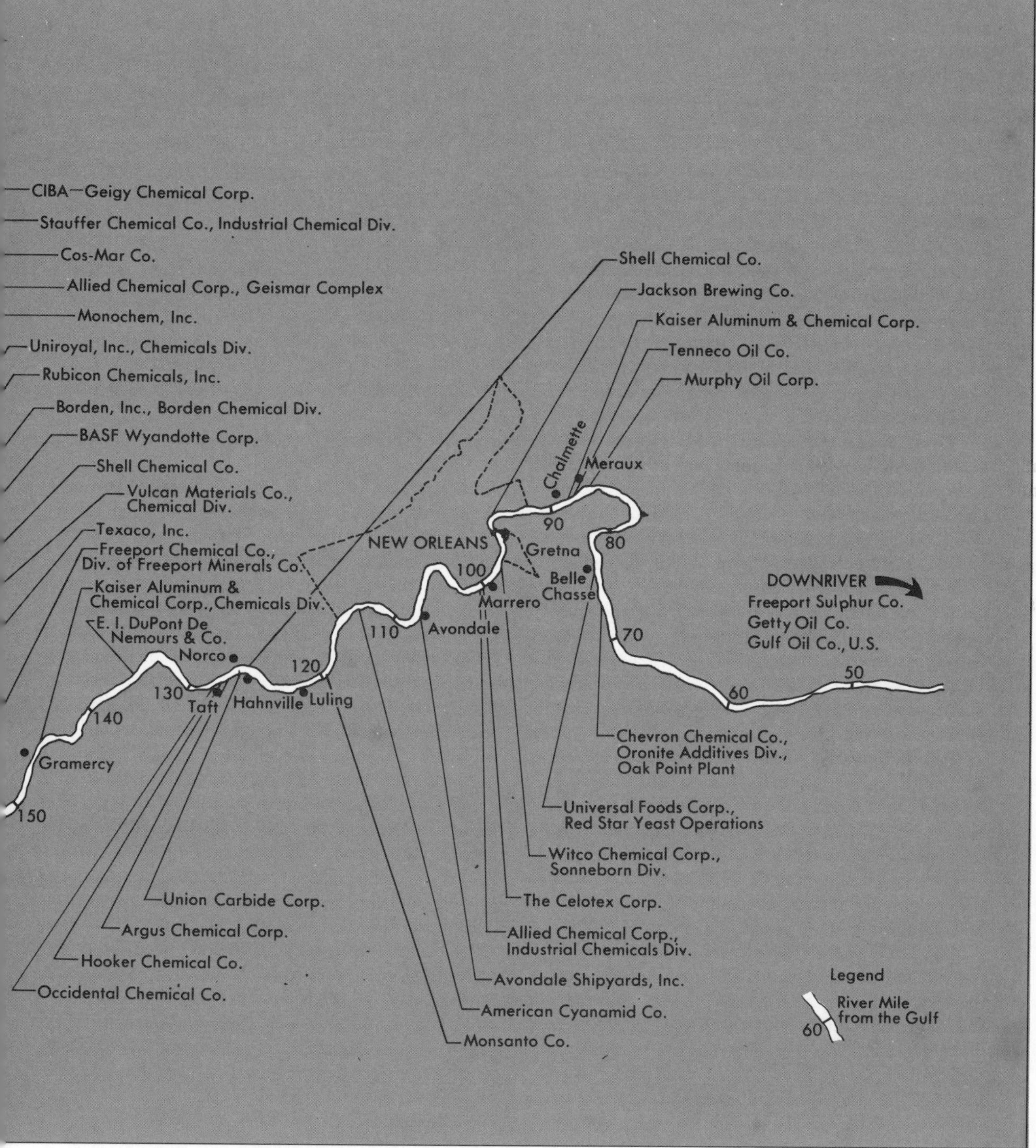

The mighty Mississippi carries the pollution of numerous industries. Near the river's mouth is the drinking water intake pipe for the people of New Orleans. (*From* Water Pollution *by Julian McCaull and Janice Crossland. © 1974 by Scientists' Institute for Public Information. Reproduced by permission of Harcourt Brace Jovanovich, Inc.*)

parted from it. This vast distribution enterprise has been under way for millions of years, leveling mountains, enriching the sea. In the past century, however, the waters of the Mississippi have become mixed with chemical debris from modern farms and waste matter excreted from factories and sewage plants—from the people and the industries processing along the Mississippi's banks the riches of the great Midwest farm belt, which the river helped to create.

New Orleans is the last major city along the 4,000 miles (6,437 kilometers) of riverbank in the system. Thus it is downstream from 40 percent of the nation, from a majority of its farms, factories, refineries, sewage outfalls, pulp plants, chemical laboratories. Yet, when the water of the Mississippi reaches New Orleans—laden with fertilizers, insecticides, feedlot wastes, topsoil, mine slag, dyes, acids, heavy metals, and industrial chemicals—the city pumps it into the municipal water system and the people drink it.

For decades now, New Orleans tap water has been notoriously unpalatable, but little attention was paid to its quality until recently. The water was yellowish, with an oily consistency and a strong taste. Some days it had an offensive odor. In 1967, markets had to stop selling fish caught near New Orleans because they had a repulsive taste. Experiments showed that a fish immersed in Mississippi water from the region was inedible within seventy-two hours.

In 1972, the Federal Water Pollution Control Administration identified forty-six organic compounds in the area's water. They found that several were toxic, and at least three were carcinogenic. Most troublesome of all, they estimated that their discoveries probably represented only 2 percent of the total chemical load. The Environmental Protection Agency (EPA) reacted by proclaiming that Mississippi drinking water was dangerous, especially for the elderly and children.

Very little attention was paid to these developments; the studies seemed to sink into bureaucratic murk. But in 1974 Dr. Robert Harris of the Environmental Defense Fund offered evidence linking New Orleans' drinking water with the city's extraordinary cancer rate, which is 32 percent above the national average. In response, the city health director claimed that drinking New Orleans water was no more hazardous than driving a car. It had probably never occurred to the average citizen that drinking city water could involve a risk comparable to traveling at 55 miles (88 kilometers) per hour on a crowded highway.

Since the Harris study, several agencies and colleges have conducted their own analyses of the river, ferreting out more chemicals each time. The number of proven organic chemicals passed one hundred in the mid-1970s, and a city official has predicted that the total may reach nine hundred. The three most common heavy metals found in the water were chromium, zinc (neither of which is clearly dangerous, although zinc is toxic to fish), and lead, which can be lethal in even a brief exposure to the human body. In 1970 one chemical plant in Baton Rouge discharged as much as 3,700 pounds (1,665 kilograms) of lead into the Mississippi on a single day. Under pressure from the EPA, the company had reduced its lead effluent to about 300 pounds (135 kilograms) per day within a year.

Among the chemicals detected in the river, several have been proven cancer-causing in laboratory animals: benzene, carbon tetrachloride, dichloroethyl ether, ethyl benzene, and dimethyl sulfoxide. Their effects on people are not yet fully understood.

Among the disturbing findings reached so far is the curious fact that some of the dangerous chemicals found in the drinking water did not come from the river. They were created unwittingly at the city water-treatment plant. Chlorine added as a disinfectant was reacting with other chemicals to create several compounds from the class called trihalomethanes, including chloroform, a suspected carcinogen. Ironically, the one action taken by the city to protect its citizens from contaminated water was further endangering them.

At the time of this writing, little progress had been made toward improving the situation. The EPA in 1979 proposed two new regulations, one to limit the use of chlorine in treatment plants, the other to encourage installation of granular activated-carbon filters on all city water systems. The steps are part of a national program by the EPA, since the problems experienced in New Orleans are common to many cities in the United States, although to a lesser degree. (One other site of severe problems is Cincinnati, where EPA scientists have verified the presence of at least seven hundred artificially introduced chemicals in Ohio River water.)

Meanwhile, regional EPA monitoring of river water continues, and when dangerous levels of a specific chemical are detected, those industries suspected of contributing to the problem are notified. Most of them respond quickly to suggestions that their effluent volume be reduced, but there is no direct control over their actions, and there are no proposals to regulate the waste chemical materials at their source, the factory and sewage outfall. An EPA chemist in Washington, D.C., ventured that it would not make sense to take such a step since contamination of the river comes from several other sources, such as accidental shipping spills and both urban and rural runoff. In the meantime, New Orleans residents wonder about the hazards of a simple drink of water, and on Bourbon Street tourists are encouraged to quench their thirst with alcohol and avoid the risk.

M.R.

A RECIPE FOR TAP WATER

Editor's Note: *Most municipal drinking water in the United States and many other countries is elaborately treated before it's piped to citizens. Although the recipe for tap water varies from city to city, the basic process is similar. Detroit* Free Press *science writer Judith Serrin describes how Detroit mixes a drink of water.*

Here is the recipe for the most popular drink in town.

Start with raw branch water, as in bourbon-and-branch. Drop it through a funnellike device. Shake it up a bit. Strain it to remove large impurities, like fish and trees. Add some chlorine to kill the germs. Add some fluoride, so the drink's good for your teeth. Funnel some more. Add aluminum sulfate to settle the dirt. Add charcoal, if needed, to kill bad tastes. Let set several hours. Filter it and add some more chlorine. Let set some more. Pour into a glass and drink it neat.

Total cost of ingredients: in Detroit, $1.83 per 1,000 cubic feet [28 cubic meters] for the first 10,000 cubic feet [284 cubic meters] a month, with discounts after that.

Number served: 4.2 million people, 46 percent of the state's population.

You've made yourself a drink of water.

The process is a bit more complicated than the recipe might seem. It involves chemists' manuals and federal regulations, not bartenders' guides. And even the most popular pub at Happy Hour could not compete with the demand that the Detroit Metro Water Department does: an average daily consumption of 169 gallons [640 liters] a person, according to 1975 statistics, served in ninety-seven communities in Michigan over 1,654 square miles [4,284 square kilometers]. There is, of course, no last call. In an average twenty-four hours, 695.3 million gallons [2.6 billion liters] of water are served. The record, set July 9, 1974, is 1.3 billion gallons [4.9 billion liters] a day.

The consumption is not steady, but rather comes in gushes and trickles. Water department charts, for example, show what are known around the department as "TV peaks," the surges that come when millions of consumers get up from their chairs at the same time, say during a commercial break, to get a glass of water or to use the bathroom.

One out of every 100 gallons [378 liters] of water that flows in the Detroit River, water department statistics show, is sucked into the Detroit water supply system. Most of this water is taken in at the eastern end of Belle Isle, where Lake St. Clair flows into the Detroit River, through what looks like an ordinary government building but is actually an ornate sieve.

Generally, according to John P. Kanters, water department director, more treatment is needed in the springtime than at any other time of the year. "It's due to natural causes," he explained. "You're getting a lot of runoff from snow melting and you're having heavy rains. You've also had a long period of time when the water's been moving a minimum speed under a cover of ice." The spring breakup stirs up the water, he said, and it picks up more than the normal amount of contaminants.

Detroit's water department is counting on its existing filters, plus the relative purity of the raw water from the river, to enable it to meet federal regulations requiring cities to remove synthetic organic chemicals from drinking water on the grounds that the chemicals may cause cancer. The alternative would be to install expensive activated charcoal filters.

SOURCE: By Judith Serrin, reprinted with permission from the Detroit *Free Press,* May 28, 1978.

NOT A DROP TO DRINK

While billions of people flush their toilets with treated tap water, more than a billion others have no safe water to drink. Millions more have little opportunity to wash themselves, their clothes, their food, and their utensils, even though such elementary sanitation could prevent deaths from disease. Nine tenths of the rural populations in the developing world have no access to safe latrines or sewage systems. This has an immediate effect on people's health, as wells become contaminated by fecal seepage. In rural India, for example, 70 percent of the wells show a high count of coliform bacteria, a condition indicating that more dangerous bacteria are also present.

A *harratin* (former black slave) draws water from a small well in Mauritania for cattle. (*FAO/A. Defever*)

Mining Water

Water is a tiny part of the earth's volume, and fresh water an even smaller portion (see "Water Facts," page 116). Most of the fresh water is locked up in the polar ice caps. What is left over is mostly groundwater—water contained underground, between bedrock and topsoil. Only three one thousandths (0.3 percent) of all the earth's water is available for humans to drink. All the rest is either too expensive to reach or unfit to consume.

The crisis of water comes about because, while human population soars and industry and agriculture use ever more water, the amount of usable water has not changed in most places. Where water is most abundant today, it is often so badly polluted, sometimes with near-permanent pollutants, that it is unusable as drinking water. (See "The Hudson River," page 327.)

Originally, nearly all humans drank surface water, from rivers, streams, and lakes. Now, however, many areas of the world get all their water from wells that tap groundwater supplies. There is far more groundwater than surface fresh water (more than eighty times more), and it is often purer than surface water, since it has been filtered through intervening layers of rock and soil. But groundwater has usually been accumulating for hundreds or even thousands of years, at very slow rates. In places all over the world people are now using up groundwater faster than it can be replaced—mining it as a nonrenewable resource, at least on a human time scale.

Running on Empty

In areas with little surface water, such as the western half of the United States, mining water is a common practice. Half of all drinking water in the United States is from groundwater; 82 billion gallons (310 billion liters) of groundwater are drawn up every day, mostly for agriculture and industry. Twenty-one billion gallons (79 billion liters) of this groundwater will not be replaced for many human lifetimes. The United States is increasing its groundwater withdrawals by 4 percent a year.

When groundwater is withdrawn too fast, all kinds of problems crop up. If the groundwater is near the coast, salt water may seep in, making the wells useless. Stream flows are often reduced, and ponds and bogs dry up. The ground may cave in after the water is pumped out. Of course, the biggest concern is that the water will run out.

In the world as a whole, there would be enough fresh drinking water for everyone if it were evenly distributed. But fresh water, like other natural resources, is spottily distributed. Most population centers grew up around a water source, but some devised elaborate methods to import water.

Los Angeles, California, and Phoenix, Arizona, grew to unnatural size because of long aqueducts from distant rivers. As the cities grew in their desert locations, they demanded ever more water, and now they sometimes suffer water shortages.

Irrigation is another technically unnatural use for distant water. Because of it deserts bloom—there are golf courses and rice fields in southwestern U.S. deserts. As water becomes more scarce and precious, our priorities for using it will have to be reexamined. We may have to go back to the "dry-farming" days of no irrigation, carefully selecting and breeding native desert plants. The cities in the desert may shrink as people move back to more accessible water supplies. We will certainly be more aware of water—and the need to conserve it—in the future.

WATER SUPPLY AROUND THE WORLD

Bangladesh

Bangladesh lies in the delta formed by the convergence of the Ganges and Brahmaputra rivers. The nation receives heavy rainfall during the monsoon season and seems an unlikely spot for a water supply problem. But since the land is flat, overpopulated and to a large extent deforested, floods are common. (See "The Himalayas," page 189.) The soil erodes in the monsoon season, and the people are too poor to fertilize it in the dry season. Although the vast majority of the people are rural, the countryside has almost no sanitation and most wells are polluted. Bangladesh finds itself in conflict with its neighbors over use of the rivers' water.

India

Most of India's people do not have safe drinking water within a mile from their homes. The supply of surface water is dependent on the erratic weather, and most rivers in India are polluted. (The major exception is the Ganges, which, because it is sacred to Hindus, cannot be polluted.) Most of the nation's groundwater is inaccessible to the small hand pumps of the farmers, so water near the surface is being used up quickly, especially in southern India. Poor sanitary habits as well as contaminated water supplies contribute to severe health problems. Even where clean water is available, people often collect it in dirty containers or put contaminated fingers in it before it is drunk.

Among the many waterborne diseases that are all too common in India are amebiasis and amebic dysentery, infectious hepatitis, severe diarrhea and other gastrointestinal diseases, fluorosis and bone deformations from toxins in the water, and endemic cholera, which periodically spreads from Lower Bengal to the rest of India.

Libya

In the desert nation of Libya, rich with oil, the water table in some coastal regions is falling 10 feet (3 meters) a year. The population of Libya is growing steadily, and the main water source is still the ancient aquifers, which yield mostly small amounts of rather poor-quality water. This overpumping has allowed sea water from the Mediterranean to seep into wells. The Libyans hope that desalting sea water will provide them with enough fresh water in the future.

Egypt

Egypt has a critical population growth rate, which is putting great pressure on its inadequate amount of arable land. Since the Aswan Dam was built, irrigation water has been plentiful—and also more necessary than ever, since the Nile

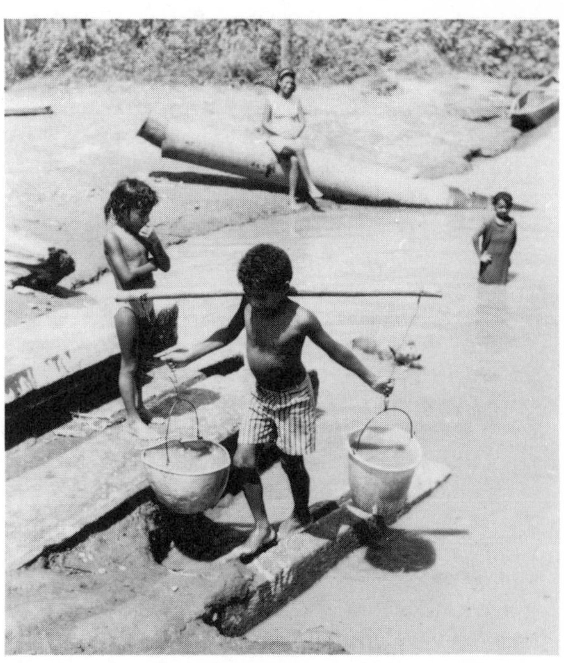

A young boy hauls water from a river near Santa Marta, Colombia. About 70 percent of the country's rural population has no access to clean water. (*World Bank/Edwin G. Huffman*)

no longer waters and fertilizes the fields every year with its flood (see "The Aswan High Dam," page 173). Also, as irrigation water evaporates, it leaves behind salts that eventually build up to the point where plants can no longer grow in it. Since the dam was built, much of the water that normally would flow downstream simply evaporates from Lake Nasser. The reduced amount of fresh water reaching the Nile Delta has allowed Mediterranean sea water to infiltrate this most fertile area of Egypt.

Israel

Israel has made the Negev Desert bloom, but it too is approaching a water crisis. Half the country's water supply comes from groundwater that is decreasing because of rapid withdrawals. Conservation of water has always been emphasized in Israel, so there are now programs to purify and reuse waste water. Many planners predict that these programs will have to accelerate to make up for the loss of other water sources. (See "The Negev Desert, Israel," page 84.)

Thailand

Pollution, due partly to growing prosperity, is spreading throughout Thailand. The rainfall is seasonal and undependable, and more and more upstream water is being diverted for agriculture and industry from the Chao Phraya, Thailand's main river. Bangkok is at the mouth of the Chao Phraya, and two thirds of the city's water comes from the river. The water system in Bangkok is inadequate and floods are common. Specialists have concluded that there is not enough water in the Chao Phraya to meet all existing and proposed needs; many believe a serious water shortage will hit Bangkok in the near future.

The Soviet Union

While there is no lack of clean fresh water in the Soviet Union, most of it is in Siberia. The fastest-growing part of the Soviet Union, though, is the burgeoning population of the Central Asian republics, where desertlike conditions prevail. For several years, the Soviets have been seriously discussing a project to channel part of the northward flow of certain Siberian rivers into the arid regions of the country's southern border. If followed through, this would be perhaps the most ambitious water project of all time, and would certainly have noticeable effects on at least the local climate. (See "Changing Climate," page 19.)

Australia

Near the growing southwest Australian city of Perth, the Swan Coastal Plain faces possible dehydration in the not-too-distant future. This swampy, sandy lowland, presently a home to many animals and birds, as well as a recreation area for southwest Australians, could be destroyed by further withdrawal of groundwater to supply Perth.

In Queensland, a big sugarcane industry in the Burdekin Delta uses large amounts of groundwater for irrigation. The area is quite dry and sugarcane production is expanding; therefore, more and more water is being withdrawn. The water table is dropping and seawater is entering the aquifers, affecting water supplies for smaller farms.

J.S.

HOW YOU USE WATER (IF YOU LIVE IN THE UNITED STATES)

Direct Personal Use — Eight percent of the nation's total, or 160 gallons per person per day, is used for personal and home activities:

Average Amount of Water Required	*Activity*
3 to 5 gallons	Flushing a toilet
3 gallons	Shaving with a blade, leaving the water running
5 gallons per minute	Taking a shower
8 gallons	Cooking (three meals)
8 gallons	Cleaning house
10 gallons	Washing the dishes (three meals)
20 to 30 gallons	Washing clothes
30 to 40 gallons	Taking a bath

Agricultural Use — About 33 percent of the nation's total, or 600 gallons per person per day, is used in farm and ranch operations:

Average Amount of Water Required	*Food Produced*
40 gallons	One egg
80 gallons	One ear of corn
150 gallons	One loaf of bread
230 gallons	One gallon of whiskey
375 gallons	Five pounds of flour
2,500 gallons	One pound of beef

Industrial Use—About 59 percent of the nation's total, or 1,040 gallons per person per day, is consumed in the production of material goods:

Average Amount of Water Required	*Product*
7 to 25 gallons	One gallon of gasoline
35 gallons	One pound of steel
280 gallons	One Sunday newspaper
300 gallons	One pound of synthetic rubber
1,000 gallons	One pound of aluminum
100,000 gallons	One new car

NOTE: About 720 gallons per person per day is used as cooling water for electrical power plants.

Reprinted from G. Tyler Miller, Jr., *Living in the Environment: Concepts, Problems, and Alternatives,* Wadsworth Publishing Co., 1975.

DRINKING LORE

- The average human has about 50 quarts (45 liters) of water in his or her body. Most of this water is found between the cells, bathing and lubricating them. The wettest part of the body: blood, which is 83 percent water. The driest: tooth enamel at 2 percent.
- Most people would die if they lost only 12 percent of this water.
- Among animals, the amount of water in the body usually depends on the conditions of a habitat. Desert-dwellers survive with less water than marine animals. The kangaroo rat (a desert rodent) is about 65 percent water. A jellyfish is about 95 percent water. Some others: chicken, 74 percent; lobster, 79 percent; earthworm, 80 percent.
- Some more water proportion facts: a baked sunflower seed, only about 5 percent water, is the driest food consumed by humans. Watermelon, at 97 percent, is the wettest.
- Historically, drinking water has carried many dangerous diseases, including typhoid, cholera, and dysentery. In 1900, in the United States alone, there were 35,379 reported deaths from typhoid. Seventy-five years later there were only 375 cases of typhoid reported, the decrease attributable to the improvement in public water supplies.
- However, even with today's water purification systems, there are about 4,000 cases of waterborne diseases a year in the United States.
- A National Academy of Sciences study of 161 contaminants in U.S. drinking water found 22 suspected carcinogens, one confirmed human carcinogen (vinyl chloride), 6 organic chemicals associated with possible birth defects, and 61 substances for which data were too scarce to label them as harmful or harmless.
- The U. S. Safe Drinking Water Act of 1974 sets standards for the amounts of several contaminants to be allowed in municipal drinking water, including radioactivity, several pesticides, and heavy metals. Water suppliers must notify the public health department and water users if these contaminants exceed allowable limits.
- In 1975, approximately 179 million Americans received their water from central-supply systems. Another 33 million obtained water from private supplies (usually wells). By the year 2000 central supply systems are expected to serve 242 million people, while 26 million will depend on private supplies.
- Half the drinking water in the United States comes from surface waters and the other half comes from groundwater.
- The chemical fluoride is added to water supplies in some parts of the United States and other countries to prevent tooth decay. Small quantities of fluoride (about 1 part per million) prevent tooth decay but amounts markedly above or below this level result in poor tooth development. Controversy also exists over whether the constant intake of fluoride at unpredictable levels, according to individual taste and local circumstances, could be carcinogenic. Although major health organizations have endorsed the use of fluoride in drinking water, a number of communities and European nations have rejected it.

M.R. and M.P.

Wavemakers:

THE STREAM WALKERS

One hot July day in 1978, David Brook pulled on his rubber hip boots and waded into the murky waters of Woodbridge Creek. Though it was to be the first of more than thirty visits to that troubled stream, what he found there that day is still clear in his memory.

Acting on a tip from a resident of Woodbridge, a town of 22,000 in central New Jersey, Brook was on the trail of an industrial polluter who, the resident claimed, had turned the headwaters of the creek, once teeming with life, into a biological desert.

Though the diminutive Brook, sloshing through the muck and the brambles, looked more like a lost Boy Scout than a hard-nosed investigator, he and his fellow "stream walkers" are seasoned, and successful, environmental detectives. In a year they will traverse hundreds of miles of New Jersey's rivers and streams, on foot and by canoe, searching out polluters who are violating the clean water laws of the United States.

The New Jersey Public Interest Research Group, which sponsors the unique stream-walking project, is an environmental-action organization funded by nearly twenty thousand college students from campuses around the state. It's one of twenty-three such groups in the United States, all based on a model proposed by consumer advocate Ralph Nader.

The notion of padding and paddling through New Jersey's waterways looking for polluters, according to Guy Calcerano, research director for the stream-walking program, evolved after passage of the Federal Water Pollution Control Act amendments in 1972—a tough set of laws designed to clean up American waterways.

"The way we have used water resources in this country has had a sad history," says Calcerano. "The new clean-water laws sought to correct the mistakes of the past, but without people in the field the mistakes will continue. The major weakness of the water-pollution laws is a lack of enforcement staff."

So, since 1975, rain or shine, summer or winter, stream walkers have hitched up their waders and launched their canoes in a relentless search for illegal polluters. The technique does have certain advantages.

"What's good about stream walking is that it's completely clandestine," says Brook, who heads a stream-walking project in New Jersey's Middlesex County. "We're walking down streams below the level of the property, and we can see a lot without being seen. We like to have industries think we're everywhere at once." The stream-walking program has been remarkably effective. Brook estimates that in two years stream walkers have uncovered two hundred violations of the clean water act in one New Jersey county alone.

Brook views his work as a supplement to that of the state and federal environmental agencies. But, more often than not, the agencies themselves feel some heat from the young clean-water crusaders.

"Agencies definitely respond to public pressure," says Brook. "A large part of our job is to make sure that state and federal officials keep pestering polluters to clean up their act."

The sight that greeted Brook as he trudged his way up the tainted waters of Woodbridge Creek that July day in 1978 was a case in point. When he reached the lake at the headwaters of the stream, Brook discovered that the local resident's lurid description of the pollution there was accurate.

"The first thing I noticed was that the bottom of the pond was bright orange and there were dead trees everywhere," says Brook. "Nothing was living, it was a wasteland." He also noticed a black, oily discharge entering the lake from a nearby manufacturer of recycled wire.

"It was the most flagrant case of pollution I had ever seen. It was very obvious that the company knew what they were doing and didn't care. And as I began to dig, that became even more clear."

Water-quality tests conducted by the stream walkers revealed that wastewater spewing from the plant was highly acidic and riddled with toxic chemicals. After some quick investigative work Brook and his cohorts were astonished to discover that the wire company had been wantonly violating clean-water laws for twenty years.

Though state and local officials had repeatedly warned the company it was violating pollution laws, and had taken plant executives to court three times (the company pleaded guilty each time), the despoliation continued. Frustrated by the company's recalcitrance and his own agency's lack of will to pursue the case aggressively, one environmental official wrote in a 1967 memorandum: "There is nothing in this problem that a well-placed kick and a bomb wouldn't solve."

Eleven years later, Brook and his fellow stream walkers dedicated themselves to delivering that kick to the government. Brook returned to the plant site again and again, collecting samples, recording discharges, and submitting his findings to federal officials. When a year had passed, and no action was taken against the wire company, Brook called a press conference. With dramatic flair the publicity-conscious stream walker marched to the devastated lake and, with an entourage of reporters close on his heels, recounted the long legacy of environmental abuse and bureaucratic neglect.

The next day the company's discharge stopped. Two months later a federal district court fined the wire manufacturer $300,000 for water pollution violations, or $10,000 for each of Brook's thirty visits to the site during which he documented the illegal discharges.

Brook still isn't satisfied with his victory. Three hundred thousand dollars, he says, is a light penalty for twenty years of pollution. But there have been some side benefits to the stream walkers' persistence in the case.

"People in the state and federal government are very interested in us now," says Brook with a smile. "They're afraid we're going to have another press conference." B.P.B.

Stream walkers tracking pollution in Assunpink Creek, Trenton, New Jersey. (*N. J. Public Interest Research Group/Al Pfeiffer*)

GREAT BREATHING DISASTERS

The average adult inhales once every five seconds, taking in about 5 quarts (4.7 liters) of air. Today, in industrialized areas, that also means inhaling minute amounts of pollutants, thousands of which pour into the atmosphere every second of every day. In most cases, the effects are not immediately observable. But in a few instances, unusual weather conditions have intensified the air pollution, resulting in major disasters.

The Meuse River Valley

The first mass fatality from industrial air pollution was in Belgium's high-cliffed Meuse River Valley in early December, 1930. For three days a lid of cold air trapped smoke from the valley's steel mills, concentrating it over thickly populated towns. Sixty people died and several thousand became violently ill. There was no precedent for killer air; residents were frightened and shocked. Some speculated that the valley had been sprayed with a poisonous gas or that fumes had leaked from one of the plants. An English biologist suggested that the bubonic plague had broken out.

The Belgian government appointed a commission to investigate. It concluded that thirty chemical waste gases, released regularly by the factories, had been confined and concentrated by weather conditions, creating the lethal air. But the government failed to warn other countries that a particular combination of factory smoke and weather could cause death. If they had, a frightfully similar accident in Donora, Pennsylvania, might have been averted.

Donora, Pennsylvania

Over the coal-mining community of Donora in October 1948 hovered a pocket of bad air. Steam locomotives burning soft coal emitted clouds of smoke on their daily runs along the Monongahela River, and plants producing wire, steel, and sulfuric acid added to the deadly air. A high-pressure condition brought cold air into the area. Rain clouds added a lid of fog and moisture, keeping the toxic gases confined within the hills of Donora for more than five days. When the fog lifted, twenty persons had died. Forty-two percent of the population—5,910 persons—had become ill. As in most air-pollution cases, the elderly and smokers were most strongly affected. Damaged or weakened respiratory systems make them more susceptible to breathing ailments than most of the population. But even football players at a local high school were forced to drop out of a game with chest pains and shortness of breath. A veterinarian reported that two dogs, seven chickens, two canaries, and two rabbits also died from the smoke. As in the Meuse Valley, Donora officials attributed the disaster to the pollution from industrial complexes and unusual weather conditions. The pollution, they said, was a combination of toxic agents.

A follow-up study, conducted ten years later, showed the incident's long-term effects. Donora residents who became violently ill at the time of the smog had a higher death and illness rate than others in town.

London

On December 4, 1952, a mass of cold air reached the city of London, keeping home fireplaces working overtime. The smoke from them was condensed in the moisture of London's fog, covering the city for five days like a blanket. The air caused choking, stinging eyes, and skin irritation. Visibility dropped so low that a ferry collided with an anchored vessel in the River Thames, automobiles crashed into trains, and traffic was brought to a standstill.

During the week ending December 13, the lives of 2,851 persons above the usual death rate had been lost. Another 1,224 deaths were attributed to the fog in the following weeks, and it is believed that the fog caused about eight thousand other related deaths. The British Committee on Air Pollution stated in its report: "The number of deaths over and above those normally expected in the last three weeks of December indicates that some four thousand people died of the 'smog.' "

Contributing to the disaster were the estimated 2,000 tons of sulfur dioxide and sulfur pollutants emitted daily by thousands of coal-burning industrial furnaces and home-heating systems.

The fatal 1952 smog prompted London officials to initiate preventive measures. Tighter restrictions on coal-burning furnaces, limited use of soft coal, and the enforcement of antipollution laws have substantially reduced the smog.

Although the laws lessen the possibility of another incident, they do not eliminate all the causes. Only four years later, London was the victim of another "smog." Although it lasted only eighteen hours, the smog caused a thousand deaths above the usual death rate.

Los Angeles

Since 1943 residents of Los Angeles have been concerned about their dirt-filled air, and according to a California State Health Department survey, they have reason to be. About three fourths of the population in the metropolitan areas of Southern California experience burning and irritation of their eyes during peak hours of smog, the survey said. In Los Angeles, it is not fireplaces that damage the atmosphere, it is automobiles. Exhaust wastes and the strong rays of the California sun create the smog (a mixture of ozone, oxides of nitrogen, and peroxidized organic compounds). Automobiles, which are heavily used, and tall city buildings, which prevent the pollutants from dispersing, can create a deathtrap in most large metropolitan areas.

In late August and early September of 1955, a week-long heat wave struck Los Angeles. The intense ultraviolet rays and the automobile exhaust combined to produce irritating chemicals. The death rate among persons sixty-five and older rose from an average of about 70 to 317 a day. Asthma and bronchitis reached epidemic levels.

Health officials, recognizing the seriousness of the smog, began to study the problem. Enlisting the aid of specialists, they examined the photochemical action of the sun on vehicle exhaust gases. Supported by the results of these studies, California government officials have led the United States in placing restrictions on automobile exhaust levels. Although this has reduced pollutants released into the air by each vehicle, it has been nearly offset by an increasing number of vehicles on the road.

Piscataway, New Jersey

On September 16, 1971, in Piscataway, New Jersey, local high school students were affected by pollutants released from automobiles and factories. The town, 30 miles (48 kilometers) southwest of New York, is located near seven major state and federal highways. Factories, including chemical plants, line many of these routes. A wind blew across the factories and highways, picking up polluted air. Accumulating all morning, the smog engulfed an area 25 miles (40 kilometers) long and 10 miles (16 kilometers) wide by midafternoon. At a high school 8 miles (13 kilometers) from the highways, students practicing football experienced tearing, breathing difficulties, and chest pains. Similar symptoms occurred at six other athletic fields within 20 miles (32 kilometers) of the first school.

Tests the morning after indicated that seven high school students had disturbed liver functions and two had suffered heart damage. No information was available on the death rates of the populations in the affected areas. The low content of one enzyme, cholinesterase (involved in transmission of nerve impulses), in the blood indicated that pesticides being manufactured in the area influenced the activity of this enzyme.

The total number of lives lost in these disasters would seem to be insignificant when compared to the fatality counts associated with such disasters as earthquakes, hurricanes, and floods. But the numbers are misleading. It is often difficult to prove beyond doubt that air pollution was the cause of death, especially when it merely administered the final blow to a person already ill. The figures also do not include the countless people whose health has been slowly eroded through years of ingesting polluted air, though their death may be specifically attributed to an illness made possible by their weakened conditions. Until it is possible to tally these indirect effects, air pollution will continue to take lives quietly—more like a thief than a killer.

J.M.R.

CUBATÃO: WORLD'S MOST POLLUTED TOWN?

One of Latin America's largest petrochemical centers and one of the most polluted communities on earth, Cubatão, Brazil rests atop coastal lowlands intersected by four lifeless rivers and under a venomous mist fed by 1,000 tons of toxic gases daily and trapped by a 2,000-foot (600-meter) range of hills just inland.

The mayor of this city of 80,000 inhabitants, located 20 miles (32 kilometers) southeast of Sao Paulo, refuses to live here, and a group of state functionaries left when their request for gas masks was turned down.

A government environmental group once labeled Cubatão "the valley of death," a description that has become starkly apt with figures recently turned up by Dr. Alberto Pessoa de Souza, the city's director of health. According to Dr. Souza, 40 of every 1,000 babies born here are dead at birth and another 40 perish within a week. The majority of the victims, Dr. Souza said, are deformed.

Atmosphere of Poison

Florivaldo de Oliveira Cajé, a member of the city council and president of its environmental commission, said the number of miscarriages was rising dramatically while the average weight of normally born infants had decreased markedly.

Many of the mothers come from Vila Parisi, a boggy slum a foot and a half (a half meter) below sea level surrounded by three of Cubatão's twenty-four industries. A pollution-monitoring machine set up there by state authorities broke down under the intensity of the contamination in 1977 after only a year and a half of service.

The residents, it found, were being showered with a constant barrage of 1,200 particulates per cubic meter, more than twice what the World Health Organization says produces "excess mortality" after twenty-four hours of exposure. The figures proved statistically that the atmosphere could not support human life. Fifteen thousand people live there today.

According to the test results, Cubatão's 50-square-mile (130-square-kilometer) area was being bombarded daily by 473 tons of carbon monoxide, 182 tons of sulfur dioxide, 148 tons of particulate matter, 41 tons of nitrogen oxide and 31 tons of hydrocarbons. A survey conducted this year revealed that of 40,000 emergency medical calls in Cubatão, 10,000 were for tuberculosis, pneumonia, bronchitis, emphysema, asthma, and assorted nose and throat ailments.

A Matter of Priorities

These findings would prompt protests and action in nations of the industrialized world, but in developing countries environmental concerns usually stand little chance against national goals of speedy growth and the reluctance to worsen balance of payments difficulties by importing costly antipollution equipment.

In a recent statement, Franco Benoffi, managing director of the Fiat-owned FMB Steel Company said: "Foundry work is unavoidably polluting work, and it is no longer accepted by highly unionized workers of the so-called developed countries. As is well known, in the developed countries an extremely strong emphasis—I don't say if correctly or not—is placed on the pollution problem. In view of these considerations, the iron foundry is an activity more suitable to third world countries."

Cubatão's affliction, much of which comes from the giant foundry of the Paulista Steel Company, is being aggravated. In the first six months of 1980, emergency calls for respiratory problems in Vila Parisi rose by 50 percent because fertilizer plants switched to more sedimentary rock, whose shavings slip more easily through chimney filters into the air. Many of the victims were children who had to be revived with oxygen pumps.

The director of the national office for environmental protection, Paulo Nogueira Neto, has suggested moving the 15,000 Vila Parisi inhabitants to a less pernicious place nearby. Mr. Cajé said this arrangement was acceptable only if accompanied by installation of antipollution equipment. "Why should we punish people who can't adapt to irresponsible industries rather than punish irresponsible industries who won't adapt to people?" Mr. Cajé argued.

Most of the contamination is generated by fully owned Brazilian companies, but Dow Chemical, Du Pont, Union Carbide, and French and German multinational concerns are reported to add to the problems.

Life in Cubatão

The twelve-year-old state unit responsible for reducing pollution has the power to fine offending industries, but statistics on its actions are not publicly available. Visible evidence suggests forcefully that the agency is lax.

One of Cubatão's dead rivers is covered with billowing suds from detergents, another boils from the effect of the chemicals dumped into it, and a third is so hot that its course can be traced by the rising steam that snakes through a fetid field of refuse. Fish retrieved from the nearby ocean outlet have been found blind and skeletally deformed from having ingested mercury in the tributaries. Mr. Cajé recalled frolicking and catching fish with his hands in the same waters before the first refinery opened twenty-five years ago.

Smoke rolls forth from scores of stacks in blue, yellow, red, charcoal, and white, turning the air a jaundiced gray and invading the nostrils with a sickening mixture of acrid odors. There are no birds, no butterflies, and no insects of any kind, and when it rains on particularly windless days, the drops burn the skin.

The industries of Cubatão have given the city the highest average per capita income of any city in Brazil, though the fact that the profits do not reach most of the city's inhabitants is attested to by the fact that 35 percent live in shantytowns like Vila Parisi with no social services. These worker colonies are characterized by small rundown cabins with a cot inside known as a "hot bed." A nighttime laborer sleeps in it by day while his daytime counterpart occupies it by night.

Of the 55,000 workers, only one third live here. "They are the ones who simply can't afford to move elsewhere," said Carlos Frederico Soares Campos, Cubatão's mayor, whose home is in the coastal city of Santos 17 miles (27 kilometers) away.

Only one of the twenty-four industries, the Paulista Steel Company, has expressed any willingness to combat the pollution problem. "We are disposed to work for a solution," its president, Plínio Asmann, said. "But the initiative has to come from the Government."

SOURCE: Warren Hoge, "New Menace in Brazil's 'Valley of Death' Strikes at Unborn," New York *Times,* September 23, 1980 © 1980 by the New York Times Company. Reprinted by permission.

SMOG ALERT

Editor's Note: *To keep city air from reaching killer levels, the U. S. Environmental Protection Agency requires cities to do something—such as temporarily closing power plants and factories or restricting auto travel—when pollution reaches certain levels. Each city develops three sets of plans corresponding to the EPA's three categories of bad-to-worst air. If the air is bad, a "warning" is issued and the first type of plan takes effect; worse air rates an "alert," and terrible air is deemed an "emergency." The following New York* Times *article describes the scene in Los Angeles during an alert.*

Los Angeles, July 21, 1978. Until this week, smog in the Los Angeles area was the sort of material for comedians that potholes are in New York City. But now with the worst conditions in seven years, smog is no laughing matter, particularly for business, which stands to lose $5 million a day in lost production.

As an eerie grayish cloud settled over Los Angeles and surrounding communities last week, residents were advised not to exercise and to stay at home. Motorists were asked to stay off the highways and polluting industries were told to reduce their emissions.

Still, the air quality for three of the last six workdays in the area has been sufficiently poor to warrant smog alerts, affecting the production of many major industries, reducing the mobility of thousands of workers, and underscoring one of the problems of doing business in Southern California.

Today, pollution levels again were high enough to cause the South Coast Air Quality Management District to notify Los Angeles plants and refineries that they must cut back on noxious emissions by 20 percent. Yesterday a sulfur dioxide alert affected 400 plants and refineries. The notification, a spokesman for the air-quality group said, was necessary to help prevent the likelihood of a major alert like the one that crippled Los Angeles business activity on July 14. That alert affected 3,000 businesses, causing production losses estimated at $5 million.

In the first of many expected smog alerts, the Kaiser Steel Corporation voluntarily cut back its coke-oven production at one plant by one third and reduced its production in another operation by half. The Shell Oil Company shut down a solvents plant, deferred the unloading of a shipment of crude oil, and garaged its automobiles in favor of bicycles when possible.

To reduce its emissions, the Southern California Edison Company, which uses fuel oil, shifted to natural gas and was forced to bring in 60 percent of its energy, some of it hydroelectric, coal, and nuclear power, from outside the Los Angeles area.

"A repeated number of these alerts could run into millions of dollars," said a company spokesman. Natural gas is cheaper than oil, but periodic shifts to natural gas from oil could mean deferred oil shipments for Southern California Edison. "That could be costly," the company said.

Since 1955, the Los Angeles Basin—Los Angeles, Orange, Riverside and San Bernardino counties—have had a smog alert program, but this is the first time that the area has been crippled by the effects of bad air. Many employees stayed away from work, and confusion over traffic plans resulted in hard feelings at company parking lots. The second phase of the plan is aimed at reducing traffic by up to 75 percent and requires that all industries with 100 or more employees encourage the use of car pools. At most companies, parking was available only for those cars carrying three or more passengers.

About 1,200 major corporations are linked by special radio to the Air Quality Management District's headquarters. In case of alerts the agency dispatches about seventy-five air-quality inspectors who police industry compliance. During the last major alert, inspectors issued violations to more than thirty companies, including the Atlantic Richfield Corporation and the Union Oil Company. Both oil companies will be prosecuted for their failure to halt the unloading of oil tankers during the alert, the agency said.

SOURCE: Pamela G. Hollie, "Coast Smog Cuts Output," New York *Times,* July 22, 1978.

WHY YOUR CAR POLLUTES

If your car could simply burn unleaded gasoline in a mixture of 14.6 parts of air to one part of gasoline, it wouldn't pollute. Unfortunately, it wouldn't run very well either, and the gas mileage would be miserable.

That's the dilemma facing auto manufacturers, government air-pollution officials and car owners. Increasingly strict government regulations on auto emissions have spawned several antipollution systems, most of them involving devices that few car owners understand and most of them resent. In fact, in the United States thousands of car owners have destroyed their autos' pollution-control devices, intentionally or unintentionally, causing an increase in air pollution in some cities.

In the 1960s the growing number of research reports linking health problems to smog and smog to auto exhausts made an obvious case for government control of the tailpipe. In the 1950s, California, where photochemical smog had brought death and disease to many city dwellers, was the first state in the United States to act. It set emission standards as early as 1961 and has consistently imposed stricter standards than the rest of the United States. The U.S. government followed with emission standards in 1968, coupled with a schedule that tightens the standards every few years until 1982. Since 1968, environmentalists and auto companies have engaged in a tug of war with the Environmental Protection Agency (EPA), the environmentalists demanding strict adherence to the standards and the companies claiming the standards couldn't be met and begging (usually successfully) for more time.

The problem of air pollution and the controversy over exhaust control has raged through the media, yet few people understand exactly why a car pollutes and how it can be made to stop. Consider an old car (a "pre-emission-control car," as the EPA would call it), say, a 1972 medium-size American car. This car mixes air and gas in its

(The Cousteau Society)

carburetor at a ratio of about 13 or 14 parts of air to one part of gas, a richer mix than the 14.6-to-1 ratio required for fuel to burn completely. If the fuel did burn completely, the car would emit nothing but carbon dioxide and water. Unfortunately the air-to-gas mix that burns best is not the mix that makes the car run best. At an efficient mix, the car would shake and sputter; it wouldn't have much power. "You could plot on a graph one line showing how much fuel is burned at various air-to-fuel mixes and another line showing increasing power for the car," said an EPA engineer. "Where those lines intersect is the air-to-fuel mix used in most cars."

So this 1972 American car emits some unburned fuel—hydrocarbons, carbon, a small amount of sulfur (an impurity in gasoline), and "tars" (heavy, poor-burning components of gasoline and oils). The carbon combines with oxygen to form poisonous carbon monoxide. Similarly the sulfur combines with oxygen to form sulfur dioxide, a notorious pollutant, most of which comes not from autos but from fossil-fuel-burning power plants. During combustion the engine gets hot enough to unite nitrogen and oxygen from the air into nitrogen oxides, also emitted through the tailpipe. Nitrogen oxides are a major ingredient in smog; they are the chemicals that, when warmed by the sun, set off the series of reactions that lead to several harmful pollutants.

A pre-emission-control car, the EPA estimates, releases 8.7 grams of hydrocarbons per mile, 87.0 grams of carbon monoxide, and 3.5 grams of nitrogen oxides. These figures are in excess of the "ultimate" standards required by the Clean Air Act: 0.41 grams per mile of hydrocarbons, 3.4 of carbon monoxide, and 0.4 of nitrogen oxides.

Also floating out of the tailpipe are tiny specks of lead, long known as a poison that can cause anemia, kidney disease, mental retardation, blindness, and death. Not enough lead is emitted by autos to kill anyone outright, but researchers have found that lead from auto exhausts can coat heavily traveled city streets, causing a health problem for the urban children who play there (especially those who don't follow their parents' advice not to put things that have touched the street into their mouths).

Lead is not actually part of gasoline; it's an additive that hikes the octane rating. Technically, octanes are hydrocarbons that prevent the air-fuel mix in the cylinder from exploding spontaneously before being ignited by the spark plug. Otherwise the mixture might explode prematurely, causing the engine to "knock." Unfortunately, octanes are expensive. However, oil and auto companies discovered that a small amount of lead added to gasoline produces the same effect as octanes. During the 1960s 4.17 billion pounds (1.9 billion kilograms) of lead were added to gasoline sold in the United States, 60 percent of which passed through tailpipes into the air.

What can the owner of an older car do to reduce pollution? There are two improvements possible, but neither will reduce emissions enough to meet new-car standards. First, keep the car tuned up. Second, experiment with unleaded gasoline. Government and industry studies show that a well-tuned car gets 3 to 4 percent better gas mileage than an out-of-tune one. Although older cars were designed for leaded gas, many can use unleaded. A try-out tank of unleaded gas won't hurt an older car; if the engine knocks, switch back to regular. Unleaded gas, though it costs more, saves money on auto maintenance.

But these measures were not enough to relieve cities of pollution from their growing loads of traffic. State governments stepped in with regulations to protect health. The first regulations in California in 1961 merely involved the control of crankcase vapors, which were vented into the air. Manufacturers simply sealed off the crankcase and added a device that routed the vapors through a tube to the carburetor, where they were fed back into the cylinders and burned. From the mid-1960s through the early 1970s, manufacturers met U.S. emission standards by simply injecting air into the exhaust, producing a blowtorch effect that burned extra fuel. They also retarded the spark. This reduced emissions, but at a cost in fuel economy—as much as 25 percent in some big cars in 1973–74—right at a time when motorists were lining up at the gas pumps and gas prices were skyrocketing.

In 1975 a new method of pollution control was introduced, the catalytic converter, accompanied by a host of complementary systems including high-energy ignition to make the sparks hotter, intake manifold heaters to warm fuel and air for the carburetor, and an improved air pump to ensure sufficient oxygen for the converter. With the converter, emission control was taken out of the engine and moved into the exhaust system, allowing engineers to retune the engine for better performance and mileage.

The converter is a sausage-shaped bulge in the exhaust system, usually located under the floor beneath the front passenger's feet. Inside the converter most of the carbon monoxide and hydrocarbons from the engine are transformed into carbon dioxide and water vapor. The full name of the converter, oxidizing catalytic converter, describes how it works. It transforms pollutants by oxidizing them, adding an oxygen molecule. The inside surface of the converter is coated with a thin layer of the catalyst metal, usually a combination of platinum and palladium. Some converters contain thousands of tiny catalyst-coated beads, others are folded like a honeycomb. Carbon monoxide, hydrocarbons, and oxygen molecules rush into the interior, hit the metal surface, and stick there, next to each other, until the oxidation process forces them to rearrange themselves. But a problem remains. Nitrogen oxides escape the converter unchanged. To make them harmless they must be *reduced*—the opposite of oxidation—that is, they must surrender an oxygen molecule.

For a device the size of a breadbox to carry out two chemically opposite processes constantly is quite a trick, but Volvo has done it. In its Series 240 cars, sold in California, Volvo introduced the three-way converter, which adds a second catalyst, rhodium, to reduce nitrogen oxides. American manufacturers are considering similar converters or the development of a second converter to reduce nitrogen oxides.

Catalytic converters work, but they have faced a rocky road to public acceptance. They were met by a spate of complaints: that they got too hot, had a "rotten egg odor," and reduced performance. Tests by manufacturers and the EPA debunked these claims. But there are problems. For one thing, catalysts depend on nonrenewable resources: platinum, palladium, and rhodium imported from South Africa and the Soviet Union. Though converters from junkyards are recycled, an EPA engineer admitted this dependency is a weakness in the system. "With ten million cars a year being produced in the United States, it could be a problem in years to come," he said.

Another problem is that converters produce small amounts of a few pollutants that a car without a converter would not emit. One of these is corrosive sulfuric acid—the acid in acid rain. (Most atmospheric sulfuric acid, however, derives from industrial sources and power plants. See "The Trespassing Poison," page 186.) Another is hydrogen cyanide, the gas used in the gas chambers of Nazi Germany. EPA tests have shown that, as of 1980, neither of these pollutants was emitted in large-enough amounts to be a health threat.

The converter itself is an amazingly simple and effective device, but like Achilles it has a great weakness. It can be completely destroyed by three tankfuls of leaded gas. In 1979 the EPA found that many service stations were flouting the law, which imposes penalties up to $10,000 for putting leaded gas into a car equipped with a converter. Motorists, enticed by the lower price of leaded gas, were filling up with it, assuming oil companies were cheating them by charging extra to take lead *out* of gas. However, switching to leaded gas, according to the EPA, is like trying to save money by never changing the oil—it catches up with you in the end. Not only does leaded gas ruin the catalyst, a $300 piece of equipment, it shortens the life of the exhaust system and spark plugs. Leaded gas contains corrosive hydrochloric acid, which eats away these parts. A muffler lasts about 30,000 miles (48,270 kilometers) with leaded gas, 60,000 miles (96,540 kilometers) with unleaded gas. Spark plugs are good for 10,000 to 15,000 miles (16,090 to 24,135 kilometers) on leaded gas, 30,000 to 40,000 miles (42,270 to 64,360 kilometers) on unleaded gas, according to the EPA.

Why does gas without lead cost more? Lead was put into gas because it is a cheap and effective antiknock compound. Without lead, oil companies were forced to search for an alternative to eliminate "knock." They experimented with manganese and a few other metals, which the EPA rejected because they also caused pollution. They settled on alcohol and organic compounds, but these alternatives demand an expensive processing step. Also, unleaded gas must be handled separately from leaded gas to prevent contamination. This all amounts to a price increase of about two cents a gallon.

The catalytic converter was the American car companies' answer to emission standards, but it's not the only answer. Some Japanese Honda Civic models use two carburetors and two combustion chambers to reduce emissions. The German Volkswagen Rabbit uses a fuel-injection system to measure the proper air-to-fuel ratio. The Swedish Volvo couples its three-way converter with fuel injection and a highly sophisticated computer that calculates the necessary air-to-fuel ratio. All these systems work well on small cars.

M.P.

WHAT'S IN THE AIR YOU'RE BREATHING?

Sulfur oxides, particulates, nitrogen oxides, carbon monoxide, hydrocarbons, photochemical oxidants—you read about them in newspaper stories or hear about their daily concentrations on the radio. What are these chemicals, where do they come from, and what do they do?

The most important air pollutants come from burning of fossil fuels—coal and oil—either in industrial plants or in vehicles. Each source has its characteristic pollutants. The smokestacks of industry release sulfur oxides and particulates (very fine dusts). From the tailpipes of vehicles and the smokestacks of industries come carbon monoxide, hydrocarbons, and nitrous oxides. Once released into the atmosphere, these chemicals don't just mingle, they are often transformed into an array of harmful substances.

Investigations into the health effects of a particular pollutant sometimes come to grief because the substance under investigation has turned into a different chemical between its entry into the air and its arrival in the human lungs. Photochemical smog, the plague of sunny cities like Los Angeles, is an ever-changing soup of chemicals produced when sunlight changes the nature of auto-exhaust pollutants. Smog (smoke and fog) is a recognized health threat. It begins with auto exhaust and sunlight, then undergoes complicated metamorphoses that have proven very difficult to control. Another example: sulfur dioxide rises from smokestacks, but the sulfuric acid that falls in acid rain and the sulfate dust that lodges in our lungs are mixed in the atmosphere.

In the United States, cars, trucks, industries, power plants, and other sources spewed out into the air 194 million metric tons of pollutants in 1977—that's a ton for every man, woman, and child in the country. This floating mass of pollutants is only a small fraction of the total air mass, but many of these substances enter our lungs as

Like an airborne buoy, a plastic bag filled with helium marks a section of air over Los Angeles, California, for a study of pollutants. (*EPA Documerica/Gene Daniels*)

we breathe our daily 33 pounds (15 kilograms) of air. These pollutants, of course, are not evenly dispersed. Once airborne, they follow weather changes, sometimes circling around cities or riding prevailing wind patterns along well-established routes, falling to the earth perhaps hundreds of miles away from their original source.

Air pollution is one of the oldest environmental issues; complaints and government controls date back at least to the fourteenth century when King Edward I of England forbade coal-burning while parliament was in session because the air had become so thick with smoke that it was hampering the work of government. Air pollution was a rallying point on Earth Day in 1970, but over the following decade many people grew bored with the subject or assumed that the problem, in the United States at least, was on its way to a solution through legislation and stricter pollution controls. Indeed, the National Wildlife Federation's Environmental Quality Index report on the 1970s showed air quality to be the only pollution problem that showed improvement. Unfortunately, the problem is still with us and it is changing in nature. Over a seven-year period in the United States, emissions of sulfur oxides and suspended particles—the coal and oil smoke from power plants and industries—dropped, but pollutants from autos and trucks remained about the same, and nitrogen oxide emissions increased. The number of cities struggling with the problem is getting larger: Bratislava, Slovakia; São Paulo, Brazil; Mexico City, Mexico; Athens, Greece; New Delhi, India; Hong Kong; Ankara, Turkey.

So, though we are making progress, the pollutants are still with us. Below are profiles of the most notorious.

Sulfur Oxides

The reputation as the most toxic of the air pollutants falls on sulfur oxides, especially when combined with floating particulates. That may be because we have been producing, breathing, and studying them longer than the others; they were responsible for London smogs in the fourteenth century and have been the deadly ingredient in most air-pollution disasters.

Sulfur is a nonmetallic element found in nature either free or combined with other elements. It is an impurity in fossil fuels only. When these fuels are burned, sulfur combines with oxygen in the air to produce sulfur oxides. Most of the sulfur combines with two oxygen molecules to become sulfur dioxide (SO_2), a heavy, pungent, colorless gas that then combines easily with water vapor. That produces sulfurous acid (H_2SO_3), a corrosive, colorless substance. Sulfurous acid joins easily with one more oxygen molecule, and the result is a highly corrosive, irritating mist: sulfuric acid (H_2SO_4).

The visible effects of this invisible atmospheric haze are impressive. Sulfur oxides yellow the leaves of plants, dissolve marble, and eat away iron and steel. They limit visibility and cut down light from the sun. They are blamed, together with accompanying particulates, for increases in respiratory infections, asthma attacks, and other diseases.

Eighty-two percent of the sulfur dioxide in the air comes from fossil-fuel smokestacks, and two thirds of those smokestacks belong to utility companies. Smaller amounts of sulfur dioxide arise from various industrial processes, such as copper smelters. As energy use grew during the 1960s, so did sulfur-dioxide emissions from power plants, increasing 92 percent during that decade. The 1970s saw stricter air-pollution controls, but the U.S. government also drew up plans to burn more high-sulfur coal to offset our dependence on foreign oil.

Particulates

The danger lies in their size: They are too tiny. Particulates are minute dusts or liquids floating on air currents. Most of them are too small to be seen and too small for the protective systems of your nose, throat, or lungs to screen out. With no effective obstacles to their penetration, they travel into the air sacs of the lungs, where they can block oxygen utilization. Worse yet, many types of particulates are composed of, or coated with, highly toxic substances. They can carry chemicals deep into the lungs that might otherwise have been trapped by mucus in the upper airways. These fine and varied particles are lumped into the category "Total Suspended Particulates" (TSP) by air-pollution people who recognize their common ability to elude the body's defense system.

The tiniest of particulates are called "aerosols," because they easily remain suspended, drifting on air currents over great distances. Aerosols measure less than a micron in diameter (a micron is equal to 1/1,000 of a millimeter or 1/25,000 of an inch; a particle ten microns in diameter can be seen by the naked eye). Although 47 percent of these tiny particles come originally from manufacturing processes and 34 percent from combustion. Larger particulates—"coarse" particles (larger than ten microns)—are composed mainly of soil and rock fragments tossed into the air by

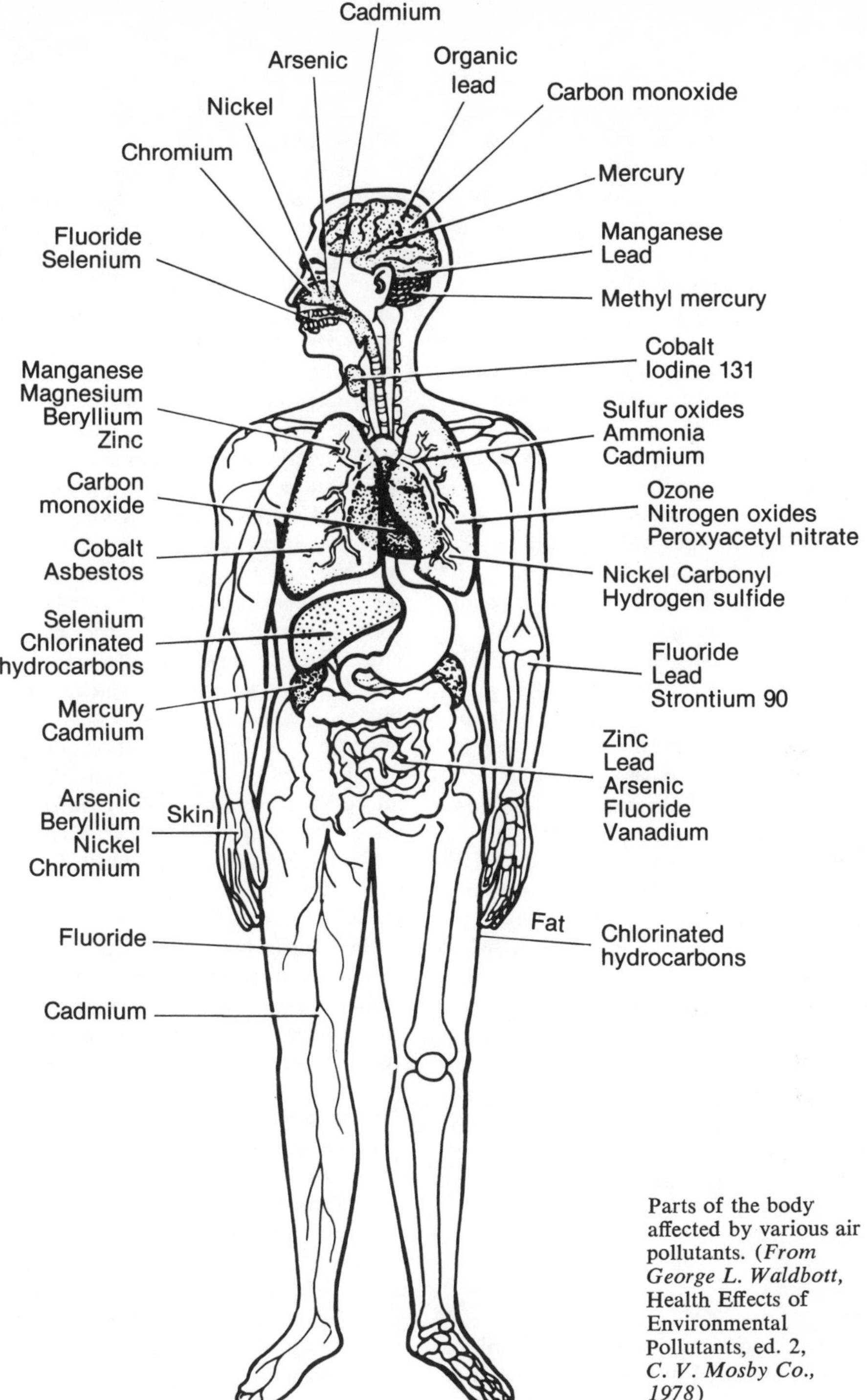

Parts of the body affected by various air pollutants. (*From George L. Waldbott,* Health Effects of Environmental Pollutants, ed. 2, *C. V. Mosby Co., 1978*)

industrial processes, such as stone-crushing operations, agricultural practices, or such natural events as erosion and volcanic eruptions.

Industrial urban areas are plagued more by fine than by coarse particles in the air, and most of the fine particles—60 to 80 percent—were formed right in the air by the chemical reaction between gases.

Carbon Monoxide

Carbon (C) is the major component of fossil fuels. Carbon monoxide (CO) is formed when fuel is incompletely burned (oxidized) because of a shortage of oxygen. When ample oxygen is present, CO_2 (carbon dioxide) is produced instead. This is a harmless product of respiration.

A high concentration of carbon monoxide can kill very quickly; at lower concentrations it causes dizziness, headaches, and fatigue. Red blood cells in the lung's air sacs bind carbon monoxide instead of oxygen, reducing the amount of oxygen the blood can carry to cells. Carbon monoxide, a colorless and odorless gas, is especially dangerous to persons with heart disease, because it forces the heart to pump harder to move enough oxygenated blood to vital organs.

Almost two thirds of the carbon monoxide in the air comes from the internal combustion engines of vehicles. United States auto-emissions standards required a drastic cutback by 1981 in the amount of CO emitted. While an average car used to produce 87 grams per mile (54 grams per kilometer) of CO in pre-emission-control days, it will be required to emit no more than 3.4 grams per mile (2 grams per kilometer) in the future.

Fortunately, once in the air, carbon monoxide is usually chemically dispersed and is slowly converted to CO_2, broken down, or trapped by natural processes. Its danger lies in its presence in high concentration along congested city streets and expressways and its contribution to the formation of photochemical smog.

The catalytic converter, now installed on new cars in the United States, oxidizes carbon monoxide to form carbon dioxide. As of 1978, the CO levels in thirteen U.S. cities had declined 36 percent, according to the Council on Environmental Quality, but other cities showed little or no decline. Los Angeles, famous for its auto-induced pollution, showed a slight increase. More efficient vehicular engines are likely to reduce this problem in the future. Meanwhile, it will take about ten years for the world's older, more polluting cars to wear out and be replaced by less polluting models.

Hydrocarbons

Most liquid fossil fuels are made up of carbon and hydrogen chains called hydrocarbons. Octane is such a substance, made up, as its name implies, of eight carbon atoms and eighteen hydrogen atoms. Fuel efficiency is measured as octane rating. Unburned fuel evaporating into the atmosphere contributes to pollution and many states now require special traps and vacuum devices on fuel delivery pumps and tanks to reduce hydrocarbon release in the atmosphere. Hydrocarbon pollutants are converted into toxic substances by the action of sunlight.

Nitrogen Oxides

Nitrogen (N_2) is the colorless, tasteless, odorless gas that forms 78 percent of the atmosphere. At high temperatures, however, nitrogen combines with oxygen to form a number of compounds known as nitrogen oxides. These have been called "jet age pollutants," because only countries with advanced industry and transportation systems suffer from them. Actually, industrial production is responsible for only a tenth of the world's nitrogen oxides (other sources being lightning, plant decay, and bacteria), but this tenth is concentrated in populated areas, and half of it comes from the United States.

Nitric oxide, a colorless, mildly poisonous gas, is formed by nitrogen combustion with oxygen at high temperatures (1,200° F/649° C) and pressure. These conditions are met in automobile engines, electric power plants, and large industrial furnaces. Nitric oxide is relatively harmless itself, but once in the air, pairs of nitric-oxide molecules undergo a chemical reaction to form nitrogen dioxide (NO_2)—a chemical that irritates the lungs, increases respiratory infections, and reduces the oxygen-carrying capacity of the blood. Nitrogen dioxide is also emitted directly by several industries, including fertilizer and explosives manufacturing.

Harmful in itself, nitrogen dioxide also plays a major role in forming photochemical smog. In the United States, nitrogen dioxide is the only major air pollutant that increased during the first seven years of the 1970s.

Photochemical Oxidants (Smog)

There are two kinds of smog, that thick bane of certain cities. The word was originally coined to describe the contamination of coal smoke and fog common in London. When people in Los Angeles suffered their first bout with heavy, choking air in 1955, they called it smog, too. But Los Angeles smog is a different phenomenon, one that is still imperfectly understood.

Los Angeles smog—photochemical smog—is a complex cloud of constantly reacting substances. The ingredients are auto-exhaust pollutants: nitrogen oxides, hydrocarbons, and carbon monoxide. In the presence of abundant sunlight, a series of chemical reactions takes place producing a complex mixture of irritants. Ozone (O_3), a natural component of the upper atmosphere but rare in the lower, irritates lung tissue and makes people more susceptible to lung disease. It is formed in smog when sunlight splits nitrogen dioxide

(NO_2) into nitrogen oxide (NO) and atomic oxygen (O). The liberated oxygen atoms readily react with hydrocarbon and other molecules, forming new compounds. When a free oxygen atom joins an oxygen molecule (O_2)—the kind of oxygen we breathe—it forms ozone. When one joins any number of other floating chemicals, it forms a variety of exotic-sounding products, including PAN (peroxyacyl nitrate), aldehydes, hydrogen peroxide, and nitric acid—all of which represent bad news for breathers.

Investigators have found that PAN makes the eyes burn and tear, irritates lung tissue as ozone does, and can damage plants. Aldehydes, the union of hydrocarbons and free oxygen atoms, are suffocating, pungent chemicals that also irritate eyes, skin, and lungs. PAN and nitric acid are suspected of causing certain forms of cancer. Hydrogen peroxide, a product of the reaction of oxygen with water vapor, reacts with sulfur dioxide to form sulfuric acid, the acid in acid rain.

Smog can hang for days over a city, building up a high concentration of harmful chemicals, or it can ride the wind, its chemical content changing as it moves. For example, a study that tracked oxidants on prevailing winds 185 miles (298 kilometers) from New York City to northeastern Massachusetts found that the highest ozone concentration formed over southwestern Connecticut.

Clearly the most obvious way to control photochemical smog is to control the ingredients in auto exhaust. In the United States, auto-emission controls have slightly reduced the amounts of hydrocarbons and carbon monoxide in the air, leading to an overall reduction in photochemical smog. But nitrogen-oxide emissions from vehicles and smokestacks alike have increased. Whether your air is getting more or less smog-ridden depends on where you live. In the United States, for example, Dayton's air-pollution levels have skyrocketed, while Fort Lauderdale's have plunged. Los Angeles, photochemical smog's mother city, showed fairly constant levels between 1973 and 1976. M.P.

WORST AIR POLLUTERS

The following table records emissions of major air pollutants in the United States during 1977 and provides an overall picture of the sources of air pollution.

U.S. EMISSION ESTIMATES, 1977
(in millions of metric tons per year)

Source Category	*TSP*	*SO_x*	*NO_x*	*VOC*	*CO*
Transportation	1.1	0.8	9.2	11.5	85.7
Highway vehicles	0.8	0.4	6.7	9.9	77.2
Non-highway vehicles	0.3	0.4	2.5	1.6	8.5
Stationary fuel combustion	4.8	22.4	13.0	1.5	1.2
Electric utilities	3.4	17.6	7.1	0.1	0.3
Industrial	1.2	3.2	5.0	1.3	0.6
Residential, commercial, and institutional	0.2	1.6	0.9	0.1	0.3
Industrial processes	5.4	4.2	0.7	10.1	8.3
Chemicals	0.2	0.2	0.2	2.7	2.8
Petroleum refining	0.1	0.8	0.4	1.1	2.4
Metals	1.3	2.4	0	0.1	2.0
Mineral products	2.7	0.6	0.1	0.1	0
Oil and gas production and marketing	0	0.1	0	3.1	0
Industrial organic solvent use	0	0	0	2.7	0
Other processes	1.1	0.1	0	0.3	1.1
Solid waste	0.4	0	0.1	0.7	2.6
Miscellaneous	0.7	0	0.1	4.5	4.9
Forest wildfires and managed burning	0.5	0	0.1	0.7	4.3
Agricultural burning	0.1	0	0	0.1	0.5
Coal-refuse burning	0	0	0	0	0
Structural fires	0.1	0	0	0	0.1
Miscellaneous organic solvent use	0	0	0	3.7	0
Total	12.4	27.4	23.1	28.3	102.7

TSP—total suspended particles
SO_x—sulfur oxides
NO_x—nitrogen oxides
VOC—volatile organic compounds
CO—carbon monoxide

NOTE: A zero indicates emissions of less than 50,000 metric tons per year.

SOURCE: "National Air Quality, Monitoring, and Emissions Trends Report, 1977," U. S. Environmental Protection Agency, 1978.

K.F.

14

Living Quarters

SHELLS

No house should ever be on *any hill or on anything. It should be* of *the hill, belonging to it, so hill and house could live together each the happier for the other.*

FRANK LLOYD WRIGHT
An Autobiography 1932

Une maison est une machine-à-habiter.
(*A house is a machine for living in.*)

LE CORBUSIER
(CHARLES ÉDOUARD JEANNERET)
Vers une Architecture 1923

For 600 million years, working in the darkness and cold liquid winds several hundred feet deep in tropical seas, one of the earth's most successful architects has drawn elements from the surrounding water to fashion sturdy, practical, efficient homes. So symmetrical and graceful are the living quarters built by the chambered nautilus that its pearly shell is prized by humans and displayed on pedestals like sculpture. It is photographed, X-rayed, and painted. It is celebrated in poetry. But whatever its value to people, to the nautilus the shell is most important as shelter. For one thing, it is not easily bitten through. That is important in the sea. The shell is also hydrodynamic and buoyant. It is constructed of local materials. And it is never obsolete, since the design allows for the natural growth of the inhabitant.

Like many land and sea animals, early human beings looked to the environment for their building materials. They ingeniously constructed dwellings that took advantage of the comforting aspects of the environment—the sun in winter and cool breezes in summer—and blocked the more violent elements—wind, driving rain, and cold. Using local materials they fashioned practical, efficient shelters. Thick walls in traditional desert houses block the outside heat; porous walls in tropical rain forests admit cool breezes. The domed snow house of the Eskimo withstands driving arctic winds. The wind scoop roof of homes in Hyderabad, Pakistan, captures wind to cool the house. (See "Houses Around the World," page 661.) As architecture expanded from a necessity to an art, the planners of ancient cities continued to use the environment to their

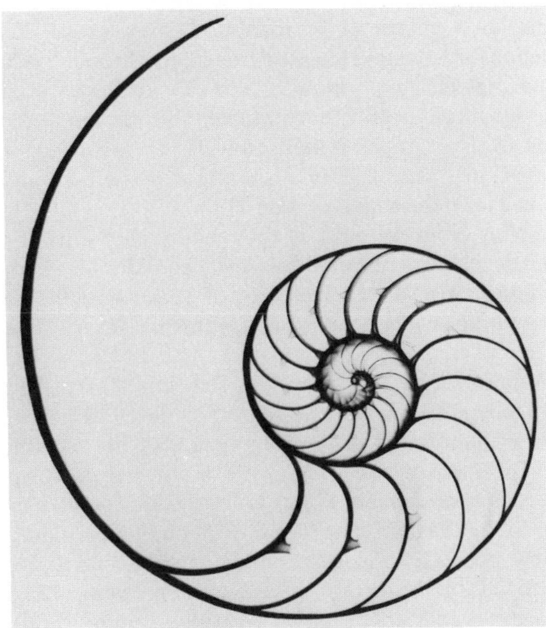

(*Richard C. Murphy*)

advantage by orienting buildings to soak up heat from the sun. (See "Solar Homes," page 644.)

But when twentieth-century skyscraper and climate-control technology arrived, the intimacy between architects and the environment was broken (see "Skyscraper Architecture: The Edifice Complex," page 665). The same office building or house could be erected in the sweltering heat of Riyadh or the frigid cold of Oslo, since it was sealed from the outer world and pumped full of heat or cooled by fossil-fuel-driven mechanisms. In the United States there arose Cape Cod homes in the desert and haciendas in New England. Not only was cheap energy necessary for their temperature-control systems, but petroleum-derived products made up the skin, flesh, and bones of many of these buildings.

Today, as energy becomes more expensive, many architects are relearning the wisdom of their ancient predecessors: how to capture natural energy sources, how to build in harmony with the seasons, the climate, and the entire envelope of nature surrounding a structure.

This chapter of the *Almanac* brings together some thoughts, some history, and some data on human living quarters because nearly every environmental issue can be linked with human housing. First, it is vital that we recognize the "biology" of the built environment, which is an inextractable part of nature's own plumbing and power systems. A house is a temporary stop along the water cycle, an exchange point for energy, a link in uncountable food webs, since the nourishment that enters its doorways in grocery sacks and floods away through its drainpipes has come from all over the world and is headed back to everywhere via the global ocean.

Without the energy demands of our buildings there might be no widespread development of nuclear power, no worries over the burning of coal. The dangerous pressures building over access to oil reserves would be partly relieved. With different waste-disposal systems, the flow of sewage and toxic substances to the sea would diminish. Careful planning could prevent the waste of wilderness and croplands beneath sprawling developments.

There is a broader concern in this chapter, too, because the actual boxes we live in as individuals cannot be separated from the clustering of boxes that produces aggregations as small as a village or as mammoth as a major city. And these settlements, these collections of boxes plugged together through grids of water, transportation, telephones, electricity, sewage, and so on, are strained by increasing population growth, as more people accumulate and as landless rural poor become jobless urban poor. In Los Angeles the result is an inefficient sprawl; in Tokyo it is crowded conditions; in Caracas it is a shantytown shell around a wealthy central city; in Calcutta it is a wretched lack of sanitation.

The failures of some cities to sustain the health and spirit of their people have caused utopians and developers to build "planned communities" with mixed success, to fantasize about building cities in the frontiers of space and the ocean, and to design ecology-minded communities like Hamilton, California. (See "The Invented Village," page 681.)

But another movement seems to be gaining strength where there is no freedom to begin anew. In the United States, convinced that some cities have grown too unwieldy to be very effective, neighborhood groups are springing up and their plans could work a significant change on urban life. The idea is to fragment the megalopolis into smaller, more workable cells capable of generating some of their own energy, growing some of their own food, rehabilitating their own buildings, planting their own urban forests. Like the new appreciation of "primitive" architecture, this is a revival of an old form of city life. Until the Industrial Revolution began, large cities were collections of small villages, with garden plots, livestock, small shops, community wells. Sumer, Babylon, Athens, Rome, and other great ancient cities were sizable living systems made up of community cells. In 1740, about 725,000 people lived in London, then the largest city in the world, yet it was an accumulation of neighborhoods, each with its own industries and commercial areas.

The German philosopher Friedrich von Schelling called architecture "frozen music." In the heady rush toward modernism and development during the past few decades, priceless older buildings and neighborhoods—the concertos and symphonies of past generations—have been callously razed. In response, citizen's organizations have formed to rehabilitate and preserve the old music. The physical structure of a community imposes itself on the character of life within it, in the way that the key and time signatures determine the mood of a musical composition. As space and fuel grow scarcer and humanity grows more abundant, the ingenuity of our builders, architects, and engineers will produce a new frozen music around us. It may turn out to be clashing and shrill. But perhaps it will be lyrical, harmonious, and, like the appropriate structures of the nautilus, beautiful.

M.R.

WHERE IT COMES FROM, WHERE IT GOES

From the front it's a pleasant white wood-frame house on an older residential street in an affluent, burgeoning commuter suburb. From the backyard the view opens to encompass a southern Connecticut salt marsh through which meanders Ash Creek, a polluted tidal stream. Beyond it one glimpses Long Island Sound, and at night one sees the flashing red Penfield Light that marks a reef and a cluster of dangerous rocks named "the Cows."

Four *Almanac* staff members live here on Riverside Drive in Fairfield, Connecticut (Mary Paden, managing editor; Bruce Ballenger, Wave-vice called a "heatolator" that is supposed to ordinator; and karin negoro, art director). Our house could be anywhere.

We try to practice what we preach: We recycle cans, bottles, and newspapers; we keep the thermostat at 58° F (14° C) and even bought a device called a "heatolator" that is supposed to throw heat from the fireplace back into the room. We open the drapes in the morning to let in the sun and close them at night to keep heat in. In the summer we don't exactly keep up with our neighbors' grass-cutting schedules, but then we don't over-fertilize our lawn, allowing the runoff to pollute Ash Creek, either.

We are what you might call commuter ecologists. But like most middle-class people around the world, we expect—depend on—certain conveniences. We like the lights to go on at the flip of a switch and water to shoot out of the faucets at a touch and the heat to kick on when the winds howl across the marsh and the garbage to disappear on Tuesday mornings and the toilets to flush away wastes discreetly. Yet these conveniences, which we casually include in the phrase "standard of living," are tightly linked to some of our most pressing environmental problems: energy, solid waste, water pollution.

Wondering exactly what impact our house had on the local environment, we probed its supply and relief systems, something anyone can do with a telephone directory and a sense of curiosity. We found that our impact was not entirely local. Like most of the U. S. Northeast, we depend for much of our electrical generation and heating fuel on oil imported from the Middle East. Our electric utility is hooked into a grid that covers six New England states, so that in a power shortage we can get electricity from any of several plants, including controversial nuclear ones. Clean water from our faucet depends on the health of a 94-square-mile watershed that is suffering from overdevelopment. Our garbage is filling up a tidal marsh and pollutes the remaining marsh as it decays and seeps into the water. We found some of the systems linked in unexpected ways. The Town of Fairfield has contracted to sell its garbage to a resource recovery plant that will in turn sell some of it to our utility to use as fuel. When that system goes into effect our garbage will return to us as light.

Of course volumes could be written about each of these systems and they are documented in internal company and government reports and local newspaper articles. We made a limited inquiry into each system just to find out where things come from and where they go.

WHERE IT COMES FROM/WHERE IT GOES

The Garbage

Our garbage is whisked away once a week by County Refuse, a small private company based in a town about fifteen miles east of us. Fairfield is a mecca for free enterprise in garbage collection: twenty small companies with a total of forty-two trucks compete for the trash of 59,000 people, charging about $7.50 a month per house. The trucks are weighed at the town dump and charged $2.50 per ton to drop their collections. Some people pinch pennies and haul their own garbage; the town logged about 64,000 cars and 24,000 pickup trucks bringing garbage to the dump in 1978. All in all, 40,000 tons of garbage arrive at the dump each year—about two thirds of a ton for every town resident. If we are batting average, our four-person household contributed nearly three tons of garbage to the Fairfield dump during the time we worked on the *Almanac*. And, if we threw out the same kinds of things most Fairfielders did, our trash consisted mostly of paper (38 percent), followed by food wastes (14 percent), yard trimmings (15 percent), glass (10 percent), and metal (10 percent).

The dump (now a landfill) was sited in 1950 on forty acres of a salt marsh, an unfortunate choice because thirty years of decay and leaching have now polluted the state-owned Pine Creek estuary that surrounds it on three sides. The garbage has been piled ten, twenty, and in places thirty feet above ground level, interspersed with layers of dirt and sludge from the sewage-treatment plant. Each afternoon a thirty-four-ton compactor smashes down the layer of trash and a payloader covers it with dirt. The landfill smells "obnoxious," according to a sanitary engineer who works there, and like many other landfills in fast-growing Connecticut, is almost full.

The town, well aware of these problems, contracted in 1977 with a resource-recovery plant in the nearby industrial city of Bridgeport to sell its garbage. The scheme seemed like the ultimate in recycling: turning trash into electricity. The trash would be taken to a plant operated by the Connecticut Resources Recovery Commission where it would be separated into glass, aluminum, ferrous metals, and "other." The "other," about 50 percent of the trash, would be ground into a gray powder called "Eco Fuel II" and sold to our utility, United Illuminating. The utility would mix it with No. 6 fuel oil and burn it in its 84-megawatt Bridgeport Harbor Station Unit I plant, saving up to 600,000 barrels of oil per year. If Eco Fuel II is cheaper than oil, the utility promises to pass its share of the savings to its customers.

But in early 1980 the resource-recovery plant was more than a year behind schedule, still working out technical problems. One sticky problem was sulfur. It is added as part of the grinding process that turns the trash into powdery fuel, but it pollutes the air when the fuel is burned. Plant technicians were experimenting with how much sulfur they could add and still meet air quality standards.

Another option, of course, is recycling paper, cans, and bottles to reduce the volume of solid waste and to save energy and materials. A recycling station at the dump collects these materials, but ironically the town has made few efforts to encourage recycling because it now needs to generate at least 38,000 tons of trash each year to fulfill its contract to the resource-recovery plant. The Town of Fairfield is even worried that Connecticut's returnable bottle bill, which took effect in 1980, will reduce its trash below the amount it contracted to deliver.

While many communities have private recycling operations, about three hundred in the United States have municipal recycling systems in which all residents separate their garbage into four bags, paper, glass, metal, and "other," for regular pickup. The first three are sold to companies that reprocess the materials.

Once the resource-recovery center starts buying its trash, Fairfield plans to turn its dump into a park, including a golf course and mounds for skiing, as has been done successfully in other places. The process involves more than planting grass and trees on the highly fertilized site. The chemistry of decay going on beneath the layers of dirt can produce pockets of combustible methane gas and areas of collapse. But there are other pioneers in landfill reclamation, such as the famous Mount Trashmore, a ski slope built on a hill of garbage in Norfolk, Virginia, and Fairfield can learn from their examples.

The Lights

United Illuminating (UI), a medium-size utility based about thirty miles northeast of Fairfield, dates back to only a few years after Thomas Edison invented the electric light bulb. During the 1880s, two utilities formed to provide street lighting in nearby cities, and in 1899 merged into United Illuminating. Its history is similar to most American utilities. Its earliest plants were coal-fired and they were built in rapid succession to keep up with post-World War II demand for electric power. By 1957, the utility reports, 192,000 customers were consuming 1.5 billion kilowatt-hours of electricity—fifteen times as much as the 100 million kilowatt-hours used in 1918. By the 1970s only 4 percent of the utility's output went to street lighting; the rest was used by residential customers (38 percent), businesses (33 percent), and industry (25 percent).

In the late 1960s, pressured by environmental regulations on the dirty coal fuel, the utility switched to oil, most of it imported from foreign countries, and invested $9.2 million in pollution-control equipment. In the 1960s it also bought into the newest energy technology: nuclear power, with a 9.5 percent share in the Connecticut Yankee Atomic Power Plant, a small plant with a good safety and production record through 1979. Despite loud protests from antinuclear groups and some customers, the utility recently bought into four new nuclear power plants including the infamous Seabrook in New Hampshire, where nonviolent demonstrations by local residents and antinuclear groups made national headlines. In 1980 United Illuminating generated 92 percent of its electricity from oil fuel and 8 percent from nuclear power.

As oil prices skyrocketed in the 1970s, the utility gained permission from the Connecticut Public Utilities Commission to pass on fuel-price increases to customers. As a result the average electric bill has climbed from $10 per month in 1970 to $35 per month in 1980. The utility's recent bids for rate hikes have been denounced by the Connecticut Citizen Action Group (CCAG), a neighborhood organizing group, which charges that UI is investing in more expensive nuclear plants than will be needed given a slowing increase in demand for electric power. The consumer counsel in the state Department of Public Utilities Control agrees. The utility has a cash-flow problem, a staff member of the counsel's office explained.

Optimistically assuming that the demand for electric power would continue to grow at 7 percent a year, as it did in the early 1970s, the utility invested in nuclear plants. However, by 1980 demand was growing at only 2 percent a year. Meanwhile construction delays and inflation boosted the cost of building nuclear plants. (Seabrook construction estimates went from $1.4 billion to $2 billion over a few years.) Contractors were demanding payment. So were the oil companies, as oil prices doubled between 1978 and 1980, going from $12 to $25 per barrel. With its assets tied up in nonproducing nuclear plants, the utility was hard pressed to pay its oil bill. It pushed for a $30-million rate hike in 1978, but was granted only $17 million by the Department of Public Utilities Control. Since then it has put 5 percent of its interest in Seabrook up for sale, hoping to get about $30 million.

United Illuminating rates are higher than Northeast Utilities—the state's giant, heavily nuclear utility. But, while Northeast offers the best rates now, the consumer counsel staffer said it may be the most expensive utility in the year 2000 when costs from nuclear waste disposal and plant decommissioning could be added to the rates.

Tracing the actual path of our electricity is much more complicated than following the garbage to the dump. A flip of the light switch could bring electricity generated at the original plant, Steel Point Station, built in Bridgeport in 1923 (now oil-fired), or from the old Yankee nuclear plant, or in fact from almost any plant in New England, since all are hooked together by transmission lines and computers under a system called the New England Power Exchange (NEPEX). Formed in 1971, NEPEX is meant to "insure the efficient and reliable utilization" of power throughout the six New England states.

Nor is it easy to trace the source of the imported oil burned at Steel Point. Texaco is the major supplier, but where the oil comes from —the Middle East, Venezuela, Mexico—varies according to shifts in global economics, politics,

"I NOTICE YOU'RE NOT QUOTING THOREAU SO MUCH ANYMORE."

and internal decisions at Texaco and other suppliers.

Meanwhile the U. S. Department of Energy is pressuring New England utilities to unhook themselves from foreign oil and switch back to U.S. coal. Although most of United Illuminating's plants began as coal-burners, switching back to coal would be costly, requiring as much as $100 million each. The consumer counsel calls the switch a "terrible move" that would further degrade Connecticut air quality.

The Heat

About once a month during the fall and winter, Superior Fuel Company drives a tank truck up our drive and fills a tank in our basement with No. 2 fuel oil. The source of this oil is "very confusing," even to Superior manager Jim Horhan. It comes from Exxon, which gets it "from the Arabs or from domestic sources, whichever is most economical." Superior is a thirty-year-old distributor, one of about sixty companies along the southwest shore of Connecticut. It has fourteen trucks and fifty employees, who spend most of their time on the road filling furnace tanks. In the winter of 1980 rising fuel prices were a source of concern to Superior's manager as well as to its customers. The price per gallon has risen from about 57¢ in December 1978 to $1.08 in December 1980. Price is a hot topic at meetings of the regional association of fuel oil dealers. "We are worried that people won't be able to pay," Horhan said. "We have to carry accounts. We aren't like gas stations, where people pay cash. If the winter is hard, some people will be unable to pay and we will have to carry the accounts, which costs us money."

The Water

Our water comes from the tranquil and aptly named Hemlock Reservoir only ten miles from our house. Hemlock in turn is connected to the larger Saugatuck Storage Reservoir to the north, which is fed by creeks and streams that meander through southern Connecticut. The system's three distribution reservoirs and six storage reservoirs in its ninety-four-square-mile watershed were created by damming streams beginning in the 1920s. Like many water suppliers, the Bridgeport Hydraulic Company has had to abandon some sources over the years as they became polluted, and one of its main problems today is keeping its reservoirs clean in the face of increasing development near their shores.

The Hemlock Reservoir is indeed bordered on one side by a magnificent stand of hemlocks whose roots filter out excess nutrients and pollutants as they move through the soil toward the lake. In other places, however, public roads bend alarmingly near the shore (oil and salt runoff from roads pollutes water), and private homes with septic tanks pose a potential source of pollution.

Bill Lyon's job is to inspect the watershed for potential trouble spots and to respond to pollution emergencies. The state health code requires that the hydraulic company make an annual survey noting possible hazards to the drinking water. The most common hazards Lyon finds as he travels the water system are faulty septic tanks and erosion from new housing developments. There are a few local problems he keeps an eye on—manure runoff from stables, leaking oil from home fuel tanks or gas stations—but his main concern is development. "There is a direct correlation between increasing population and the deterioration of water quality," he said.

Although the 20 percent of watershed land owned by the Bridgeport Hydraulic Company is under tight development restrictions, privately owned land is not. There are, of course, requirements for septic tank placement, but construction erosion, as in most places, is loosely inspected and controlled. When Lyon spots a problem he notifies the offender and the local health department. Does the system work? "That's a tough question," Lyon said. "Sometimes it does, sometimes it doesn't."

Although most of the watershed development is residential, Lyon occasionally responds to a chemical spill or a traffic accident in which a car has crashed into the reservoir, leaking gasoline. Hydraulic company workers do what they can to contain the spill, notify the state Department of Environmental Protection, and hire a contractor to finish the job.

From Hemlock Reservoir the water flows through a large pipe to a treatment plant only a few hundred feet away. There the water is tested for bacteria, several toxic chemicals and heavy metals, and turbidity (suspended solids). Chlorine is added to kill bacteria, lime to reduce acidity, a zinc phosphate corrosion inhibitor to keep the pipes clean, and fluoride to prevent tooth decay. (As in many places, the addition of fluoride provoked controversy. It was added after a statewide public referendum in the 1960s.)

In compliance with the Federal Safe Drinking Water Act of 1974, water lab technicians test the water at several points for purity and notify the state health department if it doesn't meet federal standards. So far Hemlock water has passed the test, according to John Herlihy of the lab, and he attributes this to Lyon's detective work in the watershed. Watershed inspecting, he said, "is an effective program. Without this check there could be serious problems." Some types of pollution, toxic chemicals for example, just can't be screened out entirely at a treatment plant, he said. They must be prevented from entering the watershed in the first place.

Thirty million gallons (113 million liters) a day flow from the Hemlock Reservoir, through the treatment plant, then to pipes, one of which ends at our house. Hemlock, its sister reservoirs, and a few wells supply 390,000 people in southern Connecticut with water at the flip of a faucet.

The Sewage

Our house had a septic tank until 1953, when the neighborhood sewer was built. The owner paid $696.90 to hook into the municipal waste system, a price that had tripled for homeowners who received sewers under a $14-million project to install thirty-five miles of pipe in a newer section of town in 1980. Slightly more than half the city of Fairfield has sewers, and there are no plans to finish the job, according to an employee of the sewer commission. Homes on large lots—two acres or more—simply don't need sewers, she said, since they have adequate room for a septic drainfield.

Like many municipalities, Fairfield took advantage of the river of federal money that poured into sewer grants in the 1960s and 1970s in response to clean-water legislation. But many small towns found the new sewers a mixed blessing. Rapid development followed the sewer lines, often in strips along roads leading out of town, away from central business areas. And as contractors and politicians took advantage of the burst of federal funds, sewer scandals became so common that many fledgling local reporters broke into the front page with stories of corruption and kickbacks. (Fairfield is pleased with its current contractor, who actually expects to complete the job ahead of schedule.) By the late 1970s some cities began refusing federal sewer money, preferring to stick with septic tanks and to shun development.

Fairfield has two sewer systems: one for sewage and one for storm water. Cities that cut costs by combining storm and sewage lines find that a heavy rain can overfill the sewage-treatment plant, forcing operators to release some of the wastewater directly into the environment without treatment.

Our sewage-treatment plant, located next to the landfill, was built in 1952, a year after the first sewer lines were installed. It works on the principle of "activated sludge with anaerobic digestion," a type that fell out of vogue for a while, but it is now making a comeback, according to James Feher, superintendent of Water Pollution Control.

Feher is a proud booster of the small plant. He was the first worker hired when it began operation and worked his way up to superintendent. "It used to be called the 'sewer plant,' he quipped, "but then nobody would talk to you. Now we call it Water Pollution Control." Feher has spent every workday for twenty-seven years at the plant, watching it expand in 1965 and 1972 to its present capacity of 9 million gallons per day, listening to other city planners deride the plant's process and advocate a switch to incinerators, then quietly chuckling as rising fuel prices increased costs at the incinerators and planners began again touting digesters. The planners' original problem with digesters was that they require careful control and biological monitoring and can be easily upset by an influx of acidic or toxic industrial wastes.

Feher says he keeps industrial wastes out of his plant unless they are pretreated by the industry. The Fairfield Sewer Commission sets standards on what type of waste can enter the plant and Feher's workers test it for compliance as it comes in. The sewage flows first through mechanical claws that trap solids, then to a settling tank where suspended particles settle to the bottom. Ninety percent of the waste is removed here and the cleaned water is sent through a pipe that extends three quarters of a mile into Long Island Sound. The solid waste is transformed into harmless sludge by adding anaerobic bacteria.

The sludge looks like mud when it leaves the plant at the rate of 12 to 14 wet tons per day (2 dry tons) and is trucked to the landfill, where bulldozers spread it on the ground. Fairfield's sludge is excellent fertilizer—low in metals and high in nitrogen. As it ages in the landfill, it turns to the consistency of peat. Some Fairfield residents collect it as free fertilizer for their lawns and gardens, and the Parks and Recreation Department uses it to reclaim worn-out parkland. But most of it piles up and, as nitrogen seeps out, contributes to the pollution of Pine Creek Estuary.

It's a wintry Friday evening in Fairfield. A post-Christmas turkey dinner is being cooked in our electric oven that works on power from either imported oil or a nuclear plant. We are listening to Mozart on a stereo fired by the same, sitting comfortably in a dining room most likely heated by Arabian oil, drinking coffee made from Hemlock Reservoir water. Later we will send turkey scraps and wrappings to the overfull landfill and pour a dishpan of water into James Feher's water pollution control plant.

Easily, unthinkingly, we use systems that reach thousands of miles from our house, employ thousands of people, consume or pollute natural resources, and influence local and world economics and politics.

Are we overwhelmed by our impact? Do we feel guilty? Not really. We admire our colleagues who compost their garbage to grow their food, use windmills to generate electricity, and use solar energy for heat. But we haven't the means or the time right now to become self-sustaining.

What we can do is become vocal. We are not pawns of overwhelming systems; we are one of the reasons these systems exist and we have every right and reason not only to inquire into our support systems, but to express our approval or disapproval of how they are managed. If we don't want nuclear-powered turkey, we must tell United

Illuminating and join with organized antinuclear groups to protest. If we want our garbage turned into electricity, we must express support for the concept and monitor the snags. We also have a responsibility. If we see a gas station leaking oil into our drinking-water supply, we should tip off watershed inspector Bill Lyon.

It's not always easy, of course, to forge the kind of systems we want, but it's possible, and sometimes it's even fun.

M.P.

Wavemakers:

FRIENDLY, FIGHTING NEIGHBORHOODS

Every weekday morning—and most weekends—Karen Santana arrives at her cluttered office, situated unobtrusively over a decaying movie theater, and settles behind her wide desk. The routine day starts with a bitter cup of instant coffee, and then she begins her phone calls.

"Hello, Pat, this is Karen. I'm just calling to find out what you thought of the meeting last night."

The conversation can last a minute or an hour—whatever it takes to gauge the organizational pulse of the community group she works for. Santana, a slight, twenty-five-year-old woman with piercing eyes and a quick smile, will work well into the night, making phone calls to the group's members, planning agendas for future meetings, and designing flyers to publicize them. In many ways, it is a job that might appear similar to that of a precinct captain, or some other caretaker of a political party's local machinery. Both jobs entail long hours of organizing, but there the similarities end.

Karen Santana is a community organizer in East Hartford, Connecticut—an aging, working-class suburb that is host to, among other things, one of the United States' biggest aerospace firms—and the long hours she puts in at the small office on Main Street are not on behalf of a political party or local candidate. Santana, and the citizens she works for in East Hartford, are promoting a different brand of political activism. Though it may begin on a neighborhood block or reach as far as the halls of Congress, this new activism remains firmly rooted in the community. Because it has so far defied traditional political categorization, the new phenomenon has been labeled several things, among them "the neighborhood movement" or the push for "grassroots democracy." Whatever its label, neighborhood activism is sweeping the United States and keeping full-time organizers like Karen Santana very busy.

The foundation of this movement is the community organization, and though these organizations may vary in nature, most get their start when powerless individuals organize to attack a specific problem that affects their neighborhood's quality. Once politically baptized by local fights, neighborhood groups frequently take on issues—like utility rates and heating-oil costs—that formerly seemed beyond their control.

The East Hartford Citizen Action Group (EHCAG), for example, organized its first block club around the issue of speeding trucks, which were illegally barreling through a residential neighborhood. Confrontations with city officials over the issue provided the inexperienced EHCAG leadership with its first lesson in the dynamics of power: Organized citizens have much more political clout than individuals. The speeding truck victory, though a seemingly small issue, helped energize formerly apathetic neighbors into community activists, and convinced many that city hall can be beaten. With local success under their belt, EHCAG activists later fought a proposed $135-million rate increase that threatened to boost annual utility bills by $60. In coalition with other groups around the state, EHCAG managed to slash $45 million from the increase.

The key to the political success of neighborhood groups, say their leaders, is strong organization. "There aren't many vehicles for blue-collar workers and poor people to feel that they can do anything," said Gail Cincotta, a former homemaker who now heads National People's Action, a coalition of neighborhood groups. "That's what organization does, it gives a sense of control and dignity."

Across the United States this new cadre of community leaders, having gained insight into the workings of the political system through their community organizations, are initiating grassroots

efforts to reverse the decline of urban neighborhoods. And in many places, they are succeeding. These examples are not atypical:

- In Brooklyn, New York, the Hoyt Street Block Association turned a vacant lot, once strewn with garbage and debris, into an ornamental garden replete with wrought-iron fences and winding paths. (For another urban gardening success story, see "Pioneers on the Bronx Frontier," page 675.)
- In Detroit, Michigan, residents of Hobart Street, a lonely outpost of residential homes in an area overwhelmed by urban renewal, singlehandedly stopped the bulldozers from razing their homes until they secured an agreement from city officials that low-income housing would be built in its place. They got their housing and the community has stayed together.
- The Chicago-based Citizen Action Program, a multiracial coalition of community groups, defied the powerful city political machine and halted construction of the Mayor's favorite new highway scheme—the massive Crosstown Corridor Expressway. The proposal was never revived.
- And in South Philadelphia, Pennsylvania, a feisty woman named Mamie Nichols encouraged her local community group, Point Breeze Federation, Inc., to help rebuild the deteriorating neighborhoods. The financing for the renovation came from grants—$1.5 million in 1980–81—that the group solicited from government sources and from property owners.

Though this sampling of neighborhood projects is inspiring testimony to the initiative of community organizers, a new level of activity that transcends city boundaries is beginning to emerge. The groups are beginning to discover each other, and they are forging broad alliances that, in the words of one observer, will "help refashion our political and social imaginations in the 1980s, with untold but enormous consequences for the future."

The discovery that many neighborhood problems—issues like housing, crime, unemployment, energy rates, and pollution—have solutions that cannot be found at city hall, has led to the formation of new state and national coalitions of community organizations. One of the largest of these—the Association of Community Organizations for Reform Now (ACORN)—has affiliates in nineteen states. ACORN's entry into the national political scene began at the midterm national conference of the Democratic Party in 1978, when one thousand of the group's community activists marched to the convention center demanding new national policies that would help the poor and the cities.

National People's Action, representing community organizations in 39 states and 104 urban areas, has already won passage, over opposition of the banking industry, of federal legislation that helps limit neighborhood "redlining," or mortgage discrimination in urban areas. The group vows to return to Washington, D.C. in busloads until a stronger bill is passed.

Christened in local battles with city hall, the neighborhood activists are showing no hesitancy in taking on, with equal determination, the corporate giants that they believe threaten their community's survival. For example, members of the Boston chapter of the statewide Massachusetts Fair Share, saddled with high property taxes and declining city services, went after local corporations that were delinquent in paying their taxes. One airline company, they discovered, owed $9 million. After intense public pressure by Fair Share leaders, the airline paid up and the Mayor agreed to post the group's "most wanted" posters of other corporate tax delinquents on downtown bulletin boards. Groups in California, Ohio, Illinois, and Maryland are waging similar battles over utility-rate reform, mass transportation issues, and housing.

Whether this new insurgence of neighborhood power can breathe new life into aging cities is uncertain. But the social chemistry that has given rise to the movement—the strong need for people to gain some measure of control over their lives and their communities—is likely to continue to generate local experiments in self-reliance.

B.P.B.

SOLAR HOMES

Every home is a solar home. People think they heat their homes with firewood, oil, or other fuels, but 95 percent of their warmth comes from sunlight. In a sunless world, each dwelling would be 400° F below zero (—240° C) before the furnace was turned on.

DENIS HAYES
Worldwatch Paper 15, 1977

In the fifth century B.C. the Greeks made deliberate use of solar energy to heat their homes. The streets of the ancient city of Priene were laid out to allow all homes maximum exposure to the sun's rays. The Romans also oriented homes and public baths for optimal solar access and developed transparent windows that both allowed the sun's heat to enter and prevented it from dissipating. Ken Butti and John Perlin have collected historical examples of solar technology (*A Golden Thread: Twenty-five Hundred Years of Solar Architecture and Technology;* Cheshire Books, 1980) that reveal solar energy as a long-practiced technology that we temporarily forgot.

The Greeks and Romans, and many others since them, used what we now call "passive" solar design. They used no special apparatus or machinery, but designed their buildings so that the entire structure worked as a solar collector. Sunlight entered through windows on the south wall; the stone, brick, or adobe walls and floor stored heat, releasing it slowly during the night; and all parts of the building that did not admit sun were designed to prevent heat from escaping. Windows were recessed or protected by an overhang to keep out the high hot summer sun. And the thick walls, capable of storing the sun's heat, could also block it out in the summer.

These simple principles have been generally ignored in recent years as buildings were oriented and designed with little attention to the sun. Almost no one noticed because oil was cheap and heating bills relatively low. A few perceptive people, however, revived the art of passive solar design. Without significant extra expense they built homes that used considerably less energy with no extra equipment or maintenance. They set an example that all builders can easily follow.

Any new home can incorporate passive solar heating simply by being constructed to face in the proper direction. For optimal heating, of course, large south-facing windows and a well-planned heat-storage system are important. Residents of existing homes can take advantage of passive solar heating by letting the sun shine in southern windows and covering the others with drapes or shutters for insulation.

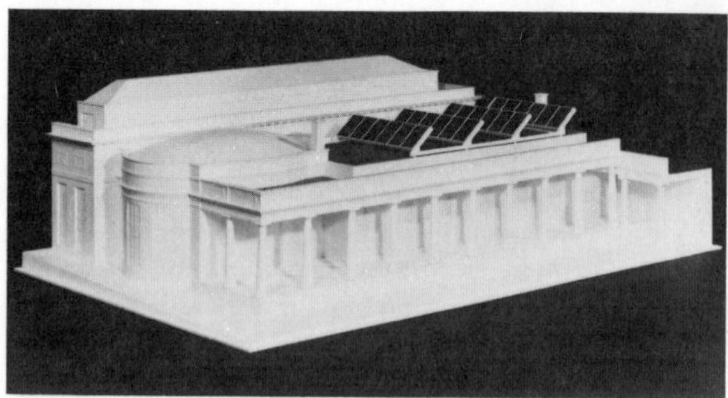

Model of the solar White House. In 1979, President Jimmy Carter installed solar panels on the White House to aid in water heating. (*White House Photo*)

Of course you *can* spend money on passive solar heat. Attaching a greenhouse with some means of heat storage to the south wall of your house can amplify solar heat collection. And if you plant vegetables in the greenhouse, you can save money on both food and heating bills. At the New Alchemy Institute, fish ponds in the greenhouse double as a heat-storage medium and another food source (see "The New Alchemists," page 446). Imaginative do-it-yourselfers have used water-filled black steel drums and beer cans for heat storage.

"Active" solar systems, on the other hand, use specially designed solar collectors and mechanical circulation systems to provide even more heat.

Active systems are still expensive and require periodic maintenance. They work best and are most economical when they are part of the original design of a house. Their initial cost is greater than that of a fossil-fuel system, but because the fuel is free, the system can pay for itself in several years. Although many solar architects prefer to work with passive designs, which are simpler and more economical, active collectors have received the most publicity.

Buildings can be retrofitted with active solar systems only if the building's orientation and structure are suitable. If the roof does not have a south face with a slope appropriate for its latitude, the solar collector will not work efficiently. Many people, in their enthusiasm for saving energy, buy solar systems without considering the situation of their building. Also, not all solar collectors are equal. As solar energy becomes popular, solar-equipment dealers spring up, running the gamut from honest to "shady." A $10,000 system might collect nothing but air pollution.

The most successful active solar system is the solar water heater. The simplest water heater—used by millions of homes in Japan—consists of a 50-gallon (189-liter) black vinyl bag placed on a platform on the roof. The device works well as long as the temperature is above freezing; it lasts for two to four years and costs less than ten dollars. A slightly more sophisticated system that used blackened water tanks inside a glass-covered wooden box was popular in the United States around 1900. Today's systems involve flat glass boxes containing tubing through which water circulates. The sun-heated water is piped through coils in the hot-water tank, warming the water without touching it, and is then recycled through the solar collector. During the winter, antifreeze can be added to the circulating water to prevent freezing.

The following homes illustrate the long history and innovative designs of solar architects. Solar energy is not just a flat glass box on the roof. It is an awareness of the sun's gift of warmth, an awakening that can inspire the architecture of the future.

The typical New England "salt box" home is actually a passive solar design. The main rooms are in the front of the house, which usually faces south to catch sunlight. The back is lower and steeply sloped to minimize the chilling effect of north winds in winter. Vines growing on the traditional lattice that covers much of the front of the house help to block summer sun but allow winter sun to enter. (*From* A Golden Thread, *by Ken Butti and John Perlin, 1980*)

Greenhouses were very popular among wealthy Europeans in the nineteenth century. They were often attached to the south side of homes to capture sunlight and help supply heat. Even city homes like this one in London made use of the greenhouse. (*From* A Golden Thread, *by Ken Butti and John Perlin, 1980*)

The Massachusetts Institute of Technology designed a "hybrid" home in 1948 that combined active and passive systems. Solar collectors combined with plenty of double-paned, south-facing windows provide 80 percent of the house's winter heating needs. (*M.I.T. Historical Collections*)

Karen Terry designed and built this distinctive passive solar home near Sante Fe, New Mexico. The back of the building is built into the hillside to preserve heat, and the adobe walls provide heat storage. Some of the inside walls are lined with barrels of water to improve their heat-retaining ability. (Water is an excellent heat-storage material, taking a long time to release its energy.) Two wood stoves provide occasional backup heat when necessary. (*Jon Naar*)

Tom Smith's home in Lake Tahoe, California, is a passive design that was actually cheaper to build than conventional homes in the neighborhood. The greenhouse collects the sun's heat, and natural convection currents of warm air circulate throughout the house. To obtain a loan and obey local building codes, Smith installed an electric baseboard heater, but he hasn't used it. A wood stove provides extra heat when necessary. The backfill that supports the house also serves to store heat, and an air vent is imbedded in the earth to cool warm summer air. During a very cold February his electricity bill for a hot-water heater and appliances was one quarter that of a neighbor with a home of similar size. (*Scott Kline Photography*)

THE WHOLE HOUSE CONSERVATION QUIZ

I. Multiple Choice

1. What does Btu stand for?

a. Basic temperature unit: the unit used in measuring the difference between indoor and outdoor temperatures in order to calculate real heat loss.
b. British thermal unit: the amount of heat required to raise the temperature of a pint of water one degree Fahrenheit. It is the standard measure of energy.
c. Baggy thermal underwear: keeps you warm and doesn't bind.

2. What is weatherstripping?

a. Removing weathered paint from the exterior of a house before covering with insulated siding.
b. Removing baggy thermal underwear in hot weather.
c. Material for sealing cracks in window and door frames to keep in heat.

3. Insulation material consists of . . .

a. fiber glass.
b. goose down.
c. asbestos.
d. urethane foam.
e. All of the above.

4. In the typical two-story, single-family house, the most heat is lost . . .

a. up the fireplace chimney and furnace flue.
b. through the walls, joints, and cracks.
c. through the windows.
d. through the attic or roof.
e. through electric outlets and switches.
f. None of these.
g. All of these.

5. A conventional wood-burning fireplace with a roaring fire in it . . .

a. keeps the whole house warm.
b. cools the house and makes the furnace run longer.
c. is a powerful aphrodisiac.

6. A wood-burning fireplace can be made more efficient by . . .

a. covering with a tempered glass screen.
b. installing a tighter damper.
c. placing an iron stove on the hearth.
d. using a tubular grate that returns heated air to the room.
e. All of the above.
f. None of the above.

7. *Better use of solar energy can reduce home heating and cooling costs . . .*
   a. only if expensive equipment is installed.
   b. only in warm climates that don't need much heat anyway.
   c. only in new, specially designed houses.
   d. in most buildings.
   e. in all buildings.
   f. only where conventional energy costs are extremely high.
   g. only where the residents are numb to pain.

II. True Or False, More Or Less

1. The home refrigerator is more efficient now than twenty years ago. _____

2. A 100-watt light bulb is a highly energy-efficient light source. _____

3. A self-cleaning oven is an energy-saver. _____

4. Your water heater, set at 160° F (71° C), is just right for a hot bath. _____

5. Showers and baths use the same amount of hot water. _____

6. The automatic dishwasher is very wasteful of energy and water compared to washing by hand. _____

7. Major energy savings can only be had at great initial expense, or with great discomfort. _____

III. More Choices

1. *Which of the following factors need* not *be considered in designing a new house for efficient energy use?*
   a. Northern and southern exposures.
   b. Types of trees planted around the house.
   c. Size of windows and doors.
   d. Types of glass panes and doors installed.
   e. Latitude north or south of the equator.
   f. Strength of prevailing winds.
   g. Proximity of mass transit lines.
   h. Cost per Btu (see Question I.1) of available sources of energy.
   i. Hours of sunlight per year.
   j. Likely number of occupants of house.
   k. Path of migrating waterfowl.

2. *Which of the following energy-saving steps should you take first?*
   a. Insulate your attic or roof.
   b. Wrap insulation around your hot-water pipes and air ducts.
   c. Don baggy thermal underwear and turn off the furnace. (In summer, strip for hot weather.)
   d. Modernize your furnace and air conditioner and clean all filters, coils, valves, etc.
   e. Install storm windows.
   f. Install weatherstripping on all doors and windows.
   g. Take a shower.
   h. It depends on you, your house, and your community.

3. *The person who can help you save the most energy—and money—the soonest is which of the following?*
   a. The President of the United States of America.
   b. Your representative in Congress, Parliament, etc.
   c. An energy auditor.
   d. A friendly banker.
   e. Your local hardware supplier.
   f. You.

ANSWERS

I. Multiple Choice

1. b. It's a very small amount of energy. The United States uses several quadrillion of them ("quads") each year.

2. c. It's available in many types for every purpose and is usually very easy to put in place.

3. e. All of these materials are used in different types of insulation for different purposes. Only goose down, among these choices, is suitable for insulating humans (and geese) from the cold.

4. d. The attic and roof lead the list with 27 percent of the heat loss, but all are significant, including electrical outlets and switches at 10 percent.

5. b. Sad but true in many cases unless special efforts are made to reduce the fire's air intake and exhalation of heat up the chimney. See next question.

6. e. All of these modifications make the fireplace more efficient, at varying initial costs.

7. e. Yes, just letting more sun in during cold weather, and keeping it out in summer by drawing or closing curtains and drapes, reduces demand on the heating and cooling systems in your house.

II. True Or False, More Or Less

1. False. The modern refrigerator's walls are thinner; the motor tends to heat the cabinet more; the "frost-free" feature increases energy use, as does increased size, especially if the increased freezer capacity is left empty.

2. False. Only 5 percent of the energy used by a 100-watt incandescent light bulb is converted to light—the remainder is dissipated as heat.

3. True. Better-insulated walls and doors make the self-cleaning oven operate more efficiently than the standard models.

4. False. Ouch! Turn it down 20° F (11° C) or more and save.

5. False. Showers use less, but the bather(s) can recoup some energy by letting the water in the tub warm and humidify the bathroom, before pulling the plug.

6. False. Not necessarily, if the machine is only operated when full and turned off before the "dry" cycle. Then open the door to let the dishes drip dry and warm the kitchen.

7. False! Many energy-saving devices are inexpensive to buy and "pay for themselves" very quickly in reduced fuel and electricity bills. Examples: a showerhead that cuts hot water use; a clothesline instead of a dryer; weatherstripping materials; and heavier curtains on the windows. As for the discomfort, these devices and other techniques described above, when taken together can save as much energy as turning the thermostat down. When it comes to major purchases, there is help available: energy audits to determine the most urgent need among various choices and financial assistance from government agencies and public utilities. Sooner or later, conservation measures always pay for themselves. And as prices rise for all types of fuel, the payoff comes *sooner*.

III. More Choices

1. k. This factor should be taken into consideration so as not to disturb migratory patterns by building on wetlands, for instance, but it has no bearing we can think of in terms of energy efficiency. All the others do.

2. h. Many factors lead to setting the right priorities in home energy-conservation measures. The first should always be getting accurate information about your house, your geographic and weather conditions, and financial resources available in your community.

3. f. The others might be of some help, but the initiative must be taken by the person with the most to gain.

R.B.

WATTS IT TAKE?

Energy is wasted—expensive energy—whenever it is produced where it is not needed or in a form that is not useful. Here are some common ways of wasting energy:

- Leaving a light on in an empty room
- Leaving an air conditioner on to cool a house while you're on vacation
- Boiling a full pot of water for one cup of tea
- Running a tubful of water when a shower will do
- Not fixing a leaky faucet

The *Almanac* staff calculated the cost of a few wasteful practices at the rate of 10 cents per kilowatt-hour (the price in New York City in 1979):

- A short shower with a needle spray head costs

5 cents while a full, hot bath costs 45 cents. If you replace an everyday bath with an everyday shower you can save $140.00 a year (roughly 160 gallons of fuel oil).

- A slow drip from your hot-water faucet costs $7.53 per year. A fast drip costs $75.26. A continuous trickle can cost a whopping $115 a year.
- Leaving only one 200-watt ceiling light on for six hours a day costs $43.80 a year.
- Boiling a full teapot (six cups) of water twice a day for a year costs $11.98. Boiling only one cup in the pot twice a day costs $5.38.

Saving energy means practicing conservation at home. Conservation does not rule out convenience—no one's suggesting we all give up electricity or hot water. The idea is to become aware of what conveniences cost instead of taking them for granted. It also means using them in the most efficient way possible—and buying new electrical appliances with efficiency in mind. One thing is certain: The more labor-saving devices you have, the more energy it takes to run them.

Consumers in the United States will soon get help in identifying how much electricity their appliances are using. Under a recent U. S. Federal Trade Commission (FTC) ruling, all appliances manufactured in the United States must have labels showing their "energy efficiency rating." The labels must also provide estimates of the highest and lowest efficiency ratings for similar size (competitive) products and estimated yearly utility costs. By evaluating this information, the aware consumer can buy the most efficient appliance available in a given category. The FTC hopes the labels will encourage manufacturers to make all appliances as energy-efficient as possible.

Even without the labels, there are several general rules.

- *Refrigerators and freezers*

  If you're buying a new refrigerator or freezer, consider a manual rather than automatic defrost model. The manual defrost feature will save you a significant amount of electricity each year—enough to pay for the entire unit in four or five years!
- *Top-loading or front-loading freezers*

  Top-loading models keep the cold in more efficiently than front loaders. And with both your refrigerator and freezer, remember to open the doors as briefly as possible. The more warm air you let in, the sooner the unit will frost up.
- *Ovens*

  While self-defrosting refrigerators waste energy, self-cleaning ovens save energy. Self-cleaning ovens are better insulated and therefore use less energy than ordinary ovens. They save work too!
- *Television sets*

  You might not think of your TV set as an appliance but it, too, needs a continuous supply of electricity. If you're buying a new set, remember that black-and-white models require less energy than color sets, smaller screens naturally need less than larger screens, and instant-on models use more than standard models. Another benefit: You'll get fewer X rays from the smaller black-and-white models.
- *Lights*

  In general, the greatest waste occurs when a small quantity of energy is lost over a long period of time. For example, electric lights that are small in wattage compared to, say, an electric motor can actually waste more energy. That's because we tend to leave lights on for hours at a time. In contrast, the "surge" of electricity that appliance motors need when starting up lasts only a few seconds.

  If you leave a night light burning, use the smallest bulb available. For other lights, consider dimmer switches for lights that don't require full brightness all the time. In brightly lit areas, fluorescent lights are more efficient than incandescent light bulbs. For bulbs under 100 watts, there is no significant savings in switching to fluorescent.
- *Pots and pans*

  Choosing the right cooking pot can save surprising amounts of energy. Wide-bottom pots, for example, collect heat faster than smaller ones—so the pot is on the burner a shorter time. Similarly, thin-walled aluminum or copper pots heat more quickly than thick-walled ceramic ones.

  Other cooking tips: A good electric frying pan uses less energy than a regular pot on an electric stove. Similarly, a pressure cooker saves energy by cooking faster than a conventional pot.
- *Toasters*

  Ovens are big energy users. For that reason, it's more efficient to use a toaster or toaster oven for small items.

"NUMBSKULL — YOU JUST SMASHED HALF THE SOLAR-HEAT PANELS ON OUR ROOF!"

(© *1980, by Sidney Harris*)

- *Dishwashers*

If you wash dishes by hand, remember that running water is often wasted water. Wash dishes in a batch and then rinse them off. Don't leave the water running during this operation, which wastes both water and the energy used in heating it.

If you use a dishwasher, turn it on only with a full load and turn it off before the dry cycle. The dishes will dry anyway—they'll just take a bit longer.

- *Baths and showers*

Showers save water compared to baths. And of course, shorter showers save more than longer ones. Obviously, cooler showers consume less energy than hotter ones. Sharing a shower can cut consumption in half.

E.B.

WATT BUDGETS

This chart gives a rough approximation of the cost of operating common household appliances. Electricity used by your appliances will vary according to the wattage and efficiency of the particular model. The price of electricity also varies depending on where you live. The cost used here is ten cents per kilowatt hour, the rate in New York City in 1979.

Appliance	*Average Wattage*	*Cost Per Use*	*Average Cost Per Year*
Refrigerator			
12 cubic feet, manual defrost	241	–	$ 72.80
14 cubic feet, frostfree	615	–	182.90
Electric range	12,200	–	117.00
Freezer (15 cubic feet, frostless)	440	–	176.10
Washing machine	512	$0.025/use	10.30
Clothes dryer	4,856	.03 /use	99.30
Dishwasher	1,200	.06 /use	36.30
Television (black and white)	55	.005/hour	12.00
Television (color)	200	.02 /hour	44.00
Stereo	109	.01 /hour	10.90
Air conditioner (10,000 Btu)	1,250	.125/hour	139.00
Humidifier	177	.02 /hour	16.30
Coffee percolator	850	.015/use	9.60
Clock	2	–	1.70
Electric blanket	177	.08 /day	14.70
Hair dryer	38	.01 /use	1.40
Toaster	1,146	.005/use	3.90
Vacuum	600	.06 /hour	4.60

SOURCES: Edison Electric Institute, New York State Department of Energy.

OIL DAY LONG

Editor's Note: *Few of us realize how much oil we use that has nothing to do with our car or furnace. We asked Mike Maza, a Detroit writer, to spend a day at home keeping track of the petroleum-based products he encountered.*

7:00 A.M.—I awake feeling smug. I lead a decidedly nonplastic life, so I have no worries that my image is at risk in keeping track of all the petroleum derivatives I encounter in an average day. Plastics, after all, are the biggies in home petrochemicals. But one worry lingers: Will I come up with enough items to make a convincing list? Perhaps I should keep the evening clear for an emergency visit to K-Mart . . .

7:10 A.M.—I have my first item. These sheets I'm stretching between are 50 percent polyester, a fiber produced from ethylene, a petrochemical obtained mostly from natural gas feedstocks and cracked refinery gas.

7:11 A.M.—I know the exact time because it's displayed on the styrene plastic face of the clock radio, which is housed in a styrene case. Styrene is another ethylene derivative.

7:20 A.M.—I think I've just witnessed a petrochemical chain reaction. A re-enactment: Searching for my glasses on the bedside table (made of ABS plastic), my fingers mistook a rubberized plastic lamp cord for the rubberized plastic temple-piece of my glasses. Still somewhat sleep-bleared, I tugged at the cord, jerking the styrene base of the reading lamp into the business end of a plastic ballpoint pen that, like its brother-in-plastic the pinball flipper, pivoted on the table top, whacking a polystyrene button recently separated from its satin-simulating but nonetheless polyester shirt. This button, in flight, overshot the petroleum-derived bedside rug of nylon-wool blend, plinked onto the petroleum-derived, vinyl-asbestos floor tile, and skidded across the petroleum-derivative waxed surface to a heating grate through which it dropped, never to be seen again.

7:21 A.M.—One footnote on the above item. ABS is acrylonitrile-butadiene-styrene. Styrene we've met. Butadiene is produced from butylenes and butane, both byproducts of petroleum refining. It is also used in synthetic rubbers. Acrylonitrile is made primarily from propylene, a light hydrocarbon separated from crude in the refining process. Some propylene is produced as a co-product in the manufacture of ethylene.

7:22 A.M.—A second footnote: Waxes come from paraffin, a heavy residue of crude. (See "Roots: A Gallon of Gasoline," page 235.) A truth of the petrochemical industry is that it's hard to tell where the refinery ends and the chemical plant begins. It may also be true that chemists have learned to make use of every petroleum fraction except the odor.

7:40 A.M.—Flash: I look at the world through petrochemical lenses. Yes indeed, eyeglass lenses from plastic.

7:50 A.M.—I'm bound for a jog through the park. Gym shorts, T-shirt, and socks are all of 50-percent-polyester fabric. The shoes are petro products from the ground up. Synthetic rubber soles. Polyethylene insole. Plastic foam pads. Nylon upper. The suede trim, presumably, is not human-made.

The sweatband stretches to fit my head because of its synthetic rubber fibers. Like the waistband of my undies, come to think of it.

7:51 A.M.—I almost stepped over the morning paper without realizing it was pulped using petro-detergents and printed in inks that combine petroleum solvents with carbon black.

(Carbon black is one of the few important inorganic chemicals found in crude. The others include the most abundant petrochemical, ammonia, which goes into fertilizer, and sulfur, which ends up in matches, among other things.)

8:20 A.M.—While jogging I saw Mrs. X., a neighbor who lives with the help of a plastic heart valve. She was carrying a vinyl purse and pushing a collapsible stroller of nylon, which contained her granddaughter. The child was holding a plastic baby bottle and wearing a plasticized disposable diaper. More: In the park, tennis players volleyed balls of petroleum over a net of petroleum on a court of asphalt from petroleum. Couldn't check the tags on their clothes, but unless I miss my guess . . .

Also: One Frisbee abandoned in the grass. And packaging debris—plastic cups, plastic wraps, a half-pint milk carton coated with wax.

9:00 A.M.—My wife is off to work and my daughter to school, carrying her lunchbox by its plastic handle. Inside: one sandwich wrapped in polyethylene film, soup in a plastic thermos bottle (probably of polyurethane), and one plastic spoon.

We do try to reuse them.

I'm beginning to feel defensive.

9:05 A.M.—I take the plastic drip basket off the coffeepot, lift the pot from the plastic coffee maker by its plastic handle and pour myself a cup.

9:45 A.M.—Out of the bathroom with more for the list. Soap made from the fatty acid components of paraffin. Shampoo containing propylene glycol. I brushed my teeth with one styrene-handled, nylon-bristled brush, my hair with another. My toothpaste probably contains formaldehyde, a petroleum product now suspected of being a carcinogen. I shaved with a plastic-handled razor loaded with a double blade set in plastic. Shaving cream contains petro-products. And in the medicine chest and the bathroom closet I found a score of petroleum-derived products. Nail polish and its remover. Rubbing alcohol. Drugs and cosmetics containing alcohols and other petro-products, packaged in plastic tubes, vials, and jars. Hand lotion. Deodorant. Bubble bath. Lipstick. Cough syrup. Pool toys of plastic. Petroleum jelly.

9:55 A.M.—Yearning for distraction, I slide a plastic cassette of Mylar audio tape—a polyester film—out of its plastic storage container and into the tape deck. Plastic meter faces covered by plastic lenses. Who knows how many feet of synthetic rubber insulation on the wires inside?

Back to the bathroom for two tablets of acetyl salicylic acid—aspirin, also derived from petroleum.

10:00 A.M.—I seek refuge in work. The typewriter keys are plastic. The ribbon is nylon. The "carbon film" is Mylar.

1:00 P.M.—Time for a break. I need a paper clip. And I'm hungry.

When the desktop paper clip font dries up, a stray can usually be found in that centrally located family repository we call the junk drawer.

Opening it is almost like striking oil. Three quarters of a crayon (burnt umber), a plastic whistle, two red checkers, a cracked protractor, a ballpoint pen (dry), two penless ballpoint caps, one capless ballpoint pen pocket-clip fragment. Also: an unopened box of wax birthday candles, one comb (minus three large middle teeth), a cat's flea collar, the tail section of one toy airplane, two hair rollers, one die, and (ouch) a pushpin. A plastic-coated playing card, a guitar pick, an empty disposable lighter, a rain hat in its plastic pouch, a swizzle stick, two poker chips, an eraser estranged from its pencil, a plastic nametag holder, a plastic bag containing two balloons, and one pair of children's scissors of styrene plastic. But no paper clip.

Back to the bathroom. Four plastic-tipped hairpins purloined from their plastic box do the job nicely.

1:35 P.M.—Lunch is yesterday's leftover salad, greens and tomatoes gone soggy, but still quite tasty in a homemade French dressing. That's with *vegetable* oil. I sense a temporary respite from petroleum in the food before me. Of course, it did come out of the plastic-lined refrigerator.

2:00 P.M.—The kitchen faucet is leaking hot water—probably a bad washer. In the basement I can't help seeing the ammonia, the laundry detergent, the "sponge" mop in the plastic pail. One synthetic rubber washer from the plastic drawer that hangs below the styrene plastic rack holding plastic-handled screwdrivers and longnose pliers with handles covered in PVC—polyvinyl chloride, an ethylene derivative by way of vinyl chloride, another plastic on the carcinogen suspect list.

2:30 P.M.—I sit down again on my PVC-covered chair to type my list on my plastic typewriter keys. And so on.

6:00 P.M.—By evening my record keeping begins to falter. I lose track of time, and jot down only words. Phonograph records. Stereo earphone pads. Toilet seat. Toilet brush. Picture frame. Mirror handle. Waste basket. Drinking straws. Cannister lids.

I know I could find more if I combed the house, room to room. Telephone. Some coat hangers. But what's the use? The list will grow repetitious: more clothing, household cleaners, furniture, a ruler, a camera case.

Near midnight I give up and go to bed. I fall asleep to the sound of rain on the roof. In my dreams a contractor recites the specifications for a new roof: a layer of polyfoam sheet insulation, three plies of asphalt-saturated roofing felt, a hot asphalt seal.

In my dream I smile, and pay him with plastic money.

M.M.

DOES YOUR LAWN POLLUTE?

Editor's Note: *The first efforts to stop water pollution concentrated on the obvious sources: industrial and sewage pipes. However, as researchers continued to track down pollution sources, they discovered some that were very close to home. A $5.2-million study of Long Island, New York, for example, exposed some surprising villains—a fertilizer spreader used on the lawn; the laundry room, with its stain and spot removers; family dogs, being walked in the gutters near street drain pipes. The results of the Long Island investigation say a lot about how we supply ourselves with drinking water and dispose of our wastes.*

The study, one of the first of its kind anywhere, looked beyond toilet wastes as the main source of pollution and beyond sewage treatment plants as the solution, and considered the effects of anything that is disposed of or leaks into the ground. Although its scope was confined to Long Island, which gets all of its drinking water from wells, its findings have broad implications for many parts of the world. These findings indicate that sewers are not a complete or satisfactory answer to water pollution. Instead, they show that if people want to keep their bays and ocean fronts clean enough for swimming and shellfishing, and their drinking water supplies pure, they cannot foul their own nests.

Such a study needed to be done on Long Island, not only because the drinking water comes from underground, but because much of the island is not sewered. Septic tanks or cesspools are the rule. Ten years ago, most experts believed that all of Suffolk County, which covers the eastern portion of Long Island, would eventually require sewers. Accordingly, a massive sewer project was undertaken; many now say it was a massive mistake. In part because of the cost of the sewage system and in part because of challenges by environmentalists, the regional planning board was given the task of developing a study of all the alternatives.

The results of the study were startling. It found, for example, that the principal source of pollutants in the Great South Bay, the most productive natural hard clam factory in the world, was dog feces. The feces, it turned out, were washed into the bay by every rainfall. One recommendation of the study, therefore, is an end to mere curb-your-dog ordinances. "We may have to set up grassed areas to be used by defecating dogs, rather than to allow them on streets or sidewalks," said Aldo Andreoli, a member of the study group's technical staff and a public health engineer with the Suffolk County Health Department.

Storm water runoff in general was found to be a significant source of marine pollution. In addition to dog feces, the runoff contains lead from car exhausts and many other substances spilled onto the streets. Therefore, one traditional way of dealing with storm water runoff—collecting it in catch basins connected directly by pipes to lakes or bays—should be changed, according to the report.

The study found that lawn fertilizer, not human wastes, was the leading contributor of nitrates to Long Island's groundwater. "People will have to get used to having lawns that are not as lush but which don't require as much feeding," said Andreoli. The study recommends that homeowners be urged to plant lawns of fescue grass rather than bluegrass, which not only requires heavy fertilizing but a lot of watering besides.

The study also identifies chemical solvents as the source of halogenated and aromatic hydrocarbons, which are known to be toxic or which have been listed as suspected carcinogens in drinking water. The Nassau County Health Department has a list of 500 substances that fall into this category, among them common household spot and stain removers. Not enough is known as yet about how quickly or in what quantities such removers seep into the groundwater.

The evidence is clearer, however, for another category of such products—septic tank and cesspool cleaners. New York State Attorney General Louis J. Lefkowitz is seeking assurances from manufacturers that they will not sell these products on Long Island. If they will not agree voluntarily, a legislative ban will probably be sought.

Andreoli said homeowners will get along nicely without the cleaners. "For the average household, what is needed is periodic pumping of the septic tank, perhaps once a year," he said. This kind of regular maintenance, he said, would not only eliminate the need for the chemical solvents, but increase the life of the septic tank by perhaps 50 percent.

But perhaps the most far-reaching finding of the study was that not all land should be used by human beings in the same way. A hydrogeologic examination of Long Island showed that a drop of water falling near the south shore will never find its way into the wells that supply drinking water. Instead, it will travel horizontally through the ground out into the bays.

But rain falling in the center of Long Island will travel straight down, deep into the aquifers. Thus, the study recommended that wherever possible, the central parts of Long Island be gently used by people. Where land is developed, zoning should allow no more than one dwelling for every 2 acres (0.8 hectares). On the south shore, in contrast, much higher densities would not adversely affect the water supply.

Formal acceptance of the study by government agencies will mean that no federally funded construction projects would be permitted on Long Island unless they conform with the study's recommendations. Passage of new dog control ordinances or educational campaigns to tell homeowners to give up their bluegrass lawns will have to come from local town and county governments. To people such as Mr. Andreoli, not doing so carries a very high risk. "Not only might we end up ruining our own water supply, but that of future generations as well," he said.

THE WATERLESS WATER CLOSET

Flushing away human wastes in a swirl of water is taken for granted in so many parts of the world that it is difficult to imagine doing it any other way. But such a system depends on virtually unlimited supplies of water and it wastes potentially useful resources.

The problem of squandered water, though, is not a new one. In nineteenth-century London, cisterns that supplied water closets had only an on-off valve, resulting in tremendous water waste. Addressing this problem, Thomas Crapper invented the Valveless Water Waste Preventer. It soon became—and remains—the standard flush toilet for much of the world. For this singular accomplishment, the English knighted Sir Thomas, while Americans made his name a part of the vernacular.

This marvelous device upon which so many have come to depend requires about 13,000 gallons (49,210 liters) of water to carry away the mere 165 gallons (625 liters) of body waste produced by one person each year. In a more recent effort to curb this demand, the state of California adopted legislation outlawing any toilet that consumes more than 3.5 gallons (13.2 liters) per flush, thus cutting in half the usage of the standard 7-gallon (26-liter) version.

Carrying off wastes is of course only part of the problem. Once polluted, the water must go somewhere. For centuries, the standard solution was simply to dump it into the nearest river, sea, or lake. Those upstream emptied raw sewage with little thought for those downstream. English castles discharged the sewage directly into their moats, where it presumably provided one more deterrent to prospective invaders.

In modern times, it became increasingly apparent that some form of wastewater treatment was necessary. Cities with extensive networks of sewage-collection pipes (in 1863, the Paris system had about 3,500 kilometers of pipe) began to attach simple treatment plants to the outfalls of these collection systems. As suburbanization spread out from central cities, many more networks of pipes, pumps, and plants were constructed.

In the United States today, for example, 70 percent of the population is served by sewers and 92 percent of these systems feed into wastewater treatment plants. Currently, the U. S. Environmental Protection Agency (EPA) is providing grants of $4.8 billion annually to cities and towns for the construction or upgrading of complex systems in what has been called the largest civil works project ever attempted in the history of the world.

These sophisticated systems are costly to build and maintain, plagued with operational problems, and are large consumers of energy. And all of these resources are being expended, remember, so that perfectly good fertilizer (human excrement) can be combined with pure drinking water, flushed away underground to installations that separate it back into its component parts, whereupon the water is poured back into the nearest body of water and the resulting sludge is dumped into the ocean, spread over the land, or burned.

Fortunately, there are some sensible alternatives to this costly and wasteful process that are attracting increasing attention in many parts of the world. None of them involves new principles or high technology.

Septic Tanks

The septic tank is well known in suburban and rural settings where municipal sewering has been prohibitively expensive. It is a small, underground treatment plant into which wastewater flows and solid materials are settled out. The resulting effluent travels from the septic tank into a large underground drainage area called a leaching field, where it slowly percolates down through the soil, becomes purified, and enters the water table in ultimate recycling.

The system is fairly dependable and ecologically acceptable as long as certain requirements are met. These include sufficient land area, a porous type of soil adequate for filtration, a source of water, and periodic cleaning out of the tank itself. If the household using the septic tank also depends on well water, care must be taken to make sure that the wastewater is completely purified before it enters that portion of the water table supplying the well.

In the United States, many people were introduced to septic tanks following World War II when the flight of urban dwellers out of the central cities began in earnest. In a majority of these suburban communities, the common practice was to depend on septic tanks until the rising development density of a neighborhood produced unsanitary conditions, such as the pollution of neighbors' wells and a bubbling up of the inadequately treated wastewater to the surface during heavy rainstorms. At this point, investments in municipal sewering were made.

One of the interesting features of septic tanks is that they can be used effectively as the basis of a zoning requirement to restrict development above a certain density. Conversely, municipal sewering can open up an area to much more intensive development. So, human waste-disposal systems can inadvertently influence community patterns.

Dry Toilets

The compost toilet is another viable alternative to our present sewer systems based on water as the medium of disposal. It too comes from an old idea: combining heat, oxygen, and humidity to decompose organic wastes into carbon dioxide and water vapor which can be vented harmlessly to the outside atmosphere. It requires no water or chemicals and very little energy. The residue of this decomposition process represents only 5 percent of the original waste mass, in the form of an odor-free material that becomes nutrient-rich topsoil or humus.

There are at least two compost toilets being marketed in Europe and the United States; both are Swedish in origin: the Mullbank and the Clivus Multrum.

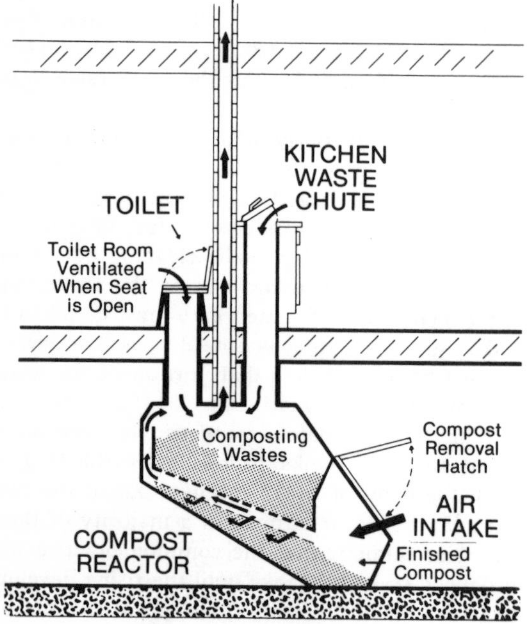

(*Clivus Multrum USA, Inc.*)

The toilet itself is a seat, with cover, on top of a wide chute leading down to the compost chamber. Bathroom wastes fall by gravity to the chamber below, which may be just under the toilet unit or in a separate unit in the basement. A small fan draws air through the chamber and vents it into a long pipe leading out through the roof. This provides the necessary oxygen for the composting process and also vents away odors and the carbon dioxide and water vapor produced. Once a year or so, the accumulated material in the bottom of the unit is removed from a tray and disposed of in the garden or around the shrubbery. There is no odor to this residue and it appears no different than soil.

The Clivus Multrum is designed to be a complete processing system for a family of four or five. More than one toilet can be hooked up to it but each must have its own straight, vertical chute to a fiber-glass tank in the basement. The tank also accepts organic garbage from the kitchen, which has its own chute. The Multrum costs about $2,000 plus installation and is perhaps better suited for new homes or low-rise apartments specifically designed to accommodate it, although it has been successfully installed in existing structures.

The Mullbank is a smaller, individual unit that is both cheaper to buy (less than $1,000) and cheaper to install. It does not accept garbage and has both a fan for ventilation and a small heating unit to make sure the compost pile maintains the required temperature—between 72° F and 98° F (22° C–37° C).

The composting action that takes place will be slowed down or stopped by such things as extremes in temperature or the addition of household chemicals. Excess moisture or lack of air results in the process going anaerobic (operating without oxygen) the way a septic tank does, with resulting undesirable odors.

For all this apparent fragility, however, it is not likely that the composting process will be permanently halted and, when the undesirable conditions are removed, the active bacteria quickly multiply back to normal levels.

Since the compost toilet is essentially a waterless system, some arrangement must be made to dispose of wastewater from kitchen and bathroom sinks, washing machines and dishwashers—commonly referred to as "gray water." The previously installed sewage system or septic tank will take care of this gray water very nicely, since total wastewater volume has now been reduced by 50 percent or more.

Abby Rockefeller, of the Chase Manhattan Bank branch of the family, is the U.S. distributor for Clivus Multrum. She and Carl Lindstrom, son of the inventor of the device, have been experimenting for several years with a system that recycles gray water through a rough stone filter to remove hair, lint, small bits of food and the like, and then pipes it into a small greenhouse where it is filtered through the same soil in which plants are growing. Excess purified water that is not taken up by the plant life is simply piped off into a dry well where it returns to the water table. A similar system could presumably be arranged without actually including a greenhouse—for those not possessing green thumbs.

Although the waterless water closet is still a suspicious novelty to most planners and developers, some communities lacking sewers are looking more closely at composting. As sewer costs increase and water supplies become both more scarce and more costly, a trend to waterless water closets can be expected to grow. At some point, the compost toilet or its future equivalent may become as compelling an idea as Thomas Crapper's flush toilet did in the late nineteenth century. R.N.

LIVING ON THE LOVE CANAL

Not far from where newlyweds gaze dreamily at mists rising from the thunder of Niagara Falls is a neighborhood of abandoned houses and shattered hopes. More than irony haunts this place. There is also the disturbing sense that this deserted neighborhood—the area they call Love Canal—stands as a silent warning: It could happen again.

Though Love Canal, a neighborhood of Niagara Falls, New York, has been called "an environmental time bomb gone off," what happened there didn't occur in a spectacular explosion. The neighborhood was poisoned, slowly; the agents of its demise—toxic chemicals buried decades ago—bubbling from the ground, tainting the water, and filling the basements of the modest single-family homes with invisible, but poisonous gases.

There were early warnings of what was to come. Chemical odors were persistent, but not unusual. Love Canal residents were accustomed to the smell of nearby chemical plants. Though children and animals periodically developed rashes and chemical burns, Niagara Falls officials told concerned parents that the skin disorders "were nothing to worry about." And there were the unexplained personal tragedies—birth defects, miscarriages, and central-nervous-system disorders. Love Canal families quietly suffered, and wondered to themselves why their middle-class neighborhood, once envisioned by its namesake William Love as a turn-of-the-century model city, could be visited by so much unhappiness.

Karen Schroeder, one of the earliest inhabitants of a new home along the abandoned canal that Love, a misbegotten entrepreneur, built to service the model city that never was, recalls that decades ago the area was serenely rural. "We used to swim in the canal, and there was fishing and boating too." More families moved in, many of whom worked at nearby chemical plants. One of those companies, Hooker Chemical and Plastics Corp., also had designs for the Love Canal. The canal itself offered an ideal site, they thought, for the disposal of chemical wastes.

Sometime in the 1940s, Hooker began dumping 55-gallon (208-liter) drums of wastes in the canal. In 1953 the canal had served its purpose, was covered with clay and topsoil, and sold to the local Board of Education for the paltry sum of $1. The rest of the 300-yard-long (274-meter) dump site was sold to a developer; the neighborhood needed more room to grow.

One thing the community needed, city officials reasoned, was a new elementary school, and the reclaimed dump site was a convenient and available location. Hooker executives claim they warned the city that the dump contained toxic chemicals, 22,000 tons worth, and the warning was ignored. (Hooker officials, however, were careful to word the deed for the site to exempt them from liability for what happened there.) Former Love Canal resident Bonnie Snyder faults the Board of Education with gross negligence. "They knew what those chemicals were. They should have realized that at some time something was going to happen."

It did. The water from several years of heavy rain and snow began to seep into the clay vault containing the rusting drums of waste. Though Hooker claims the dump would have remained secure if the construction on the site had not scraped away some of the clay cap, some observers believe that it was just a matter of time. "The problem was going to develop anyway," said one Hooker critic. "Landfills are just playing games with time."

Rotting drums began to emerge from the chemical grave in the school playground and the backyards of some homes. Karen Schroeder recalled that her backyard swimming pool suddenly rose a foot and a half out of the ground. When they removed the pool the Schroeders discovered a pond underneath with a colorful chemical slick. Love Canal resident Pat Bulka said that she went through four sump pumps in her attempt to remove chemical-tainted spring runoff from her basement. "The water was burning the motors out, just eating them up."

Alarmed residents began to understand that their problems were not simply personal ones, the entire neighborhood was being poisoned. They began to complain.

Few city or state officials were ready to listen to Love Canal residents' unfolding tale of the tragedy until an enterprising young reporter from the Niagara Falls *Gazette* began to ask questions. In the course of investigating conditions at Love Canal, journalist Mike Brown began to note the unusually high incidence of health defects among residents. He recalled one woman who greeted him at her home in a wheel chair. Her doctors were puzzled at her condition because, for no obvious reason, she simply became weaker and weaker. The woman, he discovered, operated a beauty parlor in her basement. He suspected chemical poisoning.

There were many other victims. Members of the Bulka family have chronic hearing problems, abnormally high white blood cell counts, and Pat Bulka's sister, who spent much time in the basement washing clothes, has had four miscarriages. Ann Hillis says her son has respiratory problems, asthma, skin rashes, and is hyperactive. His symptoms, she claims, disappear when he is away from the family's home at Love Canal.

With Brown's help, Love Canal residents organized to pressure local, state, and federal officials to look into the problem. In 1977 and 1978 more than one hundred stories appeared in the *Gazette* exploring the conditions there, and residents stepped up pressure on government offices. Finally, in April 1978, the state health commissioner authorized a study of Love Canal that confirmed the existence of hazardous levels of a broad array of toxic chemicals including benzene and seven other carcinogens in the basements of homes on or near the dump site. The report also pointed dramatically to an incidence of miscarriages and birth defects three times normal, and widespread liver damage in local adults. Several months later, Love Canal, once the vagary of a turn-of-the-century entrepreneur and later the suburban dream of some modest middle-class families, was declared a disaster area by the President of the United States.

By the spring of 1980, 239 families had been evacuated from the area on or near the Love Canal and relocated and the U. S. Environmental Protection Agency recommended evacuating 710 more. The vacant homes stand as testimony to the folly of careless disposal of toxic wastes. Lois Gibbs, president of the Love Canal Homeowners Association, and one of those homeowners not included in the first evacuation, argued for two years that many other families should also be relocated. State and federal government agencies squabbled over the necessity and cost of purchasing the remaining homes. Most of the families couldn't afford to move, despite the danger, without selling their homes. When members of the Homeowners Association took to the streets to dramatize their demand for relocation, there were sixteen arrests, and still no action.

Clean-up of the Love Canal, which some experts estimate could cost $150 million, is under way, but the work may be just beginning. Hooker Chemical has identified several additional chemical dumps, one possibly more hazardous than the Love Canal site, under a ball field near another elementary school in Niagara Falls, near the city's water-treatment plant, and at a 16-acre (4-hectare) landfill near Niagara University. The company has also admitted burying up to 3,700 tons of trichlorophenol, which contains the deadly chemical dioxin (TCDD), at several sites throughout Niagara County. In early 1980, both the State of New York and the federal government filed multimillion-dollar lawsuits against Hooker over these dumps (see "Cases in Point," page 580).

The problem is clearly much larger than Love Canal. Federal officials believe that there may be more than eight hundred sites in the United States that could be as dangerous as the debacle in Niagara Falls, and some even worse. Perhaps they can be cleaned up, but not easily. And what of the neighbors of these chemical time bombs? Can their disrupted lives and dreams be as easily repaired? In the aftermath of the tragedy at Love Canal, remaining residents confronted another problem—hordes of the curious, driving by in tightly closed automobiles who came to stare at the infamous neighborhood. Perhaps it's more than morbid gawking that lures them there. Perhaps there is also a nagging uncertainty—could their neighborhood be next? B.P.B.

A TALE OF TWO HOUSES

In the 1940s, an American builder named William Jaird Levitt designed a low-cost, attractive home that could be assembled quickly. Since energy was abundant and cheap in those post-War years, the Levitt house—or one of the hundreds of variations on the idea that ultimately appeared—and its heating and cooling systems could be erected almost anywhere, regardless of climate. The design soon spread throughout the United States; it was ideal for an expanding home-construction industry that could reap substantial profits by building mass-housing projects based on a single design, and it solved the problem of young families looking for affordable homes in which to raise the millions of postwar "baby-boom" children of the 1950s and 1960s. The most famous of the new housing developments was Levittown, New York, built in 1947; nearly all of the U.S. suburban "tract" home projects built over the years are its descendants.

The rise of these sprawling developments influenced the pattern of American life-styles for the next forty years: encouraging an exodus from cities, dependence on the automobile, the growth of highways. (See "The Hidden Costs of Sprawl," page 263.) Within each house, energy use doubled or tripled during that time as newly affluent suburbanites riding on an expanding economy bought freely from the new inventory of household conveniences: air conditioners, electric dishwashers, huge refrigerators, and gadgets to do almost anything electrically from opening cans to slicing meat. The suburban dream was based on cheap energy.

Meanwhile, in Europe, postwar development was more restrained. There were suburbs, but energy-conserving traditions reaching back hundreds of years still guided most builders. There is little difference in the standard of living between Europeans and Americans of comparable income, but there is a *huge* difference in their household energy consumption. The drawings compare two highly stereotyped American and European homes, pointing out specific differences in energy use.

Doors: The front door of a common European home leads to a vestibule with a second door leading to the living room. This is more than a place for guests to wipe their feet. It helps keep cold air from entering the house and warm air from escaping. Americans like arches and large open spaces, but most European houses have doors on all rooms, enabling rooms not in use to be closed off and left unheated.

Kitchen Gadgets: While small electric appliances are not huge energy consumers (see "Watts It Take?" page 649), they are more prolific in most middle-class American kitchens.

Stoves: American stoves may come in designer colors and the ovens may clean themselves, but European stoves often do double duty as hot-water heaters. A coil of pipe passing through the oven carries stove-heated water to the kitchen sink and to the upstairs bathroom.

Laundry: Front-loading washing machines, which require less soap and water than top-loading models, are popular in Europe. Clothes are usually dried in the "drying room," which contains the hot-water storage tank, eliminating the need for a clothes dryer.

Refrigerators: The average European refrigerator is 7.8 cubic feet (0.22 cubic meters), using about 550 kilowatt-hours of electricity per year. The typical U.S. refrigerator of the same size uses about 1,100 kilowatt-hours per year, but many Americans opt for a larger frostfree refrigerator that at 17 cubic feet (0.48 cubic meters) uses 1,700 kilowatt-hours per year.

Bathrooms: Books have been written about the American fondness for warm, luxurious, and numerous bathrooms. Although the bathroom is used only a few hours a day, it's usually heated all day and a 40- to 60-gallon supply (151 to 227 liters) of water is kept constantly hot in case it's needed. The traditional European bathroom calls for more planning by the user, but is cleverly designed to save energy. It employs a space heater, rather than uniform central heating, or it might have an electric night storage heater, which is run at night when electric rates are lower and releases heat slowly during the day. A flash hot water heater heats enough water for a bath or shower when the bather turns it on.

Fireplaces: During the days of cheap central heating, American builders installed fireplaces only as decoration, if at all. Even functional fireplaces were designed for atmosphere, not heat. They allow heat to escape quickly up the chimney and may even result in a net loss of heat as the embers are dying—the updraft pulls most of the fire's hot air up the chimney. Although the fire does produce some heat, the cold air enter-

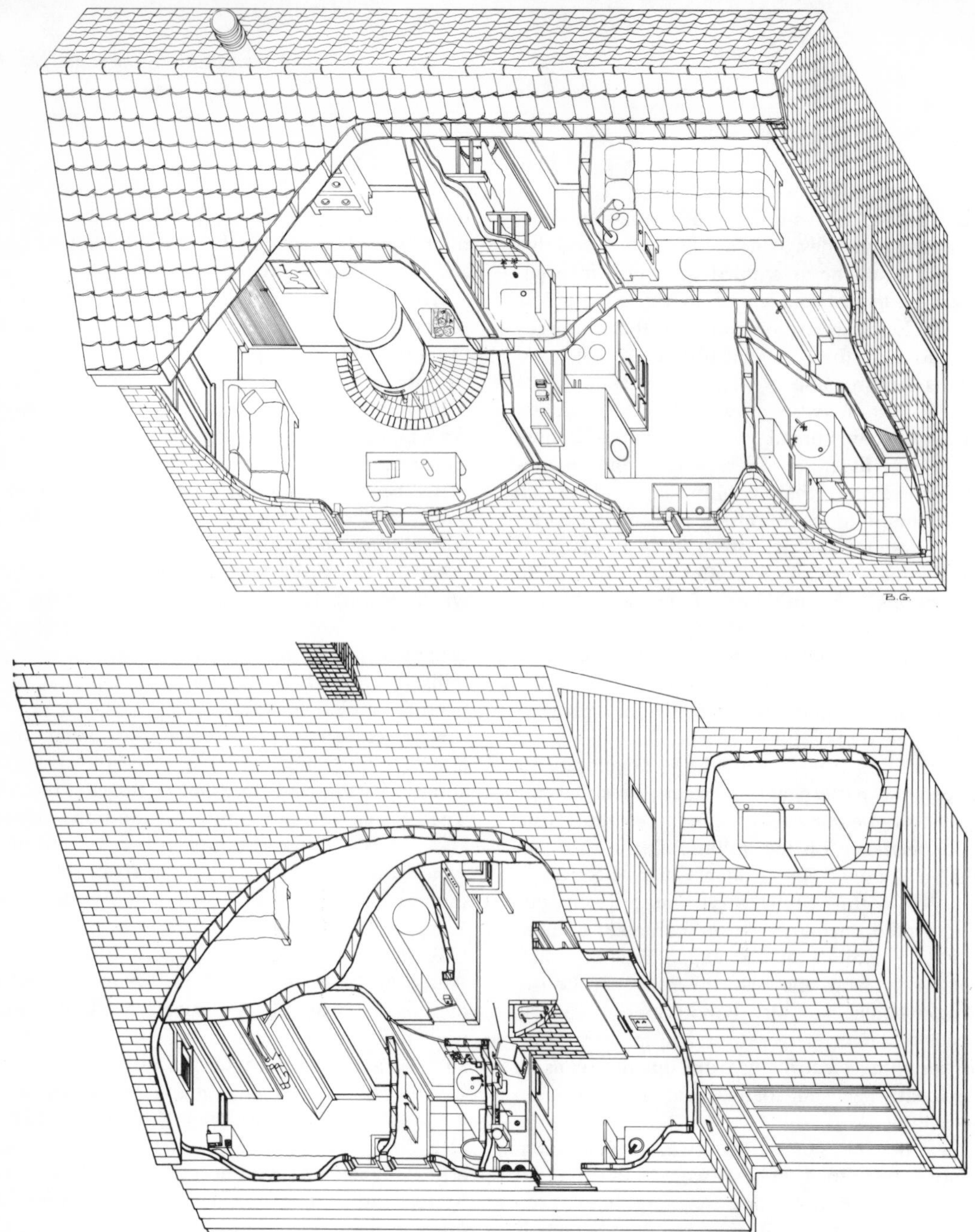

A common style of European home at top, a variation on the American Levitt home below.

ing the house to replace what goes up the chimney results in a net heat loss. Unless the hearth is fitted with doors that can be tightly closed as the smoke from embers goes up the chimney, and unless there is some circulation device to shoot hot air into the room while the fire is burning, the American fireplace does more to heat the air above the house than the air in the living room. The Finnish fireplace common in many European homes, on the other hand, is lined with metal walls that slowly release heat into the room and with vents that circulate air past the fire and then back into the room.

Bedrooms: American bedrooms often feature electric blankets that use a kilowatt-hour of electricity each night. Traditional European bedrooms still rely on the ceramic hot water bottle placed under the covers shortly before bedtime to warm the bed. Quilts and comforters hold in body heat throughout the night.

Size: The average American house is much larger than its European counterpart, and therefore more difficult to heat or cool.

The American Institute for Architects estimates that by 1990 the United States could cut its energy use by one third by modifying existing buildings and designing new buildings to conserve energy. Europeans, though far ahead of Americans in energy conservation, still see room for improvement.

B.G., K.F.

HOUSES AROUND THE WORLD

An anthropology textbook written in the United States in the 1960s expressed puzzlement over a seeming enigma among so-called primitive peoples. Why, it asked, have tribal peoples not concentrated as much interest on housing as they have on myth-making, religion, art, song, and dance? The Navaho Indians were taken as an illustration, living in "wood and dirt hogans" while making intricate sand paintings and performing elaborate nine-day chants. But when one examines the efficiency of the hogan, it is clear what the Navahos were up to. They had designed an extraordinarily functional and sophisticated structure. The adobe roof of a hogan kept the intense desert heat from penetrating the interior, while providing cool shade and storing up heat which was released automatically all night to counter the chill.

A Navaho hogan in Arizona. (*National Archives*)

Recently, the traditional hogan, developed over many generations, has been modified so that it is easier to build. The timber and adobe roof has been replaced by one made of sawed lumber and asphalt shingles. The new hogans can be built more quickly, but they don't work. They are too hot in the afternoon, too cold at night.

Many groups of people learned over the centuries to build with nature, to build *within* nature. The site of a home was carefully picked for its access to resources; the orientation was precisely chosen to take full advantage of natural sources of heating, shading, and ventilation. The shape was measured against the climate, so that in Scandinavia, the roof was made too steep for snow to accumulate, and in Dahomey, too porous for heat to build up. Windows were designed to direct light, almost like spotlights, to working areas. Trees were planted where they would provide windbreaks during the windy season and shade during the summer. By wintertime they were leafless so that no ray of warming sunshine was deflected.

Observations of seasons, solar angles, rainfall, wind, insects, and other important phenomena accumulated over generations, providing local builders with an unwritten catalog of environmental considerations. In some parts of the world, designs grew elaborate. Traditional houses in Baghdad featured first-floor rooms built with thick masonry walls which sealed in coolness. During the summer, families lived in these rooms and spent their evenings in adjacent courtyards. In the winter, the families moved upstairs, where walls of light wood and glass acted like solar collectors to warm the home.

Although in many parts of the world tribal peoples have traded their traditional dwellings for modern houses, a few still build with the wisdom and materials of their ancestors. The following are examples of houses intricately adapted to their environments.

M.R.

Cliff Houses

The island of Santorini, in the Aegean Sea, is a partially submerged volcanic cone. The sea has filled the area where lava once flowed and cliffs rise steeply seven hundred feet above the bay. Some of the island's residents have taken advantage of these cliffs by carving houses into the soft rock. Whitewashed like other traditional Greek buildings, these houses protect their inhabitants from the harsh summer sun and the cold winter winds. The surrounding rock varies in temperature much less than the air and moderates both summer heat and winter cold. Only one side is exposed to severe changes in temperature.

Cliff houses were also built by Native Americans in North America for protection from enemies and the climate. The homes at Mesa Verde, Colorado, are sophisticated four- and five-story buildings built in large caves on the face of a cliff. The cave opening faces south, shading the buildings from the high summer sun but allowing the low winter sun to enter and warm the buildings. (The Mesa Verde houses are buildings built into a cave, while the Santorini homes are caves with added facades.)

Cliff houses present obvious problems—lack of water and sanitation facilities, light, and ventilation. And expansion of a dwelling is difficult because tunneling one way or the other could break through a neighbor's wall. But, for cliff dwellings, houses at Mesa Verde and Santorini are remarkably sensible, efficient, and hospitable.

B.G., K.F.

The Cliff Palace in Mesa Verde National Park, Colorado, was once an Indian "apartment house" with more than 200 rooms. (*EPA Documerica/Boyd E. Norton*)

Cliff houses, Santorini.

Desert Houses

The desert climate is hostile because of its extreme variation between hot days and cold nights and the limited resources of building materials. Some desert areas also have cold or even wet winters. In the African Sahel, where there is a rainy season, the village people build earthen houses with small, high windows.

The heavy walls have good "thermal lag," meaning they slowly gather heat during the day, keeping the house from getting hot quickly, and slowly release the heat at night when it is cool. The small windows prevent too much sun from entering the house and raising the temperature, and their high placement permits light to enter as deeply into the house as possible so that people can work inside.

The nomadic tribes of Niger, Mali, and Mauritania had to abandon their traditional work of raising livestock because the drought from 1968 to 1973 destroyed most of the grazing land. (See "Engineering a Famine," page 193.) They were forced to settle in villages and to adopt earthen houses for the rainy season. During the summer, however, they set up their traditional tents beside the house. The tents of lamb's wool blankets are kept as low as possible for protection from windstorms. They are so low, in fact, that the people actually developed "knee dancing" as an art form. White linen is hung inside to make the interior brighter, and the tent sides are pinned open at night to allow the cool air to enter.

Buildings of adobe, stone, and stucco are common throughout the world. In warmer climates where the roof is not needed for heat retention, thatched roofs provide good insulation from daytime sun but do not store heat which would overheat the house at night.

B.G., K.F.

A North African desert house, with a nomadic tribal tent outside.

Snow Houses

Eskimos, faced with frigid Arctic temperatures, no conventional building materials, and the need to travel great distances in search of food, developed the famous snow house, or igloo.

In two hours an Eskimo can build a house with blocks of snow. The blocks are placed in a rising spiral, rather than concentric circles, to make the structure sturdier. One snow block is replaced by an ice block to allow some light to enter. The entrance tunnel faces away from prevailing winds and has a double vestibule to prevent cold air from blowing in. Sled dogs are tied near the entrance to preheat whatever air does enter, while the body heat of the human occupants melts the snow on the inner surface of the dome that later freezes to form a heat-reflective coating of ice

An eskimo ice house.

much like foil insulation. Furs are hung along the walls for more insulation, and sleeping platforms are built near the top where the warm air rises. Body heat and a small oil lamp are the only sources of heat.

Canadian soldiers using snow houses reported temperatures around 45° F (7° C) at the bed platform level when the outside temperature was −60° F (−51° C). In 1979, the recommended night temperature for a house in the United States was 55° F (13° C).

K.F.

Stilt Houses

In the tropical rainforests of Thailand the dry season is hot and humid, and even the rainy season can be stifling. The houses are built on poles about 10 feet (3 meters) above the ground. Elevating the houses improves ventilation, provides protection from animals, insects, and periodic floods. A sloping grass roof with a large overhang stops both rain and sun without storing heat. Porous walls keep out sunlight but allow ventilation. People tend to gather on the shaded porch, the coolest place, in the afternoon.

Variations of this house are found in Africa

A stilt house in Thailand.

and the southeastern United States. In South Africa some tribes use woven fiber mats for walls. The fiber of these mats allows ventilation in dry weather, but expands in wet weather to form a tight, nearly waterproof wall. Other tribes use detachable walls that can be arranged according to wind direction.

Although the bamboo used in these houses is flexible enough to bend in the wind without breaking, these structures are often destroyed in storms. Better modern materials could prevent this without too much additional cost.

B.G., K.F.

New Houses from Old Materials

Experiments in India are showing that housing costs can be dramatically reduced by using local materials such as bamboo and secondary timber. The Regional Research Laboratory in Assam has pioneered a novel construction technique combining these materials with ordinary cement mortar.

First, walls and roofs of pretreated split bamboo are fixed to timber framing. The split bamboo matting is then plastered. Houses built this way have an aesthetic quality and an expected life of about fifteen years.

A house with kitchen, bathroom, and toilet, complete with water fittings and electricity, with an area of 355 square feet (33 square meters) costs approximately $600. This is one third to one half the cost of more conventional low-cost housing (brick with either galvanized iron or asbestos cement roof sheeting).

K.F.

LIVING QUARTERS LORE

- The first cities arose about 5,500 years ago in lower Mesopotamia between the Tigris and Euphrates rivers.
- The total human demand for housing or shelter grows each year by a staggering amount. We

"LISTEN, IF YOU'RE EVER IN THE NEIGHBORHOOD..."

An experimental house by Michael Reynolds made of "building blocks" composed of used beverage cans. Eight steel cans are wired together and then covered with adobe. (*EPA Documerica/David Hiser*)

are adding about 80 million people per year to the planet. That is a new population the size of Pakistan needing homes, energy, water, and sanitation systems.

- By the year 2000 it is estimated that about 40 percent of the human population, or 2.5 billion people, will be living in major cities.
- About 20 percent of our total energy use is devoted to space heating, that is heating homes, offices, and all of the rest of our human-made structures.
- The energy used in making approximately 60 million disposable containers used yearly in the United States could heat 2.5 million homes, or the equivalent of the energy needs of Pittsburgh, San Francisco, Boston and Washington, D.C.
- It has been estimated that if all of the residents of California traded in their freezers for the most energy-efficient model, it could eliminate the need for all of the power supplied by one nuclear power plant.
- Complete insulation of a home can cut heating bills by as much as 40 percent.
- As a power source for appliances like hot-water heaters or dishwashers, natural gas is, in most cases, more economical than electricity. A dollar's worth of natural gas generates three times as much heat as a dollar's worth of electricity.
- A wood-burning fireplace is another inefficient energy source when compared to an airtight wood-burning stove. A cord of wood purchased at ninety dollars is equivalent, with its 5 percent efficiency, to paying ten dollars a gallon for oil, while the 65 percent efficiency of the stove would reduce the price to the equivalent of eighty cents a gallon.
- The median sale price of an American house in 1980 was about $78,000 according to the MIT–Harvard Joint Center for Urban Studies. This compares to a median price of $23,400 in 1970.
- Rising 110 stories, the World Trade Center Towers in New York are second only to Chicago's Sears Tower in height. The Towers contain 43,600 windows; 200,000 tons of steel; 274,000 lights (32,500 now removed to save energy); and enough concrete for a five-foot-wide sidewalk to Washington, D.C. Each day they hold 50,000 workers, produce 50 tons of garbage, use more than 2 million gallons of fresh water, and burn enough electricity to supply a U.S. city of 100,000 people.

World Trade Towers under construction, August 1971. (*Port Authority of New York and New Jersey*)

The buildings' internal systems suffer from the inefficiencies of inappropriate scale. Air-conditioning is divided into 34-story zones, so that if one office wants cooler air, all 34 floors have to be cooled. The smallest unit of lighting that can be turned on illuminates a quarter of an acre.

T.C.

SKYSCRAPER ARCHITECTURE: THE EDIFICE COMPLEX

It is sometimes called the "built environment" —the constructions fashioned by humanity throughout the ages to provide shelter. In recent decades, builders of human living quarters have appeared to wield engineering magic, as they erect structures unlike anything ever seen on earth. Modern buildings commonly rise so high that people now sleep farther above the ground than any human being had ever been before the invention of the hot-air balloon. Standing at a

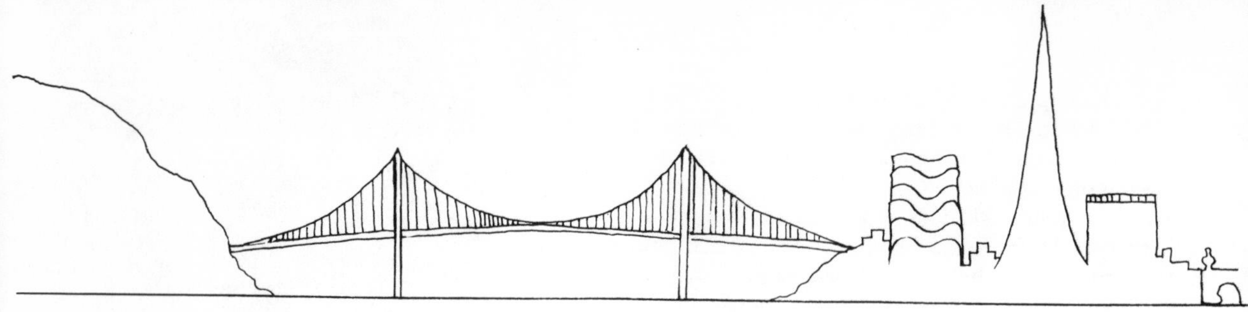

sealed window in shirtsleeves, they can watch a blizzard outside that would have threatened the lives of earlier peoples.

Modern architecture, however, is entering a period of criticism and review. In the United States, where many of the techniques of modern architecture were developed, fully *40 percent* of national energy consumption is used for buildings—to construct them, to manufacture their components, and to heat, cool, and illuminate them. In an age of energy scarcity, the marvels of recent architecture threaten to become unaffordable monstrosities of waste. The problem is not that people have recently lacked for new inventions but that we forgot the old inventions.

The history of human architecture is one of adaptation to local circumstances and local materials. Ingenious builders of the past were limited to one or two stories—seldom more than six—by the strengths and weights of building materials, and by the fact that no one wanted to climb hundreds of feet daily. But despite these constraints, builders managed to fashion immense, graceful, dramatic buildings—the Taj Mahal, the Temple at Angkor Wat, the great cathedrals of Europe, the public buildings of Greece and Rome, the temple towers of the Maya.

Advancing Backward

In the last century, many of the limitations on building were overcome by technological advances. These enabled architects to modify building design in revolutionary ways.

- *Elevators* The first elevator was installed in New York City in 1857 by its inventor, Elisha Otis. Compared to modern elevators it was slow, traveling vertically at forty feet per minute, but it made practical the idea of buildings that would rise higher than six stories. Modern express elevators move at 1,200 feet (366 meters) per minute.
- *Steel* Until the introduction of iron (and later steel) as a building material in the latter half of the nineteenth century, masonry walls had to support the weight of tall buildings. Above about sixteen stories the walls grew too thick to make rising higher practical. With the advent of strong steel girders, the walls no longer had to bear all of the weight; the steel skeleton accomplished that. Architects were free to think of walls as a skin, and to design for attractiveness rather than strength. The shape and size of a building became almost unlimited.
- *Light and Ventilation* After World War II, elaborate and enormous mechanical systems for heating, cooling, ventilating, and lighting appeared. Buildings could have a larger interior volume because work space was no longer limited to the reach of sunlight and breezes through windows. The immediate result: more rentable floor space in commercial buildings.
- *Glass Walls* With the need for a rigid exterior "bearing wall" eliminated by steel framework, architects were free to wrap their buildings in glass, which looked tidy, admitted more light, and provided a pleasant view. The need for insulation from heat and cold, an age-old problem, was overcome by internal temperature-

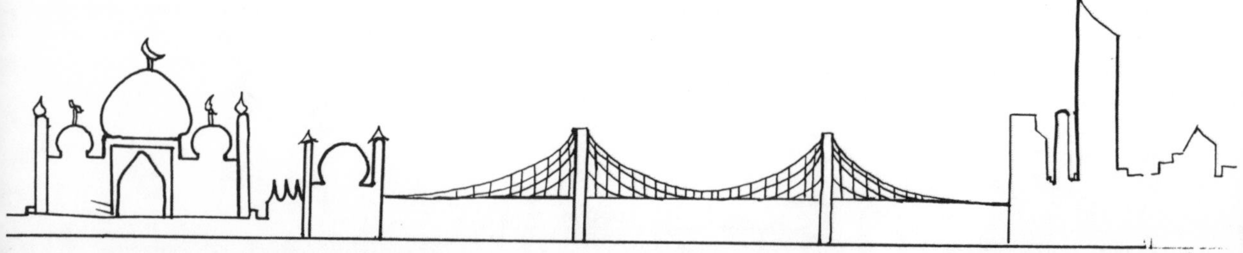

control systems, which were, of course, great consumers of energy. The glass wall came to be known, because of its nature as a thin, largely decorative wrapping, as a "curtain wall."

- *Flexible Space* Steel skeletons created large, column-free expanses within buildings. The walls on each floor were no longer fixed, no longer part of the structural system. As the needs of an office changed, so did the walls. Since the locations of partitions could no longer be counted upon, the lighting and ventilating needs could not be predicted. Therefore the mechanical equipment of the building had to be able to serve all parts of the building equally well. Lighting systems were made of uniform intensity, wasting light where no tasks were ever performed. And a special heating system was developed to keep the entire building at a uniform temperature.
- *Terminal Reheating* The idea was to create a huge heating and air-conditioning system capable of adapting to conditions on each floor. The goal was noble, but the method seems incredible in the energy-conscious world of today. At a central location, air is uniformly cooled to between 55° F and 60° F (13° C and 16° C), then blown through a system of ducts to each floor, where it is *reheated* to the desired temperature of each office.
- *Synthetic Materials* As structures were changing, so were the building and decorative materials within them. Steel window supports are now aluminum, asphalt tile and linoleum have given way to vinyl asbestos and sheet polyvinyl chloride. Linseed oil has been replaced by polysulphide in caulkings. Cotton and wool for drapes and carpets have been replaced by fiber glass, polyester, and acrylic. Plywood and wood often remain only as photographic veneers under plastic laminate surfacing. There are undeniable advantages to all of these materials, but many require more energy to produce than the product they replace. A pound of aluminum, for example, uses five times as much energy in production as a pound of steel. Although aluminum is stronger per pound than steel, its energy efficiency is still less.

As a result of the above developments and others, the design of a building no longer necessarily needed to express the purpose of a building. Building shape and surface ceased to relate to the activities within, and energy was used to create artificial, but comfortable, conditions.

As one result, the same building design patterns can be seen in Juneau, New Delhi, Berlin, Phoenix, Singapore, Tokyo, or Mexico City.

Holes in the Theory

Simultaneously, architecture grew more and more inefficient. The glass walls permitted the rapid penetration and escape of warmth and coolness. The windows couldn't be opened, eliminating the possibility of natural cooling and ventilation. As buildings got bigger, more space was given up to the mechanical plant for heating, cooling, ventilation, and elevators. The heat of

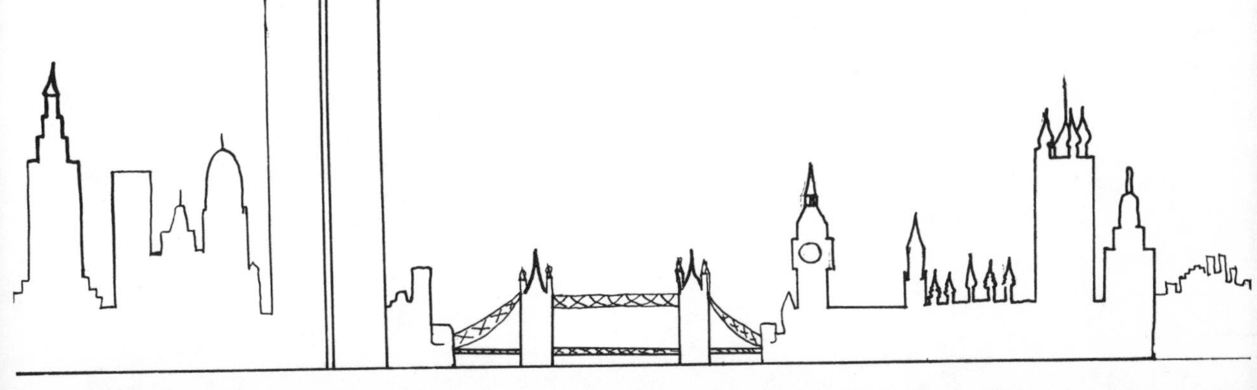

this machinery added to the heat of the building, increasing the need for air conditioning. As the air-conditioning system cools the building, it creates its own heat, which is vented outside where it heats the atmosphere. The city gets hotter and the cycle continues. Because cities have so little vegetation, which holds moisture and then cools the air through evaporation, they do not experience as much cooling at night, and so-called "heat islands" are created.

Since the introduction of the first glass-walled building, Lever House in 1952 in New York City, urban energy consumption has skyrocketed. A study of New York office buildings found that between 1950 and 1969 energy use per square foot doubled.

Remodeling Architecture

Changing course, when the global architecture and building establishment is deeply entrenched in its ways, is not an easy accomplishment. The impetus behind the modern style is strong, and buildings, unlike automobiles or furniture, are designed to stand for fifty years or more, so that there is a long time lag for significant change. In most cases, there are no immediate savings attached to energy efficiency for the people who design, build, and own office buildings. The developer erects a building and sells it, concerned principally with construction costs. The purchaser wants a maximum amount of rentable space, and if energy costs rise, passes the increases on to tenants.

An obstacle to change that may be even more intractable is the system of codes which govern such things as the brightness of lighting and the number of ventilation "air changes" per hour in offices. The codes are established by engineering societies and craft unions *within* the building and manufacturing industries. Thus, the people who are selling and installing the equipment are determining how much energy buildings require. Not surprisingly, the codes have recommended more air changes and stronger illumination over the years.

Perhaps the major obstacle to putting modern buildings on an energy diet is that peoples' expectations have risen with the wizardry of technology. For example, in the United States, before World War II, people were willing to live without air conditioning. Now it is considered a birthright among generations reared in modern apartment houses and offices.

There are, however, stirrings of changes to come. Energy performance standards are being developed, detailed materials research by energy specialists is underway, and energy "auditors" are being consulted before, as well as after, many new commercial buildings go up.

The ancient closeness between builders and the environment is being revived, too. The new IBM Plaza in Southfield, Michigan, has shiny walls facing west and south to reflect summer sun and black walls facing north and east to absorb solar heat in the winter. Chances are that the new design challenges imposed by energy limitations will have a stimulating effect on aesthetics, too, since responding to climate and function will force architects to develop new forms. Cities could bloom with new appearances that are distinctive reflections of their environment. Buildings need to adapt to the environment like living organisms in order to survive and prosper.

In a recent article in *Architectural Record,* architect Donald Watson characterized the changing nature of his profession:

> Architects once studied the rules of proportion for the styles and the orders of the classical temples of antiquity. The earth is now that temple: the rules are those of building and living within the limits of the earth's balance of resources and energy.

K.F., B.G., and M.R.

THE TEN HIGHEST BUILDINGS

	Feet	*Meters*
1. Sears Tower Chicago, Illinois	1,454	443
2. World Trade Center New York, New York	1,369	417
3. Empire State Building New York, New York	1,250	381
4. Standard Oil (Indiana) Chicago, Illinois	1,136	346
5. John Hancock Center Chicago, Illinois	1,107	337
6. El Paso Tower Houston, Texas	1,049	320
7. Chrysler Building New York, New York	1,046	319
8. Eiffel Tower Paris, France	984	300
9. First Bank Tower Toronto, Ontario	970	295
10. American International New York, New York	952	290

SOURCES: Information Please Almanac 1980, World Almanac 1980, People's Almanac

THE ALMOST-SOLAR SKYSCRAPER

The Citicorp Center, rising 914 feet (279 meters) above midtown Manhattan, is a blazing silver tower crowned with a southward-sloping roof, which was intended to accommodate a super solar panel. The tower was built between 1973 and 1975 by the holding company that owns Citibank (the former First National City Bank) New York's largest, to serve as its corporate headquarters. Designed by architect Hugh Stubbins, the complex, comprising the tower, a smaller office building, and a church, strives for the most modern in every detail: an underground mall of restaurants and boutiques, an airy open galleria rising through the heart of the office building, and a total design for energy efficiency up to the very top—where it stopped short of embracing the sun as a source of power. The reasons its distinctive rooftop did not become the world's first skyscraper solar collector reveal some of the difficulties in bringing solar energy to the big city in the mid-1970s.

(*Citicorp Center*)

Best of Intentions

The tower was already under construction when installing solar panels on its roof was first proposed. Originally, the roof was to slope westward and form glassed-in terraces for residences at the top. The residence idea was discarded, but the sloping roof was kept in the design, and at the same time, 1974, technical studies began for a rooftop solar collector.

The plan called for solar-generated energy to assist primarily in the air-conditioning system for the top twenty-five floors of the building, and, secondarily, to contribute to the hot-water supply. In modern tall buildings air-conditioning is required almost the year round. The sealed glass skin on a modern skyscraper lets in light and heat (direct solar energy) but does not let out the hot air: The windows don't open; lights, office machines, elevators, and people generate enough heat within such a building to make the temperature uncomfortably high. (See "Skyscraper Architecture," page 665.)

To combat the overheating problem, the Citicorp tower employs several energy-saving innovations. It shares energy with another Bank-owned building across the street; only 46 percent of the building's surface is glass, which is reflective and double-glazed; the remaining surface is reflective insulated aluminum; the lighting wattage throughout the building is about half that of conventional designs; and a computerized energy-management system further reduces waste.

These design features, of course, do not eliminate the enormous air-conditioning demand of the tower, created by its "terminal reheat" system. Air-conditioning systems first cool the air *below* a comfortable temperature to condense hot air, squeezing water out of it, thus reducing its humidity. When pumped into the building, this air must be *reheated* to suit the human occupants. (See "Skyscraper Architecture," page 665.)

The solar collector system proposed for the Citicorp Center was designed to dehumidify warm air, eliminating the need to reheat superchilled air. In the system, hot, humid, outdoor air is drawn into a "conditioner" where it is sprayed with a desiccant (triethylene glycol) that causes water in the air to condense. The dehumidified but still warm air moves on to an ordinary air-conditioning system, but the water-desiccant solution is pumped to a "concentrator" where it is sprayed on coils heated by the solar collector. The water evaporates and is borne away by warm, dry air exhausted from inside the building. The desiccant returns to the conditioner and is used to dehumidify more incoming air. The solar dehumidifier reduces air-conditioning energy use when it is greatest—in summer—by using solar energy when it is most available.

Right System, Wrong Year

In the first rough estimates by the Massachusetts Institute of Technology and Consolidated Edison Company, the privately held utility serving New York City and surroundings, the installation cost was put at $900,000, the annual energy savings at $47,000. Citicorp spent $90,000 to redesign the roof to face south and $20,000 on the feasibility studies in 1974 and 1975. However, later estimates put the installation price tag closer to $2 million, including all related electrical wiring, platforms for workers, and consultants' fees. Considering the cost of the alternative (steam power from Con Ed), the collector was judged to be worth only $237,000 in savings over the coming decades, far less than it would have cost to build. Since the investment could not be returned in full in that time, the project was rejected.

If all the figures and projections in these estimates are accepted as the most accurate available at the time, the reason for the decision not to install a thermal solar collector atop the Citicorp Center can be stated simply: bad timing. First, turning the roof to face the sun was not contemplated until after the design was complete, orders had been placed, and contracts signed.

Second, the building was under construction when the solar equipment manufacturing industry was in its infancy. Solar companies in 1974 and 1975 had limited production capacity. In fact, an order from Citicorp for 20,000 square feet of solar collector panels would have represented nearly 3 percent of the medium-temperature collectors manufactured in the United States in 1975. It should not have been surprising to the builders that bids received from solar manufacturers were few and sometimes vague. The same order would have represented only about 0.4 percent of medium-temperature collectors produced in the United States three years later.

Finally, competing fossil-fuel prices were lower in 1975 than they are today. The same decision, at the higher fuel prices of the 1980s, might have gone to solar rather than oil-consuming steam generation. (One ironic factor was the relatively efficient design of the Citicorp building. A more wasteful structure, needing more air-conditioning, would have found the alternative solar system more economical.)

Though this opportunity to use solar energy in an urban setting has passed, Citicorp has not abandoned the concept. Solar *thermal* energy has been set aside, but in 1979 the company expressed an interest in placing photovoltaic cells on the roof, to convert sunlight directly into electricity to run its lights, office machines, and elevators.

R.B.

FLOATING CITIES

Will some future cities float on the water like lilies, be self-contained habitats unlike any terrestrial cities? Will they be kinetic, disposable, able to be added to and subtracted from, towed elsewhere as the needs arise? Perhaps, as population increases, humankind will look to the oceans for more "land."

Marine architects in Scandinavia, Germany, and Holland have developed floating platforms and artificial islands as extensions of land to which growing industry may move. Other builders are already planning cities so that sociological, psychological, and economic needs can be met in ways that blend rather than intrude upon their fluid environment. Kiyonori Kikutake is such an architect. For the Okinawa Fair of 1975 he

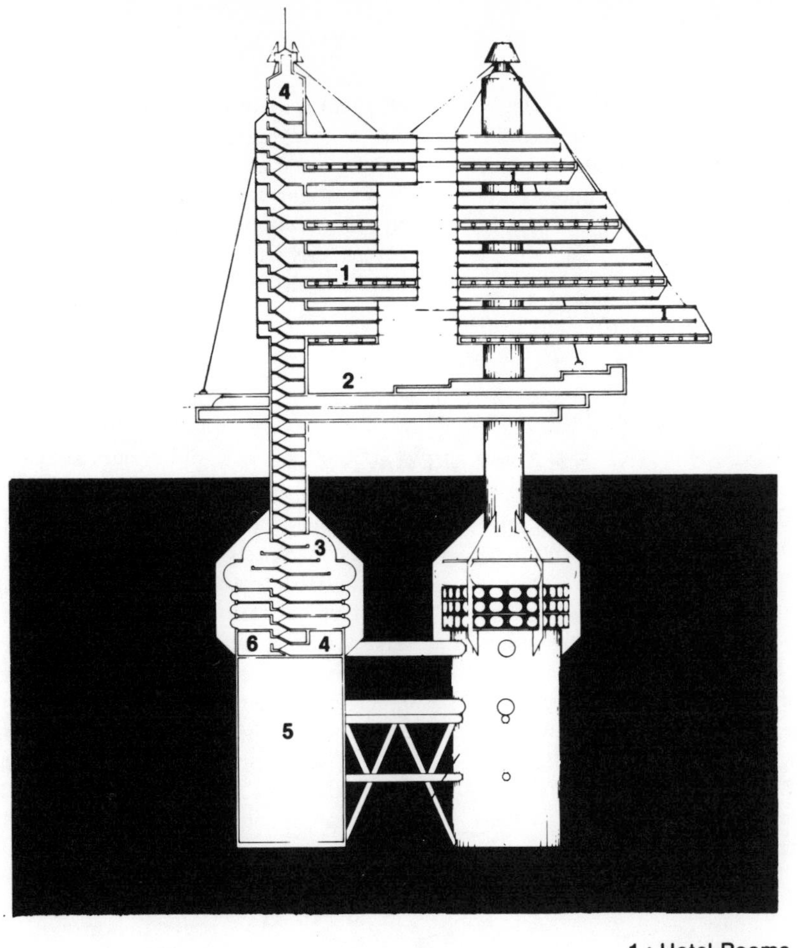

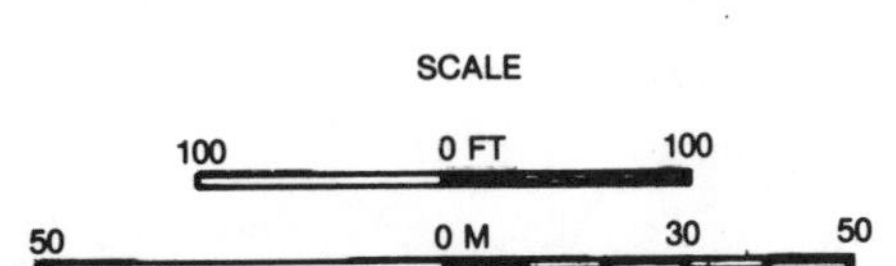

Based on technology developed for offshore oil platforms, floating cities could accommodate housing, industry, and recreation. (*University of Hawaii/Oceanic Institute, Hawaii*)

designed a demonstration floating city with restaurants and an industrial power plant. John Craven, an engineer at the University of Hawaii, devotes his efforts to developing ocean thermal energy conversion (see "OTEC," page 23), convinced that once this power source is operational, floating cities cannot be far behind.

Floating cities would extend comfortable living to the surface of the sea and preserve land for farming, for open space, for wildlife habitat, and for human recreation. (The potentials for marine pollution might be great, however, and would have to be considered carefully.) Sea-city industry could be situated below the water line or on separate platforms to allow treatment of their wastes. Like the hotel, apartment, and commercial complexes in many large cities, a floating city would be compact and convenient. Power, sewage, gas, and transportation lines would be short, and therefore energy-saving.

Built on platforms of prestressed, reinforced concrete, a floating city would be only a few stories high, with modular, interchangeable units. It would be near enough to shore to allow quick access, but not so close as to be obtrusive.

To most, floating cities seem as futuristic as living on the moon. In fact, all the technology necessary has been demonstrated at the necessary scale. Offshore oil platforms have demonstrated that we can build stable structures on water to house people comfortably for extended periods.

Would sea-city residents be perpetually seasick? Probably not. During a heavy storm, inhabitants of an offshore oil platform usually feel little motion.

Craven is aware that the idea of living in a city at sea is not easy for most people to accept. It does seem a quantum leap into the future. But we have taken such leaps before, ready or not. Now that Japan has launched *MESA,* a 300-ton, 430-passenger ferry capable of a smooth ride in heavy seas, comfortable transportation to the future sea city is ready. Within a decade, Craven thinks, the city will be there too.

L.W., M.P.

SHANTYTOWNS

The fast-growing cities of the developing nations are usually surrounded by large shantytowns where the poorest new arrivals to the city live.

These migrants from the poverty-stricken rural areas come to seek their fortune in the cities. When they find no housing available to them, they are forced to build their own shacks on any open land. Often the land they invade is unused precisely because it is not suitable for building. In the marshland near the Bay of Bengal, for example, a huge shantytown has grown up. These marshlands are a breeding ground for mosquitoes, and malaria is rife.

Other shantytowns arise on the sides of steep hills. Stripped of vegetation, the soil on these hills becomes extremely unstable. Hundreds of shanty houses wash down the hills in landslides after heavy tropical rains.

Shantytowns, because of crowding and lack of water pipelines and cooking facilities, are also subject to frequent fires. When firefighting equipment arrives, there is often not enough water pressure, and the trucks cannot fit through the narrow passages between houses. In Manila, in the Philippines, thousands of shanties burn down every year.

Once squatters have found land to build on, word quickly spreads. Almost overnight the open

Shantytown in El Salvador (*World Bank/Jaime Martin*)

land is covered with new shelters built by the invaders. At first they use anything at hand, and some houses are nothing but cardboard boxes with corrugated tin roofs to keep off the rain. As the shantytown becomes more settled, through the passage of time, the residents build more permanent structures around the first shelters.

Depending on the attitude of the local government, the shantytown sooner or later acquires a water-spigot (usually a communal one that serves dozens of families), latrines, and sometimes electricity. The owners of the land often are hostile to the squatters. In India, for example, a squatter cannot be evicted once he has put a lintel over his window, so owners try to knock down the walls before the squatter can finish building.

Some governments, unable to prevent squatters from acquiring new land, try to control the development of their settlements by providing certain open sites with services. Then squatters can move in and build what they want. A more expensive approach is to build core houses with a room and a bath. Squatters can add on to this well-constructed model.

The poverty and exploding population in the developing countries has led to a severe urban housing shortage around the world. In many large cities, like Caracas, Venezuela, more than half the population lives in shantytowns that have become permanent. Large sections of Rio de Janeiro, Manila, and Lagos, to name only three cities, are given over to vast stretches of these makeshift slums. In Calcutta, even shantytowns are a luxury not all can afford; an estimated two hundred and fifty thousand people sleep on the sidewalks every night.

B.G. and J.S.

RECYCLED COMMUNITIES

The World Bank is doing it in slums in developing nations, the British government is doing it in historic sections of London, local community groups are doing it in the impoverished Lower East Side of New York City. Recycling buildings has become a popular activity in urban and rural areas, in developed and developing nations. Whole communities are being brought back to life through the labor of local residents and the aid of governments and other organizations.

When the World Bank began its efforts in 1972 to improve living conditions in developing nations, its program was to supply land and services such as roads and water, with the hope of encouraging people to build new homes and create a new community. This approach was based on the assumption that existing slums and shantytowns were hopelessly disorganized and beyond redemption. A study done in Zambia, however, revealed that these neighborhoods were actually well-organized into cooperative markets, credit unions, schools, and political groups. In the Pinto Salinas area of Caracas, about one third of the residents use their homes as a place of business. In spite of their apparent poverty, many shantytowns are actively functioning social and economic entities.

Building entirely new communities is disruptive and expensive. The World Bank learned that money would be much more effectively used improving existing communities that already have a strong social structure. Residents can use the skills they have to help one another, and money used to install floors or replace metal walls with brick will go much farther than money spent in new housing. But, the approximately $1 billion lent by the World Bank since 1972 is not enough to make a difference. The capital needed to improve housing is the energy and skills of local people. Money is effective only if it triggers this energy, which stimulates the local economy and

Squatters' huts in Lusaka, Zambia, are being replaced by more substantial dwellings constructed by local residents in a project financed by the World Bank. (*World Bank/Edwin G. Huffman*)

preserves the most valuable resource—a sense of community.

London has a different story. The British government has led the way in a program of "gentrification," which restores historic old neighborhoods such as Covent Garden and Islington. Preserving the old buildings provides a feeling of continuity, maintains a useful "museum" of architectural styles, and contributes character and diversity to the city. The scale of the neighborhoods is more intimate and convenient because they were built before people depended on automobiles. Similar programs are underway in the *Marais* section of Paris and in the seventeenth-century neighborhoods along the canals of Amsterdam.

(*World Bank/Edwin G. Huffman*)

Gentrification raises a number of troubling questions, however. Once historic buildings are restored, they usually become very fashionable and expensive, so that the people who live in a decaying old neighborhood cannot afford to remain there once it is restored. Speculators often buy old buildings, drive out renters, restore the building, and then charge exorbitant rents. Buildings are saved, but communities are destroyed.

The United States has developed a pilot program designed to prevent the displacement of low-income groups from reviving neighborhoods. When the government takes possession of a building for unpaid taxes, it offers the building for a nominal fee to local "homesteaders," who promise to renovate the building themselves and thereby pay for it with "sweat equity." As in the developing nations, human energy is the capital investment.

(*World Bank/Edwin G. Huffman*)

Communities have also developed their own programs. In Minneapolis, the Project for Pride in Living began by promoting a self-help housing improvement program and now oversees a tool-lending library, a housing-purchase counseling program, and a construction training and employment program. New York City's Interfaith Adopt-a-Building group has renovated more than ninety buildings, including the now-famous East Eleventh Street apartment house—the first solar- and wind-powered building in Manhattan.

Neighborhood organizations are crucial in the recycled housing movement. Better homes are not enough to re-create a community. Collective enterprises such as schools, stores, churches, industry, and entertainment must also be nurtured, and can only be kept healthy by cooperative effort. One of the advantages of rebuilding an old neighborhood is that these expensive facilities already exist and can be easily rehabilitated. Indeed, the most significant social drawback of new suburban housing is the lack of cultural and entertainment establishments essential to a sense of community. Old neighborhoods, built to accommodate the bustling and vigorous life of the street that existed before the age of the automobile, still encourage social interaction.

Recycling buildings, like recycling paper or glass, makes good economic and environmental sense. Fewer raw materials are used, less land is paved over, less energy is used. Many old buildings were designed to conserve heat. New York City's Urban Homesteading Assistance Board estimated in 1976 that a two-bedroom housing unit would cost $45,000 to build, $32,000 to be renovated by a contractor, and only $15,000 to be owner-renovated.

The psychological and emotional benefits, however, may be even more important. Humans need the stimulation of diversity, the aesthetic pleasure of forgotten styles, the connection with our neighbors, and the connection with our past. We can benefit from the awareness that our forebears left us good buildings, and that we have worked hard, individually and collectively, with our own hands, to maintain them.

K.F.

Wavemakers:

PIONEERS ON THE BRONX FRONTIER

Irma Fleck, cofounder and president of New York City's Bronx Frontier Development Corporation, stands just over 5 feet tall in her high heels. She has discerning brown eyes, red hair, two grandchildren, and thirty years of experience working in Bronx community affairs. She describes herself as "a treasure hunter, sort of like a scavenger." She gestures at several items bolted to the office wall: "This one is a wheel from a sewing machine, that's a piece from one of my husband's musical instruments. Over there is a press mold. I found them rusty and old. I polished them up."

Irma's eye for spotting the sow's ear—and her ability to turn it into a silk purse—are major forces behind the three-year-old, $300,000 operation aptly called the Bronx Frontier. One of its major tasks is transforming vacant city lots into gardens and parks by using fertile soil that the organization makes from garbage. To make the soil—compost, actually—the Bronx Frontier has enlisted the help of a seven-story-high, forty-kilowatt windmill.

The ambitious goal of the Bronx Frontier is to redevelop the devastated South Bronx, a large New York City neighborhood that fell prey to abandonment, bulldozers, and arsonists—turning whole sections into moonscapes of broken bricks and rubble. Irma Fleck saw it a different way. She envisioned the smoldering debris as a great natural resource in disguise. With some decent topsoil, she reasoned, the broken bricks could act as drainage for vegetable and flower gardens that would green over all the bald spots—500-acres (200-hectares) worth—in the South Bronx.

Upon preliminary investigation, Irma discovered a large problem: the price of topsoil for the abandoned acreage. "Let's not talk in acres, I'm a city girl," says Irma impatiently explaining the dilemma. "It would have cost about $40,000 a block —and that was out of the question. If you can't buy something, you make it. Composting was the answer—and I figured we could do it with vegetable remains from Hunts Point Market, the largest vegetable market in the country, sitting right here under our noses in the South Bronx."

During 1976, while these ideas were sprouting

in Irma's mind, a compatriot entered her life—Jack Flanagan—a young cop from New York City's 41st Precinct, the infamous "Fort Apache" in the South Bronx. Irma had worked with Jack briefly in the past. Bumping into him again that year at a cocktail party, she asked him, "Jack, do you know anything about composting?" Jack was a vegetarian and firm recycling advocate. "As a matter of fact, I have a compost pile in my backyard," he answered. Irma Fleck had found a partner.

Fleck and Flanagan complemented each other, though they made a decidedly odd couple. Jack was twenty-nine at the time, half Irma's age. But when it came to ideas, Fleck and Flanagan were on the same wavelength.

Plans for the Bronx Frontier so excited Jack that he took a leave of absence from the Police Department, where he was a community-affairs specialist. Flanagan immediately set about organizing support for the project within the constituencies he knew best: street and community people. Irma, on the other hand, worked the politicians and business types she had come to know during her long career in philanthropy. "We'd go to the places where we felt comfortable," says Irma. "Jack doesn't much like to dress up in a suit and tie. I love to go to dinners and I do very well at them, especially if there are men my own age and I can flirt a bit." Irma believes the Bronx Frontier would never have happened if it weren't for Jack's perseverance and ability to get things done. Jack credits Irma's charm and impeccable track record. Greening the South Bronx with vegetable remains had sounded crazy to just about everyone from the top down.

Irma Fleck and Jack Flanagan. (*Bronx Frontier Development Corporation*)

After a year of filling out forms and writing proposals, the Bronx Frontier won a $55,000 grant from the Community Services Administration, a federal agency. The Frontiersmen then hired Curtis Suerth, a genial 34-year-old, cigar-smoking plant biologist who gave up a university post to oversee the composting operation. Later that year, a fourth member joined the team—Joan Pipolo—a longtime South Bronx resident and organizer. In a recycled bookmobile dubbed "the Chuck Wagon," Pipolo began cruising the community, spreading the garden and good-nutrition message.

Despite its good reputation and the presence of a Ph.D. biologist on the Frontier team, the compost operation took a grueling year to launch. Myriad city and state authorities—departments of Health, Sanitation, Ports and Terminals—demanded exhaustive proof that composting wasn't a health hazard. Through sheer doggedness, the numerous permits and licenses were won, and the chosen demonstration site—a 3.7-acre (1.6-hectare) former junkyard on the East River—was readied for start-up. In May 1978, the first load of Hunts Point refuse was slowly transforming to humus in the springtime sun.

By the end of that year, Bronx Frontier was in high gear: the composting process had been proved viable to the tune of about 50 tons of vegetable waste per day; a "green team" of specialists was developing ten community gardens with the soil; the Chuck Wagon had reached thousands of school children, senior citizens, and street people. The Frontier people had demonstrated some important directions for urban dwellers in the coming age—an age that would be predicated, they believed, on conservation, recycling, and re-education.

In 1979, Bronx Frontier started to plan scaling up the composting to 200 tons a day. Turning one percent of New York City's solid waste into valuable topsoil is a move calculated to create jobs for community workers as well as just enough profit to make the operation self-sustaining. (The Frontier's budget now includes contributions from foundations as well as a grant from the Community Services Administration.)

Quadrupling the size of the compost heaps

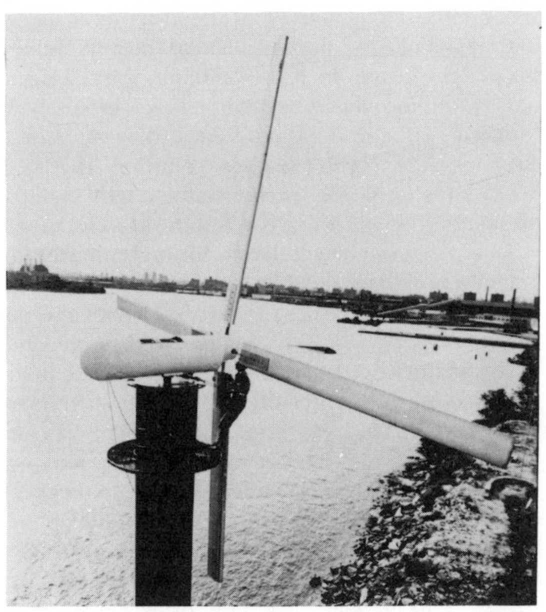

The wind machine operated by the Bronx Frontier Development Association. (*Greig Cranna*)

would require auxiliary power to speed the process along. But using electricity seemed to contradict the spirit of the whole undertaking, Curtis Suerth believed. He and Jack Flanagan were working the compost piles one windy day in 1978, when a perfect solution occurred to them: a windmill.

To that end, the Bronx Frontier successfully enlisted the help of the Energy Task Force, the New York group that had built the city's first residential windmill. The Frontier machine is another original—the first urban commercial windmill on the East Coast. Its price tag was $34,000, paid for by the Community Services Administration. After the money came in, Energy Task Force wind specialist Ted Finch joined the Bronx Frontier staff as full-time director for the wind project.

Twenty-six-year-old Finch, whose fascination with birds' wings as a child and travels through rural Scandinavia had led him to major in wind energy at experimental Hampshire College, was the perfect fifth member of the Bronx Frontier leadership team. When word came from the city that the windmill's storage batteries had to be housed in a separate explosion-proof bunker—a facility for which the Community Services grant had made no provision—Finch demonstrated typical Bronx Frontier ingenuity. A separate facility for the batteries? Why not combine its function with something else? And so the Community Services Administration was coaxed into funding another proposal for a solar-heated battery house just big enough to double as a display area for examples of alternative technology. Beside the center sits New York City's first solar-heated outhouse with composting toilet.

Success breeds bustle, and projects at the Bronx Frontier proliferated like wildflowers. More than a partial solution to New York's critical waste problem, more than a way to green a dilapidated neighborhood, the Bronx Frontier embodies a new urban consciousness. As Irma puts it, "We can't waste land, garbage, anything. If you take a look at something and think, 'this looks bad,' don't stop there. Turn it around. Turn it upside down. You might be surprised—it could look pretty good."

J.W.

BICYCLE CITIES

As fuel prices rise and urban air pollution and congestion worsen, millions of people around the world are rediscovering the joys and advantages of the bicycle as a fast, maneuverable, inexpensive, and independent method for getting around. And nowhere are the bicycle's benefits as apparent as in auto-choked cities; today's urban cyclist commutes, shops, and visits friends by bike as well as biking for weekend recreation. A number of cities are trying to help cyclists and these efforts are attracting the attention of planners. Here are the world's nine greatest bicycling cities:

SHANGHAI, CHINA. The world's largest city is also the world's premier bicycling metropolis, with an estimated 2.5 million bike trips every day. Along the wide boulevards in Shanghai (and in Peking, which also rates top honors) it is a common sight to see a phalanx of bicyclists twenty abreast pedaling their one-speeds, totally engulfing the occasional car that ventures past. (In all of China there are only 37,000 automobiles, compared with 120 million in the United States.) Most of Shanghai's 50,000 motorized vehicles are buses and trucks, but much freight and passenger service is provided by heavily loaded "tricycle trucks" and "pedi-cabs." Senior citizens ride, too, and handicapped persons can obtain hand-cranked bicycles that don't require leg power.

Shanghai is also home of the world's largest bicycle-production facility, the mammoth Forever Bicycle Factory that turns out 1.7 million units a year. One item the Forever plant doesn't manufacture, however, are locks—the Chinese never lock their bikes.

Are the streets of Shanghai quieter than those of Western cities that are clogged with noisy trucks and motorcycles? No, says Ethel Weichbrod of the U.S.-China Peoples Friendship Committee. "The few cars in Shanghai are so worried about hitting a bicyclist that they honk their horns continuously. It's as noisy there as New York."

DELFT, THE NETHERLANDS. The Netherlands is the undisputed bicycle leader among Western countries. The small nation has 5,300 miles (8,530 kilometers) of exclusive bike lanes, and Holland's 14 million citizens own 8 million bikes (compared to only 4 million cars). Every day 5 million men, women, and children cycle to their daily destinations. According to Lester Brown's *Running on Empty* (Norton, 1979), a book on alternatives to the auto, nearly half of all commuting is by bicycle in some Dutch cities.

A bikeway in Rijswijk, The Netherlands. Bicycles are a high priority in countries like The Netherlands, where crowding and dependence on foreign oil are major problems. (*CEES Mastenbroek*)

One of those cities is Delft, located midway between Rotterdam and The Hague (two other outstanding bicycle locales). Delft has taken the position that cities are for people, not cars, and has made many modifications to encourage cycling and walking instead of driving. Streets have been rebuilt with frequent curves, flower planters, and benches; parking has been restricted; and—as also in Göteborg, Sweden—access between different portions of the downtown neighborhoods has been blocked to cars. Meanwhile, bicycles are permitted to ride both directions on one-way auto streets, and special bike-only drawbridges have been erected over the canals at key locations.

One of the most famous Dutch bicycling experiments took place in the country's largest metropolis, Amsterdam, several years ago. There, a radical political party purchased several hundred bicycles, painted them white, and announced that anyone could use them at any time as long as they were again left on the street for the next person's use. Although the bikes were eventually worn out, a similar "red-and-white" plan has been adopted in Bremen, Germany (see following page) and free "yellow bikes" are available in France's bike capital, La Rochelle.

When Holland's urban cyclists need a rural respite, they can take their bicycles to one of the world's most interesting national parks, the Hooge Veluwe, which is crisscrossed by wilderness bicycle paths and which also contains an art museum in the woods, featuring two hundred paintings by Van Gogh.

STEVENAGE, ENGLAND. Thirty-two miles north of London lies Stevenage, a town of 72,000, which calls itself "Britain's First and Finest New Town." It can also boast of what is probably the top urban cycleway system in the world. Bicyclists have at their disposal a 24-mile (39-kilometer) bikeway network plus 100 miles of pedestrian paths, neither of which crosses auto roads once. (In fact, the entire city lacks a single traffic light.) At intersections, autos circulate on "roundabouts"—traffic circles—while bikes and pedestrians use tunnels under the roadways. (A similar system, with seventy tunnels, was recently installed in Västerås, Sweden, vastly improving safety and convenience in that bike-oriented town, too.) Although the population density of Stevenage is greater than that of London, it has no traffic congestion. Even better, no cyclist has ever been killed in the town's thirty-three-year history, and Stevenage's bicycle injury rate is one quarter that of the rest of the country. Other English cities—notably Oxford, Cambridge, and York—have a higher rate of cycling, but Stevenage may be a vision of the future.

BREMEN, GERMANY. Bremen's red-and-white bike scheme (those are the city's official colors) is the first in Germany, and is likely to become a model for other urban areas to follow. The original two hundred bicycles were freely available; when too many of them were damaged or lost, a small fee (one mark) was instituted for all-day use. The bikes all have large baskets to encourage shopping use, and the rental stations are located near parking garages. The number of red-and-white bikes is being increased to five hundred. According to bicycle activists Fritz Neubauer and Marilyn Schapiro, Bremen has 380 miles (610 kilometers) of bicycle paths and bicycles make up 20 percent of the city's traffic. Bremen was also the site of the successful court case that allowed bicycles to use the auto-free pedestrian malls commonly found in German city centers.

On weekends, Bremen cyclists can board special bike-carrying trams that take them to the end of the line and allow for lengthy rides through the countryside without having to cross through the city.

DAVIS, UNITED STATES. Ironically, the car capital of the world—California—contains the unquestioned bike capital of the United States —Davis. Located 20 miles (32 kilometers) west of Sacramento, Davis could have followed the lead of scores of other fast-growing California cities during the 1960s. Instead, the townspeople stood up against sprawl, far-distant shopping centers, and endless parking lots, and demanded safe bicycle routes and a human-scale city. In a class by itself in the United States, Davis has virtually as many bikes as residents; year-round, fully one quarter of all city trips are by bike, while in the summer the number rises as high as 90 percent. In fact, in Davis bicycle congestion actually becomes a problem—finding a bike-parking space downtown and on the campus of the University of California is often difficult. Moreover, several major intersections became so clogged during some university class breaks (three thousand cyclists were counted at one) that Davis followed the Stevenage example and constructed a number of roundabouts. Davis is one of the few cities in the United States that requires housing developers to construct off-street bicycle paths as part of the development—and it is probably the only town its size not to have a single parking meter in the city center.

NEW YORK, UNITED STATES. New York is a great place to visit but you wouldn't want to bicycle there, right? Perhaps. But New York has earned itself a top bicycle rating because of the astonishing number of innovations and experiments that are taking place there. And while you may not have the nerve to ride in the "Big Apple," twenty thousand commuters—and hundreds of thousands of weekenders—do, making it America's bicycling capital in volume. In fact, during an eleven-day transit strike in April 1980, more than two hundred thousand New Yorkers bicycled to work—an all-time record for a United States city.

New York's greatest achievement is that the city's two premier green spaces—Central Park in Manhattan and Prospect Park in Brooklyn—are auto-free areas for much of the year. In the summer, cars may use the parks' roads only during rush hours and not at all on weekends. (This may soon be expanded to a year-round policy.) Various other roads, including the lovely Bronx River Parkway and the Grand Concourse, are closed to cars on Sundays. New York has also pioneered in taking roadway from cars and giving it to bikes. Most recently, one lane on the Queensboro Bridge was given to cyclists, bringing to four the number of major bridges that can be crossed by bike. (In the United States, bridge use is often prohibited to bikes.)

In addition, two forms of mass transit allow bicycles on board—the subway line that runs under the Hudson River to New Jersey, and the aerial tramway that connects Manhattan with Roosevelt Island. (Roosevelt Island, the "Little Apple," is a new town in the East River that has virtually eliminated auto traffic.) New York also boasts two outstanding annual cycling events—the 35-mile (56-kilometer), five-borough tour sponsored by the Youth Hostel and drawing ten thousand participants, and the "Apple Lap," a 75-mile (121-kilometer) European-style bike race through the city, with police closing sections of streets minutes before the speeding pack of racers arrive and opening them up again after they pass.

Unfortunately, New York destroyed its very best bike route. When a portion of the decrepit

West Side Highway collapsed and the mayor closed the whole road to cars, it rapidly became a major bicycling and jogging route. Although the fate of the elevated highway is still being debated, a key section of roadway was demolished, rendering the route useless for commuters.

Downtown, congestion is so severe that 1,200 of the city's messenger and delivery persons get around by bike. But not everyone favors the two-wheelers: Not too long ago the Taxi Association unsuccessfully petitioned the City Council to ban all bikes from Manhattan!

OTTAWA, CANADA. In the summertime, fully 4 percent of Ottawa's federal employees commute by bike, making Canada's capital its cycling capital, too. Many of them ride on the 30 miles (48 kilometers) of separated bikeways, much of it along the Rideau Canal. What do the commuting cyclists do during Ottawa's long, cold, and snowy winter? They *skate* to work—fifty thousand of them daily using that same canal, which is kept smooth and clean by a squad of sweepers and a nightly flooding with fresh water.

In sharp contrast to Ottawa is the situation in Montreal where cyclists have fought unsuccessfully for several years for the simple right to cross the St. Lawrence River. Despite militant confrontations with angry bikers, the city has refused to create safe bike access to any of the five bridges, or to convert an ice-regulation barrier to a bike river crossing, or even to allow bicycles on the Metro line that crosses under the river.

DODOMA, TANZANIA. Africa is not a hotbed of bicycling, even though the rapidly developing continent could avoid many of the transportation mistakes that were made by auto-dazzled planners in Europe and the United States. One exception is Tanzania, whose president, Julius Nyerere, is taking his country's oil shortage so seriously that he has ordered his ministers to bike to work. He has also pledged that Tanzania's largest city, Dar es Salaam, will ultimately turn into a bicycling city "second only to Peking." The smaller town of Dodoma, however, may have an even brighter future. Slated to become the country's new capital by 1990, Dodoma's metamorphosis has been extensively planned by firms from Europe and North America. The Canadians who mapped out the transportation plan have decided to base it almost solely on buses and bicycles, according to John Dowlin, coordinator of The Bicycle Network. Reportedly, Nyerere also plans to limit car imports to three hundred per year for his entire nation.

TOKYO, JAPAN. Cycling has become such a passion in and around Tokyo that some angry Japanese refer to bicycles as the newest form of pollution. According to a New York *Times* report, "Every day millions of men, women, and children pedal off to work, to school, or on their errands. But when they arrive, having consumed no fossil fuel and emitted no fumes, they have no place to put the bikes, so they leave them anywhere—in the streets, by the tracks at stations, along fences, in front of doors, all over sidewalks and crosswalks, and on top of one another."

With annual sales of over 5 million, Japan's bicycle population has grown to 47 million. Tokyo's most severe bicycle congestion is around the city's 2,200 railroad stations where many commuters shift from pedal power to the outstanding rapid transit system. Downtown bicycle use is not as heavy as in China, Holland, or Denmark, although the beautiful boulevard that surrounds the Imperial Palace is closed to cars on Sundays. Also, foreigners are often astounded to see Japanese caterers pedaling to their destination holding trays of food high over their heads.

What to do about Japan's bicycle pollution? The government has responded by subsidizing the construction of huge seven-story bike-parking garages near the largest railroad stations. But one Tokyo ward came up with a simpler, if long-term, solution to the problem of illegally parked bicycles: spraying them daily with water in the hope that rust will succeed where the police have failed.

Honorable Mentions

Portland, Oregon, has the world's best bicycle map, a meticulously detailed, color-coded rating of every street for rideability, taking into account such factors as lane width, traffic volume, hills, congestion, and intersections. In *London,* fifty Members of Parliament belong to the Commons Cycling Pool, which has a collection of bicycles on loan from the British Cycling Bureau. Every road-maintenance and road-improvement project in *Seattle, Washington,* must be reviewed by the city's full-time bicycle coordinator so that bike improvements can be made at the same time. *Palo Alto, California,* requires that all new office and apartment buildings provide secure bicycle-storage facilities at the rate of at least one bike space for every ten auto spaces. And finally, *Boston, Massachusetts,* is the starting point for U. S. Bicycle Route 1, a 65-mile network of little-used roads leading to Cape Cod—with "Bikeway 1" signs the whole length. U. S. Interstate highway system—watch out!

P.H.

THE INVENTED VILLAGE

The *Pacific Sun,* the weekly regional newspaper of California's Marin County, had planned a cover story on *Star Wars* producer George Lucas, who lives in Marin. Lucas cancelled a planned interview at the last minute, so writer Joanne Williams suggested interviewing Sim Van der Ryn, the California State Architect at the time, who had just moved to the county. She contacted him and made an appointment. As she was leaving to meet him, editor Steve McNamara suggested that she ask if he had any good ideas for Hamilton.

Hamilton is the abandoned Hamilton Air Force Base in northern Marin. When it was closed in 1974, local real estate developers suggested that the site be converted into a regional airport that would serve nearby San Francisco and create a real estate boom. Residents of the city of Novato organized to oppose the airport, which they saw as a source of noise and traffic problems. Besides, only 2 percent of the Bay Area's airline passengers came from the area. Novato voters elected a city council and a representative to the county board of supervisors who were against the airport.

The only alternative to the airport plan was a little-known suggestion for a housing redevelopment project. Van der Ryn knew nothing about the controversy, but was currently working on designs for communities that would use renewable sources of energy and would be as energy efficient as possible. McNamara told Van der Ryn about the Hamilton airport plan and Van der Ryn agreed to create a plan for a solar village at Hamilton. While he was working on the plan, McNamara was writing articles in the *Sun* about the necessity for imagination and vision in using the Hamilton site. The most popular proposal at that time was a plan for a shopping center.

Van der Ryn's proposal, which appeared in the *Sun* in March 1979, is an ambitious and comprehensive plan for an energy-conscious community.

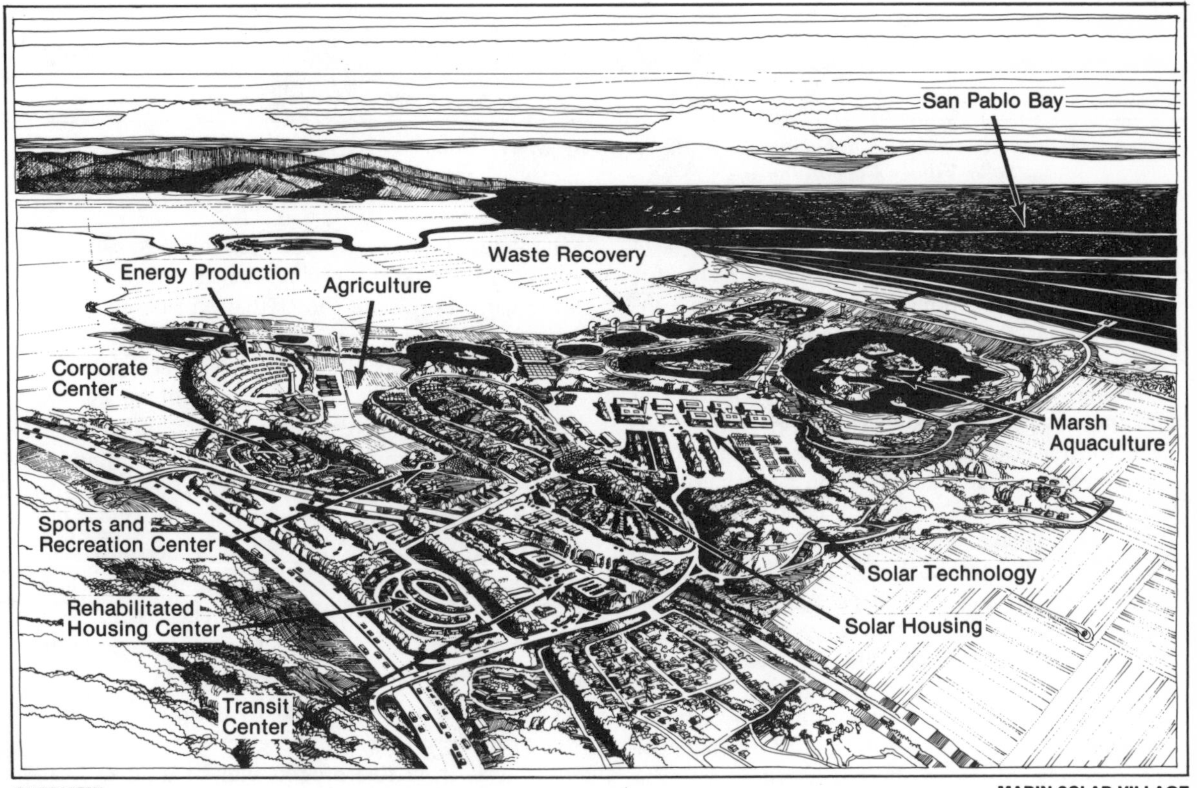

(*Gordon Ashby/Marin Solar Village Corporation*)

Artist's rendering of townhouses in the planned Marin Solar Villages. (*Gordon Ashby/ Marin Solar Village Corporation*)

The 1,271-acre (507-hectare) site is to have 2,500 residents. New townhouses with space for a private patio, garden, or greenhouse will incorporate passive solar design that provides 80 to 100 percent of heating and cooling. Existing buildings will be remodeled for use by elderly and low-income people. Roads within Hamilton Village will be designed to accommodate only electric-powered public transportation and emergency vehicles. All private cars will be parked at the edge of the village, and internal movement will be by foot, bicycle, golf cart, or shuttle bus. Only 15 percent of the land will be paved for roads (35 percent is typical), so that more land will be available for other uses, and air pollution and noise will be lessened.

Transportation will also be reduced by providing jobs within the village for about 50 percent of the residents. Much of the space within existing structures and hangars will be used by local businesses involved in research or manufacture of solar and other small-scale technologies. Seventy acres (28 hectares) beside the freeway are set aside for a corporate center that will be available for administrative, research, or production facilities of an environmentally responsive corporation.

Energy use in the food system will be cut by setting aside 100 acres (40 hectares) of land for commercial organic truck farms and community gardens that will provide cheap, fresh food for the residents. Solar greenhouses will allow for year-round farming, and fish will be raised in open ponds and solar greenhouse tanks (see "The New Alchemists," page 446). The farms will be fertilized by the community's wastewater after it has been biologically purified.

Cogeneration (see "Cogeneration," page 44) will produce power for the electric vehicles, and waste heat from this process will be used to heat greenhouses and fish ponds. Finally, 600 acres (240 hectares) of land that is below sea level will be restored to its original condition as saltwater marsh.

By building townhouses rather than detached dwellings, heating and cooling costs are cut by 40 percent, costs of material and construction are reduced, and less land is used. Locally produced food will save money and energy by eliminating the need for transportation, distribution, and processing. Fossil-fuel use will be 50 to 80 percent lower than in traditional communities. And energy savings are only one advantage. Residents will spend less time commuting to work and shopping. They will eat cheaper and fresher food, endure less noise, see less asphalt, breathe cleaner air, and enjoy the satisfaction of living in close harmony with the earth.

Marin County residents had been active during the 1960s in the struggle to save their area from reckless development and machine politics. Political enthusiasm waned during the 1970s when all the campaigns were *against* something—the Vietnam War or nuclear plants or dams or pesticides. Steve McNamara thought people might respond to the opportunity to be *for* something, so he organized Friends of Solar Village.

In eight weeks there were two thousand members and every meeting drew a crowd. The U. S. Department of Energy approved a planning grant and, as of 1981, the Hamilton Village plan was still being discussed as a viable option for the abandoned base.

K.F.

"WEATHERSTRIPPING."

(*©1980, by Sidney Harris*)

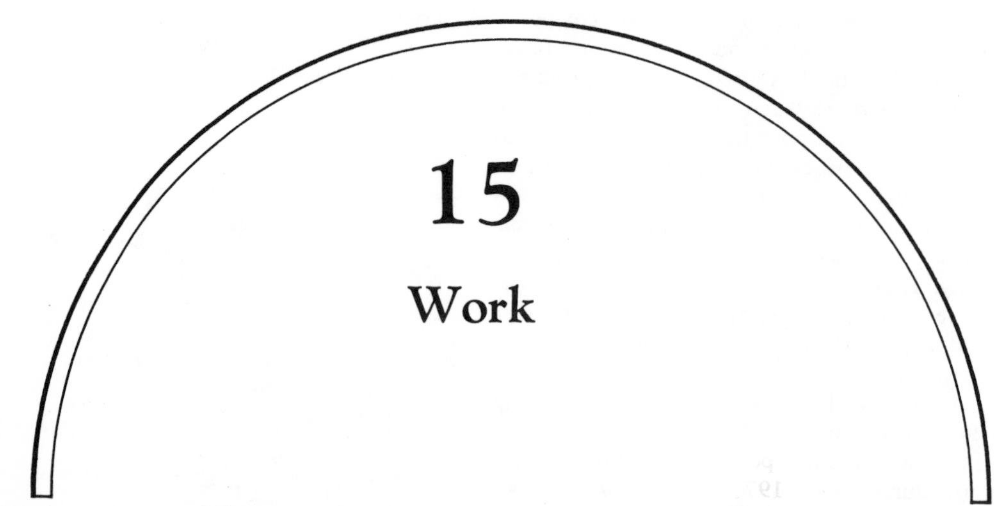

15

Work

Work, try as we might, cannot be avoided. It is our medium of exchange, our marketable product, our great common ground. Even those who are rich enough to avoid holding down their own jobs are not above the consequences of someone else's work; at the very least, they are rich *because* of someone else's work.

Work is a challenge that some of us enjoy a good day's worth of, that many of us don't get paid enough for. And that work requires an array of creative, manual, and mental skills that are, in their range, a tribute to our versatility. But our varied work is not without impact on our health and our environment.

In this chapter the *Almanac* examines the links between some of our work activities and our environmental equilibrium. We praise some heroes and heroines of the workplace: Gilbert Pugliese, who refused to dump the wastes from his plant into the Cuyahoga River in Ohio; Pete Seeger, one of America's favorite folksingers, whose music brought hope to early struggling unionists and inspiration to environmentalists.

We also look at the relationship between the labor and environmental movements, which had cooperated in the early 1970s but which eventually threatened to separate because pollution-control and economic growth were seen as incompatible. Now there are tentative advances by environmentalists who view the hazards of the workplace environment as a legitimate part of their movement and by workers who see environmental and energy conservation policies creating more, if somewhat different, jobs. We explore both some invisible dangers in the workplace and some of the new jobs on the horizon of a more environmentally conscious world.

We also look at some "odd jobbers" whose work, whether it is stalking wildlife in New York City, monitoring fish catches on a wind-whipped shipdeck in the North Atlantic, or prospecting sites for windmills, not only pleases them but also makes a difference to the rest of us.

In order to enhance the quality of life for all humanity, we cannot simply protect diverse and beautiful biological systems. We must also enhance the environments of home, community, and workplace, on which so much of our sustenance, fulfillment, and dignity depend.

P.D.

ARE YOU DYING TO MAKE A LIVING?

Work, as we have said, cannot be avoided by most of us. And, until recently, neither could we sidestep the hazards of the workplace—the liquids, dusts, abrasives, lubricants, polishes, dyes, and virtually countless other substances that we handle in the course of doing our jobs, and that we may not even suspect of being dangerous. But the evidence of occupational dangers has grown substantially, and pressure from labor unions, as well as public interest groups in the United States and elsewhere, has stimulated regulations to enhance safety. Some are controversial, and the laws are often resisted by management. They are sometimes spottily enforced.

There were 104 million workers in the United States as of 1979 and about 1.65 billion worldwide. And while we may not all be doing the most dangerous jobs, we are very dependent on those who do.

Here the *Almanac* has compiled a list of visible and invisible hazards.

Agricultural Workers

Dairy farmers show higher incidences of bladder cancer than the rest of the population, while nondairy farmers demonstrate a high risk of melanoma of the skin. Farm workers are almost constantly exposed to pesticides, of which there are about eight thousand different types, including the infamous kepone. Though kepone use is restricted in the United States, 9 million pounds (4 million kilograms) of it are being stored by the U.S. government until a suitable disposal method can be found. The product, which has caused nerve damage and sterility in workers who handled it, can still legally be produced for export.

Arsenic, another well-known poison, is also a component of insecticides and has been linked to skin and lung cancers. "Farmer's lung," yet another danger, can be fatal. It results from inhaling fungal spores in moldy hay. Farmers in many parts of the world are still exposed to carcinogenic pesticides like DDT and aldrin, which have been banned for general use in the United States. In addition, agricultural workers are exposed to lead, mercury, and asbestos, all proven to be dangerous materials. They also face countless allergies and bacteriological diseases that accompany the handling of animals and plants. Agriculture workers also risk mechanical accidents in connection with the operation of heavy machinery.

Auto Workers

Auto workers face exposure to lead, mercury, and several carcinogens in all stages of automobile production, including the foundry process, vinyl-seat-cushion manufacture, painting, battery handling, and gasoline refining. In the United States, *one fourth of all jobs* are related to the automobile industry—making, repairing, or fueling automobiles.

Barbers, Hairdressers, and Cosmetologists

This group, exposed to an array of solvents and chemicals, has exhibited a higher-than-average rate of cancer of the ovary, uterus, and lymph glands, which could be related to the chemical composition of hair-spray products and dyes.

Roof Workers

Roofers, as well as road builders, are regularly exposed to hot pitch and asphalt, which contain the residue of refined coal tar and crude petroleum. The chemicals and volatile vapors in both are strongly suspected of being carcinogenic. Each batch of roofing material is different in composition, so a consistent analysis is difficult. Also, since many workers free-lance their services and move from job to job, tracing the population at risk is extremely difficult. One rarely sees these workers using protective clothing or masks of any kind, although many report frequent problems of skin irritation, nausea, and dizziness.

Plastics Workers

This population frequently handles polyvinyl chloride, for which the basic ingredient is vinyl chloride. In 1974, the industry released the information that many workers exposed to vinyl chloride were dying of angiosarcoma, a form of liver cancer that has no symptoms until the disease is well along and appears to have no cause other than exposure to vinyl chloride. Vinyl chloride is present everywhere, from stereo records to plastic wrap to ballpoint pens, but the danger is in the production of the products, not in their use. At each stage of production there is potential for gas leakage, and in most large plastics plants there is a low level of vinyl chloride gas throughout the building. The greatest danger is to the workers who clean the giant vats of vinyl chloride residue. When standards to prevent vinyl chloride exposure were implemented in the United States, the plastics industry predicted massive lay-offs because of the costs of complying with the law, but the predicted decline in the industry did not take place.

Coke-Oven Workers

The coke oven is used in steel-making, both to produce fuel for the blast furnace and to capture chemical by-products of the coal-burning process. Those who work around the oven exhibit a lung cancer rate twice as high as other steelworkers, and even higher incidences of kidney and bladder cancers. In a study of black workers, the cancer rate was three times as high as the general population, a difference due probably to the fact that blacks are more often assigned the least desirable positions, such as working on the top of the oven, where emission levels are highest. Those working five or more years on top of the oven had a lung cancer rate ten times that of other steelworkers.

Coal Miners

Besides the mechanical dangers of mining, such as cave-ins, coal miners regularly risk progressive lung deterioration, called "black lung." In this disease, coal dust gathers on the lung air sacs, causing emphysema, lung scarring, and eventual heart failure. Generally, black lung does not show up on X rays until it is well advanced. Ironically, the mechanization of coal mining in the twentieth century has contributed to higher incidences of black lung because mining machines generate more raw dust. There is considerable controversy over the dust standard in the United States, and naturally, increased coal production will focus more discussion on the problem.

Cotton Workers

The disease known as byssinosis, or "brown lung," effects textile workers in the United States. It is a debilitating lung disease not unlike black lung in its effects. First noted in 1877, it was not until 1964 that any serious research was done in the United States. That year Dr. Arend Bouhoys, who had a grant from the U. S. Public Health Service, was denied entry to textile mills by their owners; he finally conducted his study in a cotton mill located within an Atlanta, Georgia, federal penitentiary. Bouhoys discovered an extremely high incidence of byssinosis in that population, sparking a long controversy over cotton dust standards. (See "Blue Jeans," page 221, for more on brown lung.)

Radiation Workers

This group is deployed throughout the economy, in medical occupations, military research and development, industrial radiography, the nuclear energy industry, and scientific research. Except for those employed in nuclear power plants, monitoring is minimal, though anyone with significant radiation contact should wear a dosimeter badge that records radiation accumulation. Some tasks at nuclear power plants have been designated "hot jobs," those where exposure is highest. There have been reports of temporary workers, called "jumpers," who are hired to do short jobs in highly irradiated areas, such as making repairs in a plant that malfunctioned, accumulating dosages that would bring permanent workers close to their annual limit. Temporary workers in nuclear plants move from job to job and there is no official record of their exposure history; no hiring official would know whether they had exceeded their annual limit. Since pay rates for temporary workers are high, there is considerable temptation to avoid safe limits and lie about exposure.

Radiation workers at most sites are woefully ill-informed about the dangers of the jobs they do and may fail to understand the serious consequences of radiation. Excess radiation, which disrupts cell structure at the molecular level, has been linked to many cancers, including leukemia, malignancies of the breast, thyroid gland, colon, lymph glands, and pancreas. In many cases, cancers have appeared where radiation exposure took place ten to twenty years prior to diagnosis. In the 1950s, X rays were widely administered for diagnostic and treatment purposes, exposing thousands of medical personnel to amounts of radiation now considered unsafe. There are very few statistical data on international nuclear-worker exposure, and limits vary from nation to nation.

Lead Workers

Lead is a by-product of metal grinding, smelting, scrap metal recycling, battery making, and a variety of other industries. Its danger was recognized by Pliny the Elder in ancient Rome, who recommended that workers who handled lead wear masks made of animal bladders. Though lead occurs naturally in trace amounts in the body, introduced lead is exclusively a poison and can cause everything from dizziness to kidney disease, anemia to sterility.

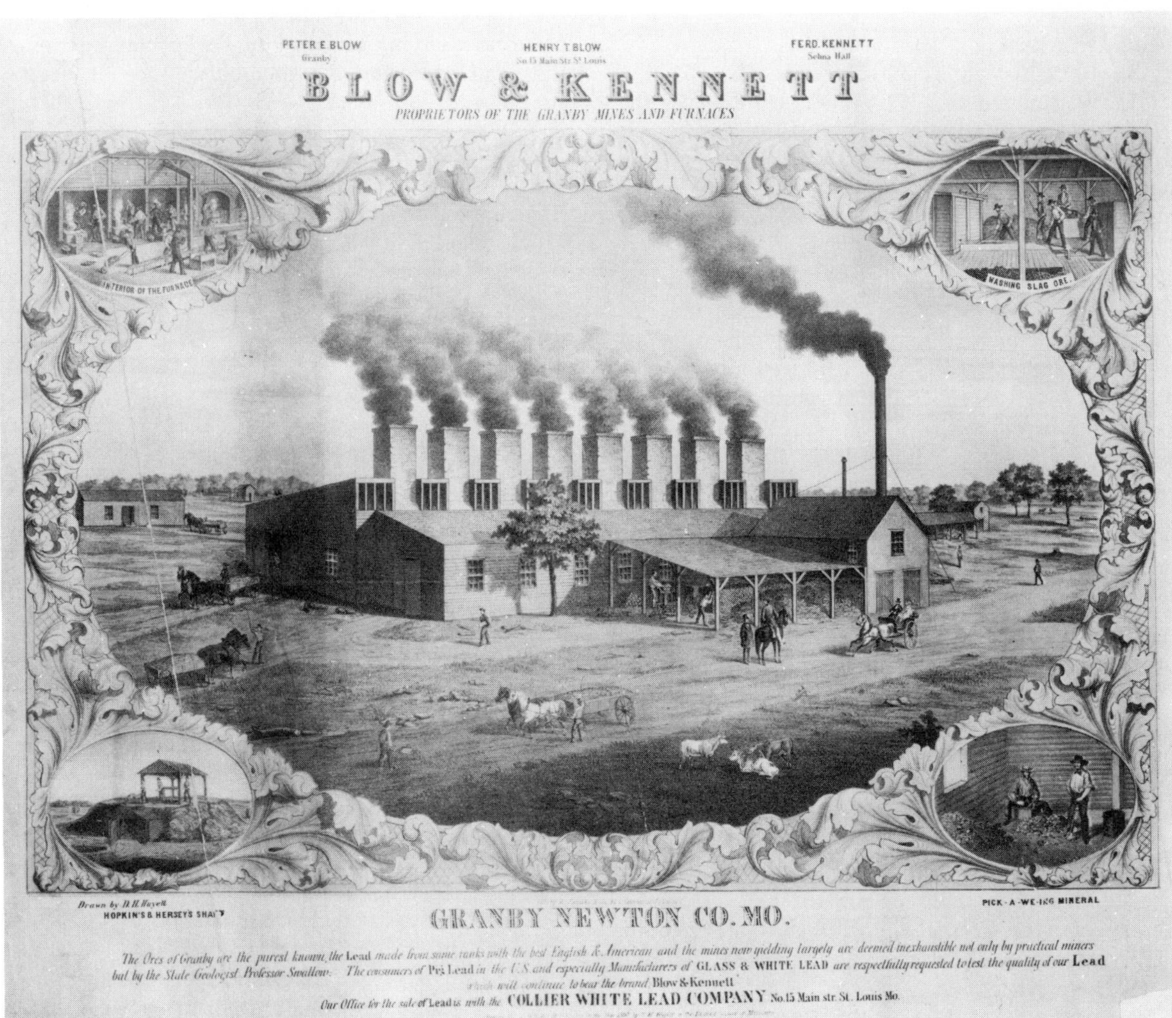

Once a symbol for progress and prosperity, smoke-belching factories are now a source of concern to both workers and environmentalists. The drawing shows a lead furnace in Missouri in 1860. (*Library of Congress*)

Chemical Workers

Of the approximately 70,000 chemicals commercially available, about 1,500 of them are suspected of causing cancer (although only several hundred have actually been tested). Most of these substances cross occupational lines, affecting thousands of workers beyond those involved in chemical production. For example, benzene, which is handled by some 600,000 people, including petrochemical workers, oil refinery workers, dye users, distillers, artists, and shoemakers, has been linked clearly with leukemia and aplastic anemia.

Toluene (TDI), a chemical that has become prevalent in the last twenty years, can be found in almost all polyurethane plastics as well as in adhesives and rubber, insulation, and soft-sole shoes. The population of workers exposed to toluene is approximately 40,000. TDI is virtually certain to irritate any human tissue it touches, but most recently it has been linked with extreme and irreversible lung damage.

Bischloromethylether (BCME), which has been linked to lung cancer, is used in a wide variety of industrial processes, although its use was restricted in 1974. The occupational dangers associated with handling these and thousands of other substances have only begun to be explored.

Child Workers

In 1979, the International Labor Organization (ILO) estimated that 52 million children in the world under the age of fifteen were working, of the 1.4 billion children that age worldwide. (The ILO advises this estimate may be low, since statistical reliability varies so much from country to country.) Some children begin working at the age of four or five. Much of this child labor occurs in agriculture, where young children come in contact with dangerous pesticides and other chemicals. In the United States, children of migrant workers have been found harvesting foods recently sprayed with proven carcinogens. Elsewhere, children are employed in the handmade-carpet industry (because their nimble fingers make tighter thread knots), where they are exposed to fabric dusts; in the leather industry, where they handle dangerous glues and dyes; and in the metalworking industry, where solvents are especially dangerous to children because of vapor toxicity. Intensive exposure to hazardous substances can be even more harmful to children than to adults because of their faster metabolism, as well as the fact that their body's accumulation of these substances starts earlier. The ILO reported significant use of child labor in such countries as Italy, Nigeria, Argentina, Mexico, Peru, India, and Greece, although it is generally conceded that child labor occurs to some extent in every country in the world. Investigators, both U.S.-sponsored observers and interested journalists, report observing children busy at all levels of work, carrying loads of bricks to construction sites and exploring the tiny cul-de-sacs of deep coal mines. P.D.

"I'm sorry, Bert, but I'm the only one well enough to go on strike." *(From* The Doomsday Fun Book, *edited by Edward Goldsmith. Cartoon by Richard Willson. © EcoSystems, 1977.)*

THE POISONING OF ISAAC NEWTON

In 1692, Isaac Newton suffered from severe insomnia, poor digestion, amnesia, depression, and delusions of persecution. For the next two years he had little contact with people except for a few old friends to whom he occasionally wrote irrational letters. In a letter to John Locke he tried to account for his melancholic withdrawal: "The last winter by sleeping too often by my fire I got an ill habit of sleeping and a distemper which this summer has been epidemical put me further out of order, so that when I wrote to you I had not slept an hour a night for a fortnight together & for 5 nights together not a wink."

Historians have not been successful in finding the cause of Newton's distemper.

Now, two investigations published in *Notes and Records of the Royal Society of London* (1979) suggest that Newton's breakdown had a chemical cause. Laila W. Johnson and Myron L. Wolbarsht of the Duke University Eye Center, and P. E. Spargo of the University of Capetown, and C. A. Pounds of the Central Research Establishment in Aldermaston, have independently proposed that Newton's illness was chiefly the result of poisoning by the materials he used in his chemical and optical experiments. Over the years before his breakdown, Newton did many experiments in alchemy with a wide variety of metals, including lead, arsenic, antimony, and mercury. Most of the experiments involved heating the metals in large open vessels, in furnaces and over candles, undoubtedly exposing him continually to toxic vapors. Moreover, the symptoms of his illness are those of metallic poisoning.

Newton also had the early chemist's penchant for tasting the products of his experiments. On 108 separate occasions he recorded in his notebooks that he had tasted materials, whose flavors he described as ranging from "tastless" to "sweetish" and "saltish" to "strong stiptic vitriolique tast." And he not only inhaled and ingested toxic materials but also handled and rubbed them, so lead, arsenic, antimony, and mercury, and compounds of them, probably entered his body through his skin. Another source of toxic material may have been the dark red paint, with cinnabar (mercury sulfide) as its chief pigment, that had been freshly applied to the walls of his room in London at about the time of his breakdown.

To test the hypothesis that Newton suffered from metallic poisoning, Spargo and Pounds analyzed (by the ultrasensitive modern techniques of neutron-activation analysis and atomic absorption spectrophotometry) four surviving samples of Newton's hair. All four samples showed unusually high concentrations of lead, antimony, and mercury. Although it cannot be known with certainty that all the samples are authentic, two of them provided by the current Earl of Portsmouth have a strong claim to being so. The daughter of Newton's niece Catherine Barton married John Conduitt, whose daughter, also named Catherine, married John Wallop, the first Earl of Portsmouth. The two locks of hair, along with other Newton relics and manuscripts, have been passed down from generation to generation in the Portsmouth family.

Excerpted from "Science and the Citizen," *Scientific American,* December, 1979.

CANCER

- Estimates vary widely, but it is now generally agreed that environmental factors contribute to or directly cause about 80 percent of all cancer cases.
- About 20 percent of all cancers are believed to be *occupationally* related.
- Cancers can develop five years or more after exposure to a carcinogen.
- Cancer as of 1980 accounted for 405,000 deaths per year in the United States alone, 3,000,000 worldwide.
- Cancer costs the United States approximately $15 billion a year in hospital expenses and lost worker productivity.

P.D.

WORKPLACE LORE

- Percival Pott, an English surgeon, is generally credited with the first observation of occupational cancer. In 1775, he reported a high incidence of scrotal cancer among chimney sweeps. The sweeps had been exposed, many from a very young age, to coal combustion products.
- Animal bladders were used by slaves in ancient Rome as masks to screen out toxic vapors from various occupational contacts.
- Glass-grinders in the sixteenth century suffered from a lung disease then termed "grinders' disease," but which probably was silicosis, a disease prevalent in the United States among silica-sand blasters.
- Twenty-one million workers in the United States—one in four—are exposed to known health hazards on the job.
- Five million workers are injured in the United States each year in job-related accidents.
- The British Rail System had approximately 8,500 asbestos-lined railway cars in service in 1968, and embarked on a $59 million program to replace the linings with plastic foam. Workers in the program must wear protective space-suit clothing, work while breathing through filters or air hoses, and be decontaminated in an air-locked "asbestos house" before leaving work every day.
- In 1967, the staff of *The New Yorker* magazine threatened to leave their offices if the building owner refused to suspend the Muzak system in the elevator.

P.D.

UBIQUITOUS ASBESTOS

In 430 B.C. Pausanias, a Greek geographer, described lamp wicks made of asbestos, which was called "Carpathian flax" at the time. The Romans used the same material as a cremation cloth for holding the ashes of ranking officials. Charlemagne supposedly impressed visitors by passing an asbestos tablecloth through a flame in order to clean off crumbs.

Asbestos is the name commonly given to a group of fibrous silicate minerals that are among the strongest fibers in the world. Since asbestos fibers resist heat and friction, they are invaluable wherever fire is to be avoided.

That asbestos, however, is dangerous to human health has been known at least since the times of the ancient Greeks and Romans, who left references in their writings to lung malfunction among slaves who had the unenviable job of weaving asbestos into cloth. But this information lay dormant for centuries. In the 1890s, asbestos received some attention, and in 1930 a study published in London demonstrated a link between asbestos mining and respiratory disease in asbestos miners. Many other studies followed, strongly suggesting a link between asbestos exposure and increased cancer risk. One important study done in 1964 by Dr. Irving Selikoff of Mt. Sinai Hospital in New York City established irrefutable evidence of an increased incidence of lung cancer among asbestos insulation workers, sometimes as high as eight times that expected for the average population.

Though asbestos has been linked to many forms of cancer, its closest tie is to mesothelioma, an untreatable fatal malignancy of the lining of the lung and stomach. The disease was so rare until asbestos became widely used that it was not internationally classified or even recognized as a separate cancer. And virtually every case of it, as of 1979, can be traced to some form of asbestos exposure. Workers who have even minimal exposure to asbestos are in direct danger, but facts about asbestos are chilling for everyone, because asbestos is a commonplace material.

- Asbestos is almost everywhere. It may be found in the brake linings of almost every vehicle, in clutch facings, floor tile, roofing, paints, ceilings, pipe insulations, boilers, walls, ship bulkheads, potholders, lining of air-conditioning ducts, theater curtains, papier-mâché, playground surfaces—in at least 3,000 products.
- There is no legal restriction on the use of asbestos in food, except in drugs that are ingested. So asbestos filters may be used in the processing of beer, wine, liquor, fruit juices, sugar, lard, cider, spices, vinegar. It is used in pesticides and can be absorbed into food through particles in water and air.
- Asbestos particles can travel hundreds of miles from their source, either in water or through the air, once they are released into the environment.
- Asbestos fibers do not decompose in the body for many years, if ever. The fibrils can be seen only with an electron microscope. There are about one million to an inch (400,000 to a centimeter), compared to about 1,600 human hairs to the same inch.
- The fibers of asbestos also cause asbestosis, or "white lung," which causes shortness of breath, lung scarring, and eventual death by heart failure (or even by severe bronchitis that scarred lungs are too worn to resist).
- Some amount of asbestos fiber is found in the lungs of virtually every person in the United States.
- There are natural sources of asbestos—from water erosion of asbestos-bearing rocks, for example—but secondary sources, like building demolition, are more dangerous because they produce higher concentrations of unsettled fiber.
- Cancer from exposure to asbestos may not dis-

A worker pouring asbestos compounds breathes through a filter mask attached to a recording device on his belt. The device measures and records the amount of particles in the air he breathes. (*Courtesy Shop Talk Productions, Inc.*)

play symptoms for about fifteen years, and disease may occur many decades after exposure. Exposure to asbestos need not be continuous to cause cancer.

- Since World War II, between 8 million and 11 million workers have been exposed to asbestos, including 1.6 million workers employed in asbestos product manufacturing, 2 million automobile workers, and 3.5 million shipyard workers. In contrast, the number of miners exposed directly during asbestos mining is only about 600.
- Of the workers exposed since World War II, 2 million may die of asbestos-related cancers, according to estimated projections.
- Asbestos workers who smoke cigarettes are eight times more likely to have lung cancer than nonsmoking asbestos workers. And cigarette-smoking asbestos workers are ninety-two times more likely to develop lung cancer than nonsmokers in the general population who are not exposed to asbestos.
- Cases of mesothelioma have been observed even in the families of asbestos workers, who are exposed to the asbestos fibers brought home daily on the worker's clothing.
- As early as 1938 the U. S. Public Health Service recommended that asbestos exposure in industry be limited, but no law was passed until 1970, and many consider it to be too lenient.
- Methods for limiting exposure to asbestos include coating asbestos blocks to prevent flaking or spraying the work area to reduce dust. There are also alternative materials that may be used, such as glass-reinforced cement, fibrous glass, and polyurethane; synthetic alternatives exist but have been called "exotic and expensive" by a U.S. government publication on the subject.
- It is estimated that if all dangerous asbestos exposure were eliminated tomorrow, 67,000 deaths from previous exposure would still occur every year for the next thirty years.

P.D.

WHERE TO FIND OUT MORE ABOUT SAFETY IN THE WORKPLACE

You suspect a chemical that you work with daily is hazardous. Where do you turn to document your suspicions? If you belong to a union, that's the place to start. If not, then there are several nongovernmental organizations that might be helpful. This list, though far from comprehensive, is a beginning.

- NATURAL RESOURCES DEFENSE COUNCIL, 122 East 42nd Street, New York, NY 10017, (212) 949-0049.
Publications: *Amicus* (quarterly to members, $15/year), *NRDC Newsletter,* and numerous miscellaneous reports.

The Natural Resources Defense Council is a ten-year-old national environmental organization with broad concerns including environmental carcinogens.

- URBAN ENVIRONMENT CONFERENCE, 1302 18th Street NW, Washington, D.C. 20036, (202) 466-6040.
Publications: Miscellaneous pamphlets.

The Urban Environment Conference is a coalition of environmental, labor, and minority groups active in environmental health issues. Though not an organization of individual members, it is a useful source of up-to-date information on occupational and health rules.

- ENVIRONMENTALISTS FOR FULL EMPLOYMENT, Room 300, 1785 Massachusetts Avenue NW, Washington, D.C. 20036, (202) 347-5590.
Publications: Miscellaneous reports and pamphlets (membership $7.50/year).

Environmentalists for Full Employment is a coalition of environmental organizations that lobby for occupational-safety and health legislation and promote job-creating environmentally sound industries.

- LABOR OCCUPATIONAL HEALTH PROJECT, Institute of Industrial Relations,

University of California, Center for Research and Education, 2521 Channing Way, Berkeley, CA 94720, (415) 642-0323.

General information on occupational health. Distributes film and filmstrips.

- YOUR LOCAL "COSH"

Committees on Occupational Safety and Health (COSH) are organized locally by unions and health professionals. They work to coordinate activities, disseminate information, and cooperate with enforcement agencies—activities vary with locale. You might find out how to contact your local COSH through your regional office of the U. S. Department of Labor.

B.L.

KEY TO ORGANIZATION SYMBOLS:

 pursues environmental litigation

 has a lobbying program

 engages in public education and/or research

 has local chapters or involved in grassroots organizing

UNIONS AND THE ENVIRONMENT

The foreman was emphatic: "I'm telling you to pump it in the river or go home." Gilbert Pugliese, a millwright at Cleveland's Jones and Laughlin Steel Corporation (J&L) balked at the foreman's order, though he was well aware that his refusal to trigger the release of plant wastes into the Cuyahoga River would probably cost him his job.

The task Pugliese refused to carry out was routine, though in all likelihood illegal. Waste oil from a steel rolling operation collected in sumps under the plant and periodically had to be flushed. Proper disposal dictated that the oil be pumped into drums, but J&L Steel Corporation found it more convenient to dump the oil—usually in the middle of the night—into the already ailing Cuyahoga River.

Two years earlier Gilbert Pugliese had taken a similar stand, firmly declining to push the button that would vent the waste. "Anyone with a conscience, who is concerned about the health and welfare of himself and his family, is concerned about this," he said. But the corporations "just keep on stalling, polluting the waterways and air. So one day you take a stand." That day was June 5, 1969, and though the company, already under pressure from federal officials for other pollution violations, threatened the fifty-one-year-old Pugliese with suspension for his defiance, they quietly dropped the matter.

For two years management was careful to avoid asking Pugliese to pump the oil into the river, but on July 14, 1971, while local union officials were away in Washington negotiating a new contract, the plant foreman again demanded that Pugliese push the button. He refused and was immediately suspended, though he was later rehired after nationwide publicity about the incident sparked sharp protests from union officials and co-workers.

Unions on the Environmental Bandwagon

Pugliese's defiance was hailed as an encouraging indication that organized labor, and workers in general, were beginning to embrace the new ecological consciousness.

There were, of course, other encouraging signs. On Earth Day, 1970, the late Walter Reuther, then president of the 1.8-million-member United Auto Workers union (UAW), the nation's second largest union, declared that "the environmental crisis has reached such catastrophic proportions that I think the labor movement is now obligated to raise this question at the bargaining table in any industry that is in any measurable way contributing to man's deteriorating environment." Several large U.S. unions also became active in a "Breather's Lobby" that pushed for air pollution legislation, and labor signed on to the 1969 Citizen's Crusade for Clean Water, which successfully sought increased funding for sewage-treatment plant facilities. As John Yolton, an official of the UAW's Department of Conservation and Recreation, put it, "We helped start the hullabaloo of the early 1970s."

Leonard Woodcock, then president of the United Auto Workers (UAW), speaking to a conference of union representatives and environmentalists in Onaway, Michigan, 1976. (*UAW*)

The endorsement of the fledgling ecology crusade by much of organized labor made sense. Workers were often the primary victims of pollution, both in their workplaces and in their neighborhoods. They had the most to gain by its cleanup. Unfortunately, it quickly became evident that while workers clearly benefit from pollution cleanup, they might also pay the greatest price for it. The workers seemed trapped in a "no-win" situation—forced to choose between losing their health or losing their jobs.

Environmental Blackmail

On February 16, 1971, the Union Carbide Corporation announced that it wanted to close its Marietta, Ohio, ferroalloys plant because it was too expensive to install equipment to meet new clean-air standards there. The closing would throw about 625 employees out of work. Local union officials were shocked. The president of the Oil, Chemical, and Atomic Workers (OCAW), which represents a portion of the Union Carbide workers, called the company's bluff: "We resent the fact that Union Carbide is using our members as pawns in its resistance to clean up the air around Marietta," he charged. An official of the local Allied and Technical Workers, which also represents members at the plant, sided with the company, urging that the government "ought to give the company more time." The Union Carbide ploy was an early example of what came to be called "environmental blackmail." At Union Carbide it very nearly worked.

Such threats by management left workers—and their unions—increasingly in the crossfire between environmentalists and industrialists. Organized labor, which had so far supported environmental goals, quickly realized the potential costs.

Several unions fought back against environmental blackmail, drafting resolutions that decried the practice and lobbying for legislation that would provide economic protection for workers who lost their jobs because of pollution controls. These efforts generally went nowhere, and many unions that had been staunch supporters of environmentalists became cautious.

"The environmental movement has been too slow to grasp the social and economic aspects of the environmental issue which [it] has so effectively brought to national attention," said Leonard Woodcock, who succeeded Reuther as president of the UAW in 1971. "In failing to come to grips with the politics of the environment, they have exposed themselves, as well as the working men and women who should be their strongest allies, to the trap being set for them by corporate polluters."

A Falling Out

Environmentalists were mostly sympathetic to labor's pleas that they grapple with the jobs issue. But with one notable exception—the passage of a California Redwoods National Park expansion bill, which provided for retraining and compensation of displaced workers—environmental groups failed to go beyond rhetorical support for the fate of workers affected by environmental policies. And with the recession of 1974–75, which sent millions of American workers into unemployment lines, the environmental activism of organized labor suffered a severe decline.

While the labor movement was preoccupied with protecting the economic security of its members, environmentalists were having troubles of their own. The political momentum of the early 1970s was slowing as the furor over the "ecological crisis" began to cool. It became increasingly clear that without the political support of organized labor, further gains would be elusive.

Rebuilding the Alliance

Reflecting this political maturation, Environmentalists for Full Employment (EFE) was formed in Washington, D.C., in 1975. Sponsored by about one hundred environmental and community groups, EFE was created to begin building bridges to unions by actively endorsing labor issues, most notably labor-law reform and full employment legislation, and by promoting job-creating environmental programs. EFE has added a measure of sophistication to environmental groups' dealings with organized labor—something most union officials say is sorely needed.

"We've been straight with the unions we work with," says EFE staff member Gail Daneker. "We work with them on their issues when we can, and don't when we can't, and we expect the same thing in return." The bottom line for the unions, Daneker believes, is the organization's "commitment to a full-employment economy and a different system of distributing the wealth created by workers in this country."

"That," she says, "is why unions are willing to work with us."

The Workplace Environment

While attempting to marshal labor support for wilderness and wildlife preservation and clean air and water in the early 1970s, environmentalists frequently gave lip service to the environmental problems of the workplace. Ecologist Barry Commoner popularized the issue early, but the environmental movement was slow to pick it up. That too began to change as environmental activists started to realize the extent to which workers are exposed to pollutants in the plant (see "Are You Dying to Make a Living?" page 685). Those who came to see the health and safety environment *inside* the plant as an environmental issue began to build strong alliances with workers.

Unions responded favorably to the involvement of environmentalists in the workplace environment, and at least one labor official, Peg Seminaro of the AFL-CIO's Department of Occupational Health and Safety, believes that this involvement is the key to winning rank-and-file support for measures to clean up pollution outside the plant.

"Environmentalists are never going to get anywhere until workers are involved at the community level: the environmental activism [of the union] is going to have to come from the bottom up," she says. "As the link between the workplace environment and the community environment becomes clearer—by exposure to information and action on occupational health—workers will be increasingly open to environmental issues outside the plant."

Bargaining for Better Air

Though Gilbert Pugliese's refusal to punch the button releasing pollutants into the Cuyahoga River dramatized the extent to which many individual workers shared the environmental awakening that swept the nation, the activism of union locals on environmental problems outside their plants has been limited. However, several international unions and their locals *did* agree to take on community environmental problems in the early 1970s, and vowed to carry demands for pollution control to the bargaining table. The UAW, the OCAW, and the International Brotherhood of Pulp, Sulfite, and Paper Mill Workers (now the United Paper Workers) were among the unions that urged locals to try to win concessions from management on environmental cleanup, both inside and outside the plant. Although the unions made some progress on workplace pollution control, worker demands for protection of the community environment were decisively quashed; management claimed workers had no legal right to negotiate for controls outside the plant.

However, environmentally minded unions continued to press for pollution controls. For example, rank-and-file members of United Steel Workers Local 1010 in Gary, Indiana, recently won an agreement requiring Republic Steel to reduce graphite levels both inside and outside the plant, an important legal breakthrough.

The union has also gone beyond the bargaining table to intervene in a permit case, insisting that Republic Steel clean up its old plants before being given a pollution-control permit for a new mill. The Steel Workers' Environment Committee has also tackled—often in alliance with local environmental groups—a variety of other issues, supporting antinuclear activists battling a proposed nuclear power plant in the area and conservationists lobbying to expand the nearby Indiana Dunes National Lakeshore (see "The Dune Defenders," page 396).

Lingering Doubts

Despite encouraging signs of cooperation, the environmental and labor movements still have disagreements. Some union leaders remain troubled by many environmentalists' lack of concern for the economic plight of workers. "Look, most people don't like to work. But keeping the job they have is imperative, given the lack of real options for most of our members," says Anthony Mazzocchi, health and safety director of the OCAW. "The reason we don't support a moratorium on nuclear power is that nobody is willingly going to dig their own economic grave. And let's face it, most discussions [by environmentalists] of what's going to happen if a plant shuts down for environmental reasons are very abstract."

John Yolton of the UAW, who has a long history of working with environmental groups, faults many environmentalists for failing to understand that the primary function of a union is to assure economic security for its members. "Environmentalists always come to unions expecting the union to listen to their studies and support their environmental position. Instead, environmentalists must understand that the unions' responsibility is fundamentally an economic one."

The Energy-Crunch Cupid

Though economic hard times threaten to chill the labor/environment alliance in the 1980s, energy may be the issue that will forge the two movements into a closer political relationship than ever before. Alarmed by the impact of escalating energy costs, many unions are becoming increasingly open-minded about environmentalists' alternatives, particularly solar power. Nuclear energy is under fire from a growing number of labor unions—at least six international unions have passed resolutions calling for a slowdown or moratorium on nuclear construction—and even the pronuclear unions are becoming suspicious of workplace radiation hazards at atomic plants. In what one environmental leader called "a turning point for both movements," environmental groups recently lent active support to the pronuclear OCAW in a health and safety strike at a Portsmouth, Ohio, nuclear enrichment plant. In addition, over sixty environmental, labor, and community groups have formed the nationwide Citizen Labor Energy Coalition, which is billed as "a movement to equalize the assault being made on us by the energy companies."

The First Law of Alliances

The 1980s may yet prove that organized labor and environmentalists have learned a thing or two about working together. For its part, labor has learned to take the environmental movement seriously, as a sympathetic ally with popular and often relevant concerns. As for environmentalists, most have learned that in the world of political alliances, like the world of ecology, there is no such thing as a free lunch.

B.P.B., M.C.S

Wavemakers:

PETE SEEGER—WE ALL LIVE HERE

For forty-one years—since the summer he acted the part of a cow in a puppet troupe organizing striking dairy farmers—folksinger Pete Seeger has been fighting for the causes he believes in: for the labor movement since the 1940s, for civil rights since the 1950s, and against war and for environmentalism since the 1960s.

At sixty-two he is as thin as a banjo; a singer, songwriter, and radical activist who scurries rather than walks, Seeger performs a staggering average of two hundred benefit concerts a year, often for environmental causes. But it wasn't always so.

"Up until about 1960 I was still thinking that an interest in nature was kind of frivolous in view of the pressing need to push for peace and get rid of poverty and racism and so on," he says. "And then, in 1962, I read Rachel Carson's *Silent Spring*, and I came to the conclusion that the poor might inherit the earth, but what they inherit could be such a poisonous garbage dump that it might not be worth saving."

In 1966 he helped found Hudson River Sloop Clearwater, Inc., an environmental organization that grew to include five thousand members com-

Folksinger-union activist-environmentalist Pete Seeger chats with a young friend on the dock next to the *Clearwater*. (*Marty Gallanter*)

mitted to cleaning up the Hudson River in New York. (See "Saving a River with a Song," page 329).

As a young man Seeger devoted much of his boundless energy to the labor movement, singing at union rallies for copper miners in Montana, for autoworkers in Detroit, for lumberjacks in Minnesota, and for countless other union causes around the country, sometimes making the rounds with singer Woody Guthrie. Environmentalists, he believes, can learn an important lesson from the labor movement.

"In many ways the struggles are similar," he says. "You print leaflets and pass them out free, write articles, make speeches, and organize rallies. But the labor movement usually worked very much on a local basis, around a specific factory that had to be lined up, and until recently I don't think the environmental movement has been shrewd enough to adopt this tactic."

Environmentalists are making the mistake many intellectuals have made for years, according to Seeger. "Through the printed page they often skip community organizing, and instead they reach their friends all across the country."

"Environmentalists have failed to recognize one of the crucial things movements do," he says. "That is to dig into neighborhood activity and make the issue a matter of crucial importance to a neighborhood. This was the appeal that could be made to workers in a coal mine or a steel mill: to say, 'We live here and we work here and we've got to stick together.' "

He decided several years ago to devote less time singing for "my mostly middle-class audience" in concert halls around the United States and "devote more time to cleaning up my own back yard," as he calls it, focusing his energies on specific problems in the Hudson Valley. Seeger lives in Beacon, a small riverside village almost midway between New York City and Albany. He tells of the time a few years ago when he sang for a union at a General Electric Company plant on the upper Hudson. The plant had been contaminating the river with toxic PCBs (polychlorinated biphenyls). Accompanying Seeger was a young pathologist from the New York State Department of Environmental Conservation whose superiors had ignored his warning on the hazards of PCBs for years.

"The workers were cordial but cool at first," Seeger recalls. "The company had told them that the plant would have to close down if environmentalists made the company clean up."

But the pathologist explained to them the health hazards of PCBs, told them the precautions they should be taking, and for the first time many of them realized it was they themselves who were in danger, not just the fish.

"Not only did the United Electrical Workers local get behind the cleanup effort," says Seeger, "but the cleanup actually generated jobs at the plant." And when he sang for the union's installation of officers a year later, he was warmly received.

He tells the story not to congratulate himself—the ongoing PCB cleanup is the work of many environmental groups—but to make the point that environmentalists can allay suspicions and form bonds with working people by joining directly with the people in a threatened workplace.

"Some groups will say, 'Oh, that's not for us, we've got to save the redwoods,' " says Seeger. "But if you're not interested in saving the environment of the workplace, why, you're not going to reach these people. Very slowly the rank and file [of unions] are awakening to their mistake in ignoring environmental concerns, and I'm glad to see some environmental groups are now waking up to their own mistake of ignoring the environment of the working place for so long.

"I think the environmental movement will really move ahead when they work more on a neighborhood basis, as they did in Seabrook, as they did in stopping Project Sanguine in Wisconsin, and so on.

"We all live here," says Seeger. "We've got to stick together."

D.O'R.

COME POLLUTE US

"Come pollute us," appealed a group of Brazilian officials quoted in a 1977 *Wall Street Journal* column. "We need industry."

American Cyanamid Corporation, for one, responded almost immediately by opening a Malathion pesticide plant in Brazil early in 1978, after new exposure standards for American workers had been proposed by the U. S. National Institute for Occupational Safety and Health (NIOSH) in 1976. Studies indicated possible brain and nerve damage in the 75,000 U.S. workers occupationally exposed to the pesticide each year.

In Brazil, Cyanamid joined the Dow Chemical Company, which already had a plant in São Paulo producing picloram, the key ingredient in a lethal pesticide unregistered for use in the United States, carrying the space-age trade name Tordon-155.

Running Away

They are called "runaway shops"—businesses fleeing regulation for places where the labor is cheap, cooperative, and unorganized. With the Environmental Protection Agency (EPA) belatedly imposing pollution controls and the Occupational Safety and Health Administration (OSHA) moving forcefully—in some cases—to guarantee workers' safety and health, many hazardous U.S. industries are moving to countries where environmental requirements are minimal or nonexistent.

The motivation is profit. A study published by McGraw-Hill shows that, in percentage of total capital expenditures, companies in developing countries spend less than half of what is required in the United States on pollution control and worker safety.

Dow and American Cyanamid are among numerous other U.S. companies taking advantage of a unique Brazilian scheme—"hazardous-pay increments" for three levels of occupational hazard determined by the government. This scheme has the effect of making hazardous work economically attractive to the largely unskilled work force, and forcing workers to take pay cuts if they opt for less hazardous conditions.

Many countries actively recruit U.S. industries displaced by government regulation or high labor costs. They have established "Free Trade Zones," enclaves where companies are given tax and regulatory exemptions to produce goods primarily for export. According to Barry Castleman, an environmental consultant in Washington, D.C., a whole range of industries, like the lead, zinc, and copper refiners, the steel and asbestos producers, and the benzene-dye manufacturers, are running away to these countries at top speed.

The Amatex Corporation, for instance, closed a new asbestos yarn mill in Norristown, Pennsylvania, in 1973 (only six years after it opened) because OSHA established strict workplace standards for airborne asbestos fibers.

By December 1974, Amatex was importing one fourth of all the asbestos used in the United States from its two plants in Mexico, where there are no specific regulations protecting workers from asbestos particles or for the control of asbestos air and water pollution.

By 1978 the Asbestos Textile Institute reported that its membership of seven primary producers of asbestos in 1972 had diminished to three, while the U. S. Commerce Department recorded that asbestos imports from Mexico, Taiwan, and Brazil had increased more than 100 percent.

Take the Money and Run

Often the hazardous runaway is encouraged by U.S. tax laws. Foreign profits of U.S. corporations are exempt from taxation until they are remitted to this country. This situation encourages multinational corporations to relocate plants, deduct the expenses of the moves, and transfer the foreign profits to other foreign operations—in effect, encouraging further relocations.

On top of this, a corporation can receive insurance from the government-supported Export-Import Bank and Overseas Private Investment Corporation (OPIC) when setting up shop overseas. For example, after OSHA found high rates of lung cancer among U.S. smelter workers exposed to arsenic extracted from copper and proposed strict arsenic exposure limits in 1976, the Amax Corporation got backing from OPIC for a 25-percent-share in a nickel-copper smelting complex in Botswana. Then Amax received help from the U. S. Agency for International Development program in planning construction of the Botswana smelter and the infrastructure necessary to support it.

Dumping hazardous production on foreign countries takes its toll in the United States. The Department of Labor registers 449,702 people who in the past four years have received $707 million in Trade Adjustment Assistance, a federal program designed to supplement unemployment benefits for those thrown out of work by plant relocations or import competition.

A NIOSH study completed in 1975 concluded: "Foreign facilities, which may be owned by domestic companies, typically have a competitive advantage over domestic producers since they do not have to pay for environmental controls capable of meeting the OSHA standards."

This boomerang effect is especially pronounced in the case of pesticides. A General Accounting Office report determined in June 1979 that dangerous pesticides banned or regulated for use in the U.S. have been appearing in large quantities in fruits and vegetables imported by the United States from countries with minimal controls over pesticide production and use.

The cycle, as in the global ecosystem, is continuous: Like the pesticides that return as residues on produce, the runaway hazardous industry comes back to haunt.

M.S.

KAREN SILKWOOD

All movements have martyrs. In the United States the most famous martyr of the anti-nuclear-power struggle is Karen Silkwood. Her face has been printed on posters and screened on T-shirts. Her legend is sung in folk songs. The anniversary of her death is marked by memorial services in many parts of the country.

Karen Silkwood, whose death remains a mystery. (*Karen Silkwood Fund*)

Early in the fall of 1975, a handful of people formed Supporters of Silkwood (SOS) in Washington, D.C., to draw attention to the strange events surrounding Karen Silkwood's death in a car crash on November 13, 1974. With other groups, including the Oil, Chemical, and Atomic Workers Union (OCAW), the National Organization for Women (NOW), and the National Emergency Civil Liberties Fund, they supported a lengthy legal case claiming Silkwood's former employer, Kerr-McGee Nuclear Fuel Corporation, was responsible for her contamination by deadly plutonium. They did not claim the company was responsible for her mysterious death, though suspicious circumstances pointed to the company and were used as a rallying point by her supporters.

The court decision, handed down by a federal jury three years after her death, set a precedent that could deeply affect the future of the nuclear industry. For the first time a court found nuclear companies liable for radioactive contamination of people away from the plant site, even if the company has followed government safety standards. This means people whose health or property is damaged by radioactive releases from a nuclear plant or industry can sue the company. The Price-Anderson Amendment to the Atomic Energy Act of 1959, which sets limits on how much nuclear companies and the government will pay in damages from a nuclear meltdown, had limited the liability to damage done during a serious accident. The Silkwood decision removed that limitation.

The Early Days

At the time of her death Karen Silkwood was a laboratory technician at the Kerr-McGee Cimarron plant near Oklahoma City. Oklahoma-based Kerr-McGee was founded in 1929 by Senator Robert S. Kerr and energy expert Dean A. McGee to drill for oil. As the nuclear industry developed, the company branched into uranium mining and processing. In the early 1970s the Cimarron plant began processing plutonium fuel pins for an experimental liquid metal fast-breeder reactor at Hanford, Washington. Silkwood's job involved working with radioactive materials, including plutonium.

At the time of her hiring, Silkwood joined the Oil, Chemical, and Atomic Workers (OCAW) local, following in the footsteps of her grandfather, who had been a union activist.

Working for the Union

In the spring of 1974, Silkwood was elected an officer in OCAW. She began to notice and record safety lapses, accidents, and leaks of nuclear material. The following summer she and others noticed a production speedup (often involving twelve-hour shifts) and a further decline in attention to safety standards. On the last day of July, air-sample filter papers from the lab in which Silkwood was working showed there had been a leak of radioactive gas during her shift. Tests of her urine showed some contamination.

In late September Silkwood and two other union representatives carried their complaints to national union officials in Washington, D.C. Mostly on the basis of Silkwood's notes, they made serious allegations about the health and safety standards at the Kerr-McGee plant. They also charged that the company was falsifying quality control information—marking up with black felt-tip pens the X-ray negatives of the welds on the fuel pins. The next day the union delegation carried its complaints to the Atomic Energy Commission (now the Nuclear Regulatory Commission). A national OCAW official, Steve Wodka, asked the local group to return and continue documenting its charges. Silkwood became obsessed with conditions at the plant. She carried a notebook constantly.

Contaminated

On November 5, Silkwood routinely checked her hands on a scanner after removing them from the "glove box," a protective box with built-in gloves used for handling radioactive materials. They showed contamination as did her arms and coveralls. She had to go through decontamination, which involved three scrubbings with a mixture of strong bleach and laundry detergent. The next day she still showed contamination and went through the decontamination procedure again.

The following day the company decontamination squad was sent to check her apartment and found it hot with radioactive contamination, which was concentrated in the kitchen and bathroom, even in bologna and cheese in the refrigerator. Silkwood waited in a car outside with company lawyers while the squad, dressed in radiation-proof suits, ripped up the carpet, removed the refrigerator and kitchen cabinets, and took her clothes and personal belongings for burial. Silkwood later called her parents from a phone booth and tearfully said she thought she might be dying from radiation.

A check of Silkwood and her roommate (who also worked at the plant) the next day revealed that neither was in immediate danger of radiation poisoning. Silkwood's test recorded a dose of plutonium still within federal safety limits.

Somewhat reassured, Silkwood returned to work on November 13. She attended a union meeting that evening and afterward planned to meet with Steve Wodka and David Burnham, a reporter from the New York *Times*, to document her charges of safety hazards and falsification of documents at the plant. At the union meeting she clutched a notebook and folder, which she implied contained the evidence. After the meeting she drove toward a nearby Holiday Inn to meet the union official and the reporter.

Tragedy and a Missing Memo

Seven miles down the road, Silkwood's 1973 Honda ran off the left side of the road, traveled about 250 feet along the shoulder and flew about 20 feet through the air smashing into a concrete culvert wall. Karen Silkwood was killed on impact. The notebook and folder she clutched so carefully at the union meeting were never recovered.

The highway patrol investigation concluded she had fallen asleep at the wheel. A private accident investigator, however, discovered a fresh dent in the rear of her car, which he said contained traces of metal, possibly from another car. Supporters theorize she was run off the road by someone who then recovered the folder and notebook, but they have not been able to prove their allegations. Her death was ruled accidental.

At the 1979 civil trial, Kerr-McGee lawyers argued that Silkwood had stolen plutonium from the plant to use as false evidence for her charges, and in the process accidentally contaminated herself. The jury agreed with Silkwood family attorneys that she had been contaminated through the negligence of Kerr-McGee and awarded her heirs $10.5 million.

B.K.

ODD JOBS

There are jobs and jobs, and what is odd to some of us is all in a day's work to others. Here the *Almanac* meets some environmental odd jobbers, whose day's work probably never proceeds the same way twice.

Fish Watchers

"Sometimes all you see around you is ice. Once I was out and our warmest day was −14° C, that's about 7° F. That was the warmest, and all our processing is done on deck before the fish are down in the hold. It can get pretty cold."

"Cold" hardly sounds frigid enough to describe the winter ocean in the North Atlantic, but fish trawling is an all-year-round operation, and so fishery observing is too. Michael Cox, age twenty-four, is a watcher, not a fisher.

So is Carol MacGillirray, also twenty-four, who joined the program after working with the Canadian Department of Fisheries onshore. "It's great work, but being away from home for so long means you lose touch with a lot of people." Her being female in a male-dominated field hasn't provoked any awkward situations, and MacGillirray has been out on both Russian and Japanese boats. "I was less an oddity on the Russian boat. It had five other women aboard."

In 1977, Canada declared a 200-mile limit on its fisheries, and required that any vessel fishing within that area be issued licenses only after agreeing to fish within quotas and regulations established by the Canadian government. In order to secure the license, fishing trawler captains must agree to house a Canadian observer on board for the duration of the voyage, *and* to pay the observer's salary and expenses. If a country refuses these terms, it may lose the right to fish in Canadian waters. (A similar program exists in the United States, and Australia was considering instituting one as of 1980.) Countries that fish Canada's waters include Bulgaria, Japan, Poland, Cuba, the Soviet Union, East and West Germany, Spain, Portugal, France and Romania. The observer's purpose is to gather information about fishing stocks for use by the Canadian Department of Fisheries and to monitor the extent to which the fishing ships, including Canadian ships, comply with fishing regulations.

Canada employs approximately 140 observers —15 of them are women—who have ranged in age from twenty to sixty and in background from graduate degrees in environmental science to many weather-beaten years of commercial fishing. The Canadian government provides observers with training in marine biology, navigation, and marine law. The observer's salary is about $100 a day while at sea.

A typical foreign trawler voyage lasts about thirty days, and the long days at sea are the most difficult part of the job as far as Cox is concerned. "You're out there alone on a ship where practically no one speaks your language, so you kind of have to be your own best friend. But the flip side is that you get to live among different kinds of people for a long time, people you might not otherwise get to meet. Plus, I like the work."

On board, the observer must be available more or less around the clock, depending on when the fishing is done. His or her job is to gather detailed information about the length, weight, age, sex, maturity, species, and numbers of the fish caught, so the observer has to be on hand when the catch is hauled in even if it's during the dead of night. The observer is also a "watchdog" to make sure the ship is not overfishing and that its equipment is up to standard. This can be tricky, since the observer has no police power. If wrongdoing is noted, the information must be sent, sometimes in code, to the authorities, who dispatch a patrol boat to the site immediately. For these monitoring reports, the observers are occasionally considered "spies," but both Cox and MacGillirray insist that an observer's presence on board is met with almost total cooperation from the crew. "I can be struggling to measure some sample and a crew member will come along and watch out of curiosity. The next thing I know he's giving me all kinds of help," says Cox. According to MacGillirray, "About the only noncooperation I've had is sometimes the crew won't let me pick up a basket of fish because they think it's too heavy, but you can work with that."

Observer work can be especially complicated if the ship's captain is unfamiliar with the local waters. For example, a trawler might pull in a load of fish, silver hake for example, but along come other fish as well. Such "by-catches" are strictly limited. If the observer's data show that the ship is approaching its by-catch quota, the captain must move the ship to another part of the sea where the by-catch population might be lower, even though the quota for the desired fish might not have been reached yet. Sometimes ship captains resist moving from a productive fishing area, but in general observers can be convincing. Language can be a problem, but all the observers master some international sign language, they draw pictures, and often the radio officer speaks some English. "Between us all we work it out," Cox chuckles. "It can be pretty hilarious sometimes."

To pass the proverbial long hours at sea, the observers mix with the crew as much as possible. Cox tells the story of an at-sea bridge session: "I play bridge a lot at home, and once, on a Polish vessel, the crew managed to get their question across as to whether I played bridge, because apparently the Polish also play bridge a lot. They taught me how to say the suits of the cards in Polish and the numbers one to seven. Then through the game there was a lot of communication going on, all without any language. That impressed me."

As far as the distinctly non-Canadian menu served by Russian, Japanese, and other trawler chefs is concerned, both Cox and MacGillirray seem to thrive. Cox summed it up. "It's great but different. You really get the whole range. I like it, but then I'm a less conservative eater than most people from the Maritime Provinces. We have a reputation for sticking close to what we can eat at home."

P.D.

Wind Prospectors

Just being windy some of the time is not enough. At least not according to wind prospectors, whose job it is to search out locations where windmills might be used to produce energy.

According to Richard Simon, of Global Weather Consultants, Inc., one year's air flow data are usually needed in order to determine whether a site is suitable for a windmill, or wind turbine, as the device is properly known. An average year-round wind of 14 miles (23 kilometers) an hour is a minimum requirement. The wind prospector also has to check the upper limits of the wind in any given spot, since too high a wind—45 to 60 miles per hour (72 to 97 kilometers)—requires shutting down or "braking" the turbine lest it be blown apart.

The prospector, who is hired by a government, a utility company, an institution, or an individual, sometimes acts on local information by visiting a site he or she has heard is windy. But the breeze rarely blows as consistently as people think. According to Simon, the layperson overestimates the average year-round windspeed by as much as a factor of two.

Since "hard" wind data are scanty, the prospector scouts a likely region looking for definite physical signs of windiness, like tree branches or other vegetation blown in one direction. After that, the prospector strategically places sensitive measuring devices to record air patterns. Simon placed twenty-five such instruments around a 7,000-square-mile (18,100-square-kilometer) area in Southern California that he was "staking."

Richard Simon, a "wind prospector," adjusts an anemometer with which he measures wind speed. (*Courtesy Richard Simon*)

Eventually the prospector can decide where the turbine should be placed.

Small mills can power a private home, but larger ones seem more promising economically. One example is a U.S. government experimental mill at Block Island, Rhode Island, which stands 160 feet (49 meters) high, topped by what looks like a giant, gleaming airplane propeller. The average annual wind at Block Island is 17 miles (27 kilometers) per hour, with blasts over 100 miles (160 kilometers) per hour registered during the winter. If successful over the long term, the Block Island turbine could generate enough electricity for fifty families. It is similar to other mills operating in New Mexico and Puerto Rico, also erected by the U. S. Department of Energy. Larger turbines that could generate enough power for a thousand families are currently being designed and tested.

Simon sees as much, if not more, promise for wind energy as for direct solar technology. Turbines generate energy that can be stored for use on days without wind, and they can be easily connected to existing electrical grids. However, because of its variability, the real value of wind is to save the burning of gas and oil to generate electricity. Cautious optimists predict that by the year 2000 wind technology could provide between 3 and 5 percent of all electrical power in the United States.

As for training in wind prospecting, a background in engineering and meteorology helps. Simon had both, studying under one of the leading meteorologists in the United States, but he still says he "just fell into the wind" because it looked like a good idea.

P.D.

Energy Auditors

Austin Randolph, with ten years of experience in the energy business, is a kind of Sherlock Holmes for energy, an auditor for New York City's Con Edison company, one of the largest electric-power utilities in the world. Randolph's job is to detect energy leaks in houses and make recommendations for how they can be eliminated.

In the course of a day, Randolph explores several houses. "For us, each house is a challenge and you never know what you are going to find. The idea is to motivate the customer to improve energy efficiency. Sometimes we are in and out of a house in a few minutes, sometimes it takes hours. I've been in houses with forty rooms, some with three rooms. Once I was in a small bungalow, a 30-foot-square (9-meter-square) house, and was there for four hours because the customer was really prepared and had a lot of pertinent questions."

The questions have to do with consumption and distribution of energy, how to cut use, how to improve floor, wall, and ceiling insulation, thermostat control, hot water systems. Randolph says, "We give emphasis to the living envelope—the walls, windows, and doors."

The auditor locates energy escape routes and the audit report shows what it will cost to fix the problem, and how much energy and money will be saved by fixing it. For example, installing door weatherstripping might cost $44 and save $32 a year in energy costs, a payback period of about one and a half years. Most calculations are done by computer, and the homeowner then studies the figures and decides what investments are worthwhile. The audit itself costs $10.

Con Edison also uses thermogram photography. In this operation, an airplane flies in parallel lines over the area of the home at an altitude of about 1,600 feet (488 meters) while a technician takes infrared photographs. Well-insulated homes appear in black or dark shades, homes with escaping heat reveal themselves in light shades. The thermograms are matched up to area maps and the utility company invites homeowners to a thermogram screening to view their houses. According to Randolph, customers who have had their houses audited usually come to these meetings.

In 1979, about 44 percent of the people audited by Con Edison in New York City and nearby Westchester County took action to plug their energy leaks. Mainly, the energy auditor hopes to raise the "consciousness" of the homeowner, since many are completely ignorant of how energy systems in homes work. In the United States, federal legislation requires that all utility companies in all fifty states make energy audit services available, and eventually audits may be mandatory in apartment buildings and commercial space.

Randolph thinks energy audits should be done on houses *before* they are built. "If customers would show us their plans, we could make a big difference before it is too late."

P.D.

Whale Builders

Designing, hammering, soldering, welding, sculpting, refining—Larry Foster and company build whales. They build them to scale, life size,

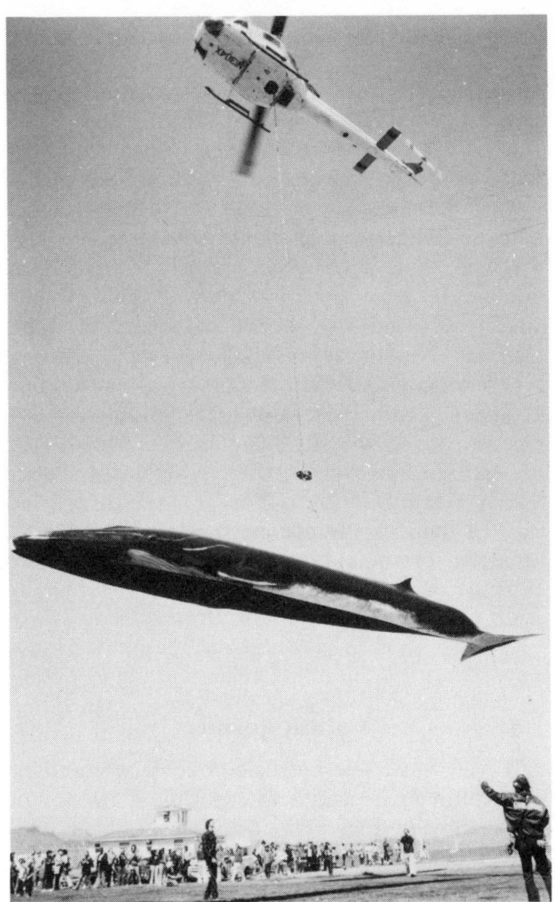

"Pheena," a model of a fin whale, arrives by helicopter at a display site. She's one of many whales built by General Whale. (*General Whale*)

some up to 50 feet (15 kilometers) long, composed of steel and fiber glass or ferrocement, weighing one ton. They build them to exhibit, to educate, to entertain, to demonstrate. Mainly they build whales because seeing the great leviathans alive, in their own liquid territory, is impossible for most people. The models are as close as most of us will come to understanding the magnitude of the whale, and the success of any save-the-whale campaign depends on that understanding.

Depending on the size of the whale commissioned—and General Whale, Foster's group, usually works only on contract to museums, schools, or exhibition centers—there can be from two to six builders at work. In their work, there is a union of engineering, design, art, and love of the whale. The first stage is whale design, and one of Foster's major problems when he started whale building was the lack of information about live whales in the water. Most photography had been done on whaling ships, and there were only pictures of dismembered and bloated whales. So Foster began investigating and collecting from every available source, including archives and libraries. He located unique photo collections including some pictures that had been taken as harpooned whales were dying in the water. The result is that General Whale now claims museum-quality accuracy.

Once the model is designed, the plans are turned over to sculptors who mold the whale and builders who put the whale together. The process is much like constructing a boat, since although these whales will never hit the water, they must be strong enough to withstand travel to exhibitions and be flexible enough to represent accurately a whale's movements.

Pheena, a 50-foot (15-kilometer) fin whale model that occasionally travels by helicopter, weighs a ton—a living fin whale weighs about 65 tons—and was built of 2,570 linear feet (784 meters) of steel, 3,000 square feet (84 square meters) of fiber glass, two and a half barrels of resin, and 50 pounds (23 kilograms) of fiber glass reinforcing pellets. Pheena took 1,900 worker-hours to build.

General Whale's models all go on tour, some around the entire United States, carrying the message that live whales are endangered. The models visit schools, parks, and fairs, where visitors may touch, rub against, or even climb aboard them. People learn to the maximum extent possible, short of swimming along with one, what it is like to be close to a whale.

Though General Whale probably could branch out and produce models of dolphins, otters, manatees, and other marine species, Larry Foster et al. reckon there is enough whale work for the foreseeable future. They will be "sticking to whales" until the creatures are better understood and strictly protected. (For a review of the whale's plight see "Whales," page 286.)

P.D.

Urban Environmental Conservation Officer

Michael O'Hara is one of several conservation officers assigned to monitor and protect the wildlife of—believe it or not—New York City. And while it may seem peculiar to be stalking alligator, whale, and tortoise among the concrete and glass and subways and shops, that is exactly what O'Hara does, in addition to several other unusual and unpredictable daily tasks including the enforcement of state regulations concerning air and

Lt. Donald Brewer of New York City's conservation police looks over some confiscated artifacts made from the skins or teeth of endangered species. (*New York State Department of Environmental Conservation*)

water pollution, illegal dumping of toxic wastes, and wetlands protection.

A primary responsibility of the urban conservation force is to police and eliminate the trade—hardly unique to New York—in illegal animal products, items like shoes molded from the skins of reptiles found on the endangered species list, or buttons punched from the shells of threatened turtle species, or furs peeled from rare animals, or ivory elephant tusks and whale teeth carved into trinkets. Lieutenant Donald Brewer, who is in charge of the New York City force, works out of an office that is a veritable storeroom of seized items, all tagged and numbered, ready to be traced back along the circuitous trail from the wilderness through poachers to the swift dealers and retailers who pass them along, occasionally unaware that the goods are illegal and banned from import in the United States.

The conservation police dip into the city's water system too, checking the rivers and bays for contaminated fish, lobsters (there are lobsters, they claim, in the East River and Lower New York Bay) and other crustaceans, even periodically visiting the famous Fulton Fish Market unannounced to ensure that fishermen are not selling undersized or diseased wares.

Occasionally, Brewer's team is dispatched to rescue a confused raccoon or opossum from one of the city's cemeteries or parks, or to help rehabilitate no-longer-wanted exotic pets, like the wolf that had never acquired wilderness survival skills because it grew up in a Park Avenue duplex apartment. And very occasionally, surprised but charmed New Yorkers phone Brewer's office to report an unusual animal sighting. For example, in Alley Pond Park along the north edge of Queens, one of the city's five crowded, heavily industrialized boroughs, a wild red fox was spotted by an astonished New Yorker. Apparently less startled than its discoverer, the fox trotted away serenely, presumably to continue roaming successfully along the byways of America's largest city.

P.D.

Catfish Farmers

If you have low-nutrient "buckshot" land, as they call it in the southeastern United States, you can't grow cotton, rice, or soybean. You can't grow much of anything, but you *can* grow catfish.

Farmers in the Mississippi area flood these less productive lands to create ponds and holding areas between 3 and 8 feet (1 to 2.5 meters) deep, stocking them with fingerlings, or baby catfish. The fish are fed a combination of fish meal, soybean, and grain. It takes about 1.7 pounds (.77 kilogram) of feed to grow one pound (.45 kilogram) of catfish, which is a reasonably efficient conversion of protein when one considers that it takes about 16 pounds (7.25 kilograms) of grain to produce one pound of beef in a feedlot. (See "How to Make a Cow," page 590, and "Aquaculture," page 609.)

On the farm, fingerlings mature to the 1-pound (.45-kilogram) size in five to seven months, whereas in the wild the same process takes three to four years. In all, it takes eighteen to twenty-four months from the time an egg is hatched to produce a 1.5-pound (.68-kilogram) market-size fish. And the process appears ecologically sound and safe—poor land that needs no chemical applications is put to use growing renewable resources that feed people.

David Pearce, president in 1979 of Catfish Farmers of America, a trade organization, became interested in catfish through a relative who

Harvesting catfish at an Alabama catfish farm. (*Alabama Farm Bureau Federation*)

had been "playing with these catfish ponds as a hobby. I saw it had as much potential as any other crop we could grow here."

Pearce's day is much like any other farmer's. His "fields," however, are water, which he must keep clean and oxygen-rich. In summer months, when water oxygen levels drop, catfish farmers monitor the levels twice a day, using waterwheel aerators when necessary. "Otherwise, you can lose a pond of fish overnight," according to Pearce. Water must also be carefully maintained at the right temperature and kept free of extra food, fish waste products, and other contaminants. The fish themselves are fed once a day but otherwise need little attention once they leave the hatchery. The catfish farmer might operate his own hatchery, or buy fingerlings from someone else.

There are now about 35,000 acres (14,100 hectares) of land in Alabama and Mississippi devoted to catfish farming, and about two thousand catfish farmers. These farmers have also become public relations specialists in some cases, developing markets for the fish outside the southeastern United States, which is the traditional catfish-eating belt. The industry has grown about 25 percent a year since 1974, and shows no signs of shrinking. According to Mark Freeman of the Agriculture Department of the State of Mississippi, "We are getting more fish per acre, and more acres turned over to fish farming; production is up, and everybody involved is making money. It's great to work in a business where everyone gets a whack at the bat." That means to the farmer about 70¢ per pound of fish, $1.65 per pound to the wholesaler, and about $1.99 to the consumer. (With catfish, as with most other crops, the farmer's share is not the greatest portion of the retail price.)

According to catfish connoisseurs, the fish makes good eating. Long a favorite in the South, catfish are becoming popular in places like Kansas City and Oklahoma City, and catfish farmers are hoping the demand will grow "up North." "Right now," says Freeman, "we can't grow enough fish to supply our old customers, let alone look for new ones. We're not even selling fish as far north as Washington, D.C., yet."

As for the taste of catfish, Freeman has definite opinions: "Farm-raised catfish are on the menu of that first meal served in heaven, and you don't even have to wait to enjoy it." P.D.

CONSERVATION CREATES JOBS

Early in the environmental movement, when laws began to regulate pollution in the United States, industrial employers argued that in order to pay the costs of compliance, workers would have to be laid off, the general *standard* of living would go down, and the general *cost* of living would go up. Those who argued for a clean environment were considered elitists who were alienated from the needs of the working class. This attitude rippled, and continues to ripple, through the developing countries, where job creation is a prime necessity and where getting ahead is almost always equated with getting big, which almost always means getting dirty.

It's true that conservation *costs* jobs. But it's also true that it *creates* jobs, more jobs than are lost. When a company decides to close an old plant rather than refit it with pollution controls, workers are unfortunately displaced (as they are when an industry switches to a new technology). But matching all the jobs lost against all the jobs created by the pollution-control industry in the United States results in a net job gain. For example, as customers shun large cars, some auto assembly plants shut down. But as the industry switches to smaller cars and as more money is invested in mass transit, more jobs are created. The trick is to speed "switchover" and keep the new jobs in the same neighborhood as the old.

Since the early 1970s, environmental agencies have consistently shown that programs to protect natural resources, clean air and water, and conserve energy in fact nourish the economy, stimulate sensible growth, and create jobs—all kinds of skilled, unskilled, professional, blue- and white-collar jobs.

Economic transitions are always difficult, but the need for conservation demands a shift from energy-intensive to labor-intensive production. And that means more jobs. Study after study has borne this out. Following is a smattering of findings.

- Pollution control standards have directly cost 21,000 jobs since 1971. As of late 1979 another 24,000 jobs were in jeopardy. Most industrial facilities that closed rather than comply with environmental regulations were only marginally economically successful before the regulations were imposed. According to the U. S. Environmental Protection Agency (EPA) and the President's Council on Environmental Quality (CEQ), about one million people have been employed as a result of environmental regulations since 1970, about 300,000 of whom were in specialized positions, such as "air analyst."
- As of late 1979 in the United States alone, pollution control directly accounted for 700,000 jobs, 280,000 of which are in the private sector.
- The U. S. Senate Commerce Committee has estimated that $1.6 billion in subsidies and loan guarantees for energy-saving home retrofitting would generate about 400,000 jobs.
- The Sheet Metal and Air Conditioning Contractor's Association calculated that retrofitting three million homes to 60 percent solar energy dependence would generate 12.2 million hours per year of work for ten years.
- The U. S. Federal Energy Administration (FEA) reported in "Project Independence," 1977, that a national returnable-for-deposit container law would not only conserve energy and resources but result in a net employment increase of approximately 118,000 jobs.
- A major study by the California Public Policy Center in 1978 found that an all-out attempt to use solar energy in that state between 1981 and 1990 would create 376,815 direct and indirect jobs per year, ranging from sheet metal assemblers to plumbers to salespersons to architects, as well as save $1.3 billion a year in unemployment benefits and $10 billion a year in exported capital, including money to buy oil.
- A U. S. Congressional subcommittee estimates that "crash" conversion to solar energy and intensive conservation measures would generate 2.9 million jobs, after subtracting jobs lost in industries dependent on fossil fuels. The new jobs would be mainly in installation. The purchasing power freed by resulting reduced fuel consumption could generate *still another 1.8 million jobs.*
- In 1975, it was estimated by Dr. Bruce Hannon of the Center for Advanced Communication at the University of Illinois that if $5 billion a year were shifted from the U. S. National Highway Fund (which had spent $275 billion between 1956 and 1975) to railroad and other mass-transit construction, there would be a net 3.2 percent increase in the transportation-construction job sector.

- In 1976, the F.E.A. studied the natural gas consumption of 34,372 private homes. It determined that through modest home improvement:

  — 1.2 trillion cubic feet of natural gas could be saved by 1985, an amount equal to a major discovery of gas in the Alaskan North Slope.
  — consumers would save $1.7 to $2.3 billion in heating costs.
  —the installation work would *create 487,000 jobs* over seven years, both in manufacturing and local installation.

- According to the CEQ, the costs of air and water pollution cleanup resulting from legislation will add only 0.1 to 0.2 percent to the inflation rate until 1986, while lowering the unemployment rate 0.2 to 0.4 percent. (The cleanup has both negative and positive effects on business investment, the balance of trade, disposable incomes, and corporate profits, though none of these economic measures considers the value of improved health and other human benefits of cleaner air or water.)
- Manufacturers sold $1.8-billion worth of equipment used to clean air and water in the United States alone in 1977, and the industry is growing twice as fast as any other U.S. industry.
- The energy crisis has generated new business ventures for many companies:

  — General Electric is developing a long-lasting lightbulb, investing $20 million in research, $20 million in production, yielding two hundred to three hundred new jobs.
  — IBM sold 50 percent more of its monitoring systems to control energy use for lighting, cooling, and heating buildings in 1979 than in 1978, and the entire industry is expected to expand to $850 million per year by 1985 from $450 million in 1979.
  — Some companies that had been facing slowdown in the aerospace industry have shifted to energy management; others have revived old product lines, like ceiling fans and windmills, while others are branching out into entirely new areas, such as the conversion of sugar and other organic waste into fuel.

- The Seabrook Nuclear Power Station in New Hampshire will cost about $2.5 billion to install and will employ thousands of construction workers, *but* the power plant will employ only approximately two hundred workers once it is running.

"HAVE A NICE WEEKEND, EVERYBODY! DON'T BLOW YOUR PAYCHECK IN ONE PLACE!"

- The ratio of tradesperson jobs to professional scientist jobs is 2:1 for the nuclear power industry but 9:1 for the solar industry.
- Jobs in solar energy tend to favor small businesses. Of the approximately six hundred companies producing solar units in 1979, fewer than fifty employed more than thirty persons, and more than two hundred had no more than two employees. (This situation is rapidly changing. See "The Business of the Sun Also Rises," page 503.) P.D.

INVESTING IN JOBS

The growth of various industries is not equal in the eyes of workers. As the table below shows, the same capital investment would create ten to twenty times as many jobs in the textile industry, service sector, or retail trade as it would in public utilities or petroleum.

Capital Investment Per Employee	*Industry*
$108,000	Petroleum
105,000	Public utilities
41,000	Chemicals
31,000	Primary metals
24,000	Stone, clay, glass
19,500	All manufacturing (average)
18,000	Food & related products
11,000	Textile mill production
11,000	Wholesale and retail trade
9,500	Services
5,000	Apparel & other fabricated industries

SOURCE: The Conference Board, N.Y.C., *Capital Invested,* Road Maps of Industry #1799, New York, January 1977.

WORKERS ON THE CORPORATE BOARD

Editor's Note: *In Europe, a system has emerged in which workers share in their company's economic and labor decisions, making it possible for workers to wield more influence over their work environment. The following article by Lucy Komisar, which appeared in the Bergen* Record *in New Jersey, describes the system.*

Werner Willutzki has a comfortable office at the headquarters of Hoesch Works in Dortmund, West Germany. It's the tenth-largest steel company in the world, and Willutzki's office looks like that of any high-level executive.

But Willutzki is not a company officer. He represents labor on the board of the Hoesch steelworks and heads the works council for fifty thousand employees at the billion-dollar Hoesch conglomerate. Forty-two years old, a slight, balding man with large, angular glasses, he keeps a worker's eye on the company's economic fortunes and labor policies.

At a steelworks' board meeting, for example, management proposed closing two plants with five hundred workers. Willutzki and the other labor delegates delayed the decision and demanded a "social plan" for the workers about to be dismissed. Their consent was necessary, for the workers control half the board seats.

That kind of worker power might be unusual in the United States, but it is standard in West Germany—and, to a lesser degree, elsewhere in Western Europe—where worker participation from the shop floor to the boardroom has altered corporate life. The concept is called "co-determination" and it has brought the country unrivaled labor peace and been a major factor in a thriving economy that is the envy of the world.

Co-determination has not meant the end of capitalism in West Germany. Far from it. But it has improved conditions for workers within the market system and cushioned the impact of economic disruption.

Workers participate at two levels. They elect a third to a half of a company's directors and they vote for plant-level works councils. The directors choose the management board and meet several times a year to pass on such major issues as investment policy. The works councils have substantial power over hiring and firing, pay structure, and work rules.

Corporate and labor leaders give the system considerable credit for Germany's high productivity growth (4 percent) and low unemployment rate (only 3.4 percent). Americans, meanwhile, suffered from a productivity growth rate in 1979 of *minus* 1.2 percent and unemployment of 5.7 percent. One reason for this is the difference in the two countries' strike rates: the U.S. rate is fifteen times Germany's.

But co-determination has never won more than a foothold in the United States. Its first big premier is at the Chrysler Corporation where the United Auto Workers (UAW) negotiated a seat on the board in exchange for giving up raises and vacation time to help keep the company from bankruptcy in 1979. UAW attempts to negotiate a board seat prior to the financial crisis at Chrysler had failed.

In Germany, co-determination is accepted across the political spectrum. "We hope we have ended once and for all the class struggle notion and replaced it with a partnership," said Dr. Henning Wehener, international secretary of the Christian Democratic Union.

Co-determination on corporate boards is ironically a gift of the British, whose own strike-ridden system leads Germans to refer disparagingly to "the British disease." After World War II the British occupation forces in the industrial Ruhr backed the bids of trade unions for power in order to keep pro-Nazi industrialists from regaining control.

The works councils, dating to the 1920s, were abolished by Hitler but revived after the war. They give workers equal say with management over such issues as piece rates, job evaluation, working hours, overtime, manpower policies, training, occupational safety, and welfare plans. Hiring, firing, promotion, allocation of work, and transfers all need the advance consent of the works council. Conflicts are settled by labor courts.

Sometimes worker delegates can reduce the scope of layoffs. When Volkswagen wanted to build a plant in the United States in 1976, it faced the prospect of strikes by German workers whose jobs would be lost. In a compromise, production of cars for the U. S. market was divided 60-40 between the United States and Germany and no VW workers in Germany were laid off.

Manfred Paul, a thirty-six-year-old mechanic who has worked at Hoesch for twenty-two years, described the effect of the system on his life. "We have become conscious," he said. "Men used to come to work like corpses with their heads hanging. Now they come with their heads up. They have the security of their jobs and salaries and the right to discuss what goes on in their jobs."

Co-determination has not eliminated unions; 43 percent of the German work force belongs to twenty national labor unions, all but one of which are organized along industrial lines such as chemicals, public services, construction, and trade and commerce. Agreements are worked out nationally for whole industries. Having workers on the corporate boards has taken much of the game playing out of labor negotiations.

"Labor representatives have all the information management has," said Hans Metthoefer, West German minister of finance. "If you sit down at the bargaining table, you know what management knows and management knows what you know. You start at a different level. You know what is possible."

For all the benefits of the system, neither side is completely happy with the co-determination law, which was a compromise. Business fears it goes too far and mounted an unsuccessful legal challenge to it a few years ago. Unions think it does not go far enough.

In the United States the works council idea is most closely approached by an experiment at the Harman International Industries rear-view-mirror factory in Bolivar, Tennessee. There a committee of UAW workers and managers make decisions about job structure, work environment, and production for 1,300 employees. The project was initiated by the company's president, Sydney Harman, former Undersecretary of Commerce, and Irving Bluestone, UAW vice-president, after the two had attended Labor Department seminars on improving working life.

Perhaps when workers see how their jobs are affected by decisions about products, marketing, purchasing, and pricing, Bluestone has said, they will demand to take part in those decisions as well.

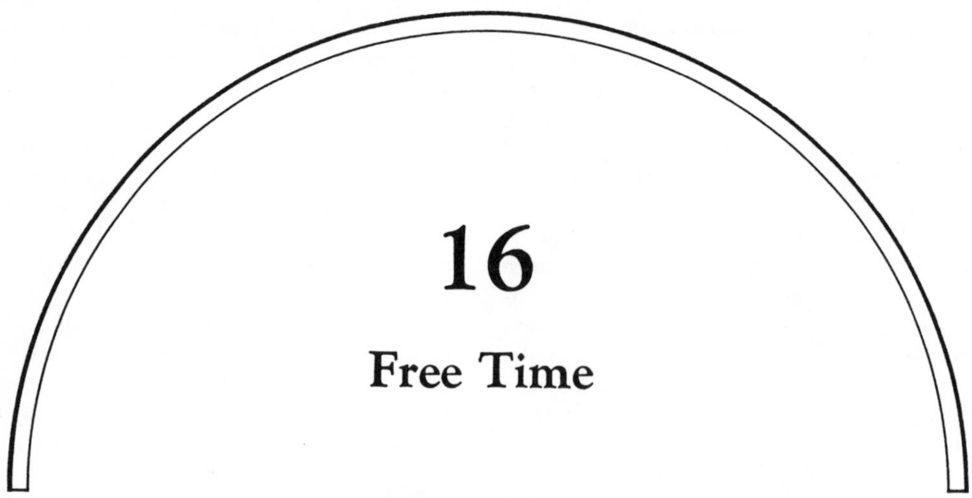

16

Free Time

Free time is the time we do with as we please. It is our time to relax, to create, to explore, to share joys with others. These hours present a great challenge. They are ours to use to shape our lives, our minds, and our world. Our creative energies can be applied to improving ourselves and our surroundings or to having harmless fun. Or they can be used destructively. Or they can simply be wasted.

Individual free time is a relatively modern concept and is still found mostly in industrialized countries, where a middle class has been freed from the constant work of daily sustenance. In these places, people have more choices about how to spend their leisure time, and those choices often take them beyond the traditional activities of family and community.

In this chapter we explore two dimensions of this newfound individual free time. First we look at some environmental effects of our play. Then we explore the nature of free time itself, its promise and its challenge. Of course there are many other dimensions—duties, pastimes, entertainment, sports, hobbies—the possibilities are vast.

Physical Escapes

Often we use a block of free time, a vacation, to get away and recharge ourselves for the work year. We often seek unspoiled natural places—sandy beaches, tropical islands, national parks, ancient slow-paced cities, or cities that have become accustomed to amusing tourists. Somehow it helps those who slush through winters in grimy northern cities just to dream about visiting these milder places. But when we go there en masse, year after year, we bring many of the pressures we are trying to escape. In "Tourist Detractions" we look at some of the most popular vacation spots in the world, not from a traveler's perspective but from the point of view of the people who live there, and from an environmental angle, examining both the benefits and costs tourism has brought. Next we look at our parks, places around the world we have set aside as public showcases of the environment. As millions flee the pressing cities and suburbs for a few days or weeks with "nature," they often find instead a small suburb of campers with radios blaring. Even worse is our impact on the land and its creatures as off-road vehicles erode gullies and create patches of desert, as campers strip vegetation for campsites and firewood. We look at how park authorities are trying to accommodate the press of nature-lovers and still preserve nature.

In pointing out some of the environmental abuses of our fun-seeking, we are not suggesting that everyone stay home, but rather that we travel as respectful, undemanding guests, since all places are the home of other living things.

Exploring Happiness

The second cluster of stories explores the potential of our free time. Often we spend it in quest of fun or happiness, so we examine those elusive concepts. "Great Adventures" looks at recent explorers, people who shunned the tourist routes to travel in unexpected and creative ways, experimenting with new machines and rediscovering old places. They inspire others to explore in perhaps smaller ways, or at least to take comfort in the fact that exploration is alive and well.

Robert Pirsig, author of *Zen and the Art of Motorcycle Maintenance,* gives advice that might apply to tourists and stay-at-homes, as well as to the long-distance sailors he writes about. Stripped of the constant, passive flow of entertainment offered by modern culture, he finds not an escape from reality, but reality itself—the ancient realities of sun, wind, and water, and the inner reality of the human facing them alone.

Finally, Captain Cousteau offers his thoughts on happiness too. It is found, he says, not in the pursuit of status or thrills but in the simple, though often difficult, act of extending oneself to understand the natural world and sharing selflessly with other humans.

Caring, sharing, exploration, and discovery, of course, are not limited to free time. Many people integrate them so thoroughly that the distinction between work and free time becomes meaningless. We discuss these concepts here because our thoughts often turn to them in our free time, our own time, the time allotted to us to fashion moments of quality.

M.P.

A Cousteau Society diver photographs a starfish and sea urchins on a reef. Many such reefs have been denuded by souvenir-hunting tourists. (*The Cousteau Society*)

TOURIST DETRACTIONS

Suppose you were to receive the gift of an untouched, white sand beach, which stretched along a clear, silky sea. You would have certain options. You might hoard the gift, rush immediately to the site, build a beach cottage, and retire there. A public-spirited option would be to declare the site a national park. But there is another likely option: assessing the profitability of this virgin territory, occupying it in the commercial sense, building a hotel and introducing tourism to this private place.

Of course, there are few such "undiscovered" places left in the world. Tourism has established itself almost everywhere already. Whether the sites are beaches, mountains, forests, scenic overlooks, or ancient ruins, development has inevitably followed discovery, for economic and commercial reasons. And regardless of how sensitive or well-planned the development is, what is once discovered is never the same again.

The economic lure of tourism is logical. About 260 million people were international tourists in 1978. According to the United Nations, international tourism increased 75 percent between 1967 and 1977, accounting for $54.4 billion in receipts to countries involved, or about 5 percent of the world's foreign trade. Approximately 13 percent of this revenue was spent in developing countries.

Tourism provides employment for construction workers, taxi drivers, guides, translators, waiters, waitresses, maids, hotel managers, entertainers. Some of the jobs it provides are exclusive to tourism. For example, if Hawaiian musicians couldn't play traditional hula music for tourists sipping mai tais with pineapple sticks at Waikiki Beach, they might not have a livelihood as musicians at all.

But there is a great deal more to tourism than what the tourist enjoys, a great deal beyond what the developer initiates. Tourism has bestowed fame and fortune on many of the world's most beautiful and treasured spots, but not without exacting a price. It has shattered what Lawrence Durrell has called "the spirit of place"—that elusive, ephemeral quality that makes a place feel as it feels, seem as it seems. Tourism has contributed to social unrest by placing "have" tourists conspicuously in the midst of "have not" local inhabitants. Most importantly, perhaps, tourism can spoil or mar the attractive natural environment that made tourism feasible in the first place. The following tales of tourism are what the travel brochures leave out.

Acapulco: "Private Enterprise Gone Mad"

This famous resort on the south coast of Mexico began to develop during the late 1920s because of the superb beach-ringed bay. Land at the time cost as little as three cents an acre. John Paul Getty was said to have purchased 900 acres (364.5 hectares) in 1940 for less than $30. By the 1950s the spot was permanently on the road to development; hotels sprang up from bay end to bay end, often without restrictions on style or size. By 1973 about 1.5 million annual visitors were lodged in about twelve thousand hotel rooms, but by then the growth had begun to level off.

Luxury and Squalor

According to Fred P. Boesselman, who studied the area extensively for his book *In the Wake of the Tourist,* the side effects of tourism in Acapulco have been denigrating. The resident population has grown even faster than the number of visitors, with estimates ranging up to a 20-percent increase per year as people from rural areas migrated to Acapulco looking for work. Their makeshift residences cover the hills. Now the once-quiet fishing village has a permanent population of three hundred thousand. Although unemployment is high, and many people end up hawking trinkets and begging pesos, the influx continues.

Indiscriminate Growth

Unabashed luxury was designed into Acapulco's hotels. The adjacent town just grew. The lean-tos dotting the hills are unserviced by sewers, potable water, electricity, schools, or recreation facilities. Public health is poor. An open canal in the town carries runoff to the bay, while the hotels plan and build their own services. "There is no sense of community here, no sense that what one hotel does affects everybody. This place is private enterprise gone mad," a local businessman complained to Boesselman.

The Bay of Acapulco, with its stretches of wide beach, is obscured by development. The green

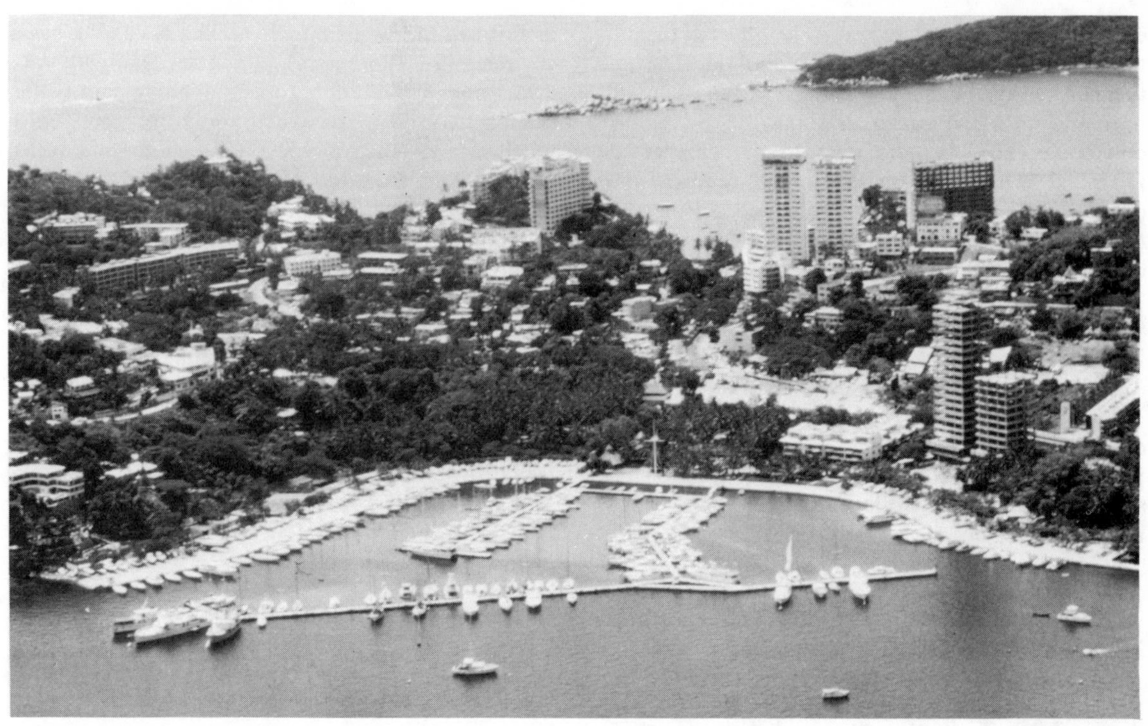

Acapulco, Mexico, one of the country's most popular, and developed, resorts. (*Mexican Government Tourism Office*)

hills are pitted with erosion. There are few breathing spaces of greenery.

In the mid-1970s, a Plan Acapulco was developed under the joint administration of several of Mexico's federal ministries. It emphasizes sewage treatment, but it also includes such improvements as a local bus system, upgrading the local market, a tourist institute for training hotel workers, and houses for low-income people.

Boesselman concludes that while Acapulco is probably not sorry it attracted tourists, and while many legitimate benefits have accrued, Acapulco does demonstrate above all else the phenomenon of over-development.

The Hawaiian Islands: The Blight of Discovery

In these isolated, lush, world-famous volcanic islands, tourism is the number-one industry. Tourism began at famous Waikiki Beach in the aftermath of World War II and grew remarkably fast: 110,000 overnight (or longer) visitors in 1955, 2,829,000 by 1975, 3,500,000 in 1978. Of the islands' 48,000 hotel rooms—the number is expected to double by the year 2000—over 50 percent are owned by local companies, 24 percent by mainland companies, about 20 percent by foreign companies, mainly Japanese.

The Price

Annual revenues from Hawaiian tourism is reported by the tourist industry to be over $1 billion. But Hawaii pays for this rich industry in congestion, pollution, and a general increase in the cost of living for the average Hawaiian. Land, always scarce and costly on the islands, has become relentlessly more expensive. In 1980, new housing in Hawaii cost $100 a square foot, almost double the cost of housing on the East Coast of the United States, and new houses in Honolulu were priced about $40,000 higher than the national average.

Covering the Reefs

The increased building for hotels and housing has had a secondary effect on the underwater coral formations, for which Hawaii is famous. For one thing, the ground cover has largely been removed for development, permitting dirt and sand to erode into the ocean, suffocating reefs and the aquatic life they support. This has, according to many divers, severely altered formations in Kaneohe Bay, outside Honolulu. The increased sewage, which is all too often dumped untreated into the ocean, has had an extremely deleterious effect on the reefs in the vicinity of Diamond Head, also on Oahu. Off remote, less developed islands like Lanai and the Big Island of Hawaii, diving remains magnificent, wooing more divers setting the "discovery" cycle in motion.

Shadow on the Outer Islands

Tourism sprawl is most widespread in Honolulu, but it is certainly most noticeable on the outer islands, dots of land rising from the Pacific, cast in the minds of millions by movies and travel posters as paradise found. Kauai, for example, is a virtual garden of foliage-dressed rolling hills and sweeping beaches, and even a trace amount of tourism has a lasting effect. The Na Pali Coast, 15 miles (24 kilometers) of hidden "hanging valleys" and deep rain forest opening onto the ocean, had been accessible only by foot until tourism arrived. At first, only cautious adventurers hiked into Na Pali, but now helicopters and small planes buzz the beaches to provide sightseers with a glimpse of Eden, and some even fly in to deposit campers and hikers for a few vacation days with nature, some of whom leave not only footprints in the sand but also discarded tuna cans, paper, garbage, and sundry other items. Though Na Pali will probably remain safe from extensive development (it has been designated the Na Pali Archaeological District), the trend toward more visitors is an unmistakable sign of the widening tourism picture throughout Hawaii. It exemplifies the potential blight of discovery.

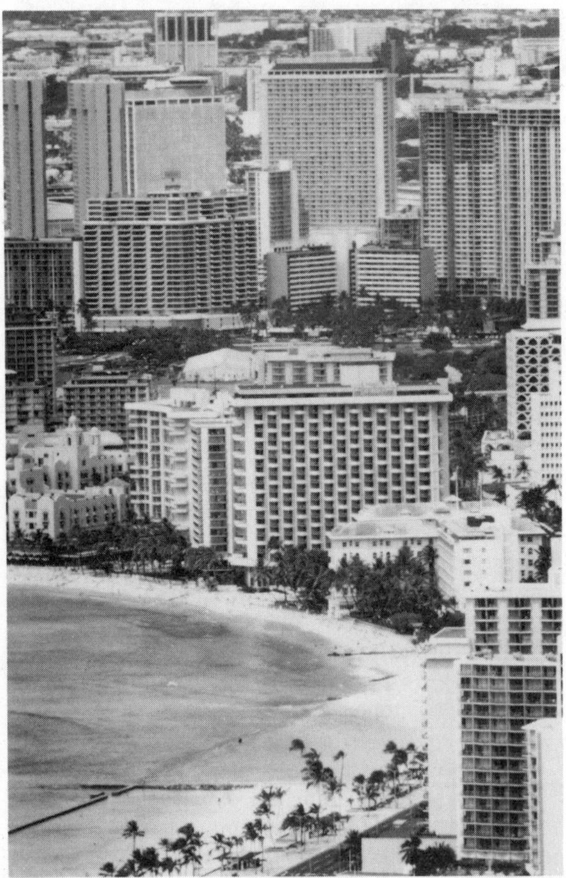

Waikiki District of Honolulu, Hawaii. Development brought jobs, but also congestion, pollution, and a soaring cost of living. (*EPA Documerica/Charles O'Rear*)

The Greek Islands: What Everybody Knows, Even in Absentia

"Greece," wrote Henry Miller, "is what everybody knows, even in absentia, even as a child, or as an idiot, or as a not-yet-born."

During ancient times, Greeks traveled around their own country on religious pilgrimages to the Parthenon in Athens, Poseidon's temple at Cape Sounion, the Oracle at Delphi. Eventually temples lost religious significance, fell into ruin, became secular objects of curiosity to foreigners. Upper-class archaeologists, mostly wealthy foreigners, excavated all over the country, turning up long-forgotten cities and still more temples. Unfortunately, they also carried off many of the best decorative sculptures.

During the nineteenth and early twentieth centuries, the number of visitors to Greece was not more than the country could comfortably absorb. But in the 1950s, Greece was finally "discovered" in the commercial sense. In 1950, Greece received approximately 37,000 visitors; by 1979 over 5 million visited. Income realized from this influx has increased 196 percent since 1974, hitting $1.3 billion in 1979.

The Price

Greek tourism authorities are concerned that their industry may have developed too fast. Native Greece is virtually eclipsed in the summer months. Constitution Square in Athens, the city's focal point, has practically no Greeks in it, except those who are serving the tourists or attempting to sell them something. The Parthenon has been so worn down by tourists' shoes that much of the temple is now closed to visitors; the main road in Delphi is so crowded with tourist buses that people have to zigzag around them to cross the street.

A traditional evening ritual of the Greeks, the *volta,* or walk through town for the purposes of seeing or being seen, is dominated by tourists in July and August. In some small villages, the presence of foreigners has inhibited the *volta* altogether, and the locals just sit and let the tourists "cruise."

This particular effect is especially sad, since the hospitality of Greece has been legend during the past century of tourism. Hardly a vacationer returned without stories of new Greek friends, of Greek homes opened warmly to him or her, of invitations for coffee or candied fruits, which are the traditional gestures of welcome. But, at the moment, there are so many foreigners in Greece that hospitality is strained.

Heavy Sea

The very environmental masterpieces that have haunted poets and lured visitors since antiquity are also now imperiled, and the spirit of the Greek islands gradually diffuses into a mesh of hotel complexes and tourist shops selling third-rate handicrafts. The romantic Aegean Sea, in some places still so clear that bottom pebbles can be distinguished 75 feet (23 meters) above, breathes heavily, clogged by pollution and the floating garbage thrown overboard from yachts, cruise ships, and merchant vessels. Without strict new controls (which are slowly being adopted), Greece stands to lose the unique marriage between its culture and its seas and land. Nowhere is the fragility of this union more obvious than on the Greek islands—there are 160 of them, indented with coves, beaches, and *limanakia* (little harbors)—which are the soul of Greece. Already tourism has marked some indelibly, and it casts a hungry eye on the rest. What is true of Crete, Mykonos, and Rhodes may eventually be true of all.

The North Coast of Crete

Crete was the island of Zorba, where men with thick mustaches wore baggy trousers tucked into heavy black boots, and knives displayed like jewelry tucked into their waist bands. It is the largest of the Greek islands, craggy and wild, but made famous mainly by the remnants of the Minoan civilization, which dates from 1400 B.C. Early tourism here was largely confined to the exploration of ruins. Until 1973, the airport on Crete was a simple strip of macadam parallel to the main road. Passenger baggage was collected onto a cart, which was pulled across the road manually to the one-room "terminal." There, in a disorganized but good-natured melée, it was claimed by passengers who had to yell out their tag numbers, or yank their bags from the bottom of the heap. Today there is an international airport, with direct flights arriving from England, Western Europe, and Scandinavia. Jets whisk one to Athens on the mainland in less than thirty minutes. There are 5,600,000 visitors per year.

The road along the north coast, where some of the island's best and longest sandy beaches can be found, has become a virtual boulevard of high-rise hotels, some with as many as one thousand beds. Hoteliers compete with each other for the best land, building up ten stories because the adjacent hotel has only nine. One hotel company greedily built a hotel next to a cement factory, assuming tourists could be lured there anyway, if the brochures showed one side of the building only. The area, plagued by water shortages under the best of conditions, must suspend supply in the summer months for hours at a time. Now developers are shifting to the remote south coast, which grows less remote each day.

Mykonos

Mykonos epitomizes Greece. The island's port town rambles with narrow streets; charming round-roof houses, repainted white each year, reflect the bright Aegean sun. The windmills of Mykonos, used for irrigation and milling, are virtually national symbols. The island's handicrafts, notably its heavy white wool sweaters, are sold in shops around the world.

Visitors first came to Mykonos because of its proximity to Delos, a rocky uninhabited island covered by classical ruins. Tourism in the region began around 1930, and visitors rented rooms either in two very small hotels or in the homes of local residents. Gradually at first, and then rapidly after 1967, when the military government strongly encouraged investment in tourism, it proceeded to the point where now, in summer, foreign visitors nearly double the year-round Greek population of 4,000. About 75 percent of the tourist services, hotels, and shops are owned by non-Mykonians.

From the beginning, Mykonos attracted an elite, sophisticated clientele. "Beautiful people" found Mykonos, using the privacy of the beaches for nude bathing and other behavior which, although acceptable along the Riviera, horrified the more traditional local Greeks. Sometimes, Greek families preferred not to swim at all rather than to frequent their own beaches, where the tourist presence made them uncomfortable.

Since the 1950s, water supply in Mykonos has been a major problem. The pumping of sewage, mostly by hotels, into septic tanks has contaminated some groundwater. To date, no satisfactory sewage system exists and water occasionally has to be purchased from outside the island.

While tourism has benefited the people who live on Mykonos to the extent that they have more cash to spend, the island offers them little to spend it on, and few future prospects. Most jobs are in tourism—waiting on tables, cleaning rooms, checking in guests. Consequently, the young people of the island want to leave. The better off, though still not wealthy, shopkeepers and restaurant owners of Mykonos can now travel to Athens once a year because of their new income; there, they see "modern" architecture, "modern" goods. They bring these ideas home, modernizing Mykonos but ironically jeopardizing at the same time the unspoiled quality that has lured free-thinking tourists in the first place. How much of Mykonos to "preserve" and how much to "develop" remains in question.

Sanibel: The Irony of Planning

Sanibel island lies 0.5 miles (0.8 kilometers) off the west coast of Florida, in the Gulf of Mexico. With the neighboring island of Captiva, it forms a natural crescent barrier between the open sea and the Florida mainland. The island is a bird haven and natural catchment of shells of great variety and color. In fact, Sanibel, reputed to be one of the three best beaches in the world for shelling, hosts an annual shell fair, a ritual begun forty years ago. But today, finding shells is more and more difficult. With tourism its number-one industry, Sanibel is an island overrun.

Shell-Less

When the first shell fair was held, Sanibel was virtually unknown to any but the permanent residents, who fished for a living, and a few long-term visitors who spent the winter on the island. Slowly development came to Sanibel, where no laws controlled it. In 1974, residents incorporated Sanibel city, thereby gaining the administrative status necessary to establish laws to monitor growth, and in fact Sanibel was the first U.S. city east of the Mississippi to pass a rate-of-growth ordinance. There is a maximum density law permitting only five housing units per acre, a maximum height law permitting no building higher than 45 feet (13.7 meters), and a maximum pace of growth, permitting only 180 single family dwelling units per year.

But, ironically, the building control laws did not really hinder development, though they did change its direction. By weeding out construction that would overwhelm the esthetics of the island, the laws made what was developed especially attractive. Though the current voting population is low, the population is swollen by day visitors and long-term tourists. Where there were 4,662 visitors per year in 1974, five years later there were approximately 11,000. The two-lane highway leading on and off the island is, in season, bumper-to-bumper with cars.

Of course, controlled, attractive development is better for a barrier island's ecology than rampant development, but it creates its own kind of pernicious cycle. As Dick Workman of the Sanibel-Captiva Conservation Foundation described it: "You can't stop change, but you can guide it, and we have learned a lot in the process." Word of Sanibel's appeal spread, attracting new batches of tourists for whom the "natural system" was not enough. It was soon embellished with bars and a disco, and according to visitors who've known Sanibel for years, the essential character of the island has changed completely.

The land-use controls add costs in construction, so developers recoup their investments by selling the apartments and hotels at a high cost, setting off a spiral that drives the value of real estate so high that middle- and working-class Sanibel residents can't afford to rent there, or to pay property taxes—and they can't resist the high prices offered for their land. With more people, all other costs go up. More people need more fresh water, a problem on any island, and so a desalination plant was installed in 1979—water cost $3 for every 1,000 gallons (3,785 liters), plus an installation charge of about $2,000. A sewage treatment plant was built that complements local septic-tank facilities, and all garbage must now be hauled off the island to a mainland fill by a private carter.

And not every visitor to Sanibel treads lightly on the fragile barrier island ecosystem. Beaches are now picked clean of shells. Many visitors, frustrated because beaches are bare, pick living crustaceans and mollusks at low tide, tearing them from their habitat. This further depletes the living ocean, leaving still fewer shells to wash up naturally, interfering with the reproduction cycle that would produce new generations of shellfish. A New York *Times* article in March 1979 described how a tourist "shelled" the walkway of a private garden, digging out its decorative shells, because the natural shelling along the beaches had been disappointing.

Sanibel has mounted a shelling control program to educate visitors about the danger of overshelling, especially the taking of live species, but any law restricting shelling would be virtually unenforceable.

East Africa: Wildlife on Display

The diversity of animal life in Africa has long lured tourists to the safari, first with guns and now with cameras as well. It all started with small cadres of wealthy Europeans visiting Africa through the nineteenth and early twentieth centuries, covering ground slowly, with many bearers and the classic "white hunter" as guide. Today, tourism is one of East Africa's major industries.

One can now photo-safari by the month, week, day, practically even by the hour, traveling from wildlife park to wildlife park by car, zebra-striped minibus, Land-rover, or even by private airplane. Gone, unless the tourist requests the pleasure of roughing it, are the tough trappings of safari, stuffy tents with fresh water supplied only in buckets. East African game lodges are among the most luxurious hotels in the world, and virtually every tourist to Africa returns home vividly describing the uniquely peaceful sensation of sipping a cool drink while sitting in the dark on a raised hotel balcony, listening to the rustling and ruffling of the nighttime forays of animals below.

Call of the Wild

In East Africa tourism *is* wildlife. True, some tourists come for the beaches, and some to buy art, but most visit to view the mixed animal population of mammals, reptiles, birds, and amphibians, which dates to before the Ice Age. It is the world as it once was. What they do not see is the effect of tourism on the land, animals, and people of East Africa.

According to the Sierra Club, national parks in Kenya, Zambia, Uganda, and Tanzania total approximately 38,000 square miles (98,420 square kilometers), an area the size of the New England states. Outside the borders of the parks, local inhabitants are mainly agricultural workers and farmers. As of 1978, the gross national product

A Japanese tourist photographs a Masai woman at a special "tourist village" in Kenya. (*UNEP*)

per capita was $225 in Tanzania, $420 in Zambia, $150 in Uganda. These farmers try to eke out a living from marginal lands; the best, most arable land is already under cultivation.

Pressure to transfer some park lands to farmers is great. In the meantime, farmers are prohibited from hunting any game in the parks to supplement their food supply, so animals and people are both restrained by unnatural boundaries. Consequently, the local farmers tend to view tourism skeptically and somewhat resentfully, since they themselves see little benefit from it, except the occasional tip from an eager tourist paying for the privilege of photographing them.

Fenced In and Out

For the animals, parks are confining. In Tsavo, the largest national park in Africa, the elephant population has dropped from about 40,000 to 20,000 because of a combination of drought and overpopulation within confined land space. The land resources of Tsavo could not sustain the population, which had been underestimated when the park was established. Elephants must migrate in order to find new forage, and in Tsavo food became scarce. Elephants that leave the park—there are no fences—are dangerous nuisances to farmers and are likely to be shot. (See "Tsavo National Park, Kenya," page 85.)

Predator animals suffer too, because they compete for territory with livestock. As wilderness is converted to ranchland, smaller animals lose their habitat and dwindle in number; therefore predators lose their natural prey. So they are forced to stalk more available prey, like sheep and cows, which earns the likes of the cheetah, lion, and leopard even less favor from the farmers. For them, wild animals are to be respected from a distance, and battled to the death if they come too close. Allotting special land for these animals, and making it off-limits to humans, is difficult to explain to someone who hasn't enough to eat.

One Hundred Wedding Headdresses, C.O.D.

Tourism also dilutes the local traditions of Africa. Distinctive and vibrant tribal customs and arts are pressed into tourist service—what were once specially carved and painted masks, fashioned for a wedding or other feast, are now mass-ordered and produced by the hundreds. In the meantime, prices for these "real" arts soar in galleries on famous boulevards around the world, though the "real" artists see hardly a fraction of the price on the retail tag.

Meanwhile, tourists continue to arrive, and East Africa wrestles with the forces of imbalance. In a now well-known essay on touring in East Africa, the writer Francis du Plessix Gray described how so many tourists converged on the same potential photo, that the object of their lenses was scared off:

> After we have watched them for some twenty minutes the cheetahs have approached to about 130 yards of their prey coming close to the distance from which they make their famous 60 m.p.h. dash for the kill. But as they reach the critical moment minibuses start crashing about them; tourists leaning on the open rooftops of their vehicles, cameras poised, urge their drivers to get the closest possible view of the kill. Startled by the commotion the impalas race about in circles and cough out their warning message . . . The cheetahs must know better than we that they have lost their chance for dinner but they go on stalking for a few minutes, as if to finish their pose. And then, amid the clicking of some fifty cameras the lead scout turns away from the impalas. The three slink off into the plain. Their fragile rib cages seem terribly thin in the dusk, the black markings of their cheeks—like rivulets of black tears—seem to express their frustrated hunger.

P.D.

Reprinted from *The Golden Hordes* by Louis Turner and John Ash, St. Martin's Press, Inc., 1976.

SOME TOURISM FACTS

Water

- 350 to 400 gallons (1,327 to 1,516 liters) of water, enough for approximately ten baths, are used in one average resort hotel room per day.
- An eighteen-hole golf course that requires irrigation consumes up to a million gallons (3,790,000 liters)—15,000 baths—per day.

Power

- A resort hotel consumes 3.25 to 3.75 kilowatt-hours of electricity per room per day. This is an amount equivalent to burning a 100-watt bulb constantly for thirty-seven hours.

Sewage and Drainage

- A resort area requires a sewage flow capacity of 255 to 275 gallons (1,042 liters)—about seven baths—of water per day per room. Drainage requirements are about 1,800 gallons of water per day—about forty-five baths—for each acre of developed land (16,844 liters for each hectare).

Adapted from Charles Kaiser, Jr. and Larry C. Helber, *Tourism, Planning, and Development*, CBI Publishing, 1978.

OLD-TIME TOURISTS

Tourist towns are not a modern phenomenon, nor are many of the elements we associate with tourism.

- The great cities of ancient Greece developed resorts on their peripheries to cater to the upper class. Antioch had Daphne, famous for its springs and its oracle of Apollo; Alexandria had Canopus, on a branch of the Nile. A canal gave easy access to the delights of Canopus, and boating parties, often complete with singers and musicians, were extremely popular. The rich also had villas on the shore of Lake Mareotis. Such escapes from the stresses and ennui of the urban life were very necessary to the Alexandrians. Their city was overcrowded, and suffered considerable racial tension among Greeks, Jews, and Egyptians who lived in separate sections of town.

- Although the peripheral resorts of the Greco-Roman cities grew out of a desire to escape, to pursue a simpler life of fishing, boating, and bathing, they soon became extensions of metropolitan excess. Like Canopus, Baiae, on the north shore of the Bay of Naples, became a favorite target of criticism for its luxury and moral laxity. Seneca found it so intolerable that he left after only a day. Baiae, however, remained popular until the fall of the Western Empire in the fifth century A.D.
- The principle of the souvenir snapshot was established long before the appearance of the camera. The Grand Tourist in Rome would pose to have his portrait painted against a distinctive backdrop such as the Colosseum or the Forum. The Roman souvenir portrait developed into a minor industry, providing a useful source of income not only for local artists but also for foreign artists who had come to Rome to study the glories of antiquity.
- Eighteenth-century Italy developed what was probably the first package tour. A *vetturino* was a kind of guide or one-person tour operator who, for a lump sum, organized the transport of passengers and luggage with prearranged stops along the way to the destination. Board, lodging, and wayside meals were included. The *vetturino* was proverbially dishonest, but his clients were seldom troubled by bandits.
- The French Riviera began developing its fame as a winter resort at the end of the nineteenth century. It soon attracted wealthy and eccentric visitors. A certain Prince Tcherkovsky, who had a villa at Cimiez, for example, maintained a staff of eighty-seven. Of these, forty-eight were gardeners whose chief task was to change every flower in their master's garden each night, so that he might be spared the boredom of viewing the same arrangement on two consecutive mornings.
- A suntan is now sported proudly as a symbol of health and leisure, but it was not considered healthful until the value of vitamin D was discovered in the 1920s. Still, a suntan was not considered fashionable among leisured, affluent whites until much later: they considered sunbathing a proletarian form of recreation associated with darker peoples and lower classes. In ancient Rome, aristocratic women used silk to screen the rays of the sun, and nineteenth-century women shaded themselves with parasols.

SOURCE: Louis Turner and John Ash, *The Golden Hordes*, St. Martin's Press, 1976.

LEISURE LORE

In 1978–79:

- American consumers spent $180 billion on leisure activities, or one of every eight consumer dollars.
- Americans spent $12.6 billion on foreign travel.
- There were 210 million recreational visits to national parks in the United States, and 225 million spectators at major sporting events.
- Ninety-eight percent of all households in the United States had at least one television set; 13 million households had cable TV connections, which cost $1 billion in annual fees.
- Americans spent $12 billion on stereos, televisions, home computers, and other electronic leisure items.
- Walt Disney World in Florida drew 14 million visitors; its precursor, Disneyland in California, drew 11 million.

- One out of every three consumer dollars spent on food in the United States was spent in restaurants.
- Americans spent $1.3 billion going to the movies.
- Broadway theaters in New York City had a landmark year, drawing over 10 million patrons.
- Sixty-two million Americans attended at least one live theater performance.
- Seventy-eight million Americans made at least one museum visit.
- Sixty-nine percent of the United States population read; 39 percent read newspapers and magazines but *not* books, the other 30 percent read books and periodicals.
- The "typical reader" has read eight books in six months, spending about $18 for them. Most purchases are of paperbacks, though nearly half of all paperback readers also buy hardcover.

SOURCES: *U. S. News and World Report,* Jan. 1979; The New York *Times,* November, 1978.

CROWDING THE WILDS

Much of our once unexplored wilderness has gone public. Lake Solitude in Grand Teton National Park is commonly called "Lake Multitude," and in Montana's Glacier National Park some employees call one trail the "Garden Wall freeway." The Appalachian and Pacific Crest trails are jammed in the summer. So many people rafted down the Grand Canyon's Colorado River in the early 1970s that the National Park Service has had to set strict limits on the traffic. In 1973, almost sixteen thousand people climbed Mt. Whitney, the highest U.S. peak outside Alaska.

"Loving nature to death" is not unique to the United States. Europe's pockets of wilderness suffer the same problems of overuse and in Japan the impact of hundreds of thousands of city-dwelling nature-lovers has become a major problem, especially on holidays. The Japanese have always loved their mountainous scenery, but now, with most Japanese living in metropolitan areas, more people try to go into less wilderness than ever before. Japanese park rangers report that in spite of people's obvious love for nature, they litter beautiful spots, then watch curiously when patrols come through to pick up the trash.

The Search for Nature

Unfortunately, too many people all looking for solitude and quiet in the same place destroy the very qualities that make the wilderness attractive in the first place. No backcountry hiker likes to wake up and see another bright orange tent several feet away. And people who visit the national parks for a glimpse of nature are often disconcerted to find that other "escapees" have merely transplanted their urban habits to the woods—public campsites are often equipped to permit the hook-up of portable televisions.

The growing number of people entering wilderness areas has meant that park rangers see more examples of ignorant damage to the land. For instance, when hikers take shortcuts up switchbacks the steeper path they use wears quickly away into a gully.

There are several ways to lessen the damage of too many visitors. The wilderness can be restricted—fewer people let in. It can be "hardened," or protected against the people who do come. A combination of these methods can protect the most fragile areas while guiding most traffic to hardened places. There is also the alternative of allowing no human use at all.

To harden the wilderness means to pave the trails, build bridges, fireplaces, shelters, and latrines, increasing the carrying capacity of an area. In Yosemite National Park, there are even two backcountry sewage-treatment plants.

Hardening the wilderness does decrease the damage. People who walk on paved trails can't erode the soil. Cement fireplaces and wood shelters keep meadows from being blackened and scarred. Latrines prevent pollution of the groundwater. If hordes of campers and hikers visit an area, hardening the wilderness is the least damaging way to accommodate them. But a hardened wilderness is not a pure wilderness.

Restricting the Wilderness

An approach that may make more sense in the long run is the permit system. At any one time

"DON'T COMPLAIN TO ME — THEY'RE YOUR DESCENDENTS, NOT MINE."

only a certain number of people are allowed to visit an area. The number is limited because the amount of use an area can take without damage is also limited. The permit system gives rangers a chance to instruct hikers on wilderness etiquette.

An adjunct of the permit system is the restriction of certain *types* of activities in a wilderness area. For instance, snowmobiles may be forbidden because they disturb the wildlife. In the Boundary Waters Canoe Area in northern Minnesota, a continuing controversy rages over whether motorboating and certain other activities should be excluded.

The writer Edward Abbey has gone one step further than the permit system. He has proposed that some wilderness areas be closed permanently to all humans, and left in truly primeval condition. Some countries have come close to this with scientific reserves where only biologists and wildlife specialists are allowed. In Europe, ironically, leaving some wilderness areas alone would destroy their character because humans have already made significant alterations. The famous Luneburg heath of West Germany is a beautiful expanse of rosy heather. To keep the pine forest from taking over, sheep were reintroduced to the heath. Now they are an essential part of the area's natural balances, and human management must continue.

There is one advantage to the crowds that now head for the wilderness at every holiday: the same multitude that is threatening to "overlove" the wilderness can become a powerful force to save it by joining groups that lobby for wilderness protection and by writing directly to government officials.

J.S.

RECREATION MACHINES

Whenever they have a free weekend, George and his brother Sam load their motorbikes on a pickup and follow the Los Angeles freeways out of town. The suburbs fall away as the desert begins to dominate the horizon. They leave the car, mount the bikes, and tear off into the vast expanse of open land. They leap rises and shoot down gullies, enjoying an exhilaration unknown during the work week.

Like many, they seek renewal in the wilderness.

But unlike most of the other visitors to the wild, who are mostly hikers and campers, bikers bring a certain amount of destruction. Their spinning tires tear at the fragile desert soil, uprooting plants, exposing loose soil to wind that blows it into the air and to rain that washes it into streams.

The equivalent of dirt bikes in northern climates is the snowmobile, the machine that allows winter access to the most remote spots despite deep snow. Consistently they prove their worth to people living in isolated communities during winter, but when used for sport they have brought the wrath of property owners and people pursuing quieter winter sports such as cross-country skiing. On a winter weekend in Michigan, for example, one can see a parade of snowmobiles being carried by trailers up Interstate 75 to the north woods. There, property owners complain that snowmobilers vandalize remote vacation homes, run over saplings in orchards, and leave their trails littered with beer cans.

Although the environmental damage they cause is far less than that caused by dirt bikes, snowmobiles do upset northern ecology. Many northern woods and meadows become crisscrossed with snowmobile trails of compacted snow. The effect of compacting is to make the soil beneath the snow colder—by as much as 27° F (15° C)—than ground under surrounding snow. With their winter insulation gone, many small burrowing animals under the trails freeze. And the compacted snow of the trails thaws later than surrounding snow, affecting the growth cycle of plants beneath. Also, the loud noise made by snowmobiles startles wildlife.

The coastal equivalent is the dune buggy, swooping down dunes, tearing away fragile beach grasses that hold the sand in place, setting the dune up for a "blowout" by strong winds. And they drive out wildlife. The Back Bay National Wildlife Refuge, more than 4,000 acres (1,620 hectares) of barrier island along the Virginia coast, has lost much of its shore wildlife as a result of dune buggies and cars invading the beaches and dunes. According to a 1974 report by the Defenders of Wildlife and the Friends of the Earth, "This heavy use has completely eliminated shore nesting birds. Migratory birds no longer breed on the beach. Ghost crabs, once numbering in the millions, are no longer found, and loggerhead turtles, which used to bury their eggs in the sand, can no longer do so for the sand is too compacted for them to dig in."

In the past decade all forms of outdoor recreation have increased in the United States, but none so much as motorized off-road vehicles (ORVs), according to "Off-Road Vehicles on Public Land," a 1979 report by the U. S. Council on Environmental Quality (CEQ). The government estimated that about 44 million Americans used about 10 million ORVs in 1977.

Accordingly, a recent Gallup poll showed 23 percent of those surveyed wanted more places for ORV use while about half of those surveyed wanted ORVs restricted to fewer places.

Starting Lines

According to the CEQ, the phenomenon began, oddly enough, "in a bomb-shattered section of Hamamatsu, Japan, in 1947. There, in a board shack, Soichiro Honda, a forty-one-year-old mechanic and college dropout, removed a small motor from a war-surplus field generator and strapped it to a bicycle. He sold enough of these improvised motorbikes to exhaust his supply of surplus generator motors and was soon designing his own motorbike." Throughout the 1950s the Honda company improved its design and in the 1960s began marketing the bikes in the United States. Honda overcame the sinister, tough image the motorcycle had gained during the 1950s in the United States by showing ads that depicted clean-cut, middle-class youths riding down serene country roads, leaping gulleys, or splashing through streams. Honda, recognizing the U.S. dependence on cars for transportation, emphasized that bikes were for recreation. Americans went for the lightweight, relatively inexpensive motorbikes. By 1976 they had purchased 5.4 million of them from Honda and its competitors.

In the 1950s in Germany, the refinement of a light, two-stroke engine made the mass production of snowmobiles practical. Several Canadian and American manufacturers enjoyed a booming business during the 1960s and 1970s. By 1979 there were about 2.2 million snowmobiles in the United States and one million in Canada. (There are also about 250,000 dune buggies and more than three million four-wheel-drive vehicles in the United States according to the CEQ report.)

Passing from Behind

The mushrooming popularity of ORVs caught most government land-use planning agencies off guard. ORVs are barely mentioned in major reports during the 1960s and early 1970s by the U. S. Department of Interior's Bureau of Outdoor

Recreation (now called the Heritage Conservation and Recreation Service) or the U. S. Bureau of Land Management (BLM), which manages much of the Western public land being damaged by ORVs. By the late 1970s scientists and government agencies had begun to study the effects of ORV use and to try to devise plans to accommodate both foot and motorized recreation. By 1980 much of the damage had been documented and various plans formed to restrict the use of ORVs to certain areas. But by then ORV users formed a large and vocal constituency, used to roaming freely and unwilling to abide by restrictions. And government agencies lack the personnel to police huge tracts of desert, beach, or woods to catch unauthorized ORV enthusiasts.

According to the CEQ report "ORVs have damaged every kind of ecosystem found in the United States: sand dunes covered with American beach grass on Cape Cod; pine and cyprus woodlands in Florida; hardwood forests in Indiana; prairie grasslands in Montana; chaparral and sagebrush hills in Arizona; alpine meadows in Colorado; conifer forests in Washington; arctic tundra in Alaska. In some cases the wounds will heal naturally; in others they will not, at least for a millennium."

The scarred hills of the arid West near large population centers are perhaps the most severely damaged. The U. S. Geological Survey has found ORVs can cause staggering soil erosion. A semiarid region southeast of San Francisco, the Panoche Hills, was open to ORV use for three years, then closed. Four years later geologists estimated that soil was still being lost from the ORV area at an annual rate of nearly 7 tons per acre (2.5 metric tons per hectare), while erosion from undisturbed land in the same area was too small to measure, according to a 1978 *Smithsonian Magazine* article. The eroded soil causes further problems, swirling in the air during dust storms and washing into small streams where it chokes aquatic life.

The Noisiest Issue

The author of the 1979 CEQ report began his preface: "Off-road vehicles are an extremely touchy issue. In fact, of the several issues which arise out of public land-use decisions—grazing, surface mining, water diversion, forest cutting, and wilderness designation—none, in this author's experience, is as volatile as off-road vehicles." Ironically, even when Americans can agree to preserve a wilderness from development they are divided on whether it should be used as a playground for their machines.

CEQ's author clearly delineates the issue: "Nonmotorized recreationists, especially the ones who seek peace and quiet, demand *freedom* from these machines while motorized recreationists demand a place to *enjoy* their machines. But there is a third party involved in the conflict—the land, specifically the land that is held in trust for all U.S. citizens by our agent, the federal government. Of course the land is silent. It cannot speak for itself. At the end of my research I reached one inescapable conclusion: Too few federal land managers are effectively representing the interests of the land and the plants and creatures who live upon it."

M.P., J.S.

GREAT ADVENTURES

Even in an age when the globe is well-mapped and widely populated, when tourists have overwhelmed places that charmed or threatened early explorers, there are still people exploring. Some of them spend years preparing for a chance to break away from the civilized routine, to try out a new way of travel or an old, now uncommon way, or perhaps to do something alone that no one has done alone before. Governments, private industry, and research institutes have taken over much of the expensive exploration of our last frontiers—outer space and the undersea world—but individual explorers are resourceful, sometimes setting new records, sometimes rediscovering old places. They are people from all nations and all walks of life who have followed the advice of British explorer Sir Edmund Hillary (first to climb Mount Everest and first to make an overland tractor journey to the South Pole): "You don't have to be a fantastic hero to do certain things. You can just be an ordinary chap, sufficiently motivated to do interesting and challenging things."

Most adventurers are pleasantly surprised by the selfless kindnesses they often receive en route or by warm popular welcomes upon completing a successful challenge. They inspire a vicarious thrill in people, who, for whatever reason, can't be adventurers at the moment but know that their lives are richer because somebody else is. Somebody like them.

The adventures described below are a sampling of many undertaken during the 1970s.

Inventing Travel Machines

For a while it seemed there was nothing to do but refine the great transportation breakthroughs of the turn of the century: internal combustion automobiles, airplanes, engine-driven ships. And the last great frontier, space, seemed to belong only to highly financed government projects. But backyard Leonardos have continued to tinker with travel machines. Spurred by the fuel crisis, many attempt to design vehicles and vessels that operate on cheap or free fuel. (See also "Windships," page 25, and "Reinventing the Automobile," page 438.) Only one person, as far as we know, is designing a "people's rocket" to open space to the average thrillseeker.

The Solar Balloon

The hot-air balloon has changed little since 1783 when the Montgolfier brothers, sons of a French paper manufacturer, launched two Parisians in a taffeta balloon. Early balloons ascended when the air inside them was heated (in modern times by propane burners) or when lighter-than-air hydrogen or helium was pumped into them. But hot-air balloons could only carry enough fuel to stay aloft for about three hours, hydrogen balloons were dangerously flammable, and helium is expensive. In 1979 another paper manufacturer, Frederick Eshoo, flew the first successful sun-powered balloon over Albuquerque, New Mexico, for four hours, ten minutes, and seventeen seconds at an altitude of 12,500 feet (3,800 meters). Eshoo sees his invention as a prototype for a new generation of aircraft and space vehicles powered by the sun. Previous experimental solar balloons had proved slow and hard to maneuver. Eshoo solved these problems by creating a balloon that is black on one side and transparent on the other. The transparent side acts like a lens, focusing sunlight on the black side, which absorbs and retains the heat. When the transparent side is turned toward the sun, the balloon heats and rises; when the black side faces the sun, with a reflective outer layer, the interior air cools and the balloon descends.

Eshoo, a 49-year-old pilot who has experimented with a number of odd flying machines, is delighted with the innovation. As a balloon pilot and inventor, he said, "I am slowing down in speed, but speeding up in the brain."

Pedaling Through the Air

Twenty-six-year-old California biologist Bryan Allen also made aviation history in 1979 with a more strenuous but equally fuel-independent flying machine: he pedaled the 75-pound (34-kilogram) aircraft *Gossamer Albatross* across the English Channel at an altitude of 10 to 15 feet (3 to 5 meters). The flight, backed by a twenty-two-

The *Gossamer Albatross*

man team lead by the craft's inventor, aeronautical engineer Dr. Paul B. MacCready, collected a $220,000 prize offered by British industrialist Henry Kremer for the first human-powered flight across the Channel.

In his log of the two-hour and fifty-nine-minute flight, published in *National Geographic* magazine, Allen describes the machine: "Above me the huge transparent wing extends 94 feet [28.7 meters], slightly more than the wingspan of a DC-9. In front, mounted on a lightweight pole, hangs the stabilizer by which I can control my direction. Behind me is the 13-foot [4-meter] pusher propeller, connected by a reinforced plastic chain to a bicycle sprocket beneath my seat in the cockpit."

To maintain a cruising speed of 12 to 14 miles (19 to 23 kilometers) per hour, Allen had to pedal constantly at 80 to 90 rpm, generating about a third of a horsepower.

Like most adventurers, Allen had a moment when determination overcame fatigue: "Four miles to go or four hundred. I'm fading now and know it . . . I talk to myself and sense that my friends below me are talking too: Don't give up now, you *can* do it! As I waver between hope and despair, the radio crackles again: 'Altitude six inches, six inches; get it up, you've got to get it up!' "

Why do it? The question is always asked by the unadventurous. Designer MacCready answered: "A great challenge and fun." And the hope of contributing a new form of transportation: "Our research could mean a more efficient surface transportation and improved ultralight aircraft," he said.

The Volksrocket X-17

There are those who say it could only happen in the gadget-conscious, invention-crazed, space-exploring United States. There, in the backyard of his California home, Captain Robert C. Truax, sixty-one, U. S. Navy (Ret.), is building a rocketship. He is building it out of junkyard parts scavenged from disassembled obsolete U.S. spacecraft, and he has every intention of shooting a paying customer on a ten-minute, thrill-packed fling 50 miles (80 kilometers) into the stratosphere. Truax will work the controls from the ground.

Truax has an instinct for the dramatic. He built the jet-powered motorcycle that was to carry stuntman Evel Knievel across Idaho's Snake River Canyon (the jump aborted when the parachute opened prematurely—not Truax's fault). The two most likely candidates for the first people's space shot are a far cry from the familiar, cool, methodical astronauts who pilot government rockets. One is an Incan Rosicrucian who made a fortune in tortillas, and the other a stunt man and stage manager of a rock group. Both are interested in the publicity.

But if anyone has the proper background to build a backyard rocket, it is Truax, who conceived, organized, and directed the U. S. Navy's first rocket project. He was a career rocketman, counting as colleagues Wernher von Braun and a group of space visionaries such as Bob Bussard.

Truax considers the NASA space shuttle a clumsy design and prefers his tiny, sleek Volksrocket X-17: 24 feet (7.3 meters) long, 3,100 pounds (1,406 kilograms) at lift off, a single-stage, liquid-fueled, reusable rocket. Like Alan Shepard's first U.S. space flight, it will arc into space and splash down in the Pacific Ocean, where cutters and divers will retrieve both astronaut and rocket.

In 1979, Truax was testing the device at a local airfield in California's Santa Clara Valley. Financing is his main problem and he's leaving that to his first passenger: whoever comes up with $100,000 will be the first nongovernment astronaut.

But Truax sees his project as more than an amusement for publicity-seeking millionaires. He plans to cut the price of a trip to $10,000 and expects the lure of space to entice many at that price. Why will they go? "People are incurable optimists," he told *Omni* magazine. "The X-17 is no more dangerous than the Indy 500, where people risk their lives for paltry rewards."

While most of us still think of space as exotic, Truax sees himself as only a few steps ahead of the rush. "Within fifty years, at least fifty thousand people will be living in space. And way downstream, in a thousand years, there'll be more people living in space than on earth."

But right now his rewards are in his ship. In an industry as complex and specialized as rocketry, for one man to design and build his own spacecraft is an amazing accomplishment. "Here I can see the whole picture and get my hands dirty," he said. "I'm probably the envy of all the engineers in the aerospace industry."

Re-exploring Old Ways

Some look for adventure through old, slower ways of travel, re-exploring traditional routes with a fresh perspective. The Strait of Hormuz in the Persian Gulf, one of the world's busiest and most strategic shipping lanes, is an unlikely spot for an explorer, but Thor Heyerdahl saw it from the deck of a reed ship built on a 3,500-year-old design. Driving across the United States is no longer an adventure worth publicizing, but Peter and Barbara Jenkins *walked* from New York to New Orleans to Oregon, seeing modern America at a Lewis and Clark pace. Equipped with new or old technology, or with just packs and free spirits, these explorers found excitement and wonder on well-worn paths.

Sailing into the Past

It started with the question of how ancient peoples might have moved around the globe. Did cultures on one continent influence those on another? Had forgotten voyagers preceded Leif Ericson, Columbus, and Magellan? Norwegian Thor Heyerdahl has made a career of exploring possible ancient routes in vessels of historic design. "I have spent the better part of my life trying to disprove that the sea was a barrier to human travel and cultural exchange," he wrote in *National Geographic* magazine.

Heyerdahl's first experimental voyage was in the now-famous *Kon-Tiki,* an Inca-type balsa log craft he sailed from South America to Polynesia. In 1970 he sailed the *Ra II,* an Egyptian papyrus-reed boat, from Africa to Barbados. In 1978 he completed a third voyage, in the *Tigris,* a boat built of reed bundles after a design of the ancient Sumerians.

Beginning about 3500 B.C., the Sumerian civilization flourished for a thousand years at the juncture of the Tigris and Euphrates rivers, the alleged site of the Garden of Eden, now part of the country of Iraq. Its influence spread overland through Asia Minor to the Mediterranean, but Heyerdahl wondered if the Sumerians had played a part in the "almost simultaneous birth of seemingly independent civilizations in Mesopotamia, Egypt, and the Indus Valley."

Unlike the *Kon-Tiki* and *Ra II* expeditions, both "drift" voyages dependent on favorable winds and currents, the voyage of the *Tigris* had to be navigated through the Persian Gulf, the Arabian Sea, and the Gulf of Aden, areas now thick with oil tankers. From his study of ancient records, Heyerdahl was convinced Sumerian captains had the navigational ability to follow this route.

Flying a United Nations flag, with a crew of ten men from nine nations, the *Tigris* set sail from the juncture of the Tigris and Euphrates into the Persian Gulf in November 1977. Built of reeds by local craftsmen, her double hull "took the sea like a giant sieve simply straining the waves and allowing them to pass harmlessly back into the sea," wrote Heyerdahl.

Though occasionally stranded on reefs, lashed by storms, and nearly sideswiped by tankers, the *Tigris* visited ports in Oman and the Indus Valley, where Heyerdahl found ghostly remnants of Sumerian culture.

After 144 days afloat and 4,200 miles (6,759 kilometers) of travel, the Tigris landed in Djibouti in the war-torn Gulf of Aden. The international crew, which had journeyed so far in friendship, set her afire, with sails set, outside the harbor. "In that gesture," Heyerdahl wrote, "we sought to appeal to men of reason to resume the cause of peace in a corner of the world where civilization first dawned."

Walking Across America

While re-creating an ancient voyage may take years of planning and considerable financial backing, taking a long walk is within the reach of anyone with sufficient stamina, a lot of free time, and an inclination to experience civilization and nature slowly. Peter Jenkins set off on such a journey from upper New York State in 1974 and trekked for eight months to New Orleans, where he stopped briefly to work on an oil rig. There he met and married Barbara Pennell, who had never camped out in her life, but who gamely struck out with him to walk for two and a half years across seven states to reach the Pacific at Florence, Oregon. Stopping often to earn money, they worked for a Cajun alligator trapper in the swamps of Louisiana, waited tables in a Dallas Mexican restaurant, worked on a cattle ranch in Colorado (where they spent a snowy winter in a log cabin in the Rocky Mountains), and as ranch hands in Idaho. The young couple walked through scorching desert heat protected only by umbrellas clipped to their packs, through breathtaking Colorado mountain passes, and through Oregon blizzards. They suffered from heat and cold, from blisters and fatigue, and from mud-splashing motorists. (Once, in Utah, Barbara and a part-time fellow traveler, Peter's sister, were struck by a car that skidded off the road. Luckily, shielded by their packs, they were not seriously injured.)

On January 18, 1979—five years after Peter set out—the couple were met in Florence, Oregon, by 150 friends and relatives who shared the last mile of their walk to the Pacific. "When we got to the edge of the water, we couldn't stop," Peter wrote. "We kept on walking right up to our waists. Everyone was yelling, laughing, crying, and hugging each other. . . . We'd done what we set out to do—and much more. Our own personal odyssey had somehow come to have a special significance for all these wonderful laughing people around us."

Ballooning the Atlantic

It was in balloons that humans first realized the dream of flying, but after almost three hundred years of flights for experiment, sport, and science, no one had ever flown a balloon across the Atlantic. In August 1978 three Albuquerque, New Mexico, businessmen-turned-balloonists finally did it. They floated above the clouds for six days from Presque Ilse, Maine, to Paris, France.

Balloons were abandoned for commercial potential at the turn of the century, but the dreams they inspired in eighteenth-century Europeans have been revived by balloon sport enthusiasts. Albuquerque, because of its favorable weather conditions, has become the world capital of ballooning. The thing about balloons, enthusiasts say, is that they are quiet and their successful flight depends on the pilot's ability to ride favorable winds. He or she can control vertical maneuvers, but must know where and when to find the best wind and pressure to make horizontal progress.

New Mexicans Ben Abruzzo and Maxie Anderson attempted a transatlantic crossing in 1977 but went down in a storm off Iceland. The next year, joined by Larry Newman, they tried again in the *Double Eagle II*. Thirteen other balloonists had tried it before them. Most of the balloons were ditched at sea; two vanished; one burst in the air. Five of those attempting the crossing had died.

The crew consulted extensively with meteorologists and had a ground crew relaying weather data so they could vary altitude to take advantage of the best winds. Still, there were uncertain moments. Once the balloon mysteriously descended from 20,000 feet to 4,000 feet (6,096 meters to 1,219 meters) in mid-Atlantic. For about a third of the flight they were above 15,000 feet (4,572 meters), breathing oxygen and bundled against the zero-degree (−20° C) temperature. Despite the quiet, there was little time to contemplate the clouds. They reported that radio communications, navigation, ballast planning and execution, updating logs, and housekeeping took up 90 percent of their waking hours.

As they floated toward Paris, ground authorities offered a landing at Le Bourget airfield, where Lindberg had ended his transatlantic flight, but they opted for a less populated area, settling on a farm field near the small village of Miserey. As they had passed over England, villagers had poured into the streets flashing mirrors in a signal of salute. Now throngs of well-wishers jammed the roads around Miserey to welcome them.

"Frankly, until we landed, I never understood fully what had motivated me," Abruzzo wrote in *National Geographic*. "People may not be able to picture themselves in a spacecraft to the moon or beyond, but they can see themselves in a balloon. They can feel with us that when mankind stops crossing frontiers or achieving new goals, [we will] stagnate and move backward instead of forward. That moving forward was, for me, the long-hidden motive of our voyage."

Going It Alone

For some there is joy in teamwork; for others there is singular pleasure in a solo accomplishment. The book of world records keeps track of the first team to explore an area or accomplish a feat, then gives a separate distinction to the first person to do it alone. Yet the motivation of the soloist mystifies many. For some it's the reward of distinction. For others it is the fulfillment of self-discovery. One sailor, asked why he had sailed alone for many years, replied, "I couldn't get anyone to go with me."

Sailing Alone Around the World

In 1522, Magellan (who died en route) and his crew proved one could sail around the world. In 1898, Joshua Slocum proved one could do it alone.

"The profound peace and contentment which Captain Slocum discovered as he and little *Spray* sailed westward across the rolling Pacific, she with a necklace of foam at her forefoot and he, hat in hand, curtseying to the moon, has provided a beacon for sailors everywhere," wrote a contributor to the *Spray*, the newsletter of the Slocum society founded in the 1950s to encourage long-distance cruising. Several men repeated Slocum's feat, but it wasn't until the 1970s that women, long barred from traditional sailing craft and shunned by yacht clubs, sailed around the world alone.

Australian Ann Gash was a fifty-three-year-old grandmother when she set out across the Indian Ocean in 1975 in the 26-foot (7.8-meter) Swedish-built folkboat *Ilimo*. Despite a pounding storm, she rounded the Cape of Good Hope and sailed north along the coast of Africa. In the port of Accra, Ghana, her supplies were stolen and her boat damaged by a tug. Discouraged, she accepted passage for herself and *Ilimo* on a freighter to England. From there she continued her voyage around the world. The deck passage, however, disqualified her as the first solo woman circumnavigator.

Krystyna Chojnowska-Liskiewicz, a forty-year-old Polish naval architect, did complete a two-year solo circumnavigation in the 31-foot (9.3-meter) sloop *Mazurek* a year after Gash returned home. She left the Canary Islands in March 1976 heading across the South Atlantic, through the Panama Canal and across the Pacific to Tahiti and Australia, where she laid over from December to May. Throughout the summer of 1977 she sailed along the Great Barrier Reef and the eastern coast of Australia, but in July she fell ill and had to be airlifted from a small port and taken to a hospital. By August she was back aboard, preparing for the long voyage across the Indian Ocean. She crossed successfully, rounded the Cape of Good Hope, and returned to the Canary Islands in the spring of 1978.

With only two years of sailing experience, an English woman, Naomi James, twenty-nine, set out from London in 1977 aboard the 53-foot (16.2-meter) sloop *Express Crusader* to attempt a *non stop* single-handed circumnavigation, but she was forced to abandon the non-stop goal to put in for repairs several times. She suffered two knockdowns, the collapse of her port shrouds, and fiercely cold and windy weather in the southern ocean. She was the first woman to circumnavigate by way of the old clipper ship routes around the three great capes: the Cape of Good Hope, Southwest Cape of Stewart Island, and Cape Horn. For this accomplishment she was named "Dame Commander of the Order of the British Empire" by Queen Elizabeth II in 1979. Her book recounting the voyage, *Alone Around the World* (called *At One With the Sea* in England and Canada) became a best seller and an inspiration for female sailors.

Alone at the Pole

Naomi Uemura might be called a professional explorer. At thirty-seven years of age when he set off to become the first person to reach the North Pole alone in 1978, he had already scaled the highest peaks in North America, South America, and Africa, rafted 3,700 miles (6,000 kilometers) down the Amazon, dogsledded more than 7,450 miles (12,000 kilometers) from Greenland to Alaska (the longest solo dogsled trip on record), and climbed Mount Everest with the first Japanese expedition to reach the summit.

He has traveled with companions and traveled alone. "Sharing a project means sharing the satisfaction from it," he told *National Geographic*. "I want to do a project all by myself." The project he chose was perhaps the coldest and loneliest this side of outer space. He set out by dogsled from Cape Columbia, north of Greenland, and spent the next eight weeks chopping his way over jagged ice, encouraging his dogs across dangerous cracks, sheltering the four pups one of his sled dogs gave birth to, and, once, having a frighteningly close encounter with a polar bear. Alone he struggled across 500 miles (800 kilometers) of ice-covered Arctic Ocean silently competing with a team from Nihon University in Tokyo, also headed for the pole.

Shifting ice presented many dangers. "I notice an ice peak fifty meters to the north, moving majestically in a southeast direction," he wrote. "The world around me seems to move like a revolving stage in a giant clockwise manner."

Once he was trapped on a block of ice that separated from adjoining ice, then cracked twice leaving him on a small, dangerous island. As a current jammed the island against more solid ice he raced the dogs across the gap and made it.

Uemura was backed up by planes dropping supplies and periodically bringing fresh sled dogs and by a satellite navigation system that kept track of him through a transmitter on his sled. But the day he reached the pole, atmospheric conditions prevented proper transmissions and he had to confirm his position with a traditional sextant. He was disappointed to learn that the university team beat him to the Pole, but consoled himself: "It is the Arctic I must challenge, not my countrymen." As he was airlifted back to a base camp, Uemura reviewed his fifty-five grueling days alone on the ice. What kept him going, he said, was "the thought of countless people who had helped and supported me, and the knowledge that I could never face them if I gave up."

M.P.

THE CRUISING BLUES

Editor's Note: *Many people dream of taking an extended vacation either between jobs or after retirement. Some picture a remote cabin, others an adventurous trip. For sailors, it's a long cruise, perhaps an ocean crossing. But many who attempt their dream vacation abruptly stop and rush back to the once-hated routine. In this article, originally published in* Esquire *magazine, Robert Pirsig (author of* Zen and the Art of Mortorcycle Maintenance), *describes the psychological shift necessary to wean oneself from a daily fix of "civilization," to confront one's inner demons, and to finally appreciate one's place in the great order of things.*

Their case was typical. After four years of hard labor their ocean-size trimaran was launched in Minneapolis at the head of Mississippi navigation. Six and one half months later they had brought it down the river and across the gulf to Florida to finish up final details. Then at last they were off to sail the Bahamas, the Lesser Antilles, and South America.

Only it didn't work out that way. Within six weeks they were through. The boat was back in Florida up for sale.

"Our feelings were mixed," they wrote their home-town paper. "Each of us had a favorite dream unfulfilled, a place he or she wanted to visit, a thing to do. And most of us felt sheepish that our 'year's escape' had shrunk to eight months. Stated that way, it doesn't sound as if we got our money's worth for our four years' labor.

"But most of us had just about all the escape we could stand; we're overdosed on vacation. Maybe we aren't quite such free spirits as we believed; each new island to visit had just a bit less than its predecessor.

"And thoughts were turning to home."

Change the point of origin to Sacramento or Cincinnati or any of thousands of places where the hope of sailing the world fills landlocked, job-locked dreamers; add thousands of couples who have saved for years to extend their weekends on the water to a retirement at sea, then sell their boats after six months; change the style and size of the boat, or the ages and backgrounds of the participants, and you have a story that is heard over and over again in cruising areas—romantic dreams of a lifetime destroyed by a psychological affliction that has probably ended the careers of more cruising sailors than all other causes put together: cruising depression.

The depressed will offer a number of excuses for their disillusionment: things always seem to be breaking down on the boat, money is running short, people are unfriendly. But eventually they make a statement along these lines: "All this is just running away from reality. You never realize how good that friendly old nine-to-five office job can be. Just little things—like everyone saying hello each morning or the supervisor stopping by to get your opinion because he really needs it. And seeing old friends and familiar neighbors and streets you've lived near all your life. Who wants to escape all that? Perhaps what cruising teaches more than anything else is an appreciation of the real world you might otherwise think of as oppressive."

This last symptom—the desire to "get back to reality"—is one I've found in almost every case of cruising depression and may be the key to the whole affliction. If one bears down on this point a little it begins to open up and reveal deeper sources of trouble.

One first has to ask where those who are depressed got the idea that cruise sailing was an escape from reality. Who ever taught them *that?* What exactly do they *mean?* Scientists and philosophers spend their entire working lives puzzling over the nature of reality, but now the depressed ones use the term freely, as though everyone should know and agree with what they mean by it.

As best I can make out, reality for them is the mode of daily living they followed before taking to the water; unlike cruise sailing, it is the one shared by the majority of the members of our culture. It usually means gainful employment in a stable economic network of some sort without too much variance from what are considered the norms and mores of society. In other words, back to the common herd.

The illogic is not hard to find. The house-car-job complex with its nine-to-five office routine is common only to a very small percentage of the earth's population and has only become common to this percentage for the last hundred years or so. If this is reality, have the millions of years that preceded our current century all been unreal?

An alternate—and better—definition of reality

can be found by naming some of its components . . . air . . . sunlight . . . wind . . . water . . . the motion of waves . . . the patterns of clouds before a coming storm. These elements, unlike twentieth-century office routines, have been here since before life appeared on this planet and they will continue long after office routines are gone. They are understood by everyone, not just a small segment of a highly advanced society. When considered on purely logical grounds, they are more real than the extremely transitory life-styles of the modern civilization the depressed ones want to return to.

If this is so, then it follows that those who see sailing as an escape from reality have got their understanding of both sailing and reality completely backwards. Sailing is not an escape but a return to and a confrontation of a reality from which modern civilization is itself an escape. For centuries, man suffered from the reality of an earth that was too dark or too hot or too cold for his comfort, and to escape this he invented complex systems of lighting, heating, and air conditioning. Sailing rejects these and returns to the old realities of dark and heat and cold. Modern civilization has found radio, TV, movies, nightclubs, and a huge variety of mechanized entertainment to titillate our senses and help us escape from the apparent boredom of the earth and the sun and wind and stars. Sailing returns to these ancient realities.

For many of the depressed ones, the real underlying source of cruising depression is that they have thought of sailing as one more civilized form of stimulation, just like movies or spectator sports, and somehow felt their boat had an obligation to keep them thrilled and entertained. But no boat can be an endless source of entertainment and should not be expected to be one.

It follows that the best way to defeat cruising depression is never to run from it. You must face into it, enter it when it comes, just be gloomy and enjoy the gloominess while it lasts. You can be sure that the same mechanism that makes depression unavoidable also makes future elation unavoidable.

It sounds strange, but some of my happiest memories are of days when I was very depressed. Slow monotonous gray days at the helm, beating into a wet freezing wind. Or a three-day dead calm that left me in agonies of heat and boredom and frustration. Days when nothing seemed to go right. Nights when impending disaster was all I could think of. I think of those as "virtuous days," a strange term for them that has a meaning all its own.

Virtue here comes from childhood reading about the old days of sailing ships when young men were sent to sea to learn manliness and virtue. I remember being skeptical about this. "How could a monotonous passage across a pile of water produce virtue?" I wondered. I figured that maybe a few bad storms would scare hell out of the young men and this would make them humble and manly and virtuous and appreciative of life ever afterward, but it seemed like a dubious curriculum. There were cheaper and quicker ways to scare people than that.

Now, however, with a boat of my own and some time at sea, I begin to see the learning of virtue another way. It has something to do with the way the sea and sun and wind and sky go on and on day after day, week after week, and the boat and you have to go on with it. You must take the helm and change the sails and take sights of the stars and work out their reductions and sleep and cook and eat and repair things as they break and do most of these things in stormy weather as well as fair, depressed as well as elated, because there's no choice. You get used to it; it becomes habit-forming and produces a certain change in values. Old gear that has been through a storm or two without failure becomes more precious than it was when you bought it because you know you can trust it. The same becomes true of fellow crewmen and ultimately becomes true of things about yourself. Good first appearances count for less than they ever did, and real virtue—which comes from an ability to separate what merely looks good from what lasts and the acquisition of those characteristics in one's self—is strengthened.

But beyond this there seems to be an even deeper teaching of virtue that rises out of a slow process of self-discovery after one has gone through a number of waves of danger and depression and is no longer overwhelmingly concerned about them.

Every cruising sailor knows that the long ocean hours at the helm, far from the stimulation of civilization, are not blank hours. A flow of thought comes: first a review of incidents of the previous day or week (few as they may be), later the older memories of months or years past, sometimes interrelated with new insights. New ideas seem to pop up from nowhere because the rigid patterns of thought that inhibited them are now weakened.

Then eventually the empty nights dredge out deeper thoughts, forgotten thoughts repressed years ago: old injustices, ancient feelings of personal doubt, remorse, hatred, fear. You must face them again and again until they die away like the thoughts preceding them.

This self that one discovers is in many ways a person one would not like one's friends to know about; a person one may have been avoiding for years, full of vanity, cowardice, boredom, self-pity, laziness, blamingness, weak when he should be strong, aggressive when he should be gentle, a person who will do anything not to know these things about himself—the very same fellow who has been having problems with cruising depression all this time. I think it's in the day-after-day, week-after-week confrontation of this person that the most valuable learning of virtue takes place.

But if one will allow it time enough, the ocean itself can be one's greatest ally in dealing with this person. As one lives on the surface of the empty ocean day after day after day and sees it sometimes huge and dangerous, sometimes relaxed and dull, but always, in each day and week, endless in every direction, a certain understanding of one's self begins slowly to break through, reflected from the sea, or perhaps derived from it.

This is the understanding that whether you are bored or excited, depressed or elated, successful or unsuccessful, even whether you are alive or dead, all this is of *absolutely no consequence whatsoever*. The sea keeps telling you this with every sweep of every wave. And when you accept this understanding of yourself and agree with it and continue on anyway, then a real fullness of virtue and self-understanding arrives. And sometimes the moment of arrival is accompanied by hilarious laughter. The old reality of the sea has put cruising depression in its proper perspective at last.

By Robert Pirsig, from *Esquire* magazine, May 1978. Reprinted with permission.

Wavemakers:

A CELEBRATION OF PLACE

Ralph Carpentier, bundled in a parka, strides across the sand into a gray shingled building perched on a dune overlooking the Atlantic Ocean. A discrete sign, creaking in the wind, announces the East Hampton Marine Museum.

It is a second home to Carpentier, as it is to many in the diverse group that makes up the community of East Hampton on the sandy eastern tip of Long Island, New York. The Marine Museum, which had been a barracks during WW II, is also a testament to the potentials of using one's free time to create something that will serve an entire community, that will preserve local history, that will encourage a spirit of sharing among people who are thrust together by the happenstance of occupying the same village or neighborhood. The story of Carpentier's association with the museum illustrates how involvement in a personal goal can come to blur the distinctions between work and free time, between history and the present, between the individual and the community that envelops him or her.

Now in his late forties, Carpentier, a painter, came to East Hampton in his mid-twenties to teach art. He also fished in the summer to supplement his income, like many other artists, and did odd jobs such as carpentry and boat repair. In his snatches of free time he accumulated a wealth of knowledge about the community and its physical environment.

The community is a curious mix of entrenched local fishers, old whaling families, writers, artists, and more recently, newly wealthy executives and professionals. The residents of East Hampton, like locals almost everywhere, have developed a familiarity with and appreciation for their environment, in this case the windswept duney tail of an island, peaceful in summer and desolate in winter. The story is repeated from farm villages to urban ghettos. Wherever humans make a home, they integrate themselves into its surrounding environs and they often also make a community.

The roots of East Hampton are deep, reaching back to five English families who settled around Accabonac Harbor (from which they derive the name "Bonakers") in the 1600s. They and their descendants have made a living for more than three hundred years fishing for scallops, clams, and oysters, farming and doing any odd jobs that shifting economics presented. They stuck together

so closely that University of Chicago researchers in the early 1950s found some Bonakers who still spoke a dialect resembling middle English. The Bonakers were followed by whalers, who settled in the village and accumulated fortunes during the East Coast's heyday of whaling. In the 1880s summer people from New York sought out the town, riding the length of Long Island by carriage and steamer. About the same time, artists and poets clustered into a colony there, attracted by the serenity and low cost of living in the fishing village.

Today, East Hampton maintains a reputation among New Yorkers as an exclusive community, a town of well-connected people—the kind of people who have little trouble getting what they want. Within the community sharp class lines still appear, but in many cases they have been blurred by a sense of place: those who live there, no matter how they live or when they came, are part of it.

It was an odd mix at first, the simple fishers, the old whaling families, the rich summer residents, and the progressive artists. "We used to go to the beach to lie in our bathing suits and there would be the Bonakers in their waders and slickers with their fishing nets," recalled Marta Vivas, a long-time resident who moved there to be with her husband, sculptor Wilfrid Zogbaum, in 1957. "We would just look at each other. It had never occurred to them to lie down on the beach. To them it was a place to catch food."

When the artists tried a hand at fishing to supplement their sporadic incomes, the Bonakers watched at first in amusement and later with respect as one by one the newcomers learned the ways of the water. Although the Bonakers considered them eccentric and different, the first few waves of artists and poets did little to disrupt the status quo. "Artists tend to bring out what is beautiful in a place, to see the joy of a place," Vivas said. "Even looking at a run-down shack, they see style and structure."

Later, when a new influx of affluent professionals built large houses of strikingly different architectural style along the low dunes, the slow sense of rhythm of the place began to change. But long-time residents, even as they deprecate the intruders, reflect that in time the land will probably absorb this group of strangers as it has the previous groups.

Ralph Carpentier never meant to be absorbed by East Hampton. He went there to teach and be with other artists, but after almost thirty years of painting, fishing, boatbuilding, sharing the spring fish festivals, the housewarmings, the funerals, and the politics of the town, he has become one of its moving spirits.

"I never meant to be what I became," he said. "I meant, like so many, to go in another direction. I never gave up being an artist, but something happened along the way."

One day he was asked to help design an event to celebrate the fishing history of the area, something that would draw even the independent Bonakers. Carpentier exploited ties with both artists and fishers, inspiring one fisherman to make a model of his dragger, another to rig up his sharpie for demonstration, others to bring and explain their gear. Artists designed exhibits and posters and writers worked on a catalog. Merchants donated time and money.

"I suppose every little community does this," Carpentier said. "But it was wonderful. In the end we had an incredible party to celebrate our success."

The momentum of the celebration moved many to push for a permanent marine museum. After many false starts and differences of opinion, the museum emerged. It is one example of what a community, with its members working together in their off hours, can do for itself. Out of attics and sheds came the artifacts of the old whaling days. Small traditional workboats were discovered and restored. Carpentier painted pictures on the walls depicting the items in use.

Today the town's elder craftsmen and craftswomen come here to carve and paint; to stuff fish-shaped pillows and make other offbeat items for the museum gift shop. The basement, lined with model ships and instructional displays, is the meeting room and classroom—the setting for everything from poetry readings to courses in celestial navigation.

Separate from the museum, but an important part of it, is "The Boat Shop," where the tradition of designing and building wooden workboats adapted to local waters is preserved and knowledge is passed on to students. Carpentier asked fishermen what they wanted in a small workboat. Wide combings, a large cockpit, shallow draft, they said. He designed a model; they critiqued it; he modified it; they built it. They will build more, paying only for supplies.

As visitors walk up the stairs of the museum to its second-floor exhibit, they pass a gallery of enlarged photos culled from family albums. The grandfathers and great grandfathers pose by their nets and fish boxes at the bottom of the stairs. Ascending, one passes through the generations; faces change against the unchanging background of the

bay. Near the top are pictures of younger fishermen, many of whom frequent the museum.

One portrait, midway up the stairwell, depicts a group of fishermen seated stiffly, dressed in their turn-of-the-century Sunday best—all the way down to their hips. Despite the formality of the portrait-taking, they had come shod in their hip-high, rubber fishing boots.

There is something invigorating about a community celebrating itself, its traditions, its resources, its ancestors, its way of life, its quality of life. Perhaps it is the quality of life that inspires the celebration and the celebration that enhances the quality of life.

As museum director, Carpentier draws a salary now. But in the early years, the center was a dream he pursued in his spare time. The distinction between work and free time is blurry to him now. "When you are involved in this way, when it is purposeful, then your life is one whole: your work and play directed toward the same end. You feel very fortunate. It isn't sacrifice at all. Then it is fun."

M.P. with M.V.

THE EXPLORATION OF HAPPINESS

Happiness is the only sanction of life; where happiness fails, existence remains a mad lamentable experiment.

George Santayana

The concept of happiness has become almost as ethereal, and surely as elusive, as the legendary end of the rainbow. Full of color, full of promise, it is sought by everyone but can be described by few. Those who finally reach the spot where they thought they would find it often discover that there's nothing there; they realize, sometimes too late, that they had been looking in the wrong places all the time.

Even essayists and philosophers have edged away from the subject of happiness; those few who have discussed it describe it as little more than a specter, a puckish spirit that taunts us into pursuing it and then vanishes just when we think we have it within grasp. "We are convinced," wrote a cynical Samuel Johnson, "that happiness is never to be found; and each believes it possessed by others, to keep alive the hope of obtaining it for himself." In the end, many of us have glumly accepted the conclusions of secluded religious scholars—that happiness, if deserved, will be attainable only in the next world, not in this one.

There is foolishness in these matters, however; and it should be ascribed not to those who search for happiness, but to those who assume that happiness is abstract and out of reach. We readily declare psychiatry, psychology, even sexology to be "sciences," even though they are largely subjective studies, based on opinions about theoretical recesses of the mind. Yet anyone who would suggest that the study of happiness is at least equally complex, fascinating, worthy of investigation and contemplation would be promptly cast from the gates of academia and denounced as a dreamer.

A Science of Joy

The idea of formally studying happiness, however, is not such a crazy one; it is, in fact, elegantly logical when seen in perspective. The psychologist, whose endeavors are judged to be vital to society, is a dreamer, too. The only difference between a psychologist and an explorer of happiness is that one studies nightmares and the other visions. The psychologist's job is to identify what is bad for us, the emotional sparks that inflame our minds with neuroses and fears. The "happiologist," on the other hand, searches for the common denominator of happiness and then outlines the trends that can be developed to make happiness attainable and even widespread.

Obviously, the job requires all the concentration and intricacies of thought any scholar can muster. But the study of happiness is far from unmanageable; the most productive place to start is with a review of the dead ends humans have pursued, thinking they would lead to happiness but discovering only a vacuum.

The Roots of Deception

The directions civilization took to bring us to our present position seemed rational enough. Survival requires the fulfillment of certain essential needs—shelter, food, clothing. And the attainment of these sustaining components of living generated a certain sense of relief, of security, of comfort. The leaders of industry during its initial surges in the nineteenth century capitalized on this deep-seated human hunger for goods that would ease the burdens and uncertainties of life. Under a moral pretext they set out to mass produce every item imaginable that would hold the promise of filling the needs of humanity. The ancient wisdom passed down by poets and sages throughout recorded history was ignored; happiness through material wealth was promoted.

In our time this trend has become an obsessive drive. How and why did this happen? Advertising vividly illustrates part of the problem. Advertising and industry are commensals; each supports and nurtures the other. Industrial moguls have long known that people would attempt to buy happiness if they thought they could. Advertisers fashioned ways to convince them it was possible. By linking their products to goals that people confused with happiness, they were able to sell more products than people could rationally use. Their promises are rarely subtle: this car will make you powerful; this garment will make you beautiful; this vacation will give you status; this toothpaste will make you sexy; this deodorant will give you security; this wrist watch will bring you admiration. Buy some sparkling piece of junk, logic implies, and you will be happy. But this lures us into solipsism; it tells us that if we accumulate ornaments for our egos, we will find happiness.

But the sad truth is that egomaniacs are never happy. We have shaped a civilization that in turn has shaped us, making us a species of introverts. We are now obsessed with, and consumed by, choices—choosing which goods we should buy, which salaried jobs we should go after, what kinds of goals we should relentlessly pursue to find happiness. Yet the only kind of happiness these choices offer is a contrived, artificial mirage of happiness that quickly vanishes.

The Wealth of the Universe

Fumbled attempts at attaining happiness need not be regarded as chronicles of despair, for there is one shining truth, one valuable piece of wisdom, that we can gain by examining our mistakes. Introversion and egomania lead only to hollow pleasures. Happiness will never be attained with self obsession; instead, it is easily and comfortably and joyfully available with *self extension*. We enrich our own souls when we reach out to the souls of others, to gather and appreciate and absorb not the manufactured wealth of society but the natural wealth of the universe.

- *Extension by knowledge*. The exhilarating quest for discovery, the search to find what magic lies beyond the stars and inside the atom, is at once wonderfully insatiable and wonderfully satisfying. We cannot find happiness in contemplating ourselves; but we can find it in contemplating infinity. Reaching out, with our imaginations, toward its majesty, it will in turn embrace us and inspire us.
- *Extension by love*. The trappings of society, the products we are supposed to buy and the films by which we are supposed to be entertained, are meant to convince us that the quest for physical pleasure will lead to love and thus to

happiness. The modern obsession with sex, however, serves only to separate two people, with each concentrating only on quenching individual desires. True love generates passion; it does not depend on it. It requires no reciprocal obligations and need not always even be returned; for one person can extend himself or herself by taking joy simply in the existence of another. Tenderness, complicity, the courage to cherish someone, are the true elements of love, whether it be love of a father for a son, a brother for a sister, of lovers, or of friends.

- *Extension by sharing.* The difference between the word "sharing" and the word "charity" is far greater than semantic. Charitable people merely listen to their own music; sharing people participate in a symphony, mingling their notes with those of others, caught up in the intoxicating excitement of creating a grand crescendo in unison.
- *Extension by creation.* Giving birth, writing a book, piecing together a machine, building a chair—the person who creates gains the distinctive feeling of playing a role that is bigger than himself or herself. Those who make no attempt to create, who will not take a part of themselves, whether it be an embryo, a thought, a skill, to make a new entity, will try vainly in other ways to become something but will be nothing. They will remain miserable.

All these methods of self extension have one thing in common: The people who extend themselves are participators, players, not just single beings. They use their imagination, their wit, their intellect to find ways of joining themselves with the universe and with the rest of humanity. They see themselves not as single cells in an ocean of humanity; they see humanity functioning as a single cell.

The protection of the environment, of course, is intimately connected to the quest for happiness. When we perceive our oneness with humanity, it is easy to perceive humanity's oneness with the environment. Even the salinity of our bodies is a legacy of our marine origins, as the first living cell took shape from ocean waters. Safeguarding the environment, then, is a way of extending ourselves in every way possible—by knowledge, by love, by sharing, by creation. We can find happiness in protecting the world around us not only because we cherish it for its awesome beauty, power, mystery, but because we cherish our fellow humans, those who live today and those who will live tomorrow, living beings who, like ourselves, will increasingly depend on the environment, for happiness and even for life itself.

PART VII

MAKING WAVES

17

Of Means and Ends

THE WAY IT WAS, THE WAY IT IS

It began with the click of shutters and the whir of TV cameras; flashbulbs flashed and floodlights bathed the celebrants in an attentive glare. It captured them holding teach-ins, staging mock trials for polluters, burying automobiles, and baking whole wheat bread. Reporters filled notepads with accounts of their demonstrations, and their message was duly recorded. It was a day of pedagogy, of irony, of passionate concern. Perhaps most of all, it was a day of symbolism. And a remarkable thing occurred—millions of people believed, despite all the hype and the clatter, that something important was happening. "And that's the way it is," intoned Walter Cronkite, "April 22, 1970. Earth Day."

Perhaps it is overstatement to say that the media were midwives to the American environmental movement that day a decade ago. Many of the organizations that made the event possible were established years before, and by the late 1960s many of them were already locked in battles to turn ecological concern into new laws and new lifestyles. But for millions of Americans—for those who participated and for those who did not—the first Earth Day was the dawn of a new environmental conscience. Some measure of that remarkable environmental awakening can be found in the opinion polls. In 1965, only 35 percent of Americans polled believed that water pollution was a serious problem where they lived. By June 1970, merely two months after Earth Day, that figure had risen to 74 percent. When asked in 1965 whether they would be willing to spend anything at all on pollution control, only three or four out of ten Americans said yes. By 1971, well over 50 percent of those polled agreed to pay more in taxes to finance pollution cleanup. "A miracle of public opinion has been the unprecedented speed and urgency with which ecological issues have burst into American consciousness," said one pollster. "Alarm about the environment sprang from nowhere to major proportions in a few short years."

Backed by this surge in popular support, the early 1970s were a golden period for the environmental "movement." In the United States new laws were passed protecting the environment: the Clean Water and Clean Air Acts, the National Environmental Policy Act, laws protecting wildlife and expanding wilderness, and a spate of environmental protection bills were passed in states and communities as well. Memberships in environmental organizations soared, and "ecology" became a favorite word for political speechwriters. Across the Atlantic, Europeans embraced the new environmental ethic, though some argue that political machinery there was slower to respond. In some ways, Europe was farther along than the United States—many of its citizens had long ago learned to accommodate the everyday realities of limited resources.

But then, as the decade of the 1970s closed, the initial surge of environmental spirit began to slow down. Membership in environmental organizations began to level off, and many small, local groups faded. Special interest groups, first surprised by the political tenacity of the environmental movement and then wiser to its tactics, launched a counteroffensive. Some adopted a public relations veneer of environmentalism, while sinking more and more money into lobbying efforts to undermine environmental laws. And they met with some success. In 1977, the Clean Water and Clean Air Acts, legislative landmarks for the environmental movement when passed, were diluted by weakening amendments. The SST, grounded by environmental campaigns in 1971, flew again at several U.S. airports five years later. Rampant energy development—increased strip mining and offshore drilling, the easing of nuclear plant restraints, and the rush to synthetic fuels—occupied the minds of the professional politicians, and for many of them environmental protection became an afterthought. Some political observers wondered out loud whether environmentalism was a fad that had run its course; the more cynical among them filed an obituary for the environmental movement.

Chilled by the gloomy political climate, environmentalists began to take stock of where they were going, and in the process they discovered something remarkable: the public still strongly believed in what they were trying to do. The most recent public opinion polls bear this out; the "miracle of public opinion" in the early 1970s, they reveal, has turned to rock-hard support in the 1980s.

This chapter of the *Almanac,* "Of Means and Ends," explores how the citizens of the planet can begin that process. It intentionally takes a mostly political perspective because we believe it is in the political arena that many of the obstacles to environmental responsibility have arisen, and there they must ultimately be overcome. Though we spend much time in the United States, we will also journey to Europe to examine the often unique approaches used by environmentalists on that continent, comparing their style and strategies with those of the American environmental movement. We will look at some unorthodox approaches to environmental action that may inspire and amuse, and the serious new strategies that are being fashioned to cope with the political realities of the 1980s.

"Of Means and Ends" is a pause, a chance to reflect on ten years of progress in cleaning up the environment, and an opportunity to look ahead, applying the experiences of the past to a new decade of environmental action. There is nothing certain about the work ahead, except that it will be difficult and vital.

B.P.B.

CANDIDATES FOR THE ENVIRONMENT

Two months after the 1977 municipal elections in Paris, the city's radiowaves were suddenly invaded by a startling broadcast. "Green radio, local radio's first broadcast ecology manifesto . . ." spouted an enthusiastic voice. Headquartered in a Paris apartment unknown to the authorities, the pirate broadcasters were airing the first program of what they called "Radio Verte" (Green Radio).

The transmission lasted thirty-seven minutes and featured music, commentary by prominent ecologists, and plenty of static. Listeners in Paris who caught the outlaw program were enchanted nonetheless. The French "Green Party" had made good on a campaign promise by taking to the airwaves with their ecological message, and they had successfully defied the state broadcast monopoly. It was both a political victory and a political point.

Three days later the Greens readied their second broadcast. That one never reached its waiting audience. A red police helicopter hovered overhead and jammed the transmission.

That the government went to the trouble to stymie the fledgling broadcast is in itself significant. The Green Party had apparently become a political force to be reckoned with. In the 1977 French elections, Green candidates garnered a respectable 12 percent of the popular vote.

The Inside – Outside Debate

The entrance of environmentalists into the electoral fray marks the emergence of a new strategy, one that relies less on the outside pressure from environmental groups and more on getting environmentalists inside, in the seats of power. In many ways, it is a less radical strategy and it has critics even among its allies. As one environmental organizer put it, "Once an environmentalist gets elected, he or she will inevitably wind up under the thumb of the special interests. It's the way the system works. That same environmentalist could be much more effective on the outside, applying the pressure."

Other environmentalists critical of the electoral approach say it will sap the movement of what they feel are more important grassroots organizing efforts. West German antinuclear activist Michael Lucas writes that "in the upswing of electoralism, a large portion of the energy, the imagination, and political work that could otherwise go into extending the grassroots organizational structure of the movement through direct-action tactics will be channeled into campaigns."

Jacques Cousteau campaigning for ecology candidates popularly called "the Greens" in France, 1978. (*The Cousteau Society*)

Despite these misgivings, the European environmental movement has increasingly embraced the electoral strategy, creating new ecology parties and running candidates for everything from mayor to member of Parliament.

A New Political Philosophy

In many ways, the ecology parties have allowed —or even forced—the environmental movement to broaden its outlook, and apply a sort of "ecological logic" to myriad problems including employment, women's rights, government organization, and foreign relations. Britain's Ecology Party, for example, issued a manifesto calling for community-based crime control, a reduction in Britain's exploitation of resources of developing countries, economic conversion of industry to job-creating small business, and preventive health care.

This new analysis of old problems has caused a stir in the established and ideologically well-defined world of European politics. Though quickly dismissed by the Right as "eco-nuts," the environmental parties have the sympathetic Left somewhat mystified. There are some in the ecology parties who feel they must find a home in the established Left, but the thrust of the new parties has been to establish an "autonomous political presence."

"The right-left split has lost much of its meaning in the ecological struggles," said Brice Lalonde, a leader of the French party Europe-Ecologie. "This is why the ecological movement is defined as an autonomous movement. It doesn't want to make the same mistakes as the left and suffer the same setbacks. . . . And the fact is that the parties and the trade unions are proving incapable of taking charge of the problems we are putting forward."

The key differences between the ecologists and their friends on the Left come on the issues of decentralization, nuclear power, and economic growth. The Communists in several European countries are unbendingly pronuclear, and the Socialists, though softening their pronuclear stance, still have a penchant for centralized state control. Both groups generally take a traditional view of economic growth, believing that an expanding economy is key to creating jobs for workers.

The popularity of some of the ecology parties may in fact be based less on the appeal of their positions than the desire of the electorate to vote *against* the established parties. A poll taken by the French weekly *L'Express* revealed that 55 percent of those voting for a Green candidate did so because he or she was not backed by a traditional party.

The Greens Take Root

But whatever the reason, the ecology parties are winning a following, and are sending a tremor through the already shaky balance of European politics. Though the French and West German environmental parties won only 4.4 percent and 3.2 percent of the national vote respectively in 1979 elections, leaders of the established parties, who often rule with a majority of only a few percentage points, are clearly worried. Both Willy Brandt, leader of West Germany's Social Democratic Party, and Maurice Schumann, an official of the French Gaullist Party, attribute a slide in their electorate support to the rise of the environmental parties. In Britain, where the Ecology Party averaged a mere 1.6 percent average of the votes cast for the fifty-three seats it contested, the conservative *Daily Telegraph* called the environmental party "one of the fastest emerging political forces in the West."

Electoral fever has also struck the U.S. environmental movement, though with less fervor, with the creation of the Citizens Party by environmentalist Barry Commoner and other progressives. But in a nation so totally dominated by two major parties, the third-party effort is in for rough going. Its success, say party organizers, will hinge in part on winning over America's growing antinuclear movement, which has the grassroots activists to aid Citizen Party organizing efforts. At this point, it's unclear whether the antinuclear movement is ready to shift from direct-action strategies to engage in traditional party politics.

The American antinuclear movement is not alone in this quandary. Many European activists fear that the inevitable losses a minor party faces at the polls will hurt the image of the movement, or that the traditional parties will simply co-opt and dilute environmental issues. Whatever their future, the rise of ecology parties has had an undeniable impact on traditional political analysis; with its "ecological logic" it has added a new dimension—some say a revolutionary one—to world politics. As that first broadcast of Radio Verte suggested: "Our purpose is not to add words to other words, institutionalized speeches to noninstitutionalized speeches. . . . We want to urge people to do something else . . . urge them to walk off the beaten path."

B.P.B.

GRASSROOTING THE MOVEMENT

In his speech before the Regional Highway Transportation Congress in Niagara Falls, New York, William Huebner paused to delight in how nice it was to be among friends.

"This may well be the first friendly audience I have faced in the past four months," said Huebner. As Public Relations head of Connecticut's most outspoken highway lobby, he had until then been spending much of his time tangling with environmentalists over proposed interstates.

Then came a boast: "But if need be, I could have flooded this meeting room with two hundred hard-hat construction workers and two hundred citizens, all supporting the construction and completion of the interstate highway system. Because we in Connecticut have developed a strategy of activism to counter the activists."

Huebner's strategy was, as he put it, "to parallel the opposition's program"—in a word, to *organize.*

The Roots of Grassrooting

In U.S. politics, the wielding of influence has traditionally been a fairly straightforward affair. When special interests had a particular ax to grind they simply summoned a lobbyist, made a few well-placed phone calls to key officials, or picked up the tab for a few political campaign bills. When environmentalists came on the political scene in the early 1970s, lacking the resources to play the game the traditional way, they by necessity chose a different strategy. Like the civil rights and antiwar groups that preceded them, they found their political clout coming from "grassroots" activism. Riding high on a wave of popular support, environmental groups were able to storm legislators' offices with letters, phone calls, and sometimes people. Local ecology groups sprouted everywhere in the favorable social climate, and many politicians, quick to sense changing political winds, adopted environmentalism with almost patriotic fervor.

This display of grassroots political power took industry by surprise. Environmental laws to clean up the air and water were passed, and corporate lobbyists, though still able to water things down a bit, often could not halt the political momentum toward pollution control.

In the mid-1970s, though public opinion polls indicated that support for strong environmental protection remained solid, the activist fervor began to cool. "There was an influx of members to local environmental groups in the early 1970s," notes one long-time environmental activist, "but then membership began to level off." As the grassroots activism waned, so did the environmental movement's political clout, and special interest lobbies quietly began to undermine environmental laws.

Buying a Movement

Businesses opposed to regulation began to make political gains, in part by bolstering their traditional lobbying programs, sinking more cash into political action committees to pay campaign bills, increasing the number of lobbyists, buttonholing lawmakers, and expanding their PR efforts. But business groups also began to recognize the political clout of "grassroots" activism, and in their own way, they began to imitate the tactics of environmentalists.

Huebner's pro-highway lobby, for example, organized its own citizen groups. They issued press releases, drafted testimony for their leaders, and arranged media coverage for their demonstrations against environmentalists. The U.S. nuclear industry launched a similar "citizen action" campaign on a nationwide scale following the Three Mile Island nuclear plant accident.

A 137-page manual recently distributed to electric utilities across the country bluntly acknowledged the new grassroots emphasis: "The energy industry is discovering that citizens with pro-energy messages are often . . . more effective spokespeople [than executives]. Industry's return on a small investment of supporting citizen activities can be extremely high." Toward that end, "pro-energy citizen groups" are being bankrolled by the nuclear industry under the well-designed veneer presented to the public; however, many of these so-called citizen groups are largely composed of nuclear industry employees. (See "Phony Environmental Groups," page 782.) Still other business lobby groups are using expensive computer technology to generate letters, telegrams, and phone calls to "targeted" politicians in their effort to weaken environmental policies.

Going Home Again

All of this has had an impact on the environmental lobby, particularly in the U.S. capital. There, shifting political fortunes have caused many environmentalists to reassess their political strategies in the 1980s. If there is one thing activists seem to agree on, it is that the environmental movement must revitalize its own grassroots base. Echoing this sentiment, chairperson Byron Kennard launched the event celebrating the tenth anniversary of Earth Day—Earth Day '80—by proclaiming: "It is now time to recognize that the strength of the environmental movement is in those American communities where it has its roots." His remark was made, ironically enough, at a Washington, D.C., press conference.

Some environmentalists predict that the major fights of the 1980s will radically shift away from Washington, D.C., to the states and towns across the nation. "I think we will see the demise of the Washington mentality in the 1980s," says Peter Harnik, a veteran activist who helped organize the first Earth Day in 1970. "In fact, we may see the demise of a lot of Washington groups. The pendulum is swinging away from Washington, and on both the policy side and the decision-making side the focus is shifting to the states. The Washington environmental groups are, for the most part, in holding patterns, they are not breaking new ground. That new ground has to be broken on the state, regional, and local levels."

Organizations or Issues?

Though there is a broad consensus that this renewed grassroots environmental activism needs to occur, a debate is brewing about what form it should take. Some environmentalists, including Joe Lamson of the Northern Rockies Action Group (NRAG), argue that new and existing local groups should focus on "constituency building"—identifying local issues that touch the direct interest of a broad variety of people, many of whom never considered themselves environmentalists before, encouraging them to become active in environmental groups.

"Those environmental groups that continued to grow through the 1970s put an emphasis on grassroots organizing: working on issues that people were interested in, not those that had no local support," says Lamson. Environmental issues that spark broader participation will expand the membership of the organization and ultimately give it more political clout, according to Lamson. In the West, groups like the Wyoming Outdoor Council are taking up issues like utility-rate reform to win new members. Other groups are organizing ranchers and farmers against transmission lines and mining operations.

Some environmentalists, however, are critical of this "direct interest" organizing approach, arguing that it tends to dilute the broader environmental goals and make the organization more important than its issues. "One thing that characterizes the environmental movement is its goal-oriented, outwardly objective approach to things," says Jeffrey Knight, of Friends of the Earth. "We try to put effort into working on issues, not organization. The issues are not those that are normally dealt with by community-based groups. The environmental issues that affect people's lives are still pretty fuzzy." It is easy to understand the pollution of a local river, but a threat to the ozone layer is largely abstract to most people.

Knight says that while Friends of the Earth plans to put more effort into organizing new local branches, the group "wants to take a more flexible approach. . . . We don't try to force new organizations in areas that already have plenty, and we don't want to interfere with individuals who want to continue to work as individuals."

"I'd like to see more work on connections between solid local groups and national groups," he adds. "They can help each other out, without having to reinvent the wheel."

Whatever techniques they settle on to mobilize grassroots support again—and it will likely be an amalgam of organizing approaches—environmentalists will have a tough time changing a political climate that has made it easier for politicians to weaken air and water standards and to forge ahead with potentially destructive new energy projects. Money will, as always, be a nagging problem. One observer estimates that public-interest groups spend roughly three tenths of 1 percent of the amount spent by business groups on grassroots lobbying alone.

But if the public opinion polls are right, communities across the nation should still prove fertile ground for environmental activism. And with a little recultivation, that grassroots support promises to continue bearing fruit.

B.P.B.

COALITIONS THAT STUCK

The political wilderness has often been unkind to the lonely wanderer, and of late many environmentalists, traditionally independent sorts, have been seeking out fellow travelers. In the jargon of the lobbyist, this is called "coalition politics," and the environmental movement has increasingly embraced the strategy as it faces the 1980s.

Environmentalists have frequently had difficulty forging working relationships with each other, much less with other groups. But many activists say that the severe political and economic climate of the 1980s is helping to nurture new dialogue between environmentalists and those other constituencies; old antagonisms are fading as new alliances are struck.

Coalitions are not a new phenomenon in the relatively young environmental movement. In the 1970s environmental groups formed alliances with labor on such issues as toxic substances control legislation and with community groups on urban parks and recreation measures. But these were, for the most part, marriages of the moment. As soon as the specific issue was decided, the coalitions dissolved. Not infrequently, the partners in these agreements felt used. "[Environmentalists] always come to unions expecting them to listen to their studies and support their environmental positions," complains one labor official. Environmental groups, he says, seldom offered to become likewise involved in issues close to the heart of labor. (See "Unions and the Environment," page 692.)

Reaching Out

There are signs that this is changing, as economic anxieties, strategic foreign policy moves, and fragmented special interests change the political realities of the 1980s. "The environmental movement is moving from protest to broader advocacy," observed Vernon Jordan, Jr., president of the National Urban League, a major black advocacy group. "In that respect it resembles the changes in the civil rights movement. Both have been affected by the new realities. Both find the new realities moving them closer together."

The coalitions being forged as a result of these "new realities" reach from the nation's capital all the way down to the grassroots; these examples give some measure of the breadth and scope of the new alliances:

- A "City Care" conference in Detroit, co-sponsored by the Sierra Club and the National Urban League, drew hundreds of environmentalists and community activists. They endorsed plans to form new environmentalist-city alliances that would promote such things as urban gardening, protection of neighborhoods from toxic wastes, and reinvestment in downtown urban areas.
- The Citizen/Labor Energy Coalition, formed in 1978, has united unions, environmentalists, and community groups to promote, among other things, renewable energy development and conservation.
- In Montana, environmentalists joined with ranchers, Native Americans, farmers, and union members to form the Montana Committee for an Effective Legislature in a joint effort to elect progressive, and environmentally responsive, candidates.
- Members of a United Steel Workers local in Indiana are fighting side by side with environmentalists opposing a proposed nuclear power plant in the area and seeking to expand the Indiana National Lakeshore.
- In a move that one environmental leader said "showed that the ecology movement has something concrete to offer the unions that we're willing to deliver," antinuclear activists joined workers striking over health and safety conditions at a Portsmouth, Ohio, nuclear enrichment plant. The antinuclear groups supported the union despite its outspoken support for nuclear power.
- And the Urban Environment Conference, a nine-year-old coalition of labor, minority, and environmental groups, played a key role in winning tougher federal rules limiting carcinogens in the workplace.

To Be Pure, Or to Win?

The effect of these alliances is, quite simply, to maximize political clout. Most environmentalists admit that there is sometimes a cost to coalition politics; in order to win the support of powerful allies, goals may have to be molded to meet their objections. And for some, that is too great a price to pay.

"Coalition politics is something that environmental groups will emphasize in the 1980s, but mostly coalitions with other environmental groups, like the Alaska Coalition," says one staff member at the San Francisco-based Friends of the Earth. "Coalitions with other consitituencies will happen too, but they imply a watering down of our goals to reach consensus. We will seek labor support, for example, but not to the extent that it forces us to reduce our goals for political expediency."

To that, another environmentalist responds: "There's a way to go it alone, and be pure, and lose a lot. And then you can go it in a coalition and lose some, but still basically serve your social and environmental goals."

The Alaska Coalition, formed in 1977 to lobby for passage of a bill that would set aside 170 million acres (69 million hectares) of the state's wilderness for parks and refuges, was indeed an impressive demonstration of the effectiveness of environmental organizations working together. Composed of every major national environmental lobbying group, the Alaska Coalition was, in the words of one observer, "a mind-boggling success." The groups shared funds, office space, and staff for the effort, developed phone banks, and sent teams of organizers to mobilize grassroots support. It paid off. As the bill to preserve Alaskan lands wound through Congress, the President and Secretary of Interior set aside 110 million acres (49.5 million hectares) of land from development.

How Shall We Hang?

It is likely that both kinds of alliances will take shape in the 1980s: environmental groups will join on some big issues, and reach out to a variety of constituencies on others. Potential allies among labor, minority, and community groups abound, and they seem more open to environmentalists' advances than ever before. It remains to be seen whether these new coalitions merely reflect political opportunism in an era of social and environmental retrenchment, or the frank realization that common goals bind them together over the long haul. If nothing else, perhaps Benjamin Franklin's dictum applies: "We must indeed all hang together, or, most assuredly, we shall all hang separately."

B.P.B.

Wavemakers:

THE HOLY ALLIANCE OF BELO HORIZONTE

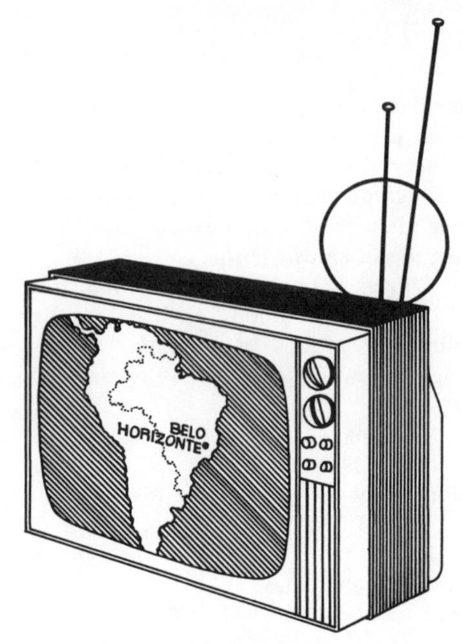

In 1972, factory workers in heavily industrialized Belo Horizonte, Brazil's third-largest city, pressured the government to install filters on the stacks of local industry to reduce dust levels in the area. The filters were ultimately installed, but with burgeoning industrial production the city's air pollution problem has persisted at unbearable levels. Thick layers of dust settle on the rooftops of houses near the industrial area, and by World Health Organization (WHO) standards, pollution in the city air was five times the acceptable level even with the filters. All of this has had a profound effect on the health of residents, 50 percent of whom suffer from asthma, allergies, and bronchitis.

In 1978, an unusual alliance formed to combat the dirty air. Actors who star in a soap opera on national television joined forces with local leaders of the Roman Catholic Church, and together they are dramatizing the problem and agitating for change. For example, the Church in Belo periodically holds well-attended Ecological Masses that focus attention on the air pollution problem and organizes Ecological Processions through the streets of Belo to demonstrate support for pollution control. Every evening on national television, 10 million Brazilians are treated to a portrayal of the struggle in the dramatic serial "Warning Signal," which depicts factory workers suffering from debilitating pollution because of the callous disregard of the factory's owner. Periodically the actors, along with their film crews, travel to Belo to participate in the ecological demonstrations, and the real-life scenes are incorporated into the drama.

All of the publicity is adding momentum to the movement for pollution cleanup, say its leaders, and most optimistically predict that this holy alliance will soon succeed in clearing the air over Belo Horizonte.

B.P.B.

ENVIRONMENTAL LITIGATION: THE END OF A FRONTIER?

The major arena for environmental battles in the United States was the courtroom during the 1970s; writs and briefs were the environmental movement's premier weapons. With the legislative groundwork laid by tough new U.S. environmental laws like the Clean Air and Water Acts and the National Environmental Policy Act, environmental lawyers erected formidable legal obstacles to dam projects and destructive developments, and they forced environmental compliance by polluting industries.

Now some environmentalists, including attorneys, believe that, although litigation will continue to be used effectively, it is not enough, and broad-based political support is needed to ensure the long-term success of any campaign.

They stress that the judicial process is only one branch of government and that the political mood must keep step; if not, legislatures will write new statutes that reverse favorable court decisions.

"If the courts say a law means something broader than the legislative body intended, they (the legislature) can always change it back," said Samuel Sage, director of the Sierra Club's Atlantic Chapter. "The opinion polls show the public is more and more committed to environmental issues," and yet political leaders don't recognize it, said Sage.

Changing the Rules of the Game

The fight over the Trans-Alaska pipeline provides a good example of "how you can win in court and lose in Congress," said John Sims, staff attorney at Public Citizen's Litigation Group in Washington, D.C. In that case, the Wilderness Society won an injunction against building the pipeline because it didn't meet federal environmental safeguards. But Congress just passed a special statute to allow the pipeline's construction.

In addition, say the experts, judges are themselves swayed by political opinion and can't be expected to hand down decisions that diverge widely from the current mood.

"Litigation can be a tactic in winning, but no one should have the illusion that major litigation is going to be successful unless there is political clout behind it," says the former director of a citizens' organization in New England that is involved in grassroots environmental organizing. "The battles of the eighties are going to be won on what citizen organizing we do, the breadth of the constituencies we put together."

According to Peter Hertzberg, staff attorney in Washington for the Sierra Club, "The role of litigation is going to be to *maintain* the victories, rather than *make* the victories, like in the sixties and seventies." The broad gains made so far in the courts are threatened, says Hertzberg, because industry continues to challenge regulatory mechanisms.

A Legal Labyrinth

"We're in a different phase of the environmental movement," he says. "The programs are there, but in the implementation of programs, industry has the upper hand. Say all the chemical industry decides, 'Let's take up an appeal'—they can ball up the regulations. You have to do many more cases than in the past. The whole regulatory scheme is becoming more complicated."

He cited as an example a 1972 Sierra Club suit that sought to have the Environmental Protection Agency rewrite eleven words in the preamble to the Clean Air Act. Although the club won its initial suit, industry appealed and the case became a legal nightmare leading to an act of Congress and then to more suits and appeals, one of which included a stack of briefs several feet high from one hundred parties—more than the District of Columbia Circuit Court had ever heard in a single case.

When the issue was finally settled, the EPA had written sixty pages of resolutions to replace the original eleven words. "We're down to such fine issues it's impossible for any side to claim victory," said Hertzberg. "Here's an example where litigation had an impact, at least at first, but now because of such detailed regulation, it's hard to see what's going on."

Echoing the laments of other environmental attorneys who find themselves fighting rearguard actions in court, Hertzberg added, "It's just not like the old days—it's not the frontier anymore."

L.B.

ENVIRONMENTAL MEDIATION

Environmental lawsuits are often bitterly fought battles waged at considerable cost, producing partial solutions that satisfy no one. Into the fray have stepped those who offer a peaceful alternative—the new cadre of environmental mediators, who say negotiation can often replace litigation, saving the high cost of courtroom conflict and yielding better results.

Born in the early 1970s, the young field of environmental mediation has been criticized when applied to national issues, but on the local level where there are specific conflicts the concept has gained widespread recognition for resolving disputes and hammering out agreements at the bargaining table.

In the Snohomish River Basin east of Seattle, Washington, for instance, controversy raged in 1973 over a dam designed by the U. S. Army Corps of Engineers (see "The Super-Engineers," page 462) to control flooding. Farmers and other interests who favored flood control were pitted against a coalition of environmental and citizens' groups who feared urban sprawl on the reclaimed flood plain.

Appointed by Governor Daniel Evans, two mediators sought to achieve a settlement. After receiving nominations from dozens of citizens, they selected a bargaining panel that represented all factions in the controversy, including a Sierra Club member, a farmer, a shopkeeper, and a Boeing engineer. The panel members struggled under the guidance of the mediators for eight months, until December 1974, when they signed a set of recommendations for modified flood control.

Four years later, a more formal agreement was signed by representatives of the state, two counties, thirteen cities and towns, and the Tulalip Indian Tribe. The mediation-forged agreement set up comprehensive planning for the nearly 2,000-square-mile (5,180-square-kilometer) basin.

In another case, an attorney for the National Wildlife Federation was assigned to help a South Carolina naturalist save the breeding ground of the endangered Bachman's warbler from timber-cutting by the U. S. Forest Service.

"Instead of a confrontation we prevailed on both sides to put together a three-person panel of experts to mediate the dispute," Federation counsel Robert J. Golden told *Audubon* magazine.

"The panel (which included biologists from the

"I'm an environmentalist. I suppose that frightens you."

(*Drawing by Weber.* © *1977,* The New Yorker *Magazine, Inc.*)

Forest Service, Fish and Wildlife Service, and the Wildlife Society) was established, did its homework, held a hearing, and made its recommendations—essentially, that logging in some stands of pine was okay, but not in bottomland hardwood stands. A result which left the antagonists satisfied and the dispute settled—without the cost, delay, and aggravation that courtroom litigation entails."

Whatever the success of mediation in local disputes, it has received some criticism in larger arenas. Some environmentalists were alarmed in 1977, for instance, when sixty representatives of environmental groups and industry, brought together in the industry-sponsored National Coal Policy Project, delivered a set of recommendations that would allow "high walls" left by strip mining to remain ungraded in some Western farm regions and would permit tall stacks to replace emission controls on older coal-burning plants.

The recommendations "do not represent a 'legitimate consensus' on these issues," said Richard Ayers of the Natural Resources Defense Council in a letter to one environmental participant in the project. The tall stacks "were not, and would not be, supported as compromises by the thousands of individuals and hundreds of organizations across the country who spent years working on proposed amendments to the Clean Air Act."

Despite criticism like Ayers's and fears that cooperation may unwittingly become co-option, the concept of environmental mediation appears to be gaining ground. Centers have opened to provide information, train mediators, and mediate specific disputes. Among these are the Office of Environmental Mediation at the University of Washington, founded by Gerald W. Cormick, who mediated the Snohomish Basin dispute along with Jane McCarthy and has been called the father of the concept; and RESOLVE, the Center for Environmental Conflict Resolution, in Palo Alto, California, headed by John Busterud, a former chairman of the Council on Environmental Quality.

Supporters believe the work of centers and individuals like these may hasten the day when the environmental movement loses its antagonistic image and gains the support of new segments of the population. Critics maintain that concessions are unacceptable when health and the environment are at stake. Either way, those now confused by the bitter rhetoric from both sides in environmental fights may find themselves inspired by the forging of alliances, and by reasonable discussions.

L.B.

FLACKS BY ANY OTHER NAME

flack\\ *'flak*\\ n, [*origin unknown*]:
one who provides publicity; var. of
FLAK (*antiaircraft guns*).

The ecological cause that some may say was made "an instant movement" by the elaborate media coverage following Earth Day in 1970 has entered a new stage of media consciousness. Many environmental groups have shifted from the hit-or-miss publicity approaches that characterized much of their communication in the early 1970s to an emphasis on somewhat more sophisticated—albeit low-cost—public relations (PR) strategies.

Publicity, which aims simply to maximize public exposure of an issue, has for some environmental groups given way to *PR,* which more selectively focuses public attention, and opinion, to serve political and organizational ends.

Fighting Fire with Fire

Why the new public relations initiative? Most environmentalists say it has evolved out of the frustrations of continually running up against adept corporate PR campaigns that can quickly cool public opinion on some issues. Ohio and Washington environmentalists, for example, faced a $2.6-million media blitz engineered by the beverage industry to crush public support for bottle bill initiatives in those states. Environmental groups in Long Beach, California, battling a proposed oil terminal and pipeline project were outspent forty-eight to one by Standard Oil Company, whose massive PR assault led to the defeat of an initiative that would have halted the plan. A PR spokesperson for the oil company admitted that the campaign was costly, but predicted that such heavily financed media campaigns are "going to happen more and more."

Many environmentalists also credit their growing interest in PR to a realization that more creative—and persuasive—ways are needed to get their message across to a public suffering from post-1970s ennui with environmental rhetoric. (For more on environmental persuasion, see "How to Say It," page 775.) In fact, Herbert Gunther, director of the Public Media Center, a San Francisco-based public interest advertising firm with a long history of involvement in environmental issues, argues that many national environmental groups have become "fossilized" and have lost the ability to talk to the general public.

"There seems to be a conscious decision to concentrate on the converted, and no longer attempt to convert," he adds.

To counter this trend and to "meet fire with fire," environmental media experts are appearing. Community Media, an environmental PR consulting and training group founded in Washington, D.C. in 1979, reports a steady stream of business from environmental groups. The Public Media Center says it now works with 100 to 150 groups a year, the bulk of them community-based. Many state and regional citizen groups have chosen to hire their own full-time PR experts, a shift in priorities that is especially significant in light of the tight financial constraints that limit staff additions to most such organizations. And those organizations that can't afford to hire their own full-time PR person are turning to groups, like Community Media, which can give them training in the fine points of press release writing, production of public service advertisements, and communications campaign strategy.

Low-Budget Flacking

The duties of these new full-time environmental PR specialists differ little from those of their corporate counterparts. According to one communications expert in a statewide environmental group, the bulk of his time is spent working with the news media, preparing press statements, answering reporters' queries, and planning news "events." For this reason many journalists view them as simply a new generation of "flacks"—a somewhat derogatory term used by reporters to describe publicists who try to influence news coverage.

Environmentalists' public relations campaigns, however, are usually severely limited by the lack of money. This, in part, accounts for the heavy reliance by environmental groups on the "free" access to the news media in getting their message across. It also means that environmental PR people turn to low-cost alternative communications—things like flyers, bumper stickers, posters, and newsletters. Most of these are homemade creations, often the product of an ailing mimeograph machine, endless sheets of cheap press-apply lettering, and a fair measure of graphic skill.

Gathering Friends, Teaching the Media

With the growing emphasis on "constituency building," or a broadening of the political base of the grassroots organizations, PR is seen as a tool to help redefine issues so that they have greater appeal. For example, the Northern Rockies Action Group (NRAG), an environmental consulting organization based in Montana, has helped environmentalists in the area develop broad communications campaigns on such issues as coal development and land use, campaigns that have helped forge coalitions among ranchers, agricultural interests, Native Americans, and environmental groups. "You shouldn't define issues in such narrow terms that they don't appeal to other constituencies," says Joe Lamson, NRAG media strategist. "If you do, where are you going to go—just to the true believers? That's just crazy. You won't develop any kind of political force."

Despite the increasing sophistication of many environmental groups in dealing with the news media, there are some critics who argue that the press, by its very nature, will often get it wrong. A recent Conservation Foundation report complains that the "media's preference for conflicts and crises often leads to sensationalized and overly simplistic reporting." The Tellico Dam controversy in Tennessee, which most press accounts treated as a humorous story about a minuscule endangered fish holding up the progress of a multimillion-dollar construction project, is, critics say, a case in point. Environmentalists charged that the dam project was an economic boondoggle, designed to enrich a few land speculators, that threatened to flood forever valuable cropland and to cause needless social disruption in a rustic region dotted with small farms, many of which had been in the hands of their owners for generations. (See "The Tellico Dam," page 584.) The economic and social aspects of the Tellico Dam construction, which most environmentalists viewed as the most compelling reasons to halt the project, became obscured by a flurry of press reports that portrayed the issue as a controversy over the fate of the snail darter, a small minnow threatened with extinction by the dam.

Some environmental PR experts disagree with those who blame the media. "The Tellico Dam controversy was, if anything, a case study of unwitting PR blunders by environmentalists," says Diane MacEachern, director of Community Media. "The press focused on the snail darter because the environmental groups involved largely failed to provide a dramatic PR focus on the other economic and social issues. I don't recall ever seeing the faces of the people threatened with displacement by the dam on the TV news. I did see, however, environmentalists wearing T-shirts emblazoned with snail darters sporting Jaws-like teeth."

There are indeed limitations imposed by the media on the kinds of messages they view as palatable news. Reporters do have a penchant for dramatic, simple, and timely events. Some complex ecology issues may not be conducive to that kind of coverage—and some would be ill-served by the tailoring required to meet those demands. The small but growing cadre of PR-savvy environmentalists argue, however, that if active public involvement in ecological protection is the aim, then the skillful use of the mass media remains the best bet.

B.P.B.

VOLUNTARY SIMPLICITY

Some years ago, writer Barbara Garson told of her introduction to recycling, which at the time was something of a daily ritual for those who professed to be concerned about ecology. In search of a location for her Portland, Oregon, day-care center, Garson found a couple who offered her use of the first floor of their home. The homeowners were also recyclers, so after the children's snacks, the adult overseers at the center would, with great moral purpose, peel the labels off juice cans, flatten them for recycling, and collect half-chewed apple cores for composting.

As Garson tells it, her sudden divorce from this ecological ritual came one day while she was washing the label off a grape juice bottle. "What kind of nonsense is this?" she declared. "I've got fifteen kids to take care of, and here I am washing labels off bottles when a machine is slapping them on faster than all the good women of Portland can possibly peel them off." Swept away by this sudden insight she went further with the heresy: "Either it's right to paste paper labels on bottles or it's wrong. If it's wrong you don't sit there scraping them off. You go down to the factory and make them stop. Rip out the evil, root and branches."

The Life-Style Question

Recycling was one of the more visible symbols of the new resource-conscious life-style being urged by environmentalists in the early days of the environmental movement. Composting, gardening, using mass transit, eating healthful food, and just living simply were proposed as essential personal strategies for dealing with the emerging environmental crisis. To some life-style change advocates, they were fundamental political solutions as well. In part, it was "practicing what you preach." But mostly, the emphasis on life-style change reflected the belief among environmentalists that in order to restore ecological harmony, sweeping societal changes were needed, beginning with the way each person lives.

For many environmentalists, flattening cans for recycling and putting bricks in toilet tanks to conserve water were the beginning of other kinds of involvement in environmental action. A few, like Garson, came to view this obsession with individual ecological responsibility as a diversion from fighting for important institutional changes to halt pollution. Others, who jumped into the political fray of lobbying, litigation, and social action simply discovered that they no longer had time to bake their own bread or peel the labels off grape juice bottles. But other environmentalists shunned political conflict and chose to continue their individual efforts at ecological living, to varying degrees and in a variety of ways, content to live out their commitments and perhaps set an example.

Small Is Popular

The publication in 1973 of British economist E. F. Schumacher's book *Small Is Beautiful,* which urged a return to simple community-based economies and an end to spiraling consumption of ephemeral goods, provided a compelling vision for many of these social experimenters, and even attracted many new converts as the U.S. economy foundered. In fact, a 1975 Harris poll found that more than three quarters of the American public agreed that "when the alternative is posed between changing our life-style to have less consumption of physical goods, on the one hand, and enduring inflation and unemployment on the other," life-styles must change. Another Harris poll two years later proved that this acceptance of life-style change was not an aberration, and in fact suggested that Americans were having a remarkable change of heart about the nation's traditional vision of unimpeded economic and industrial growth. According to the 1977 poll, a whopping 79 percent of those surveyed would place a greater emphasis on "teaching people how to live more with basic essentials" than on "reaching higher standards of living." Fifty-nine percent would put "a real effort into avoiding doing those things which cause pollution" over "finding ways to clean up the environment as the economy expands."

Outwardly Simple, Inwardly Rich

The social chemistry that is reflected by this shift in attitudes, say some observers, is giving rise to a new social movement in the United States and other developed countries. It is, as they put it, a movement toward "voluntary simplicity." And according to the Stanford Research Institute (SRI), a California research group that has extensively studied the phenomenon, the movement may involve as many as five million people in the United States alone.

This new preoccupation with the simple life, or as SRI puts it, "living in a way that is outwardly simple and inwardly rich," is very much a product of the environmental movement's emphasis on ecological life-style. The voluntary simplicity movement is propelled by a sense of urgency about growing resource shortages, environmental pollution, and declining natural beauty. It has, however, evolved beyond simply recycling cans and composting garbage. The concept of ecological living has grown to embrace an emphasis on personal growth, community, and self-determination; it is, to borrow a word from ecologists, a much more *holistic* way of living.

A New Social Order?

To call voluntary simplicity a movement may be a bit premature, but there is plenty of evidence of something afoot. The remarkable growth of home gardening, the interest in natural foods, the increasing number of small alternative businesses, the personal growth groups, the use of solar energy, and even the popularity of simple, durable clothing are all indicators of a shifting public attitude. But the movement has no leaders, no clear agenda, and no organized constituency. Despite this, SRI researchers predict that as many as 60 million people in the United States could choose the simple life in the next twenty years. If cultural currents do move dramatically in that direction, the social and political implications will be profound.

"Widespread adoption of the social goals and characteristics implied by the value themes underlying voluntary simplicity," says an SRI report, "would surely mark a deep and perhaps permanent alteration in the nature of the American dream. The eventual result could be the creation of a social order that is as different from the present as the industrial era was different from the Middle Ages."

With the decentralization of institutions implied by the voluntary simplicity movement, the push for that way of life "would likely be driven by political activism at a grassroots level," the SRI report adds. The spread of neighborhood organizations in the United States and elsewhere may be a manifestation of this grassroots activism. (See "Friendly, Fighting Neighborhoods," page 642.)

If it is indeed the beginning of a profound change in our way of life, the voluntary simplicity movement may mark the success of the life-style strategists in convincing society to accommodate the environmental crisis. In fact, there's probably a good chance that Barbara Garson's polite recyclers are still peeling the labels off of juice cans. By now they may also be making their own clothing, using a flushless toilet, and biking to work. And, if SRI is right, five million other Americans are doing the same thing.

B.P.B.

ECOTAGE

"Polluters Beware!" suggests the spirit of some environmental defenders who are no longer content to deal in lawsuits and letters to their congressmen. They've turned outlaw, become prankster-guerrillas who strike with a tactic dubbed "ecotage."

Take, for example, "The Fox" of Aurora, Illinois, who took to ecotage and assumed his outlaw name after watching the Fox River he had fished as a boy become a poisoned stream. To a large segment of Aurora, he has now become something of a folk hero.

One day, according to Chicago syndicated columnist Mike Royko, The Fox entered the eighteenth-floor executive offices of U. S. Steel carrying a bottle of foul-smelling, repulsive liquid he'd collected from one of the company's drains along the river.

"Good afternoon," he said to the secretary who greeted him. "I'm from the Fox Foundation for Conservation Education, and we have an award for U. S. Steel for their outstanding contributions to our environment." Whereupon The Fox unscrewed the top of the bottle and dumped the sludge on U. S. Steel's immaculate white carpet. As he walked from the office, he stopped to slap a bumper sticker supplied by one of his admirers onto the glass entrance door. It read: "Go Fox, Stop Pollution." Departing expeditiously before security could be alerted, he hailed a cab and escaped.

It was not The Fox's first exploit, nor his last. During the clandestine career he began in 1970, he has plugged the drainpipes and capped the smokestacks of many polluting companies. He plastered the front walls and windows of the McWhorter Chemicals Company with "buckets of a thick resinous muck" they had dumped in the Fox River, according to *Saturday Review* magazine. He posted signs in windows all over Gary, Indiana, with messages like, "I Can't Stop Killing Your Environment. I Need the Profits. U. S. Steel." He's never been caught, although there have been a few narrow escapes and a bullet directed his way once. Whenever he strikes he explains his motives by leaving notes with suggestions like, "Why not put your engineers on this problem and eliminate your pollution?" And he always signs them "The Fox."

A Last Resort

Although The Fox may be the best-known of the ecotage raiders, having received national publicity, he is not alone in his use of the tactic. When Environmental Action, the Washington, D.C.-based organization that coined the term "ecotage," held a contest for the most imaginative ecotage missions, it was so impressed by the thousands of replies from all fifty states and several foreign countries that it published a book in 1972 titled *Ecotage!*

Ecotage may be seen by some amused newspaper readers as a capricious lark, but to the people who perform it and to their targets, it is serious business. It is defended by its perpetrators as the tool of normally law-abiding citizens who've become so frustrated with a system of laws that allows environmental destruction that they are sometimes willing to commit misdemeanors in the hope that publicity will bring pressure to stop such abuse. Ecotage tactics aren't always illegal, but they are always private, defiant, symbolic gestures that call public attention to a problem—and usually embarrass a polluter. They are a serious affront to the image of the organization under attack. In fact, a rumor circulated in the early 1970s that several companies had offered rewards for The Fox's capture.

Is ecotage effective? Conclusive evidence is hard to come by, but it's safe to say publicity is a powerful tool. The Fox claims some companies have made improvements following his raids. And a group of ecotage raiders called "Eco-Commandos '70" maintained that pollution-control officials became more effective in Dade County, Florida, after a particularly embarrassing action by that group in 1970.

Bottles and Balloons as Weapons

The Eco-Commandos sought to publicize the nature of Miami's sewage treatment facilities, which consisted of a plant that ground up sewage and piped it raw into the ocean 12,000 feet (3,660 meters) from shore. There, because it was carried by freshwater, it rose to the surface. Officials had long maintained that winds and tides carried the sewage out to sea, but the Eco-Commandos doubted it.

They took a boat to where the pipe spewed out its sewage—an area dubbed "The Rose Bowl" by local residents—and released seven hundred watertight bottles. Every bottle contained a note and two mail-in cards, one to Florida's governor and the other to the editor of the Miami *News,* which read:

> "This card was placed in a drift bottle released directly over the end of the Miami Beach sewer outfall which dumps raw, untreated sewage into the ocean. This drift bottle was found by (name, address). It was found at (location). This drift bottle was moved by the same wind and currents that move the raw sewage. THIS IS WHERE MIAMI'S SEWAGE GOES."

Twelve days later, the *News* had received seventy cards from various locations on Florida's coast, including twenty-three from Hollywood, eight from Fort Lauderdale, one from Vero Beach, which is 120 miles (193 kilometers) from Miami, and one from Melbourne, 140 miles (225 kilometers) distant.

In Southern California, antinuclear activists used a similar ploy to alert local residents to the potential dangers of the much-publicized Diablo Canyon nuclear power plant being built by Pacific Gas and Electric Company in San Luis Obispo County, not far from a known earthquake fault. Organizers held a day-long protest event, during which they released hundreds of black balloons. Attached to each was a note that made a definite impression on people who found one of the balloons near their home. "If you found this balloon," the message said, "you are directly downwind from the nuclear plant under construction. If an accident occurs and a cloud of radioactive material is released from the plant, your home will be in its path."

After another Eco-Commando action in Miami, residents and tourists who arrived early at four beaches one July Fourth found big red signs that read: "DANGER—POLLUTED—NO FISHING—NO SWIMMING. POTENTIALLY DANGEROUS CONCENTRATIONS OF PATHOGENIC BACTERIA HAVE BEEN FOUND AT OR NEAR THIS LOCATION. SWIMMERS AND FISHERMEN RISK INFECTION AND DISEASE. DO NOT REMOVE THIS NOTICE." Officials had soon removed the eight hundred signs, but not before they had roused the curiosity of thousands of people.

Those on the receiving end of such tactics will continue to cry "foul" and call ecotage proponents criminals, and they will often be right, at least in part, but they will be countered by people like one Eco-Commando, quoted in *Ecotage!:* "Although we have committed a couple of misdemeanors—we consider the risks worthwhile. Our crimes are minuscule compared to the hundreds of crimes that are being committed daily on our environment. We honestly believe we are fighting for our lives."

The Fox also contributed insight into the motivations of ecotage raiders, Royko reported in a column, when he was in a bar one night talking to strangers about the environment. One of them said, "You're really a nut when it comes to the environment, aren't you?"

"Sure," said The Fox. "I'm a nut about the environment because I don't know any other place to live."

L.B.

EUROPE AND AMERICA: A CONTRAST OF ENVIRONMENTAL STYLES

Editor's Note: *In 1979, Thomas Burke, director of Friends of the Earth (FOE) in the United Kingdom, spent three months traveling the breadth of the United States, taking stock of the U.S. environmental movement. The article that follows, which first appeared in FOE's publication* Not Man Apart, *chronicles his observations of the differences—and similarities—between environmental action in Europe and the United States. He finds that the political landscapes of the two continents differ in interesting ways, and that by necessity environmentalists on each side of the Atlantic have chosen different paths through the terrain.*

The most striking difference between the European and American contexts is the amount of information in the public domain. There are a number of reasons for this: in Europe corporate disclosure laws are weaker, libel laws are stronger, thus discouraging investigative journalism; the right of the press to publish is not constitutionally enshrined; the academic community is smaller and less generously funded and thus less willing to involve itself in the public discussion of potentially controversial issues. Above all, no equivalent of the Freedom of Information Act exists. Indeed, a number of countries have Official Secrets Acts which specifically prohibit the unauthorized release of much official information.

Serving Different Masters

In addition to these formal barriers to the flow of information to the public are significant attitudinal differences. Most important, European civil servants tend to see themselves—and to be seen by most citizens—as the servants of "authority" as embodied in the "State." To a much greater extent, American public servants are seen, and see themselves, as just that: servants of the people. These attitudinal differences produce very different responses on the part of officials to requests for information and very different expectations on the part of environmental activists. Few French environmentalists would see much value in visiting the Quai d'Orsay to inquire about the French government's position on, for example, the forthcoming non-proliferation treaty review. The effect of lack of information in the public domain is to stifle informed debate and to encourage polarization of views.

This dynamic is enhanced in Europe by the prevalence of unitary governments in which legislative and executive functions are essentially combined and in which the judiciary plays a much smaller role in defining "policy." Thus European parliaments are generally weaker in their policy-making and oversight roles than Congress. Because of much stronger party discipline, there is little room for legislative initiative by individual representatives.

Few equivalents of semi-autonomous government agencies, such as the Nuclear Regulatory Commission or the Environmental Protection Agency, exist. Access to the courts is much more restricted, and the judiciary conceives of its role more as administrator of justice than as interpreter of law. In short, the opportunities for environmentalists to engage usefully in the policy-making process are much reduced in Europe.

Lawsuits vs. White Papers

This difference in the availability of opportunities to influence policy has led to major differences in the approach of European and American groups to environmental protection. One way of characterizing this is to say that American environmentalists have perceived their task as building a strong barrier of legal constraints to the operation of economic, industrial, energy, and other policies, so as to prevent those policies from damaging the environment. In the United States, laws enacted by Congress often lead the middle ground in politics via the major legislative victories—the Clean Air Act, the Clean Water Act, the Nuclear Non-Proliferation Act, etc. Attitudes often change to confrom to the law.

In Europe, the law almost inevitably lags behind the middle ground; attitudes must change before legal initiatives will succeed. American environmentalists describe their successes over the past ten years by pointing to the development of the impressive body of environmental law. In response to the same question, European environmentalists point to changes in government spending, resolutions at party conferences, government white papers, and other indications of shifts in public policy.

Drama vs. Gray Detail

The emphasis of American environmentalists on the role of legislation has been very marked. In many ways this leads to a more confrontational style of environmental politics; battle lines and arenas are clearly drawn and the tone of the public debate accompanying major legal or legislative battles is distinctly adversarial. European environmentalists talk much less frequently of winning and losing. From a European point of view, immersed in the grayness, detail, and slow pace of consensus politics, the advantages and drama of the U.S. context are immediately apparent. However, the pace and drama of environmental action in the United States can also be beguiling. It now seems clear that the wall of legal policy constraints in the United States is coming under increasing pressure from a beleaguered economy.

If U.S. environmentalists are to continue to make gains in the future to compare with the successes of the past, more of their effort may need to be devoted to the slow task of shifting the middle ground of public policy. Conversely, European environmentalists may find that they need to devote more effort to structural problems such as freedom of information or the committee structure of the European parliament.

The Other Great Issues

What I sense is *common* to environmentalists in both Europe and the United States is an uncertainty about the future. In ten years the environment has become a major political issue throughout the West and environmentalists on both sides of the Atlantic have made significant gains. But in both the United States and Europe the funding foundations are beginning to turn their attention elsewhere and the political price of achievements in the face of worsening economies is growing. On both sides of the Atlantic the importance of the environmental non-governmental organizations is widely recognized. However, it may now be time to rethink our relevance: to examine carefully what, if anything, we have to say on other great issues of our time—unemployment, inflation, for instance; to discover what contribution we can make to solving the growing crises of Western democracy.

Reprinted from *Not Man Apart,* January, 1980, by permission of Friends of The Earth.

18

Organizing

"DON'T MOURN, ORGANIZE!"

The day before he was to stand in front of a Utah firing squad in 1915, accused of a murder that many said was a frame-up orchestrated by copper-mining bosses, the legendary labor organizer Joe Hill was reported to have sent a telegram to his union's headquarters in Chicago. The message was simple: "Don't mourn, organize!" It later became a marching song for the labor movement and an inspiration to millions working to fashion a better world. In this section of the *Almanac* we take Joe Hill's advice, and explore the first steps to turning environmental concern into organized environmental action.

We have asked four experienced activists to share their thoughts on organizing a local environmental group, finding the funds to get it started and to keep it going, and searching out the facts to set it on the right course. The final article, "Building a Coalition," tells the tale of several statewide environmental campaigns, some that succeeded and some that failed, and highlights the lessons we can learn from each.

Though their thoughts are not the last word on fund raising, organizing, researching, and launching an environmental campaign—an entire encyclopedia could be devoted to those subjects—the provocative insights of these four activists provide useful guidance to people faced with a local issue that deserves action, and interesting reading for anyone who wants to know how it's done.

B.P.B.

GETTING STARTED

Editor's Note: *To sift down through the towering stacks of flyers, files, and reports that have long since overwhelmed Mary Mushinsky's desk is something of an archaeological revelation. Her accumulations are a record of six years of environmental activism, and every layer reveals something about many of the major issues the environmental movement has faced through those years. Wetlands protection, the bottle bill, agricultural preservation, solid waste disposal, all of these issues were the focus of her efforts as a full-time researcher, lobbyist, and organizer for Connecticut's largest environmental group. In "Getting Started" Mary Mushinsky tells of her most recent foray.*

Roberta Friedman, a doctor's wife in the small town of North Haven, Connecticut, discovered one day in 1979 that the pleasant community she had chosen for raising her children was to become the home of a supermall, a giant shopping center to be constructed on a nearby floodplain.

At the same time, Alma Engels and several of her neighbors finally found out why the government wished to condemn their homes—to widen the road that would service the supermall.

Several phone calls later, a handful of concerned residents gathered in Roberta's home. What to do next? How to begin to fight? They were groping for the basic techniques of getting started.

1. **Choosing an Issue.** For Roberta and Alma, the issue was already chosen. They saw the supermall as a clear and present danger to their homes and their small town. But even to an observer watching from the sidelines, the mall fit the criteria for a good organizing issue.

   It was immediate. People knew the developer was close to breaking ground for the project.

   It was deeply felt. Neighborhoods, wetlands, and even their very homes were endangered.

   It was widely felt. The mall, by increasing traffic and heightening the possibility of floods, would affect several hundred households.

   It was clear-cut. The lines were clearly drawn between residents who sought to protect the flavor of their town and an out-of-state developer who sought to make a sizable profit.

2. **Recruiting.** The original core of seven or eight worried residents faced the immediate job of increasing their ranks, for no elected official would listen to so small a group. Against a foe like this developer, only the power of numbers would work.

Several techniques were used to find likely supporters. *House meetings* were set up in core members' homes to which ten to fifteen neighbors were invited for refreshments and a recruitment speech. *Slides and photos* of the areas to be damaged were shown. Core-group members set *speaking engagements* before clubs and associations. They circulated anti-mall *petitions* from house to house. They devised a *fact sheet* on the mall and the new group they were forming, encouraging people to call them for more information. At each step—house meeting, speech, petition—the goal was always *to collect new names and enlarge the organization.*

3. **Establishing a Presence.** A new organization makes a name for itself by establishing a reputation as the best *information source* on the issue, by appearing before government bodies and the press in *visible intervention,* and by *winning victories and then claiming public credit for them.*

Settling on the name Stop the Mall (STM), the new group assigned several members to gather all the environmental, economic, and social data available and to compile them into a series of "white papers" for press and fellow STM members. The group's leaders gave interviews to reporters and began to organize a file of press clippings and notices of government regulatory actions on the issue.

At each stage of the regulatory process to be carried out before the mall could be constructed, Stop the Mall pleaded its case with both facts *and* the political pressure of a large, visible crowd of supporters. And when each small victory was won —even a delay is a victory in a development case —STM issued press statements and flyers to its members claiming credit.

4. **Fund raising.** Flyers, postage, phone calls, newspaper advertisements, and chartered buses are costly, but they are the working tools of an action organization. How to pay for them? (See also "Funding the Fight," page 763.)

STM decided that *dues-paying memberships* were key. Membership carried with it financial responsibility toward the fledgling group; the most dedicated mall fighters became members. From a wider group of less dedicated but sympathetic townspeople, other funds were obtained through *social-event fund raisers* like parties and the *sale of campaign paraphernalia* such as bumper stickers. When supplies were needed (paper goods, printing) the group first looked to sympathetic merchants for *supply donations.*

5. **Using Experienced Advice.** Awesome as a particular environmental battle may seem, someone somewhere probably has fought it before. If not, it may have been studied by some researcher.

Roberta Friedman persistently tracked down experienced advisers. The Connecticut Fund for the Environment, a legal group, pointed out federal wetlands regulations that applied to this case. A Yale University graduate student assembled a report summarizing laws covering the mall. And

the Connecticut Citizen Action Group, an activist group that had successfully fought regulatory cases, offered to train STM members in the legislative process and other political skills such as publicity, research, and organizing.

6. **Widening Your Base.** In environmental battles, a limited number of people may be affected directly enough to join the organization. To reach out farther the group must identify other *allies and constituencies* and explain how joining the battle might benefit them.

Stop the Mall found its most important ally in the nearby city of New Haven, which would lose $22 million in retail sales to the mall by 1985. And in North Haven itself STM identified several constituencies: environmentalists concerned about wetlands destruction and air pollution; flood victims who were veterans of frequent floods already caused by floodplain development; homeowners near the mall, facing as many as 28,000 additional vehicles per day on their streets; small merchants who were unable to compete with a supermall; and historic preservationists who were worried that access roads would destroy historic homes.

7. **Creating Leaders.** Like many activist groups, Stop the Mall at first coalesced around one strong leader, Roberta Friedman. But the group knew that a long, tiring fight lay ahead, and STM would need several individuals who could take turns speaking for the group at public hearings, talking to reporters, running meetings, and recruiting new members. Other members were encouraged to polish their leadership skills, to create a *pool of leaders* for STM.

8. **Creating Active Membership.** The forces seeking to build the mall could not be defeated by a paper organization. Stop the Mall's membership had to be active, informed, and totally supportive of its leaders' battle strategies.

To encourage active participation, major campaign *activities were divided* so that each member shared some responsibility. A simple *newsletter* kept members abreast of new developments. And all major campaign decisions were backed by the *consensus* of members at STM planning meetings.

9. **Using Symbols of Identity.** To inspire its own members and at the same time establish an ever-present reminder of its cause, an organization needs symbols of its presence. Stop the Mall developed a hexagon logo after the familiar "STOP" traffic sign and used it on membership cards, stationery, placards, and lapel badges.

10. **Following a Plan.** A looming threat tends to focus the view of the environmental activist narrowly, first on the short-term goal of reacting to each move of the enemy, then on the long-term goal of winning. But the activist must look at wider goals.

Short term: the campaign goals. Stop the Mall first analyzed the regulatory steps in the mall's path and created an activity timetable to match the developer's. Frequently, STM would initiate its own action (for example, a surprise meeting with a regulatory official) rather than merely react. And the group also added realistic recruitment and fund-raising goals to its timetable.

Long term: protecting our rights. Stop the Mall, a single-issue group, might have chosen not to continue after the battle was won. But to guard the community from the next danger, organizing can include leaving some fragments of the organization in place. The threats will not stop; the protective vigil must not either.

M.MU.

FINDING THE FACTS

Editor's Note: *The targets of his investigations, which span years of activism with civil rights, environmental, and neighborhood groups, are quite familiar with Scott Hempling's research work, though they may not know him by name. He has a flair for uncovering the unexpected conflict of interest, the embarrassing contradiction, and even the outright illegality of actions by business and government decision-makers. In this article he tells us how it's done.*

It may seem, at times, that truth matters little when David meets Goliath. Individuals, even with the facts on their side, frequently find themselves on the losing side of an issue because of the lobbying and financial power of special interests. To experience this is, for most citizen activists, a bitter lesson in political realities.

But while facts alone seldom determine the outcome of a bitterly fought environmental issue, the right information, used at the right time and the right place, can have a dramatic impact. Environmentalists need to be well-informed, they need to be accurate, they need to be right. But what's also needed is a new way of looking at how facts can be used in an environmental campaign.

In 1973, the Chicago-based group Citizens for a Better Environment (CBE) was locked in a bitter fight with United States Steel Corporation over its air and water pollution violations. While federal officials had tried to crack down on the company, their efforts were frustrated by a recalcitrant management, which relied on layoff threats if strict pollution controls were enforced, as well as claims that the company had, in fact, undertaken its own cleanup efforts.

CBE researcher Barry Greever realized that the political stalemate could only be broken if U. S. Steel could be publicly embarrassed, forcing it to back down from its spurious claim of environmental responsibility.

Knowing that all corporations are required by federal law to report oil spills to the U. S. Coast Guard, Greever quickly checked the records to determine how many spills into Lake Michigan were reported by U. S. Steel. Armed with that information, Greever suspected U. S. Steel was underreporting the spills to other federal agencies. All corporations, he recalled, were required to file "10-K" reports with the federal Securities and Exchange Commission (SEC). Among other things, these public documents provide information to prospective investors about potential risks they may be taking by sinking money into the company. Would the oil spills be reported in the "10-K"? Indeed they were, and Greever discovered, when comparing them with Coast Guard figures, that U. S. Steel had in fact lied to the SEC about the number of oil spills for which it claimed responsibility.

CBE realized that it now had damaging information on the company, but Greever wanted to bolster the group's case with evidence, in understandable terms, of U. S. Steel's disregard for federal environmental laws and the laxity of federal officials in enforcing them. The "10-K" reports again helped provide part of the answer. Quickly studying the SEC reports, Greever compiled a list of all the environmental violations for which the company paid a fine, and compared this figure with the total fines that the government could have levied. With a little more figuring Greever calculated that U. S. Steel had paid, on the average, a startling one tenth of 1 percent of the maximum penalty for its environmental violations.

When the results of Greever's research forays hit the Chicago newspapers, U. S. Steel officials were taken by surprise, the public was outraged, and the government—a bit sheepishly—moved in to force the company to clean up.

What to Look For, Where to Look

Greever calls this quick and purposeful fact-finding in an environmental campaign "tactical research." It is not an exercise in blind information-gathering. The facts are pursued with a purpose in mind: uncovering a conflict of interest, a violation of law, lackadaisical enforcement, or embarrassing contradictions in policy or public positions. Citizens for a Better Environment, for example, hoped to uncover information that would illuminate contradictions between U. S. Steel's *claims* of environmental responsibility and company *practices*. Barry Greever was fortunate enough to find evidence so compelling that it helped to force a pollution cleanup effort. It's not always that easy—sometimes the facts are there, and sometimes they aren't.

A surprising amount of information about individuals and corporations is filed in public records in government offices. You have every right to read these documents. They are sometimes difficult to decipher, but once you crack the code, the information flows freely. Clerks are often helpful if you ask for assistance. The key, of course, is knowing what to look for and where to look.

Conflicts of Interest. Highway proponents, dump operators, discharging companies, and other potential engineers of environmental pollution frequently enjoy a cozy relationship with government regulators and lawmakers. A high-rise apartment builder may do business with a member of your Zoning Board of Appeals. An offshore drill operator may have contributed to the mayoral campaign of your state environmental protection commissioner. A former legislative leader may be testifying before a committee whose chair he or she appointed. Conflicts of interest, both legal and illegal, sometimes abound, and your controversial exposé may stymie a project that threatens the environment.

Where to look:

1. Check the present and past *occupation* of decision-makers by looking at your local newspaper's clipping files, or in the city directory in your public library.
2. Learn about the *property ownership* of decision-makers by visiting the tax assessor's office in his or her home town. That information should be available for the asking.
3. Look at *campaign contributions* received by politicians by going to the Secretary of State's office or the town clerk.
4. To find out about the *business relationships* of local decision-makers and those who might benefit from their decisions, ask the town clerk for a look at local "business certificates," or check the "corporation records" in the Secretary of State's office.

Embarrassing Contradictions in Company Policy. Your corporate target may contribute to the American Cancer Society and the Fresh Air Fund, yet make decisions that endanger the air you breathe. Or perhaps its glossy annual report lauds its participation in the Chamber of Commerce's Welcoming Committee, yet its decision to allow seepage of dangerous substances into local water supplies has made new residents of your neighborhood feel most unwelcome. Contradictions like these help break down a facade of moral righteousness.

Where to look:

1. Read the company's *annual report to the stockholders* (available at the company's headquarters and in certain business libraries), or check its *"10-K" annual report,* which is available from the U. S. Securities and Exchange Commission's regional or Washington, D.C., offices. For larger companies they might be found at a good public or university library. The "10-K" report lists legal violations as well as financial data.
2. Find out the *occupations of the company's directors* by reading the annual reports and the proxies, which are also required by the Securities and Exchange Commission.
3. Determine whether the company is up to date on its local property tax payments by checking with your local *tax collector.*

Outright Violations of Environmental Regulations. State and local governments issue a variety of permits that allow companies certain levels of environmental pollution. Permits for discharges, noise, disposal sites, transporting of dangerous substances, use of pesticides, wetlands development, and many other activities, in addition to state and local regulations relating to environmental protection, all provide you with the legal standards with which to assess a company's activities.

Where to look:

1. Check the *Securities and Exchange Commission* reports cited earlier.
2. *Court records,* which are usually indexed by plaintiff and defendant, sometimes provide clues to past violations that may merit follow-up.
3. Look at *permit applications* and other records at your local or state environmental protection offices.

Poor Enforcement. An action that threatens the environment often involves two parties: the company responsible for the action and the governmental official who allows it to happen. Poor enforcement of existing legislation and regulations occurs in a number of ways:

- undetected violations
- chronic violators who escape penalties
- unanswered complaints

and can stem from a variety of causes:

- insufficient staff
- lack of affirmative inspection procedures

- "revolving door" between the regulators and the regulated industry
- meddling by politicians in a regulating agency's activities

Whether intentional or accidental, poor enforcement leaves an open invitation to corporate environmental abuse.

Where to look:

1. Examine the enforcement agency's *budget* to see if it allots adequate staff to environmental programs it claims are critical.
2. Compare the reports filed by the *agency's inspectors* with the actual conditions at the site of environmental pollution.
3. Compare the *penalties* levied by the enforcement agency for any violations with the maximum fines allowed by statute. Do they differ greatly?

Contradictions in Government Policy. Government officials sometimes say one thing, and then do another. A much-heralded state transportation plan calling for mass-transit expenditures sits on the commissioner's shelf as he studies the new $500 million highway plans on his desk. Legislation requiring the state to evaluate the impact of large developments on urban areas lies dormant as the state pours money into a giant suburban shopping mall that promises to drain downtown of much of its trade. A governor promises rapid detection of illegal dumps, yet allocates only enough money for three full-time inspectors. By comparing plans to laws, laws to regulations, and any of these to actual departmental operations, an environmental researcher can often find strong contradictions that raise suspicions about a regulator's credibility.

Where to look:

1. Many state agencies are required to develop *"comprehensive plans"* to outline priorities for the coming year. Are these consistent with their public stances?
2. Compare *agency regulations* with the original language in the laws they were designed to implement.
3. Check the *letter files* that an agency keeps on each of its projects. Do these reveal internal disagreement about an agency's policies?

Contradictions in a Public Official's Behavior. A candidate can speak out against toxic wastes in a poisoned community, yet quietly vote to cut the budget of the chief enforcement agency. A bureaucrat issuing permits to build highway segments can make contradictory decisions in similar cases. Citizens who expose such contradictions can spark the curiosity of members of the community and interest them in pursuing a government target.

Where to look:

1. Check old newspaper clippings for a politician's previous *campaign statements* and promises.
2. Transcripts of legislative *floor debates* are easily available to the environmental researcher. Does a politician say one thing in the legislature and another to your group?
3. How did legislators vote on issues related to the environment? Check the *voting transcripts,* which are also available at legislative information offices.

Evidence of Damage. Cancer rates. Poisoned wells. Pollution disasters. Dying crops. Sometimes the most powerful facts are those that document the actual environmental tragedies. Although these facts often require scientific research, the results can galvanize an entire community into action.

Where to look:

1. If new research is required, try to enlist the aid of the appropriate faculty at the nearest college or university.
2. Most states offer some simple services such as *soil testing* through the Cooperative Extension Service and *well-water testing* through the state health department. You send the sample; they send the results.
3. State and federal environmental agencies do innumerable *scientific studies* that may be useful for comparison or to point out trends. For example, many states do a periodic assessment of surface-water quality and take regular air pollution samples from set stations.
4. Also check the *thesis-title files* at nearby universities. It's a long shot, but a graduate student may have just spent three years studying the topic that interests you.

Once You've Found It, How Do You Use It?

So you have found the ultimate conflict of interest. You have discovered the pattern of ignorance on the part of the state agency or the environmental abuse by a local business. How do you tell the world? You might want to tie the release of your findings to your group's activities. Perhaps a *press release* can slip out a few of your key points, and also announce your first organizational meeting. (See "Making the Papers," page 769.) Or maybe you want to saturate the affected neighborhood with *flyers,* which contain a *fact sheet* that concisely states the key points of your research. You might opt for a formal presentation, releasing a *research report* that accompanies your formal *testimony* at a public hearing. *Charts and other visuals,* when you have numbers to present, always help.

Whatever way you choose to publicize your findings, realize that only rarely do facts alone turn the tide in an environmental battle. It often takes lobbying, grassroots organizing, and a fair measure of just plain persistence. But arm yourself with the facts; there really is no substitute for being right.

S.H.

WHAT THE FACTS CAN DO

- **Facts Can Arouse People.** When you've caught a company operating an illegal dump in your town, and then learn that it has done so undetected in ten other towns in your state, you can expect that angered neighbors will have many questions for both the company and the government agency that regulates it.
- **Facts Can Document Suspicions About Corporate or Official Abuse.** A local zoning official who is found to have done business for ten years with a company now seeking a zoning variance to build a multimillion-dollar mall can expect a lot of questions from your group.
- **Facts Can Weaken the Opposition by Exposing Contradictions.** When people learn that a highway department official denied a permit in his old legislative district but allowed one in your neighborhood, they will be interested in bringing the matter to his attention.
- **Facts Can Focus Conflicts on Those Responsible for Environmental Abuse.** When people learn that a utility company president earns $200,000 a year while claiming that the utility can ill-afford a $100,000 investment in pollution control, you can be sure that they'll have good reason to go with their two hundred neighbors to his office for a chat.
- **Facts Can Win a Group More Attention and More Credibility.** When your group makes its first dramatic discovery of corporate abuse, you become the source of information for many in town.
- **Facts Can Attract New Groups to a Traditionally "Narrow" Issue.** Research demonstrating that a company fouling a river also exposes its employees to asbestos will add workers and their relatives to a group initially involving only homeowners living along the polluted water.

S.H.

FUNDING THE FIGHT

Editor's Note: *"People who recognize that it takes thousands of dollars to fight the interests that threaten the environment," says the author of the article that follows, "also must recognize that they have a responsibility to help raise some of that money." In four years of grassroots fund raising from the Carolinas to New England, Bill Bloss has helped add nearly $175,000 to the campaign coffers of citizen organizations. In this article, he tells how he did it.*

A successful fund-raising effort does more than just help a public-interest group meet expenses. First of all, it proves to anyone who may be watching—politicians, governmental agencies, corporations—that your group and its issues are popular. Successful fund raising gives your group legitimacy, particularly when done at a grassroots level. Second, your group will almost certainly be able to recruit active members from among your donors. Contributing, for some people, leads to greater involvement.

It is always advisable to convince as many people as possible to contribute to your campaign. Though it may be possible to get several very large gifts—if you're extremely lucky, you may be able to raise your goal from just a few people —don't stop there. Try to tie as many people as you can into the group through contributions, giving your cause more people with a stake, a financial investment, in the campaign. The fight, in a democracy, is more easily won by many participants each doing a small part than by a few participants doing everything.

There are generally two categories of fund-raising activities: those which take little time and energy to plan and have relatively small returns, and those which take much time, capital, and energy, but which usually return more funds. The following is a brief description of some tried-and-true fund-raising ideas:

- A local group should start off with a small event almost certain to make *some* money, to give its members a victory. The most likely event is the *bake sale,* in which expenses are kept to a minimum (assuming the baked goods are donated), and your profits can be 100 percent of revenues. If you're going to hold one, be sure to let your local media know about it. One local group fighting completion of an expressway through a residential area set up tables full of cakes and pies in front of idle bulldozers parked near the edge of the neighborhood. Residents whose homes were threatened by the highway came to the sale in droves; the group sold every crumb, making enough to pay for computer projections on environmental damage from the proposed highway. Local media gave the sale lavish attention on the six o'clock news and in the newspaper.
- Another modest but effective means of raising money is a bazaar. It doesn't really matter what you sell, as long as it's legal and someone wants it. Options include *book sales* and *tag sales. Plant sales* are particularly effective for city-based environmental groups.
- A group with a more sizable following might consider publishing an *"ad book."* For example, a coalition fighting for increased use of solar energy raised $1,400 by selling space in its convention brochure. Nearly every manufacturer and retailer in the region bought an ad, perhaps because they were fearful of losing business to rivals who bought ads, or were anxious to promote a good environmental image for their businesses.
- *Dances, dinners, or cocktail parties* can serve the twin purposes of raising money and getting many of your members and potential members under the same roof. It's usually easy to find local musicians who will donate their time to a worthwhile effort, and a church or municipal hall might be willing to provide free space.
- *Raffles* nearly always make money, but don't attempt one unless your group has a lot of members who will actually sell tickets. Buyers won't come to you. You should be able to get prizes donated, in return for some publicity, and you should never pay more than wholesale for a prize. A bicycle shop may be willing to donate a ten-speed racer to a group fighting highway expansion; a canoe would be an appropriate prize if the fight is against damming a free-flowing river.
- *Auctions* often attract great crowds. The Greenpeace Foundation raised $13,000 in 1979 from an auction of celebrities' belongings, and used the money in its save-the-whales campaign. Articles sold included art works and stage costumes. A black leather jacket worn by actor John Travolta in the movie "Grease" went for $1,400. Your group may not have access to the closets of stars, but it doesn't hurt to appeal to local celebrities, such as a politician or sports figure.
- *Door-to-door canvassing* is a high-profit, nearly foolproof way to raise large sums of money, but it requires a fairly high level of expertise, usually a professional fund-raiser. However, canvassing may be done on a small scale. A public-interest group in North Carolina, faced with a $2,000 bill for printing a handbook on the dangers of a certain insecticide, recruited volunteer college students to work a few hours each week. They raised enough to pay off the bill in one month—with enough left over to sponsor a statewide membership retreat. Any group has the constitutional right to canvass in the United States, as long as its workers aren't paid. Be sure to let the media and the police know you're going to be around.

  On a larger scale, canvassing has enabled dozens of groups to expand their budget and staff significantly. The Connecticut Citizen Action Group (CCAG), started by Ralph Nader in 1971, increased its budget in four years from $80,000 to $600,000. Most of the increase, according to executive director Marc Caplan, can be attributed to canvassing. Besides being a good money-raiser, canvassing has educational benefits. Members of your group who go door to door can counter the claims of your opponents, and personally encourage those who want to get more involved to join your group.
- *Direct mail campaigns,* particularly for smaller groups, can be described in two words: expensive and risky. Unless you have access to a list of people interested in causes like yours, you'll be lucky to get a 3 percent return on appeals. If more than 5 percent contribute, you should

consider changing professions: you're a blue-ribbon fund-raiser.

- Many groups treat membership dues as a primary source of funding, and with good reason: if your members aren't willing to invest financially in the fight, chances are they won't be willing to invest their time. A financial contribution is generally the lowest level of involvement an organizer might expect. Set up a dues scale, but let people know that there's no "free lunch."
- Most fund-raising methods discussed here are relatively time-consuming. Some groups, which seem to lose patience with tag sales, dances, and canvassing, resort to applying for grants, which they see as a quick and neat source of unlimited funds. But for most groups, grants are unrealistic. They are never quick. Months or years are necessary to identify sources, write proposals, and wait for decisions. Grants rarely, if ever, bring in new members. Most important, grants usually have restrictions on their use; far better to be accountable to your members than to the government or to corporations, which are responsible for most grants.

There's plenty of money in the world to fund your fight. Sometimes it may be tricky to get that money in your group's bank account, but it is never impossible, assuming you are working on popular and important issues. Without money, the fight cannot be won.

W.M.B.

Several useful guides to fund raising:

- Joan Flanagan, *The Grass Roots Fundraising Book,* $5.25, The Youth Project, 1000 Wisconsin Avenue NW, Washington, D.C. 20007.
- David Grubb and David Zwick, *Fundraising in the Public Interest,* $5.00, Public Citizen, Inc., P.O. Box 194904, Washington, D.C. 20036.
- *Helping NOW Grow—Fundraising,* Chicago Chapter, National Organization for Women, Room 1501, 53 West Jackson, Chicago, IL 60604.
- Elizabeth B. Peterson, *Spend Less, Raise More. A Cost-Conscious Look at Direct-Mail Fund Raising,* $1.00, Direct Mail Fundraisers Association, 810 Seventh Avenue, New York, NY 10019.
- Nancy Mitiguy, *The Rich Get Richer and the Poor Write Proposals,* $5.00, Citizen Involvement Training Project, 138 Hasbrouck, University of Massachusetts, Amherst, MA 01003.

W.M.B.

BUILDING A COALITION

Editor's Note: *Diane MacEachern has spent years helping environmental groups fashion campaign and public relations strategies.* Almanac *managing editor Mary Paden, who contributes to this piece, has joined MacEachern on occasion, advising grassroots groups in the U. S. Midwest on environmental campaign strategy. In this article, Paden and MacEachern tell how the game is played.*

Few issues epitomize the ups and downs of environmental campaigns better than the "bottle battle"—the fight for deposit legislation in the United States. Since at least 1953, environmentalists and consumers have attempted to eliminate throwaway soda and beer bottles and cans by requiring a minimal deposit on all beverage containers.

Most attempts to pass deposit legislation have been made through state legislatures, and have failed. One veteran of the deposit battle estimates that the issue has probably been introduced in every state legislature an average of five times. Yet, only five states—Oregon, Vermont, Iowa, Connecticut, and Delaware—have been successful in enacting state-wide controls on throwaways through the legislative process.

Beginning in 1970 in Washington State, deposit proponents, frustrated by the legislative quagmire, gathered enough petition signatures to have the issue put to a popular vote. The special interests —bottle and can manufacturers, distributors, and some supermarkets—that had kept deposit bills bottled up in legislative committees spilled into the public arena with well-financed campaigns against the proposals. In this case, the anti-deposit forces won, yet national opinion polls showed the American public favored deposit legislation. In 1976, the proposal was placed on the ballot in four states: Michigan, Maine, Massachusetts, and

Colorado. In Michigan and Maine it passed easily. In Massachusetts it lost by a small margin and in Colorado it was defeated two to one.

Why had it passed in some states and failed in others? Analyzing their campaigns afterward, organizers in all four states came to the same conclusion: the successful campaigns had been those organized by broad-based coalitions. Where a small group of environmentalists had tried to go it alone, they had failed. It was a clear lesson in the importance of coalition building.

Organizing and running a coalition is no easy task. Because they are made up of diverse, autonomous groups, coalitions are harder to direct than any single organization. It can be like trying to get a roomful of politicians from different parties to agree on the wording of a resolution. The secret of successful coalitioning, according to experienced organizers, is to develop a *framework* within which to make decisions, communicate with each other, and share funds. And, of course, like any group involved in a campaign, a coalition should start out with a clear sense of its goals and overall strategy.

The Common Goal

Sometimes in the confusion of a campaign, people lose sight of their goal. It must be simple and understandable. In the case of the bottle battles it was simply to get people to vote for the bottle bill. Some coalition members, however, might have pursued a long-range goal of convincing people of the need for resource conservation, while others might have been quite satisfied with the goal of reducing litter along the highways. No problem, if both groups channel their energies into getting people to vote yes on the bottle bill. But, if the first group diverts attention to newspaper recycling and the second group attacks the bureaucracy of the Highway Department's litter cleanup operation, they are no longer supporting the common goal of the bottle bill.

The Clear-Cut Issue

Some issues are better than others for coalition-building. The bottle bill, according to Pamela Deuel, an Environmental Action lobbyist, was "the perfect issue."

"People had only to vote yes or no," she said. "There was no complicated technology to grasp, no numerous phases to implement, no difficulty understanding who was on each side of the issue and why." Campaign workers in Maine agreed: "We found that simplification is the key to reaching the public." It is easier to build a coalition around a simple, clear-cut issue. Issues that are heavily intertwined with technical or economic intricacies, such as nuclear power or the conversion of military facilities to peacetime uses, are more difficult. So are issues that seem remote from the public and the goals of local groups, such as oil tanker regulations for the open ocean. Bottles are something everyone has in the home, something everyone has seen strewn along the roadside.

The Overall Strategy

The real challenge in coalition building is developing a winning strategy. A coalition must offer different groups different reasons to support it. In the case of the bottle bill, it *would* conserve resources, so environmental groups could talk to their members about that. It *would* reduce litter, so more conservative community groups could campaign on that facet. And it *would* prevent cans from winding up in agricultural fields, so farmers could talk about that. The point is to key each facet of the issue to the interests of a particular audience always keeping in mind the ultimate goal. For example, the bottle coalition in Michigan guessed accurately that residents of the state proud of its reputation as an outdoor sports paradise were offended by roadside litter. The group geared many of its campaign ads to that. They also knew that Detroiters, sensitive to the maxim "when the nation catches cold, Detroit catches pneumonia," were concerned about jobs. The opposition, mainly bottle and can manufacturers, wooed several unions into their coalition by convincing them that the bottle bill would cause the loss of jobs. Bottle bill advocates countered with studies showing the bill had increased the number of jobs in other states.

Making Decisions

To be united, the coalition must have an internal method of making and implementing decisions. Groups come testily into coalitions, each wary of giving up too much autonomy, of being ruled by another group, of not getting proper credit for its contributions. One of the first tasks is for the groups to decide exactly who will have what authority. Who pays for what? Who handles the money? Who is authorized to say what to the press? Every organization, especially a coalition, needs individuals responsible for particular day-to-day decisions. Organizers must also devise a quick system to keep all members alerted to new developments. Groups used to working independently forget to inform each other of their actions. It can result in embarrassing moments for a coalition spokesperson. Phone chains to key members and mimeographed newsletters are usually the simplest techniques.

Sharing the Spoils

As a campaign gets underway, it often attracts resources: volunteers, contributions, and donations of materials. Coalition members often fall into dispute about how to use these resources, and as a result, often squander them. Figure out, before the volunteers' calls start, specific tasks for volunteers of varying skills, so they won't be greeted by confusion. Every campaign needs writers, speakers, graphic designers, door knockers, and (always) envelope stuffers. Marshal volunteer skills and connections efficiently.

Money is always a problem. Proponents of deposit legislation in Massachusetts were outspent fifty to one. Michigan's coalition raised $117,000 to pit against the opposition's $1.3 to $3 million. Coalitions should watch their money at both ends, by hiring or appointing a fund raiser to keep the coffers full and a bookkeeper to document where it goes. Someone should be appointed to authorize daily office, printing, and mailing expenses—and to keep a sharp eye out for the best deals.

The tactics above work. They may seem simple on paper but they are often forgotten in the heat of a campaign. A good coalition can win the race, but it requires careful steering, a constant eye on the road, and regular internal maintenance.

D.M., M.P.

19

Communicating

We devour it at the breakfast table, or take it with us on the train to work. We come home to it in the evening and may take another dose before going to bed. Some people are hooked, others only mildly so. But everyone has some appetite for the news. It is served to us in a variety of ways—in newspapers, on radio and TV, in magazines, and in the local weekly that's stuffed in our mailbox, whether we want it or not. Collectively, they are called the mass media, and most experts agree that for citizens of the industrialized world, they are the primary sources of information on the issues of the day, including the state of the environment.

Several years ago a researcher decided to find out where the media get that information. He asked San Francisco Bay-area reporters and editors to cite the origins of local environmental news stories that appeared over a twelve-day period. Of the 200 environmental news stories carried by San Francisco Bay-area media during those twelve days, 51 were entirely based on PR handouts: press releases, film clips, and business news services. Another 54 were the partial products of PR initiatives: the public relations person suggested the story through a phone call, press release, or personal visit, and the reporter followed it up. In other words, *over half* of the environmental news stories were initiated, or written, by PR experts. Who are these behind-the-scenes pseudo-journalists? Another study suggests the answer. Of the 457 press releases on environmental issues received by one San Francisco radio station, nearly three quarters were from government and industry. Environmental groups contributed 14 percent.

The implications are obvious. If environmentalists are going to influence public opinion, they must learn to work with the mass media. That, in part, is what this section of the *Almanac* is all about. In "Communicating" we follow the odyssey of an environmental press release that made the papers and ultimately influenced policy. During the journey we pause to examine the elements of effective newswriting. We explore the nature of a news event, and the sometimes off-beat approaches environmentalists can use to ensure success. And we look at the public relations tactics of industry when it sets out to defend itself from reproaches.

The news media are but one, admittedly important, means for the environmental movement to communicate its message. In this section we consider other alternatives such as advertising and film. We take a close look at what has traditionally been one of the movement's most effective communication tools—the letter. Persuasion, a science that is a favorite of governments and advertisers, can be useful to environmentalists as well. We explore how some of its principles can be applied to environmental communication.

Communicating is what we do every day. This section of the *Almanac* looks into how defenders of the environment can do it better.

B.P.B.

MAKING THE PAPERS

Like a cop on a beat, Julie Mannarino routinely made the rounds at the offices of the state environmental department. These were intelligence missions, of a sort, and her government footpatrols occasionally produced valuable inside information.

But usually her trips to the department were little more than opportunities to renew old ties with some middle-level officials, friendly and often useful relationships that had developed during her five years as environmental lobbyist and researcher for one of the United States' oldest and largest statewide environmental organizations—the Connecticut Citizen Action Group (CCAG).

John T. Donlon and Stephen T. Thorick were two such friends. Both were air pollution control engineers in the department's Air Compliance Unit and both were, like Mannarino, committed to protecting the environment.

When Mannarino dropped by their office on her usual department rounds one late November day in 1978, Donlon and Thorick were steaming.

The cause of their consternation that day was a permit applied for by the state transportation department, which would clear the way for the widening of an interstate highway in western Connecticut. The permit was required by state environmental law because the highway indirectly, by attracting large numbers of cars, contributes to the smog problem. The permits, which need approval by the environmental agency, are largely based on traffic projections routinely supplied by none other than the transportation department.

Officials at the environmental agency were ready to grant the permit since transportation officials claimed in their application the highway widening would not increase traffic, or pollution, at all.

Donlon and Thorick thought this claim to be "ludicrous" because it ignored the simple fact that new highways both attract more cars and spur new development, and hence cause additional air pollution. The two engineers were not only suspicious of the bureaucratic reasoning used to justify the widening project. They also believed it was being pushed through at the behest of a multinational chemical company that was building new offices in nearby Danbury.

Donlon and Thorick were pondering what to do when Julie Mannarino walked in. Since the air pollution permit review was largely based on self-serving statistics supplied by the transportation department, the engineers told her they wanted to expose the environmental review process as an exercise in futility. They discussed the possibilities. They could simply appeal to their superiors. They quickly rejected that idea. Earlier appeals had resulted in the admonishment that it was against department policy to reject figures from transportation officials. They could call a friendly reporter with their complaints. Better, but would the story have impact if it appeared in one newspaper? Why not, Mannarino suggested to the disconsolate bureaucrats, pen your objections in a formal inter-office memorandum and supply a copy to CCAG? Her organization, she assured them, would see to it their story would make the papers across the state.

A Donlon and Thorick memorandum, Julie Mannarino realized, was an unusually good publicity opportunity. The memo Mannarino received, courtesy of the two frustrated bureaucrats, *was* news to most reporters. The story was new, was interesting, credible, it was pegged to a discrete event or action. Controversy over the air pollution program had already received some press attention, and this was a new angle to the story. Donlon and Thorick were credible sources—and even more so since their charges were contained in an official department memorandum. And when Mannarino glanced at the four-page memo, she *knew* the story was interesting. In one of the many hard-hitting and quotable phrases it contained, the two engineers charged that the permit program was "a sham on the public and an embarrassment to the department." Best of all, for Mannarino and her organization, the story was theirs to control, to get credit for, and to use to press the issue.

Though hundreds of press releases cross reporters' desks in a week, the release is still a most effective weapon in the publicist's arsenal.

Boiled down to basics, the press release is a ghost-written news story. The survival rate of press releases is low; about 10 percent of them find their way to the pages of the newspaper or the set of the TV newscast.

The fate of your news release can be greatly enhanced by paying strict attention to the rather rigid rules of content and format. First off, the release has to be "news" (unless you're trying to peddle a feature release, which is notoriously hard to get into print). News is defined by journalists, but some helpful criteria for assessing the news potential of your story are: it's new, no one has said it or heard it before; something has happened or is about to; it affects a lot of people or an identifiable group of people; it's timely; someone important is involved; it's unusual, humorous, or ironic; there's a human interest angle; or it's a local variation on a theme already receiving media attention.

If you meet some, or all, of these criteria, your story is newsworthy and the media will be interested. Environmentalists, particularly local activists, seldom have spectacular news for release. More often than not it's an announcement of a meeting, a fund-raiser, or a local campaign. Those releases can make the papers, but on page thirty-five, not page one.

Though the publicist carefully constructs the release, emphasizing some points and not others, it still must read like a news story. The first, or "lead" paragraph, contains the most newsworthy point and succeeding paragraphs elaborate with supporting information and quotes. The best way to learn this newswriting style is to read the newspaper and imitate the standard "inverted pyramid" structure of the articles. When your release, unchanged, sounds like a story from Associated Press, then the style is right.

The *look* of a news release does not change from year to year. In fact, reporters are notoriously intolerant of any format innovation; they want it typed, double-spaced, no longer than two pages, with short one or two-sentence paragraphs and the name and number of a contact person who can answer their questions. Press release writers should also note that they are written in the past tense (someone announced, charged, said) and all information that is not accepted fact must be attributed. For credibility's sake, a formal, printed letterhead for your releases helps immensely.

On November 23 the release on the Donlon and Thorick memorandum was finished. The lead paragraph of the release gave prominent mention to CCAG, clearly crediting the organization for disclosing the internal memo and targeting the commissioner of the environmental department in a call for action. The thrust of the paragraph, however, was the engineers' own charge that the air pollution review for new highways was a "sham."

The rest of the release was largely based on the allegations contained in the memorandum along with generous quotes from CCAG's executive director. One urged that the air pollution permit program be "a real one, rather than a paper-shuffling, prolonged bureaucratic exercise with a foregone conclusion."

The only question that remained was one of timing. When should the story officially become "news"? Several factors were considered: which day would have the least other news to compete with the story, and which of the major media should get it first?

A "slow" news day can occur anytime, but some days of the week are more predictable than others. The weekend is normally fairly slow, but at the same time press coverage is more limited then because of a reduction in news staff, particularly at the TV and radio stations. Monday morning is often better. Though the papers are somewhat smaller that day and the space for news more limited, editors are often starved for fresh stories and broadcast news staffs are at full strength. The release was slated for Monday, November 27.

With their differing deadlines it is impossible for all the news media—particularly newspapers—to use the story at the same time. Which should be allowed to break the story first? In Connecticut, the largest daily, the Hartford *Courant,* is a morning newspaper. Boasting a circulation of over 200,000 and a base in the capital city, the *Courant* is widely considered the most influential paper in the state. It is also regularly clipped in the early hours of the morning by TV assignment editors lining up stories to cover that day. There are, on the other hand, more afternoon papers in the state, though their readership is somewhat smaller.

Because of its circulation and its influence on state politics, Julie Mannarino settled on Monday morning for the release, allowing the Hartford *Courant* and other morning papers to use it first.

On Thursday night CCAG's press release was mailed, with a copy of the four-page memorandum attached, to over one hundred daily newspapers, weeklies, and radio and TV stations. Four days later, what started as a friendly discussion between two frustrated officials and an aggressive environmentalist would become reading material at breakfast tables around the state.

The storm broke as expected on Monday morn-

CCAG News Release

CONNECTICUT CITIZEN ACTION GROUP BOX G, HARTFORD, CT 06106

FOR RELEASE:
Monday, November 27, 1978
AM Papers

CONTACT:
Bruce Ballenger
527-7191

SMOG REVIEW LABELED "SHAM," CCAG URGES ACTION

Urging immediate action by state Department of Environmental Protection (DEP) Commissioner Stanley Pac, the Connecticut Citizen Action Group (CCAG) today disclosed an internal DEP memo in which two pollution control engineers label the agency's own review of the air pollution impacts of new highways "a sham on the public and an embarassment to the Department."

The memorandum, written by two officials in DEP's Air Compliance unit, charges that DEP is forced to rely on sometimes "absurd" traffic projections supplied by the state Department of Transportation (DOT) when analyzing the air pollution impacts of new highways.

John T. Donlon and Stephen T. Thorick, both air pollution control engineers in DEP, charged that the Department's air pollution review staff "finds itself with having to accept (DOT) traffic projections which in some cases border on the absurd, and with performing equally absurd air quality analyses whose outcomes can only be as valid as the traffic data on which they are based."

The two cited the DEP's recent approval of the widening of I-84 in Danbury in which air pollution projections are identical whether the expressway is widened or not.

Donlan and Thorick labeled that conclusion as "ludicrous, "because the expanded highway will promote new development that will increase air

--more--

C.C.A.G. 130 Washington St., Hartford, 06106 (203)527-7191 Fairfield County: 64 Wall St., Norwalk Ct. 06850 (203)866-4410 ing. The Hartford *Courant*'s front page story bore the headline "Highway Pollution Reviews by DEP Criticized in Memo." Ultimately, the story was carried by both wire services, over fifty of the state's radio stations, and appeared on two TV newscasts. It was, by any measure, a publicity coup. The memo, was used by environmentalists in a legal challenge to block construction of another new road in western Connecticut.

Stung by attacks from environmentalists, including the disclosure about the weakness of the highway pollution review program, the commissioner of the environmental department put his signature to a statement agreeing never again to suggest publicly that new highways *reduce* pollution. The press, of course, was assembled by environmentalists to witness the signing.

B.P.B.

PSEUDO AND OTHER EVENTS

In 1976 a Canadian consumer rights group literally wrapped the local city hall in shiny red tape, then charged that the city was dragging its heels on consumer protection. To dramatize inhuman prison conditions, a U. S. Midwestern group held its press conference in front of the monkey cage at the zoo, pointing out that the county budgeted more money for monkeys than for prisoners. And on the U. S. West Coast an environmental group collected one day's litter from a nearby fast-food franchise, and met with reporters on top of the pile.

What these three happenings have in common, of course, is that they are all irresistible to the media. It is hard to imagine a station or newspaper—whatever its stand on consumer rights, prison conditions, or fast-food joints—that would pass up the chance to cover such a story.

Social historian Daniel Boorstin has coined the term "pseudo-event" to describe events that take place solely because the mass media are likely to report them. Like most of us, Boorstin doesn't like pseudo-events. He thinks reporters should dig for real events instead, the ones that usually happen in private. But digging for news takes time and effort, exposes the reporter to charges of news bias, and seldom leads to zippy TV footage. As a rule the media find it easier and safer to cover an obviously public occurrence designed to be reported: a pseudo-event.

Established and prestigious sources have no trouble arranging pseudo-events to suit the media. A city hall press conference, a congressional committee hearing, or a corporate groundbreaking seem obviously deserving of media attention. But low-power sources often need something a little more seductive. Unlike the mayor, you might schedule a formal press conference and find nobody there from the press.

The news media cover what they consider newsworthy. If you represent a powerful institution or a viewpoint that's strongly supported by the media, what you *are* is automatically newsworthy. If you're immersed in a hot public battle that has dominated the front page for days, what you *say* is automatically newsworthy. The rest of the time the media will judge your newsworthiness by what you *do*. Hence the emphasis on novelty, whimsy, human interest, and hype in most successful nonestablishment pseudo-events.

This doesn't mean you have to bomb a building or drape yourself in an American flag. The Weathermen and the Yippies were masters of the polarizing pseudo-event, the sort that wins plenty of publicity but very little sympathy. That's no good if your goal is to build a broader constituency. Look instead for a pseudo-event that is symbolically appropriate, one that will focus attention on your issue, not on your radicalism or your rudeness. If you decide to wrap city hall in red tape, clean up the tape when you're done.

Some other tips on pseudo-events:

1. Get your membership organized and involved in the organizing. A large turnout is essential to many pseudo-events—a disciplined turnout.
2. Don't let the issues get lost in the hubbub. Use speakers, both experts and ordinary members, who can articulate the substance behind the pseudo-event. Have a handout ready that explains the issues to passers-by.
3. Let the media know in advance what you're doing. You don't have to reveal your gimmick, but make sure they understand that there will

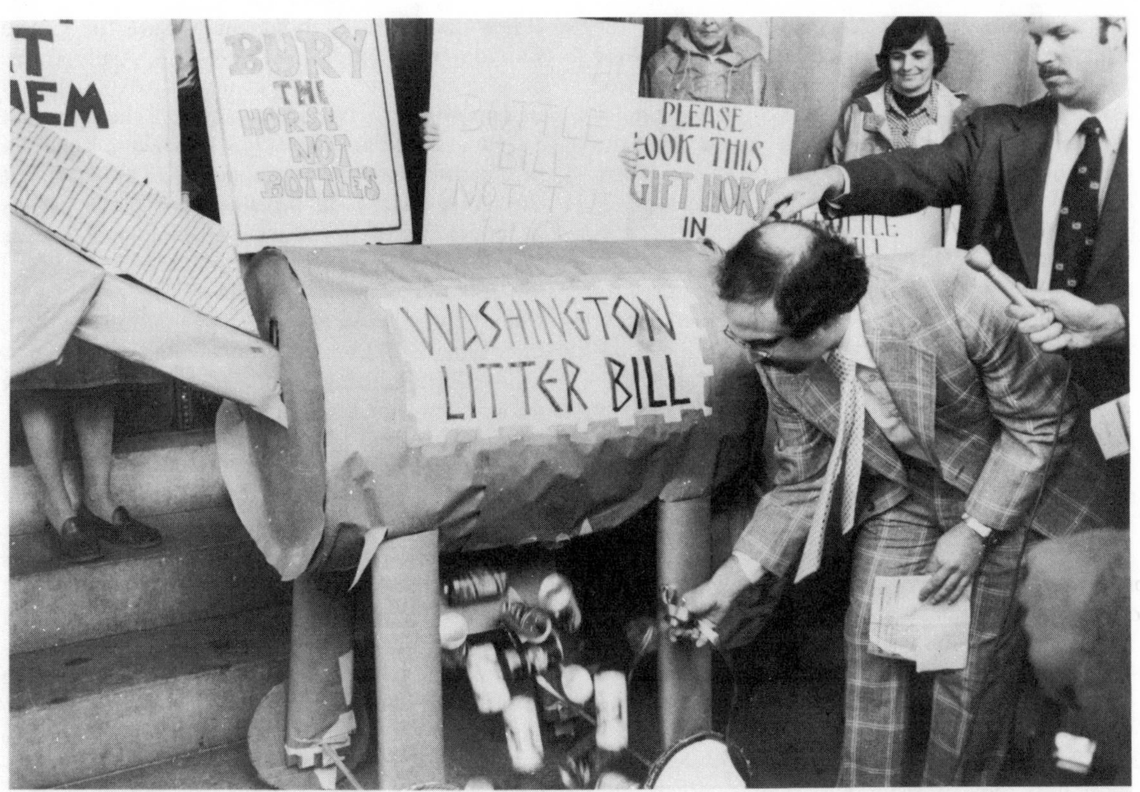

To attract attention to a piece of industry-sponsored legislation that environmentalists feared would scuttle their returnable-bottle bill, a group of Connecticut activists built a Trojan horse and rolled it in front of the state capitol. When invited reporters had gathered, a spokesperson for the activists opened a trap door in the belly of the horse and out tumbled a heap of beverage cans and bottles. Like this Trojan horse, he explained, the industry litter bill was a ploy, not designed to solve the litter problem but filled with more of the same. The event made newscasts and headlines across the state and helped doom the industry bill. (*Timothy Kelly/Courtesy Bruce Ballenger*)

be good pictures and good copy. If possible, get the advice of a friendly reporter on scheduling.

4. If you have any doubts about your pseudo-event, check it out with the police and an attorney. An unplanned confrontation with the authorities is sure to focus attention on the wrong issues.
5. Have a press release ready for newspapers that didn't show, and an audio "feed" for radio stations.
6. Don't do it again. Last month's pseudo-event won't go over well if done again this month.
7. Don't call it a pseudo-event. Reporters like to think they're covering the news.

By Dr. Peter M. Sandman, reprinted with permission from *Access* magazine. Dr. Sandman teaches Environmental Communication at Cook College, Rutgers University, New Jersey.

POSTAL PROTESTS

One day in 1963, Leo Rothschild, a New York lawyer and conservationist, sat down to write a letter to the editor of his local newspaper, the New York *Times*. It began simply: "The highlands of the Hudson are now in danger of major damage. They constitute one of the scenic treasures of the nation, and they should be preserved for all time."

Three years earlier, Consolidated Edison, the utility that supplies electricity to the sprawling New York metropolitan area, quietly initiated plans to build a new hydroelectric plant 40 miles (64 kilometers) up the Hudson River. The site they chose for the project, a place called Storm King Mountain, was ideal from the utility's standpoint. It was largely unpopulated, there was ample space for the pumped storage reservoirs, and though some blasting would be required in the granite face of the mountain, utility engineers were confident that it presented no major problem.

As it turned out, there *was* a problem. The place that Con Ed chose to mold to meet the electricity needs of New York City was a place of striking beauty, one of the last unspoiled waterways in the northeastern states.

When Rothschild sat down to pen his plea to save Storm King, the hydro project was well on the way to becoming a *fait accompli.* The U. S. Federal Power Commission had already given Con Ed the go-ahead, and all the right politicians were solidly behind the project. Rothschild's letter to the New York *Times* seemed like a cry in the wilderness. But it was a *good* letter: it was short and to the point; it was urgent yet rational, describing the basic details of the project so clearly that the reader couldn't miss the aesthetic implications; and it ended with a clear call-to-arms.

"We cannot allow the most beautiful part of one of the most beautiful of the world's rivers to be desecrated," he concluded. "I hope that public indignation can be aroused and a movement started to save the river."

When the letter was printed, the response was immediate. The New York *Times* quickly followed Rothschild's letter with an editorial against the Storm King project. Alarmed residents along the river, many of whom were unaware of Con Ed's plans, began to organize the Scenic Hudson Preservation Conference, a group to oppose the project. (See "Saving a River with a Song," page 329.) And national environmental organizations signed on to lend support. Before long, it became a national issue, with contributions pouring in from across the country. Environmentalists battled the plant in the courts and at hearings for more than a decade. The plant was never built. Not bad for one brief letter and a postage stamp.

Environmentalists are prolific letter writers. Well-organized letter-writing campaigns aimed at triggering a deluge of postal protests have, in fact, been an integral part of virtually every national environmental campaign in the 1960s and 1970s. When the Sierra Club sought to save the Grand Canyon from flooding by the U. S. Army Corps of Engineers, the group generated 20,000 letters in opposition to the project. (See "The Ads that Saved a Canyon," page 778.) When a coalition of environmental groups launched an effort to halt the Trans-Alaska oil pipeline, tens of thousands of letters and telegrams were received by Congress and Department of Interior officials in a postal onslaught that was sustained for two years. Though the pipeline battle was ultimately lost, that same coalition of groups later organized a similar letter-writing campaign to support setting aside millions of acres of Alaskan land for wilderness areas. That grassroots support, say organizers, was instrumental in getting the land preserved.

With the power of the pen amply demonstrated by these earlier fights, some environmental groups have developed alert systems to trigger letters and telegrams from citizens. The National Wildlife Federation, for example, can send out 7,500 "action alerts" to its membership in little more than twenty-four hours. Business groups, quick to catch on to a good thing, have developed more sophisticated systems for generating letters in targeted Congressional districts. At the push of a computer button, corporate lobbying groups like the Business Roundtable can generate the names of local business leaders in targeted Congressional districts who can be relied on to send letters to politicians opposing new environmental laws.

On a more local level, the numbers become less important. "Our legislators can get five letters and think there's a public mandate," notes an activist in sparsely populated Montana. And sometimes, as Leo Rothschild's letter demonstrates, a single letter, eloquently and persuasively worded, can have a dramatic impact.

In 1978, eight Oregon women wrote a letter that ultimately reached into the hearts of an international public, and triggered a landmark decision by the United States Environmental Protection Agency (EPA) to ban the use of several herbicides in the Pacific Northwest region.

"We are eight women who have lived in the Alsea area," their letter began. "We are virtually surrounded by Forest Service, BLM (Bureau of Land Management), and private timber lands, all of whom have sprayed literally thousands of acres for years with dioxin-containing herbicides in the spring months."

"The eight of us," read the next, startling paragraph, "have suffered a total of 10 miscarriages in the spring months, starting in 1973."

The letter, sent to a number of federal agencies the women believed might help, went on to give details of the miscarriages, herbicide spraying dates, and data implicating the toxic chemicals with health effects. Accompanying their letter, the women sent charts and research documenting their suspicions (see "Birth Defects," page 418).

Not long after they received the letter, the EPA sent a team of epidemiologists to investigate the women's complaints, and in March 1979, the agency ordered a temporary ban on the sale or use of two of the offending herbicides.

The letter from the women in Alsea followed some of the best-known rules for letter-writing. They had done their homework; they could quote from a Forest Service Environmental Impact Statement to support their claims; and they bent over backward, despite their personal tragedies, to make the tone of the letter cooperative as well as impassioned. Their purpose was impossible to miss; their personal plea impossible to ignore. They stood up for what they believed in a very courageous way, and they began with little more than time, paper, and some stamps.

J.M.V., B.P.B.

HOW TO WRITE THAT LETTER

"Dear Editor . . ." is an easy beginning for a free forum that can reach millions of readers. A letter to your local legislator may have an audience of one, but if persuasively worded or in the company of a hundred others expressing similar sentiments, it can have an impact.

1. Keep your letter short and to the point. One page can do it.
2. Stress your main point. Say it at least twice.
3. Show that you are knowledgeable about the subject. Give references and reasons for your position.
4. For letters to the editor, make reference to news articles, editorials, or other letters already published on the same issue. That will improve the chances of your letter getting into print.
5. Ask for some kind of action. Tell readers what you want them to do.
6. Make your letter relevant by bringing it down to a local level. Tell people how this issue will affect their lives.
7. Be personal. Don't be afraid to be emotional.
8. Don't threaten.
9. Try to be positive. Talk about the good along with the bad. It's depressing enough just reading the front page.
10. If you can, type the letter on your business or personal letterhead.

J.M.V.

HOW TO SAY IT

How to say it has, in the past, seldom been an issue for most environmentalists. Like other well-intentioned crusaders, the environmental movement hoped to move potential allies by naked truth, and nothing more. In that spirit antinuclear activists preached a gospel of hard and scary facts, such as the number of deaths that could result from a serious nuclear plant accident; recycling advocates recited the startling statistics on how much garbage the average family tosses out each year; and financially strapped environmental groups periodically sent useful fund-raising letters to their members predicting imminent collapse unless yet another donation was hurried through the mails.

All of these things may be true: the dangers of a nuclear accident are frightful indeed, we are prodigious generators of solid waste, and most environmental groups are continually on a financial precipice. Such appeals *can* be motivating to those already heavily committed to the fight in question—but a common response from the uncertain masses is to discredit (or ignore) the antinuclear movement for making such dramatic and unpleasant claims, to ceremoniously package garbage in neat trash bags instead of recycling, and to withhold a donation from an environmental group that seems to be going under anyway.

In the world of mass communication, in which hundreds of messages compete for attention each day, being right is not enough. It is all in how you say it, when you say it, and to whom. Politicians know this, and advertisers do, too. Perhaps it is time the planet's protectors too learned how to present their case honestly *and* persuasively. It's not an issue of giving up on truth or facts. It is a matter of whens, whiches, and hows: when to tell which facts and how to present them; when and how to appeal to legitimate emotion; and, sometimes, when it's better to say nothing at all. The bottom line, of course, is never to tell a lie. It's a matter of telling the truth in a way that will inspire and motivate rather than bore or repulse the listener. What this all means, in essence, is that environmentalists need to learn the technology of persuasion.

Though the science of persuasion is a twentieth-century phenomenon, its researchers have accumulated a prodigious literature. Prodded by impatient advertisers and propaganda-prone governments, study after study has explored the techniques of persuasive communication, everything from how many times a phone number should be repeated in a thirty-second ad to enhance audience recall, to how a government can persuade homemakers to use cheaper meats during wartime.

Determining how to communicate effectively, however, is largely intuitive. The following quiz is an opportunity to test your "persuasion savvy," your ability to motivate someone to do something. That is, after all, the goal. It's nice if you can inform and educate people, but unless you can motivate them to *do* something you can't save whales or awaken the public to the dangers of nuclear power or run successful recycling centers or accomplish any other change. We think there is one best answer to each of the following questions.

1. As part of a local campaign to recruit members for a national "Save the Whale" group, you are asked to design a poster. Which of the following three designs will work best?
   a. This poster—in full color—captures the death throes of a bloodied sperm whale. In the foreground a stern environmentalist in a small Zodiac boat glares at the reader while pointing at the dying whale. Superimposed in the slogan: "What have you done lately about the thousands of whales slaughtered like this every year? Join Whale Defenders, Inc."
   b. Half the poster pictures a smiling corporate executive, meticulously attired in a three-piece suit, seated in his plush office. Superimposed is the following copy: "THE CLAIM: 'Our company is concerned. We have spent millions to protect the environment and at great cost to this company we are no longer involved in whaling.'" The other half of the poster pictures a giant whaling ship, red with blood of butchered whales. Superimposed is the following copy: "THE TRUTH: This pirate whaler—responsible for the slaughter of 3,000 whales in 1979—sells 80 percent of its 'processed' whale flesh to the man who is 'no longer involved in whaling.' Help Whale Defenders stop this ship. And this man."
   c. The poster captures a humpback diving with only its tail protruding over a glassy sea. Its wide fluke provides an artistic background for this slogan, in bold letters: "This is the end of the humpbacks . . . unless you help the Whale Defenders turn things around."

2. You are designing a local newspaper ad that you hope will generate opposition to a proposed nuclear power plant in your area, which is predominantly rural. You also hope to recruit members for your regional safe-energy group. Which ad would work best?
   a. A sketch of a nuclear power plant with an overlay graphic of a "ONE WAY" traffic sign. The slogan: "Nuclear power can kill. Do you want to be caught on this one-way street? Join Citizens for Safe Energy."
   b. A picture of Herman Olsen, a prominent local farmer, standing next to the windmill he recently built to supply power to his dairy barn. This quote is superimposed: "I don't know much about nuclear power. But I'm learning and, frankly, it scares me a little. Now this windmill, that's something I can understand. It's pretty cheap, I can fix it myself, and it works. For me the choice is easy. I'm against the nuclear power plant. I'm a member of Citizens for Safe Energy."
   c. A large question mark superimposed on a photograph of the site of the proposed nuclear power plant. The question mark is surrounded by quotes from famous scientists, political leaders, and activists, all of which question nuclear safety. The slogan: "If all these people have questions about nuclear power, shouldn't you? For answers, join Citizens for Safe Energy."

3. You are writing a fund-raising letter seeking contributors to your solar energy lobbying organization. You're hard up for money. Which appeal would be most effective?

a. "Once again, the Solar Lobby Center desperately needs your help. We depend on people like you if we are to continue our important work for another year."
b. "An all-out assault by special interests on the Solar Lobby Center's legislative package left us far short of our goals. Next year we can win at the Capitol, but only with your help."
c. "Max Higgins is a lobbyist for the Petrol Oil Co. He hopes you don't contribute to the Solar Lobby Center."

4. You are designing a flyer to encourage local residents to attend a hearing on a utility rate hike. Which of the following should be at the top of the flyer in bold black letters?
   a. RATE HIKE HEARING TUESDAY NIGHT!
   b. YOUR VOICE COUNTS. LET'S HEAR IT TUESDAY!
   c. YOU CAN STOP YOUR UTILITY BILL FROM INCREASING BY $60 A YEAR!

5. You have just opened a recycling center in your town, and you're about to launch a publicity campaign urging residents to participate. You have developed the following publicity materials for the campaign: 1) a public service announcement (PSA) for television featuring a famous actress and her family, who live in the area, flattening cans and washing bottles; 2) an attractive detailed brochure outlining the energy and solid waste savings from recycling; and 3) a press release announcing the center's opening, as well as its hours and requirements. Which one of the following sequences would maximize the effectiveness of each item?
   a. Send out the press release to local papers, then mail the brochure to town residents, and finally run the PSA on TV.
   b. Mail the brochure to residents, then air the PSA, and finally run the press release.
   c. Air the PSA, publish the press release, and hand out the brochures at the recycling station.

The Answers

1. The first persuasion riddle—the "Save the Whale" poster—provides some interesting insight into a classic communication dilemma faced by environmentalists: Should we try to make people feel guilty? Or angry?

   Though all three posters communicate a sense of urgency about the plight of whales, persuasion research accumulated over years of study supports "b" as the appeal most likely to work. It was fashionable, particularly in the days of blossoming ecological consciousness, for environmentalists to make people terribly guilty for the sorry state of the environment. (A classic example is a cartoon in which the character Pogo, surveying a littered landscape, says, "We have met the enemy and he is us.") Poster "a" relies heavily on guilt, harshly asking its audience "What have *you* done lately" about slaughtered whales. Poster "b," on the other hand, attempts to make the reader *angry*. Unlike guilt, a feeling that is internally directed; anger is directed outward, in this case at an opponent who is portrayed as dishonest, getting rich on the flesh of dead whales.

   A recent study, which examined the behavior of students after watching an emotion-packed film on endangered wildlife, revealed that those feeling predominantly guilty were willing to take an action (signing a petition) immediately after the film, but once having relieved their guilt, were not interested in the issue a month later. The angry students, on the other hand, took immediate enthusiastic action and when surveyed a month later, were even angrier about the issue and willingly took a second action. The conclusion? Design honest messages that make people angry enough to do something; don't design messages that make them feel guilty about not having done it.

   Poster "c," which is beautiful but less dramatic, is probably less effective. The whaling issue, quite legitimately, is a natural for an emotional appeal. The positive image, the whale diving on the glassy sea, might touch the emotions, but the slogan is defeating. If this is the end of the humpbacks, why bother? It makes one feel sad—but powerless.

2. When should environmentalists use fear appeals? That's a question for the antinuclear movement, which is fond of such messages, to ponder. Newspaper ad "a"—"Nuclear power can kill"—relies heavily on fear, and for that reason the ad will be a flop. Strong fear appeals, several studies suggest, work *only* when they are 1) delivered by a credible source, 2) are concerned with the audience's loved ones, and 3) offer an opportunity to relieve the fear. This ad flunks on all counts.

   Poster "c" is better, but not great. All of

those famous scientists, political leaders, and activists don't really mean beans in a small town where they would likely be viewed as "outsiders."

Poster "b" is best. The believability of a message is directly tied to the credibility of the source. Herman Olsen, the prominent farmer, is ideal in this respect. Most residents will feel he is one of them, sharing the same fears, and, in this case, the same values and the same caution—in short, he is credible. Olsen's message is also positive, not simply "no" to nuclear power, but "yes" to alternative energy.

3. Writing a fund-raising letter is tricky. There are all sorts of specialized, tested techniques for writing them (like using more "you's" than "we's"), but most of the common principles of persuasion research apply. Appeal "a" falls short: who wants to give money to a group that seems embarrassed to ask for it, and implies that even if you do contribute, they'll probably be in the same fix next year? Appeal "b" is better, but should instead focus on legislative victories, not defeats. They would be more positive, more upbeat, and more persuasive. The best appeal is "c"; there's the element of David beating Goliath, and it benefits from an existing mistrust of "Big Oil" that is probably strongly felt by Solar Lobby Center members. The letter using this approach might also describe legislation that the Center passed despite the all-out lobbying efforts of Max Higgins. Tell the reader why he is so worried. Unlike alternatives "a" and "b," this appeal focuses on success, not failure. And it's fun.

4. Sometimes the straightforward approach can be effective. It speaks directly to the immediate issue at hand—keeping electric bills from going up. (Answer "c.")

5. The question here is one of timing. Dr. Peter M. Sandman, who specializes in environmental communication at Rutgers University, offers some interesting insight into this. He suggests a "two-tiered approach to communication." First, make people want to act, then "cement" that motivation with relevant information that helps them do so. In this case, the public service announcement, featuring the well-liked actress and family, should be motivating—it suggests that recycling is fun, that it is a worthwhile collective effort for families, and that it is endorsed by an admired local resident. In contrast, the press release supplies information that is relevant only to people who have already decided they want to recycle (how, when, etc.).

The information in the brochure—how recycling saves energy and reduces solid waste—provides the incentive people need to keep on recycling. The Sandman theory suggests that sequence "c" is best. The PSA should be aired first, motivating residents to try recycling, quickly followed up by the press release, which provides relevant logistical information to those committed to giving it a try. Once at the recycling center residents will likely ask for the brochure themselves. Having made the effort to come they will be interested in learning all the other reasons that recycling is such a good thing. The brochure contains relevant information to help "cement" their behavior. The strategy works, says Sandman. He tested it at a recycling station.

B.P.B.

THE ADS THAT SAVED A CANYON

In 1966, it looked as if the United States government was going to flood the Grand Canyon. Influential politicians, including the U. S. Secretary of the Interior, claimed that dams in the canyon would increase the water supply to the southwestern United States and made the argument that the flooding would allow tourists to get a close look at the canyon walls from boats. Congress seemed ready to authorize the dams.

The Sierra Club, which until then had not been particularly political, believed that the public, which was beginning to show signs of environmental concern, would be outraged if it knew what was being planned for the canyon. But the news media had not been picking up the story. As a last-ditch effort, the group hired a small San Francisco advertising agency to design a series of ads that would inform and incite the public.

The first ad, a full page in the Sunday New York *Times,* was headlined, "Only you can stop the Grand Canyon from being flooded for profit." It was accompanied by two thousand words of text explaining the issue. The ad not only urged people to express their outrage, but it was the first environmental ad to provide coupons to be clipped and mailed to Congress, the Secretary of the Interior, and the Sierra Club.

Flooding the Flooders

"Stewart Udall [then Secretary of the Interior] said that never in history had there been as much mail on an environmental issue. . . . He was amazed," says Jerry Mander, a partner in the firm that did the ad. Udall received an incredible twenty thousand pieces of mail.

But there were startling repercussions to this unique publicity move. Within forty-eight hours of the ad's appearance, the Sierra Club received a telegram in which the Internal Revenue Service, citing the ad in the *Times,* denied the group its tax-exempt status because it was now lobbying, an activity denied tax-exempt groups. The Club was audited and its status changed. Ultimately, the Club set up a separate, tax-exempt Sierra Club Foundation, which does research, while the Club itself continues to lobby.

However, the ad had served its purpose. The news media began to cover the issue, and the ad inspired the largest public outcry on an environmental issue to that date. The ad also contained a Sierra Club membership coupon. And, within a few years, the Sierra Club's membership had more than doubled, bringing in revenue to pay for the ad and to buy more ads in other publications. Probably the most famous read, "Should we flood the Sistine Chapel so that tourists can get closer to the ceiling?"

These ads were run for two years. Because of the strong public response, the Grand Canyon flooding proposal never passed.

For the Price of a Stamp

Peter Sandman, who teaches environmental communication at Cook College of Rutgers University (See "How to Say It," page 775), puzzled over the success of the unusually wordy ads. "Unlike conventional ads, they were not designed to persuade people," he said. "They were successful because they were aimed at people who already believed passively, but had never done anything about it. At the time, there was a cadre of people who did not want to flood the Grand Canyon, who didn't like the Army Corps of Engineers, who were vaguely into environmental causes and into politics. What Mander did, with large ads that were clever, attention-attracting, yet full of words and information, was to ask something of people who formerly did nothing about their feelings. The ads showed them that they were part of a large group, gave them ammunition to argue their environmental beliefs, told them exactly what they could do to help, and gave them a way (with the coupons) to be effective and useful for the price of a postage stamp."

Unedited News

Mander feels that the same factors that made the Grand Canyon ads work can be applied to other environmental advertising. "Ads can be a catalyst," he says. "If the media won't pick up a story, a group can alert the public by speaking to them directly in ads . . . you can get newspeople to report the story by giving it to them in the ad. You become the press. A good ad can have a ripple effect."

Mander and others later founded a nonprofit group called Public Media Center (PMC), which designs "alternative" advertising. There are other such public interest advertising groups throughout the United States.

Although not all campaigns can be as successful as the Grand Canyon fight, such ads still give the valuable opportunity, says Mander, "to speak directly to the world, unedited."

Noncommercial Commercials

The price of using ads as a forum, however, is high. Print media are under no obligation to devote free space to worthy causes.

On the other hand, broadcast media are. The Fairness Doctrine of the Federal Communications Commission (FCC) requires that broadcasters provide coverage of all sides of "controversial issues of public importance" and devote time to local public affairs issues. Many stations accomplish this, in part, by offering free "advertising" to community groups. For the most part, broadcasters shun these "public service announcements" (PSAs) if they might set off a new controversy, since then factions on all sides of the issue would demand equal time. Nor are they required to air any group's views on an already-hot issue through a public service announcement; they may decide, for example, to have someone represent the view on a talk show instead. More often than not, stations run noncontroversial PSAs under a broad federal mandate to air them as a public service. Unfortunately, PSAs are rarely aired during prime listening or viewing time, which is sold at the highest rates and is reserved for paying customers. Still, PSAs are free. They can be as simple as a three-sentence script sent to a radio announcer to read on the air or as complicated as a sixty-second TV spot professionally produced. Sometimes local stations will even offer technical assistance to a group to produce a PSA.

Most of the PSAs used by American media are supplied or endorsed by the National Advertising Council, which favors established and non-controversial groups such as the Boy Scouts and the American Lung Association. However, since the FCC scrutinizes each station's service to the community at license-renewal time, stations have an incentive to accept PSAs from local groups.

"PSAs are a good way to publicize meetings, build your name recognition and credibility, urge small changes in people's personal behavior, or focus attention on impending decisions," Sandman said. "For any individual, social action begins with baby steps: coming to a meeting, exercising a right, even beginning to think about an issue. Sometimes all you can do with an ad is get the process started and hope that the change will lead them to seek out more information and then try more ambitious sorts of action."

S.D., J.S., M.P.

THE ART OF CORPORATE IMAGE-MAKING

Many corporate executives call it a necessary response to a "pressure-cooker" political environment. Others are more blunt, terming it an effective way for business "to cope with some of the knees in the groin." Besieged by environmentalists, consumer advocates, and civil rights activists, corporations are turning increasingly to expanded public relations programs to help defend their battered image and blunt the reproaches of bothersome critics.

Public relations, of course, is old hat to the business world. But while PR departments used to spend most of their time conjuring up ways to sell products, the new PR approach also has them fashioning campaigns to polish the company image and even to influence public policy.

"PR used to be mainly how to get information into the media without having to pay for it," one corporate executive told *Business Week* recently. "We're now talking about much more sophisticated attempts to interact on issues."

The PR campaigns are indeed more sophisticated. But they don't always work.

PR in a Pinch at Three Mile Island

The 1979 Three Mile Island nuclear plant accident was potentially the industry's waterloo. From the outset, the public relations department of Metropolitan Edison (the plant's operators) knew they were on the front lines of a possible PR disaster. After confusing reporters for several days with contradictory statements, they had lost most of their credibility with the press. Like good soldiers faced with defeat, Met Ed's tiny PR staff called in reinforcements. They hired big guns from Chicago—Hill and Knowlton, the largest U.S. public-relations firm. They cloistered in a suite at the Hershey Motor Lodge, near the ailing plant, to plan a strategy. What should they say to three hundred besieging reporters, most of whom felt that Met Ed had lied to them about the seriousness of the accident? Beer was ordered to calm frayed nerves, and hours later, when everyone was suitably relaxed, ideas for handling the PR nightmare began to emerge. Some of them centered not on how to deal with the swarm of reporters, but on how to *avoid* them. Someone suggested handing out press packets, thus avoiding further face-to-face questions. Another suggested distributing a list of emergency "Met Ed communications phone numbers" to journalists but then leaving the phones off the hook.

After a long evening, punctuated by more room-service beer deliveries, the meeting took on a boisterous flavor. That fact was not overlooked by two Philadelphia *Inquirer* reporters who stood, notepads in hand, outside the closed doors of the suite, overhearing and recording long snatches of conversation. The journalists listened for eight hours, posing for passersby sometimes as an arguing married couple, sometimes as potential lovers engaged in a game of cat and mouse. No one interrupted them. Their account of the secret strategy meeting appeared in a lengthy Sunday article about the accident and quickly became a favorite humor story among other reporters on the scene. Instead of upgrading its image, Met Ed's press people had provided a new barroom tale, and the joke was on them. None of the tactics suggested at the meeting were implemented.

Ads Gone Awry

The advertising copywriters on Madison Avenue know a good thing when they see one, and when the environmental fervor began to catch on in the early 1970s, the ad people were quick to jump on the bandwagon. In 1970 one observer estimated that the budget for corporate environmental advertising during a six-month period was nearly $1 billion. What did they sell? Mostly claims about their environmental responsibility—the millions being spent on new pollution controls, the programs to preserve wildlife habitat, and the participation in community litter cleanup efforts. Some businesses engineered advertising appeals that tied their products to ecological concern: the low emission gasoline, the trash-masher that saved landfill space, and the low-suds, low-phosphate detergents.

Some of these ads, while perhaps excessively self-promotional and opportunistic, were basically accurate in their claims. Others were deceptive. Some were outright lies.

In early 1970, the Idaho-based Potlatch Forests Corporation launched a new advertisement that featured a beautiful photograph of a rushing, stone-studded stream. It looked just like a pristine mountain trout stream ought to look. Under this pleasing picture was the headline: IT COST US A BUNDLE BUT THE CLEARWATER RIVER STILL RUNS CLEAR.

Potlatch Forests, Inc., has a pulp and paper plant on the Clearwater and Snake rivers, and at the time, the company was discharging tons of organic pollutants into their waters. The U.S. government was not too pleased with this state of affairs, and after it cited the company for pollution violations, Potlatch announced *plans* to spend $9.6 million on environmental controls. At the time the ad appeared, that financial outlay had yet to become reality.

Most commercial media gladly accept—and aggressively seek out—advertising dollars, and while advertisers' claims are sometimes scrutinized, rarely do the media go to the trouble to check out the accuracy of an ad the way *Newsweek* did with Potlatch. Tipped off that the Clearwater River may not be as clear as the company claimed it to be, *Newsweek* sent a photographer to take a picture of the river below the plant. Mired in foul-smelling wastes, it was, they realized, hardly the pristine stream pictured in the ad. That photograph, *Newsweek* discovered, was taken 50 miles (80 kilometers) upstream.

When the deception was uncovered, Potlatch suffered no pangs of conscience. The company simply pulled all its "environmental" advertising. "We tried our best," claimed Potlatch's president. "You just can't say anything right anymore—so to hell with it."

McDonald's Worm Caper

Imagine this conversation between the head of a giant fast-food corporation and the director of its office of public relations.

"We've got a problem," mutters the boss.

"Nothing we can't handle, sir," replies his PR man with a toothy, press-conference grin. "What's the problem?"

"It's the rumor again."

The smile fades on the face of the director of the office of public relations. "Which rumor?" he asks. "The one about ground insect parts in the hamburger buns, or sawdust in the milk shakes?"

"No, no. It's much worse," says the boss, drumming his fingers on the desk top. "It's the worm rumor."

If the PR man is wise to the art of rumor control, he's aware that there are three strategies the PR department can pursue to put an end to the insidious notion that their hamburgers contain red worms. He can ignore it, and hope that truth will triumph in the face of the obvious absurdity. He can deal with it indirectly by rebutting the rumor with vague, euphemistic references, and limiting the PR offensive to the region in which it's circulating. Or he can launch an all-out nationwide attack in hopes of stamping out the worm rumor wherever it may rear its ugly head.

When McDonald's Corporation faced this very rumor several years back, it chose option two.

The worm rumor got its start in the summer, McDonald's officials told the *Wall Street Journal,* following the circulation of similar suspicions about the contents of a competitor's hamburger. A company investigation suggested Chattanooga, Tennessee, as its place of origin, and by fall sales at McDonald's outlets throughout the southeastern states had fallen by 20 percent. Company officials, blaming the worm rumor as a partial cause for the precipitous sales decline, decided to launch a PR counteroffensive.

Calling a press conference in Atlanta, Georgia, and carefully avoiding naming the offending creature, McDonald's officials vehemently refuted the spurious charge that its hamburgers contained, as they put it, "protein additives." To add weight to this denial, company spokespeople produced a letter from the U. S. Secretary of Agriculture that backed their claim, and letters from officials at the TV networks verifying that no talk show host, nor any other broadcast celebrity for that matter, had referred to the worm rumor as anything but a rumor. It was, to any rational observer, a very convincing demonstration.

McDonald's experience with rumor-mongering is not unique. There was, for example, the rumor about a certain popular bubble gum that was supposed to contain spider eggs and cause cancer. The gum manufacturer spent between $50,000 and $100,000 on advertising to dispel that one. It even hired private investigators to track down the perpetrator. And then there was the rumor, which later became the subject of a lawsuit, that roaches were found in a Coca-Cola bottle. The company took the head-on approach to shatter that one: a witness in court testified that even if the insects did enter a coke bottle, they would do no harm, and to prove his point, he ate a few for the jury.

B.P.B.

PHONY ENVIRONMENTAL GROUPS

At first glance, the groups look unimpeachable: the National Environmental Health Association, Americans for Energy Independence, Keep America Beautiful. Their names, their public relations literature, and sometimes even their activities show them to be defenders of the environment. A closer look, however, reveals a hidden purpose.

They are examples of scores of associations, institutes, and other organizations that appear to act in the public interest, but actually derive their support from, and further the interests of, industry. Whether oriented toward the environment, consumerism, or other issues, they are accused by legitimate public-interest advocates of being wolves in sheep's clothing—in some cases using deceptive titles and credentials to push industry propaganda, in other cases promoting projects that produce little benefit and distract attention from authentic groups whose budgets are minuscule by comparison.

The National Environmental Health Association, for example, sounds as if it may promote reduction of unhealthy pollutants, but in fact it represents the "single-service" industry of paper-plate and plastic-ware manufacturers, according to Environmental Action, a Washington D.C.-based citizen group. When the U. S. Environmental Protection Agency (EPA) published a report proposing ways to discourage throwaway tableware, the association issued a resolution charging EPA with "regressive" ideas about public health.

Americans for Energy Independence is not exactly a coalition of citizens concerned with dependence on foreign oil, according to a 1977 article in *The Nation,* but is instead an advocate of nuclear power supported mostly by Westinghouse and other nuclear manufacturing companies.

"Eco" Fronts

The ethical questions that bear on industry "front groups" are not always clear-cut, and the

"WE'RE INCAPABLE OF MAKING A MORAL JUDGEMENT, BUT WE ALSO HAVE A DESPERATE NEED TO EXPRESS OURSELVES."

groups are not always blatant misrepresentations; in some cases, these organizations can have certain positive effects. Keep America Beautiful, for instance, is as familiar as Smokey the Bear after twenty-six years of promoting programs to help communities clean up litter. No doubt its 109 corporate members and contributors, many of whom are packagers and container manufacturers, point with pride to their "contributions to the environment."

Environmentalists ask them two questions: first, aren't the thousands of Keep America Beautiful volunteers being asked to pick up litter caused largely by the wasteful packaging procedures of the group's supporters? And second, don't the organization's enthusiastic cleanup campaigns deflect public awareness from a more effective but less profitable tactic of reducing waste at its source, by using returnable bottles and trimming packaging?

"What the corporate philosophy is [for supporting Keep America Beautiful], I can't tell you," says Ed Regenye, a public relations representative of the organization. "What I can tell you is that it's a good program and that it works."

Consulting the Rule Books

What are the criteria for a "real" public-interest group? According to R. Michael Cole, legislative director of Common Cause, a true public-interest group is "an organization representing a broad constituency that is not represented by traditional economic interests."

The influence of what have come to be called "phony" groups reaches all levels of public opinion. Newspaper readers, for example, are likely to encounter articles like those that quoted testimony about food additives and pesticides from scientists employed by a group called the Council for Agricultural Science and Technology. Though its name is suitably scientific sounding, the council is anything but objective; 60 percent of the group's operating budget is paid by large corporations including Dow Chemical, Agrico Chemical Company, and General Mills, according to *Nutrition Action* magazine.

Legislators are affected by groups like the Calorie Control Council, which placed an advertisement in the Washington *Post* urging readers to let congressmen "know how you feel about the proposed ban on saccharin . . . Phone him! Write him! . . . It's up to you to make this experiment in democracy really work." No mention was made in the ad that the council was an association of dietetic food and drink producers, and when asked why not, the council's advertising agency claimed it was "an oversight."

While this ad was being run, along with two subsequent ads containing the same "oversight," more letters were received in Washington concerning saccharin than on "any issue since the Cambodian bombing," said a representative of the advertising firm.

The issues raised by these ads promoted Thomas Stanton, a Ralph Nader attorney, to remark: "Once again corporate abuse is setting the stage for government intervention. This could be a very fruitful area for an investigation by the U. S. Federal Trade Commission."

Whether official action will ever seek to lessen the impact of bogus public-interest groups is open to question. But it's apparent that in a corporate society, public-spirited citizens attracted to a cause need to read the fine print—if they can find it.

L.B.

THE TWELVE LARGEST U.S. ENVIRONMENTAL GROUPS

Many of these groups are undoubtedly familiar—most have made names for themselves in the courts, in the halls of Congress, in classrooms, and in other environmental theaters in the United States and around the world. These are among the largest citizen-supported environmental groups, but by no means the only ones carrying the banner. The smaller, grassroots organizations, which are too numerous to list, are also the lifeblood of the movement. We list these groups as a measure of the breadth and verve of environmental consciousness.

Organization	*1980 Membership*	*Budget*
National Wildlife Federation 1412 16th Street NW Washington, D.C. 20036	4.1 million	$29 million (1979)
National Audubon Society 950 Third Avenue New York, NY 10022 With offices worldwide.	400,000	$14.7 million (1980)
Sierra Club 530 Bush Street San Francisco, CA 94108	177,708	$9.5 million (1980)
Cousteau Society 777 Third Avenue New York, NY 10017 Membership Center: 930 21st Street Norfolk, VA 23517 With offices also in Los Angeles, Paris, France, and Monaco.	160,000	$4.5 million (1979)
Fund for Animals 40 West 57th Street New York, NY 10019 With offices also in Toronto, Canada.	125,000	$880,364 (1978)
Animal Protection Institute P.O. Box 22505 5894 Southland Park Drive Sacramento, CA 95882	115,000	$1.76 million (1980)
Union of Concerned Scientists 1384 Massachusetts Avenue Cambridge, MA 02238	90,000	$1.1 million (1979)
The Wilderness Society 1901 Pennsylvania Avenue NW Washington, D.C. 20006	50,000	$1.75 million (1980)
Natural Resources Defense Council 122 East 42nd Street New York, NY 10017	47,000	$3.1 million (1979)
Environmental Defense Fund 475 Park Avenue South New York, NY 10016	46,000	$1.9 million (1980)
Friends of the Earth 529 Commercial Street San Francisco, CA 94111 With twenty-three other offices in: Australia, Austria, Belgium, Canada, El Salvador, England, France, West Germany, Greece, Ireland, Italy, Japan, Malaysia, Mexico, Netherlands, New Zealand, Portugal, Scotland, Spain, Sweden, Switzerland, Thailand, and Yugoslavia.	25,000	$1 million (1980)
Environmental Action 1346 Connecticut Avenue NW Washington. D.C. 20036	22,000	$500,000 (1980)

L.B.

THE STRATEGY OF THE DOLPHIN

It is an unavoidable fact of international life that the decision-makers in governments everywhere are most influenced by vested interests with extravagant lobbying budgets and by organizations with enormous memberships. Those of us who love the sea, who recognize the blood relationship of all earth's beings, who see on this Water Planet a growing threat to our most fundamental biological machinery, do not command the money and power of even a single major multinational corporation. But we can wield the formidable power of our numbers, the strength of a great unified crowd of citizens of the planet.

How sad and how alarming is the rate of environmental devastation! We ourselves are increasingly threatened by toxic debris and lethal miscalculations.

It is unbelievable. It is unacceptable.

We must stop this stupidity, and the most effective weapon we have as citizens—as parents—is the sheer force of our numbers. That is the strategy of the dolphin when threatened by an animal

(*The Cousteau Society*)

armed with greater strength and size. Pursued by a large shark a pack of dolphins will suddenly turn en masse, dive below the shark and drive their blunt noses into its belly, one after another. It is the perfect strategy. With no ribs or diaphragm to protect its vital organs, the shark is vulnerable. For all of its power, the shark is defeated by intelligence and the force of numbers. It is the weaponry of the peacemakers and the common people throughout history.

Let me offer a final thought. For all the darkness that presently confronts us and our descendants, there is no reason to give up. There is every reason to take up the fight, because we have within our grasp the power of the people to force the right decisions. The more people, the more power, the more hope.

On behalf of the future generations whose legacy we are squandering, let us begin to make waves—forcing decision-makers to protect and to nurture the environment. How can we accomplish this? We can rise as a human family and compel the powerful and the profit-only-minded to consider life the greatest priority. We can take our inspiration from the dolphins, who defend themselves and their offspring through an instinct to mass together in the face of danger . . . and to attack power with wisdom.

Index

B

D

E

F

G

H

I

J

M

N

O

P

Q

R

S

T

V

X

Y

Z